The Sunday Telegraph

GOLF COURSE GUIDE
—— TO ——
BRITAIN & IRELAND

Introduction by Mark Reason

16th Edition

MACMILLAN

The publishers would like to acknowledge the contribution of the following:

Editorial
*Jon Ryan; Mark Reason for all his editorial work; Jim Bruce-Ball, John Gibb
and Mark Salter for course reviews and all round help*

Editorial co-ordination and typesetting
Penrose Typography, Maidstone, Kent

Advertising
*Enquiries about advertising in this book should be addressed to
Barry Hood on 020 8949 7687*

First published 1968 by William Collins, Sons & Co Ltd, London
This edition published 2004 by Macmillan
an imprint of Pan Macmillan Ltd
20 New Wharf Road, London N1 9RR
Basingstoke and Oxford
Associated companies throughout the world
www.panmacmillan.com

ISBN 1 4050 4170 6

1 3 5 7 9 8 6 4 2

A CIP catalogue record for this book is available from the British Library.

Printed and bound in Great Britain by Bath Press

CONTENTS

INTRODUCTION
by Mark Reason

Following a year when Prince Andrew was Captain of the Royal and Ancient and Royal Troon hosted the Open Championship, it seemed a fitting idea to feature the royal golf courses of Britain and Ireland in the 16th edition of *The Sunday Telegraph Golf Course Guide*. And the more you find out about the history of royal golf, from duffers and drinkers to dab hands and stinkers, the more fascinating the whole business becomes.

Golf's first brush with royalty was not altogether encouraging. In 1457 James II of Scotland told his subjects to stop messing about with the game because it was interfering with the archery practise necessary if the country was to repel the English. But matters soon improved.

James IV of Scotland was a bit of a player, Henry VIII's courtiers were once described as "busy with the golf" and Mary Queen of Scots was criticised for playing "golf and pall-mall in the field beside Seton" a day or so after her husband Darnley was murdered. Still, if there is a better balm for grief than golf I haven't yet come across it.

In the seventeenth century James I granted a monopoly to golf ball manufacturers in England in order to counter the thriving Dutch export business and maybe Tony Blair should consider something similar if the Dunlop 65 is ever to make a nostalgic come back.

It was presumably with one of these English balls that James I's son almost hit his tutor Isaac Newton and thus deprived the world of the discovery of gravity. James II was also a keen player and Charles I is reputed to have been playing golf at Holyrood when news of the Irish rebellion reached him in 1641.

And so through the centuries the royal family has become ever more supportive of golf. You may wonder why there is not a Royal Marylebone Cricket Club or a Royal All England Club, and one can only suppose that there simply wasn't the same historical span of royal enthusiasm for those games, even though tennis crops up once or twice in Shakespeare.

The advantages to golf of royal patronage, as bestowed by both William IV and Queen Victoria in the nineteenth century are fairly obvious, but there were also advantages to be had from playing golf if you were a royal.

The future Edward VII – and "nature had not made the king's figure suitable for driving a long ball", according to one description – once played a game against Lionel Hewson, a captain in the South Irish horse, at Royal Curragh. Afterwards Hewson observed, "At the first hole I was six inches from the hole and he was ten yards. He remarked, 'I always count two on the greens to avoid putting'."

Edward VIII might have done well to employ a similar tactic. When he was the Prince of Wales, he made it through to the semi-final of the Parliamentary Handicap at Walton Heath. Edward took four putts on one hole, but still contrived to beat the accommodating Lady Astor.

Edward's talent did not always match his enthusiasm. When he drove himself in as Captain of the R&A he hit such a dreadful shot that it came nowhere near the expectant caddies who were awaiting a souvenir some way down the fairway.

Instead Willie Petrie dived out of the nearby club-making shop and snaffled the ball for himself. Eight years later when the future George VI drove himself in the caddies were reported as standing "disloyally close to the tee". But they were again foiled when the Duke got a good drive away.

The caddying fraternity eventually recovered their losses from the future Edward VIII when five of them conspired to give him a hole-in-one at Royal Wimbledon. Choosing a hole with a blind tee shot, the four who were on active duty got one of their colleagues to hide on the other side of the hill and pop HRH's ball into the hole when it came over the brow. The result was record tips for the caddies, headline news and considerable celebration.

But then the royal golf courses have always been particularly good at celebrating. Maybe it was because the early royal clubs, of which the Royal Perth Golfing Society was the first to receive the title in 1833 beating the R&A by a year, often had strong Masonic connections, thereby guaranteeing a certain indulgence from the local constabulary.

Royal Perth indeed had a huge hollow silver club from which people swigged rather in the manner of the modern yard of ale. Royal Worlington has the pink jug, consisting of one bottle of French champagne and one measure each of Benedictine, brandy and Pimms No.1. Whilst Royal Epping Forest was sufficiently indulgent to let the local ARP wardens use its bar during World War II, although they then had to ask them not to visit quite so frequently due to an alarming and sudden beer shortage.

Other royal clubs had more significant aggravations to deal with during the war. Royal Jersey, one of the most long standing royal clubs outside Scotland, was almost wiped out by the trenches, gunpits, concrete blockhouses and gravel heaps (as large as half a million tons) deemed necessary hazards by the Germans in the days before Bernhard Langer.

But the invading force couldn't obliterate the history of the club thanks to the cunning of the captain who hid the club records and trophies behind a false wall whilst stashing the golf clubs in a remote warehouse.

Not all the royal clubs were able to survive, however. Royal Isle of Wight, Royal Eastbourne Ladies and Royal Ashdown Ladies are now deceased, whilst Royal Cornwall's clubhouse became a café. (Royal) Curragh has neither died nor had its royal title rescinded, but chooses not to use the name.

As a result Royal Dublin is the only existing true royal club in Eire. Royal Tara appears on lists, but bestowed the title upon itself as a nod to the nearby hills of Tara where the Irish kings used to live.

The right to the royal title is granted by a sovereign or a member of the royal house, the most recent recipient being Royal Troon (1978), the only one to have been given the status in the reign of the present monarch.

Often the impetus is geographical. For instance there are five royal clubs in East Anglia, three more than in the whole of Wales (Royal Portcawl and Royal St David's). The reason is probably that the future Edward VII spent a lot of time at Sandringham and was not averse to the occasional round of golf.

Sometimes the army was instrumental in the process. There are many such courses in Britain and even more overseas. But however the title came about, they all have intriguing stories to tell. And who knows, such is the interest of the present Duke of York, a far more accomplished player than some of his predecessors, that there may be one or two more by the end of the decade.

(*The Sunley Book of Royal Golf* by Sir Peter Allen was a source of much useful information in the course of our research for the current golf guide)

Mark Reason, who also introduces each region, is Golf Correspondent of The Sunday Telegraph.

ROYAL GOLF CLUBS ABROAD
by Mark Reason

Although the United States now bestrides the game like a giant mollusc, it is a slightly humbling thought for Americans that golf came to Canada well ahead of their own development of the game. Indeed golf came to India before the game really got going in the States and Royal Calcutta is the oldest titled course outside Britain, a product of Commonwealth and Empire.

The course once stood on the site of Calcutta International Airport at Dum Dum, before a new one was hacked out of the jungle. But although Calcutta was granted royal status in 1912, it wasn't until 34 years later that the first Indian members were admitted. The other great course of India, Royal Bombay, no longer exists although the silver medal that it presented to the R&A in 1845 is still played for at the Spring Meeting.

Royal Montreal and Royal Quebec also have considerable history. The two clubs used to hold matches to which the members would travel overnight on riverboat steamers. The Centennial of Golf in North America notes with some levity, "The unofficial records state that these journeys were characterised by long hours of blissful slumber, a prodigious consumption of lemonade and a complete absence of card games".

Royal Ottawa and Royal Colwood on Vancouver Island are Canada's other two royal courses, although Australia has the largest contingent with eight. In the face of such abundance it is strange that New Zealand does not possess a single royal course.

Royal Adelaide is Australia's oldest club to be given royal status, although Royal Melbourne is its most highly regarded and unfortunately also its snootiest. Given Melbourne's airs and graces it must be pointed out that when Lieutenant Governor Sir John Madden reopened the course in 1901 he turned up in top hat and tails and promptly hit an air shot.

There are many quirks to the royal courses, but few better the local rule at the 12th hole of Royal Queensland. Due to the building of a bridge the tee-shot has to be played through an arch, but relief is granted if the player misses the gap.

South Africa's four royal courses (at Cape Town, Johannesburg, Durban and Port Alfred) also had their hazards. The original greens at Royal Port Alfred were built by convict labour and formed from shell grit, Royal Johannesburg's President was imprisoned under sentence of death and its first captain also jailed and Royal Cape is aerated by mole snakes.

Fortunately they are considerably less harmful than the snakes that used to congregate in the rocks by the fourth tee of Royal Harare. Any ball finishing in those rocks was deemed to be lost. At least Harare was surrounded by fences. In 1919 a leopard was shot between the fourteenth and fifteenth holes of Royal Nairobi.

Royal Malta's hazards were rather more man-made, although not by the golf course architect. The original nine-hole course was built amongst the walls and ditches of the island's historic fortifications. Something a little "toey" could easily finish lodged in one of the 20ft walls that lined the fairways.

The Far East is also colonised by royal golf courses. Sri Lanka, Singapore and Malaysia all have courses that were granted royal status as does Royal Hong Kong. Designated the best player in our group (not much of an honour, as it happens) I was given a golf ball with which to play the opening shot of our round at Royal Hong Kong. The thing disappeared off in a trail of red smoke before exploding, much to the mirth of the locals whose local joke shop must still have much 19th century stock.

There are other countries that bestow royal titles. Belgium (Henry Cotton was the professional at Royal Waterloo in the thirties) and Spain have several such clubs. Baghdad and Teheran had royal courses that have not survived the new regimes, the sultans have ennobled several in Malaysia, King Hassan II of Morocco was a player and patron and even Samoa and Nepal have royal courses.

Membership of a royal club in Britain will not entitle you to play these latter courses, but it does facilitate playing rights at all those courses around the world elevated by the British Royal Household. That turns out to be both quite a privilege and a hazard.

The clubhouse at Royal Quebec Golf Club

THE ROYAL HOUSEHOLD GOLF CLUB

by Mark Reason

The nine-hole course in Windsor Park is probably the most difficult to get on in the world as it is for members of the Royal Household and staff to play on. The secrecy surrounding it implies that it is either the best course in the world or the worst. When Sir Peter Allen tried to gain access for *The Sunley Book of Royal Golf,* the Lord Chamberlain's office turned down the request on security grounds.

So like Sir Peter Allen we are forced to go to Sir Frederick Ponsonby's *Recollections of Three Reigns* for a brief synopsis of the golf course's genesis, the result of King Edward VII's enthusiasm for the game.

Ponsonby writes, "I asked Mr Mure Ferguson, a distinguished amateur player who had laid out a course called New Zealand at Woking, to come down and sketch the Windsor Castle links. He came down and took infinite trouble. We had men with stakes to mark the right and left of each bunker, and a man with a tape measure. Mure Fergusson succeeded in laying out nine good holes ending up just below the East Terrace, and I gave instructions to the farm bailiff to have the bunkers made."

What follows is Windsor Castle meets Fawlty Towers. Two months later Ponson-by received a furious letter from the King saying that the park had been ruined and that the bunkers should be obliterated. The man who had constructed the 'bunkers' didn't have a clue as to what was required and "the result was that the ground looked like a graveyard with tombstones dotted around … He said that he proposed to make the last bunker in the shape of a Victoria Cross with flowers." Inevitably he was sacked and the work was saved by the local pro from Datchet. A favoured few were allowed onto the course including Ben Sayers, who once exclaimed "very good direction, Your Majesty" after the King had hideously topped a drive.

There is also a nine hole parkland course at Balmoral, with two tees at each hole to allow the possibility of playing a slightly manufactured 18 holes. You could combine the courses at Windsor and Balmoral to come up with a genuine eighteen holes, but the walk from the ninth green to the tenth tee would be an awful strain. Perhaps Colin Montgomerie could be persuaded to play the course on behalf of charity – there are plenty who would give generously to the cause to see Monty take on a walk like that.

THE BRITISH EMPIRE OF GOLF
by John Gibb

Golf is one of a lasting legacies of the British Empire. In every continent, in every big city we visit, the chances are that somewhere close by is a tricky little eighteen holes which was built by the Scots. Nineteenth century Scots were like moles. Unable to stop digging they would spend their lives laying railways or excavating mines or something industrious, and during the weekends, they'd build themselves a golf course to remind them of home. If you go to Venice for instance, there's a lovely old links at the end of the Lido carved out of wasteland in the 20s by someone from Glasgow called Cruikshank. The original Greenbrier in West Virginia was built by homesick Scottish railwaymen laying a line between Washington and Charleston. The eminent Tollygunge Club in Calcutta was laid out by Sir William Cruikshank, another Scot, and the sublimely eccentric course at Naldera near Simla was the personal creation of the viceroy, Lord Curzon. The legendary Colt, architect of St Cloud in Paris was also responsible for Sunningdale and Swinley Forrest. Admittedly he was English but there was almost certainly a bit of Scot in him somewhere.

So arrive in any city in Europe and you'll find a well established golf course nearby, probably designed or set up by the British, and, faced with hours of shopping or a morning trudging round St. Mark's Square, what a welcome alternative a round of golf on an unfamiliar course will be.

The English have long been expert at the actual business of clubs. They loved them because it afforded them the pleasure of creating a gathering of like minded middle class people and allowed them to arrange things in such a way as to make it impossible for the lower classes to get in. Heaven. Clubs need secretaries, subservient staff and, above all, Rules. The first ground rule in the book at the National Golf Links of America in Long Island, a classic Knickerbocker golf club created by the great, bald, plus foured, dog hating Scotsman Charles Blair MacDonald, says, 'Dogs shall not be allowed in the clubhouse or on the club grounds. Violators of this rule are subject to a fine of $25.'

Golf clubs abroad have stuck with the system invented by the British, reluctantly adapting the regulations to allow women in to the club where necessary, and the rules of the game administered by the Royal and Ancient Golf Club of St. Andrews stand unchallenged wherever you go. That is why we can rest assured that if we make the effort to get a game next time we find ourselves in a foreign city with nothing to do, the odds are that a visit to the local golf club will be a reassuring and familiar experience.

Our ancestors have thus been responsible for providing us all with a little bit of home wherever we wander. Well seasoned travellers should never leave Britain without a letter from the Secretary of their club introducing them to the Secretary of the course in whichever city they find themselves. The Americans have MacDonald's to remind them of home. We have golf.

From Paris to Budapest ...
a range of city gem courses

Rome

I love Fiuggi. It's about forty minutes drive from Rome towards Lazio. There's a spa, the water of which is apparently patronised by the Vatican and has been shown to successfully relieve the Pope's kidney-stones. Sadly, the communist mayor of Fiuggi built the course above the source of the priceless water, simultaneously prohibiting the use of fertilisers and weed-killers. The fairways are thus a mixture of grass and dandelion and in the spring the rough is a riot of wildflowers. In spite of this, Fiuggi is a unique golfing experience. Narrow, with small greens, it is a serious test of golf. Only around 6,000 metres long, it is the lush rough which makes it tricky and the blue, often snow capped Appenine hills which make it memorable. Tel: (39) 0 7755 15250

Geneva

About ten miles up on the north side about half way to Lausanne, is The Domaine Imperial. It was designed by Pete Dye, and although American in style it's not one of those long slogs and is only 6346 metres from the championship tees. The club is on the banks of the lake with views across to the Alps. This a shot-makers course with heavily defended greens and a series of long, narrow, tree lined par fours. The club-house, a Napoleonic Villa once the home of the Emperor's brother, is comfortable and the green fees, food and drink are, of course, expensive. It's easy to walk it

and anyway, they won't hire you a buggy without a note from your doctor. Tel: (41) 022 999 0600

Paris

Golf de St Cloud is just across the Periferique from the Bois de Boulogne. There are two Colt designed courses, Le Vert is recognised as the more senior, although Le Jaune, shorter and built later, should not be sniffed at. St. Cloud is a lovely old Belle Epoque club, where the Duke of Windsor was a member. For years they preserved his locker with the old co-respondent shoes and knickerbockers, just as they were when he died. It is a senior parkland course through wooded rough with steep slopes and tight, narrow fairways and they've played the French Open here many times. It is particularly beautiful in the Autumn with the views across the City and the Eiffel tower coming into view above the trees.
Tel: (33) 01 47 010185

Edinburgh

Around ten miles to the east of Edinburgh, Royal Musselburgh, next to the sublime and exclusive Muirfield is a short parkland course with only one par 5. It was originally designed by James Braid and updated by Mungo Park in 1939. It's owned by the Scottish Union of Railworkers and opened for business in 1774, although golf was played on these links long before that. The clubhouse was once a hunting lodge and it has a secret tucked away on the first floor where a priceless collection of historic golf memorabilia has been amassed by the Union and has become one of their most valuable assets. Musselburgh is friendly, you'll always get a game, and it's a joy to play. The beer's subsidised too. Tel: (44) 01875 810 276

Venice

The 75 year old Club Venezia at Alberoni on the Lido has one of the loveliest courses in Europe. The American industrialist and golf addict, Henry Ford, suggested to the hotelier Count Volpi di Misurata in 1924 that 'a golf club in Venice might be a good idea.' The Count hired a Glaswegian called Cruikshank who produced nine holes by the end of the 1920s. The course was finished off in 1950 by C.K. Cotton.

The course has matured into a wonderland of pine, olive grove, oak and exotic woodland, alive with wildlife and crisscrossed with tidal inlets. Although, at 6,200 metres, it is not long, it is tricky and narrow, bending and twisting and testing you out with small, subtle greens and sloping fairways. The credentials of the Venezia are impeccable. The Duke of Windsor used to play here and Arnold Palmer holds the course record of 67. They've played the Italian open here three times.

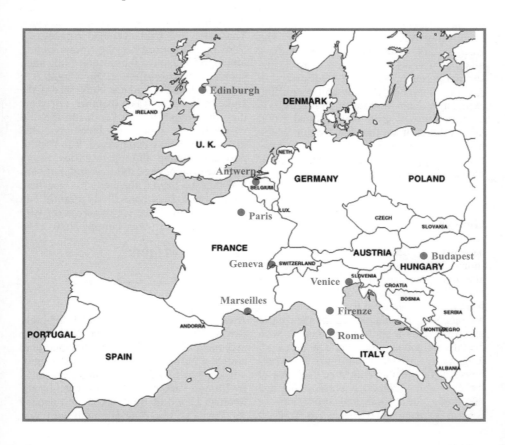

Johnny Miller, at the height of his powers, was leading by two strokes in the final round in 1974, when the eighteenth did for him and he put his ball out of bounds and lost by one stroke. Tel: (39) 041 731 333.

Marseilles

Fregate, up in the hills between Marseilles and Toulon is one of the hidden jewels of the south of France. Laid out in 1930, it has never been easy. A tight par 72 with precipitous, winding fairways and wonderful views out over the Mediterranean, Fregate keeps you on your toes. Designed by Ronald Fream, the course is set amongst vineyards and olive groves and, I believe, is one of the most beautiful courses in France. After you've played it, you won't forget the 397, narrow par four tenth which runs through a pinewood with the sea below and the fairway sloping to your right. It takes your breath away. It's not just the course you'll remember though, it's the food in the clubhouse and the immaculate greens. Tel: 9330 0494 293800.

Firenze

The Florence Cub in Ugolino, high up in the Chianti landscape, was formed in 1889 and is the oldest golf club in Italy. It's posh and the founders were the British and American Ambassadors, the Duke and Duchess of Sutherland and a long list of Italian nobility. There's an old photograph of an elegant woman golfer in a saucy bonnet hanging behind the bar and I had a feeling it was Joyce Wethered, but discovered later that she was Margery Maquey Caccia, the Secretary's handsome wife photographed smiting an athletic spoon from the fifth fairway in 1920.

The course, designed by the Englishmen Gammon and Bland, runs around the crest of a hillside and the steep sloping fairways make it a test to be reckoned with. Ugolino has pedigree as well as age.

This was where Bernard Langer won his epic battle with Severiano Ballesteros in the play off for the Italian Open in '83. While I enjoyed the course, I won't forget the après golf in the old bar where I was served the best plate of pasta I have ever eaten. Tel: (39) 055 2301 009.

Antwerp

I have a feeling that some youths from Knokke le Zoute managed to achieve something heroic in a Eurovision song contest in the seventies. But it's golf that matters here. I once played the course with Florie Van Donc and he said it was one of the great European courses. This is tight and tricky, especially when the wind is blowing. It is well worth a visit in the spring or autumn. The course was designed in the early nineteenth century by the great H.S. Colt, and it's a genuine links. In the winter, it's a stinker, in fact it's probably one of the best seaside courses in Europe. There are seven rooms where you can stay in the clubhouse and the food is marvellous. Tel: (32) 050 60 12 27.

Budapest

The Old Lake Golf And Country Club at Tata about 40 miles from Budapest was built eight years ago in the Gerecse foothills on the hunting estates of Count Eszterhazy. The 5,800 metre course is carefully looked after; there's even a Scottish teaching pro called Damian MacPherson. I loved the way the holes have been laid out; individually designed and enclosed in the forest.

This course is not simple; the Hungarians are uninhibited about sharp angled dog legs and tight approach shots; but it's beautiful to look at and refreshing to play 18 holes unencumbered by American style lakes and ravines. The Diana Hotel a few yards from the clubhouse in Eszterhazy's old hunting lodge has a deep understanding of the needs of tired, hungry golfers. Tel: (36) 34 587 620.

LINKS COURSES

GOLFING HOTELS

From Cornwall to St Andrews, a selection of good places to stay at or near some of the great golf courses across the UK

Five Lakes Resort
Colchester Road, Maldon, Essex CM9 8HX
Tel: 01621 862316   Fax: 01621 862315
E-mail: enquiries@fivelakes.co.uk
4-Star hotel with two 18-hole golf courses, plus golf academy and floodlit driving range.

The Springs Hotel & Golf Club
Wallingford Road, North Stoke, Wallingford,
Oxfordshire OX10 6BE
Tel: 01491-836687   Fax:01491-836877
E-mail: info@thespringshotel.com
Attractive Tudor-style country house with 18-hole par 72 golf course. Set in landscaped gardens, overlooking a spring-fed lake in the heart of the Thames Valley.

Barnham Broom Hotel & Golf Club
Honingham Road, Barnham Broom, Norwich
NR9 4DD
Tel: 01603 759393
52 en-suite bedrooms with two 18-hole golf courses plus golf school, indoor golf simulator and leisure facilities including swimming pool.

Rudding Park Hotel & Golf Club
Follifoot, Harrogate, North Yorkshire HG3 1JH
Tel: 01423 871350   Fax: 01423 872286
E-mail: sales@ruddingpark.com
Rudding Park is an ideal venue for the discerning golfer. The contemporary award-winning AA 4 Red Star hotel and AA 2-Rosette Clocktower Restaurant, coupled with the magnificent 18-hole, par 72, parkland golf course, ensures a relaxing break.

Petwood Hotel
Woodhall Spa, Lincolnshire LN10 6QF
Tel: 01526 352411   Fax: 01526 353473
E-mail: reception@petwood.co.uk
Delightful Edwardian country house hotel, set in 30 acres of gardens and woodland. Ideally placed for Woodhall Spa Golf Course.

Metropole Hotel
Portland Street, Southport PR8 1LL
Tel: 01704 536836   Fax: 01704 549041
E-mail: metropole.southport@btinternet.com
2-Star hotel, centrally situated and close to Royal Birkdale and 5 other championship courses.

Crusoe Hotel
2 Main Street, Lower Largo, Fife KY8 6BT
Tel: 01333 320759
E-mail: relax@crusoehotel.co.uk
Great waterside location with own harbour just 10 minutes from St Andrews. In the heart of golf country with Lundin Links, Crail, Ladybank and St Andrews close by.

Caer Beris Manor
Builth Wells, Powys LD2 3NP
Tel: 01982 552601   Fax 01982 552506
E-mail: caerberismanor@btinternet.com
First built in 1093, Caer Beris Manor has been transformed into a 3-Star real country house hotel, adjacent to the 18-hole parkland course at Builth Wells.

The Chequers Inn
Chequers Lane, Fladbury, Nr Pershore, Worcs
WR10 2PZ
Tel: 01386 860276   Fax: 01386 861286.
Good food and accommodation in the relaxing atmosphere of a country inn, with easy access to several golf courses including Broadway, The Vale and Evesham.

Devere Slaley Hall Hotel
Hexham, Nr Newcastle Upon Tyne NE47 OBY
Tel: 01434 673350   Fax: 01434 673962.
E-mail: slaley.hall@devere-hotels.com
International golf resort.

Piperdam Golf & Leisure Resort
Fowlis, Dundee, Angus DD2 5LP
Tel: 01382 581374   Fax: 01382 581102
E-mail: golf@piperdam.com
Twenty 4-Star Lodges close to the Osprey Par 72 Golf Course.

Lostwithiel Hotel, Golf & Country Club
Lower Polscoe, Lostwithiel, Cornwall
PL22 OHQ
Tel: 01208 873550   Fax: 01208 873479
E-mail: reception@golf-hotel.co.uk
Close to the Eden Project, this fine hotel is set amongst 150 acres of undulating countryside and has a superb 18-hole golf course with floodlit driving range.

Tewkesbury Park Hotel
Lincoln Green Lane, Tewkesbury, Gloucestershire
GL20 7DN
Tel: 01684 295405   Fax: 01684 292386
*Set in 176 acres of parkland, which includes an
18-hole championship golf course, this Victorian
manor house has panoramic views of the
Gloucestershire countryside.*

Heronston Hotel
Ewenny Road, Bridgend, South Wales
CF35 5AW
Tel: 01656 668811   Fax: 01656 767391
E-mail: heronston@bestwestern.co.uk
*Situated in the heart of Glamorgan, the Heronston
Hotel offers 75 en-suite bedrooms, with Leisure
Club, and is just minutes from Royal Porthcawl
and a dozen other excellent golf clubs.*

Highbullen Hotel
Chittlehamholt, Umberleigh, North Devon
EX37 9HD
Tel: 01769 540561   Fax: 01769 540492
E-mail: info@highbullen.co.uk
*Luxury hotel with award winning golf course set in
richly wooded parkland, with breathtaking views
towards Dartmoor and Exmoor.*

Bovey Castle
Bovey Castle, Dartmoor National Park, Devon
TQ13 8RE
Tel: 01647 445016. Fax: 01647 445020.
E-mail: enquiries@boveycastle.com
*Built in 1907, Bovey Castle offers luxurious
accommodation in the heart of Dartmoor National
Park, with a championship golf course designed as
a companion to Gleneagles and Turnberry.*

Marriott Worsley Park Hotel
Worsley Park, Worsley, Manchester. M28 2QT.
Tel: 0161 975 2000   Fax: 0161 799 6341
E-mail: golfsales.worsleypark1
@marriotthotels.co.uk
*Superb dining facilities and 158 en-suite bedrooms
set in the historical Worsley Park, plus 18-hole par
71 championship parkland golf course.*

Deer Park Hotel and Golf Courses
Howth, Co Dublin, Republic or I reland
Tel: (01) 832 2624   Fax: (01) 839 2405
E-mail: sales@deerpark.iol.ie
*With spectacular views over Dublin Bay and the
North-Eastern coastline and 80 superb en-suite*

*rooms, Deer Park is also Ireland's largest golf
complex with 4 courses to choose from.*

Carlyon Bay Hotel
St Austell, Cornwall PL25 3RD
Tel: 01726 812304
*4-Star (AA/RAC) hotel in stunning cliff top loca-
tion, with 2 pools, tennis, health and beauty, plus
superb 18 hole championship golf course (free to
residents).*

The Bell Hotel
The Quay, Sandwich, Kent CT13 9QB
Tel: 01304 613388. Fax: 01304 615308.
*The Bell is the perfect golfers' base, close to Royal
St George, Prince's and Royal Cinque Ports clubs.
Situated in a delightful historic area The Bell
offers comfort, relaxation and friendly service.*

Fairways Hotel
Seafront, Porthcawl CF36 3LS
Tel: 01656 782085   Fax: 01656 785351
*3-star (AA/RAC) recently refurbished 18th-century
building with individually designed en-suite rooms.
Within easy reach of Royal Porthcawl and Pyle
and Kenfig Golf Courses.*

Aldwark Manor Hotel
Aldwark, Nr Alne, York YO61 1UF
Tel: 01347 838146   Fax: 01347 838867
*This 60 bedroom Victorian manor was built in
1856, and is set in 120 acres of beautiful parkland
with the River Ure meandering through the
grounds, and an 18-hole par 72 course with
island greens.*

Coulsdon Manor Hotel
Coulsdon Court Road, Old Coulsdon, Nr Croydon,
Surrey CR5 2LL
Tel: 020 8668 0414   Fax: 020 8668 3118
E-mail: coulsdonmanor@marstonhotels.com
*This 35 bedroom, 4-star hotel was built in the
1850's and is set in 140 acres of parkland with an
excellent 18 hole, par 70 golf course.*

Hellidon Lakes Hotel
Hellidon, Daventry, Northamptonshire
NN11 6GG
Tel: 01327 262550   Fax: 01327 262559
*51 en-suite bedrooms set in glorious unspoilt
countryside with gently rolling hills and valleys,
plus an amazing 27 hole championship golf
course.*

HOW TO USE THE GUIDE

The country is divided into regions. There are some strange anomalies which are caused primarily by some courses belonging to golf unions that do not necessarily correspond to local government boundaries.

There is a comprehensive index, if you know the name of the club you want to find out about. Each club has a phone number, postal address and relevant travel directions plus a brief description of the type of course.

There is also a separate listing of links courses. Although this is the indeterminate land on which the game originated, even now links golf is still pretty much exclusive to Britain and Ireland. We have reflected that by listing 'links courses' with their locations.

We have tried to indicate to golfers when they will be welcome at each course and whether individuals or societies are allowed. There is also a short description of the catering facilities each club provides.

Unless separate telephone numbers are supplied for Secretary, Professional, etc., the main telephone number will reach all departments

It is, of course, a common courtesy to telephone any club you plan to visit to check both the availability of the date you plan to play and also any restrictions which may be placed on visitors. In the main it is recommended to make a tee-off time reservation, thus preventing any frustrating delays at the courses. Always remember to leave plenty of time to get to the course – it will improve your enjoyment and almost certainly your play!

Most clubs provide catering facilities for societies and many make a point of offering special packages that include both refreshments, food and golf. Again it is vital to ring in advance to check prices and the times that kitchens are open as well as the range of services on offer.

Prices. This is the main bone of contention with every golfer. Every care has been taken to list accurate prices for a round or a day ticket, but it is quite usual for the green fees to change from season to season and often from day to day. Some clubs offer special twilight fees, while others habitually charge more at weekends and on Bank Holidays.

Again it is vital that golfers check the prices, which can sometimes rise quite dramatically, before they step into the car or before they plan a trip. Often clubs are open to negotiating special deals but this is more likely to be achieved before rather than after arriving at the course.

All the information on green fees, club policy on visitors, societies, catering, etc has been gleaned from the secretaries, managers and professionals and *The Sunday Telegraph* thanks them for their time.

Comments. *The Sunday Telegraph* welcomes feedback on the book and comments on courses that readers visit. We would also be keen to hear of alterations, errors or extensions regarding any of the courses. Comments should be addressed to The Publisher, Telegraph Books, 1 Canada Square, Canary Wharf, London E14 5DT.

KEY TO COURSE DETAILS

☎ Telephone	† Visitors	🛍 Societies
▭ Email	ⵊ Practice Ranges	🍽 Catering
⛁ Website	Ⅰ Green Fees	⛌ Hotels

℧ Telegraph Open Fairways Club

KEY TO THE MAPS

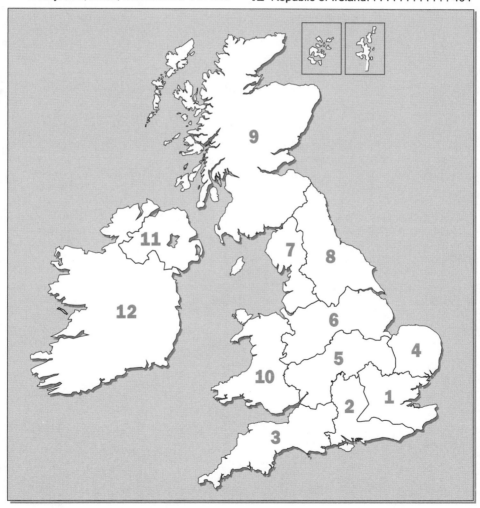

LONDON AND THE HOME COUNTIES

1A

Surrey, Kent, South London

Here lies an abundance of royal land and so it is no surprise that this region should have no fewer than five royal courses in Wimbledon, Mid-Surrey, Blackheath, St George's and Cinque Ports. Blackheath is believed to have been golfing land as far back as the early 17th century and Wimbledon is one of the oldest royal clubs in England.

Many people's initial expectations of Surrey are probably prosaically similar to those of CS Lewis when he arrived there for the first time. He had been told that Surrey was "suburban". Instead Lewis discovered, "little hills, watered valleys, and wooded commons which ranked by my Wyvernian and Irish standards as forests; bracken everywhere; a world of red and russet and yellowish greens".

It is fertile land on which to build golf courses and once people got started – Woking was founded in 1893 by "a few mad barristers" – there was no stopping them. Willie Park, JF Abercromby, James Braid and JH Taylor began designing all over the county.

Even in those years before the Great War, when men were men and women were voteless, there were limits to what was tolerable. Fed up with discrimination, one Mrs Lubbock decided that if men were so determined to keep her off Surrey's golf courses on a Sunday then she would go ahead and build her own. West Hill was the child of her determination.

West Hill and the Addington – one of the best courses within London's immediate sprawl and much improved in its condition since its more derelict years of recent times – are a cause of debate between two of golf's greatest writers. Henry Longhurst believed the Addington's par three thirteenth to be the best short hole on inland Britain. A perfectly struck shot into this green represented "the sweetest satisfaction that golf has to offer".

Bernard Darwin was a West Hill man. To him the par three fifteenth, flanked by trees, was the best in England. There is an obvious scenic similarity between the two holes so perhaps Longhurst's and Darwin's difference is not as great as it might seem.

Surrey is bulging with superb holes and courses. Sunningdale, Wentworth and Walton Heath – each has two first rate courses. Any of Worplesdon, Hindhead, St George's Hill, Coombe Hill and Hankley Common would be the feature course of a lesser golfing county.

Kent may not have quite so many five star courses as Surrey, but the best in the county are amongst the best in the country. Royal St George's remains the only Open Championship venue south of Lancashire. It can be a swine when the wind blows, but even then you have to admire its grandeur through gritted teeth. As Bill Deedes said, "You can be in the soup at St George's, but it is delicious". So is the beer served in proper tankards.

Neighbouring Prince's is another good test while Royal Cinque Ports has staged two Open Championships and been denied three more by war and salt water. The other Kent links not to be missed is Littlestone.

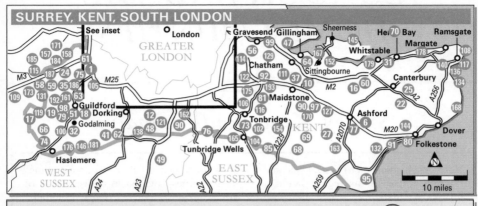

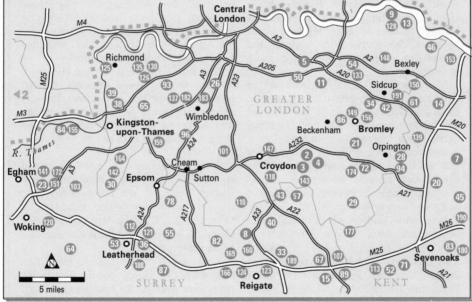

1A 1 **Abbey Moor**
Green Lane, Addlestone, Surrey,
KT15 2XU
☎ 01932 570741, Fax 577111,
Pro 570765, Rest/Bar 570293
Leave M25 at Junction 11 and proceed
on St Peter's Way towards Weybridge:
take right turn at large roundabout
towards Addlestone on A318, then over
railway bridge; take 2nd turning right at
small roundabout into Green Lane;
course 0.5 mile on right.
Public parkland course.
Pro Paul Tigwell; Founded 1991
Designed by David Walker
9 holes, 5104 yards, S.S.S. 66
† Welcome WD and WE; advisable
to book early.
⌶ WD £10; WE £11.50.
⌷ Any time; terms on application.
🍽 Full Bar.
🏷 White Lodge.

1A 2 **The Addington**
205 Shirley Church Road, Croydon,
Surrey, CR0 5AB
🖥 theaddgc@dialstart.net
☎ 020 8777 1055, Fax 6661
Through Addington Village, 2.5 miles
from East Croydon.
Heather, Bracken, Silver Birch and
Pine.
Founded 1913
Designed by JF Ambercromby
18 holes, 6338 yards, S.S.S. 71
† WD only.
⌶ WD £65.
⌷ WD only; terms on application.
🍽 Restaurant and Bar.

1A 3 **Addington Court**
Featherbed Lane, Croydon, Surrey,
CR0 9AA

KEY							
1	Abbey Moor	40	Coulsdon Manor	78	Horton Park CC	117	Prince's
2	The Addington	41	The Cranleigh Golf and	79	Hurtmore	118	Purley Downs
3	Addington Court		Leisure Club	80	Hythe Imperial	119	Puttenham
4	Addington Palace	42	Cray Valley	81	Kings Hill	120	Pyrford
5	Aquarius	43	Croham Hurst	82	Kingswood Golf & CC	121	Redhill & Reigate
6	Ashford (Kent)	44	Cuddington	83	Knole Park	122	Redlibbets
7	Austin Lodge	45	Darenth Valley	84	Laleham	123	Reigate Heath
8	Banstead Downs	46	Dartford	85	Lamberhurst	124	Reigate Hill
9	Barnehurst	47	Deangate Ridge	86	Langley Park	125	Richmond
10	Bearsted	48	Dorking	87	Leatherhead	126	Richmond Park
11	Beckenham Place Park	49	The Drift	88	Leeds Castle	127	The Ridge
12	Betchworth Park	50	Dulwich & Sydenham Hill	89	Limpsfield Chart	128	Riverside
13	Bexleyheath	51	Dunsfold Aerodrome	90	Lingfield Park	129	Rochester & Cobham Pk
14	Birchwood Park	52	Edenbridge G&CC	91	Littlestone	130	Roehampton
15	Bletchingley	53	Effingham	92	The London	131	Roker Park
16	Boughton	54	Eltham Warren	93	London Scottish	132	Romney Warren
17	Bowenhurst	55	Epsom	94	Lullingstone Park	133	Royal Blackheath
18	Bramley	56	Falcon Valley	95	Lydd	134	Royal Cinque Ports
19	Broadwater Park	57	Farleigh Court	96	Malden	135	Royal Mid-Surrey
20	Broke Hill	58	Farnham	97	Marriott Tudor Pk CC	136	Royal St George's
21	Bromley	59	Farnham Park	98	Merrist Wood	137	Royal Wimbledon
22	Broome Park CC	60	Faversham	99	Mid-Kent	138	Rusper
23	Burhill	61	Fawkham Valley	100	Milford	139	Ruxley
24	Camberley Heath	62	Foxhills Club and Resort	101	Mitcham	140	St Augustine's
25	Canterbury	63	Gatton Manor	102	Moatlands	141	St George's Hill
26	Central London GC	64	Goal Farm Par 3	103	Moore Place	142	Sandown Golf Centre
27	Chart Hills	65	Guildford	104	Nevill	143	Selsdon Pk Hotel & GC
28	Chelsfield Lakes	66	Hampton Court Palace	105	New Zealand Golf Club	144	Sene Valley
29	Cherry Lodge		Golf Club	106	Nizels	145	Sheerness
30	Chessington	67	Hankley Common	107	North Downs	146	Shillinglee Park
31	Chestfield	68	Hawkhurst	108	North Foreland	147	Shirley Park
32	Chiddingfold	69	Hemsted Forest	109	Oak Park	148	Shooters Hill
33	Chipstead	70	Herne Bay	110	Oaks Sports Centre	149	Shortlands
34	Chislehurst	71	Hever Castle	111	Oastpark	150	Sidcup
35	Chobham	72	High Elms	112	Pachesham Park Golf	151	Silvermere
36	Clandon Regis	73	Hilden		Centre	152	Sittingbourne & Milton
37	Cobtree Manor Park	74	Hindhead	113	Park Wood		Regis
38	Coombe Hill	75	Hoebridge Golf Centre	114	Pedham Place	153	Southern Valley
39	Coombe Wood	76	Holtye	115	Pine Ridge Golf Centre	154	Staplehurst Park
		77	Homelands B'golf Centre	116	Poult Wood	155	Sunbury
						156	Sundridge Park
						157	Sunningdale
						158	Sunningdale Ladies
						159	Surbiton
						160	Surrey National
						161	Sutton Green
						162	Tandridge
						163	Tenterden
						164	Thames Ditton & Esher
						165	Tunbridge Wells
						166	Tyrrells Wood
						167	Upchurch River Valley
						168	Walmer & Kingsdown
						169	Walton Heath
						170	Weald of Kent
						171	Wentworth
						172	West Byfleet
						173	West Hill
						174	West Kent
						175	West Malling
						176	West Surrey
						177	Westerham
						178	Westgate & Birchington
						179	Whitstable & Seasalter
						180	Wildernesse
						181	Wildwood
						182	Wimbledon Common
						183	Wimbledon Park
						184	Windlemere
						185	Windlesham
						186	The Wisley
						187	Woking
						188	The Woldingham Club
						189	Woodcote Park
						190	Woodlands Manor
						191	World of Golf (Jack
							Nicklaus GC)
						192	Worplesdon
						193	Wrotham Heath

☎ 020 8657 0281, Fax 8651 0282,
Sec 8651 0282, Pro 8657 0281,
Rest/Bar 8657 0281
2 miles E of Croydon off the B281 in
Addington Village.
Undulating parkland course.
Pro Gordon Dawson; Founded 1931
Designed by F. Hawtree Snr
✳ Two-tier range.
✝ Welcome.
♦ WD £17; WE £20.
☞ Welcome by prior arrangement;
catering packages available.
◉ Full catering facilities.
⬥ Selsdon Park.

1A 4 **Addington Palace**

Gravel Hill, Addington Park, Croydon,
Surrey, CR0 5BB
☎ 020 8654 3061, Fax 8655 3632,
Pro 8654 1786, Sec 8654 3061, Bar
8654 2650, Rest 8655 1290
2 miles east of Croydon on the A212.
Undulating parkland course.
Pro Roger Williams; Founded 1927
Designed by JH Taylor
18 holes, 6304 yards, S.S.S. 71

✝ Welcome if accompanied by a
member.
♦ WD £35; everyone welcome;
members only at weekends, no charge.
☞ Welcome Tues, Wed, Fri; details
on application; £57.
◉ Bar and catering facilities.
⬥ The Selsdon Park.

1A 5 **Aquarius**

Marmora Road, Honor Oak, London,
SE22 ORY
✉ aquariusgolfclub@btopenworld.com
☎ 020 8693 1626, Pro 8693 1811
Set around and on top of an
underground reservoir.
Pro Fred Private; Founded 1912
9 holes, 5465 yards, S.S.S. 66
✝ Welcome with members.
♦ WD £10; WE £10.
⬥ Bromley Court, Queens at Crystal
Palace.

1A 6 **Ashford (Kent)**

Sandyhurst Lane, Ashford, Kent,
TN25 4NT

☎ 01233 620180, Fax 622655,
Pro 629644, Sec 622655,
Rest/Bar 620180
Welcome with handicap certs.
Parkland course.
Pro Hugh Sherman; Founded 1903
Designed by CK Cotton
18 holes, 6263 yards, S.S.S. 70
✝ Course is 1.5 miles from Junction
9 on the M20.
♦ WD £24; WE £40.
☞ Tues, Thurs; packages available;
£25-~£45.
◉ Bar and restaurant.

1A 7 **Austin Lodge** ♛

Upper Austin Lodge Road, Eynsford,
Kent, DA4 OHU
✉ greghaenen@hotmail.com
☎ 01322 863000, Fax 862406
A225 to Eynsford station; course is in
road behind station.
Rolling parkland course.
Pro Greg Haenen; Founded 1991
Designed by Peter Bevan & Mike
Walsh
18 holes, 7200 yards, S.S.S. 73

🏌 Driving range.
† Welcome.
£ WD £22; WE £30 to 13.00, £22 after 13.00.
↻ Mon-Fri; WE after 12.00.
🍴 Meals and bar.
🛏 Castle, Eynsford.

1A 8 Banstead Downs
Burdon Lane, Belmont, Sutton, Surrey, SM2 7DD
📧 bdgc@online.co.uk
☎ 020 8642 2284, Fax 8642 5252, Pro 8642 6884, Rest/Bar 8624 9286
On A217 North from M25 Junction 8.
Downland course.
Pro Ian Golding; Founded 1890
Designed by JH Taylor/J Braid
18 holes, 6194 yards, S.S.S. 69
🏌 Practice area.
† Welcome WD; WE with member only.
£ WD £35.
↻ Welcome, Thurs only; full day's golf and catering £57.
🍴 Full clubhouse facilities.

1A 9 Barnhurst
Mayplace Road East, Bexleyheath, Kent, DA7 6JU
☎ 01322 551205, Fax 528483, Sec 523746, Rest/Bar 552952
N of Crayford town centre.
Mature inland course.
Founded 1904
Designed by James Braid
9 holes, 5474 yards, S.S.S. 68
† Welcome.
£ WD £8.45; WE £11.55.
↻ Welcome; terms available on application.
🍴 Full facilities and function room.
🛏 Swallow, Bexleyheath.

1A 10 Bearsted
Ware Street, Bearsted, Kent, ME14 4PQ
☎ 01622 738389, Fax 735608, Pro 738204, Sec 738198, Rest/Bar 738389
M20 to Junction 7 and follow Bearsted Green signs.
Parkland course.
Pro Tim Simpson; Founded 1895
Designed by Golf Landscapes
18 holes, 6486 yards, S.S.S. 71
† Welcome with handicap certs.
£ WD £32; WE £37 with members only.
↻ Tues-Fri; 36 holes of golf, coffee, lunch and dinner; £59.50.
🍴 Full facilities.

🛏 The Hilton, Tudor Park, Great Danes.

1A 11 Beckenham Place Park
Beckenham Hill Road, Beckenham, Kent, BR3 5BP
☎ 020 8650 2292, Fax 8663 1201, Pro 8650 2292, Sec 8464 1581
1 mile from Catford towards Bromley, right at Homebase.
Parkland course.
Pro Jon Good; Founded 1932
18 holes, 5722 yards, S.S.S. 68
† Welcome.
£ WD £15; WE £22.
↻ Terms on application.
🍴 Meals and snacks.
🛏 Bromley Court.

1A 12 Betchworth Park
Reigate Road, Dorking, Surrey, RH4 1NZ
🖳 www.betchworthparkgc.co.uk
📧 manager@betchworthparkgc.co.uk
☎ 01306 882052, Fax 877462, Pro 884334, Sec 882052, Rest/Bar 889802/885929
Course is 1 mile E of Dorking on A25, entrance is opposite garden centre.
Parkland course.
Pro A Tocher; Founded 1913
Designed by Harry S Colt
18 holes, 6285 yards, S.S.S. 70
🏌 Large practice ground.
† Welcome except Tues am, Sat and Sun am.
£ WD £35 (after 4pm £19); WE £45 (after 4pm £25).
↻ Mon and Thurs; packages including meals available; terms on application.
🍴 Full catering facility.
🛏 White Horse.

1A 13 Bexleyheath
Mount Road, Bexleyheath, Kent, DA6 8JS
☎ 020 8303 6951, Fax 8303 6951, Sec 8303 6951, Rest/Bar 8303 4232
1 mile from Bexleyheath station off Upton road.
Undulating course.
Founded 1907
9 holes, 5239 yards, S.S.S. 66
† Welcome WD.
£ WD £20.
↻ Welcome WD by appointment.
🍴 Full bar and catering facilities, except Mon.
🛏 Marriott.

1A 14 Birchwood Park
Birchwood Road, Wilmington, Dartford, Kent, DA2 7HJ
🖳 www.birchwoodparkgc.co.uk
📧 info@birchwoodparkgc.co.uk
☎ 01322 662038, Fax 667283
Off A20 or M25 at Swanley turn-off.
Parkland course.
Pro Cranfield Gilf Academy; Founded 1990
Designed by Howard Swan
18 holes, 6364 yards, S.S.S. 71
🏌 41 bay floodlit range.
† Welcome.
£ WD £18; WE £23.
↻ Welcome WD; WE limited to pm, contact Sec; terms on application.
🍴 Full facilities.
🛏 Stakis.

1A 15 Bletchingley   ♜
Church Lane, Bletchingley, Surrey, RH1 4LP
🖳 www.bletchingleygolf.co.uk
📧 info@bletchingleygolf.co.uk
☎ 01883 744666, Fax 744284, Pro 744848, Rest/Bar 742943
From M25 Junction 6 take A25; course 3 miles.
Parkland course.
Pro Alasdair Dyer; Founded 1993
18 holes, 6513 yards, S.S.S. 71
† Welcome.
£ WD £28; WE £38.
↻ Welcome by appointment, terms on application.
🍴 Bar and restaurant.
🛏 Priory, Redhill.

1A 16 Boughton
Brickfield Lane, Boughton, Nr. Faversham, Kent, ME13 9AJ
☎ 01227 752277, Fax 752361, Pro 751112, Rest/Bar 751414
At intersection of the A2/M2 follow signs for Boughton and Dunkirk.
Upland course.
Pro Trevor Dungate; Founded 1993
Designed by P Sparks
18 holes, 6551 yards, S.S.S. 71
🏌 15.
† Welcome.
£ WD £18 WE £24.
↻ Welcome; terms on application.
🍴 Bar and restaurant.
🛏 White Horse Inn.

1A 17 Bowenhurst
Mill Lane, Crondall, Nr Farnham, Surrey, GU10 5RP
☎ 01252 851695, Fax 852039, Pro 851344
M3 Junction 5.4 miles on A287 to Farnham.

Royal Blackheath

Golf was played on Blackheath as early as the beginning of the seventeenth century, but the precise origins of the club are somewhat uncertain due to the loss of records in a fire at the end of the eighteenth century.

Even the royal title comes with a degree of uncertainty. The title was certainly granted by Edward VII in 1901, but earlier records show that the club was already known as Royal Blackheath as far back as 1857. Maybe it was so good that they dubbed it twice.

Originally there were five holes, but in 1844 a new 7-hole design was put down. Measuring some 2,565 yards it must have been quite a slog. The course record (over 21 holes) was 95, set in 1910 at a time when most 18-hole records were under 70.

In 1923 the club moved to crown land in Eltham Park where it remains today. And the feature of a visit to Royal Blackheath is the 17th century clubhouse (or Eltham lodge) and its horde of trophies, china and fine paintings.

With the best will in the world (something that is a feature of the professional and his staff) the course is not of the same standard. It is soggy in the winter and, with a couple of odd walks from green to tee and its back and forth layout, almost municipal in feel. As a parkland course it cannot, for example, compare with Royal Mid-Surrey on the other side of London.

Too many holes lack the lining of trees that would really define them, but having said all that there are still one or two gems along with golf's traditional railway line running alongside the fifth. The most talked about hole (if not necessarily the best) is the eighteenth, an uphill par four dogleg left to the clubhouse. The tempter is that in theory the green is drivable. The penalty for failure is a hedge that runs across the course 20 yards or so short of the green and from which there is no escape except to drop under penalty.

At least there is further relief close to hand. There is a hatch in the side of the clubhouse which opens up into a bar, so having foraged about in the hedge, at least you can lay your hands on a drink immediately afterwards.

As in rugby football Blackheath's position in the game is one of great historical significance. The club presented a trophy to Royal Calcutta, assisted the development of Royal North Devon and Royal Liverpool and was the winner of the first ever national golf championship to be played.

The event was staged at St Andrews in 1857 and on their way to victory Blackheath beat Royal Perth, Innerleven, Edinburgh Bruntsfield and then the R&A in the final, 6 holes representing the least of their winning margins. George Glennie, who held the amateur record at St Andrews for almost 20 years, and a Lieutenant J.C. Stewart of the 72nd Highlanders were responsible for victory, presumably finding the grass of their native Scotland a doddle after the stony soil and gravel pits of Blackheath. — **Mark Reason**

Parkland course.
Pro Adrian Carter; Founded 1994
Designed by N Finn/G Baker
9 holes, 4210 yards, S.S.S. 60
🏌 20.
† Welcome.
☂ WD £11; WE £14.
⛳ Welcome by arrangement with
Sec.
🍽 Function facilities.

1A 18 **Bramley**
Bramley, Nr Guildford, Surrey, GU5 0AL
✉ secretary@bramleygolfclub.co.uk
☎ 01483 892696, Fax 894673,
Pro 893685, Rest/Bar 893042
3 miles S of Guildford on A281.
Parkland course.
Pro Gary Peddie; Founded 1913
Designed by Charles Mayo
(redesigned by James Braid)
18 holes, 5990 yards, S.S.S. 69
🏌 Members only 10.
† Welcome with member.
☂ WD £35; WE Members only.
Round 36 holes £40.
⛳ Contact Sec; full bar and catering
with driving range and practice area;
£43-£58.
🍽 Full catering and grill menu.
⛳ Harrow, Compton; Parrot, Shalford.

1A 19 **Broadwater Park**
Guildford Road, Farncome, Nr
Godalming, Surrey, GU7 3BU
☎ 01483 429955, Fax 429955,
Pro 429955, Sec 429955,
Rest/Bar 429955
On A3100 between Godalming and
Guildford.
Par 3 parkland course.
Pro K Milton; Founded 1989
Designed by KD Milton
9 holes,1301 yards, S.S.S. 27
🏌 16.
† Welcome
☂ WD £4.95; WE £5.75.
⛳ Not available.
🍽 Bar and snacks.
⛳ The Manor Inn.

1A 20 **Broke Hill**   ☎
Sevenoaks Road, Halstead, Kent,
TN14 7HR
🖥 www.brokehillgolf.co.uk
☎ 01959 533225, Fax 532880,
Pro 533810, Rest/Bar 533810
Close to M25 Junction 4 opposite
Knockholt station.
Parkland course/downland.
Pro Chris West; Founded 1993

Designed by D Williams
18 holes, 6374 yards, S.S.S. 71
† Welcome WD.
☂ WD £35.
⛳ Societies welcome Mon to Fri but
not weekends.
🍽 Full clubhouse facilities.
⛳ Post House, Borough Green;
Bromley Court Hotel; Brands Hatch.

1A 21 **Bromley**
Magpie Hall Lane, Bromley, Kent,
BR2 8JF
☎ 020 8462 7014
A21 2 miles S of Bromley.
Public parkland course.
Pro Alan Hodgson
9 holes, 5158 yards, S.S.S. 67
† Welcome WD.
☂ WD £5.60; WE £7.35.
⛳ Welcome by appointment; terms on
application.
🍽 Limited.

1A 22 **Broome Park CC**   ☎
Broome Park Estate, Barham,
Canterbury, Kent, CT4 6QX
🖥 www.broomepark.co.uk
✉ broomeparkgolf@compuserve
.com
☎ 01227 830728, Fax 832591,
Pro 831126, Sec 830728
Just off A2 E of Canterbury.
Parkland course.
Pro Tienie Britz; Founded 1982
Designed by Donald Steel
18 holes, 6580 yards, S.S.S. 72
🏌 6.
† Welcome.
☂ WD £40; WE £50.
⛳ Welcome by prior arrangement;
terms on application.
🍽 Full facilities.

1A 23 **Burhill**   ☎
Walton-On-Thames, Surrey, KT12
4BL
☎ 01932 227345, Fax 267159,
Pro 221729
M25 Junction 10; off A3 London-bound
towards Byfleet on the A245.
Parkland course.
Pro Lee Johnson; Founded 1907
Designed by Willie Park
2 x 18 holes, 6179/6597 yards, S.S.S.
71/72
🏌 6 plus grass range.
† Welcome weekdays only.
☂ £75 per day; £60 per round.
⛳ By prior arrangement only; terms
on application.

🍽 Full facilities.
⛳ Oatlands Park Hotel, Weybridge.

1A 24 **Camberley Heath**
Golf Drive, Camberley, Surrey,
GU15 1JG
🖥 www.camberleyheathgolfclub
.co.uk
✉ info@camberleyheathgolfclub
.co.uk
☎ 01276 23258, Fax 692505,
Pro 27905, Sec 23258,
Rest/Bar 23258
Off A325 Portsmouth road between
Bagshot and Frimley.
Pine and heather course.
Pro Glenn Ralph; Founded 1913
Designed by HS Colt
18 holes, 6637 yards, S.S.S. 70
🏌 Driving range.
† Welcome WD only.
☂ WD £52.
⛳ Welcome weekdays by
appointment; terms available on
application.
🍽 Full facilities.
⛳ Frimley Hall Hotel.

1A 25 **Canterbury**   ☎
Scotland Hills, Canterbury, Kent,
CT1 1TW
✉ cgc@freeola.com
☎ 01227 453532, Fax 784277,
Pro 462865, Sec 453532,
Rest/Bar 781871
1 mile from town centre on A257 road
to Sandwich.
Parkland course.
Pro Paul Everard; Founded 1927
Designed by HS Colt
18 holes, 6249 yards, S.S.S. 70
🏌 Buggies available for hire.
† Welcome if carrying handicap
certs.
☂ WD £36; WE £40.
⛳ Welcome Tues and Thurs;
minimum 12, 36 holes, light lunch, 3-
course evening meal, £50 per person
Discounts for larger groups.
🍽 Full facilities and bar.
⛳ Many in Canterbury, recommend
County Hotel.

1A 26 **Central London GC**
Burntwood Lane, Wandsworth, London,
SW17 0AT
🖥 www.clgc.co.uk
✉ golf@glgc.co.uk
☎ 020 8871 2468, Fax 8874 7447,
Pro 8871 2468, Rest/Bar 8871 2468
Take Garratt Lane from A3 in

Wandsworth, Burntwood Lane is off Garratt Lane after Earlsfield.
Parkland course.
Pro Jeremy Robson; Founded 1992
Designed by Patrick Tallack
9 holes, 4468 yards, S.S.S. 62
⌇ 14 bays floodlit.
† Welcome anytime.
[WD £9.50; WE £11.50.
⌇ By arrangement.
⦿ Function and conference facilities.
⌇ In Wimbledon.

1A 27 Chart Hills ☎
Weeks Lane, Biddenden, Kent, TN27 8JX
⌁ www.charthills.co.uk
☎ 01580 292222, Fax 292233
M20 to Junction 8; follow signs to Leeds Castle before turning on to A274 through Sutton Valence & Headcorn; 7 miles turn into Weeks Lane.
Parkland course.
Pro Peter Chandler; Founded 1993
Designed by Nick Faldo
18 holes, 7086 yards, S.S.S. 72
⌇ 20 grass bays; putting green; short practice area.
† Tue/Thur/Fri am; limited times WE.
[Summer £50; winter £39.50.
⌇ Restricted; full facilities including lunch and coffee; £75-£105.
⦿ Full facilities.
⌇ Great Danes; Forstal B&B.

1A 28 Chelsfield Lakes
Court Road, Orpington, Kent, BR6 9BX
⌁ www.chelsfieldgolf.co.uk
▤ cdo@chelsfieldgolf.co.uk
☎ 01689 896266, Fax 824577, Rest/Bar 896266
From M25 J4 follow signs to Orpington; course 300 yds from 2nd roundabout.
Parkland course.
Pro Nigel Lee; Founded 1993
Designed by MRM Leisure
18 holes, 6110 yards, S.S.S. 69
⌇ Full driving range facilities.
† Welcome.
[18-hole course: WD £17; WE £22.
9-hole course: WD £4; WE £5.
⌇ Welcome by prior application; minimum 8; golf and catering packages available; terms on application.
⦿ Full clubhouse facilities.
⌇ Brands Hatch Thistle Hotel.

1A 29 Cherry Lodge ☎
Jail Lane, Biggin Hill, Kent, TN16 3AX
⌁ www.cherrylodgegc@aol.com

▤ info@cherrylodge.co.uk
☎ 01959 572250, Fax 540672, Pro 572989, Sec 572250, Rest/Bar 572250
3 miles N of Westerham off A233.
Parkland course.
Pro Nigel Child; Founded 1970
Designed by John Day
18 holes, 6593 yards, S.S.S. 73
⌇ Driving range.
† WD by prior arrangement; with a member only at WE.
[WD £35; WE £20.
⌇ Welcome by arrangement.
Packages from £35.
⦿ Full bar and restaurant facilities available.
⌇ Kings Arms, Westerham.

1A 30 Chessington ☎
Garrison Lane, Chessington, Surrey, KT9 2LW
⌁ www.chessingtongolf.co.uk
☎ 020 8391 0948, Fax 8397 2068, Opposite Chessington South station, very near Chessington Zoo.
Parkland course.
Pro Mark Janes; Founded 1983
Designed by Patrick Tallack
9 holes, 1761 yards, S.S.S. 30
⌇ 18.
† Everyone welcome.
[WD £7.50; WE £9.
⌇ Welcome; terms on application.
⦿ Full facilities.
⌇ Seven Hills; Oatlands Park.

1A 31 Chestfield ☎
103 Chestfield Road, Whitstable, Kent, CT5 3LU
⌁ www.chestfield/golfclub.co.uk
▤ secretary@chestfield/golfclub.co.uk
☎ 01227 794411, Fax 794454, Pro 793563
0.5 mile S of A299 at Chestfield stn.
Parkland course, with sea views.
Pro John Brotherton; Founded 1924
Designed by James Braid and Abe Mitchell
18 holes, 6208 yards, S.S.S. 70
⌇ Practice green; practice area.
† WD Call for availability.
[WD £25 Round; £30 day.
⌇ Welcome WD; packages available; terms on application.
⦿ Facilities available.
⌇ Marine, Tankerton.

1A 32 Chiddingfold
Petworth Road, Chiddingfold, Surrey, GU8 4SL

☎ 01428 685888, Fax 685939, Pro 8681381
Take A283 off A3 and course is 10 minutes away, 50 yards S of Chiddingfold
Downland course
Pro Gary Wallace; Founded 1994
Designed by J Gaunt & P Alliss
18 holes, 5568 yards, S.S.S. 67
⌇ 4.
† Welcome.
[WD £16; WE £22 summer/WD £13; WE £20 winter.
⌇ Welcome, packages available; terms on application.
⦿ Full facilities; conference suite.
⌇ Lythe Hill.

1A 33 Chipstead ☎
How Lane, Coulsden, Surrey, CR5 3LN
⌁ www.chipsteadgolf.co.uk
▤ office@chipsteadgolf.freeserve.co.uk
☎ 01737 555781, Fax 555404, Pro 554939
Follow signs to Chipstead from the A217. M25 take Junction 7 or 8.
Undulating parkland course.
Pro Gary Torbett; Founded 1906
18 holes, 5504 yards, S.S.S. 67
† Welcome WD.
[WD £30 per round, after 4pm £20.
⌇ Welcome WD by appointment; terms on application.
⦿ Lunch served; booking required. Bar snacks.
⌇ Reigate Manor, Hotel Heathside in Burgh Heath.

1A 34 Chislehurst ☎
Camden Place, Camden Park Road, Chislehurst, Kent, BR7 5HJ
☎ 020 8467 055, Fax 8295 0874, Pro 8467 6798, Sec 8467 2782, Rest/Bar 8467 2888
0.5 miles from Chislehurst station.
Parkland course.
Pro Jon Bird; Founded 1894
18 holes, 5106 yards, S.S.S. 65
† Welcome WD; with a member at WE.
[WD £30; WE £30.
⌇ Welcome Mon-Fri; 36 holes £35.50.
⦿ Full facilities.

1A 35 Chobham ☎
Chobham Road, Knaphill, Woking, Surrey, GU21 2TZ
⌁ www.chobhamgolfclub.co.uk

info@chobhamgolfclub.co.uk
☎ 01276 855584, Fax 855663,
Pro 855748
Take the A322 from the M3 J3 towards
Guildford; at the first roundabout take
the A319 to Chobham, course is 2
miles on right towards Knaphill.
Wooded parkland with lakes.
Pro Tim Coombes; Founded 1994
Designed by Clive Clark & Peter Alliss
18 holes, 5959 yards, S.S.S. 69
✝ Members' guests welcome only in
midweek.
⌁ WD £16.50 before 2.00pm.
⌁ Welcome by appointment; terms
on application.
⏲ Restaurant, bar and function rooms.

1A 36 Clandon Regis
Epsom Road, West Clandon, Nr
Guildford, Surrey, GU4 7TT
⌁ www.clandonregisgolfclub.co.uk
☎ 01483 224888, Fax 211781,
Pro 223922
Course is four miles E of Guildford on
the A246.
Parkland course.
Pro Steve Lloyd; Founded 1994
Designed by D Williams
18 holes, 6412 yards, S.S.S. 71
✝ Welcome by prior arrangement.
⌁ WD £30; WE £40 (by
arrangement).
⌁ Welcome by prior arrangement;
terms on application.
⏲ Full bar and restaurant.

1A 37 Cobtree Manor Park
Chatham Road, Maidstone, Kent,
ME14 3AZ
☎ 01622 753276, Rest/Bar 751881
Take A229 from M20.
Municipal parkland course.
Pro Paul Foston; Founded 1984
Designed by F Hawtree
18 holes, 5611 yards, S.S.S. 67
✝ Welcome.
⌁ Guest rate WD £15.50; WE £18.50.
If registered WE £15 and WD £11.
⌁ Terms on application.
⏲ Available.
☜ Holiday Inn, Rochester;
Bridgewood Manor Hotel, Rochester;
Maidstone Hilton, Maidstone.

1A 38 Coombe Hill
Golf Club Drive, Kingston, Surrey,
KT2 7DF
⌁ www.coombehillgolfclub.com
✉ thesecretary@coombegillgolf
.demon.co.uk

☎ 020 8336 7600, Fax 8336 7601,
Pro 8949 3713, Sec 8336 7600,
Rest/Bar 8942 2284
1 mile W of New Malden on A238.
Undulating, tree-lines.
Pro Craig Defoy; Founded 1911
Designed by JF Abercromby
18 holes, 6293 yards, S.S.S. 71
✝ WD by prior arrangement.
⌁ WD £80 summer, £50 winter.
⌁ Welcome by prior arrangement
with Sec; terms on application.
⏲ Restaurant and bar.
☜ Kingston Lodge.

1A 39 Coombe Wood
George Road, Kingston Hill, Kingston-
on-Thames, Surrey, KT2 7NS
⌁ www.coombewoodgolf.com
✉ cwoodgc@ukonline.co.uk
☎ 020 8942 0388, Fax 8942 5665,
Pro 8942 6764, Rest/Bar 8942 3828
From the A3 take A308 (E) or A238 (W).
Mature parkland course.
Pro Phil Wright; Founded 1904
Designed by Tom Williamson
18 holes, 5299 yards, S.S.S. 66
✝ Visitors welcome 7 days
(weekends pm only).
⌁ WD £25; WE £35.
⌁ Welcome Wed, Thurs, Fri;
packages available from £25.
⏲ Full bar and restaurant facilities
available.
☜ Kingston Lodge.

1A 40 Coulsdon Manor ℃
Coulsdon Court Road, Old Coulsdon,
Surrey, CR5 2LL
⌁ www.marstonhotels.com
✉ coulsdonmanor@
marstonhotels.com
☎ 020 8668 0414, Fax 8668 3118,
Pro 8660 6083, Sec 8660 6083
Just off A23, 2 miles S of Croydon, 2
miles N of M25 and M23.
Parkland course.
Pro James Leaver; Founded 1926
Designed by H S Colt
18 holes, 6037 yards, S.S.S. 68
✝ Welcome.
⌁ WD £15.95; WE £19.95.
⌁ Welcome by prior arrangement;
terms on application.
⏲ Full facilities.
☜ Coulsdon Manor.

1A 41 The Cranleigh Golf ℃
and Leisure Club
Barhatch Lane, Cranleigh, Surrey,
GU6 7NG

⌁ www.cranleighgolfandleisure.co.uk
☎ 01483 268855, Fax 267251,
Pro 277188
Take A281 out of Guildford, 1 mile
through Cranleigh take Ewhurst road,
then turn into Barhatch Road and
Barhatch Lane.
Parkland course.
Pro Trevor Longmuir; Founded 1985
18 holes, 5648 yards, S.S.S. 67
✝ 10 bay driving range (7 covered).
✝ Welcome WD; restrictions WE.
⌁ WD £30; WE £33.
⌁ Welcome WD, WE subject to
availability; terms on application.
⏲ Bar, restaurant, snacks, banquets.
☜ The Cranley Hotel, The Random
Hall.

1A 42 Cray Valley
Sandy Lane, St Paul's Cray, Orpington,
Kent, BR5 3HY
☎ 01689 839677, Fax 891428,
Pro 837909, Rest/Bar 871490
Leave the A20 off Ruxley roundabout;
course is on Sandy Lane, 0.5 miles on
left.
Parkland course.
Pro Stephen Lee, Raphael
Piannandrea; Founded 1972
Designed by Golf Centres Ltd
18 holes, 5669 yards, S.S.S. 67
✝ Pay and play.
⌁ WD £16.75; WE £22.
⌁ Bookings requested 7 days in
advance.
⏲ Bar and restaurant.

1A 43 Croham Hurst
Croham Road, South Croydon, Surrey,
CR2 7HJ
⌁ www.chgc.co.uk
✉ secretary@chgc.co.uk
☎ 020 8657 5581, Fax 8657 3229,
Pro 8657 7705, Rest/Bar 8657 2075
1 mile from S Croydon; from M25 exit
6 N on to A22, take B270 to
Warlingham at roundabout, then B269
to Selsdon; at traffic lights turn left into
Farley Road, clubhouse is 1.75 miles
on left.
Parkland course.
Pro Matthew Paget; Founded 1911
Designed by James Braid & Sons
18 holes, 6290 yards, S.S.S. 70
✝ Welcome by arrangement,
handicap certs required.
⌁ WD £40; WE £50.
⌁ Welcome Wed, Thurs, Fri by
arrangement; terms on application.
⏲ Full facilities every day 10am-6pm;
banqueting.
☜ Selsdon Park.

1A 44 **Cuddington**
Banstead Road, Banstead, Surrey,
SM7 1RD
🖳 www.cuddinggc.co.uk
📧 cuddingtongc@aol.com
☎ 020 8393 0952, Fax 8786 7025,
Pro 8393 5850, Sec 8393 0952,
Rest/Bar 8394 2827 (catering)
200 yards from Banstead station.
Parkland course.
Pro Mark Warner; Founded 1929
Designed by H S Colt
18 holes, 6394 yards, S.S.S. 70
 🕴 Welcome if carrying handicap
certs.
 Ⓘ WD £45; WE £55.
 ⟋ Welcome Thurs; full day's golf and
meals, including dinner; £72.50.
 🍽 Full catering service.
 ⟅ Heathside; Driftbridge.

1A 45 **Darenth Valley**
Station Road, Shoreham, Nr
Sevenoaks, Kent, TN14 7SA
🖳 www.darenth-valley.co.uk
📧 darenthvalleygolfcourse@
shoreham2000.fsbusiness.co.uk
☎ 01959 522944, Fax 525089,
Pro 522922
Along A225 Sevenoaks – Dartford
Road, 4 miles N of Sevenoaks.
Parkland course.
Pro David Copsey; Founded 1973
18 holes, 6258 yards, S.S.S. 71
 🕴 Welcome; bookings daily. No
members.
 Ⓘ WD £17.50; WE £25.
 ⟋ Welcome by prior arrangement
with office; terms available on
application, societies welcome Mon-Fri
and some weekends.
 🍽 Bar meals, society catering,
functions (up to 150 persons).

1A 46 **Dartford**
Dartford Heath, Dartford, Kent, DA1 2TN
📧 dartfordgolf@hotmail.com
☎ 01322 223616, Pro 226409,
Sec 226455, Rest/Bar 223616
0.5 miles from A2 Dartford-Crayford
turn-off.
Park/heathland course.
Pro John Gregory; Founded 1897
Designed by James Braid
18 holes, 5591 yards, S.S.S. 69
 🕴 WD with handicap certs; with
member only at WE.
 Ⓘ WD £21.
 ⟋ Mon and Fri by prior arrangement;
full day's package of golf and catering,
including evening meal; £50.
 🍽 Full clubhouse facilities.

 ⟅ Swallow, Bexleyheath; The Stakis,
Dartford Bridge.

1A 47 **Deangate Ridge**
Hoo, Rochester, Kent, ME3 8RZ
☎ 01634 251180, Fax 250537,
Pro 251180, Sec 251950,
Rest/Bar 254481
A228 from Rochester to Isle of Grain,
then road signposted to Deangate.
Municipal parkland course.
Pro Richard Fox; Founded 1972
Designed by Hawtree & Sons
18 holes, 6300 yards, S.S.S. 71
 Ⓘ 11.
 🕴 Welcome anytime; bookings
essential at WE.
 Ⓘ WD £12.10; WE £16.
 ⟋ Welcome; terms available on
application.
 🍽 Lunch and dinner served.

1A 48 **Dorking**   ☏
Chart Park, Dorking, Surrey, RH5 4BX
🖳 www.dorkinggolfclub.co.uk
📧 dorkinggolfclub@ukgateway.net
☎ 01306 886917, Rest/Bar 885914
1 mile S of Dorking on A24.
Parkland course.
Pro Allan Smeal; Founded 1897
Designed by James Braid
9 holes, 5163 yards, S.S.S. 65
 🕴 Welcome WD; WE after 12.00.
 Ⓘ WD £15; WE after 2.00 £20.
 ⟋ Welcome by prior arrangement.
 🍽 Restaurant and bar.
 ⟅ Burford Bridge, Boxhill.

1A 49 **The Drift**
The Drift, East Horsley, KT24 5HD
🖳 www.driftgolfclub.com
📧 info@driftgolfclub.co.uk
☎ 01483 284641,
Fax 284642, Pro 284772,
Rest/Bar 284641
On B2039 East Horsley road off A3.
Woodland course.
Pro Mark Smith; Founded 1975
Designed by H Cotton/R Sandow
18 holes, 6425 yards, S.S.S. 72
 🕴 WD; WE after 12.
 Ⓘ Terms on application.
 ⟋ Mon-Fri by appointment.
 🍽 Full restaurant and bar.
 ⟅ Jarvis Thatcher Hotel, E Horsley;
Hautboy, Ockham.

1A 50 **Dulwich & Sydenham Hill**
Grange Lane, College Road, London,
SE21 7LH

📧 dulwichgc@hotmail.com
☎ 020 8693 3961, Fax 2481,
Pro 8491
Off S Circular road at Dulwich College
and College Road.
Parkland course.
Pro David Baillie; Founded 1894
18 holes, 6008 yards, S.S.S. 69
 🕴 Welcome all week with handicap
certs.
 Ⓘ WD £25; WE £35.
 ⟋ Welcome WD by prior
arrangement; terms available on
application.
 🍽 Lunch daily, dinner by
appointment.

1A 51 **Dunsfold Aerodrome**
British Aerospace, Dunsfold
Aerodrome, Nr Godalming, Surrey,
GU8 4BS
☎ 01483 265403
12 miles S of Guildford on A281.
Parkland course.
Founded 1965
Designed by John Sharkey
9 holes, 6099 yards, S.S.S. 69
 🕴 With member only.
 Ⓘ Member's responsibility.
 ⟋ Welcome from British Aerospace.
 🍽 Bar and snacks.

1A 52 **Edenbridge G & CC**   ☏
Crouch House Road, Edenbridge,
Kent, TN8 5LQ
☎ 01732 867381, Fax 868060
Travel N through Edenbridge High
Street, turn left into Stangrove Road (30
yds before railway station), at end of the
road turn right, course is on the left.
Undulating meadowland course.
Pro Mark Chatfield; Founded 1975
Designed by D Williams
18-hole and 1 x 9-hole, 6601 yards,
S.S.S. old course 72
new course 68
 Ⓘ Practice 14.
 🕴 Welcome.
 Ⓘ WD £20; WE £30; Academy £5
 ⟋ Welcome by appointment;
packages available; terms on
application.
 🍽 Clubhouse bar and catering
facilities available.

1A 53 **Effingham**
Guildford Road, Effingham, Surrey,
KT24 5PZ
🖳 www.effinghamgolfclub.com
📧 secretary@effinghamgolfclub
.com

☎ 01372 452203, Fax 459959,
Pro 452606
On A246 8 miles E of Guildford.
Downland course.
Pro Stephen Hoatson; Founded 1927
Designed by HS Colt
18 holes, 6524 yards, S.S.S. 71
† WD only by arrangement;
handicap certs required.
[WD £40-£55.
☾ Welcome Wed, Thurs and Fri;
terms on application.
🍽 Lunch, tea, evening meal, snacks,
etc.
☛ Ramada (East Horsley); Preston
Cross (Great Bookham).

1A 54 **Eltham Warren**
Bexley Road, Eltham, London, SE9 2PE
⛳ www.elthamwarrengolfclub.co.uk
🖥 secretary@elthamwarren.idps
.co.uk
☎ 020 8850 1166, Pro 8859 7909,
Sec 8850 4477, Rest/Bar 8850 1166
0.5 miles from Eltham Station on A210.
Parkland course.
Pro Gary Brett; Founded 1890
9 holes, 5874 yards, S.S.S. 68
† Welcome on WD.
[WD £28, WE £28.
☾ Thurs only; green fees, morning
coffee, ploughman's lunch, evening
meal; £42.
🍽 Full bar and catering.
☛ Swallow, Bexleyheath.

1A 55 **Epsom**   ♼
Longdown Lane South, Epsom, Surrey,
KT17 4JR
⛳ www.epsomgolfclub.co.uk
🖥 enquires@epsom golfclub.co.uk
☎ 01372 721666, Fax 817183,
Pro 741867, Rest/Bar 723363
Course is 0.5 miles south of Epsom
Downs Station on the road to Epsom
College.
Downland course.
Pro Ron Goudie; Founded 1889
18 holes, 5658 yards, S.S.S. 68
† Welcome except before noon on
Tues, Sat and Sun.
[WD £29; WE £32.
☾ Welcome WD except Tues, and
WE pm; min 12, max 40; packages
available; terms on application.
🍽 Full clubhouse facilities.
☛ Heathside hotel.

1A 56 **Falcon Valley**
Gay Dawn Farm, Fawkham, Longfield,
Kent, DA3 8LY

☎ 01474 707144, Fax 707911,
Pro 707144, Sec 707144,
Rest/Bar 707144
Take A20 off Junction 3 of M25
towards Brands Hatch and turn left
towards Fawkham/Longfield.
Wooded parkland course.
Pro Cameron McKillop; Founded 1986
Designed by Greg Turner
9 holes, 6547 yards, S.S.S. 72
⛳ Large practice area.
† Welcome WD, after 1pm at WE.
[WD £20; WE £27.50.
☾ Welcome midweek; packages
available; terms on application.
🍽 Bar and restaurant.
☛ Brands Hatch Hotel; Brands Hatch
Thistle.

1A 57 **Farleigh Court**   ♼
Old Farleigh Road, Farleigh, Surrey,
CR6 9PX
🖥 enquiries @farleighcourt.co.uk
☎ 01883 627711 (enquiries)/627733
(pro shop), Fax 627722,
Pro 627733, Sec 627711,
Rest/Bar 627711
Ten minutes from Croydon town
centre.
Inland links.
Pro Scott Graham; Founded 1996
Designed by John Jacobs
27 (Visitors 9) holes, 6409 (Visitors
3255) yards, S.S.S. 72
⛳ 20.
† Welcome 7 days.
[Terms available on application.
☾ Welcome.
🍽 Restaurant, bar and function
rooms.

1A 58 **Farnham**
The Sands, Farnham, Surrey,
GU10 1PX
⛳ www.grahamecowlishaw.co.uk
🖥 grahameproshop@aol.com
☎ 01252 783163, Fax 781185,
Pro 782198, Sec 782109,
Rest/Bar 782342
On A31 from Runfold.
Heathland, pines, parkland course.
Pro Grahame Cowlishaw; Founded 1896
18 holes, 6447 yards, S.S.S. 71
† Welcome WDs.
[WD £40.
☾ Wed, Thurs, Fri only; 2 rounds of
golf, coffee and roll on arrival, snack
lunch and evening meal; golf clinics
available; £66.
🍽 Bar and restaurant facilities
available.
☛ Hogs Back Hotel.

1A59 **Farnham Park**
Folly Hill, Farnham, Surrey,
GU9 0AU
☎ 01252 715216, Rest/Bar 715216
On A287 next to Farnham Castle.
Parkland course.
Pro Darren Bryant; Founded 1966
Designed by Henry Cotton
9 holes, 1163 yards, S.S.S. 54
† Public pay and play.
[WD £4.80; WE £5.50.
☾ By prior arrangement.
☛ The Bush Hotel, Farnham.

1A 60 **Faversham**   ♼
Belmont Park, Faversham, Kent,
ME13 0HB
⛳ www.favershamgolfclub.co.uk
🖥 manager@favershamgolfclub
.co.uk
☎ 01795 890561, Fax 890760,
Pro 890275, Sec 890561,
Rest/Bar 890251
Leave M2 at Junction 6, A251 to
Faversham, then A2 Sittingbourne for
0.5 mile, turn left at Brogdale Road,
and then follow signs.
Parkland course.
Pro Stuart Rokes; Founded 1902
18 holes, 6030 yards, S.S.S. 69
† WD; only with member WE and
BH and with handicap cert.
[WD £30; WE £30.
☾ By arrangement; terms on
application.
🍽 All facilities available.

1A 61 **Fawkham Valley
(formerly Corinthian GC)**
Gay Dawn Farm, Fawkham, Longfield,
Kent DA3 8LY
☎ 01474 707144, Fax 707911
Take A20 off J3 of M225 towards
Brands Hatch and turn left towards
Fawkham/Longfield.
Wooded parkland.
Pro Nigel Willis; Founded 1986
Designed by Greg Turner
9 holes, 6547 yards, S.S.S. 72
⛳ Large practice area.
† Welcome WD; after 1pm WE.
[WD £20; WE £27.50.
☾ Welcome midweek; packages
available; terms on application.
🍽 Bar and restaurant.
☛ Brands Hatch Hotel; Brands Hatch
Thistle.

1A 62 **Foxhills Club and Resort**
Stonehill Road, Ottershaw, Surrey,
KT16 0EL

Royal Cinque Ports

Royal Cinque Ports is a great course of simple pleasures. There can be few better ways of spending a summer's evening than on the links of Deal unless, by chance, there happens to be a mini cyclone blowing in as happened to me recently. We were forced to shelter under the lip of the bunker by the 12th green whilst our golf balls were blown off the putting surface by the force of the storm. Until then the weather had been almost calm.

That story in itself is almost a metaphor for Deal. The first 10 holes are relatively benign – which is not to say unchallenging – and then you begin the turn for home. It is because of the finish that Bernard Darwin wrote, "Deal is a truly great course. I incline myself to think it is the most testing and severe of all the Championship courses." Just ten minutes along the coast road from Royal St George's, there is little doubt that Deal would have hosted far more than its two Open Championships were it not for bad weather (the course was due to stage the Open in both 1938 and 1949 but high tides damaged the greens beforehand) and the lack of extra ground on which to pitch all a modern Open's attendant paraphernalia.

Deal is now engaged in a rethink. It has brought the running of the club into the modern era and is intent on a programme of renovation and restoration on the course itself. It has scarcely gone to seed, but Deal hopes one day soon to attract some of Britain's great competitions back to its links.

Amongst the mighty whom Deal has humbled in the past is the great Walter Hagen. In 1920 he swept into town certain that he was about to win his first Open Championship. As it happened he failed to break 80 in any of his four rounds and is reputed to have had a side bet with his partner over the final eighteen holes as to which of them would finish last.

The local mullahs stroked their beards. They said that Hagen hit the ball too high to prevail on a windy links like Deal. Hagen retorted, "There are no bunkers in the air". Gravity responded by ensuring that both the great American and his ball still came down to earth. "I tried too hard, just like any duffer might play," said Hagen in conclusion.

Even Henry Cotton, who once subdued the giant of St George's, said of Deal, "It is possible at nearly every hole to place a ball bang in the middle of the fairway and then find yourself in such an awkward position that a successful shot can scarcely be played."

If any of this sounds at all off putting, don't be turned away. One of the delights of Deal is that however foreboding the course can appear on occasions, the club itself offers an unpretentious welcome. It has none of the self appointed grandeur of some of the other royal courses.

It is perhaps no great surprise then that Cinque Ports got in a bit of a muddle over the granting of its royal status. After the Prince of Wales played there in 1910, the club asked for his patronage and use of the royal title. By now the Prince had become King George V and although he granted royal patronage it did not come with the royal title. In all innocence the club assumed the title and it wasn't until 39 years later that the error came to light and King George VI agreed to bestow royal status. — **Mark Reason**

www.foxhills.co.uk
events@foxhills.co.uk
☎ 01932 872050, Fax 874762,
Pro 704465, Mgr 704466,
Bookings 704444, Rest/Bar 704480
From the M25 Junction 11 follow the
signs for Woking; at the 2nd
roundabout take the 3rd exit into
Foxhills Road.
Treelined course.
Pro R Summerscales; Founded 1972
Designed by F Hawtree
Bernard Hunt 18; Longcross 18 holes,
Bernard Hunt 6883; Longcross 6743
yards, S.S.S. Bernard Hunt 73;
Longcross 72
† Welcome WD if carrying handicap
certs.
Ⅰ WD £75.
♳ WD only; packages available;
driving range facilities; from £60.
¶●¶ Full clubhouse facilities.
♺ Four star hotel on site.

1A 63 **Gatton Manor** ☏

Ockley, Dorking, Surrey, RH5 5PQ
www.gattonmanor.co.uk
gattonmanor@enterprize.net
☎ 01306 627555, Fax 627713,
Pro 627557
Course is 1.5 miles SW of Ockley on
the A29.
Parkland course.
Pro Rae Sergeant; Founded 1969
Designed by DB & DG Heath
18 holes, 6653 yards, S.S.S. 72
Ⅰ 5 mats.
† Welcome except Sun until 10.15am.
Ⅰ WD £25; WE £35 (winter £20/
£25).
♳ Welcome WD; coffee, lunch, dinner,
36 holes of golf; conference facilities,
tennis with gym and health suite;
£32–£62.
¶●¶ Bar and restaurant.
♺ Gatton Manor.

1A 64 **Goal Farm Par 3**

Gole Road, Pirbright, Surrey,
GU24 0PZ
☎ 01483 473183
1 mile from Brookwood station off A322
towards Pirbright.
Parkland course.
Founded 1977
9 holes, 1128 yards, S.S.S. 48
† Welcome except Thurs am or Sat
am.
Ⅰ WD £4.90; WE £5.20.
♳ Welcome.
¶●¶ Bar and bar snacks.
♺ Lakeside.

1A 65 **Guildford** ☏

High Path Road, Merrow, Guildford,
Surrey, GU1 2HI
☎ 01483 563941, Fax 453228,
Pro 566765, Rest/Bar 531842
Course is 2 miles E of Guildford on the
A246.
Downland course.
Pro PG Hollington; Founded 1886
Designed by James Braid
18 holes, 6090 yards, S.S.S. 70
† Welcome WD; members' guests
only at WE.
Ⅰ WD £30; WE £30.
♳ Welcome by prior arrangement;
packages including practice areas and
indoor practice rooms and snooker;
terms available on application.
¶●¶ Full bar and catering facilities
available.
♺ White Horse; Angel.

1A 66 **Hampton Court Palace Golf Club**

Hampton Wick, Kingston-upon-
Thames, KT1 4AD
www.hcpgc.com
hamptoncourtpalace@
americangolf.uk.com
☎ 020 8977 2423, Fax 8614 4747,
Pro 8977 2658, Rest/Bar 8977 6645
Entrance to Home Park is through
Kingston Gate at Hampton Wick
roundabout.
Parkland course/links.
Pro Len Roberts; Founded 1895
18 holes, 6611 yards, S.S.S. 71
† Welcome.
Ⅰ WD only £30.
♳ Welcome with prior appointment;
packages available; terms on
application.

1A 67 **Hankley Commom**

Tilford Road, Tilford, Farnham, Surrey,
GU10 2DD
www.hankley.co.uk
☎ 01252 792493, Fax 795699,
Pro 793761
Off M3 or A3 to Farnham, along A31
Farnham by-pass to lights; left to
Tilford.
Heathland course.
Pro P Stow; Founded 1896
Designed by James Braid
18 holes, 6438 yards, S.S.S. 71
Ⅰ Practice ground.
† Welcome only with telephone
booking and handicap certs.
Ⅰ WD £55; WE £70.
♳ Tues, Wed; packages available;
£78/£90.

¶●¶ Full catering and bar.
♺ Bush, Farnham; Frensham Ponds;
Pride of Valley, Churt.

1A 68 **Hawkhurst** ☏

High Street, Hawkhurst, Cranbrook,
Kent, TN18 4JS
☎ 01580 754074/752396, Fax
754074, Pro 754088
On A268 3 miles from A21 at Flimwell,
0.5 mile from junction with A229.
Undulating parkland course.
Pro Tony Collins; Founded 1968
Designed by Rex Baldock
9 holes, 5791 yards, S.S.S. 68
† Welcome weekdays; only with
member at weekends.
Ⅰ WD £20; WE £24 after noon.
♳ Welcome by prior arrangement;
mostly Fri; £18.
¶●¶ By arrangement.
♺ Royal Oak, Tudor Court; Queens.

1A 69 **Hemsted Forest**

Golford Road, Cranbrook, Kent,
TN17 4AL
www.hemstedforest.co.uk
golf@hemstedforest.co.uk
☎ 01580 712833, Fax 714274,
Pro 712833, Rest/Bar 715771
Off A262 at Sissinghurst; turn right at
Bull towards Benenden; 1 mile on left.
Tree-lined parkland course.
Pro Karl Steptoe; Founded 1969
Designed by John D Harris
18 holes, 6295 yards, S.S.S. 70
† Welcome except Mon.
Ⅰ WD £25; WE £30.
♳ Welcome Tues-Fri; packages
available from £19.50.
¶●¶ Full clubhouse facilities.
♺ Kennel Holt; The George.

1A 70 **Herne Bay**

Eddington, Herne Bay, Kent,
CT6 7PG
☎ 01227 373964, Pro 374727,
Rest/Bar 374097
Off A299 Thanet road at Herne Bay–
Canterbury Junction.
Parkland course/links.
Pro F Scott; Founded 1895
Designed by James Braid
18 holes, 5567 yards, S.S.S. 66
Ⅰ Practice green.
† Welcome WD, and afternoons at
WE.
Ⅰ WD £18; WE £28.
♳ By prior arrangement; terms on
application.
¶●¶ Full facilities.

1A 71 Hever Castle ☏

Hever, Edenbridge, Kent, TN8 7NP
🖥 www.hevercastlegolfclub.co.uk
✉ mail@hevercastlegolfclub.co.uk
☎ 01732 700771, Fax 700775,
Pro 701008, Rest/Bar 700016
Course is off the A21 between
Sevenoaks and Edenbridge adjacent
to Hever Castle.
Parkland course, with water hazards.
Pro Peter Parks; Founded 1992
Designed by Dr Peter Nicholson
18 holes (Kings and Queens), 7002
yards, S.S.S. 74 Par 72
9 holes (Princes), 2784 yards, Par 35
ⵏ Practice range, putting green and
chipping area.
† Welcome after 11 am on Kings and
Queens Championship course.
Ⅰ 18: WD £40; WE £60
9: WD £15; WE £20.
☞ By prior appointment WD only; golf
packages with coffee, lunch and dinner
available £38-£68.
🍽 Restaurant and bars.
💤 Hever Hotel adjacent on site.

1A 72 High Elms

High Elms Road, Downe, Kent,
BR6 7SI
☎ 01689 858175, Pro 853232,
Rest/Bar 861813
5 miles out of Bromley off the A21 to
Sevenoaks.
Public parkland course.
Pro Peter Remy; Founded 1969
Designed by Fred Hawtree
18 holes, 6221 yards, S.S.S. 70
ⵏ Practice ground.
† Welcome.
Ⅰ WD £12.30; WE £16.10.
☞ Welcome WD only; terms on
application.
🍽 Full meals and snacks.
💤 Bromley Court.

1A 73 Hilden ☏

Rings Hill, Hildenborough, Kent,
TN11 8LX
☎ 01732 833607, Fax 834484,
Rest/Bar 838577
Course is off the A21 towards
Tunbridge Wells adjacent to
Hildenborough station.
Parkland course.
Pro Nicky Way; Founded 1994
9 holes, 1558 yards, S.S.S. 54
ⵏ 36.
† Welcome.
Ⅰ WD £5.95; WE £7.50.
☞ Welcome; terms on application.
🍽 Full facilities.

1A 74 Hindhead

Churt Road, Hindhead, Surrey,
GU26 6HX
🖥 www..the-hindhead-golf-club.co.uk
✉ secretary@the-hindhead-golf-club
.co.uk
☎ 01428 604614, Fax 608508,
Pro 604458
1.5 miles N of Hindhead on the A287.
Heathland course.
Pro Ian Benson; Founded 1904
18 holes, 6356 yards, S.S.S. 70
† Welcome WD; by appt WE.
Ⅰ WD £42; WE £52.
☞ Wed, Thurs only; 36 holes of golf,
coffee, snack lunch, evening meal;
£78.50.
🍽 Full catering and bar.
💤 Mariners, Farnham; Devils Punch
Bowl, Hindhead; Frensham Pond.

1A 75 Hoebridge Golf Centre

Old Woking Road, Old Woking, Surrey,
GU22 8JH
🖥 www.hoebridge.co.uk
✉ info@hoebridge.co.uk
☎ 01483 722 611, Fax 740369,
Pro 722611, Sec 720256
On B382 between Old Woking and
West Byfleet.
Public parkland one par 3 course; one
18-hole course; one 9-hole course.
Pro Craig bufoy; Founded 1982
Designed by John Jacobs
Hoebridge 18 holes; Sheycopse 9
holes; Maybury 18 holes,
Hoebridge 6536; Sheycopse 2294
holes; Maybury 2280 Yards, S.S.S.
Hoebridge 71; Sheycopse 31;
Maybury 54
ⵏ Practice range 41 floodlit bays.
† Welcome 7 days per week.
Ⅰ Hoebridge WD £18.75, WE
£24.75; Sheycopse WD £10, WE £11;
Maybury WD £8, WE £8.
☞ WD by prior arrangement, Health
and Fitness terms on application.
🍽 Restaurant and bar facilties.
💤 Travel Inn nearby.

1A 76 Holtye

Holtye Common, Cowden, Kent,
TN8 7ED
🖥 www.holtye.com
✉ secretary@holtye.com
☎ 01342 850635, Fax 850576,
Pro 850957, Sec 850576
On the A264 1 mile S of Cowden.
Forest/heathland course.
Pro K Hinton; Founded 1893
9 holes, 5325 yards, S.S.S. 66
ⵏ 3/4 bays under cover.

† Welcome Mon, Tues, Fri;
Restrictions Wed and Thurs
mornings.
Ⅰ WD £18; WE £20.
☞ By prior arrangement; terms on
application.
🍽 Catering and bar facilities.
💤 White Horse Inn (next door).

1A 77 Homelands Bettergolf Centre

Ashford Road, Kingsnorth, Kent,
TN26 1NJ
🖥 www.bettergolf.co.uk
✉ isj@bettergolf.co.uk
☎ 01233 661620, Fax 720553
M20 Junction 10 following signs for
International station until 2nd
roundabout, turn left where course is
signposted.
Parkland course.
Pro Tony Bowers; Founded 1995
Designed by Donald Steel
9 holes, 4410 yards, S.S.S. 64
ⵏ 14 floodlit.
† Public pay as you play.
Ⅰ WD £8 for 9 holes £12 for 18; WE
£10 for 9 holes £16 for 18.
☞ Welcome; bar snacks, driving
range, academy pitch and putt; terms
on application.
🍽 Bar with drinks and snacks; BBQs
can be arranged.
💤 Many in area, contact club for
details.

1A 78 Horton Park Country Club

Hook Road, Epsom, Surrey,
KT19 8QG
☎ 020 8393 8400, Fax 8394 1369
M25 Junction 9; follow signs to
Chessington, turning right at Malden
Rushett lights. 2 miles, then left into
Horton Lane.
Parkland course.
Pro Martyn Hurst/Stewart Walker /
John Terrill; Founded 1987
18; 9 holes, 6028; 1637 yards, S.S.S.
70
ⵏ Practice area/Floodlit driving bays.
† Bookings WD; WE.
Ⅰ Terms on application.
☞ Welcome; packages include golf
and lunch/dinner.
🍽 Restaurant, bar, private suites.
💤 Chalk Lane Hotel, Epsom.

1A 79 Hurtmore

Hurtmore Road, Hurtmore, Surrey,
GU7 2RN

HortonPark
Golf & Country Club

Attractive parkland course situated within a picturesque country park with water hazards and lakes.
Eating facilities: bar food, restaurant and function room. *Visitors:* welcome.
Society Meetings: Welcome weekdays and weekend afternoons.
Tel: 020 8393 8400 • Pro Shop: 020 8394 2626 • Fax: 020 8394 1369
Professional: Martyn Hirst • General Manager: Anthony Picariello
Hook Road, Epsom, Surrey KT19 8QG • E-mail: hortonparkgc@aol.com

☎ 01483 426492, Fax 426121, A3 Guildford, M25 (15 minutes), A3 exit Guildford to Portsmouth.
Undulating parkland course with seven large lakes.
Pro Maxine Burton; Founded 1992
Designed by Peter Alliss and Clive Clark
18 holes, 5530 yards, S.S.S. 67
⚐ Practice nets; putting green.
† Welcome all times; bookings by phone.
Ⓛ WD £13; WE £19.
⚐ Welcome by appointment.
🍴 Full facilities available.
🛏 Squirrel.

1A 80 **Hythe Imperial**
Princes Parade, Hythe, Kent, CT21 6AE
🖥 www.hytheimperialgolfclub.co.uk
☎ 01303 267554, Fax 267554, Pro 233745
Turn off M20 to Hythe, to E end of seafront.
Seaside links course.
Pro Gordon Ritchie; Founded 1950
9 holes, 5560 yards, S.S.S. 68
⚐ Practice area, chipping and putting green.
† Welcome; handicap certificate required.
Ⓛ WD £15; WE £20.
⚐ Welcome by prior appointment; terms on application.
🍴 Hotel/club bar.
🛏 Hythe Imperial 4 star on site with full leisure facilities.

1A 81 **Kings Hill**
Kings Hill, West Malling, Kent, ME19 4AF
🖥 www.kingshill-golfclub.com
📧 khatkhgolf@aol.com
☎ 01732 875040, Fax 875019, Pro 842121, Sec 875040, Rest/Bar 875040
From M20 Junction 4 take A228 towards Tonbridge.
Heathland course.
Pro David Hudspith; Founded 1996
Designed by David Williams
18 holes, 6622 yards, S.S.S. 72

Ⓛ 6.
† Welcome WD; WE with member.
Ⓛ WD £30.
⚐ Welcome by appointment; £37–£53.
🍴 Full bar and catering.

1A 82 **Kingswood Golf & CC**
Sandy Lane, Tadworth, Surrey, KT20 6NE
☎ 01737 832188, Fax 833920, Pro 832334, Rest/Bar 832316
From A217 take Bonsor Drive (A2032) to Kingswood Arms. Club 0.25 miles down Sandy Lane.
Parkland course.
Pro Terry Sims; Founded 1938
Designed by James Braid
18 holes, 6904 yards, S.S.S. 73
⚐ Driving range, practice area.
† Welcome but WE restrictions.
Ⓛ WD £40; WE £55.
⚐ Welcome; terms on application.
🍴 Bar and restaurant.
🛏 Club will provide list.

1A 83 **Knole Park**   ♛
Seal Hollow Road, Sevenoaks, Kent, TN15 0HJ
🖥 www.knoleparkgolfclub.co.uk
📧 secretary@knolepark.fsnet.co.uk
☎ 01732 452150, Fax 463159, Pro 451740, Sec 452150, Rest/Bar 452021
0.5 miles from Sevenoaks town centre.
Parkland course.
Pro Phil Sykes; Founded 1924
Designed by JA Abercromby
18 holes, 6246 yards, S.S.S. 70
† Welcome after 9am WD.
Ⓛ WD £35.
⚐ Tues, Thurs, Fri by appt. £73.
🍴 Full facilities.
🛏 Donnington Manor Hotel, Dunton Green.

1A 84 **Laleham**
Laleham Reach, Chertsey, Surrey, KT16 8RP
🖥 www.laleham-golf.co.uk
📧 secretary@laleham-golf.co.uk
☎ 01932 564211, Fax 564448, Pro 562877, Rest/Bar 502188

From M25 Junction 11 take A320 to Thorpe Park roundabout then to Penton Marina and signposted.
Parkland course.
Pro Hogan Scott; Founded 1908
18 holes, 6211 yards, S.S.S. 70
† Welcome with handicap certs.
Ⓛ WD £22.
⚐ Mon, Tues, Wed; catering facilities; £21-£48.50.
🍴 Full facilities.

1A 85 **Lamberhurst Golf Club**
Church Road, Lamberhurst, Kent, TN3 8DT
🖥 www.lamberhurstgolfclub.com
📧 secretary@lamberhurstgolfclub.com
☎ 01892 890591, Fax 891140, Pro 890552, Sec 890591, Rest/Bar 890241
6 miles S of Tunbridge Wells on A21; turning on to B2162 at Lamberhurst.
Parkland course.
Pro Brian Impett; Founded 1890
Designed by Fran Pennik
18 holes, 6275 yards, S.S.S. 70
† Welcome WD, and pm at WE.
Ⓛ Summer rate WD £25 per round; WE £40 per round – winter rates WD £25 per round WE £25 per round.
⚐ Welcome Tues, Wed and Thurs, April to October; 36 holes, coffee, lunch and 3-course dinner; min 16, max 36; £56.
🍴 Full clubhouse facilities.
🛏 Pembury Resort, Pembury; George & Dragon, Lamberhurst.

1A 86 **Langley Park**
Barnfield Wood Road, Beckenham, Kent, BR3 6SZ
🖥 www.langleyparkgolf.co.uk
☎ 020 8658 6849, Fax 8658 6310, Pro 8650 1663, Rest/Bar 8650 2090
1 mile from Bromley South station.
Parkland course.
Pro Colin Staff; Founded 1910
Designed by JH Taylor
18 holes, 6488 yards, S.S.S. 71
† Welcome WD by arrangement with Pro shop. WE only with member.

⌇ WD £30 round, £40 day; WE members only.
⟳ Wed and Thurs only; maximum 24 Thurs; 36 holes
of golf, lunch and dinner; £58.
⫶⊙⫶ Full bar and restaurant.
⟿ Bromley Court Hotel.

1A 87 **Leatherhead**
Kingston Road, Leatherhead, Surrey, KT22 0EE
⬓ www.lgc/golf.co.uk
✉ professional@lgcgolf.co.uk
☎ 01372 843966, Fax 842241, Pro 843956
From M25 J9 take A243 towards London, course entrance 500 yards.
Parkland course.
Pro Simon Norman; Founded 1903
18 holes, 6203 yards, S.S.S. 70
⌇ Practice area.
† Welcome by appointment; WE not before 12 noon.
⌇ WD £37.50; WE £37.50.
⟳ Welcome; terms available on application.
⫶⊙⫶ Restaurant, brasserie, bar.
⟿ Woodlands Park (Oxshott).

1A 88 **Leeds Castle**
Leeds Castle, Maidstone, Kent, ME17 1PL
⬓ www.leeds-castle.co.uk
✉ stevepurves@leeds-castle
.co.uk
☎ 01622 880467, Fax 735616, Pro 880467, Sec 880467
M20 Junction 8 and follow signs to Leeds Castle on A20.
Parkland course.
Pro Steve Purves;
Founded 1933
Designed by Neil Coles
9 holes, 2681 yards, S.S.S. 33
† Can book 6 days ahead; no jeans please.
⌇ WD £11; WE £13.
⟳ WD only; terms on application.
⟿ Tudor Park, Maidstone.

1A 89 **Limpsfield Chart**
Limpsfield, Oxted, Surrey, RH8 0SL
☎ 01883 722106, Sec 723405, Rest/Bar 722106
Course is on the A25 between Oxted and Westerham, over the traffic lights 300 yards on right, east of Oxted.
Heathland course.
Founded 1889
9 holes, 5718 yards, S.S.S. 69
⌇ Practice net.

† WD welcome; WE by prior arrangement or with member.
⌇ WD £20; WE £22.
⟳ Can be arranged; terms on application.
⫶⊙⫶ Meals served.
⟿ Kings Arms (Westerham).

1A 90 **Lingfield Park** ♛
Racecourse Road, Lingfield, Surrey, RH7 6PQ
☎ 01342 834602, Fax 836077, Pro 832659, Sec 834602
From A22 at E Grinstead take the B 2028 to Lingfield.
Parkland course.
Pro Chris Morley; Founded 1987
18 holes, 6487 yards, S.S.S. 72
⌇ 20.
† Welcome WD, WE by appt.
⌇ WD £38; WE £52.
⟳ Welcome by prior arrangement; packages include golf and catering; call for information.
⫶⊙⫶ Full facilities available.
⟿ Felbridge; Copthorne.

1A 91 **Littlestone**
St Andrew's Road, Littlestone, New Romney, Kent, TN28 8RB
⬓ www.littlestonegolfclub.org.uk
✉ secretary@littlestonegolfclub
.org.uk
☎ 01797 363355, Fax 362740, Pro 362231, Rest/Bar 362310
In New Romney on A259 between Brenzett and Hythe; 15 miles S of Ashford.
Links course.
Pro Andrew Jones; Founded 1888
Designed by Laidlaw Purves
18 holes, 6486 yards, S.S.S. 72; Blue Course: 18 holes, 6676 yards, S.S.S. 73
⌇ Driving range.
† Welcome by prior arrangement WD and WE.
⌇ WD £39; WE £55.
⟳ Welcome WD; golf and catering packages; from £55.
⫶⊙⫶ Full facilities.
⟿ Romney Bay House; Broadacre; Rose and Crown; White House B&B.

1A 92 **The London** ♛
South Ash Manor Estate, Ash, Nr Sevenoaks, Kent, TN15 7EN
⬓ www.londongolf.co.uk
✉ golf@londongolf.co.uk
☎ 01474 879889, Fax 879912
Off A20 near Brands Hatch at W Kingsdown.

Parkland course; inland links.
Pro Bill Longmuir/Paul Stewart; Founded 1993
Designed by Jack Nicklaus & Ron Kirby
Heritage 18; International 18 holes, Heritage 7208; Int 7005 yards, S.S.S. Heritage 72; Int 74
⌇ Driving range.
† Welcome only if accompanied by a member and by prior arrangement.
⌇ Heritage WD £00; WE N/A. International WD £70; WE £75.
⟳ Corporate days arranged.
⫶⊙⫶ Restaurant bar, function rooms and coffee shop.
⟿ Brands Hatch Thistle; Brands Hatch Place; Holiday Inn, Maidstone.

1A 93 **London Scottish**
Windmill Enclosure, Wimbledon Common, London, SW19 5NQ
⬓ www.londonscottishgolfclub.co.uk
✉ secretary.lsgc@virgin.net
☎ 020 8789 1207, Fax 8789 7517, Rest/Bar 8788 0135
1 mile from Putney station.
Heathland course.
Pro Steve Barr; Founded 1865
Designed by Tom Dunn
18 holes, 5458 yards, S.S.S. 66
† Welcome WD, except BH; must wear red upper garment.
⌇ WD from £10.
⟳ Welcome except WE; terms on application.
⫶⊙⫶ Lunch served, dinner if ordered.
⟿ Wayfarer.

1A 94 **Lullingstone Park**
Park Gate Rd, Chelsfield, Orpington, Kent, BR6 7PX
☎ 01959 533793, Fax 534129, Rest/Bar 532928
Signposted from M25 Junction 4.
Municipal parkland course.
Pro Mark Watt; Founded 1923
Designed by Fred Hawtree
18 holes, 6779 yards, S.S.S. 72
⌇ 32.
† Welcome.
⌇ WD £14; WE £18.60.
⟳ Welcome by prior arrangement; terms on application.
⫶⊙⫶ Bar and restaurant.
⟿ Thistle (Brands Hatch).

1A 95 **Lydd** ♛
Romney Road, Lydd, Romney Marsh, Kent, TN29 9LS
⬓ www.lyddgolfclub.co.uk
✉ info@lyddgolfclub.co.uk

Lingfield Park Golf Club

Racecourse Road, Lingfield, Surrey RH7 6PQ

Boasting a splendid 18 hole golf course and a 300 acre racecourse, Lingfield Park is set in complete privacy in 500 acres of beautiful Surrey countryside.

The golf course provides a challenging 72 standard scratch course, 6487 yards in length, whilst the racecourse is the busiest in England with over 75 meetings per year.

With ponds, streams and a variety of mature trees featured throughout the course, Lingfield Park provides an unforgettable test of golf. All this complemented by a range and practice ground, modern Clubhouse, informal bar and lounge area, and a restaurant open daily for Lunch or Dinner in relaxed surroundings overlooking the golf course.

Golf Operations Manager/Professional: Chris Morley   Email: cmorley@lingfieldpark.co.uk
Tel (Office): 01342 834602   Fax (Office): 01342 836077   Pro Shop Tel: 01342 832659

☎ 01797 320808, Fax 321482,
Pro 321201
Take Ashford exit off M20 and follow
A2070 signs to Lydd Airport. At
Brenzett turn left (B2075), club on left.
Links type course.
Pro Miss Stuwart; Founded 1993
Designed by M Smith
18 holes, 6517 yards, S.S.S. 71
ⁱ 25 floodlit.
♦ Welcome.
⌶ WD £17; WE £25.
⌁ Welcome only by prior
appointment; terms available on
application.
⦿ Bar and restaurant.

1A 96 Malden
Traps Lane, New Malden, Surrey,
KT3 4RS
✉ maldengc@lwcdial.net
☎ 020 8942 0654, Fax 8936 2219,
Pro 8942 6009, Rest/Bar 8942 3266
0.5 miles from New Malden station,
close to the A3 between Wimbledon
and Kingston.
Parkland course.
Pro Robert Hunter; Founded 1926
Designed by Alex Herd
18 holes, 6295 yards, S.S.S. 70
♦ Welcome WD; WE restrictions.
⌶ WD £30; WE £50.
⌁ Subject to availability midweek.
⦿ Full clubhouse facilities.
⌂ Kingston Lodge.

1A 97 Marriott Tudor Park   ☞
Hotel & CC
Ashford Road, Bearsted, Maidstone,
Kent, ME14 4NQ
⌇ www.marriotthotels.co.uk
/tudorpark
☎ 01622 734334, Fax 735360,
Pro 739412, Sec 739412,
Rest/Bar 734334

Follow A20 Ashford road; 3 miles from
Maidstone centre.
Parkland course.
Pro Nick McNally; Founded 1988
Designed by Donald Steel
18 holes, 6041 yards, S.S.S. 69
ⁱ 6 bays.
♦ Welcome with handicap certs.
⌶ WD £25; WE £35.
⌁ Welcome WD by appointment.
⦿ Hotel and restaurant.
⌂ Marriott Tudor Park.

1A 98 Merrist Wood   ☞
Coombe Lane, Worplesdon, Guildford,
Surrey, GU3 3PE
✉ mwgc@merristwood.co.uk
☎ 01483 238890, Pro 884050,
Rest/Bar 884048
Off A323 at Worplesdon.
Parkland/woodland course.
Pro Andrew Kirk; Founded 1997
Designed by David Williams
18 holes, 6909 yards, S.S.S. 73
♦ Welcome WDs.
⌶ WD £35.
⌁ Welcome by appointment.
⦿ Bar and restaurant facilities.
⌂ Worplesdon Place.

1A 99 Mid-Kent
Singlewell Road, Gravesend, Kent,
DA11 7RB
☎ 01474 568035, Fax 564218,
Pro 332810, Rest/Bar 352387
On A227 after leaving A2 signposted
Gravesend.
Parkland course.
Pro Mark Foreman; Founded 1909
Designed by Frank Pennink
18 holes, 6218 yards, S.S.S. 70
ⁱ Practice range – irons only.
♦ Welcome WDs if members of a
club with handicap certs; WE with
member only.

⌶ WD £35/£25 (day/round); WE not
available.
⌁ Terms on application; Tues only.
⦿ Full facilities.
⌂ Manor; Tolgate.

1A 100 Milford
Milford, Nr Guildford, Surrey, GU8 5HS
⌇ www.americangolf.com
✉ milford@americangolf.uk.com
☎ 01483 419200, Fax 419199,
Pro 416291
From A3 take Milford exit and head for
station.
Parkland course.
Pro Paul Creamer; Founded 1993
Designed by Peter Alliss, Clive Clark
18 holes, 5960 yards, S.S.S. 69
ⁱ 8.
♦ Welcome.
⌶ WD £20; WE £25 after 12 noon.
⌁ Welcome; from £35.
⦿ Full clubhouse facilities.
⌂ Inn on the Lake.

1A 101 Mitcham
Carshalton Road, Mitcham Junction,
Surrey, CR4 4HN
☎ 020 8648 1508, Fax 8648 4197,
Pro 8640 4280, Sec 8648 4197
A237 off A23, by Mitcham Junction
station.
Meadowland course.
Pro Jeff Godfrey; Founded 1886
18 holes, 5935 yards, S.S.S. 68
♦ Welcome by appointment WD; pm
only at WE.
⌶ WD £16; WE £16.
⌁ Terms on application.
⦿ Full facilities.
⌂ Hilton, Sutton Croydon.

1A 102 Moatlands   ☞
Watermans Lane, Brenchley, Kent,
TN12 6ND

Royal Mid-Surrey

Having played over one thousand rounds of golf at Royal Mid-Surrey I think I can say that it is a course (or courses) that I know well. And the biggest compliment that I can pay it is that over all that time I have never become weary with familiarity or been anything other than hopeful and enthusiastic standing on the first tee.

The outer course has not changed much over the 25 years that I was a member. The two tiered green at the seventh was lost to a botched reconstruction job and there was a summer when the rough was grown so ludicrously high that the professional shop must have done record trade in golf balls. But other than that and some new bunkering and planting it has stayed pretty much the same.

How underrated a golf course the outer at Mid-Surrey is. It is rich with landmarks. The exile rugby clubs of Scotland and Wales bordered the second hole. The Chinese pagoda looms behind the fourth green. The fifth, sixth and seventh are bordered by Kew Gardens, the ninth, fifteenth and sixteenth by the river Thames (although you would need a slice of monumental proportions to reach the river).

The cedar tree to the left of the 12th fairway is approaching its 500th year and a shanked second down the fourteenth can put you in the gardens of what was once the observatory, where Sir William Herschel, discoverer of Uranus, served as its first director. RMS is rich with landmarks, but not so generous about giving up pars.

The clubhouse was also one of the finest in Britain and full of priceless paintings, photographs and artefacts. Tragically it burned to the ground in 2001 and with it the club lost a part of its soul. The cause of the fire has never been conclusively established, although one theory has it that some linseed-oil soaked rags that had been used to ready the outdoor furniture for the spring spontaneously combusted.

The new clubhouse was finished at the end of 2003 and to some of us it jars. A mass of metal and glass it seems like an intruder on crown land. Some friends described it as looking like a young offender's institute, but maybe it will grow into itself.

The club has a lengthy royal tradition. Not only is it a tenant on crown land (Henry V founded a Carthusian monastery here, traces of which lie under the 14th and 15th fairway), but George III ordered the building of the observatory, the future Edward VIII became captain in 1926, the year that his father King George V granted the royal title, and the current Duke of York is a strong supporter of the club.

RMS's golfing associations are just as rich. The great J.H. Taylor (the famous painting of him sadly went in the fire) was professional for over 40 years and was succeeded in the job by Henry Cotton. And the club was home to Pam Barton, perhaps England's most celebrated woman amateur after Joyce Wethered, who was both British and American Ladies champion in 1936 at the age of 19. Tragically Barton was killed whilst serving in the war, otherwise who knows what she might have gone on to achieve.

The club has an extraordinary history. It will be interesting to see what it makes of the future. — **Mark Reason**

www.moatlands.com
moatlandsgolf@btconnect.com
☎ 01892 724400, Fax 723300,
Pro 724252, Rest/Bar 724555
From A21 take B2160 to Paddock
Wood traveling through Matfield.
Parkland course.
Pro Simon Wood; Founded 1993
Designed by K Saito
18 holes, 7060 yards, S.S.S. 74
🏌 15.
† Welcome WD; pm at WE.
⌁ WD £29; WE £39.
⌁ Welcome Mon–Fri, terms on appl.
🍴 Clubhouse bar and restaurant.
⌁ Ramada Jarvis Resort.

1A 103 **Moore Place**
Portsmouth Road, Esher, Surrey,
KT10 9LN
www.moore-place.co.uk
☎ 01372 463533, Fax 463533,
Pro 463533, Rest/Bar 463532
On A3 Portsmouth road, 0.5 mile from
centre of Esher towards Cobham.
Public undulating parkland course.
Pro Nick Gadd; Founded 1926
Designed by Harry Varden
9 holes, 2078 yards, S.S.S. 61
† Welcome.
⌁ WD £6.30; WE £8.00.
⌁ Welcome WD; terms on
application.
🍴 Full facilities.
⌁ The Haven Hotel.

1A 104 **Nevill**
Benhall Mill Road, Tunbridge Wells,
Kent, TN2 5JW
www.nevillgolfclub.co.uk
manager@nevillgolfclub.co.uk
☎ 01892 525818, Fax 517861,
Pro 532941, Rest/Bar 527820
S of Tunbridge Wells on A21.
Parkland course.
Pro Paul Huggett; Founded 1914
Designed by CK Cotton
18 holes, 6349 yards, S.S.S. 70
† Welcome with handicap certs.
⌁ WD £30; WE £40.
⌁ Welcome Wed, Thurs; terms on
application.
🍴 Full facilities.
⌁ Spa Hotel, Tunbridge Wells.

1A 105 **New Zealand Golf Club**
Woodham Lane, Addlestone, Surrey,
KT15 3QD
☎ 01932 345049, Fax 342891,
Pro 349619
On A245 from W Byfleet to Woking.
Wooded heathland course.

Pro V Evelvidge; Founded 1895
Designed by Muir-Ferguson/Simpson
18 holes, 6012 yards, S.S.S. 69
† Welcome by appointment.
⌁ Terms on application.
⌁ Welcome by appointment; terms
on application.
🍴 Full facilities.

1A 106 **Nizels**
Nizels Lane, Hildenborough, Nr
Tonbridge, Kent, TN11 8NU
www.clubhaus.com
nizels.membership@clubhaus
.com
☎ 01732 833138, Fax 835492,
Pro 838926
Take the A21 southbound from M25
Junction 5; then take the B245 towards
Tonbridge. At roundabout head for
Hildenborough and the first right is
Nizels Lane.
Parkland course.
Pro Neil Thirkill; Founded 1992
Designed by Paul Way
18 holes, 6297 yards, S.S.S. 71
† Welcome except am WE.
⌁ WD £25; WE £30.
⌁ Welcome by prior arrangement;
minimum 12. Call Alison Ronaldson.
🍴 Full facilities and bar.
⌁ Rose & Crown, Tonbridge; Philpots
Manor, Hildenborough.

1A 107 **North Downs**   ⌇
Northdown Road, Woldingham, Surrey,
CR3 7AA
www.northdownsgolfclub.co.uk
info@northdownsgolfclub.co.uk
☎ 01883 652057, Fax 652832,
Pro 653004, Rest/Bar 653298
Travel 2 miles north of the M25 Junction
6 to the roundabout, take the 5th exit to
Woldingham (2 miles); the clubhouse is
0.5 mile through village on left.
Parkland course.
Pro Mike Homewood; Founded 1899
Designed by JJ Pennink
18 holes, 5857 yards, S.S.S. 68
† Welcome WD with handicap certs
or; WE after 3 pm (summer), after
noon (winter).
⌁ WD £30; WE £25.
⌁ WD, half or full day (half-day only
Thurs); terms available on application.
🍴 Restaurant, snacks.
⌁ Travel Inn (M25, Clacket Lane);
Wesleyan Hotel, Warlingham.

1A 108 **North Foreland**
Convent Road, Broadstairs, Kent,
CT10 3PU

Bpre342845@aol.com
☎ 01843 862140, Fax 862663,
Pro 604471
A28 from Canterbury, or A2/M2/A299
from London to Kingsgate via
Broadstairs; course 1.5 miles from
Broadstairs station.
Seaside/clifftop course; links course.
Pro Neil Hansen; Founded 1903
Designed by Fowler and Simpson
18 holes, 6430 yards, S.S.S. 71; Short
course: 18 holes, 1752 yards, par 3
† Prior booking, not Sun, Mon, Tues
am; handicap certs required; short
course unrestricted.
⌁ WD £30; WE £40; Short: WD £6;
WE £7.50.
⌁ Welcome by appointment; terms
on application.
🍴 Full clubhouse facilities.
⌁ Castle Keep.

1A 109 **Oak Park**
Heath Lane, Crondall, Nr Farnham,
Surrey, GU10 5PB
☎ 01252 850850, Fax 850851,
Pro 850066
Course is 1.25 miles off the A287
Farnham-Oldham road; and 5 miles
from M3 Juntion 5.
Woodland course; also 9-hole Village
Parkland course.
Pro Gary Murton; Founded 1984
Designed by Patrick Dawson
18 holes, 6318 yards, S.S.S. 70
† Welcome.
⌁ WD £20; WE £28; 9-hole course:
WD £10; WE £12.
⌁ Welcome by appointment.
🍴 Conservatory bar, restaurant with
cocktail bar.
⌁ Bishops Table; Bush, both Farnham.

1A 110 **Oaks Sports Centre**
Woodmansterne Road, Carshaton,
Surrey, SM5 4AN
www.oaksportscentre.co.uk
☎ 020 8643 8363, Fax 8770 7303,
Pro 8643 8363, Sec 8642 7103,
Rest/Bar 8643 8363
Course is on the B2032 past
Carshalton Beeches station, the Oaks
Sports Centre signposted N of the
A2022, halfway between the A217 and
the A237.
Public parkland course.
Pro Craig Mitchell/Michael Pilkington;
Founded 1982
Designed by Alphagreen
18 holes, 6033 yards, S.S.S. 69
🏌 16 bays.
† Welcome.

ⅼ WD £15.25; WE £18.
🖝 Welcome by appointment; terms on application.
🍽 Restaurant and bar.
🍷 The Post House,Croydon.

1A 111 **Oastpark**
Malling Road, Snodland, Kent, ME6 5LG
☎ 01634 242818, Fax 240744, Pro 242661, Rest/Bar 242659
On A228 close to M20 Junction 4 and M2 Junction 2.
Parkland course.
Pro David Porthouse; Founded 1992
Designed by Terry Cullen
9 holes, 2833 yards, S.S.S. 68
† Welcome.
ⅼ WD 9 £7. WD 18 £12. WE 9 £8 WE 18 £14.
🖝 Welcome WD and after 11am at WE; minimum 8; from £15.
🍽 Full clubhouse facilities.
🍷 Swan; Larkfield Priory; Forte Crest.

1A 112 **Pachesham Park Golf Centre**
Oaklawn Road, Leatherhead, Surrey, KT22 0BT
🖥 info@pacheshamgolf.co.uk
☎ 01372 843453
M25 Junction 9; A244 towards Esher.
Parkland course.
Pro Phil Taylor; Founded 1991
Designed by Phil Taylor
9 holes, 5608 yards, S.S.S. 67
ⅼ 33 bays.
† Welcome; book 48 hours ahead.
ⅼ WD £9; WE £10.50.
🖝 Welcome by appointment; terms on application.
🍽 Full facilities.
🍷 Woodlands Park.

1A 113 **Park Wood**
Chestnut Avenue, Tatsfield, Westerham, Kent, TN16 2EG
🖧 www.parkwoodgolf.co.uk
🖥 mail@parkwoodgolf.co.uk
☎ 01959 577744, Fax 572702, Pro 577177, Rest/Bar 577740
From the centre of Westerham take Oxted Road then turn right onto the B2024, go under M25 to the top of the hill; course is right and immediate right again.
Parkland and lakes course.
Pro Nick Terry; Founded 1994
Designed by R Goldsmith
18 holes, 6835 yards, S.S.S. 72
† Welcome.
ⅼ WD £22; WE £24.

🖝 Welcome Mon-Fri.
🍽 120-seat restaurant, Full bar.
🍷 Kings Arms (Westerham).

1A 114 **Pedham Place Golf Club**
London Road, Swanley, Kent, BR8 8PP
🖧 www.ppgc.co.uk
🖥 golf@ppgc.co.uk
☎ 01322 867000, Fax 861646
Junction 3 M25, A20 towards Brands Hatch.
Links style course.Pro F Hanlon/ R Mitchell.
Designed by John Fortune.
9 hole: 1097 yards, Par 3; 18 hole: 6047 or 6044 yards, Par 72
ⅼ 40 bays floodlit; £2 for 40 balls
† Welcome.
ⅼ Par 3: WD £6, WE £7.50; 18-hole: WD £18, WE £25; discount seniors and junios.
🖝 Welcome.
🍽 Restaurant and bar.
🍷 Travel inns off M25.

1A 115 **Pine Ridge Golf Centre**
Old Bisley Road, Frimley, Camberley, Surrey, GU16 5NX
🖧 www.pineridgegolf.co.uk
🖥 enquiry@pineridgegolf.co.uk
☎ 01276 675444, Fax 678837, Pro 675444, Rest/Bar 675444
5 mins from M3 Junction 3; location map available on request.
Public pine-forested course.
Pro Peter Sefdon; Founded 1992
Designed by Clive D Smith
18 holes, 6012 yards, S.S.S. 72
ⅼ 36.
† Welcome.
ⅼ WD £20; WE £26.
🖝 Welcome WD, min 12; terms on application.
🍽 Bar and restaurant, all day.
🍷 Lakeside; Frimley Hall.

1A 116 **Poult Wood**
Higham Lane, Tonbridge, Kent, TN11 9QR
☎ 01732 364039, Fax 353781, Sec 364039, Rest/Bar 366180
Course is 1 mile N of Tonbridge off the A227.
Municipal wooded course.
Pro Chris Miller; Founded 1972
Designed by Fred Hawtree
18 holes, 5569 yards, 9 holes, S.S.S. 67; 9 holes, 1281 yards
† Welcome; booking required for 18.
ⅼ Prices on application.

🖝 Welcome WD by appointment; terms on application.
🍽 Restaurant and bar.
🍷 Langley; Rose & Crown.

1A 117 **Prince's Golf Club** ♔
Sandwich Bay, Sandwich, Kent, CT13 9QB
🖧 www.princesgolfclub.co.uk
🖥 office@princesgolfclub.co.uk
☎ 01304 611118, Fax 612000, Pro 613797
M2, A2 to A256 then follow signs for Sandwich; course signposted.
3 loops of 9 holes; Links course.
Pro Derek Barbour; Founded 1906
Designed by Sir Guy Campbell & John Morrison
27 holes, 7145 yards, S.S.S. 72
ⅼ Driving range.
† Welcome 7 days a week.
ⅼ WD £40-£60; WE £50-£70.
🖝 Welcome by appointment.
Packages available from £45.
🍽 Spike bar; restaurant.
🍷 The Bell; The Blazing Donkey, Ham; Royal, Deal.

1A 118 **Purley Downs**
106 Purley Downs Road, South Croydon, Surrey, CR2 0RB
🖧 www.purleydownsgolfclub.co.uk
🖥 info@purleydownsgolfclub.co.uk
☎ 020 8657 1231, Fax 8651 5044, Pro 8651 0819, Sec 8657 8347, Rest/Bar 8657 1231/8657 8142
3 miles S of Croydon on A235.
Downland course.
Pro Graham Wilson; Founded 1894
18 holes, 6275 yards, S.S.S. 70
† Welcome WD. WE with members.
ⅼ WD £30; WE £15 with a member.
🖝 Welcome Mon, Thurs; terms on application.
🍽 19th hole bar, lounge bar and restaurant.
🍷 Selsdon Park; Trust House Forte; Croydon Hilton.

1A 119 **Puttenham**
Heath Road, Puttenham, Guildford, Surrey, GU3 1AL
🖧 www.puttenhamgolfclub.co.uk
🖥 enquiries@puttenhamgolfclub.co.uk
☎ 01483 810489, Fax 810988, Pro 810277, Rest/Bar 811087
Off A31 Hogs Back at Puttenham sign (B3000).
Tight heathland course.
Pro Dean Lintott; Founded 1894
18 holes, 6220 yards, S.S.S. 70

Driving range.
Welcome WD by prior arrangement; with a member only at WE.
WD £32; WE no green fees, invitation with members only.
Welcome Wed, Thurs, Fri; terms on application (or see website).
Full catering and bar.
Hogs Back Hotel.

1A 120 Pyrford
Warren Lane, Pyrford, Woking, Surrey, GU22 8XR
pyrford@americangolf.uk.com
01483 723555, Fax 729777, Pro 751070
From A3 take Ripley/Wisley exit (B2215) through Ripley, follow signs for Pyrford.
Inland links.
Pro Darren Brewer; Founded 1993
Designed by Peter Alliss & Clive Clark
18 holes, 6256 yards, S.S.S. 70
Welcome.
WD £40; WE £45.
Welcome; from £45.
Full bar and catering.
Cobham Hilton.

1A 121 Redhill & Reigate
Clarence Lodge, Pendleton Road, Redhill, Surrey, RH1 6LB
redhillandreigategolfclub@btopenworld.com
01737 240777, Fax 242117, Pro 244433, Rest/Bar 244626
1 mile S of Redhill between A23 and A25.
Wooded parkland course.
Pro Warren Pike; Founded 1887
Designed by James Braid
18 holes, 5272 yards, S.S.S. 68
Welcome WD and after 11am at WE.
WD £15; WE £25.
Welcome by prior arrangement; packages available from £37.50.
Full facilities.
Reigate Manor.

1A 122 Redlibbets
Manor Lane, West Yoke, Ash, Sevenoaks, Kent, TN15 7HT
www.golfandsport.co.uk
redlibbets@golfandsport.com
01474 872278, Fax 879290, Pro 4872278, Sec 4 879190
Take the A20 exit from the M25 towards Brands Hatch, course is on

Paddock side next to Fawkham Manor Hospital, 8 miles from Sevenoaks.
Parkland course.
Pro Ross Taylor; Founded 1996
Designed by J Gaunt
18 holes, 6639 yards, S.S.S. 72
Welcome. With a member weekends only.
WD £40 (without a member), WD £15; WE £25.
Mon,Tues, Thurs; terms available on application.
Full facilities.
Brands Hatch Place.

1A 123 Reigate Heath
Reigate Heath, Reigate, Surrey, RH2 8QR
www.reigateheathgolfclub.co.uk
reigateheath@surreygolf.co.uk
01737 242610, Fax 249226, Sec 226793
1.5 miles W of Reigate on Flanchford Road off A25.
Heathland course.
Pro Barry Davies; Founded 1895
9 holes, 5658 yards, S.S.S. 67
Practice ground.
Welcome in midweek.

Royal St George's

It didn't take long for the world's finest golfers to discover at the 2003 Open Championship that Royal St George's can be an unforgiving soul. Tiger Woods lashed his opening tee shot of the Championship into the right rough. The next time he saw his ball was in a picture in one of the next day's tabloids, having been retrieved long after Woods had given up the search.

His countryman Jerry Kelly took an 11 at the same hole before remarking, "I've hit shots out of that wet grass all week and they've come out fine. I just hit six of them that didn't come out. When people ask me how did you make an eleven, I'll say I made a 30-footer, man."

I wonder what Woods and Kelly made of the remark of Walter Hagen, the winner of the Open here in 1922 and '28. Hagen said, "The first nine holes – tremendous fun, not very good golf. Second nine holes – tremendous golf, no fun at all."

Or the words of Bernard Darwin who wrote, "A fine spring day, with the larks singing as they seem to sing nowhere else; the sun shining on the waters of Pegwell Bay and lighting up the white cliffs in the distance, this is as nearly my idea of heaven as is to be attained on any earthly links." Thomas Levet, the runner-up at the 2002 Open, put it another way. The Frenchman said, "The course is a big monster."

Apart from the capricious bounces for which Royal St George's is renowned, consider also the fate of the Irishman Harry Bradshaw in 1949. In the second round his ball finished in a bottle. Without a referee at hand to give him a ruling, Bradshaw played the ball as it lay, shut his eyes to avoid the splintering glass and gave the bottle a whack. It cost him a six. He would lose to Bobby Locke in a play-off.

Hopefully Bradshaw found solace in the clubhouse bar that, with its "tankards of ale from the wood", is one of the finest in the country and must have helped the club to the royal title that Edward VII bestowed in 1902.

Although the original design of holes like the Maiden (once the Jungfrau) and Hades and Corsets has gone, St George's is still a tease. From the fourteenth hole on it provides one of the most testing finishes in golf.

Darwin, a former president of the club, wrote of the old 17th, "Those who love the hopes and fears of a lucky bag will enjoy the seventeenth, where the hole lies in a deep dell with sharply sloping sides. Man can direct the ball into the dell but only Providence can decide its subsequent fate." The modern pros did not enjoy the hopes and fears of a lucky bag one little bit.

Thomas Bjørn, the man who threw away the 2003 Open, tempted fate when he said, "When I set foot here the other day I knew straight away that a lot of guys don't have a hope and they were going to be home on Friday because they can't deal with the bounces and they don't have the game."

Yet with a list of past Sandwich champions that includes Harry Vardon, Hagen, Henry Cotton, Sandy Lyle and Greg Norman, wonderful ball strikers obviously get luckier than most. Given the equipment available to him then it is almost impossible to believe that in 1934 Cotton opened with rounds of 67 and 65.

— **Mark Reason**

WD £25; WE n/a.
Wed, Thurs; max 30; terms on app.
Full facilities.
Cranleigh Hotel, Reigate.

1A 124 Reigate Hill

Gatton Bottom, Reigate, Surrey,
RH2 0TU
www.reigatehillgolfclub.co.uk
01737 646070, Fax 642650,
Pro 646070, Sec 645577,
Rest/Bar 64577
Course is 1 mile from J8 of the M25.
Parkland course.
Pro Christopher Forsyth; Founded 1995
Designed by D Williams
18 holes, 6175 yards, S.S.S. 70
12.
WD, WE after 12 noon.
WD £25; WE £35.
Welcome by appointment; terms
on application.
Full facilities.
Bridge House, Reigate Hill; The
Priory, Nutfield.

1A 125 Richmond

Fulwood Court, Long Lane, Staines,
Middx, TW19 7AS
020 8940 1463, Fax 8332 7914,
Pro 8940 7792
On A307 1 mile S of Richmond, look
for Sudbrook Lane on left.
Parkland course.
Pro Nick Job; Founded 1891
Designed by Tom Dunn
18 holes, 5785 yards, S.S.S. 69
WD by app.; WE with members.
WD £27; WE £25.
Tues, Thurs, Fri by appointment;
terms on application.
Bar snacks, lunches every day.
Petersham; Richmond Gate.

1A 126 Richmond Park

Roehampton Gate, Richmond Park,
London, SW15 5JR
www.richmondparkgolf.co.uk
info@richmondparkgolf.co.uk
020 8876 3205, Fax 8878 1354,
Pro 8876 1795
Inside Richmond Park; enter through
Roehampton Gate off Priory Lane.
Parkland courses.
Pro David Bown; Founded 1923
Designed by Hawtree & Sons
Duke's 18 holes, 6036 yards, S.S.S. 68
Prince's 18 holes, 5868 yards. S.S.S.
69
18 not floodlit.
Pay and play course.

WD £18; WE £21.
Welcome.
None.
Richmond Gate Hotel.

1A 127 The Ridge

Chartway Street, East Sutton,
Maidstone, Kent, ME17 3JB
ridge@americangolf.uk.com
01622 844382, Fax 844168,
Pro 844243
From M20 Junction 8 take B2163 to
Sutton Valence.
Old apple orchards.
Pro James Cornish; Founded 1993
Designed by Tryton Design Ltd
18 holes, 6214 yards, S.S.S. 70
Handicap certs required; midweek
only.
WD £30; WE £18 (pm, with
members only).
Tues, Thurs, welcome by prior
appointment; golf and catering; £35-£57.
Full catering facilities.

1A 128 Riverside

Summerton Way, Thamesmead,
SE28 8PP
enquiries@thamesview-golf.fsnet
.co.uk
020 8310 7975, Pro 0785 586
4485
Course is off the A1, 10 mins from
Blackheath, 15 mins from Bexleyheath;
near Woolwich.
Pay-as-you-play on reclaimed
marshland.
Pro Graeme Wilson; Founded 1991
Designed by Heffernan & Heffernan
9 holes, 5482 yards, S.S.S. 66
30.
Welcome subject to reasonable
standard of golf.
WD £6.50; WE £8.50.
Welcome by appointment WD, only
small societies WE; terms on
application.
2 bars, à la carte.
Black Prince (Bexleyheath);
Swallow.

1A 129 Rochester & Cobham Park

Park Pale by Rochester, Kent, ME2 3UL
www.rochesterandcobhamgc.co.uk
rcpgc@talk21.com
01474 823411, Fax 824446,
Pro 823658, Sec 823411,
Rest/Bar 823412
3 miles E of Gravesend east exit for
Cobham, Higham & Shoreham off A2.

Parkland course.
Pro Iain Higgins; Founded 1891/1997
Designed by Donald Steel
18 holes, 6597 yards, S.S.S. 72
10 + excellent practice facilities.
WD with handicap certs; WE with
member only.
WD £35 per round £45 per day;
WE members only.
Tues and Thurs; packages
available; £42-£70.
Full catering facilities.
Inn on the Lake, A2; Tolgate Motel,
Gravesend.

1A 130 Roehampton

Roehampton Lane, London,
SW15 5LR
www.roehamptonclub.co.uk
admin@roehamptonclub.co.uk
020 8480 4200, Fax 8480 4265,
Pro 8876 3858, Rest/Bar 8480 4225
Just off the South Circular road
between Sheen and Putney.
Private members parkland course.
Pro Alan Scott; Founded 1901
18 holes, 6065 yards, S.S.S. 69
Members' guests only.
WD £25; WE £34.
Welcome by members' Introduction
only; terms available on application.
Restaurant, bar and function
rooms.

1A 131 Roker Park

Holly Lane, Aldershot Road, Guildford,
Surrey, GU3 3PB
01483 236677, Fax 232324,
Sec 232324, Rest/Bar 237700
2 miles W of Guildford on A323.
Parkland course.
Pro Kevin Warn; Founded 1992
Designed by WV Roker
9 holes, 6074 yards, S.S.S. 72
12.
Public pay and play course.
WD £8.50; WE £10 and BH for 9
holes £17.50 for 18 holes. WD £14.50
for 18 holes. £12.50 unlimited use in
winter.
WD preferable; minimum 12; WD
£12; WE £15.
Facilities available.
Worpelson Hotel.

1A 132 Romney Warren

St Andrew's Road, Littlestone, New
Romney, Kent, TN28 8RB
01797 362231, Fax 363511,
Pro 362231, Sec 362231,
Rest/Bar 366613

Take A259 to New Romney, turn right into Littlestone Road and after 0.5 miles into St Andrew's Road.
Links course.
Pro Andrew Jones; Founded 1993
Designed by JD Lewis, BM Evans
18 holes, 5126 yards, S.S.S. 65
↟ Practice ground.
♦ Welcome with booking.
↳ WD £15; WE £20.
↷ Apply at Pro shop; from £14.

1A 133 **Royal Blackheath** ☏
Court Road, Eltham, London, SE9 0LR
⬡ www.rbgc.com
✉ jan@rgbc.com
☎ 020 8850 1795, Fax 8859 0150, Pro 8850 1763, Rest/Bar 8850 1042
J3 M25-A25 to London; 2nd lights turn right; club is 600 yards on right.
Parkland course; oldest known in world.
Pro Richard Harrison; Founded 1608
Designed by James Braid
18 holes, 6219 yards, S.S.S. 70
↟ Chipping and putting area.
♦ Welcome midweek by arrangement with handicap cert; WE only with member.
↳ WD £45, £60 (for the day); WE no fees.
↷ Welcome Mon-Fri by appointment; from £65.
🍽 Full catering and bar facilities.
🛏 Bromley Court, Bromley Clarendon, Blackheath.

1A 134 **Royal Cinque Ports**
Golf Road, Deal, Kent, CT14 6RF
⬡ www.royalcinqueports.com
✉ rcpgcsec@aol.com
☎ 01304 374007, Fax 379530, Pro 374170
Follow coast road through Deal to end and turn left on to Godwyn Road, at the end turn right on to Golf Road.
Seaside links course.
Pro Andrew Reynolds; Founded 1892
Designed by Tom Dunn, Guy Campbell, James Braid
18 holes, 6754 yards, S.S.S. 71
♦ Welcome WD except Weds; WE by appointment; handicap certs required.
↳ WD £75; WE £85.
↷ Welcome WD by prior appointment; terms available on application.
🍽 Full facilities; dress code required.
🛏 Royal; Kings Head, both Deal; Bell, Sandwich.

1A 135 **Royal Mid-Surrey**
Old Deer Park, Richmond, Surrey, TW9 2SB
⬡ www.rmsgc.co.uk
✉ secretary@rmsgc.co.uk
☎ 020 8940 1894, Fax 8332 2957, Pro 8939 0148, Sec 8940 1894
On A316 300 yards before the Richmond roundabout heading to London.
Parkland courses.
Pro Philip Talbot; Founded 1892
Designed by JH Taylor
Inner: 18; Outer: 18 holes, Inner: 5544; Outer 6345 yards, S.S.S. Inner: 68; Outer: 69
♦ WDs with handicap cert; WE only with a member.
↳ WD £70; WE (for member's guests only) £24.50.
↷ Contact Sec; terms available on application.
🍽 Lunches served every day except Mon; bar and snacks available.
🛏 Richmond Hill; Richmond Gate.

1A 136 **Royal St George's**
Sandwich, Kent, CT13 9PB
⬡ www.royalstgeorges.com
✉ bookings@royalstgeorges.com
☎ 01304 613090, Fax 611245, Pro 615236, Sec 613090, Rest/Bar 617308
2 miles E of Sandwich on road to Sandwich Bay.
Open Championship 2003; Links.
Pro Andrew Brooks; Founded 1887
Designed by Dr Laidlaw Purves
18 holes, 7102 yards, S.S.S. 74
↟ Driving range.
♦ Welcome midweek but with maximum 18 handicap; cert required.
↳ WD £95-£130 per day. Winter rate (1 Nov-1 Mar) £65 (inc 2-course lunch)
↷ £150.
🍽 Full facilities.

1A 137 **Royal Wimbledon**
29 Camp Road, Wimbledon, SW19 4UW
⬡ www.rwgc.co.uk
✉ secretary@rwgc.co.uk
☎ 020 8946 2125, Fax 8944 8652, Pro 8946 4606, Sec 8946 2125, Rest/Bar 8946 0055
0.75 mile from War Memorial in Wimbledon Village.
Heathland course.
Pro David Jones; Founded 1865
Designed by Harry Colt
18 holes, 6348 yards, S.S.S. 70
↟ Driving range.
♦ By prior arrangement; handicap certs required; WD only.

↳ £60.
↷ Wed, Thurs only; terms on application.
🍽 Full facilities.
🛏 Cannizaro House Hotel.

1A 138 **Rusper** ☏
Rusper Road, Newdigate, Surrey, RH5 5BX
☎ 01293 871871, Fax 871456, Pro 871871, Rest/Bar 8714143
M25 exit 9 and A24 towards Dorking, follow signs to Newdigate and Rusper.
Parkland course.
Pro Janice Arnold; Founded 1992
Designed by S Hood
18 holes, 6224 yards, S.S.S. 72
↟ Driving range.
♦ Welcome.
↳ WD £17.50; WE £20.
↷ Welcome with prior arrangement.
🍽 Bar and meals.
🛏 Ghyll Manor, Rusper.

1A 139 **Ruxley**
Sandy Lane, St Paul's Cray, Orpington, Kent, BR5 3HY
⬡ www.americangolf.co.uk
☎ 01689 839677, Fax 891428, Pro 871490, Rest/Bar 871490
M20 exit 1, follow signs to St Paul's Cray and then signs to course.
Parkland course.
Pro Stephen Lee; Raphael Giannandrea; Founded 1973
Designed by Gilbert Lloyd
18 holes, 5712 yards, S.S.S. 68
↟ 30.
♦ Public pay and play.
↳ WD £16.75; WE £22.
↷ Welcome; terms available on application.
🍽 Facilities available.

1A 140 **St Augustine's**
Cottington Road, Cliffsend, Ramsgate, Kent, CT12 5JN
✉ sagc@ic24.net
☎ 01843 590333, Fax 590444, Pro 590222
On B2048 off Ramsgate to Sandwich road.
Parkland course.
Pro Derek Scott; Founded 1907
Designed by Tom Vardon
18 holes, 5254 yards, S.S.S. 66
♦ Welcome with handicap certs.
↳ WD £25; WE £30.
↷ Welcome by appointment; from £25-£40.
🍽 Clubhouse facilities.

Jarvis Marine, Ramsgate; Blazing Donkey, Ham; Bell Inn, Sandwich.

1A 141 St George's Hill
Golf Club Road, St George's Hill, Weybridge, Surrey, KT13 0NL
www.stgeorgeshillgolfclub.co.uk
admin@stgeorgeshillgolfclub.co.uk
01932 847758, Fax 821564, Pro 843523
B374 towards Cobham, 0.5 miles from station.
Wooded heathland courses.
Pro AC Rattue; Founded 1913
Designed by HS Colt
27 holes, 6513 yards, S.S.S. 71
† Welcome Wed, Thurs, Fri by prior appointment.
WD £80 per round £105 per day.
Wed, Thurs, Fri only £137.50 to £154.
Full facilities available.
Oatlands Park Hotel; Hilton, Cobham.

1A 142 Sandown Golf Centre
More Lane, Esher, Surrey, KT10 8AN
01372 461234, Pro 469260, Sec 461234, Rest/Bar 461280
In centre of Sandown Park racecourse.
Parkland course.
Cranfield Golf Academy; Founded 1967
Designed by John Jacobs
9 holes, 5656 yards, S.S.S. 68
† Welcome.
WD £7; WE £9.
Welcome.
Facilities available.
Haven Hotel, Sandown.

1A 143 Selsdon Park Hotel & GC
Addington Road, Sanderstead, South Croydon, Surrey, CR2 8YA
www.principalhotels.co.uk
020 8657 8811 ext 659, Fax 8657 3401, Pro 8657 8811 ext 694
Take A2022 towards Selsdon. Hotel entrance is 0.5 miles opposite Junction with Upper Selsdon Road.
Parkland/downland course.
Pro Malcolm Churchill; Founded 1929
Designed by JH Taylor
18 holes, 6473 yards, S.S.S. 71
6.
† Welcome by prior arrangement.
WD £27.50; WE £32.50.
Welcome by prior arrangement; terms on application.
Catering in hotel.
Selsdon Park.

1A 144 Sene Valley
Sene, Folkestone, Kent, CT18 8BL
www.sceneatsene.cwc.net
01303 268513, Fax 237513, Pro 268514
M20 Junction 12, take A20 towards Ashford and left at 1st roundabout.
Downland course.
Pro Nick Watson; Founded 1888
Designed by Henry Cotton
18 holes, 6196 yards, S.S.S. 70
† Welcome with handicap certs.
WD £25; WE £30.
Welcome with prior arrangement.
Catering and bar facilities.
Sunny Bank House.

1A 145 Sheerness
Power Station Road, Sheerness, Kent, ME12 3AE
thesecretary@sheernessgc.freeserve.co.uk
01795 662585, Fax 668180, Pro 583060
M2/M20 to A249 to Sheerness.
Seaside course.
Pro Leon Stanford; Founded 1909
18 holes, 6460 yards, S.S.S. 71
† WD welcome; WE with a member.
WD £20; WE £25.
Welcome WD by prior arrangement; from £34.
Clubhouse bar and catering facilities available.
Kingsferry GH, Isle of Sheppey.

1A 146 Shillinglee Park
Chiddingfold, Godalming, Surrey, GU8 4TA
www.shillinglee.co.uk
01428 653237, Fax 644391, Sec 6532377
Leave A3 at Milford, S on A283 to Chiddingfold; at top end of green turn left along local road, then after 2 miles turn right signposted Shillinglee; entrance to course on left after 0.5 mile.
Public undulating parkland course.
Pro Mark Dowdell; Founded 1981
Designed by Roger Mace
9 holes, 2516 yards, S.S.S. 64
† Welcome, book in advance.
WD £8.50; WE £9.50.
Welcome; terms on application.
Bar and restaurant 8.30am-6pm (3pm Sun); evening meals and parties by arrangement.
Lythe Hill.

1A 147 Shirley Park ☎
194 Addiscombe Road, Croydon, Surrey, CR0 7LB
www.shirleyparkgolfclub.co.uk
secretary@shirleyparkgolfclub.co.uk
020 8654 1143, Fax 8654 6733, Pro 8654 8767, Sec 8654 1143, Rest/Bar 8654 1143
On A232 1 mile E of E Croydon station.
Parkland course.
Pro Michael Taylor; Founded 1914
Designed by Tom Simpson/Herbert Fowler.
18 holes, 6210 yards, S.S.S. 70
† Welcome WD and Sunday pm.
WD £38; Sun £45.
Various packages available.
Full catering and bar.
Croydon Park Hotel.

1A 148 Shooters Hill
Lowood, Eaglesfield Road, London, SE18 3DA
020 8854 6368, Fax 8854 0469, Pro 8854 0073, Sec 8854 6368, Rest/Bar 8854 1216
Just past water tower on A207 Shooters Hill.
Hilly parkland/woodland course.
Pro Dave Brotherton; Founded 1903
Designed by Willie Park
18 holes, 5721 yards, S.S.S. 68
† Welcome WD with handicap cert.
WD £22; £27 all day Mon-Fri.
Tues, Thurs only; terms on application.
Full clubhouse facilities.
Clarendon, Blackheath.

1A 149 Shortlands
Meadow Road, Shortlands, Kent, BR2 0DX
020 8460 2471, Pro 8464 6182
2 miles S of Bromley.
Parkland course.
Founded 1894
10 holes, 5261 yards, S.S.S. 66
† With member only and handicap cert.
£15 (18 holes); £10 (9 holes).
By arrangement; terms on application.
Bar and catering.
Bromley Court.

1A 150 Sidcup
7 Hurst Road, Sidcup, Kent, DA15 9AE
sidcupgolfclub@tiscali.co.uk
020 8300 2864, Pro 8309 0679, Sec 8300 2150, Rest/Bar 8302 8661
A222 off A2, 400 yards N of station.

Founded 1891
Designed by H Wilson
9 holes, 5571 yards, S.S.S. 68
♦ Welcome; WE with member only; handicap certs required, smart casual dress.
Ⓘ WD £18.
♦ Welcome; terms on application.
Ⓘ Bar, restaurant, except Mon.
⊸ Marriott, Bexleyheath.

1A 151 Silvermere
Redhill Road, Cobham, Surrey, KT11 1EF
⊶ www.dougmcclellangolf.com
✉ claire@silvermere.freeserve.uk
☎ 01932 584300, Fax 58401,
Pro 584323, Rest/Bar 584333
At Junction 10 of M25 and A3 take A245 to Byfleet; Silvermere is 0.5 mile.
Parkland course.
Pro Doug McClelland; Founded 1976
18 holes, 6404 yards, S.S.S. 71
Ⓘ 32.
♦ Welcome WD; WE by appointment from Apr-Oct.
Ⓘ WD £22; WE £35 (slots £130).
⊘ Welcome WD; terms on application.
Ⓘ Bar, restaurant.
⊸ Hilton National, Cobham.

1A 152 Sittingbourne & Milton Regis
Wormdale, Newington, Sittingbourne, Kent, ME9 7PX
⊶ www.sittingbournegolfclub.com
✉ sittingbourne@golfclub.totalserve.co.uk
☎ 01795 842261, Fax 844117,
Pro 842775, Sec 842261,
Rest/Bar 842261
1 mile N of exit 5 off M2 on A249.
Chestnut Street, Dalaway.
Undulating course.
Pro John Hearn; Founded 1929
Designed by Harry Hunter
18 holes, 6295 yards, S.S.S. 70
♦ Welcome WD if carrying handicap certs.
Ⓘ WD £28.
⊘ Welcome Tues and Thurs; terms on application.
Ⓘ Facilities available.
⊸ Coniston, Sittingbourne; Newington Manor.

1A 153 Southern Valley Golf Course
Thong Lane, Shorne, Gravesend; Kent, DA12 4LF
⊶ www.southernvalley.co.uk

✉ info@southernvalley.co.uk
☎ 01474 568568, Fax 360366,
Pro 568568, Sec 740026
1/3 mile off A2 south of Gravesend.
Exit signposted to Chalk/Thong.
Links style.
Pro Larry Batchelor; Founded 1999
Designed by Richardson/Weller.
18 holes, 6100 yards, S.S.S. 69
♦ Yes.
Ⓘ WD £16.50, WE £19.
⊘ Yes.
Ⓘ Yes.
⊸ Manor Hotel, Gravesend; Inn on the Lake, Gravesend.

1A 154 Staplehurst Golf Centre
Craddock Lane, Staplehurst, Kent, TN12 0DR
☎ 01580 893362, Fax 893373
Course lies 9 miles south of Maidstone on the A229 Hastings Road, turning on to Headcorn Road at Staplehurst and then right into Craddock Lane.
Parkland course.
Pro Colin Jenkins; Founded 1993
Designed by John Sayner
9 holes, 6114 yards, S.S.S. 70
Ⓘ Open Range.
♦ Welcome.
Ⓘ WD £12; WE £13.
⊘ Welcome terms on application.
Ⓘ Bar and snacks.
⊸ Bell Inn, The George at Cranbrook.

1A 155 American Golf at Sunbury
Charlton Lane, Shepperton, Middx, TW17 8QA
✉ sunbury@americangolf.uk.com
☎ 01932 770298, Fax 789300,
Pro 771414
2 miles from M3 Junction 1.
Public parkland course.
Pro Alistair Hardaway; Founded 1992
Designed by Clive Clark/Peter Alliss
27 holes, 5103 yards, S.S.S. 65
♦ Welcome; golf shoes must be worn.
Ⓘ WD £14; WE £20.
⊘ Welcome by appointment; terms on application.
Ⓘ Bar and restaurant facilities in 16th century clubhouse.
⊸ Warren Lodge Hotel, Moat House.

1A 156 Sundridge Park
Garden Road, Bromley, Kent, BR1 3NE
⊶ www.spgc.co.uk
✉ secretary@spgc.co.uk
☎ 020 8460 0278, Fax 8289 3050,
Pro 8460 5540, Sec 8460 0278,
Rest/Bar 8460 1822/8289 3060

N of Bromley on A2212.
Parkland courses.
Pro Stuart Dowsett; Founded 1901
Designed by Willie Park
East 18. West 18 holes, East 6538. West 6019 yds, S.S.S. East 71. West 69.
♦ Welcome WD; WE only with a member.
Ⓘ WD £55; WE £55 with a member only.
⊘ Welcome WD by prior appointment; terms available on application.
Ⓘ Full catering and bar.
⊸ Bromley Court.

1A 157 Sunningdale
Ridgemount Road, Sunningdale, Surrey, SL5 9RR
⊶ www.sunningdale-golfclub.co.uk
☎ 01344 621681, Fax 624154,
Pro 620128
From M3 J3 or M25 J13; take A30.
Heathland courses.
Pro Keith Maxwell; Founded 1900
Designed by HS Colt (New), W Park (Old)
New 18. Old 18 holes, New 6703 Old 6609 yards, S.S.S. New 73. Old 72
Ⓘ Driving range.
♦ Mon-Thurs only; with max 18 handicap and letter of introduction.
Ⓘ WD £95 (New); £125 (Old); £160 WE (Both).
⊘ Tues, Wed, Thurs only; min 20 players, max 20 handicap; £205.
Ⓘ Full catering and bar.
⊸ Berystede Hotel.

1A 158 Sunningdale Ladies
Cross Road, Sunningdale, Surrey, SL5 9RX
✉ slgolfclub@tiscali.co.uk
☎ 01344 620507, Sec 620507,
Rest/Bar 620507
S of A30 600 yards W of Sunningdale level crossing.
Heathland course.
Founded 1902
Designed by Edward Villiers/HS Colt
18 holes, 3616 yards, S.S.S. 60
Ⓘ Practice net.
♦ Welcome with handicap certs but not before 11am at WE.
Ⓘ WD £22 (men £22); WE £25 (men £25).
⊘ Societies; terms on application.
Ⓘ Full facilities, not Sun.

1A 159 Surbiton
Woodstock Lane, Chesington, Surrey, KT9 1UG

☎ 020 8398 3101, Fax 8339 0992,
Pro 8398 6619, Rest/Bar 8398 2056
From the A3 westbound take the
Esher/Chessington turn-off, turn left to
Claygate, and club is 400 yds on right.
Parkland course.
Pro Paul Milton; Founded 1895
18 holes, 6055 yards, S.S.S. 69
† Welcome WD only; handicap certs
required; members' guests only at WE.
Ⅼ WD £30; WE £17.
⌇ Welcome by prior arrangement;
terms on application.
🍽 Full facilities.
⌁ Haven, Esher; Travelodge.

1A 160 Surrey National Golf ☎ Club

Rook Lane, Chaldon, Surrey, CR3 5AA
⌁ www.surreynational.co.uk
✉ caroline@surreynational.co.uk
☎ 01883 344555, Fax 344422
M25 Jt, take M23 N. Soon after M23
becomes A23 turn right into Dean Lane
then left into Rook Lane. Course
approx. 1.5 miles on left..
Parkland.
Pro David Kent/Wayne East; Founded
1999.
Designed by David Williams
18 holes, 6858 yards, S.S.S. 73, Par 72
Ⅰ 300 yard driving range; short game
practice area; putting green.
† Welcome WD (anytime); WE after
11 am.
Ⅼ WD £25, WE £28.
⌇ Welcome WD/WE.
🍽 Spike bar and function rooms.
⌁ Enquire with club.

1A 161 Sutton Green ☎

New Lane, Sutton Green, Nr Guildford,
Surrey, GU4 7QF
⌁ www.ssuttongreengc.co.uk
✉ admin@suttongreengc.co.uk
☎ 01483 747989, Fax 750289,
Pro 766849, Sec 747898
Midway between Guildford and Woking
on A320.
Parkland with water features.
Pro Tim Dawson; Founded 1994
Designed by Laura Davies and D
Walker
18 holes, 6400 yards, S.S.S. 70
Ⅰ Grass covered.
† WD; after 1pm at WE.
Ⅼ WD £40; WE £50.
⌇ Welcome WD; packages available.
🍽 Full catering and bar.
⌁ Forte Post House, Guildford;
Cobham Hilton; Worplesdon Place.

1A 162 Tandridge

Oxted, Surrey, RH8 9NQ

⌁ www.tandridgegolfclub.com
✉ secretary@tandridgegolfclub.com
☎ 01883 712274, Fax 730537,
Pro 713701, Sec 712274,
Rest/Bar 712273
From M25 Junction 6, take A22 and
the A25.
Parkland course.
Pro Chris Evans; Founded 1924
Designed by H S Colt
18 holes, 6250 yards, S.S.S. 70
Ⅰ Driving range.
† Welcome Mon, Wed, Thurs.
Ⅼ WD £59, after 12 noon £40.
⌇ Welcome Mon, Wed, Thurs; £83.
🍽 Full clubhouse facilities.

1A 163 Tenterden

Woodchurch Road, Tenterden, Kent,
TN30 7DR
⌁ www.tenterdengolfclub.co.uk
✉ enquiries@tenterdengolfclub
.co.uk
☎ 01580 763987, Fax 763430
Take A28 to Tenterden and at St
Michaels take B2067.
Woodland course.
Pro Kyle Kelsall; Founded 1905
18 holes, 6152 yards, S.S.S. 69
Ⅰ Practice ground.
† Welcome by appointment; with
member at WE.
Ⅼ WD £28; WE £28.
⌇ Contact secretary; terms on
application.
🍽 Catering facilities and bar.
⌁ White Lion; Little Silver.

1A 164 Thames Ditton & Esher

Scilly Isles, Portsmouth Road, Esher,
Surrey, KT10 9AI
☎ 0208 3981551
Off A3 by Scilly Isles roundabout (0.25
mile from Sandown Park Race Course).
Parkland course.
Pro Robert Jones; Founded 1892
9 holes, 2537 yards, S.S.S. 33
Ⅰ Practice green 2 Driving nets
† Welcome Mon-Sat and Sun pm.
Ⅼ WD £12; WE £14.
⌇ Max 28 booked in advance with
Sec; terms on application.
🍽 Bar and snacks available.

1A 165 Tunbridge Wells ☎

Langton Road, Tunbridge Wells, Kent,
TN4 8XH
☎ 01892 536918, Pro 541386,
Sec 536918, Rest/Bar 523034
Behind Marchants Garage next to Spa
Hotel.

Undulating parkland course.
Pro Mike Barton; Founded 1889
9 holes, 4725 yards, S.S.S. 62
† Welcome.
Ⅼ WD £15.75; WE £26.25.
⌇ Contact Sec; terms on application.
🍽 By arrangement.
⌁ Spa; Periquito, Royal Wells.

1A 166 Tyrrell's Wood ☎

The Drive, Tyrrell's Wood,
Leatherhead, Surrey, KT22 8QP
☎ 01372 376025, Fax 360836,
Pro 375200, Rest/Bar 360702
2 miles SE of Leatherhead off the A24;
M25 Junction 9, 1 mile.
Undulating course.
Pro Simon Defoy; Founded 1924
Designed by James Braid
18 holes, 6063 yards, S.S.S. 70
† Welcome WD.
Ⅼ WD £35.
⌇ Welcome by appointment; from
£40.
🍽 Full clubhouse facilities.
⌁ Burford Bridge Hotel.

1A 167 Upchurch River Valley

Oak Lane, Upchurch, Sittingbourne,
Kent, ME9 7AY
☎ 01634 360626, Fax 387784,
Pro 379592, Rest/Bar 378116
From M2 Junction 4 take A278
Gillingham road; then A2 for 2.5 miles
towards Rainham.
Moorland/seaside courses.
Pro Roger Cornwell; Founded 1991
Designed by David Smart
18 holes, 6237 yards, S.S.S. 70;
9 holes, 3192 yards, par 60
Ⅰ 24.
† Welcome; book 2 days in advance.
Ⅼ WD £11.45; WE £14.45.
⌇ Welcome WD; min of 12 in party;
terms on application.
🍽 Restaurant and bar facilities
available.
⌁ Newington Manor; Rank Motor
Lodge.

1A 168 Walmer & Kingsdown ☎

The Leas, Kingsdown, Deal, Kent,
CT14 8EP
✉ kingsdown.golf@gtwiz.co.uk
☎ 01304 373256, Fax 382336,
Pro 363017, Sec 373256,
Rest/Bar 373256
Off A258 Dover to Deal road; follow
signs to Kingsdown from Ringwould,
signposted thereon.
Downland with views of English
Channel.

Pro M Paget; Founded 1909
Designed by James Braid
18 holes, 6444 yards, S.S.S. 71
♦ Welcome by appointment with Pro.
[WD £25; WE £30.
⌣ Welcome by appointment; terms
on application.
🍽 Full catering and bar.

1A 169 **Walton Heath**
Off Deans Lane, Walton-on-the-Hill,
Tadworth, Surrey, KT20 7TP
🖳 www.whgc.co.uk
🖥 secretary@whgc.co.uk
☎ 01737 812380, Fax 814225,
Pro 812152, Sec 812380,
Rest/Bar 813777
From the M25 exit at Junction 8 and
take the A217, London bound. After the
2nd roundabout turn left into Mill Road
and at the next junction left into
Dorking Road. Deans Lane is 1.5 miles
on right.
Heathland course.
Pro Ken MacPherson; Founded 1903
Designed by Herbert Fowler.
Old: 18. New: 18 holes, Old: 7063.
New: 7026 yards, S.S.S. Old: 73. New
72.
♦ By appointment only.
[WD £80 (before 10.30am), £70
(after 10.30am); WE £90.
⌣ By prior arrangement only; terms
on application.
🍽 Full facilities in clubhouse.
🛏 Club can provide list.

1A 170 **Weald of Kent**
Maidstone Road, Headcorn, Kent,
TN27 9PT
🖳 www.weald-of-kent.co.uk
🖥 info@weald-of-kent.co.uk
☎ 01622 890070, Fax 891671,
Pro 890866, Sec 891793, Rest/Bar
891793
7 miles from Maidstone on A274.
Parkland course.
Pro paul Fosten; Founded 1991
Designed by John Millen
18 holes, 5954 yards, S.S.S. 70
⚑ Driving range.
♦ Public pay and play course.
[WD £16; WE £20.
⌣ Welcome; from £14.
🍽 Catering and bar facilities; full on-
site kitchen for functions.
🛏 Own 19 bedroom hotel.

1A 171 **Wentworth**
Wentworth Drive, Virginia Water,
Surrey, GU25 4LS

🖳 www.wentworthclub.com
☎ 01344 842201, Fax 842804,
Pro 846306, Sec 842201,
Rest/Bar 846300
21 miles SW of London on A30/A329
Junction.
Heathland courses.
Pro D Rennie; Founded 1924
Designed by HS Colt
East: 18 holes, 6198 yards, S.S.S. 70;
West: 18 holes, 6957 yards, S.S.S. 74;
Edinburgh: 18 holes, 6979 yards,
S.S.S. 73
♦ Welcome WD by appointment.
[WD.
⌣ Welcome by appointment Mon-
Thurs; min 20; from £115. Driving
range, caddies, buggies and golf
clinics.
🍽 Top-class catering facilities
available.
🛏 16 rooms available at course.

1A 172 **West Byfleet**
Sheerwater Road, West Byfleet,
Surrey, KT14 6AA
☎ 01932 345230, Fax 340667,
Pro 346584, Sec 343433
On A245 in West Byfleet.
Woodland course.
Pro David Regan; Founded 1906
Designed by Cuthbert Butchart
18 holes, 6211 yards, S.S.S. 70
♦ Welcome by appointment, no WE.
[WD £50.
⌣ Welcome Mon, Tues, Wed; £72.
🍽 Full clubhouse facilities.
🛏 Holiday Inn,Woking.

1A 173 **West Hill**
Bagshot Road, Brookwood, Surrey,
GU24 0BH
🖳 www.westhill/golfclub.co.uk
🖥 secretary@
westhill/golfclub.co.uk
☎ 01483 474365, Fax 474252,
Pro 473172, Rest/Bar 472110/474365
5 miles W of Woking on A322.
Heathland course.
Pro John Clements; Founded 1909
Designed by Willie Park/Jack White
18 holes, 6368 yards, S.S.S. 70
⚑ Practice ground.
♦ Welcome WD with handicap certs;
WE only with member.
[WD summer £75 day, £55 round;
winter £40.
⌣ WD except Wed, by prior
arrangement; packages available.
🍽 Full facilities and bar; jacket and
tie required in dining room.
🛏 Worplesdon Place, Perry Hill.

1A 174 **West Kent**
West Hill, Downe, Orpington, Kent,
BR6 7JJ
🖳 www.wkgc. co.uk
🖥 golf@wkgc.co.uk
☎ 01689 851323, Fax 858693,
Pro 856863, Sec 851323,
Rest/Bar 853737
A21 to Orpington, head for Downe
village; leave on Luxted Lane for 300
yards then right into West Hill.
Woodland course.
Pro Chris Forsyth; Founded 1916
18 holes, 6385 yards, S.S.S. 70 Men
74 Women
♦ Welcome WD with letter from Sec
or handicap cert; should phone in
advance.
[WD £35.
⌣ Welcome by appointment; terms
on application.
🍽 Full facilities.
🛏 Kings Arms, Westerham.

1A 175 **West Malling**
London Road, Addington, Maidstone,
Kent, ME19 5AR
☎ 01732 844785, Fax 844795,
Pro 844022, Sec 844785
Course is off the A20, 8 miles NW of
Maidstone.
Parkland courses.
Pro Duncan Lambert; Founded 1974
Hurricane: 18 holes, 6256 yards,
S.S.S. 70; Spitfire: 18 holes, 6142
yards, S.S.S. 70
⚑ 13.
♦ Welcome WD; WE afternoon.
[WD £25; WE £30.
⌣ Welcome by appointment; terms
on application.
🍽 Full facilities.
🛏 Larkfield.

1A 176 **West Surrey**
Enton Green, Godalming, Surrey,
GU8 5AF
🖳 www.wsgc.co.uk
🖥 westsurreygolfclub@btinternet
.com
☎ 01483 421275, Fax 415419,
Pro 417278, Rest/Bar 419786
0.5 miles SE of Milford Station.
Wooded parkland course.
Pro A Tawse; Founded 1910
Designed by Herbert Fowler
18 holes, 6482 yards, S.S.S. 71
⚑ 1 range for members/guests.
♦ By appointment with Sec.
[WD £35; WE £40.
⌣ Welcome Wed, Thurs, Fri by
appointment; £72.

Royal Wimbledon

"A wonderful place is this new Wimbledon course", Bernard Darwin wrote in 1910. "For as soon as we are on it, all signs of men, houses and omnibuses, and other symptoms of a busy suburb disappear as if by magic, and a prospect of glorious solitary woods stretches away into the distance in every direction". The same holds true today.

Just 20 minutes from the heaving metropolis of London, you can weave your way through Wimbledon Common's maze of country lanes to arrive at Royal Wimbledon Golf Club – a true haven, where the gentle pursuit of golf is all. Passing the Common, a horde of gentlemen in red jumpers will be seen playing a round of golf, and it is a common misconception that these are the Royal Wimbledon members. No, these are the players from Wimbledon Common Golf Club, a society that has been entirely separate from their neighbours since 1915.

The history of the two clubs dates back to 1864 when some members of the London Scottish Rifle Volunteers, who were posted nearby, met on Wimbledon Common to form the London Scottish Golf Club.

By 1874 civilian membership had increased to 250 (compared to the Corps's 50) and by 1881 the rift between civilians and Corps had reached breaking point and by Feb 3 1881 a breakaway club had been formed. The civilians were advised to rename their club, respecting the fact that they were more from the Wimbledon end of the Common and that they weren't very Scottish. The then Prince of Wales, who was a patron of the club, came to their rescue by allowing them to add the prefix "Royal" to their name. Thus, on June 6 1882, the Royal Wimbledon Golf Club was formed.

Royal Wimbledon golfers now had their own club and their own rules – but they still shared the course with two other clubs, walkers and picnic parties. In 1907, Willie Park started work on designing their own course, on 240 acres of Warren Farm, that adjoined the Common, and the two clubs began their separate lives.

Their neighbours on the Common were forced to wear red jackets after residents complained that they could not see the dangers that now lurked around every corner in Wimbledon – it even became illegal to hook, slice or shank there.

Since 1924, Royal Wimbledon's layout has barely altered and its finishing stretch remains a treat for all visitors. The 16th hole remains the course's signature – an elevated tee offering a stunning view of what still looks like common land. The left-hand bunkers seem unimportant from up high but can easily be reached with a tee shot pulled too far to the left. Avoid the bunkers, and a tricky approach shot awaits from the valley to an elevated, narrow green, overlooked by some stunning South London property. All the greens have to be read with care at Royal Wimbledon. There are few gimmes here.

Then follows what appears to be a straightforward par-three at 17. The hole is short and the green is huge – what can go wrong? But anything less than your best strike from the tee may leave you in some very deep greenside bunkers – and the green has a horrendous slope from back to front which has been three-putted by the very best. The last is a great finishing hole, a slight dog-leg right to left but only 350 yards away so that grand clubhouse, offering a beer and a sandwich is only minutes away. Once ensconced in the bar, it is hard to leave, knowing that you have to get back out to the clamour of London life. Darwin was right. This is a "wonderful place". – **Jim Bruce-Ball**

🍽 Full catering facilities.
🛏 Inn on the Lake.

1A 177 Westerham
Valence Park, Brasted Road,
Westerham, Kent, TN16 1LJ
🖳 www.westerhamgc.co.uk
✉ jon.wittenburg@westerhamgc.co.uk
☎ 01959 567100, Fax 567101
On A25 between Brasted and
Westerham Village.
Woodland course.
Pro James Marshall; Founded 1997
Designed by David Williams
18 holes, 6272 yards, S.S.S. 72
🏌 Driving range; short game practice
area; buggies available.
† Welcome.
ℾ Mon-Thur £29 round, £45 day; Fri
£32 round, £50 day; WE/BH after noon
£36.
🝆 Welcome by appointment.
🍽 Restaurant, bar and function room.
🛏 Jarvis Fellbridge.

1A 178 Westgate & Birchington
176 Canterbury Road, Westgate-on-
Sea, Kent, CT8 8LT
✉ wandbgc@btopenworld.com
☎ 01843 831115, Pro 831115,
Sec 831115, Rest/Bar 833905
0.25 miles from Westgate station off
A28.
Clifftop links.
Pro Roger Game; Founded 1893
18 holes, 4889 yards, S.S.S. 64
† Welcome after 10am Mon-Sat;
after 11am Sun.
ℾ WD £17; WE £20 both prices
inclusive of insurance.
🝆 Welcome by appointment; Thurs
preferred; terms on application.
🍽 Clubhouse facilities.
🛏 The Promenade Travel Lodge.

1A 179 Whitstable & Seasalter
Collingwood Road, Whitstable, Kent,
CT5 1EB
✉ wasgc@btconnect.co.uk
☎ 01227 272020, Fax 280822,
Sec 272020, Rest/Bar 272020
On A290 to Whitstable.
Seaside links course.
Founded 1910
9 holes, 5357 yards, S.S.S. 63
† By arrangement.
ℾ WD £20; WE £20.
🝆 Not welcome.
🍽 Full catering facilities.
🛏 Marine Hotel, Tankerton.

1A 180 Wildernesse
Seal, Sevenoaks, Kent, TN15 0JE

🖳 www.wildernesse.co.uk
✉ golf@wildernesse.co.uk
☎ 01732 761526, Fax 763809,
Pro 761527, Sec 761199,
Rest/Bar 761526
Off A25 in Seal village.
Rolling parkland course.
Pro Craig Walker; Founded 1890
Designed by W Park
18 holes, 6482 yards, S.S.S. 71
† Handicap cert. required; not WE.
ℾ WD £40.
🝆 Apply to Sec; terms on application.
🍽 Bar and restaurant.

1A 181 Wildwood Country ⚑ Club
Horsham Road, Alfold, Cranleigh,
Surrey, GU6 8JE
🖳 www.wildwoodgolf.co.uk
✉ enquiries@wildwoodgolf.co.uk
☎ 01403 753255, Fax 752005
On A281 Guildford to Horsham road
10 miles from Guildford.
Parkland course.
Pro Mark Dowdell; Founded 1992
Designed by Martin Hawtree
27 holes, 6655 yards, S.S.S. 72
🏌 7 mat and 9-hole par 3 course.
† Welcome.
ℾ WD £35; WE £50.
🝆 Welcome WD; packages available;
from £29 after 12 pm.
🍽 Full catering and bar.
🛏 Random Hall, Slinfold.

1A 182 Wimbledon Common
19 Camp Road, Wimbledon Common,
London, SW19 4UW
🖳 www.wcgc.co.uk
✉ secretary@wcgc.co.uk
☎ 020 8946 0294, Fax 8947 8697,
Pro 8946 0294, Sec 8946 7571,
Rest/Bar 8946 0294
1 mile NW of War Memorial past Fox
and Grapes.
Links type wooded course.
Pro J S Jukes; Founded 1908
Designed by Tom and Willie Dunn
18 holes, 5438 yards, S.S.S. 66
† Welcome WD; must wear plain red
top.
ℾ WD £15 (Mon £10).
🝆 Welcome Tues-Fri by appointment;
terms on application.
🍽 Full facilities.
🛏 Canizaro House.

1A 183 Wimbledon Park
Home Park Road, Wimbledon, London,
SW19 7HR
🖳 www.wpgc.co.uk

✉ secretary@wpgc.co.uk
☎ 020 8946 1250, Fax 8944 8688,
Pro 8946 4053, Rest/Bar 8946 1002
Near Wimbledon Park District Line tube.
Parkland course.
Pro Dean Wingrove; Founded 1898
Designed by Willie Park
18 holes, 5492 yards, S.S.S. 66
🏌 Practice area and indoor nets.
† Welcome WD with handicap certs.
ℾ WD £50.
🝆 Welcome Tues, Thurs by
appointment; terms available on
application.
🍽 Full facilities available except Mon.
🛏 Canizaro House.

1A 184 Windlemere
Windlesham Road, West End, Woking,
Surrey, GU24 9QL
☎ 01276 858727, Pro 858727
Take A322 from Bagshot towards
Guildford; turn left on A319 towards
Chobham, course is on left opposite
Gordon Boys School.
Gently undulating public parkland
course.
Pro David Thomas; Founded 1978
Designed by Clive D Smith
9 holes, 2673 yards, S.S.S. 34
🏌 13.
† Open to public on payment of
green fees.
ℾ WD £9; WE £10.50.
🝆 By appointment with Pro; terms on
application.
🍽 Bar snacks always available.

1A 185 Windlesham ⚑
Grove End, Bagshot, Surrey, GU19 5HY
🖳 www.windleshamgolf.com
✉ admin@windleshamgolf.com
☎ 01276 452220, Fax 452290,
Pro 472323
At Junction of A30 and A322.
Parkland course.
Pro Lee Mucklow; Founded 1994
Designed by Tommy Horton
18 holes, 6650 yards, S.S.S. 72
🏌 3 covered bays. 10 outdoor.
† Welcome except before noon at
WE; handicap certs required.
ℾ WD £30; WE £35.
🝆 Welcome Mon-Fri by prior
appointment; terms available on
application.
🍽 Bar and restaurant.
🛏 Pennyhill Park; Hilton; Berrystead.

1A 186 The Wisley
Mill Lane, Ripley, Nr Woking, Surrey,
GU23 6QU

www.wisleygc.com
reception@wisleygc.com
☎ 01483 211022, Fax 211622,
Pro 211213
Exit A3 at Ockham, Send and Ripley,
3rd exit from the roundabout and first
left into Mill Lane.
Parkland course 3 x 9 holes.
Pro Denis Pugh; Founded 1991
Designed by Robert Trent Jones, Jr.
27 holes, 6858 yards, S.S.S. 73
⌇ Large practice ground.
† Private members' club.
⌀ None.
⦿ Full clubhouse catering and bar
facilities.

1A 187 **Woking**
Pond Road, Hook Heath, Woking,
Surrey, GU22 0JZ
☎ 01483 760053, Fax 772441,
Pro 769582, Sec 760053,
Rest/Bar 760053
Off A322 after West Hill GC.
Oldest heathland course in Surrey.
Pro Carl Bianco; Founded 1893
Designed by Tom Dunn
18 holes, 6340 yards, S.S.S. 70
† WD with a handicap cert; WE only
with member.
⌇ WD £60.
⌀ By appointment with 12 months'
notice.
⦿ Full facilities.
⌲ Worplesdon Place, Worplesdon.

1A 188 **The Woldingham** ℭ
Club (formerly Duke's Dene)
Haliloo Valley Road, Woldingham,
Surrey, CR3 7HA
☎ 01883 653501, Fax 653502,
Pro 653541
From M25 Junction 6 towards
Caterham; at roundabout take
Woldingham exit.
Valley course, we guarantee no
tempgreen.
Pro Phil Harrison; Founded 1996
18 holes, 6393 yards, S.S.S. 70
⌇ Practice range.

† Welcome except after 12 at WE.
⌇ WD £30; WE £40; accept 2 for 1
vouchers.
⌀ Welcome WD.
⦿ Bar and brasserie; weddings/
conferences/functions.

1A 189 **Woodcote Park** ℭ
Meadow Hill, Bridleway, Coulsdon,
Surrey, CR5 2QQ
www.woodcotepgc.co.uk
info@woodcotepgc.co.uk
☎ 020 8668 2788, Fax 8660 0918,
Pro 8668 1843, Rest/Bar 8660 0176
2 miles N of Purley on Coulsdon-
Wallington road.
Parkland course.
Pro Raith Grant; Founded 1912
18 holes, 6682 yards, S.S.S. 72
⌇ Practice Area.
† Welcome by appointment and with
handicap certs, not WE.
⌇ WD £35.
⌀ Welcome by appointment; Varied
society prices.
⦿ Catering and bar facilities.

1A 190 **Woodlands Manor**
Tinkerpot Lane, Sevenoaks, Kent,
TN15 6AB
☎ 01959 523805, Pro 524161,
Sec 523806
Off A225, 4 miles NE of Sevenoaks, 5
miles S of M25 Junction 3.
Undulating parkland course.
Pro Phil Womack; Founded 1928
Designed by N Coles, J Lyons
18 holes, 6037 yards, S.S.S. 68
† Welcome WD; not WE.
⌇ WD £21.
⌀ Welcome Mon-Fri by appointment;
terms on application.
⦿ Meals served.
⌲ Thistle (Brands Hatch).

1A 191 **World of Golf (Jack**
Nicklaus Golf Centre)
Sidcup by-pass, Chislehurst, Kent,
BR7 6RP
www.worldofgolf-uk.co.uk

sc.worldofgolf@line1.net
☎ 020 8309 0181, Fax 8308 1691
Course is on the main A20 London
Road.
Driving Range.
Pro David Young
Designed by M Gillet
⌇ Practice range, 54 bays floodlit.
† Driving range open to public.
⦿ Café Bar.
⌲ Stakis, Nr Dartford Tunnel.

1A 192 **Worplesdon**
Heath House Road, Woking, Surrey,
GU22 0RA
☎ 01483 472277, Fax 473303,
Pro 473287, Sec 472277
Leave Guildford on A322 to Bagshot,
6 miles turn right into Heath House Rd.
Heathland course.
Pro Jim Christine; Founded 1908
Designed by JF Abercromby
18 holes, 6440 yards, S.S.S. 71
† Welcome WD only by prior
arrangement.
⌇ WD £55 (Nov-Feb £32).
⌀ Welcome WD by prior
appointment (except Tues); terms on
application.
⦿ Bar and Catering Facilities Daily.
⌲ Worplesdon Place.

1A 193 **Wrotham Heath**
Seven Mile Lane, Borough Green,
Sevenoaks, Kent, TN15 8QZ
☎ 01732 884800, Fax 887370
Off A20 near junction with A25.
Woodland/heathland course.
Pro Harry Dearden;
Founded 1906
Designed by Donald Steel
18 holes, 5954 yards, S.S.S. 69
† Welcome WD with handicap certs,
not WE or BH without member.
⌇ WD £25.
⌀ Welcome Fri only; terms on
application.
⦿ Full catering by arrangement with
caterer.
⌲ Post House.

1B

Hertfordshire, Essex, Middlesex, North London

The north London belt is an area of grand houses to which golf courses have become attached, but there is only one royal club. Epping Forest, like several of the Scottish clubs, is a royal private members club that uses an adjoining public golf course.

Henry Cotton, the winner of three Open Championships, might not have thought too much of such fraternisation. Cotton wore "silk monogrammed shirts and drove a large motor car, which he had a tendency to park opposite a sign saying 'No parking' ". He served as the professional at Royal Waterloo and Royal Mid-Surrey and his exhibitionism did much to put Ashridge on the map (it's in Hertfordshire) when he was employed as that club's professional in 1937, five years after its foundation.

The four woods which he used to win the Open Championship at Carnoustie that same year are in display in the club house, although they will soon have to move home as Ashridge expands from its current modest building. Cotton would doubtless have been pleased to see the club barging its way into the twenty-first century. His professionals' shop went about its business as immodestly as possible.

When you survey the par four ninth hole at Ashridge the line of the drive is not an obvious one and the green does not come into consideration until hopefully the second shot. Unless you are Cotton. He devised a low hooker to take maximum advantage of the downslope, kicking onto the green over 350 yards away.

With three reachable par fives in the final six holes Ashridge offers an encouraging finish to those who have so far held their score together. It is a pleasure to play although some of the greens, up with the best in the area, take a fair bit of reading.

Along the road Berkhamsted has some unusual hazards to overcome. Accuracy off the tee is a prerequisite although there are no bunkers to bother about. An ancient earthwork called Grim's Dyke provides the natural obstacle on seven of the holes, once again raising a finger at those who like to scatter sand all over the place.

In Essex, Thorpe Hall has been the home club of Sir Michael Bonallack for several years and Thorndon Park, designed by Harry Colt, is a lush course with lots of intrigue once the nondescript opening hole is out of the way.

For some bizarre reason many of these courses to the north of London are dominated by huge houses. Thorndon Park has a neo-classical mansion, Hanbury Manor is the site of a former convent, now a luxury hotel, and Moor Park is the home of a Grade 1 listed historic building that is inconceivably grand. Happily Moor Park's two golf courses are rather better conceived than the attack on Arnhem – the subject of the film *A Bridge Too Far* – which was planned here.

The High Course is considered to be the better of the two courses. Unusually it finishes with a par three, but the real scandal was caused by the pond beside the eighth green, inserted long before water features became all the rage. Just up the road Sandy Lodge, the club at which John Jacobs was a pro, also finishes with a par three.

North London's principal courses are Highgate, Hampstead, Hendon, Fulwell and Mill Hill. Soft spikes are recommended for Mill Hill, not because the course has a reputation for aridity, just the opposite in fact, but to negotiate the scuttle across a busy dual carriageway necessary to reach the first tee.

1B 1 **Abbey View**

Holywell Hill, Westminster Lodge, St
Albans, Herts, AL1 2DJ
☎ 01727 868227, Pro 868227,
Sec 868227
In centre of St Albans.
Public parkland course.
Pro Roddy Watkins; Founded 1990
Designed by Jimmy Thomson
9 holes, 1383 yards
† Open to public at all times.
Ⅼ WD £5.50; WE £5.50.
⚸ Welcome; terms on application.
⧯ Tea/coffee on site; cafe in main
centre.

1B 2 **Abridge G & CC**

Epping Lane, Stapleford Tawney,
Essex, RM4 1ST
⚏ www.abridgegolf.com
✉ info@abridgegolf.com
☎ 01708 688396, Fax 688550,
Pro 688333, Sec 688396,
Rest/Bar 688367
M11 from London exit 5 via Abridge;
from the N, M11 exit 7 via Epping.
Parkland course.
Pro Stuart Layton; Founded 1964
Designed by Henry Cotton
18 holes, 6686 yards, S.S.S. 72
† Welcome WD and WE pm;
handicap certs required.
Ⅼ WD £35; WE £45.
⚸ Mon, Wed and Fri; terms on
application.
⧯ Available every day.
⛴ Post House, Epping.

1B 3 **Airlinks** ♛

Southall Lane, Hounslow, Essex,
TW5 9PE
☎ 020 8561 1418, Fax 8813 6284,
Pro 8561 1418,
Rest/Bar 8561 1418
M4 Junction 3 on to A312 and A4020;
part of David Lloyd Tennis Centre.
Public meadowland/parkland course.
Pro Tony Martin; Founded 1984
Designed by P Alliss
18 holes, 5813 yards, S.S.S. 68
Ⅰ 24.
† Welcome; some restrictions at
weekends.
Ⅼ WD £12; WE £18.
⚸ Welcome Mon-Fri; fees negotiable.
⧯ Bar snacks, hot and cold meals
available.
⛴ London Airport hotels nearby.

1B 4 **Aldenham G & CC** ♛

Church Lane, Aldenham, Nr Watford,
Herts, WD25 8NN

✉ info@aldenhamgolfclub.co.uk
☎ 01923 853929, Fax 858472,
Pro 857889
M1 Junction 5 on to A41, left at
roundabout to B462 and then into
Church Road.
Parkland course.
Pro Tim Dunstan; Founded 1975
18; 9 holes, 6480; 2350 yards,
S.S.S. 71
† Welcome WD but afternoon only at
WE.
Ⅼ WD £26; WE £35.
⚸ Welcome WD and WE afternoons;
Full catering packages and 36 holes of
golf; from £58.
⧯ Full facilities.
⛴ Watford Hilton National; Jarvis
International.Premier Lodge; Red Lion;
Elstree Inn.

1B 5 **Aldwickbury Park** ♛

Piggottshill Lane, Harpenden, Herts,
AL5 1AB
⚏ www.aldwickburyparkgolfclub.com
✉ enquiries@
aldwickburyparkgolfclub.com
☎ 01582 760112, Fax 760113,
Pro 760112, Sec 765112,
Rest/Bar 766463
10 mins from M1 Junction 9 on road
between Harpenden and
Wheathampstead.
Parkland course.
Pro James Jones; Founded 1995
Designed by K Brown/M Gillett
18 holes, 6352 yards, S.S.S. 70
† Welcome WD; WE after 12.
Ⅼ WD £26; WE £32.
⚸ Welcome WD; 36 holes, coffee and
biscuits, lunch, 3-course dinner; other
packages available; £55.
⧯ Full catering and bar.
⛴ Harpenden House.

1B 6 **Amida Golf Hampton**
(formerly Twickenham Park)

Staines Rd, Twickenham, Middx,
TW2 5JD
✉ info@crocodilesports.co.uk
☎ 0208 783 1648
On A305 near Hope and Anchor
roundabout.
Municipal parkland course.
Pro Suzy Watt; Founded 2004
Designed by Charles Lawrie
9 holes, 6076 yards, S.S.S. 69
Ⅰ Teaching Academy; virtual golf.
† Welcome.
Ⅼ WD £10.
⚸ Welcome by arrangement; catering
packages available; terms on
application.

⧯ Full licensed bar, snacks, function
room.
⛴ Richmond Gate.

1B 7 **Arkley** ♛

Rowley Green Road, Barnet, Herts,
EN5 3HL
⚏ www.arkleygolfclub.co.uk
✉ secretary@arkleygolfclub.co.uk
☎ 020 8449 0555, Fax 8440 5214,
Pro 8440 8473, Sec 8449 0394,
Rest/Bar 8449 0394
Off A1 at Arkley.
Parkland course.
Pro Martin Porter; Founded 1909
Designed by James Braid
9 holes (18 tees), 6046 yards, S.S.S. 69
† Welcome WD but with members
only at WE.
Ⅼ WD £25.
⚸ Welcome Wed and Fri; terms on
application.
⧯ Full catering facilities except Mon.

1B 8 **Ashford Manor** ♛

Fordbridge Road, Ashford, Middx,
TW15 3RT
⚏ www.amgc.co.uk
✉ secretary@ashfordmanorgolfclub
.fsnet.com
☎ 01784 257687, Fax 420355,
Pro 255940, Sec 424644,
Rest/Bar 424641/424642
Off A308 between Staines and Sunbury.
0.5 miles from Fordbridge roundabout.
Wooded parkland course.
Pro Ian Partington; Founded 1898
Designed by Tom Hog.
18 holes, 6352 yards, S.S.S. 71
† Welcome WD with handicap certs.
Ⅼ WD £35, £40 for the day.
⚸ Welcome WD by prior
arrangement; golf, morning coffee,
lunch, afternoon tea, dinner.
⧯ Full catering facilities.
⛴ Shepperton Moathouse; The Ship,
Shepperton.

1B 9 **Ashridge** ♛

Little Gaddesden, Berkhamsted, Herts,
HP4 1LY
⚏ www.ashridgegolfclub.ltd.uk
✉ info@ashridgegolfclub.ltd.uk
☎ 01442 842244, Fax 843770,
Pro 842307, Sec 842307,
Rest/Bar 842379
4 miles N of Berkhamstead on B4506.
Wooded parkland course.
Pro Andrew Ainsworth; Founded 1932
Designed by Sir Guy Campbell/Colonel
Hotchkin
18 holes, 6580 yards, S.S.S. 71

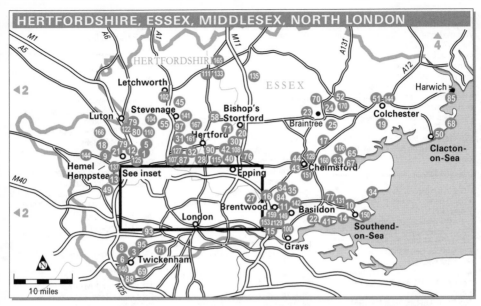

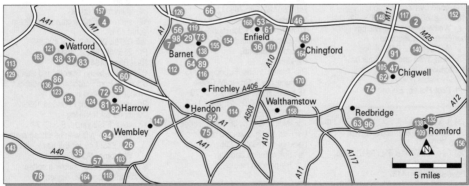

🏌 14.
† Welcome WD only.
🍸 WD on application.
🔁 WD only; terms on application.
🍴 Full facilities.

1B 10 **Ballards Gore** ☎

Gore Road, Canewdon, Essex, SS4 2DA
☎ 01702 258917, Fax 258571,
Pro 258924, Sec 258917
From London via A127 to Southend
Airport, then through Rochford on to
Great Stambridge road; course 1.5
miles from Rochford centre.
Parkland course.

Pro Richard Emery; Founded 1980
Designed by D and JJ Caton
18 holes, 6845 yards, S.S.S. 73
† Welcome WD; guest of member
only at WE, Sun after 2pm.
🍸 WD £30 round, £35 day.
🔁 WD by arrangement with Sec,
subject to availability; terms on
application.
🍴 Bar and restaurant; private functions.
🔁 Renouf.

1B 11 **Basildon**

Clay Hill Lane, Basildon, Essex,
SS16 5JP

✉ basildongc@onetel.net.uk
☎ 01268 533297, Fax 284163,
Pro 533352
On A176 S of Basildon via either A127
or A13.
Undulating wooded parkland.
Pro Mike Oliver; Founded 1967
Designed by A H Cotton
18 holes, 6236 yards, S.S.S. 70
† Welcome; book tee time in
advance.
🍸 WD £10.80; WE £17.50.
🔁 Welcome, packages by prior
arrangement; terms on application.
🍴 Restaurant and bar.
🔁 Haywain; Campanile, Basildon.

KEY							
		35 The Burstead	70 Gosfield Lake	104 Little Hay Golf Complex	139 Stanmore
1	Abbey View	36 Bush Hill Park	71 Great Hadham	105 Loughton	140 Stapleford Abbotts
2	Abridge G & CC	37 Bushey G & CC	72 Grim's Dyke	106 Maldon	141 Stevenage
3	Airlinks	38 Bushey Hall	73 Hadley Wood	107 Malton	142 Stock Brook Manor
4	Aldenham G & CC	39 C & L Golf & CC	74 Hainault Forest	108 Manor of Groves G & CC	143 Stockley Park
5	Aldwickbury Park	40 Canons Brook	75 Hampstead	109 Maylands Golf & CC	144 Stocks
6	Amida	41 Castle Point	76 Hanbury Manor G& CC	110 Mid-Herts	145 Stoke-by-Nayland
7	Arkley	42 Chadwell Springs	77 Hanover	111 Mill Green	146 Strawberry Hill
8	Ashford Manor	43 Channels	78 Harefield Place	112 Mill Hill	147 Sudbury
9	Ashridge	44 Chelmsford	79 Harpenden	113 Moor Park	148 Theydon Bois
10	Ballards Gore	45 Chesfield Downs	80 Harpenden Common	114 Muswell Hill	149 Thorndon Park
11	Basildon	46 Cheshunt	81 Harrow Hill	115 The Nazeing	150 Thorpe Hall
12	Batchwood Hall	47 Chigwell	82 Harrow School	116 North Middlesex	151 Three Rivers Golf & CC
13	Batchworth Park	48 Chingford	83 Hartsbourne G & CC	117 North Weald Golf Club	152 Toot Hill
14	Belfairs Park	49 Chorleywood	84 Hartswood	118 Northwood	153 Top Meadow
15	Belhus Park (Thurrock)	50 Clacton-on-Sea	85 Harwich & Dovercourt	119 Old Fold Manor	154 Trent Park
16	Bentley	51 Colchester	86 Haste Hill	120 Orsett	155 Tudor Park Sports Gd
17	Benton Hall	52 Colne Valley (Essex)	87 Hatfield London CC	121 Oxhey Park	156 Upminster
18	Berkhamsted	53 Crews Hill	88 Hazelwood	122 Panshanger	157 Verulam
19	Birch Grove	54 Crondon Park	89 Hendon	123 Perivale Park	158 Wanstead
20	Bishop's Stortford	55 Danesbury Park	90 The Hertfordshire	124 Pinner Hill	159 Warley Park
21	Boxmoor	56 Dyrham Park	91 High Beech	125 Porters Park	160 Warren
22	Boyce Hill	57 Ealing	92 Highgate	126 Potters Bar	161 Welwyn Garden City
23	Braintree	58 East Herts	93 Hillingdon	127 Redbourn	162 West Essex
24	Braintree Towerlands	59 Edgewarebury	94 Horsenden Hill	128 Regiment Way	163 West Herts
25	Braxted Park	60 Elstree	95 Hounslow Heath	129 Rickmansworth	164 West Middlesex
26	Brent Valley	61 Enfield	96 Ilford	130 Risebridge (Havering)	165 Whaddon Golf Centre
27	Brentwood	62 Essex Golf & CC	97 Knebworth	131 Rochford Hundred	166 Whipsnade Park
28	Brickendon Grange	63 Fairlop Waters	98 Laing Sports Club	132 Romford	167 Whitehill
29	Bridgedown	64 Finchley	99 Lamerwood	133 Royston	168 Whitewebbs
30	Briggens House Hotel	65 Five Lakes Hotel	100 Langdon Hills	134 Ruislip	169 Woodford
31	Brocket Hall	66 Forest Hills	101 Lee Valley	135 Saffron Walden	170 Woolston Manor
32	Brookmans Park	67 Forrester Park	102 Letchworth	136 Sandy Lodge	171 Wyke Green
33	Bunsay Downs	68 Frinton	103 Limetrees Park Golf	137 Shendish Manor	
34	Burnham-on-Crouch	69 Fulwell	Course	138 South Herts	

1B 12 Batchwood Hall

Batchwood Tennis And Golf Centre,
St Albans, Herts, AL3 5XA
☎ 01727 833349, Fax 850586,
Pro 844250
NW corner of St Albans; 5 miles S of
M1 Junction 9.
Parkland course.
Pro Mark Flitton; Founded 1935
Designed by J H Taylor
18 holes, 6509 yards, S.S.S. 71
⌇ 18-hole putting green.
† Welcome.
⌐ WD £10; WE £13.
⌁ Welcome by prior arrangement;
packages available; tennis courts; 2
squash courts; fitness gym; dance
studio.
⦿ Bar and restaurant.
⌁ Aubry Park.

1B 13 Batchworth Park

London Road, Rickmansworth, Herts,
WD3 1JS
⌂ www.crownsportplc.com
✉ bpgc@crownsportplc.com
☎ 01923 711400, Fax 710200,
Pro 714922
From M 25 Junction 17 towards
Rickmansworth to the Batchworth
roundabout; course 400 yards.
Parkland course.
Pro Steven Proudfoot; Founded 1996
Designed by Dave Thomas

18 holes, 6723 yards, S.S.S. 72
⌇ Practice range for members/guests.
† Private; members and guests only.
⌐ Not available.
⦿ Bar and restaurant.
⌁ Jarvis Watford.

1B 14 Belfairs Park (Southend-on-Sea)

Starter's Hut, Eastwood Road North,
Leigh-On-Sea, Essex, SS9 4LR
☎ 01702 252345, Pro 520202
4.5 miles from Southend centre;
Eastwood Rd links A127 and A13. Set
in Belfairs Park.
Parkland/Woodland course.
Pro Martin Foreman; Founded 1926
Designed by HS Colt
18 holes, 5840 yards, S.S.S. 68
† Unrestricted; bookings every day,
week in advance or on day.
⌐ WD £10; WE £15.80.
⌁ Welcome; terms available on
application.
⦿ Public restaurant.
⌁ Westcliff Hotel.

1B 15 Belhus Park (Thurrock)

Belhus Park, South Ockendon, Essex,
RM15 4QR
☎ 01708 854260, Fax 854260,
Pro 854260, Sec 852907,
Rest/Bar 852907
A13 to Avely.

Parkland course.
Pro Jamie Gowan; Founded 1972
Designed by Frank Pennink
18 holes, 5589 yards, S.S.S. 69
⌇ 12; floodlit.
† Bookings can be made at course
WD; in advance by phone WE
(booking card required).
⌐ WD £10.00; WE £15.
⌁ Welcome; terms on application.
⦿ Bar and restaurant.
⌁ Thurrock Hotel.

1B 16 Bentley

Ongar Road, Brentwood, Essex,
CM15 9SS
☎ 01277 373179, Fax 375097,
Pro 372933
On A128 between Brentwood and
Ongar.
Parkland course with water hazards.
Pro Nick Garrett; Founded 1972
Designed by Alec Swan
18 holes, 6709 yards, S.S.S. 72
† Welcome WD.
⌐ WD £22.
⌁ Welcome WD; terms on
application.
⦿ Full catering facilities.
⌁ The Holiday Inn Brentwood.

1B 17 Benton Hall

Wickham Hill, Witham, Essex, CM8 3LH

www.clubhaus.com
☎ 01376 502454, Fax 521050
Off A12 at Witham; course is well
signposted.
Woodland course.
Pro C Fairweather; Founded 1993
Designed by Alan Walker and Charlie
Cox
18 holes, 6495 yards, S.S.S. 72
† Welcome by prior arrangement.
[Terms on application.
◔ Welcome WD by prior
arrangement; packages available; from
£37.50.
🍴 Clubhouse facilities.

1B 18 Berkhamstead
The Common, Berkhamstead, Herts,
HP4 2QB
📧 barryh@berkhampsteadgc.co.uk
☎ 01442 865832, Fax 863730,
Pro 865851, Rest/Bar 870965
1 mile N of Berkhamstead.
Heathland course.
Pro John Clarke; Founded 1890
Designed by GH Gowring (1890-92
Founder)
18 holes, 6605 yards, S.S.S. 72
† Welcome with handicap certificate.
[WD £30; WE £40.
◔ Welcome Wed and Fri.
🍴 Meals and bar facilities.
🛏 Hemel Hempstead Post House.

1B 19 Birch Grove
Layer Road, Colchester, Essex,
CO2 0HS
☎ 01206 734276, Fax 734276,
Pro 734276, Sec 734103
On B1026 3 miles S of Colchester.
Parkland course.
Pro C Laitt; Founded 1970
Designed by Course owners
9 holes, 4546 yards, S.S.S. 63
† Welcome.
[£10 9 holes; £13 18 holes.
◔ Welcome by arrangement.
🍴 Full facilities.
🛏 Kingsford Park Hotel.

1B 20 Bishop's Stortford ☎
Dunmow Road, Bishop's Stortford,
Herts, CM23 5HP
www.bsgc.co.uk
📧 bofice@bsgc.co.uk
☎ 01279 654715, Fax 655215,
Pro 651324, Sec 654715,
Rest/Bar 461779
From M11 Junction 8 follow signs to
Bishop's Stortford; course is 1.5 miles
on left.
Well-established, undulating, parkland.
Pro Steve Bryan; Founded 1910

Designed by James Braid
18 holes, 6404 yards, S.S.S. 71
🏌 Practice ground.
† Welcome with handicap certs; not
at WE and Ladies Day (Tues).
[WD £30 (round), £39 (day); WE
guest of members only.
◔ Welcome by prior arrangement;
varied packages available (minimum
12); Tues (Ladies' day) exc; special
winter deals; from £35-65.
🍴 Full restaurant and bar bistro.
🛏 Hilton, Stansted Airport; Downhall,
Hatfield Heath.

1B 21 Boxmoor
18 Box Lane, Hemel Hempstead,
Herts, HP3 0DJ
☎ 01442 242434
On A41 0.75 miles from Hemel
Hempstead station.
Undulating parkland course.
Founded 1890
9 holes, 4812 yards, S.S.S. 64
† Welcome except Sun.
[WD £10; WE £15.
◔ Welcome with month's notice.
🍴 Limited service; meals available by
prior arrangement.
🛏 Boxmoor Lodge.

1B 22 Boyce Hill
Vicarage Hill, South Benfleet, Essex,
SS7 1PD
📧 secretary@boycehillgolfclub.co.uk
☎ 01268 793625, Fax 750497,
Pro 752565, Sec 793625,
Rest/Bar 793102
7 miles W of Southend-on-Sea; A127
to Rayleigh Weir (3 miles from course);
A13 to Victoria House Corner (1 mile
from course).
Undulating parkland course.
Pro Graham Burroughs; Founded 1922
Designed by James Braid
18 holes, 6003 yards, S.S.S. 69
† Welcome WD; WE with member;
handicap certs required and 24 hours
notice.
[WD £30.
◔ Thurs only; terms available on
application.
🍴 Service 7.30am-8pm.
🛏 Crest Maisonwyck.

1B 23 Braintree ☎
Kings Lane, Stisted, Braintree, Essex,
CM7 8DA
www.braintreegolfclub.freeserve.uk
📧 manager@
braintreegolfclub.freeserve.co.uk
☎ 01376 346079, Fax 348677, Pro
343465, Sec 346079, Rest/Bar 346079

A120 eastbound after Braintree by-pass,
1st left, 1 mile to course, signposted.
Parkland course.
Pro Tony Parcell; Founded 1891
Designed by Hawtree and Son
18 holes, 6228 yards, S.S.S. 69
† Welcome; handicap certs required
Sat and Sun pm.
[WD £25, WE £42 – round or day.
◔ By arrangement all WD except
Tues am.
🍴 Meals served.
🛏 White Hart.

1B 24 Braintree Towerlands
Panfield Rd, Braintree, Essex, CM7 5BJ
www.towerlands.co.uk
☎ 01376 326802, Fax 552487
Course is 1 mile NW of Braintree on
the B1053.
Picturesque parkland course.
Founded 1985
Designed by GR Shiels/Golf
Landscapes
9 holes, 5559 yards, S.S.S. 68
† Welcome.
[WD £10; WE £12.
◔ Welcome by appointment; contact
C W Hunnable; terms on application.
🍴 Clubhouse facilities.
🛏 Old House; Old Court, Hare and
Hounds.

1B 25 Braxted Park
Braxted Park, Witham, Essex,
CM8 3EN
☎ 01376 572372, Fax 892840,
Pro 572372, Sec 572372,
Rest/Bar 572372
1.5 miles off A12 near Kelvedon.
Parkland course.
Pro John Hudson; Founded 1953
Designed by Sir Allen Clark
9 holes, 5704 yards, S.S.S. 68
† Public pay as you play WD;
members only WE.
[WD £13.
◔ Welcome WD; terms on
application.
🍴 Restaurant, bar.
🛏 Braxted Park; Rivenhall.

1B 26 Brent Valley
Church Road, Hanwell, London,
W7 3BE
☎ 020 8567 4230, Pro 8567 1287,
Sec 8567 4230
A4020 Uxbridge Road, Hanwell, on to
Greenford Ave then on to Church Rd.
Public meadowland course.
Pro Peter Bryant; Founded 1938
Designed by P Alliss and D Thomas

18 holes, 5446 yards, S.S.S. 66
† Welcome.
℩ WD £10; WE £14.95.
⚲ Organised via the Pro; terms on application.
🍽 Restaurant from 8am.
⚑ Ealing Common.

1B 27 **Brentwood Golf Centre**
Ingrave Road, Brentwood, Essex, CM14 5AE
🖳 www.discountgolfstore.co.uk
☎ 01277 214830, Fax 200601, Pro 218714, Sec 218850, Rest/Bar 218850
Take M25 Junction 29 then take A127 to Southend. Turn up the A128 towards Brentwood. Then go over 2 round-abouts. Course is 100 yards on the left.
Parkland course.
Pro Steve Cole; Founded 1965
18 holes, 6192 yards, S.S.S. 69
† Municipal course.
℩ WD £10; WE £15.
⚲ Welcome WD; meals and 18 or 36 holes, coffee on arrival; £25-£35.
🍽 Facilities available.
⚑ Brentwood Post House.

1B 28 **Brickendon Grange** ♔
Brickendon, Nr Hertford, Herts, SG13 8PD
🖳 www.brickendongrangegc.co.uk
🖳 play@brickendongrangegc.co.uk
☎ 01992 511258, Fax 511411, Pro 511218, Sec 511258, Rest/Bar 511228
3 miles S of Hertford near Bayford Br station.
Undulating parkland course.
Pro G Tippett; Founded 1968
Designed by CK Cotton
18 holes, 6394 yards, S.S.S. 70
† Welcome WD; handicap certs required.
℩ WD £35.
⚲ WDs except Wed; terms on application.
🍽 Bar lunches.
⚑ White Horse.

1B 29 **Bridgedown**
St Albans Road, Barnet, Herts, EN5 4RE
☎ 020 8441 7649, Fax 8440 2757, Pro 8440 4009
1.5 miles from M25 Junction 23 at South Mimms exit.
Parklands course.
Pro Lee Jones; Founded 1994
Designed by Seve Ballesteros
18 holes, 6626 yards, S.S.S. 72

† Welcome.
℩ WD £15; WE £17.
⚲ Welcome by prior arrangement; terms on application.
🍽 Bar and catering facilities available.
⚑ Travel Lodge, J23 off M25.

1B 30 **Briggens House Hotel**
Stanstead Road, Stanstead Abbots, Ware, Herts, SG12 8LD
🖳 www.corushotels.com/briggenshouse
☎ 01279 829955, Fax 793685, Pro 793742, Sec 793742, Rest/Bar 793742
Situation on A414 between Harlow and A10.
Parkland course.
Pro Alan Battle; Founded 1988
9 holes, 5582 yards, S.S.S. 69
† Welcome at all times.
℩ WD £10 for 9 holes £15 for 18 holes; WE £12 for 9 holes, £17 for 18 holes. Discounts for on site hotel residents.
⚲ Terms on application.
🍽 Full facilities available.
⚑ On site.

1B 31 **Brocket Hall**
Brocket Hall, Welwyn Garden City, Herts, AL8 7XG
🖳 www.brocket-hall.co.uk
☎ 01707 368808, Fax 390052
On B653 to Wheathampstead off A1 (M) Junction 4.
Parkland/woodland course.
Pro Keith Wood; Founded 1992
Designed by Peter Alliss/Clive Clark/Donald Steele
36 holes, 7016 yards, S.S.S. 73
⚑ 15; Faldo Golf Institute.
† Members' guest only.
⚲ Corporate days can be arranged; terms on application.
🍽 Clubhouse restaurant and bar facilities.
⚑ Melbourne Lodge.

1B 32 **Brookmans Park**
Golf Club Road, Hatfield, Herts, AL9 7AT
🖳 clubbpc@aol.com
☎ 01707 652487, Fax 661851, Pro 652468, Sec 652487, Rest/Bar 652459
10 min from M25 through Potters Bar.
Parkland course.
Pro Ian Jelley; Founded 1930
Designed by Hawtree & Taylor
18 holes, 6460 yards, S.S.S. 71

† Welcome by prior arrangement not WE.
℩ WD £30.
⚲ Welcome Wed/Thir only, terms on application.
🍽 Full facilities, bar and catering.
⚑ Brookmans Park Hotel.

1B 33 **Bunsay Downs**
Little Baddow Road, Woodham Walter, Nr Maldon, Essex, CM9 6RW
☎ 01245 222648, Sec 222648, Rest/Bar 222369
Leave A414 at Danbury towards Woodham Water; course 0.5 W of village.
Gently undulating meadowland.
Pro Henry Roblin; Founded 1982
9 holes, 5864 yards, S.S.S. 68. Also Badgers course: 9 holes, 5864 yards, par 27.
⚑ Practice facilities.
† Welcome.
℩ WD £11; WE £13.00.
⚲ Welcome WD except BH; packages available.
🍽 Full facilities all week.
⚑ Blue Boar in Mouden, Pondlands Park.

1B 34 **Burnham-on-Crouch** ♔
Ferry Road, Creeksea, Burnham-on-Crouch, Essex, CM0 8PQ
🖳 burnhamgolf@hotmail.com
☎ 01621 782282, Fax 784489, Sec 782282, Rest/Bar 785508
1 mile before entering Burnham on B1010.
Undulating parkland course.
Founded 1923
Designed by Howard Swan (2nd 9)
18 holes, 6056 yards, S.S.S. 69
† Welcome WD and after 2pm WE.
℩ WD £26.
⚲ Welcome WD except Thurs am; Full catering facilities; from £27.
🍽 Full bar and restaurant facilities.

1B 35 **The Burstead**
Tye Common Road, Little Burstead, Billericay, Essex, CM12 9SS
☎ 01277 631171, Fax 632766
Leave A127 at Research Centre/Laindon exit; 1st exit at roundabout and then right into Dunton Road; left into Rectory Road.
Parkland course.
Pro Keith Bridges; assisted by D Bullock; Founded 1993
Designed by Patrick Tallack
18 holes, 6275 yards, S.S.S. 70
† Welcome WD and Sat, Sun pm.
℩ WD £19; WE £25.

⚲ Welcome WD by prior arrangement; packages available; from £19.
🍽 Clubhouse bar and restaurant facilities.
🛏 Trust House Forte and Camponile, both A127; Hill House.

1B 36 Bush Hill Park
Bush Hill, Winchmore Hill, London, N21 2BU
🖳 www.bushhillgolfclub.co.uk
☎ 020 8360 5738, Fax 8360 5583, Pro 8360 4103
0.5 mile S of Enfield town.
Parkland course.
Pro Adrian Andrews; Founded 1895
18 holes, 5767 yards, S.S.S. 68
† Welcome WD except Wed am.
Ⅼ WD £27.
⚲ On application, except Wed.
🍽 Bar snacks, restaurant service.
🛏 West Lodge.

1B 37 Bushey Golf & CC   ₢
High Street, Bushey, Herts, WD23 1TT
☎ 020 8950 2283, Fax 8386 1181, Pro 8950 2215, Rest/Bar 8950 2283
On A411, 1.5 miles from M1/A411 Junction.
Parkland course.
Pro Graham Atkinson; Founded 1980
Designed by Donald Steel
9 holes, 6120 yards, S.S.S. 69
Ⅰ 30.
† Welcome WD except Wed, Thurs am; WE and Bank Hols after 3.30pm.
Ⅼ WD £11 WE £13.
⚲ Maximum 50 by arrangement; not available Wed or Thurs mornings; terms on application.
🍽 Meals served.
🛏 The Hilton.

1B 38 Bushey Hall   ₢
Bushey Hall Drive, Bushey, Herts, WD23 2EP
🖳 www.golfclubuk.co.uk
📧 info@golfclubuk.vo.uk
☎ 01923 222253, Fax 229759, Pro 225802, Sec 222253, Rest/Bar 222253
1 mile SE of Watford.
Undulating parkland course.
Pro Ken Wickham; Founded 1886
Designed by Robert Stewart Clouston
18 holes, 6099 yards, S.S.S. 69
† Welcome; must book at reception.
Ⅼ WD £26; WE £33.
⚲ Welcome WD; terms on application.
🍽 Full facilities.

1B 39 C & L Golf & Country Club
West End Road, Northolt, Middx, UB5 6RD
☎ 020 8845 5662, Fax 8841 5515
Junction of West End Road and A40, travelling from London; opposite Northolt Airport.
Parkland course.
Pro Richard Kelly; Founded 1991
Designed by Patrick Tallack
9 holes, 2251 yards
† Welcome; no jeans or T-shirts; golf shoes only.
Ⅼ WD £4.50; WE £7.00.
⚲ Welcome WD; terms on application.
🍽 Bar restaurant, banqueting hall available.
🛏 Master Brewer.

1B 40 Canons Brook
Elizabeth Way, Harlow, Essex, CM19 5BE
🖳 www.canonsbrook.co.uk
📧 sjl.canonsbrook@btclick.com
☎ 01279 421482, Fax 626393, Pro 418357, Sec 421482, Rest/Bar 425142
1 mile W of Harlow Town station.
Parkland course.
Pro A McGinn; Founded 1963
Designed by Sir Henry Cotton
18 holes, 6763 yards, S.S.S. 73
† Welcome WD.
Ⅼ WD £24.
⚲ Welcome Mon, Wed, Fri; golf and catering; £45.
🍽 Full catering facilities.
🛏 Churchgate Hotel; Moat House.

1B 41 Castle Point
Sommes Avenue, Canvey Island, Essex, SS8 9FG
☎ 01268 510830, Pro 510830, Sec 696298, Rest/Bar 511149
A13 to Southend right on A130 to Canvey Island at Saddlers Farm roundabout over Waterside farm roundabout to Sommes Ave, course on left.
Public seaside links course.
Pro Michael Otleridge; Founded 1988
Designed by Golf Landscapes
18 holes, 6096 yards, S.S.S. 69
Ⅰ 24 bays floodlit.
† No restrictions booking required; WE smart attire.
Ⅼ WD £10; WE £14.30.
⚲ On request telephone in advance terms on application.
🍽 Bar and Restaurant facilities available.
🛏 Crest; Basildon; Oyster Fleet.

1B 42 Chadwell Springs
Hertford Road, Ware, Herts, SG12 9LE
☎ 01920 461447, Pro 462075
On A119 between Hertford and Ware.
Parkland course.
Pro Mark Wall; Founded 1975
Designed by J H Taylor
9 holes, 3209 yards, S.S.S. 71
† Welcome WD: WE by arrangement.
Ⅼ WD £10; WE £15.
⚲ Welcome Mon; terms on application.
🍽 Full facilities.
🛏 Salisbury, Hertford; Moat House, Ware.

1B 43 Channels   ₢
Belsteads Farm Lane, Little Waltham, Chelmsford, Essex, CM3 3PT
🖳 www.channelsgolf.co.uk
📧 info@channelsgolf.co.uk
☎ 01245 440005, Fax 442032, Pro 441056
Course is two miles NE of Chelmsford off the A130.
Undulating parkland course.
Pro Ian Sinclair; Founded 1974
Designed by Henry Cotton
Belsteads: 9. Channels: 18 holes, Belsteads: 4779. Channels: 6376 yards, S.S.S. Belsteads: 63. Channels: 71
Ⅰ Driving range.
† Welcome anytime.
Ⅼ Belsteads £20; Channels(Mon-Fri only) £32.
⚲ Welcome WD; packages involve playing both Channels and Belsteads courses; £28-£62.
🍽 Full catering facilities.
🛏 County Hotel, Chelmsford.

1B 44 Chelmsford
Widford Road, Chelmsford, Essex, CM2 9AP
🖳 www.chelmsfordgc.co.uk
📧 office@chelmsfordgc.co.uk
☎ 01245 256483, Fax 256483, Pro 257079, Rest/Bar 250555
Off A414 Chelmsford road.
Parkland course.
Pro Mark Welch; Founded 1893
Designed by Harry Colt (1924)
18 holes, 5981 yards, S.S.S. 69
† Welcome WD only.
Ⅼ WD £38.
⚲ Welcome Wed and Thurs only; terms on application.
🍽 Full facilities.
🛏 South Lodge, Chelmsford.

1B 45 Chesfield Downs   ₢
Jack's Hill, Graveley, Herts, SG4 7EQ
☎ 01462 482929, Fax 485753

Channels
'The Perfect Golf Venue'

Set in over 300 acres of stunning Essex parkland countryside, Channels offers 27 holes with a fully computerised irrigation system, excellent greens and numerous water holes - something that has made it one of the top courses in Essex.

Channels, Belsteads Farm Lane, Little Waltham, Chelmsford, Essex CM3 3PT
Tel: **01245- 440005**   Fax: **01245- 442032**
Email: **info@channelsgolf.co.uk**   **www.channelsgolf.co.uk**

From A1M follow signs on B197 to Graveley. Southbound exit A1m at Junction 8 and head for B197 northbound.
Parkland course.
Pro Jane Fernley/Henry Arnott; Founded 1991
Designed by Jonathan Gaunt
18 holes, 6646 yards, S.S.S. 71
↑ Everyone welcome.
⌁ WD £16; WE £24.
⌁ Welcome; various packages available; terms on application.
⍩ Full facilities.
⌁ Balckmore Hotel, Little Wymondley.

1B 46 Cheshunt
Park Lane, Cheshunt, Herts, EN7 6QD
⌁ www.broxbourne.gov.uk
⌁ refer to website
☎ 01992 624009, Fax 636403, Sec 624009, Rest/Bar 633610
From M25 Junction 25 towards Cambridge. 2nd junction 1st set of traffic lights take left filter.
Municipal parkland course.
Pro David Banks; Founded 1976
⌁ Practice area with 10 bays specifically for irons use/nets-both.
↑ Visitors welcome at any time advisable to phone for availability at weekends.
⌁ WD £14.50 (pm £10); WE £19.50.
⌁ By arrangement; terms on application.
⍩ Cafe service all day.
⌁ Marriott.

1B 47 Chigwell ☏
High Road, Chigwell, Essex, IG7 5BH
⌁ www.chigwellgolfclub.co.uk
⌁ info@chigwellgolfclub.co.uk
☎ 020 8500 2059, Fax 8501 3410, Pro 8500 2384
On A113, 13.5 miles NE of London or M25,Juntion 26.

Undulating parkland course.
Pro Ray Beard; Founded 1925
Designed by Hawtree Taylor
18 holes, 6279 yards, S.S.S. 70
↑ Welcome Mon-Thurs with handicap certs; only with member at WE.
⌁ WD £35.
⌁ Welcome Mon, Wed and Thurs by prior arrangement; terms on application.
⍩ Bar and catering facilities.
⌁ Prince Regent; Roebuck Holiday Inn Express.

1B 48 Chingford
Bury Road, Chingford, London, E4 7QJ
☎ 0208 5292107, Pro 85295708
In Station Road, 150 yards S of Chingford station.
Public Forest course.
Pro John Francis; Founded 1888
Designed by James Braid
18 holes, 6342 yards, S.S.S. 69
↑ Welcome; red outer garment must be worn.
⌁ WD £10.40; WE £14.25.
⌁ Welcome by appointment; terms on application.
⍩ Snacks, no bar; cafe available next to club.
⌁ Ridgeway (Chingford).

1B 49 Chorleywood
Common Road, Chorleywood, Herts, WD3 5LN
⌁ chorleywood.gc@btclick.com
☎ 01923 282009; Fax 286739
1 mile from J18 of M25; 0.2 mile from Chorleywood Station (Metropolitan Line).
Wooded heathland course on common land.
Founded 1890
9 holes, 5686 yards, S.S.S. 67
↑ Welcome, handicaps required; WD except Tues/Wed am; WE restrictions apply – please phone for availability.
⌁ WD £20; WE £25.

⌁ Small societies welcome; terms on application.
⍩ Bar and catering.

1B 50 Clacton-on-Sea ☏
West Road, Clacton-On-Sea, Essex, C015 1AJ
⌁ www.clactongolf.com
⌁ clactongolfclub@btclick.com
☎ 01255 421919, Fax 424602, Pro 426304, Sec 421919, Rest/Bar 424793
On the seafront at Clacton.
Parkland links course.
Pro Stuart Levermore; Founded 1892
Designed by Jack White
18 holes, 6532 yards, S.S.S. 71
⌁ Practice areas.
↑ Welcome WD; WE restrictions apply.
⌁ WD £20; WE £25.
⌁ Welcome WD; full day of golf plus lunch and dinner; £45.
⍩ Full facilities and bar.
⌁ Kingcliff; Plaza; Chudleigh.

1B 51 Colchester ☏
Braiswick, Colchester, Essex, CO4 5AV
☎ 01206 852946, Fax 852698, Pro 853920, Sec 853396
0.75 miles NW of Colchester North station on the B1508.
Parkland course.
Pro Mark Angel; Founded 1907
Designed by James Braid
18 holes, 6307 yards, S.S.S. 70
↑ Welcome with handicap certs.
⌁ WD £20; WE £30.
⌁ Welcome by arrangement; terms on application.
⍩ Full facilities.
⌁ George Hotel; Rose & Crown; both Colchester.

1B 52 Colne Valley (Essex) ☏
Station Rd, Earls Colne, Essex, CO6 2LT

www.club-noticeboard.co.uk/
colnevalley
enquiries@colnevalleygolfclub.co.uk
☎ 01787 224343, Fax 224126,
Pro 224343, Sec 224343,
Rest/Bar 224343
10 miles W from A12/A1124 Junction.
Parkland course.
Pro James Gurry/Robert Taylor;
Founded 1991
Designed by Howard Swan
18 holes, 6301 yards, S.S.S. 70
† Welcome midweek and after
11.00am at WE with prior arrangement.
no earlier than 7 days.
ℝ WD £25; WE £30.
⌕ Welcome; in-house catering
corporate days for up to 200; football
table; terms available on application.
🍽 Restaurant and bar.
⌂ Bull Hotel; Forte Posthouse; Marks
Tey Hotel.

1B 53 Crews Hill
Cattlegate Road, Crews Hill, Enfield,
Middx, EN2 8AZ
gmchgc@aol.com
☎ 020 8363 6674, Fax 8363 2343,
Pro 8366 7422, Sec 8363 6674,
Rest/Bar 8363 6674
Off A1005 Enfield to Potters Bar road
into East Lodge Lane, turn right into
Cattlegate Road.
Parkland course.
Pro Neil Wichelow; Founded 1921
Designed by H Colt
18 holes, 6244 yards, S.S.S. 70
† Must be members of a recognised
golf club; WE and BH only with a
member.
ℝ WD £36, WE £40; 2-for-1 available
with voucher.
⌕ Welcome with advance booking;
terms on application.
🍽 Full facilities, except Mon.
⌂ Royal Chase.

1B 54 Crondon Park
Stock Road, Stock, Essex, CM4 9DP
☎ 01277 841115, Fax 841356,
Pro 841887, Rest/Bar 841386
Off the B1007 outside the village of
Stock.
Parkland course.
Pro Paul Barham/Freddy Sunderland;
Founded 1984
Designed by M Gillett
18 holes, 6585 yards, S.S.S. 71
† Welcome.
ℝ WD £20; WE £30.
⌕ WDs only, full clubhouse facilities;
POA.
🍽 Full bar and restaurant.

⌂ South Lodge; County Hotel; Miami
Hotel, all Chelmsford.

1B 55 Danesbury Park
Codicote Road, Welwyn Garden City,
Herts, AL6 9SD
☎ 01438 840100, Fax 846109
0.5 miles from A1M Junction 6 on
B656 to Hitchin.
Parkland course.
9 holes, 4150 yards, S.S.S. 60
† Restrictions at weekends; by prior
arrangement only.
ℝ WD £12.
⌕ By arrangement only.
🍽 Facilities; meals by arrangement.

1B 56 Dyrham Park
Galley Lane, Barnet, Herts, EN5 4RA
☎ 020 8440 3904, Pro 8440 3904,
Sec 8440 3361
2 miles outside Barnet near Arkley, off
A1 and M25.
Parkland course.
Pro Bill Large; Founded 1963
Designed by C K Cotton
18 holes, 6428 yards, S.S.S. 71
† Only as guest of member or
member of golf society.
ℝ Golf society rate: WD £25; WE £35.
⌕ Wed only; two rounds golf, light
lunch and dinner or lunch and afternoon
tea; terms available on application.
🍽 Full restaurant facilities.
⌂ Post House.

1B 57 Ealing Golf Club 1923 Ltd
Perivale Lane, Greenford, Middx,
UB6 8SS
www.ealinggolfclub.com
junemackison@hotmail.com
☎ 020 8997 0937, Fax 8998 0756,
Pro 8997 3959, Sec 8997 0937 x1
Off A40 W opposite Hoover building.
Parkland course.
Pro David Barton; Founded 1898
Designed by H S Colt
18 holes, 6216 yards, S.S.S. 70
† Welcome WD only, phone for
advance booking.
ℝ WD £37.
⌕ Advanced booking only; terms on
application.
🍽 Full facilities.
⌂ Travel Inn (Metro) Greenford.

1B 58 East Herts
Hamels Park, Buntingford, Herts, SG9
9NA
www.ehgc.co.uk

secretary@ehgc.fsnet.co.uk
☎ 01920 821978, Fax 823700,
Pro 821922, Rest/Bar 821923
On A10 N of Puckeridge.
Parkland course.
Pro Glen Culmer; Founded 1899
18 holes, 6456 yards, S.S.S. 71
† WDs with handicap certs; WE with
member only.
ℝ WD £30 round, £40 day.
⌕ Terms available on application; 18
holes of golf, bar, catering; £65.00.
🍽 Full facilities.

1B 59 Edgewarebury
Edgeware Way, Edgeware, Middx,
AL4 0BR
☎ 020 8958 3571, Fax 958 2000,
Sec 8905 3393
On A41 between Edgeware and Elstree.
Pitch and putt course.
Founded 1946
9 holes, 2090 yards, S.S.S. 27
† Welcome 9am until dusk; no
booking necessary.
ℝ WD £4; WE £4.50.
⌕ Welcome; terms on application.
🍽 No facilities.
⌂ Edgewarebury Hotel.

1B 60 Elstree   ℭ
Watling Street, Elstree, Herts,
WD6 3AA
☎ 020 8953 6115, Fax 8207 6390
On A5183 between Elstree and
Radlett.
Parkland course.
Pro Marc Warwick; Founded 1984
18 holes, 6556 yards, S.S.S. 72
ℝ 60.
† Welcome WD and after midday at
WE. Conference rooms available. Also
functions, weddings, bar mitzvahs etc.
ℝ WD £20; WE £25.
⌕ Welcome WD except Wed, by prior
arrangement; minimum 8 players in
party; golf and catering packages
available; In golf Simulator room; from
£15.
🍽 Full catering and bar.
⌂ Edgewarebury Hotel, Elstree;
Oaklands, Boreham Wood; North Me.

1B 61 Enfield   ℭ
Old Park Road South, Enfield, Middx,
EN2 7DA
www.enfieldgolfclub.co.uk
enfieldgolf@destmail.co.uk
☎ 020 8366 4492, Fax 8342 0381,
Sec 8363 3970, Rest/Bar 8363 3970
Leave the M25 at Junction 24; take the
A1005 to Enfield, turn right at the

roundabout in Slades Hill, then the first left into Old Park View, at the end of the road turn right into Old Park Road South. Parkland course.
Pro Lee Fickling; Founded 1893
Designed by James Briad
18 holes, 6154 yards, S.S.S. 70
† WD, except Tue.
⌶ WD £28.
⌔ WD only with references; full clubhouse facilities; from £30.
🍴 Full catering facilities.
🛏 West Lodge Park, Cockfosters; Royal Chase, Enfield.

1B 62 Essex Golf & CC ☏
Earls Cone, Nr Colchester, Essex, Plumbridge, CO6 2NS
🖧 www.clubhaus.com
☎ 01787 224466, Fax 224410
On B1024 2 miles N of A120 at Coggeshall.
Parkland course.
Pro Lee Cocker; Founded 1990
Designed by Reg Plumbridge
18 holes, 6982 yards, S.S.S. 73
⌶ 20.
† Also 9-hole academy course, par 34. Welcome by prior arrangement.
⌶ WD £25; WE £30.
⌔ Welcome WD by prior arrangement; packages available; health and beauty facilities; terms on application.
🍴 Restaurant and bar, also has poolside cafe.
🛏 The Lodge.

1B 63 Fairlop Waters
Forest Rd, Barkingside, Ilford, Essex, IG6 3HN
🖧 www.wigginsplc.co.uk
☎ 020 8501 1881, Pro 8500 9911
Signposted from M11 along the A12; near Fairlop station (Central Line).
Public Heathland course.
Pro Paul Davies; Founded 1968
Designed by John Jacobs
18 holes, 6281 yards, S.S.S. 69
⌶ Practice range 36 bays; floodlit.
† Welcome; tidy dress required.
⌶ WD £10.95; WE £15.50.
⌔ Welcome WD prior arrangement; sailing; childrens play area; country parks, terms available on application.
🍴 Bar;Daitons American Diner; 2 Banqueting suites.
🛏 Granada Travel Inn (Redbridge).

1B 64 Finchley
Nether Court, Frith Lane, Mill Hill, London, NW7 1PU

🖧 www.finchleygolfclub.co.uk
✉ secretary@finchleygolfclub.co.uk
☎ 020 8346 2436, Fax 8343 4205, Pro 8346 5086
2 miles from M1 Junction 2.
Parkland course.
Pro David Brown; Founded 1929
Designed by James Braid
18 holes, 6411 yards, S.S.S. 71
⌶ Practice Area.
† By arrangement only.
⌶ WD £28; WE £37.
⌔ Terms on application.
🍴 Full facilities.

1B 65 Five Lakes Hotel ☏
Colchester Rd, Tolleshunt Knight, Maldon, Essex, CM9 8HX
🖧 www.fivelakes.co.uk
✉ enquiries@fivelakes.co.uk
☎ 01621 862326, Fax 862320, Pro 862326
Off A12 at Kelvedon take B1023 to Tiptree following tourist signs.
Parkland course.
Pro Gary Carter; Founded 1991
Designed by N Coles MBE
2 x 18 holes, 6751 lakes course; 6181 links course yards, S.S.S. 73/70
⌶ 8 bay driving range.
† Welcome.
⌶ WD £29; WE £38, lakes course; WD £22; WE £29, links course.
⌔ By arrangement packages available.
🍴 Two restaurants available; also light snacks and refreshments.
🛏 Five Lakes.

1B 66 Forest Hills
Newgate Street Village, Herts, SG13 8EW
☎ 01707 876825
5 mins from M25 jct 25 at Cuffley.
Hilly parkland course.
Pro Craig Easton; Founded 1994
Designed by Mel Flannagan
9 holes, 6440 yards, S.S.S. 71
† Welcome.
⌶ WD £15; WE £20.
⌔ By arrangement packages available.
🍴 Chinese Restaurant available in clubhouse.

1B 67 Forrester Park
Beckingham Road, Great Totham, Near Maldon, Essex, CM9 8EA
☎ 01621 891406, Fax 891406, Pro 891406, Sec 891406, Rest/Bar 891406
Off A12 at Rivenhall End, follow signs to Great Braxted until B1022. Turn right to Maldon, course is 1.8 miles on left.

Undulating woodland course.
Pro Gary Pike; Founded 1968
Designed by DAH. Everett & TR Forrester-Muir
18 holes, 6073 yards, S.S.S. 69
† Welcome by arrangement.
⌶ WD £19; WE £20; twilight rates available £10. WD after midday and at WE.
⌔ Societies welcome. Pre booking essential. Prices may vary.
🍴 Full facilities available.
🛏 Rivenhall Hotel.

1B 68 Frinton ☏
1 The Esplanade, Frinton-on-Sea, Essex, CO13 9EP
🖧 www.frintongolfclub.com
✉ frintongolf@lineone.net
☎ 01255 674618, Fax 682450, Pro 671618
18 miles E of Colchester on Frinton seafront.
Seaside course, links type.
Pro PeterTaggart; Founded 1895
Designed by Tom Dunn (1895)/Willie Park Jnr (1904)
18 holes, 6265 yards, S.S.S. 70
† Welcome by prior arrangement with Sec.
⌶ WD £32; WE £35.
⌔ Welcome Wed, Thurs and some Fri by arrangement with Sec; catering by arrangement; £25-45.
🍴 Facilities available.
🛏 Rock Hotell.

1B 69 Fulwell
Wellington Road, Hampton Hill, Middx, TW12 1JY
🖧 www.fulwellgolfclub.co.uk
✉ secretary@fulwellgolfclub.co.uk
☎ 020 8977 2733, Fax 7732, Pro 3844, Rest/Bar 3188
2 miles S of Twickenham on A311 opposite Fulwell bus station.
Meadowland course.
Pro Nigel Turner; Founded 1904
Designed by JT Morrison
18 holes, 6544 yards, S.S.S. 71
† Welcome WD; book via Pro shop.
⌶ WD £30.
⌔ Welcome by prior arrangement; terms on application.
🍴 By arrangement.
🛏 The Winning Post.

1B 70 Gosfield Lake
The Manor House, Hall Drive, Gosfield, Halstead, Essex, CO0 1SE
🖧 www.gosfield-golf-club.co.uk
✉ gosfieldlakegc@btconnect.com

☎ 01787 474747, Fax 476044,
Pro 474488, Rest/Bar 474400
7 miles N of Braintree on A1017;
1 mile W of Gosfield village.
Parkland course.
Pro Richard Wheeler; Founded 1988
Designed by Sir Henry Cotton; Howard
Swan
18 holes, 6756 yards, S.S.S. 72
† Welcome.
ℂ WD £30; WE £35.
⌇ Welcome; 36 holes; lunch carvery;
from £42.
🍽 Full catering facilities.
⌂ Bull in Halstead.

1B 71 Great Hadam ☎
Great Hadam Rd, Much Hadam, Herts,
SG10 6JE
☎ 01279 843558
5 mins on the B1004 off the A120 and
M11 at Junction 8.
Meadowland course.
Pro Kevin Lunt; Founded 1993
18 holes, 6854 yards, S.S.S. 73
✐ All-weather driving range, 15 bays, 3
practice holes, practice bunker. Hadham
Health Club; Kevin Lunt Golf College.
† Welcome every day except before
noon at WE.
ℂ Call for details.
⌇ Welcome WD except Wed;
packages available from £19.
🍽 Two bars, fully licensed dining area.
⌂ Down Hall, Hatfield Heath; Hilton
International.

1B 72 Grim's Dyke
Oxhey Lane, Hatch End, Pinner,
Middx, HA5 4AL
🖧 www.club-noticeboard.com/
grimsdyke
✉ grimsdykegolfclub@hotmail.com
☎ 020 8428 4539, Fax 8421 5494,
Pro 8428 7484, Rest/Bar 8421 4539
On the A4008 between Hatch End and
Watford.
Gently undulating parkland.
Pro Lee Curling; Founded 1910
Designed by James Braid
18 holes, 5590 yards, S.S.S. 67
✐ Practice green.
† Welcome WD.
ℂ WD £30.
⌇ Welcome Tues-Fri; 36 holes 2
meals; £60.
🍽 Full catering facilities.

1B 73 Hadley Wood ☎
Beech Hill, Barnet, Herts, EN4 0JJ
🖧 www.hadleywoodgc.com
✉ gen.mgr @hadleywoodgc.com

☎ 020 8449 4328, Fax 8364 8633,
Pro 8449 3285
Off A111 Cockfosters road a mile from
M25 Junction 24.
Parkland course.
Pro Peter Jones; Founded 1922
Designed by A MacKenzie
18 holes, 6457 yards, S.S.S. 71
✐ 300 yards practice area.
† Welcome WD with handicap certs.
ℂ WD £36.
⌇ Welcome Mon, Thurs and Fri;
terms on application.
🍽 Full catering and bar facilities
available.
⌂ West Lodge Park, Cockfosters.

1B 74 Hainault Forest
Chigwell Row, Hainault, Essex, IG7 4QW
🖧 www.essexgolfcentres.com
✉ info@essexgolfcentres.com
☎ 020 8500 2131, Pro 8500 2131,
Sec 8500 2131, Rest/Bar 8500 8333
Off the A12.
Parkland course.
Pro Chris Hope; Founded 1912
Designed by JH Taylor
2 x18 hole courses, 6545/5886 yards,
S.S.S. 72/69
✐ 22 bay illuminated range.
† Welcome pay and play course.
ℂ WD £16.00; WE £21.00.
⌇ Welcome by prior arrangement;
packages available.
🍽 Meals and bar service.

1B 75 Hampstead
Winnington Rd, Hampstead, London,
N2 0TU
☎ 020 8455 0203, Fax 8731 6194,
Pro 8455 7089
400 yards down Winnington Road near
Kenwood House.
Undulating parkland course with
mature trees.
Pro Peter Brown; Founded 1893
Designed by Tom Dunn
9 holes, 5822 yards, S.S.S. 68
† Welcome with handicap certs or
letter of introduction; restrictions Tues
and WE.
ℂ WD £30; WE £35.
⌇ Not available.
🍽 Not available.

1B 76 Hanbury Manor
Ware, Herts, SG12 0SD
🖧 www.hanbury-manor.com
✉ golf.hanburymanor@marriotthotels
.co.uk
☎ 01920 487722, Fax 487692,
Pro 885000, Sec 885000

J25 off M25, take A10 N for 12 miles.
Parkland course.
Pro David Ingram; Founded 1990
Designed by Jack Nicklaus
18 holes, 7016 yards, S.S.S. 74
† Welcome if hotel resident or
member's guest.
ℂ Hotel residents: WD/WE £85,
Summertime. WD/WE £50 Wintertime.
⌇ Welcome by prior arrangement
with the golf co-ordinator; terms on
application.
🍽 Hotel and clubhouse facilities.
⌂ Marriott Hanbury Manor.

1B 77 Hanover
Hullbridge Rd, Rayleigh, Essex,
SS6 9QS
☎ 01702 232377, Fax 231811
Down A130 past Carpenters Arms
Roundabout. Right down Rawreth Lane.
Undulating course.
Pro Tony Blackburn; Founded 1991
Designed by Reg Plumbridge
18 holes, 3700 yards, S.S.S. 61
† Welcome.
ℂ WD £12.50; WE £17-£50.
⌇ Welcome midweek; afternoons at
WE; terms on application.
🍽 Full catering facilities including
carvery and bar.
⌂ Master Brewer Hillingdon.

1B 78 Harefield Place
The Drive, Harsfield Place, Uxbridge,
Middx, UB10 8AQ
☎ 01895 272457, Fax 810262, Pro
237287, Sec 272457, Rest/Bar 272457
B467 towards Ruislip off off at A40 1st
left down The Drive.
Undulating parkland.
Pro Cameron Smillie
18 holes, 5677 yards, S.S.S. 68
† Welcome.
ℂ WD £12.50; WE £18.50.
⌇ Welcome midweek afternoons; at
WE terms on application.
🍽 Full catering facilities; including
carvery and Bar.
⌂ Master Brewer.

1B 79 Harpenden
Hammonds End, Redbourn Lane,
Harpenden, Herts, AL5 2AX
🖧 www.harpendengolfclub.co.uk
✉ office@harpendengolfclub.co.uk
☎ 01582 712580, Fax 712725,
Pro 767124, Sec 817520,
Rest/Bar 462014
On A487 Redbourn road.
Parkland course.
Pro Mr Peter Cherry; Founded 1894

Designed by Hawtree & Taylor
18 holes, 6277 yards, S.S.S. 70
♦ Welcome WD except Thurs; with a member at WE.
Ⅰ WD £30 round, £40 day.
♐ Welcome WD except Thurs; £55-£70.
⦿ Full facilities.
⬳ Gleneagles Harpenden; Harpenden House Hotel.

1B 80 Harpenden Common
Cravells Road, East Common, Harpenden, Herts, AL5 1BL
⬡ www.hcgc.co.uk
⬛ admin@hcgc.co.uk
☎ 01582 711320, Fax 711321, Pro 460655, Rest/Bar 711322
Course is 4 miles N of St Albans on the A1081.
Parkland course.
Pro D Fitzsimmons; Founded 1931
Designed by Ken Brown (1995)
18 holes, 6214 yards, S.S.S. 70
♦ Welcome WD.
Ⅰ WD £25.
♐ Welcome on Thurs and Fri; package rates from £31-£55.
⦿ Full facilities.
⬳ Gleneagles Harpenden.

1B 81 Harrow Hill
Kenton Road, Harrow, Middx, HA1 2BW
⬡ www.harrowhillgolfcourse.co.uk
☎ 020 8864 3754
Off main Harrow by-pass near Northwick Park roundabout.
Simon Bishop; Founded 1982
Designed by S Teahan
9 holes, 850 yards
♦ Public beginners par 3.
Ⅰ WD £4; WE £5.
⦿ Cold soft drinks and sweets available.

1B 82 Harrow School
Harrow School Golf Club, c/o Masters' Room, 5 High St, Harrow-on-the-Hill, Middx, HA1 3JE
☎ 020 8872 8000
Parkland course.
Founded 1976
Designed by Donald Steel
9 holes, 3690 yards, S.S.S. 57
♦ Members guests' only.
Ⅰ WD/WE £8.

1B 83 Hartsbourne Golf and Country Club
Hartsbourne Ave, Bushey Heath, Herts, WD23 1JW

⬡ www.hartsbournegolfclub.co.uk
⬛ GM@hartsbournegolfclub.co.uk
☎ 0208 421 7272, Fax 950 5357, Pro 421 7266
Turn off A411 at entrance to Bushey Heath village 5 miles SE of Watford.
Parkland course.
Pro Reeves Weedon; Founded 1946
Designed by Hawtree and Taylor
18 and 9 holes, 6385 and 5773 yards, S.S.S. 70 Par 70
♦ Members' guests only.
Ⅰ WD £20 WE £30.
♐ Welcome WD only catering packages available.
⦿ Full catering and bar facilities.
⬳ Hilton National.

1B 84 Hartswood
King George's Playing Fields, Ingrave Road, Brentwood, Essex, CME14 5AE
☎ 01277 214830, Pro 218714, Sec 218850
On A128 Ingrave Rd, 1 mile from Brentwood.
Parkland course.
Pro Steve Cole; Founded 1965
18 holes, 6192 yards, S.S.S. 69
♦ Municipal course.
Ⅰ WD £10; WE £15.
♐ Welcome WD, minimum 20; meals and 18 or 36 holes, coffee on arrival; £25-£35.
⦿ Full facilities.

1B 85 Harwich & Dovercourt
Station Rd, Parkeston, Harwich, Essex, CO12 4NZ
☎ 01255 503616, Fax 503323
Turn left off the A120 roundabout for Parkston village; course is 100 yards on left.
Parkland course.
Founded 1906
9 holes, 5900 yards, S.S.S. 69
♦ WD welcome if carrying handicap certs; WE welcome only if guests of a member.
Ⅰ WD £20.
♐ Welcome by prior arrangement; catering by prior arrangement.
⦿ Clubhouse facilities.
⬳ Tower; Cliff both at Dovercourt. Pier Hotel, Harwich.

1B 86 Haste Hill
The Drive, Northwood, Middx, HA6 1HN
☎ 01923 825224, Fax 826485
On A404 at Northwood.
Tree-lined parkland course.
Pro Cameron Smilie; Founded 1930.

18 holes, 5797 yards, S.S.S. 68
♦ Welcome; book in advance.
Ⅰ WD £13.50; WE £19.50.
♐ Welcome; terms on application.
⦿ Facilities available.
⬳ Tudor Lodge, Eastcote.

1B 87 Hatfield London CC
Bedwell Park, Essendon, Hatfield, Herts, AL9 6JA
☎ 01707 642624, Fax 646187, Pro 642624
A1000 from Potters Bar B158 towards Essendon.
Undulating parkland course.
Pro Norman Greer; Founded 1976
Designed by Fred Hawtree
18 holes, 6385 yards, S.S.S. 70
Ⅰ Practice area. Par 3 pitch and putt. Practice green.
♦ Welcome by advance booking.
Ⅰ WD £17; WE £27.
♐ Welcome; terms on application.
⦿ Full facilities.

1B 88 Hazelwood
Croysdale Ave, Sunbury-on-Thames, Middx, TW16 6QU
☎ 01932 770981, Fax 770933, Pro 770932, Rest/Bar 783496
1 mile from M3 Junction 1.
Parkland course.
Pro Francis Sheridan; Founded 1993
Designed by Jonathan Gaunt
9 holes, 5660 yards, S.S.S. 67
Ⅰ 36 bay driving range.
♦ Welcome.
Ⅰ WD £7.50; WE £9.50.
♐ Welcome by arrangement; terms on application.
⦿ 11 am - 7 pm.

1B 89 Hendon
Ashley Walk, Devonshire Rd, Mill Hill, London, NW7 1DG
⬛ londongolfclub@globalnet.co.uk
☎ 020 8346 6023, Fax 8343 1974, Pro 8346 8990, Rest/Bar 8349 0728
From Hendon Central take Queens Rd through Brent St continue to roundabout take 1st exit on left club 0.5 miles on left in Devonshire Rd.
Parkland course.
Pro Matt Deal; Founded 1903
Designed by HS Colt
18 holes, 6266 yards, S.S.S. 70
Ⅰ Metro Centre (5 min).
♦ WD advise to book in Summer.
Ⅰ WD £30 WE £35.
♐ By arrangment.
⦿ Bar/Rest.
⬳ Holiday Inn (Brent Cross).

1B 90 The Hertfordshire
Broxbournebury Mansion, White Stubbs
Lane, Broxbourne, Herts, EN10 7PY
🖧 www.americangolf.com
✉ hertfordshire@
americangolf.uk.com
☎ 01992 466666
M25 Junction 25 take A10 towards
Cambridge. Take A10 exit for Turnford
and then A1170 to Bell Lane. Turn left
Bell Lane becomes White Stubbs
Lane. Course is on the right.
Parkland course.
Pro Adrian Shearn; Founded 1995
Designed by Jack Nicklaus (his first
pay and play course In Europe)
18 holes, 6388 yards, S.S.S. 70
🏌 Practice range, 30 bays floodlit.
✝ Welcome WE 7.30-11.30 am
members only.
Ⅼ WD £30; WE £35.
⌔ Welcome; corporate days available;
health club, indoor swimming pool,
tennis club, golf academy with chipping
green; terms available on application.
🍽 Restaurant and bar.
🛏 The Cheshunt Marriott.

1B 91 High Beech
Wellington Hill, Loughton, Essex,
IG10 4AH
☎ 020 8508 7323
5 mins from M25 Junction 26 at
Waltham Abbey.
Parkland course.
Pro Clark Baker; Founded 1963
Two 9-hole courses, 1477/847 yards,
S.S.S. par 3
🏌 Practice nets.
✝ Public pay and play.
Ⅼ WD £3.70; WE £4.70.
⌔ Everyone welcome.
🍽 No facilities.
🛏 The Swallow, Waltham Abbey.

1B 92 Highgate
Denewood Road, London, N6 4AH
🖧 www.highgategolfclub.
freeserve.co.uk
✉ secretary@
highgategolfclub.freeserve.co.uk
☎ 020 8340 1906, Fax 8340 9152,
Pro 8340 5467, Sec 8340 3745,
Rest/Bar 8240 1906
Off Hampstead Lane near Kenwood
House, turn into Sheldon Ave then 1st
left into Denewood Rd.
Parkland course.
Pro RobinTurner/DarrenTurner;
Founded 1904
18 holes, 5985 yards, S.S.S. 69
✝ Welcome WD (after noon on Wed);
no visitors at WE.

Ⅼ WD £30.
⌔ Welcome Tues, Thurs, Fri; terms
on application.
🍽 Full facilities 12-8pm.

1B 93 Hillingdon
18 Dorset Way, Hillingdon, Middx,
UB10 0JR
✉ hillingdongolfclub@lineone.net
☎ 01895 233956
Turn off A40 to Uxbridge past
RAF station up Hillingdon Hill, turn
left at Vine Public House into Vine
Lane.
Undulating parkland course.
Pro Phil Smith; Founded 1892
Designed by Harry Woods & Chas E
Stevens
9 holes, 5490 yards, S.S.S. 68
✝ Welcome WD except Thurs pm;
WE with a member only after 12.30pm.
Ⅼ WD £15.
⌔ Welcome Mon by prior
arrangement; special golf and catering
packages available; from £25.
🍽 Bar and catering facilities available.
🛏 Master Brewer; Old Cottage.

1B 94 Horsenden Hill
Woodland Rise, Greenford, Middx,
UB6 0RD
☎ 0208 902 4555, Pro 07958 947
409, Rest/Bar 0208 900 9181
Signposted off Whitton Ave East at the
rear of Sudbury Golf club.
Public undulating parkland course.
Pro Jeff Quarshie; Founded 1935
9 holes, 1632 yards, S.S.S. 28
🏌 Practice area.
✝ Welcome no restrictions.
Ⅼ WD £4.40; WE £6.40.
⌔ Welcome any time by prior
arrangement.
🍽 Bar and restaurant.

1B 95 Hounslow Heath
Staines Rd, Hounslow, Middx, TW4 5DS
☎ 020 8570 5271, Fax 8570 5205
A315 main road between Hounslow
and Bedfont on left hand side.
Heathland course.
Pro Jo Smith; Founded 1979
Designed by Fraser Middleton
18 holes, 5901 yards, S.S.S. 68
🏌 Practice green, Putting area.
✝ Welcome.
Ⅼ WD £9.25; WE £13.40.
⌔ Welcome by arrangement; terms
on application.
🍽 No bar; snacks and soft drinks
available.

🛏 Several available in Hounslow or
Heathrow.

1B 96 Ilford
291 Wanstead Park Rd, Ilford, Essex,
IG1 3TR
☎ 020 8554 0094
0.5 mile from Ilford railway station.
Parkland course.
Pro Stuart Dowsett; Founded 1908
18 holes, 5297 yards, S.S.S. 66
🏌 Practice area.
✝ Welcome with advance booking;
restricted Tues and Thurs; Sat
10.30am-12.30pm Sun 12.30pm-
1.30pm.
Ⅼ WD £15; WE £19.
⌔ Welcome WD by prior
arrangement with Sec; terms available
on application.
🍽 Restaurant available most days.
🛏 Woodford Moat House.

1B 97 Knebworth
Deards End Lane, Knebworth, Herts,
SG3 6NL
✉ knebworth.golf@virgin.net
☎ 01438 812752, Fax 815216,
Pro 812757
1 mile S of Stevenage on B197 leave
A1M at Junction 7.
Undulating parkland.
Pro Garry Parker; Founded 1908
Designed by Willie Park
18 holes, 6492 yards, S.S.S. 71
✝ Welcome WD.
Ⅼ WD £37 round and day.
⌔ Welcome Mon, Tues and Thurs
only; terms on application.
🍽 Full catering and bar.

1B 98 Laing Sports Club
Rowley Lane, Arkley, Barnet, Herts,
EN5 3HW
☎ 020 8441 6051
Off A1 S at Borehamwood.
Parkland course.
Designed by Employees of John Laing
and members
9 holes, 4178 yards, S.S.S. 60
✝ Welcome by prior arrangement;
weekend restrictions.
Ⅼ WD £8; WE £8.
⌔ Packages available.
🍽 Bar and English and Japanese
restaurant.

1B 99 Lamerwood Country ☏
Club
Codicote Rd, Wheathampstead, Herts,
AL4 8GB

☎ 01582 833013, Fax 832604
5 miles W of A1 jct 4 on B653.
Woodland/parkland course.
Pro Matthew Masters; Founded 1996
Designed by Mr Sinclair
18 holes, 6588 yards, S.S.S. 73
🏌 11 floodlit bays.
♦ Welcome by prior arrangement.
⌐ WD £25; WE £37.
⌒ Packages available.
🍽 Bar and English/Japanese
restaurant.

1B 100 Langdon Hills Golf ☞ and Country Club

Lower Dunton Road, Bulphan, Essex,
RM14 3TY
☎ 01268 548444, Fax 490084,
Pro 544300, Sec 548444,
Rest/Bar 548444
Course is 8 miles from M25 Junction
30; take the A13 E towards Tilbury
after approx 7 miles turn off on the
B1007 towards Horndon on the Hill;
after approx 1 mile turn left into Lower
Dunton Rd.
Parkland course.
Pro Terry Moncur; Founded 1991
Designed by MRM Sandow
27 holes, 9558 yards, S.S.S. 71
🏌 Practice range 22 bays; floodlit.
♦ Welcome WD; not before 10.30am
WE.
⌐ WD £20 approx; WE £22 approx.
Pre-booking required 5 days in
advance maximum with pro shop.
⌒ Welcome WD by prior
arrangement; European School of golf;
special packages; function suite; terms
on application.
🍽 Bar and restaurant.
⌒ Langdon Hills.

1B 101 Lee Valley

Edmonton, London, N9 0AS
☎ 020 8803 3611, Fax 8884 4975,
Pro 8803 3611, Sec 8364 7782,
1 mile N of North Circular Road
Junction with Meridian Way.
Public parkland course with large lake
and river.
Pro Richard Gerken; Founded 1974
18 holes, 4902 yards, S.S.S. 64
🏌 Practice range 20 bays; floodlit.
♦ Open to public every day no
restrictions.
⌐ WD £12.00; WE £15.00.
⌒ Welcome WD only; max 30
persons.
🍽 Breakfast until midday, bar and bar
snacks daily.
⌒ Holt Whites Hotel Enfield.

1B 102 Letchworth ☞

Letchworth Lane, Letchworth, Herts,
SG6 3NQ
☎ 01462 683203, Fax 484567
1 mile S of Letchworth off A505.
Parkland course.
Pro Steve Allen; Founded 1905
Designed by Harry Vardon
18 holes, 6181 yards, S.S.S. 69
🏌 Large practice area with open
driving range bays.
♦ Welcome WD; restrictions Tues.
⌐ WD £28.
⌒ Welcome Wed, Thurs and Fri; 36
holes of golf snack lunch and dinner;
£58.
🍽 Full clubhouse facilities.
⌒ Ambassador, Letchworth;
Letchworth Hall.

1B 103 Limetrees Park Golf Course

Ruislip Rd, Northolt, Middx, UB5 6QZ
☎ 020 8845 3180, Fax 8842 0542,
Pro 087074590289
0.5 miles S of Polish War Memorial on
A4180.
Parkland course.
Pro Neil MacDonald/Michael Stanger;
Founded 1982
9 holes, 5836 yards, S.S.S. 69
🏌 Driving range 20 floodlit bays
♦ Welcome.
⌐ WD £7.25; WE £8.75.
⌒ Welcome WD; unlimited golf
2-course lunch.
🍽 Bar and catering facilities.

1B 104 Little Hay Golf Complex

Box Lane, Bovingdon, Hemel
Hempstead, Herts, HP3 0QD
✉ chris.gordon@dacorum.gov.uk
☎ 01442 833798, Fax 831399,
Pro 833798, Rest/Bar 831378
Just off A41 turn left at first traffic lights
past Hemel Hempstead station; 1.5
miles up hill, complex on right.
Public parkland pay and play course.
Pro Nick Allen
Designed by Hawtree & Son
18 holes, 6311 yards, S.S.S. 70
🏌 Practice range 22 bays; floodlit.
♦ Welcome.
⌐ WD £13; WE £17.
⌒ Welcome by prior arrangement;
bookings accepted on the day after
8.30am by phone; golf and catering
packages available on request; terms
on application.
🍽 Full meals.
⌒ Bobsleigh.

1B 105 Loughton

Clay's Lane, Debden Green, Loughton,
Essex, IG10 2RZ
☎ 020 8502 2923
From M25 Junction 26 take A121
towards Loughton; 3rd exit at
roundabout; first turning on left.
Undulating parkland course.
Founded 1982
9 holes, 4652 yards, S.S.S. 63
🏌 Practice field.
♦ Welcome.
⌐ WD £7 (9) £12 (18); WE £8 (9)
£14 (18).
⌒ Terms available on application.
🍽 Facilities available but limited.
⌒ The Bell, Epping; The Swallow,
Watham Abbey.

1B 106 Maldon

Beeleigh, Langford, Maldon, Essex,
CM9 6LL
✉ maldon.golf@virgin.net
☎ 01621 853212, Fax 855232
2 miles NW of Maldon on B1019. Turn
off at Essex waterworks.
Parkland course.
Founded 1891
9 holes, 6253 yards, S.S.S. 70
🏌 Practice area.
♦ Welcome WD; with a member only
at WE.
⌐ WD £15.
⌒ Welcome; maximum of 32;
packages; terms on application.
🍽 Clubhouse catering and bar.
⌒ Blue Boar, Maldon.

1B 107 Malton

Malton Lane, Meldreth, Royston, Herts,
SG8 6PE
🖳 www.maltongolf.co.uk
✉ info@maltongolf.co.uk
☎ 01763 262200, Fax 262209
A10 towards Cambridge turn at
Melbourne towards Meldreth; 4 Miles.
Parkland course.
Founded 1994
18 holes, 6708 yards, S.S.S. 72
🏌 Driving range; 10 bays.
♦ Everyone welcome.
⌐ WD £10; WE £16.
⌒ Welcome; packages available;
from £13.
🍽 Bar and bar snacks.
⌒ Cambridge Motel.

1B 108 Manor of Groves ☞ Hotel Golf Country Club

High Wych, Sawbridgeworth, Herts,
CM21 0JU
🖳 www.monorofgroves.com
✉ info@manorofgroves.com

☎ 01279 600777, Fax 726972,
Pro 603543, Sec 603539
On A1184 to High Wych; leave M11 at
Junction 7.
Parkland course.
Founded 1991
Designed by S Sharer
18 holes, 6237 yards, S.S.S. 71
⚲ Putting green; 80 bed hotel; health
complex.
† Welcome WD; pm at WE.
£ WD £24; WE £25 during summer,
reduced winter.
⚘ Welcome WD; packages arranged
for parties; from £26.
🍽 Full hotel facilities.
🛏 Manor of Groves Hotel.

1B 109 Maylands Golf & CC
Colchester Road, Harold Park,
Romford, Essex, RM3 0AZ
☎ 01708 342055, Fax 373080,
Pro 346466, Sec 342055
Rest/Bar 342055
1 mile W of M25 Junction 28.
Parkland course.
Pro S Hopkin/R Cole Touring;
Founded 1936
Designed by Colt Alison and Morrison
18 holes, 6361 yards, S.S.S. 70
† WD Welcome with prior
arrangement and handicap certs.
£ WD £20.
⚘ Mon, Wed and Fri; packages
available; terms on application.
🍽 Full catering facilities.
🛏 Brentwood Post House; Mary
Green Manor.

1B 110 Mid-Herts
Lamer Lane Gustard Wood,
Wheathampstead, St Albans, Herts,
AL4 8RS
⌨ www.mid-hertsgolfclub.co.uk
✉ secretary@mid-hertsgolfclub.co.uk
☎ 01582 832242, Fax 834834
6 miles N of St Albans on B651.
Parkland course.
Pro Barney Puttick; Founded 1892
18 holes, 6060 yards, S.S.S. 69
⚲ Practice area.
† Welcome except Tues morning
and Wed afternoon.
£ WD £25, day pass £35.
⚘ Welcome Thurs and Fri; terms on
application.
🍽 Catering and bar facilities.
🛏 Hatfield Lodge Hotel.

1B 111 Mill Green
Gypsy Lane, Welwyn Garden City,
Herts, AL7 4TY
⌨ www.americangolf.com
✉ millgreen@americangolf.uk.com
☎ 01707 276900, Fax 276898,
Pro 270542
Off A100 Welwyn Garden City, past
Bush Hall, at lights turn left, 2nd right
and then into Gypsy Lane.
Parkland/woodland course.
Pro Ian Parker; Founded 1993
Designed by Peter Alliss & Clive Clark
18 holes, 6615 yards, S.S.S. 72
⚲ Practice range grass.
† Everyone welcome.
£ WD £19 (Mon £15); WE £25.
⚘ Welcome by prior arrangement;
packages available; par 3 course;
terms on application.
🍽 Full catering and bar.
🛏 Jarvis Comet Hatfield.

1B 112 Mill Hill ☎
100 Barnet Way, Mill Hill, London,
NW7 3AL
☎ 020 8959 2339, Fax 8906 0731,
Pro 8959 7261
From Junction of A1/A41 going N
immediately filter right and cross into
Marsh Lane after 0.5 mile turn left
into Hankins Lane leading to club-
house; going S 1 mile from Stirling
Corner.
Parkland course.
Pro David Beal; Founded 1925
Designed by JF Abercromby (1931
remodelled by HS Colt)
18 holes, 6247 yards, S.S.S. 70
⚲ Practice area with driving area.
† Welcome WD; WE reservations
only.
£ WD £25; WE £30.
⚘ Welcome Mon, Wed, Fri (except
BH); terms on application.
🍽 Facilities daily.
🛏 Jarvis; Hilton National; Welcome
Lodge.

1B 113 Moor Park
Rickmansworth, Herts, WD3 1QN
⌨ www.moorparkgc.co.uk
✉ enquiries@moorparkgc.co.uk
☎ 01923 773146, Fax 777109,
Pro 774113
1 mile SE of Rickmansworth off
Batchworth roundabout on A4145.
Parkland course.
Pro L Farmer; Founded 1923
Designed by H.S. Colt
High: 18 holes, 6713 yards, S.S.S. 72;
West: 18 holes, 5815 yards, S.S.S. 68
† WDs only with handicap certs.
£ WD West £45; High £72.50.
⚘ Welcome WD only; packages
available; terms on application.
🍽 Full restaurant facilities.

1B 114 Muswell Hill ☎
Rhodes Ave, Wood Green, London,
N22 7UT
☎ 020 8888 1764, Fax 8889 9380
1 mile from Bounds Green tube station
1.5 miles from N Circular Rd.
Undulating parkland course.
Pro David Wilton; Founded 1893
18 holes, 6432 yards, S.S.S. 70
⚲ Limited practice area.
† WD; WE and BH limited bookings
through Pro.
£ WD £30.
⚘ Welcome WD by arrangement;
packages available; terms on application.
🍽 Meals and snacks bar.
🛏 Raglan Hall.

1B 115 The Nazeing
Middle Street, Nazeing, Essex,
EN9 2LW
☎ 01992 893915, Fax 893882,
Pro 893798, Sec 893798
On B194 in Nazeing.
Parkland course.
Pro Robert Green; Founded 1992
Designed by Martin Gillett
18 holes, 6598 yards, S.S.S. 72 off the
whites
⚲ 18.
† Welcome after 8.30am WD and 12
at WE.
£ WD £20; WE £28 PMs only. Mon
£16 only.
⚘ Welcome WD with a minimum of
12 players; packages involving
breakfast lunch and dinner and 18, 27
or 36 holes can be arranged.
🍽 Full catering and bar.
🛏 Swallow Hotel; Waltham Abbey.

1B 116 North Middlesex ☎
The Manor House, Friern Barnet Lane,
Whetstone, London, N20 0NL
⌨ www.northmiddlesexgc.co.uk
✉ office@northmiddlesexgc.co.uk
☎ 020 8445 1604, Fax 8445 5023,
Pro 8445 3060, Sec 8445 1604,
Rest/Bar 020 8445 1732
Course is 5 miles south of M25
Junction 23 between Barnet and
Finchley.
Parkland course.
Pro Freddy George; Founded 1905
Designed by Willie Park Jnr
18 holes, 5594 yards, S.S.S. 67
† Welcome by prior arrangement.
WE after 12.30 pm.
£ WD £25; WE £30 summer. WD
£20; WE £25 winter.
⚘ Welcome WD by prior
arrangement with Secretary.
🍽 Full clubhouse facilities available.

1B 117 North Weald GC
Rayley Lane, North Weald, Essex,
CM16 6AR
☎ 0199 2522118, Fax 522881
On A414 Chelmsford road from M11
Junction 7.
Parkland course.
Pro David Rawlings; Founded 1996
Designed by D Williams
18 holes, 6377 yards, S.S.S. 70
⚑ Driving range and practice areas.
† Welcome; book with Pro.
⌞ WD £20; WE £27.50.
⚐ Welcome by prior arrangement
with Sec; bar and restaurant facilities.
🍽 Bar and restaurant.

1B 118 Northwood   ℧
Rickmansworth Rd, Northwood, Middx,
HA6 2QW
✉ jenny@ngcnorthwood.co.uk
☎ 01923 821384, Fax 840150,
Pro 820112
0.25 miles S of Northwood on A404.
Parkland course.
Pro C Holdsworth; Founded 1891
Designed by James Braid
18 holes, 6535 yards, S.S.S. 73
⚑ Practice area.
† Welcome WD.
⌞ WD £28.
⚐ Welcome Mon and Thurs;
packages available; terms on
application.
🍽 Full catering facilities.
⚑ Tudor Lodge, Eastcote; The Barn,
Ruislip.

1B 119 Old Fold Manor   ℧
Old Fold Lane, Hadley Green, Barnet,
Herts, EN5 4QN
🖳 www.oldfoldmanor.co.uk
✉ manager@oldfoldmanor.co.uk
☎ 0208 440 9185, Fax 441 4863,
Pro 440 7488, Sec 440 9185
On A1000 1 mile N of Barnet close to
M25 Junction 23.
Heathland course.
Pro Peter McEvoy; Founded 1910
18 holes, 6260 yards, S.S.S. 71
† Welcome with handicap certs.
⌞ WD £25; WE £30.
⚐ Welcome Thurs and Fri; packages
for golf and catering available; £60.
🍽 Full clubhouse facilities.
⚑ Hadley Hotel; West Lodge.

1B 120 Orsett
Brentwood Rd, Orsett, Essex,
RM16 3DS
✉ orsettgc@aol.com
☎ 01375 891352, Fax 892471,
Pro 891797, Sec 893409

4 miles NE of Grays on the A128.
Heathland/parkland course.
Pro Paul Joiner; Founded 1899
Designed by James Braid
18 holes, 6603 yards, S.S.S. 72
⚑ Practice area, netted bays.
† Welcome.
⌞ WD £30.
⚐ Welcome, Mon, Tues and in
afternoon on Wed; packages include
all meals.
🍽 Full catering and bar facilities.
⚑ Orsett Hall; Stifford Moat House
Near Grays.

1B 121 Oxhey Park
Prestwick Rd, South Oxhey, Watford
Herts, WD1 6DT
☎ 01923 248312
2 miles SW of Watford.
9 holes, 1637 yards, S.S.S. 58
† Welcome.
⌞ £10.00.

1B 122 Panshanger
Old Herns Lane, Welwyn Garden City,
Herts, AL7 2ED
☎ 01707 333350, Fax 390010,
Pro 323443, Sec 333312,
Rest/Bar 333312
Off B1000 close to A1 1 mile NE of
town.
Municipal undulating parkland course.
Pro Mick Corlass/Bryan Lewis;
Founded 1975
18-hole main course 9-hole pitch and
put holes, 6347 yards, S.S.S. 70
⚑ 2.
† Welcome; no restrictions.
⌞ WD £13.30; WE £18.50.
⚐ Welcome by prior arrangement;
terms on application.
🍽 Lunch every day.
⚑ Tewinbury Farm, Beefeater,
Stanborough.

1B 123 Perivale Park
Stockdove Way, Argyle Road,
Greenford, Middx, UB6 8TJ
☎ 020 8575 7116
Between Greenford and Perivale,
entrance from Argyle Rd.
Public parkland course.
Pro Peter Bryant; Founded 1932
9 holes, 2733 yards, S.S.S. 67
⚑ Practice area.
† Welcome.
⌞ WD £6; WE £8.
⚐ No societies.
🍽 Café serving meals, tea, coffee,
etc; no bar.
⚑ Kenton Hanger Hill.

1B 124 Pinner Hill
South View Rd, Pinner Hill, Middx,
HA5 3YA
🖳 www.pinnerhillgc.co.uk
✉ pinnerhillgc@uk2.net
☎ 020 8866 0963, Fax 8868 4817,
Pro 8866 2109
1 mile W of Pinner Green.
Parkland course.
Pro Mark Grieve; Founded 1928/47
Designed by JH Taylor/Hawtree
18 holes, 6388 yards, S.S.S. 70
⚑ Putting greens and practice area.
† Welcome WD particularly Wed and
Thurs.
⌞ WD £30; Wed & Thurs £15; WE £30
⚐ Welcome WD for groups of 12-40
players; package of full meals and full
day's golf; £40-£42.
🍽 Full facilities.
⚑ Barn House Eastcote; Harrow
Hotel; Frithwood GH Northwood.

1B 125 Porters Park
Shenley Hill, Radlett, Herts, WD7 7AZ
🖳 www.porterspark.com
✉ info@porterspark.fsnet.co.uk
☎ 01923 854127, Fax 855475,
Pro 854366, Rest/Bar 856262
From M25 Junction 22 to Radlett via
A5183 turn at railway station 0.5 mile
to top of Shenley Hill.
Undulating parkland course.
Pro David Gleeson; Founded 1899
18 holes, 6313 yards, S.S.S. 70
⚑ Practice area.
† Welcome WD; handicap certs
required, phone 24 hours in advance;
member guest only at WE.
⌞ WD £30.
⚐ Wed, Thurs only; min 20 max 50;
£68 inc. Full catering available for
societies.
🍽 Breakfast (pre-ordered), bar menu.
⚑ Red Lion.

1B 126 Potters Bar
Darkes Lane, Potters Bar, Herts,
EN6 1DE
🖳 www.pottersbargolfclub.com
✉ info@pottersbargolfclub.com
☎ 01707 652020, Fax 655051
1 mile N of M25 Junction 24 close to
Potters Bar station.
Parkland course.
Pro G A'ris/J Harding; Founded 1924
Designed by James Braid
18 holes, 6291 yards, S.S.S. 70
† Welcome WD with handicap certs.
⌞ WD £27.50.
⚐ Welcome WD except Wed; full
lunch and dinner with 36 holes of golf.
🍽 Full clubhouse facilities.

Royal Epping Forest

A Royal course in Essex? Surely not. But that is to pander to the stand-up comedian's view of the county. Royal Epping Forest has a history to be proud of and wonderful links to Royalty and the past of the great game.

Founded in 1888, Royal Epping Forest Golf Club is the oldest golf club in Essex playing on a course built on land that was once the hunting grounds of Henry VIII and Queen Elizabeth I.

It is one of only two Royal Clubs that play over a public golf course, the other being the Royal and Ancient at St Andrew's.

More history? Certainly. The land where the course sits was also where the highwayman Dick Turpin roamed in the 1730's.

But now to the confusing part of Royal Epping Forest – the only club in Essex to carry the Royal title. The 18 holes are actually Chingford Golf Course and is home to three clubs – Chingford, Chingford Ladies and Royal Epping Forest. All three play their golf on the course but each has its own private clubhouse.

The public nature of the land can lead to the occasional wandering of blissfully unaware families into the firing line. Hence one of the course's more interesting rules – players must wear an item of red clothing to identify themselves as golfers.

The PGA Professional and Course Manager is Andy Traynor who keeps a supply of suitable red shirts, slip-overs or jumpers in the club shop that can be hired at £3 per round. As the extremely helpful Mr Traynor, who has his own website – www.andytraynorpgapro.co.uk – offering full details of green fees and bookings, points out the garment must be red, not burgundy, pink or orange.

A mere 20 minutes by train from London's Liverpool Street station Royal Epping's course is not long – it measures 6,432 yards – but provides a test for golfers of all abilities with narrow tree-lined fairways and small sloping greens.

The course, as it is within the boundaries of Epping Forest, falls under the control of The Corporation of London. – **Jon Ryan**

1B 127 Redbourn ☏
Kinsbourne Green Lane, Redbourn,
Herts, AL3 7QA
🖳 www.redbourngolfclub.com
📧 golfclubsecretary@
redbourngolfclub.com
☎ 01582 793493, Fax 794362,
Sec 794888, Rest/Bar 793363
Off A5183 turn into Luton Lane and
club is 0.5 miles. Approx. 1 mile from
J10 of M1.
Parkland course.
Pro Stephen Hunter; Founded 1971
Designed by H Stovin
18 holes, 6506 yards, S.S.S. 71
⏸ Practice range, 20 bay target range.
† Welcome with prior bookings
accepted 3 days in advance. After 12
noon WE.
⏸ WD £26; WE £32.
🖧 Welcome WD; full golfing day on
18-hole course; Golf clinics golf ranger
buggies; £26-£53.
🍽 Full restaurant and bar facilities.

1B 128 Regiment Way
Pratts Farm Lane, Little Waltham,
Chelmsford, Essex, CM3 3PR
🖳 www.channelsgolf,co,uk
📧 info@channelssgolf.co.uk
☎ 01245 361100, Fax 442032,
Rest/Bar 362210
On A130 off the A12 at Boreham.
Parkland course.
Pro D March; Founded 1995
Designed by Richard Stubbings
9 holes, 4887 yards, S.S.S. 64
⏸ Practice range, 16 bays floodlit.
† Welcome; pay and play.
⏸ 9 holes: WD £10; WE £11.
18 holes: WD £14; WE £16.
🖧 Welcome by arrangement.
🍽 Snack facilities. Restaurant and
bar.

1B 129 Rickmansworth
Moor Lane, Rickmansworth, Herts,
WD3 1QL
☎ 01923 775278
0.5 miles S of Rickmansworth on A4145.
Undulating parkland course.
Pro Alan Dobbins; Founded 1944
Designed by HS Colt
18 holes, 4493 yards, S.S.S. 62
† Welcome.
⏸ WD £9.60; WE £13.80.
🖧 Welcome with prior appointment;
terms on application.
🍽 Available in the Fairway Inn.
🛏 Long Island Hotel.

1B 130 Risebridge (Havering)
Risebridge Chase, Off Lower Bedfords
Road, Romford, Essex, RM1 4DG

☎ 01708 741429, Pro 741429,
Sec 727376, Rest/Bar 727376
From A12 Gallows Corner; left and
then left again.
Parkland course.
Pro Paul Jennings; Founded 1972
Designed by FW Hawtree
18 holes, 6271 yards, S.S.S. 71
⏸ Driving Range; 15 bays; 9-hole
pitch and putt.
† Welcome anytime.
⏸ WD £11.00; WE £14.50.
🖧 Welcome by prior arrangement
with Pro; packages available; terms on
application.
🍽 Full clubhouse catering.
🛏 Forte Lodge Brentwood.

1B 131 Rochford Hundred
Rochford Hall, Hall Rd, Rochford,
Essex, SS4 1NW
☎ 01702 544302, Fax 541343,
Pro 548968
On B1013 off the A127.
Parkland course.
Pro Graham Hill; Founded 1893
Designed by James Braid
18 holes, 6176 yards, S.S.S. 71
† Welcome with handicap certs,
except Sun.
⏸ WD £30; WE £40.
🖧 Welcome; packages available
include 36 holes of golf and meals.
🍽 Full clubhouse facilities.

1B 132 Romford
Heath Drive, Gidea Park, Romford,
Essex, RM2 5QB
☎ 01708 740986, Fax 752157,
Oro 749393
1.5 miles from Romford centre off A12.
Parkland course.
Pro Chris Goddard; Founded 1894
Designed by James Braid
18 holes, 6410 yards, S.S.S. 71
⏸ Practice field.
† WD with handicap certs and by
arrangement with Pro; with member
only at WE.
⏸ WD £27.50.
🖧 Welcome by prior arrangement;
packages available; terms on
application.
🍽 Facilities available.
🛏 Coach House.

1B 133 Royston ☏
Baldock Road, Royston, Herts,
SG8 5BG
🖳 www.roystongolfclub.co.uk
📧 roystongolf@btconnect.com
☎ 01763 242696, Fax 246910,
Pro 243476

On A505 on outskirts of town to W
course on Therfield Heath.
Heathland course.
Pro Sean Clark; Founded 1892
Designed by Harry Vardon.
18 holes, 6042 yards, S.S.S. 70
⏸ Practice area; putting green.
† Welcome WD; WE with member
only.
⏸ WD £30.
🖧 By prior arrangement with Sec;
packages available; terms on
application.
🍽 Full clubhouse dining facilities.
🛏 Old Bull Inn; The Banyers.

1B 134 Ruislip
Ickenham Rd, Ruislip, Middx, HA4 7DQ
☎ 01895 638835, Rest/Bar 638081
Course is opposite West Ruislip Tube
station.
Parkland course.
Pro Paul Glozier/Paul Hendrick;
Founded 1936
Designed by Sandy Herd
18 holes, 5571 yards, S.S.S. 67
† Public pay and play.
⏸ WD £13.50; WE £19.50.
🖧 Terms on application: contact
01923 825224.
🍽 Facilities available.
🛏 Barn Ruislip.

1B 135 Saffron Walden
Windmill Hill, Saffron Walden, Essex,
CB10 1BX
🖳 www.philipdavis.co.uk (pro);
www.swgc.com (club)
📧 golf@philipdavis.co.uk (pro);
office@swgc.com (club)
☎ 01799 522786, Fax 520313,
Pro 527728
Take the B184 from Stumps Cross
roundabout on the M11 (exit at
Junction 9) course entrance is just
before entering town.
Parkland course.
Pro Philip Davis; Founded 1919
18 holes, 6606 yards, S.S.S. 72
⏸ Practice range, 9 bays.
† Welcome WD with handicap certs;
with member WE and BH.
⏸ 18 holes £35; 27/36 holes £45.
🖧 Welcome Mon, Wed, Thurs; terms
on application.
🍽 Food available all day; reservations
recommended for evening meals.
🛏 Saffron Hotel.

1B 136 Sandy Lodge
Sandy Lodge Lane, Northwood, Middx,
HA6 2JD
🖳 www.sandylodge.com

▨ lesleydiamond@sandylodge.co.uk
☎ 01923 825429, Fax 824319,
Pro 825321
Off A404 adjacent to Moor Park
underground station.
Inland links.
Pro J Pinsent; Founded 1910
Designed by Harry Vardon
18 holes, 6328 yards, S.S.S. 71
❚ 17 bays.
† Welcome WD by prior arrangement.
❚ WD £25 till April; May-October £35.
↻ Welcome Mon and Thurs; full
catering and bar facilities; £28-£40.
◉ Full clubhouse facilities.
↬ Hilton National, Watford; Bedford
Arms, Rickmansworth.

1B 137 **Shendish Manor** ☂
Shendish Manor, London Road,
Apsley, Hemel Hempstead, Herts,
HP3 0AA
☎ 01442 251806, Fax 230683
3 miles from M25 Junction 20 on
A4251. M1 Junction 8 is 5 miles away.
Parkland course.
Pro Murray White; Founded 1984/96
Designed by Henry Cotton
18 holes, 5660 yards, S.S.S. 67
❚ Pitch and Putt area.
† Welcome by prior arrangement.
❚ WD £15; WE £20.
↻ Welcome WD and by special
arrangement at WE; packages
available include 18-hole course,
health club, 9-hole pitch and putt,
conference and banqueting rooms.
Lessons also available; from £21.
◉ Full clubhouse facilities with
private function rooms.

1B 138 **South Herts**
Links Drive, Totteridge, London,
N20 8QU
⊞ www.southhertsgolfclub.co.uk
☎ 020 8445 0117, Fax 8445 7569,
Pro 8445 4633, Sec 8445 2035,
Rest/Bar 8445 0117/8446 3951
On Totteridge Lane 2.5 miles E of A1M
at Mill Hill.
Parkland course.
Pro R Mitchell; Founded 1899
Designed by Harry Vardon
18 holes, 6432 yards, S.S.S. 71
† Welcome with handicap of 24 or
less.
❚ WD £30; WE £40.
↻ Welcome Wed, Thurs and Fri;
terms on application.
◉ Full clubhouse catering and bar
facilities.
↬ Queens Moat House Boreham
Wood; South Mimms Post House.

1B 139 **Stanmore**
Gordon Avenue, Stanmore, Middx,
HA7 2RL
☎ 020 8954 2599, Fax 8954 6418,
Pro 8954 2646, Sec 8954 2599,
Rest/Bar 8954 4661
Between Stanmore and Belmont off
Old Church Lane.
Parkland/woodland course.
Pro VR Law; Founded 1893
18 holes, 5860 yards, S.S.S. 68
† Welcome WD – reduced rates on
Mon and Fri.
❚ £15 Mon and Fri; £18 Tue, Wed,
Thu; £25 Sat/Sun.
↻ Welcome Mon-Fri. Various
packages available from £36.50.
◉ Full catering service and bar.

1B 140 **Stapleford Abbotts**
Horseman's Side, Tysea Hill,
Stapleford Abbotts, Essex, RM4 1JU
▨ staplefordabbotts@
americangolf.uk.com
☎ 01708 381108, Fax 386345,
Pro 381278
Course is 3 miles from M25 Junction
28 off the B175 Romford to Ongar
road; left at Stapleford Abbots, up
Tysea Hill.
Parkland course.
Pro Dean Vickerman; Founded 1972
Designed by Howard Swan
18 holes, 6501 yards, S.S.S. 72
❚ Practice ground x 2.
† Welcome.
❚ Terms on application.
↻ Welcome by prior arrangement;
packages available; sauna; function
room; also Friars course: 2280 yards
par 3; Priors course: 5720 yards.
◉ Full bar and restaurant facilities.
↬ Post House Harlow.

1B 141 **Stevenage**
Aston Lane, Aston, Stevenage, Herts,
SG2 7EL
☎ 01438 880424, Fax 880040,
Pro 438424, Sec 880322,
Rest/Bar 880223
Leave A1(M) Stevenage South then on
A602 to Hertford, course signposted
about 1.5 miles.
Parkland course.
Pro Steve Barker; Founded 1967
Designed by John Jacobs
18 holes, 6341 yards, S.S.S. 71
❚ Practice range 24 bays; floodlit.
† Welcome every day; book in
advance.
❚ WD £11.80; WE £15.50.
↻ Welcome WD; packages available;
terms available on application.

◉ Full meals and bar snacks.
↬ Roebuck.

1B 142 **Stock Brook Manor Golf & CC**
Queens Park Avenue, Stock, Billericay,
Essex, CM12 0SP
▨ events@stockbrook.com
☎ 01277 653616, Fax 633063
M25 Junction 28 then A12 to
Gallywood/Billericay exit following the
B1007 to Stock.
Parkland course.
Pro Kevin Merry; Founded 1992
Designed by Martin Gillett
27 holes, 6728 yards, S.S.S. 72
❚ Driving range and practice areas.
† Welcome.
❚ WD £25; WE £30.
↻ Welcome by prior arrangement;
country club facilities; bowls; tennis;
gym facilities. swimming pool.
◉ Full clubhouse facilities.
↬ Trust House; Basildon.

1B 143 **Stockley Park** ☂
Uxbridge, Middx, UB11 1AQ
⊞ www.stockleyparkgolf.com
▨ info@stockleyparkgolf.com
☎ 020 8813 5700, Fax 8813 5655,
Rest/Bar 8813 5701
Course is 5 mins from Heathrow
airport and 2 mins from the M4
Junction 4 towards Uxbridge.
Hilly parkland American style
championship course.
Pro Stuart Birch; Founded 1993
Opened by Nick Faldo
Designed by Robert Trent Jones Snr
18 holes, 6754 yards, S.S.S. 71
❚ Practice nets; chipping green;
putting green
† Welcome, pay as your play, correct
attire required.
❚ Summer WD £25; WE £35.
↻ Welcome WD; booked in advance
packages available; terms available on
application; limited WE.
◉ Bar and Restaurant .
↬ Novotel; Crowne Plaza; Many in
Heathrow area.

1B 144 **Stocks**
Stocks Road, Aldbury, Near Tring,
Herts, HP23 5RX
⊞ www.stocksgolf.co.uk
▨ rdarling@stocksgolf.co.uk
☎ 01442 851341, Fax 851253,
Pro 852511, Sec 852504
From either J20 of M25 or J11 of M1
follow signs to Tring. Then follow signs
to Aldbury.

Stockley Park
Golf Course

Pay & Play

Located 1 mile from Junction 4 of the M4 (Heathrow Airport) the 18 hole, 6754 yard, par 72 course is set in 248 acres of undulating parkland.

Designed by Robert Trent Jones Senior, best known for his design work at the Augusta National and other courses, such as Valderama. Stockley Park Golf course is one of the best draining courses in the South.

The Clubhouse, Stockley Park, Uxbridge, Middlesex, UB11 1AQ
Tel: 020 8813 5700   Fax: 020 8813 5655   Pro Shop: 020 8561 6339
info@stockleyparkgolf.com   www.stockleyparkgolf.com

Parkland course.
Pro Peter Lane; Founded 1993
Designed by Mike Billcliff
18 holes, 7016 yards, S.S.S. 74
🏌 Practice ground; putting green; chipping area.
† Welcome WD any time, WE after 12 noon; handicap certs required.
⌐ WD £35; WE £45.
🛒 WD by prior arrangement; terms on application.
🍽 Full club and hotel facilities available.
🛏 Stocks.

1B 145 Stoke-by-Nayland   ☎
Keepers Lane, Leavenheath,
Colchester, Essex, CO6 4PZ
🖥 www.stokebynaylandcub.co.uk
✉ info@golf-club.co.uk
☎ 01206 262836, Fax 263356,
Pro 262769, Sec 265815
Off A134 on B1068 between
Colchester and Sudbury.
Parkland.
Pro Kevin Lovelock; Founded 1972
Designed by W Peake
18 holes, 6498 yards, S.S.S. 71
🏌 Covered practice range 20 bays.
† Welcome at all times with handicap certs.
⌐ WD £22; WE £27.50.
🛒 Welcome WD; 36 holes of golf on 2 courses plus driving range and full facilities; from £40.
🍽 Full clubhouse facilities available.
🛏 Stoke by Nayland Club Hotel.

1B 146 Strawberry Hill
Wellesley Rd, Strawberry Hill,
Twickenham, Middx, TW2 5SD
🖥 www.shgc.net
☎ 0208 894 0165, Fax 898 0786,
Pro 898 2082, Sec 894 0165,
Rest/Bar 894 1246
Near Strawberry Hill BR station.
Parkland course.

Pro Peter Buchan; Founded 1900
Designed by JH Taylor
9 holes, 4762 yards, S.S.S. 62
† Welcome WD only.
⌐ WD £18 per round; £25 all day;
April to October; £11 per round with a member; £18 all day.
🛒 Fri only; maximum 25; terms on application.
🍽 Bar and catering facilities available.

1B 147 Sudbury
Bridgewater Rd, Wembley, Middx,
HA0 1AL
🖥 www.sudburygolfclubltd.co.uk
✉ enquiries@sudburygolfclubltd .co.uk
☎ 0208 902 3713, Fax 3713,
Pro 7910
At Junction of Bridgewater Rd (A4005) and Whitton Ave East (A4090).
Undulating parkland course.
Pro Neil Jordan; Founded 1920
Designed by H Colt
18 holes, 6277 yards, S.S.S. 70
† Welcome WD with handicap certs; Mon open day (no handicap certs required); WE as a guest of member only.
⌐ WD £25.
🛒 Welcome; please contact for details.
🍽 Full catering service bar.
🛏 The Cumberland Harrow.

1B 148 Theydon Bois   ☎
Theydon Rd, Epping, Essex,
CM16 4EH
✉ theydonbois@btconnect.co.uk
☎ 01992 813054, Fax 815602,
Pro 812460, Sec 813054
1 mile S of Epping on B1721.
Woodland course; no par 5s.
Pro Richard Hall; Founded 1897
Designed by James Braid
18 holes, 5487 yards, S.S.S. 68

🏌 Practice area.
† Welcome with handicap certs.
⌐ WD £26; WE £26 after 2pm.
🛒 Welcome Mon, Tues, Fri; £35.
🍽 Full clubhouse facilities available.
🛏 The Bell, Theydon Bois.

1B 149 Thorndon Park
Ingrave, Brentwood, Essex,
CM13 3RH
🖥 www.thorndonparkgolfclub.com
✉ tpgc@btclick.com
☎ 01277 811666, Fax 810645,
Pro 810736, Sec 810345,
Rest/Bar 811666
Course is 2 miles SE of Brentwood on the A128.
Parkland course.
Pro Brian White; Founded 1920
Designed by H Colt
18 holes, 6492 yards, S.S.S. 71
† Welcome WD and Sun after 1.00pm; with member WE; handicap certs required.
⌐ WD £45.
🛒 Welcome Mon, Tues and Fri; terms on application.
🍽 Meals served WD.
🛏 Post House.

1B 150 Thorpe Hall
Thorpe Hall Ave, Thorpe Bay, Essex,
SS1 3AT
✉ sec@thorpehallgc.co.uk
☎ 01702 582205, Fax 584498,
Pro 588195
4 miles E of Southend on Sea, on seafront at Thorpe Bay.
Parkland/meadowland course.
Pro Bill McColl; Founded 1907
18 holes, 6319 yards, S.S.S. 71
† Welcome on WD by prior arrangement.
⌐ WD £40.
🛒 Fri only; maximum party of 40; catering by arrangement; terms available on application.

🍽 Full catering facilities available.
🛏 Rosylin Hotel.

1B 151 **Three Rivers Golf & Country Club**
Purleigh, Nr Chelmsford, Essex, CM3 6RR
🖥 www.clubhaus.com
☎ 01277 653616, Fax 01621 828060,
Pro 01621 828631, Sec 01621 828631,
Rest/Bar 01621 828631
From the M25 Junction 29 take the A127 and then the A132 to South Woodham Ferrers. Follow the signs for Cold Norton. Course is 4 miles.
Parkland/new heathland course.
Pro Phil Green; Founded 1973
Designed by Fred Hawtree
18 holes, 6500 yards, S.S.S. 71
† Welcome.
[WD £20; £15 as a guest; WE £25. £18 as a guest.
⌕ Welcome by prior arrangement; combination of 18, 27, 36 holes, video analysis, clubhouse and private rooms; squash and tennis; from £20.
🍽 Full facilities.
🛏 Three Rivers.

1B 152 **Toot Hill**
School Road, Toot Hill, Ongar, Essex, CM5 9PU
☎ 01277 365523, Fax 364509,
Pro 365747, Sec 365523,
Rest/Bar 366221
2 miles off A414 between N Weald and Ongar.
Parkland course.
Pro Mark Bishop; Founded 1991
Designed by Martin Gillett
18 holes, 6053 yards, S.S.S. 69
[5 indoor bays and grass area.
† Welcome, WE after 1.30pm by prior arrangement.
[WD £25; after 1.30pm WE £30.
⌕ Welcome Tues and Thurs; packages include lunch and/or dinner; from £34.
🍽 Full catering facilities.
🛏 Post House, Epping

1B 153 **Top Meadow**
Fen Lane, North Ockendon, Essex, RM14 3PR
🖥 www.topmeadow.co.uk
📧 info@topmeadow.co.uk
☎ 01708 859545
Off B186 in North Ockendon.
Parkland course.
Pro Roy Porter; Founded 1986
18 holes, 6227 yards, S.S.S. 72
[Practice range.

† Welcome WD; only with member at WE.
[WD £12 inc breakfast.
⌕ Welcome WD by advance booking; terms on application.
🍽 Bar and restaurant.
🛏 On site hotel.

1B 154 **Trent Park**
Bramley Road, Southgate, London, N14 4UW
📧 trentpark@americangolf.uk.com
☎ 020 8367 4653, Fax 8366 4581,
Pro 8367 4653
200 yards from Oakwood underground station between Barnet and Enfield on A110.
Parkland course.
Pro Ray Stocker; Founded 1973
18 holes, 6200 yards, S.S.S. 69
[Practice range; video teaching bay and range heaters.
† Public course (booking available).
[WD £14; WE £17.50. Different rates for members.
⌕ Welcome; restaurant and bar facilities; driving range; buggies; video analysis; terms on application.
🍽 Full facilities available.

1B 155 **Tudor Park Sports**
Clifford Rd, New Barnet, Herts, EN5 9ND
☎ 020 8449 0282
Off Potters road.
Public parkland course.
9 holes, 3772 yards, S.S.S. 58
[Driving range and practice area.
† Welcome.
[WE & WD £4 (9) £7 (18).
⌕ Apply for details.
🍽 Clubhouse for members only.

1B 156 **Upminster**
114 Half Lane, Upminster, Essex, RM14 1 AU
🖥 www.upminstergolfclub.com
📧 secretary@upminstergolfclub.com
☎ 01708 222788, Fax 222484,
Pro 220000, Sec 222788,
Rest/Bar 220249
On A127 towards Romford from M25 Jct 29.
Parkland course.
Pro Steve Cipa; Founded 1927
Designed by HA Colt
18 holes, 6013 yards, S.S.S. 69
† Welcome WD prior arrangement.
[WD £25.
⌕ Welcome Wed- Fri by prior arrangement some small societies possible Mon and Tues.

🍽 Full clubhouse facilities.
🛏 Post House Brentwood.

1B 157 **Verulam**
London Rd, St Albans, Herts, AL1 1JG
🖥 www.verulamgolf.co.uk
📧 genman@verulamgolf.co.uk
☎ 01727 853327, Fax 812201,
Pro 861401, Sec 853327,
Rest/Bar 839016
Turn off London Road A1081 at railway bridge.
Parkland course.
Pro Nick Burch; Founded 1905
Designed by James Braid/upgrade by D Steel
18 holes, 6448 yards, S.S.S. 71
† Welcome WD; WE with member.
[WD £25 (Mon £20).
⌕ Tues and Thurs only by arrangement with Sec; Full day golf and catering packages available; from £62.
🍽 Full facilities.
🛏 Apple Hotel; Sopwell House.

1B 158 **Wanstead**　　　　　🅒
Overton Drive, Wanstead, London, E11 2LW
🖥 www.wanstead.golf.org.uk
📧 wgclub@aol.com
☎ 020 8989 3938, Fax 8532 9138,
Pro 8989 9876, Sec 8989 3938,
Rest/Bar 8530 1315/8989 0604
Close to Wanstead Tube station.
Parkland/heathland course.
Pro David Hawkins; Founded 1893
Designed by James Braid
18 holes, 6015 yards, S.S.S. 69
† Welcome Mon, Tues and Fri.
[WD £30.
⌕ Welcome Mon, Tues and Fri; facilities include 36 holes of golf, lunch and dinner; £50.
🍽 Full clubhouse facilities.

1B 159 **Warley Park**　　　　🅒
Magpie Lane, Little Warley, Brentwood, Essex, CM13 3DX
🖥 www.warleyparkgc.co.uk
📧 enquiries@warleyparkgc.co.uk
☎ 01277 224891, Fax 200679,
Pro 200441, Rest/Bar 231352
Off B186.
Parkland course.
Pro Kevin Smith; Founded 1975
Designed by R Plumbridge
27 holes, 6232 yards, S.S.S. 69
† Welcome WD only.
[WD £30.
⌕ Welcome WD; packages available; terms available on application.

🍴 Restaurant bar and spike bar.
🛏 Holiday Inn; New World Inn; Marygreen Manor.

1B 160 **Warren**
Woodham Walter, Maldon, Essex, CM9 6RW
🖳 www.warrengolfclub.co.uk
📧 warrengolfclub@hotmail.com
☎ 01245 223258, Fax 223989, Pro 224662
A414 6 miles E of Chelmsford towards Maldon.
Undulating parkland course.
Pro David Brooks; Founded 1934
18 holes, 6263 yards, S.S.S. 70
🏌 Practice ground.
🏌 Welcome WD; booking essential.
🏌 WD £30.
⛳ Mon, Tues, Thurs, Fri; packages available; terms available on application.
🍴 Full facilities 7 days.
🛏 Pontlands Park; Blue Boar.

1B 161 **Welwyn Garden City**
Mannicotts, High Oaks Rd, Welwyn Garden City, Herts, AL8 7BP
📧 dharvey@btconnect.com
☎ 01707 325243, Fax 393213, Pro 325525, Sec 325243 x202
1 mile N of Hatfield from A1M Junction 4.
Parkland course.
Pro Richard May; Founded 1922
Designed by Hawtree & Son
18 holes, 6074 yards, S.S.S. 69
🏌 Practice area.
🏌 Welcome by arrangement.
🏌 WD £25; WE £35.
⛳ Welcome Wed and Thurs; 36 holes, coffee, lunch and dinner; £60.
🍴 Full clubhouse bar and catering.

1B 162 **West Essex** ☎
Bury Rd, Sewardstonebury, Chingford, Essex, E4 7QL
🖳 www.westessexgolfclub.co.uk
📧 sec@westessexgolfclub.co.uk
☎ 020 8529 7558, Fax 8524 7870, Pro 8529 4367, Sec 8529 7558, Rest/Bar 8529 1029/8529 0517
1.5 miles N of Chingford station.
Parkland course.
Pro Robert Joyce; Founded 1900
Designed by James Braid
18 holes, 6289 yards, S.S.S. 70
🏌 Welcome WD except Tues am.
🏌 WD £35.
⛳ Welcome Mon, Wed and Fri; package includes coffee, lunch, dinner and 36 holes of golf plus driving range; £58.

🍴 Bar and catering facilities.
🛏 Swallow Hotel Waltham Abbey.

1B 163 **West Herts**
Cassiobury Park, Watford, Herts, WD3 3GG
☎ 01923 236484, Fax 222300, Pro 220352, Rest/Bar 224264
Off A412 between Watford and Rickmansworth.
Parkland course.
Pro Charles Gough; Founded 1890
Designed Morris & MacKenzie
18 holes, 6528 yards, S.S.S. 71
🏌 2.
🏌 Welcome.
🏌 WD £38; WE £48.
⛳ Welcome Wed, Fri; Full facilities; £72.
🍴 Full facilities.

1B 164 **West Middlesex**
Greenford Rd, Southall, Middx, UB1 3EE
🖳 www.westmiddxgolfclub.co.uk
📧 westmid.gc@virgin.net
☎ 020 8574 3450, Fax 8574 2383, Pro 8574 1800, Rest/Bar 8843 0224
At Junction of Greenford and Uxbridge road.
Parkland course.
Pro T Talbot; Founded 1891
Designed by James Braid
18 holes, 6119 yards, S.S.S. 69
🏌 Practice area.
🏌 Welcome.
🏌 WD £24 (Mon £13 Wed £15).
⛳ Welcome; golf and catering.
🍴 Full catering and bar.
🛏 Bridge Hotel. Greenford.

1B 165 **Whaddon Golf Centre**
Church Street, Whaddon, Royston, Herts, SG8 5RX
☎ 01223 207325, Fax 207325, Pro 207325, Sec 207325, Rest/Bar 207325
4 miles N of Royston off A1198
Parkland course.
Pro G Huggett; Founded 1990
Designed by Richard Green
9 holes, 905 yards, S.S.S. par 3
🏌 14.
🏌 Public pay and play.
🏌 WD £3.50; WE £4.
⛳ Welcome; terms on application.
🍴 Bar snacks.

1B 166 **Whipsnade Park**
Studham Lane, Dagnall, Herts, HP4 1RH
🖳 www.whipsnadeparkgolf.co.uk
📧 whipsnadeparkgolf@btopenworld .com

☎ 0144 2842330, Fax 842090, Pro 842310
Between Studham and Dagnall.
Parkland course.
Pro Darren Turner; Founded 1974
18 holes, 6704 yards, S.S.S. 72
🏌 Grass driving range.
🏌 Welcome WD; WE with member.
🏌 WD £27.
⛳ Welcome Tues, Wed, Thurs, Fri; coffee, 2 rounds of golf with lunch and 4-course dinner; £59.
🍴 Full catering facilities.
🛏 Moat House, Markyate.

1B 167 **Whitehill** ☎
Dane End, Ware, Herts, SG12 0JS
📧 whitehillgolfcentre@btinternet.com
☎ 01920 438702, Fax 438891, Pro 438326, Sec 438495
4 miles N of Ware just off A10.
Parkland course.
Pro M Belsham; Founded 1990
Designed by Golf Landscapes
18 holes, 6681 yards, S.S.S. 72
🏌 25 bay floodlit driving range.
🏌 Welcome with handicap certs.
🏌 WD £21; WE £25.50.
⛳ Welcome WD; maximum 16 at WE; golf and catering packages available; £20-40.
🍴 Full facilities.
🛏 County Ware; Vintage Corner, Puckeridge.

1B 168 **Whitewebbs**
Whitewebbs Lane, Enfield, EN2 9HH
☎ 020 8363 4454, Fax 8366 2257, Pro 8363 4454, Sec 8363 2951, Rest/Bar 8363 2951
1.5 miles from M25 Junction 25.
Public parkland course.
Pro Gary Sherriff; Founded 1932
18 holes, 5507 yards, S.S.S. 68
🏌 Welcome; book 6 days in advance.
🏌 WD £12.50; WE £15.50.
⛳ Welcome by arrangement; café on site; nature trails and horse riding; packages available on application.
🍴 Public café on site.
🛏 Royal Chase.

1B 169 **Woodford**
2 Sunset Ave, Woodford Green, Essex, IG8 0ST
📧 office@ woodfordgolfclub.fsnet.co.uk
☎ 020 8504 0553, Fax 8559 0504, Pro 8504 4254, Sec 8504 3330, Rest/Bar 8504 0553
11 miles northeast of London; 2 miles N of North Circular Road on A11.

Forest course.
Pro Richard Layton; Founded 1890
Designed by Tom Dunn
9 holes, 5867 yards, S.S.S. 68
♥ Welcome except Tues am; Sat or
Sun am; red clothing must be worn.
⌐ WD £15; WE £15 (£9 twilight).
⌐ Welcome by prior arrangement
with Sec; packages including meals
can be arranged; terms available on
application.
⦿ Dining facilities bar.
⌐ Packfords, Woodford Green.

1B 170 Woolston Manor   ☎
Woolston Manor, Abridge Road,
Chigwell, Essex, IG7 6BX
⌐ www.woolstonmanor.co.uk

⌐ golf@woolstonmanor.co.uk
☎ 020 8500 2549, Fax 8501 5452,
Pro 8559 8272
From M11 Junction 5 take the A113;
course is 1 mile on between Abridge
and Chigwell.
Parkland course.
Pro Paul Eady; Founded 1994
Designed by Neil Coles
18 holes, 6408 yards, S.S.S. 71
⌐ 18 floodlit.
♥ Welcome.
⌐ WD £25 after 10.30; WE £35 after
12.
⌐ WD welcome by prior
arrangement; terms on application.
⦿ Full catering and bar facilities.
⌐ Marriott Hotel, Waltham Abbey.

1B 171 Wyke Green
Syon Lane, Isleworth, Middx,
TW7
5PT
⌐ www.wykegreengolfclub.co.uk
⌐ office@wykegreen.golfagent
.co.uk
☎ 020 8560 8777, Fax 8569 8392,
Pro 8847 0585, Rest/Bar 8847 1956
0.5 miles N of A4 near Gillettes corner.
Flat parkland course.
Pro Neil Smith; Founded 1928
Designed by Hawtree and Taylor.
18 holes, 6189 yards, S.S.S. 70
♥ Welcome on WD only.
⌐ WD £28; WE £30.
⌐ Welcome Tues, Thurs; minimum
12 players.
⦿ Full catering facilities and bar.

THE SOUTH

2A

Hampshire, Sussex, Isle of Wight

Maybe it will one day return, but by 1961 the little Royal Isle of Wight Club was reduced to only a dozen members and had to be abandoned to picnickers and dog-walkers. Its demise left Royal Ashdown Forest, Royal Eastbourne and Royal Winchester as the region's surviving standard bearers.

Rye, however, stands above them all and until recently thought of itself as royalty, being incredibly hard to get onto unless you were related to a member or bore an uncanny resemblance to the Duke of York. The club used to boast a steward who was the rudest man in Sussex, but things have improved greatly even if a day at Rye is still far from just a golfing experience.

If three of you turn up to play you may be asked to play a Rye threesome, whereby each of you plays his own ball over six holes while the other two join forces playing alternate shots against the single. But whatever game you play, Rye is a course worth playing it on, perhaps the most varied and surprising of all the English links.

The course is a mix of classic and quirky seaside golf with a loop of holes around the turn that are a little more inland in character. It is the home of the President's Putter, an Oxbridge competition of past and present Blues, played early in the year preferably with a scattering of snow on the ground and a mild gale in the air.

Perhaps the eighteenth best sums up Rye's character. The tee shot is difficult enough to an elevated fairway. Then further along the hole the lesser golfers amongst us can stand trembling in fear of a pull hook, a shot that threatens to shatter the windows of the club house and the glasses of pink gin inside. The daunting finish only loses its peril when the visitor is informed (usually at the end of his round) that the windows are made from bullet-proof glass.

A more gentle resident of Sussex is Royal Ashdown Forest, a golf course with no bunkers. Bernard Darwin wrote, "Nature had been kind in supplying a variety of pits and streams to carry". It also left a fair bit of thick grass and heather behind. This is Winnie-the-Pooh country, although as "a bear of very little brain" it is hard to imagine Pooh breaking par around Ashdown Forest.

An absorbing course, Ashdown Forest is a severe rebuttal of those people who smear golf courses with vast sandy beaches, seemingly unaware that these no longer present a hazard to the half decent player. Liphook, in Hampshire, is another course that makes a point about golf architecture. Arguably the outstanding course in the county, Liphook was designed by AC Croome, a man who was schoolteacher, golfer, writer and many things besides.

The assumption that the best golfers make great course designers seems as sensible as the notion that master bricklayers make great architects. It is a point rather well made by Liphook and Croome.

Some of the other courses in this region that are well worth a visit are North Hants, the home of Justin Rose; Osborne, a nine hole parkland course on the Isle of Wight that runs through the grounds of Osborne House, Queens Victoria's favourite royal retreat; East Sussex National, a course slightly in the American style that offers a big welcome; West Sussex, a much shorter traditional course with several stunning par threes.

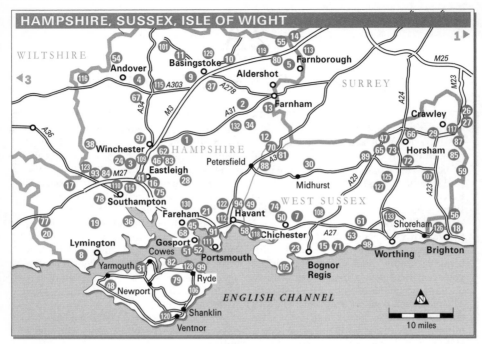

HAMPSHIRE, SUSSEX, ISLE OF WIGHT

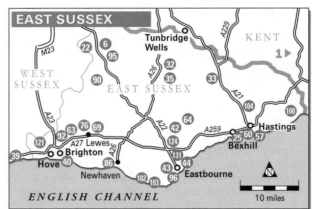

EAST SUSSEX

2A 1 **Alresford**

Cheriton Road, Tichborne Down,
Alresford, Hants, SO24 0PN
www.alresfordgolf.co.uk
secretary@alresford-
golf.demon.co.uk
01962 733746, Fax 736040,
Pro 733998, Rest/Bar 733067
One mile S of Alresford.
Downland/parkland course.
Pro Malcolm Scott; Founded 1890
Designed by Scott Webb Young
18 holes, 5622 yards, S.S.S. 68
Covered practice area.
Anytime Mon-Fri, after 12 pm WE.
WD £25, WE £40, full day £35.
Welcome by prior arrangement
with sec, terms on application.
Full facilities.
The Swan, Alresford.

2A 2 **Alton**

Old Odiham Road, Alton, Hants,
GU34 4BU
www.altongolfclub.org.uk
richardkeeling@pgai.psbusiness
.co.uk
01420 82042/86518, Pro 86518
On B3349 Alton to Odiham road, turn
off at Golden Pot.
Parkland course.

Pro Paul Brown; Founded 1908
Designed by James Braid
9 holes, 5744 yards, S.S.S. 68
Welcome, restrictions on Sun.
WD £18, WE £22.
Welcome by prior arrangement,
bar catering, PGA professional,
practice area; terms on application.
Full facilities.
Wheatsheef Inn, Alton House,
Grange Hotel.

2A 3 **Ampfield**

Winchester Road, Ampfield, Romsey,
Hants, SO51 9BQ
01794 368480, Pro 368750
A31 Winchester to Romsey Road
opposite Keats restaurant, next stop
White Horse Public House.
Parkland course.
Pro Richard Benfield; Founded 1965
Designed by Henry Cotton
18 holes, 2478 yards, S.S.S. 53

KEY							
1	Alresford	28	Corhampton	57	Hastings	85	Paxhill Park
2	Alton	29	Cottesmore	58	Hayling Golf Club	86	Peacehaven
3	Ampfield Par 3 G & CC	30	Cowdray Park	59	Haywards Heath GC	87	Pease Pottage GC
4	Andover	31	Cowes	60	Highwoods		& Driving Range
5	Army Golf Club	32	Crowborough Beacon	61	Hill Barn	88	Petersfield
6	Ashdown Forest Hotel	33	Dale Hill Hotel	62	Hockley	89	Petworth Golf Club
7	Avisford Park	34	Dean Farm (Kingsley)	63	Hollingbury Park	90	Piltdown
8	Barton-on-Sea	35	Dewlands Manor GC	64	Horam Park	91	Portsmouth
9	Basingstoke	36	Dibden	65	Horsham Golf Park	92	Pyecombe
10	Basingstoke Golf Centre	37	Dummer	66	Ifield G & Country Club	93	Romsey
11	Bishopswood	38	Dunwood Manor GC	67	Leckford & Longstock	94	Rowlands Castle
12	Blackmoor	39	The Dyke Golf Club	68	Lee-on-the-Solent	95	Royal Ashdown Forest
13	Blacknest	40	East Brighton	69	Lewes	96	Royal Eastbourne
14	Blackwater Valley	41	East Horton Golf Centre	70	Liphook	97	Royal Winchester
15	Bognor Regis	42	East Sussex	71	Littlehampton	98	Rustington Golf Centre
16	Botley Park Hotel	43	Eastbourne Downs	72	Mannings Heath	99	Ryde
	& Country Club	44	Eastbourne Golfing Park	73	Mannings Heath Hotel	100	Rye
17	Bramshaw	45	Fleetlands	74	Marriott Goodwood Park	101	Sandford Springs
18	Brighton & Hove	46	Fleming Park		Golf & Country Club	102	Seaford
19	Brokenhurst Manor	47	Foxbridge	75	Meon Valley Hotel	103	Seaford Head
20	Burley	48	Freshwater Bay		Golf & Country Club	104	Sedlescombe
21	Cams Hall Estates Golf	49	Furzeley	76	Mid-Sussex		(Aldershaw)
22	Chartham Park	50	Goodwood	77	Moors Valley Golf Centre	105	Selsey
23	Chichester Golf Centre	51	Gosport & Stokes Bay	78	New Forest	106	Shanklin & Sandown
24	Chilworth Golf Centre		Golf Club	79	Newport	107	Singing Hills Golf Course
25	Cooden Beach	52	Great Salterns GC	80	North Hants	108	Slinfold Park G & CC
26	Copthorne	53	Ham Manor Golf Club	81	Old Thorns	109	South Winchester
27	Copthorne Effingham	54	Hampshire	82	Osborne	110	Southampton
	Park	55	Hartley Wintney GC	83	Otterbourne GC	111	Southsea
		56	Hassocks Golf Club	84	Paultons Golf Centre	112	Southwick Park

113	Southwood		
114	Stoneham		
115	Test Valley		
116	Tidworth Garrison		
117	Tilgate Forest Golf		
	Centre		
118	Tournerbury		
119	Tylney Park		
120	Ventnor		
121	Waterhall		
122	Waterlooville		
123	Wellow		
124	Wellshurst Golf &		
	Country Club		
125	West Chiltington		
126	West Hove		
127	West Sussex		
128	Westridge		
129	Weybrook Park		
130	Wickham Park		
131	Willingdon		
132	Worldham Park		
133	Worthing		

---

† Welcome but advisable to telephone first.
Ⅰ WD £9 WE £15.50.
♨ Welcome by arrangement; function room; terms on application.
🍽 Bar and catering by arrangement.
🛏 Potters Heron, Ampfield.

2A 4 **Andover**

51 Winchester Road, Andover, Hants, SP10 2EF
🔗 www.andovergolfclub.co.uk
📧 play@andovergolfclub.co.uk
☎ 01264 358040, Fax 358040,
Pro 324151, Rest/Bar 323980
Turn off A303 at Wherwell/Stockbridge turning; take Andover direction, golf course 0.5 mile on right.
Downland course.
Pro Derrick Lawrence; Founded 1907
Designed by JH Taylor
9 holes holes, 6096 yards, S.S.S. 69
† Welcome.
Ⅰ Terms on application.
♨ Welcome.
🍽 Full facilities .
🛏 White Hart Hotel, Andover.

2A 5 **Army Golf Club**

Laffan's Road, Aldershot, Hants, GU11 2HF
🔗 www.whichgolfclub.com/army
📧 agc@ic24.net
☎ 01252 337272, Fax 337562,
Pro 336722, Rest/Bar 336776

Access from Eelmoor Bridge off A323 Aldershot – Fleet Rd.
Heathland course.
Pro Graham Cowley; Founded 1883
18 holes, 6550 yards, S.S.S. 71
† Welcome on WD by prior arrangement; WE members and guests only.
Ⅰ WD £26; WE Visitors with a member only.
♨ Welcome by prior arrangement.
🍽 Facilities available.
🛏 Trust House Forte, Farnborough; Potters International, Farnborough.

2A 6 **Ashdown Forest Hotel**

Chapel Lane, Forest Row, E Sussex, RH18 5BB
☎ 01342 824866, Fax 824869
3 miles S of East Grinstead on A22 in village of Forest Row, East on B2110, Chapel Lane 4th on the right.
Heathland/Woodland course.
Pro Martyn Landsborough; Founded 1985
Designed by Horace Hutchinson (1930s) Henry Luff (1965)
18 holes, 5606 yards, S.S.S. 67
† Welcome but advisable to phone first, particularly at WE.
Ⅰ WD £16; WE £21.
♨ Welcome by prior arrangement; full facilities; terms on application.
🍽 Full restaurant service; bar snacks; banqueting facilities for up to 100.
🛏 Ashdown Forest.

2A 7 **Avisford Park Hilton**

Yapton Lane, Walberton, Arundel, W Sussex, BN18 0LS
☎ 01243 554611, Fax 552485
On A27 4 miles W of Arundel, 6 miles E of Chichester.
Parkland course.
Founded 1985/1997
18 holes, 5390 yards, S.S.S. 67
Ⅰ Practice area.
† Welcome, pay as you play.
Ⅰ WD £15 WE £18.
♨ Welcome by prior arrangement.
🍽 Bar and catering.
🛏 Hilton, Aviston Park.

2A 8 **Barton-on-Sea**

Milford Road, New Milton, Hants, BH25 5PP
🔗 www.barton-on-sea-golf.co.uk
☎ 01425 615308, Fax 621457,
Pro 611210, Sec 615308,
Rest/Bar 610189
From New Milton take B3058 towards Milford on Sea; club is signposted about 0.75 miles on the right.
Cliff Top Links course.
Pro Peter Rodgers; Founded 1897
Designed by J Hamilton Stutt
27 holes, 6296 yards, S.S.S. 70
† Welcome with handicap certificates by prior arrangement.
Ⅰ WD £36; WE £41.
♨ Welcome by arrangement.
🍽 Snacks and teas available, other catering by arrangement.
🛏 Chewton Glen.

2A 9 **Basingstoke**
Kempshott Park, Kempshott,
Basingstoke, Hants, RG23 7LL
☎ 01256 465990, Fax 331793, Pro
351332
3 miles West of Basingstoke on A30
M3 Junction 7.
Parkland course.
Pro Guy Shoesmith; Founded 1928
Designed by James Braid
18 holes, 6334 yards, S.S.S. 70
⏴ Practice area for members only.
† Welcome WD, WE with a member.
⏴ Prices on application.
⏴ Welcome Wed and Thur packages
available.
⏴ Full clubhouse facilities available.
⏴ Wheatsheaf.

2A 10 **Basingstoke Golf Centre**
Worting Road, West Ham,
Basingstoke, Hants, RG22 6PG
☎ 01256 350054, Pro 350054
M3 Junction 7, 0.5 miles from
Basingstoke town centre.
Public parkland course.
Pro Matthew Skinner; Founded 1985
9 holes, 908 yards
⏴ Practice range 24 bays.
† Everyone welcome.
⏴ WD £2.70 WE £3.20.
⏴ No societies. Course is open to
public only.
⏴ Confectionery Machine.
⏴ Travel Inn in leisure park next door.

2A 11 **Bishopswood**
Bishopswood Lane, Tadley, Hants,
RG26 4AT
⏴ www.bishopswoodgolfcourse.co.uk
⏴ david@
bishopswoodgolfcourse.co.uk
☎ 0118 9815213, Fax 9408606,
Rest/Bar 9408603
6 miles North of Basingstoke.
Proprietary parkland course.
Pro Stephen Ward; Founded 1976
Designed by Blake and Phillips
9 holes, 6474 yards, S.S.S. 71
⏴ Practice range 12 bays, floodlit.
† Welcome WD.
⏴ WD £12, for 9; WD £18 for 18.
Reduced rates for OAPs and juniors.
⏴ Welcome WD by arrangement, full
facilities.
⏴ Bar snacks and restaurant.
⏴ Romans.

2A 12 **Blackmoor**
Firgrove Road, Whitehill, Bordon,
Hants, GU35 9EH
⏴ www.blackmoorgolf.co.uk

⏴ admin@blackmoorgolf.co.uk
☎ 01420 472775, Fax 487666, Pro
472345
Located on A325 between Petersfield
and Farnham, at Whitehill crossroads
turn left into Firgrove Rd, Blackmoor is
1000 yards on right.
Parkland/heathland course.
Pro Steve Clay; Founded 1913
Designed by HS Colt
18 holes, 6164 yards, S.S.S. 69
⏴ Practice ground.
† Welcome WD, members' guests
only at WE.
⏴ WD £35 round, £47 day.
⏴ Welcome Mon/Wed/Thurs and Fri
by arrangement, packages available.
⏴ Full facilities.

2A 13 **Blacknest Golf and
Country Cub**
Binstead Road, Binstead, Alton, Hants,
GU34 4QL
☎ 01420 22888, Fax 22001,
Pro 22888, Rest/Bar 22888
Take A31 to Bentley, then the Bordon
road, course is 2 miles on right.
Parkland/heathland course.
Pro Tony Cook; Founded 1992
Designed by P Nicholson
18 holes, 6038 yards, S.S.S. 69
⏴ Practice range, 13 bays, gym.
† Welcome; no jeans.
⏴ WD £20; WE £25.
⏴ Welcome by arrangement; full
facilities.
⏴ Bar and restaurant.
⏴ Alton House; The Bush; The
Farnham Park.

2A 14 **Blackwater Valley**
Chandlers Lane, Yateley, Hants,
GU46 7SZ
☎ 01252 874 725, Fax 874725,
Pro 874725, Sec 874725,
Rest/Bar 874725
5 miles from Camberley on the
Reading road.
Parkland course with Lake.
Pro James Rodger; Founded 1994
Designed by Harry Allenby
9 holes, 2372 yards, S.S.S. 66
⏴ Practice range 30 bays.
† Welcome.
⏴ WD £8, WE £9.
⏴ Welcome by arrangement; full
facilities.
⏴ Full facilities.

2A 15 **Bognor Regis GC** ☎
Downview Road, Felpham, Bognor
Regis, W Sussex, PO22 8JD

⏴ www.bognorgolfclub.co.uk
⏴ sec@bognorgolfclub.co.uk
☎ 01243 821929, Fax 860719,
Pro 865209, Rest/Bar 865867
A259 Bognor Littlehampton road at
Felpham traffic lights turn left into
Downview Road.
Parkland course.
Pro Stephen Bassil; Founded 1892
Designed by James Braid
18 holes, 6238 yards, S.S.S. 70
⏴ Practice ground; indoor teaching
room with golftek and sports coach
system.
† Welcome with handicap certs WD,
with member at WE during summer.
Terms on application.
⏴ WD £25, WE £30. Call for
information.
⏴ Welcome by arrangement, tee-off
times allocated, full facilities available
£48 package.
⏴ Restaurants and bar.
⏴ The Beachcroft, Felpham.

2A 16 **Botley Park Hotel and CC**
Winchester Road, Botley,
Southampton, Hants, SO32 2UA
⏴ www.botleyparkhotel.co.uk
⏴ botleypark@macdonald-hotels
.co.uk
☎ 01489 780888, Fax 789242,
Pro 789771
NW of Botley on B3354 Winchester
Rd, within easy reach of M27 Junction
7 or M3/A33.
Parkland course.
Pro Kevin Capelhorn; Founded 1990
Designed by Charles Potterton
18 holes, 6341 yards, S.S.S. 70
⏴ Practice range 13 bays.
† Welcome by arrangement,
handicap certs or letter of introduction
required.
⏴ WD £30, WE £30.
⏴ Welcome Mon, Weds and Thurs by
arrangement, full facilities.
⏴ Full facilities, banqueting service.
⏴ Hotel in complex.

2A 17 **Bramshaw**
Brook, Lyndhurst, Hants, SO43 7HE
⏴ www.bramshaw.co.uk
⏴ golf@bramshaw.co.uk
☎ 020380 813433, Fax 813460,
Pro 813434, Rest/Bar 814628
10 miles from Southampton 1 mile
from Junction 1 M27.
Open New Forest and parkland courses.
Pro Clive Bonner; Founded 1880
Forest: 18 holes, 6517 yards, S.S.S.
71; Manor: 18 holes, 5774 yards,
S.S.S. 68

Royal Ashdown Forest

Not one for the faint-hearted: Royal Ashdown Forest promises much but gives little away. It seeks to intimidate, with its tangled mass of heather, gorse and assorted mucky stuff creeping towards you as you stand on the tees.

But in truth, the carries to the fairways are not that difficult; so a little confidence and an easy swing will take you clear. The devil is in the detail. The fairways are reasonably generous, but accuracy is essential: off them, among the heather, it is a rescue job, and usually an expensive one at that. For the high-handicapper, too, there is a real need to play to one's limitations; for the greens are usually guarded by the same tangled mass which demands a high price for arrogance. Lay up and pitch and putt.

Carved out of the Ashdown Forest in 1889 on common land leased from the Lord of the Manor, Earl De La Warr, and granted its royal charter in 1895, the unique feature is that there are no bunkers; excavations and major alterations being not permitted. But the valleys, streams, gulleys and dense vegetation make up for that. It all contributes to a stunningly beautiful setting; elevated tees giving a magnificent vista of the 6,439-yard course. Not one of the longest in the land, but as lifelong member and English Amateur champion Frank Pennick once remarked: "the yardage bears no resemblence to the length the course plays".

It was here that Bobby Locke, for the first time in recorded golf history in 1956 returned a card of 18 fours – one over at each of the "short" holes and birdies on the fives. I qualify "short" for the par-three 11th is as famous as the lack of bunkers, sitting uncomfortably at 249 yards. But even then it is mind over matter, for the carry over the horrible stuff is only 170 or so.

As for the 128-yard sixth; just try to ignore the fact that it is almost surrounded by a deep stream and gully and is known as the Island; and at the 143-yard ninth; where there is nothing but misery between tee and green.

Even the understated 312-yard 14th offers a challenge: firing blind into a well-guarded green shaped as upturned saucer, just to make things interesting.

Adding to the scenery – and just the drive to the course through the back roads in the forest is an experience – is a gentle ambience of rural England. Being common land, the common people are permitted to "take air and recreation"; walking their dogs and children; but all, at least when I was there, impeccably behaved. And I saw none strolling along with a five-iron as a walking stick. Admire, or envy the houses that nestle amid copses scattered through out the course. What price a back garden of this magnificence?

But a word or warning: as part of a conservation scheme to preserve and English heather, the club are trimming back trees, particularly silver birch, which are apparently the villains. But the end result will be more rampant, more vicious heather, from which there will be absolutely no escape. — **Mark Salter**

† Welcome WD; limited at WE.
£ Terms on application.
⌒ Welcome Mon–Fri; packages available.
🍴 Catering and bar facilities.
🛏 Bell Inn, Brook.

2A 18 Brighton and Hove ☎
Dyke Road, Brighton, E Sussex, BN1 8YJ
🖳 www.bhgolf.net
🖥 phil@bhgc68.fsnet.co.uk
☎ 01273 556482, Fax 554247, Pro 556686, Rest/Bar 507861
A23/A27 NW Brighton.
Downland course.
Pro P Bonsall; Founded 1887
Designed by James Braid
9 holes, 5710 yards, S.S.S. 68
£ Practice ground/chipping green.
† Welcome with some restrictions.
£ WD £20; WE £25.
⌒ Welcome by arrangement restaurant facilities.
🍴 Full facilities available.

2A 19 Brokenhurst Manor
Sway Road, Brockenhurst, Hants, SO42 7SG
🖳 www.brokenhurst-manor.org.uk
🖥 secretary@brokenhurst-manor.org.uk
☎ 01590 623332, Fax 624140, Pro 623092, Rest/Bar 622383
A337 to Brockenhurst then B3055 S from village centre, club 1 mile on right.
Undulating forest/parkland course.
Pro Bruce Parker; Founded 1919
Designed by HS Colt, alterations by J Hamilton
18 holes, 6222 yards, S.S.S. 70
† Welcome on Thur by prior arrangement, must have handicap certificates.
£ WD £48; WE £58.
⌒ Welcome on Thursday by prior arrangement, also small parties welcome weekends by prior arrangement.
🍴 Full facilities.

2A 20 Burley
Cott Lane, Burley, Ringwood, Hants, BH24 4BB
🖳 www.burleygolfclub.co.uk
🖥 secretary@burleygolfclub.co.uk
☎ 01425 402431, Fax 404168, Rest/Bar 403737
From A31 through Burley towards New Milton/Brockenhurst turn immediately after cricket pitch.

Open Heathland course.
Founded 1905
9 holes, 6149 yards, S.S.S. 69
† Welcome with handicap certs preferred.
£ WD £16;WE £20.
⌒ Groups up to 14 people welcome but phone in advance.
🍴 Bar and limited food available.
🛏 Burley Manor, Moorhill, White Buck.

2A 21 Cams Hall Estates Golf
Cams Hall, Fareham, Hants, PO16 8UP
🖥 camshall@americangolf.uk.com
☎ 01329 827222, Fax 827111, Pro 827732
Close to M27, Junction 11.
18-hole links course, 9-hole parkland course.
Pro Jason Neve; Founded 1993
Designed by Peter Allis & Clive Clark
18 holes, 6244 yards, S.S.S. 71;
9 holes, 3197 yards, S.S.S. 36
£ Practice range; £2 bucket of balls.
† Welcome.
£ WD £20; WE £27.50.
⌒ Welcome, subject to availability; full facilities; £21-£47 for range of packages.
🍴 Full facilities available.
🛏 Marriott Hotel, Cosham; Holiday Inn, Fareham; Solent Hotel, Whiteley.

2A 22 Chartham Park
Felcourt Road, Felcourt, East Grinstead, W Sussex, RH19 2JT
🖳 www.clubhaus.com
🖥 b.smith@clubhaus.com
☎ 01342 870340, Fax 870719, Pro 870008, Sec 870340, Rest/Bar 870340
1 mile out of E Grinstead town centre on the Lingfield road.
Mature parkland course.
Pro David Hobbs; Founded 1992
Designed by N Coles
18 holes, 6680 yards, S.S.S. 72
£ Driving range.
† Welcome but not before 2 pm at WE.
£ WD £35; WE £40.
⌒ Welcome WD; full facilities.
🍴 Full facilities.
🛏 Felbridge.

2A 23 Chichester Golf Centre
Hunston Village, Chichester, W Sussex, PO20 1AX
🖳 www.chichestergolf.com
🖥 enquiries@chichestergolf.com
☎ 01243 533833, Fax 539922, Pro 528999, Sec 536666, Rest/Bar 530777

3 miles S of Chichester (A27) on B2145 to Selsey, on left after Hunston.
Public Florida-style course with membership.
Pro Emma Fields; Founded 1990
Designed by Philip Sanders
Cathedral: 18 holes; Tower: 18 holes;
Cathedral: 6442; Tower: 6109 yards, S.S.S. Cathedral 71;Tower 71
£ Practice range, 27 bays; floodlit; academy hole; par 3 course.
† Welcome; tee reservations required; handicap certs required for Cathedral.
£ Cathedral WD £22, WE £30; Tower WD £16, WE £18.50.
⌒ Welcome by prior arrangement; society clubroom available; terms on application.
🍴 Full catering/refreshments.
🛏 Millstream (Bosham); Hunston Mill B&B (Hunston); Posthouse (Hayling Island).

2A 24 Chilworth Golf Centre
Main Road, Chilworth, Southampton, Hants, SO16 7JP
☎ 023 8074 0544, Fax 8073 3166
On A27 between Romsey and Southampton.
Parkland course.
Pro D Newing; Founded 1989
18 holes, 5837 yards, S.S.S. 69
£ 35 bays.
† Welcome.
£ WD £12; WE £15.
⌒ Welcome by prior arrangement; terms on application.
🍴 Catering facilities available.
🛏 Trusthouse Forte.

2A 25 Cooden Beach ☎
Cooden Sea Road, Cooden, Nr Bexhill On Sea, E Sussex, TN39 4TR
🖥 manager@coodenBgolfclub.force9.co.uk
☎ 01424 842040, Fax 842040, Pro 843938, Sec 842040, Rest/Bar 843936
From the A259 Eastbourne-Hastings road; follow Cooden Beach sign at Little Common roundabout; course is 1 mile further on.
Wetland course.
Pro Jeffrey Sim; Founded 1912
Designed by Herbert Fowler
18 holes, 6500 yards, S.S.S. 71
£ 4.
† Welcome with handicap certs, telephone first.
£ WD £29; WE £35.
⌒ Welcome by arrangement; full facilities; £49 package.

⬤ Full facilities available.
⬤ Jarvis Cooden Resort; Brickwall Hotel, Lansdowne Hotel.

2A 26 Copthorne

Copthorne Golf Club, Borers Arms Road, Copthorne, Crawley, W Sussex, RH10 3LL
⬤ www.copthornegolfclub.co.uk
⬤ info@copthornegolfclub.co.uk
☎ 01342 712033, Fax 717682, Pro 712405, Sec 712033, Rest/Bar 712508
M23 Junction 10; follow A264 to East Grinstead; course 3 miles on left.
Heathland course.
Pro Joe Burrell; Founded 1892
Designed by James Braid
18 holes, 6505 yards, S.S.S. 71
⬤ Welcome with handicap certs. WE only after 1pm.
⬤ WD £32; WE £34.
⬤ Mon-Fri by arrangement with Sec; full facilities available; £45-£60 packages.
⬤ Full facilities available.
⬤ Copthorne Effingham Park.

2A 27 Copthorne Effingham Park

West Park Road, Copthorne, Crawley, W Sussex, RH10 3EU
☎ 01342 716528, Fax 716039, Sec 716528, Rest/Bar 714994
From M23 Junction 10 on to A264.
Parkland course.
Pro Mark Root; Founded 1980
Designed by Francisco Escario
9 holes, 3644 yards, S.S.S. 57
⬤ Welcome with prior booking, bookings are 2 weeks in advance.
⬤ WD £9; WE £10.
⬤ Welcome by prior arrangement; terms on application.
⬤ Two restaurants and bar facilities available.
⬤ Copthorne Effingham Park; Copthorne Gatwick.

2A 28 Corhampton

Sheeps Pond Lane, Droxford, Southampton, Hants, SO32 3LP
⬤ www.corhamptongc.co.uk
☎ 01489 877279, Fax 877680, Pro 877638, Rest/Bar 878749
Right off A32 at Corhampton on B3135 for 1 mile.
Downland course.
Pro Ian Roper; Founded 1891
18 holes, 6444 yards, S.S.S. 71
⬤ Practice area.
⬤ Welcome WD; with member at WE.

⬤ WD £30.
⬤ Welcome by arrangement Mon & Thurs; full facilities; terms on application.
⬤ Lunch, teas and dinners available.
⬤ The Uplands Hotel; Little Uplands.

2A 29 Cottesmore

Buchan Hill, Pease Pottage, Crawley, W Sussex, RH11 9AT
⬤ cottesmore@americangolf.com
☎ 01293 528256, Fax 522819, Pro 535399
Take M23 Junction 11 and follow signs for Pease Pottage; course 1.5 miles on right.
Undulating meadowland and grassland courses.
Pro Callum Callam; Founded 1975
Designed by MD Rogerson
Griffin: 18 holes; Phoenix: 18 holes, Griffin: 6248; Phoenix: 5514 yards, S.S.S. Griffin: 69; Phoenix: 67
⬤ Practice area, 2 putting greens.
⬤ Welcome WD, WE and BH.
⬤ Griffin WD £22.50 Fri £26, WE £32.50; Phoenix WD £12, WE £16.
⬤ Welcome; packages to suit all needs; health club and tennis facilities; conference and function facilities.
⬤ Full restaurant, coffee shop and bar, including spike bar, facilities.
⬤ Country club has 21 bedrooms on site.

2A 30 Cowdray Park �]

Midhurst, W Sussex, GU29 0BB
⬤ www.cowdraygolf.co.uk
⬤ cowdray-golf@lineone.net
☎ 01730 813599, Fax 815900, Pro 813599, Sec 813599
About 1 mile E of Midhurst on A272.
Parkland course.
Pro Richard Gough; Founded 1904
Designed by Herbert Fowler.
18 holes, 6212 yards, S.S.S. 70
⬤ Driving range for members and guests only.
⬤ Welcome but handicap certs essential.
⬤ WD £40.
⬤ Welcome by arrangement; full facilities; terms on application.
⬤ Bar snacks daily, evening meals by arrangement.
⬤ Cowdray Park Lodge on site.

2A 31 Cowes

Crossfield Avenue, Cowes, Isle of Wight, PO31 8HN
☎ 01983 280135, Pro 280135, Sec 292303, Rest/Bar 280135

Next to Cowes High School.
Parkland course.
Founded 1909
9 holes, 5923 yards, S.S.S. 68
⬤ Welcome.
⬤ WD £15; WE £18.
⬤ Welcome; packages available; from £12.
⬤ Full clubhouse facilities.
⬤ New Holmwood; Fountain.

2A 32 Crowborough Beacon GC �]

Beacon Road, Crowborough, E Sussex, TN6 1UJ
⬤ www.crowboroughbeacongolfclub. co.uk
⬤ cbgc@eastsx.fsnet.co.uk
☎ 01892 661511, Fax 667339, Pro 653877, Rest/Bar 654016
8 miles S of Tunbridge Wells on A26.
Heathland course.
Pro Dennis Newnham; Founded 1895
18 holes, 6256 yards, S.S.S. 70
⬤ Welcome WD; handicap certs or letter of introduction required.
⬤ WD £32; WE £40.
⬤ Welcome WD by arrangement; not Thurs; terms on application.
⬤ For up to 60; breakfast available by prior arrangement.

2A 33 Dale Hill Hotel ☡

Dale Hill, Ticehurst, Wadhurst, E Sussex, TN5 7DQ
⬤ www.dalehill.co.uk
⬤ golf@dalehill.co.uk
info@dalehill.co.uk
☎ 01580 200112, Fax 201429, Pro 201090, Sec 201800,
On A21 from Tonbridge Wells.
Parkland course with lake features. Ian Woosnam course.
Pro Mark Wood; Founded 1973
Designed by Ian Woosnam.
Old: 18; Woosnam: 18 holes, Old: 5856; Woosnam: 6512 yards, S.S.S. Old: 68; Woosnam: 71
⬤ 4.
⬤ Welcome by arrangement.
⬤ Old: WD £25, WE restricted; Woosnam: WD £55, WE £65 including compulsory buggy.
⬤ Welcome by prior arrangement; restaurant, golf clinics, pool and leisure facilities; terms on application.
⬤ Restaurant and full facilities.
⬤ Dale Hill (4 star).

2A 34 Dean Farm (Kingsley)

Main Road, Kingsley, Bordon, Hants, GU35 9NG

Royal Eastbourne

Royal Eastbourne, as you stroll to the first tee of the Devonshire course, presents itself as a compliant and willing partner: The vista is magnificent, cut to edge of the South Downs, winding its way around the nine-hole Hartington course and Eastbourne College's driving range; the fairways mostly separated by thin slices of troublesome vegetation. The open-plan, bowl-like arrangement shows a hive of activity; little figures meandering down the fairways, crossing and turning like a slow-motion ballet.

The 422-yard first stretches away invitingly, a slight left-to-right slope to Paradise Drive; the second perhaps a little more testing; only 266 yards from the back markers, but with a stiff climb; a slightly more threatening drift from left to right. Once there, it provides a great view of Old Eastbourne, the sea and the cliffs to the south.

Then it hits you and reveals its true, almost malicious nature: The club members, with some wry pride, claim it as "the worst hole in Sussex". The third, of a yardage of just 333 – 666 would be more appropriate – is approached blind over a quarry. Nasty trick. But it slides down the sides of the Downs, the fairway a mere fantasy before it tumbles down a steep bank. Anything vaguely right, even a bad bounce off the vicious slope, and it is a pitching wedge back up; at least the green is sunk into a bowl so you can go for it.

From thereon in, right is wrong. For the most part a good draw is hugely beneficial.

Ultimately, Royal Eastbourne becomes a stern test; always willing to punish, and often requiring great precision, and always the dreaded slopes to consider: It is of little comfort that there are five par-threes and three par-fives in a lay-out of 6,074 yards. There are some stiff climbs; either to the tee or to the green. The first short hole; the 159-yard eighth offers a miserly target high above the tee, the banks looming ominously in front as you line up the tee shot, and little relief for the wayward; the 192-yard 13th too requiring precision for it falls away down a steep bank to the left. (Time to change that draw).

Four of the par-threes lie in the back nine; including two to end the day, although the 17th is a a long 210 yards, up the hill. The course was founded in 1887 in the year of Queen Victoria's golden jubilee and following patronage by her grandson, Prince Albert Victor, was granted its title that year.

It is on land leased from the Duke of Devonshire, and his house provides a spectacular backdrop to the 16th green. Even there on a 507-yard dog-leg, the right hand side is out of bounds in his garden. The ninth, too turns a corner to the right and rises to an old folly; where the atmosphere is very much one of demure teas overlooking the beautiful spread to the sea; a world of charm and tranquility.

Whatever difficulties the course presents, the effect is heightened when the wind comes up, sweeping over the Downs and out to sea; for the most part, from right to left. Just what you really need if you are slicing or fading. For fade you will. – **Mark Salter**

☎ 01420 489478, Pro 489478,
Sec 489478, Rest/Bar 489478
On B3004 between Alton and Bordon
on W side of Kingsley.
Parkland course.
Founded 1984
Designed by GW Doggrell
9 holes, 1399 yards, S.S.S. 29
† Public pay and play.
ⅼ WD £5; WE £5.
⌁ Not available.

2A 35 Dewlands Manor Golf Course
Cottage Hill, Rotherfield, Crowborough,
E Sussex, TN6 3JN
☎ 01892 852266, Fax 853015,
Pro 852266, Sec 853015
0.5 mile S of village of Rotherfield just
off B2101 to Five Ashes, 10 miles from
Tunbridge Wells.
Parkland/meadowland course.
Pro Nick Godin; Founded 1991
Designed by RM and Nick Goding
9 holes, 3186 yards, S.S.S. 70
† Welcome all year; 15 minute tee
intervals.
⌁ Small business groups welcome,
maximum 50 persons; full facilities;
terms on application. Corporate days
also available.
🍽 Bar, light snacks at all times,
special orders by arrangement.
⌁ Spa; Royal Wells (Tunbridge
Wells).

2A 36 Dibden
Main Road, Dibden, Southampton,
Hants, SO45 5TB
⌨ www.nfdc.gov.uk/golf
☎ 023 80207508, Pro 80845596,
Sec 80207508, Rest/Bar 80845060
Turn off A326 at Dibden roundabout,
course situated 0.5 mile on right.
Public parkland course.
Pro John Slade; Founded 1974
Designed by J Hamilton Stutt
27 holes, 5931 yards, S.S.S. 69
ⵌ Practice range, 20 bays; floodlit
(also 9-hole par 3 course).
† Welcome; no restrictions.
ⅼ WD £10.75; WE £13.50.
⌁ Welcome by arrangement with Pro;
full facilities; terms on application.
🍽 Full facilities.
⌁ Four Seasons; Pilgrim; Fountain
Court.

2A 37 Dummer   ☎
Basingstoke, Hants, RG25 2AR
⌨ www.dummergc.co.uk
✉ golf@dummergc.co.uk

☎ 01256 397888, Fax 397889,
Pro 397950, Sec 397888
M3 exit 7.
Parkland course.
Pro A Fannon, Scott Watson and David
Chivers; Founded 1993
Designed by Peter Alliss & Clive Clark
18 holes, 6407 yards, S.S.S. 71
ⵌ 11 bays covered.
† Welcome.
ⅼ WD £30; WE £34; visitors after
12.00.
⌁ Welcome by arrangement; full
facilities; terms on application.
🍽 Full facilities.
⌁ Audley's Wood; Hilton National
(Basingstoke), The Wheatsheaf.

2A 38 Dunwood Manor Golf Club
Danes Road, Awbridge, Romsey,
Hants, SO51 0GF
⌨ www.dunwood-golf.co.uk
✉ admin@dunwood-golf.co.uk
☎ 01794 340549, Fax 341215,
Pro 340663, Sec 340549,
Rest/Bar 340549
Off A27 Romsey to Salisbury road;
after 2 miles turn right at Shootash
crossroads into Danes Road; club is
800 yards on left.
Undulating parkland course.
Pro Heath Teschner; Founded 1972
18 holes, 5474 yards, S.S.S. 68
ⵌ Practice area.
† Welcome WD by arrangement.
ⅼ WD £26 summer.
⌁ Welcome Mon/Tues/Thurs/Fri all
day and Wed pm; packages available.
🍽 Facilities available.
⌁ Luxury farmhouse and lodge
accommodation available; details on
request. Abbey Hotel; Bell Inn.

2A 39 The Dyke Golf Club
Devil's Dyke, Dyke Road, Brighton,
E Sussex, BN1 8YJ
⌨ www.dykegoldclub.co.uk
✉ secretary@dykegolfclub.
org.uk
☎ 01273 857296, Fax 857078,
Pro 857260, Sec 857296,
Rest/Bar 857230
A27 Brighton by-pass; follow directions
for Devil's Dyke; course 2.5 miles west
of by-pass.
Downland course.
Pro Richard Arnold; Founded 1906
Designed by Fred Hawtree
18 holes, 6627 yards, S.S.S. 72
ⵌ Practice area and net.
† Welcome by prior arrangement;
Sat/Sun not before 12 noon.

ⅼ WD £28; WE £35.
⌁ Welcome by prior arrangement; full
facilities available; packages from
£44.50.
🍽 Full facilities.
⌁ Tottington Manor, nr Henfield.

2A 40 East Brighton   ☎
Roedean Road, Brighton, E Sussex,
BN2 5RA
☎ 01273 604838, Fax 680277, Pro
603989, Sec 604838, Rest/Bar 621461
1.5 miles east of Palace Pier, just off
A259 behind Brighton Marina.
Undulating downland course.
Pro Mark Stewart-William; Founded 1894
Designed by James Braid
18 holes, 6020 yards, S.S.S. 69
† Welcome WD except Tues am;
WE and Bank Holidays after 11am.
ⅼ WD from £25; WE from £30.
⌁ Welcome Mon-Fri, except for Tues
am, by arrangement.
🍽 Full facilities available.
⌁ Old Ship; Grand; Metropole.

2A 41 East Horton Golfing Centre
Mortimers Lane, Fair Oak, Eastleigh,
Hants, SO50 7EA
☎ 023 806 02111, Fax 96280
From M27 Junction 7 follow signs for
Fair Oak.
Parkland course.
Pro Trevor Pearce; Founded 1993
Greenwood:18; Parkland:18 holes,
Greenwood: 5920; Parkland 5097
yards, S.S.S. Greenwood: 70;
Parkland: 70
ⵌ Practice range, 15 bays; floodlit.
† Welcome; 7 day advance booking
system.
ⅼ WD £13; WE £16.
⌁ Welcome everyday by prior
arrangement.
🍽 Bar and restaurant facilities.
⌁ Marwell Lodge; Botley Grange.

2A 42 East Sussex National
Little Horsted, Uckfield, E Sussex,
TN22 5ES
⌨ www.eastsussexnational.co.uk
✉ golf@eastsussexnational.co.uk
☎ 01825 880088, Fax 880066,
Pro 880256, Gen Mgr 889233,
Rest/Bar 880224
Situated on the A22 between East
Grinstead and Eastbourne just outside
Uckfield.
Superior parkland courses, both to
championship standards.
Pro Sarah Maclennan; Founded 1989

Designed by Robert E Cupp
East:18; West:18 holes, East: 7138;
West: 7154 yards, S.S.S. East 74;
West 74

🏌 30 bays, 8 covered, 2 covered with video room.
♦ Welcome.
ℾ Terms on application.
⌁ Welcome with handicap certs.
🍴 Full catering and entertaining as well as bar facilities, sauna and steam rooms.
🛏 Opening summer 2005.

2A 43 Eastbourne Downs

East Dean Road, Eastbourne,
E Sussex, BN20 8ES
☎ 01323 720827, Fax 412506, Pro 732264, Sec 720827, Rest/Bar 730809
0.5 miles W of Eastbourne on the A259.
Downland course.
Pro Terry Marshall; Founded 1908
Designed by JH Taylor
18 holes, 6601 yards, S.S.S. 72
🏌 Practice range.
♦ Welcome.
ℾ WD £18 round, £23 day; WE £30.
⌁ Welcome WD; some WE by arrangement; packages available.
🍴 Full clubhouse facilities.
🛏 Landsdown.

2A 44 Eastbourne Golfing ⚷ Park

Lottbridge Drove, Eastbourne,
E Sussex, BN23 6QJ
☎ 01323 520400, Fax 520400, Pro 506500, Rest/Bar 504134
East side of Eastbourne, turn left at Tesco.
Parkland course.
Pro Barrie Finch; Founded 1993
Designed by David Ashton
9 plus blue tees for back 9 holes, 5046 yards, S.S.S. 63 Par 66
🏌 Practice range, 22 bays, floodlit all-weather driving range; £2.20 for 42 balls, Range cards available with great discounts.
♦ Welcome.
ℾ 9 holes £9, 18 holes £15, all day golf £18; Junior, OAP & students £8 for 9 holes, £12 for 18 holes (WE no concessions + 9 holes £10, 18 holes £16).
⌁ Welcome by arrangement; full facilities; terms on application.
🍴 Full facilities.
🛏 Wish Tower Hotel.

2A 45 Fleetlands

Defence Aviation Repair Organisation,
Fleetlands, Fareham Road, Gosport,
Hants, PO13 0AA

🖳 www.john.watmore.btinternet.co.uk
☎ 02392 544384, Sec 543662, Rest/Bar 544457
Off A32 2 miles S of Fareham.
Parkland course.
Founded 1963
9 holes, 4852 yards, S.S.S. 64
♦ Welcome with a member.
ℾ WD £7; WE £9.
⌁ None.
🍴 Bar.

2A 46 Fleming Park

The New Club House, Paffield Avenue,
East Leigh, Hants, SO50 9NL
☎ 023 80512797, Fax 80651686
A27/M27, turn off at Eastleigh sign,
1 mile to course.
Parkland course.
Pro Chris Strickett; Founded 1973
Designed by Charles Lawrie
18 holes, 4380 yards, S.S.S. 61
♦ Welcome.
ℾ Terms on application.
⌁ Terms on application to Sec; full facilities; packages available.
🍴 Bar snacks and meals.
🛏 Holiday Inn; Gateway.

2A 47 Foxbridge

Foxbridge Lane, Plaistow Road,
Kirdford, nr Billingshurst, W Sussex,
RH14 0LB
☎ 01403 753303, Pro 01798 872218
Take B2133 from Billingshurst to Loxwood; then take Plaistow Road and course is signposted.
Parkland course.
Pro Steven Hall; Founded 1991
Designed by P Clark
9 holes, 6236 yards, S.S.S. 70
♦ Welcome.
ℾ WD £24; WE £30.
⌁ Welcome WD by arrangement; full facilities; terms on application.
🍴 Full facilities and bar available.
🛏 Lythe Hill Hotel; Checkers Blue.

2A 48 Freshwater Bay

Afton Down, Freshwater Bay, Isle of Wight, PO40 9TZ
📧 fbgc_iow@yahoo.co.uk
☎ 01983 752955
3 miles from Yarmouth on A3055 overlooking Freshwater Bay.
Seaside downland course.
Founded 1893
18 holes, 5725 yards, S.S.S. 68
🏌 Practice area.
♦ Welcome after 9.30am on WD and 10:30am on Sun.
ℾ WD £22; WE £26.

⌁ Welcome by arrangement; after 9.30am on WD and 10:30am on Sun; full facilities; terms on application.
🍴 Full catering facilities; licensed bar.
🛏 Albion, Country Garden, Farringford.

2A 49 Furzeley

Furzeley Road, Denmead, Hants,
PO7 6TX
☎ 023 92231180, Fax 92230921, Pro 92231180, Sec 92231180, Rest/Bar 92231180
2 miles NW of Waterlooville.
Parkland course.
Pro Derek Brown; Founded 1993
Designed by M Sale
18 holes, 4454 yards, S.S.S. 61
♦ Welcome, bookings taken 2 days in advance.
ℾ WD £12; WE £13.50.
⌁ Welcome; packages available; terms on application.
🍴 Available.

2A 50 Goodwood

Kennell Hill, Goodwood, Chichester,
W Sussex, PO18 0PN
🖳 www.goodwood.co.uk
☎ 01243 755130, Fax 755135, Pro 755133, Rest/Bar 755132
3 miles NE of Chichester on road to racecourse.
Downland course.
Pro Damon Allard; Founded 1892
Designed by James Braid
18 holes, 6434 yards, S.S.S. 71
♦ Welcome with handicap certs.
ℾ WD £40 (£20 with a member); WE £50 (£25 with member).
⌁ Welcome Wed/Thurs only; minimum 16; full facilities.
🍴 Full facilities available.

2A 51 Gosport & Stokes Bay

Fort Road, Alverstoke, Gosport, Hants,
PO12 2AT
☎ 023 92581625, Fax 92527941, Pro 92587423, Sec 92527941, Rest/Bar 92580226
M27 to Fareham; A32 Gosport; Haslar Bridge to Haslar Road to Fort Road.
Links course.
Founded 1885
9 holes, 5999 yards, S.S.S. 69
♦ Welcome.
ℾ Terms on application.
⌁ Welcome by arrrangement; full facilities.
🍴 Full facilities.

↩ The Old Lodge; The Alverbank; The Anglesey (all in Alverstoke).

2A 52 Great Salterns Golf Course

Burrfields Road, Portsmouth, Hants, PO3 5HH
☎ 023 92664549, Fax 92650525, Sec 92668667
2 miles off M27/A27/A3 on A2030 road into Portsmouth.
Municipal meadowland course.
Pro Terry Healy; Founded 1935
18 holes, 5575 yards, S.S.S. 67
⚐ Practice range, 24 bays; floodlit.
† Welcome.
☒ WD £12; WE £15.
⚐ Welcome by arrangement; catering available in adjacent farmhouse pub; terms on application.
🍽 Available in adjacent farmhouse pub.

2A 53 Ham Manor Golf Club

West Drive, Angmering, Littlehampton, W Sussex, BN16 4JE
🖳 www.shammanor.co.uk
🖂 secretary@hammanor.co.uk
☎ 01903 783288, Fax 850886, Pro 783732, Rest/Bar 775653
Off A259 between Littlehampton and Worthing.
Parkland course.
Pro Simon Buckley; Founded 1936
Designed by HS Colt
18 holes, 6267 yards, S.S.S. 70
† Welcome with handicap certs.
☒ WD £30; WE £40.
⚐ Welcome Thurs by arrangement; full facilities; packages available.
🍽 Full facilities.
↩ Arundel Hotel; Lamb Inn, Angmering.

2A 54 Hampshire Golf Club ♨

Winchester Road, Goodworth Clatford, Andover, Hants, SP11 7TB
🖳 www.thehampshiregolfclub.co.uk
🖂 enquiry@thehampshiregolfclub .co.uk
☎ 01264 357555, Fax 356606, Sec 356606
From Andover take the Stockbridge road on the A3057, course is 0.5 mile S of Andover.
Downland course.
Pro Ian Powell; Founded 1993
Designed by T Fiducia & A Mitchell
18 holes, 6146 yards, S.S.S. 71.
Par 3 course, 1056 yards
⚐ Practice range, covered bays.
† Welcome.

☒ WD £17, WE £25.
⚐ Welcome by arrangement; full facilities; packages available; terms on application.
🍽 Full facilities.
↩ White Hart (Andover).

2A 55 Hartley Wintney

London Road, Hartley Wintney, Hook, Hants, RG27 8PT
🖳 www.hartleywintneygolfclub.com
🖂 office@hartleywintneygolfclub.com
☎ 01252 844211, Fax 844211, Pro 843779, Rest/Bar 842214
A30 between Camberley (5 miles) and Basingstoke (12 miles).
Parkland course.
Pro Martin Smith; Founded 1891
18 holes, 6240 yards, S.S.S. 71
⚐ Practice range.
† Welcome.
☒ WD £30; WE £35.
⚐ Welcome by arrangement; full facilities; packages available; terms on application to Pro.
🍽 Comprehensive menu available.
↩ Hook House Hotel, Hook.

2A 56 Hassocks

London Road, Hassocks, W Sussex, BN6 9NA
🖳 www.hassocksgolfclub.co.uk
🖂 hgc@hassocksgolfclub.co.uk
☎ 01273 846630, Fax 846070, Pro 846990, Rest/Bar 846949
Take A273 towards Hassocks from Brighton; club is between Hassocks and Burgess Hill.
Parkland course.
Pro Charles Ledger; Founded 1995
Designed by P Wright
18 holes, 5698 yards, S.S.S. 68
⚐ Driving range; irons only.
† Welcome anytime; tee time booking recommended.
☒ WD £15; WE £19.95.
⚐ Welcome by arrangement with Sec; full facilities.
🍽 Full facilities.
↩ The Birch Hotel, Haywards Heath; Hickstead Hotel, Bolney.

2A 57 Hastings

Battle Rd, St Leonards-on-Sea, E Sussex, TN37 7BP
🖳 www.hastingsgolfclub.com
🖂 mark@hastingsgolfclub.com
☎ 01424 852981, Fax 854244
A2100 from Battle to Hastings, 3 miles NW of Hastings.
Municipal undulating parkland course.
Pro Charles Giddings/Sean Creasy;

Founded 1973
Designed by Frank Pennink
18 holes, 6248 yards, S.S.S. 70
⚐ Practice range, 14 bays; floodlit.
† Welcome; no restrictions WD; booking system in use at WE 7am-10.30am.
☒ WD £14; WE £17.50.
⚐ Welcome Mon-Fri; full facilities; terms on application.
🍽 Full facilities.
↩ Beauport Park.

2A 58 Hayling Golf Club

Links Lane, Hayling Island, Hants, PO11 0BX
🖳 www.haylinggolf.co.uk
🖂 hgcltd@aol.com
☎ 023 924 64446, Fax 61119, Pro 64491, Rest/Bar 63712
From Havant Junction on A27 take A3023 to SW corner of Hayling Island.
Links course.
Pro R Gadd; Founded 1883
Designed by JH Taylor/Tom Simpson
18 holes, 6521 yards, S.S.S. 71
⚐ Practice range, putting green; 2 covered driving nets.
† Welcome with handicap certs.
☒ WD £40; WE £55.
⚐ Welcome Tues/Wed by prior arrangement; full facilities.
🍽 Full facilities.
↩ Newton House Hotel; Broad Oak Country Hotel.

2A 59 Haywards Heath

High Beech Lane, Haywards Heath, W Sussex, RH16 1SL
🖂 haywardsheath.golfclub@virgin.net
☎ 01444 414457, Fax 458319, Pro 414866, Sec 414457, Rest/Bar 414310
1.5 miles north of Haywards Heath on the Ardingly road.
Parkland course.
Pro Michael Henning; Founded 1922
Designed by Donald Steel
18 holes, 6204 yards, S.S.S. 70
⚐ 8.
† Welcome with handicap certs.
☒ WD £26; WE £36.
⚐ Welcome by prior arrangement with the secretary; packages from £38.
🍽 Full facilities.

2A 60 Highwoods

Ellerslie Lane, Bexhill on Sea, E Sussex, TN39 4LJ
🖳 www.highwoodsgolfclub.co.uk
🖂 secretary@highwoodsgolfclub .co.uk
☎ 01424 212625, Fax 218866, Pro 212770, Rest/Bar 219600

Off A259 from Eastbourne or Hastings;
2 miles from Bexhill; from Battle, A269
via Ninfield, turn right in Sidley.
Parkland course.
Pro Mike Andrews; Founded 1925
Designed by JH Taylor
18 holes, 6218 yards, S.S.S. 70
† Welcome with handicap certs; no
visitors Sun before noon unless with
member.
⌢ WD £30; WE £35.
⌢ Welcome by prior arrangement;
full facilities; terms on application.
⦿ Full facilities.
⌐ Cooden Resort.

2A 61 **Hill Barn** ☎
Hill Barn Lane, Worthing, W Sussex,
BN14 9QE
✉ info@hillbarngolf.com
☎ 01903 237301, Fax 217613,
Rest/Bar 233918
N of Worthing off Norwich Union
roundabout on A27, take last exit
before the Brighton exit; course is
signposted.
Municipal downland course.
Pro Fraser Morley; Founded 1935
Designed by Hawtree & Son
18 holes, 6224 yards, S.S.S. 70
† Welcome.
⌢ WD £15; WE £17.50.
⌢ Welcome 7 days a week; minimum
12; terms on application.
⦿ Full catering service 7 days a
week up to 4.30 pm.
⌐ Beach; Ardington & Chatsworth.

2A 62 **Hockley**
Twyford, Winchester, Hants, SO21 1PL
⌁ www.hockleygolfclub.com
✉ secretary@hockleygolfclub.com
☎ 01962 713165, Fax 713612, Pro
713678, Rest/Bar 714572
Leave M3 at Junction 11 and follow
signs for Twyford.
Downland course.
Pro G Stubbington; Founded 1914
Designed by James Braid
18 holes, 6296 yards, S.S.S. 70
† Welcome anytime.
⌢ WD £35; WE £50.
⌢ Welcome Wed/Fri by prior
arrangement; full facilities.
⦿ Full facilities every day except Mon.
⌐ Winchester Royal Hotel; Harestock
Lodge; Potters Heron.

2A 63 **Hollingbury Park**
Ditchling Road, Brighton, E Sussex,
BN1 7HS
⌁ www.hollingburypark.co.uk

☎ 01273 552010, Fax 552010/6,
Pro 500086
1 mile from Brighton, astride the
Downs between A23 London Rd and
A27 Lewes Rd.
Public undulating downland course.
Pro Graeme Crompton; Founded 1908
Designed by J Braid and J H Taylor
18 holes, 6400 yards, S.S.S. 71
† Welcome anytime.
⌢ WD £14; WE £19.
⌢ Welcome WD; full facilities; terms
on application.
⦿ Full restaurant facilities.
⌐ Old Ship; Preston Resort.

2A 64 **Horam Park**
Chiddingly Road, Horam, Heathfield,
E Sussex, TN21 0JJ
⌁ www.horamparkgolf.co.uk
✉ angie@horamgolf.freeserve.co.uk
☎ 01435 813477, Fax 813677
Off M25 at Junction 6; A22 to
Eastbourne; A267 to Heathfield; before
reaching Horam, take Chiddingly road,
200 yards on right.
Parkland course with lakes.
Pro Giles Velvick; Founded 1985
Designed by Glen Johnson
9 holes, 6128 yards, S.S.S. 69 (19 tee
positions)
⌁ 16 bay floodlit; 5 hole pitch & putt.
† Welcome 7 days a week.
⌢ 9 holes: WD £9; WE £11.50.
18 holes: WD £16.50; WE £18.
Discounts for juniors and seniors.
⌢ Specialists in society and
corporate days.
⦿ Full facilities.
⌐ The Boship Hotel, Hialsham.

2A 65 **Horsham Golf Park**
Denne Park, Horsham, W Sussex,
RH13 7AX
☎ 01403 271525, Fax 274528
A24 between Horsham and
Southwater; off Hop-Oast roundabout.
Parkland course.
Pro Alex Paterson; Founded 1993
9 holes, 4122 yards, S.S.S. 60
⌁ Practice range; £2.50 bucket of balls.
† Welcome at all times.
⌢ WD £7; WE £8.
⌢ Welcome by arrangement; full
facilities.
⦿ Full facilities.

2A 66 **Ifield Golf and Country
Club**
Rusper Road, Ifield, Crawley, West
Sussex, RH11 0LN

☎ 01293 520222, Fax 612973,
Pro 523088, Sec 520222,
Rest/Bar 520222
M23 Junction on the outskirts of
Crawley near Gossops Green.
Parkland course.
Pro Jon Earl; Founded 1927
Designed by Bernard Darwin
18 holes, 6330 yards, S.S.S. 70
† Welcome WD but should phone in
advance.
⌢ WD £30 round, £40 day.
⌢ Society Bookings taken for 16
people or more; coffee, buffet lunch, 3-
course dinner in carvery and 36 holes
of golf; £55.
⦿ Full Facilities.
⌐ Ifield Court Hotel.

2A 67 **Leckford**
Leckford, Stockbridge, Hants,
SO20 6JF
✉ golf@leckfordestate.co.uk
☎ 01264 810320
2.5 miles north of Stockbridge on
Andover road.
Downland course.
Pro Tony Ashton; Founded 1932 (old
course)/1987 (new course)
9:9 holes, 6394:4562 yards, S.S.S.
72:66
† Yes – please phone.
⌢ WD £11; WE/BH £15.
⌢ Welcome by prior arrangement.
⦿ None.

2A 68 **Lee-on-the-Solent**
Brune Lane, Lee-on-the-Solent, Hants,
PO13 9PB
⌁ www.leeonthesolentgolfclub.co.uk
✉ enquiries@leeonthesolentgolfclub
.co.uk
☎ 023 925 51170, Fax 54233,
Pro 51181, Rest/Bar 50207
3 miles South of M27 Junction 11.
Heathland course.
Pro Rob Edwards; Founded 1905
Designed by JH Taylor
18 holes, 5962 yards, S.S.S. 69
⌁ Practice range.
† Welcome WD.
⌢ WD £36.
⌢ Welcome Thur by prior
arrangement.
⦿ Full Clubhouse facilities.
⌐ Holiday Inn, Fareham.

2A 69 **Lewes** ☎
Chapel Hill, Lewes, E Sussex,
BN7 2BB
☎ 01273 483474, Fax 483474,
Pro 473245, Rest/Bar 473245

East of town centre on A27.
Downland course.
Pro Paul Dobson; Founded 1896
18 holes, 6220 yards, S.S.S. 70
† Welcome weekdays and after 2pm
at weekends.
Ⓘ WD £28; WE £36.
↻ Welcome; terms on application.
Ⓘ Full bar and restaurant facilities.
↪ White Hart Hotel, Lewes.

2A 70 Liphook
Wheatsheaf Enclosure, Liphook,
Hants, GU30 7EH
✉ liphookgolfclub@btconnect.com
☎ 01428 723271, Fax 724853
I mile south of Liphook on B2070 (old
A3).
Heath and heather course.
Pro Ian Mowbray; Founded 1922
Designed by Arthur Croome
18 holes, 6167 yards, S.S.S. 69
† Welcome with handicap certs but
not on Tue and only PM at WE.
Ⓘ WD £39, Sat £47, Sun £56.
↻ Welcome Wed, Thur, Fri; min 16,
max 36; terms on application.
Ⓘ Bar, bar snacks and restaurant
facilities.

2A 71 Littlehampton
Rope Walk, Riverside West,
Littlehampton, W Sussex, BN17 5DL
✉ www.littlehamptongolf.co.uk
✉ lgc@talk21.com
☎ 01903 717170, Fax 726629,
Pro 716369
From Littlehampton take the A259
Bognor Regis Road; take the first left
after New River Bridge, follow signs for
the golf club.
Seaside links course.
Pro Guy Mc Quitty; Founded 1889
18 holes, 6226 yards, S.S.S. 70
† Welcome at any time; after 12
noon on Sun with handicap certificates.
Ⓘ WD £30; WE £35.
↻ Welcome WD; full facilities; terms
on application.
Ⓘ Full facilities.
↪ Bailiff's Court; Norfolk Arms.

2A 72 Mannings Heath ♉
Fullers, Hammerpond Road, Mannings
Heath, Horsham, W Sussex,
RH13 6PG
✉ www.manningsheath.com
✉ enquiries@manningsheath.com
☎ 01403 210228, Fax 270974,
Sec 210228, Rest/Bar 210228
2 miles south of Horsham on A281
from Junction 11 on the M23; 4 miles

along Grouse Road; turn right at T
junction.
Undulating wooded course.
Pro Clive Tucker; Founded 1905
Designed by D Williams
Kingfisher course: 18 holes, 6217
yards, S.S.S. 70; Waterfall course: 18
holes, 6412 yards, S.S.S. 73 off white
tees
† Visitors with handicaps preferred
but everyone welcome.
Ⓘ Prices on application.
↻ Welcome; full catering available,
tennis, steam rooms and practice
facilities; Societies from £45.
Ⓘ Full facilities.
↪ South Lodge.

2A 73 Manningsheath Hotel
Winterpit Lane, Lower Beeding,
Horsham, W Sussex, RH13 6LY
✉ www.manningsheathhotel.
com
✉ info@manningsheathhotel.
com
☎ 01403 891191, Fax 891499,
Sec 891191, Rest/Bar 891191
From the M23 take A2110 to
Handcross, through village and right at
Red Lion Pub, approx 2 miles past
garage on right (Church Lane) then 1st
left into Winterpit Lane.
Public parkland course.
Founded 1991
Designed by P Webster
9 holes, 3335 yards
† Welcome at all times.
Ⓘ WD £10 WE £10.
↻ Welcome, corporate days
available.
Ⓘ Bar, lounge and restaurants.
↪ Mannings Heath Hotel on site.

2A 74 Marriott Goodwood ♉
Park Golf & CC
Goodwood, Nr Chichester, W Sussex,
PO18 0QB
✉ golfgoodwood@marriotthotels
.co.uk
☎ 01243 775537, Fax 520120,
Pro 520117, Sec 520117,
Rest/Bar 520117
3 miles north of Chichester.
Parkland course.
Pro Adrian Wratting; Founded 1989
Designed by Donald Steel
18 holes, 6650 yards, S.S.S. 72
Ⓘ 15.
† Welcome.
Ⓘ WD/£35; 2 for 1 accepted + £60
tee time for up to 4 players.
↻ Welcome; packages available for
golf, catering and hotel; aerobic studio,

swimming pool, tennis, gym, driving
range; from £55.
Ⓘ Full facilities, restaurant and sports
cafe bar.
↪ Marriott Goodwood Park.

2A 75 Meon Valley Hotel ♉
Golf & CC
Sandy Lane, Shedfield, Southampton,
Hants, SO32 2HQ
✉ www.marriotthotels.co.uk
✉ golf.meonvalley@
marriotthotels.co.uk
☎ 01329 833455, Fax 834411,
Pro 832184, Sec 833455,
Rest/Bar 836826
Off M27 at Junction 27, take Botley
exit A334 towards Wickham; course is
on Sandy Lane.
Wooded parkland course.
Pro Rod Cameron; Founded 1978
Meon: 18 holes, 6520 yards, S.S.S.
71; Valley: 9 holes, 2879 yards
Ⓘ 8 covered,7 uncovered.
† Book in advance.
Ⓘ WD £38; WE £45.
↻ Welcome; parties catered for;
terms on application.
Ⓘ Full facilities.
↪ Meon Valley Country Club.

2A 76 Mid Sussex ♉
Spatham Lane, Ditchling, E Sussex,
BN6 8XJ
✉ www.midsussexgolfclub.co.uk
✉ admin@midsussexgolfclub.co.uk
☎ 01273 847815, Fax 847812,
Pro 846567, Sec 841835,
Rest/Bar 845644
1 mile east of Ditchling on Lewes Road.
Parkland course.
Pro Neil Plimmer; Founded 1995
Designed by D Williams Partnership
18 holes, 6446 yards, S.S.S. 71
Ⓘ Practice range, grass tees
available.
† Welcome WD and afternoons at
WE.
Ⓘ WD £23; WE £30.
↻ Welcome on WD; restaurant and
practice facilities.
Ⓘ Full Facilities.
↪ Many in the Brighton area.

2A 77 Moors Valley Golf Course
Horton Road, Ashley Heath, Ringwood,
Hants, BH24 2ET
✉ www.moors-valley.co.uk
✉ golfcentre@moorsvalley
.fsnet.co.uk
☎ 01425 479776 (reception),
Fax 471656, Rest/Bar 480448

A31 through Ringwood, right at roundabout to Ashley Heath, course 2 miles on the right.
Parkland/heathland course.
Coaching Pro Michael Torrens; Founded 1988
Designed by Martin Hawtree
18 holes, 6337 yards, S.S.S. 70
⌁ Practice facilities plus short course.
† Welcome.
⌁ Offpeak £1; peak £19.
⌁ Welcome after 11am.
⦿ Full bar and catering facilities.
⌁ On request.

2A 78 New Forest
Southampton Road, Lyndhurst, Hants, SO43 7BU
☎ 01238 028 2752, Fax 2484
On the A 35 between Ashurst and Lyndhurst.
Forest heathland course.
Pro Colin Murray; Founded 1888
Designed by Peter Swann
18 holes, 5772 yards, S.S.S. 68
† Welcome.
⌁ WD £15; WE £18.
⌁ Welcome but must book in advance; bar and lounge facilities.
⦿ Full facilities.

2A 79 Newport
Near Shide, Newport, Isle of Wight, PO30 3BA
☎ 01983 525076
On A 3056 Newport Sandown Road half a mile from Newport.
Downland course.
Founded 1896
Designed by Guy Hunt
9 holes, 5660 yards, S.S.S. 68
† Welcome with Handicap certs.
⌁ Terms on application.
⌁ Welcome by arrangement; catering packages available by special arrangement with caterer; from £12.
⦿ Bar and catering facilities.

2A 80 North Hants
Minley Road, Fleet, Hants, GU51 1RF
☎ 01252 616443, Fax 811627, Pro 616655
Half a mile north of Fleet station on B3013, Junction 4A on M3
Heathland course.
Pro Steve Porter; Founded 1904
Designed by James Braid
18 holes, 6519 yards, S.S.S. 72
† Welcome by prior arrangement with Sec; letter off introduction and handicap certs required.

⌁ WD £32.
⌁ Welcome Mon to Fri by arrangement with Sec; full facilities; packages available; terms on application.
⦿ Lunch, tea, dinner; pre-booking required.
⌁ Various in Fleet, Camberley and Farnborough.

2A 81 Old Thorns   ℭ
Old Thorns, Weavers Down, Longmoor Road, Liphook, Hants, GU30 7PE
✉ info@oldthorns.com
☎ 01428 724555, Fax 725063
Signposted from A3 at Griggs Green.
Parkland course.
Pro Keiran Stevensons; Founded 1982
Designed by Commander John Harris; adapted by Peter Alliss and Dave Thomas
18 holes, 6533 yards, S.S.S. 71
⌁ 2.
† Welcome.
⌁ WD £35; WE £40.
⌁ Welcome any day; corporate and society days can be arranged; packages available; function rooms.
⦿ European and Japanese restaurants.
⌁ Old Thorns.

2A 82 Osborne
Osborne House Estate, East Cowes, Isle of Wight, PO32 6JX
☎ 01983 295421, Sec 295431
1 mile from Red Funnel Terminal in grounds of Osborne House.
Parkland course.
2 holes opened for Royal household in 1892; extended to 9 by Osborne House Governor in 1904
9 holes, 6398 yards, S.S.S. 70
⌁ Practice nets, practice green.
† Welcome by prior arrangement except Tues, Sat and Sun am.
⌁ Terms on application.
⌁ Welcome by arrangement but a maximum of 24; bar and restaurant facilities; terms on application.
⦿ Facilities available.
⌁ Memories, East Cowes; Wheatsheaf, Newport; Albert Cottage, York Avenue, East Cowes.

2A 83 Otterbourne Golf Club
Poles Lane, Otterbourne, Nr Winchester, Hants, SO21 1DZ
☎ 01962 775225
On A31 between Hursley and Otterbourne villages.

Parkland course.
Founded 1995
9 holes, 1939 yards, S.S.S. 30
⌁ Open practice range.
† Public pay and play.
⌁ WD £4; WE £5.
⌁ None.
⦿ None.

2A 84 Paultons Golf Centre
Salisbury Road, Ower, Romsey, Hants, SO51 6AN
✉ paultons@americangolf.co.uk
☎ 023 8081 3345, Fax 3993, Rest/Bar 4622
Exit 2 off M27 in direction of Ower, left at 1st roundabout, then right at The Vine Hotel, then signposted.
Parkland course.
Pro Mark Williams; Founded 1993
18 holes, 6238 yards, S.S.S. 70
⌁ Practice range 24 bays; floodlit.
† All welcome at all times.
⌁ Available on request.
⌁ Welcome by arrangement; full facilities; terms on application.
⦿ Bars and restaurant.
⌁ The Vine Hotel (500 yards).

2A 85 Paxhill Park   ℭ
East Mascalls Lane, Lindfield, Haywards Heath, W Sussex, RH16 2QN
🖳 www.paxhillpark.com
✉ johnbowen@paxhillpark.fsnet.com
☎ 01444 484467, Fax 482709, Pro 484000
2 miles outside Haywards Heath on Lindfield Road.
Parkland course.
Pro Marcus Green; Founded 1990
Designed by Patrick Tallack
18 holes, 6117 yards, S.S.S. 69
⌁ 5.
† Welcome WD and after 12 noon at WE.
⌁ WD £17; WE £22.
⌁ Welcome Mon-Fri; full facilities but no food on Mon evenings; from £45.
⦿ Full facilities except evenings unless prior arranged.
⌁ Birch Hotel, Haywards Heath.

2A 86 Peacehaven
Brighton Road, Newhaven, E Sussex, BN9 9UH
✉ golf@peacehavengc.freeserve.co.uk
☎ 01273 514049, Pro 512602
On A259 1 mile W of Newhaven.
Undulating downland course.
Pro Ian Pearson; Founded 1895
Designed by James Braid

9 holes, 5488 yards, S.S.S. 67
† Welcome WD; after 11.30am WE and BH.
ℓ WD £15; WE £20.
⌁ Welcome WD; full facilities; terms on application.
⏵ Available WE; by prior arrangement WD.

2A 87 Pease Pottage Golf Club

Buchan Hill, Horsham Road, Crawley, W Sussex, RH11 9SG
☎ 01293 521706, Fax 518428
Leave M23 at Junction 11, then course is signposted from large roundabout.
Public parkland course.
Pro David Blair; Founded 1986
Designed by Adam Lazar
9 holes, 3511 yards, S.S.S. 60
⌇ Practice range, 26 bays; floodlit.
† Welcome.
ℓ WD £8.50; WE £11.
⌁ Welcome by arrangement; full facilities; terms on application.
⏵ No Restaurant.
⏩ Cottismore Hotel.

2A 88 Petersfield

Tankerdale Lane, Liss, Hants, GU33 7QY
▤ greghughes@18global.com
☎ 01730 895165, Fax 894713, Pro 895216, Sec 895165, Rest/Bar 895324
Off A3 between Petersfield/Midhurst & Liss exit.
Parkland course.
Pro Greg Hughes; Founded 1892; New course 1997
New course designed by Martin Hawtree
18 holes, 6450 yards, S.S.S. 71
† Welcome with handicap certificates.
ℓ WD £25; WE £30.
⌁ Welcome Mon, Wed and Fri; modern new clubhouse facilities; terms on application.
⏵ Full facilities.
⏩ Concord Hotel.

2A 89 Petworth Golf Club

London Road, Petworth, W Sussex, GU28 9LX
⌁ www.petworthgolfcourse.co.uk
▤ info@petworthgolfclurse.co.uk
☎ 01798 344097, Fax 344097, Pro 07932 163941, Sec 01730 817707, Rest/Bar 01732 163941
1.5 miles N of Petworth on A283.
Parkland course over farmland.
Pro Mr Little; Founded 1989
Designed by Chris Duncton
18 holes, 6191 yards, S.S.S. 69

† Welcome.
ℓ £11 (18 holes), £8.50 (9 holes) – anytime.
⌁ Welcome; new clubhouse opened 1999 with full facilities; terms on application.
⏵ Full facilities in new clubhouse.
⏩ B&B on course; Stonemasons Arms, Petworth.

2A 90 Piltdown

Piltdown, Uckfield, E Sussex, TN22 3XB
▤ piltdowngolf@lineone.net
☎ 01825 722033, Fax 724192, Pro 722389
1 mile W of Maresfield on the A272.
Heathland course.
Pro J Partridge & A Milligan; Founded 1904
Designed by J Rowe, GM Dodd, Frank Pennink
18 holes, 6076 yards, S.S.S. 69
⌇ Driving range.
† Welcome by arrangement.
ℓ WD £32. WE £32 round, £42 day.
⌁ Welcome Mon, Wed and Fri; packages available; terms on application.
⏵ Full facilities.

2A 91 Portsmouth

Crookhorn Lane, Widley Waterlooville, Hants, PO7 5QL
☎ 023 92372210, Fax 92200766, Pro 92372210, Sec 92201827, Rest/Bar 92375999
1.5 miles from A3(M), junction of Purbrook/Leigh Park.
Parkland course.
Pro Jason Banting; Founded 1972
Designed by Hawtree
18 holes, 5760 winter card summer card yardage6139 yards, S.S.S. 70
† Welcome with prior booking.
ℓ WD £10.50; WE £13.50.
⌁ Welcome at any time by prior arrangement; packages available.
⏵ Bar and restaurant facilities.
⏩ Innlodge Hotel.

2A 92 Pyecombe

Clayton Hill, Pyecombe, Brighton, E Sussex, BN45 7FF
▤ pyecombegc@btopenworld.com
☎ 01273 845372, Fax 843338, Pro 845398, Sec 845372, Rest/Bar 844176
Off A23 at Hassocks and Pyecombe.
Filter left on to A273 and course is 300 yds on right.
Downland course.
Pro Chris White; Founded 1894

Designed by James Braid.
18 holes, 6221 yards, S.S.S. 70
⌇ Practice green. Practice nets.
† Welcome.
ℓ WD £25; WE £30.
⌁ Welcome by prior arrangement; terms on application.
⏵ Full facilities.
⏩ Club can advise.

2A 93 Romsey

Romsey Road, Nursling, Southampton, Hants, SO16 0XW
⌁ www.romseygolfclub.com
▤ mike@romseygolf.co.uk
☎ 023 80734637, Fax 80741036, Pro 80736673, Rest/Bar 80732218
2 miles SE of Romsey on A3057 Southampton Road, near M27/M271 Junction 3.
Wooded parkland course.
Pro Mark Desmond; Founded 1900
Designed by Charles Lawrie
18 holes, 5856 yards, S.S.S. 68
† Welcome WD.
ℓ WD £27.50.
⌁ Welcome by arrangement Mon, Tues and Thurs; full facilities; terms on application.
⏵ Full facilities.
⏩ Travel Inn, Nursling; Novotel, Southampton.

2A 94 Rowlands Castle ℡

Links Lane, Rowlands Castle, Hants, PO9 6AE
☎ 023 924 12784, Fax 13649, Pro 12785, Rest/Bar 12216
3 miles on the B2149 off Junction 2 of the A3M.
Parkland course.
Pro P Klepacz; Founded 1902
Designed by HS Colt
18 holes, 6612 yards, S.S.S. 72
† Welcome except for Sat.
ℓ WD £30; WE £35.
⌁ Welcome Tues and Thurs by prior arrangement; packages include 36 holes plus lunch and dinner; £41-£45.
⏵ Full facilities.
⏩ Brook Fields Hotel, Emsworth.

2A 95 Royal Ashdown Forest

Chapel Lane, Forest Row, E Sussex, RH18 5LR
⌁ www.royalashdown.co.uk
▤ office@royalashdown.co.uk
☎ 01342 822018, Fax 825211, Pro 822247, Sec 822018, Rest/Bar 823014; West Course 824866

A22 East Grinstead-Eastbourne Road,4.5 miles S of East Grinstead turn left in Forest Row opposite church on to B2110 to Hartfield, after 0.5 mile turn right into Chapel Lane, top of hill turn left, over heath to clubhouse. Undulating heathland course with views over forest.
Pro Martyn Landsborough; Founded 1888
Designed by James Braid.
Old: 18 holes, 6463 yards, S.S.S. 71; West: 18 holes, 5606 yards, S.S.S, 69
⌐ Practice area for members and visitors only.
† Welcome by arrangement only; restrictions at WE and BH.
Ⅼ Old: WD £45; WE £60. West: WD £22; WE £26.
⌐ Welcome by prior arrangement; catering; full facilities, except Mon.
⍟ Lunch, tea; casual visitors requested to book in advance or before teeing off.
⌐ Ashdown Park Hotel, Wych Cross;Forest; Brambletye, Chequers, Forest Row.

2A 96 **Royal Eastbourne** ☏
Paradise Drive, Eastbourne, E Sussex, BN20 8BP
⌐ www.regc.co.uk
✉ sec@regc.co.uk
☎ 01323 729738, Fax 729738, Pro 736986, Rest/Bar 730412
0.5 miles from Town Hall.
Downland course.
Pro Alan Harrison; Founded 1887
18 holes, 6118 yards, S.S.S. 69
⌐ 9-hole course, 4294 yards, S.S.S. 61.
† Welcome but handicap certs needed on the Devonshire course.
Ⅼ WD £25; WE £30 (2003 rates).
⌐ Welcome on WD only; golf, lunch and 3-course dinner; £40-£50.
⍟ Full facilities.
⌐ Grand; Lansdowne; Chatsworth, all in Eastbourne.

2A 97 **Royal Winchester** ☏
Sarum Road, Winchester, Hants, SO22 5QE
⌐ www.royalwinchestergolfclub.com
✉ manager@royalwinchestergolfclub.com
☎ 01962 852462, Fax 865048, Pro 862473, Sec 852462, Rest/Bar 851694
Take M3 to Junction 11 and at Pitt roundabout follow sign to Winchester until roundabout, first turn off into Chilbolton Ave, first turning left into Sarum Road, mile up the road on the right is the golf club.

Downland course.
Pro Steve Hunter; Founded 1888
Designed by HS Colt and AP Taylor
18 holes, 6216 yards, S.S.S. 70
† Welcome WD; with a member only at WE. Not bank holidays.
Ⅼ WD £33.
⌐ Mon, Tues afternoon £42 and Wed only by prior arrangement; £55.
⍟ Full facilities.

2A 98 **Rustington Golf Centre** ☏
Golfers Lane, Angmering, Littlehampton, W Sussex, BN16 4NB
⌐ www.rgcgolf.com
☎ 01903 850790, Fax 850982
A259 at Rustington, between Worthing and Chichester.
Public parkland course, membership avail.
Pro Granfield Golf Academy; Founded 1995
Designed by David Williams P'ship
9 holes, 5735 yards, S.S.S. 68
⌐ Practice range, 30 covered bays, 6 outdoor bays.
† Welcome 7:00am to 9pm 7 days a week; bookings taken.
Ⅼ 18 holes £16.50. 9 Holes £10.50.
⌐ Welcome by arrangement; full facilities; terms on application.
⍟ Coffee shop serving hot and cold lunches; licensed bar.

2A 99 **Ryde**
Binstead Road, Ryde, Isle of Wight, PO33 3NF
✉ secretary@rydegolfclub.freeserve.co.uk
☎ 01983 614809, Fax 567418, Sec 614809, Rest/Bar 614809
Main Ryde-Newport road.
Parkland course.
Founded 1895
Designed by Hamilton Stutt.
9 holes, 5772 yards, S.S.S. 68, Par 70.
† Welcome; not Wed 10-2.30 or Sun am.
Ⅼ WD £18; WE £20.
⌐ Welcome WD except Wed; contact Sec; facilities and packages by arrangement; terms on application.
⍟ By arrangement.
⌐ Newlands.

2A 100 **Rye**
New Lydd Road, Camber, Rye, E Sussex, TN31 7QS
☎ 01797 225241, Fax 225460, Pro 225218, Sec 225241

From Rye take the A259 to New Romney; 2 miles out of town turn right towards Camber; course is 1.5 miles on right.
Links course.
Pro Micheal Lee; Founded 1894
Designed by HS Colt
27 holes, 6308 yards, S.S.S. 71
† Introduced by member only.
Ⅼ Not available.
⌐ None.
⍟ Full facilities.
⌐ Hope; Anchor; Mermaid, all in Rye.

2A 101 **Sandford Springs** ☏
Wolverton, Tadley, Hants, RG26 5RT
☎ 01635 296800, Fax 296801, Pro 296808
Off the A339 at Kingsclere between Basingstoke and Newbury.
Picturesque varied course overlooking 5 counties.
Pro Gary Edmunds; Founded 1988
Designed by Hawtree & Son
27 holes: Woods 6222 yards, S.S.S. 70; Lakes 6005 yards, S.S.S. 69
† Welcome WD, bookingavailable; WE subject to availability.
Ⅼ WD £23.
⌐ Society and Company days welcome by prior arrangement.
⍟ Full bar and restaurant facilities.
⌐ Hilton National, Basingstoke & Newbury.

2A 102 **Seaford Golf Club**
Firle Road, Seaford, E Sussex, BN25 2JD
⌐ www.seafordgolfclub.co.uk
✉ secretary@seafordgolfclub.co.uk
☎ 01323 892442, Fax 894113, Pro 894160
1 mile N of Seaford on A259.
Downland course.
Pro D Mills; Founded 1887
Designed by JH Taylor
18 holes, 6551 yards, S.S.S. 71
† Open.
† Welcome by arrangement.
Ⅼ WD £28; WE £33.
⌐ By arrangement; terms on request.
⍟ Full facilities available.
⌐ Dormy House.

2A 103 **Seaford Head**
Southdown Road, Seaford, E Sussex, BN25 4JS
☎ 01323 894843, Pro 890139, Sec 894843, Rest/Bar 894843
S of A259, 12 miles from Brighton.
Public seaside course.

Royal Winchester

There is a quirkiness about Royal Winchester that starts with the drive down a one-horse country lane in which old-fashioned courtesy comes into play if all are to reach their destinations; and quite thematic in the circumstances.

But it is worth the effort, for the course has the air of a lost world, a Serengeti in the Downs just a couple of miles south of the historic City of Winchester, ancient capital of England, and just off the roaring M3 artery with its ceaseless flow of juggernauts and fast cars. It is a tranquil park with an understated grandeur and a gentle reserve.

There is a code here: no changing in the car park – an increasingly rare sign nowadays – no practice swings on the tees and a bar set aside for those gagging for a drink while still in the clothes in which they started their round (assuming you have changed your shoes). Protocol is important in this, the oldest, and the only Royal club in Hampshire. The title was confirmed by King George V in 1913; but as members are quick to point out, the title was granted by the Duke of Connaught in 1893, only for the pedantic Home Office to contest the issue.

It is slightly disconcerting not having a practice swing, especially on the first; but driving nets are set aside so you can warm up. It certainly focuses the mind, especially as you gaze down the first fairway from the elevated tee, a gentle 284-yards straight and true. The lush meadow-grass fairways are immaculate, and the greens, based on soft sand which aids drainage, seem to embrace the ball with love; once there, it's up to you to make the best of it.

The subtle delights of the course appear first at the 351-yard second hole; where you are required to produce a decent drive of 180-odd yards to a rising fairway, a bunker sits on the left at 190. The green is nowhere to be seen, but a short stroll up will reveal that the fairway drops away dramatically to the bowl-like green, which gives you a chance if you are a bit short.

And while those contours are emphatic, it is the more subtle slopes that define the course: the short third runs down to the green, but an over-enthusiastic shot will run away at the back. It is the use of the slopes which can make or break your day, so the accuracy of the approach shot is important.

All the holes present themselves as attainable targets; yet every now again, something unusual crops up to make you stop and stare: the 162-yard seventh requires a brave shot over mounds and bunkers on to a green which can carry you away to the left. The 479-yard par-five ninth involves threading the ball through the mounds and over the rough half-way along and immediately after comes the wonderful par-five 490-yard 10th, which needs two good shots and then a delicate approach to a green set high above you. Just don't pull it, otherwise you start all over again, and from the left it is a formidable climb.

The back nine is fairly bracing: the "short" 11th stands at 192 yards from the back tees; the par-four 13, at a formidable 451 yards, needs a cracking drive to reach the fairway; and the par-five 16th touches 500 yards. Still, you get to admire the magnificent houses that line the course. At least the close is more gentle; drving homewards from a high tee and across a road, and then over the bizarre pot-bunker, known as the bomb crater, immediately before the green.

Given that the course is built on the chalk downs, drainage is not a problem; but given the course's altitude the wind will be a debilitating factor when it gets up. It could change the course of your day.
– **Mark Salter**

Pro Tony Lowles; Founded 1887
18 holes, 5848 yards, S.S.S. 68
♦ Welcome at all times.
⌶ WD £15; WE £18 and bank
holidays £18.
⌁ Welcome; full facilities; terms on
application Mon-Fri.
⏹ Light snacks.
⌁ Traslyn, Clear View.

2A 104 Sedlescombe – James Andrews School of Golf
Kent Street, Sedlescombe, Battle,
E Sussex, TN33 0SD
⌸ www.golfschool.co.uk
⏹ golf@golfschool.co.uk
☎ 01424 871700, Fax 871712
On main A21 near Sedlescombe.
Parkland course.
Pro James Andrews; Founded 1991
18 holes, 6321 yards, S.S.S. 70
⌶ Practice range, 25 bays; floodlit.
♦ Welcome.
⌶ WD £20; WE £25.
⌁ Full facilities; terms on application.
⏹ Bar and restaurant.
⌁ On-site golf lodge

2A 105 Selsey
Selsey Country Club Ltd, Golf Links
Lane, Selsey, Chichester, W Sussex,
PO20 9DR
⏹ golf@selseycountryclub.co.uk
☎ 01243 602203, Fax 602203
On B2145 7 miles S of Chichester.
Seaside course.
Pro Percy Carter; Founded 1908
Designed by JH Taylor.
9 holes, 5848 yards, S.S.S. 68
♦ Welcome.
⌶ WD £14; WE £18.
⌁ Small societies welcome; full
facilities; terms on application.
⏹ Lunch and snacks; private
functions.

2A 106 Shanklin & Sandown
The Fairway, Sandown, Isle of Wight,
PO36 9PR
☎ 01983 403217, Fax 403217,
Pro 404424, Rest/Bar 403170
Off main Sandown & Shanklin road at
Lake (A3055).
Heathland course.
Pro Peter Hammond; Founded 1900
Designed by Dr J Cowper, James
Braid
18 holes, 6062 yards, S.S.S. 69
♦ Welcome with handicap certs;
restrictions at WE before lunch.
⌶ WD £27.50; WE £33.

⌁ Welcome on WD except Tues by
prior arrangement; packages available;
terms on application.
⏹ Full facilities available.

2A 107 Singing Hills Golf Course
Albourne, Hassocks, W Sussex,
BN6 9EB
⌸ www.singinghills.co.uk
⏹ info@singinghills.co.uk
☎ 01273 835353, Fax 835444
On the B2117 off the A23.
Parkland course with 3 x 9 holes
(River, Valley & Lake).
Pro Wallace Street; Founded 1992
Designed by Richard Hurd (Sandow)
27 holes, 6079 yards, S.S.S. 71
⌶ Practice range, 15 bays.
♦ Welcome.
⌶ From WD £23; WE £31 (18 holes).
⌁ Welcome for groups of more than
12; prices and packages vary each day.
⏹ Restaurant and bar facilities
available.
⌁ Hickstead Hotel, Bolney; Birch
Hotel, Haywards Heath.

2A 108 Slinfold Park Golf & Country Club ☏
Stane Street, Slinfold, Horsham, W
Sussex, RH13 0RE
⌸ www.slinfoldpark.co.uk
⏹ info@slinfoldpark.co.uk
☎ 01403 791555, Fax 791465, Pro
791555, Sec 791154, Rest/Bar 791154
4 miles W of Horsham, with direct
access from A29, there are also fast
road connections from the N via the
M25 and the A24. Slinford Park is also
conveniently situated from the South
coast or in either direction via the
A272.
Parkland course.
Pro Tony Clingan; Founded 1992
Designed by John Fortune
27 holes, 6418 yards, S.S.S. 71
⌶ Practice range, 19 bays floodlit.
♦ Welcome.
⌶ WD £25; WE £25.
⌁ Welcome Mon-Fri although some
restrictions on Tues; full facilities; from
£30.
⏹ Full facilities.
⌁ Random House, Slinfold.

2A 109 South Sea
Burrfields Road, Portsmouth, Hants,
PO3 5HH
☎ 023 926 64549, Fax 50525,
Sec 68667

2 miles off M27/A27/A3 on A2030 road
into Portsmouth.
Municipal meadowland course.
Pro Terry Healy; Founded 1935
18 holes, 5575 yards, S.S.S. 67
⌶ Practice range, 24 bays; floodlit.
♦ Welcome.
⌶ WD £10.50; WE £13.50.
⌁ Welcome by arrangement; catering
available in adjacent farmhouse pub;
terms on application.
⏹ Available in adjacent farmhouse
pub.

2A 110 South Winchester ☏
Pitt, Winchester, Hants, SO22 5QW
⌸ www.southwinchester.com
☎ 01962 877800, Fax 877900,
Pro 840469, Sec 877800,
Rest/Bar 877800
S of Winchester on Romsey road.
Championship style links course.
Pro Richard Adams; Founded 1993
Designed by D Thomas, P Alliss, C
Clark
18 holes, 7100 for men 5981 for ladies
yards, S.S.S. par 72 men par 74
women
⌶ Practice range for teaching and
members only.
♦ Guests of members only.
⌶ Visitors £25 WD £40 WE.
⌁ Welcome; terms on application.
⏹ Full bar and dining facilities. Bistro
and Carvery open to visitors.
⌁ Lainstone Hotel; Royal Hotel; Hotel
du Vin.

2A 111 Southampton
Golf Course Road, Bassett,
Southampton, Hants, SO16 7AY
☎ 023 80760546, Pro 80768407,
Rest/Bar 80767996
N end of city, off Bassett Ave, halfway
between Chilworth roundabout and
Winchester Rd roundabout.
Municipal parkland course.
Pro Jon Waring; Founded 1935
18 holes, 6213 yards, S.S.S. 70
⌶ Also a 9-hole course.
♦ Welcome.
⌶ WD £8.20; WE £11.30.
⌁ Welcome by arrangement; full
facilities; terms on application.
⏹ Breakfast, lunch, bar snacks.
⌁ Hilton (Chilworth).

2A 112 Southwick Park
Pinsley Drive, Southwick, Fareham,
Hants, PO17 6EL
☎ 023 92370683, Fax 92210289,
Pro 92380442, Sec 92380131

B2177 to Southwick village.
Parkland course.
Pro J Green; Founded 1977
Designed by Charles Lawrie
18 holes, 5992 yards, S.S.S. 69
† Strictly by prior arrangement.
Ⅼ Not available.
⌁ Welcome by prior arrangement; 36
holes with coffee, lunch and dinner;
£40.
🍴 Full bar and dining facilities.

2A 113 Southwood
Ively Road, Farnborough, Hants,
GU14 0LJ
☎ 01252 548700, Pro 548700,
Sec 548700,
Rest/Bar 515139
0.5 miles W of Farnborough.
Parkland course.
Pro Matt Robbins; Founded 1976
Designed by Hawtree & Son
18 holes, 5738 yards, S.S.S. 68
† All Welcome.
Ⅼ Terms on application.
⌁ Welcome on WD; full facilities
available; terms on application.
🍴 Full facilities.
🛏 Potters International, Aldershot.
The Monkey Puzzle, Farnborough.

2A 114 Stoneham
Monks Wood Close, Southampton,
Hants, SO16 3TT
🖥 www.stonehamgolfclub.org.uk
✉ richard.penley-martin
@stonehamgolfclub.org.uk
☎ 023 8076 9272, Fax 6320,
Pro 8397, Sec 8397
Close to M3 and M27.
Undulating parkland course with
heather.
Pro Ian Young; Founded 1908
Designed by Willie Park
18 holes, 6392 yards, S.S.S. 70
Ⅰ Indoor and outdoor practice areas.
† Welcome by arrangement.
Ⅼ Terms on application.
⌁ Welcome Mon, Thurs and Fri by
prior arrangement.
🍴 Full facilities.
🛏 Hilton, Southampton.

2A 115 Test Valley   ℡
Micheldever Road, Overton,
Basingstoke, Hants, RG25 3DS
🖥 www.testvalleygolf.com
✉ testvalley@testvalleygolf.com
☎ 01256 771737, Rest/Bar 772080
2 miles S of Overton village junction
with B3400, or 1.5 miles N of A303
from Overton turn-off.
Inland links course.

Pro Alastair Briggs; Founded 1992
Designed by D Wright
18 holes, 6883 yards, S.S.S. 72
Ⅰ 6.
† Welcome WD and WE; advisable
to phone first.
Ⅼ WD £18; WE £24.
⌁ Welcome 7 days; full facilities.
🍴 Full bar and dining facilities; dining
room for up to 100.
🛏 White Hart, Overton.

2A 116 Tidworth Garrison
Bulford Road, Tidworth, Wilts, SP9 7AF
🖥 www.tidworthgolfclub.co.uk
✉ tidworth@
garrison-golfclub.fsnet.co.uk
☎ 01980 842301, Fax 842301, Pro
842393, Rest/Bar 842321
A338 Salisbury to Marlborough into
Bulford Road.
Tree-lined downland course.
Pro Terry Gosden; Founded 1908
Designed by Donald Steel
18 holes, 6320 yards, S.S.S. 70
† Welcome.
Ⅼ WD/WE £33.
⌁ Welcome Tues and Thurs; full
facilities and packages on application.
🍴 Full catering facilities.
🛏 Red House Hotel, Parkhouse
Motel.

2A 117 Tilgate Forest Golf Centre
Titmus Drive, Crawley, W Sussex,
RH10 5EU
☎ 01293 530103, Fax 523478
M23 Junction 11 for Pease Pottage,
follow main road to Crawley, at 1st
roundabout turn right, follow signs.
Public parkland course.
Pro Sean Trussell; Founded 1983
Designed by Huggett and Coles
18 holes, 6359 yards, S.S.S. 70
Ⅰ Practice range, 36 bays. Also a 9-
hole course.
† Welcome.
Ⅼ WD £14.80; WE £19.60.
⌁ Welcome Mon-Thurs; full facilities;
terms on application.
🍴 Restaurant and bar all day.
🛏 Holiday Inn (Crawley).

2A 118 Tournerbury
Tournerbury Lane, Hayling Island,
Hants, PO11 9DL
☎ 023 9246 2266, Pro 92462266,
Sec 92462266
Off A27 on Hayling Island.
Seaside course.
Pro Robert Brown; Founded 1994

Designed by Robert Brown
9 holes, 5912 yards, S.S.S. 68
Ⅰ Practice range, 16 bays; floodlit.
† Welcome; pay and play.
Ⅼ WD £8.00 WE £9.30 9 HOLES;
WD£12.50 WE£15 for 18 holes.
⌁ Welcome by arrangement.
🍴 None; local pub.
🛏 Forte Post House.

2A 119 Tylney Park
Rotherwick, Hook, Hants,
RG27 9AY
☎ 01256 762079, Fax 763079,
Pro 762079, Sec 762079,
Rest/Bar 762079
Take M3 to Junction 5 amd then 2
miles to Rotherwick via Hook or
Newnham. Take M4 Junction 11 and
then A33 and B3349 to Rotherwick.
Mature parkland course; fine specimen
trees; practice areas.
Pro Chris de Bruin; Founded 1974
Designed by W Wiltshire
18 holes, 6200 yards, S.S.S. 69
† Welcome on WD; WE telephone
for availability.
Ⅼ WD £27; WE £33.
⌁ Welcome Mon to Thurs inc; 36
holes of golf plus coffee, lunch and
dinner max £49; alternative packages
available throughout golfing year.
🍴 Full facilities.
🛏 Tylney Hall; AA hotels in Hook.

2A 120 Ventnor
Ventnor Golf Club, Steephill Down
Road, Ventnor, Isle of Wight, PO38
1BP
☎ 01983 853326
On A3055 to Ventnor.
Undulating downland course.
Founded 1892
12 holes, 5767 yards, S.S.S. 68
† Welcome; not before 1pm Sun.
Tees closed until 12pm Mon. Mon 11 til
1pm closed.
Ⅼ WD £17; WE £20.
⌁ Welcome by arrangement.
🍴 Bar and bar snacks.
🛏 Eversly; Bonchurch Manor;
Mayfair, Shanklin.

2A 121 Waterhall
Waterhall Road, Brighton, E Sussex,
BN1 8YN
☎ 01273 508658
3 miles N of Brighton off A27.
Hilly downland course.
Pro Graham Crompton; Founded 1923
18 holes, 5713 yards, S.S.S. 68
† Welcome.

WD £12; WE £17.
Welcome; full catering facilities and packages on request; terms on application.
Restaurant and bar.

2A 122 Waterlooville
Cherry Tree Avenue, Waterlooville, Hants, PO8 8AP
www.waterloovillegolfclub.co.uk
secretary@waterloovillegolfclub
.co.uk
023 922 63388, Fax 924 42980, Pro 922 56911, Sec 922 42990
Rest/Bar 922 42987/8
A3(M) Junction 3 take B2150 to Waterlooville; at 1st roundabout take exit for Hurstwood. Cherry Tree Ave is approx. 1.2 miles from roundabout.
Parkland course.
Pro John Hay; Founded 1907
Designed by Henry Cotton
18 holes, 6602 yards, S.S.S. 72
Practice area.
Welcome WD.
WD £30 round, £35 day.
Welcome Thurs with prior arrangement with Sec.; 36 holes of golf; coffee on arrival, light lunch and evening meal; other packages also available; £48.
Full catering and bar facilities.
Hilton National.

2A 123 Wellow
Ryedown Lane, East Wellow, Romsey, Hants, SO51 6BD
01794 322872, Fax 323832, Pro 323833
Take M27 to Junction 2 then A36 for 2 miles to Whinwhistle road, then 1.5 miles to Ryedown Road.
Parkland course; 27 holes, three 9s: Ryedown, Embley, Blackwater.
Pro Neil Bratley; Founded 1991
Designed by W Wiltshire
27 holes, 5966 yards
Welcome.
WD £17; WE £21.
Welcome on WD; 27 holes, full catering; terms on application.
Full catering available.
Vine Hotel, Ower Romsey; Bramble Hill, Bramshaw.

2A 124 Wellshurst Golf & Country Club
North Street, Hellingly, Hailsham, E Sussex, BN27 4EE
www.wellshurst.com
info@wellshurst.com
01435 813636, Fax 812444, Pro 813456

From the A22, Take A267 Heathfield on the left 2/3 miles is the golf course.
Parkland course.
Pro M Jarvis; Founded 1992
Designed by Golf Corporation
18 holes, 5771 yards, S.S.S. 70
Practice range, 8 bays and 2 bunker bays.
Public pay and play.
WD £18; WE £22.
Welcome; packages available. Full fitness room and gym, sauna etc.
Available.
Boship Farm Hotel, Hailsham.

2A 125 West Chiltington
Broadford Bridge Road, West Chiltington, Pulborough, W Sussex, RH20 2YA
01798 812115, Fax 812631, Pro 812115
On A29 proceed south and turn left at Advesane.
Undulating parkland course.
Pro Geoffrey Cotton; Founded 1988
Designed by Brian Barnes and Max Faulkner
18 (additional short course of 9 holes) holes, 5877 yards, S.S.S. 69
Welcome.
WD £17; WE £19.
Welcome by arrangement; terms on application.
Full facilities.
Roundabout Hotel, W Chiltington; Chequers Hotel, Pulborough.

2A 126 West Hove
Church Farm, Hangleston Valley Drive, Hove, E Sussex, BN3 8AN
info@westhovegolf.co.uk
01273 419738, Fax 439988, Pro 413494, Rest/Bar 413411
On A27 Brighton by-pass at the Hangleton Interchange.
Downland course relocated in 1990.
Pro Darren Cook; Founded 1910/1991
Designed by Hawtree
18 holes, 6226 yards, S.S.S. 70
Practice range, 18 bays.
Welcome.
WD £25; WE £30.
Welcome; packages available for groups; terms on application.
Full bar and catering.
Grand Hotel.

2A 127 West Sussex
Golf Club Lane, Pulborough, W Sussex, RH20 2EN
www.westsussexgolf.co.uk
secretary@westsussexgolf.co.uk
01798 872563, Fax 872033, Pro 872426, Sec 872563, Rest/Bar 874019

1.5 miles E of Pulborough on A283.
Heathland course.
Pro Tim Packham; Founded 1931
Designed by Sir Guy Campbell, Major CK Hutchison
18 holes, 6223 yards, S.S.S. 70
Practice range, 15 bays.
Welcome WD only, not Fri; prior book and handicap certs required.
WD £60 (18 holes), £75 (36).
Welcome Wed and Thurs; full facilities; terms available on application.
Lunch and tea.
Amberley Castle; Roundabout, West Chiltington.

2A 128 Westridge
Brading Road, Ryde, Isle of Wight, PO33 1QS
www.westridgegc.co.uk
westgc@aol.com
01983 613131, Fax 567017
A3054 Ryde to Sandown road 2 miles S of Ryde.
Flat parkland course.
Pro Mark Wright; Founded 1992
9 holes, 3554 yards, S.S.S. 58
Practice range, 19 bays floodlit.
Welcome.
WD £8.50; WE £9.50 (9 holes).
Welcome by arrangement; terms on application.
Bar and food available.
Several in area.

2A 129 Weybrook Park
Rooksdown Lane, Basingstoke, Hants, RG24 9NT
01256 320347, Fax 812973, Pro 333232, Rest/Bar 331159
2 miles NW of town centre between A339 and A340.
Parkland course.
Pro Anthony Dillon; Founded 1971
18 holes, 6468 yards, S.S.S. 70
Practice range, grass.
Welcome by arrangement.
POA.
Welcome by prior arrangement.
Available.

2A 130 Wickham Park
Titchfield Lane, Wickham, Fareham, Hants, PO17 5PJ
www.crown-golf.co.uk
wpgc-sales@crown-golf.co.uk
01329 833342, Fax 834798, Rest/Bar 836356
2 miles N of Fareham off M27 Junction 10.
Parkland course.
Pro Scott Edwards; Founded 1995
Designed by J Payne

18 holes, 5733 yards, S.S.S. 67
- ⚐ 12 bay driving range.
- ✝ Public pay and play.
- ⚑ WD £14; WE £17 from pm Sun.
- ⚐ Welcome by prior arrangement WD; packages available; society room.
- 🍽 Clubhouse facilities.

2A 131 Willingdon
Southdown Road, Eastbourne,
E Sussex, BN20 9AA
- 🖳 www.wgc.demon.co.uk
- 📧 secretary@willingdongolfclub.co.uk
- ☎ 01323 410981, Fax 411510, Pro 410984, Sec 410981, Rest/Bar 410983
2 miles N of Eastbourne off A22.
Downland course.
Pro Troy Moore; Founded 1898
Designed by JH Taylor; modernised by Dr MacKenzie 1925
18 holes, 6044 yards, S.S.S. 69
- ✝ Welcome WD.

⚑ WD £25 WE £28.
⚐ By prior arrangement WD except Tues; packages available; terms on application.
🍽 By arrangement.
🛏 Grand; Queens; Lansdown.

2A 132 Worldham Park
Blanket Street, East Worldham, Alton,
Hants, GU34 3AG
- ☎ 01420 543151, Sec 544606
Take A31, then A3004 to Bordon; course on right.
Parkland course.
Pro Jon Le Roux; Founded 1994
Designed by F Whidborne
18 holes, 6196 yards, S.S.S. 68
- ✝ Pay and play.
- ⚑ WD £12; WE £15.
- ⚐ Welcome 7 days a week; terms on application.
- 🍽 Full bar and catering.

🛏 Alton Hotel; Swan Hotel; Grange Hotel, Holybourne.

2A 133 Worthing
Links Road, Worthing, W Sussex,
BN14 9QZ
- 🖳 www.worthinggolf.co.uk
- 📧 worthinggolf@easynet.co.uk
- ☎ 01903 260801, Fax 694664, Pro 260718
On A27 near Junction with A24.
Downland courses.
Pro Stephen Rolley; Founded 1905
Designed by H Vardon
18/18 holes, 6530/5243 yards, S.S.S. 72/66
- ✝ Welcome except at WE April-Oct.
- ⚑ WD £35; WE £40.
- ⚐ Welcome by arrangement; day's golf and catering arrangements; from £63.
- 🍽 Full facilities.
- 🛏 Winsor House; Rosedale GH; Ardington Hotel.

2B

Berkshire, Buckinghamshire, Oxfordshire

For far too long the people in these three shires thought that they had far better things to be getting on with in life than golf. The game was regarded as the unspeakable in pursuit of the unhittable. Their resistance was futile. Little by little courses began to appear. Now, like Surrey, the land is fertile with golf.

Perhaps the royal influence was irresistible. King Edward VII had a course laid out in the grounds of Windsor Castle and in 1977 the Ascot Heath Golf Club was allowed to resurrect the royal title that had died back in 1922.

And then there is the club that was king for a day. It would be hard to think of a more pleasant place on which to spend a summer's day than the Berkshire, near Ascot. The Berkshire has two courses, the Red and the Blue. Primary courses named after primary colours because the powers-that-were did not want to imply that one was superior to the other.

If someone took a popular vote, however, the Red would just about nudge it. It is most unusual in consisting of six par threes, six par fives and six par fours.

It is not just the quality of the Berkshire's courses that make for such a wonderful day out, the club is also renowned for its lunches.

Just over the road Swinley Forest really is a hidden gem. The signposting to a course masked by trees is desultory, but when you stumble upon it the reward is ample. The heathland course is a joy, but perhaps the most memorable part of the experience is the clubhouse atmosphere. You are very clearly a guest, although a most welcome one, but many of the members lurk like "pot plants left over from the Edwardian era", seemingly reluctant to come out into the vulgar sunlight of the twenty-first century.

Oxfordshire has many excellent clubs. It would be hard to pick a favourite out of Frilford Heath, Tadmarten and Huntercombe. Frilford, described by Darwin as "a wonderful oasis in a desert of mud" has three courses, colour coded like the Berkshire. Again the Red probably just shades it.

Tadmarten, according to Harry Vardon, has a divine spark. When Vardon was asked if a golf course could be built on Wiggington Hill he replied, "God made it to be a golf course". It is a short course, but a tight course. A ball missing the fairway has not that much hope of an instant recovery. It is more than likely to finish in the gorse or broom under penalty of a drop.

Huntercombe opens with an ordinary looking par three down the hill, although clubbing can be deceptive, but after that gets better and better. Just out of Frilford's and Tadmarten's earshot, Huntercombe is a favourite of the three.

Although opened as recently as 1976 Woburn is now the best known course – or three – in Buckinghamshire. A few years back the British Masters was played over the Marquess, the most recent of the three courses, and it held up very well to all the attention, even when Thomas Levet of France went on his hilarious victory lap around the seventeenth green after winning a multiple play-off. The Duke's, the oldest of the three, starts and finishes well but can be a little humdrum in the middle. The Duchess is slightly easier but still very popular.

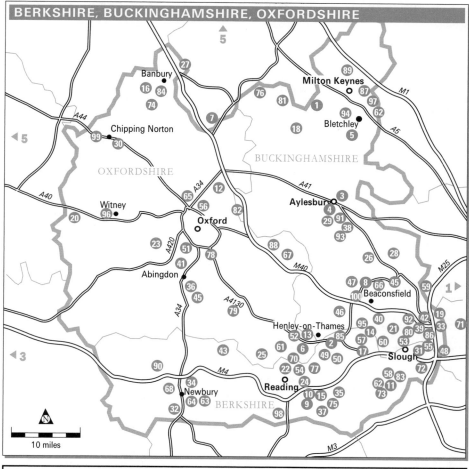

BERKSHIRE, BUCKINGHAMSHIRE, OXFORDSHIRE

KEY

1	Abbey Hill	19	The Buckinghamshire	40	Flackwell Heath
2	Aspect Park	20	Burford	41	Frilford Heath
3	Aylesbury	21	Burnham Beeches	42	Gerrards Cross
4	Aylesbury Park	22	Calcot Park	43	Goring & Streatley
5	Aylesbury Vale	23	Carswell Golf & CC	44	Hadden Hill
6	Badgemore Park	24	Castle Royle	45	Harewood Downs
7	Banbury	25	CavershamHeath GC	46	Harleyford Golf
8	Beaconsfield	26	Chartridge Park	47	Hazlemere Golf &
9	Bearwood	27	Cherwell Edge		Country Club
10	Bearwood Lakes	28	Chesham & Ley Hill	48	Heathpark GC
11	The Berkshire	29	Chiltern Forest	49	Henley Golf Club
12	Biecester Golf and	30	Chipping Norton	50	Hennerton
	Country Club	31	Datchet	51	Hinksey Heights
13	Billingbear Park	32	Deanwood Park	52	Huntercombe
14	Bird Hills	33	Denham	53	Huntswood
	(Hawthorn Hill)	34	Donnington Valley	54	Hurst
15	Blue Mountain Golf		Hotel	55	Iver
	Centre	35	Downshire	56	Kirtlington
16	Brailes	36	Drayton Park	57	Lambourne
17	Braywick	37	East Berkshire	58	Lavender Park Golf
18	Buckingham	38	Ellesborough		Centre
		39	Farnham Park (Bucks)	59	Little Chalfont

60	Maidenhead Golf Club	80	Stoke Poges Golf Club
61	Mapledurham	81	Stowe
62	Mill Ride	82	Studley Wood
63	Newbury & Crookham	83	Swinley Forest
64	Newbury Golf Centre	84	Tadmarton Heath
65	North Oxford	85	Temple
66	Oakland Park	86	Thorney Park
67	The Oxfordshire	87	Three Locks
68	Parasampia Golf and	87	Waterstock
	Country Club	89	Wavendon Golf Centre
69	Princes Risborough	90	West Berks
70	Reading	91	Weston Turville
71	Rectory Park	92	Wexham Park
72	Richings Park	93	Whiteleaf
73	Royal Ascot	94	Windmill Hill
74	Rye Hill	95	Winter Hill
75	Sandmartins	96	Witney Lakes
76	Silverstone	97	Woburn
77	Sonning	98	Wokefield Park
78	Southfield	99	The Wychwood
79	Springs Hotel & Golf	100	Wycombe Heights
	Club		Golf Centre

2B 1 Abbey Hill Golf Centre
Two Mile Ash, Milton Keynes, Bucks,
MK8 8AA
🖳 www.abbeyhillgc.co.uk
📧 info@abbeyhillgc.co.uk
☎ 01908 563845, Fax 569538,
Sec 562566
2 miles S of Stony Stratford.
Parkland course.
Pro C Iddon; Founded 1982
18 holes, 6025 yards, S.S.S. 69; 9 hole
par 3
⌇ Practice range, 21 bays floodlit.
† Public pay and play.
⌇ Available on application.
⤷ Welcome WD; golf and catering
packages.
🍽 Available.
⤷ Friendly Hotel, Milton Keynes.

2B 2 Aspect Park　　　　　　　☏
Remenham Hill, Remenham, Henley
On Thames, Oxon, RG9 3EH
🖳 www.aspectgolf.com
📧 enquiries@aspectgolf.com
☎ 01491 578306, Fax 578306,
Rest/Bar 410308
On A4130 Henley-Maidenhead road
0.75 miles from Henley.
Historic parkland course.
Pro Terry Notley; Founded 1988
Designed by Tim Winsland
18 holes, 6559 yards, S.S.S. 71
⌇ 6 bays covered, 6 open.
† Welcome.
⌇ WD £20; WE £25.
⤷ Welcome; terms on application.
🍽 Facilities available.
⤷ Red Lion.

2B 3 Aylesbury Golf Centre
Hulcott Lane, Bierton, Aylesbury,
Bucks, HP22 5GA
☎ 01296 393644, Rest/Bar 423350
1 mile N of Aylesbury on the A418
Leighton Buzzard road.
Parkland course.
Pro Richard Wooster; Founded 1992
Designed by TS Benwell
18 holes, 5965 yards, S.S.S. 69
⌇ Practice range, 30 floodlit bays.
† Welcome.
⌇ WD £10; WE £15.
⤷ Welcome at all times; terms on
application.
🍽 Facilities available.
⤷ Forte Crest; Holiday Inn.

2B 4 Aylesbury Park
Aylesbury Park Golf Club, Andrew's
Way, Aylesbury, Bucks, HP17 8QQ
☎ 01296 399196, Fax 336830

Just off A418.
Parkland course.
Founded 1996
Designed by Hawtree & Son
18 holes, 6150 yards, S.S.S. 69
† Welcome at all times.
⌇ WD £14; WE £20.
⤷ Welcome at all times; terms on
application.
🍽 Bar and servery.
⤷ Forte Post House; Hartwell
House.

2B 5 Aylesbury Vale　　　　　　☏
Stewkley Road, Wing, Leighton
Buzzard, Beds, LU7 0UJ
🖳 www.avgc.co.uk
📧 info@avgc.co.uk
☎ 01525 240196, Fax 240848
Course lies three miles W of Leighton
Buzzard between Wing and Stewkley.
Parkland course.
Pro James Pugh; Founded 1990
Designed by D Wright/Mick Robinson
18 holes, 6612 yards, S.S.S. 72
⌇ 9.
† Welcome with prior booking.
⌇ WD £17; WE £25.
⤷ Welcome midweek.
🍽 Meals and bar facilities.

2B 6 Badgemore Park　　　　　☏
Badgemore, Henley on Thames,
Oxon, RG9 4NR
🖳 www.badgemorepark.com
📧 info@badgemorepark.com
☎ 01491 637300, Fax 576899,
Pro 574175
1 mile North West from centre of
Henley-on-Thames.
Parkland course.
Pro J Dunn; Founded 1972
Designed by Bob Sandow
18 holes, 6129 yards, S.S.S. 69
† Welcome WD (except Tues am)
and WE afternoons only.
⌇ Fees on request from Pro
Shop/Secretary.
⤷ Welcome WD(wed, Thur, Fri only);
full catering facilities for lunch and
dinner; £39-£60.
🍽 Full facilities, management training
centre, overnight accommodation
available; function rooms.

2B 7 Banbury
Aynho Road, Adderbury, Banbury,
Oxon, OX17 3NT
📧 office@banburygolfcentre.co.uk
☎ 01295 812880, Fax 810056, Pro
812880, Sec 810419, Rest/Bar
810419

5 miles S of Banbury on the B4100;
10 mins from M40 Junction 10.
Parkland course.
Pro Stuart Kier; Founded 1994
Designed by Reed/Payn.
27 holes, 6536 yards, S.S.S. 71
† Welcome.
⌇ WD £17; WE £22 (18 holes).
⤷ Welcome by prior arrangement;
terms available on application.
🍽 Clubhouse facilities.

2B 8 Beaconsfield Golf Club
Seer Green, Beaconsfield, Bucks,
HP9 2UR
📧 secretary@beaconsfieldgolfclub
.co.uk
☎ 01494 676545, Fax 681148,
Pro 676616
Off M40 on to A355 Amersham road
adjacent to Seer Green/Jordans
railway station.
Parkland course.
Pro Michael Brothers; Founded 1902
Designed by HS Colt
18 holes, 6493 yards, S.S.S. 71
⌇ Practice range, 6 bays.
† Welcome WD with handicap
certificates.
⌇ WD £36 round, £50 day.
⤷ Welcome Tues and Wed.
🍽 Full facilities.
⤷ Bellhouse.

2B 9 Bearwood
Mole Road, Sindlesham, Berks,
RG11 5DB
☎ 0118 9761330, Pro 9760156,
Sec 9760060
On B3030 1.5 miles N of Arborfield
Cross.
Parkland course.
Pro Bayley Tustin; Founded 1986
Designed by B Tustin
9 holes, 5600 yards, S.S.S. 68
⌇ 10 bay covered driving range,
two chipping greens and practice
bunkers.
† Welcome WD; with member at
WE.
⌇ WD £18; WE £22 (18 holes).
⤷ Small societies welcome by prior
arrangement.
🍽 Facilities and special packages
available.
⤷ Reading Moat House.

2B 10 Bearwood Lakes
Keepers Cottage, Bearwood Road,
Wokingham, Berks, RG41 4SJ
🖳 www.bearwoodlakes.co.uk
📧 golf@bearwoodlakes.co.uk

BADGEMORE PARK GOLF CLUB
Badgemore, Henley-on-Thames, Oxon RG9 4NR
In the heart of the Chilterns, superb challenging 18 hole mature parkland course. Offering a friendly welcome to all golfers. S.S.S. 69, chipping green, 2 putting greens, practice nets and bunkers. Visitors and Societies welcome. C19th Clubhouse with restaurant, spike bar; en suite accommodation available. PGA Professional Jonathan Dunn (01491 574175). Large car park. Ideally located close to M4 & M40.
Tel: 01491 637300   Fax: 01491 576899   Email: info@badgemorepark.com

☎ 0118 9797900, Fax 97972911, Pro 9783030, Sec 9797900, Rest/Bar 9797900
Half a mile S of M4 Junction 10 for Wokingham & Sindlesham.
Woodland course.
Pro Tim Waldron; Founded 1995
Designed by Martin Hawtree
18 holes, 6857 yards, S.S.S. 72
⌁ Practice ground.
† Members and guests only.
⌙ WD £30; WE £35.
⌁ Not allowed.
🍴 Full facilities for members and guests.
🛏 The Moat House.

2B 11 The Berkshire
Swinley Road, Ascot, Berks, SL5 8AY
☎ 01344 621495, Fax 623328, Pro 622351
On A332 between Ascot and Bagshot, off J3 M3.
Heathland course.
Pro Paul Anderson; Founded 1928
Designed by Herbert Fowler
2 x 18 holes, 6379/6260 yards, S.S.S. 71/71
⌁ Lessons by arrangement with Pro.
† Welcome WD by prior arrangement with the secretary.
⌙ WD £75 1 round, £100 for two.
⌁ Welcome by prior arrangement; packages available.
🍴 Full clubhouse facilities.
🛏 Berystede; Cricketers; Royal Foresters.

2B 12 Bicester Golf and Country Club
Chesterton, Bicester, Oxon, OX26 1TE
🖥 bicestergolf@ukonline.co.uk
☎ 01869 241204, Fax 240754, Pro 242023
1 mile from M40 exit 9 by A41 towards Bicester, 2nd left, left again at Red Cow, 150 yards on right.
Meadowland course.
Pro Julian Goodman; Founded 1973
Designed by RR Stagg
18 holes, 6229 yards, S.S.S. 70
⌁ Practice ground.

† Welcome.
⌙ Prices on application.
⌁ By arrangement; min 16 persons; full facilities.
🍴 Bar and bar snacks and full restaurant.
🛏 Littlebury (Bicester).

2B 13 Billingbear Park Golf Course
The Straight Mile, Wokingham, Berks, RG40 5SJ
🖳 www.billingbeargolf.co.uk
☎ 01344 869259, Fax 869259, Pro 869259, Sec 869259, Rest/Bar 869259
From M4 Junction 10 take A329M to Binfield; after Coppid Beech roundabout, left at Travelodge lights; then left into Foxley Lane; left at T junction to mini roundabout, then right for 1 mile.
9 hole Parkland course; second 9 hole course, par 3 with feature waterholes.
Pro Martin Blainey; Founded 1980
9 holes, 5750 yards, S.S.S. 68
† Pay and play; advance booking available.
⌙ Terms on application.
⌁ Welcome by arrangement only.
🍴 None; clubhouse planned; excellent pub 5 mins away.
🛏 Coppid Beech.

2B 14 Bird Hills
Drift Road, Hawthorn Hill, Maidenhead, Berks, SL6 3ST
🖳 www.birdhills.co.uk
🖥 info@birdhills.co.uk
☎ 01628 771030, Fax 631023, Pro 07973 324203/635153
M4 Junction 8/9; take A330 towards Bracknell for 2.5 miles; course on right at crossroads.
Parkland course.
Pro Nick Slimming; Founded 1984
Designed by Clive D Smith
18 holes, 6176 yards, S.S.S. 70
⌁ Practice range, 36 floodlit bays.
† Welcome subject to club competitions; pay as you play.
⌙ WD £17; WE £22.

⌁ Welcome WD; packages available; terms on application.
🍴 Extensive facilities including baronial function room.
🛏 Holiday Inn, Maidenhead; Frederick's Maidenhead; Thames Riviera, Maidenhead.

2B 15 Blue Mountain Golf Centre
Wood Lane, Binfield, Bracknell, Berks, RG42 4EX
☎ 01344 300200, Fax 360960
At Binfield on the A322 off the A329.
Parkland course with lake features.
Founded 1992
18 holes, 6097 yards, S.S.S. 70
⌁ Practice range, 33 bays; floodlit with video and tuition.
† Welcome any day.
⌙ WD £16; WE £22.
⌁ Welcome.
🍴 Full restaurant and hospitality facilities.

2B 16 Brailes
Sutton Lane, Lower Brailes, Banbury, Oxon, OX15 5BB
🖳 www.brailes-golf-club.co.uk
🖥 office@brailes-golf-club.co.uk
☎ 01608 685633, Fax 685205, Pro 685633, Sec 685336, Rest/Bar 685611
On B4035 4 miles from Shipston on Stour towards Banbury.
Parkland/meadowland course.
Pro Alastair Brown; Founded 1992
Designed by Brian A Hull
18 holes, 6304 yards, S.S.S. 70
⌁ Practice area, 14 bays.
† Welcome.
⌙ WD £25; WE £35.
⌁ Welcome Mon, Tues, Fri and afternoons on Wed and Thurs; lunch and dinner available; from £30.
🍴 Full facilities and bar.
🛏 The George at Lower Brailes.

2B 17 Braywick
Braywick Road, Maidenhead, Berks, SL6 1DH
☎ 01628 676910
On A308 Maidenhead-Windsor road.

Parkland course.
Pro Mike Upcott; Founded 1992
Designed by Mike Upcott
9 holes, 2514 yards, S.S.S. 55
⚑ Practice and driving range.
♟ With member only.
☼ £8 Full Day.
♪ Terms on Application.
🍴 By arrangement.
🛏 Oakley Court.

2B 18 **Buckingham**
Tingewick Road, Tingewick,
Buckingham, Bucks, MK18 4AE
☎ 01280 815566, Fax 821812, Pro
815210, Rest/Bar 813282
2 miles SW of Buckingham on A421.
Parkland course.
Pro Gregor Hannah; Founded 1914
18 holes, 6068 yards, S.S.S. 69
♟ Welcome WD.
☼ WD £30 (day ticket).
♪ Welcome Tues and Thurs; bar,
restaurant, conference facilities, full
day's golf.
🍴 Full facilities.
🛏 Beales Hotel; Villiers.

2B 19 **Buckinghamshire**   ☏
Denham Court Drive, Denham, Bucks,
UB9 5PG
🖥 www.buckinghamshiregc.com
✉ golf@bucks.dircon.co.uk
☎ 01895 835777, Fax 835210, Pro
836814, Sec 836804
Follow signs to Denham Country Park
from M40 Junction 1 or M25 Junction 16.
Gently undulating parkland course.
Pro John O'Leary; Founded 1992
Designed by John Jacobs
18 holes, 6880 yards, S.S.S. 73
⚑ Up to 12 grass driving, extensive
short game practice area.
♟ Mon–Thurs.
☼ WD £80; WE £90 and Bank
Holidays.
♪ By prior arrangement only; full
catering and bar facilities; lunch and
dinner; £90-£130; winter £65.
🍴 Catering and clubhouse bar and
Restaurant Heron Fine Dining.
🛏 The Bull Hotel and the Bellhouse
both in Gerrards Cross.

2B 20 **Burford**
Burford, Oxon, OX18 4JG
🖥 www.burfordgc.co.uk
✉ robin@burfordgc.firenet.co.uk
☎ 01993 822583, Fax 822801, Pro
822344, Sec 822583, Rest/Bar 822149
19 miles W of Oxford at junction of A40
and A361 at Burford roundabout.

Parkland course.
Pro Michael Ridge; Founded 1936
Designed by J H Turner.
18 holes, 6408 yards, S.S.S. 71
♟ By arrangement.
☼ Apply for details.
♪ By arrangement.
🍴 Full facilities.
🛏 Several.

2B 21 **Burnham Beeches**
Green Lane, Burnham, Slough, Berks,
SL1 8EG
🖥 www.bbgc.co.uk
✉ enquiries@bbgc.co.uk
☎ 01628 661448, Fax 668968,
Pro 661661, Sec 661448,
Rest/Bar 661150
M40 exit Beaconsfield Junction 2,
follow signs to Slough, A355 as far as
Farnham Royal at second mini
roundabout, turn right and follow
Burnham signs (not Burnham
Beeches) to Green Lane.
Parkland course.
Pro Ronnie Bolton; Founded 1891
18 holes, 6449 yards, S.S.S. 71
♟ Welcome WD; at WE only with
member.
☼ WD £40.
♪ Welcome Wed, Thurs, Fri; full
catering facilities; from £62.
🍴 Full facilities except Mon.

2B 22 **Calcot Park**
Bath Road, Calcot, Reading, Berks,
RG31 7RN
✉ info@calcotpark.com
☎ 01189 427124, Fax 453373, Pro
427797, Rest/Bar 414952
1.5 miles from M4 Junction 12 on A4.
Parkland course.
Pro I J Campbell; Founded 1930
Designed by HS Colt
18 holes, 6283 yards, S.S.S. 70
♟ Welcome WD.
☼ WD £40.
♪ Welcome WD.
🍴 Full facilities.
🛏 Calcot Hotel (www.calcotpark.com
for details).

2B 23 **Carswell Golf & Country
Club**
Carswell Home Farm, Carswell,
Faringdon, Oxon, SN7 8PU
🖥 www.carswellgolfandcountryclub
.co.uk
✉ info@carswellgolfandcountryclub
.co.uk
☎ 01367 870422, Fax 870592,
Pro 870505, Rest/Bar 870472

Off A420 near Faringdon, midway
between Swindon and Oxford.
Parkland course.
Pro Steve Parker; Founded 1993
Designed by Ely Brothers
18 holes, 6183 yards, S.S.S. 70
⚑ Practice range, 19 bays covered
floodlit.
♟ Welcome at all times.
☼ WD £18; WE £25.
♪ Welcome WD only; full facilities;
terms on application.
🍴 Full facilities in attractive
clubhouse.
🛏 Carswell Country Club Hotel rooms.

2B 24 **Castle Royle**
Bath Road, Knowl Hill, Reading, Berks,
RG10 9XA
🖥 www.clubhaus.com
✉ castleroyle.retail@clubhaus.com
☎ 01628 829252, Fax 829299,
Pro 825442, Golf Ops Mgr 825442,
Rest/Bar 820711
From M4 Junction 8/9 follow A4 signs
to Reading and course is 2.5 miles.
Inland links course.
Pro Robert Watts; Founded 1992
Designed by Neil Coles
18 holes, 6828 yards, S.S.S. 73
⚑ Function room available for hire,
golf tuition for non members, 24000 sq
ft health and fitness cub, driving range.
♟ Members and their guests only.
☼ Not applicable.
🍴 Facilities available.
🛏 Bird in Hand; Holiday Inn,
Maidenhead.

2B 25 **Caversham Heath Golf ☏
Club**
Mapledurham, Reading, RG4 7UT
🖥 www.cavershamgolf.co.uk
✉ golf@cavershamgolf.co.uk
☎ 0118 947 8600, Fax 8700,
Pro 9400
In Mapledurham on
Oxfordshire/Reading border, just
outside Reading.
Slightly hilly.
Pro Carl Rutherford.
Designed by David Williams.
18 holes, 7151 yards
⚑ Driving range.
♟ Yes.
☼ WD £29, WE £40.
♪ Yes.
🍴 Restaurant.
🛏 In Caversham.

2B 26 **Chartridge Park**   ☏
Chartridge, Chesham, Bucks, HP5 2TF

www.cpgc.co.uk
☎ 01494 791772
From M25 Junction 19 take A41 W to
Aylesbury until Chesham sign.
Parkland course.
Pro Peter Gibbins; Founded 1989
Designed by John Jacobs
18 holes, 5580 yards, S.S.S. 67
† Welcome with booking.
Ⅼ WD £30; WE £35.
Welcome by arrangement;
unlimited golf and catering.
Full catering facilities.
Club can recommend.

2B 27 Cherwell Edge
Chacombe, Banbury, Oxon, OX17 2EN
cegc@ukonline.co.uk
☎ 01295 711591, Fax 713674,
Pro 711591, Sec 711591,
Rest/Bar 711591
3 miles E of Banbury, A442 to
Northampton; 1.5 miles E of M40
Junction 11.
Parkland course.
Founded 1983
Designed by Richard Davies
18 holes, 5947 yards, S.S.S. 68
Practice range, 18 bays; floodlit.
† Welcome any time.
Ⅼ WD £12; WE £16.
Welcome by arrangement; full
facilities; £48 full day.
Lunches, bar snacks, evening
meals.
Whatley Arms.

2B 28 Chesham & Ley Hill
Ley Hill, Chesham, Bucks, HP5 1UZ
www.lhggolfclub.co.uk
☎ 01494 784541, Fax 785506,
Rest/Bar 783652
Course is off the A41 on the B4504 to
Ley Hill.
Parkland course.
Founded 1900
9 holes, 5296 yards, S.S.S. 65
† Welcome Mon and Thurs all day;
afternoon Wed and all day Fri until 4pm.
Ⅼ WD £15.
Welcome on Thurs by prior
arrangement; full catering facilities and
36 holes of golf; various menus; from
£39.
Restaurant and packages.
Crown, Old Amersham.

2B 29 Chiltern Forest
Aston Hill, Halton, Aylesbury, Bucks,
HP22 5NQ
www.chilternforest.co.uk
secretary@chilternforest.co.uk

01296 631267, Fax 632709, Pro
631817, Rest/Bar 630899
Between Aylesbury, Tring & Wendover.
Wooded hilly course.
Pro Andy Lavers; Founded 1920
18 holes, 5760 yards, S.S.S. 70
† Welcome WD; with member at WE.
Ⅼ WD £30; £30 2-for-1 with a
Telegraph ticket.
Welcome Tue, Wed and Thurs; full
day of golf, lunch and dinner; £45.
Full facilities.
Red Lion, Wendover; Forte,
Aylesbury.

2B 30 Chipping Norton
Southcombe, Chipping Norton, Oxon,
OX7 5QH
chipping.nortongc@virgin.net
☎ 01608 641150, Fax 645422, Pro
643356, Sec 642383, Rest/Bar 644321
Follow A44 to Evesham from Oxford
and turn left at Chipping Norton sign;
club 50 yards.
Downland course.
Pro Neil Rowlands; Founded 1890
18 holes, 6241 yards, S.S.S. 70
Practice area.
† Welcome WD; with members at
WE.
Ⅼ WD £32; WE £16 with a member.
Welcome WD by prior
arrangement; morning coffee, buffet
lunch and evening meal with full day of
golf (27 or 36 holes).
Full facilities.
Crown & Cushion; White Hart; Fox,
all Chipping Norton.

2B 31 Datchet
Buccleuch Road, Datchet, Slough,
Berks, SL3 9BP
www.datchetgolfclub.co.uk
secretary@datchetgolfclub.co.uk
☎ 01753 543887, Fax 541872,
Pro 545222, Sec 541872
Close to Slough and Windsor, easy
access from M4.
Parkland course.
Pro Ian Godleman; Founded 1890
Designed by J H Taylor
9 holes, 6087 yards, S.S.S. 70
† Welcome WD.
Ⅼ WD £20.
Small societies welcome by prior
arrangement; full facilities.
Bar snacks and lunches available.
The Manor.

2B 32 Deanwood Park
R Snook And Son, Baydon Road,
Stockcross, Newbury, Berks, RG20 8JS

deanwood@newburyweb.net
☎ 01635 572820, Fax 572827, Pro,
572822, Sec 572824, Rest/Bar 572828
From the A4 take the B4000 towards
Stockcross; the course lies 500 yards
on the right.
Parkland course.
Pro James Purton; Founded 1995
Designed by Col. Dion Beard
9 holes, 4228 yards, S.S.S. 60
10 bays.
† Welcome with prior booking.
Ⅼ WD £14.50; WE £17.50.
Welcome by prior arrangement; full
practice, clubhouse facilities; packages
available; terms on application.
Bar and restaurant facilities
available.
Elcot Park; The Vineyard.

2B 33 Denham
Tilehouse Lane, Denham, Uxbridge,
Middx, UB9 5DE
club.secretary@
denhamgolfclub.co.uk
☎ 01895 832022, Fax 835340, Pro
832801
From M40 take Uxbridge/Gerrards
Cross turn off on to A40 towards
Gerrards Cross; right on to A412
towards Watford; 2nd turning left.
Parkland course.
Pro Stuart Campbell; Founded 1910
Designed by HS Colt
18 holes, 6462 yards, S.S.S. 71
† Welcome Mon-Thurs by prior
arrangement.
Ⅼ 18: £55; 18+: £75
Welcome Tues, Wed, Thurs by
prior arrangement; from £130 for full
day's package and £73 for half a day.
Full facilities; lunches served daily.
Bull, Gerrards Cross.

2B 34 Donnington Valley Hotel
Donnington Valley Golf Club, Snells
Moore Common, Newbury, Berks,
RG14 3BG
www.donnigtonvalleygolfclub
.co.uk
☎ 01635 568140, Fax 568141, Pro
568142, Sec 568140
Off the Old Oxford Road N of Newbury.
Parkland course.
Pro Martin Balfour; Founded 1985
Designed by Mike Smith
18 holes, 6358 yards, S.S.S. 71
† Welcome.
Ⅼ WD £24; WE £32.
Welcome by prior arrangement;
packages on request.
Full facilities.

Donnington Valley Hotel (on site).

2B 35 Downshire
Easthampstead Park, Wokingham, Berks, RG11 3DH
downshiregc@ bracknell\forest.golf.uk
01344 302030, Fax 301020
Between Bracknell and Wokingham off Nine Mile Ride.
Municipal parkland course.
Pro Wayne Owers/Tim Neil; Founded 1973
Designed by F Hawtree
18 holes, 6416 yards, S.S.S. 71
Practice range, 30 bays covered, floodlit.
Welcome.
WD £17.60; WE £21.75.
Welcome by arrangement.
Full bar and restaurant.
Ladbroke Mercury; St Annes Manor.

2B 36 Drayton Park
Stevington Rd, Abingdon, Oxon, OX14 4LA
draytonpark@btclick.com
01235 528989, Fax 525731, Pro 550607, Rest/Bar 539339
2 miles S of Abingdon off A34.
Parkland course.
Pro Martin Morbey; Founded 1992
Designed by Hawtree & Co
18 holes, 5503 yards, S.S.S. 67
Practice range, 21 bays; floodlit
Also 9 holes, 776 yards, par 3.
Welcome.
WD from £17.95; WE from £19.95.
Welcome; packages available.
Full bar and dining facilities.
Abingdon Four Pillows, Milton Travel Lodge.

2B 37 East Berkshire
Ravenswood Avenue, Crowthorne, Berks, RG45 6BD
01344 772041, Fax 777378
M3 Junction 3 towards Bracknell and follow Crowthorne signs to railway station.
Heathland course.
Pro D Kelly; Founded 1903
Designed by P Paxton
18 holes, 6344 yards, S.S.S. 70
Welcome WD.
WD £40.
Welcome Thurs and Fri only; golf, lunch and dinner; £65.
Clubhouse facilities.
Waterloo.

2B 38 Ellesborough
Wendover Road, Butlers Cross, Aylesbury, Bucks, HP17 0TZ
01296 622114, Pro 623126, Rest/Bar Bar 622375 Rest.623514
On B4010 1 mile W of Wendover.
Undulating downland course.
Pro Mark Squire; Founded 1906
Designed by James Braid
18 holes, 6283 yards, S.S.S. 71
Welcome WD except Tues.
Terms on application.
Welcome by prior arrangement; packages available for full day's golf and catering; from £62.
Full clubhouse facilities available.
Red Lion, Wendover.

2B 39 Farnham Park
Park Road, Stoke Poges, Slough, Berks, SL2 4PJ
01753 647065, Pro 643332, Rest/Bar 643335
M4 Junction 5 take A355 to Farnham Pump; at 2nd roundabout turn right into Park Road.
Parkland course.
Pro Paul Warner; Founded 1977
Designed by Hawtree & Sons
18 holes, 6172 yards, S.S.S. 69
Public pay and play.
WD £10; WE £13.50.
Welcome Tues and Thurs; terms on application.
Full clubhouse facilities available.
Burnham Beeches.

2B 40 Flackwell Heath
Treadaway Road, Flackwell Heath, High Wycombe, Bucks, HP10 9PE
www.flackwellheathgolfclub.co.uk
info@flackwellheathgolfclub.co.uk
01628 520929, Fax 530040, Pro 523017, Rest/Bar 520027
Off A40 High Wycombe-Beaconsfield road at Loudwater roundabout; 1.5 miles from M40 Junction 3 or 4.
Undulating heathland course.
Pro Paul Watson; Founded 1905
Designed by Sherlock J Turner.
18 holes, 6211 yards, S.S.S. 70
Practice facilities are available.
Welcome WD with handicap certs.
WD £25.
Welcome Wed & Thurs only.
Full facilities Tues-Sun; limited Mon.
Bellhouse; Papermill.

2B 41 Frilford Heath
Oxford Road, Frilford Heath, Abingdon, Oxon, OX13 5NW
secretary@frilfordheath.co.uk

01865 390864, Fax 390823, Pro 390887
3 miles W of Abingdon on A338.
Parkland/heathland course.
Pro Derek Craik; Founded 1908
Designed by JH Taylor, CK Cotton and S Gidman
3 x 18 holes, 6884; 6006; 6728 yards, S.S.S. 73; 69; 72
Welcome with handicap certs.
WD £55; WE £75.
Welcome WD; packages using 3 golf courses available; £70-£90.
Full clubhouse facilities available.
Four Pillars; Upper Reaches, both Abingdon; Westwood Hotel, Oxford.

2B 42 Gerrards Cross
Chalfont Park, Chalfont St Peter, Gerrards Cross, Bucks, SL9 0QA
secretary@gxgolf,co.uk
01753 883263, Fax 883593, Pro 885300, Rest/Bar 278513
Off A413 at Gerrards Cross.
Wooded parkland course.
Pro Matthew Barr; Founded 1922
Designed by Bill Pedlar
18 holes, 6212 yards, S.S.S. 70
Welcome WD with handicap certs.
WD £40.
Welcome on Thurs and Fri with handicap certs; terms on application.
Full facilities.
Bull; Bellhouse Gerrards Cross The Ethorpe.

2B 43 Goring & Streatley
Rectory Road, Streatley, Reading, Berks, RG8 9QA
01491 873229, Fax 875224, Pro 873715
On A417 Wantage Road 0.25 miles from the Streatley crossroads.
Parkland course.
Pro Jason Hadland; Founded 1895
18 holes, 6320 yards, S.S.S. 70
Welcome WD; WE with member.
WD £35.
Welcome by prior arrangement; packages available; from £55.
Full restaurant facilities.
Swan Diplomat, Streatley; Miller at Mansfield, Goring.

2B 44 Hadden Hill
Hadden Hill Golf Club, North Moreton, Didcot, Oxon, OX11 9BJ
www.haddenhillgolf.co.uk
info@haddenhillgolf.co.uk
01235 510410, Fax 511260, Rest/Bar 510656
On A4130 E of Didcot.

FRILFORD HEATH GOLF CLUB

Visitors and Societies are warmly welcomed to Frilford Heath Golf Club, one of a select group of complexes able to boast 54 holes of championship golf. Founded in 1908 on traditional heathland it offers a true test of golf on three distinctive course layouts. The recently enlarged and refurbished clubhouse also provides a warm and attractive atmosphere for refreshment and dining. For details please contact - **Frilford Heath Golf Club, Abingdon, Oxon OX13 5NW. Tel: 01865 390864**

Parkland course.
Pro Ian Mitchell; Founded 1990
Designed by Michael V Morley
18 holes, 6563 yards, S.S.S. 71
⚡ Practice range, 20 bays; floodlit.
✝ Welcome; telephone to reserve tee time.
🍴 WD £17; WE £22.
⟳ Welcome WD by arrangement; packages available; telephone for details.
🍴 Full bar and restaurant.
🍷 George; Springs, both Wallingford; George; White Hart, both Dorchester.

2B 45 Harewood Downs

Cokes Lane, Chalfont St Giles, Bucks, HP8 4TA
🖳 www.hdgc.co.uk
✉ secretary@hdgc.co.uk
☎ 01494 762184, Fax 766869, Pro 764102, Sec 762184
Course lies 2 miles E of Amersham on the A413.
Rolling tree-lined parkland course.
Pro GC Morris; Founded 1907
18 holes, 5958 yards, S.S.S. 69
✝ Welcome with advance application.
🍴 WD £38, £40 per day; WE £38: £45.
⟳ Welcome; 2 rounds of golf and full day's catering with refreshment hut; £63.50.
🍴 Full clubhouse facilities are available.

2B 46 Harleyford Golf Club ☎

Harleyford estate, Henley Road, Marlow, Bucks, SL7 2SP
🖳 www.harleyfordgolf..co.uk
✉ info@harleyfordgolf.co.uk
☎ 01628 816161, Fax 816160, Pro 816162, Sec 816172, Rest/Bar 816165
Course is on the A4155 Marlow-Henley road two miles from Marlow town centre.
Downland course.
Pro Lee Jackson; Founded 1996
Designed by Donald Steel
18 holes, 6798 yards, S.S.S. 72
⚡ Driving range for use by members; full practice areas.
✝ Welcome by arrangement.

🍴 Terms on application.
⟳ Welcome by prior arrangement; minimum 12 maximum 60; winter and summer packages available; terms on application.
🍴 Full clubhouse facilities.
🍷 Danesfield Housel Crown Plaza.

2B 47 Hazlemere Golf Club ☎

Penn Road, Hazlemere, High Wycombe, Bucks, HP15 7LR
🖳 www.hazlemeregolfclub.co.uk
✉ enquiry@hazlemeregolfclub.co.uk
☎ 01494 719300, Fax 713914, Pro 710396
B474 between Beckham Field and Hazlemere.
Parkland course.
Pro P Harrison; Founded 1982
Designed by Terry Murray
18 holes, 5807 yards, S.S.S. 69
⚡ Practice area for members.
✝ Welcome.
🍴 WD £30; WE £40.
⟳ Welcome; packages available; from £45.
🍴 Full restaurant and bar facilities.
🍷 White Harte, Beaconsfield; Bellhouse; Bull, Gerrards Cross; Crown, Amersham.

2B 48 Heathpark GC

Stockley Rd, West Drayton, Middx, UB7 8BQ
☎ 01895 444232, Fax 445122
In carpark of Crowne Plaza Hotel at M4 Junction 4.
Undulating heath/parkland course.
9 holes, 3856 yards, S.S.S. 62
✝ Welcome.
🍴 Pay and play: £7.
⟳ Limited facilities.
🍴 Tea and snacks only; hotel close by with full bar and restaurant facilities.

2B 49 Henley

Harpsden, Henley on Thames, Oxon, RG9 4HG
🖳 www.henleygc.com
✉ henleygolfclub@btinternet.com
☎ 01491 575742, Fax 412179, Pro 575710, Rest/Bar 575781

1 mile SW of Henley; off A4155 Henley-Reading road.
Parkland course.
Pro Mark Howell; Founded 1907
Designed by James Braid
18 holes, 6239 yards, S.S.S. 70
✝ Welcome WD with handicap certs and prior arrangement; WE with member.
🍴 WD £33.
⟳ Wed and Thurs only; packages available; £70.
🍴 Full clubhouse facilities.

2B 50 Hennerton ☎

Crazies Hill Road, Wargrave, Reading, Berks, RG10 8LT
🖳 www.hennertongolfclub.co.uk
☎ 0118 9401000, Fax 9401042, Pro 9404778
Off A321 into Wargrave village; club signposted.
Parkland course.
Pro William Farrow; Founded 1992
Designed by Col. Dion Beard
9 holes, 5460 yards, S.S.S. 67
⚡ Practice range, 7 bays.
✝ Welcome with prior booking.
🍴 WD £12, WE £15 (9 holes), WD £17, WE £20 (18 holes).
⟳ Welcome; terms on application.
🍴 Full bar and restaurant facilities.

2B 51 Hinksey Heights

South Hinksey, Oxford, Oxon, OX1 5AB
🖳 www.oxford-golf.co.uk
✉ clay@oxford-golf.co.uk
☎ 01865 327 775, Fax 736930
Off the A34 at Oxford between the Botley and Hinksey Hill interchanges.
Heathland and links type course with water coming into play.
Pro David Bolton; Founded 1996
Designed by David Heads
18 (also 9-hole par 3), 7023 yards, S.S.S. 74
✝ Welcome any time.
🍴 WD £15; WE and BH £20.
⟳ Welcome any time by prior arrangement.
🍴 Fully licensed bar providing home cooked meals and snacks.
🍷 Oxford Holiday Inn.

Royal Ascot

For 117 years Royal Ascot Golf Club has enjoyed one of the most striking settings in the middle of the racecourse. For a week every year play is suspended while the Royal race meeting takes place but the members have always accepted that minor irritation with alacrity.

However the decision to rebuild the racecourse has meant an upheaval to test the most patient of Royal Ascot members. The new plans for racing mean that the Ascot jump track will be moved to a line where the current clubhouse stands.

All this has meant that since September 2003 their course has been restricted to nine holes while they await the completion of a new 18-hole course across the Winkfield Road. Work started on the new course in January and it is planned that it will be open for members in August 2004 and by the spring of 2005 the club hopes that visitors will be able to use the new course.

The Royal Ascot authorities have agreed to pay for the course while the golf club is funding their new clubhouse. "The Royal club is 117 years old but golf was played on the present land before that. A lot of our history was lost in a fire around 30 years ago and we are still trying to complete our old records. While we have been around for a considerable time it is not as long as there has been horse-racing here", said Keith Wetherell a director of Royal Ascot.

The members have mixed feelings over the new course. There is sadness for the end of the heathland of their former home but an excited anticipation over the new course – a mixture of pasture and woodland.

"It will be a different course. It covers 150 acres of land as opposed to the 50 acres of our old course and it will be rather longer than our previous 18 holes but I think it is a more testing course. Our members will have to reacquaint themselves with trees as there is woodland and some copses, not something that they have been used to. They will be on very much of a learning curve when the new course opens.

"The whole thing has been going on for some time now and we have been through despondency as well as elation but there really was no alternative for us. We will be sad to leave but very keen to get playing on our new course", said Mr Wetherell.

The traffic congestion brought about by Royal Ascot races, which are scheduled to return from their temporary home at York in 2006, may mean that the golfers will be denied unlimited access for the week, but that is nothing new and will be forgotten when they get to play a full 18 holes.

Club captain Malcolm Reid said: "We are very sorry to be leaving the Heath with all its history but we are going to have a magnificent new set-up".

One feature that remains unaffected is Royal Ascot Cricket Club, the close neighbours of the golf club, they will continue to play in the middle of the redesigned racecourse. – **Jon Ryan**

2B 52 **Huntercombe**
Huntercombe, Nuffield, Henley On Thames, Oxon, RG9 5SL
☎ 01491 641207, Fax 642060, Pro 641241
On A4130 6 miles from Henley towards Oxford.
Woodland/heathland course.
Pro David Ressin; Founded 1901
Designed by Willie Park Jnr
18 holes, 6311 yards, S.S.S. 70
† Welcome WD; no 3 or 4 balls.
⌊ WD £28/40.
⟲ Welcome Tues and Thurs only.
🍽 Restaurant and bar facilities.
⌂ White Hart, Nettlebed.

2B 53 **Huntswood Golf Course**
Taplow Common Road, Burnham, Slough, Berks, SL1 8LS
🖥 www.huntswoodgolf.com
☎ 01628 667144, Fax 663145
Off M4 Junction 7; turn left at round-about and then right at next mini-roundabout; straight on for 1.5 miles and course is just past Grovefield Hotel.
Wooded valley course.
Pro Neil Pagett; Founded 1996
18 holes, 5229 yards, S.S.S. 65
† Welcome.
⌊ WD £15; WE £18.
⟲ Welcome by prior arrangement with club manager Mark Collard; packages available; terms on application.
🍽 Full bar and catering; Sun lunches.

2B 54 **Hurst**
Hurst Grove, Sandford Lane, Hurst, Reading, Berks, RG10 0SQ
☎ 0118 9344355, Sec 9344355
Between Reading and Twyford signposted from Hurst village.
Parkland course.
Pro Justin Hennesey; Founded 1977
9 holes, 6308 yards, S.S.S. 70
⌶ Practice green.
† Welcome.
⌊ WD £6.50; WE £8 OAP £4 Mon-Fri
⟲ Welcome by prior arrangement.
🍽 Bar facilities.

2B 55 **Iver Golf & Leisure**
Hollow Hill Lane, Iver, Bucks, SL0 0JJ
☎ 01753 655615, Fax 654225
Near Langley station.
Parkland course.
Pro Jim Lynch; Founded 1984
Designed by Garreth Davies.
9 holes, 2573 yards, S.S.S. 66;
9 hole short course, 1407 yards, Par 29
⌶ Practice range, 18 bays, 9 covered.
† Welcome.

⟲ Welcome; packages available; terms on application.
🍽 Full facilities.
⌂ Marriott.

2B 56 **Kirtlington**
Kirtlington Golf Club, Kirtlington, Kidlington, Oxon, OX5 3JY
🖥 www.kirtlingtongolfclub.co.uk
✉ info@kirtlingtongolfclub.co.uk
☎ 01869 351133, Fax 351143, Pro 0800 587 2489
On A4095 to Kirtlington off M40 J9.
Parkland course.
Pro Andy Taylor; Founded 1995
Designed by Graham Webster
27 holes: 18 holes, 6107 yards, S.S.S. 69; 9 holes, 1546 yards, Par 30
⌶ Practice range, 12 bays, grass and covered; practice putting/chipping green.
† Welcome.
⌊ WD £20; WE £25.
⟲ Welcome; packages available; terms on application.
🍽 Full facilities.

2B 57 **Lambourne**
Dropmore Road, Burnham, Slough, Berks, SL1 8NF
☎ 01628 666755, Fax 663301, Pro 662936, Rest/Bar 606716
From M4 Junction 7 to Slough and Burnham; M40 Junction 2 to Burnham.
Parkland course.
Pro David Hart; Founded 1991
Designed by Donald Steel
18 holes, 6771 yards, S.S.S. 72
⌶ Practice range, grass.
† Welcome WD with handicap certs.
⌊ Terms on application.
⟲ Not welcome.
🍽 Full clubhouse facilities available.
⌂ Burnham Beeches.

2B 58 **Lavender Park**
Swinley Road, Ascot, Berks, SL5 8BD
🖥 www.lavenderparkgolf.co.uk
✉ lavenderparkgolf@yahoo.co.uk
☎ 01344 893344, Pro 893344, Sec 893344, Rest/Bar 893344
On A329 opposite the Royal Foresters Hotel.
Parkland course.
Pro David Johnson; Founded 1974
9 holes, 2248 yards, S.S.S. 56
⌶ Practice range, 26 bays; floodlit.
† Welcome any time.
⌊ WD from £5; WE from £8.
⟲ Welcome by prior arrangement.
🍽 Full bar and catering facilities available.
⌂ Royal Foresters.

2B 59 **Little Chalfont**
Lodge Lane, Chalfont St Giles, Bucks, HP8 4AJ
☎ 01494 764877, Fax 762860, Pro 762942, Sec 764877, Rest/Bar 764877
From M25 Junction 18 take A404 towards Amersham; course first left after garden centre.
Parkland course.
Pro Mike Dunne; Founded 1982
Designed by James Dunne
9 holes, 5852 yards, S.S.S. 70
† Welcome by prior arrangement.
⌊ WD £11.50; WE £13.50.
⟲ Welcome by arrangement; package includes day's golf and full catering; £30.
🍽 Bar and clubhouse.
⌂ White Hart.

2B 60 **Maidenhead Golf Club**
Shoppenhangers Road, Maidenhead, Berks, SL6 2PZ
☎ 01628 624693, Fax 624693, Pro 624067, Sec 624693, Rest/Bar 620545
Off A404 signposted Henley.
Parkland course.
Pro S Geary; Founded 1896
18 holes, 6364 yards, S.S.S. 70
† Welcome WD; not afternoons on Fri. WE by prior arrangement.
⌊ WD £30; WE £35.
⟲ Welcome Wed and Thurs; terms on application; winter society.
Packages are £27.50 for food and golf on Mon-Thurs.
🍽 Full catering and bar facilities.
⌂ Fredericks; Holiday Inn.

2B 61 **Mapledurham**   ☏
Chazey Heath, Mapledurham, Reading, Berks, RG4 7UD
☎ 0118 9463353, Fax 9463363
Off A4074 NW of Reading 1.5 miles from Mapledurham village.
Undulating parkland course.
Pro Simon O'Keefe; Founded 1992
Designed by MRM Sandow
18 holes, 5621 yards, S.S.S. 67
⌶ Practice range.
† Welcome.
⌊ WD £15; WE £18.
⟲ Welcome by prior arrangement; packages available; terms on application.
🍽 Bar and restaurant facilities available.
⌂ Holiday Inn, Caversham.

2B 62 **Mill Ride**   ☏
Mill Ride Estate, Mill Ride, Ascot, Berks, SL5 8LT

🖳 www.mill-ride.com
☎ 01344 891494, Fax 886820,
Pro 886777, Sec 886777
From Ascot take A329 until lights, then right into Fernbank Road, which leads to Mill Ride.
Blend of parkland and links course.
Pro T Wylde; Founded 1991
Designed by Donald Steel
18 holes, 6762 yards, S.S.S. 72
ℹ Driving range; full practice facilities.
♣ Welcome by prior arrangement.
ℓ WD £50; WE £75.
☝ Welcome; terms on application.
🍽 Full catering and club facilities.
🛏 Royal Berkshire, Ascot; Berystede, Sunningdale.

2B 63 **Newbury & Crookham** ⚤
Burys Bank Road, Greenham,
Thatcham, Berks, RG19 8BZ
🖳 www.newburygolf.co.uk
📧 steve.myers@newburygolf.co.uk
☎ 01635 40035, Fax 40045, Pro 31201
4 miles SE of Newbury.
Wooded parkland course.
Pro David Harris; Founded 1873
Designed by JH Turner
18 holes, 5940 yards, S.S.S. 69
♣ Welcome WD.
ℓ WD £30 round, £35 day.
☝ Welcome by prior arrangement; terms on application.
🍽 Full clubhouse facilities.
🛏 Hilton, Newbury; Carnavon Arms, Burghclere.

2B 64 **Newbury Golf Centre**
Newbury Racecourse Plc, Newbury Racecourse, Newbury, Berks, RG14 7NZ
🖳 www.mitchgolf@ukf.net
📧 mitchgolf@ukf.net
☎ 01635 551464
Signposted off the A34 for racecourse/conference centre.
Parkland course.
Pro Nick Mitchell; Founded 1994
18 holes, 6500 yards, S.S.S. 70
ℹ Practice range, 20 floodlit bays.
♣ Welcome.
ℓ WD £15; WE £20.
☝ Welcome by prior arrangement.
🍽 Full catering facilities available.
🛏 Hilton National.

2B 65 **North Oxford Golf Club**
Banbury Road, Oxford, Oxon, OX2 8EZ
☎ 01865 554924, Fax 515921, Pro 553977

Between Kidlington and N Oxford 2.5 miles N of the city centre.
Parkland course.
Pro Robert Harris; Founded 1907
18 holes, 5456 yards, S.S.S. 67
♣ Welcome WD.
ℓ WD £25.
☝ Welcome by prior arrangement; packages available; terms on application.
🍽 Full facilities.
🛏 Moat House; Linton Lodge; Randolph.

2B 66 **Oakland Park**
Bowles Farm, Three Households, Chalfont St Giles, Bucks, HP8 4LW
☎ 01494 877333, Fax 874692, Pro 871277, Sec 871277, Rest/Bar 877323
Beaconsfield Junction off M40; course is off A413 Amersham road.
Parkland course.
Pro Alistair Thatcher; Founded 1994
Designed by J Gaunt
18 holes, 5208 yards, S.S.S. 66
ℹ Driving range.
♣ Welcome 7 days subject to availability.
ℓ WD/WE £25 (Twilight fees available).
☝ Welcome WD; terms on application.
🍽 Facilities available.
🛏 Bellhouse Hotel.

2B 67 **The Oxfordshire**
Rycote Lane, Thame, Oxon, OX9 2PU
🖳 www.theoxfordshiregolfclub.com
📧 info@theoxfordshiregolfclub.com
☎ 01844 278300, Fax 278003, Pro 278505
M40 Junction 7 turn right on to A329; club is 1.5 miles on right.
Championship parkland course; hosted B&H International Open 1996–99.
Pro Neil Pike; Founded 1993
Designed by Rees Jones
18 holes, 7187 yards, S.S.S. 75
ℹ Driving range – for members and golfers playing on the day only.
♣ Members' guests only.
ℓ WD £80; WE £100 (WE pm only).
☝ Welcome.
🍽 Outstanding clubhouse bar and catering facilities.
🛏 Manoir aux Quatre Saisons, Great Milton; Oxford Belfry, Milton Common.

2B 69 **Parasampia Golf & Country Club**
Donnington Grove, Donnington, Newbury, Berks, RG14 2LA
🖳 www.parasampia.com

📧 enquiry@parasampia.com
☎ 01635 581000, Fax 552259, Pro 551975
Follow signs to Donnington Castle off A34; after 2.5 miles, Grove Road is on the right.
Moorland/parkland course.
Pro Gareth Williams; Founded 1993
Designed by Dave Thomas
18 holes, 7108 yards, S.S.S. 74
ℹ Practice area (Bring your own balls).
♣ Must become day member.
ℓ WD £30; WE £35.
☝ Welcome; full facilities, tennis courts, lake fishing; from £36.
🍽 Japanese and English restaurant.
🛏 Donnington Grove Hotel (onsite).

2B 69 **Princes Risborough**
Lee Road, Saunderton Lee, Princes Risborough, Bucks, HP27 9NX
☎ 01844 346989, Fax 274838, Pro 274567
7 miles NW of High Wycombe on A4010.
Parkland course.
Pro Simon Lowry; Founded 1990
Designed by Guy Hunt
9 holes, 5522 yards, S.S.S. 66
ℹ Practice ground, tuition with Pro available by prior arrangement.
♣ Welcome.
ℓ WD £16; WE £21.
☝ Welcome by prior arrangement; packages available; terms on application.
🍽 Full clubhouse facilities available.
🛏 Rose and Crown, Saunderton.

2B 70 **Reading**
Kidmore End Road, Emmer Green, Reading, Berks, RG4 8SG
🖳 www.readinggolfclub.com
📧 secretary@readinggolfclub.com
☎ 0118 9472909, Fax 9464468, Pro 9476115, Sec 9472909, Rest/Bar 9472169
2 miles N of Reading off Peppard Road.
Parkland course.
Pro Scott Fotheringham; Founded 1910
Designed by James Baird
18 holes, 6212 yards, S.S.S. 70
♣ Welcome Mon-Thurs.
ℓ WD £30.
☝ Welcome Tues-Thurs; catering packages available; terms on application.
🍽 Full catering and bar facilities available.
🛏 Holiday Inn.

2B 71 **Rectory Park**
Northolt Golf Club Ltd, Huxley Close,
Northolt, Middx, UB5 5UL
☎ 020 88415550, Fax 88424735,
Pro 88458555, Sec 88415550,
Rest/Bar 88415550
Course is off the Target roundabout on
the M40, then the fourth turning on the
left.
Parkland course.
9 holes, 3000 yards, S.S.S. 52
✝ Welcome.
Ɩ Pay and play; £5.
⌂ No facilities.
🍽 Snack bar.

2B 72 **Richings Park**
North Park, Iver, Bucks, SL0 9DL
🖳 www.richingspark.co.uk
☎ 01753 655370, Fax 655409,
Pro 655352
From M4 Junction 5 head towards
Colnbrook; turn left at the lights to Iver.
Parkland course.
Pro Robert Mullane; Founded 1995
Designed by Alan Higgins
18 holes, 6094 yards, S.S.S. 69
ƛ Practice range, 12 bays; academy
course, tuition available.
✝ Welcome WD.
Ɩ WD £22.
⌂ Welcome by arrangement;
packages available; terms on
application.
🍽 Restaurant and function room
available.
↪ Marriott.

2B 73 **Royal Ascot**
Winkfield Road, Ascot, Berks, SL5 7LJ
📧 golf@royalascotgc.fsnet.co.uk
☎ 01344 625175, Fax 872330, Pro
624656, Sec 625175, Rest/Bar 622923
Inside Ascot racecourse.
Heathland course.
Pro Alastair White; Founded 1887
Designed by JH Taylor
9 holes, 5008 yards, S.S.S. 64
ƛ Yes.
✝ Members' guests only.
🍽 Restaurant.
↪ Royal Berkshire; Berystede.

2B 74 **Rye Hill**
Milcombe, Banbury, Oxon, OX15 4RU
☎ 01295 721818, Fax 720089, Pro
721818, Sec 721818, Rest/Bar 721818
Off A361 between Banbury and
Chipping Norton, take road signposted
Bloxham.
Links style hillside course; 2 holes
redesigned in late 1998.

Pro Tony Pennock; Founded 1993
18 holes, 6916 yards, S.S.S. 73
✝ Welcome.
Ɩ WD £20; WE £25.
⌂ Welcome by prior arrangement;
packages available; terms on
application.
🍽 Full facilities.
↪ White Horse.

2B 75 **Sandmartins** ☏
Finchampstead Road, Finchampstead,
Wokingham, Berks, RG40 3RQ
🖳 www.sandmartins.com
📧 sandmartins@sandmartins.com
☎ 0118 9792711, Fax 9770282, Pro
9770265
1 mile S of Wokingham & 4 miles from
Reading on B3016.
Parkland first 9; links style back 9.
Pro Andrew Hall; Founded 1993
Designed by ET Fox
18 holes, 6212 yards, S.S.S. 70
✝ Welcome WD.
Ɩ WD £30.
⌂ Welcome; minimum 12 in summer;
various packages available with dining
facilities in the Georgian style
clubhouse; terrace; video analysis;
terms on application.
🍽 Full clubhouse catering and bar
facilities.
↪ Stakis St Annes Manor.

2B 76 **Silverstone** ☏
Silverstone Road, Stowe, Buckingham,
Bucks, MK18 5LH
☎ 01280 850005, Fax 850156
5 miles beyond race track on
Silverstone road from Buckingham and
Stowe.
Farmland course.
Pro Rodney Holt; Founded 1992
Designed by David Snell
18 holes, 6558 yards, S.S.S. 72
ƛ Practice range, 11 bays.
✝ Welcome.
Ɩ WD £18; WE £25.
⌂ Welcome WD by prior
arrangement; private dining room;
swing analysis; terms on application.
🍽 Full bar and restaurant facilities.
↪ White Hart, Buckingham; Green
Man, Syresham; Travelodge, Towcester.

2B 77 **Sonning**
Duffield Road, Sonning, Reading,
Berks, RG4 6GJ
🖳 www.sonning-golf-club.co.uk
📧 secretary@sonning-golf-club.co.uk
☎ 0118 9693332, Fax 9448409, Pro
9692910, Rest/Bar 9272055

S of A4 between Reading and
Maidenhead.
Parkland course.
Pro Richard MacDougall; Founded 1914
18 holes, 6366 yards, S.S.S. 70
✝ Welcome WD if carrying handicap
certs.
Ɩ WD £30-£40.
⌂ Welcome Wed; terms on
application.
🍽 Full clubhouse catering facilities
available.
↪ The Great House, Sonning.

2B 78 **Southfield** ☏
Hill Top Road, Oxford, Oxon, OX4 1PF
🖳 www.southfieldgolfclub.com
📧 sgcltd@btopenworld.com
☎ 01865 242158, Fax 728544,
Pro 244258
1.5 miles SE of Oxford city centre off
B480.
Undulating and picturesque parkland
course.
Pro Tony Rees; Founded 1875
Designed by James Braid (1875),
Redesigned H Colt (1923)
18 holes, 6320 yards, S.S.S. 70
✝ Welcome WD; with a member WE.
Ɩ Terms on application.
⌂ Welcome but must make prior
arrangement in writing; the home of
Oxford University GC, Oxford City and
Oxford Ladies; terms available on
application.
🍽 Full catering facilities are available
in Southfield restaurant.
↪ Randolph Hotel; Eastgate Hotel,
both Oxford; Travel Inn, Cowley.

2B 79 **Springs Hotel and Golf** ☏
Club
Wallingford Road, Noth Stoke,
Wallingford, Oxon OX10 6BE
🖳 www.thespringshotel.com
📧 golfclub@thespringshotel.com
☎ 01491 827315, Fax 827312,
Pro 827310
2 miles SW of Wallingford on B4009
(15 miles SE of Oxford; 12.5 miles NW
of Reading).
Parkland course.
18 holes, 6470 yards, Par 72
ƛ Short game practice area; practice
nets; putting green..
Ɩ WD £29; WE £35.
↪ 31-room Springs Hotel on site (tel:
01491 836687; fax: 836877).

2B 80 **Stoke Park Club (home of**
Stoke Poges Golf Club)
Park Road, Stoke Poges, Slough,
Berks, SL2 4PG
🖳 www.stokepark.com

info@stokepark.com
☎ 01753 717171, Fax 717181,
Pro 717172, Sec 717172,
Rest/Bar 717172
Take the exits from the M4 or A4 into
Slough, head for Stoke Poges Lane,
then into Park Road.
Parkland course.
Pro Stuart Collier; Founded 1909
Designed by HS Colt
27 holes, 6787 yards, S.S.S. 71
⚑ 15.
♦ Welcome.
⚑ WD £125; WE £200 (18 holes);
winter prices on application.
⚘ Society and corporate days
welcomed; various packages and
prices available on application to the
events organiser; terms on
application.
⚑ Full facilities.
⚘ Bellhouse; Bull, Gerrards Cross;
Copthorne, Slough; Chequers Inn,
Woburn Common.

2B 81 **Stowe**

Stowe School, Buckingham, Bucks,
MK18 5EH
⚑ www.stowe.co.uk
✉ bkemp@stowe.co.uk
☎ 01280 818280, Fax 818186,
Sec 818282
At Stowe school.
Parkland course.
Founded 1974
9 holes, 4573 yards, S.S.S. 63
♦ Private; members only.
⚑ WD £10; WE £10.

2B 82 **Studley Wood**   ♱

Straight Mile Road, Horton-cum-
Studley, Oxford, Oxon, OX33 1BF
⚑ www.studleywoodgolf.co.uk
✉ admin@swgc.co.uk
☎ 01865 351122, Fax 351166,
Pro 351122, Sec 351144,
Rest/Bar 351174
From M40 Junction 8 take A40 to
Headington roundabout; follow signs to
Horton-cum-Studley.
Woodland course.
Pro Tony Williams; Founded 1996
Designed by Simon Gidman
18 holes, 6315 yards, S.S.S. 71
⚑ Practice range, 13 bays.
♦ Welcome.
⚑ WD £34; WE £44; winter fees on
application.
⚘ Welcome only by prior
arrangement.
⚑ Restaurant and function room;
spike bar.
⚘ Studley Priory.

2B 83 **Swinley Forest**

Bodens Ride, Ascot, Berks, SL5 9LE
✉ swinleyfgc@aol.com
☎ 01344 620197, Fax 874733, Pro
874811, Sec 874979
2 miles S of Ascot.
Heathland course.
Pro S Hill; Founded 1909
Designed by HS Colt
18 holes, 6062 yards, S.S.S. 70
⚑ Driving range.
♦ Members' guests only.
⚑ WD/WE £80.
⚘ By introduction of a member only;
packages £150.
⚑ Clubhouse bar and catering.
⚘ Royal Berkshire; Highclere;
Berystede.

2B 84 **Tadmarton Heath**

Banbury, Oxon, OX15 5HL
⚑ www.thgc.btopenwold.com
✉ thgc@btopenworld.com
☎ 01608 737278, Fax 730548,
Pro 730047, Sec 737278,
Rest/Bar 737278
5 miles SW of Banbury off B4035.
High heathland course.
Pro Tom Jones; Founded 1922
Designed by Major C K Hutchison
18 holes, 5917 yards, S.S.S. 69
♦ Welcome WD by prior
arrangement.
⚑ WD £39.
⚘ Welcome WD except Thurs by
arrangement; 36 max; full day's golf,
coffee, lunch and dinner; £61.
⚑ Full facilities.
⚘ Banbury Manor; Wheatley Hall;
Cromwell Lodge.

2B 85 **Temple**

Henley Road, Hurley, Maidenhead,
Berks, SL6 5LH
✉ templegolfclub@btconnect.com
☎ 01628 824795, Fax 828119, Pro
824254, Rest/Bar 824248
Five mins from J4 M40 or J8/9 M4;
A404 then A4130; entrance r/hand side
of A4130.
Chalk downland course.
Pro James Whiteley; Founded 1908
Designed by Willie Park Jnr
18 holes, 6266 yards, S.S.S. 70
⚑ Practice area.
♦ By appointment only.
⚑ WD £40; WE £50.
⚘ By prior appointment; packages
available on request; coffee, lunch,
dinner all available.
⚑ Full clubhouse catering facilities.
⚘ Compleat Angler, Marlow; Bell Inn,
Hurley.

2B 86 **Thorney Park**

Thorney Mill Road, Iver, Bucks, SL0 9AL
⚑ www.thorneypark.com
☎ 01895 422095, Fax 431307,
Rest/Bar 436547
Off A4 at Langley into Parlaunt Road.
Parkland course.
Pro Andrew Killing; Founded 1993
Designed David Walker.
18 holes, 5731 yards, S.S.S. 68
⚑ Practice area; putting green.
♦ Welcome.
⚑ WD £19.50; WE £22 (18 holes).
⚘ Welcome; terms on application.
⚑ Restaurant.
⚘ Any Heathrow hotel.

2B 87 **Three Locks**

Partridge Hill, Great Brickhill, Milton
Keynes, Bucks, MK17 9BH
⚑ www.threelocks.co.uk
☎ 01525 270470, Fax 270470, Pro
270050, Sec 270470, Rest/Bar 270696
3 miles from Leighton Buzzard on
A4146.
Parkland course with several water
hazards.
Pro Gareth Harding; Founded 1992
Designed by MRM Sandow/P Critchley
18 holes, 6025 yards, S.S.S. 68
♦ Welcome; booking strongly
recommended.
⚑ WD £18.50; WE £23.
⚘ Welcome with prior booking;
various packages available to cover
day's golf and catering; terms on
application.
⚑ Full catering facilities available.
⚘ Limited accommodation on site.

2B 88 **Waterstock**   ♱

Thame Road, Waterstock, Oxford,
Oxon, OX33 1HT
⚑ www.waterstockgolf.co.uk
✉ wgc_oxfordgolf@btinternet.com
☎ 01844 338093, Fax 338036
Direct access from M40 Junction 8 and
Junction 8a on to A418 Thame road.
Parkland course.
Pro Paul Bryant; Founded 1994
Designed by Donald Steel
18 holes, 6535 yards, S.S.S. 71
⚑ 22 bays and floodlit.
♦ Welcome.
⚑ WD £18.50; WE £22.
⚘ Welcome by prior arrangement;
packages available for groups of up to
70; terms on application.
⚑ Bar and grill facilities.
⚘ Belfry (01844 279381), Milton;
County Inn; Travelodge, both
Wheatley. Days Inn-Junction 8a M40
(0800 0280 400).

2B 89 Wavendon Golf Centre ☎
Lower End Road, Wavendon, Milton
Keynes, Bucks, MK17 8DA
✉ jackbarker@btinternet.com
☎ 01908 281811, Fax 281257,
Pro 281011, Sec 281297
M1 Junction 13 to A421, 1st left at
r/bout; take1st left into Lower End Rd.
Parkland course.
Pro Greg Iron; Founded 1989
Designed by John Drake/Nick Elmer
18 holes, 5570 yards, S.S.S. 69
🏌 Driving range; 9-hole par 3 course.
2x9 hole pitch and putt. 9-hole
academy course.
† Public pay & play.
🏌 WD £12; WE £17.50.
⟳ Contact events co-ordinator.
🍴 Facilities; carvery, bar & bar snacks.
🛏 The Bell-Woburn.

2B 90 The West Berkshire
Chaddleworth, Newbury, Berks,
RG20 7DU
☎ 01488 638574, Fax 638781, Pro
638851
M4 Junction 14 follow signs to RAF
Welford.
Downland course.
Pro Paul Simpson; Founded 1975
Designed by R Stagg
18 holes, 7001 yards, S.S.S. 73
🏌 Yes and practice area.
† Welcome; afternoons only at WE.
🏌 WD £20; WE £30.
⟳ Welcome by prior arrangement;
packages available; terms on
application.
🍴 Full facilities.
🛏 Queens, E Gaston; The Crab,
Chiveley; Littlecote House, Hungerford.

2B 91 Weston Turville ☎
New Road, Weston Turville, Aylesbury,
Bucks, HP22 5QT
☎ 01296 424084, Fax 395376, Pro
425949
2 miles from Aylesbury between Aston
Clinton and Wendover.
Parkland course.
Pro Gary George; Founded 1975
18 holes, 6008 yards, S.S.S. 69
† Welcome except Sun am.
🏌 Terms on application.
⟳ Welcome WD, some WE, by prior
appointment; terms available on
application.
🍴 Lunches and evening snacks.
🛏 Holiday Inn.

2B 92 Wexham Park
Wexham Street, Wexham, Slough,
Berks, SL3 6ND

🖥 www.wexhamparkgolfcourse.co.uk
✉ wexhamgolf@freenetname.co.uk
☎ 01753 663271, Fax 663318
2 miles from Slough towards Gerrards
Cross; follow signs to Wexham Park
Hospital; 200 yrds from hospital.
Parkland course.
Pro John Kennedy; Founded 1977
Designed by Emil Lawrence and David
Morgan
18 holes, 5251 yards, S.S.S. 66;
9 holes, 2727 yards, S.S.S. 34;
9 holes, 2219 yards, S.S.S. 32
🏌 36 bays, 18 covered.
† Welcome.
🏌 18: WD £13; WE £17. 9: WD £8;
WE £9.50
⟳ Welcome; full catering facilities;
terms on application.
🍴 Bar and catering facilities.

2B 93 Whiteleaf
Upper Icknield Way, Whiteleaf, Bucks,
HP27 0LY
✉ whiteleafgc@tiscali.co.uk
☎ 01844 343097, Fax 275551,
Pro 345472, Sec 274058,
Rest/Bar 343097
From Monks Risborough turn right into
Casden Road and 100 yards on turn
right into Whiteleaf village; course 0.25
miles on left.
Hilly Chilterns course.
Pro Ken Ward; Founded 1904
9 holes, 5391 yards, S.S.S. 66
† Welcome WD and with member at
WE.
🏌 WD £20, £12 with member; WE
£12 only with member.
⟳ Welcome on Thurs by prior
arrangement; special packages
available.
🍴 Full facilities.
🛏 Red Lion; Whiteleaf; Rose &
Crown, Saunderton.

2B 94 Windmill Hill
Tattenhoe Lane, Bletchley, Milton
Keynes, Bucks, MK3 7RB
☎ 01908 631113, Fax 630034,
Pro 378623, Sec 366457,
Rest/Bar 630660 main number
Off A421 through Milton Keynes
towards Buckingham, M1 Junction 13
northbound 14 southbound.
Parkland course.
Pro Colin Clinghan; Founded 1972
Designed by Henry Cotton
18 holes, 6720 yards, S.S.S. 72
🏌 Practice range; 23 indoor, 6
outdoor bays, 3 putting greens, all year
round greens.
† Welcome.

🏌 WD £11; WE £15.
⟳ Welcome WD and after 11am at
WE; packages available for catering
and golf; from £10.50.
🍴 Full clubhouse facilities available.
🛏 Forte Crest, Milton Keynes;
Shenley, Bletchley.

2B 95 Winter Hill ☎
Grange Lane, Cookham, Maidenhead,
Berks, SL6 9RP
☎ 01628 527613, Fax 527479,
Pro 527610, Rest/Bar 527811
M4 Junction 8/9 through Maidenhead
to Cookham; club signposted.
Parkland course.
Pro Roger Frost; Founded 1976
Designed by Charles Lawrie
18 holes, 6408 yards, S.S.S. 71
† Welcome WD; with members at
WE afternoons.
🏌 Terms on application; £31 round.
⟳ Welcome Wed and Fri; packages
can be arranged; terms on
application.
🍴 Full facilities.
🛏 Spencers, Cookham.

2B 96 Witney Lakes ☎
Downs Road, Witney, Oxon, OX29
0SY
🖥 www.witney-lakes.co.uk
✉ resort@witney-lakes.co.uk
☎ 01993 893000, Fax 778866,
Pro 893011, Rest/Bar 893012
Course is W of Witney on the B4047
Burford road, 1.5 miles from town
centre.
Lakeland style course.
Pro Adam Souter; Founded 1994
Designed by Simon Gidman
18 holes, 6675 yards, S.S.S. 71
🏌 Practice range, 24 bays; floodlit.
† Welcome.
🏌 WD £18; WE £25.
⟳ Welcome; various packages
available; £28-£44.
🍴 Full clubhouse facilities.
🛏 Four Pillars, Witney.

**2B 97 Woburn Golf And
Country Club**
Little Brickhill, Milton Keynes, Bucks,
MK17 9LJ
🖥 www.woburngolf.com
✉ enquiries@woburngolf.com
☎ 01908 370756, Fax 378436,
Pro 626600
Course is four miles W of M1 Junction
13; half mile E of Little Brickhill, A5.
Woodland course.
Pro Luther Blacklock; Founded 1976

Designed by Charles Lawrie (Duke's/Duchess), Alex Hay (Marquess).
Duke's: 18 holes, 6975 yards, S.S.S. 74; Duchess: 18 holes, 6651 yards, S.S.S. 72; Marquess: 18 holes, 7214 yards, S.S.S. 72
⌁ Practice range.
† Welcome WD by prior arrangement.
⌐ Terms on application.
⌘ Welcome WD by prior arrangement; terms available on application.
🍽 Full clubhouse catering, restaurant and bar facilities.
⌁ The Inn at Woburn.

2B 98 **Wokefield Park** ☎
Mortimer, Reading, Berkshire, RG7 3AG
⌨ www.golf-isc.co.uk
✉ wokefieldgolf@initialstyle.co.uk
☎ 01189 334072
Exit from the M4 at Junction 11 and take the A33 towards Basingstoke. At first roundabout, take first exit, golf course is 2.5 miles down this road on the right.

Mature parkland course built in an American style.
Pro Gary Smith; Founded 1998
Designed by Jonathan Gaunt
18 holes, 7000 yards, S.S.S. 73
⌁ Driving range, 14 bays.
† Welcome any time.
⌐ WD £30; WE £45.
⌘ Welcome by prior arrangement.
🍽 3 restaurants.
⌁ Own accommodation: 300 rooms and full leisure facilities for residents.

2B 99 **The Wychwood** ☎
Lyneham, Chipping Norton, Oxon, OX7 6QQ
✉ golf@lynehamgc.freeserve.co.uk
☎ 01993 831841, Fax 831775, Pro 831841, Sec 831841, Rest/Bar 832011
1 mile off A361 Chipping Norton to Burford Road.
Parkland course with water hazards.
Pro James Fincher; Founded 1992
Designed by D Carpenter, A Smith
18 holes, 6707 yards, S.S.S. 72
⌁ 15.
† Welcome; after 11am at weekends; booking 3 days in advance.
⌐ WD £20; WE £24.

⌘ Welcome; full day's golf and catering; scorecard and scoreboard administration available; terms on application.
🍽 Full facilities.
⌁ Mill, Kingham; Crown & Cushion; Kings Arms, both Chipping Norton.

2B 100 **Wycombe Heights Golf Centre** ☎
Mobile Home Park, Rayners Avenue, Loudwater, High Wycombe, Bucks, HP10 9SW
☎ 01494 816686, Fax 816728
Exit M40 at Junction 3, A40 to High Wycombe, right in Rayner Avenue after half a mile.
Parkland course.
Pro Joseph Awuku; Founded 1991
Designed by John Jacobs
18 holes, 6253 yards, S.S.S. 72
⌁ Practice range, 24 floodlit bays.
† Pay and play.
⌐ Terms on application.
⌘ Welcome WD by prior arrangement; packages available.
🍽 Bar, restaurant, family room.
⌁ Post House Forte; Cressex; Alexandria.

THE SOUTH WEST

3A

Cornwall, Devon, Channel Islands

The royal, the ancient and the new can each be found in the region, occasionally even on the same golf course. Royal North Devon, aka Westward Ho!, is the oldest seaside course in England. Yet despite all that tradition, in 1934 a lady called Gloria Minoprio shocked the Western world by turning up to play golf at Westward Ho! in a pair of trousers, an event that Henry Longhurst recorded for posterity.

More recently Royal North Devon and neighbouring Saunton devised a match between the two clubs. The players teed up on the first at Saunton, played along the beach until they reached the narrowest part of the estuary, a carry of 170 yards, entered Westward Ho! near the eighth green and holed out on the eighteenth green. A tee peg was allowed for each shot or, in the case of the rocks along the shore, three polo mints. The 'hole' stretched seven miles and the winning pairing required just 61 strokes.

Golf in the area has come a long way since the pre-Monoprio days at Royal North Devon when players used to solve the problem of deteriorating holes by cutting a new one with a dinner knife and marking it with a gull's feather. Jack Nicklaus used rather more up to date equipment to build St Mellion in Cornwall, a course that is politely described as challenging.

Among the most loved of Cornish courses is St Enedoc. Sir John Betjeman once composed a poem on the subject of a birdie he achieved there. But if ever he hit his ball into the Himalayas that protect St Enedoc's sixth hole, alleged to be the largest sand dune on a British course, he was not moved to verse by that experience. With 326 miles of coastline and a climate that wavers between temperate and extremely cross Cornwall is full of first rate golf courses. Trevose and West Cornwall (often called Lelant) are amongst the best of them.

An even severer hazard than the Himalayas is the belief of some Cornish folk that everyone originating outside the county border is a foreigner. When one holidayer told an inquisitive local that he was from London, the overheard reply was, "Then either you are a pixie or a homosexual". Maybe such wacky independence is why no Cornish course has yet acquired royal status.

The same is not true of the Channel Islands who boast two royal courses and two regal golfers in Harry Vardon and Ted Ray, both of whom hailed from Jersey. It seems extraordinary that two winners of the US Open should both hail from an island more famous for its tomatoes than its golf courses.

Another US Open winner Tony Jacklin, who had found the British mainland rather too taxing, was made an honorary member of La Moye after he took up residency on the island. La Moye and Royal Jersey are both excellent links courses, although they can get pretty congested in the summer. Over the water Royal Guernsey is another fine course that has been known to suffer from the same problem.

Devon has its perils too – "they were the footprints of a gigantic hound" – but its courses tend to be slightly less crowded. The East Course at Saunton is the most highly regarded – when he was secretary of the R&A Sir Michael Bonallack is said to have harboured a dream of bringing an Open Championship to the course.

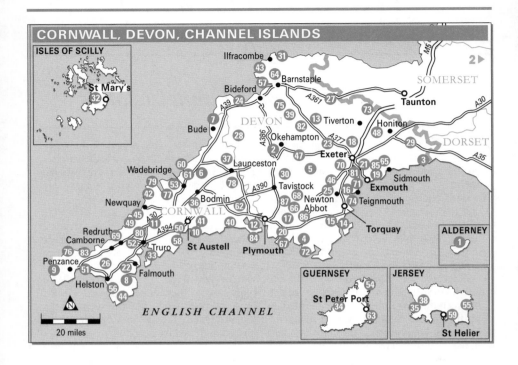

KEY					
1	Alderney	29	Honiton	59	St Clements
2	Ashbury	30	Hurdwick	60	St Enodoc
3	Axe Cliff	31	Ilfracombe	61	St Kew
4	Bigbury	32	Isles of Scilly	62	St Mellion International
5	Bovey Castle	33	Killiow Park	63	St Pierre Park Hotel
6	Bowood	34	La Grande Mare	64	Saunton
7	Bude and N Cornwall	35	La Moye	65	Sidmouth
8	Budock Vean Hotel	36	Lanhydrock	66	Sparkwell
9	Cape Cornwall Golf & Country Club	37	Launceston	67	Staddon Heights
		38	Les Ormes Golf and Leisure	68	Tavistock
10	Carlyon Bay Hotel			69	Tehidy Park
11	Carvynick	39	Libbaton	70	Teign Valley
12	China Fleet Country Club	40	Looe	71	Teignmouth
13	Chulmleigh	41	Lostwithiel Hotel G & CC	72	Thurlestone
14	Churston	42	Merlin	73	Tiverton
15	Dainton Park	43	Mortehoe & Woolacombe	74	Torquay
16	Dartmouth Golf & Country Club	44	Mullion	75	Torrington
		45	Newquay	76	Tregenna Castle Hotel
17	Dinnaton	46	Newton Abbot (Stover)	77	Treloy
18	Downes Crediton	47	Okehampton	78	Trethorne
19	East Devon	48	Padbrook Park (Cullompton)	79	Trevose Country Club
20	Elfordleigh Hotel Golf & Leisure			80	Truro
		49	Perranporth	81	Warren
21	Exeter Golf & CC	50	Porthpean	82	Waterbridge
22	Falmouth	51	Praa Sands	83	West Cornwall
23	Fingle Glen	52	Radnor Golf Centre	84	Whitsand Bay Hotel Golf and Country Club
24	Hartland Forest Golf & Leisure Park	53	Roserrow		
		54	Royal Guernsey	85	Woodbury Park Golf & Country Club
25	Hele Park	55	Royal Jersey		
26	Helston Golf and Leisure	56	Royal Naval Air Station Culdrose	86	Wrangaton
27	Highbullen Hotel			87	Yelverton
28	Holsworthy	57	Royal North Devon		
		58	St Austell		

A beautiful 18-hole course overlooking the sea in South Devon

BIGBURY GOLF CLUB

Bigbury-on-sea, South Devon TQ7 4BB; Club Pro (01548) 810412, Secretary (01548) 810557

No golfer visiting the South Hams should miss the opportunity of playing at Bigbury. It's an ideal holiday course - challenging enough for low handicappers but not too daunting for the average golfer. There are outstanding views from almost everywhere on the course - with Dartmoor to the North, the river Avon running near a number of holes and breathtaking scenes of Bantham beach and Burgh Island.

3A 1 Alderney
Route des Carrieres, Alderney, Guernsey, Channel Islands, GY9 3YD
☎ 01481 822835, Fax 823609, Sec 823981
1 Mile E of St Annes.
Undulating seaside course.
Designed by Frank Pennink
9 holes, 4964 yards, S.S.S. 65
† Welcome at all times; except competition days.
⌊ WD from £22.50; WE from £27.
⌗ Welcome by arrangement WD and WE; for special events catering available.
⍾ All day; arrangement for large parties.

3A 2 Ashbury
Higher Maddaford, Southcott, Okehampton, Devon, EX20 4NL
☎ 01837 55453, Fax 55468, Pro 55453, Sec 55453, Rest/Bar 55453
Leaving Okehampton, take Okehampton-Holsworthy Road A3079 and turn right to Ashbury; course half mile on right.
Hilly parkland course.
Pro Reg Cade; Founded 1991
Designed by DJ Fensom, Ashbury course
54 holes, 5351/5374/5628 yards, S.S.S. 68; 18 holes, 2019 yards, Par 3
⌶ 8 Bays.
† Welcome; normal dress codes

apply; half-price if playing with a member; booking essential.
⌊ WD £20; WE £25.
⌗ Essential to book at least 2 weeks in advance; no societies April – October; March packages available; terms on application.
⍾ Full facilities lunch available.
⍾ Manor House Hotel, Okehampton; golf free to hotel guests.

3A 3 Axe Cliff
Squires Lane, Axmouth, Seaton, Devon, EX12 4AB
☎ 01297 24371, Pro 21754, Rest/Bar 217549
Off A3052 Axmouth-Seaton Road.
Coastal/parkland course.
Pro Mark Dack; Founded 1884
Designed by James Braid.
18 holes, 5969 yards, S.S.S. 70
† Welcome.
⌊ WD £18; WE £22.
⌗ Welcome by prior arrangement; packages available; terms on application.
⍾ Bar and restaurant facilities.
⍾ Seaton Heights Hotel; Anchor Hotel; Dolfin Hotel; Garlands Hotel, Beer.

3A 4 Bigbury
Bigbury-On-Sea, Bigbury, South Devon, TQ7 4BB
⌸ www.bigburygolfclub.com
☎ 01548 810412, Fax 810207, Pro 810412, Sec 810557

Turn off the A379 Kingsbridge/Plymouth road near Modbury, on to the B3392; follow signs to Bigbury-on-Sea which lead to the course.
Seaside/parkland course.
Pro Simon Lloyd; Founded 1923
Designed by JH Taylor
18 holes, 5896 yards, S.S.S. 68
⌶ Practice ground and practice green.
† Welcome, but essential to belong to a golf club, handicap certs preferred.
⌊ WD £28; WE £35.
⌗ Bookings taken in advance for Tues and Thurs; handicap certs preferred; see website for details.
⍾ Full Facilities.
⍾ Cottage Hotel, Hope Cove; Thurlestone Hotel, Thurlestone; Royal Oak, Bigbury.

3A 5 Bovey Castle
Bovey Castle, Dartmoor National Park, Devon, TQ13 8RE
☎ 01647 445000, Fax 440961
On B3212 towards Mortonhampstead.
Spectacular championship course built around 2 rivers.
Pro Richard Lewis; Founded 1926
Designed by Peter de Savary and Donald Steel (2003)
18 holes, 6303 yards, S.S.S. 69
† Welcome but must book start time.
⌊ £100 per round (+VAT) for non-residents.
⍾ Bar and dining room.
⍾ Accommodation at Bovey Castle.

3A 6 Bowood
Lanteglos, Camelford, Cornwall,
PL32 9RF
🖥 www.bowoodpark.com
📧 golf@bowoodpark.com
☎ 01840 213017, Fax 212622
3A39 through Camelford to Valley
Truckle, then right on to B3266
Boscastle-Tintagel road, 1st left after
garage towards Lanteglos; entrance
0.5 mile on left.
Parkland course with woodland, lakes.
Pro John Phillips; Founded 1992
18 holes, 6692 yards, S.S.S. 72
⌶ Practice range available.
† Welcome with handicap certs.
I WD £30; WE £35.
⌁ Welcome anytime by arrangement;
full facilities available; terms on
application.
🍽 Full facilities.
🔊 Lanteglos Country House Hotel;
Bowood Park Hotel.

3A 7 Bude and North　　　　　☎
Cornwall Golf Club
Burn View, Bude, Cornwall, EX23 8DA
🖥 www.budegolf.co.uk
📧 secretary@budegolf.co.uk
☎ 01288 352006, Fax 356855,
Pro 353635, Rest/Bar 353176
Through the Bude one-way system on
A39 and turn right and right again to
the Golf Club; 1 min from town centre.
Seaside links course.
Pro John Yeo; Founded 1891
Designed by Tom Dunn
18 holes, 6057 yards, S.S.S. 70
† Welcome.
I WD £25; WE £30.
⌁ Some societies are welcome but
not at WE; available depending on
numbers; terms on application.
🍽 Wide selection of meals available
throughout the day.
🔊 Many in local area.

3A 8 Budock Vean Hotel
Budock Vean, Mawnan Smith,
Falmouth, Cornwall, TR11 5LG
📧 relax@budockvean.co.uk
☎ 01326 250288, Pro 250102
On main road between Falmouth and
Helston; head for Mawman Smith
approx 1.5 miles on left.
Undulating parkland course.
Founded 1932

Designed by James Braid, D. Cook
and PH Whiteside
9 holes, 5222 yards, S.S.S. 65
† Welcome with handicap certs;
phone for start time am only.
I Day Ticket: Mon-Sat £18; Sun £20.
⌁ Welcome; full facilities; phone prior.
🍽 Full facilities available.
🔊 Budock Vean.

3A 9 Cape Cornwall Golf and
Country Club
Cape Cornwall, St Just, Penzance,
Cornwall, TR19 7NL
🖥 www.capecornwall.com
📧 info@capecornwall.com
☎ 01736 788611, Fax 788611
3A3071 to St Just-in-Penwith, left at
memorial clock, 1 mile down road on left.
Coastal parkland course.
Founded 1990
Designed by Bob Hamilton
18 holes, 5650 yards, S.S.S. 68
† Welcome 7 days a week.
I WD £20; Fri/Sat/Sun £25.
⌁ Welcome by arrangement; full bar all
WE, lunch 12am-2pm, dinner 7-9.30pm.
🍽 Full facilities.
🔊 The Boswedden Hotel/B&B.

DARTMOUTH GOLF & COUNTRY CLUB

BLACKAWTON, NR DARTMOUTH, DEVON TQ9 7DE

Tel: 01803 712686   Email: info@dgcc.co.uk   Website: www.dgcc.co.uk

Dartmouth Golf & Country Club set in 225 acres of wonderful rolling Devon countryside, just five miles from Dartmouth, is one of the region's premier golf & leisure resorts.

- 3 Star hotel with 35 fabulous en-suite bedrooms
- 18 hole Championship golf course (voted within the top 80 courses in Great Britain & Ireland)
- a 9 hole Dartmouth course
- driving range
- a superb health & leisure suite, complete with swimming pool, sauna, steam room, spa, health & beauty treatments, sunbed, gymnasium and physiotherapy clinic.

Open daily to non members. Society groups welcome. 3 Day Golf Breaks from £120.00 per person.

3A 10 Carlyon Bay Hotel

The Club House, Sea Road, Carlyon Bay, St Austell, Cornwall, PL25 3RD
✉ info@carlyonbay.com
☎ 01726 814250, Fax 814250, Pro 814228
Main Plymouth-Truro road, 1 mile W of St Blazey.
Parkland course.
Pro Mark Rowe; Founded 1926
Designed by J Hamilton Stutt
18 holes, 6597 yards, S.S.S. 71
⚐ Handicap certs required; phone pro shop for start times.
▯ Varies from £25-£39 depending on season.
⚐ Welcome by arrangement.
🍽 Full facilities available.
⌂ Carlyon Bay.

3A 11 Carvynick Golf & Country Club

Summercourt, Newquay, Cornwall, TR8 5AF
🖳 www.carvynick.co.uk
✉ info@carvynick.co.uk
☎ 01872 510716, Fax 510172, Rest/Bar 510544
Off A30 at Summercourt exit on the road towards Newquay.
Parkland course.
Pro Eric Randle
9 holes, 2492 yards, S.S.S. 66
⚐ Welcome at all times.
▯ 9 holes £5; 18 holes £8; reduced rates for players staying in the cottages.
⚐ Welcome.
🍽 Evenings only after 6.30 pm.

3A 12 China Fleet Country Club

North Pill, Saltash, Cornwall, PL12 6LJ
🖳 www.china-fleet.co.uk
✉ sales@china-fleet.co.uk
☎ 01752 848668, Fax 848456
1 mile from Tamar Bridge, leave A38 before tunnel and follow signs.

Parkland course.
Pro Nick Cook; Founded 1991
Designed by Martin Hawtree
18 holes, 6551 yards, S.S.S. 72
⚐ Welcome by prior arrangement only.
▯ WD £25; WE £30.
⚐ By arrangement with Sec; full facilities available.
🍽 Full Facilities.
⌂ Accommodation available, telephone for details.

3A 13 Chulmleigh

Leigh Road, Chulmleigh, Devon, EX18 7BL
🖳 www.chulmleighgolf.co.uk
✉ chulmleighgolf@aol.com
☎ 01769 580519
From Barnstaple follow Tourist Route Exeter signs; from Exeter follow A377 Crediton road, continue through Crediton, after approx 12 miles turn right into Chulmleigh.
Meadowland course.
Founded 1976
Designed by JWD Goodban OBE
Nov-March: 9 hole, par 3, 1450 yards; April-Oct: 18 holes, 2310 yards, S.S.S. 54
▮ Practice areas.
⚐ Welcome.
▯ £8.50 (£7.50 before 10am); reductions for juniors.
⚐ Welcome by arrangement; bar and light snacks available.
🍽 Bar and light snacks.
⌂ Cottage for rent, phone for details.

3A 14 Churston Golf Club

Dartmouth Road, Churston Ferrers, Brixham, Devon, TQ5 0LA
🖳 www.churstongolfclublimited.co.uk
✉ smanager@churstongc.freeserve .co.uk
☎ 01803 842751, Fax 845738, Pro 843442, Sec 842751

5 miles south of Torquay along the main road towards Brixham.
Clifftop course.
Pro Neil Holman; Founded 1890
Designed by HS Colt
18 holes, 6208 yards, S.S.S. 70
⚐ Welcome with handicaps certs.
▯ WD £30; WE £35; concessions apply.
⚐ Mon, Thurs and Fri only; minimum 12; reductions for 50+; bar, restaurant, pro shop, function and conference room; terms on application.
🍽 Restaurant facilities.
⌂ Grand Hotel, Torquay; Imperial Hotel, Torquay; Redcliffe Hotel, Paignton; Berry Head Hotel, Brixham; Torcroft Hotel.

3A 15 Dainton Park

Totnes Road, Ipplepen, Newton Abbot, Devon, TQ12 5TN
☎ 01803 815000, Rest/Bar 815005
2 miles south of Newton Abbot on the A381.
Parkland course.
Pro Martin Tyson;
Founded 1993
Designed by Adrian Stiff
18 holes, 6307 yards, S.S.S. 70
▮ Practice range, 12 bays; floodlit.
⚐ Unrestricted access.
▯ WD £22; WE £25.
⚐ Groups of 12 or more welcome; bar and catering available as well as practice ground; £15.
🍽 Full bar and catering service.
⌂ Passage House, Kingsteignton; Seven Stars, Totnes; Sea Trout Inn, Totnes.

3A 16 Dartmouth Golf & Country Club

Blackawton, Nr Dartmouth, Devon, TQ9 7DE
🖳 www.sdgccx.co.uk
✉ info@dgcc.co.uk

☎ 01803 712686, Fax 712628,
Pro 712650, Sec 712016
Off A3122 between Totnes and
Dartmouth, 5 miles W of Dartmouth.
Moorland/parkland course.
Pro Steve Dougan; Founded 1992
Designed by Jeremy Pern
18 holes, 6663 yards, S.S.S. 74
⌡ 18.
† Welcome; phone for starting times.
⌐ WD £30; WE £40.
♺ Welcome by arrangement; full
facilities available. Also a 9-hole
course; terms on application.
⋈ Bar meals, restaurant, function
room.
⌐ On site, 3 star, 35 bedrooms, en
suite.

3A 17 **Dinnaton** ☎
Dinnaton Fitness & Golf, Blachford
Road, Ivybridge, Devon, PL21 9HU
⌐ www.mccaulays.com
⌐ sales@mccaulays.com
☎ 01752 892512, Fax 698334,
Pro 690020
Leave A38 at Ivybridge; head to town
centre; follow signs to club from r/bout.
Parkland course.
Pro David Ridyard; Founded 1987
Designed by Cotton & Pink
9 holes, 4089 yards, Par 64
† Welcome. No handicap required.
⌐ WD/WE £7.50 (9 holes).
WD/WE £11 (18 holes)
♺ Welcome.
⋈ Snacks available for societies,
prior organisation required.

3A 18 **Downes Crediton** ☎
The Clubhouse, Hookway, Crediton,
Devon, EX17 3PT
⌐ www.downscreditongc.co.uk
⌐ secretary@downscreditongc.co.uk
☎ 01363 773025, Fax 775060, Pro
774464
Leave A377 Exeter to Crediton road, 8
miles NW of Exeter at Crediton station;
turn left at crossroads to Hookway.
Parkland course with water.
Pro Scott Macaskill; Founded 1976
18 holes, 5954 yards, S.S.S. 69
† By arrangement and with
handicap certs.
⌐ WD £25; WE £28.
♺ Welcome by arrangement;
catering facilities available; terms on
application.
⋈ Meals& snacks;coffee available.

3A 19 **East Devon**
Links Rd, Budleigh Salterton, Devon,
EX9 6DG

⌐ secretary@edgc.co.uk
☎ 01395 443370, Fax 445547,
Pro 445195, Rest/Bar 442018
M5 junction 30; follow signs to
Exmouth and the course is on the right
as you enter Budleigh Salterton.
Clifftop, heathland course.
Pro Trevor Underwood; Founded 1902
18 holes, 6239 yards, S.S.S. 70
⌡ Long practice area.
† Welcome by prior arrangement
and with handicap certs.
⌐ £30 for 18 holes; £40 for 36.
♺ Welcome on Thurs only; bar and
restaurant as well as practice facilities;
£30 per round.
⋈ Restaurant and bar.
⌐ Recommendations available from
secretary.

3A 20 **Elfordleigh Hotel Golf** ☎
and Leisure
Colebrook, Plympton, Plymouth,
Devon, PL7 5EB
⌐ elfordleigh@btinternet.com
☎ 01752 336428, Fax 344581, Pro
348425
Off A38 5 miles NE of Plymouth, 2
miles from Marsh Mills roundabout.
Parkland course.
Pro Dominik Naughton; Founded 1932
Designed by JH Taylor
18 holes, 5664 yards, S.S.S. 67
† Welcome with handicap certs.
⌐ WD £25; WE £30.
♺ Terms on application.
⋈ Full facilities available.
⌐ Elfordleigh Hotel.

3A 21 **Exeter Golf & CC** ☎
Countess Wear, Topsham Road,
Exeter, Devon, EX2 7AE
⌐ www.exetergcc.co.uk
⌐ info@exetergcc.fsnet.co.uk
☎ 01392 874139, Fax 874914,
Pro 875028, Sec 874639, Rest/Bar
874139
Exit 30 off M5; follow road marked
Topsham; course4 miles SE of Exeter.
Parkland course.
Pro Mike Rowett; Founded 1895
Designed by James Braid
18 holes, 5980 yards, S.S.S. 69
† Welcome with handicap certs; not
on Tues mornings or Sats; booking
advisable.
⌐ WD £30; WE £35 per round.
♺ Welcome on Thurs only; function
room, four bars and spike bars;
players' guests welcome; terms on
application.
⋈ Full catering facilities available
from 8.00am.

⌐ Buckerell Lodge; Countess Wear
Lodge; Devon Motel.

3A 22 **Falmouth**
Swanpool Road, Goldenbank,
Falmouth, Cornwall, TR11 5BQ
⌐ falmouthgc@onetel.net.uk
☎ 01326 314296, Fax 317783, Pro
311262
Half a mile west of Swanpool beach
on the road to Maenporth.
Seaside parkland course.
Pro Bryan Patterson; Founded 1894
18 holes, 6061 yards, S.S.S. 70
⌡ Practice range; driving range.
† Welcome.
⌐ WD/WE £30.
♺ Welcome by prior arrangement;
bar, lunch and tea facilities; terms on
application.
⋈ Available.
⌐ Royal Duchy; Meudon Vean; Park
Grove.

3A 23 **Fingle Glen Golf Hotel**
Tedburn St Mary, Exeter, Devon,
EX6 6AF
⌐ www.ukgolfer.com/fingle
⌐ fingle.glen@btinternet.com
☎ 01647 61817, Fax 61135,
Pro 61718, Sec 61817,
Rest/Bar 61817
4 miles from Exeter on the A30 to
Okehampton, 400 yards from Fingle
Glen Junction.
Parkland course.
Pro K Pitts; Founded 1989
Designed by W Pile
9 holes, 4747 yards, S.S.S. 63
⌡ 12.
† Welcome.
⌐ WD £8.50; WE £10 (9 holes).
WD £13.50; WE £16 (18 holes).
♺ Welcome; golfing packages can
be arranged; terms on application.
⋈ Bar, lounge and restaurant.
⌐ Own accommodation on site.

3A 24 **Hartland Forest Golf** ☎
& Leisure Parc
Woolsery, Bideford, Devon, EX39 5RA
☎ 01237 431442, Fax 431734
6 miles S of Clovelly off A39.
Parkland course.
Founded 1987
Designed by Alan Cartwright.
18 holes, 5870 yards, S.S.S. 69
† No restrictions except acceptable
standard of golf; dress code applies.
⌐ WD/WE £20; booking advisable.
♺ Welcome by arrangement; full
facilities available.

Royal Guernsey

With a card measuring just 6,215 yards, including a par five of 438 yards and five par fours of under 350 yards, it might be thought that Royal Guernsey (founded in 1890 and a royal golf club just a year later) was a course for the faint hearted. But this is a Mackenzie Ross design. And the man responsible for Dornoch and Pinehurst was almost bound to bring another version of his cruel beauty to the Channel Islands.

Norman Wood, the current professional of Royal Guernsey, beat Lee Trevino 2&1 in the 1975 Ryder Cup – "he was very quiet until he went one down, then it was as if someone pressed a switch and off he went, you couldn't shut him up" – and arrived on Guernsey via Turnberry and Sandy Lane in Barbados (it's a tough life, but someone's got to do it). Wood says, "It's a links course but, after the watering system was introduced following the drought of '76 when everything got burned, there is a softer inland feel to the fairways. But the rough gets pretty thick in the summer, there is gorse on just about every hole on the front nine, we've always got a wind and there are some fairly sandy lies if you miss the fairways. But the key to scoring is the short game (one visitor said chipping in the summer was like a game of pinball). The greens are tricky. Four of the par fours used to be par fives, so their greens were designed to challenge shorter pitch shots. The fact that the course record is 64 (the par is 70) shows you how tough it can be although our golf manager Bobby Eggo (who

played in the 1987 Walker Cup with Colin Montgomerie) is still off +3 and regularly gets round in under par."

Other less contemporary hazards include German pillboxes left over from the war, a couple of Martello Towers by the 15th and 16th greens and wandering commoners who retain a right of access. Until two years ago the golfer also had to contend with half a dozen cows because for £1 a year the locals could exercise their grazing rights. Wood feels with a sense of regret that the cows are unlikely to return even though the animals were tethered to prevent them from invading the greens.

Sadly the inhabitants of Guernsey didn't manage to tether the Germans who invaded during the Second World War. The "gentle Hun", as he was ironically referred to, marched into the clubhouse, threw the secretary's records out of the window, set fire to them and then gutted the building. Gentle like a maggot.

The Germans did not succeed in destroying the island's golfing history however. Henry Cotton's mother was a Guernsey woman and Herbert Jolly, Royal Guernsey's most renowned golfer, played in the inaugural Ryder Cup along with Ted Ray, the captain, and Aubrey Boomer, making three Channel Islanders from a team of eight. Astounding. Jolly obviously chose to ignore King John's Charter that decreed that no Guernsey man could serve outside the island except to rescue the King or help with the recapture of the mainland. — **Mark Reason**

Bar. Limited food service: enquire in advance.

38 luxury units of accommodation available on site sleeping 207.

3A 25 Hele Park
Ashburton Road, Newton Abbot, Devon, TQ12 6JN
01626 336060, Fax 332661
On edge of Newton Abbot on the A383 Newton Abbot-Ashburton road.
Parkland course.
Pro J Langmead; Founded 1992
Designed by M Craig/N Stanbury
9 holes, 5168 yards, S.S.S. 65
Practice range, floodlit driving range and outdoor grass tees.
Welcome.
WD from £9.50; WE from £10.50.
Welcome on application to the secretary; terms on application.
Full facilities.
Passage House, Kingsteignton, Newton Abbot.

3A 26 Helston Golf and Leisure
Wendron, Coverack Bridges, Helston, Cornwall, TR13 0LX
01326 572228, Fax 52228, Rest/Bar 565103
1 mile N of Helston on B3297 Redruth road.
Short park and downland course, par 3.
Founded 1988
18 holes, 2100 yards, S.S.S. 54
Welcome anytime.
WD/WE £6.
Welcome by prior arrangement.
Full facilities available at Whealdream Bar.
Lyndale Guesthouse, Helston.

3A 27 Highbullen Hotel
Chittlehamholt, Umberleigh, Devon, EX37 9HD
www.highbullen.co.uk
info@highbullen.co.uk
01769 540561, Fax 540492, Pro 540530
10 mins west on A361 from South Molton.
Parkland course.
Pro Paul Weston; Founded 1960
Designed by Hugh Neil. New extension by M Neil & H Stutt
18 holes, 5455 yards, S.S.S. 66
Welcome; free for hotel guests.
WD £16; WE £18.
By arrangement.
Restaurant open everyday; Bar snacks also.
Highbullen Hotel.

3A 28 Holsworthy Golf Club
Killatree, Holsworthy, Devon, EX22 6LP
www.holsworthygolfclub.co.uk
hgcsecretary@aol.com
01409 253177, Fax 253177, Pro 254771
1.5 miles out of Holsworthy on the A3072 Bude Road.
Parkland course.
Pro Graham Webb; Founded 1937
18 holes, 6062 yards, S.S.S. 69
Very welcome.
WD/WE up to £25.
By arrangement; packages available; terms on application.
Clubhouse facilities.
Court Barn, Clawton.

3A 29 Honiton
Middlehills, Honiton, Devon, EX14 9TR
01404 44422, Fax 46383, Pro 42943, Sec 44422, Rest/Bar 47167
1 mile S of Honiton off the A35.
Parkland course.
Pro A Cave; Founded 1896
18 holes, 5902 yards, S.S.S. 68
Welcome by arrangement.
WD £24; WE £30.
Welcome on Thurs; terms on application.
Bar facilities available.
Space for 10 touring caravans available.

3A 30 Hurdwick
Tavistock Hamlets, Tavistock, Devon, PL19 0LL
01822 612746
Signposted from centre of Tavistock; course is one mile N of Tavistock on Brentor road.
Parkland course.
Founded 1988
Designed by Hawtree
18 holes, 5302 yards, S.S.S. 67
Welcome at any times; dress code applies.
WD £15; WE £15.
Welcome; packages available; 36 holes of golf and lunch available from £18.
Lunch and snacks.
Bedford Hotel, Tavistock; Castle Inn, Lydford.

3A 31 Ilfracombe
Hele Bay, Ilfracombe, North Devon, EX34 9RT
www.ilfracombegolfclub.com
ilfracombe.golfclub@virgin.net
(tee bookings) 01271 863328, Fax 867731, Pro 863328, Sec 862176, Rest/Bar 862675
Course is one mile from Ilfracombe towards Combe Martin on the A399 coast road.
Undulating heathland course with spectacular views.
Pro Mark Davis; Founded 1892
Designed by TK Weir
18 holes, 5893 yards yards, S.S.S. 69
3 bay, covered with ball dispenser.
Welcome by prior arrangement, particularly in the summer.
WD £20; WE £25.
Welcome by prior arrangement with the secretary; terms on application.
Full clubhouse facilities.
Club can recommend in local area.

3A 32 Isles of Scilly
St Mary's, Isle of Scilly, TR21 0NF
01720 422692, Sec 423103
1.5 miles from Hugh Town in St.Mary's.
Heathland/seaside course.
Founded 1904
Designed by Horace Hutchinson
9 holes, 6001 yards, S.S.S. 69
Welcome; phone one hour before on Sunday.
WD £19; WE £19. twilight golf £10.
Available.
Star Castle Hotel.

3A 33 Killiow Park
Killiow, Kea, Truro, Cornwall, TR3 6AG
office@killiow.fsnet.co.uk
01872 270246, Fax 240915, Sec 240915, Rest/Bar 270246
Leave Truro on A39 Truro/Falmouth road, turn right at first roundabout 3 miles from Truro, clearly signposted thereafter.
Picturesque parkland course.
Founded 1987
18 holes, 5274 yards, S.S.S. 68
8 indoor and 3 outdoor.
Welcome after 8.30am; advisable to book in high season.
WD £15.50; WE £15.50.
Welcome.
Bar and Restaurant.
The Alverton Manor.

3A 34 La Grande Mare Country Club
Vazon Coast Road, Castel, Guernsey, Channel Islands, GY5 7LL
www.lgmguernsey.net

HIGHBULLEN HOTEL Golf & Country Club

A superb award winning golf course set in richly wooded parkland, Highbullen boasts breathtaking views towards the Devon landscapes of Dartmoor and Exmoor. It's easy-walking 5,570 yards, par-68 provides an excellent test of golf for the accomplished player without creating an unfair or unrewarding challenge for the novice.

Highbullen Hotel • Chittlehamholt • Umberleigh • North Devon • EX37 9HD
Telephone: 01769 540561   Facsimile: 01769 540492   eMail: info@highbullen.co.uk

---

✉ lgmgolf@cwgsy.net
☎ 01481 253544, Fax 255194,
Pro 253432, Rest/Bar 256576
On the west coast of Guernsey at Vazon Bay.
Parkland course.
Pro Matt Groves; Founded 1994
Designed by Hawtree
18 holes, 5112 yards, S.S.S. 66
⚑ Practice area and green.
† Welcome.
⌊ WD £27; WE £29.
⤳ Book in advance; restaurant and bar; hotel has 5 crowns; terms on application.
🍴 Bar, restaurant and hotel.
⌁ La Grande Mare Hotel.

3A 35 La Moye
La Moye, La Route Orange, St Brelade, Jersey, Channel Islands, JE3 8GQ
☎ 01534 743401, Fax 747289, Pro 743130, Sec 743401, Rest/Bar 742701
2 miles W of airport off Route des Orange.
Links course.
Pro Mike Deeley; Founded 1902
Designed by James Braid
18 holes, 6664 yards, S.S.S. 72
⚑ 1 driving range.
† Welcome by prior arrangement.
⌊ WD £45; WE and bank holidays £50.
⤳ Welcome by prior arrangement WD only; £5 booking fee per person; Restaurant facilities available.
🍴 Full clubhouse restaurant and bar facilities.
⌁ Atlantic; L'Horizon, both St Brelade.

3A 36 Lanhydrock ☎
Lostwithiel Rd, Bodmin, Cornwall, PL30 5AQ

⊞ www.lanhydrock-golf.co.uk
✉ golfing@lanhydrock-golf.co.uk
☎ 01208 73600, Fax 77325,
Pro 73600, Sec 73600,
Rest/Bar 73600
1 mile south of Bodmin.
Parkland course.
Founded 1992
Designed by J Hamilton Stutt
18 holes, 6100 yards, S.S.S. 70
⚑ Driving range.
† Welcome.
⌊ From £22 to £45.
⤳ Welcome; packages available for groups of 16 and above players; private suite available with own bar facility.
🍴 Full facilities.

3A 37 Launceston ☎
St Stephen's, North Street, Launceston, Cornwall, PL15 8HF
☎ 01566 773442, Fax 777506, Pro 775359, Sec 773442, Rest/Bar 773442
1 mile N of Launceston on Bude road (B3254).
Parkland course.
Pro John Tozer; Founded 1927
Designed by J. Hamilton Stutt
18 holes, 6415 yards, S.S.S. 71
† Welcome by arrangement.
⌊ WD £20; WE £20.
⤳ Welcome WD by arrangement; full facilities; terms on application.
🍴 Available by prior arrangement.
⌁ White Hart.

3A 38 Les Ormes Golf and Leisure
Le Mont à la Brune, St Brelade, Jersey, Channel Islands, JE3 8FL
⊞ www.lesormes.je
✉ mikegraham@localdial.com
☎ 01534 744464, Fax 499122, Pro 497000, Sec 497006, Rest/Bar 497010

Course is five minutes from Jersey Airport following the signs for St Brelade.
Parkland course.
Pro Andrew Chamberlain; Founded 1996
9 holes, 5018 yards, S.S.S. 66
⚑ Practice range, 17 bays, 4 very modern indoor tennis courts.
† Welcome.
⌊ WD £13; WE £16.
⤳ Welcome by prior arrangement.
🍴 Full catering facilities.
⌁ Many in Jersey; contact local tourist board.

3A 39 Libbaton
High Bickington, Umberleigh, Devon, EX37 9BS
✉ gerald.herniman@tesco.net
☎ 01769 560269, Pro 560167
A377 to Atherington and then B3217 to High Bickington.
Parkland course.
Pro Sarah Burnell; Founded 1988
Designed by Col P Badham
18 holes, 6481 yards, S.S.S. 71
⚑ Practice range.
† Visitors and societies welcome at all times. Advanced booking for tees advisable.
⌊ WD £20; WE £24.
⤳ Welcome all week including WE; golf, coffee, snack lunch, evening meal.
🍴 Full catering facilities available all day.
⌁ Northcote Manor, Umberleigh; Exeter Inn, Chittlehamholt.

3A 40 Looe
Bin Down, Looe, Cornwall, PL13 1PX
☎ 01503 240239, Fax 240864
Course is three miles E of Looe just off the B3253.
Parkland/downland course.
Pro A MacDonald; Founded 1933
Designed by Harry Vardon
18 holes, 5940 yards, S.S.S. 69

Royal Jersey

No wonder it was just a matter of months after its foundation that Jersey came by its royal title. After all Queen Victoria was such an admirer of this piece of land that she insisted that Grouville Bay be referred to with a royal prefix. And the locals will tell you that although Harry Vardon was the son of a gardener and possessed the giant horny hands that you might expect of someone with such earthy genes, he was golfing majesty.

So at its first annual meeting in December 1878 it was unanimously agreed that Jersey should ask for royal status. One month later the reply came back via Queen Victoria, the Home Secretary and the Lieutenant Governor of Jersey "that the Jersey Golf Club may be permitted to assume the title of 'Royal'."

Soon after its formation the club was home to some of the greatest players to have ever played the game. Nodding sages will tell you out of the corner of their mouths that Vardon would play in the morning, have a spot of lunch and then play a second round where he would drive into the divots that his irons had left earlier in the day. Despite such fairytales it is hard to argue that Vardon was not the greatest British golfer of all time. Not only did he win six Open Championships, but out of three US Open starts he won once, lost in a play-off and finished second by a shot. Nick Faldo and Henry Cotton have their admirers, but it is hard to argue against Vardon particularly when you consider that he lost many years of his golfing prime to two bouts of tuberculosis and World War I. The extraordinary thing is that to date there are only two other British US Open Champions in Ted Ray and Tony Jacklin and the former was also a Jerseyman whilst the latter made his

home there. Ray was good enough to be admired by Bobby Jones.

The first hole is a ferocious challenge of 468 yards, the opening tee shot having to be laced between the remains of Fort Henry and two German pillboxes. It is a tribute to the fortitude of the club that the course is considerably more likely to outlive the pillboxes, because it looked doomed by the German invasion of Jersey in the Second World War.

Proclamations were pinned up on the island which alleged that "Certain incidents have occurred in which on the part of the inhabitants of the Island acts have been committed which were against the interests of the Army of Occupation." It is not detailed whether a cleverly sliced three iron onto the eyebrows of a German soldier was one such act, but if it was it was punishable by death. The Germans precluded the possibility by banning golf and Royal Jersey became a huge warehouse for barbed wire, concrete blockhouses, mines, trenches, light railways and gravel dumps. But the invading force didn't get to melt down the club trophies which were hidden behind a false wall, whilst the members' golf clubs were hidden in a warehouse on the other side of the island.

Inevitably it took a while for the course to recover, but it has now been going strong again for a number of years, the front nine running alongside the coast and the second nine dotted with bracken and gorse and more inland in feel. After all that it had been through it was deserved that Royal Jersey's centenary should be commemorated by a set of postage stamps, perhaps the only golf club to have earned such a distinction. — **Mark Reason**

⚹ Practice ground.
† Welcome.
Ⅎ Price on application.
⤴ Welcome but minimum of 8 players; catering packages available; from £18; special society weekend rates available; details on application.
🍽 Facilities available.
⤴ Call club for details.

3A 41 Lostwithiel Hotel ☎ Golf & Country Club
Lower Polscoe, Lostwithiel, Cornwall, PL22 0HQ
⤴ www.golf-hotel.co.uk
✉ reception@golf-hotel.co.uk
☎ 01208 873550, Fax 873479, Pro 873822
On the A390 from Plymouth to Lostwithiel.
Parkland course.
Pro Tony Nash;
Founded 1991
Designed by Stewart Wood
18 holes, 5984 yards, S.S.S. 72
⚹ Practice range, 6 undercover bays; floodlit.
† Welcome.
Ⅎ WD £25; WE £29.
⤴ Welcome; golf from only £15; coffee and lunch, evening meal and day's golf from £28; terms on application.
🍽 Full facilities.
⤴ 21 country-style bedrooms on site with tennis courts, indoor swimming pool and gym.

3A 42 Merlin ☎
Mawgan Porth, Newquay, Cornwall, TR8 4DN
☎ 01841 540222, Fax 541031
On coast road between Newquay and Padstow. After Mawgan Porth take St Eval Road.
Heathland course.
Founded 1991
Designed by Ross Oliver
18 holes, 6210 yards, S.S.S. 71
⚹ Practice range, 6 covered bays; buggy, trolley and club hire.
† No restrictions.
Ⅎ WD/WE £16.
⤴ Welcome by prior arrangement; includes golf only; lunch and dinner are available at special rates.
🍽 Bar and Restaurant.
⤴ Merrymoor Inn; Whitelodge; Sea Vista, all Mawgan Porth; Falcon, St Mawgan.

3A 43 Mortehoe & Woolacombe
Easewell, Mortehoe, Devon, EX34 7EH
⤴ www.easewellfarm.co.uk
☎ 01271 870225, Fax 870225, Pro 870566
1 mile before Mortehoe on the Ilfracombe road.
Parkland with superb sea views.
Founded 1992
Designed by Hans Ellis/David Hoare
9 holes, 4638 yards, S.S.S. 63
† Welcome.
Ⅎ WD £7; WE £7; £12 for 18 holes.

⤴ Welcome with pre-booking; terms on application.
🍽 Bar and restaurant
⤴ Woolacombe Bay; Watersmeet; Lundy House; Rockham Bay.

3A 44 Mullion ☎
Cury Cross Lanes, Helston, Cornwall, TR12 7BP
✉ secretary@ mulliongolfclub.plus.com
☎ 01326 240276, Fax 240685, Pro 241176, Sec 240685, Rest/Bar 241231
S of Helston on A3083 towards The Lizard past Culdrose Naval Air station.
Parkland/links course.
Pro P Blundell; Founded 1895
Designed by W Sich
18 holes, 6037 yards, S.S.S. 70
† Welcome with handicap certs.
Ⅎ WD £25; WE £30 (or bank holidays).
⤴ Welcome with prior arrangement; packages available; terms on application.
🍽 Full catering and bar available.
⤴ Polurrian; Mullion Cove; Angel.

3A 45 Newquay Golf Club ☎
Tower Road, Newquay, Cornwall, TR7 1LT
✉ newquaygolfclub@smartone .co.uk
☎ 01637 874354, Fax 874066, Pro 874830, Sec 874354, Rest/Bar 872091
Adjacent to Fistral Beach; signposted.

ROSERROW GOLF & COUNTRY CLUB Tel: 01208 863000

Roserrow, St Minver, Wadebridge, Cornwall PL27 6QT   www.roserrow.co.uk   e-mail: mail@roserrow.co.uk

Nestling in over 400 acres of unspoilt countryside near Rock and the Camel Estuary, Roserrow's 6507 yard 18 hole course offers a congenial atmosphere of quiet seclusion against a beautiful backdrop. Considered one of Cornwall's favourite society venues, both visitors and societies are warmly welcomed. Additionally, Roserrow boasts extensive self-catering accommodation, tennis courts, heated indoor swimming pool, sauna, steam room, spa and fitness suite.

Seaside links course.
Pro Mark Bevan; Founded 1890
Designed by HS Colt
18 holes, 6150 yards, S.S.S. 69
⚑ Welcome; handicap certificates required.
▌ WD £25; WE £25.
⚘ By arrangement only; full facilities; terms on application.
🍽 Bar and restaurant.
⌂ Bristol; Esplanade, Narrowcliff.

3A 46 Newton Abbot ☎
(Stover Golf Club)
The Club House, Stover, Newton Abbot, Devon, TQ12 6QQ
☎ 01626 352460, Fax 330210, Pro 362078
Off A38 at Drumbridges and turn towards Newton Abbot on the A382; course is 300 yards on right.
Wooded parkland course.
Pro Malcolm Craig; Founded 1931
Designed by James Braid
18 holes, 5764-5527 yards, S.S.S. 68
⚑ Welcome with handicap certs unless with a member.
▌ WD £28 or £32 per day; WE £32 or £35 per day.
⚘ Thurs only; full catering facilities to order; terms on application.
🍽 Bar and restaurant.
⌂ Dolphin; Edgemoor, both Bovey Tracey.

3A 47 Okehampton ☎
Tors Road, Okehampton, Devon, EX20 1EF
🖥 www.okehamptongc.co.uk
📧 okehampton@btconnect.com
☎ 01837 52113, Fax 52734, Pro 53541, Sec 52113, Rest/Bar 659334
Enter town centre from A30 and follow signs from the main lights.
Parkland course.
Pro Ashley Moon; Founded 1913
Designed by JH Taylor
18 holes, 5268 yards, S.S.S. 66
⚑ Welcome but only by prior arrangement; booking essential.
▌ WD and Sunday £17-20; WE £20.
⚘ Welcome by prior arrangement; Group discounts available; terms on application.

🍽 Available.
⌂ Fox and Hounds, Bridestowe; White Hart, Okehampton.

3A 48 Padbrook Park ☎
Cullompton, Devon, EX15 1RU
🖥 www.padbrookpark.co.uk
📧 padbrookpark@fsmail.net
☎ 01884 38286, Fax 34359.
Pro 07762 033140
Exit 28 of the M5; follow signs through Cullompton towards Exeter; across roundabout and then first on right.
Parkland course.
Pro Stewart Adwick/Ross Troke;
Founded 1991
Designed by Bob Sandow
9 holes, 6108 yards, S.S.S. 69
⚑ Welcome but must pre-book tee time.
▌ WD £15; WE £18.
⚘ Welcome with prior arrangements; full catering for society and corporate packages; terms on application.
🍽 Bar and restaurant.
⌂ On-site hotel under construction.

3A 49 Perranporth ☎
Budnic Hill, Perranporth, Cornwall, TR6 0AB
🖥 www.perranporthgolfclub.com
📧 perranporth@golfclub92 .fsnet.co.uk
☎ 01872 573701, Fax 573701, Pro 572317, Rest/Bar 572454
Take Perranporth road off the A30; course is on the right when entering town.
Links course with panoramic views.
Pro Derek Michell; Founded 1927
Designed by James Braid
18 holes, 6252 yards, S.S.S. 72
⚑ Welcome with prior booking.
▌ Day ticket: WD £25; WE £30.
⚘ Welcome with booking; packages can be arranged; terms on application.
🍽 Bar and restaurant.
⌂ Ponsmere, Perranporth; White Lodge, Mawgan Porth.

3A 50 Porthpean
Porthpean, St Austell, Cornwall, PL26 6AY

☎ 01726 64613
Off A390 2 miles from St Austell.
Parkland course.
Founded 1992
Designed by R Oliver/A Leather
18 holes, 5184 yards, S.S.S. 67
⚐ Practice range, 9 bays; floodlit range.
⚑ Welcome.
▌ WD £12; WE £12.
⚘ Welcome by prior arrangement; packages available; terms on application.
🍽 Clubhouse facilities.
⌂ Cliff Head; Pier House; Porth Avallen.

3A 51 Praa Sands ☎
Germoe Crossroads, Praa Sands, Penzance, Cornwall, TR20 9TQ
🖥 www.praasandsgolfclub.com
📧 praasandsgolf@aol.co.uk
☎ 01736 763445, Fax 763399
7 miles east of Penzance on A394 to Helston.
Seaside parkland course.
Founded 1971
2 x 9 holes, 4122 yards, S.S.S. 60
⚑ Welcome except Sun mornings.
▌ 9 holes £11; 18 holes £16; day ticket £21.
⚘ By arrangement; packages available; terms on application.
🍽 Meals and snacks; licensed bar.
⌂ Queens Hotel, Penzance; Meundon Hotel, Falmouth.

3A 52 Radnor Golf Centre
Radnor Road, Redruth, Cornwall, TR16 5EL
🖥 www.radnorgolfski.fsnet.co.uk
☎ 01209 211059, Fax 211059
Take A30 from Redruth to Porthtowan; after 200 yards turn right; golf centre on left after 1 mile.
Heathland course with gorse.
Pro Gordon Wallbank; Founded 1988
Designed by Gordon Wallbank
9 holes, 1312 yards, S.S.S. men 52 ladies 56
⚐ 4 indoor, 3 outdoor.
⚑ Pay and play.
▌ WD £8.00; WE £8.00 (18 holes). £5.00 (9 holes).

Royal North Devon Golf Club

Championship Course: 18 holes - White 6723 yards par 72; Yellow 6424 yards par 72; Ladies 5703 yards par 73.

Play England's oldest Golf Course (1864) and afterwards visit the Golf Museum.

Enjoy good food in comfortable surroundings.

e-mail: info@royalnorthdevongolfclub.co.uk   website: www.royalnorthdevongolfclub.co.uk

Westward Ho!, Bideford, Devon EX39 1HD   Tel: 01237 473817 (Secretary)   01237 477598 (Professional)

⌁ Welcome.
🍽 None.
↩ The Inn for all Seasons.

3A 53 Roserrow Golf & ₲
Country Club
Roserrow, St Minver, Wadebridge,
Cornwall, PL27 6QT
✉ mail@roserrow.co.uk
☎ 01208 863000, Fax 863002
From Wadebridge take the B3314
towards Polzeath.
Heathland course.
Pro Nigel Sears; Founded 1997
18 holes, 6507 yards, S.S.S. 72
🏌 13.
† Welcome anytime.
Ɩ £18 (low season); £35 (high).
⌁ Welcome by prior arrangement.
🍽 Full bar meals and brasserie.
↩ Own accommodation.

3A 54 Royal Guernsey
L'Ancresse Vale, Guernsey, Channel
Islands, GY3 5BY
🖥 www.royalguernseygolfclub.com
✉ bobby@rggc.co.uk
☎ 01481 247022, Fax 243960,
Pro 245070, Sec 246523
3 miles north of St Peter Port.
Seaside links course.
Pro Norman Wood; Founded 1890
Designed by MacKenzie Ross
18 holes, 6215 yards, S.S.S. 70
🏌 Driving range.
† Welcome; restricted times on
Thurs/Sat morning; no visitors on Sun.
Ɩ WD/WE £40.
⌁ Not welcome.
🍽 Coffee, afternoon teas and meals
available.
↩ Peninsular Hotel.

3A 55 Royal Jersey
Le Chemin Au Greves, Grouville,
Jersey, Channel Islands, JE3 9BD
🖥 www.royaljersey.com
✉ thesecretary@royaljersey.com
☎ 01534 854416, Fax 854684, Pro
852234, Rest/Bar 851042
4 miles east of St Helier on road to
Gorey.
Links course.

Pro David Morgan; Founded 1878
18 holes, 6100 yards, S.S.S. 70
† Welcome between 10am-noon and
2pm-4pm on WD & after 2.30pm at WE.
Ɩ WD/WE £50.
⌁ Apply in writing to Sec; full
catering by prior arrangement with
Steward.
🍽 Bar and catering facilities.

3A 56 Royal Navy Air Station
Culdrose
RNAS Culdrose, Helston, Cornwall,
TR12 8QY
☎ 01326 552413, Sec 573929
3A3083 1 mile from Helston towards
Lizard.
Flat parkland course built around part
of airfield.
Founded 1962
14 holes holes, 6132 yards yards,
S.S.S. 70
† Must be accompanied by club
member.
Ɩ Terms on application.
⌁ Welcome by arrangement.
🍽 Clubhouse bar and hot/cold
snacks available.

3A 57 Royal North Devon ₲
Golf Links Road, Westward Ho,
Bideford, Devon, EX39 1HD
🖥 www.royalnorthdevongolfclub.co.uk
✉ info@royalnorthdevongolfclub
.co.uk
☎ 01237 473817, Fax 423456,
Pro 477598, Rest 423234, Bar 473824
Take M5 to A361 and go through
Northam Village to Sandymere road
and then into Golf Links Road.
Links course.
Pro Richard Herring; Founded 1864
Designed by 'Old' Tom Morris
18 holes, 6653 yards, S.S.S. 72
🏌 Indoor practice facility.
† Welcome with handicap certs.
Ɩ WD £34; WE £40.
⌁ Welcome; bar, restaurant, snooker
room; terms on application.
🍽 Full facilities.
↩ Broomhayes Manor, Westward
Ho!; Culloden House, Westward Ho!;
Riversford Hotel, Northam.

3A 58 St Austell ₲
Tregongeeves Lane, St Austell,
Cornwall, PL26 7DS
☎ 01726 72649, Fax 71978,
Pro 68621, Sec 74756
1 mile out of St Austell on the A390
Truro road; signposted.
Heathland/parkland course.
Pro Tony Pitts; Founded 1911
18 holes, 6089 yards, S.S.S. 69
🏌 8 bay driving range.
† Must be a member of a golf club
and hold handicap cert.
Ɩ WD £20; WE £22.
⌁ Welcome by appointment except
on WE; restaurant and lounge bar;
meals to be arranged with the
caterer.
🍽 Full catering facilities.
↩ The White Hart.

3A 59 St Clements
Jersey Recreation Grounds Co Ltd,
Plat Douet Road, St Clement, Jersey,
Channel Islands, JE2 6PN
☎ 01534 721938, Fax 721012
Close to St Helier.
Meadowland course.
Founded 1913
9 holes, 4138 yards
† Welcome every day except before
11.30 Tues and 1.30pm Sun.
Ɩ WD/WE £12.
⌁ Welcome by arrangement.
🍽 Buffet bar and restaurant.
↩ Hotel de Normandy, Merton.

3A 60 St Enodoc
Rock, Wadebridge, Cornwall,
PL27 6LD
☎ 01208 863216, Fax 862976,
Pro 862402, Sec 862200
6 miles NW of Wadebridge.
Links course.
Pro Nick Williams; Founded 1890
Designed by James Braid
18 holes, 6243 yards, S.S.S. 70
🏌 Basic driving range.
† Welcome; max handicap 24 on
Church course. No restrictions on other
course.
Ɩ WD £38; WE £45 for Church
course; £15 for Holywell course.

Royal North Devon

Royal North Devon claims to be the oldest links course in the world still playing on the original land and apart from the addition of about 400 yards at the beginning of 2004, not too much has changed. Bernard Darwin wrote, "Without entering into invidious comparisons there is, for the fun and adventure of the game, no more ideal piece of golfing country in the world".

'The Bay Challenge' is typical of the fun and adventure of a course also named 'Westward Ho!' after the Charles Kingsley novel that was written just down the road. 'The Bay Challenge' is a foursomes competition between Saunton and Royal North Devon that involves staring at the first tee of Royal North Devon and holing out on the eighteenth green at Saunton. Given that there is a whacking expanse of water between the two courses, as well as several other obstacles, it is quite a feat just to complete the challenge.

The trick is to wait for the right tide, although even then a carry of 220–230 yards is required. Given the severe nature of some of the terrain players were originally allowed to tee up each shot with a stack of polo mints, but these days a normal tee peg is used. The clubs tried to replay the challenge in the millennium year, but they have always needed the help of the marines to get across the water and in this age of commerce the marines wanted payment for the use of their machinery.

You might have thought that the golf course itself presented enough challenges, without looking for even more. Sheep and horses still roam the land although if your ball finishes in an area where these animals have found relief then you too are entitled to obtain relief from what might be termed "ball in motion".

Cate's bunker runs across the fourth hole and is one of the widest in the world and a "bit of a beast" according to pro Richard Herring. He adds that the course is also defended by a wind that can require a player to hit a 9-iron from 190 yards downwind and a driver 160 yards into the teeth.

And then there are the sea rushes that run alongside the 10th, 11th and 12th holes. Their vast spikes can impale a ball and have been known to do such damage that this stretch of holes is referred to by the locals as their own amen corner. Herring has considered mounting a driving range dispenser on the eleventh tee and reckons he would make a fortune from the amount of reloads that this drive necessitates.

The record of 65 over the extended course was set by Paul Waring in the 2004 West of England Strokeplay, but far more impressive was the 65 of Dick Champion back in 1953, an achievement he had 50 years of life left to enjoy. The fact that in the first 100 years of the club's history only four scores under 70 were registered in the Club's medal competition is a measure of Champion's achievement.

Although it has had its ragged years in the past, the course is now tended to with the love and care that you would expect from a head greenkeeper who is a local lad just retired from county golf after captaining Devon to victory in the county finals in 2003 and who plays off a handicap of one.

He is in charge of historic land. The royal title was granted in 1867, the Duke of York was president in 2000 and most notable of all perhaps, Royal North Devon was home to John Henry Taylor, five times the Open champion, who died here at the age of 93 and was born just up the road in the village of Northam. – **Mark Reason**

SAUNTON GOLF CLUB
Two Championship Links Course

Visitors and Societies Welcome (Handicap Certificates **are** required)
Excellent Bar and Restaurant facilities (all green fees include a complimentary meal voucher)

Tel: **01271 812436**   Email: **info@sauntongolf.co.uk**   **www.sauntongolf.co.uk**

 Welcome by prior arrangement; meals can be arranged through restaurant.
 Full restaurant and bar.

3A 61 St Kew
St Kew Highway, Nr Wadebridge, Bodmin, Cornwall, PL30 3EF
☎ 01208 841500, Fax 841500
Main A30 Wadebridge to Camelford road; course two and a half miles north of Wadebridge.
Parkland course.
Pro Nick Rogers; Founded 1993
Designed by D Derry
9 holes holes, 4543 yards, S.S.S. 62
 Practice range, covered.
 Welcome at all times.
 WD £13; WE £13.
 Welcome by arrangement; discounts on application; catering available; terms on application.
 Full facilities.
 Bodare Hotel, Daymer Bay; Molesworth Arms, Wadebridge; St Moritz, Trebetherick.

3A 62 St Mellion International
St Mellion Hotel Golf and Country Club, St Mellion, Saltash, Cornwall, PL12 6SD
 www.st-mellion.co.uk
 stmellion@americangolf.uk.com
☎ 01579 351351, Fax 350537, Pro 352002, Rest/Bar 352005
3 miles south of Callington on A388.
Parkland course; former home of Benson & Hedges Masters.
Pro D Moon; Founded 1976
Designed by Jack Nicklaus; old course designed by J Hamilton Stutt
Nicklaus: 18 holes, 6651 yards, S.S.S. 72; Old course: 18 holes, 5782 yards, S.S.S. 68
 6 undercover, 30 turf bays.
 Welcome.
 Nicklaus: WD £50, WE £50 Old Course; WD £35, WE £35.
 Welcome subject to availability; coffee, 18 holes of golf, 3-course club meal packages available.
 Full catering, coffee shop, grill room.
 Own lodge and hotel.

3A 63 St Pierre Park Hotel
Rohais Road, St Peter Port, Guernsey, Channel Islands, GY1 1FD
 www.stpierrepark.co.uk
 enquiries@stpierrepark.co.uk
☎ 01481 727039, Fax 712041, Rest/Bar 428282
1 mile west of St Peter Port on Rohais Road.
Hilly course with water hazards.
Pro Roy Corbet; Founded 1982
Designed by Tony Jacklin
9 holes, 2610 yards, S.S.S. 50
 Driving range.
 Welcome.
 WD £13; WE £15 (9 holes).
 Welcome; packages available, terms on application.
 Full facilities at the hotel.
 St Pierre Park Hotel.

3A 64 Saunton
Braunton, Devon, EX33 1LG
 www.sauntongolf.co.uk
 trevor@sauntongolf.co.uk
☎ 01271 812436, Pro 812013, Sec 812436, Rest/Bar 812436
On B3231 from Braunton to Croyde, 7 miles from Barnstaple.
Two traditional links courses.
Pro Albert MacKenzie; Founded 1897
Designed by Herbert Fowler (East), Frank Pennick (West)
East: 18 holes, 6373 yards, S.S.S. 73; West: 18 holes, 6138 yards, S.S.S. 72
 Driving range.
 Welcome with handicap certificates.
 2003 fees: £50 (18 holes); £70 (36 holes); All inclusive of a meal voucher; 2004 prices on application
 Welcome by arrangement; full facilities available.
 Full restaurant facilities.
 Saunton Sands; Kittiwell House, Woolacombe Bay.

3A 65 Sidmouth
Cotmaton Road, Sidmouth, Devon, EX10 8SX
☎ 01395 516407, Rest/Bar 513023
Take station road to Woodlands Hotel and then turn right into Cotmaton Road.
Undulating parkland course.
Pro Gaele Tapper; Founded 1889
18 holes, 5068 yards, S.S.S. 65
 Welcome by prior arrangement with the Pro.
 WD £20, WE £20; packages on request.
 Welcome – terms on application.
 Full Facilities.

3A 66 Sparkwell
Welbeck Manor Hotel, Sparkwell, Plymouth, Devon, PL7 5DF
☎ 01752 837219, Fax 837219, Rest/Bar 837374
A38 from Plymouth, turn left at Plympton then signposted to Sparkwell.
Parkland course.
Founded 1993
9 holes, 5772 yards, S.S.S. 68
 Welcome; pay as you play course.
 WD £7; WE £8.
 Welcome; full facilities available.
 Full bar and restaurant facilities.
 Welbeck Manor.

3A 67 Staddon Heights
Plymouth, Devon, PL9 9SP
 www.staddon-heights.co.uk
 golfclub@staddon-heights.co.uk
☎ 01752 402475, Fax 401998, Sec ext 22
Club is five miles south of the city near the Royal Navy aerials.
Parkland cliff-top course; no par fives.
Pro Ian Marshall; Founded 1904
18 holes, 5845 yards, S.S.S. 68
 Welcome if carrying handicap certificates.
 WD £20, WE £24.
 Welcome with prior arrangement and handicap certificates; catering available; £25.
 Bar Available.

3A 68 Tavistock
Down Rd, Tavistock, Devon, PL19 9AQ
 www.tavygolfclub.org.uk
 tavygolf@hotmail.com
☎ 01822 612049, Fax 612344, Pro 612316, Sec 612344

From town centre take Whitchurch Road, turn left at Down Road. Moorland course.
Pro Dominic Rehaag; Founded 1890
18 holes, 6495 yards, S.S.S. 71
† Welcome on weekdays by prior arrangement; must be accompanied by member at weekend.
 WD £26; WE £32.
 Welcome by prior arrangement; minimum 20; terms on application.
 Full clubhouse facilities.
 Bedford.

3A 69 Tehidy Park
Tehidy, Camborne, Cornwall, TR14 0HH
☎ 01209 842208, Fax 843680,
Pro 842914, Rest/Bar 842557
Off A30 at Camborne exit; follow Portreath signs to club; 2 miles north-east of Camborne.
Parkland course.
Pro James Dumbreck; Founded 1922
18 holes, 6241 yards, S.S.S. 71
 Practice Area.
† Welcome with handicap certs; day ticket, WD £25.50, WE £30.50.
 WD £22.50 WE £27.50.
 Welcome with handicap certificates; packages available.
 Full bar snacks/meals available.

3A 70 Teign Valley Golf Club
Christow, Exeter, Devon, EX6 7PA
☎ 01647 253026, Pro 253127
From M5 to A38 Plymouth road taking exit marked Teign Valley.
Parkland course.
Pro Scott Amiet; Founded 1995
Designed by David Nicholson
18 holes, 5913 yards, S.S.S. 68
† Welcome.
 WD from £17, WE from £20.
 Welcome; packages available; discounts for larger groups; catering packages arranged; terms on application.
 Full bar and catering facilities.
 Ilsington; Passage House; club manager can arrange local B&Bs.

3A 71 Teignmouth
Teignmouth Golf Club, Teignmouth, Devon, TQ14 9NY
 www.teignmouthgolfclub.co.uk
 info@teignmouthgolfclub.co.uk
☎ 01626 777070, Fax 777304,
Pro 772894, Rest/Bar 773614
2 miles from Teignmouth on B3192.
Heathland course.
Pro Robert Selley; Founded 1924
Designed by Dr Alister MacKenzie

18 holes, 6083 yards, S.S.S. 69
† Must be members of a club and have handicap certificates.
 WD from £25 WE from £27.50.
 Welcome Thurs by arrangement; full facilities available.
 Full facilities available.
 London; The Bay Hotel.

3A 72 Thurlestone Golf Club
Thurlestone, Kingsbridge, Devon, TQ7 3NZ
☎ 01548 560405, Fax 562149,
Pro 560715, Sec 560405,
Rest/Bar 560405
Seaward side of A379 Kingsbridge-Salcombe road.
Clifftop course.
Pro Peter Laugher; Founded 1897
Designed by H S Colt.
18 holes, 6340 yards, S.S.S. 70
† Welcome, must have handicap certificates.
 WD/WE £32.
 None.
 Available.
 Thurlestone Hotel; Cottage Hotel.

3A 73 Tiverton
Post Hill, Tiverton, Devon, EX16 4NE
 tivertongolfclub@lineone.net
☎ 01884 252187, Fax 251607,
Pro 254836, Rest/Bar 252114
5 miles from Junction 27 on M5 towards Tiverton on A373; take first exit left on dual carriageway through Samford Peverell to Halberton.
Parkland/meadow course.
Pro Michael Hawton; Founded 1931
Designed by James Braid
18 holes, 6236 yards, S.S.S. 71
† Welcome with letter of introduction or handicap certificates, not Wednesday, weekends, Bank Holidays or competition days.
 WD £21, WE £31.
 By prior arrangement.
 Lunch and teas available.
 Parkway House Hotel, Lower Town, Sampford Peverell.

3A 74 Torquay
Petitor Road, Torquay, Devon, TQ1 4QF
 www.torquaygolfclub.corg.uk
 torquaygolfclub@skynow.net
☎ 01803 314591, Fax 316116,
Pro 329113, Rest/Bar 313438
North of Torquay on A379 Teignmouth road on outskirts of town.
Parkland course.
Pro Martin Ruth; Founded 1910

18 holes, 6175 yards, S.S.S. 69
 Practice nets.
† Welcome with handicap certificates.
 WD £25.50; WE £32.50.
 Welcome by prior arrangement.
 Full Facilities.

3A 75 Torrington
Weare Trees, Torrington, Devon, EX38 7EZ
 theoffice@torringtongolf.fsnet.co.uk
☎ 01805 622229, Fax 623878
Between Bideford and Torrington.
Heathland course.
Founded 1895/1932
9 holes, 4429 yards, S.S.S. 62
† Welcome.
 WD£12; WE £12.
 Welcome by prior arrangement to secretary; terms on application.
 Facilities available.

3A 76 Tregenna Castle Hotel ℡
St Ives, Cornwall, TR26 2DE
☎ 01736 795254, Fax 796066,
Sec 797381
In grounds of Tregenna Castle Hotel, signposted to left just before St Ives on A3074 from Hayle.
Parkland course.
Founded 1982
18 holes, 3478 yards, S.S.S. 58
† Welcome.
 WD£13.50; WE £13.50.
 Welcome by prior arrangement; full facilities; terms on application.
 Full bar and restaurant.
 Tregenna Castle.

3A 77 Treloy
Newquay, Cornwall, TR8 4JN
☎ 01637 878554, Fax 871710
On A3059 St Columb Major-Newquay road, 3 miles from Newquay.
Public heathland/parkland course.
Founded 1991
Pro Designed by MRM Sandow
9 holes, 4286 yards, S.S.S. 62
† Welcome.
 WD £12.50; WE £12.50.
 Welcome.
 Bar, full facilities.
 Barrowfield; California Hotel, Newquay.

3A 78 Trethorne Golf Club ℡
Kennards House, Launceston, Cornwall, PL15 8QE
 www.trethornegolfclub.com
 jen@trethornegolfclub.com

TREVOSE GOLF & COUNTRY CLUB

Constantine Bay, Padstow, Cornwall. Tel: **(01841) 520208** Fax: **(01841) 521057**
Email: **info@trevose-gc.co.uk** **http://www.trevose-gc.co.uk**

- Championship Golf Course of 18 holes, S.S.S.71. Fully automatic watering on all greens.
- 2 x 9 hole courses. One 3100 yards, par 35; the other 1369 yards, par29.
- Excellent appointed Clubhouse with Bar and Restaurant providing full catering facilities. A/C throughout.

- Superior accommodation in 18 flats, 7 chalets, 6 bungalows and 4 cabins. Daily rates available. Mid-week bookings encouraged.
- **OPEN ALL YEAR.**
- 3 hard tennis courts.
- Heated swimming pool open from mid May to mid September.

- In addition to Membership for Golf and tennis, Social Membership of the Club is also available with full use of the Clubhouse facilities.
- 6 glorious sandy bays within about a mile of the Clubhouse, with pools, open sea and surf bathing.
- 8 miles from Civil Airport.
- Daily flights to and from London Gatwick.
- **SOCIETIES WELCOME.**

☎ 01566 86903, Fax 86981,
Pro 86903, Sec 86903,
Rest/Bar 86903
2 miles west of Launceston, 200 yards off the A30 on the A395.
Parkland course.
Pro Mark Boundy; Founded 1993
Designed by F Frayne
18 holes, 6432 yards, S.S.S. 71
⚑ Practice range, floodlit driving range and 9 bays.
♦ Welcome.
⌾ WD £28; WE £28.
⌁ Welcome; £15 for 18 holes.
⊙ Available.
⌂ Guest House on site.

3A 79 **Trevose Golf and** ⚷
Country Club
Constantine Bay, Padstow, Cornwall, PL28 8JB
⌸ www.trevose-gc.co.uk
✉ info@trevose-gc.co.uk
☎ 01841 520208, Fax 521057,
Pro 520261
Course is four miles west of Padstow off the B3276.
Seaside links course.
Pro Gary Alliss; Founded 1925
Designed by HS Colt
18 holes, 6608 yards, S.S.S. 71
⚑ Driving range under construction.
♦ Welcome; 3 and 4 ball matches restricted; phone first.
⌾ WD £38; WE £38 (summer).
⌁ Welcome anytime, except from July to September; full facilities available.
⊙ Full facilities.
⌂ Own self-contained accomodation available; phone for details.

3A 80 **Truro** ⚷
Tresawls Road, Truro, Cornwall, TR1 3LG
☎ 01872 272640, Fax 278684,
Pro 276595, Sec 278684

On edge of Truro adjacent to Treliske Hospital on the A390 Truro to Redruth road.
Undulating parkland overlooking Truro; no par fives.
Pro Nigel Bicknell; Founded 1937
Designed by Colt, Alison & Morrison
18 holes, 5306 yards, S.S.S. 66
♦ Welcome if carrying handicap certificates.
⌾ WD £20, WE £25.
⌁ Welcome; inclusive price on application.
⊙ Two bars and a restaurant.
⌂ The Brookdale; The Golf View.

3A 81 **Warren** ⚷
Dawlish Warren, Dawlish, Devon, EX7 0NF
⌸ www.dwgc.co.uk
✉ secretary@dwgc.co.uk
☎ 01626 862255, Fax 888005,
Pro 864002, Sec 862255,
Rest/Bar 862493
12 miles south of Exeter off the A379.
Links course.
Pro Darren Prowse; Founded 1892
Designed by J Braid & Sir Guy Campbell
18 holes, 5912 yards, S.S.S. 68
♦ Welcome.
⌾ WD £25; WE £28.
⌁ Welcome by application; terms on application.
⊙ Bar and meals available.
⌂ Langstone Cliff; Sea Lawn Lodge.

3A 82 **Waterbridge**
Down St Mary, Crediton, Devon, EX17 5LG
⌸ www.waterbridge.fsnet.co.uk
☎ 01363 85111, Pro 83406
Off A377 Barnstaple road, 1 mile after Copplestone.
Parkland course.
Pro David Ridyard; Founded 1992
Designed by David Taylor

9 holes, 3910 yards, S.S.S. 64
♦ WD £7; WE £8 (9 holes).
⌾ As above.
⌁ Welcome by arrangement; packages available; terms on application.
⊙ Licensed café bar with light meals.
⌂ New Inn, Crediton.

3A 83 **West Cornwall**
Church Lane, Lelant, St Ives, Cornwall, TR26 3DZ
✉ ian@westcornwallgolfclub.fsnet.co.uk
☎ 01736 753401, Pro 753177,
Rest/Bar 753319
Take A30 to Lelant, right at Badger Inn.
Links course.
Pro Jason Broadway; Founded 1889
Designed by Rev Tyack
18 holes, 5884 yards, S.S.S. 69
⚑ Practice ground.
♦ Welcome with handicap certificates.
⌾ Prices on application.
⌁ Welcome; catering to be negotiated; snooker.
⊙ Restaurant, snack bar and bar.
⌂ Badger Inn, Lelant.

3A 84 **Whitsand Bay Hotel** ⚷
Seaview Cottage, Finnygook Lane, Portewrinkle, Cornwall, PL11 3BU
⌸ www.whitsandbayhotel.co.uk
✉ whitsandbay@btconnect.com
☎ 01503 230276, Fax 230329,
Pro 230788
On B3247 6 miles off A38 from Plymouth.
Clifftop course.
Pro S Poole; Founded 1905
Designed by William Fernie of Troon
18 holes, 5885 yards, S.S.S. 69
♦ Handicap certificates except for residents.
⌾ WD £20; WE £22.50.
⌁ Welcome; bar and leisure facilities; terms on application.
⌂ Whitsand Bay.

3A 85 Woodbury Park Golf and Country Club ☎
Woodbury Castle, Woodbury, Exeter, Devon, EX5 1JJ
🔗 www.woodburypark.co.uk
✉ golfbookings@woodburypark.co.uk
☎ 01395 233382, Fax 233384, Pro 233500
From M5 J30, take A3052 Sidmouth road, turn right onto B3180, after approx. 1 mile turn right to Woodbury, then immediately turn right to course.
Parkland course.
Pro Alan Richards; Founded 1992
Designed by J Hamilton Stutt
18 holes, 6905 yards, S.S.S. 73
🏌 16 bays (covered).
† Welcome with handicap certificates.
[Prices on application.
⌢ Welcome by prior arrangement; catering packages by arrangement; 9-hole Acorn course: 4582 yards, par 65; terms on application.

🍽 Full facilities.
🛏 55 4 star bedrooms + Swiss style lodges on site with leisure complex.

3A 86 Wrangaton
Golf Links Road, Wrangaton, South Brent, Devon, TQ10 9HJ
☎ 01364 73229, Fax 73229, Pro 72161, Rest/Bar 73001
Turn off A38 between South Brent and Bittaford at Wrangaton Post Office.
Moorland/parkland course.
Pro Glenn Richards; Founded 1895
Designed by Donald Steel
18 holes, 6083 yards, S.S.S. 69
🏌 Practice area.
† Welcome with handicap certificates or member of recognised club; no beginners.
[WD £20; WE £20.
⌢ Welcome by arrangement.

🍽 Bar and catering.
🛏 The Coach House Inn; Glazebrook.

3A 87 Yelverton ☎
Golf Links Road, Yelverton, Devon, PL20 6BN
🔗 www.yelvertongc.co.uk
✉ secretary@yelvertongc.co.uk
☎ 01822 852824, Fax 854869, Pro 853593, Sec 852824, Rest/Bar 852824
Off A386, 8 miles north of Plymouth.
Moorland course.
Pro Tim McSherry; Founded 1904
Designed by Herbert Fowler
18 holes, 6353 yards, S.S.S. 71
† Welcome with handicap certificates.
[WD £30; WE £40.
⌢ Welcome with handicap certificates; full bar/restaurant facilities.
🍽 Restaurant and bar.
🛏 Moorland Links Hotel; Burrator Inn; Rosemount Guest House.

3B

Somerset, Dorset, Wiltshire and South Avon

When Bath became England's leading rugby club in the 1980's county golf was not high on the list of Somerset's sporting priorities. Burnham and Berrow remained one of the country's finest links courses, but after that there was plenty of pause for thought. This is not royal golfing land.

But when David Dixon won the silver medal for the leading amateur at the 2001 Open Championship he reminded everyone of the progress the game has made in some of the less acknowledged golfing parts of the country.

Dixon emerged from Enmore Park Golf Club near Bridgewater. Boosted by a gentleman who made a small fortune out of keeping central heating systems quiet, Enmore Park is typical of many a less famous club that now has a flourishing junior section.

Wiltshire is another county without a great golf reputation that is starting to attract investment. Peter Green, a friend and adviser to Dixon, is the affable professional at Manor House Golf Club. The course was designed by Peter Alliss and Clive Clark and is located in one of England's most picturesque towns. Apart from its beauty, Castle Combe is remarkable for its absence of television aerials. They were all replaced by cable when the 1967 film *Dr Doolittle* was shot in the town.

Another relatively new course to the area is Bowood. With one par five of 600 yards it is unsociably long off the back tees, particularly in winter when it can get a bit boggy. But on the holes where the designers didn't get overly excited there are challenges and views to absorb the golfer. The course is set beside the Great Park, 2,000 acres that were originally laid out by Capability Brown.

The modernist fingers of Alliss have done much progressive prodding in this part of England, but they began their golfing activities at Ferndown in Dorset where his father was the professional. In contrast to Bowood, you don't have to be a mighty hitter to cope with Ferndown, just a good golfer. The heather, birch and pines are reminiscent of some of Surrey's lovelier courses.

Dorset is the richest golfing county in this region. Parkstone, a course which like Ashridge has five par fives and five par threes, and Broadstone are both high quality lay-outs, although the last time I was at Broadstone the bar was invaded by the navel-pierced and Stetson-wearing in preparation for a line-dancing evening. Queens Park is one of the best public courses in England and the Isle of Purbeck has some of the finest views and some absorbing holes that include the signature fifth, with its terrifying blind drive.

The finish to one of the most exposed of the courses in the area, Came Down's eighteenth hole has views of Egdon Heath, the "great inviolate" hero of Thomas Hardy's *The Return of the Native*. "The sea changed, the fields changed, the rivers, the villages, and the people changed, yet Egdon remained." It has even proved fairly resistant to golf course designers.

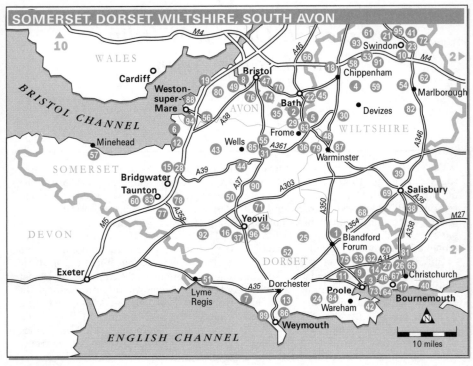

SOMERSET, DORSET, WILTSHIRE, SOUTH AVON

WALES

Cardiff

Weston-super-Mare

BRISTOL CHANNEL

Minehead

SOMERSET

Bridgwater

Taunton

DEVON

Exeter

Lyme Regis

ENGLISH CHANNEL

Bristol

Bath

AVON

Wells

Frome

Warminster

WILTSHIRE

Swindon

Chippenham

Marlborough

Devizes

Yeovil

Blandford Forum

Dorchester

Poole

Wareham

Weymouth

Bournemouth

Christchurch

Salisbury

DORSET

10 miles

KEY

1	The Ashley Wood Golf Club	32	Ferndown
2	Bath Golf Club	33	Ferndown Forest
3	Bournemouth & Meyrick Park	34	Folke
4	Bowood Golf & Country Club	35	Fosseway Country Club
5	Bradford-on-Avon	36	Frome
6	Brean	37	Halstock
7	Bridport & West Dorset	38	Hamptworth Golf & Country Club
8	Bristol & Clifton	39	High Post
9	Broadstone	40	Highcliffe Castle
10	Broome Manor	41	Highworth Golf Centre
11	Bulbury	42	Isle of Purbeck
12	Burnham & Berrow	43	Isle of Wedmore
13	Came Down	44	King Weston
14	Canford Magna	45	Kingsdown
15	Cannington	46	Knighton Heath
16	Chedington Court	47	Knowle
17	Chichester	48	Lafarge (Westbury)
18	Chippenham	49	Long Ashton
19	Clevedon	50	Long Sutton
20	Crane Valley	51	Lyme Regis
21	Cricklade Hotel & Country Club	52	Lyons Gate
22	Cumberwell Park	53	Manor House Golf Club (at Castle Combe)
23	Defence Academy	54	Marlborough
24	Dorset Golf & Country Club	55	Mendip
25	Dorset Heights	56	Mendip Spring
26	Dudmoor	57	Minehead & West Somerset
27	Dudsbury	58	Monkton Park Par 3
28	Enmore Park	59	North Wilts
29	Entry Hill	60	Oake Manor
30	Erlestoke Sands	61	Oaksey Park
31	Farrington	62	Ogbourne Downs
		63	Orchardleigh
		64	Parkstone

65	Parley Golf Centre
66	The Players Club
67	Queen's Park (Bournemouth)
68	Rushmore
69	Salisbury & South Wiltshire
70	Saltford
71	Sherborne
72	Shrivenham Park
73	Solent Meads Golf for All
74	Stockwood Vale
75	Sturminster Marshall
76	Tall Pines
77	Taunton & Pickeridge
78	Taunton Vale
79	Thoulstone Park
80	Tickenham
81	Two Riversmeet
82	Upavon (RAF)
83	Vivary
84	Wareham
85	Wells (Somerset)
86	Wessex Golf Centre
87	West Wilts
88	Weston-super-Mare
89	Weymouth
90	Wheathill
91	The Wiltshire Golf and Country Club
92	Windwhistle
93	Woodbridge Park
94	Worlebury
95	Wrag Barn Golf & Country Club
96	Yeovil

3B 1 The Ashley Wood Golf Club

Wimborne Road, Blandford Forum, Dorset, DT11 9HN

📧 ashleywoodgolfclub@hotmail.com

📞 01258 452253, Fax 450590, Pro 480379, Sec 452253, Rest/Bar 450190

Half a mile from Blandford.
Parkland course; two par fives in first three holes.
Pro John Shimmons; Founded 1896
Designed by Patrick Tallack
18 holes, 6276 yards, S.S.S. 70

🚹 Welcome weekdays.

💷 WD £25.

🛎 Welcome Weekdays by prior application to Secretary.

🏨 Anville (Pimperne).

3B 2 Bath Golf Club ⓣ

Sham Castle, North Road, Bath, Avon, BA2 6JG

📞 01225 463834, Fax 331027, Pro 466953, Sec 463834, Rest/Bar 425182

One and a half miiles south east off A36 Warminster road.

BOWOOD
GOLF & COUNTRY CLUB

Set in the heart of 'Capability' Brown's Great Park and the 2,000 acre estate of Bowood House and Gardens.

- Corporate Golf Events
- Society Golf Days
- Conferencing/Activities
- Queenwood Golf Lodge
- Social Events
- Wedding Ceremonies & Receptions.

Bowood Golf and Country Club, Derry Hill, Calne SN11 9PQ
Tel: **01249 822228**   Fax: **01249 822218**
E-mail: **golfclub@bowood.org**   Website: **www.bowood.org**

Downland course.
Pro Peter Hancox; Founded 1880
Designed by HS Colt
18 holes, 6438 yards, S.S.S. 71
𝅘 4.
† Welcome, handicap certificates required.
⌶ WD £30/£36; WE £36/£40.
⟳ Welcome Wed and Fri only; coffee, 18 holes, £25.
⦿ restaurant, bar snacks.
⤳ Bath; Beafort; Dukes; Spa.

3B 3 **Bournemouth & Meyrick Park**
Central Drive, Meyrick Park, Bournemouth, Dorset, BH2 6LH
⚏ www.clubhaus.com
☎ 01202 786040, Fax 786020, Rest/Bar 786000
In centre of Bournemouth.
Picturesque parkland course (Meyrick Park).
Pro David Miles; Founded 1890
18 holes, 5461 yards, S.S.S. 69
† Welcome; advisable to book up to 7 days in advance.
⌶ WD £17.50; WE £20.50.
⟳ Welcome by prior arrangement; packages available; full facilities.
⦿ Bars and restaurant.
⤳ 17 bedroom lodge.

3B 4 **Bowood Golf and Country Club**   ₢
Derry Hill, Calne, Wilts, SN11 9PQ
⚏ www.bowood.org
✉ golfclub@bowood.org
☎ 01249 822228, Fax 822218
Off the A4 between Chippenham and Calne.
Parkland course.
Pro Max Taylor; Founded 1992
Designed by Dave Thomas
18 holes, 7317 yards, S.S.S. 72
𝅘 Practice range, 10 bays, floodlit; 3 hole Academy course.

† Welcome on weekdays and after 12 noon weekends.
⌶ Prices on application.
⟳ Welcome by prior arrangement; special rates on Monday.
⦿ Full facilities.
⤳ Queenwood Golf Lodge; Bowood Golf and CC.

3B 5 **Bradford-on-Avon**
Avon Close, Bradford on Avon, Wilts, BA15 1JJ
☎ 01225 868268
From Bardford towards Trowbridge on left near Police Station.
Picturesque parkland course next to River Avon.
Founded 1991
9 holes, 2109 yards, S.S.S. 61
† Welcome anytime; pay and play.
⌶ £6 for 9 holes; £10 for 18 holes.
⟳ Welcome by prior arrangement.
⦿ None.

3B 6 **Brean**   ₢
Coast Road, Berrow, Burnham on Sea, Somerset, TA8 2QY
⚏ www.brean.com
✉ admin@brean.com
☎ 01278 751595, Fax 752102, Pro 752111, Sec 752103
Follow tourist signs for Brean Leisure Park from Junction 22 off M5.
Meadowland course.
Pro David Haines; Founded 1973
Designed by Brean Leisure Park
18 holes, 5715 yards, S.S.S. 68
† Welcome at all times except competition days.
⌶ WD £18; WE £20.
⟳ Welcome weekdays and after 1pm at weekends; packages available from £20.
⦿ Facilities available.
⤳ Accomodation available on the Brean Leisure Park.

3B 7 **Bridport and West Dorset**   ₢
Burton Road, Bridport, Dorset, DT6 4EP
⚏ www.bridportgolfclub.org.uk
✉ B_Wdgc@btinternet.com
☎ 01308 421095, Fax 421095, Pro 421591, Rest/Bar 421998
One mile east of Bridport on B3157 towards Burton Bradstock.
Clifftop links course.
Pro David Parsons; Founded 1891
Designed by CSP Salmon/1996 modified by F Hawtree
18 holes, 5729 yards, S.S.S. 67
𝅘 Driving range.
† Welcome; dress codes apply.
⌶ WD £22; WE £22.
⟳ Welcome; bookings must be made in advance; packages can be arranged to meet individual requirements; terms on application.
⦿ Full facilities.
⤳ Haddon House, West Bay.

3B 8 **Bristol and Clifton**   ₢
Beggar Bush Lane, Failand, Bristol, Avon, BS8 3TH
⚏ www.bristolgolf.co.uk
✉ mansec@bristolgolf.co.uk
☎ 01275 393474, Fax 394611, Pro 393031, Sec 393474, Rest/Bar 393117
Junction 19 off M5, 4 miles along A369 to Bristol, turn right at traffic lights, then further 1.5 miles.
Parkland course.
Pro Paul Mitchell; Founded 1891
18 holes, 6316 yards, S.S.S. 70
𝅘 Driving range.
† Welcome weekdays with handicap certificates; restrictions at weekends.
⌶ WD £35; WE £40.
⟳ Welcome by arrangement on Thurs only; full facilities available.
⦿ Full facilities.
⤳ Redwood Lodge.

3B 9 **Broadstone**
Broadstone Dorset Golf Club,
Wentworth Drive, Broadstone, Dorset,
BH18 8DQ
🖳 www.broadstonegolfclub.com
📧 admin@broadstonegolfclub.com
☎ 01202 692595, Fax 642520,
Pro 692835, Rest/Bar 693363
Take A349 from Poole to the village;
the club is signposted off the main
roundabout.
Heathland course.
Pro Nigel Tokley; Founded 1898
Designed by Tom Dunn (1898) & HS
Colt (1920)
18 holes, 6315 yards, S.S.S. 70
† Members may introduce one guest
per round.
Ⅰ WD £40/round. WE subject to
booking/availability.
⌁ Welcome but there are restricted
times so it is essential to phone in
advance.
🍴 Full bar and restaurant facilities.

3B 10 **Broome Manor**
Pipers Way, Swindon, Wilts,
SN3 1RG
☎ 01793 495761, Fax 433255,
Pro 532403, Rest/Bar 490939
Take junction 15 off M4 and follow
signs; course 2 miles off motorway.
Parkland course.
Pro Barry Sandry; Founded 1976
Designed by Hawtree & Son
18 & 9 holes, 6283 & 2690 yards,
S.S.S. 70 & 33
Ⅰ Practice range and 34 bays.
† Pay and play course.
Ⅰ 9 holes £11.60; 18 holes £19.10.
⌁ Welcome Monday to Friday; 27
holes, driving range and most
packages include first tee video and
analysis; £20-£50.
🍴 Full facilities.

3B 11 **Bulbury Woods Golf Club**
Halls Road, Lytchett Minster, Poole,
Dorset, BH16 6HR
☎ 01929 459574, Fax 459000
Just off A35, one mile after Bakers
Arms roundabout. Three miles from
Poole centre.
Woodland course.
Pro David Adams; Founded 1989
Designed by J Sharkey
18 holes, 6313 yards, S.S.S. 70
† Welcome subject to availability.
Ⅰ WD £16; WE £22.
⌁ Welcome by prior arrangement.
🍴 Full à la carte and bistro menu.
📍 On site accomodation.

3B 12 **Burnham & Berrow**
St Christopher's Way, Burnham-on-
Sea, Somerset, TA8 2PE
🖳 www.burnhamandberrowgolfclub
.co.uk
📧 secretary@
burnhamandberrowgolfclub.co.uk
☎ 01278 783137, Fax 795440, Pro
784545, Sec 785760, Rest/Bar 783137
M5 Junction 22; 1 mile N of Burnham.
Seaside links; also has a 9-hole course.
Pro Mark Crowther-Smith; Founded
1890
18 holes, 6759 yards, S.S.S. 73
Ⅰ Practice area (own balls required).
† Must be members of golf clubs
with handicaps of 22 and under.
Ⅰ Championship course: WD £45
(18), £60 (36); WE £60 (18).
Channel course (9 hole): £15/day.
£50 for 27 holes (18 Championship, 9
Channel).
⌁ Terms on application.
🍴 Full facilities.
📍 Batch Farm, Lympsham; Lulworth
GH, Warren GH, both Burnham on
Sea.

3B 13 **Came Down**
Dorchester, Dorset, DT2 8NR
☎ 01305 812531, Fax 813494
2 miles S of Dorchester off A354.
Undulating downland course.
Pro Nick Rodgers; Founded 1896
Designed by JH Taylor
18 holes, 6244 yards, S.S.S. 71
† Welcome by arrangement with
handicap certs; midweek after 9am;
Sun after 11am.
Ⅰ Terms on application.
⌁ Welcome by arrangement on Wed;
packages available approx £32; full
facilities.
🍴 Bar and restaurant.
📍 Rembrandt (Weymouth); Junction
Hotel (Dorchester).

3B 14 **Canford Magna**
Knighton Lane, Wimborne, Dorset,
BH21 3AS
☎ 01202 592552, Fax 592550,
Sec 592505
Off the A341 Magna road near the
Bearcross roundabout on the main
A348 Ringwood road.
Parkland course.
Pro Martyn Cummins; Founded 1994
Designed by Howard Swan
45 holes, 6495, 6173 and 2754 yards,
S.S.S. 70:71
Ⅰ 6-hole Academy course and
driving range; 9-hole par 3 course.
† Welcome.

Ⅰ Prices on application.
⌁ Welcome by prior arrangement;
Cygnet Suite available for corporate
hire.
🍴 Two bars and a restaurant.
📍 Contact local tourist board.

3B 15 **Cannington**
Cannington College, Nr Bridgewater,
Somerset, TA5 2LS
☎ 01278 655050
Leave the M5 at Junction 23. Take the
A38 to Bridgewater; course is 4 miles
from Bridgewater on the A39 road to
Minehead.
Links/parkland course.
Pro Ron Macrow; Founded 1993
Designed by Martin Hawtree
9 holes 18 tees, 6072 yards,
S.S.S. 68
Ⅰ New Driving Range10 floodlit bays.
Two-ball practice balls.
† Welcome.
Ⅰ 9 hole: £9.50 WD, £12.50 WE;
18 hole: £14 WD, £18.50 WE.
⌁ Apply to Pro; terms on application.
🍴 Clubhouse facilities.

3B 16 **Chedington Court**
South Perrott, Beaminster, Dorset,
DT8 3HU
📧 chedingtoncourtgolfclub@
waitrose.com
☎ 01935 891413, Fax 891217,
Pro 891413, Sec 891413,
Rest/Bar 891413
0.5 mile E of South Perrott on A356
Crewkerne-Dorchester road.
Parkland course.
Founded 1991
Designed by D Hemstock; D Astill
18 holes, 5924 yards, S.S.S. 70
Ⅰ Driving range and practice area.
† Welcome; properly dressed.
Ⅰ WD £16; WE £20.
⌁ Welcome by arrangement; terms
on application.
🍴 Bar and Catering facilities
available all day.
📍 The Stage Coach, Crewekerne.

3B 17 **Chichester**
Iford Bridge Sports Centre, Barrack
Rd, Christchurch, Dorset, BH23 2BA
☎ 01202 473817
Off the A35 between Bournemouth and
Christchurch.
Parkland course.
Pro Laurence Moxon; Founded 1977
9 holes, 4360 yards, S.S.S. 61
Ⅰ Practice range.

† Welcome.
[WD £6.40; WE £7.25.
⟳ Welcome by prior arrangement;
also tennis, bowling.
🍽 Full bar facilities.
🛏 Contact local tourist board.

3B 18 Chippenham
Malmesbury Road, Chippenham, Wilts,
SN15 5LT
🖳 www.chippenhamgolfclub.co.uk
🖥 chippenhamgc@onetel.net.uk
☎ 01249 652040, Fax 446681,
Pro 655519, Sec 652040,
Rest/Bar 443481
From M4 Junction 17 take A350
towards Chippenham; course on right
before town.
Parkland course.
Pro Bill Creamer; Founded 1896
18 holes, 5600 yards, S.S.S. 67
🏌 Practice fairway.
† Everyone welcome.
[WD £22; WE £27.
⟳ Welcome Tues, Thurs, Fri by prior
arrangement; full day of golf and
catering packages available.
🍽 Clubhouse facilities.
🛏 Travel Inn overlooks 1st fairway.

3B 19 Clevedon
Castle Road, Clevedon, North
Somerset, BS21 7AA
🖳 www.clevedongolfclub.co.uk
🖥 clevedongc.sec@virgin.net
☎ 01275 874057, Fax 341228,
Pro 874704, Rest/Bar 341443
Leave the M5 at Junction 20 and follow
the signs to Portishead; turn right into
Walton Road then Holly Lane.
Hilltop course overlooking Bristol
Channel.
Pro Robert Scanlan; Founded 1891
Designed by JH Taylor
18 holes, 6557 yards, S.S.S. 72
† Welcome with handicap certs.
[WD £28; WE £40.
⟳ Welcome; must book in advance
and minimum of 12; terms on
application.
🍽 Facilities and bar.
🛏 Walton Park; Highcliffe House.

3B 20 Crane Valley ☎
The Club House, Verwood, Dorset,
BH31 7LE
🖥 crane-valley@hoburne.com
☎ 01202 814088, Fax 813407
On B3081 Verwood to Cranborne
Road.
Parkland course featuring lakes and
River Crane.

Pro Darrel Ranson; Founded 1992
Designed by Donald Steel
18 holes, 6400 yards, S.S.S. 7;
9 hole woodland course, 2100 yards.
🏌 Covered driving range.
† Welcome at all times.
[Terms on application.
⟳ Welcome by appointment.
🍽 Restaurant and bar facilities.
🛏 St Leonards Hotel.

3B 21 Cricklade Hotel &
Country Club
Common Hill, Cricklade, Near
Swindon, SN6 6HA
🖳 www.crickladehotel.co.uk
🖥 info@crickladehotel.co.uk
☎ 01793 750751, Fax 751767,
Rest/Bar 750751
B4040 Cricklade-Malmesbury road 15
mins from M4 Junctions 15/16.
Parkland course.
Pro Ian Bolt; Founded 1990
Designed by Ian Bolt/C Smith
9 holes, 3660 yards, S.S.S. 57
† Welcome Mon-Fri; WE must be
accompanied by a member.
[WD £16 WE must be guest of
member £10 charge.
⟳ Welcome; terms available on
application.
🍽 Full bar and restaurant facilities.

3B 22 Cumberwell Park
Bradford on Avon, Wilts, BA15 2PQ
🖳 www.cumberwellpark.com
🖥 enquiries@cumberwellpark.com
☎ 01225 863322, Fax 868160,
Pro 862332, Sec 863322,
Rest/Bar 863322
M4 Junction 18; take A46 to Bath and
then A363 to Bradford-on-Avon.
Parkland course.
Pro John Jacobs; Founded 1994
Designed by Adrian Stiff
27 holes, Park 6123, Wood 6405, Lake
6040 yards, S.S.S. Park 71 Wood 70
Lake 71
🏌 8 undercover, 10 outdoors;
teaching facilities also available.
† Welcome.
[WD £26; WE £32.
⟳ Welcome Mon-Fri; 27 holes of golf
plus 3-course private dinner and coffee
on arrival; prices on application. Winter
and summer brochure available
🍽 Bar and restaurant.
🛏 Bath Spa Hotel; Leigh Park;
Combe Grove Manor.

3B 23 Defence Academy
Swindon, Wilts, SN6 8LA

☎ 01793 785725
In the grounds of the Defence
Academy on A420 1 mile NE of
Shrivenham.
Parkland course.
Founded 1953
18 holes, 5684 yards, S.S.S. 69
🏌 Practice green.
† Restricted access; welcome with
member.
[WD £10; WE £10.
⟳ Welcome WD subject to
availability.
🍽 Coffee and soft drinks.

3B 24 The Dorset Golf & ☎
Country Club
Bere Regis, Nr Poole, Dorset, BH20 7NT
🖳 www.dorsetgolfresort.com
🖥 admin@dorsetgolfresort.com
☎ 01929 472244, Fax 471294,
Pro 473915, Sec 473911
A35 or A31 50 Bere Regis take Wool
road and signs to the club.
Parkland course.
Pro Derwyn Honan; Founded 1978
Designed by Martin Hawtree
18 holes, 7029 yards, S.S.S. 74;
9 holes, 5032 yards, S.S.S. 64
🏌 Practice range; floodlit & covered.
† Welcome with prior reservation.
[Lakeland: WD £35, WE £39;
Woodland: WD £24, WE £28.
⟳ Welcome any day with reservation;
combination of courses and catering
on application; from £18.
🍽 Full facilities.
🛏 Own accommodation in the Dorset
Golf Hotel – luxury log homes with log
stoves and sauna; includes free golf.

3B 25 Dorset Heights
Belchalwell, Blandford Forum, Dorset,
DT11 0EG
☎ 01258 861386
On A357 Sturminster Newton-
Blandford road.
Woodland course.
Founded 1991
Designed by Project Golf (DW Asthill)
18 holes, 6138 yards, S.S.S. 70
† Welcome with prior arrangement.
[Terms on application.
⟳ Welcome by prior arrangement;
packages available; restaurant; terms
on application.
🍽 Restaurant and bar.
🛏 Crown Hotel, Blandford.

3B 26 Dudmoor
Dudmoor Farm Rd, Christchurch,
Dorset, BH23 6AQ

☎ 01202 473826, Fax 480207
Off A35 W of Christchurch.
Woodland course.
Founded 1974
9 holes, 1575 yards
† Welcome anytime.
[Terms on application.
⌒ Welcome by arrangement.
🍽 Snacks and soft drinks.
🛏 Avon Causeway.

3B 27 Dudsbury ℭ
64 Christchurch Road, Ferndown,
Dorset, BH22 8ST
🖳 www.thedudsbury.co.uk
✉ giles@dudsbury.demon.co.uk
☎ 01202 593499, Fax 594555,
Pro 594488
On B3073 off A348 from Ferndown.
Parkland course.
Pro Kevin Spurgeon; Founded 1992
Designed by Donald Steel
18 holes, 6904 yards, S.S.S. 73
⟂ 8.
† Welcome with prior booking.
[WD £34; WE £39.
⌒ Welcome; packages available from
secretary; 6-hole par 3 course; terms
on application. Spikes and lounge bar.
⌒ function room and restaurant.
🛏 Dormy Hotel; Bridge House.

3B 28 Enmore Park
Enmore, Bridgewater, Somerset,
TA5 2AN
🖳 www.golfdirector.com/enmore
✉ golfclub@enmore.fsnet.co.uk
☎ 01278 671481, Fax 671740, Pro
671519, Rest/Bar 671244
M5 to Junction 23 or 24; follow A38 to
Bridgewater; A39 to Minehead then left
to Spaxton/Durleigh; left at reservoir
and course is 2 miles on the right.
Parkland course.
Pro Nigel Wixon; Founded 1906
Designed by Hawtree and Son
18 holes, 6411 yards, S.S.S. 71
⟂ Practice ground.
† Welcome but handicap certs
required at WE.
[WD £25; WE £35.
⌒ Mon, Thurs or Fri with advance
booking; 27-hole packages available;
from £25.
🍽 Full facilities.

3B 29 Entry Hill Golf Course
Entry Hill, Somerset, BA2 5NA
☎ 01225 834248
Take A367 Wells road from city centre;
fork left into Entry Hill Road after 1
mile; course is 0.5 mile on right.

Parkland course.
Pro Tim Tapley; Founded 1984
9 holes, 2078 yards, S.S.S. 61
† Welcome; book up to 7 days in
advance for WE, Bank Holidays and
peak periods.
[WD and WE 9 holes £7 18 holes
£11; concessions for juniors and
seniors.
⌒ Welcome.
🛏 Aquae Sulis; Ayrlington; Cranleigh.

3B 30 Erlestoke Sands
Erlestoke, Devizes, Wilts, SN10 5UB
🖳 www.erlestokesands.co.uk
✉ office@erlestokesands.co.uk
☎ 01380 830300, Fax 831284, Pro
831027, Sec 831069, Rest/Bar 830507
On B3098 off A350 at Westbury
signposted Bratton; course 6 miles on
left before village of Erlestoke, (3
miles) on right after Erlestoke village.
Pro Michael Walters; Founded 1992.
Designed by Adrian Stiff
18 holes, 6406 yards, S.S.S. 71
⟂ Driving range.
† Welcome.
[WD £25; WE £30.
⌒ Preferably WD by prior
arrangement; full facilities.
🍽 Full facilities.

3B 31 Farrington ℭ
Marsh Lane, Farrington Gurney,
Bristol, BS39 6TS
🖳 www.farringtongolfclub.net
✉ info@farringtongolfclub.net
☎ 01761 451596, Fax 451021,
Pro 451046
Course is 12 miles S of Bristol on the
A37.
Parkland course with lakes.
Pro Jon Cowgill; Founded 1993
Designed by Peter Thompson
18 holes, 6716 yards, S.S.S. 72
⟂ Practice range 16 bays covered;
floodlit.
† Welcome; advisable to phone in
advance for weekends.
[WD £20; WE £30.
⌒ Welcome WD only; 2 courses
driving range, spikes bar, restaurant
and private suite seating 150; BBQ
area; terms on application.
🍽 Bar and restaurant.
🛏 Hunstrete House, Hunstrete;
Harnham House, Paulton; Ston,
Easton.

3B 32 Ferndown
119 Golf Links Rd, Ferndown, Dorset,
BH22 8BU

✉ ferndowngc@lineone.net
☎ 01202 874602, Fax 873926
A31 to Trickett's Cross and A348 to
Ferndown.
Heathland course.
Founded 1913
Designed by Harold Hilton (Old Course)
18 holes, 6452 yards, S.S.S. 71
† With prior permission.
[Handicap certs required; limited
WE. WD £50; WE £60.
⌒ Tues and Fri only; full facilities;
9-hole course: 5604 yards.
🍽 Full facilities all week.
🛏 Coach House Motel; Dormy;
Bridge House.

3B 33 Ferndown Forest
Forest Links Road, Ferndown, Dorset,
BH22 9QE
🖳 www.ferndownforestgolf.co.uk
✉ golf@ferndownforestgolf.co.uk
☎ 01202 876096, Fax 894095,
Pro 876096, Sec 876477,
Rest/Bar 894990
Midway between Ringwood and
Wimborne directly off the Ferndown
by-pass A31.
Parkland course.
Pro Mike Dodd; Founded 1993
Designed by G Hunt & R Grafham
18 holes, 5094 yards, S.S.S. 65
⟂ Practice range floodlit bays with
targets.
† Everyone welcome.
[WD £13; WE £15.
⌒ Welcome; catering facilities; from £9.
🍽 Full bar and restaurant facilities
available.
🛏 Coach House Motel, Ferndown.

3B 34 Folke Golf Centre
Alweston, Sherborne, Dorset, DT9 5HR
☎ 01963 23330
From Sherborne head towards
Sturminster Newton; 2 miles from
Sherborne turn off towards Folke;
course is 200 yards away.
Parkland course.
Founded 1991
9 holes, 2847 yards, S.S.S. 66
⟂ Practice range 10 covered bays;
floodlit.
† Welcome.
[WD £11; WE £13.
⌒ Welcome by prior arrangement;
terms on application.
🍽 Sandwiches, snacks; bar.

3B 35 Fosseway Country ℭ
Charlton Lane, Midsomer Norton, Bath,
Somerset, BA3 4BD

⠿ www.centurionhotel.com
⌨ centurion@
centurionhotel.demon.co.uk
☎ 01761 412214, Fax 418357,
Rest/Bar 417711
10 miles S of Bath on the A367.
Parkland course.
Founded 1971
Designed by CK Cotton and F
Pennink
9 holes, 4565 yards, S.S.S. 67
† By prior arrangement.
Ⓛ WD £15; WE £15.
⌘ Terms on application.
⦿ Facilities.
⌁ Centurion Hotel (on site).

3B 36 Frome
Critchill Manor, Frome, Somerset,
BA11 4LJ
⠿ www.fromegolfclub.fsnet.co.uk
⌨ fromegolfclub@yahoo.co.uk
☎ 01373 453410, Fax 453410
Take A361 from Frome towards
Shepton Mallet; at Nunney Catch
roundabout follow signs to course.
Parkland course.
Pro Lawrence Wilkin; Founded 1992
18 holes holes, 5466 yards, S.S.S. 67
Ⓘ 16 bay covered floodlit range
† Welcome.
Ⓛ WD £17; WE £19.
⌘ Welcome; contact club for details.
⦿ Licensed bar and light
refreshments.

3B 37 Halstock Golf Enterprises
Common Lane, Nr Yeovil, Somerset,
BA22 9SF
⌨ halstock.golf@freeuk.com
☎ 01935 891689, Fax 891839,
Rest/Bar 891747
300 yards from centre of Halstock
village turn right at green, signposted.
Parkland course.
Founded 1988
18 holes, 4351 yards, S.S.S. 63
Ⓘ Driving range.
† Welcome.
Ⓛ WD £12 (18) £7 (9); WE £14 (18)
£8.50 (9).
⌘ Welcome by arrangement; terms
on application.
⦿ Light refreshments available.

3B 38 Hamptworth Golf
Hamptworth Rd, Landford, Nr
Salisbury, Wilts, SP5 2DU
⠿ www.hamptworthgolf.co.uk
⌨ info@hamptworthgolf.co.uk
☎ 01794 390155, Fax 390022,
Rest/Bar 399970

6 miles from M27 Junctions 1 and 2 off
the A36 to Salisbury; follow Landford
and then Downton road signs.
Parkland course among ancient
woodlands lakes and river.
Pro K Kuffam/M White/L Blake;
Founded 1994
18 holes, 6512 yards, S.S.S. 71
Ⓘ Full practice facilities covered bay
driving range.
† Welcome by arrangement;
handicap certs not always required.
Ⓛ WD £30; WE £30.
⌘ Welcome by arrangement.
⦿ Full facilities.
⌁ Devere Grand Harbour.

3B 39 High Post
Great Durnford, Salisbury, Wilts,
SP4 6AT
⠿ www.highpostgolfclub.co.uk
⌨ highpostgolfclub@lineone.net
☎ 01722 782356, Fax 782674,
Pro 782219
Halfway between Salisbury and
Amesbury on the A345 opposite the
Inn at High Post.
Downland course.
Pro Tony Isaacs; Founded 1922
18 holes, 6305 yards, S.S.S. 70
† Welcome WD without restriction;
handicap certs required at WE.
Ⓛ WD £30; WE £40.
⌘ Welcome WD by arrangement; full
facilities available.
⦿ Full facilities.
⌁ The Inn; High Post; Milford Hall
(Salisbury).

3B 40 Highcliffe Castle
107 Lymington Rd, Highcliffe on Sea,
Dorset, BH23 4LA
☎ 01425 272953
1 mile W of Highcliffe on A337.
Parkland course.
Founded 1913
18 holes, 4776 yards, S.S.S. 63
† Welcome if member of recognised
golf club.
Ⓛ WD £15.50 (Winter) £25.50
(Summer); WE £20.50 (Winter) £30.50
(Summer).
⌘ By prior arrangement with the
secretary; terms on application.
⦿ Clubhouse facilities.

3B 41 Highworth Golf Centre
Swindon Road,, Highworth, Wilts,
SN6 7SJ
☎ 01793 766014, Fax 766014,
Take A361 from Swindon.
Parkland course.

Pro Barry Sandry; Founded 1990
Designed by Swindon Council
9 holes, 3120 yards, S.S.S. 35
† Pay as you play.
Ⓛ £11.60 per round.
⌘ Pay as you play.
⌁ Jesmond Hotel.

3B 42 Isle Of Purbeck
Studland, Swanage, Dorset, BH19 3AB
⠿ www.purbeckgolf.co.uk
⌨ md@purbeckgolf.co.uk
☎ 01929 450361, Fax 450501,
Pro 450354
3 miles north of Swanage on the
B3351 Corfe Castle road.
Heathland course with views of Poole
Harbour.
Pro Ian Brake; Founded 1892
Designed by HS Colt
18 holes, 6295 yards, S.S.S. 71
† Welcome.
Ⓛ WD £35; WE £40.
⌘ Welcome; morning coffee;
Ploughman's lunch 2 rounds of golf
two course dinner; £48.50-£50.
⦿ Bar snacks and restaurant.

3B 43 Isle of Wedmore
Lineage, Lascots Hill, Wedmore,
Somerset, BS28 4QT
⠿ www.wedmoregolfclub.com
⌨ office@wedmoregc.
fsnet.co.uk
☎ 01934 713649, Fax 713696,
Pro 712452
Junction 22 off M5; take A38 north to
Bristol; after 5 miles turn right in Lower
Weare; follow signposts to Wedmore.
Parkland course.
Pro Graham Coombe; Founded 1992
Designed by Terry Murray
18 holes, 6009 yards, S.S.S. 68
Ⓘ Practice area.
† Welcome but after 9.30am at WE.
Ⓛ WD/WE £20; day ticket £30.
⌘ Welcome; packages available;
private function room and professional
lessons; £24-£32.
⦿ Bar and restaurant.

3B 44 King Weston
Millfield Enterprises Sports &
Recreation, Nr Glastonbury,
BA16 0YD
⠿ www.millfieldenterprises.com
⌨ info@millfieldenterprises.com
☎ 01458 444320
1 mile SE of Butleigh.
Parkland course.
Founded 1970
9 holes, 4434 yards, S.S.S. 62

† Welcome with member when not required by school.
⌜ Terms on application.
⌂ Limited.

3B 45 **Kingsdown**
Corsham, Wilts, SN13 8BS
✉ kingsdowngc@02.co.uk
☎ 01225 742530, Fax 743472,
Pro 742634, Sec 743472
5 miles E of Bath on A365.
Downland course.
Pro Andrew Butler
Founded 1880
18 holes, 6445 yards, S.S.S. 71
⌐ Practice area and driving range.
† Welcome Mon-Fri; handicap certs required.
⌜ WD £28.
⌂ Welcome Mon-Fri; full bar and catering facilities.
🍽 Bar and catering facilities.

3B 46 **Knighton Heath**
Francis Ave, Bournemouth, Dorset, B11 8NX
✉ khgc@btinternet.com
☎ 01202 572633, Fax 590774,
Pro 578275
Course is signposted from junction of A348/A3049 (at Mountbatten Arms).
Heathland course.
Pro Paul Brown
Founded 1976
Designed by Bill Freeman
18 holes, 6094 yards, S.S.S. 69
† Welcome after 9.30 WD; member's guests at WE.
⌜ WD £25; WE £18 with member.
⌂ Welcome by arrangement; minimum 12 players; packages available; from £35.
🍽 Full catering facilities.
⌐ Many in Bournemouth.

3B 47 **Knowle** ♔
Fairway, West Town Lane, Brislington, Bristol, BS4 5DF
🖳 www.knowlegolfclub.co.uk
☎ 0117 9776341, Fax 9720615,
Pro 9779193, Sec 9770660
3 miles S of City Centre on A4 to Bath or A37 to Shepton Mallett.
Parkland course.
Pro Rob Hayward
Founded 1905
Designed by Hawtree & JH Taylor
18 holes, 6016 yards, S.S.S. 69
⌐ Practice area, putting green.
† Welcome with handicap certs.
⌜ WD £22; WE £27.

⌂ Welcome on Thurs; coffee lunch; evening meal available.
🍽 Full facilities.

3B 48 **Lafarge (Westbury)**
Trowbridge Road, Westbury, Wilts, BA13 3AY
✉ chris@patbell.fsnet.co.uk
☎ 01373 828489, Pro 07660 310993,
Sec 01373 752564
Part of Lafarge Works Sport Complex.
Parkland course.
Pro Gary Sawyer; Founded 1973
9 holes, 5860 yards, S.S.S. 68
† With members only or on county card system.
⌜ Terms on application.
⌂ Welcome by prior arrangement; terms on application.
🍽 By prior arrangement.

3B 49 **Long Ashton**
Clarken Combe, Long Ashton, Bristol, BS41 9DW
🖳 www.longashtongolfclub.co.uk
✉ secretary@longashtongolfclub .co.uk
☎ 01275 392229, Fax 394395
Leave M5 at Junction 19, take A369 to Bristol, turn right into B3129 at traffic lights and then left on to B3128; club is 0.5 mile on right.
Undulating moorland/downland course.
Pro Mike Hart
Founded 1893
Designed by Hawtree & Taylor
18 holes holes, 6196 yards, S.S.S. 70
† Welcome with official club handicap certs.
⌜ WD £30; WE £35.
⌂ Welcome by arrangement; full facilities available.
🍽 Full facilities daily until 6pm; evening meals by arrangement.
⌐ Redwood Lodge.

3B 50 **Long Sutton** ♔
Long Load, Nr Langport, Somerset, TA10 9JU
🖳 www.longsuttongolf.com
✉ reservations@longsuttongolf.com
☎ 01458 241017, Fax 241022,
Pro 241017, Sec 241017,
Rest/Bar 241111
Course after Long Sutton village.
Parkland course.
Pro Andrew Hayes
Founded 1990
Designed by Patrick Dawson
18 holes, 6329 yards, S.S.S. 70

⌐ 12 bays.
† Welcome with advance tee reservation.
⌜ WD £18; WE £22.
⌂ Welcome by prior arrangement; full facilities; terms on application.
🍽 Bar restaurant and function rooms.
⌐ List can be provided.

3B 51 **Lyme Regis** ♔
Timber Hill, Lyme Regis, Dorset, DT7 3HQ
✉ bwheeler@ic24.net
☎ 01297 442963, Pro 443822,
Sec 442963, Rest/Bar 442043
Off A3052 Charmouth road 1 mile E of town.
Clifftop course.
Pro Andrew Black; Founded 1893
18 holes, 6283 yards, S.S.S. 70
⌐ Practice green.
† Welcome with handicap certificates or proof of membership of recognised club; restrictions Thurs and Sun afternoons.
⌜ WD £30; WE £23. All day £30. Morning only £25. After 2pm £20.
⌂ Welcome by arrangement not Thurs or Sun am; full facilities available.
🍽 Hot and cold snacks all day; full restaurant.
⌐ Alexander; Bay; Buena Vista; Devon; Fairwater Head; Tudor House. Fern Hill Hotel.

3B 52 **Lyons Gate Farm**
Lyons Gate, Dorchester, DT2 7AZ
☎ 01300 345239, Sec 345239,
Rest/Bar 245239
4 miles N of Cerne Abbas on A352 Sherborne-Dorchester road.
Wooded farmland/parkland course.
Founded 1991-club 1990-course
Designed by Ken Abel
9 holes,18 tees, 3834 yards, S.S.S. 60
† Welcome; no restrictions.
⌜ WD £5.00 for 9 holes. £9.00 for 18 holes.; WE £6.00 for 9 holes, £10.00 for 18 holes.
⌂ Welcome by arrangement.
🍽 Light refreshments available.
Meals by arrangement.
⌐ The Hunter's Moon, The Antelope.

3B 53 **The Manor House at Castle Coombe** ♔
Castle Combe, Wilts, SN14 7PL
🖳 www.exclusivehotels.co.uk
☎ 01249 782982, Fax 782992,
Pro 782982, Sec 782982,
Rest/Bar 782982

KNOWLE GOLF CLUB
FAIRWAY, WEST TOWN LANE, BRISLINGTON, BRISTOL BS4 5DF

Knowle is a delightful course, set in 100 acres of undulating parkland with mature trees lining many fairways to provide an excellent test of golf to players of all handicaps and renowned for the quality of its greens.

Mike Harrington, Secretary: 0117 977 0660   **Club House: 0117 977 6341**
Professional: 0117 977 9193   Fax: 0117 972 0615   Website: www.knowlegolfclub.co.uk

---

On B4039 to N of Castle Combe village. Ancient woodland/parkland course.
Pro Peter Green; Founded 1992
Designed by Peter Alliss and Clive Clark
18 holes, 6286 yards, S.S.S. 71
🏌 10.
† Welcome anytime with handicap certificatess and by making tee reservation.
⌐ WD £37.50; WE £60
⌀ Welcome by arrangement; full facilities. Two bars restaurant private dining facilities.
🍽 Bar snacks available all day.
🛏 Manor House.

3B 54 Marlborough
The Common, Marlborough, Wilts, SN8 1DU
🖳 www.marlboroughgolfclub.co.uk
✉ contactus@marlboroughgolfclub
.co.uk
☎ 01672 512147, Fax 513164,
Pro 512493
On the A346 1 mile north of Marlborough; 7 miles south of M4 exit 15.
Downland course.
Pro Simon Amor
Founded 1888
Designed by T Simpson/upgraded 1921 by H Fowler
18 holes, 6514 yards, S.S.S. 71
† Welcome with prior arrangement.
⌐ WD £26; WE £33.
⌀ Welcomed midweek particularly Tues and Thurs; numerous packages available.
🍽 Full facilities.
🛏 Castle and Ball Hotel; Ivy House Hotel both Marlborough; Parklands Hotel, Ogbourne St George.

3B 55 Mendip
Gurney Slade, Radstock, Somerset, BA3 4UT
🖳 www.mendipgolfclub.co.uk
✉ secretary@mendipgolfclub.co.uk
☎ 01749 840570, Fax 841439,
Pro 840793
3 miles N of Shepton Mallett off A37.
Undulating downland course.
Pro Adrian Marsh; Founded 1908

Designed by H Vardon with extension by F. Pennink
18 holes, 6381 yards, S.S.S. 71
† Welcome.
⌐ WD £25; WE £30.
⌀ Welcome by arrangement Mon & Thurs; full facilities.
🍽 Full facilities.
🛏 Stone Easton Park Hotel.

3B 56 Mendip Spring ☎
Honeyhall Lane, Congresbury, North Somerset, BS49 5JT
☎ 01934 852322, Fax 853021,
Rest/Bar 853080
Take A370 from M5 Junction 21 to Congresbury.
Parkland/water features; also 9-hole lakeside course.
Pro John Blackburn/Robert Moss;
Founded 1991
Designed by Terry Murray
18 holes, 6334 yards, S.S.S. 70
🏌 14 bays.
† Welcome by prior arrangement.
⌐ WD £24; WE £27.
⌀ Welcome; full catering facilities; halfway house facilities for refreshments buggies; terms on application.
🍽 Full facilities.

3B 57 Minehead and West ☎
Somerset
The Warren, Minehead, Somerset, TA24 5SJ
🖳 www.mineheadgolf.co.uk
✉ secretary@mineheadgolf.co.uk
☎ 01643 702057, Fax 705095,
Pro 704378
Course at end of seafront.
Links course.
Pro Ian Read
Founded 1882
Designed by Johnny Alan
18 holes, 6228 yards, S.S.S. 71
🏌 Practice green.
† Welcome.
⌐ WD £26; WE £30.
⌀ Welcome on written application; full facilities.
🍽 By prior arrangement with caterer; snacks always available.
🛏 York; Northfield; Marshfield.

3B 58 Monkton Park Par 3
Chippenham, Wilts, SN15 3PE
🖳 www.pitchandputtgolf.com
☎ 01249 653928, Pro 653928,
Sec 653928
Into Chippenham, past railway station, turn right.
Parkland course.
Pro Mel Dawson; Founded 1960
Designed by M Dawson
9 holes, 990 yards, S.S.S. 27
† Welcome.
⌐ WD £4.00; WE £4.00; concessions apply.
⌀ Welcome.
🍽 Refreshments available.

3B 59 North Wilts
Bishops Cannings, Devizes, Wilts, SN10 2LP
🖳 www.northwiltsgolf.com
✉ secretary@northwiltsgolf.com
☎ 01380 860257, Fax 860877,
Pro 860330, Sec 860627,
Rest/Bar 860257
Take A361 Devizes to Swindon road and after 3 miles turn to Calne.
Downland course.
Pro Graham Laing; Founded 1890/1972
Designed by H Cotton
18 holes, 6414 yards, S.S.S. 71
† Welcome by prior arrangement.
⌐ WD £30 day; WE £35 round.
⌀ Welcome WD by prior arrangement; brochure and price list available; terms available on application.
🍽 Clubhouse facilities.
🛏 Bear, Devizes; Landsdown, Calne.

3B 60 Oake Manor ☎
Oake, Taunton, Somerset, TA4 1BA
🖳 www.oakemanor.com
✉ russell@oakemanor.com
☎ 01823 461993, Fax 461995,
Rest/Bar 461992
5 minutes from Junction 26 off M5.
Lakeland course with water features on 10 out of 18 holes, breathtaking views of the Quantock and Blackdown hills.
Pro Russell Gardner; Founded 1993

Designed by Adrian Stiff
18 holes, 6109 yards, S.S.S. 70
⌇ 11 bays, covered; also two
Academy practice holes and short
game area
† Welcome; phone 01823 461993 to
reserve start time.
⌇ WD £22; WE £25.
♐ Welcome; contact golf manager
Russell Gardner; from £20. Function
rooms.
♦ bar and restaurant, function suites
for up to 250 people, air conditioned
clubhouse.
♐ Rumwell Manor.

3B 61 Oaksey Park
Oaksey, Nr Malmesbury, Wilts,
SN16 9SB
✉ johnscooper@btinternet.com
☎ 01666 577995, Fax 577174
Off A419 between Swindon and
Cirencester, west of Cotswold Water
Park.
Public parkland course.
Pro David Carrol
Founded 1991
Designed by Chapman & Warren
9 holes, 2904 yards, S.S.S. 69
⌇ 8 Driving bays.
† Welcome.
⌇ WD £8; WE £10. 18 Holes WD
£12 WE £15.
♐ Welcome; full facilities; terms on
application.
♦ Full facilities.
♐ Oaksey Park Country Cottages
Hotel (10 farm cottages).

3B 62 Ogbourne Downs
Ogbourne St George, Marlborough,
Wilts, SN8 1TB
✉ www.ogdgc.co.uk
☎ 01672 841327, Pro 841287
Junction 15 off M4; course on A345.
Downland course.
Founded 1907
Designed by Taylor; Hawtree and
Cotton
18 holes, 6363 yards, S.S.S. 71
† Welcome with handicap certs.
⌇ WD £25; WE £35.
♐ Terms on application from
secretary; bar; dining room; ball hire;
buggy hire.
♦ Full Bar and restaurant facilities.
♐ Parklands Hotel; Ogbourne St
George.

3B 63 Orchardleigh
Frome, Somerset, BA11 2PH
✉ trevor@orchardleigh.co.uk

☎ 01373 454206, Fax 454202,
Pro 454206, Sec 454200,
Rest/Bar 454200
On the A362.
Parkland course.
Pro Ian Ridsdale;
Founded 1995
Designed by Brian Huggett
18 holes, 6810 yards, S.S.S. 73
⌇ 3 practice putting greens + mat
and grass practice range.
† Welcome.
⌇ WD £30; WE £40.
♐ Welcome; terms available on
application.
♦ Bar and restaurant.
♐ The Full Moon at Rudge.

3B 64 Parkstone ☎
49a Links Road, Parkstone, Poole,
Dorset, BH14 9QS
✉ www.parkstonegolfclub.co.uk
✉ admin@parkstonegolfclub.co.uk
☎ 01202 707138, Fax 706027,
Pro 708092, Sec 707138,
Rest/Bar 708025
On A35 between Bournemouth and
Poole; signposted left off Bournemouth
road.
Links course.
Pro Martyn Thompson; Founded 1910
Designed by Willie Park and James
Braid
18 holes, 6250 yards, S.S.S. 70
⌇ 1 bay for members' use only.
† Welcome with handicap
certificates.
⌇ Terms on application.
♐ Welcome but booking is
essential.
♦ Full catering facilities.

3B 65 Parley Court
Parley Green Lane, Hurn,
Christchurch, Dorset, BH23 6BB
☎ 01202 591600, Fax 579043
Opposite Bournemouth International
Airport.
Parkland course.
Founded 1992
9 holes, 4938 yards, S.S.S. 64
† Everyone welcome.
⌇ WD £6.50 for 9 holes, £9 for
18 holes; WE £7.50 for 9 holes, £10
for 18 holes.
♐ Welcome by arrangement; full
facilities.
♦ Full catering facilities.
♐ Avon Causeway, Dormy Hotel.

3B 66 The Players Club ☎
Codrington, Bristol BS37 6RX

✉ www.theplayersgolfclub.com
✉ enquiries@theplayersgolfclub.com
☎ 01454 313029, Fax 323446,
Pro 311818
1 mile from J18 of M4. From Motorway
take A46 towads Stroud for 200
yards, turn left on B4465. Club less
than ½ mile on right.
Inland American links.
Pro Paul Barrington; Founded 2002
Designed by Adrian Stiff
18 holes, 6376–7607 yards, S.S.S. 72
(six sets of tees).
⌇ Driving range; 9-hole academy
course; 2 putting greens.
† Welcome at all times.
⌇ Mon–Thur £70; Fri–Sun £90; club
operates 2-for-1 scheme.
♐ Welcome WD only.
♦ Full clubhouse facilities.
♐ Compass Inn, 1 mile from club.

3B 67 Queen's Park
(Bournemouth)
Queens Park West Drive,
Bournemouth, Dorset, BH8 9BY
☎ 01202 396198, Fax 396817,
Pro 396817, Sec 302611,
Rest/Bar 394466
Off Wessex Way in Bournemouth.
Parkland course.
Pro R Hill; Founded 1906
18 holes, 6090 yards, S.S.S. 69
⌇ Putting green.
† Welcome.
⌇ WD £17; WE £20; concessions
apply.
♐ Welcome, prior booking essential.
♦ Full catering.
♐ Embassy; Wessex; Marsham Court.

3B 68 Rushmore ☎
Tollard Royal, Salisbury, Wilts,
SP5 5QB
✉ www.rushmoregolfclub.co.uk
✉ andrea@rushmoregolfclub.co.uk
☎ 01725 516326, Fax 516437,
Pro 516326, Sec 516391,
Rest/Bar 516466
12 miles from Salisbury off the A354
Blandford road through Sixpenny
Handley; course is just before Tollard
Royal.
Parkland course.
Pro Sean McDonagh; Founded 1994
18 holes, 6200 yards, S.S.S. 67
⌇ 6 bays.
† Welcome.
⌇ WD £20; WE £25.
♐ Welcome by prior arrangement.
♦ Full menu available.

3B 69 Salisbury & South Wiltshire
Netherhampton, Salisbury, Wilts, SP2 8PR
✉ mail@salisburygolf.co.uk
☎ 01722 742645
On A3094 2 miles from Salisbury and from Wilton.
Downland course.
Pro John Cave; Founded 1888
Designed by JH Taylor; extra 9 holes by S Gidman 1991
27 holes, 6485 yards, S.S.S. 71
† Welcome.
୮ WD £25; WE £40.
⌁ Welcome by arrangement; full facilities.
⚑ Full facilities.
⌁ Rose & Crown Kings Arm, both Salisbury; Pembroke Arms, Wilton.

3B 70 Saltford ☎
Golf Club Lane, Saltford, Bristol, BS31 3AA
☎ 01225 873513, Fax 873525, Pro 872043, Sec 873513, Rest/Bar 873220
Off A4 between Bath and Bristol.
Meadowland course.
Pro Dudley Millensted; Founded 1904
18 holes, 6046 yards, S.S.S. 70
∬ Practice ground.
† Welcome with handicap certs.
୮ WD £24; WE £32.
⌁ Welcome Mon and Thurs by arrangement; full facilities.
⚑ Full facilities.
⌁ Grange (Keynsham); Crown; Tunnel House.

3B 71 Sherborne
Higher Clatcombe, Sherborne, Dorset, DT9 4RN
✉ sherbornegc@btconnect.com
☎ 01935 814431, Fax 814218, Pro 812274, Sec 814431, Rest/Bar 812475
1 mile N of Sherborne off B3145.
Parkland course.
Pro Alistair Tresidder; Founded 1894
Designed by James Braid
18 holes, 6415 yards, S.S.S. 71
∬ Practice area members only.
† Welcome with handicap certs.
୮ WD £25; WE £36.
⌁ Welcome Tues and Wed only; full playing practice and dining facilities; terms available on application.
⚑ Full facilities.
⌁ Sherborne Hotel; Eastbury; Antelope.

3B 72 Shrivenham Park
Pennyhooks, Shrivenham, Swindon, Wilts, SN6 8EX
☎ 01793 783853
Off A420 between Swindon and Oxford.
Parkland course.
Pro Tony Pocock; Founded 1969
Designed by Glen Johnson
18 holes, 5769 yards, S.S.S. 69
† All Welcome.
୮ WD £14; WE £18.
⌁ Welcome anytime with prior booking; packages available.
⚑ Facilities available.
⌁ Blunsdon House.

3B 73 Solent Meads Golf for All
Rolls Drive, Nr Hengistbury Head, Bournemouth, Dorset, BH6 4NA
✉ golfforallltd@aol.com
☎ 01202 420795, Pro 396198, Rest/Bar 420795
Off Broadway close to Hengistbury Head.
Par 3 links course.
Pro Roddy Watkins; Founded 1968
18 holes, 2182 yards + 9 hole pitch & putt
∬ Practice range 10 bays (5 covered).
† All Welcome; pay and play.
୮ WD/WE £7.20, concessions apply.
⌁ Welcome.
⚑ Refurbished café.

3B 74 Stockwood Vale
Stockwood Lane, Keynsham, Bristol, BS18 2ER
🖵 www.stockwoodvale.com
✉ stockwoodvalegc@netscapeonline.co.uk
☎ 0117 9866505, Fax 9868974, Pro 9866505, Sec 9860509, Rest/Bar 9866505
In Stockwood Lane off A4.
Undulating parkland course.
Pro John Richards; Founded 1991
Designed by J Wade & M Ramsay
18 holes, 6031 yards, S.S.S. 71
∬ 16.
† Welcome with prior reservation.
୮ WD £15; WE £17.
⌁ Welcome by prior arrangement; terms on application.
⚑ Restaurant and Bar snacks available.
⌁ Grange Hotel, Keynsham.

3B 75 Sturminster Marshall
Moor Lane, Sturminster Marshall, Dorset, BH21 4AH
☎ 01258 858444
In village centre on the A350 midway between Blandford and Poole.
Parkland course.
Pro Graham Howell; Founded 1992
Designed by John Sharkey
9 holes, 4882 yards, S.S.S. 65
∬ New driving range for 2002.
† Welcome.
୮ WD/WE £12 (18 holes), £8 (9 holes).
⌁ Welcome with prior bookings accepted 7 days in advance; terms on application.
⚑ Full facilities.

3B 76 Tall Pines Golf Club ☎
Cooks Bridle Path, Downside, Backwell, Bristol, BS48 3DJ
☎ 01275 472076, Fax 474869, Pro 472076, Rest/Bar 474889
Take A38 or A370 from Bristol and course is next to Bristol International Airport.
Woodland/parkland.
Pro Alex Murray; Founded 1990
Designed by Terry Murray
18 holes, 6067 yards, S.S.S. 69
† Welcome; not Sat/Sun a.m..
୮ WD/WE £18.
⌁ Welcome; full facilities; terms on application.
⚑ Bar and restaurant.
⌁ Accommodation on site.

3B 77 Taunton & Pickeridge ☎
Corfe, Taunton, Somerset, TA3 7BY
✉ sec@taunt-pickgolfclub.sagehost.co.uk
☎ 01823 421537, Fax 421742, Pro 421790, Rest/Bar 421876/421840
B3170 4 miles S of Taunton through Corfe village then first left.
Undulating course.
Pro Gary Milne; Founded 1892
Designed by Hawtree
18 holes, 6015 yards, S.S.S. 69
† Welcome WD; handicap certs required.
୮ WD £24; WE £35.
⌁ Welcome by arrangement; full facilities.
⚑ Full facilities.
⌁ Castle.

3B 78 Taunton Vale
Creech Heathfield, Taunton, Somerset, TA3 5EY
🖵 www.tauntonvalegolf.co.uk
✉ tvgc@easynet.co.uk
☎ 01823 412220, Fax 413583, Pro 412880

Just off A361 junction with A38 exits 24 or 25 from the M5.
Parkland course.
Pro Martin Keitch; Founded 1991
Designed by John Pyne
18 holes, 6177 yards, S.S.S. 70.
9 holes, 2004 yards, Par 32
⚲ 10 bays, floodlit.
† Welcome; dress code applies.
⌶ WD £20; WE £25.
⌀ Welcome WD; terms on application.
⦿ Full facilities.
⌇ Walnut Tree (North Petherton); Castle (Taunton); Falcon (Henlade); Tudor (Bridgwater).

3B 79 **Thoulstone Park**
Chapmanslade, Nr Westbury, Wilts, BA13 4AQ
☎ 01373 832825, Fax 832821, Pro 832808
3 miles NW of Warminster on the A36.
Parkland course.
Pro Tony Isaacs; Founded 1991
Designed by MRM Sandow
18 holes, 6312 yards, S.S.S. 70
⚲ 20.
† All welcome.
⌶ WD £10; WE £20.
⌀ Welcome; terms on application.
⦿ Full facilities.
⌇ Granada Lodge, Warminster. Travel Lodge, Beckington.

3B 80 **Tickenham**
Clevedon Rd, Tickenham, N Somerset, BS21 6RY
⬚ www.tickenhamgolf.co.uk
✉ info@tickenhamgolf.co.uk
☎ 01275 856626
Take M5 Junction 20 and follow signs for Nailsea; course on left after Tickenham.
Pro Andrew Sutcliffe; Founded 1994.
Designed by A Sutcliffe
9 holes, 3836 yards, S.S.S. 58
⚲ Practice range 24 bays floodlit.
† Welcome.
⌶ WD £7; WE and after 4pm £9 (9 holes).
⌀ Welcome by arrangement; catering and bar facilities; driving range; teaching academy; terms on application.
⦿ Bar club room.
⌇ Redwood Lodge.

3B 81 **Two Riversmeet**
Stony Lane South, Christchurch, Dorset, BH23 1HW
☎ 01202 477987, Fax 470853, Sec 477987, Rest/Bar 477987

Signposted from the centre of Christchurch.
Public seaside course.
Founded 1986
Designed by local authority
18 holes, 1591 yards
† Pay and play.
⌶ WD £5.10; WE £5.10.
⌀ Welcome; terms on application.
⦿ Bar and restaurant.
⌇ Many by the seaside; list available from the club.

3B 82 **Upavon (RAF)** ☏
Andover Rd, Upavon, Nr Pewsey, Wilts, SN9 6BQ
⬚ www.upavongolfclub.co.uk
✉ play@upavongolfclub.co.uk
☎ 01980 630787, Fax 635419, Pro 630281
On the A342 1.5 miles SE of Upavon village.
Undulating chalk downland course.
Pro Richard Blake; Founded 1918/1997
18 holes, 6407 yards, S.S.S. 71
⚲ Practice range.
† Welcome on WD and afternoon at WE.
⌶ WD £26; WE £36; 2 for 1 operated at all times.
⌀ Welcome WD; from £21 per head.
⦿ Bar and restaurant.

3B 83 **Vivary**
Vivary Park, Taunton, Somerset, TA1 3JW
☎ 01823 289274, Pro 333875
Centre of Taunton in Vivary Park.
Parkland course.
Pro Mike Steadman; Founded 1928
Designed by Herbert Fowler
18 holes, 4620 yards, S.S.S. 63
† Welcome.
⌶ WD £8.50; WE £8.50.
⌀ Welcome on WD only; contact Pro; terms on application. Catering on application.
⦿ Full restaurant and bar facilities.
⌇ Corner House; Castle.

3B 84 **Wareham** ☏
Sandford Rd, Wareham, Dorset, BH20 4DH
⬚ www.warehamgolfclub.com
✉ admin@warehamgolfclub.com
☎ 01929 554147, Fax 557993, Sec 557994, Rest/Bar 557995
N of Wareham off A351 between Sandford and Wareham.
Mixture of parkland and heathland course; fine views.

Pro Gary Prince; Founded 1908
Designed by C Whitcome
18 holes, 5753 yards, S.S.S. 68
⚲ Practice area.
† Welcome WD after 9.30am; WE after 1pm.
⌶ WD £22, £28 day pass; WE £25.
⌀ Welcome WD; packages available; group prices negotiable; full facilities for dining.
⦿ Full bar and catering.
⌇ Worgret Manor; Springfield; Priory; Kemps.

3B 85 **Wells (Somerset)** ☏
East Horrington Rd, Wells, Somerset, BA5 3DS
✉ secretary@wellsgolfclub99.freeserve.co.uk
☎ 01749 675005, Fax 683170, Pro 679059, Sec 683171, Rest/Bar 683172
E of Wells off B3139.
Parkland course.
Pro Adrian Bishop; Founded 1893
18 holes, 6053 yards, S.S.S. 69
⚲ Practice range, 10 bays floodlit.
† Welcome.
⌶ WD £24; WE £30.
⌀ Welcome on Tues and Thurs by prior arrangement; packages available; from £33.
⦿ Full facilities.
⌇ Swan; White Hart, both Wells; Charlton House, Shepton Mallet.

3B 86 **Wessex Golf Centre**
Radipole Lane, Weymouth, Dorset, DT4 9HX
☎ 01305 784737
Off Weymouth bypass behind the football club.
Parkland course.
Pro J Bevan; Founded 1980
9 holes, 1432 yards, S.S.S. 30
⚲ Practice range available.
† Public pay and play.
⌶ WD/WE £4.50.
⌀ No restrictions.
⦿ None at all.

3B 87 **West Wilts**
Elm Hill, Warminster, Wilts, BA12 0AU
⬚ www.westwiltsgolfclub.co.uk
✉ westwiltsgc@btopenworld.com
☎ 01985 213133, Fax 219809, Pro 212110, Bar 212702
1 mile ff A350 N or Warminster signposted to Town Centre.
Chalk Downland course.
Pro Simon Swales; Founded 1891
Designed by JH Taylor

18 holes, 5754 yards, S.S.S. 68
⚑ Practice ground and indoor net available.
† Welcome except Sat; must have handicap cert.
⚐ WD £25 round, £30 day; WE £30 round, £40 day.
⚒ Wed only; package details available on request.
⚑ Full catering service.
⚑ Bishopstrow House; The Full Moon at Rudge.

3B 88 Weston-super-Mare ⚔
Uphill Rd North, Weston-Super-Mare, N Somerset, BS23 4NQ
⚐ www.westonsupermaregolfclub.com
✉ karen@wsmgolfclub.fsnet.co.uk
☎ 01934 626968, Fax 621360,
Pro 633360, Sec 626968
M5 to Junction 21 and then follow road to seafront.
Links course.
Pro M Laband; Founded 1892
Designed by T Dunn, A McKenzie
18 holes, 6208 yards, S.S.S. 70
† Welcome; handicap certs required.
⚐ WD £36; WE £54. 2 for 1 offer.
⚒ Welcome; terms on application.
⚑ Full bar and restaurant facilities.
⚑ Beachlands; Commodore; Rozel; Timbertops.

3B 89 Weymouth ⚔
Links Rd, Weymouth, Dorset, DT4 0PF
⚐ www.weymouthgolfclub.co.uk
✉ weymouthgolfclub@aol.com
☎ 01305 784994, Fax 788029,
Pro 773997, Sec 773981,
Rest/Bar 773981
1 mile from Weymouth town centre.
Parkland course.
Pro Des Lochrie; Founded 1909
Designed by James Braid
18 holes, 5963 yards, S.S.S. 69
⚑ Practice area.
† Welcome if carrying handicap certs.
⚐ WD £24; WE £30.
⚒ Welcome WD; catering always available.
⚑ Full facilities.
⚑ Several offer reduced rates – enquire from club.

3B 90 Wheathill
Somerton, Somerset, TA11 7HG
⚐ www.foremostonline.co.uk/wheathill
✉ wheathill@wheathill.fsnet.co.uk

☎ 01963 240667, Fax 240230
Take A37 towards Yeovil; at village of Lydford on Fosse turn left; course 1 mile on right.
Parkland course.
Pro Andrew England and John Geymer; Founded 1993
Designed by J Payne
18 holes, 5351 yards, S.S.S. 66
⚑ Practice ground; Academy course; 8 hole par 3.
† Welcome.
⚐ WD £15; WE £20.
⚒ Welcome by arrangement; full facilities.
⚑ Full facilities.
⚑ The Bear, Street.

3B 91 The Wiltshire Golf and Country Club ⚔
Vastern, Wootton Basset, Swindon, Wilts, SN4 7PB
✉ tracey@the-wiltshire.co.uk
☎ 01793 849999, Fax 849988
Course is on the A3102 one mile S of Wootton Bassett close to the M4 Junction 16.
Pro Kevin Pickett; Founded 1991
Designed by Peter Alliss/Clive Clark
18 holes, 6519 yards, S.S.S. 72
⚑ Practice range; practice ground.
† Welcome by prior arrangement.
⚐ WD £25; WE £35.
⚒ Welcome by arrangement; golf and catering packages can be arranged; terms on application.
⚑ Full clubhouse facilities.
⚑ 32 bed hotel.

3B 92 Windwhistle
Cricket St Thomas, Near Chard, Somerset, TA20 4DG
☎ 01460 30231, Fax 30055
Course is on the north side of the A30 five miles from Crewkerne; three miles from Chard; opposite a wildlife park; follow signs from the M5 Junction 5.
Downland/parkland course.
Pro Duncan Driver; Founded 1932
Designed by JH Taylor (1932) and Leonard Fisher (1992)
18 holes, 6470 yards, S.S.S. 71
⚑ 12.
† Welcome but best to phone first.
⚐ WD £18; WE £22.
⚒ Welcome by arrangement; full facilities.
⚑ Full facilities.

3B 93 Woodbridge Park
Longmans Farm, Brinkworth, Chippenham, Wilts, SN15 5DG

☎ 01666 510277
Between Swindon and Malmesbury on B4042.
Meadowland course.
Pro Mark Whitby;
Founded 1984
18 holes, 6089 yards, S.S.S. 70
† Welcome anytime.
⚐ From WD £10; WE £12.
⚒ Welcome by arrangement.
⚑ Full facilities.

3B 94 Worlebury ⚔
Monks Hill, Worlebury, Weston-Super-Mare, Avon, BS22 9SX
⚐ www.worleburygc.co.uk
✉ secretary@worleburygc.co.uk
☎ 01934 625789, Fax 621935,
Pro 623932, Sec 625789,
Rest/Bar 623214
From M5 Junction 21 follow old road to Weston-super-Mare; turn right at Milton Church.
Hilltop parkland course.
Pro Gary Marks;
Founded 1908
Designed by W Hawtree & Son
18 holes, 5936 yards, S.S.S. 69
† Everyone welcome.
⚐ WD £20; WE £30.
⚒ Welcome by prior arrangement; terms on application.
⚑ Bar and restaurant facilities.
⚑ Commodore; Beachlands.

3B 95 Wrag Barn Golf ⚔
Shrivenham Rd, Highworth, Wilts, SN6 7QQ
⚐ www.wragbarn.com
✉ info@wragbarn.com
☎ 01793 861327, Fax 861325
10 miles from M4 Junction 15; take A419 towards Cirencester left turn to Highworth; follow A361 to Highworth; then 3rd exit at roundabout on to B4000 to Shrivenham; course is 0.5 miles to the right.
Parkland course.
Pro Barry Loughrey;
Founded 1990
Designed by Hawtree & Sons
18 holes, 6348 yards, S.S.S. 72
⚑ Driving range, covered.
† Welcome; restrictions apply in afternoon at WE so it is advisable to phone first.
⚐ WD £30; WE £35.
⚒ Welcome WD by arrangement.
⚑ Full bar and restaurant, catering for companies, parties, receptions.
⚑ Blunsdon House Hotel; Jesmond House (Highworth).

3B 96 Yeovil
Sherborne Road, Yeovil, Somerset,
BA21 5BW
🖳 www.yeovilgolfclub.co.uk
📧 secretary@yeovilgolfclub.co.uk
☎ 01935 475949, Fax 411283, Pro
473763, Sec 422965, Rest/Bar 431130
1 mile from town centre towards
Sherborne on A30.

Parkland course; also 9-hole course
available.
Pro Geoff Kite;
Founded 1919
Designed by Fowler & Alison (18
holes); STRI (9 holes)
18 holes holes, 6144 yards, S.S.S.
70
⌇ 20 bays floodlit.

† Welcome but ring for tee times.
⌇ WD £25; WE £30 (Nov–Mar).
WD £30; WE £40 (Apr–Oct).
↻ Welcome Mon, Wed, Thurs and
Fri; packages available to be
arranged.
🍽 Full facilities.
↝ Ludgate House, Ilchester.

EAST ANGLIA

4

Suffolk, Norfolk

It is either because East Anglia has so many great courses or because the future Edward VII spent so much time at Sandringham and knew so many of the local players that a quarter of England's royal courses are to be found in the region.

But although the latter is certainly the real reason, East Anglia is still a great golfing landscape. After all, this is Bernard Darwin country. Bernard, who had as many worthwhile things to say about golf as Charles did about natural sciences, learned to play the game at Felixstowe Ferry, a bleak links course dominated by its Martello tower.

He is said to have hit his last shots at Aldeburgh before declaring, "Now I can retire gracefully from this unspeakable game". Between the two events he travelled and wrote great distances.

This is his description of the journey to Royal West Norfolk, more commonly called Brancaster. "We get out at Hunstanton station and drive a considerable number of miles along a nice, flat, dull east country road till we get to the tranquil little village, with a church and some pleasant trees. In front of the village is a stretch of grey-green marsh, and beyond the marsh is a range of sandhills, and that is where the golf is."

That is where the golf is. He could not have put it better. Sand dunes, railway sleepers, salt marsh, marram grass, Brancaster makes you feel as if you have been playing a century of golf on this same spot without ever wanting to leave. The clubhouse, dressed in a wooden windcheater, is one of the cosiest in the country.

Also mentioned in Darwin's journey, Hunstanton is a championship course that runs between the sea and the river Hun. It is an out-and-back links with superlative greens. It is also the course where Robert Taylor, a visitor from Scraptoft in Leicestershire, holed in one at the 188-yard 16th hole with a one iron. Nothing too remarkable in that, except that he had a hole-in-one at the same hole on the following day, this time with a six iron. The next day he was offered rather skinny odds of a million to one to repeat the feat and promptly plonked it in the hole again.

Along the coast Royal Cromer and Sheringham are both excellent courses, but their greens are not as reliable as Hunstanton's. Sheringham is where Joyce Wethered, one of the game's greatest players, is reputed to have said, "What train" after holing a winning putt to the background accompaniment of a locomotive. The same story, but with a different cast, is often attached to Lytham. They are likely both true. Driving inland Norwich probably owes its royalty more to the influence of its first President, Mr J.J.Coleman of mustard fame, than to its notability but it is still a fair course.

If Suffolk does not quite match the splendour of Norfolk it still has a lot of good golf about it. Royal Worlington is argued to be the world's greatest nine-hole course. Whilst Aldeburgh, a heathland course with deep bunkers and nine par fours over four hundred yards, would be an appropriate setting for one of Benjamin Britten's more fiendish works such as *The Turn of the Screw*.

Woodbrige and Thorpeness are also good tracks, but Suffolk's most famous course is according to some just half a course – the nine holes of Royal Worlington.

4 1 Aldeburgh ☏

Saxmundham Road, Aldeburgh,
Suffolk, IP15 5PE
☎ 01728 452408, Fax 452937,
Pro 453309
From the A12 N of Ipswich take the
A1094 to Aldeburgh; course is six
miles E of the A12.
Open heathland course; no par 5s
Pro Keith Preston; Founded 1884
Designed by John Thompson/Willie
Fernie
27 holes, 6350 yards, S.S.S. 71
⌇ Practice green; putting green;
practice ground.
† Welcome by prior arrangement.
⌇ WD £40; WE £50 before 12 am;
After 12 WD, £35 WE £60.
⌁ Welcome by prior arrangement;
terms on application. Also a 2114-yard,
9-hole course with SSS 62.
⌾ Clubhouse facilities.
⌁ Wentworth; White Lion; Brudenell.

4 2 Alnesbourne Priory

Priory Park, Nacton Road, Ipswich,
Suffolk, IP10 0JT
⌂ www.priory-park.com
✉ jwl@prior-park.com
☎ 01473 727393, Fax 278372
From A14 take Ransomes Europark
exit and follow signs to Prior Park.
Parkland course.
Founded 1987
9 holes, 1760 yards, S.S.S. 58
† Public pay and play (closed Tues).
⌇ WD £10; Sat £11; Sun £12.
⌁ Course available for hire every
Tues; packages available, adventure
playground; terms on application.
⌾ Bar and restaurant.
⌁ Courtyard Marriott approx. 1 mile.

4 3 Barnham Broom ☏

Honingham Road, Barnham Broom,
Norwich, Norfolk, NR9 4DD
⌂ www.barnham-broom.co.uk
☎ 01603 759393, Fax 758224
9 miles SW of Norwich.
River valley setting
Pro Adrian Rudge; Founded 1977
Designed by Frank Pennink (Valley),
Donald Steel (Hill)
Hill: 18. Valley: 18 holes, Hill: 6495.
Valley 6483 yards, S.S.S. Hill: 72.
Valley 71
† Welcome by prior arrangement.
⌇ WD £40; WE £40.
⌁ Many golfing breaks and corporate
packages available; complete hotel,
conference and golfing leisure breaks
available at the hotel.
⌾ Full club and hotel facilities.
⌁ Barnham Broom Hotel.

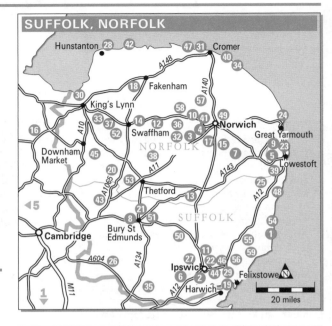

SUFFOLK, NORFOLK

KEY		20	Feltwell	41	Royal Norwich
1	Aldeburgh	21	Flempton	42	Royal West Norfolk
2	Alnesbourne Priory	22	Fynn Valley	43	Royal Worlington &
3	Barnham Broom	23	Gorleston		Newmarket
4	Bawburgh	24	Great Yarmouth & Caister	44	Rushmere
5	Beccles	25	Halesworth	45	Ryston Park
6	Brett Vale	26	Haverhill	46	Seckford Golf Centre
7	Bungay & Waveney Valley	27	Hintlesham Hall	47	Sheringham
8	Bury St Edmunds	28	Hunstanton	48	Southwold
9	Caldecott Hall	29	Ipswich	49	Sprowston Park
10	Costessey Park	30	King's Lynn	50	Stowmarket
11	Cretingham	31	Links Country Park	51	Suffolk Golf & Country Club
12	Dereham	32	Mattishall	52	Swaffham
13	Diss	33	Middleton Hall	53	Thetford
14	Dunham Golf Club	34	Mundesley	54	Thorpeness
	(Granary)	35	Newton Green	55	Ufford Park Hotel
15	Dunston Hall	36	Norfolk Golf & Country Club	56	Waldringfield
16	Eagles	37	RAF Marham	57	Wensum Valley Hotel Golf &
17	Eaton	38	Richmond Park		Country Club
18	Fakenham	39	Rookery Park	58	Weston Park
19	Felixstowe Ferry	40	Royal Cromer	59	Woodbridge

4 4 Bawburgh ☏

Glen Lodge, Marlingford Road,
Bawburgh, Norfolk, NR9 3LU
⌂ www.bawburgh.com
✉ info@bawburgh.com
☎ 01603 740404, Fax 740403,
Pro 742323
Off the Norwich southern by-pass
(A47) at the Royal Norfolk Showground
Junction; follow road to Bawburgh.
Parkland/heathland course
Pro Chris Potter; Founded 1978
Designed by John Barnard
18 holes, 6209 yards, S.S.S. 70
⌇ 14 floodlit.
† Welcome.
⌇ WD £25; WE £28.
⌁ Welcome by prior arrangement;
normal packages involve 18-36 holes;
lunch and evening meal; terms on
application.
⌾ Full clubhouse facilities.
⌁ Park Farm, Hethersett.

4 5 Beccles

The Common, Beccles, Suffolk,
NR34 9BX
☎ 01502 712244, Sec 714616
Leave A146 Norwich-Lowestoft road at
Sainsbury's roundabout.
Parkland course; formerly Wood Valley.

Founded 1899
9 holes, 5562 yards, S.S.S. 67
† Welcome; with member Sun am.
[WD £8; WE £10.
⟳ Welcome with prior notice; terms
on application.
🍽 Clubhouse facilities.
🛏 King's Head; Waveney House,
both Beccles.

4 6 Brett Vale
Noakes Road, Raydon, Ipswich,
Suffolk, IP7 5LR
🖳 www.brettvalegolf.com
📧 info@brettvalegolf.com
☎ 01473 310718
2 miles off A12 along B1070, 6 miles
north of Colchester.
Parkland; stunningly beautiful.
Founded 1993
Designed by Howard Swan
18 holes, 5813 yards, S.S.S. 70
⟋ 7.
† Welcome preferably by prior
arrangement.
[WD £22, WE £28, £22 after 2pm.
⟳ Welcome by prior arrangement;
terms on application.
🍽 Full clubhouse facilities.
🛏 The County Hotel, Copdock.

4 7 Bungay & Waveney   ℭ
Valley
Outney Common, Bungay, Suffolk,
NR35 1DS
🖳 www.club-noticeboard.co.uk
📧 bungaygolf@aol.com
☎ 01986 892337, Fax 892222
Signposted from A 143 Bungay by-
pass.
Heathland course.
Pro A Collison; Founded 1889
Designed by James Braid
18 holes, 6044 yards, S.S.S. 69
⟋ Practice area.
† Welcome by arrangement.
[Terms on application.
⟳ Welcome by prior arrangement;
discounted day rates and green fees
for groups of more than 20.
🍽 Clubhouse facilities.

4 8 Bury St Edmunds
Tuthill, Bury St Edmunds, Suffolk,
IP28 6LG
🖳 www.club-noticeboard.co.uk/
burystedmunds
📧 info@burygolf.co.uk
☎ 01284 755979, Fax 763288
Bury West exit off A14 for Bury St
Edmunds; 0.25 miles down B1106 to
Brandon.

Parkland course.
Pro Mark Jillings; Founded 1924
Designed by Hawtree (9 holes); Ray
(18 holes)
18 holes, 6678 yards, S.S.S. 72
† Welcome WD; WE with a
member.
[WD £30.
⟳ Welcome WD by arrangement;
also a pay and play 9-hole course;
terms on application.
🍽 Full clubhouse facilities.
🛏 Butterfly.

4 9 Caldecott Hall
Caldecott Hall, Beccles Road, Fritton,
Norfolk, NR31 9EY
🖳 www.caldecotthall.co.uk
☎ 01493 488488, Fax 488561
5 miles SW of Great Yarmouth on
A143 Beccles Road.
Parkland course.
Pro Syer Shulver; Founded 1994
18 holes, 6685 yards, S.S.S. 72
⟋ 20.
† Welcome by prior arrangement.
[WD £20; WE £26.
⟳ Welcome by prior arrangement;
discounts available for groups of
10 or more; terms available on
application. Also a 9-hole par 3
course.
🍽 Full clubhouse facilities.
🛏 Caldecott Hall Hotel and Spa.

4 10 Costessey Park   ℭ
Old Costessy, Norwich, Norfolk,
NR8 5AL
🖳 www.costesseypark.com
📧 cpgc@ljgroup.com
☎ 01603 746333, Fax 746185,
Pro 747085, Sec 746333,
Rest/Bar 746333
Course is off the A1074 at the Round
Well public house three miles W of
Norwich.
Parkland/river valley course.
Pro Andrew Young; Founded 1983
Designed by Frank MacDonald
18 holes, 5900 yards, S.S.S. 69
† Welcome; only after 11am at WE.
Handicaps required.
[WD/WE £30.
⟳ Welcome by prior arrangement;
terms on application.
🍽 Full catering and bar facilities
available.

4 11 Cretingham
Cretingham, Woodbridge, Suffolk,
IP13 7BA
☎ 01728 685275, Fax 685488

2 miles from the A1120 at Earl Soham;
10 miles N of Ipswich.
Parkland course.
Pro Neil Jackson; Founded 1984
18 holes, 5024 yards; 9 hole practice
course
† Welcome.
[WD £14; WE £16.
⟳ Welcome by arrangement; catering
packages available; snooker; pitch &
putt; swimming pool; tennis; caravan
park.
🍽 Full restaurant and licensed bar
available.
🛏 Swiss-style log cabins.

4 12 Dereham
Quebec Road, Dereham, Norfolk,
NR19 2DS
☎ 01362 695900, Fax 695904,
Pro 695631, Sec 695900
0.5 miles out of Dereham on B1110.
Parkland course.
Pro R Curtis; Founded 1934
9 holes, 6225 yards, S.S.S. 70
† Welcome by prior arrangement.
[Terms on application.
⟳ Welcome by arrangement;
packages available; terms on
application.
🍽 Clubhouse facilities.
🛏 Phoenix; Kings Head; George.

4 13 Diss   ℭ
Stuston Common, Diss, Norfolk,
IP21 4AA
🖳 www.club-noticeboard
.co.uk/diss
📧 sec.dissgolf@virgin.net
☎ 01379 642847, Fax 644586,
Pro 644399, Sec 641025
Course is one mile W of the A140 at
Scole, half-way between Norwich and
Ipswich.
Commonland course.
Pro Nigel Taylor; Founded 1903
18 holes, 6262 yards, S.S.S. 70
⟋ 15 bay covered and floodlit, 1
miles from clubhouse.
† Welcome; WE only as the guest of
a member.
[WD £28; £32 per day.
⟳ Welcome WD by prior
arrangement.
🍽 Full facilities available.
🛏 Park Hotel, Diss. Cornwallis
Country Hotel, Broome.

4 14 Dunham Golf Club
Little Dunham, Nr Swaffham, King
Lynn, Norfolk, PE32 2DF
🖳 www.dunhamgolfclub.com

Royal Cromer

A bit like the royals themselves, Cromer has taken something of a battering over the years, yet it remains a thoroughly enjoyable diversion and the grandeur of its environs are still there to be admired.

The club was granted its royal patronage before any golf was played on the course when HRH Edward Prince of Wales gave it such status on Christmas Day 1887. The course opened on January 2 1888.

Situated between the seaside towns of Cromer and Overstrand on the north-east corner of Norfolk, and jutting out into the North Sea, the course stands 320 feet above the town's sandy beaches and is backed by a hinterland of rolling wooded and bracken-covered hills. However, the disadvantage of its positioning has been severe coastal erosion and has led to significant changes that have shaped the course today.

The spectacular views now begin at the sixth hole – a 457-yard par-four which can play a lot longer when the wind gets up in Norfolk – which it does frequently, even on what appears to be a glorious, calm summer's day. The sixth is rated as the hardest hole on the course but the vista more than makes up for any troubles you encounter here. It is called Cliff Hanger and vertigo sufferers may be advised not to let their ball wander to the right-hand side of the fairway.

The stretch of holes from 13th to finish will endure longest in the memory. The 13th is a great par-three across a gully, then the lighthouse comes into view as you stand on the next tee. The course used to start pointing out towards this famous landmark but, under the current Frank Pennick design it is the 14th – and one of the most talked-about, photographed and filmed holes in golf. Its beauty and its challenge attracted Tony Jacklin to visit the course as he made a journey around Britain to play his "favourite 18 holes". The fomer Open and US Open winner entertained the Norfolk locals when he dropped in by helicopter on his whirlwind tour of the country.

Jacklin walked off with a four, which is a good score for any golfer here. First is a daunting drive uphill over scrubby gorse, then an approach shot down the hill and off to the left, where the green sits next to the famous lighthouse. The 15th is the inverse of the 14th, requiring another strong drive – often against the wind – and over gorse, of course. Then the hole bends round to the right and the up the hill. Another beautiful view awaits on the 16th, this time the short par-four, which runs along a hog's back, offers views over Cromer Town, most of the course and Overstrand. If you have lost your bearings during the round, you can find them again here.

The 17th is a very short par-three at only 119 yards, but it offers little respite because the green cannot be seen from the tee. Finally, the 18th is a grand finishing hole, again with the lighthouse in view.

It was the *Daily Telegraph* journalist Clement Scott who brought Cromer to the attention of the public when, in 1883, he wrote an article by "a holiday maker" entitled Poppyland. Scott was using the newly-built railways to explore the East Coast in his search for "solitude, fine air, scenery and seclusion".

Cromer had then just developed into a town from a small fishing village and was attracting the middle classes pursuing leisure activities. Scott looked down on Cromer from Lighthouse Hill and wrote: "In aimless fashion I strolled ... wild flowers in profusion around me, poppies predominating everywhere, the hedgerows full of blackberry blossom and fringed with meadowsweet; the bees busy at their work as I pursued my solitary way". People read Scott's words and flocked to the area and they still do today, in search of a taste of England's past – a splendid royal retreat. –
Jim Bruce-Ball

☎ 01328 701718, Sec 701906, Rest/Bar 701906
On A47 at Necton/Dunham crossroads.
Parkland with lakes.
Pro Gary Potter; Founded 1987
Designed by Mr Jim Harris
9 holes, 4852 yards, S.S.S. 67
🏌 Indoor practice facility available.
† Welcome.
🍽 Terms on application. WE 18-holes £16, WD 18-holes £12.
⌁ Welcome by prior arrangement. Weekends included.
🍽 Full bar and snack facilities available.

4 15 Dunston Hall ☏
Dunston Hall, Ipswich Road, Norwich, Norfolk, NR14 8PQ
☎ 01508 470178
On the main A140 Ipswich road; 10 minutes drive from Norwich city centre.
Meadowlands course.
Pro Peter Briggs; Founded 1994
Designed by M Shaw (1998 extension)
18 holes, 6319 yards, S.S.S. 70
🏌 22.

† Welcome but booking essential, priority to members and hotel guests.
🍽 WD £25; WE £30.
⌁ Welcome by prior arrangement; catering packages; conference facilities; leisure and health centre.
🍽 Full clubhouse facilities.
⌁ Dunston Hall on site.

4 16 Eagles
39 School Road, Tilney All-Saints, King's Lynn, Norfolk, PE34 4RS
🖳 www.eagles-golf.co.uk
🖳 shop@eagles-golf.co.uk
☎ 01553 827147, Fax 829777, Pro 827147, Rest/Bar 829000
Off A47 between King's Lynn and Wisbech.
Parkland course.
Pro Nigel Pickerell; Founded 1992
Designed by David Horn
9 holes and a par 3 course, 4284 yards, S.S.S. 61
🏌 20.
† Welcome. 2 floodlit tennis courts on astro turf, also for 5-a-side football.
🍽 WD £7.95 9 holes; £11.95 18 holes; WE £8.95 9 holes £14.75 18 holes.
⌁ Welcome by arrangement; catering facilities available by negotiation; terms

on application.
🍽 Facilities available.
⌁ Bufferfly; Park View, both King's Lynn.

4 17 Eaton
Newmarket Road, Norwich, Norfolk, NR4 6SF
🖳 www.eatongc.co.uk
🖳 administrator@eatongc.co.uk
☎ 01603 451686, Fax 451686, Pro 452478, Rest/Bar 452881
Off A11 1 mile S of Norwich.
Predominantly parkland course.
Pro Mark Allen; Founded 1910
18 holes, 6118 yards, S.S.S. 70
Ladies 5262 yards S.S.S. 70.
† Welcome WD; only after 11.30 on WE.
🍽 WD £30; WE £40.
⌁ Welcome by arrangement; terms on application.
🍽 Bar and catering facilities.
⌁ Red Lion, Eaton.

4 18 Fakenham Sports Centre
Hempton Road, Fakenham, Norfolk, NR21 7NY
🖳 brian.watson6@btinternet.com
☎ 01328 863534, Pro 855678, Sec 855678, Rest/Bar 862867

Course is on the B1146 from Dereham or the A1067 from Norwich.
Parkland course.
Pro Colin Williams; Founded 1981
Designed by Charles Lawrie
9 holes, 6245 yards, S.S.S. 71
♣ Welcome; restrictions Sat/Sun a.m.
Ⅰ WD £22.50; WE £28.
♂ Welcome by arrangement.
|●| Bar and restaurant in Sports Centre.
⬟ Wensum Lodge; Crown; Limes.

4 19 Felixstowe Ferry
Ferry Road, Felixstowe, Suffolk, IP11 9RY
♨ www.felixstowegolf.co.uk
✉ secretary@felixstowegolf.co.uk
☎ 01394 286834, Fax 273679, Pro 283975
A14 to Felixstowe, following signs for the golf course and yacht centre.
Links course.
Pro Ian MacPherson; Founded 1880
Designed by Henry Cotton & Sir Guy Campbell
18 holes, 6260 yards, S.S.S. 70;
9 holes, 2986 yards, S.S.S. 69;
9-hole Pay & Play Kingsfleet Course, 5972 yards, Par 70
Ⅰ Large practice area.
♣ Welcome WD.
Ⅰ Terms on application.
♂ Welcome WD by arrangement;
catering packages.
|●| Full catering facilities.
⬟ Elizabeth Hotel, Orwell; self-catering flats above clubhouse for rent.

4 20 Feltwell
Thor Ave, Feltwell, Thetford, Norfolk, IP26 4AY
♨ www.club-noticeboard.co.uk
✉ secretary@feltwellgolfclub.co.uk
☎ 01842 827644, Fax 827644, Pro 829089
Off B1112 Lakenheath-Feltwell road just before Feltwell village.
Inland links course.
Pro Christian Puttock; Founded 1972
9 holes, 6488 yards, S.S.S. 71
♣ Welcome.
Ⅰ WD £16; WE £25.
♂ Welcome WD; by arrangement;
terms on application.
|●| Bar and catering except Mon.
⬟ Brandon House, Brandon; Comfort Inn, Northwold.

4 21 Flempton
Flempton, Bury St Edmunds, Suffolk, IP28 6EQ

☎ 01284 728291
4 miles NE of Bury St Edmunds on A1101 to Mildenhall.
Breckland course.
Pro Mark Jillings; Founded 1895
Designed by JH Taylor
9 holes, 6240 yards, S.S.S. 70
♣ Welcome WD with handicap certs;
weekends by prior arrangement.
Ⅰ WD £30 all day.
♂ Limited availability.
|●| By arrangement.
⬟ Priory & Angel, Bury St.Edmunds;
The Riverside, Mildenhall.

4 22 Fynn Valley ☎
Witnesham, Ipswich, Suffolk, IP6 9JA
♨ www.fynn-valley.co.uk
✉ enquiries@fynn-valley.co.uk
☎ 01473 785267, Fax 785632, Pro 785463, Rest/Bar 785202
From A14 or A12 take A1214 and then B1077 to N of Ipswich.
Parkland course.
Pro P Wilby/K Vince/A Lucas/S Dainty;
Founded 1991
Designed by Antonio Primavera
18 holes, 6310 yards, S.S.S. 70;
9-hole par 3 course
Ⅰ Floodlit and undercover 22 driving range bays and 18-hole putting green.
♣ Welcome except before 10.30am Sun; Ladies day Wed.
Ⅰ WD £22; WE £25.
♂ Welcome WD; catering and golf packages available; special offer between Oct-Mar £19 – 18 holes of golf & 1 course lunch.
|●| Excellent restaurant.
⬟ Novotel, Ipswich; Travel Lodge, Claydon; Salthouse Harbour Hotel.

4 23 Gorleston
Warren Road, Gorleston, Great Yarmouth, Norfolk, NR32 6JT
♨ www.gorlestongolfclub.co.uk
✉ manager@gorlestongolfclub.co.uk
☎ 01493 661911, Fax 661911, Pro 662103, Rest/Bar 441922
Off A12 between Great Yarmouth and Lowestoft.
Clifftop course.
Pro N Brown; Founded 1906
Designed by JR Taylor
18 holes, 6391 yards, S.S.S. 71
♣ Welcome with handicap certs.
Ⅰ WD £25; WE £30.
♂ Welcome by prior arrangement; full golf and catering package; terms on application.
|●| Full clubhouse catering facilities.
⬟ The Cliff, Gorleston; Potters HH, Hopton.

4 24 Great Yarmouth & Caister
Beach House, Caister-on-Sea, Great Yarmouth, Norfolk, NR30 5TD
♨ www.caistergolf.co.uk
✉ office@caistergolf.co.uk
☎ 01493 728699, Fax 728831, Pro 720421, Rest/Bar 720214
From Yarmouth N to Caister-on-Sea.
Links course.
Pro Martyn Clarke; Founded 1882
Designed by T Dunn/HS Colt
18 holes, 6330 yards, S.S.S. 70
Ⅰ Practice field.
♣ Welcome; handicap certs preferred.
Ⅰ WD £30; WE £35.
♂ Welcome by prior arrangement;
packages available; dining room, TV lounge, snooker; terms available on application.
|●| Full catering and bar facilities available.
⬟ Imperial; Burlington; Caister Old Hall.

4 25 Halesworth ☎
Bramfield Road, Halesworth, Suffolk, IP19 9XA
♨ info@halesworthgc.co.uk
☎ 01986 875567, Fax 874565, Pro 875697
On A144 off the A12 1 mile N of Darsham.
Parkland; formerly St Helena GC.
Pro S. Harrison; Founded 1990
Designed by JW Johnson
27 holes, 6580 yards, S.S.S. 72
Ⅰ 10 covered floodlit bays.
♣ Welcome.
Ⅰ WD £18, WE £22.
♂ Welcome by prior arrangement;
Full day packages available; company days organised; also 9-hole par 33 course available; terms on application.
|●| Full clubhouse facilities.
⬟ The Angel.

4 26 Haverhill ☎
Coupals Road, Haverhill, Suffolk, CB9 7UW
♨ www.club-noticeboard.co.uk
✉ haverhillgolf@coupalsroad.fsnet.co.uk
☎ 01440 761951, Fax 761951, Pro 712628, Rest/Bar 710311
Leave Haverhill on A1307 towards Colchester and turn second left after railway viaduct; first right into Coupals Road.
Parkland course.
Pro Nick Duc; Founded 1973
Designed by Charles Lawrie and Philip Pilgrim

18 holes, 5929 yards, S.S.S. 69
/ Practice range.
† Welcome.
⌐ WD £25; WE £34.
⌐ Welcome by prior arrangement.
⏀ Bar facilities & catering available.
⌐ Woodlands.

4 27 Hintlesham Hall ☏
Hintlesham, Ipswich, Suffolk, IP8 3NS
⌐ www.hintleshamhallgolfclub.com
⌐ office@hintleshamhallgolfclub.com
☎ 01473 652761, Fax 652750,
Pro 656006
4 miles W of Ipswich; 10 mins from
A12 or A14.
Parkland course.
Pro Alistair Spink; Founded 1991
Designed by Hawtree & Sons
18 holes, 6062 off yellows 6602 off
whites yards, S.S.S. 72
† Welcome with handicap
certificates.
⌐ WD£36; WE £44.
⌐ Welcome WD by prior
arrangement with the secretary;
packages available; spa; sauna; steam
room.
⏀ Full bar and restaurant service.
⌐ Hintlesham Hall.

4 28 Hunstanton
Golf Course Road, Old Hunstanton,
Norfolk, PE36 6JQ
⌐ hunstanton.golf@eidosnet
.co.uk
☎ 01485 532811, Fax 532319,
Pro 532751, Sec 532811,
Rest/Bar 533932
On the North Norfolk coast; take
the A149 Cromer Road through
Old Hunstanton and follow signs to
club.
Links course; 2 ball only.
Pro James Dodds; Founded 1891
Designed by George Fernie; updated
by J Braid
18 holes, 6759 yards, S.S.S. 72
† Welcome from 9.30am to
11.30am and after 2pm on WD in
summer; 10.30am-11am and after 2pm
at WE.
⌐ WD £60; WE £70 summer. WD
£40; WE £50 winter.
⌐ Welcome by prior arrangement,
but 2 ball play only; packages
available; Full facilities; terms on
application.
⏀ Full catering facilities from 11am to
4.30pm Otherwise by prior
arrangement.
⌐ The Lodge; Le Strange Arms,
Hunstanton; Lifeboat Inn, Thornham.

4 29 Ipswich
Purdis Heath, Bucklesham Road,
Ipswich, Suffolk, IP3 8UQ
⌐ www.ipswichgolfclub.com
⌐ mail@ipswichgolfclub.com
☎ 01473 728941, Fax 715236,
Pro 724017, Rest/Bar 727474
3 miles E of Ipswich off A14.
Heathland course with pine trees.
Pro S Whymark; Founded 1895/1927
Designed by James Braid, Hawtree &
Taylor
27 holes, 6435 yards, S.S.S. 71
† Welcome WD by arrangement; WE
as member's guest only.
⌐ WD £35; WE £40.
⌐ Welcome by prior arrangement;
packages including breakfast, lunch
and dinner available.
⏀ Full catering facilities.
⌐ Marriott Courtyard.

4 30 King's Lynn
Castle Rising, King's Lynn, Norfolk,
PE31 6BD
⌐ www.club-noticeboard.co.uk
⌐ klgc@eidosnet.co.uk
☎ 01553 631654, Fax 631036,
Pro 631655, Sec 631654,
Rest/Bar 631656
On A149 King's Lynn to Hunstanton,
turn at Castle Rising.
Well drained wooded course.
Pro John Reynolds; Founded 1923/1975
Designed by Alliss & Thomas
18 holes, 6609 yards, S.S.S. 73
/ Practice range.
† Welcome with handicap certificate
by prior arrangement with Pro.
⌐ WD £45; WE £55.
⌐ Welcome Thurs and Fri
only; catering available from society
menu; minimum 12. Enquiries
welcome.
⏀ Full facilities.
⌐ Knights Hill Hotel, Grimston
Road/Grange Hotel (Wooton Rd).

**4 31 The Links Country
Park Golf Course**
Sandy Lane, West Runton, Cromer,
Norfolk, NR27 9QH
⌐ www.links-hotel.co.uk
⌐ sales@links-hotel.co.uk
☎ 01263 838383, Fax 838264,
Pro 838215
Off the A149 road.
Coastal course with heath; 300 yards
from sea.
Pro Andrew Collison; Founded
1899/1903
Designed by JH Taylor (1903 when 18
holes)

9 holes, 4842 yards, S.S.S. 64
† Welcome.
⌐ WD £22.50; WE £27.50 summer
WD £15 WE £20 winter.
⌐ Welcome with prior arrangement;
full catering and golf packages; hotel
on site with pool, sauna, sun bed and
tennis course; terms on application.
⏀ Full catering facilities.
⌐ ETB 4 Crown Links Country Park
Hotel.

4 32 Mattishall
South Green, Mattishall, Dereham,
Norfolk, NR20 3JZ
☎ 01362 850111, Sec 850464
B1063 to Mattishall; right at church;
course 1 mile on left from Dereham.
If one comes from Norwich turn left
at church and course is 1.5 miles on
left.
Parkland course.
Founded 1990
Designed by Mr Todd
9 holes, 18 tees, 6170 yards, S.S.S.
69, par 70 men, par 72 ladies
/ Pitch and putt.
† Welcome.
⌐ Terms on application.
⌐ Limited availability.
⏀ Limited.
⌐ Phoenix, E Dereham; Wensum
Valley Golf Club, Taverham.

4 33 Middleton Hall
Hall Orchards, Middleton, Nr King's
Lynn, Norfolk, PE32 1RH
⌐ www.middletonhall.co.uk
⌐ middleton/hall@btclick.com
☎ 01553 841800, Fax 841800,
Pro 841801, Sec 841800,
Rest/Bar 841800
On A47 between King's Lynn and
Swaffham.
Parkland course.
Pro Steve White; Founded 1989
Designed by D Scott
18 holes, 6007 yards, S.S.S. 69
/ 6.
† Welcome.
⌐ WD £25; WE and BH £30.
⌐ Welcome by prior arrangement;
golfing and catering packages available;
carvery available for 30 or more players.
⏀ Full catering and bar facilities
available.
⌐ Butterfly; Knight's Hill, both King's
Lynn.

4 34 Mundesley
Links Road, Mundesley, North Norfolk,
NR11 8ES

Royal Norwich

Sometimes the press does have its uses. In August 1893, Norwich's newspaper, the *Eastern Daily Press*, published a letter from a man calling himself Trueflight, demanding that his city form a golf club. "Will not some energetic sportsman sound the trumpet-call, summon a meeting, and earn for himself the eternal gratitude of would-be golfers?" he asked.

Col. A C Dawson wrote back to the newspaper asking for an audience with Trueflight (soon to be revealed as a Mr Richard Jewson, a future Lord Mayor of Norwich) and within three months a club was formed on land just outside the city, bisected by the Drayton Road. The then Mayor of Norwich, Mr A R Chamberlain despatched a letter to the Duke of York, later King George V, asking him to patronise the club. The Duke obliged and Royal Norwich began its history.

Drayton Road still bisects the course's two nines, giving Royal Norwich two Road Holes, though sadly neither can compete with the St Andrews original. Indeed, getting away from the road and into the parkland is where Royal Norwich is at its best. And the very best can be found at the eighth.

It is the only "original" hole, a source of much pride among members – and rightly so. Measuring 420 yards, it demands a straight drive down the valley (taking care to avoid others teeing off at the fourth) before you can take on your shot of the round into "The Glade" – a two-tiered green flanked by the woods. Underclub and three-putting is more than likely.

The par-three ninth is similarly surrounded by fir trees, maintaining the feel of No 8. It is the shortest hole on the course and definitely birdie-able (well, if this hack can, anyone can).

Indeed, this is the part of the course where you must believe your card can really improve. Fast approaching are 12 and 13 and, as John Hudson will certify, these are holes where you can save yourself a few shots. In 1971 Hudson from Hendon, then 25, played in the Martini International Club Tournament here and managed a feat as yet unsurpassed in professional golf when he holed-in-one at 12 and 13. The 12th you can accept – a 198-yard par-three – but at the 13th you may just scratch your head in wonder.

They call this one Hades. The tee is elevated and offers a wonderful view of Norfolk – but not the hole. All that confronts you as you face the hole, driver in hand, is a valley of gorse. But have faith. Swing slowly, hit straight and when you get down to the fairway, you'll discover it is not so hell-ish after all. However a steady approach is still required to stop the ball rolling off the banks of the green. Okay, so you may not ace it – but console yourself in the knowledge that Hudson did not win in 1971 – Bernard Gallacher did.

There is something of a "no-nonsense" feel about Norwich and its premier golf club. As you enter the city along Colman's Road, a sign alerts you to the fact that you are entering a "fine city". The road is named after the famous mustard manufacturers of Norwich. Indeed, a 1909 advertisement reproduced in the club's centenary celebration book tells golfers who have braving the elements out on Royal Norwich: "You need not be afraid of the weather if you go straight home to a hot bath with a tablespoonful of Colman's Mustard added".

Norwich is indeed a fine city and Royal Norwich is a fine golf course. – **Jim Bruce-Ball**

☎ 01263 720279, Fax 720279, Sec 720095, Rest/Bar 720279
Turn off Mundesley-Cromer road at Mundesley church.
Undulating parkland with fine views.
Pro Terry Symmons
Founded 1901
Designed by Harry Vardon (in part)
9 holes, 5377 yards, S.S.S. 66
⚑ Driving range.
† Welcome WD except Weds; after 11.30am at WE.
⌣ WD £20 per round £26 per day; WE £25 after 11.30.
⌣ Welcome as with guests; catering by prior arrangement; terms on application.
🍽 Clubhouse bar and catering facilities.
⌐ Manor House, Mundesley.

---

4 35 Newton Green
Newton Green, Sudbury, Suffolk, CO10 0QN
⌂ www.newtongreengolfclub.co.uk
🖥 info@newtongreengolfclub.co.uk
☎ 01787 377217, Fax 377549, Pro 313215, Rest/Bar 377501
Course is on the A134 three miles E of Sudbury.
Moorland course.
Pro Tim Cooper
Founded 1907
18 holes, 5947 yards, S.S.S. 68
† Welcome 7 Days.
⌣ Terms on application.
⌣ Welcome by prior arrangement.
🍽 Bar and restaurant facilities.
⌐ Mill Hotel, Sudbury.

---

4 36 Norfolk Golf & CC ♉
Hingham Road, Reymerston, Norwich, Norfolk, NR9 4QQ
⌂ www.the-norfolk.co.uk
☎ 01362 850297, Fax 850614, Pro 850297, Rest/Bar 850297

Signposted from B1135.
Parkland course; was Reymerston GC.
Pro T Varney; Founded 1993
Designed by Adas
18 holes, 6609 yards, S.S.S. 72
⚑ Practice range, golf academy.
† Welcome with prior arrangement.
⌣ WD £19; WE £23.
⌣ Welcome WD; full golf, catering and leisure packages; terms on application.
🍽 Full facilities; function room.
⌐ White Hare, Hingham; Mill, Yaxham.

---

4 37 RAF Marham
King's Lynn, Norfolk, PE33 9NP
⌂ www.rafmarham.co.uk
☎ 01760 337261, Sec 337261 ext 7422
7 miles SE of King's Lynn near Narborough.
Parkland.
9 holes, 5967 yards, S.S.S. 69
† Restricted; apply on ext 7262.
⌣ £14.
⌣ Restricted access, MOD land, apply on 01760 337261 ext 7062.

---

4 38 Richmond Park ♉
Saham Road, Watton, Thetford, Norfolk, IP25 6EA
⌂ www.richmondpark.co.uk
☎ 01953 881803, Fax 881817, Pro 886104, Sec 881803, Rest/Bar 881803
Course is at bottom of Watton High Street.
Parkland course.
Pro Alan Hemsley
Founded 1990
Designed by R Jessup, R Scott
18 holes, 6289 yards, S.S.S. 70
⚑ 4 bay driving range available, call for details.
† All welcome, special offers at selected times.

⌣ WD £22 per round, WE £30 then £20 after 2pm.
⌣ Welcome WD by prior arrangement; coffee on arrival, light lunch and 3-course dinner; other packages available.
🍽 Full facilities.
⌐ Accommodation on site.

---

4 39 Rookery Park
Carlton Colville, Lowestoft, Suffolk, NR33 8HJ
⌂ www.club-noticeboard.co.uk
🖥 office@rookeryparkgolfclub.co.uk
☎ 01502 509190, Fax 509191, Pro 515103, Rest/Bar 574009
Course is two miles W of Lowestoft on the A146.
Parkland course.
Pro Martin Elsworthy
Founded 1975
Designed by Charles Lawrie
18 holes, 6714 yards, S.S.S. 72; 9-hole par 3 course
† Only visitors with handicaps welcome.
⌣ WD £30; WE £35.
⌣ Welcome by prior arrangement except Tues; packages by arrangement; snooker.
🍽 Full facilities.
⌐ Carlton Manor, Broadlands.

---

4 40 Royal Cromer ♉
145 Overstrand Road, Cromer, Norfolk, NR27 0JH
⌂ www.royalcromergolfclub.com
🖥 general.manager@royal-cromer.com
☎ 01263 512884, Fax 512430, Pro 512267, Sec 512884, Rest/Bar 512884
1 mile E of Cromer on the B1159 coast road close to the Cromer lighthouse.
Undulating clifftop course.
Pro Lee Patterson; Founded 1888

Designed by James Braid
18 holes, 6508 yards, S.S.S. 72
♦ Welcome WD and after 11am most
WE.
♀ Terms available on application.
♂ Welcome WD by prior
arrangement.
⦿ Daily facilities.
⟿ Cliftonville; Roman Camp Inn;
Anglia Court; Red Lion; Virginia Crt.

4 41 Royal Norwich
Drayton High Road, Hellesdon,
Norwich, NR6 5AH
⧉ www.royalnorwichgolf.co.uk
✉ mail@royalnorwichgolf.co.uk
☎ 01603 429928, Fax 417954,
Pro 408459, Sec 429928,
Rest/Bar 429928
On A1067 3 miles from Norwich on
Fakenham road.
Mature undulating Parkland course.
Pro Dean Futter
Founded 1893
Designed by JJW Deuchar 1893;
J Braid 1924
18 holes, 6603 yards, S.S.S. 72
♦ Welcome; bookings necessary at
WE.
♀ Available upon request.
♂ Welcome; book through general
manager; packages available; catering
and golf facilities; from £40.
⦿ Bar and restaurant facilities
available.
⟿ Norwich Sports Village; Ramada
Jarvis; Garden House; Stower Grange;
Hilton; Anglia Court.

4 42 Royal West Norfolk
Brancaster, King's Lynn, Norfolk,
PE31 8AX
☎ 01485 210223, Fax 210087,
Pro 210616, Sec 210087
Course is seven miles E of
Hunstanton; in Brancaster village turn
at the Beach/Broad Lane Junction with
the A149; course one mile.
Historic links course.
Pro S Rayner
Founded 1892
Designed by Holcombe Ingleby
18 holes, 6428 yards, S.S.S. 71
♀ Practice range.
♦ By arrangement with the secretary;
not last week of July or August or first
week of September.
♀ WD £65; WE £75.
♂ Welcome but prior booking
essential.
⦿ Full facilities.
⟿ Hoste Arms, Burnham Market;
Titchwell Manor, Titchwell.

4 43 Royal Worlington & Newmarket
Golf Links Road, Worlington, Bury St
Edmunds, Suffolk, IP28 8SD
☎ 01638 712216, Fax 717787,
Pro 715224, Sec 717787,
Rest/Bar 712216
6 miles NE of Newmarket on A14 then
A11 towards Thetford; follow signs to
Worlington.
Inland links course.
Pro Malcolm Hawkins; Founded 1893
Designed by HS Colt
9 holes, 6210 yards, S.S.S. 70
♀ Pratice ground, net, chipping area,
putting green.
♦ WD only.
♀ WD £55 before 2pm, £40 after
2pm (summer), 12pm (winter). No WE.
♂ Welcome Tues and Thurs by
arrangement; catering packages; limit
36 players, from £60 (foursomes golf
only).
⦿ Full clubhouse facilities.
⟿ Worlington Hall; Riverside,
Mildenhall.

4 44 Rushmere   ☏
Rushmere Heath, Ipswich, Suffolk,
IP4 5QQ
⧉ www.club-noticeboard.co.uk
✉ rushmeregolfclub@talk21.com
☎ 01473 725648, Fax 273852,
Pro 728076, Rest/Bar 719034
3 miles E of Ipswich off A1214
Woodbridge road.
Heath and commonland course.
Founded 1927
18 holes, 6262 yards, S.S.S. 70
♦ Welcome WD and after 2.30pm
WE; handicap certs required and proof
of membership of another club.
♀ WD/WE £30.
♂ Welcome by arrangement;
packages available; terms on
application.
⦿ Full clubhouse facilities.
⟿ Marriott; Posthouse.

4 45 Ryston Park
Ely Road, Denver, Downham Market,
Norfolk, PE38 0HH
⧉ www.club-noticeboard.co.uk
✉ Joeflogdell@rystonparkgc
.fsnet.co.uk
☎ 01366 382133, Fax 383834
On A10 1 mile S of Downham Market.
Parkland course.
Founded 1933
Designed by J Braid
9 holes, 6310 yards, S.S.S. 70
♦ Welcome WD; with members at
WE.

♀ Terms on application.
♂ Welcome; maximum 60; catering
packages available from the steward;
terms on application.
⦿ Full facilities.
⟿ Castle Hotel, Downham Market.

4 46 Seckford Golf Centre
Seckford Hall Road, Great Bealings,
Woodbridge, Suffolk, IP13 6NT
⧉ www.seckfordgolf.co.uk
✉ info@seckfordgolf.co.uk
☎ 01394 388000, Fax 382818, Pro
446191, Sec 446193, Rest/Bar 446192
Off A12 at Woodbridge Junction.
Parkland course.
Pro Simon Jay; Founded 1991
Designed by Johnny Johnson
18 holes, 4936 yards, S.S.S. 64
♀ Practice grund; putting green;
practice bunker.
♦ Welcome at all times.
♀ WD £20; WE £30/£20, Twilight
£15.
♂ Welcome by prior arrangement;
apply for information.
⦿ Terrace restaurant.
⟿ Seckford Hall Hotel; Bull Hotel.

4 47 Sheringham
Weybourne Road, Sheringham,
Norfolk, NR26 8HG
⧉ www.sheringhamgolfclub.co.uk
✉ sgc@seccare43.net
☎ 01263 823488, Fax 825189,
Pro 822980, Sec 823488,
Rest/Bar 822038
From the A148 follow the signs into
Sheringham; left at roundabout; club
0.5 miles.
Clifftop links course.
Pro M W Jubb; Founded 1891
Designed by Tom Dunn
18 holes, 6464 yards, S.S.S. 71
♀ Practice green.
♦ Welcome with prior booking.
♀ WD £40; WE £45.
♂ Welcome with prior arrangement;
terms on application.
⦿ Clubhouse facilities.

4 48 Southwold
The Common, Southwold, Suffolk,
IP18 6TB
☎ 01502 723234, Fax 723635,
Pro 723790, Sec 723248,
Rest/Bar 723234
From A12 Henham to Blythborough;
take A1095 to Southwold.
Heathland course.
Pro Brian Allen; Founded 1884
Designed by J Braid

Royal West Norfolk

The sea occasionally gets the better of Royal West Norfolk, or Brancaster as it is more familiarly known, but not too many golfers have such staying power. The north Norfolk coast can be a bleak and bitter spot, but it can also be one of the most beautiful spots in England when the flat light bounces off the water channels running through the marshes. If golfers have a soul, then it is sure to be touched by Brancaster.

The story behind the evolution of the golf course is that the Prince of Wales (the future Edward VII) was out shooting snipe on the marshes near Sandringham when his companion remarked that the area would be ideal for golf. From a start like that royal patronage was an absolute guarantee.

Brancaster is an old fashioned course and all the better for it. There are no huge shots, except those that are dictated by the wind. The bunkers – and there are several large cross bunkers, often revetted by railway sleepers as you might find at Prestwick, say – are a punishment for a bad shot, rather than a minor inconvenience designed to make the golf course look pretty in aerial photographs. The turf is spare, requiring the golfer to nip the ball off the top with little room for error. The fairways are narrow and require accuracy rather than brute force. And the greens are small and pacey, a case of the concise requiring the precise.

Every time that you play Brancaster it is like the tingle of a hot bath after a fresh Autumn day of russets, yellows, oranges and bonfire smoke. I know that all sounds pretty tosspot-ish, but imagine something cosy bashing up against the edges of nature and you will get an idea of Brancaster. The par threes are superb, the 8th is a par five unlike any other in the world and the par fours can take your game to the limit right from the start, even if the finish is slightly weak. The real finish, however, is anything but weak. Anyone who wants to find out what a golf clubhouse should be like, must visit Brancaster. This is not a building better suited for locking up local government, but a wooden refuge from the elements. I don't know if it creaks when the wind really gets up, but it certainly should do.

And the elements can get fairly violent around this part of the country. The sea is constantly trying to beat up the land and invades so regularly that the course can become partly cut off. There is no point trying to fight it, so managed retreat is the preferred option. The lifeboat house just 150 yards up the coast and the presence of deep holes filled with soft sand that are bottomless and can take a man right down, tell of how lethal this bit of coastline can be.

But with all the dangers the sea also brings its beauty. The unbroken reach of North Sea to the north pole brings with it an extraordinary light and its relationship with the marshes nurtures the flowers and the birds, as well as providing a rich environment for samphire, the profits from which sustains some of the local community.

This really is a blessed and cursed spot. – **Mark Reason**

9 holes, 6052 yards, S.S.S. 69
⚐ Practice green.
† Welcome.
£ WD £26; WE £28. Daily rate £35.
⚐ Welcome by arrangement;
packages available; terms on
application.
⚑ Clubhouse facilities.
⚐ Swan; Crown; Cricketers; Pier
Avenue Hotel.

4 49 Sprowston Manor ℭ
(Marriott)
Wroxham Road, Sprowston, Norwich,
NR7 8RP
⚐ www.marriotthotels.com
☎ 01603 254290, Fax 788884,
Pro 254290, Rest/Bar 254292
On A1551 Norwich to Wroxham road;
10 minutes from city centre.
Parkland course.
Pro G Ireson; M Borrett, C Jefferson,
R Lewis; Founded 1980
18 holes, 6543 yards, S.S.S. 68
⚐ 27 bays.
† Welcome.
£ WD £30; WE £35.
⚐ Welcome by prior arrangement;
Full package of golf and catering,
including morning coffee, lunch and
dinner. Inclusive golf breaks.
⚑ Full catering facilities.
⚐ Sprowston Manor.

4 50 Stowmarket
Lower Road, Onehouse, Stowmarket,
Suffolk, IP14 3DA
⚐ www.club-noticeboard.co.uk
☎ 01449 736473, Fax 736826,
Pro 736392, Rest/Bar 736733
Course is 2.5 miles south-west of
Stowmarket off the B1115 Stowmarket-
Bidlestone road.
Parkland course.
Pro Duncan Burl; Founded 1962
18 holes, 6107 yards, S.S.S. 69
⚐ 12.
† Welcome after 9.15am with
handicap certs, except Wed.
£ WD £31; WE £37.
⚐ Welcome Thurs and Fri.
⚑ Full facilities.
⚐ Cedars.

4 51 Suffolk Golf & CC ℭ
Fornham St Genevieve, Bury St
Edmunds, Suffolk, IP28 6JQ
⚐ www.the-suffolk.co.uk
✉ thelodge@the-suffolk.co.uk
☎ 01284 706777, Fax 706721
From A14 take B1106 to Fornham.
Parkland course.

Pro Steven Hall; Founded 1969
18 holes, 6077 yards, S.S.S. 70
† Welcome by prior arrangement.
£ WD £25; WE £30.
⚐ Society packages and residential
breaks available.
⚑ Full clubhouse catering facilities
available.
⚐ 41 en-suite bedrooms.

4 52 Swaffham ℭ
Cley Road, Swaffham, Norfolk,
PE37 8AE
⚐ www.swaffhamgc.supanet.com
✉ swaffhamgc@supanet.com
☎ 01760 721611,
Fax 725485/721621, Sec 721621
1 mile out of town on Cockley Cley
road; signposted in market place.
Heathland course.
Pro Peter Field; Founded 1922
18 holes, 6554 yards, S.S.S. 71
⚐ Practice green; 7 acre practice
ground.
† Welcome WD; with member at
WE.
£ All day £35; from 12 noon £25,
4pm £15. Winter rate: £15 any time,
Nov-March inclusive.
⚐ Welcome WD by arrangement.
⚑ Full catering.
⚐ George Hotel; Horse & Groom
Hotel.

4 53 Thetford
Brandon Road, Thetford, Norfolk,
IP24 3NE
⚐ www.club-noticeboard.co.uk
✉ sally@thetfordgolfclub.co.uk
☎ 01842 752258, Fax 752662,
Pro 752662, Sec 752169, Rest/Bar
764742
Just off A11 on B1107.
Wooded heathland course.
Pro Gary Kitley; Founded 1912
Designed by CH Mayo, Donald Steel
18 holes, 6879 yards, S.S.S. 73
⚐ Practice green.
† Welcome WD with handicap certs;
weekend with member only.
£ Terms on application. Without
member £40.
⚐ Welcome Wed, Thurs, Fri only;
packages available; terms on
application.
⚑ Full facilities.
⚐ Bell; Thomas Paine; Wereham
House.

4 54 Thorpeness ℭ
4 54 Thorpeness ℭ
Thorpeness Hotel & Golf Club,
Lakeside Avenue, Thorpeness, Suffolk,
IP16 4NH

⚐ www.thorpeness.co.uk
✉ info@thorpeness.co.uk
☎ 01728 452176, Fax 453868,
Pro 454926, Sec 452176,
Rest/Bar 452176
25 miles N of Ipswich on A12; then
B1094 to Aldeburgh and then B1069 to
Thorpeness.
Coastal heathland course.
Pro Frank Hill; Founded 1922
Designed by James Braid
18 holes, 6241 yards, S.S.S. 71
⚐ 3.
† Welcome if carrying handicap
certs.
£ WD £25; WE £30.
⚐ Welcome; packages available;
catering facilities, snooker; lounge,
function room; tennis courts; terms on
application.
⚑ Restaurant, patio bar, lounge.
⚐ 30-room hotel on site; guests have
priority tee-times.

4 55 Ufford Park Hotel ℭ
Yarmouth Road, Ufford, Woodbridge,
Suffolk, IP12 1QW
⚐ www.uffordpark.co.uk
✉ uffordparkltd@btinternet.com
☎ 01394 382836, Fax 383582,
Pro 382836
Course is two miles N of Woodbridge
on the B1438.
Parkland with ponds.
Pro S Robertson; Founded 1991
Designed by Phil Pilgrim
18 holes, 6300 yards, S.S.S. 70
⚐ Practice; driving nets.
† Welcome by arrangement.
£ WD £20; WE £30.
⚐ Welcome on WD; packages
available; leisure facilities inc pool,
spa, sauna, gym; terms on application.
⚑ Full facilities.
⚐ Ufford Park Hotel on site.

4 56 Waldringfield
Newbourne Road, Waldringfield,
Woodbridge, Suffolk, IP12 8PT
⚐ www.club-noticeboard.co.uk/
waldringfield
☎ 01473 736768, Fax 736436,
Pro 736417
3 miles NE of Ipswich.
Heathland course.
Founded 1983
Designed by P Pilgrim
18 holes, 7863 yards, S.S.S. 70
⚐ Practice area and net.
† Welcome WD; after 11am WE.
£ WD £22; WE £26.
⚐ Welcome WD by prior arrangement;
day tickets are available from £22.50
and £25 on WE. Terms on application.

Royal Worlington and Newmarket

Royal Worlington and Newmarket Golf Club achieved its royal patronage in 1895 when the then Prince of Wales agreed to become President of the club that was then only five years old. Many Cambridge undergraduates remember it fondly as the course where they cut their competitive teeth in the game, though many still refer to it sentimentally as Mildenhall, rather than give it its full title.

Unusually for the royals, it has only ever had nine holes. One of the attractions of that is that you get a second chance at every hole. The converse is that the second time around you know much more and your mind has the opportunity to magnify the difficulties. This, however, is said to be the best nine-hole course in the world and the truth of this dictum makes it worth playing again and again.

Patric Dickinson felt the need to defend the reputation of "the sacred nine" when he wrote: "If ever a man declares: 'nine holes are not enough; real golf requires 18', let him be reminded of Mildenhall, for there is no more difficult feat of real golf in this country, probably anywhere in the world".

It is difficult to exaggerate a nine-hole course. Worlington is set on heathland, with stands of pine trees forming natural divisions between some of the fairways. The opening par-five might unkindly be described as nondescript, but at least it allows the golfer to get swinging in preparation for what is to follow.

The second is an oxymoron, "a long short hole" that can make or break the good bad golfer. Dickinson described difficulty of finding the green to being "like pitching on to a policeman's helmet". It is well over 200 yards long and made all the more difficult by the green sloping away on all sides. Even the truest of drives to the heart of the green is sometimes not enough to score well.

The greens are quick too, aided by the sandy Suffolk soil that allows a round to be played here all the year round. One of the more popular topics of conversation in the clubhouse after an afternoon's golf is generally how many putts each golfer made. To keep in the twenties is something to brag about – so long as you are playing the nine holes twice.

The fifth is one of the most memorable holes on the course. At 155 yards, it seems innocuous enough, but the three-level green is long and narrow, set on a promontory with steep slopes on either side. A former captain of the club is said to have driven the green and walked off with an eight on his card.

Astute bunkering and awkward swales around some greens offer a challenge to all standards of golfer. Peter Alliss recalls that four Ryder Cup players played an exhibition match here some 40 years ago, and the best round among them was a 74.

This is the sort of course where the inclusion on the card of the bogey for each hole, as well as par, strikes you not as affectation, but as a reminder that this is a club which prides itself on tradition and propriety. There is nothing stuffy about the club, and every aspect of its clubhouse exhibits the same warmth and austerity. Visitors are provided with a standard issue tankard and a ration of IPA.

Henry Longhurst wrote a piece entitled "Golftopia". In it he described his ideal, and imaginary course. The more you see of Worlington, and Longhurst saw a fair bit of it, the more you imagine that he had this famous nine-hole course in mind. – **Jim Bruce-Ball**

🍽 Full facilities.
🛏 Marriott Courtyard, Ipswich.

---

4 57 **Wensum Valley Hotel Golf & Country Club**
Beech Avenue, Taverham, Norwich,
Norfolk, NR8 6HP
☎ 01603 261012, Fax 261664,
Pro 261012, Sec 261012,
Rest/Bar 261012
Take the A1067 Fakenham to
Taverham road.
Parkland course; golf school.
Pro Peter Whittle; Founded 1989
Designed by BC Todd
Valley: 18 holes, 6223 yards; S.S.S.
70; Wensum: 18 holes,6037 yards;
S.S.S. 69
† Welcome.
[WD £20; WE £20 (day ticket that
includes a bar meal of up to £5).
🔗 Welcome; packages on request;
TV lounge, pool table; bowling green.
Other leisure facilities can be
organised; conference facilities; golfing
breaks available; terms on application.

🍽 Clubhouse facilities; Morton
Restaurant; Wensum suite; bars.
🛏 Hotel on site.

---

4 58 **Weston Park**   ♉
Weston Longville, Norwich, Norfolk,
NR9 5JW
🖥 www.weston-park.co.uk
💻 golf@weston-park.co.uk
☎ 01603 872363, Fax 873040,
Pro 872998, Rest/Bar 876306
9 miles NW of Norwich off A1067
Norwich-Fakenham road.
Parkland course.
Pro Michael Few; Founded 1993
Designed by Golf Technology
18 holes, 6603 yards, S.S.S. 72
📏 Practice ground.
† Welcome.
[WD £32; WE £40.
🔗 Welcome with a minimum of 12
players; packages available £25-£45;
group lessons; snooker room;
conference room.
🍽 Full restaurant facilities.
🛏 Wensum Country Hotel.

---

4 59 **Woodbridge**
Bromeswell Heath, Woodbridge,
Suffolk, IP12 2PF
🖥 www.woodbridgegolfclub.com
💻 woodbridgegc@anglianet
.co.uk
☎ 01394 382038, Fax 382392,
Pro 383213, Sec 382038,
Rest/Bar 383212
2 miles E of Woodbridge on A1152.
Heathland course.
Pro C Elliott; Founded 1893
Designed by F Hawtree
27 holes, 6299 yards, S.S.S. 71
† Welcome WD with handicap
certs. 9-hole course open all week to
visitors.
[WD £42 18-hole course, £18 9-
hole course.
🔗 Welcome WD by prior
arrangement; maximum 36; packages
available; from £37.
🍽 Catering facilities available
9am to 5.30pm or by prior
arrangement.
🛏 Crown & Castle, Orford; The Bull
Hotel, Woodbridge.

SOUTH MIDLANDS
5A

Bedfordshire, Northamptonshire, Cambridgeshire, Leicestershire

Henry Longhurst learned his golf at Bedford Golf Club, or the Bedfordshire as it is now more grandly known. He wrote, "It was a flat, lush hundred-acre meadow, bounded by the Midland Railway, the River Ouse, the Girls High School hockey field, the allotments, a cornfield and Mr Somebody's garden". As it happened all these boundaries were to the golfer's left, so in years to come, when someone hit a shot with a touch of involuntary fade, it was said "to have a bit of Bedfordshire on it".

The Bedfordshire is greatly improved from those muddy days, indeed Longhurst called its advancement a "miracle", but his description makes the point about a lot of the golf in the area. Flat and muddy, much of the Midlands makes for mundane golf untouched by royalty.

Dunstable Downs is an exception that proves the rule. Because of its elevation and chalky subsoil it has some of the best fairways in Britain. It can be a testing walk but it has several dramatically elevated tees. Standing on the eleventh you can see six counties. There is a gliding school nearby so do not be surprised to see your ball carried off on a thermal.

John O'Gaunt is another decent course, although it leans rather heavily in favour of par fours (there are 13 of them), and Aspley Guise & Woburn Sands, just over the county border from Woburn, is a well-maintained heathland course.

Cambridgeshire is not blessed with too many top golf courses and many a divot (the name for Cambridge's second team) has crossed the Suffolk border to play their golf at Royal Worlington. But Gog Magog, three and a half miles outside Cambridge and with over a hundred years of history, is well worth a visit. Named after some rare bumps in the fen landscape, the Gogs has a hilly start and a hilly finish with a flat stretch between.

Northamptonshire is another of those counties that has welcomed a big name with a big design in order to raise its golfing profile. Johnny Miller excavated a lake to shape the land to create Collingtree Park. It is another of those long, American-style courses designed to accommodate championships more than the average golfer.

More to many people's taste is Northamptonshire County, often used for regional qualifying into the Open Championship.

Leicestershire has received a little more recognition as a golfing county following the emergence of Gary Wolstenholme, the only Briton to have played on four winning Walker Cup teams. Having left it late to learn his golf in Leicestershire Wolsten-holme is helping to raise the profile of Kilworth Springs, a course that is nearly always open for play, quite a recommendation in a county that often has to turn to the dreaded rubber mat in the winter.

Tree lined Longcliffe is the most highly regarded of Leicestershire's courses, but The Leicestershire itself is a good place for spotting county cricketers and international rugby players out for a hack. It has a couple of severe doglegs, a feature that seems something of a regional trait as Peterborough Milton and Hinckley are also remembered for their doglegs.

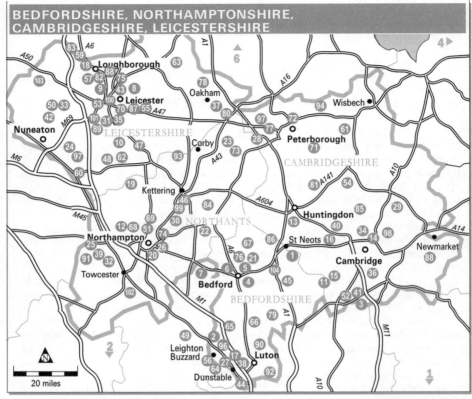

BEDFORDSHIRE, NORTHAMPTONSHIRE, CAMBRIDGESHIRE, LEICESTERSHIRE

KEY			
1	Abbotsley	26	Delapre Park
2	Aspley Guise & Woburn Sands	27	Dunstable Downs
3	Barkway Park	28	Elton Furze
4	Beadlow Manor Hotel	29	Ely City
5	Bedford & County	30	Embankment
6	The Bedford Golf Course	31	Enderby
7	The Bedfordshire	32	Farthingstone Hotel G & LC
8	Beedles Lake	33	Forest Hill
9	Birstall	34	Girton
10	Blaby	35	Glen Gorse
11	Bourn	36	Gog Magog
12	Brampton Heath	37	Greetham Valley
13	Brampton Park	38	Griffin
14	Cambridge	39	Hellidon Lakes Hotel and CC
15	Cambridge Meridian	40	Hemingford Abbots
16	Cambridgeshire Moat	41	Heydon Grange G & CC
17	Chalgrave Manor Golf Club	42	Hinckley
18	Charnwood Forest	43	Humberstone Heights
19	Cold Ashby	44	Ivinghoe
20	Collingtree Park	45	John O'Gaunt
21	Colmworth & N Beds	46	Kettering
22	Colworth	47	Kibworth
23	Corby	48	Kilworth Springs
24	Cosby	49	Kingfisher CC
25	Daventry & District	50	Kingstand
		51	Kingsthorpe
		52	Kingsway
		53	Kirby Muxloe

54	Lakeside Lodge	80	RAF North Luffenham
55	The Leicestershire	81	Ramsey
56	Leighton Buzzard	82	Rothley Park
57	Lingdale	83	Rushcliffe
58	Links	84	Rushden
59	Longcliffe	85	St Ives
60	Lutterworth	86	St Neots
61	March	87	Scraptoft
62	Market Harborough	88	Shelthorpe
63	Melton Mowbray	89	Six Hills
64	Mentmore	90	South Beds
65	Mount Pleasant	91	Staverton Park
66	Mowsbury	92	Stockwood Park
67	Northampton	93	Stoke Albany
68	Northamptonshire County	94	Thorney Golf Centre
69	Oadby	95	Thorpe Wood
70	Old Nene Golf & Country Club	96	Tilsworth
71	Orton Meadows	97	Ullesthorpe
72	Oundle	98	Waterbeach Barracks
73	Overstone Park	99	Wellingborough
74	Park Hill	100	Western Park
75	Pavenham Park	101	Whetstone
76	Peterborough Milton	102	Whittlebury Park Golf & Country Club
77	RAF Cottesmore	103	Willesley Park
78	RAF Henlow	104	Wyboston Lakes
79			

5A 1 Abbotsley Golf Hotel and Country Club

Eynesbury Hardwicke, St Neots, Cambs, PE19 6XN

📧 abbotsley@americangolf.uk.com

☎ 01480 474000, Fax 403280, Abbotsley Pro 477669, Cromwell Pro 215153

2 miles SE of St Neots leaving A428 at Tesco roundabout.

Parkland course.

Pro Steve Connolly; Founded 1976
Designed by Derek Young, Vivien Saunders, Jenny Wisson
Abbotsley: 18 holes, 6311 yards, S.S.S. 72; Cromwell: 18 holes, 6087 yards, S.S.S. 69

Ⓘ 21-bay floodlit driving range.

† Welcome; restrictions at WE (Abbotsley); 7-day bookings availability for tee times.

Ⓛ Terms on application.

♻ Welcome by prior arrangement; packages available; tailored to suit individual needs, prices on request; residential packages; residential golf schools: Denise Hastings and Vivian Saunders.

🍴 The Garden restaurant and choice of bars.

🛏 Hotel on site; 42 well-appointed, en suite bedrooms.

5A 2 Aspley Guise & Woburn Ⓣ Sands

West Hill, Aspley Guise, Beds, MK17 8DX

☎ 01908 583596, Fax 583596, Pro 582974, Sec 583596

2 miles W of M1 Junction 13 between Aspley Guise and Woburn Sands

Undulating parkland course.

Pro Colin Clingan; Founded 1914
Designed by Sandy Herd
18 holes, 6079 yards, S.S.S. 70

† Welcome WD; WE as member's guest.

Ⓛ WD £38 per day £28 for 18 holes; WE £38 per round £50 per day by prior arrangement only.

♻ Welcome Wed and Fri; April to October; catering and golf packages available; from £55.00 for an all day package.

🍴 Full catering facilities 7 days a week.

🛏 Moore Place.

5A 3 Barkway Park

Barkway Park Golf Club, Nuthampstead Road, Barkway, Royston, Herts, SG8 8EN

☎ 01763 848215, Pro 849070

On B1368 5 miles S of Royston

Gently undulating links course.

Pro Jamie Bates; Founded 1992
Designed by Vivien Saunders
18 holes, 6997 yards, S.S.S. 74

† Welcome; WE tee times cannot be booked until Fri pm.

Ⓛ WD £10; WE £15.

♻ Welcome by prior arrangement; packages available; function room; pool table and darts; terms on application.

🍴 Full facilities. Practice area.

🛏 Vintage Puckeridge; Flintcroft Motel.

5A 4 Beadlow Manor Hotel

Beadlow, Nr Shefford, Beds, SG17 5PH

📧 beadlow@kbnet.co.uk

☎ 01525 860800, Fax 861345, Pro 861292

On the A507 between Ampthill and Shefford; 1.5 miles W of Shefford.

Parkland course.

Pro G Dixon; Adrienne Englemann; Founded 1973
Designed by Baron Manhattan
18 holes, 6072 yards, S.S.S. 69

Ⓘ Practice range, 25 bays floodlit; buggies and clubs for hire.

† Welcome.

Ⓛ Terms on application.

♻ Welcome by prior arrangement; several golf and catering packages available; health club; conference rooms; terms on application.

🍴 Bar, restaurants.

🛏 33 room hotel on site.

5A 5 Bedford and County Ⓣ

Green Lane, Clapham, Bedford, Beds, MK41 6ET

📧 olga@bedcounty.fsnet.co.uk

☎ 01234 352617, Fax 357195, Pro 359189, Sec 352617, Rest/Bar 354010

Off the A6 N of Bedford before Clapham village.

Parkland course.

Pro Roger Tattersall; Founded 1912
18 holes, 6420 yards, S.S.S. 70

† Welcome WD; with a member at WE.

Ⓛ WD £26.

♻ Welcome WD except Wed; all day golf packages available; from £50.

🍴 Full facilities.

🛏 Woodlands Manor.

5A 6 The Bedford Golf Ⓣ Course

Carnoustie Drive, Great Denham Golf Village, Biddenham, Bedford, MK40 4FF

🖥 www.kolengolf.com

📧 thebedford1@ukonline.co.uk

☎ 01234 320022, Fax 320023, Pro 353653, Sec 330559, Rest/Bar 348822

1.5 miles W of Bedford A248 Northampton Road.

American design, well bunkered, many lakes.

Pro Zac Thompson; Founded 1998
Designed by David Pottidge
18 holes, 6305 yards, S.S.S. 72

Ⓘ Grass driving range, up to 30 people.

† Welcome WD; as members' guests at WE.

Ⓛ WD £30; WE £40-£50

♻ Welcome WD; full clubhouse facilities; green fee plus catering.

🍴 Full clubhouse facilities.

🛏 Shakespeare; Swan; Moat House.

5A 7 Bedfordshire Golf Club Ⓣ

Spring Lane, Stagsden, Bedford, MK43 8SR

🖥 www.bedfordshiregolf.com

📧 david@bedfordshiregolf.com

☎ 01234 822555

On A422 between Milton Keynes and Bedford.

Hilly, crossways.

18 holes – 6565 yards, 9-hole par 3

† Yes but not a WE unless with member; 9-hole at all times.

Ⓛ Enquire for fees.

♻ Yes.

🍴 Dining room, function suite.

🛏 Shakespeare Hotel, Bedford; Swan Revived, Newport Pagnell; Post House, Newport Pagnell Road.

5A 8 Beedles Lake

Broome Lane, East Goscote, Leics, LE7 3NQ

☎ 0116 2606759, Fax 2604414, Pro 2606759, Sec 2604414 (tel/fax), Rest/Bar 2607086

Between A46 Leicester-Newark road and A607 Leicester-Melton Mowbray.

Parkland course.

Pro Sean Bryne; Founded 1993
Designed by D Tucker
18 holes, 6641 yards, S.S.S. 72

Ⓘ 17; practice range.

† Welcome at all times.

Ⓛ WD £12; WE £16 (2003 fees).

♻ Welcome any time WD; WE after 11a, with prior arrangement with Mgr).

🍴 Clubhouse facilities.

5A 9 Birstall Ⓣ

Station Road, Birstall, Leicester, Leics, LE4 3BB

🖥 www.birstallgolfclub.co.uk

Beedles Lake Golf Centre
170 Broome Lane · East Goscote · Leicestershire LE7 3WQ
Tel: **0116 260 6759** (Pro)   Tel: **0116 260 7080** (Steward)   Tel/Fax: **0116 260 4414** (Golf Manager)
MEMBERSHIPS AVAILABLE
SOCIETY PACKAGES AVAILABLE (Mon - Fri from £18.00; Sat & Sun from £23.00)
VISITORS WELCOME

suechilton@btconnect.com
0116 267 4322, Fax 4322,
Pro 5245, Rest/Bar 4450
Off A6 3 miles N of Leicester city.
Parkland course.
Pro David Clark; Founded 1901
18 holes, 6213 yards, S.S.S. 70
† Welcome – WE by arrangement
with Pro.
⌊ WD £25-£30.
⌀ Welcome Wed and Fri by prior
arrangement; reductions for groups of
more than 12; snooker; billiards; prices
on application.
⦿ Full facilities except Mon.
⌐ Contact club for details.

5A 10 **Blaby**
Lutterworth Road, Blaby, Leics.,
LE8 3DP
www.blabygolfcourse.com
0116 2784804
From Leicester through Blaby village;
course on the left-hand side.
Parkland course.
Pro Matt Fisher; Founded 1991
9 holes, 5312 yards, S.S.S. 66
⫾ Practice range, 27 floodlit bays;
crazy golf course.
† Welcome; pay and play.
⌊ WD and WE 9 holes £5, 18 holes £7
⌀ Welcome; special company days
available; terms on application.
⦿ Bar.

5A 11 **Bourn**
Toft Road, Bourn, Cambridge, Cambs,
CB3 7TT
01954 718057, Fax 718908, Pro
718958, Sec 718088, Rest/Bar 718057
6 miles W of Cambridge off A14
through Bourn village.
Parkland course.
Pro Craig Watson; Founded 1991
Designed by J Hull and S Bonham
18 holes, 6417 yards, S.S.S. 71
† Welcome.
⌊ WD £18; WE £25.
⌀ Welcome; full clubhouse facilities
available; terms on application.
Practice area, bring own balls; buggies
for hire.
⦿ Clubhouse facilities.
⌐ Many in Cambridge.

5A 12 **Brampton Heath**
Sandy Lane, Church Brampton,
Northampton, Northants, NN6 8AX
www.bhgc.co.uk
dcoulson@bhgc.co.uk
01604 843939, Fax 843885
3 miles N of Northampton just off A5119
Undulating heathland course.
Pro R Hudson; Founded 1995
Designed by D Snell
18 holes, 6456 yards, S.S.S. 71
⫾ PGA-approved short course;
driving range.
† Welcome at all times.
⌊ WD £16; WE £20.
⌀ Welcome WD and WE; packages
from only £16 arranged to suit.
⦿ Full facilities.

5A 13 **Brampton Park**   ℭ
Buckden Road, Brampton, Huntingdon,
Cambs, PE28 4NF
01480 434700, Fax 411145,
Pro 434705
Take A1 or A14 to RAF Brampton; club
is opposite airbase.
Meadowland course.
Pro A Currie; Founded 1991
Designed by Simon Gidman (Hawtree
& Sons)
18 holes, 6403 yards, S.S.S. 73
⫾ 10 bay floodlit
† Welcome.
⌊ Winter: WD £15, WE £35;
Summer: WD £25, WE £35.
⌀ Welcome WD; function room;
practice area; trolleys for hire; full
facilities; from £29.75.
⦿ Clubhouse facilities.
⌐ Limited accomodation on site.

5A 14 **Cambridge Golf Club**   ℭ
Station Road, Longstanton,
Cambridge, Cambs, CB4 5DR
01954 789388
10 mins N of Cambridge on B1050 off
A14.
Parkland course.
Pro G Huggett/A Engelman; Founded
1992
Designed by G Huggett
18 holes, 6736 yards, S.S.S. 74
⫾ Floodlit covered driving range and
play off grass allowed.

† Welcome.
⌊ WD £10; WE £13.
⌀ Welcome at all times; various
packages and reductions available;
terms on application.
⦿ Full clubhouse facilities.

5A 15 **Cambridge Meridian**   ℭ
Comberton Road, Toft, Cambridge,
Cambs, CB3 7RY
www.golfsocieties.com
meridian@golfsocieties.com
01223 264700, Fax 264701,
Pro 264702,
On B1046 at Toft 3 miles W of M11
Junction 12.
Parkland course.
Pro Michael Clemons; Founded 1994
Designed by P Alliss/C Clark
18 holes, 6651 yards, S.S.S. 72
† Welcome with telephone booking.
⌊ WD £16; WE £25.
⌀ Welcome WD and after 1pm WE;
range of packages available; £19-£49.
⦿ Full clubhouse catering facilities.
Practice range, large practice facilities.
⌐ University Arms Hotel; Abbotsley
Golf Hotel.

5A 16 **Cambridgeshire Moat**   ℭ
Moat House Hotel, Bar Hill,
Cambridge, Cambridgeshire, CB3 8EU
01954 780098, Fax 780010, Pro
780098, Sec 249971, Rest/Bar 249988
On A14 5 miles N of Cambridge.
Parkland course.
Pro Paul Simpson; Founded 1974
Designed by F Middleton
18 holes, 6734 yards, S.S.S. 72
⫾ Putting green; 2 nets; chipping
green.
† Everyone welcome.
⌊ Unconfirmed as yet for 2002.
⌀ Welcome; day packages can be
organised; terms on application.
⦿ Full hotel and clubhouse facilities.
Practice area, buggies and clubs for
hire; group tuition available.
⌐ Cambridgeshire Moat House,
134 en suite rooms; recent four million
pound refurbishment.

5A 17 **Chalgrave Manor**   ℭ
Dunstable Road, Toddington,
Dunstable, Beds, LU5 6JN

☎ 01525 876556, Fax 876556, Pro 876554, Sec 876556, Rest/Bar 876556
2 miles W of M1 Junction 12 on A 5120 between Toddington and Houghton Regis.
Undulating parkland course.
Pro Terry Bunyan; Founded 1994
Designed by Mike Palmer/S Rumble
18 holes, 6022 yards, S.S.S. 72
† Welcome.
Ⓘ WD £15; WE £30.
↻ Welcome midweek; full golf and catering packages can be arranged; £21-£37.
🍽 Full catering facilities.

5A 18 Charnwood Forest
Breakback Road, Woodhouse Eaves, Loughborough, Leics, LE12 8TA
🖳 www.charnwoodforestgc.co.uk
🖳 secretary@charnwoodforestgc.co.uk
☎ 01509 890259, Fax 890925
Close to M1 Junctions 22/23.
Heathland course with heather, gorse.
Founded 1890
Designed by James Braid
9 holes, 5960 yards, S.S.S. 69
ⅈ Practice green.
† Handicapped certificates required.
Ⓘ WD £20; WE £25 (summer).
↻ Welcome Wed, Thurs and Fri; full catering packages plus 27 holes of golf
Details on application.
🍽 Full catering facilities.
🖳 Friendly Hotel.

5A 19 Cold Ashby ☫
Stanford Road, Cold Ashby, Northampton, Northants, NN6 6EP
🖳 www.coldashbygolfclub.com
🖳 coldashby.golfclub@virgin.net
☎ 01604 740548, Fax 740548, Pro 740099
11 miles N of Northampton near A5199/A14 Junction 1.
Undulating parkland course with spectacular views.
Pro Shane Rose; Founded 1974
Designed by John Day extension by D Croxton 1995
27 holes, 6308 yards, S.S.S. 70
ⅈ Driving range; practice area.
† Welcome; some WE restrictions.
Ⓘ WD £15; WE £18.50.
↻ Welcome any day by prior arrangement; full day's golf and catering packages available; 27-hole course; 3 loops of 9; Winwick/Ashby par 70; Ashby/Elkington par 70; Elkington/Winwick par 70; dining room facilities; £40 WD £44 WE.
🍽 Full clubhouse facilities. Extensive practice area, buggies and clubs for hire.

🖳 Pytchley, W Haddon; Crick; Broomhill, Spratton.

5A 20 Collingtree Park
Windingbrook Lane, Northampton, Northants, NN4 0XN
🖳 www.collingtreeparkgolf.com
☎ 01604 700000, Fax 702600, Pro 701202, Rest/Bar 700000
M1 Junction 15 just past Stakis Hotel
Championship course; owned by European PGA.
Pro Henry Bareham; Geoff Pook, Alan Carter; Founded 1990
Designed by Johnny Miller
18 holes, 6908 yards, S.S.S. 73
ⅈ 26.
† Welcome with 7- day advance booking; handicap certs required.
Ⓘ Mon-Thu £20, Fri-Sun £25.
↻ Welcome with prior arrangement; full clubhouse facilities and driving range and practice ground; terms on application.
🍽 Full facilities in clubhouse.
🖳 Stakis Hotel; Swallow Hotel; Midway Hotel.

5A 21 Colmworth & N Beds
New Road, Colmworth, Bedford, Beds, MK44 2NN
🖳 www.colmworthgolfclub.co.uk
🖳 julie@colmworthg.fsnet.co.uk
☎ 01234 378181, Fax 376678
Within easy reach of A1 (10 min), M1 (20 min), A14 (15 min).
Easy walking course with water play on 6 holes.
Pro Graham Bithrey; Founded 1991
Designed by John Glasgow
18 holes, 6435 yards, S.S.S. 71.
9 holes, 611 yards, Par 3.
ⅈ 8 bay driving range; putting green.
† Welcome WD and with booking at WE after 9.30am.
Ⓘ WD £13; WE £20.
↻ Welcome every day; packages can be arranged; restaurant facilities until 2.30pm; terms on application.
🍽 Full restaurant and bar..
🖳 Self-catering holiday cottages.

5A 22 Colworth
Unilever Research Laboratory, Colworth House, Sharnbrook, Bedford, Beds, MK44 1LQ
☎ 01234 781781
10 miles N of Bedford off A6 through village of Shambrook.
Parkland course.
Founded 1985
9 holes, 5000 yards, S.S.S. 64

† Private members only.
Ⓘ Terms on application.

5A 23 Corby
Stamford Road, Weldon, NN17 3JH
☎ 01536 260756, Fax 260756, Sec 743829
A43 Corby to Stamford road 2 miles E of Weldon.
Parkland course.
Pro Jeff Bradbrook; Founded 1965
Designed by Fred Hawtree
18 holes, 6677 yards, S.S.S. 72
† Welcome.
Ⓘ WD £10.60; WE £13.70.
↻ Welcome anytime; large golf shop; packages for golf and catering available; from £9.35.
🍽 Snacks and meals available.
🖳 Hilton.

5A 24 Cosby ☫
Chapel Lane, Off Broughton Road, Cosby, Leicester, Leics, LE9 1RG
🖳 www.cosby-golf-club.co.uk
🖳 secretary@cosby-golf-club.co.uk
☎ 0116 286 4759, Fax 286 4484, Pro 284 8275
From M1 Junction 21 take B4114 for 3 miles until Cosby turning.
Parkland course.
Pro Martin Wing; Founded 1895
Designed by C Sinclair
18 holes, 6417 yards, S.S.S. 71
ⅈ Practice Range.
† Welcome midweek; member's guest only at WE.
Ⓘ WD £25 per round; £35 per day.
↻ Welcome, maximum 80 with prior arrangement; various packages available.
🍽 Full clubhouse facilities available.
🖳 Stakis Leicester, Mill on the Soar, Broughton Astley.

5A 25 Daventry & District
Norton Road, Daventry, Northants, NN11 5LS
☎ 01327 702829, Fax 702829, Sec 702829
1 mile E of the town.
Undulating meadowland course.
Founded 1908
9 holes, 5812 yards, S.S.S. 68
† Welcome; except before Sunday noon.
Ⓘ WD £12; WE £20.
↻ Welcome by prior arrangement with the Sec; packages by arrangement; discounts for more than 16 players; terms on application.
🍽 Bar and restaurant.
🖳 Britannia; Hanover.

5A 26 **Delapre Park**

John Corby Golf Ltd, Delapre Golf
Complex, Eagle Drive, Northampton,
Northants, NN4 7DU
💻 ruth@delaprenorthhampton.golf.uk
☎ 01604 764036, Fax 706378,
Sec 763957
M1 Junction 15 then 4 miles on A45.
Parkland course; also has 9-hole
Hardingstone course.
Pro J Corby/J Cuddihy; Founded 1976
Designed by J Jacobs/J Corby
🏌 Practice range 40 bays also grass
tees; 2 par 3 courses; pitch & putt
course; senior PGA professional tutor;
3 teaching pros; club hire available.
† Welcome at all times.
Ⓛ WD 9 holes £6.50, 18 holes £8.50;
WE 9 holes £7.50, 18 holes £12.50
🏌 Welcome one per day but also
welcome WE; packages can be
arranged; terms on application.
🍽 Full clubhouse catering and bar
facilities.
🛏 Swallow; Stakis; Northampton
Moat House; Courtyard by Marriott.

5A 27 **Dunstable Downs**   ☎

Whipsnade Road, Dunstable, Beds,
LU6 2NB
🌐 www.dunstable-golf.co.uk
💻 ddgc@btconnect.com
☎ 01582 604472, Fax 478700, Pro
662806, Sec 604472, Rest/Bar 604472
2 miles from Dunstable on Whipsnade
road B4541; follow signs to 'The
Downs'.
Downland course.
Pro M Weldon; Founded 1907
Designed by James Braid
18 holes, 6251 yards, S.S.S. 70
† Welcome WD; member's guests at
WE.
Ⓛ WD £28.50 per round; £40 per
day.
🏌 Welcome WD except Wed; full golf
and catering package including lunch
and dinner; half-day packages also
available. Terms on application.
🍽 Full clubhouse facilities.
🛏 Old Palace Lodge; Hertfordshire
Moat House.

5A 28 **Elton Furze**

Bullock Road, Haddon, Peterborough,
Cambs, PE7 3TT
🌐 www.eltonfurzegolfclub.co.uk
💻 secretary@eltonfurzgolfclub.co.uk
☎ 01832 280189, Fax 280299, Pro
280614, Sec 280189, Rest/Bar 280118
4 miles W of Peterborough on old
A606; leaving A1 at the
Alwalton/Showground exit.

Parkland course.
Pro Frank Kiddie; Founded 1993
Designed by Roger Fitton
18 holes, 6279 yards, S.S.S. 71
🏌 4 bays, practice range, practice
ground; buggies for hire; tuition
available.
† Welcome by prior arrangement;
handicap certs. preferred; dress codes
apply.
Ⓛ WD £22; WE £32.
🏌 Welcome by prior arrangement
with the secretary WD; golf and
catering packages available; terms
on application.
🍽 Full facilities.
🛏 Swallow, Peterborough.

5A 29 **Ely City**   ☎

Cambridge Road, Ely, Cambs,
CB7 4HX
🌐 www.elygolf.co.uk
💻 elygolf@lineone.net
☎ 01353 662751, Fax 668636,
Pro 663317, Sec 662751,
Rest/Bar 662751
1 mile S of City Centre on old A10.
Parkland course.
Pro Andrew George; Founded 1961
Designed by Henry Cotton
18 holes, 6627 yards, S.S.S. 72
† Welcome with handicap certs.
Ⓛ WD £32; WE £38.
🏌 Welcome Tues-Fri in official
organised groups; full packages
available; also practice area; snooker;
terms on application.
🍽 Full bar and restaurant facilities.
🛏 Nyton Hotel; Lamb Hotel.

5A 30 **Embankment Golf club**

The Embankment, Wellingborough,
Northants, NN8 1LD
☎ 01933 228465, Sec 224997,
Rest/Bar 228465
In the embankment area of the City
alongside the river.
Parkland course.
Founded 1977
9 holes, 3562 yards, S.S.S. 57
† Welcome with members only.
Ⓛ WD and WE £5 – must be
accompanied by a club member.
🏌 None.
🍽 Bar and limited food.
🛏 The Hind Hotel, Sheep St-
Wellingborough.

5A 31 **Enderby**

Mill Lane, Enderby, Leicester, Leics,
LE9 5LH
☎ 0116 2849388, Fax 2849388

From M1 Junction 21 to Enderby and
then follow the signs to Leisure Centre
Municipal heathland course.
Pro Chris d'Araujo; Founded 1986
9 holes, 5712 yards, S.S.S. 72
🏌 10.
† Welcome.
Ⓛ WD 9 holes £5.75, 18 holes £6.95;
WE 9 holes £6.95, 18 holes £9.25.
🏌 Welcome by arrangement.
🍽 Bar and bar snacks.
🛏 The Stakis.

5A 32 **Farthingstone Hotel**   ☎
Golf & LC

Everdon Road, Farthingstone,
Towcester, Northants, NN12 8HA
🌐 www.farthingstone.co.uk
☎ 01327 361291, Fax 361645,
Pro 361533, Rest/Bar 361560
M1 Junction 16; take signs to Weedon,
then Everdon and Farthingstone.
Woodland course.
Pro Greg Lunn; Founded 1972
Designed by M Gallagher
18 holes, 6299 yards, S.S.S. 70
🏌 Practice range and nets; buggies
for hire.
† Welcome at all times.
Ⓛ WD £17; WE £25.
🏌 Welcome any time by prior
arrangement; packages available; also
pool and snooker tables; squash court;
hotel facilities; terms on application.
🍽 Full bar; restaurant and hotel
facilities.
🛏 Farthingstone 16 en-suite twin-
bedded rooms.

5A 33 **Forest Hill**   ☎

Markfield Lane, Botcheston, Leicester,
Leics, LE9 9FJ
☎ 01455 824800, Fax 828522
2 miles from Botcheston; 3 miles SW
of the A50.
Well-wooded parkland course.
Pro Glyn Quilter; Founded 1991/1995
Designed by Alan York
18 holes, 6039 yards, S.S.S. 69
🏌 20 bays floodlit, electric trolleys
and clubs for hire; tuition available.
† Welcome.
Ⓛ WD £20; WE £25.
🏌 Welcome WD by arrangement;
packages for golf and catering
available; terms on application.
🍽 Bar; restaurant and function room.
🛏 Forest Lodge.

5A 34 **Girton**   ☎

Dodford Lane, Girton, Cambridge,
Cambs, CB3 0QE

www.club-noticeboard.co.uk
secretary@girtongolfclub
.sagehost.co.uk
☎ 01223 276169, Fax 277150
Course is 3 miles N of Cambridge on
the A14.
Flat open course.
Pro Scott Thomson; Founded 1936
Designed by Alan Gow
18 holes, 6012 yards, S.S.S. 69
† Welcome WD; with member at WE.
⌣ WD £20.
⌣ Welcome Tues-Fri by prior
arrangement; packages available;
terms on application.
🍽 Lunches and dinners served
except Mon.
⌐ Post House, Impington.

5A 35 **Glen Gorse**
Glen Road, Oadby, Leicester, Leics,
LE2 4RF
www.gggc.co.uk
secretary@gggc.co.uk
☎ 0116 271 4159, Fax 4159,
Pro 3748
On A6 Leicester-Market Harborough
road between Oadby and Great Glen,
5 miles S of Leicester.
Parkland course.
Pro Dominic Fitzpatrick; Founded 1933
18 holes, 6648 yards, S.S.S. 72
⌐ Practice area; tuition available.
† Welcome WD by arrangement; WE
with member.
⌣ WD £25; WE £10.50 with member.
⌣ WD by arrangement with
secretary; full golf and catering
facilities; terms on application.
🍽 Full catering facilities.
⌐ Premier Lodge, Oadby; Belmont
House Hotel, Leicester.

5A 36 **Gog Magog**   ☏
Shelford Bottom, Cambridge, Cambs,
CB2 4AB
www.gogmagog.co.uk
secretary@gogmagog.co.uk
☎ 01223 247626, Fax 414990,
Pro 246058
On A1307 5 miles from Cambridge. Nr
Addenbrooke's hospital.
Chalk downland course.
Pro Ian Bamborough; Founded 1901
Designed by Hawtree
⌐ 10 for members only.
† Welcome WD; booking required
Wed.
⌣ WD £37 for 18 holes (without
member) £18.50(with member) WD
£44 day rate without member & with
member £22. Juniors 1/2 price.
Handicap certs required.

⌣ Welcome WD Tues and Thurs; full
day's golf and catering package; prices
on application.
🍽 Full clubhouse facilities available.
⌐ Duxford Lodge, Duxford; many in
Cambridge.

5A 37 **Greetham Valley**   ☏
Wood Lane, Greetham, Oakham,
Leics, LE15 7NP
www.gvgc.co.uk
info@gvgc.co.uk
☎ 01780 460004, Fax 460623,
Pro 460666, Sec 460004,
Rest/Bar 460444
1 mile from A1 off the B668,
signposted Greetham.
Parkland courses with water.
Pro John Pengelly; Founded 1991
Designed by Ben Stevens Course
Design
⌐ Driving range, Par 3 and golf video
academy; 50 ClubCar buggies
available only £12 per round.
† Welcome.
⌣ 18 holes: WD £32, WE £36; WD
£48, WE £54 All Day Tickets.
⌣ Welcome WD in groups of 12 or
more.
🍽 Full restaurant and bar facilities.
⌐ Barnsdale Lodge; Barnsdale CC;
Hambleton Hall; Stapleford Park.

5A 38 **Griffin**
Chaul End Road, Caddington Village,
Luton, Beds, LU1 4AX
griffin@griffingolfclub
.fsbusiness.co.uk
☎ 01582 415573, Fax 415314,
Sec 415573 x1, Rest/Bar 415573 x2
10 mins from M1 Junction 10 or 11 via
A5 or A5056.
Parkland course.
Founded 1982
18 holes, 6240 yards, S.S.S. 70
⌐ Practice green within 2 min of the
1st tee.
† Welcome WD after 9am; WE.after
2pm
⌣ WD £14; Fri £17; WE £20.
⌣ Welcome WD; packages can be
arranged for full day's catering and
golf; from £29.
🍽 Full catering facilities.

5A 39 **Hellidon Lakes Hotel**   ☏
& Country Club
Hellidon, Daventry, Northants, NN11 6LN
www.marstonhotels.com
stay@hellidon.demon.co.uk
☎ 01327 262550, Fax 262559,
Pro 262551

15 miles from M1 Junction 16 by A45
and A361 Banbury road; turn right
before village of Charwelton.
Undulating parkland course.
Pro Gary Wills; Founded 1991
Designed by David Snell
18-hole course & 9-hole course holes,
18-hole course 6587; 9-hole course
2791 yards, S.S.S. 18-hole course 72;
9-hole course 35
⌐ Practice range; buggies and clubs
for hire; tuition available with prior
arrangement.
† Welcome; handicap certs. needed
WE.
⌣ WD £15; WE £25.
⌣ Welcome by arrangement;
packages available through the hotel;
conference facilities can be arranged; fly
fishing; tennis; health studio; swimming
pool; 4-lane tenpin bowling alley; smart
golf simulator; terms on application.
🍽 Full bar and restaurant facilities: The
Lakes Restaurant; The Brunswick Bar.
⌐ 4 – star hotel on site.

5A 40 **Hemingford Abbots**   ☏
Cambridge Road, Hemingford Abbots,
Huntingdon, Cambs, PE28 9HQ
www.astroman8.co.uk
ray/george@
astroman8.freeserve.co.uk
☎ 01480 495000, Fax 496000
Alongside A14 between Huntingdon
and St Ives.
Membership & public parkland course.
Founded 1991
Designed by Advanced Golf Services –
RD Paton
9/18 holes, 5414 yards, S.S.S. 68
⌐ Practice range; clubs for hire;
tuition available.
† Welcome.
⌣ 9 holes: WD £9; WE £11.
18 holes: WD £12.50; WE £17.
⌣ Small groups welcome by prior
arrangement.
🍽 Full catering facilities; bar and
restaurant.
⌐ St Ives; The Dolphin; Marriott;
Bridge Hotel, Huntingdon; on-site
accommodation.

5A 41 **Heydon Grange Golf &**
Country Club
Fowlmere Road, Heydon, Royston,
Herts, SG8 7NS
www.heydongrange.co.uk
heydon-grange@compuserve.com
☎ 01763 208988, Fax 208926
Leave M11 at Junction 10 on to the
A505 towards Royston; take third left
to Heydon.

Downland/parkland courses with lakes.
Pro Stuart Smith; Founded 1994
Designed by Alan Walker
Combs/Essex: 18 holes, 6336 yards.
S.S.S. 71; Combs/Herts: 18 holes,
6503 yards, S.S.S. 72; Herts/Essex: 18
holes, 6193 yards, S.S.S. 71
⌘ Practice range and practice
ground; buggies and clubs for hire;
tuition available.
† Welcome; book in advance.
⌐ Winter: 18 holes + food WD
£12.50; WE £17.50. Summer:18 holes
WD £12.50; WE £17.50.
⌁ Welcome by prior arrangement;
company days arranged; packages
available; conferences and functions
available; terms on application.
⦿ Lounge, cocktail and wine bar;
restaurants; carvery on Sun; full Indian
menu.

5A 42 **Hinckley** ℭ
Leicester Road, Hinckley, Leics,
LE10 3DR
⌕ hinckleygolfclub.com
⌨ proshop@hinckleygolfclub.com
☎ 01455 615124, Fax 890841,
Pro 615014, Sec 615014
From Hinckley Town Centre follow
signs for Earl Shinton.
Lakeland parkland course.
Pro Richard Jones; Founded 1894/1983
Designed by Southern Golf
18 holes, 6517 yards, S.S.S. 71
† Welcome WD; members of guests
WE.
⌐ WD £30.
⌁ Welcome WD with handicap certs;
packages available; terms on application.
⦿ Full catering facilities.
⌁ Sketchley Grange.

5A 43 **Humberstone Heights**
Gipsy Lane, Leicester, Leics, LE5 0TB
⌨ admin@hhgc.freeserve.co,uk
☎ 01162 997750, Fax 99569,
Pro 995570, Sec 771910 (home),
763690 (office)
Off Uppingham Rd opp. Towers Hosp.
Parkland course.
Pro Phillip Highfield; Founded 1977
Designed by Hawtree & Son
18 holes, 6343 yards, S.S.S. 70
⌘ Practice range, 30 bays; buggies
and clubs for hire, tuition available; 9-
hole par 3 course.
† Pay and play.
⌐ Winter WD £7.99; WE £9.99;
Summer WD £8.99 WE £10.99.
⌁ Terms on application.
⦿ Clubhouse facilities.
⌁ City-centre hotels in Leicester.

5A 44 **Ivinghoe**
Wellcroft, Ivinghoe, Leighton Buzzard,
Beds, LU7 9EF
☎ 01296 668696, Fax 662755,
Pro 668696, Sec 668696,
Rest/Bar 661186
4 miles from Tring and 6 miles from
Dunstable behind the Kings Head in
Ivinghoe village.
Meadowland course.
Pro Bill Garrad; Founded 1967
Designed by R Garrad & Sons
9 holes, 4508 yards, S.S.S. 62
⌘ Tuition available
† Welcome after 9am WD; after 8am
WE.
⌐ WD £9; WE £9.
⌁ Welcome WD by arrangement;
includes 36 holes of golf; coffee; light
lunch and evening meal; from £25.
⦿ Full facilities.
⌁ Rose & Crown, Tring; Stocks,
Aldbury.

5A 45 **John O'Gaunt**
John O'Gaunt Golf Club, Sutton Park,
Sandy, Beds, SG19 2LY
⌕ www.johnogauntgolfclub.co.uk
⌨ info@johnogauntgolfclub.co.uk
☎ 01767 260360, Fax 262834,
Pro 260094, Sec 260360
Between Biggleswade and Potton on
B1040.
Parkland course.
Pro Lee Scarbrow; Founded 1948
Designed by Hawtree
Carthagena: 18; The John O'Gaunt: 18
holes, Carthagena: 5869; The John
O'Gaunt: 6513 yards, S.S.S.
Carthagena: 69; The John O'Gaunt: 71
⌘ Tuition available through pro;
buggies for hire.
† Welcome with handicap certs and
by prior arrangement.
⌐ WD £50; WE £60.
⌁ Welcome WD by prior arrangement
through administrators office; package
for catering and green fees on
application; terms on application.
⦿ Full clubhouse catering.
⌁ Holiday Inn; Stratton House,
Biggleswade; Rose & Crown, Potton.

5A 46 **Kettering**
Headlands, Kettering, Northants,
NN15 6XA
☎ 01536 511104, Fax 511104,
Pro 481014, Rest/Bar 512074
S of Kettering, adjacent to A14.
Parkland course.
Pro K Theobald; Founded 1891
Designed by Tom Morris
18 holes holes, 6081 yards, S.S.S. 69

† Welcome WD; with member at WE.
⌐ WD £15-22.
⌁ Welcome Wed and Fri; full catering
and golf packages; from £40.
⦿ Full clubhouse facilities.
⌁ Kettering Park; George; Royal .

5A 47 **Kibworth** ℭ
Weir Road, Kibworth, Leicester, Leics,
LE8 0LP
☎ 0116 279 6172, Fax 2301,
Pro 2283, Sec 2301
Course is 10 miles S of Leicester off
A6.
Flat woodland/parkland course.
Pro Mike Herbert; Founded 1904/62
18 holes, 6354 yards, S.S.S. 70
⌘ Practice grass range; trolleys for
hire; tuition available from PGA
qualified professional.
† Welcome WD; WE with a member.
⌐ £25-£30 Wed.
⌁ Welcome by arrangement; golf and
catering available; from £21.
⦿ Full catering facilities.
⌁ Angel, Market Harborough.

5A 48 **Kilworth Springs**
South Kilworth Road, North Kilworth,
Lutterworth, Leics, LE17 6HJ
⌕ www.kilworthsprings.co.uk
⌨ kilworthsprings@ukonline.co.uk
☎ 01858 575082, Fax 575078,
Pro 575974, Sec 575082,
Rest/Bar 575082
Course is 5 miles from the M1 Junction
20.
Front 9: Inland links; Back 9: parkland
course.
Pro Anders Mankert
Founded 1993
Designed by Ray Baldwin
18 holes, 6718 yards, S.S.S. 72
⌘ 18.
† All Welcome. Practice ground,
2 putting greens, practice bunker, also
available video swing facilities.
⌐ WD £20; WE £22.
⌁ Welcome WD and after 12 at WE;
catering and golf packages; bar, spike
bar, private 20-seat boardroom,
restaurant, driving range; prices on
application.
⦿ Full clubhouse bar, spikes bar and
restaurant facilities.
⌁ Club can supply list.

5A 49 **Kingfisher CC**
Buckingham Road, Deanshanger,
Northants, Bucks, MK19 6DG
☎ 01908 562332, Fax 260557,
Sec 560354, Shop 560354

Course is on the A422 Buckingham road seven miles from Milton Keynes opposite the village of Deanshanger. Parkland course with lake features.
Pro Brian Mudge; Founded 1994
9 holes, 5066 yards, S.S.S. 65
🏌 Practice range, 10 bays.
† Welcome; pay and play.
£ WD 9 holes £7, 18 holes £11; WE 9 holes £11, 18 Holes £15.
⌒ Welcome by prior arrangement; corporate days organised; fishing; model steam railway; function room; terms on application.
🍽 Full facilities; 2 restaurants and 2 bars.
🛏 30 rooms.

5A 50 Kingstand
Beggars Lane, Leicester Forest East, Leicester, Leics, LE3 3NQ
☎ 0116 2387908, Fax 2388087
Off main A47 Hinkley Road; 5 mins from M1 Junction 21.
Parkland course.
Pro Simon Sherrit; Founded 1991
Designed by S.Chenia
9 holes, 5380 yards, S.S.S. 66
🏌 Practice range, 16 bays floodlit.
† Welcome.
£ WD £9; WE £10.
⌒ Welcome by prior arrangement with the professional; packages and discounts available; gymnasium.
🍽 Indian restaurant on site.
🛏 Red Cow.

5A 51 Kingsthorpe ☎
Kingsley Road, Northampton, Northants, NN2 7BU
✉ kingsthorpe.gc@lineone.net
☎ 01604 719602, Fax 719602, Sec 710610, Rest/Bar 711173
Off A508 2 miles N of Northampton town centre.
Parkland course.
Pro Paul Armstrong; Founded 1908
Designed by Charles Alison
18 holes, 5918 yards, S.S.S. 69
† Welcome with handicap certs.
£ WD £25; WE £25, with member.
⌒ Welcome; catering facilities and golf packages available; from £20.
🍽 Clubhouse catering facilities available.
🛏 Westone Hotel; Broom Hill.

5A 52 Kingsway
Cambridge Road, Melbourn, Royston, Herts, SG8 6EY
☎ 01763 262727, Fax 263298, Pro 262727

On A10 N of Royston.
Landscape farmland.
Pro Steve Brown; Founded 1991
9 holes, 4910 yards, S.S.S. 64
🏌 Practice range, 36 bays floodlit; crazy golf.
† Welcome.
£ WD £9 (18 holes); WE £12 (18 holes).
⌒ Welcome by prior arrangement; corporate days arranged; 9-hole pitch and putt; terms on application.
🍽 Bar and restaurant facilities.
🛏 Sheene Mill Hotel.

5A 53 Kirby Muxloe ☎
Station Road, Kirby Muxloe, Leicester, LE9 9EN
🖥 www.kirbymuxloe-golf.co.uk
✉ kirbymuxloegolf@btconnect.com
☎ 0116 239 3457, Fax 3457, Pro 2813, Rest/Bar 6577
From M1 Junction 21A follow signs to Kirby Muxloe.
Parkland course.
Pro Bruce Whipham; Founded 1893
18 holes, 6279 yards, S.S.S. 70
🏌 Driving range open to members and guests only
† Welcome Mon, Wed and Fri, handicap cert required.
£ £28 round, £35 day.
⌒ Welcome with handicap certs only; all day and individual round packages available; from £40.
🍽 Full clubhouse catering facilities.
🛏 Time Out Hotel, Blaby.

5A 54 Lakeside Lodge
Fen Road, Pidley, Huntingdon, Cambs, PE28 3DD
🖥 www.lakeside-lodge.co.uk
✉ info@lakeside-lodge.co.uk
☎ 01487 740540, Fax 740852, Pro 741541, Rest/Bar 740968
From A14 Cambridge-St Ives road take B1040 to Pidley.
Open parkland with 8 lakes and 15,000 trees.
Pro Scott Waterman; Founded 1991
Designed by Alister Headley
The Lodge: 18; Manor: 9; Church: 6 holes, Lodge: 6865; Manor: 2601; Church: 3290 yards, S.S.S. The Lodge: 73; Manor: 33
🏌 Floodlit covered driving range, buggies for hire, 9-hole pitch and putt course, tuition available.
† Welcome.
£ The Lodge course: WD £14, WE £22; The Manor course: WD £7, WE £9. The Church course: for 12 holes WD £7, WE £9.

⌒ Welcome any time; golf, catering and other corporate activities can be arranged (ten pin bowling); terms on application.
🍽 Full catering facilities.
🛏 On-site accommodation, 25 en suite twin rooms.

5A 55 The Leicestershire
Evington Lane, Leicester, Leics, LE5 6DJ
✉ secretary@thelgc.co.uk
☎ 0116 2738825, Fax 2731900, Pro 2736730, Rest/Bar 2731307
2 miles east of Leicester.
Parkland course; no par 5s.
Pro Darren Jones; Founded 1890
Designed by James Braid
18 holes, 6326 yards, S.S.S. 71
† Welcome with handicap certs and prior arrangement.
£ WD £24; WE £30.
⌒ Welcome with handicap certs; packages can be arranged; terms available on application.
🍽 Full clubhouse facilities.
🛏 Gables Hotel.

5A 56 Leighton Buzzard
Plantation Road, Leighton Buzzard, Beds, LU7 3JF
🖥 www.leightonbuzzardgolf.net
✉ secretary@leightonbuzzardgolf.net
☎ 01525 244800, Fax 244801, Pro 244815, Rest/Bar 244805, 244810
1 mile N of Leighton Buzzard.
Parkland/woodland course.
Pro Maurice Campbell; Founded 1925
18 holes, 6101 yards, S.S.S. 70
🏌 Practice ground.
† Welcome WD with handicap certs; WE with member.
£ WD £34.
⌒ Welcome WD except Tues (ladies day); day's golf and catering from morning coffee to evening meals; from £39 and member from £55.
🍽 Full clubhouse catering facilities.
🛏 Cock Horse Hotel.

5A 57 Lingdale
Joe Moores Lane, Woodhouse Eaves, Loughborough, Leics, LE12 8TF
☎ 01509 890703, Pro 890684, Sec 890703, Rest/Bar 890035
2 miles off M1 Junction 22 towards Woodhouse Eaves.
Parkland course.
Pro P Sellears; Founded 1967
Designed by DW Tucker & G Austin
18 holes, 6545 yards, S.S.S. 71
🏌 Practice range, practice ground; tuition available.

† Welcome.
⌐ WD/WE £30 round, £40 day.
⌐ Welcome by prior arrangement with secretary; minimum 12; day's golf and catering packages available; prices on application.
🍽 Full clubhouse facilities.

5A 58 Links Golf Course
The Links, Cambridge Road, Newmarket, Suffolk, CB8 0TG
🌐 www.club-noticeboard.co.uk /newmarket
✉ secretary@linksgc.fsbusiness.co.uk
☎ 01638 663000, Fax 661476, Pro 662395, Rest/Bar 662708
On A1304 1 mile S of Newmarket midway between racecourse entrances.
Parkland course.
Pro John Sharkey; Founded 1902
Designed by Col. Hotchkin
18 holes, 6582 yards, S.S.S. 71
† Welcome with handicap certs; not before 11.30am Sun.
⌐ WD £32; WE £36. Special winter rates WD £20; 18 holes £24W WD's 36 holes £32 WD. WE £36.
⌐ Welcome by prior arrangement; refundable booking fee of £35; catering packages; maximum 60; prices on application.
🍽 Full restaurant and bar.
🛏 Bedford Lodge.

5A 59 Longcliffe
Snells Nook Lane, Nanpantan, Loughborough, Leicestershire, LE11 3YA
✉ longcliffegolf@btconnect.com
☎ 01509 239129, Fax 231286, Pro 231450, Sec 239129, Rest/Bar 216321
1 mile from M1 Junction 23 off A512 towards Loughborough.
Heathland course.
Pro David Mee; Founded 1904
18 holes, 6672 yards, S.S.S. 73
† Welcome WD 9am-4.30pm except Tues; WE with a member.
⌐ WD £30 per round, WD £40 per day No weekend play.
⌐ Welcome WD except Tues (ladies day); packages available for groups of 12 or more; from £28 and £38 for day.
🍽 Bar, restaurant and snacks.
🛏 Quality Hotel.

5A 60 Lutterworth
Rugby Road, Lutterworth, Leics, LE17 4HN
🌐 www.lutterworthgc.co.uk
☎ 01455 552532, Fax 553586,

Pro 557199, Sec 552532, Rest/Bar 557141
On A426 0.5 miles from M1 Junction 20.
Parkland course.
Pro Roland Tisdall; Founded 1904
Designed by D Snell
18 holes, 6226 yards, S.S.S. 70
🏌 Practice range.
† Welcome WD; guests of members only at WE.
⌐ 18 holes £22 all week.
⌐ Welcome Mon,Wed and Thurs all day and Tues pm and Fri am; indoor academy; terms on application.
🍽 Clubhouse facilities.
🛏 The Denby Arms; The Greyhound, both Lutterworth.

5A 61 March
Froggs Abbey, Grange Road, March, Cambs, PE15 0YH
✉ marchgolfclub@tiscali.co.uk
☎ 01354 652364, Fax 652364, Pro 657255, Sec 652364, Rest/Bar 652364
Course is on the A141 West of the March bypass.
Parkland course.
Pro Mark Pond; Founded 1920
9 holes, 6204 yards, S.S.S. 70
† Welcome WD; guests of members only at weekends.
⌐ WD £16.50, £8.50 with a member.
⌐ Welcome WD by prior booking.
🍽 Bar facilities; meals by prior booking.
🛏 Griffin,The Oliver Cromwell.

5A 62 Market Harborough
Harborough Road, Great Oxendon, Market Harborough, Leics, LE16 8NB
☎ 01858 46384, Fax 432906
Course is one mile S of Market Harborough on the A508 towards Northampton.
Parkland course.
Pro F Baxter; Founded 1898
Updated by H Swan
18 holes, 6022 yards, S.S.S. 69
† Welcome WD; WE guests of members only.
⌐ WD £25.
⌐ Welcome WD by arrangement; inclusive packages available; from £35.
🍽 Clubhouse facilities.
🛏 Three Swans, Market Harborough; George, Oxendon.

5A 63 Melton Mowbray
Waltham Road, Thorpe Arnold, Melton Mowbray, Leics, LE14 4SD
🌐 www.mmgc.org

✉ mmgc@le144sd.fsbusiness.co.uk
☎ 01664 562118, Pro 569629, Sec 562118, Rest/Bar 562118
2 miles NE of Melton Mowbray on A607.
Undulating parkland course.
Pro Neil Curtis; Founded 1925
18 holes, 6222 yards, S.S.S. 70
† Welcome before 3pm.
⌐ WD £25; WE and BH £30.
⌐ Welcome WD by prior arrangement; golf, lunch and dinner packages can be organised; from £20.
🍽 Full catering, bar and dining facilities.
🛏 Sysonsby Knoll; George; Harborough; Stapleford Park.

5A 64 Mentmore
Mentmore, Leighton Buzzard, Beds, LU7 0UA
🌐 www.clubhaus.co.uk
☎ 01296 662020, Fax 662592, Pro 660500, Sec 662020, Rest/Bar 662020
1 mile from Cheddington, E of A41 to Aylesbury.
Parkland course.
Pro Rob Davies; Founded 1992
Designed by Bob Sandow
🏌 12.
† Welcome WD; WE booking allowed 7 days in advance.
⌐ Call to confirm.
⌐ Welcome WD; max 120; facilities; also pool, sauna, 2 tennis courts, sports bar, fitness room, Jacuzzi; £55-£75.
🍽 Full bar, restaurant facilities.
🛏 Pendley Manor; Rose and Crown, both Tring.

5A 65 The Millbrook
Millbrook Golf Club Ltd, Bedford, Beds, MK45 2JB
🌐 www.themillbrook.com
✉ info@themillbrook.com
☎ 01525 840252, Fax 406249, Pro 402269
In Millbrook Village off A507 just before Ampthill from J13 M1.
Inland links-style course.
Pro Geeraint Dixon; Founded 1980
Designed by Derek Young
18 holes, 7021 yards, S.S.S. 73
🏌 Two large practice fields.
† Restricted; phone Club Mnager Derek Cooke for details.
⌐ WD £22; WE £28.
⌐ Welcome by prior arrangement WD; golf and catering packages can be arranged; from £20.
🍽 Clubhouse facilities; restaurant and conference facilities

White Hart, Ampthill; Flitwick Manor, Flitwick; The Knife and Cleaver, Houghton.

5A 66 Mount Pleasant ☎
Station Road, Lower Stondon, Henlow, Beds, SG16 6JL
🖳 www.mountpleasantgolfclub.co.uk
📧 davidsimsmpgolf@aol.com
☎ 01462 850999, Fax 850257, Pro 850999, Sec 850999, Rest/Bar 850999
0.75 miles W of Stondon-Henlow Camp roundabout off A600 Hitchin to Bedford road; 4 miles N of Hitchin. Undulating meadowland course.
Pro Mike Roberts; Founded 1992
Designed by Derek Young
9 holes,18 tees, 6003 yards, S.S.S. 69
⌘ Practice facilities available, buggies, shoes and clubs for hire; PGA tuition available.
✝ Welcome at all times; booking advisable; can be made up to 2 days in advance.
⌐ WD 9 holes £8, 18 holes £14; WE 9 holes £10.50, 18 holes £18; OAPs: discounts of £1.50 for 9 holes; Juniors: discounts of £2.
⌑ Welcome WD; packages available; 24 maximum for full catering, 36 for buffet; terms on application.
🍽 Clubhouse bar facilities.
🛏 Sun, Hitchin.

5A 67 Mowsbury Golf and Squash Complex
Cleat Hill, Kimbolton Road, Ravensden, Bedford, MK41 8DQ
☎ 01234 771493, Fax 267040, Pro 216374, Sec 771041, Rest/Bar 771493
On B660 at northern limit of city boundary.
Parkland course.
Pro M Summers; Founded 1975
Designed by Hawtree
18 holes, 6514 yards, S.S.S. 71;72 is par for the course
⌘ 14.
✝ Welcome.
⌐ wd £10.75; WE £14.50.
⌑ Welcome anytime; golf and catering packages; driving range, squash court; terms on application.
🍽 Full facilities.
🛏 In town centre.

5A 68 Northampton
Harlestone, Northampton, Northants, NN7 4EF
🖳 www.northamptongolfclub.co.uk

golf@northamptongolfclub.co.uk
☎ 01604 845155, Fax 820262, Pro 845167, Sec 845155, Rest/Bar 845102/821905
On A428 Rugby road 4 miles from Northampton.
Parkland course.
Pro Barry Randall; Founded 1893
Designed by Donald Steel
18 holes, 6615 yards, S.S.S. 72
✝ Welcome WD; members and member's guests at WE.
⌐ WD £40.
⌑ Welcome by prior arrangement WD except Wed; packages for golf and catering available; snooker; banqueting; terms on application.
🍽 Full facilities.
🛏 Broomhill House Hotel; Heyford Manor.

5A 69 Northamptonshire County
Golf Lane, Church Brampton, Northampton, NN6 8AZ
🖳 www.countygolfclub.org.uk
📧 secretary@countygolfclub.org.uk
☎ 01604 843025, Fax 843463, Pro 842226, Sec 843025, Rest/Bar 842170
5 miles NW of Northampton in village of Church Brampton.
Heathland course with woods, gorse and streams.
Pro Tim Rouse; Founded 1909
Designed by HS Colt
18 holes, 6505 yards, S.S.S. 72
✝ Welcome by arrangement, with handicap certs.
⌐ WD £45; WE £45.
⌑ Large groups on Wed; smaller groups Thurs; terms on application.
🍽 Full catering facilities.
🛏 Broomehill; Limetrees.

5A 70 Oadby
Leicester Road, Oadby, Leicester, Leics, LE2 4AB
☎ 0116 2709052, Sec 2703828, Rest/Bar 2700215
On A6 from Leicester inside Leicester racecourse.
Meadowland municipal course; 9 holes inside adjacent Leicester racecourse.
Pro Andrew Wells; Founded 1975
18 holes, 6311 yards, S.S.S. 72
⌘ 2 nets.
✝ Everybody welcome.
⌐ Prices on application.
⌑ Welcome by prior application to the professional; welcome WD and after 12 noon WE; terms on application.

Bar meals and snacks; meals on request.
🛏 The Chase Hotel: adjacent hotel and leisure complex.

5A 71 Old Nene Golf & ☎ Country Club
Muchwood Lane, Ramsey, Huntingdon, Cambs, PE26 2XQ
☎ 01487 815622, Pro 710122, Sec 813610
1 mile N of Ramsey.
Parkland course with water hazards.
Pro Neil Grant; Founded 1992
Designed by Richard Edrich
9 holes, 5675 yards, S.S.S. 68
⌘ Practice range, floodlit; 2 piece balls; tuition available.
✝ Pay and play.
⌐ WD 9 holes £8, 18 holes £12; WE 9 holes £10, 18 holes £17.
⌑ Welcome; reductions for 12 or more players WD; packages available; terms available on application.
🍽 Bar and bar snacks available.
🛏 Several in area.

5A 72 Orton Meadows
Ham Lane, Orton Waterville, Peterborough, Cambs, PE2 5UU
🖳 www.ortonmeadowscourse.co.uk
☎ 01733 237478
On the A605 Peterborough-Oundle road 2 miles W of Peterborough.
Parkland course.
Pro Ashley Howard; Founded 1987
Designed by Dennis & Roger Fitton
18 holes, 5613 yards, S.S.S. 68
✝ Welcome; advance bookings available.
⌐ WD/WE £15.70.
⌑ Prior bookings for societies.
🍽 In adjoining steakhouse, The Granary.
🛏 Travelodge.

5A 73 Oundle ☎
Benefield Road, Oundle, Peterborough, Cambs, PE8 4EZ
🖳 www.oundlegolfclub.com
📧 oundlegc@btopenworld.com
☎ 01832 272273 (tee bookings), Fax 273267, Sec 273267, Rest/Bar 274882
On A427 Oundle-Corby road, 1.5 miles from Oundle.
Parkland course.
Pro Richard Keys; Founded 1893
18 holes, 6235 yards, S.S.S. 70
⌘ 2 practice areas; trolleys for hire; contact Pro about tuition.
✝ Welcome WD, after 10.30am WE.
⌐ WD £23 round, £30 day; WE £40.

Park Hill Golf Club

PARK HILL
Seagrave

Visitors and Societies Welcomed!

Park Hill Golf Club is one of Leicestershire's finest 18 hole Championship length golf courses. Nestled in the heart of the Leicestershire countryside, Park Hill combines the land's natural contours and water features with precisely positioned bunkers to create a challenging course with excellent playing conditions all year round.

- Championship Length Course 7219 yards Par 73
- Society and corporate golf packages available
- Restaurant serving home cooked food
- Excellent 20 bay floodlit range
- Golf cart and trolley hire available
- Conference and training facilities

Located just off the A46 north of Leicester, 10 minutes from J21a of the M1.

Park Hill Golf & Leisure Limited, Park Hill, Seagrave, Leicestershire LE12 7NG   Tel: **01509 815454**   Fax: **01509 816062**
E-mail: **mail@parkhillgolf.co.uk**   Website: **www.parkhillgolf.co.uk**

Welcome WD; golf and catering packages available; from £35.
Full clubhouse facilities.
Talbot, Oundle; Travel Lodge, Thrapston.

5A 74 **Overstone Park**
Billing Lane, Overstone, Northampton, Northants, NN6 0AP
www.overstonepark.com
enquiries@overstonepark.com
01604 647666, Fax 642635,
Pro 643555
Take A45 Northampton road to Billing Lane.
Parkland course in walled Victorian estate.
Pro Brian Mudge; Founded 1993
Designed by Donald Steel
18 holes, 6022 yards, S.S.S. 72
Practice range and practice area.
Welcome WD from 10am; WE only after 2pm.
Green fees available on application.
Welcome by prior arrangement; packages; health and leisure club.
Bar and Brasserie.
Hotel on site; 27 en suite bedrooms.

5A 75 **Park Hill** ♔
Park Hill Lane, Seagrave, Loughborough, Leics, LE12 7NG
www.parkhillgolf.co.uk
mail@parkhillgolf.co.uk
01509 815454, Fax 816062,
Pro 815775, Sec 815 454,
Rest/Bar 815885
6m N of Leicester just off A46 northbound; follow signs for Seagrave.
Parkland course; five par 5's more than 500 yards.
Pro Matthew Ulyett; Founded 1995
18 holes, 7219 yards, S.S.S. 74
20 bay floodlit range; grass bays; real greens
Welcome.
WD £22; WE and BH £26.

Welcome; need to book in advance.
Clubhouse catering facilities. open 7 days a week.

5A 76 **Pavenham Park** ♔
High Street, Pavenham, Bedford, Beds, MK43 7PE
01234 822202, Fax 826602
Course is on the A6 six miles N of Bedford.
Parkland course.
Pro Zac Thompson; Founded 1994
Designed by Derek Young/Z Thompson
18 holes, 6353 yards, S.S.S. 71
Practice range, practice area; buggies and clubs for hire.
Welcome WD; guests of members only at WE.
WD £20.
Welcome WD; full catering and golf packages; from £16.
Clubhouse facilities.

5A 77 **Peterborough Milton**
Milton Ferry, Peterborough, Cambridgeshire, PE6 7AG
www.peterboroughmiltongolfclub.co.uk
admin@peterboroughmiltongolflub.co.uk
01733 380489, Fax 380489,
Pro 380793, Sec 380489,
Rest/Bar 380204
Course is two miles W of Peterborough on the A47.
Parkland course.
Pro Mike Gallagher; Founded 1938
Designed by James Braid
18 holes, 6505 yards, S.S.S. 72
Large practice area.
Welcome with handicap certs.
WD £30; WE £30.
Welcome Tues-Fri; full catering facilities and golf packages; prices on application.

Full facilities.
Haycock, Wansford; Marriot; Moat House; Butterfly, Peterborough.

5A 78 **RAF Cottesmore**
Royal Air Force, Cottesmore, Oakham, Leics, LE15 7BL
01572 812241 EX 6706
Course is seven miles N of Oakham off the B668.
Parkland course.
Founded 1980
9 holes, 5692 yards, S.S.S. 67
With members only.
Terms on application.

5A 79 **RAF Henlow**
R A F S E E, RAF Henlow, Henlow, Beds, SG16 6DN
01462 851515 EX 7083
3 miles SE of Shefford on A505, follow signs to RAF Henlow.
Meadowland course.
Founded 1985
9 holes, 5618 yards, S.S.S. 67
Only with a member.
Terms on application.
Can be arranged through Sec.
Light refreshments available.
Bird in Hand.

5A 80 **RAF North Luffenham**
St George's Barracks, North Luffenham, Oakham, Leics, LE15 8RL
01780 720041 ext 7523
Follow signposts for MOD North Luffenham from A606, station is close to Rutland Water.
Meadowland course.
Founded 1975
12 holes 18 Tees holes, 5910 yards, S.S.S. 69
Open driving range.
With member.
Terms on application.

⚲ Can be arranged through Sec.
🍽 Bar and restaurant facilities.
⌁ George; Crown.

5A 81 **Ramsey**

Abbey Terrace, Ramsey, Huntingdon, Cambs, PE26 1DD
⌁ www.ramseyclub.co.uk
✉ admin@ramseyclub.uk.com
☎ 01487 812600, Fax 815746, Pro 813022, Sec 812600, Rest/Bar 813573
Off B660 Ramsey road from the A1 between Huntingdon and Peterborough
Parkland course.
Pro Stuart Scott; Founded 1964
Designed by J Hamilton Stutt
18 holes, 6163 yards, S.S.S. 70
🏌 Practice range, 4 large practice areas; PGA tuition available.
† Welcome WD; WE as member's guest.
⌁ WD £25.
⚲ Welcome WD only; minimum 20; 18 holes of golf and catering packages available; from £25; large well stocked pro shop, offering society prizes. Bowling green.
🍽 Clubhouse facilities.
⌁ George, Huntingdon; Bell, Stilton; Dolphin, St Ives.

5A 82 **Rothley Park** ⚑

Westfield Lane, Rothley, Leicester, Leics, LE7 7LH
⌁ www.rothleypark.com
✉ secretary@rothleypark.co.uk
☎ 0116 2302809, Fax 2302809, Pro 2303023, Sec 2302809, Rest/Bar 2302019
Off A6 N of Leicester
Parkland course
Pro Danny Spillane; Founded 1912
Designed by Hawtree
18 holes, 6476 yards, S.S.S. 71
🏌 Practice ground, tuition available
† Welcome WD except Tues; handicap certs required
⌁ WD £25
⚲ Welcome Mon, Wed, Thurs, Fri; 10 % discount for more than 40 players; full catering available; terms on application.
🍽 Full clubhouse facilities.
⌁ Rothley Court; Quorn Country Hotel; Quorn Grange.

5A 83 **Rushcliffe**

Stocking Lane, East Leake, Loughborough, Leics, LE12 5RL
✉ rushcliffegc@netscapeonline.co.uk
☎ 01509 852959, Fax 852688, Pro 852701, Rest/Bar 852209

From M1 Junction 24 take A453 towards West Bridgford; turn at Gotham, East Leake signs
Parkland course
Pro Chris Hall; Founded 1910
18 holes, 6013 yards, S.S.S. 69
🏌 4
† Welcome
⌁ WD £25 (per round) £30 per day; WE £30
⚲ Welcome WD; packages available; prices available on application; enquire with Sec. for details.
🍽 Clubhouse facilities.

5A 84 **Rushden**

Kimbolton Road, Chelveston, Wellingborough, Northants, NN9 6AN
☎ 01933 312581, Sec 418511
Course is on the A45 two miles E of Higham Ferrers.
Undulating meadowland course.
Founded 1919
10 holes, 6350 yards, S.S.S. 70
† Welcome WD except Wed pm; WE with member.
⌁ WD £18, £12 with a member.
⚲ Welcome WD, except Wed pm, by prior arrangement.
🍽 Full facilities except Mon.

5A 85 **St Ives**

Westwood Road, St Ives, Cambs, PE27 6RS
☎ 01480 468392, Fax 468392, Pro 466067, Rest/Bar 464459
Course is on B1040 off A45 in St Ives.
Parkland course.
Pro Darren Glasby; Founded 1923
9 holes, 6100 yards, S.S.S. 69
🏌 Practice ground; tuition available.
† Welcome WD; with member WE.
⌁ WD £20; WE £20.
⚲ Welcome Wed and Fri by prior arrangement; packages available; from £20.
🍽 Full clubhouse facilities.
⌁ Slepe Hall.

5A 86 **St Neots** ⚑

Crosshall Road, Eaton Ford, St Neots, Cambs, PE19 7GE
⌁ www.stneots.golfclub.co.uk
✉ office@stneots.golfclub.co.uk
☎ 01480 472363, Fax 472363, Pro 476513, Rest/Bar 474311
On B1048 off the A1.
Parkland course with water hazards.
Pro Jason Boast; Founded 1890
Designed by Harry Vardon
18 holes, 6033 yards, S.S.S. 69
🏌 Practice area available.

† Welcome WD; WE with member; handicap certs preferred.
⌁ WD £30 round, £40 day.
⚲ Welcome WD by prior arrangement; packages available; snooker; function room; terms on application.
🍽 Full clubhouse facilities.
⌁ Eaton Oak; Kings Head.

5A 87 **Scraptoft** ⚑

Beeby Road, Scraptoft, Leicester, Leics, LE7 9SJ
⌁ www.scraptoftgolf.co.uk
✉ secretary@scraptoft-golf.co.uk
☎ 0116 241 9000, Fax 9000, Pro 9138
Turn off A47 main Peterborough-Leicester road at Scraptoft at Thurnby.
Meadowland course.
Pro Simon Wood; Founded 1928
18 holes, 6151 yards, S.S.S. 70
† Welcome; dress code applies after 7pm.
⌁ WD £20; we £25.
⚲ Welcome WD by prior arrangement; packages available; terms on application.
🍽 Full facilities.
⌁ White House.

5A 88 **Shelthorpe**

Poplar Road, Loughborough
☎ 01509 267766
From Leicester on A6 turn left at first traffic lights, over island then 2nd left.
Municipal parkland course.
18 holes holes, 2054 yards yards, S.S.S. 54
† Welcome.
⌁ WD £3.30; WE £3.30.

5A 89 **Six Hills**

Six Hills Road, Six Hills, Melton Mowbray, Leics, LE14 3PR
☎ 01509 881225, Rest/Bar 889347
From M1 take A46 N; course 0.5 mile from A46.
Parkland course.
Pro Matt Alls; Founded 1986
18 holes, 5758 yards, S.S.S. 69
🏌 12 bays.
† Welcome; pay and play.
⌁ WD £12; WE £15.
⚲ Welcome but no advance booking system.
🍽 Bar and restaurant.
⌁ Ragdale Hall.

5A 90 **South Beds**

Warden Hill Road, Luton, Beds, LU2 7AE

www.southbedsgolfclub.co.uk
office@southbedsgolfclub.co.uk
☎ 01582 575201, Fax 495381,
Pro 591209, Sec 591500, Rest/Bar
596456
3 miles N of Luton on A6, signposted
into Warden Hill Road.
Undulating downland course.
Pro Eddie Cogle; Founded 1892
18 holes, 6438 yards, S.S.S. 71; 9
holes, 4914 yards, par 64
⏐ Practice area; tuition available.
✝ Welcome WD; WE by prior
arrangement.
⌐ Prices on application.
⟳ Welcome Mon, Wed and Thurs by
prior arrangement; packages available;
snooker; prices on application.
⦿ Restaurant and bar facilities
available.
⟿ Chiltern; Strathmore.

5A 91 **Staverton Park** ☎

Daventry Road, Staverton, Daventry,
Northants, NN11 6JT
www.initialstyle.co.uk
☎ 01327 302000, Fax 311428,
Pro 705506
Course is on the A425 Daventry to
Leamington road; one mile S of
Daventry.
Undulating meadowland course.
Pro Richard Mudge; Founded 1978
Designed by Comm. John Harris
18 holes, 6100 yards, S.S.S. 73
⏐ 11 bays floodlit; practice range;
tuition available; buggy hire £20; club
hire individually £1, set £7.50.
✝ Welcome.
⌐ WD £30; WE £35 (Friday inclusive)
⟳ Welcome WD by prior
arrangement; snooker; solarium; sauna;
banqueting suites; terms on application.
⦿ Full facilities at all times.
⟿ Staverton Park offers golfing
weekends.

5A 92 **Stockwood Park Golf Centre**

London Road, Luton, Beds, LU1 4LX
☎ 01582 413704, Fax 481001, Sec
431788, Rest/Bar 731421
Leave the M1 at Junction 10; go 10 A,
head towards the town centre and then
turn left at the first traffic lights.
Parkland course.
Pro Glyn McCarthy; Founded 1973
Designed by Charles Lawrie
18 holes, 6077 yards, S.S.S. 69
⏐ 24 bays floodlit; 9-hole pitch &
putt; clubs and trolleys.
✝ Welcome.
⌐ WD £9.80; WE £13.10

⟳ Welcome Mon, Tues and Thurs by
prior arrangement with Pro; packages
for catering and golf by arrangement; 9-
hole pitch and putt; terms on application.
⦿ Full facilities.
⟿ Strathmore; The Hertfordshire
Moathouse (full leisure facilities).

5A 93 **Stoke Albany**

Ashley Road, Stoke Albany, Market
Harborough, Leics, LE16 8PL
www.stokealbanygolfclub.co.uk
info@stokealbanygolfclub.co.uk
☎ 01858 535208, Fax 535505
Course is off the A427 Market
Harborough-Corby road just through
Stoke Albany.
Parkland course.
Pro Adrian Clifford; Founded 1995
Designed by Hawtree of Oxford.
18 holes, 6132 yards, S.S.S. 69
⏐ Practice ground and bunker, chipping
green and putting green; trolleys for hire.
✝ Welcome.
⌐ WD £17; WE £20.
⟳ Welcome by prior arrangement;
packages for golf and catering
available; terms on application.
⦿ Fairways Bar and Restaurant;
spike bar.
⟿ Three Swans, Market, Harborough;
Rockingham Forest, Corby.

5A 94 **Thorney Golf Centre**

English Drove, Thorney, Peterborough,
Cambs, PE6 0TJ
www.thorneygolfcentre.co.uk
☎ 01733 270570, Fax 270842,
Rest/Bar 271218
On A47 E of Peterborough
Parkland course with lakes
Pro Mark Templeman; Founded
1991/1995
Designed by A Dow/ A Hind
The Lakes:18 holes, The Fen: 18
holes; The Lakes: 6402 yards; The
Fen: 6104 yards; S.S.S. lakes 71; Fen
69; plus a 9-hole par 3 course
⏐ 12 bays floodlit; lessons available;
buggies, trolleys and clubs for hire.
✝ Welcome.
⌐ The Lakes Course: WD £14, WE
£22; The Fens Course: WD £8, WE
£10; Par 3 course: £3.25 all day.
⟳ Welcome WD; anytime on Fen;
packages available; terms on application.
⦿ Bar and restaurant.

5A 95 **Thorpe Wood**

Thorpe Wood Golf Course, Thorpe
Wood, Peterborough, Cambs,
PE3 6SE

www.thorpewoodgolfcourse.co.uk
enquiries@
thorpewoodgolfcourse.co.uk
☎ 01733 267701, Fax 332774,
Rest/Bar 267601
On A47 to Leicester 2 miles W of
Peterborough.
Parkland course.
Pro Roger Fitton/Gary Casey;
Founded 1975
Designed by Peter Alliss and
Dave Thomas
18 holes, 7086 yards, S.S.S. 74
⏐ Driving range; tuition available.
✝ Welcome.
⌐ WD £11.90; WE £15.70.
⟳ Welcome by arrangement up to a
year in advance.
⦿ The Woodman Public House (next
door).
⟿ Moat House.

5A 96 **Tilsworth** ☎

Dunstable Road, Tilsworth, Leighton
Buzzard, Beds, LU7 9PU
☎ 01525 210721, Fax 210465,
Pro 210722, Rest/Bar 210722
2 miles N of Dunstable on A5; take
Tilsworth/Stanbridge turning.
Parkland course.
Pro Nick Webb
Founded 1977
18 holes, 5306 yards, S.S.S. 69
⏐ Practice range, open all week;
tuition available; buggy and club hire.
✝ Welcome except before 10am Sun
⌐ Prices on application.
⟳ Welcome WD; terms on
application
⦿ Full facilities.
⟿ Travel Lodge.

5A 97 **Ullesthorpe Court**

Frolesworth Road, Ullesthorpe,
Lutterworth, Leics, LE17 5BZ
www.ullesthorpecourt.co.uk
bookings@ullesthorpecourt.co.uk
☎ 01455 209023, Fax 202537,
Pro 209150
Close to the M1 and M69, just off A5.
Parkland course.
Pro David Bowring; Founded 1976
18 holes, 6672 yards, S.S.S. 72
✝ Welcome WD; with members at WE.
⌐ WD £22.
⟳ Golf day packages and overnight
accommodation can be organised
through the hotel; full clubhouse and
hotel facilities for both corporate and
society golf days; from £25..
⦿ Full hotel and clubhouse facilities
available.
⟿ On-site hotel Ullesthorpe Court.

5A 98 Waterbeach Barracks
39 Engineer Regiment, Waterbeach
Barracks, Waterbeach, Cambridge,
Cambs, CB5 9PA
☎ 01223 860681, Fax 440007,
Rest/Bar 440007
Fenland course.
Founded 1972
9 holes, 6237 yards, S.S.S. 70
† HM Forces welcome; civilians must
be introduced by and play with a
member.
⌁ Terms on application.
🍴 Limited bar available.

5A 99 Wellingborough ₮
The Slips, Great Harrowden,
Wellingborough, Northants, NN9 5AD
☎ 01933 677234, Fax 679379, Pro
678752, Sec 677234, Rest/Bar 402612
Course is two miles N of
Wellingborough on the A509.
Undulating parkland course.
Pro David Clifford; Founded 1893/1975
Designed by Hawtree & Sons
18 holes, 6651 yards, S.S.S. 72
† Welcome WD.
⌁ WD £40 per round.
⌃ Welcome WD except Tues; full
day's golf, bar, restaurant, snooker;
tuition available.
🍴 Full clubhouse facilities available.
⌐ Tudor Gate, Finedon; Oak House
and Hind, both Wellingborough;
Kettering Park, Foxford at Rushden.

5A 100 Western Park
Scudamore Road, Leicester, Leics,
LE3 1UQ
☎ 0116 2995566, Fax 2995568,
Rest/Bar 875211
Off A47 2 miles W of city centre.
Parkland course.
Pro David Butler; Founded 1920
Designed by FW Hawtree
18 holes, 6518 yards, S.S.S. 70
† Welcome; must book at WE.
⌁ Winter: WD £8.99, WE £11.50;
Summer: WD £9.99, WE £12.50;
discount rate for juniors and OAPs.

⌃ Welcome by prior arrangement;
catering and golf packages available;
terms on application.
🍴 Full clubhouse facilities.
⌐ Hilton Hotel.

5A 101 Whetstone
Cambridge Road, Cosby, Leicester,
LE9 5SH
☎ 0116 2861424, Fax 2861424
4 miles from M1 Junction 21 SE of
Leicester; take A46 to Narborough then
signposts for Whetstone.
Wooded parkland course with water
features.
Pro David Raitt;
Founded 1963
Designed by Nick Leatherland
18 holes, 5795 yards, S.S.S. 68
⌁ 20 bays, Practice range.
† Welcome.
⌁ WD £15; WE £16.
⌃ Welcome by arrangement.
🍴 Full bar and catering facilities.
⌐ Time Out, Blaby.

5A 102 Whittlebury Park ₮
Golf and Country Club
Whittlebury, Towcester, Northants,
NN12 8WP
⌁ www.whittlebury.com
✉ enquiries@whittlebury.com
☎ 01327 858092, Fax 858009,
Pro 858588, Sec 858092, Rest/Bar
858092
Course is on the A413 15 mins from the
M1 Junction 15A, three miles S of
Towcester.
Parkland/lakeland course.
Pro Steve Harlock; Founded 1992
Designed by Cameron Sinclair
36 holes, 6662 yards, S.S.S. 72
⌁ 32 bay covered driving range +
indoor course; clay pigeon shooting;
archery; cricket ground; croquet lawn;
corporate hospitality; function suites.
† Welcome.
⌁ Winter: Mon £10, Tues-Fri am £20,
WE am £30; 7 days a week pm £10;
Summer rates: prices on application.

⌃ Welcome at all times by prior
arrangement; 4 x 9 loops (1905, Royal
Whittlewood, Grand Prix, Wedgewood);
terms on application.
🍴 Bars, bistros, restaurant.
⌐ On site Whittlebury Hall Hotel; 124
en-suite rooms.

5A 103 Willesley Park ₮
Measham Road, Ashby-de-la-Zouch,
Leics, LE65 2PF
⌁ www.willesleypark
✉ info@willesleypark.com
☎ 01530 414596, Fax 564169,
Pro 414820, Rest/Bar 411532
2 miles S of Ashby-de-la-Zouch on
B5006.
Parkland/heathland course.
Pro Ben Hill; Founded 1921
Designed by James Braid/CK Cotton
18 holes, 6304 yards, S.S.S. 70
⌁ Tuition available.
† Welcome with handicap certs.
⌁ WD £28 round, £40 day; WE £35,
£50 day.
⌃ Welcome Wed, Thurs, Fri; terms
on application; from £28.
🍴 Clubhouse facilities.
⌐ Royal; Fallen Knight.

5A 104 Wyboston Lakes
Great North Road, Wyboston, Bedford,
Beds, MK44 3AL
⌁ www.wybostonlakes.co.uk
✉ sales@wybostonlakes.co.uk
☎ 01480 223004, Fax 223000
Off A1 at St Neots.
Public parkland with lake features.
Pro Paul Ashwell; Founded 1981
Designed by Neil Oackden
18 holes, 5955 yards, S.S.S. 70
⌁ 12 bays floodlit; practice range;
lessons available.
† Welcome; bookings taken 7 days
in advance for WE.
⌃ Welcome WE by prior
arrangement.
🍴 Full catering facilities.
⌐ Hotel on site offers golf
packages.

5B

Gloucestershire, Warwickshire, Herefordshire and Worcestershire

Hereford must have a very good claim to being England's most beautiful county. To the south lies Symonds Yat, where Anthony Hopkins and Debra Winger in the parts of CS Lewis and Joy Gresham came to film the golden valley scene of *Shadowlands*. Symonds Yat looks over the River Wye meandering its way along the valley below. A view that inspires joy, humility and Englishness, it's the sort of spot where William Blake might have written *Jerusalem*. North west of Symonds Yat is the true golden valley lying in the shadow of the Black Mountains. To the east are the Malvern Hills from which Sir Edward Elgar derived much of his inspiration.

Many of Britain's greatest golf courses are not laid out in such beautiful countryside. That is rather the point of them. They are good at turning a scrubby bit of decaying coastal land into something useful and lovely. So finding a suitable spot to build a golf course in Hereford has been known to present quite a problem.

In a previous addition of this book Donald Steel wrote of the difficulties Ross-on-Wye had in relocating from their previous nine hole course. Originally the designer Ken Cotton wouldn't countenance building a course on the suggested site, but following a personal visit from the club committee he relented. His task entailed hacking a path through acres of woodland.

Steel wrote, "My first memory was the sight of the head woodsman, then in his eighties, fuelling a woodland fire with fresh scrub and branches and cooking a lunch of bacon and eggs on the back of a carefully cleaned shovel". Given all the woodland that had to be cleared it is not surprising that Ross-on-Wye has such narrow fairways – one professional observed that the tee shot from the tenth could only be negotiated with a rifle – but what an achievement the course is in an area almost devoid of golf for many years.

For a long while Minchinhampton, in Gloucestershire, remained just about the only course between Westward Ho! and the Worcestershire, the first of the Midlands golf clubs. Like Minchinhampton, the Worcestershire had to move from its original site on common land because all the non-golfing activity going on – from grazing sheep to picnickers – made concentration rather hazardous. There is no document of what Elgar, a member of the club, had to say about it all, but it is recorded that he once holed his second shot on the fourth hole.

Kington, the highest course in the country and devoid of bunkers, Blackwell, Abbey Park, Worcester Golf and County and Cotswold Hills are other courses of some reputation in the counties that are better known for being home to the Three Choirs Festival.

Warwickshire has a louder golfing voice if not necessarily as tuneful a one. The Forest of Arden is now the home of the British Masters and the Belfry will forever be associated with the Ryder Cup. The tenth and eighteenth holes across the lake are exciting for just those associations, but overall it is a bit of a field despite the recent modifications to the third and the fourth. Many in the Birmingham area regard Sandwell Park or King's Norton as much better value.

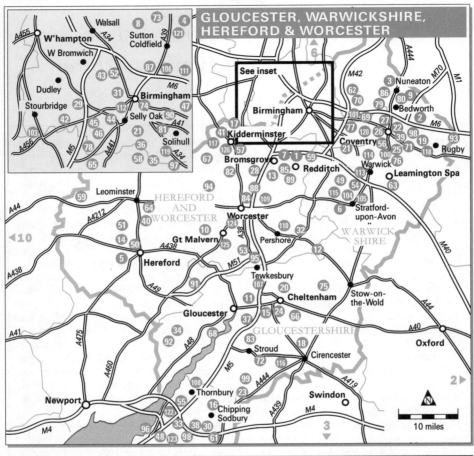

GLOUCESTER, WARWICKSHIRE, HEREFORD & WORCESTER

KEY		25	Coventry	51	Herefordshire	77	North Warwickshire	104	Stratford Oaks
1	Abbey Hotel G & CC	26	Coventry Hearsall	52	Hill Top Public Golf	78	North Worcestershire	105	Stratford-upon-Avon
2	Ansty Golf Centre	27	Cromwell Course at		Course	79	Nuneaton	106	Sutton Coldfield
3	Atherstone		Nailcote Hall	53	Hilton Puckrup Hall (98)	80	Oakridge	107	Tewkesbury Park Hotel
4	The Belfry	28	Droitwich G & CC	54	Ingon Manor G & CC	81	Olton	108	Thornbury Golf Centre
5	Belmont Lodge and Golf	29	Dudley	55	The Kendleshire	82	Ombersley	109	Tolladine
6	Bidford Grange	30	Dymock Grange	56	Kenilworth	83	Painswick	110	Vale
7	Blackwell	31	Edgbaston	57	Kidderminster	84	Perdiswell	111	Walmley
8	Boldmere	32	Evesham	58	Kings Norton	85	Pitcheroak (Kingfisher)	112	Warley
9	Bramcote Waters	33	Filton	59	Kington	86	Purley Chase G & CC	113	Warwick
10	Bransford at Bank House	34	Forest Hills	60	Ladbrook Park	87	Pype Hayes	114	Warwickshire
	Hotel	35	Fulford Heath	61	Lansdown	88	Ravenmeadow	115	Welcombe Hotel
11	Brickhampton Court	36	Gay Hill	62	Lea Marston Hotel	89	Redditch	116	Westonbirt
12	Broadway	37	Gloucester	63	Leamington & County	90	Robin Hood	117	Wharton Park
13	Bromsgrove Golf Centre	38	The Gloucestershire	64	Leominster	91	Ross-on-Wye	118	Whitefields
14	Burghill Valley	39	Grange (Marconi GC)	65	Lickey Hills (Rose Hill)	92	Royal Forest of Dean	119	Widney Manor
15	Canons Court	40	Grove Golf Centre	66	Lilley Brook	93	Rugby	120	Windmill Village Hotel
16	Chipping Sodbury	41	Habberley	67	Little Lakes	94	Sapey	121	Wishaw
17	Churchill & Blakedown	42	Hagley Country Club	68	Lydney	96	Sherdons	122	Woodlands
18	Cirencester	43	Halesowen	69	Marriott Forest of Arden	96	Shirehampton Park	123	Woodspring
19	City of Coventry	44	Handsworth	70	Maxstoke Park	97	Shirley	124	Worcester G & CC
	(Brandon Wood)	45	Harborne	71	Memorial Park	98	Shortwood Lodge	125	Worcestershire
20	Cleeve Hill	46	Harborne Church Farm	72	Minchinhampton	99	Sphinx	126	Wyre Forest
21	Cocks Moor Woods	47	Hatchford Brook	73	Moor Hall	100	Stinchcombe Hill		
22	Copt Heath	48	Henbury	74	Moseley	101	Stonebridge		
23	Cotswold Edge	49	Henley Golf & CC	75	Naunton Downs	102	Stoneleigh Deer Park		
24	Cotswold Hills	50	Hereford Municipal	76	Newbold Comyn	103	Stourbridge		

West Midlands Golf Club

www.wmgc.co.uk
Tel: 01675 444890
Fax: 01675 444890

Marsh House, Farm Lane, Barston, Solihull, West Midlands B92 0LB

New Golf Club opened June 2003

All greens and tees built to USGA Specification

18th hole is a Par 3, 150 yards to an island green (shown in picture)

Also lakeside restaurant overlooking the 18th green and the lake

5B 1 Abbey Hotel Golf & Country Club
Dagnell End Road, Redditch, Worcs, B98 9BE
⛳ www.theabbeyhotel.co.uk
✉ info@theabbeyhotel.co.uk
☎ 01527 406500, Fax 406514
On A441 Redditch to Birmingham road.
Parkland course.
Pro Rob Davies; Founded 1985
Designed by Donald Steel
18 holes, 6561 yards, S.S.S. 71
⚐ Driving range on site.
† Welcome subject to course availability.
⚑ WD 18 holes £15; WE 18 holes £23.
⚘ Welcome by prior arrangement; special packages available for members of golf club and guests of hotel; snooker; gym; swimming pool; sauna.
🍽 Brambling's restaurant and Tawney's leisure bar.
⌂ Abbey Hotel on site – 4 star, 72 bedrooms.

5B 2 Ansty Golf Centre
Brinklow Road, Ansty, Coventry, Warwicks, CV7 9JH
⛳ www.anstygc.co.uk
☎ 024 766 21341, Fax 02568, Rest/Bar 21347
From M6 Junction 2 take B4065 to Ansty; turning on to B4029 to Brinklow.
Parkland course.
Pro M Fisher; Founded 1990
Designed by D Morgan
18 holes, 6079 yards, S.S.S. 69
⚐ 18 bays; 9-hole academy course; tuition available 7 days a week; buggies and clubs for hire.
† Pay and play.
⚑ WD £11; WE £16.
⚘ Welcome with 24 hours notice.
🍽 Full facilities.
⌂ Ansty Hall; Hanover at Hinckley.

5B 3 Atherstone
The Outwoods, Colesgill Road, Atherstone, Warks, CV9 2RL
☎ 01827 713110, Sec 892568
On A5 in town centre on Coleshill Road.
Parkland course.
Founded 1894
18 holes, 6006 yards, S.S.S. 70
† Welcome; guests of members at WE.
⚑ WD £25 day.
⚘ Welcome by arrangement; packages available; full catering facilities; terms on application.
🍽 Full catering and bar.
⌂ Chapel House; Mancetter Manor, both Atherstone.

5B 4 The Belfry ℭ
The Belfry, Lichfield Road, Wishaw, Sutton Coldfield, W Midlands, B76 9PR
⛳ www.devereonline.co.uk
✉ golf.reception@thebelfry.com
☎ 01675 470301, Fax 470174, Pro 470301, Sec 470301
M42 Junction 9 follow A446 towards Lichfield and course is 1 mile on left.
Parkland course, 2002 Ryder Cup host.
Pro Peter McGovern; Founded 1977
Designed by Peter Alliss & Dave Thomas
Brabazon: 18 holes, 6393 yards, S.S.S. 71; Derby: 18 holes, 6009 yards, S.S.S. 69; PGA National: 18 holes, 6153 yards, S.S.S. 70
⚐ Practice ground; buggies (seasonal only) and clubs for hire; tuition available, group lessons available; caddies and bag carriers available.
† Welcome.
⚑ WD £135, WE £135 (Brabazon); WD £35, WE £35 (Derby); WD £70, WE £70 (PGA National).
⚘ Welcome; full championship course, clubhouse and hotel facilities; terms on application.

🍽 First-class clubhouse and hotel facilities; choice of three restaurants.
⌂ The Belfry.

5B 5 Belmont Lodge and Golf ℭ
Belmont, Hereford, Herefordshire, HR2 9SA
⛳ www.belmont-hereford.co.uk
✉ info@belmont-hereford.co.uk
☎ 01432 352666, Fax 358090, Pro 352717
1.5 miles from the centre of Hereford just off A465 Abergavenny road.
Parkland course with back 9 bordering the river.
Pro Mike Welsh; Founded 1983
Designed by R Sandow
18 holes, 6511 yards, S.S.S. 71
⚐ Practice ground; tuition available; caddy cars for hire £16.50 per round.
† Welcome.
⚑ Prices on application.
⚘ Welcome; packages can be organised; terms on application.
🍽 Full club and hotel facilities.
⌂ Belmont Lodge; self catering accomodation on site.

5B 6 Bidford Grange Golf Complex and Hotel
Bidford Grange, Stratford Road, Bidford-on-Avon, Alcester, Warks, B50 4LY
☎ 01789 490319, Fax 490998, Pro 491376
Course is off the A439 Evesham-Stratford road.
Parkland course with last 4 holes close to River Avon.
Pro Simon Leahy; Founded 1992
Designed by Howard Swan and Paul Tillman
18 holes, 7233 yards, S.S.S. 72
⚐ 16 bays, practice range.
† Welcome.

⌇ WD £15; WE £18.
⌔ Welcome; various packages available, including golf, catering, dinner and accommodation; minimum 12; from £20 – £50.
⍟ New clubhouse with spikes bar, restaurant and hotel facilities.
⍩ Bidford Grange.

5B 7 Blackwell ☏
Agmore Road, Blackwell, Bromsgrove, Worcs, B60 1PY
⌁ www.blackwellgolfclub.com
⌨ info@blackwellgolfclub.com
☎ 0121 4451994, Fax 4454911, Pro 4453113, Rest/Bar 4451781
3 miles E of Bromsgrove close to Blackwell village centre.
Parkland course.
Pro Nigel Blake; Founded 1893
Designed by H Fowler and T Simpson
18 holes, 6230 yards, S.S.S. 71
† Welcome WD; with member at WE.
⌇ WD £50.
⌔ Welcome Mon, Wed, Thurs, Fri by prior arrangement with Sec.
⍟ Full clubhouse facilities.
⍩ Perry Hall; Bromsgrove.

5B 8 Boldmere
Boldmere Municipal Golf Course, Monmouth Drive, Sutton Coldfield, West Midlands, B73 6JL
☎ 0121 354 3379, Fax 3554534, Rest/Bar 3211476
Off A452 Chester Road, 6 miles NE of Birmingham.
Parkland course.
Pro Trevor Short; Founded 1936
Designed by Bretherton
18 holes, 4474 yards, S.S.S. 62
† Everyone welcome.
⌇ WD £9.50; WE £11.
⌔ Welcome WD only.
⍟ Bar and Catering.
⍩ Parson & Clerk.

5B 9 Bramcote Waters
Bazzard Road, Bramcote, Nuneaton, Warks, CV11 6QJ
☎ 01455 220 807
5 miles SE of Nuneaton off the B4114.
Parkland course.
Pro Nic Gilks; Founded 1995
Designed by David Snell.
9 holes, 2491 yards, S.S.S. 64
⚑ Bramcote Drive (200 yards away).
† Pay and play.
⌇ 18 holes WD £14, WE £15; 9 holes WD £8, WE £9.
⌔ None.

⍟ Full clubhouse.
⍩ The Hanover International.

5B 10 Bransford at the ☏ Bank House Hotel
Bransford, Worcester, Worcs, WR6 5JD
⌨ info@bankhousehotel.co.uk
☎ 01886 833545, Fax 832461, Pro 833621, Rest/Bar 833754
Course is three miles W of Worcester on the A4013 Hereford road in Bransford village.
Florida-style course with 14 lakes and 2 island greens.
Pro Scott Fordyce/Lysa Jones; Founded 1993
Designed by Bob Sandow
18 holes, 6204 yards, S.S.S. 70
⚑ 20-bay, practice range; buggies and clubs for hire; tuition and golf clinics available.
† Welcome.
⌇ Terms on application.
⌔ Welcome; various packages including 2-night golfing break for £160; hotel and clubhouse facilities, outdoor pool, fitness centre; prices on application.
⍟ Bars, restaurants.
⍩ On site Bank House Hotel.

5B 11 Brickhampton Court
Cheltenham Road East, Gloucester, Glos, GL2 9QF
⌁ www.brickhampton.co.uk
⌨ info@brickhampton.co.uk
☎ 01452 859444, Fax 859333
On B4063 between Cheltenham and Gloucester; 3 miles from M5 J11.
Parkland course.
Pro Chris Gillick/Bruce Wilson; Founded 1995
Designed by S Gidman
18 holes, 6449 yards, S.S.S. 71
⚑ 26-bay floodlit range; Ping teaching academy; buggies for hire; corporate golf days – phone for details.
† Welcome.
⌇ Mon-Thur £21; Fri £23; WE/BH £27.50.
⌔ Welcome WD; golf and catering packages; also 9-hole Glevum course; on-course refreshments; welcome packs and golf clinics; £21-£37.50.
⍟ Clubhouse facilities, bar restaurant,
⍩ Golden Valley; Hatherley Manor; White House.

5B 12 Broadway
Broadway Golf Club, Willersey Hill, Broadway, Worcs, WR12 7LG

☎ 01386 853683, Fax 858643, Pro 853275, Rest/Bar 853561
1.5 miles E of Broadway on A44.
Inland Links.
Pro M Freeman; Founded 1895
Designed by James Braid
18 holes, 6228 yards, S.S.S. 70
⚑ 4.
† Welcome by prior arrangement except before 3pm on Sat in summer.
⌇ WD £30; WE £38.
⌔ Welcome Wed, Thurs, Fri; terms on application.
⍟ Clubhouse facilities.
⍩ Dormy House next door; Lygon Arms, Broadway.

5B 13 Bromsgrove Golf Centre
Stratford Road, Bromsgrove, Worcestershire, B60 1LD
⌁ www.bromsgrovegolfcentre.co.uk
☎ 01527 570505, Fax 570964, Pro 575886, Sec 575886, Rest/Bar 579179
1 mile from Bromsgrove town centre at junction of A38 and A448.
Gently undulating parkland course.
Pro G Long/D Wall/ C Clark; Founded 1992
Designed by Hawtree & Sons
18 holes, 5869 yards, S.S.S. 68
⚑ 35-bay covered floodlit practice range; large practice bunker; putting green.
† Pay and play.
⌇ WD £17.70; WE £23.50 (visitors). WD £15.50; WE £20.50 (associate)
⌔ Welcome by prior arrangement; group and society packages available; terms on application.
⍟ Full facilities with bar and lounge.
⍩ List available on request.

5B 14 Burghill Valley ☏
Tillington Road, Burghill, Hereford, HR4 7RW
⌁ www.bvgc.co.uk
⌨ golf@bvgc.co.uk
☎ 01432 760456, Fax 761654, Pro 760808
4 miles NW of Hereford. Built around cider orchards.
2 lakes and woods.
Pro Nigel Clarke; Founded 1991
18 holes, 6239 yards, S.S.S. 70
⚑ Practice ground; tuition and golf clinics available; buggies and clubs for hire.
† Welcome.
⌇ WD £20; WE £25.
⌔ Welcome; golf and catering packages available; from £25.
⍟ Clubhouse facilities.

5B 15 Canons Court
Canons Court Farm, Bradley,
Wotton-under-Edge, Glos, GL12 7PN
☎ 01453 843128
3 miles from M5 Junction 14 on
Wotton-under-Edge to N Nibley road.
Parkland course.
Founded 1982
9 holes, 5323 yards, S.S.S. 68
† Public pay and play.
Ⅰ WD £8; WE £10.
♂ Welcome WD; terms on
application.
🍽 Bar and bar snacks.

5B 16 Chipping Sodbury
Chipping Sodbury, Bristol, Glos,
BS17 6PU
🖳 www.chippingsodburygolfclub.co.uk
📧 info@chippingsodburygolfclub
.co.uk
☎ 01454 319042, Pro 314087,
Rest/Bar 315822
Leave M4 Junction 18 or M5 Junction
14 and from Chipping Sodbury take
the Wickwar road; first right turn.
Parkland course.
Pro Mike Watts; Founded 1906
Designed by Fred Hawtree
18 holes, 6786 yards, S.S.S. 73;
9 holes, 1076 yards
𝄡 Practice ground; tuition available;
buggies and clubs for hire.
† Welcome; after 12 noon at WE.
Ⅰ Terms on application.
♂ Welcome WD by prior
arrangement.
🍽 Full bar and meal service.
↩ Moda; Cross Hands.

5B 17 Churchill & Blakedown
Churchill Lane, Blakedown,
Kidderminster, Worcester,
DY10 3NB
☎ 01562 700018, Fax 700018,
Pro 700458, Rest/bar 700200
Off A456 3 miles NE of Kidderminster;
turn under railway viaduct in village of
Blakedown.
Undulating parkland course.
Pro Grahame Wright; Founded 1926
9 holes, 6472 yards, S.S.S. 71
† Welcome WD; WE with a member.
♂ Welcome by prior arrangement;
from £15.
🍽 Full facilities except Mon.

5B 18 Cirencester
Cheltenham Rd, Bagendon,
Cirencester, Glos, GL7 7BH
☎ 01285 652465, Fax 650665,
Pro 656124, Rest/Bar 6539390

Off A435 Cirencester-Cheltenham road
1.5 miles from Cirencester.
Undulating course.
Pro Peter Garratt; Founded 1893
Designed by James Braid
18 holes, 6055 yards, S.S.S. 69
† Welcome.
Ⅰ WD £25; WE £30.
♂ Welcome by arrangement.
🍽 Full facilities.
↩ King's Head.

**5B 19 City of Coventry
(Brandon Wood)**
Brandon Lane, Wolston, Coventry,
CV8 3GQ
☎ 024 765 43141
6 miles S of Coventry off A45.
Parkland course.
Pro Chris Gledhill
Designed by Frank Pennink
18 holes, 6610 yards, S.S.S. 71
† Welcome.
Ⅰ WD £11.35; WE £15.10.
♂ Welcome on application to
professional; terms on application.
🍽 Clubhouse facilities.
↩ Brandon Hall Hotel.

5B 20 Cleeve Hill
Cleeve Hill, Cheltenham, Glos,
GL52 3PW
🖳 www.cleevehill.com
📧 golf@cleevehill.com
☎ 01242 672592, Fax 678444
6 miles N of M5; 4 miles from
Cheltenham off A46.
Inland links course.
Pro Dave Finch; Founded 1891
18 holes, 6448 yards, S.S.S. 71
† Welcome WD; some restrictions
WE.
Ⅰ WD £15; WE £18.
♂ Welcome by prior arrangement;
catering packages; skittles alley.
🍽 Bar snacks.
↩ Rising Sun.

5B 21 Cocks Moor Woods
Alcester Rd South, Kings Heath,
Birmingham, W Midlands,
B14 6ER
☎ 0121 4443584
On A435 near city boundary.
Public parkland course.
Pro Steve Ellis;
Founded 1924
18 holes, 5769 yards, S.S.S. 68
† Welcome.
Ⅰ WD £9; WE £10.
♂ Welcome by arrangement.
🍽 Full clubhouse facilities.

5B 22 Copt Heath
1220 Warwick Rd, Knowle, Solihull,
Warwicks, B93 9LN
🖳 www.coptheathgolf.co.uk
📧 golf@copt-heath.co.uk
☎ 01564 772650, Fax 771022,
Pro 776155, Rest/Bar 777746
From M42 Junction 5 take A4141;
course 0.5 miles.
Parkland course.
Pro BJ Barton; Founded 1907
Designed by H Vardon
18 holes, 6517 yards, S.S.S. 71
† Welcome WD; restricted Sat/Sun.
Ⅰ WD/WE £40 all day.
♂ Welcome by prior arrangement
with secretary; maximum 36; terms on
application; from £40.
🍽 Clubhouse facilities.
↩ Greswolde Arms; St Johns.

5B 23 Cotswold Edge
Upper Rushmire, Wotton-under-Edge,
Glos, GL12 7PT
☎ 01453 844167, Fax 845120
On B4058 Wotton-under-Edge/Tetbury
road 8 miles from M5 Junction 14.
Meadowland course.
Pro Rod Hibbitt; Founded 1980
18 holes, 6170 yards, S.S.S. 71
† Welcome WD; WE with member.
Ⅰ WD £15; WE £20.
♂ Welcome WD by prior
arrangement; packages available; from
£30.
🍽 Full clubhouse facilities.
↩ Hunters Hall; Calcot Manor.

5B 24 Cotswold Hills   ♞
Ullenwood, Cheltenham, Glos,
GL53 9QT
🖳 www.cotswoldhills-golfclub.co.uk
📧 golf@chgc.freeserve.co.uk
☎ 01242 515264, Fax 513317,
Pro 515263, Rest/Bar 573210
3 miles S of Cheltenham.
Parkland course on limestone;
1981 English Ladies Amateur.
Pro James Latham; Founded
1902/1976
Designed by MD Little
18 holes, 6849 yards, S.S.S. 72
† Welcome by prior arrangement.
Ⅰ WD £32; WE £37.
♂ Welcome Wed and Fri; packages
available; from £30.
🍽 Clubhouse facilities.
↩ Moathouse Hotel; George Hotel;
Lilleybrook; Golden Valley.

5B 25 Coventry
St Martin's Rd, Finham Park, Coventry,
Warwicks, CV3 6PJ
🖳 www.coventrygolfcourse.co.uk

coventrygolfclub@hotmail.com
☎ 024 764 14152, Fax 766 90131,
Pro 764 11298
Close to A45/A46 Junction; take A45
towards Birmingham and left at
island.
Parkland course.
Pro Phil Weaver; Founded 1887
Designed by Tom Vardon
18 holes, 6601 yards, S.S.S. 73
† Welcome WD; with member WE.
[WD £35.
⌂ Welcome Wed and Thurs;
packages available; from £50-£55.
🍽 Clubhouse facilities.
⌐ Chesford Grange; Old Mill.

5B 26 Coventry Hearsall

Beechwood Ave, Earlsdon, Coventry,
CV5 6DF
☎ 024 767 13470, Fax 766 91534,
Pro 767 13156, Rest/Bar 767 75809
From A45/A429 towards city centre
turn into Beechwood Avenue.
Parkland course.
Pro Mike Tarn; Founded 1894/1921
18 holes, 6005 yards, S.S.S. 69
† Welcome with member.
[Terms on application.
⌂ Welcome Tues and Thurs.
🍽 Clubhouse facilities.
⌐ Hylands Hotel.

5B 27 Cromwell Course

Nailcote Hall Hotel, Nailcote Lane,
Berkswell, Warwicks,
CV7 7DE
🖰 www.nailcotehall.co.uk
📧 info@nailcotehall.co.uk
☎ 024 7646 6174, Fax 76470720
Take A452 Balsall Common Junction
from B4101 and follow brown signs
towards Tile Hall, hotel 1.5 miles on
right.
Parkland course.
Pro Sid Mouland; Founded 1994
Designed by Short Course Golf Ltd
9 holes, 1023 yards, S.S.S. 27
[Practice putting green, tution
available, leisure facilities (swimming
pool, croquet lawn, tennis, sauna).
† Welcome.
[WD £10; WE £10.
⌂ Welcome by prior arrangement;
terms on application.
🍽 Full hotel facilities.
⌐ Nailcote Hall on site.

5B 28 Droitwich Golf &
Country Club

Westford House, Ford Lane, Droitwich,
WR9 0BQ

☎ 01905 774344, Fax 797290,
Pro 770207
Off A38 1 mile N of town.
Undulating meadowland course.
Pro Chris Thompson; Founded 1897
18 holes, 5976 yards, S.S.S. 69
† Welcome WD with handicap certs;
with member at WE.
[WD £26.
⌂ Welcome Wed and Fri.
🍽 Bar meals and restaurant.
⌐ The Chateau Impney; Raven.

5B 29 Dudley

Turners Hill, Rowley Regis, Warley,
W Midlands, B65 9DP
📧 info@dudleygc.fsnet.co.uk
☎ 01384 253719, Fax 233177,
Pro 254020, Sec 233877
1 mile S of town centre.
Undulating parkland course.
Pro Guy Dean; Founded 1893
18 holes, 5730 yards, S.S.S. 68
† Welcome WD.
[WD £25.
⌂ Welcome by prior arrangement;
various packages available.
🍽 Lunch and evening meals.
⌐ Travelodge.

5B 30 Dymock Grange

The Old Grange, Dymock, Glos,
GL18 2AN
☎ 01531 890840
On A4172 off the A449 Ledbury–
Ross-on-Wye Rd.
Parkland course.
Pro Sara Foster (touring);
Founded 1995
18 holes, 4600 yards, S.S.S. 65
† Welcome with prior reservation.
[WD £10; WE £14.
⌂ Welcome by prior arrangement.
🍽 Bar.
⌐ Restaurant; fitness centre.

5B 31 Edgbaston

Edgbaston Hall, Church Rd,
Edgbaston, Birmingham, B15 3TB
☎ 0121 454 1736, Fax 2395,
Pro 3226, Rest/Bar 8141
From city centre take A38 Bristol road;
after 1.5 miles turn right into Priory
Road (B4217); after mini roundabout
club 100 yards.
Parkland course; woods and lake.
Pro J Cundy;
Founded 1896
Designed by HS Colt
18 holes, 6106 yards, S.S.S. 69
[Practice range, practice areas and
nets.

† Welcome except Sat comp days
before 2pm and Sun before 11.30am.
[WD £40; WE £50.
⌂ Welcome WD except Thurs;
packages available including private
function room, changing rooms, golf
and catering; minimum 20 maximum
100.
🍽 Extensive clubhouse facilities;
restaurant, bars and private rooms.
⌐ Copperfield House; Portland
House; Apollo; Plough & Harrow;
Marriott.

5B 32 Evesham

Craycombe Links, Fladbury Cross,
Pershore, Worcs, WR10 2QS
🖰 www.eveshamgolf.com
📧 eveshamgolf@btopenworld.com
☎ 01386 860395, Fax 861356,
Pro 861144
3 miles W of Evesham towards
Worcester on A4538.
Parkland course.
Pro Dan Cummins; Founded 1894
9 holes, 6357 yards, S.S.S. 72
[One practice ground; Two practice
greens; PGA tuition.
† Welcome with prior arrangement
WD; WE with a member.
[WD non members £20, guests of
members £10.
⌂ Welcome with prior arrangement;
terms on application.
🍽 Clubhouse facilities.

5B 33 Filton

Golf Course Lane, Filton, Bristol,
BS34 7QS
🖰 www.filtongolfclub.co.uk
📧 thesecretary@filtongolfclub.co.uk
☎ 0117 969 4169, Fax 931 4359,
Pro 969 6968, Rest/Bar 969 2021
M5 Junction 16 to A38 at Filton
roundabout turn right then first right at
lights.
Parkland course with views of Brecon
Beacons.
Pro Darren Robinson; Founded 1909
Designed by F Hawtree & Son
18 holes, 6173 yards, S.S.S. 70
† Welcome WD only; guests of
members at WE.
[WD £22.
⌂ Welcome by prior arrangement;
terms on application.
🍽 Full clubhouse facilities.
⌐ Aztec; Stakis; Premier Lodge.

5B 34 Forest Hills

Mile End Road, Coleford, Glos,
GL16 7QD

The Chequers Inn

The Chequers at Fladbury offers good food and accommodation in the relaxing atmosphere of our Country Inn. We are within easy access of several Golf Courses including Broadway, The Vale and Evesham courses.

The Chequers Inn, Chequers Lane, Fladbury, Nr. Pershore, Worcs. WR10 2PZ   Tel: 01386 860276   Fax: 01386 861286

☎ 01594 810620
Course is on the B4028 towards Gloucester, 0.5 miles from Coleford town centre.
Meadowland course.
Pro Richard Ballard; Founded 1992
Designed by Adrian Stiff
18 holes, 5674 yards, S.S.S. 67
† Welcome.
[WD £15; WE £20.
⌃ Welcome by prior arrangement; terms on application. Driving range; buggies and clubs for hire; tuition available 7 days a week; junior academy Sat morning; new juniors always welcome.
⦿ Full clubhouse facilities.

5B 35 Fulford Heath ♌
Tanners Green Lane, Wythall, Birmingham, B47 6BH
⌁ www.fulfordheath.co.uk
✉ secretary@fulfordheath.co.uk
☎ 01564 822930, Fax 822629,
Pro 822930, Sec 824758
8 miles S of Birmingham.
Parkland course.
Pro Richard Dunbar; Founded 1933
Designed by Braid/Hawtree.
18 holes, 6179 yards, S.S.S. 70
† Welcome WD; with member WE.
[WD £35 casual rate.
⌃ Welcome by arrangement on Tues and Thurs possibly one other day; golf and catering packages available; prices on application.
⦿ Clubhouse facilities.

5B 36 Gay Hill
Hollywood Lane, Hollywood, Birmingham, W Midlands, B47 5PP
⌁ www.ghgc.org.uk
✉ secretary@ghgc.org.uk
☎ 0121 430 8544, Fax 436 7796,
Pro 474 6001, Rest/Bar 436 7757
On A435 7 miles from Birmingham city centre and 3 miles from Junction 3 of the M42.
Meadowland course.
Pro Andrew Potter; Founded 1913
18 holes, 6400 yards, S.S.S. 72
† Welcome WD; WE some restrictions apply
[WD £32.

⌃ Welcome Thurs by arrangement.
⦿ Full facilities.
↬ George; Inkford House Hotel.

5B 37 Gloucester
Jarvis Hotel & CC, Robinswood Hill, Matson Lane, Gloucester, Glos, GL4 9EA
☎ 01452 411331, Fax 307212
2 miles S of Gloucester on B4073 to Painswick.
Parkland course.
Pro Peter Darnell; Founded 1976
Designed by Donald Steel
18 holes, 6170 yards, S.S.S. 69
† Welcome.
[WD £19; WE £25.
⌃ Welcome; terms on application.
⦿ Full hotel and clubhouse facilities.
↬ Jarvis Gloucester Hotel & CC.

5B 38 The Gloucestershire
The Tracy Park Estate, Bath Rd, Wick, Bristol, BS15 5RN
⌁ www.thegloucestershie.com
✉ info@thegloucestershire.com
☎ 0117 9372251, Fax 9374288
From Junction 18 on M4 head S on the A46 towards Bath; then right on the A420 to Bristol 4 miles.
Parkland course.
Pro David Morgan; Founded 1975
Designed by Golf Design
18 holes, 6430 yards, S.S.S. 71
† Welcome.
[18 holes WD £36, WE £44; Fairway greenfee WD £18 WE £22.
⌃ Welcome; packages available; terms on application.
⦿ Clubhouse facilities; two restaurants.
↬ On site hotel wth 18 en suite bedrooms.

5B 39 Grange (Marconi GC)
Copsewood, Coventry, W Midlands, CV3 1HS
☎ 024 765 62336, 764 52793
2.5 miles from Coventry on A428 Binley Rd.
Parkland course.
Founded 1924
9 holes, 6100 yards, S.S.S. 71

† Welcome WD before 2pm; except Wed; not Sat; Sun after 11am.
[WD £15; Sun £20.
⌃ Welcome by arrangement with secretary.
⦿ By arrangement only.
↬ Hilton.

5B 40 Grove Golf Centre
Fordbridge, Leominster, Herefordshire, HR6 0LE
☎ 01568 610602, Fax 616145,
Pro 615333
3 miles S of Leominster on A49.
Wooded parkland course.
Pro Phil Brooks; Founded 1994
Designed by J Gaunt/R Sandow
9 holes, 3560 yards, S.S.S. 60; extra 9 opening summer 2004
𝍦 Practice range, floodlit bays; putting green.
† Public pay and play.
[WD £4; WE £6.
⌃ Welcome any time; terms on application.
⦿ Full bar and restaurant.

5B 41 Habberley
Low Habberley, Kidderminster, Worcs, DY11 5RG
☎ 01562 745756
2 miles NW of Kidderminster.
Parkland course.
Founded 1924
9 holes, 5481 yards, S.S.S. 69
† Welcome WD if member of recognised club; WE and BH with member only.
[WD £10; WE £10.
⌃ Welcome by prior arrangement; terms on application.
⦿ Clubhouse facilities.
↬ Gainsborough; Heath Hotel.

5B 42 Hagley Country Club
Wassell Grove, Hagley, W Midlands, DY9 9JW
☎ 01562 883701, Fax 887518,
Pro 883852
4 miles S of Birmingham on A456.
Undulating parkland course.
Pro Ian Clark; Founded 1979

18 holes, 6353 yards, S.S.S. 72
† Welcome WD; WE with a member, only.
Ⅰ WD £28.
⚲ Welcome WD by prior arrangement with club manager; packages available; also squash.
◉ Bar and restaurant facilities.

5B 43 Halesowen ☏
The Leasowes, Halesowen, W Midlands, B62 8QF
✉ halesowen.gc@virgin.net
☎ 0121 501 3606, Pro 503 0593
M5 Junction 3; A456 Kidderminster, 2 miles.
Parkland course.
Pro J Nicholas; Founded 1906
18 holes, 5754 yards, S.S.S. 69
† Welcome; WE with member only.
Ⅰ WD/WE £26.
⚲ Welcome by prior arrangement with Sec; packages available for groups of 25 or more; from £18.
◉ Clubhouse facilities except Mon evening.

5B 44 Handsworth
11 Sunningdale Close, Handsworth, Birmingham, W Midlands, B20 1NP
☎ 0121 554 0599, Fax 554 6144, Pro 523 3594
Course is close to either Junction 1 of the M5 or Junction 7 of the M6 off Hamstead Hill.
Parkland course.
Pro Lee Bashford; Founded 1895
18 holes, 6267 yards, S.S.S. 70
Ⅰ Practice range; practice ground; squash; tuition available.
† Welcome WD with handicap certs; guests of members at WE.
Ⅰ WD £35.
⚲ Welcome WD by arrangement; special packages available.
◉ Full clubhouse facilities except Mon during winter times.
↩ Post House.

5B 45 Harborne
40 Tennal Rd, Birmingham, W Midlands, B32 2JE
☎ 0121 4271728, Pro 4273512, Sec 4273058
2 miles SW of city centre adjacent to M5 Junction 3.
Parkland course.
Pro Paul Johnson; Founded 1893
Designed by HS Colt
18 holes, 6235 yards, S.S.S. 70
† Welcome WD.
Ⅰ WD £35; WE £35.

⚲ Welcome by prior arrangement; terms on application; £30.
◉ Clubhouse facilities.

5B 46 Harborne Church Farm
Vicarage Rd, Harborne, Birmingham, B17 0SN
☎ 0121 427 1204
5 miles SW of Birmingham city centre.
Parkland course.
Pro Paul Johnson; Founded 1926
9 holes, 4882 yards, S.S.S. 64
† Welcome with prior booking.
Ⅰ WD £9.50; WE £11.
⚲ Welcome by prior arrangement; terms on application.
◉ Café.

5B 47 Hatchford Brook
Coventry Rd, Sheldon, Birmingham, B26 3PY
☎ 0121 743 9821, Fax 7433420, Sec 7793780
On A45 Birmingham to Coventry road, close to Birmingham airport.
Parkland course.
Pro Mark Hampton; Founded 1969
18 holes, 6120 yards, S.S.S. 69
† Welcome.
Ⅰ WD £9; WE £10.
⚲ Welcome by prior arrangement; terms on application.
◉ Full facilities.
↩ Metropole; Arden Motel.

5B 48 Henbury
Henbury Hill, Westbury-on-Trym, Bristol, Glos, BS10 7QB
☎ 0117 9500044, Fax 9591928, Pro 9502121
Leave M5 J17, 2nd exit from r/bout into Crow Lane; course at top of hill.
Pro Nick Riley; Founded 1891
18 holes, 6007 yards, S.S.S. 70
† Welcome WD with handicap certs.
Ⅰ WD and WE: non-members £25 guests of members £15.
⚲ Welcome Tues and Fri by arrangement. Tuition available; club and trolley hire.
◉ Full facilities.
↩ Many in local area.

5B 49 Henley Golf & CC ☏
Birmingham Rd, Henley in Arden, Warwicks, B95 5QA
🖥 www.henleygcc.co.uk
✉ enquiries@henleygcc.co.uk
☎ 01564 793715, Fax 795794, Pro 796868
On A3400 4 miles N of Stratford-on-Avon.

Parkland course.
Pro Neil Hyde; Founded 1993.
18 holes, 6933 yards, S.S.S. 73
Ⅰ Driving range
† Welcome by prior arrangement.
Ⅰ WD £25; WE £30.
⚲ Full packages available via Pro shop.
◉ Full Country Club facilities.

5B 50 Hereford Municipal
The Racecourse, Holmer Road, Hereford, HR4 9UD
☎ 01432 344376
A49 towards Leominster, in centre of race track.
Public parkland course.
Pro Gary Morgan; Founded 1983
9 holes, 6120 yards, S.S.S. 69
Ⅰ Practice range, practice ground; club hire £2.50; trolley hire £1.20; tuition available.
† Welcome except race days.
Ⅰ 9 holes: WD £4.25, WE £5.25; 18 holes: WE £6.50, WE £8.00; reduced green fees available for juniors and OAPs.
⚲ Welcome by prior arrangement; packages include 18 holes, coffee and 2-course meal; please ring for details.
◉ Bar and restaurant facilities.
↩ Starling Gate; Travel Inn.

5B 51 Herefordshire Golf Club ☏
Ravens Causeway, Wormsley, Hereford, HR4 8LY
🖥 www.herefordshiregolfclub.co.uk
✉ herefordshire@golf.sagehost.co.uk
☎ 01432 830219, Fax 830095, Pro 830465, Rest/Bar 830877
Off Roman Road from Hereford in direction of Weobley.
Parkland course.
Pro D Hemming; Founded 1898
Designed by Major Hutchison
18 holes, 6078 yards, S.S.S. 69
† Welcome WD; WE by arrangement.
Ⅰ WD £20; WE £25.
⚲ Welcome; terms available on application.
◉ Clubhouse facilities.
↩ The Burton Hotel; The Pilgrim Hotel; The Falcon; The Royal Oak.

5B 52 Hill Top Public Golf Course
Park Lane, Handsworth, Birmingham, W Midlands, B21 8LJ
☎ 0121 5544463
From M5 Junction 1 follow signs for Handsworth; 1st left after W Bromwich football ground.
Parkland course.
Pro Kevin Highfield; Founded 1980

18 holes, 6208 yards, S.S.S. 69
† Welcome; advisable to book a tee time.
[WD £9.50; WE £11.
⌁ Welcome WD by prior arrangement with the professional; packages available.
🍴 Full clubhouse facilities.
🛏 Post House, W Bromwich.

5B 53 Hilton Puckrup Hall ☎

Puckrup, Tewkesbury, Glos, GL20 6EL
☎ 01684 296200, Fax 850788
M50 Junction 1 towards Tewkesbury on the A38.
Parkland course.
Pro Kevin Pickett; Founded 1992
Designed by Simon Gidman
18 holes, 6189 yards, S.S.S. 70
] Practice area; tuition available; full leisure facilities (gym, pool, jacuzzi, beauty rooms etc).
† Welcome.
[WD £25; WE and BH £30.
⌁ Welcome by prior arrangement; full day and half-day packages can be arranged; £19.50-£45.
🍴 Full clubhouse facilities; restaurant for 50, licensed bar.
🛏 112-room hotel on site.

5B 54 Ingon Manor Golf & Country Club

Ingon Lane, Snitterfield, Nr Stratford-upon-Avon, Warwicks, CV37 0QE
🖳 www.ingonmanor.co.uk
🖥 info@ingonmanor.co.uk
☎ 01789 731857, Fax 731657,
Pro 731938
Course is signposted from the M40 Junction 15.
Parkland course.
Pro Paul Taylor; Founded 1993
Designed by David Hemstock Associates & Colin Geddes
18 holes, 6623 yards, S.S.S. 71
] Driving range; club; buggy; trolley and shoe hire; tuition for adults and juniors; group tuition available; practice putting green
† Welcome.
[WD £25; WE £30.
⌁ Welcome by prior arrangement; terms on application; packages available.
🍴 Full clubhouse and hotel, restaurant and bar facilities.
🛏 On site Ingon Manor Hotel.

5B 55 The Kendleshire

Henfield Rd, Coalpit Heath, Bristol, Glos, BS36 2UY
🖳 www.kendleshire.co.uk
🖥 info@kendleshire.co.uk
☎ 0117 956 7007, Fax 957 3433,
Pro 956 7000
1 mile from M32.
Parkland course with soft spikes.
Pro Mike Bessell; Founded 1997
Designed by A Stiff/P McEvoy
27 holes, 6507 yards, S.S.S. 71;
Red 3320, Yellow 3324, Blue 3029
] Grass practice range; 6 hole short course; tuition available; childrens club; YMG programmes available; OK Golf Schools; buggies; shoes and clubs for hire
† Welcome WD; WE by arrangement.
[WD £28; WE £36.
⌁ Welcome by prior arrangement; packages on request; function room for 250.
🍴 Bar and restaurant facilities available.
🛏 Post House; Emerson Green Beefeater; Juries.

5B 56 Kenilworth

Crewe Lane, Kenilworth, Warwicks, CV8 2EA
🖳 www.kenilworthgolfclub.co.uk
🖥 secretary@kenilworthgolfclub.co.uk
☎ 01926 854296, Fax 864453,
Pro 512732, Sec 858517
6 miles from Coventry.
Undulating parkland course.
Pro Steve Yates;
Founded 1889/1936
Designed by Hawtree
18 holes, 6400 yards, S.S.S. 71
] 6-hole par 3 course; tuition and golf clinics available; contact pro for details.
† Welcome by arrangement.
[WD £35; WE £45.
⌁ Welcome Wed; packages available; small conferance room; terms on application.
🍴 Clubhouse facilities.
🛏 Chesford Grange; DeMontfort.

5B 57 Kidderminster ☎

Russell Rd, Kidderminster, Worcs, DY10 3HT
🖥 info@kiddigolf.com
☎ 01562 822303, Fax 827866,
Pro 740090
Course signposted off A449 within 1 mile of town centre.
Parkland course.
Pro Nick Underwood; Founded 1909
18 holes, 6405 yards, S.S.S. 71
† Welcome WD only; WE with member.

[WD £30.
⌁ Welcome Thurs by prior arrangement.
🍴 Full facilities except Mon.
🛏 The Gainsborough; Collingdale; Stone Manor.

5B 58 Kings Norton

Brockhill Lane, Weatheroak, Alvechurch, Birmingham, B48 7ED
🖳 www.kingsnortongolfclub.co.uk
🖥 info@kingsnortongolfclub.co.uk
☎ 01564 826706, Fax 826955,
Pro 822635, Sec 826789
1 mile N of M42 J3, just off A435.
Parkland course.
Pro Kevin Hayward; Founded 1892
Designed by F Hawtree & Son
18 holes, 7019 yards, S.S.S. 74
] Practice range, 12-hole par 3 short course, PGA tuition available.
† Welcome WD.
[WD £32.
⌁ Welcome by prior arrangement; full catering and golf packages; separate reception room bar; 100-seater ball room; use of club starter; from £30.
🍴 Full clubhouse facilities.
🛏 Inkford Cottage; Pine Lodge.

5B 59 Kington

Bradnor Hill, Kington, Herefordshire, HR5 3RE
☎ 01544 230340, Fax 340270,
Pro 231320
From A44 take the B4355 Presteigne road for 100 metres and then left to Bradnor Hill.
Mountain links: highest 18-hole course in England.
Pro Andy Gealy; Founded 1925
Designed by CK Hutchinson
18 holes, 5815 yards, S.S.S. 68
] Driving range and practice area.
† Welcome with prior arrangement.
[WD £16; WE £22.
⌁ Welcome by prior arrangement with Pro shop; extensive menu and facilities available; winter packages available; prices on application.
🍴 Full catering and bar facilities.
🛏 The Burton Hotel.

5B 60 Ladbrook Park

Poolhead Lane, Tamworth-in-Arden, Warwicks, B94 5ED
🖥 secretary@ladbrookparkgolfclub.fsnet.co.uk
☎ 01564 742264, Fax 742909,
Pro 742581, Rest/Bar 742220
Take A435 to Tamworth/Portway; left into Penn Lane; then left into Broad Lane and left into Poolhead Lane.

Parkland course.
Pro Richard Mountford;
Founded 1908
Designed by HS Colt
18 holes, 6427 yards, S.S.S. 71
♦ Welcome WD; except Tues am.
╏ WD £28.
♫ Welcome by prior arrangement
with the Secretary; full golfing and
catering packages; terms on
application.
🍽 Restaurant and bar facilities.
🛏 Regency; Plough Inn.

5B 61 Lansdown
Lansdown, Bath, Avon, BA1 9BT
🖧 www.lansdowngolfclub.co.uk
📧 admin@lansdowngolfclub.co.uk
☎ 01225 420242, Fax 339252,
Sec 422138
From M4 J18 take A46 towards Bath;
at r/bout take A420 towards Bristol;
take first left & club is 2 miles on right
Parkland course.
Pro Terry Mercer; Founded 1894
Designed by Harry Colt
18 holes, 6316 yards, S.S.S. 70
♦ Welcome; handicap certs preferred.
╏ WD £23; WE £29.
♫ Welcome by prior arrangement
from £20.
🍽 Clubhouse snacks and meals.

5B 62 Lea Marston Hotel & Leisure Complex
Haunch Lane, Lea Marston, Warwicks,
B76 0BY
🖧 www.leamarstonhotel.co.uk
📧 info@leamarstonhotel.co.uk
☎ 01675 470468, Fax 470871,
Pro 470707
1 mile from M42 Junction 9 on A4097
Kingsbury rd; 1.5 miles from The Belfry.
Parkland course.
Pro Andrew Stokes; Founded 1983
Designed by JR Blake
9 holes, 7750 yards, S.S.S. 30
╏ Practice range, 26 bays floodlit;
golf simulator; tuition available.
♦ Welcome.
╏ WD £4.25; WE £5; discounts for
juniors and OAPs.
♫ Welcome by prior arrangement;
tennis; pool table; health club;
swimming pool.
🍽 Bar and restaurant facilities.
🛏 Lea Marston Hotel on site; golf
breaks call reservations for details.

5B 63 Leamington & County ☎
Golf Lane, Whitnash, Leamington Spa,
Warwicks, CV31 2QA

☎ 01926 425961, Fax 425961,
Pro 428014
6 mins from M40 towards Leamington
Spa and then take Whitnash signs.
Parkland course.
Pro Julian Mellor; Founded 1908
Designed by HS Colt
18 holes, 6410 yards, S.S.S. 71
♦ Welcome with handicap certs.
╏ WD £35; WE £40.
♫ Welcome Mon, Wed, Thurs; full
golf and catering facilities; from £29.
🍽 Clubhouse facilities.
🛏 Marriott Courtyard.

5B 64 Leominster ☎
Ford Bridge, Leominster, Hereford,
HR6 0LE
📧 leominstergolf@freeuk.com
☎ 01568 610055, Fax 610055,
Pro 611402
3 miles S of Leominster on A49.
Undulating parkland course running
alongside River Lugg.
Pro Andrew Ferriday; Founded
1903/67/90
Designed by Bob Sandow
18 holes, 6026 yards, S.S.S. 69
╏ Practice range 18 bays, next door.
♦ Welcome by arrangement.
╏ WD £15.50; WE £22.
♫ Welcome WD except Mon; 36
holes of golf; coffee, light lunch and
3-course dinner; fishing on river also
available; from £30.
🍽 Full bar and bar snacks; restaurant.
🛏 Talbot; Royal Oak.

5B 65 Lickey Hills (Rose Hill)
Lickey Hills, Rednal, Birmingham, W
Midlands, B45 8RR
☎ 0121 453 3159, Rest/Bar 3502
M5 Junction 4 or M42 Junction 1
signposted to Lickey Hills Park.
Public parkland course.
Pro Mark Toombs; Founded 1921
Designed by Carl Bretherton
18 holes, 5835 yards, S.S.S. 68
♦ Welcome.
╏ WD £9.50; WE £11.
♫ Welcome by arrangement.
🍽 Café.
🛏 Rose & Crown, 0121 453 3502.

5B 66 Lilley Brook
Cirencester Rd, Charlton Kings,
Cheltenham, Glos, GL53 8EG
📧 secretary@lilleybrookgc.fsnet.co.uk
☎ 01242 526785, Fax 256880,
Pro 525201, Rest/Bar 580715
2 miles SE of Cheltenham on A435
Cirencester road.

Parkland course.
Pro Karl Hayler; Founded 1922
Designed by MacKenzie
18 holes, 6212 yards, S.S.S. 70
♦ Welcome with handicap certs.
╏ WD £25; WE £30.
♫ Welcome WD by arrangement;
packages available; terms on
application.
🍽 Full clubhouse facilities.
🛏 Cheltenham Park; Charlton Kings.

5B 67 Little Lakes ☎
Lye Head, Rock, Beweley, Worcs,
DY12 2UZ
🖧 www.littlelakesgc.co.uk
📧 marklaing@littlelakesgc.fsnet.co.uk
☎ 01299 266385, Fax 266398,
Rest/Bar 266780
Course is on the A456 2 miles W of
Bewdley; turn left at Banbury Windows
Centre.
Undulating parkland course.
Pro Mark Laing; Founded 1975
Designed by Mark Laing
18 holes, 6278 yards, S.S.S. 70
╏ Practice range, buggies for hire,
tuition and golf clinics available
individually and on a group basis.
♦ Welcome.
╏ WD £17; WE £22.
♫ Welcome by prior arrangement;
packages available; from £28.
🍽 Lunches available.
🛏 Ramada Heath 01299 406421.

5B 68 Lydney
Lakeside Ave, Lydney, Glos,
GL15 5QA
☎ 01594 842614, Sec 843940
Entering Lydney on A48 from
Gloucester turn left at bottom of
Highfield Hill and look for Lakeside Ave
on left.
Parkland course.
Founded 1909
9 holes, 5298 yards, S.S.S. 66
♦ Welcome.
╏ WD £10m day ticket.
♫ Small societies by arrangement;
packages can be arranged.
🍽 By arrangement.
🛏 Speech House.

5B 69 Marriott Forest of Arden ☎
Maxstoke Lane, Meriden, Coventry,
Warwicks, CV7 7HR
☎ 01676 526113, Fax 526125,
Pro 0958632170, Sec 522335
Off A45 close to M42 Junction 6 or M6
South Junction 4.

Championship parkland course; site of English Open 2000.
Pro Kim Thomas; Founded 1970/91
Designed by Donald Steel
18 holes, 7134 yards, S.S.S. 71
⚑ Practice range, 6 undercover bays; teaching facility.
† Residents and visitors welcome.
Ⅰ Terms on application.
⟲ Corporate packages can be booked through golf office; 27 holes, coffee, buffet lunch, dinner, strokesaver and driving range tokens; £135.
🍴 Clubhouse and hotel facilities.
↩ Marriott Forest of Arden.

5B 70 Maxstoke Park
Castle Lane, Coleshill, Warwicks, B46 2RD
📧 sec@maxstokepark.fsnet.co.uk
☎ 01675 466743, Fax 466185, Pro 464915, Sec 466743, Rest/Bar 462158
From M6 take Coleshill road and at high street lights turn towards Nuneaton; on B4114 after 2 miles turn right into Castle Lane.
Parkland course.
Pro Neil McEwan; Founded 1898/45
Designed by Tom Marks
18 holes, 6442 yards, S.S.S. 71
⚑ Practice range; lessons available from Pro.
† Welcome with handicap certs.
Ⅰ WD £25; WE £27.50.
⟲ Welcome Tues and Thurs; packages on application; from £25.
🍴 Clubhouse facilities.
↩ Lea Marston Hotel; Swan Hotel.

5B 71 Memorial Park
Memorial Park Golf Office, Kenilworth Rd, Coventry, W Midlands
☎ 024 76675415
1 mile from the city centre.
Municipal parkland course.
Designed by John Bredemus
18 holes, 2840 yards, S.S.S. 60
† Welcome.
Ⅰ WD £3.45; WE £3.45.
⟲ Welcome; tennis courts; playground; bowling greens.
🍴 Café in park in summer.

5B 72 Minchinhampton ☎
Old Course, Minchinhampton Common, Stroud, Glos, GL6 9AQ
☎ 01453 833866, Pro 833860
Old course is on Minchinhampton Common 3 miles SE of Stroud; New course between Avening and Minchinhampton off B4014.

Parkland course.
Pro C Steele; Founded 1889 (Old); 1975 (New)
Designed by R Wilson (Old); FW Hawtree (New)
Old 18 holes, 6019 yards, S.S.S. 70; New Avening: 18 holes, 6279 yards, S.S.S. 70; Cherington: 18 holes, 6520 yards, S.S.S. 70
† Welcome (Old); Welcome by prior arrangement (New).
Ⅰ WD £12, WE £15 (Old); WD £26, WE £30 (New).
⟲ Welcome by prior arrangement; full range of packages available; terms on application.
🍴 Both clubs provide clubhouse bar and catering facilities.
↩ Amberley Inn; Bear of Rodborough; Burleigh House.

5B 73 Moor Hall ☎
Moor Hall Drive, Sutton Coldfield, W Midlands, B75 6LN
☎ 0121 3086130, Pro 3085106
From M42 take A446 to Bassets Pole roundabout; follow Sutton Coldfield road, at first lights course 200 yards on left.
Parkland course.
Pro Alan Partridge; Founded 1932
18 holes, 6249 yards, S.S.S. 70
† Welcome WD; after 12.30pm Thurs
Ⅰ WD £30.
⟲ Welcome Tues and Wed by prior arrangement.
🍴 Full facilities.
↩ Moor Hall.

5B 74 Moseley ☎
Springfield Rd, Kings Heath, Birmingham, B14 7DX
📧 admin@mosgolf.freeserve.co.uk
☎ 0121 4442115, Fax 4414662
On Birmingham ring road 0.5 miles E of Alcester road.
Parkland course.
Pro Gary Edge; Founded 1892
18 holes, 6300 yards, S.S.S. 70
† Welcome WD with letter of introduction/handicap certs.
Ⅰ WD £37.
⟲ Welcome Wed only by prior arrangement with secretary.
🍴 Full facilities.
↩ The Strathallan; Edgbaston; Oxford Hotel, Mosely; St John's Swallow, Solihull.

5B 75 Naunton Downs ☎
Naunton, Cheltenham, Glos, GL54 3AE
🖥 www.nauntondowns.co.uk

☎ 01451 850090, Fax 850091, Pro 850092
On B4068 Stow-on-the-Wold to Cheltenham road near Naunton.
Downland course.
Pro Nick Ellis; Founded 1993
Designed by Jacob Pott
18 holes, 6078 yards, S.S.S. 69
† Welcome; WE by prior arrangement.
Ⅰ WD £19; WE £27.50.
⟲ Welcome by prior arrangement; new conference room open; three astroturf tennis courts; terms on application.
🍴 Lounge; spike bars; restaurant facilities; limited Mon.
↩ Washbourne Court; The Manor; local hotels in Stow-on-the-Wold.

5B 76 Newbold Comyn
Newbold Terrace East, Leamington Spa, Warwicks, CV32 4EW
☎ 01926 421157
Off B4099 Willes road.
Parkland course.
Pro R Carvell; Founded 1972
18 holes, 6259 yards, S.S.S. 70
† Welcome.
Ⅰ WD £8.75; WE £11.75.
⟲ Welcome by prior arrangement; packages on request.
🍴 Newbold Comyn Arms (next door).

5B 77 North Warwickshire
Hampton Lane, Meriden, W Midlands, CV7 7LL
☎ 01676 522464, Fax 523004, Pro 522259, Sec 522915
Off A45 between Coventry and Birmingham.
Parkland course.
Pro Andrew Bownes; Founded 1894
9 holes, 6390 yards, S.S.S. 71
† WD only by prior arrangement.
Ⅰ WD £20.
⟲ Welcome WD by arrangement; maximum 30 players; meals available in restaurant; terms available on application.
🍴 Restaurant and bar facilities available.
↩ Manor Hotel; Strawberry Bank.

5B 78 North Worcestershire
Frankley Beeches Rd, Northfield, Birmingham, B31 5LP
☎ 0121 475 1026, Fax 476 8681, Pro 475 5721, Sec 475 1047
On A38 from Birmingham.
Parkland course.
Pro Finlay Clark; Founded 1907
Designed by James Braid

18 holes, 5950 yards, S.S.S. 68
♦ Welcome WD.
Ⅰ WD £18.50.
⚹ Welcome Tues and Thurs; terms on application.
🍽 Full facilities available.
⚑ Norwood, Kings Norton.

5B 79 Nuneaton ☎
Golf Drive, Whitestone, Nuneaton, Warwicks, CV11 6QF
☎ 024 7634 7810, Fax 76327563
M6 J3 on A444 2 miles S of Nuneaton.
Wooded undulating meadowland course.
Pro Steve Bainbridge; Founded 1906
18 holes, 6480 yards, S.S.S. 71
♦ Welcome WD; WE with member.
Ⅰ WD £25.
⚹ Welcome by prior arrangement; terms on application.
🍽 Full facilities except Mon.
⚑ Long Shoot; Chase.

5B 80 Oakridge
Arley Lane, Ansley Village, Nuneaton, Warwicks, CV10 9PH
⚏ www.oakridgegolf.fsnet.co.uk
✉ admin@oakridgeglf.fsnet.co.uk
☎ 01676 541389, Fax 542709, Pro 540542
Off B4112 3 miles W of Nuneaton.
Parkland course.
Pro Tony Harper; Founded 1993
18 holes, 6242 yards, S.S.S. 70
♦ Welcome WD; WE with member.
Ⅰ WD £16.
⚹ Welcome Mon-Thurs and Fri am.
🍽 Full meals and bar except Mon.

5B 81 Olton
Mirfield Rd, Solihull, W Midlands, B91 1JH
⚏ www.oltongolf.co.uk
✉ mailbox@oltongolfclub.fsnet.co.uk
☎ 0121 705 1083, Fax 711 2010, Pro, 705 7296, Sec 704 1936
2 miles from M42 Junction 5 on A41 towards Birmingham.
Parkland course.
Pro Charles Haynes; Founded 1893
18 holes, 6623 yards, S.S.S. 71
Ⅰ Driving range.
♦ Welcome by arrangement.
Ⅰ WD only £40.
⚹ Welcome WD by prior arrangement; terms on application.
🍽 Clubhouse facilities.

5B 82 Ombersley
Bishops Wood Road, Lineholt, Ombersley, Droitwich, Worcs, WR9 0LE

⚏ www.ombersleygolfclub.co.uk
✉ g.glenister@ombersleygolfclub.co.uk
☎ 01905 620747, Fax 620047, Rest/Bar 620621
Off A449 Kidderminster to Worcester road at A4025.
Rural parkland setting.
Pro Graham Glenister; Founded 1991
Designed by On Course Design (David Morgan)
18 holes, 6139 yards, S.S.S. 69
Ⅰ Practice range 36 bays (20 covered); chipping green; putting green; tuition available from PGA professionals; custom fit club maker Debbie Hall; open from 5am in summer; buggies and clubs for hire.
♦ Welcome; pay and play.
Ⅰ WD £16.60; WE £23.60.
⚹ Welcome; society and corporate packages; prices on application.
🍽 Restaurant bar terrace.
⚑ Hadley Bowling Green Inn.

5B 83 Painswick ☎
Painswick Beacon, Painswick, Stroud, Glos, GL6 6TL
☎ 01452 812180
On the A46 one mile N of Painswick.
Commonland course.
Founded 1891
18 holes, 4680 yards, S.S.S. 64
Ⅰ Practice range practice ground.
♦ Welcome WD and Sat; with member Sun.
Ⅰ WD £15, Sat £20.
⚹ Welcome by prior arrangement with Sec; special packages.
🍽 Bar and catering facilities.
⚑ The Painswick Hotel.

5B 84 Perdiswell
Bilford Rd, Worcester, Worcs, WR3 8DX
☎ 01905 457189, Fax 756608, Pro 754668
Off main Droitwich road, N of Worcester.
Meadowland course.
Pro Mark Woodward; Founded 1981
18 holes, 5297 yards, S.S.S. 68
Ⅰ Teaching Area; lessons available; leisure centre adjacent to course.
♦ Welcome.
Ⅰ Prices on application.
⚹ Welcome by prior arrangement; catering packages available.
🍽 Bar and snacks.

5B 85 Pitcheroak (Kingfisher)
Plymouth Rd, Redditch, Worcs, B97 4PB

☎ 01527 541054, Sec 01386 793370, Rest/Bar 01527 546063
Signposted from centre of Redditch.
Municipal parkland course.
Pro David Stewart; Founded 1973
18 holes, 4561 yards, S.S.S. 62
Ⅰ Practice range; practice area; putting green; tuition available; hire equipment available.
♦ Welcome.
Ⅰ WD £10.35; WE £11.55.
⚹ Welcome by prior arrangement.
🍽 Licensed clubhouse; bar and restaurant.
⚑ Mont Ville.

5B 86 Purley Chase Golf & Country Club
Ridge Lane, Nr Nuneaton, Warwicks, CV10 0RB
☎ 024 7639 3118, Fax 76398015, Pro 76395348
From A5 Mancetter to Atherstone road; follow signs.
Parkland course.
Pro Gary Carver; Founded 1977
Designed by B Tomlinson
18 holes, 6772 yards, S.S.S. 72
♦ Welcome WD; WE afternoons only.
Ⅰ WD £15; WE £25.
⚹ Welcome WD; various packages available; terms on application.
🍽 Full clubhouse facilities.
⚑ Hanover International; Bosworth Hall.

5B 87 Pype Hayes
Eachelhurst Rd, Walmley, Sutton Coldfield, W Midlands, B76 8EP
☎ 0121 351 1014
Off M6 Junction 6 on to Tyburn Road; 1 mile to Eachelhurst Rd.
Public parkland course.
Pro Jim Bayliss; Founded 1932
18 holes, 5927 yards, S.S.S. 68
♦ Welcome with prior booking.
Ⅰ WD £8.50; WE £9.
⚹ Welcome WD by prior arrangement.
🍽 Cafeteria.
⚑ Pens Hall.

5B 88 Ravenmeadow
Hindlip Lane, Claines, Worcester, Worcs, WR3 8SA
☎ 01905 757525, Fax 458875, Sec 458876, Rest/Bar 458876
4 miles N of Worcester off the A38; J6 M5 Motorway
Parkland course.
Pro Dean Davis; Founded 1996
9 holes, 18 tees, 5435 yards, S.S.S. 66

⌇ Practice range 10 bays floodlit; smart golf simulator; junior academy; adult and junior tuition; 9 hole pitch & putt; practice green; chipping green.
† Welcome.
⌇ 9 holes: WD £8, WE and BH £12; 18 holes: WD £10, WE and BH £15.
⌁ Welcome by prior arrangement; packages available; terms on application.
⦿ Bar and restaurant facilities.
⟼ The Founds; Star.

5B 89 Redditch
Lower Grinsty Lane, Callow Hill, Redditch, Worcs, B97 5JP
⌂ www.redditchgolfclub.com
⌸ redditchgolfclub@btconnect.com
☎ 01527 543309, Fax 547413, Pro 546372, Sec 543079
2 miles W of Redditch.
Parkland course.
Pro David Down; Founded 1913/72
Designed by F Pennink
18 holes, 6671 yards, S.S.S. 72
† Welcome; WE with members.
⌇ WD £35-£45.
⌁ Welcome by prior arrangement; catering packages and reductions available; terms on application.
⦿ Full clubhouse facilities.
⟼ The Quality Hotel; Mont Ville.

5B 90 Robin Hood
St Bernards Rd, Solihull, W Midlands, B92 7DJ
⌸ robin.hood.golf.club@dial.pipex.com
☎ 0121 706 0061, Fax 0061, Pro 0806, Rest/Bar 0159
2 miles S of M42 Junction 4 & 5.
Parkland course.
Pro A J Harvey; Founded 1893
Designed by HS Colt
18 holes, 6635 yards, S.S.S. 72
† Welcome WD.
⌇ WD £30-£35; WE £13 with member.
⌁ Welcome Tue, Thurs, Fri, with handicap certs; packages available; from £40.
⦿ Clubhouse facilities.
⟼ Arden Hotel is local.

5B 91 Ross-on-Wye
Two Park, Gorsley, Ross-on-Wye, Hereford, HR9 7UT
⌂ www.therossonwyegolfclub.co.uk
⌸ secretary@therossonwyegolfclub.co.uk
☎ 01989 720267, Fax 720212, Pro 720439, Rest 770660
5 miles N of Ross-on-Wye; close to M50 Junction 3.
Parkland course.
Pro Nick Catchpole; Founded 1903
Designed by CK Cotton
18 holes, 6451 yards, S.S.S. 73
⌇ Practice range; practice area; tuition.
† Welcome.
⌇ WD/WE £38-£48.
⌁ Welcome Wed, Thurs, Fri; packages available for 20+; deposit required; snooker tables; from £32.
⦿ Clubhouse facilities; bar and restaurant.
⟼ Chase Hotel; Royal Hotel; Chasedale Hotel; Pengethley Manor.

5B 92 Royal Forest Of Dean
Lord's Hill, Coleford, Glos, GL16 8BD
☎ 01594 832583, Fax 832584
4 miles from Monmouth; 8 miles from Ross and Chepstow.
Parkland/meadowland course.
Pro John Hansel; Founded 1973
Designed by John Day of Alphagreen Ltd
18 holes, 5813 yards, S.S.S. 69
† Welcome.
⌇ Winter WD and WE £10; Summer WD and WE £18.
⌁ Welcome by prior arrangement with the hotel; packages available for golf; catering and hotel; tennis; bowls; prices on application.
⦿ Full bar and restaurant service.
⟼ Bells Hotel on site.

5B 93 Rugby
Clifton Rd, Rugby, Warwicks, CV21 3RD
⌸ golf@rugbygc.fsnet.co.uk
☎ 01788 575134, Fax 542306, Pro 575134, Sec 542306
On Rugby-Market Harborough road on right just past railway bridge.
Parkland course.
Pro Nathanial Summers; Founded 1891
18 holes, 5614 yards, S.S.S. 67
⌇ Practice range; practice area; tuition available with two teaching pros; trolleys for hire.
† Welcome WD; WE with a member.
⌇ WD £25; WE £11 with a member .
⌁ Welcome WD by arrangement; packages available; minimum 12.
⦿ Full catering except Sun and Tues.
⟼ Carlton; Grosvenor.

5B 94 Sapey
Upper Sapey, Nr Worcester, Worcs, WR6 6XT
⌂ www.sapeygolf.co.uk
⌸ anybody@sapeygolf.co.uk
☎ 01886 853288, Fax 853485, Pro 853567/853288, Sec 853506
On B4203 between Bromyard and Stourport.
Parkland course.
Pro Chris Knowles; Founded 1990
18 holes, 5935 yards, S.S.S. 68
† Welcome.
⌇ Rowan: WD £18; WE £23. Oaks: WD £4; WE £6.
⌁ Welcome by prior arrangement; terms on application.
⦿ Clubhouse facilities.
⟼ Hundred House; The Granary.

5B 95 Sherdons
Manor Farm, Tredington, Tewkesbury, Glos, GL20 7BP
⌂ www.sherdonsgolf.co.uk
⌸ sherdonsgc@onetel.net.uk
☎ 01684 274782, Fax 275358
2 miles out of Tewkesbury on the A38; turn off at the Odessa Inn.
Parkland course.
Pro Philip Clark/John Parker; Founded 1995
9 holes, 2654 yards, S.S.S. 66
⌇ Practice range 26 floodlit bays.
† Welcome; pay and play.
⌇ 9 holes: WD £7, WE £8; 18 holes: WD £12, WE £15.
⌁ Welcome WD; WE by arrangement.
⦿ Soft drinks, coffee, snacks.
⟼ Gupshill Manor.

5B 96 Shirehampton Park
Park Hill, Shirehampton, Bristol, BS11 0UL
⌸ info@shirehamptonparkgolfclub.co.uk
☎ 0117 982 2083, Fax 982 5280, Pro 982 2488
2 miles from M5 Junction 18 on B4054 through Shirehampton.
Undulating parkland course.
Pro Brent Ellis; Founded 1904
18 holes, 5430 yards, S.S.S. 67
† Welcome.
⌇ WD £18; WE £17 (with member only).
⌁ Welcome; snacks lunch available; dinner by appointment; from £18.
⦿ Clubhouse facilities.

5B 97 Shirley
Stratford Rd, Monkspath, Shirley, Solihull, W Midlands, B90 4EW

☎ 0121 744 6001, Fax 7458220,
Pro 7454979
Towards Birmingham off M42
Junction 4.
Parkland course.
Pro S Botterill; Founded 1956
18 holes, 6507 yards, S.S.S. 71
✝ Welcome WD; with member at
WE.
⌷ WD £25; WE £25.
⌁ Welcome by arrangement;
packages available; terms on
application.
🍴 Restaurant and bar facilities.
💤 Regency Hotel.

5B 98 Shortwood Lodge
Carson's Rd, Mangotsfield, Bristol,
Glos, BS16 9LW
☎ 0117 9565501
From M32 leave at Junction for
Filton/Downend; follow signs for
Downend and Mangotsfield.
Hilly meadowland course.
Pro Craig Trewin; Founded 1975
18 holes, 5290 yards, S.S.S. 66
✝ Welcome.
⌷ WD £13; WE £16.
⌁ Welcome by prior arrangement;
packages available.
🍴 Full clubhouse facilities.
💤 Post House.

5B 99 Sphinx Club
Siddeley Ave, Coventry, Warwicks,
CV3 1FZ
☎ 024 7645 1361
4 miles S of Coventry close to main
Binley Road.
Parkland course.
Founded 1948
9 holes, 4262 yards, S.S.S. 60
✝ Welcome WD; with member at
WE.
⌷ Terms on application.
⌁ Welcome by arrangement.
🍴 Bar and bar meals.

5B 100 Stinchcombe Hill ☛
Stinchcombe Hill, Dursley, Glos,
GL11 6AQ
🖵 www.stinchcombehollgolfclub
.com
📧 stinchcombehill@golfers.net
☎ 01453 542015, Fax 549545,
Pro 543878
From A38 at Dursley; right past
post office.
Downland course.
Pro Paul Bushell;
Founded 1889
Designed by Arthur Hoare
18 holes, 5734 yards, S.S.S. 68

🏌 Practice range, putting green and
practice net, Pro available for tuition.
✝ Welcome.
⌷ WD £24; WE £35.
⌁ Welcome Mon, Wed and Fri;
catering packages available for 10 or
more players; terms on application.
🍴 Full facilities and bar.
💤 Club can provide full list.

5B 101 Stonebridge ☛
Somers Rd, Meriden, Warks, CV7 7PL
☎ 01676 522442
2 miles from M42 Junction 6.
Parkland course.
Pro Steve Harrison; Founded 1995
18 holes, 6240 yards, S.S.S. 70
🏌 Practice range, 21 bays floodlit.
✝ Welcome; bookings taken 9 days
in advance.
⌷ Mon-Thur £14, Fri £15; WE £16.
⌁ Welcome Mon to Thurs by prior
arrangement; from £20.
🍴 2 bars, restaurant and conference
facilities.
💤 Strawberry Bank.

5B 102 Stoneleigh Deer Park
The Old Deer Park, Coventry Rd,
Stoneleigh, Warwicks, CV8 3DR
☎ 0247 663 9991, Fax 765 11533,
Pro 766 39912, Rest/Bar 39331
Off A46 or A454 at Stoneleigh village.
Parkland course.
Pro Matt McGuire; Founded 1991
18 holes, 5846 yards, S.S.S. 68
🏌 Practice area.
✝ Welcome.
⌷ Mon-Thur £20; Fri £22; WE/BH £30.
⌁ Welcome with prior arrangement;
packages available; catering from
8am-9pm; also 9-hole 1251-yard par 3
course.
🍴 Catering and bar facilities.
💤 Club can recommend.

5B 103 Stourbridge
Worcester Lane, Pedmore,
Stourbridge, Glos, DY8 2RB
☎ 01384 393129, Fax 444660,
Pro 393129, Sec 395566
One mile S of Stourbridge on
B4147.
Parkland course.
Pro Mark Male; Founded 1892
18 holes, 6231 yards, S.S.S. 70
✝ Welcome WD; with member WE.
⌷ WD £28.
⌁ Welcome Tues and Thurs;
packages available; from £25.
🍴 Restaurant and bar facilities.
💤 Limes, Pedmore; Travelodge,
Hagley.

5B 104 Stratford Oaks
Bearley Road, Snitterfield,
Stratford-upon-Avon, Warwicks,
CV37 0EZ
🖵 www.stratfordoaks.co.uk
📧 admin@stratfordoaks.co.uk
☎ 01789 731980, Fax 731981,
Dir of Golf 731982, Rest/Bar 731983
On A34 to Stratford following signs to
Snitterfield.
Parkland course.
Pro Andrew Dunbar; Founded 1989
Designed by Howard Swan
18 holes, 6131 yards, S.S.S. 69
🏌 Practice range 12 floodlit covered
bays.
✝ Welcome with booking.
⌷ WD £23; WE £28.
⌁ Welcome WD by arrangement;
catering packages available.
🍴 Bar and restaurant facilities.
💤 Arden Valley; Alveston Manor.

5B 105 Stratford-upon-Avon
Tiddington Rd, Stratford-upon-Avon,
Warwicks, CV37 7BA
☎ 01789 205749, Fax 414909,
Pro 205677, Rest/Bar Bar 297296
Rest 414546
On B4089 0.5 miles from river bridge.
Parkland course.
Pro David Sutherland;
Founded 1894
18 holes, 6303 yards, S.S.S. 70
✝ Welcome WD; WE by prior
arrangement.
⌷ WD £29.50; WE £35.
⌁ Welcome Tues and Thurs by
arrangement; catering packages
available.
🍴 Full bar and catering.
💤 Many in Stratford.

5B 106 Sutton Coldfield
110 Thornhill Rd, Streetly, Sutton
Coldfield, B74 3ER
🖵 www.suttoncoldfieldgc.com
📧 sc.golfclub@virgin.net
☎ 0121 353 9633, Fax 353 5503,
Pro 580 7878, Rest/Bar 353 2014
On B4138 9 miles NE of
Birmingham.
Heathland course.
Pro Jerry Hayes; Founded 1889
Designed by Dr Alister McKenzie.
18 holes, 6541 yards, S.S.S. 71
🏌 Practice area.
✝ Welcome.
⌷ WD £30 round, £40 day; WE £40
round.
⌁ Welcome WD by arrangement.
🍴 Full clubhouse facilities.
💤 Sutton Court; Post House.

Tewkesbury Park Hotel
Golf & Country Club

Lincoln Green Lane, Tewkesbury
Gloucestershire GL20 7DN

Tel: **01684 295405**

Fax: **01684 292386**

Email:
tewkesburypark@corushotels.com

www.corushotels.com/tewkesburypark

Set in 176 acres of parkland, which includes an 18-hole championship golf course, this Victorian Manor House has been tastefully extended to offer superb accommodation, full leisure facilities and exquisite dining. Bedrooms are all en-suite with panoramic views of the Gloucestershire countryside.
A warm welcome is assured at Tewkesbury Park.

5B 107 Tewkesbury Park ☏
Hotel
Lincoln Green Lane, Tewkesbury, Glos, GL20 7DN
☎ 0870 609 6101, Fax 01684 292386, Pro 294892, Sec 299452
0.5 miles S of Tewkesbury on A38; 2 miles from M5 Junction 9.
Parkland course.
Pro Charlie Boast; Founded 1976
Designed by Frank Pennink
18 holes, 6533 yards, S.S.S. 72
⚑ Putting green; practice bunker.
† Welcome.
⌷ WD £15; WE £25 (winter) WD £25; WE £35 (summer).
⌀ Welcome WD; packages available; terms on application.
⍨ Clubhouse & hotel facilities.
⌁ 80-bedroom Tewkesbury Park Hotel on site.

5B 108 Thornbury Golf Centre
Bristol Rd, Thornbury, Avon, BS35 3XL
⌨ www.thornburygc.co.uk
✉ info@thornburygc.co.uk
☎ 01454 281144, Fax 281177, Pro 281155, Rest/Bar 281166
Off A38 at Berkeley Vale Motors; 5 miles from M4/M5.
Parkland course.
Pro Simon Hubbard; Founded 1992
Designed by Hawtree
18 holes, 6257 yards, S.S.S. 69
⚑ Floodlit driving range; 2 piece balls; 18-hole; par 3 course; teaching.
† Welcome; pay and play.
⌷ WD £18; WE £22.50.
⌀ Welcome; packages available; conference and function rooms; terms on application.
⍨ Full catering facilities.
⌁ 11-bedroom lodge on site.

5B 109 Tolladine
The Fairways, Tolladine Rd, Worcester, WR4 9BA
☎ 01905 21974

M5 Junction 6 towards Warndon; club towards Worcester city centre.
Parkland course; steep in parts.
Founded 1898
9 holes, 5432 yards, S.S.S. 67
† Welcome WD except after 4pm Wed; with member at WE.
⌷ WD £10; WE £8.
⌀ Welcome by prior arrangement; terms on application.
⍨ By prior arrangement.

5B 110 Vale ☏
Hill Furze Rd, Bishampton, Pershore, Worcs, WR10 2LZ
⌨ www.crown-golf.co.uk
✉ thevale@btinternet.com
☎ 01386 462781, Fax 462597, Pro 462520
5 miles from Evesham on A44; take Bishampton turn.
Parkland course.
Pro Caroline Griffiths; Founded 1991
Designed by M R M Sandow
18 holes, 7114 yards, S.S.S. 74
⚑ Practice range, 18 bays floodlit; 9-hole par 35 course; tuition available; equipment hire.
† Welcome.
⌷ WD £25; WE £35.
⌀ All welcome; terms on application; corporate packages can be arranged; conference and hospitality suites; terms on application.
⍨ Clubhouse.
⌁ Club can recommend.

5B 111 Walmley
Brooks Rd, Wylde Green, Sutton Coldfield, Warwicks, B72 1HR
☎ 0121 373 0029, Fax 3777272, Pro 3737103
6 miles N of Birmingham.
Parkland course.
Pro Chris Wicketts; Founded 1902
18 holes, 6559 yards, S.S.S. 72

† Welcome WD; with member WE.
⌷ WD £30.
⌀ Welcome WD; discounts available for 30+ players; from £30.
⍨ Clubhouse facilities.
⌁ Penns Hall.

5B 112 Warley
Lightwoods Hill, Smethwick, Warley, W Midlands, B67 5ED
☎ 0121 4292440, Fax 4344430
Off A465 4.5 miles W of Birmingham behind the Cock & Magpie.
Municipal parkland course; part of link card system.
Pro David Owen; Founded 1921
9 holes, 5370 yards, S.S.S. 66
† Welcome.
⌷ WD £8; WE £9; with a link card £1.50 off 18 holes; juniors WD £2-£3.25 WE £2.20-£4; discount with passports to leisure.
⌀ None.
⍨ Café.

5B 113 Warwick
The Racecourse, Warwick, Warwicks, CV34 6HW
☎ 01926 494316
In centre of Warwick racecourse.
Parkland course.
Pro Philip Sharp; Founded 1886
Designed by D.G. Dunkley
9 holes, 5364 yards, S.S.S. 66
⚑ 26 floodlit covered bays.
† Welcome except on race days.
⌷ WD £4.50; WE £5.
⌀ Welcome by arrangement.
⍨ Bar (open from 7pm).
⌁ Tudor House.

5B 114 Warwickshire ☏
Leek Woolton, Warwick, Warwicks, CV35 7QT
⌨ www.clubhaus.com

☎ 01926 409409, Fax 408409
M49 Junction 15 take A46 towards
Coventry; turn at signs for Leek
Wootton on B4115.
Parkland course.
Pro Mark Dulson; Founded 1993
Designed by K Litten
18 holes, 7407 yards, S.S.S. 74
🏌 Practice range, 25 bays, 9
covered.
† Welcome.
Ⅼ Summer: Mon-Thur £39, Fri-Sun
£49; call for winter/special rates
♧ Welcome; minimum 8; packages
available; private function suites;
buggies; coaching clinics; terms on
application.
🍽 Full restaurant and bar facilities.
🛏 De Montford, Kenilworth.

5B 115 **Welcombe Hotel**
Warwick Rd, Stratford-upon-Avon,
Warwicks, CV37 0NR
🖳 www.welcombe.co.uk
✉ sales@welcombe.co.uk
☎ 01789 299012, Fax 262665,
Sec 262665
5 miles from M40 Junction 15; 1.5
miles from Stratford on A439.
Parkland course.
Pro Carl Mason/Karen Thatcher;
Founded 1956/80
Designed by TJ McCauley
18 holes, 6288 yards, S.S.S. 70
† Welcome by prior arrangement.
Ⅼ Summer: WD £40, WE £50;
Winter: WD £25, WE £25.
♧ Welcome; packages available;
discounts available; golf clinics; floodlit
tennis courts; corporate days; snooker;
fitness room; solarium; conference
facilities; terms on application.
🍽 Full clubhouse and hotel facilities
including Trevelyan Restaurant.
🛏 Welcombe Hotel; 63 en-suite
rooms.

West Midlands Golf Club
🖳 www.wmgc.co.uk
☎ 01675 444890, Fax 444890
(See advertisement on page 177)

5B 116 **Westonbirt Girls School**
Tetbury, Glos, GL8 8QG
🖳 www.westonbirt.gloucs.sch.uk
✉ doyle@westonbird.gloucs.sch.uk
☎ 01666 880242, Fax 880364
From A433 Tetbury to Bath road turn
into Westonbirt village; opposite
Arboretum.
Parkland course.
Founded 1934

Designed by Monty Hearn
9 holes, 4504 yards, S.S.S. 61
† Welcome.
Ⅼ WD £10; WE £10 round, £20 day.
♧ None.
🛏 Hare and Hounds.

5B 117 **Wharton Park**   ☂
Long Bank, Bewdley, Worcs, DY12 2QW
🖳 www.whartonpark.co.uk
✉ enquiries@whartonpark,co.uk
☎ 01299 405222, Fax 405121,
Pro 4-5163
On A456 at west end of Bewdley by-
pass.
Parkland course.
Pro Angus Hoare; Founded 1992
18 holes, 6603 yards, S.S.S. 72
🏌 Driving range.
† Welcome.
Ⅼ WD £30; WE £35.
♧ Welcome by prior arrangement;
packages available; terms on
application.
🍽 Clubhouse facilities.
🛏 Heath Hotel.

5B 118 **Whitefields**   ☂
Coventry Rd, Thurlaston, Nr Rugby,
Warwicks, CV23 9JR
☎ 01788 815555, Fax 521695,
Sec 521800
Course is on the A45 close to junction
with the M45.
Parkland course overlooking Draycote
Water.
Founded 1992
Designed by R Mason
18 holes, 6223 yards, S.S.S. 70
🏌 Practice range, 16 bays floodlit;
18-hole putting green; tuition available.
† Welcome by prior arrangement.
Ⅼ WD £18; WE £25.
♧ 3 packages available; terms on
application.
🍽 Hotel facilities.
🛏 Whitefields; 50-room hotel on site.

5B 119 **Widney Manor**
Saintbury Drive, Widney Manor,
Solihull, W Midlands, B91 3SZ
☎ 0121 7113646
Off M42 J4 take Stratford Road and
then turn right into Monkshall Path
Road; signposted for Widney Manor.
Parkland course.
Pro Tim Atkinson; Founded 1993
Designed by Golf Design Group
18 holes, 5001 yards, S.S.S. 64
🏌 Practice range, practice area.
† Welcome.
Ⅼ WD £10; WE £13.50.

♧ Welcome WD but not before 10am
at WE; terms on application.
🍽 Full facilities.

5B 120 **Windmill Village Hotel**
Birmingham Road, Allesley, Coventry,
Warwics, CV5 9AL
🖳 www.windmillvillage.co.uk
✉ leisure@windmillvillagehotel
.co.uk
☎ 024 764 04041, Fax 04042,
Rest/Bar 04040
On A45 westbound Coventry-
Birmingham road.
Part flat part hilly course.
Pro Robert Hunter; Founded 1990
Designed by Robert Hunter.
18 holes, 5169 yards, S.S.S. 68
🏌 Warm-up nets; putting green.
† Welcome.
Ⅼ WD £15.95; WE £17.95.
♧ Welcome by arrangement;
packages available; swimming pool;
tennis courts; gym; sauna; conference
suites.
🍽 Bar and restaurant facilities.
🛏 Windmill Village on site.

5B 121 **Wishaw**
Bulls Lane, Wishaw, W Midlands,
B76 9QW
☎ 0121 313 2110
From the M42 Junction 9 take the
second left at The Belfry to the Cock
at Wishaw; the course 0.75
miles.
Parkland course.
Pro Alan Partridge;
Founded 1993
18 holes, 5729 yards, S.S.S. 68
† Welcome.
Ⅼ WD £12; WE £20.
♧ Welcome WD by arrangement;
packages available; terms on
application.
🍽 Restaurant and bar facilities
available.
🛏 Belfry; Moor Hall.

5B 122 **Woodlands**
Woodlands Lane, Almondsbury, Bristol,
BS32 4JZ
✉ woodlands@tracypark.com
☎ 01454 619319, Fax 619397,
Sec 619319
Off the A38 road at the Aztec
roundabout turning left into Woodlands
Lane.
Parkland course.
Pro Andy Lowen/Nigel Warburton;
Founded 1989
Designed by C Chapman

18 holes, 6068 yards, S.S.S. 69
� Welcome.
£ WD £12; WE £14.
⚬ Welcome by prior arrangement; terms on application.
🍴 Full clubhouse facilities.
🛏 The Range; Stakis.

5B 123 Woodspring Golf and ☏ Country Club

Yanley Lane, Long Ashton, Bristol, Avon, BS18 9LR
🖳 www.woodspring-golf.com
🖳 info@woodspring-golf.com
☎ 01275 394378, Fax 394473
On A38 near Bristol Airport.
Parkland course;
Pro Kevin Pitts; Founded 1994
Designed by P Alliss & C Clark/D Steel
27 holes, 6587 yards, S.S.S. 70
🏌 Practice range, 25 bays floodlit; snooker.
♌ Welcome.
£ WD £28; WE £32. Fairway WD £14; WE £16
⚬ Welcome; catering packages available; contact Kevin Pitts; 3 x 9 courses: Avon, Brunel, Severn; terms on application.
🍴 Full clubhouse facilities.
🛏 Swallow Royal; Redwood Lodge; Town & Country Lodge; Marriott.

5B 124 Worcester Golf & Country Club

Boughton Park, Bransford Road, Worcester, Worcester, WR2 4EZ

☎ 01905 422555, Fax 749090, Pro 422044
From M5 Junction 7 follow signs for Worcester West.
Parkland course.
Pro Colin Colenso; Founded 1898
Designed by Dr A MacKenzie (1926)
18 holes, 6251 yards, S.S.S. 70
♌ Welcome WD; guests of members only at WE.
£ WD £25.
⚬ Welcome with 12 months prior booking; catering and golf packages can be arranged; jacket and tie required in dining room; tennis; squash; from £33.
🍴 Full clubhouse, restaurant and bar facilities.

5B 125 Worcestershire

Wood Farm, Malvern Wells, Worcs, WR14 4PP
🖳 www.theworcestershiregolfclub .co.uk
🖳 secretary @theworcestershiregolfclub.co.uk
☎ 01684 575992, Fax 893334, Pro 564428, Rest/Bar 573905
Course is two miles south of Great Malvern; turn off the A449 on to the B4209.
Parkland course.
Pro Richard Lewis; Founded 1879
Designed by Colt; Mackenzie; Braid amended by Jiggins and Hawtree
18 holes, 6470 yards, S.S.S. 71
♌ Welcome; handicap certs required; no visitors before 10am WE.

£ Prices on application.
⚬ Welcome Thurs and Fri; package includes coffee, light lunch and 3-course dinner; £45.
🍴 Full catering facilities.
🛏 Abbey; Foley; Cottage in the Woods.

5B 126 Wyre Forest

Zortech Avenue, Kidderminster, Worcs, DY11 7EX
🖳 www.wyreforestgolf.co.uk
🖳 simonprice@wyreforestgolf.com
☎ 01299 822682, Fax 879433, Pro 822682 x21
Take A451 towards Stourport and course is signposted.
Parkland course.
Pro Simon Price; Founded 1994
Designed by Golf Design Group
18 holes holes, 5790 yards, S.S.S. 68
🏌 Driving range, buggies and clubs for hire; tuition available.
♌ Welcome.
£ WD £12,50; WE £17.
⚬ Welcome; terms on application; from £21.
🍴 Clubhouse facilities.
🛏 Heath; Gainsborough; Severn Manor.

6A

Shropshire, Staffordshire, Cheshire

Geographically and aesthetically Royal Liverpool sits atop the region. Newly returned to the Open roster the course and the clubhouse are almost ghostly with stories, more and more of which will reappear as the date of "Hoylake's" return approaches.

If Royal Liverpool is Cheshire's greatest course, there are still others worthy of attention. The links of Wallasey, the club associated with Dr Frank Stableford and his scoring system, Wilmslow, where crows used regularly to pick off golf balls over the final holes leading to the club emblem of a crow picking up a ball, Delamere Forest, a club that reviles the gratuitous use of trees to line fairways, and Carden Park, a fully kitted out Nicklaus project, might all win election in another constituency.

Shropshire's greatest claims to fame are probably Sandy Lyle and Ian Woosnam, both of who represented the county before they remembered that they were Scottish and Welsh respectively. Woosie's club was Llanymynech, a course that evokes the blue remembered hills of AE Housman. Constructed high on limestone outcrops Llanymynech offers views for miles around as it leads you back and forth between England and Wales. On the fourth hole the golfer drives off in Wales and holes out in England.

Sandy Lyle was raised at Hawkestone Park where later he became the touring pro. Hawkestone provides the large scale hotel golf experience without being punitively expensive. It has been an inn since 1790 although the first golf course wasn't built until the 1930's and the second added much later.

Bridgnorth is a cheerful club with a course admired by Donald Steel, but Shropshire is not exactly congested with golf. It is astonishing that two such players – Ballesteros rated Lyle as the most talented in the world and the quality of Woosnam's iron play is incontrovertible – should come up through such a relatively minor golfing county at the same time.

Neighbouring Staffordshire has its own claim to fame – aside from the sort of high quality beer that Woosie disposes of by the jugful. Diane Bailey, who grew up at Enville, was the first to captain a winning Curtis Cup team in America and Geoff Marks, a stalwart of Trentham, was the first captain of a winning Walker Cup team in America. Marks did it the hard way in 1989, having to lead his anchor man by the arm to the final tee after watching a six point lunchtime lead all but evaporate in the Georgia heat of the final afternoon singles. Jim Milligan's bogey on the last was enough to secure the half required for victory.

Enville has two courses set in woodland, the Highgate and the Lodge. The Highgate is the better thought of, an interesting contrast between some heathland holes and others dominated by trees. Trentham is a parkland course and neighbour to Trentham Park, David Gilford's old club.

Little Aston is Staffordshire's top course. Set in a pocket of reproduction suburbia it is one of Britain's finest parkland courses, a former deer park and a rare design of the great Harry Vardon.

Elsewhere in the county Beau Desert has been used for Open regional qualifiers. It is a moorland course flanked by heather and fir that requires a few carries from the tee.

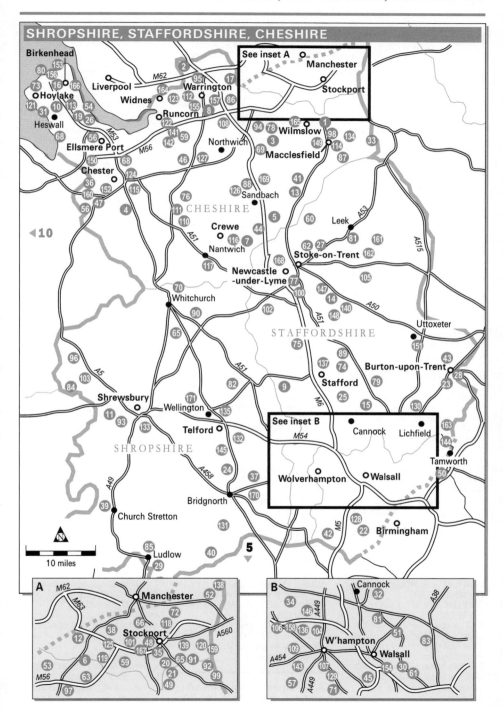

SHROPSHIRE, STAFFORDSHIRE, CHESHIRE

See inset A
Manchester
Stockport

Birkenhead
Liverpool
Widnes
Warrington
Runcorn
Hoylake
Heswall
Ellsmere Port
Chester

Wilmslow
Macclesfield
Northwich
Sandbach
CHESHIRE
Crewe
Nantwich
Leek
Stoke-on-Trent
Newcastle
-under-Lyme
Whitchurch
Uttoxeter
STAFFORDSHIRE
Burton-upon-Trent
Stafford
Shrewsbury
Wellington
Telford
See inset B
Cannock
Lichfield
Tamworth
SHROPSHIRE
Wolverhampton
Walsall
Bridgnorth
Church Stretton
Birmingham
Ludlow

10 miles

A
Manchester
Stockport

B
Cannock
W'hampton
Walsall

KEY					
		35 Cheadle	69 Heyrose	102 Onneley	137 Stafford Castle
1	Adlington Golf Centre	36 Chester	70 Hill Valley Golf & Country	103 Oswestry	138 Stamford (Stalybridge)
2	Alder Root Golf Club	37 Chesterton Valley GC	Club	104 Oxley Park	139 Stockport
3	Alderley Edge	38 Chorlton-cum-Hardy	71 Himley Hall Golf Centre	105 Parkhall	140 Stone
4	Aldersey Green Golf	39 Church Stretton	72 Houldsworth	106 Patshull Park Hotel Golf	141 Styal
	Club	40 Cleobury Mortimer GC	73 Hoylake Municipal	and Country Club	142 Sutton Hall
5	Alsager Golf & Country	41 Congleton	74 Ingestre Park	107 Penn	143 Swindon
	Club	42 Corngreaves	75 Izaak Walton	108 Peover	144 Tamworth Municipal
6	Altrincham	43 The Craythorne	76 Knights Grange Sports	109 Perton Park Golf Club	145 Telford Moat House
7	Alvaston Hall Golf Club	44 Crewe	Complex	110 Portal G & Country Club	146 Three Hammers Golf
8	Antrobus Golf Club	45 Dartmouth	77 Jack Barker's Keele Golf	111 Portal G & Country Club	Complex
9	Aqualate	46 Delamere Forest	Centre	Premier Course	147 Trentham
10	Arrowe Park	47 De Vere Carden Park	78 Knutsford	112 Poulton Park	148 Trentham Park
11	Arscott	Hotel, Golf	79 Lakeside (Rugeley)	113 Prenton	149 The Tytherington
12	Ashton on Mersey	Resort & Spa	80 Leasowe	114 Prestbury	150 Upton-by-Chester
13	Astbury	48 Didsbury	81 Leek	115 Pryors Hayes Golf Club	151 Uttoxeter
14	Barlaston	49 Disley	82 Lilleshall Hall	116 Queen's Park	152 Vicars Cross
15	Beau Desert	50 Drayton Park	83 Little Aston	117 Reaseheath	153 Wallasey
16	Bidston	51 Druids Heath	84 Llanymynech	118 Reddish Vale	154 Walsall
17	Birchwood	52 Dukinfield	85 Ludlow	119 Ringway	155 Walton Hall
18	Bloxwich	53 Dunham Forest Golf &	86 Lymm	120 Romiley	156 Warren
19	Brackenwood	Country Club	87 Macclesfield	121 Royal Liverpool	157 Warrington
20	Bramall	54 Eastham Lodge	88 Malkins Bank	122 Runcorn	158 Wergs
21	Bramhall Park	55 Eaton	89 The Manor Golf Club	123 St Michael Jubilee	159 Werneth Low
22	Brand Hall	56 Ellesmere Port	(Kingstone) Ltd	124 St Thomas's Priory GC	160 Westminster Park
23	Branston Golf & CC	57 Enville	90 Market Drayton	125 Sale	161 Westwood (Leek)
24	Bridgnorth	58 Frodsham	91 Marple	126 Sandbach	162 Whiston Hall
25	Brocton Hall	59 Gatley	92 Mellor & Townscliffe	127 Sandiway	163 Whittington Heath
26	Bromborough	60 Goldenhill	93 Meole Brace	128 Sandwell Park	164 Widnes
27	Burslem	61 Great Barr	94 Mere Golf & CC	129 Sedgley Golf Centre	165 Wilmslow
28	Burton-on-Trent	62 Greenway Hall	95 Mersey Valley	130 Seedy Mill	166 Wirral Ladies
29	Cadmore Lodge	63 Hale	96 Mile End	131 Severn Meadows	167 Withington
30	Calderfields	64 Hawkstone Park Hotel	97 Mobberley	132 Shifnal	168 Wolstanton
31	Caldy	65 Hazel Grove	98 Mottram Hall Hotel	133 Shrewsbury	169 Woodside
32	Cannock Park	66 Heaton Moor	99 New Mills	134 Shrigley Hall Hotel	170 Worfield
33	Chapel-en-le-Frith	67 Helsby	100 Newcastle-under-Lyme	135 The Shropshire	171 Wrekin
34	The Chase	68 Heswall	101 Northenden	136 South Staffordshire	

6A 1 **Adlington Golf Centre**

Sandy Hey Farm, Adlington,
Macclesfield, Cheshire, SK10 4NG
♣ www.adlingtongolfcentre.com
☎ 01625 850660, Fax 856812,
Sec 878468
Course is 1 mile South of Poynton on
the A523 Stockport-Macclesfield road.
Par 3 courses.
Pro John Watson; Founded 1992
Designed by Hawtree
Academy: 9 holes, 635 yards;
Graduate: 9 holes, 1500 yard
✗ Driving range and golf academy.
† Public pay and play.
[Academy £4.50; Graduate £7.50.
◉ Vending machines.

6A 2 **Alder Root Golf Club**　　℡

Alder Root Lane, Winwick, Warrington,
Cheshire, WA2 8RZ
☎ 01925 291919, Fax 291961,
Pro 291932
M62 Junction 9 then N on A49, turn left
at first set of lights; then 1st right into
Alder Root Lane.
Parkland course.
Pro Chris McKevitt; Founded 1993
Designed by Mr EM Millington
9 holes with 18 tees, 5834 yards,
S.S.S. 69

† Welcome by arrangement.
[WD £16; WE £18.
♂ Welcome WD by prior
arrangement; full catering and 27 holes
of golf; from £24.
◉ Bar and snacks.
↩ Winwick Quay.

6A 3 **Alderley Edge**

Brook Lane, Alderley Edge, Cheshire,
SK9 7RU
♣ www.aegc.co.uk
✉ jerry.dickson@breathemail.net.
☎ 01625 585583, Pro 584493
From Alderley Edge turn off A34 to
Mobberley/Knutsford on B5085.
Undulating parkland course.
Pro Peter Bowring; Founded 1907
Designed by TG Renouf
9 holes, 5823 yards, S.S.S. 68
† Welcome with handicap certs;
restrictions WE. Ladies day Tues.
[WD £20; WE £25.
♂ Welcome Thurs by prior
arrangement; from £30.
◉ Full catering except Mon.
↩ De Trafford Arms.

6A 4 **Aldersey Green Golf Club**

Aldersey, Chester, Cheshire, CH3 9EH

☎ 01829 782157, Pro 782157,
Rest/Bar 782453
On A41 Whitchurch road.
Parkland course.
Pro Stephen Bradbury; Founded 1993
18 holes, 6159 yards, S.S.S. 69
† Welcome.
[WD £12; WE £15.
♂ Welcome by prior arrangement; 2
packages available WD; 1 at WE;
terms on application.
◉ Bar and bar meals.
↩ Calverley Arms.

6A 5 **Alsager Golf &**　　℡
Country Club

Audley Road, Alsager, Stoke-on-Trent,
Staffs, ST7 2UR
♣ www.alsagergolfclub.com
✉ business@alsagergolfclub.com
☎ 01270 875700, Fax 882207,
Pro 877432, Sec 875700,
Rest/Bar 875700
Leave M6 Junction 16 taking A500
towards Stoke for 1 mile; first left turn
for Alsager.
Parkland course.
Pro Richard Brown; Founded 1976
18 holes, 6225 yards, S.S.S. 70
† Welcome WD; WE with member.
[WD £25.

⚲ Welcome Mon, Wed and Thurs; 3 packages available for societies; snooker; bowls; from £30.
🍽 Clubhouse facilities; banqueting available.
🛏 Manor Hotel.

6A 6 Altrincham
Stockport Road, Timperley, Altrincham, Cheshire, WA15 7LP
📧 scott-partington@hotmail.com
☎ 0161 9280761, Fax 9288542
On A560 1 mile W of Altincham.
Undulating parkland course.
Pro Scott Partington; Founded 1935
18 holes, 6385 yards, S.S.S. 71
† Welcome; advance booking at all times.
ℓ WD £8.50; WE £11.50.
⚲ Welcome.
🍽 No catering; facilities at adjacent restaurant.
🛏 Cresta Court; Woodlands Park.

6A 7 Alvaston Hall GC ☜
Middlewich Road, Nantwich, Cheshire, CW5 6PD
☎ 01270 628473, Fax 623395/628473, Pro 628473, Sec 629444, Rest/Bar 624341 x269
1 mile from Nantwich on A530 to Middlewich.
Meadowland course.
Pro Kevin Valentine; Founded 1989
Designed by Kevin Valentine
9 holes, 3708 yards, S.S.S. 59
⛳ 16.
† Welcome.
ℓ WD £8; WE £10.
⚲ Welcome WD; terms on application.
🍽 Full facilities.
🛏 Alvaston Hall Hotel.

6A 8 Antrobus Golf Club
Foggs Lane, Antrobus, Northwich, Cheshire, CW9 6JQ
☎ 01925 730890, Fax 730100, Pro 730900, Rest/Bar 730002
From A559 road off M56 Junction 10; take second left after Birch and Bottle; left into Foggs Lane.
Parkland course with water features.
Pro Paul Farrance; Founded 1993
Designed by Mike Slater
18 holes, 6220 yards, S.S.S. 71
⛳ £1 for 30 balls.
† Welcome.
ℓ WD £22; WE £25.
⚲ Welcome every day except Sat; packages available.
🍽 Full clubhouse facilities.

🛏 Park Royal, Stretton; Daresbury Park, Warrington.

6A 9 Aqualate
Stafford Road, Newport, Shropshire, TF10 9JT
☎ 01952 825343
300 yds E of junction of A41 Newport bypass and A518 Newport to Stafford Road.
Heathland course.
Pro K Short; Founded 1995
Designed in house
18 holes, 5659 yards, S.S.S. 67
⛳ 20 bay driving range, floodlit.
† Welcome.
ℓ WD £12; WE £15.
⚲ Welcome by arrangement; terms on application.
🍽 Coffee shop.

6A 10 Arrowe Park
Woodchurch, Birkenhead, Cheshire, CH49 5LW
☎ 0151 6771527, Pro 6771527, Sec 6771527, Rest/Bar 6771527
3 miles from town centre; 1 mile from M53 Junction 3 opposite Landicon Cemetery.
Municipal parkland course.
Pro Colin Disbury;
Founded 1932
27 holes, 6435 yards, S.S.S. 71
† Welcome.
ℓ WD £7.70; WE £7.70; seniors and juniors £3.85.
⚲ Welcome by prior arrangement with club Pro.
🍽 Restaurant facilities.
🛏 The Cherry Tree Hotel.

6A 11 Arscott ☜
Pontesbury, Shropshire, SY5 0XP
🖥 www.arscottgolfclub.co.uk
📧 argoco@tiscali.co.uk
☎ 01743 860114, Fax 860114, Pro 860881, Sec 860114
1 mile past Hanwood on the A488 road from Shrewsbury to Bishops Castle; signposted at Lea Cross.
Parkland course.
Pro G Sadd; Founded 1992
Designed by Martin Hamer
18 holes, 6178 yards, S.S.S. 69
⛳ Practice area.
† Welcome by prior arrangement.
ℓ WD £18; WE £22.
⚲ Welcome WD; packages including golf and catering available; from £20.
🍽 Clubhouse facilities.
🛏 Prince Rupert; Boar's Head.

6A 12 Ashton on Mersey
Church Lane, Sale, Cheshire, M33 5QQ
📧 golf@aomgc.fsnet.co.uk
☎ 0161 976 4390, Pro 973 3727, Sec 976 4390, Rest/Bar 973 3220
2 miles from Sale station.
Parkland course.
Pro Michael Williams; Founded 1897
9 holes, 6115 yards, S.S.S. 71
† Welcome except Tues (Ladies Day); can come after 4pm; also not WE.
ℓ WD £20.50.
⚲ Welcome by arrangement; terms on application.
🍽 Bar snacks and evening meals.
🛏 Mersey Farm Travelodge.

6A 13 Astbury
Peel Lane, Astbury, Nr Congleton, Cheshire, CW12 4RE
☎ 01260 272772, Fax 276420
1 mile S of Congleton off A34.
Parkland course.
Pro Ashley Salt; Founded 1922
18 holes, 6296 yards, S.S.S. 70
† Welcome with handicap certs WD; WE with a member.
ℓ WD £30 (day ticket).
⚲ Thurs only May-October; catering by prior arrangement.
🍽 Facilities available.
🛏 The Edgerton Star (0.5 mile from the golf course).

6A 14 Barlaston
Meaford Road, Stone, Staffs, ST15 8UX
🖥 www.bgc.everplay.net
📧 barlaston.gc@virgin.net
☎ 01782 372867, Fax 372867, Pro 372795
Between M6 Junction 14-15 just off A34 outside Barlaston village.
Picturesque parkland course with water hazards.
Pro Ian Rogers; Founded 1982
Designed by Peter Alliss
18 holes, 5801 yards, S.S.S. 68
⛳ Practice area.
† Welcome midweek; some WE restrictions.
ℓ WD £18; WE £32.
⚲ Welcome WD; packages for golf (maximum 27 holes), catering and prizes available; terms on application.
🍽 Bar and restaurant facilities.
🛏 Moat House; Stakis Grand, both Stoke; Stone House, Stone.

6A 15 Beau Desert
Rugeley Road, Hazel Slade, Cannock, Staffs, WS12 0PJ

☎ 01543 22626, Fax 451137,
Pro 422492, Sec 422626
On A460 between Rugeley and
Cannock near Hednesford.
Heathland course.
Pro Barrie Stevens; Founded 1921
Designed by H Fowler
18 holes, 6310 yards, S.S.S. 71
⌇ 20.
♦ Welcome by arrangement.
╏ WD £40; WE £50.
⌁ Welcome Mon-Thurs by prior
arrangement; packages available; from
£56.
|◉| Facilities available.
⌐ Little Barrow Hotel.

6A 16 **Bidston**　　　　♐

Bidston Link Road, Wallasey,
Merseyside, L46 2HR
☎ 0151 638 3412, Fax 8685
Course is close to J1 on the M53.
Parkland course/links.
Pro Mark Eagles; Founded 1913
18 holes, 6140 yards, S.S.S. 70
⌇ Moreton Hills.
♦ Welcome WD.
╏ WD £18. WE £25.00.
⌁ Welcome by prior arrangement;
packages available; terms on
application.
|◉| Full clubhouse facilities.
⌐ The Bowler Hat; The Leasowe
Castle.

6A 17 **Birchwood**

Kelvin Close, Birchwood, Warrington,
Cheshire, WA3 7PB
⌨ www.virtualgolfclub.com
✉ birchwoodgolfclub.com@
lineone.net
☎ 01925 818819, Fax 822403,
Pro 816574, Rest/Bar 818819
Off M62 at J11 taking A574 road to
Leigh and Science Park North; club
entrance just past Science Park North.
Parkland course; natural water
hazards.
Pro Paul McEwan; Founded 1979
Designed by TJ MacAuley
18 holes, 6727 yards, S.S.S. 73
♦ Welcome; restrictions on
competition days.
╏ WD £26; WE £34.
⌁ Welcome Mon, Wed, Thurs;
packages can be arranged; from £23.
|◉| Full catering facilities.
⌐ Garden Court, Woolston.

6A 18 **Bloxwich**

136 Stafford Road, Bloxwich, Walsall,
W Midlands, WS3 3PQ

✉ bloxwich.golf-club@virgin.net
☎ 01922 476593, Fax 476593,
Pro 476593 x25, Sec 476953 x20
1 mile N of Bloxwich on A34 off M6 at
Junction 10 or 11.
Parkland course.
Pro RJ Dance; Founded 1924
Designed by J Sixsmith
18 holes, 6273 yards, S.S.S. 71
♦ Welcome midweek; members
guests at WE only.
╏ WD £30; WE £35.
⌁ Welcome by prior arrangement;
reductions for groups; packages
available.
|◉| Facilities available.
⌐ Many in local area.

6A 19 **Brackenwood**

Bracken Lane, Bebington, Wirral,
Merseyside, CH63 2LY
☎ 0151 6083093
M53 Junction 4 to Clatterbridge and
Bebington.
Public parkland course.
Pro Kent Lamb; Founded 1933
18 holes, 6285 yards, S.S.S. 70
♦ Welcome.
╏ WD £7.70; WE £7.70.
⌁ Welcome by arrangement.
|◉| Thornton Hall; Village.

6A 20 **Bramall Park**

Manor Road, Bramall, Stockport,
Cheshire, SK7 3LY
✉ secbpgc@hotmail.com
☎ 0161 485 3119, Fax 7101,
Pro 2205, Sec 7101
8 miles S of Manchester (club can
provide directions from M56 and M60).
Parkland course.
Pro M Proffitt; Founded 1894
Designed by J Braid
18 holes, 6224 yards, S.S.S. 70
⌇ Practice ground.
♦ Welcome by arrangement.
╏ Terms on application.
⌁ Welcome Tues and Thurs by prior
arrangement; packages available;
terms on application.
|◉| Clubhouse catering facilities
available.
⌐ County, Bramhall; Belfry,
Handforth.

6A 21 **Bramhall**

Ladythorn Road, Bramhall, Stockport,
Cheshire, SK7 2EY
⌨ www.bramhallgolfclub.com
✉ office@bramhallgolfclub.com
☎ 0161 439 4057, Fax 0264,
Pro 1171, Sec 6092

Off A5102 S of Stockport.
Parkland course.
Pro R Green; Founded 1905
18 holes, 6340 yards, S.S.S. 70
♦ Welcome; restrictions Thurs and
WE.
╏ WD £32; WE £38.
⌁ Welcome on Wed and Fri by prior
arrangement.
|◉| Clubhouse facilities.
⌐ County Hotel, Bramhall.

6A 22 **Brand Hall**

Heron Road, Oldbury, Warley,
W Midlands, B68 8AQ
☎ 0121 5522195, Fax 5445088,
Rest/Bar 5527475
6 miles NW of Birmingham, 1.5 miles
from M5 Junction 2.
Public parkland course.
Pro Carl Yates; Founded 1901
18 holes, 5734 yards, S.S.S. 68
⌇ Practice area.
♦ Welcome; pay and play.
╏ Terms on application.
⌁ Welcome by arrangement.
|◉| Cafe, clubhouse bar.

6A 23 **Branston Golf and**　♐
Country Club

Burton Road, Branston, Burton-on-
Trent, Staffs, DE14 3DP
⌨ www.branston-golf-club.co.uk
✉ info@
branston-golf-club.co.uk
☎ 01283 543207, Fax 566984
On A5121 off A38 at Burton South.
Parkland banks of River Trent; water
on 16 holes.
Pro Richard Odell; Founded 1975
18 holes, 6697 yards, S.S.S. 72;
9 holes, 1856 yards, S.S.S. 30.
⌇ 20.
♦ Welcome WD and afternoons at
WE. March-November soft spikes only.
╏ WD £30; WE £40.
⌁ Welcome by arrangement; terms
on application.
|◉| Full catering facilities.

6A 24 **Bridgnorth**

Stanley Lane, Bridgnorth, Shropshire,
WV16 4SF
⌨ www.bridgnorthgolfclub.co.uk
✉ bridgnorth-golf@supanet.com
☎ 01746 763315, Fax 761381,
Pro 762045, Sec 763315,
Rest/Bar 763315/ 765735
On road to Broseley, 0.5 miles from
Bridgnorth.
Parkland course.
Pro Paul Hinton; Founded 1889
18 holes, 6650 yards, S.S.S. 72
♦ Welcome.

WD £24; WE £30.
Welcome Mon, Tues; Thurs, Fri; reserved tee times and packages available; from £30.
Clubhouse facilities.
Parlours Hall; Falcon; Croft.

6A 25 Brocton Hall
Sawpit Lane, Brocton, Staffs, ST17 0TH
☎ 01785 662627, Fax 661591, Pro 661485, Sec 661901
4 miles S of Stafford off A34.
Parkland course.
Pro Nevil Bland; Founded 1894/1923
Designed by Harry Vardon
18 holes, 6064 yards, S.S.S. 69
† Welcome.
WD £33; WE £40.
Welcome Tues and Thurs by prior arrangement and with handicap certs; packages for golf and catering by prior arrangement.
Full clubhouse bar and restaurant facilities.
Tillington Hall; Garth Hotel, both Stafford.

6A 26 Bromborough
Raby Hall Road, Bromborough, Wirral, Merseyside, CH63 0NW
www.bromborough-golf-club.freeserve.co.uk
sec@bromborough-golf-club.freeserve.co.uk
☎ 0151 334 2155, Fax 334 7300, Pro 334 4499, Rest/Bar 482 8903
Close to M53 Junction 5, 0.75 miles from A41 Birkenhead to Chester road; 0.5 miles from Bromborough station.
Parkland course.
Pro Geoff Berry; Founded 1903
18 holes, 6603 yards, S.S.S. 73
† Welcome WD; by arrangement WE.
WD/WE £40.
Welcome Wed; early booking essential.
Extensive catering and bar facilities.
Thornton Hall; Village.

6A 27 Burslem
Wood Farm, High Lane, Tunstall, Stoke-on-Trent, ST6 7JT
☎ 01782 837006
4 miles N of Hanley.
Parkland course.
Founded 1907
11 holes, 5360 yards, S.S.S. 66
† Welcome WD only by prior arrangement.

Terms on application.
WD by prior arrangement; catering to be arranged with the steward; terms on application.
By arrangement with the steward.

6A 28 Burton-on-Trent
43 Ashby Road East, Burton-on-Trent, Derbys, DE15 0PS
www.burtongolfclub.co.uk
thesecretary@burtongolfclub.co.uk
☎ 01283 544551, Fax 544551, Pro 562240
On A511 3 miles E of Burton-on-Trent.
Undulating parkland course with many trees.
Pro G Stafford; Founded 1894
Designed by HS Colt
18 holes, 6579 yards, S.S.S. 71
† Practice ground.
† Welcome with handicap certs.
WD £28; WE £38.
Welcome WD; catering packages available except Mon; snooker; terms on application.
Full facilities.
Stanhope Arms; Riverside, both Burton-on-Trent; Newton Park, Newton Solney.

6A 29 Cadmore Lodge
Berrington Green, Tenbury Wells, Worcester, Worcs, WR15 8TQ
info@cadmore.demon.uk
☎ 01584 810044
Off A456.
Parkland course with lakes.
Founded 1990
Designed by John Weston
9 holes, 5132 yards, S.S.S. 65
† Welcome.
WD £10; WE £14.
Welcome by prior arrangement; packages can be arranged; bowls; tennis; fishing.
Full facilities.
Hotel on site.

6A 30 Calderfields
Aldridge Road, Walsall, W Midland, WS4 2JS
☎ 01922 632243, Fax 638787, Pro 613675, Sec 640540, Rest/Bar 646888
On A454 off M6 Junctions 7 or 10.
Parkland course with lakes.
Pro David Williams; Founded 1981
Designed by Roy Winter
18 holes, 6509 yards, S.S.S. 71
† 27 floodlit; floodlit bunker and putting green.
† Welcome.

WD £18; WE £18.
Welcome every day; packages available; from £18.
Bar and restaurant facilities.
Boundary; Fairview; County.

6A 31 Caldy
Links Hey Road, Caldy, Wirral, Merseyside, CH48 1NB
www.caldygolfclub.co.uk
☎ 0151 625 5660, Fax 625 7394, Pro 625 1818, Sec 625 5660, Rest/Bar 625 5660
A540 from Chester, turn left from Caldy crossroads.
Heathland/clifftop links.
Pro Kevin Jones; Founded 1907
Designed by James Braid, John Salvesen
18 holes, 6651 yards, S.S.S. 72
† Welcome WD; Tues Ladies Day; WE with a member.
WD £40 all day; £40 one round.
Welcome Thursday by arrangement; winter packages available.
Bar snacks all day; dinner by arrangement.

6A 32 Cannock Park
Stafford Road, Cannock, Staffs, WS11 2AL
☎ 01543 578850, Pro 571091, Sec 572800
Half a mile N of Cannock on A34
Parkland course.
Pro David Dunk; Founded 1990
Designed by John Mainland
18 holes, 5149 yards, S.S.S. 65
† Welcome; telephone in advance.
WD £9; WE £11.
Welcome by prior arrangement; packages available; terms on application.
Cafeteria within leisure complex.
Roman Way; Hollies.

6A 33 Chapel-en-le-Frith
Manchester Road, Chapel-en-le-Frith, High Peak, Derbys, SK23 9UH
www.chapelgolf.co.uk
info@chapelgolf.co.uk
☎ 01298 812118, Fax 813943, Sec 813943
On the road between Whaley Bridge and Chapel.
Parkland course with water hazards.
Pro D Cullen; Founded 1905
18 holes, 6462 yards, S.S.S. 71
† Welcome by prior arrangement.
Terms on application.
Welcome by prior arrangement; 27 holes of golf; coffee and biscuits on

arrival, lunch and 4-course meal; from £39.
🍴 Full clubhouse facilities.

6A 34 **The Chase** ♛
Pottal Pool Road, Penkridge, Stafford, Staffs, ST19 5RN
🖳 www.crown-golf.co.uk
📧 chase-sales@crown-golf.co.uk
☎ 01785 712191, Fax 712692, Sec 712888
Off A34 at Penkridge/Rugeley cross roads; turn to Penkridge and course is 0.75 miles on left; from M6 Junction 12, take A5 towards Telford, then A449 followed by B5102 towards Cannock, turning left in Pottal Pool Rd after Wolgarston School.
Parkland course.
Pro Richard Stockdale; Founded 1995
Designed by John Reynolds
18 holes, 6613 yards, S.S.S. 72
🏌 Practice range, 20 bay, teaching academy, putting green, chipping green.
🚶 Welcome.
£ Mon-Thur £20; Fri-Sun £25.
⛳ Welcome by arrangement; deposit required; discounts for larger groups; video analysis; pacckages tailored to suit.
🍴 Full clubhouse facilities.
🛏 Quality Hotel, Moat House, Acton Trussel.

6A 35 **Cheadle**
Cheadle Road, Cheadle, Cheshire, SK8 1HW
☎ 0161 428 9878, Fax 428 9878, Sec 491 3873, Rest/Bar 491 3873
One and a half miles from M63 Junction 11 follow signs for Cheadle; 1 mile south of Cheadle village.
Undulating parkland course.
Founded 1885
Designed by R Renouf
9 holes, 5006 yards, S.S.S. 65
🚶 Welcome with handicap certs except Tues and Sat.
£ WD £20; WE £25.
⛳ Welcome by prior arrangement Mon, Wed, Thurs, Fri; catering packages can be arranged through the steward; no lunchtime catering on Thurs; snooker; terms available on application.
🍴 Bar and catering facilities, except Thurs.
🛏 Village, Cheadle.

6A 36 **Chester**
Curzon Park North, Chester, Cheshire, CH4 8AR

📧 secretary@chestergolfclub.co.uk
☎ 01244 677760, Fax 676667
1 mile from Chester off the A55 behind Chester racecourse.
Parkland course.
Pro George Parton; Founded 1901
18 holes, 6508 yards, S.S.S. 71
🚶 Welcome by arrangement.
£ WD £30; WE £35.
⛳ Welcome by arrangement.
🍴 Full facilities.
🛏 Many in Chester.

6A 37 **Chesterton Valley Golf Club**
Chesterton, Nr Worfield, Bridgnorth, Shropshire, WV15 5NX
☎ 01746 783682
On B4176 Dudley Telford Road.
Heathland course.
Pro Phil Hinton; Founded 1993
Designed by L Veines & M Davis
18 holes, 5671 yards, S.S.S. 67
🚶 Pay and play.
£ WD £14.50; WE £15.50.
⛳ Welcome by prior arrangement; terms on application.
🛏 The Parlors Hall, Bridgenorth.

6A 38 **Chorlton-cum-Hardy** ♛
Barlow Hall Road, Chorlton-cum-Hardy, Manchester, Lancs, M21 7JJ
🖳 www.chorltoncumhardygolclub.sagenet.co.uk
📧 chorltongolf@hotmail.com
☎ 0161 8813139, Fax 8814532, Pro 8819911, Sec 8815830
4 miles S of Manchester close to A5103/A5145 Junction.
Parkland course.
Pro David Valentine; Founded 1902
18 holes, 5980 yards, S.S.S. 69
🏌 Practice ground.
🚶 Welcome by arrangement.
£ WD £25; WE £30.
⛳ Welcome on Thurs & Fri by prior arrangement; booking form available; terms on application.
🍴 Clubhouse facilities.
🛏 Post House, Britannia, both Northenden.

6A 39 **Church Stretton** ♛
Hunters Moon, Trevor Hill, Church Stretton, Shropshire, SY6 6JH
🖳 www.churchstrettngolfclub.co.uk
📧 secretary@churchstrettongolfclub.co.uk
☎ 01694 722281, Fax 861917, Pro 722281, Sec 860679
From A49 into Church Stretton; right at top of town; first left into Cardingmill

Valley; 100 yards; bear right up Trevor Hill.
Hillside course.
Pro James Townsend; Founded 1898
Designed by James Braid
18 holes, 5020 yards, S.S.S. 65
🚶 Welcome.
£ WD £20; WE £28; winter packages.
⛳ Welcome by arrangement; some WE available; golf and catering packages by arrangement; from £18.
🍴 Clubhouse facilities.
🛏 Longmynd, Church Stretton; Stretton Hall, all Stretton.

6A 40 **Cleobury Mortimer Golf Club** ♛
Wyre Common, Cleobury Mortimer, Kidderminster, Worcs, DY14 8HQ
☎ 01299 271112, Fax 271468, Rest/Bar 271881
2 miles E of Cleobury Mortimer just off A4117; halfway between Kidderminster and Ludlow.
Parkland course.
Pro Jon Jones/Martin Payne; Founded 1993
Designed by EGU
27 holes, 6438 yards, S.S.S. 71
🏌 Practice range; nets; putting green; chipping area; digital golf coaching, please call club for information regarding courses available with the latest technology.
🚶 Welcome by arrangement.
£ WD £20; WE £30 for 18 holes Mon madness offer; Winter £10 unlimited golf; Summer £15 unlimited golf; terms on application.
⛳ Welcome by arrangement; packages involving 18, 27 and 36 holes; catering plus private function room for 90; snooker.
🍴 Spike bar, lounge bar and restaurant facilities.
🛏 Hammond House Hotel.

6A 41 **Congleton**
Biddulph Road, Congleton, Cheshire, CW12 3LZ
📧 congletongolfclub@hotmail.com
☎ 01260 273540, Fax 290902, Pro 273540, Sec 273540, Rest/Bar 273981
1 mile SE of Congleton station on A527; Congleton Biddulph road.
Parkland course.
Pro John Colclough; Founded 1898
9 holes, 5119 yards, S.S.S. 65
🚶 Welcome; Tues Ladies Day.
£ WD £21; WE £31.
⛳ Welcome Mon and Thurs by prior booking.

Stanley Hall Road, Disley, Stockport SK12 2JX

Disley Golf Club established in 1889 at the foot of the Derbyshire hills.
Possibly amongst the most scenic golf courses in England.

Secretary: **01663 764001**   Clubhouse: **01663 762071**
Professional: **01663 762884**   Facsimile: **01663 762678**

🍴 Full facilities except Mon.
🛏 Lion & Swan; Bulls Head.

6A 42 Congreaves
Corngreaves Road, Cradley Heath,
W Midlands, B64 7NL
☎ 01384 567880
2 miles E of Dudley.
Public parkland course.
Pro Carl Yates; Founded 1985
18 holes, 3979 yards, S.S.S. 61
† Welcome.
⌁ Terms on application.
⌂ Welcome by arrangement.
🍴 Full facilities.

6A 43 The Craythorne Golf ♛
Club
Craythorne Road, Stretton, Burton on
Trent, Staffs, DE13 0AZ
🖳 www.craythorne.co.uk
✉ admin@craythorne.co.uk
☎ 01283 564329, Fax 511908,
Pro 533745
300 yards from village after leaving
A38 at Stretton; follow tourist signs.
Parkland course.
Pro S Hadfield; Founded 1974
Designed by Cyril Johnson/AA Wright
18 holes, 5576 yards, S.S.S. 68
⌁ Floodlit driving range.
† Welcome by prior arrangement;
handicap certs required.
⌁ WD £28; WE £34.
⌂ Welcome by prior arrangement;
packages available; terms on
application.
🍴 Full facilities.
🛏 The Brook House.

6A 44 Crewe
Fields Road, Haslington, Crewe,
Cheshire, CW1 5TB
🖳 www.crewegolfclub.co.uk
✉ secretary@crewegolfclub.co.uk
☎ 01270 584099, Fax 256482,
Pro 585032, Rest/Bar 584227
2 m NE of Crewe station off A534.
Parkland course.
Pro David Wheeler; Founded 1911
Designed by James Braid.
18 holes, 6424 yards, S.S.S. 71
† Welcome WD; WE with a member.

⌁ WD £24 round, £30 day.
⌂ Welcome Tues; golf and catering
packages available.
🍴 Clubhouse facilities.
🛏 Hunter Lodge, Crewe Arms.

6A 45 Dartmouth
Dartmouth Golf Club, Vale Street, West
Bromwich, W Midlands, B71 4DW
🖳 www.dartmouth-golf-club.co.uk
☎ 0121 588 2131, Sec 532 4070,
Pro 07889 823549, Rest/Bar 588 5746
1.5 miles from M5/M6 Junction.
Undulating meadowland/parkland
course.
Pro Gary Kilmister; Founded 1910
9 holes (18 tees), 6036 yards, S.S.S. 69
† Welcome WD with handicap certs,
with member only at WE – phone to
book.
⌁ WD £25 (day ticket).
⌂ By arrangement with Sec;
packages available; snooker.
🍴 Full facilities.
🛏 Moat House, Albion.

6A 46 Delamere Forest
Delamere, Northwich, Cheshire,
CW8 2JE
🖳 www.delameregolf.co.uk
✉ delamere@btconnet.com
☎ 01606 883264, Fax 889444,
Pro 883307, Sec 883800
From A556 take B5152 towards
Frodsham; lane to club is 1 mile, next
to Delamere station.
Undulating heathland course.
Pro Ellis Jones; Founded 1910
Designed by Herbert Fowler
18 holes, 6305 yards, S.S.S. 71
† Welcome; restrictions at WE and
bank holidays.
⌁ WD £35 for a round. Day rate £50.
WE £50 a round from 1 Jan 2002.
⌂ Welcome by arrangement.
🍴 Bar snacks; restaurant.
🛏 Hartford Hall; Swan; Willington
Hall, Blue Cap Motel.

6A 47 De Vere Carden Park ♛
Hotel, Golf Resort & Spa
Carden Park, Chester, Cheshire,
CH3 9DQ

🖳 www.devereonline.com
✉ reservations.carden
@devere-hotels.com
☎ 01829 731000, Fax 731032,
Sec 731594, Rest/Bar 731633
On A534 east of Wrexham; 1 and a
half miles from junction with A41.
Parkland course.
Founded 1993
Designed by Course; redesigned
several times
36 holes and a par 3 9-hole course,
Nicklaus course 7010; Cheshire 6800
yards, S.S.S. 72
⌁ Practice range, also 9-hole course
available, par 3 £10; short game
practice area.
† Welcome with handicap certs.
⌁ WD/WE £45 – £65.
⌂ Welcome with handicap certs and
by prior arrangement; packages
available for golf and catering; full first
class hotel leisure and catering
facilities; terms on application.
🍴 Full first class hotel facilities.
🛏 Carden Park Hotel on site .

6A 48 Didsbury ♛
Ford Lane, Northenden, Manchester,
M22 4NQ
🖳 www.didsburygolfclub.com
✉ golf@didsburygolfclub.com
☎ 0161 998 9278, Fax 902 3060,
Pro 998 2811, Rest/Bar 998 2743
6 miles S of Manchester.
Parkland course.
Pro P Barber; Founded 1891
Designed by G Lowe (1891); G
MacKenzie (1921); D Thomas an P
Alliss (1973)
18 holes, 6273 yards, S.S.S. 70
⌁ Driving nets; practice grounds.
† Welcome with handicap certs.
⌁ WD £28; WE £32.
⌂ Welcome Thurs Fri; restricted
availability Mon; catering and golf
packages available minimum 12
maximum 80.
🍴 Full clubhouse facilties.
🛏 Post House; Brittania, Northend.

6A 49 Disley ♛
Stanley Hall Lane, Jackson's Edge,
Disley, Stockport, Cheshire, SK12 2JX

☎ 01663 762071, Fax 762678,
Pro 762884, Sec 764001
Off A6 in Disley village.
Open hillside/parkland course.
Pro Andrew Esplin; Founded 1889
Designed by James Braid
18 holes, 6015 yards, S.S.S. 69
† Welcome WD by prior
arrangement.
Ⅰ WD £25.
♂ Welcome WD by prior
arrangement; catering and golf
packages available; from £35.
⦾ Clubhouse facilities.
⛴ Stakis Moorside.

6A 50 Drayton Park
Drayton Park Golf Club Ltd, Drayton
Manor Drive, Tamworth, Staffs, B78 3TN
☎ 01827 251139, Fax 284035,
Pro 251478, Rest/Bar 287481
On A4091 at Drayton Leisure Park.
Parkland course.
Pro MW Passmore; Founded 1897
Designed by James Braid.
18 holes, 6401 yards, S.S.S. 71
† Welcome weekdays, except
Wednesday.
Ⅰ WD £38.
♂ Welcome Tues and Thurs
throughout the year by prior
arrangement with Secretary, minimum
of 12 players; catering packages can
be arranged; from £38.
⦾ Full facilities available.
⛴ Beefeater, Tamworth; Drayton
Court, Fazeley.

6A 51 Druids Heath
Stonnall Road, Walsall, W Midlands,
WS9 8JZ
☎ 01922 455595, Fax 452887,
Pro 459523
Off A452 6 miles NW of Sutton
Coldfield.
Undulating course.
Pro Glenn Williams; Founded 1973
18 holes, 6661 yards, S.S.S. 73
Ⅰ Practice area and net.
† Welcome WD and after 2pm on WE.
Ⅰ WD £30; WE £38.
♂ WD by prior arrangement.
⦾ By prior arrangement.
⛴ Barons Court; Fairlawns.

6A 52 Dukinfield
Yew Tree Lane, Dukinfield, Cheshire,
SK16 5DB
⛚ www.dukinfieldgolfclub.co.uk
✉ dgclub@tiscali.co.uk
☎ 0161 338 2340, Fax 303 0205,
Sec 368 6457

From Ashton Road 1 mile then right
into Yew Tree Lane; club 1 mile on
right on hill behind Senior Service
factory.
Hillside course.
Pro Andrew Jowett; Founded 1913
18 holes, 5338 yards, S.S.S. 66
† Welcome WD by prior
arrangement.
Ⅰ WD £18.50.
♂ Welcome by prior arrangement
with Sec.
⦾ Full clubhouse facilities except Mon.
⛴ Village, Hyde.

6A 53 Dunham Forest Golf & ♋ Country Club
Oldfield Lane, Altrincham, Cheshire,
WA14 4TY
✉ email@dunhamforestgolfclub.com
☎ 0161 9282605, Fax 9298975,
Pro 9282727
2 miles N of M56 Junction 7 towards
Manchester and course on left.
Woodland course.
Pro Ian Wrigley; Founded 1961
18 holes, 6636 yards, S.S.S. 72
Ⅰ Practice range.
† Welcome.
Ⅰ WD £40; WE £50. Out of season
WD:30. WE:35.
♂ Welcome WD except Wed;
discounts for groups of more than 20;
winter packages available.
⦾ Bar and restaurant facilities
available.
⛴ Quality; Cresta Court; Marriott.

6A 54 Eastham Lodge ♋
117 Ferry Road, Eastham, Wirral,
Merseyside, CH62 0AP
⛚ www.ukgolfer.org/clubs
/easthamlodge_m.html
✉ easthamlodge@ukgolfer.org
☎ 0151 327 3003, Fax 7574,
Pro 3008, Rest/Bar 1483
M53 Junction 5 to A41; follow signs for
Eastham Country Park.
Parkland course; was Port Sunlight GC
from 1932-76.
Pro Nick Sargent; Founded 1976
Designed by Hawtree & Sons, and
David Hemstock
18 holes, 5706 yards, S.S.S. 68
Ⅰ Port Sunlight Driving Range.
† Welcome WD; with a member only
at WE.
Ⅰ £23.50.
♂ Welcome Tues by prior
arrangement; some Mon and Fri dates
available; golf and catering packages
available. Other days by arrangement
with secretary.

⦾ Full clubhouse bar and catering
facilities.
⛴ Village Hotel & Leisure Centre.

6A 55 Eaton
Guy Lane, Waverton, Chester,
Cheshire, CH3 7PH
⛚ www.eatongolfclub.co.uk
✉ office@eatongolfclub.co.uk
☎ 01244 335885, Fax 335782, Pro
335826
3 miles SE of Chester off the A41
through the village of Waverton.
Parkland course.
Pro Bill Tye; Founded 1965
Designed by Donald Steel
18 holes, 6562 yards, S.S.S. 71
Ⅰ Practice range.
† Welcome with handicap certs.
Ⅰ WD £35; WE £45.
♂ Welcome WD except Wed by prior
arrangement; full golf and catering
packages available; from £25.
⦾ Full clubhouse facilities available.
⛴ Rowton Hall.

6A 56 Ellesmere Port
Chester Road, Childer Thornton,
Ellesmere Port, Merseyside, CH66 1QH
☎ 0151 3397689
On M53 W to A41 turn S to Chester for
2 miles; club at rear of St Paul's
Church, Hooton.
Municipal parkland/meadowland
course.
Pro Anthony Roberts; Founded 1971
Designed by Cotton, Pennink, Lawrie
& Partners
18 holes, 6432 yards, S.S.S. 71
† Welcome.
Ⅰ WD £6.70; WE £7.40; concessions
apply.
♂ Welcome with booking fee of
£1.40 per head; winter packages
available.
⦾ Full bar and restaurant.
⛴ Brook Meadow; Chimney; Village.

6A 57 Enville
Highgate Common, Enville,
Stourbridge, W Midlands, DY7 5BN
⛚ www.envillegolfclub.com
✉ secretary@envillegolfclub.com
☎ 01384 872074, Fax 873396, Pro
872585, Sec 872074, Rest/Bar 872551
6 miles W of Stourbridge on the A458
to Bridgnorth.
Woodland/heathland course.
Pro Sean Power; Founded 1935
18 holes, 6275 yards, S.S.S. 72:70
Ⅰ Practice ground.
† Welcome WD only.

[WD £30 (18 holes).
⌒ Welcome by prior arrangement and payment of £10 per player deposit; min. 12 players; 10 per cent reduction for 30 or more; terms on application.
|●| Full clubhouse catering.
⌐ The Anchor Inn, The Blakelands at Bobbington.

6A 58 Frodsham ☏
Simons Lane, Frodsham, Cheshire, WA6 6HE
🖥 www.frodshamgolfclub.co.uk
✉ office@frodshamgolfclub.co.uk
☎ 01928 732159, Fax 734070, Pro 739442
Close to M56 Junction 12; turn left at lights in Frodsham centre on to B5152.
Parkland course.
Pro Graham Tonge; Founded 1990
Designed by John Day
18 holes, 6298 yards, S.S.S. 70
† Welcome WD except for competition days; tee times booked through the shop.
[WD £36.
⌒ Welcome WD by prior arrangement with golf office; packages available; terms on application.
|●| Full bar and catering facilities available.
⌐ Forest Hills.

6A 59 Gatley
Waterfall Farm, Styal Road, Heald Green, Cheadle, Cheshire, SK8 3TW
☎ 0161 4372091, Pro 4362830, Rest/Bar 4372091
Off Yew Tree Grove and Styal Road, 2 miles from Cheadle and 1 mile from Manchester Airport.
Parkland course.
Pro James Hopley; Founded 1912
9 holes, 5934 yards, S.S.S. 68
† Welcome except Tues and Wed.
[Terms on application.
⌒ Welcome by prior arrangement with Sec or Pro.
|●| Full facilities except Mon.
⌐ Pymgate Lodge, Travel Inn at Heald Green.

6A 60 Goldenhill
Mobberley Road, Stoke On Trent, Staffs, ST6 5SS
☎ 01782 234200, Fax 234303
On A50 between Tunstall and Kidsgrove.
Parkland/meadowland course in old mine basin.
Founded 1983
18 holes, 5957 yards, S.S.S. 69

Ⅱ Practice range, practice ground; putting green.
† Welcome; booking system available.
[WD £7.00; WE £7.50.
⌒ Welcome by arrangement.
|●| Bar and restaurant.

6A 61 Great Barr
Chapel Lane, Great Barr, Birmingham, W Midlands, B43 7BA
☎ 0121 3571232, Pro 3575270, Sec 3584376
Close to M6 Junction 7, 6 miles NW of Birmingham.
Parkland course.
Pro Richard Spragg; Founded 1961
Designed by J Hamilton Stutt
18 holes, 6523 yards, S.S.S. 71
† Welcome WD.
[WD £30, £36 for the day.
⌒ Welcome Tues and Thurs by prior arrangement.
|●| Full clubhouse facilities.
⌐ Post House, The Holiday Inn.

6A 62 Greenway Hall
Stanley Road, Stockton Brook, Stoke on Trent, Staffs, ST9 9LJ
☎ 01782 503158, Fax 504259
Off A53 Stoke-Leek road at Stockton Brook.
Parkland course/heathland.
Pro Mark Armitage; Founded 1909
18 holes, 5681 yards, S.S.S. 67
† Welcome.
[WD £10; WE £12.50.
⌒ Welcome by prior arrangement; packages available; terms on application.
|●| Clubhouse facilities.
⌐ Moat House, Quality Inn.

6A 63 Hale
Rappax Road, Hale, Altrincham, Cheshire, WA15 0NU
☎ 0161 9804225, Pro 9040835
2 miles SE of Altrincham; near Altrincham Priory.
Parkland course.
Pro Alec Bickerdike; Founded 1903
9 holes, 5780 yards, S.S.S. 68
Ⅱ Practice ground.
† Welcome WD except Thurs; with member only at WE.
[WD £30.
⌒ Welcome by prior arrangement; catering available for coffee and lunch; evening meals by prior arrangement with the steward.
|●| Clubhouse facilities.
⌐ Four Seasons, Manchester Airport.

6A 64 Hawkstone Park ☏
Weston-under-Redcastle, Shrewsbury, Shropshire, SY4 5UY
🖥 www.hawkstone.co.uk
✉ info@hawkstone.co.uk
☎ 01939 200611, Fax 200311
Off A49 12 miles N of Shrewsbury or A442 12 miles N of Telford.
Parkland course.
Pro Stuart Leech; Founded 1920
Two 18-hole and one 6-hole course, 6491/6476 yards, S.S.S. 72/72
Ⅱ Practice range, 15 bays; also 6-hole par 3 academy course; putting and pitching green.
† Welcome with prior booking; handicap certs required.
[WD £34; WE £44.
⌒ Welcome by prior arrangement with Reservations office; terms on application.
|●| Full bar and restaurant facilities.
⌐ Hawkstone Park on site; golfing breaks available.

6A 65 Hazel Grove
Occupiers Lane, Buxton Road, Hazel Grove, Stockport, Cheshire, SK7 6LU
☎ 0161 4833978, Pro 4837272, Rest/Bar 4833217 Club house/ 4874399 catering
Off A6 Stockport-Buxton road.
Parkland course.
Pro Malcolm Hill; Founded 1913
18 holes, 6263 yards, S.S.S. 71
† Welcome by prior arrangement.
[WD £30; WE £35.
⌒ Welcome Thurs and Fri by prior arrangement; package includes full day of golf and catering; £38.
|●| Full clubhouse bar and restaurant facilities.

6A 66 Heaton Moor Golf Club ☏
Mauldeth Road, Stockport, Cheshire, SK4 3NX
✉ hmgc@ukgateway.net
☎ 0161 4322134, Pro 4320846
From M60 Junction 1 follow Didsbury signs and Mauldeth Rd is 1.5 miles on right.
Flat, tree-lined parkland course.
Pro Simon Marsh;
Founded 1892
18 holes, 5968 yards, S.S.S. 69
† Welcome by prior arrangement.
[Terms on application.
⌒ Welcome by prior arrangement; Thurs and Fri preferred; golf and catering packages available; from £33.
|●| Full clubhouse facilities.
⌐ Rudyard, Heaton Chapel.

6A 67 **Helsby**

Towers Lane, Helsby, Frodsham,
Cheshire, WA6 0JB
✉ secathgc@aol.com
☎ 01928 722021, Fax 725384,
Pro 725457, Sec 722021
From M56 Junction 14; follow sign to
Helsby and then right into Primrose
lane, first right into Towers Lane.
Parkland course.
Pro M Jones; Founded 1901
Designed by James Braid
18 holes, 6229 yards, S.S.S. 70
⌁ Driving range.
† Welcome WD.
☒ WD £25; WE £34.
⌁ Welcome Tues and Thurs; other
days possible by arrangement;
packages include full day's golf (£25
for 27 holes) and catering.
🍽 Full clubhouse facilities available.

6A 68 **Heswall**

Cottage Lane, Wirral, Merseyside,
CH60 8PB
⌨ www.heswallgolfclub.com
✉ dawn@heswallgolfclub.com
☎ 0151 3421237, Pro 3427431
M53 Junction 4; from roundabout, turn
into Well Lane; leads into Cottage
Lane.
Parkland course.
Pro Alan Thompson; Founded 1902
18 holes, 6554 yards, S.S.S. 72
† Welcome except Tues.
☒ WD £35; WE £40.
⌁ Welcome Wed and Fri only; winter
packages available.
🍽 Full facilities.
◄ Mollington Banastre; Thornton
Hall; Parkgate; Travelodge (Gayton);
Woodhey; Ship Hotel, Parkgate.

6A 69 **Heyrose**

Budworth Road, Tabley, Knutsford,
Cheshire, WA16 0HZ
⌨ www.heyrosegoldclub.com
✉ info@heyrosegolfclub.com
☎ 01565 733664, Fax 734578,
Pro 734267
4 miles W of Knutsford 0.5 miles along
Budworth Road off Pickmere Lane; M6
Junction 19, 1 mile.
Parkland course with ancient woodland.
Pro Colin Hiddon; Founded 1990
Designed by CN Bridge
18 holes, 6499 yards, S.S.S. 71
⌁ Putting green; driving range; swing
room.
† Welcome except before 3pm on Sat.
☒ WD £25; WE £30.
⌁ Welcome WD by prior
arrangement; from £22.50.

🍽 Clubhouse bar and restaurant.
◄ Cottons, Knutsford; Swan, Bucklow
Hill; Old Vicarage, Tabley; Travelodge,
Tabley.

6A 70 **Hill Valley Golf & Country Club**

Terrick, Whitchurch, Shropshire, SY13
4JZ
⌨ www.hill-valley.co.uk
✉ reception@hill-valley.co.uk
☎ 01948 663584, Fax 665927,
Pro 663032
Off A49/A41 Whitchurch by-pass.
Undulating parkland course.
Pro Tony Minshall; Founded 1975
Designed by P Alliss & D Thomas
36 holes, S.S.S. 73
† Welcome.
☒ WD on application.
⌁ Welcome by prior arrangement;
packages available; also East course,
5280 yards, par 66; health and leisure
centre; snooker.
🍽 Full clubhouse facilities.
◄ Motel accommodation at club;
Dodington Lodge; Terrick Hall.

6A 71 **Himley Hall Golf Centre**

Himley Park, Himley, Dudley,
W Midlands, DY3 4DF
☎ 01902 895207
From A449 Wolverhampton-
Kidderminster road to Dudley on
B4176; then into Himley Hall Park.
Public parkland course.
Pro Jeremy Nicholls; Founded 1980
Designed by DA Baker
9 holes, 6215 yards, S.S.S. 70
† Welcome.
☒ WD £6.00; WE £6.50/£9.50 Winter
prices.
⌁ Welcome by arrangement.
🍽 Cafe and hot meals.
◄ Himley House; Park Hall.

6A 72 **Houldsworth** ☎

Houldsworth Street, Stockport,
Cheshire, SK5 6BN
☎ 0161 442 1712, Fax 947 9678,
Pro 442 1714, Rest/Bar 442 9611
From M60 Junction 24 turn left up to
roundabout then take road to Reddish;
turn left at Houldsworth pub.
Parkland course.
Pro David Naylor; Founded 1910
Designed by TG Renouf
18 holes, 6247 yards, S.S.S. 69
⌁ 1.
† Welcome WD (Ladies Day Tues).
☒ WD £24; WE £30.
⌁ Welcome by prior arrangement.

🍽 Full facilities.
◄ Bredbury Hall, Bredbury Travel
Lodge, Denton; Holiday Inn Express,
Colton.

6A 73 **Hoylake Municipal**

Carr Lane, Hoylake, Wirral,
Merseyside, CH47 4BG
⌨ www.hoylake-golf.org.uk
☎ 0151 632 2956,
Rest/Bar 6326357
Off M53 10 miles SW of Liverpool
following signs for Hoylake; 100 yards
beyond Hoylake station.
Municipal parkland course.
Pro Simon Hooton; Founded 1933
Designed by James Braid
18 holes, 6321 yards, S.S.S. 70
† Welcome; book in advance at WE;
Sat from 8.30am.
☒ WD £6.50; WE £6.50.
⌁ Welcome by prior arrangement;
after 1.30pm at WE.
🍽 Hot snacks, meals and bar.
◄ Green Lodge.

6A 74 **Ingestre Park** ☎

Ingestre, Stafford, Staffs, ST18 0RE
✉ ipgc@lineone.net
☎ 01889 270845, Fax 271434,
Pro 270304, Rest/Bar 270061
Course is six miles E of Stafford off the
A51 via Great Haywood and Tixall.
Parkland course in former estate of
Earl of Shrewsbury.
Pro D Scullion; Founded 1977
Designed by Hawtree & Son
18 holes, 6352 yards, S.S.S. 71
⌁ Practice area.
† Welcome WD with handicap certs;
with member at WE.
☒ WD £25.
⌁ Welcome WD except Wed with
prior arrangement; special packages
available for 15 or more; snooker
room; lounge; from £36.
🍽 Bar and restaurant facilities
available.
◄ Garth, Tillington Hall, both
Stafford.

6A 75 **Izaak Walton**

Norton Bridge, Stone, Staffs, ST15 0NS
☎ 01785 760900
On B5026 between Stone and
Eccleshall.
Parkland course.
Pro Julie Brown; Founded 1992
Designed by Mike Lowe
18 holes, 6281 yards, S.S.S. 72
† Welcome.
☒ WD £15; WE £20.

♿ Welcome by prior arrangement; packages for catering and golf available; full facilities; terms on application.
🍽 Full clubhouse facilities.
🛏 Stone House, Stone.

6A 76 Jack Barker's Keele Golf Centre

Keele Rd, Newcastle, Staffs, ST5 5AB
🖧 www.jackbarker.com
☎ 01782 672596, Fax 714555, Rest/Bar 672182
Off M6 J5, on A525 for 2 miles.
Public parkland course.
Pro Colin Smith; Founded 1975
18 holes, 6396 yards, S.S.S. 72
🏌 Practice range, 26 bays floodlit.
† Welcome; book any time.
⌊ Terms on application.
♿ Always welcome.
🍽 Bar and meals.
🛏 Keele Hospitality Inn.

6A 77 Knights Grange Sports Complex

Grange Lane, Winsford, Cheshire, CW7 2PT
✉ knightsgrangewinsford@royalmail.co.uk
☎ 01606 552780
Course in centre of Winsford.
Public meadowland course.
Pro Graham Moore; Founded 1983
18 holes, 6010 yards, S.S.S. 67
🏌 Practice area; tennis; bowls.
† Welcome.
⌊ WD £5.50 WE £6.50 concs. apply.
♿ Welcome by prior arrangement in writing.
🍽 Hot drinks and snacks.

6A 78 Knutsford

Mereheath Lane, Knutsford, Cheshire, WA16 6HS
☎ 01565 633355, Pro 633355
2 miles from M6 Junction 19; make for Knutsford entrance to Tatton Park.
Parkland course.
Founded 1891
10 holes, 6203 yards, S.S.S. 70
† Welcome with prior reservation except Wed, Sat, Sun before 10am.
⌊ WD £25.; WE £30.
♿ Welcome Thurs by prior arrangement.
🍽 Full facilities.
🛏 Angel; Cottons; Swan.

6A 79 Lakeside

Rugeley Power Station, Rugeley, Staffs, WS15 1PR

☎ 01889 575667
Between Lichfield and Stafford.
Parkland course.
Founded 1969
18 holes, 5686 yards, S.S.S. 69
† Welcome with a member.
⌊ WD on application.
♿ By appointment.
🍽 Evening service.

6A 80 Leasowe

Leasowe Road, Moreton, Wirral, Merseyside, CH46 3RD
☎ 0151 677 5852, Fax 641 8915, Pro 678 5460
Off M53 1 mile after tunnel; 1 mile W of Wallasey village.
Links course.
Pro Andrew Ayre; Founded 1891
Designed by John Bull Jnr
18 holes, 6263 yards, S.S.S. 70
🏌 Practice area.
† Welcome WD; WE by prior arrangement.
⌊ WD £25.50 WE £30.50.
♿ Welcome by arrangement; minimum 12 players; not Sat.
🍽 Restaurant, bar and snacks.
🛏 Leasowe Castle.

6A 81 Leek

Cheddleton Rd, Leek, Staffs, ST13 5RE
☎ 01538 384779, Fax 384535, Pro 384767, Rest/Bar 381983
On A520 0.75 miles S of Leek.
Parkland course.
Pro Ian Benson; Founded 1892
18 holes, 6240 yards, S.S.S. 70
🏌 Practice facilities.
† Welcome with handicap certs.
⌊ WD £26; WE £32.
♿ Welcome Wed; golf and catering packages available. contact secretary.
🍽 Full clubhouse facilities.
🛏 Three Horse Shoes at Blackshaw Moor near Leek.

6A 82 Lilleshall Hall

Lilleshall Hall Drive, Lilleshall, Newport, Shropshire, TF10 9AS
☎ 01952 604776, Fax 604776, Pro 604104, Rest/Bar 603840
Between A41 and A5 at Sherrifhales.
Parkland course.
Pro S McKane; Founded 1937
Designed by HS Colt
18 holes, 5789 yards, S.S.S. 68
† Welcome WD/WE with a member.
⌊ WD £20; WE £15.
♿ Welcome WD by prior arrangement; terms on application.
🍽 Clubhouse facilities.

6A 83 Little Aston

Roman Road, Sutton Coldfield, W Midlands, B74 3AN
🖧 www.littleastongolf.co.uk
✉ manager@littleastongolf.co.uk
☎ 0121 353 2942, Fax 580 8387, Pro 353 0330, Rest/Bar 353 2066
4 miles NW of Sutton Coldfield off A454.
Parkland course.
Pro Brian Rimmer; Founded 1908
Designed by Harry Vardon
18 holes, 6670 yards, S.S.S. 73
† Welcome by arrangement.
⌊ Terms on application; round £60, day £75.
♿ Welcome Mon, Tues, Wed and Fri by prior arrangement; catering and golf packages available.
🍽 Full clubhouse.

6A 84 Llanymynech

Pant, Oswestry, Shropshire, SY10 8LB
🖧 www.llanymynechgolfclub.co.uk
☎ 01691 830542, Pro 830879, Sec 830983
6 miles S of Oswestry on A483; take turning at Cross Guns Inn at Pant.
Hilltop; 4th hole tee in Wales, green in England.
Pro Andrew Griffiths; Founded 1933
18 holes, 6114 yards, S.S.S. 69
† Welcome by arrangement.
⌊ WD £20 £25 day price; WE £25.
Reduction for groups.
♿ Welcome WD except Thurs; catering available by prior arrangement.
🍽 Bar and restaurant facilities.
🛏 Many in Oswestry area.

6A 85 Ludlow ♨

Bromfield, Ludlow, Shropshire, SY8 2BT
✉ ludlowgolf@barboxnet.co.uk
☎ 01584 856285, Fax 856366, Pro 856366
Course is one mile N of Ludlow off the A49.
Heathland course.
Pro Russell Price; Founded 1889
18 holes, 6277 yards, S.S.S. 70
† Welcome.
⌊ WD £20; WE/BH £25.
♿ Welcome by prior arrangement; terms on application.
🍽 Clubhouse facilities.
🛏 Feathers, Ludlow.

6A 86 Lymm ♨

Lymm Golf Club, Whitbarrow Road, Lymm, Cheshire, WA13 9AN
🖧 www.lymm-golf-club.co.uk
✉ mail@lymmgolfclub.fsnet.co.uk

Royal Liverpool

Known as Hoylake by its many friends, Royal Liverpool is one of golf's great eccentrics. The holes potter around an undistinguished flat piece of land, sometimes only finding definition through an internal out of bounds. Yet Hoylake is blissfully unaware that anyone could find it ugly. It lives in a world of its own.

It was confident of gaining royal status and when Prince Arthur accepted honorary presidency in 1871 it designated itself royal. 30 years later, on the death of Queen Victoria, the club checked up on its status and, without so much as a mild rebuke, was given "permission to continue the use of the prefix 'Royal'".

The monarchy has better taste than some. Golfers who require a reasonably sized freight train to transport their equipment, a wardrobe lady and a briefcase of yardage charts probably won't like Hoylake. The Xanadu Country Club up the road, with its sacred rivers and immeasurable caverns, is altogether a lovelier place. But not for golf.

Since 1967 a lack of spare land on which to pitch all the attendant paraphernalia has forced Hoylake off the Open roster. But the recent purchase of some school fields led to its reinstatement in 2001 and it was almost immediately granted the 2006 Open.

Bernard Darwin, fine golfer and fine writer, once wrote, "This dear flat historic expanse of Hoylake, blown upon by mighty winds, has been a breeder of mighty champions". He omits to mention rain and snow. The local fire brigade was summoned to pump water out of the bunkers during the 1932 Varsity Match, but found it an unequal struggle. Four years after the Open lost a day's play due to snow. In the middle of July.

Hoylake hums with history. Bobby Jones won the second leg of his Grand Slam on the course. John H Taylor, Walter Hagen and Peter Thomson won Open Championships here. James Braid, Harry Vardon and Jack Nicklaus has each been a runner-up. The first Amateur Championship was played at Hoylake.

Jones said of Hoylake, "This is a tight course. You can't get up there and slam away and trust to freedom of action to take care of the shot. You simply have to exercise some control of the ball". And a great deal of control of yourself. When Jamie Anderson placed a third ball down on the first tee, having put the previous two out of bounds, he said, "Ma God, it's like playing up a spout".

The members reflect the course. Their eccentric charm has gone way beyond the philosophical. In their early days they might accept Hoylake's slings and arrows with a Gallic shrug. Perhaps it is no great surprise that Arnaud Massy, still the only Frenchman to have won the Open, triumphed at Hoylake. But after a while the shrug becomes a twitch, then a flail, then a rant, before finally a sort of lunatic calm takes over.

Each year the former captains of the club assemble in an upstairs room to agree upon next year's captain. When the decision is made they come among the waiting membership below and lay a hand upon the new incumbent's shoulder.

Not so very long ago the intended got rather drunk whilst watching England defeat Wales at rugby. As he re-enacted one of the tries in the bar, various bits of his body parted company. Naturally enough the outgoing captain grabbed a bunch of flowers, headed to the hospital and after a few well chosen words about the virtues of drink, laid his hand upon the shoulder.

I am not quite sure what the story is all about, but then that's rather the point of Hoylake. – **Mark Reason**

☎ 01925 755020, Fax 755020,
Pro 755054, Rest/Bar 752177
5 miles SE of Warrington.
Parkland course.
Pro Steve McCarthy; Founded 1907
18 holes, 6304 yards, S.S.S. 70
♣ Welcome WD; Thurs ladies day, no
visitors before 2.30pm; with members
at WE.
꠸ WD £26.
☝ Welcome, usually on Wed; winter
packages.
🍽 Full meals facilities.
💤 Lymm; Statham Lodge.

6A 87 Macclesfield ☏

The Hollins, Macclesfield, Cheshire,
SK11 7EA
🖳 www.maccgolfclub.co.uk
📧 secretary@maccgolfclub.co.uk
☎ 01625 423227, Fax 260061,
Pro 616952, Sec 615845
From the southern end of the A523
(Silk Road), turn left into Windmill St.
Hillside/heathland course.
Pro Tony Taylor; Founded 1889/1901
Designed by Hawtree & Son
18 holes, 5707 yards, S.S.S. 68
♣ Welcome.
꠸ WD £30; WE £40.
☝ Welcome by arrangement;
packages available; contact Sec; terms
on application.
🍽 Full clubhouse facilities.
💤 Sutton Hall.

6A 88 Malkins Bank

Betchton Road, Malkins Bank,
Sandbach, Cheshire, CW11 4XN
☎ 01270 765931, Fax 764730,
Sec 873904, Rest/Bar 767878
1.5 miles from M6 Junction 17.
Municipal parkland course.
Pro David Wheeler; Founded 1980
18 holes, 5971 yards, S.S.S. 69
꠸ Practice area.
♣ Welcome; booking system in
operation.
꠸ WD £8.80; WE £10.30 Adults. WD
£5.30; WE £5.30 Juniors (9 holes WE
adults £7 WD £6, Juniors WD £3.90
WE £3.90).
☝ Welcome.
🍽 Bar and catering daily.
💤 Old Hall; Saxon Cross Motel.

6A 89 The Manor Golf Club ☏
(Kingstone)

Leese Hill, Kingstone, Uttoxeter, Staffs,
ST14 8QT
☎ 01889 563234
On the main Uttoxeter to Stafford road.

Parkland course.
Founded 1992
Designed by David Gough
18 holes, 5360 yards, S.S.S. 69
꠸ Practice range, 5-bay driving
range, putting green.
♣ Welcome.
꠸ Terms on application.
☝ Welcome and catering facilities.
🍽 Bar and catering facilities.

6A 90 Market Drayton

Sutton, Market Drayton, Shropshire,
TF9 2HX
☎ 01630 652266
1.5 miles S of Market Drayton.
Undulating meadowland course.
Pro Russell Clewes; Founded 1911
18 holes, 6290 yards, S.S.S. 71
♣ Welcome WD except Tues which
is Ladies Day; Sat with a member; Sun
members only.
꠸ WD £24.
☝ Welcome by arrangement.
🍽 Full facilities.
💤 Bungalow at course (sleeps six);
Bear; Corbet Arms.

6A 91 Marple ☏

Barnsfold Road, Marple, Stockport,
Cheshire, SK6 7EL
☎ 0161 427 2311, Fax 427 1125,
Pro 427 1195, Sec 427 1125
Signposted from Hawk Green.
Parkland course.
Pro David Myers; Founded 1892
18 holes, 5552 yards, S.S.S. 67
♣ Welcome except comp days.
꠸ WD £20; WE £30.
☝ Welcome by prior arrangement;
golf and catering packages available;
from £34.50.
🍽 Clubhouse facilities.
💤 Bredbury Hall Hotel.

6A 92 Mellor & Towncliffe

Mellor and Towncliffe Golf Club Ltd,
Gibb Lane, Mellor, Stockport,
Cheshire, SK6 5NA
🖳 www.mellorgolf.co.uk
☎ 0161 4279700, Pro 4275759,
Sec 4472208
Off A626 opposite Devonshire Arms on
Longhurst Lane, Mellor.
Parkland/moorland course.
Pro Gary Broadley; Founded 1894
22 holes, 5925 yards, S.S.S. 69
♣ Welcome except Sat.
꠸ WD £20; WE £27.50; Summer
Special £30 full day and meal.
☝ Welcome by prior arrangement;
winter packages available.

🍽 Full facilities except Tues.
💤 Pack Horse Inn.

6A 93 Meole Brace

Municipal Golf Course, Oteley Road,
Shrewsbury, Shropshire, SY2 6QQ
☎ 01743 364050
At Junction of A5/A49 S of Shrewsbury.
Parkland course.
Pro Nigel Bramall; Founded 1976
12 holes, 3400 yards, S.S.S. 43
꠸ 9-hole pitch and putt.
♣ Welcome; pay as you play.
꠸ Summer: WD 8.00 am to 2.50 pm
£5.75; 2.00 pm to dusk £6.40; WE/BH
7.00 am to 4.50 pm £7.65; 5.00 pm to
dusk £6.90. Winter: WD £5.10; WE
£6.10.
☝ Welcome by prior arrangement.
🍽 Drinks and confectionery machines.

6A 94 Mere Golf & Country ☏
Club

Chester Road, Mere, Knutsford,
Cheshire, WA16 6LJ
🖳 www.meregolf.co.uk
☎ 01565 830155, Fax 830713, Pro
830219
1 mile E of M6 Junction 19 on A556; 2
miles W of M56 Junction 7.
Parkland course.
Pro Peter Eyre; Founded 1934
Designed by George Duncan and
James Braid
18 holes, 6817 yards, S.S.S. 73
꠸ 6 bays open March to October.
♣ Welcome Mon, Tues and Thurs by
prior arrangement.
꠸ WD £70.
☝ Welcome Mon, Tues and Thurs by
arrangement; full range of clubhouse
facilities; golf days and golf packages;
terms on application.
🍽 Bar and restaurant service.
💤 Cottons.

6A 95 Mersey Valley ☏

Warrington Road, Bold Heath, Widnes,
Cheshire, WA8 3XL
🖳 www.merseyvalleygolfclub.co.uk
☎ 0151 424 6060, Fax 2579097
Leave M62 Junction 7; 1.5 miles on
A57 towards Warrington.
Parkland course.
Pro Andy Stevenson; Founded 1995
Designed by St Mellion Leisure
18 holes, 6374 yards, S.S.S. 70
꠸ Practice area.
♣ Welcome.
꠸ WD £18; WE £20.
☝ Welcome by arrangement; deposit
required; packages available for 18

and 27 holes of golf with meals; from
£26.
🍽 Bar and bar snacks; function suite
available.
🛏 Hillcrest, Widnes.

6A 96 Mile End
Shrewsbury Road, Oswestry,
Shropshire, SY11 4JF
🖳 www.mileendgolfclub.co.uk
✉ mileendgc@aol.com
☎ 01691 671246, Fax 670580
1 mile SE of Oswestry; signposted
from A5.
Parkland course (converted
farmland).
Pro Scott Carpenter; Founded 1992
Designed by Michael Price/D Gough
18 holes, 6194 yards, S.S.S. 69
(Yellow tees)
⚐ Practice range, 12 bays floodlit.
† Welcome.
⌇ WD £16; WE £22.
⌲ Welcome WD by prior
arrangement; terms on application.
🍽 Full clubhouse facilities.
🛏 Wynnstay; Sweeney Hall, Moreton
Lodge.

6A 97 Mobberley ⚏
Mobberley Golf Club, Burleyhurst
Lane, Mobberley, Knutsford, Cheshire,
WA16 7JZ
🖳 www.mobgolfclub.co.uk
☎ 01565 880178, Fax 880178,
Pro 880188
From M56 Junction 6 head towards
Wilmslow and after Moat House turn
right.
Parkland course.
Pro John Cheetham;
Founded 1995
9 holes, 5542 yards, S.S.S. 67
⚐ Practice range, practice area;
indoor teaching facilities.
† Welcome.
⌇ WD £14.50; WE £18.
⌲ Welcome by prior arrangement.
🍽 Bar and restaurant.
🛏 Moat House; Boddington Arms.

6A 98 Mottram Hall Hotel ⚏
Wilmslow Road, Mottram St Andrew,
Macclesfield, Cheshire, SK10 4QT
☎ 01625 820064, Fax 829135
From M56 Junction 6 follow A538
through Wilmslow; follow signposts.
Parkland/woodland course.
Pro Tim Rastall; Founded 1991
Designed by David Thomas
18 holes, 7006 yards, S.S.S. 74
⚐ 8 bays (not covered).

† Welcome with handicap certs.
⌇ WD £45; WE £50 (residents
receive a £10 reduction on fees).
⌲ Welcome by arrangement;
packages available; on-course
drink/food buggy; leisure centre.
🍽 Full clubhouse & hotel facilities.
🛏 Mottram Hall on site (133 beds).

6A 99 New Mills
Shaw Marsh, New Mills, Derbys,
SK22 4QE
🖳 www.newmillsgolfclub.co.uk
✉ carlpcross@aol.com
☎ 01663 743485, Pro 746161
0.75 miles from centre of New Mills on
St Mary Road.
Moorland course.
Pro Carl Cross; Founded 1907
Designed by David Williams
18 holes, 5665 yards, S.S.S. 68
⚐ Small practice range.
† Welcome WD and Sat mornings
except on competition days.
⌇ POA.
⌲ Welcome WD by prior
arrangement.
🍽 Bar and clubhouse catering.
🛏 Pack Horse; Sportsman; Moorside.

6A 100 Newcastle-under-Lyme
Golf Lane, Newcastle, Staffs, ST5 2QB
🖳 www.newcastlegolfclub.co.uk
☎ 01782 618526, Sec 617006
1.5 miles SW of Newcastle-under-
Lyme on A53.
Parkland course.
Pro Paul Symonds; Founded 1908
18 holes, 6331 yards, S.S.S. 71
† Welcome WD.
⌇ WD £26.
⌲ Welcome on Mon all day and Thurs
pm; packages on application; snooker.
🍽 Bar and restaurant.
🛏 Post House; Borough Arms.

6A 101 Northenden
Palatine Road, Manchester, M22 4FR
☎ 0161 9984738, Fax 9455592,
Pro 9453386, Rest/Bar 9984079
0.5 miles from M56 Junction 9; M60
Junction 5.
Parkland course.
Pro James Curtis; Founded 1913
Designed by T Renouf
18 holes, 6503 yards, S.S.S. 71
† Welcome by arrangement.
⌇ WD £28; WE £32.
⌲ Welcome Tues and Fri; packages
include 27 holes of golf; coffee and
bacon sandwich on arrival; light lunch
and dinner; from £45.

🍽 Full clubhouse facilities.
🛏 Britannia Country House; Post
House, Northenden.

6A 102 Onneley
Crewe, Cheshire, CW3 5QF
☎ 01782 750577, Sec 846759
1 mile from Woore on A51 to
Newcastle
Undulating parkland course.
Founded 1968
Designed by Geoff Marks
13 holes, 5781 yards, S.S.S. 68
† Welcome on application.
⌇ £20 per day (£10 with member).
⌲ Welcome by prior arrangement
with Sec; from £20 inc meal (min 12).
🍽 Clubhouse facilities.
🛏 Wheatsheaf.

6A 103 Oswestry
Aston Park, Oswestry, Shropshire,
SY11 4JJ
🖳 www.oswestrygolfclub.co.uk
☎ 01691 610535, Fax 610535
3 miles SE of Oswestry on A5.
Undulating parkland course.
Pro David Skelton; Founded 1903
Designed by James Braid
18 holes, 6038 yards, S.S.S. 69
⚐ Practice area.
† Welcome with handicap certs.
⌇ WD/WE £26.
⌲ Welcome Wed and Fri; packages
available; from £38.
🍽 Full clubhouse facilities.
🛏 Morton Park Lodge; The Wynstay
Hotel.

6A 104 Oxley Park
Stafford Road, Wolverhampton,
W Midlands, WV10 6DE
✉ secretary@oxleyparkgolfclub.fsnet
.co.uk
☎ 01902 425982, Pro 425445
On A449 1.5 miles S of J2 M54.
Parkland course.
Pro Les Burlison; Founded 1913
Designed by Henry Colt.
18 holes, 6228 yards, S.S.S. 71
† Welcome; only with a member at
WE in winter.
⌇ WD/WE £30.
⌲ Welcome Wed by arrangement;
snooker.
🍽 Full clubhouse catering.
🛏 Holiday Inn, Dunstall Park.

6A 105 Parkhall
Hulme Lane, Hulme, Stoke on Trent,
Staffs, ST3 5BH

☎ 01782 599584, Fax 599584,
Pro 331889
1 mile outside Longton on A50.
Public moorland course.
Pro Joe Mortimore; Founded 1989
Designed by Paul Reade.
18 holes, 4770 yards, S.S.S. 54
♦ Welcome.
Ⅰ WD £6; WE £7.
♲ Welcome by arrangement.
⑩ None.

6A 106 **Patshull Park Hotel Golf & Country Club**
Patshull Park, Burnhill Green,
Wolverhampton, W Midlands, WV6 7HR
♣ www.patshull-park.co.uk
☎ 01902 700100, Fax 700874, Pro
700342
From A41 Wolverhampton-Whitchurch
Road follow signs to Pattingham.
Parkland course.
Pro Peter Baker; Founded 1972
Designed by John Jacobs
18 holes, 6412 yards, S.S.S. 70
Ⅰ Practice ground.
♦ Welcome with handicap certs.
Ⅰ WD £30; WE £40.
♲ Welcome by prior arrangement;
packages including catering from
£29.95 per person.
⑩ Full clubhouse and hotel facilities.
↩ Patshull Park Hotel on site.

6A 107 **Penn**
Penn Common, Wolverhampton,
W Midlands, WV4 5JN
☎ 01902 341142, Fax 620504,
Pro 330472
On A449 2.5 miles W of
Wolverhampton at Penn.
Heathland course.
Pro B Burlison; Founded 1908
18 holes, 6487 yards, S.S.S. 72
♦ Welcome WD; with member at
WE.
Ⅰ WD £23 round, £24 day ticket.
♲ Welcome Mon, Wed, Fri;
reductions for groups of 20+; catering
packages available; from £22.
⑩ Full clubhouse facilities.

6A 108 **Peover**
Plumley Moor Road, Lower Peover,
Knutsford, Cheshire, WA16 9SE
♣ www. peovergolfclub.co.uk
✉ mail@peovergolfclub.co.uk
☎ 01565 723337, Fax 723311,
Pro 07967 894357
Leave M6 Junction 19 to A556; follow
signs to Plumley and Lower Peover on
Plumley Moor Rd; course is 1.5 miles.
Parkland course.

Pro Mike Grantham; Founded 1996
Designed by P Naylor
18 holes, 6702 yards, S.S.S. 72
Ⅰ Practice area.
♦ Welcome.
Ⅰ WD £23; WE £25.
♲ Welcome WD; packages available
on application; from £22.50.
⑩ Full clubhouse catering facilities
available.
↩ Belle Park.

6A 109 **Perton Park Golf Club**
Wrottesley Park Road, Perton,
Wolverhampton, W Midlands, WV6 7HL
☎ 01902 380103, Fax 326219, Pro
380073, Sec 897031
Just off the A454 Bridgnorth to
Wolverhampton Road.
Meadowland course.
Pro Jeremy Harrold; Founded 1990
18 holes, 6620 yards, S.S.S. 70
Ⅰ Practice range, 18-bay range.
♦ Welcome with tee time from starter.
Ⅰ WD £15; WE £20.
♲ Welcome by prior arrangement;
golf and catering packages available;
from £15.
⑩ Full clubhouse catering facilities
available.

6A 110 **Portal Golf & Country Club** ℡
The Champion Course, Cobblers Craft
Lane, Tarporley, Cheshire, CW6 0DJ
♣ www.portalgolf@aol.com
✉ portalgolf@aol.com
☎ 01829 733933, Fax 733928
11 miles SE of Chester off A49 near
Tarporley.
Parkland course; 3rd: Haddington's
Ground, 602 yards.
Pro Adrian Hill; Founded 1989
Designed by Donald Steel
45 holes, 7037 yards, S.S.S. 74
Ⅰ UK largest indoor golf academy.
♦ Welcome by arrangement.
Ⅰ WD £50; WE £50.
♲ Welcome by arrangement; packages
available; also Arderne course, par 71;
from £35 playing on the Premiere and
the Championship course. Arderne
course is Par 30 and is £10 a round.
⑩ Restaurant and bar facilities.
↩ The Swan, Tarporley; Wild Boar,
Beeston; Nunsmere Hotel.

6A 111 **Portal Golf & Country Club – Prem. Course**
Forest Road, Tarporley, Cheshire,
CW6 0JA
♣ www.portalpremier.co.uk
✉ portprem@aol.com

☎ 01829 733884, Fax 733666,
Pro 733703
1 mile S of Tarporley between Chester
and Northwich.
Parkland course.
Pro Judy Statham; Founded 1990
Designed by T Rouse
18 holes, 6508 yards, S.S.S. 72
♦ Welcome.
Ⅰ WD £30; WE £35.
♲ Welcome WD by prior
arrangement; on application; from £29.
⑩ Full clubhouse facilities.
↩ Swan, Tarporley; Wild Boar, Beeston.

6A 112 **Poulton Park**
Dig Lane, Croft, Warrington, Cheshire,
WA2 0SH
☎ 01925 812034, Pro 825220, Sec
822802
3 miles from Warrington off A574.
Parkland course.
Prolan Orrell; Founded 1978
9 holes, 5521 yards, S.S.S. 67
♦ Welcome by arrangement.
Ⅰ WD £17; WE £19 (to be
confirmed).
♲ Welcome by prior arrangement;
packages for golf and catering
available; minimum 8; £20-£26.
⑩ Clubhouse facilities.

6A 113 **Prenton**
Golf Links Road, Birkenhead,
Merseyside, CH42 8LW
✉ nigelbrown@prentongolfclub.co.uk
☎ 0151 609 3426, Fax 609 3421,
Pro 6081636
From M53 Junction 2 take A552
towards Birkenhead.
Parkland course.
Pro Robin Thompson; Founded 1905
Designed by Colt MacKenzie & Co
18 holes, 6429 yards, S.S.S. 71
Ⅰ Practice range, two practice areas.
♦ Welcome by arrangement.
Ⅰ WD £35; WE £40.
♲ Welcome by prior arrangement;
golf and catering packages available;
from £24.
⑩ Full clubhouse bar and catering
facilities.

6A 114 **Prestbury Golf Club**
Macclesfield Road, Prestbury,
Macclesfield, Cheshire, SK10 4BJ
✉ office@prestburygolfclub.com
☎ 01625 829388, Fax 828241, Pro
828242, Sec 828241, Rest/Bar 829388
Course is two miles NW of
Macclesfield.
Parkland course.

Pro Nick Summerfield; Founded 1920
Designed by Colt & Morrison
18 holes, 6359 yards, S.S.S. 71
☂ Welcome by prior arrangement on
WD; with a member at WE.
ℾ WD £38.
♨ Welcome Thurs; minimum 20; from
£34 pp.
🍽 Full clubhouse bar and catering
facilities.
🛏 Bridge; White House, both Prestbury.

6A 115 Pryors Hayes Golf Club ☏

Willington Road, Oscroft, Tarvin,
Chester, Cheshire, CH3 8NL
📧 info@pryors-hayes.co.uk
☎ 01829 741250, Fax 749077, Pro
740140
5 miles from Chester near Tarvin
between A54 and A51.
Parkland course.
Founded 1993
Designed by John Day
18 holes, 6074 yards, S.S.S. 69
☂ Welcome by prior booking.
ℾ WD £20; WE £25.
♨ Welcome every day by prior
arrangement; catering and golf
packages available.
🍽 Clubhouse facilities.
🛏 Willington Hall.

6A 116 Queen's Park

Queen's Park Drive, Crewe, Cheshire,
CW2 7SB
☎ 01270 662378, Pro 666724, Sec
580424
1.5 miles from town centre off Victoria
Avenue.
Parkland course.
Pro Jamie Lowe; Founded 1985
9 holes, 4922 yards, S.S.S. 64
🏌 Small practice area.
☂ Pay and play; restrictions on Wed,
Sun, Thurs so call in advance.
ℾ WD £6.50; WE £8.50 (18 holes).
♨ Welcome.
🍽 Clubhouse facilities.

6A 117 Reaseheath

Reaseheath College, Reaseheath,
Nantwich, Cheshire, CW5 6DF
🌐 www.reaseheath.ac.uk
📧 enquiries@reaseheath.ac.uk
☎ 01270 625131, Fax 625665,
Sec 613201
1 mile from Nantwich on A51 Chester
road.
Research course used for greenkeeper
training.
Founded 1987

Designed by D Mortram
9 holes, 3729 yards, S.S.S. 58
☂ Limited availability for non-
members; phone in advance.
ℾ WD £7; WE £7.
♨ Small groups; prior booking essential.
🍽 Restaurant on site WD.
🛏 Alvaston Hall Hotel.

6A 118 Reddish Vale ☏

Southcliffe Road, Stockport, Cheshire,
SK5 7EE
🌐 www.reddishvalegolfclub.co.uk
☎ 0161 480 2359, Fax 4778242,
Pro 4803824, Rest/Bar 4761521
1 mile N of Stockport off B6167
Reddish road.
Undulating course in valley.
Pro Bob Freeman; Founded 1912
Designed by Dr A MacKenzie
18 holes, 6086 yards, S.S.S. 69
☂ Welcome WD (lunchtime
restrictions); with a member at WE.
ℾ Terms on application.
♨ Welcome WD by prior
arrangement; packages available.
🍽 Restaurant and bar service.
🛏 Bradbury Hall.

6A 119 Ringway

Hale Road, Halebarns, Altrincham,
Cheshire, WA15 8SW
🌐 www.ringwaygolfclub.co.uk
📧 enquiries@ringwaygolfclub.co.uk
☎ 0161 980 8432, Fax 980 4414,
Sec 980 2630, Rest/Bar 904 9609
8 miles S of Manchester 1 mile from
M56 Junction 6 on the A538 towards
Altrincham through Hale Barns.
Parkland course.
Pro Nick Ryan; Founded 1909
Designed by Harry Colt and James
Braid
18 holes, 6482 yards, S.S.S. 71
🏌 Practice ground available.
☂ Welcome except Fri; Tues & Sat
are club competition days.
ℾ WD £35; WE £45.
♨ Welcome Thurs in summer by prior
arrangement; packages available;
corporate days organised; snooker.
🍽 Full facilities.
🛏 Cresta Court; Marriott; Bulls
Head.

6A 120 Romiley

Goosehouse Green, Romiley,
Stockport, Cheshire, SK6 4LJ
🌐 www.romilygolfclub.org
📧 office@romilygolfclub.org
☎ 0161 430 2392, Fax 430 7258,
Pro 430 7122, Rest/Bar 430 2310

On B6104 off A560 0.75 miles from
Romiley station.
Undulating parkland course.
Pro Lee Paul Sullivan; Founded 1897
18 holes, 6454 yards, S.S.S. 71
☂ Welcome except Thurs (Ladies
Day).
ℾ WD £30; WE £40.
♨ Welcome Tues and Wed by prior
arrangement.
🍽 Full clubhouse service.

6A 121 Royal Liverpool Golf Club

30 Meols Drive, Hoylake, Wirral,
Merseyside, CH47 4AL
🌐 www.royal-liverpool-golf.com
📧 bookings@royal-liverpool-golf.com
☎ 0151 6323101, Fax 6326737,
Pro 6325868, Sec 6323101,
Rest/Bar 6323102
On A540 between Hoylake and West
Kirby, off Junction 2 of the M53.
Championship links course.
John Heggarty; Founded 1869
Designed by Robert Chambers & Pro
Pro George Morris
18 holes, 7165 yards, S.S.S. 75
🏌 Practice ground.
☂ Welcome by appointment only; WE
very restricted.
ℾ WD £100; WE £130 (for 18 holes
and lunch).
♨ Welcome by prior arrangement
only; from £100, including snack lunch;
full facilities.
🍽 Full restaurant (12-2) and
clubhouse facilities.
🛏 Thornton Hall, Thornton-le-Hough;
Crabwall Manor, Mollington, Craxton
Wood, Kings Gap Court.

6A 122 Runcorn

The Heath, Clifton Road, Runcorn,
Cheshire, WA7 4SU
📧 honsec@runcorngolfclub.ltd.uk
☎ 01928 572093, Fax 574214Pro
564791, Sec 574214
M56 Junction 12; signposted off A557.
Parkland course.
Pro D Ingman
Founded 1909
18 holes, 6035 yards, S.S.S. 69
☂ Welcome WD except Tues; WE
with member; 2 for 1 vouchers
accepted.
ℾ WD £24.
♨ Welcome Mon and Fri; includes
coffee, lunch and dinner for groups
of 12 or more; various options
available.
🍽 Clubhouse facilities.
🛏 Lord Daresbury, Warrington.

6A 123 St Michael Jubilee
Dundalk Road, Widnes, Cheshire,
WA4 8BS
☎ 0151 4245636, Fax 4952124,
Pro 4246230, Sec 4246461
Close to centre of Widnes off the
Runcorn Bridge.
Public parkland course.
Pro Darren Chapman; Founded 1977
18 holes, 5667 yards, S.S.S. 68
↑ Practice area.
♦ Welcome WD; with bookings at WE.
ɤ Available on request.
⚲ Welcome by arrangement.
⦿ Full facilities.
⋐ Hillcrest.

6A 124 St Thomas's Priory Golf Club
Armitage Lane, Rugeley, Staffs,
WS15 1ED
⬚ www.st-thomass-golfclub.com
☎ 01543 492096, Fax 492096,
Sec 491911
1 mile SE of Rugeley on A513;
opposite Ash Tree Inn.
Parkland course; 14th is 601 yards.
Pro R O'Hanlon; Founded 1995
Designed by Paul Mulholland
18 holes, 5969 yards, S.S.S. 70
♦ Welcome.
ɤ WD £25; WE £30.
⚲ Welcome by prior arrangement;
terms on application.
⦿ Full clubside facilities.
⋐ Riverside Inn; Holiday Inn Express,
both Branston.

6A 125 Sale ♔
Sale Lodge, Golf Road, Sale,
Cheshire, M33 2XU
⬚ www.salegolfclub.com
✉ mail@salegolfclub.com
☎ 0161 973 1638, Fax 962 4217,
Pro 973 1730, Rest/Bar 973 3404
Close to M60 Junction 6.
Parkland course.
Pro Mike Stewart; Founded 1913
18 holes, 6150 yards, S.S.S. 69
♦ WD and Sun.
ɤ WD £25; WE £28.
⚲ Welcome by arrangement with the
Prof; golf and food packages available
on application; terms on application.
⦿ Clubhouse facilities.
⋐ Dane Lodge, Sale.

6A 126 Sandbach
117 Middlewich Road, Sandbach,
Cheshire, CW11 1FH
☎ 01270 762117, Rest/Bar 759227
Course1 mile W of Sandbach on A533.

Meadowland course.
Founded 1895
9 holes, 5295 yards, S.S.S. 67
♦ Welcome WD; WE by invitation.
ɤ £20.00 or £10.00 with a member.
⚲ Limited; by prior arrangement;
terms on application.
⦿ Full facilities except Mon.
⋐ Saxon Cross Motel; Old Hall.

6A 127 Sandiway
Chester Road, Sandiway, Northwich,
Cheshire, CW8 2DJ
⬚ www.sandiwaygolf.co.uk
✉ info@sandiwaygolf.co.uk
☎ 01606 883247, Fax 888548,
Pro 883180
On B556 14 miles E of Chester, 4
miles from Northwich.
Undulating parkland course.
Pro Bill Laird; Founded 1921
Designed by Ted Ray
18 holes, 6404 yards, S.S.S. 72
↑ Practice ground.
♦ Welcome WD except Thurs (ladies
day); WE by prior arrangement.
ɤ WD £45; WE £60.
⚲ Welcome Tues by prior
arrangement; packages available;
terms on application.
⦿ Full clubhouse facilities.
⋐ Hartland Hall; Oaklands.

6A 128 Sandwell Park ♔
Birmingham Road, West Bromwich,
W Midlands, B71 4JJ
⬚ www.sandwellparkgolfclub.co.uk
✉ secretary@sandwellparkgolfclub
.co.uk
☎ 0121 553 4637, Fax 525 1651,
Pro 553 4384, Rest/Bar 525 4151
On A41 Birmingham Road, 200 yards
from M5 Junction 1.
Heathland course.
Pro Nigel Wylie;
Founded 1895
Designed by H S Colt
18 holes, 6468 yards, S.S.S. 73
♦ Welcome WD.
ɤ WD £36.
⚲ Welcome WD by prior
arrangement; reductions for parties
over 11; catering facilities available;
from £31.
⦿ Full restaurant facilities & two bars.
⋐ West Bromwich Moat House.

6A 129 Sedgley Golf Centre
Sandyfields Road, Dudley,
W Midlands, DY3 3DL
☎ 01902 880503
Off A463 ½ mile from Sedgley town
centre near Cotwell End Nature
Reserve.

Parkland course on the side of a valley
with mature trees.
Pro Garry Mercer; Founded 1989
Designed by WG Cox
9 holes, 6294 yards, S.S.S. 70
↑ Practice range, 16 bays covered
and floodlit; chipping area.
♦ Pay and play course.
ɤ 9 holes £7.50; 18 holes £10.
⚲ Welcome by arrangement; snacks
available; terms on application.
⦿ Snacks.

6A 130 Seedy Mill ♔
Elmhurst, Lichfield, Staffs, WS13 8HE
⬚ www.clubhouse.com
✉ seedymill.sales@clubhaus.com
☎ 01543 417333, Fax 418098
3 miles N of Lichfield off A51.
Parkland course with lakes, ponds and
streams.
Pro Simon Joyce; Founded 1991
Designed by Hawtree & Sons
18 holes and a 9-hole par 3 course,
6305 yards, S.S.S. 70
↑ Practice range, 26 bays floodlit.
♦ Welcome.
ɤ WD £25; WE £30.
⚲ Welcome by prior arrangement;
limited WE access; packages available
for food and golf ranging packing
available; corporate days available;
also 9-hole Spires course, par 3; from
£24.
⦿ Full clubhouse bar and restaurant.
⋐ Little Barrow, Lichfield.

6A 131 Severn Meadows
Highley, Bridgnorth, Shropshire,
WV16 6HZ
☎ 01746 862212
10 miles N of Bewdley; 8 miles S of
Bridgenorth.
Hilly parkland course in Severn valley.
Pro Martin Payne; Founded 1989
9 holes, 5258 yards, S.S.S. 67
♦ Welcome WD; pay and play; must
book WE.
ɤ Terms on application.
⚲ Welcome by arrangement.
⦿ Clubhouse facilities.
⋐ Bull, Chelmarsh.

6A 132 Shifnal
Decker Hill, Shifnal, Shropshire,
TF11 8QL
⬚ www.shifnalgolfclub.co.uk
✉ secretary@shifnalgolfclub.co.uk
☎ 01952 460330, Fax 461127,
Pro 460457, Sec 460330
1 mile N of Shifnal close to M54
Junction 4.

Parkland course.
Pro J Flanagan; Founded 1929/1963
Designed by Frank Pennink
18 holes, 6468 yards, S.S.S. 71
⚑ 2 practice areas.
♦ Welcome WD; members only WE.
☪ WD £25.
♨ Welcome Tues, Wed and Fri;
reductions for groups of 20 or more;
terms on application.
🍽 Full clubhouse bar and catering.
🛏 Park House.

6A 133 **Shrewsbury**
Condover, Shrewsbury, Shropshire,
SY5 7BL
🖥 www.club-noticeboard.co.uk
/shrewsbury
✉ info@shrewsbury-golf-club.co.uk
☎ 01743 872976, Pro 874581,
Sec 872977
S of Shrewsbury off A49.
Parkland course.
Pro Peter Seal; Founded 1890/1972
Designed by CK Cotton, Pennink,
Lawrie & Partners
18 holes, 6205 yards, S.S.S. 70
♦ Welcome WD; after 2pm Wed;
WE between 10am-12 noon and after
2pm.
☪ WD £22; WE £25.
♨ Welcome Mon and Fri; limited
availability Tues, Thurs and Sun am;
packages can be arranged through the
professional; terms on application.
🍽 Full clubhouse facilities.
🛏 Shrewsbury Hotel, Lord Hill.

6A 134 **Shrigley Hall Hotel**
Pott Shrigley, Macclesfield, Cheshire,
SK10 5SB
🖥 www.paramount-hotels.co.uk
☎ 01625 575757, Fax 573323,
Pro 575626
Off A523 Macclesfield road; follow Pott
Shrigley from Adlington.
Parkland course.
Pro Tony Stevens; Founded 1989
Designed by Donald Steel
18 holes, 6281 yards, S.S.S. 71
⚑ Practice range.
♦ Welcome by arrangement.
☪ WD £30; Fri £35; WE £35.
♨ Welcome WD by prior
arrangement; packages can be
arranged; terms on application.
🍽 Full clubhouse and hotel facilities.
🛏 150-room Shrigley Hall Hotel on site.

6A 135 **The Shropshire**   ⚏
Muxton Lane, Muxton, Telford,
Shropshire, TF2 8PQ

🖥 www.theshropshire.co.uk
✉ sales@theshropshire.couk
☎ 01952 677800, Fax 677622,
Pro 677866, Sec 671962
From M54/A5 take B5060, turning right
at Granville roundabout; course
opposite equestrian centre.
Parkland course; 3 loops of 9 holes.
Pro Rob Gr ier; Founded 1992
Designed by Martin Hawtree
27 holes, 6637 yards, S.S.S. 72
⚑ 30 bays covered floodlit.
♦ Welcome.
☪ WD £18; WE £24.
♨ Welcome everyday; minimum 8;
catering and golf packages available;
private room; from £17.50. £15 winter
only – no winter greens.
🍽 Restaurant and two bars.
🛏 White House, Muxton; Telford Moat
House.

6A 136 **South Staffordshire**
Danescourt Road, Wolverhampton,
W Midlands, WV6 9BQ
🖥 www.southstaffsgc.co.uk
✉ manager@southstaffsgc.co.uk
☎ 01902 751065, Fax 741573,
Pro 754816
On A41 from Wolverhampton in
Tettenhall; clubhouse and course
behind cricket club.
Parkland course.
Pro Mark Sparrow; Founded 1892
Designed by Harry Vardon/HS Colt
18 holes, 6513 yards, S.S.S. 71
♦ Welcome except Tues am.
☪ WD £34; WE £45.
♨ Welcome except Tues am and WE.
🍽 Clubhouse catering and bar.
🛏 Mount; Connaught.

6A 137 **Stafford Castle**
Newport Road, Stafford, Staffs, ST16 1BP
☎ 01785 223821, Pro 212200
On A518 1 mile from Stafford Castle.
Parkland course.
Founded 1907
Designed by local lady in 1900s
9 holes, 6383 yards, S.S.S. 70 (18 tees)
♦ Welcome by arrangement.
☪ Terms on application.
♨ Welcome WD by arrangement;
terms on application.
🍽 Clubhouse restaurant and bar
facilities.
🛏 Tillington Hall.

6A 138 **Stamford Golf Club**
(Stalybridge)
Huddersfield Road, Carrbrook,
Stalybridge, Cheshire, SK15 3PY

✉ stamford.golfclub@totalise.co.uk
☎ 01457 834829, Fax 836550
On B6175 NE of Stalybridge.
Parkland/moorland course.
Pro Brian Badger; Founded 1901
18 holes, 5701 yards, S.S.S. 68
♦ Welcome WD.
☪ WD £20; WE £25.
♨ Welcome by prior arrangement,
min 12; packages include 27 holes of
golf, lunch and dinner; from £30.
🍽 Clubhouse facilities.
🛏 The Village, in Hyde.

6A 139 **Stockport**
Offerton Road, Stockport, Cheshire,
SK2 5HL
✉ info@stockportgolf.co.uk
☎ 0161 427 2001, Fax 449 8293,
Pro 427 2421, Sec 427 8369,
Rest/Bar 427 4425
Take A627 Torkington road from A6;
course 1.5 miles on right.
Parkland course.
Pro Mike Peel
Founded 1906
18 holes, 6326 yards, S.S.S. 71
♦ Welcome by arrangement.
☪ WD £40; WE £45.
♨ Welcome Wed and Thurs;
minimum 20 players; catering and golf
packages available.
🍽 Full clubhouse bar and restaurant
service.
🛏 Moorside, Disley; Britannia,
Offerton; Alma Lodge, Stockport.

6A 140 **Stone**
The Fillybrooks, Stone, Staffs,
ST15 0NB
✉ stonegolfc@onetel.net.uk
☎ 01785 813103, Sec 284875
1 mile NW of Stone on A34.
Parkland course.
Founded 1896
9 holes, 6299 yards, S.S.S. 70
♦ Welcome WD; WE only with a
member.
☪ WD £20 day/round.
♨ Welcome by arrangement; catering
packages available; terms on
application.
🍽 Clubhouse catering facilities.
🛏 Stone House.

6A 141 **Styal**
Styal Golf Club, Station Road, Styal,
Wilmslow, Cheshire, SK9 4JN
🖥 www.styalgolf.co.uk
✉ gtraynor@styalgolf.co.uk
☎ 01625 531359, Fax 416373,
Sec 530063, Rest/Bar 530063

Off M56 J5 at Manchester Airport; straight on at roundabout instead of turning to Airport; at end of Ringway road turn right into Styal Road; after 1 mile turn left into Station Rd, club on left.
Parkland course.
Pro G Traynor; Founded 1995
Designed by T Holmes
18 holes, 6172 yards, S.S.S. 70
🏌 Practice range, 24 bays, floodlit; driving range also 9-hole par 3 course.
† Welcome.
🎫 WD £21; WE £26.
⛳ Welcome by prior arrangement; packages available; from £21.
🍴 Clubhouse catering and bar.
🛏 Stanneylands; Hilton at Manchester Airport.

6A 142 **Sutton Hall**
Aston Lane, Sutton Weaver, Runcorn, Cheshire, WA7 3ED
☎ 01928 790747, Fax 759174, Pro 714872
M56 Junction 12, follow signs to Frodsham; turn left at Swingbridge for course.
Parkland course.
Pro Jamie Hope; Founded 1995
Designed by S Wundke
18 holes, 6608 yards, S.S.S. 72
† Welcome.
🎫 WD £20; WE £24.
⛳ Welcome WD; some at WE; packages for catering and golf available for groups of more than 10; groups up to 100 can be catered for.
🍴 Full catering and bar.
🛏 Forte Crest, Beechwood.

6A 143 **Swindon**
Bridgnorth road, Swindon, Dudley, W Midlands, DY3 4Pu
☎ 01902 897031, Fax 326219, Pro 896191
On B4176 Dudley to Bridgnorth road; 3 miles off A449 at Himley.
Wooded parkland course with exceptional views.
Pro Phil Lester; Founded 1974
27 holes, 6091 yards, S.S.S. 69
🏌 Practice range, 27 bays; also 9-hole course, par 3.
† Welcome.
🎫 WD £20; WE £30.
⛳ Welcome by arrangement with J Smith; terms on application.
🍴 Clubhouse facilities.
🛏 Himley Country Club, Himley.

6A 144 **Tamworth Municipal**
Eagle Drive, Tamworth, Staffs, B77 4EG

☎ 01827 709303, Fax 709304, Rest/Bar 709306
From M42 Junction 10 proceed towards Tamworth; course is signposted off the B5000 Polesworth road.
Municipal parkland course.
Pro Wiyna Illcock; Founded 1975
18 holes, 6525 yards, S.S.S. 72
† Welcome.
🎫 WD £10; WE £10.
⛳ Welcome WD by appointment.
🍴 Bar and daily catering.
🛏 Canada Lodge.

6A 145 **Telford Golf and Country Club**
Great Hay Drive, Sutton Heights, Telford, Shropshire, TF7 4DT
🖳 www.regalhotels.co.uk/telfordgolfandcountry
✉ ibarlem@aol.com
☎ 01952 429977, Fax 586602, Pro 586052, Sec 422960
Off A442 at Sutton Hill S of Telford.
Parkland course.
Pro Daniel Bateman; Founded 1975
Designed by John Harris
18 holes, 6741 yards, S.S.S. 72
🏌 8 bays, floodlit.
† Welcome.
🎫 WD £27; WE £32.
⛳ Welcome by prior arrangement.
🍴 Hotel facilities.
🛏 96 rooms on site.

6A 146 **Three Hammers Golf Complex**
Old Stafford Road, Cross Green, Wolverhampton, WV10 7PP
☎ 01902 790428, Pro 790940
From M54 Junction 2, travel N on A449 course 1 mile on right.
Parkland course.
Pro Shaun Ball and Ted Large
Designed by Henry Cotton
18 holes, 1438 yards, S.S.S. 54
🏌 23-bay floodlit range.
† Welcome.
🎫 WD £6; WE £7.
⛳ Welcome Mon-Sat.
🍴 Bar, bistro, restaurant and private dining facilities.

6A 147 **Trentham**
14 Barlaston Old Road, Stoke on Trent, Staffs, ST4 8HB
🖳 secretary@trenthamgolf.org
☎ 01782 658109, Fax 644024, Pro 657309, Rest/Bar 643623
Off A34 from Stoke to Stone, turn left at Trentham Gardens onto A5305 then first right by Nat West Bank.

Parkland course.
Pro Sandy Wilson; Founded 1894
18 holes, 6622 yards, S.S.S. 72
🏌 Practice ground.
† Welcome by prior arrangement.
🎫 WD £40; WE £50.
⛳ Welcome Mon – Fri by prior arrangement; terms available on application.
🍴 Clubhouse facilities.
🛏 Trentham Hotel; Post House Hotel; Tollgate Leisure.

6A 148 **Trentham Park**
Stoke-on-Trent, Staffs, ST4 8AE
🖳 trevor.berrisford@barbose.net
☎ 01782 658800, Fax 658800, Pro 658125, Rest/Bar 644130
Course is on the A34 four miles S of Newcastle; one mile from the M6 Junction 15.
Parkland course.
Pro Simon Lynn; Founded 1936
18 holes, 6425 yards, S.S.S. 71
† Welcome by arrangement.
🎫 WD £30; WE £35.
⛳ Welcome Wed and Fri by prior arrangement; packages for golf and catering available; from £22.50.
🍴 Clubhouse facilities.

6A 149 **The Tytherington**
Dorchester Way, Macclesfield, Cheshire, SK10 2JP
🖳 www.clubhaus.com
✉ tytherington.retail@clubhaus.com
☎ 01625 506000, Fax 506040, Pro 506003
2 miles from Macclesfield on the A523 Stockport road.
Parkland course; one of WPGA European Tour.
Pro Gav Beddow; Founded 1986
Designed by Dave Thomas and Patrick Dawson
18 holes, 6765 yards, S.S.S. 73
🏌 Driving range.
† Welcome with handicap certs.
🎫 WD £28; WE £34.
⛳ Welcome WD by prior arrangement; full facilities for golf and catering packages; private rooms; snooker and pool; health club; tennis; terms on application.
🍴 Restaurant, bars and full catering facilities.
🛏 Contact club for details.

6A 150 **Upton-by-Chester**
Upton Lane, Upton, Chester, Cheshire, CH2 1EE
☎ 01244 381183, Fax 376955

Off A41 Chester-Liverpool road near Chester Zoo.
Parkland course.
Pro Peter Gardener; Founded 1934
Designed by Bill Davis
18 holes, 5850 yards, S.S.S. 68
⚑ Putting green.
† Welcome except on competition days.
￡ £20 Full day £30.
↻ Welcome Wed, Thurs and Fri by prior arrangement.
🍽 Full clubhouse facilities.
⚐ Dene; Euromill; Mollington Banastre.

6A 151 **Uttoxeter** ☏
Wood Lane, Uttoxeter, Staffs, ST14 8JR
☎ 01889 566552, Fax 567501, Pro 564884, Rest/Bar 565108
Off B5017 Uttoxeter-Marchington road, 0.5 miles along Wood Lane just past the race course.
Parkland course with views over Dove Valley.
Pro Adam McCandless; Founded 1972
18 holes, 5801 yards, S.S.S. 70
† Welcome by arrangement.
￡ WD £24, WE £30, 50% discount with a member.
↻ Welcome by prior arrangement; packages available for groups of 10; from £23.
🍽 Catering and restaurant facilities.
⚐ White Hart; Bank House Hotel, both Uttoxeter.

6A 152 **Vicars Cross** ☏
Tarvin Road, Great Barrow, Chester, Cheshire, CH3 7HN
⚘ www.vicarscrossgc.co.uk
✉ secretary@vcgc.fsnet.co.uk
☎ 01244 335174, Fax 335686, Pro 335595
On A51 4 miles E of Chester.
Undulating parkland course.
Pro J Forsythe; Founded 1939
Designed by E Parr
18 holes, 6446 yards, S.S.S. 71
⚑ 8 indoors, 8 outdoors.
† Welcome except on competition days.
￡ WD/WE £30.
↻ Welcome Tues and Thurs, April-October except June; full golf and catering packages; from £37.50.
🍽 Full clubhouse facilities.

6A 153 **Wallasey**
Wallasey Golf Club Ltd, Bayswater Road, Wallasey, Wirral, CH45 8LA

⚘ www.wallaseygc.com
✉ wallaseygc@aol.com
☎ 0151 691 1024, Fax 638 8988, Pro 6383888
Leave the M53 at Junction 1; follow the A554 towards New Brighton, course is 0.25 miles on left.
Links course.
Pro Mike Adams; Founded 1891
Designed by Tom Morris Snr
18 holes, 6607 yards, S.S.S. 72
⚑ Practice area.
† Welcome by arrangement.
￡ WD £50; WE £65.
↻ Welcome by prior arrangement; packages for groups of 16 or more; catering available.
🍽 Clubhouse facilities.
⚐ Grove House, Wallasey.

6A 154 **Walsall**
Broadway, Walsall, W Midlands, WS1 3EY
⚘ www.walsallgolf.freeserve.co.uk
✉ golfclub@walsallgolf.freeserve.co.uk
☎ 01922 613512
Off A34 1 mile S of Walsall.
Wooded parkland course.
Pro R Lambert; Founded 1907
Designed by Dr MacKenzie
18 holes, 6257 yards, S.S.S. 70
† Welcome WD; WE as a members guest.
￡ WD £33.
↻ Welcome WD by prior arrangement; catering and golf packages available for minimum 16; from £30.
🍽 Clubhouse facilities.
⚐ Boundary; County Hotel.

6A 155 **Walton Hall**
Warrington Road, Higher Walton, Warrington, Cheshire, WA4 5LU
☎ 01925 266775, Pro 263061
Course is one mile from the M56 Junction 11.
Scenic parkland course.
Pro John Jackson; Founded 1972
Designed by Dave Thomas
18 holes, 6647 yards, S.S.S. 73
† Welcome.
￡ WD £13.50; WE £16.
↻ Welcome by prior arrangement with the Pro shop; terms on application.
🍽 Full catering facilities in season; limited in winter.
⚐ Lord Daresbury.

6A 156 **Warren**
Grove Road, Wallasey, Merseyside, CH45 0JA
☎ 0151 6398323, Pro 6395730

500 yards up Grove Rd at Wallasey Grove Rd station on left before traffic lights.
Municipal links course.
Pro Stephen Konrad; Founded 1911
9 holes, 5714 yards, S.S.S. 70
† Welcome.
￡ Prices on application.
↻ Welcome by prior arrangement.
⚐ Grove House.

6A 157 **Warrington**
London Road, Appleton, Warrington, Cheshire, WA4 5HR
⚘ www.warrington-golf-club.co.uk
☎ 01925 261620, Fax 265933, Pro 265431, Sec 261775
On A49 1 mile from M56 Junction 10.
Parkland course.
Pro Reay Mackay; Founded 1903
Designed by James Braid
18 holes, 6210 yards, S.S.S. 70
⚑ Practice ground.
† Welcome by prior arrangement.
￡ WD £27; WE £32.
↻ Welcome on Wed by prior arrangement; summer and winter packages for golf and catering.
🍽 Full clubhouse facilities.
⚐ Birchdale Hotel, Stockton Heath.

6A 158 **Wergs**
Keepers Lane, Wolverhampton, W Midlands, WV6 8UA
☎ 01902 742225, Fax 744748
Off A41, 2.5 miles from Wolverhampton
Open parkland course.
Pro Bryan Berlison; Founded 1990
Designed by CW Moseley
18 holes, 6949 yards, S.S.S. 73
† Welcome.
￡ WD £13.50; WE £17.
↻ Welcome WD; after 10am at WE; catering packages available; from £13.50.
🍽 Clubhouse catering facilities available.

6A 159 **Werneth Low**
Werneth Low Road, Hyde, Cheshire, SK14 3AF
☎ 0161 368 2503, Pro 367 9376, Sec 430 7484
Course is two miles from Hyde town centre via Gee Cross and Joel Lane.
Hilltop course.
Pro Tony Bacchus; Founded 1912
Designed by Peter Campbell
11 holes, 6113 yards, S.S.S. 70
† Welcome, except Sun.
￡ WD £20; WE £25.
↻ WD by prior arrangement.
🍽 Full catering facilities available.
⚐ The Village, Hyde.

The Wilmslow Golf Club

Great Warford
Mobberley
Knutsford
WA16 7AY

Founded 1889

Enjoy a warm, friendly welcome at our superb 18 hole (6, 607 yd) parkland course set in the heart of the Cheshire countryside.

VISITORS WELCOME Special rates for Society, Corporate & Charity events
Tel: **01565 873620**   Email: **wilmslowgolfclub@ukf.net**   Website: **www.wilmslowgolfclub.ukf.net**

6A 160 Westminster Park
Hough Green, Chester, Cheshire,
CH4 8JQ
☎ 01244 680231, Fax 680231
Course is two miles W of Chester city centre.
Parkland course.
Founded 1980
9 holes, 963 yards, S.S.S. 27
† Pay and play.
Ⅰ WD £2.50; WE £2.50 discounts for OAPs and juniors.
⌁ None.
🍽 Limited.
� Hotel Hough Green.

6A 161 Westwood (Leek)
Newcastle Road, Leek, Staffs, ST13 7AA
☎ 01538 398385, Fax 382485, Pro 398897
On A53 1 mile S of Leek.
Heathland/parkland course.
Pro Neale Hyde; Founded 1923
18 holes, 6214 yards, S.S.S. 69
Ⅰ Practice area.
† Welcome by prior arrangement.
Ⅰ WD £18; WE £20.
⌁ Welcome by prior arrangement; packages available including golf and catering; games/snooker room; from £27.50.
🍽 Full clubhouse facilities.
� The Hatcheries; Bank End Farm; Abbey Inn.

6A 162 Whiston Hall Golf Club
Whiston, Stoke on Trent, Staffs, ST10 2HZ
🖥 www.whistonhall.com
☎ 01538 266260, Fax 266820
On A52 midway between Stoke-on-Trent and Ashbourne; 3 miles from Alton Towers.
Parkland/heathland course.
Pro Derry Goodman; Founded 1971
Designed by Thomas Cooper
18 holes, 5784 yards, S.S.S. 69
† Welcome.
Ⅰ WD £10; WE £10.
⌁ Welcome by prior arrangement; packages available both WD and WE; from £12.95.
🍽 Full clubhouse facilities.
� Mansion Court Hotel.

6A 163 Whittington Heath
Tamworth Road, Lichfield, Staffs, WS14 9PW
🖥 info@whgcgolf.freeserve.co.uk
☎ 01543 432317, Fax 433962, Pro 432261
On A51 Lichfield to Tamworth road.
Heathland course.
Pro A Sadler; Founded 1886
Designed by HS Colt
18 holes, 6490 yards, S.S.S. 71
† Welcome WD with handicap certs.
Ⅰ WD £35 1 round, £50 2 rounds.
⌁ Welcome Wed and Thurs by arrangement; packages for golf and catering; maximum 40.
🍽 Full clubhouse facilities.
� Little Barrow, Lichfield.

6A 164 Widnes   ☏
Highfield Road, Widnes, Cheshire, WA8 7DT
🖥 www.widnes-golfclub.co.uk
🖥 arudder.wgc@uku.co.uk
☎ 0151 4242995, Fax 4952849, Pro 4207467
Signposted from town centre. Take signs to Autoquest Stadium, take Highfield rd and 20 yards on the left through lights.
Parkland course.
Jason O'Brien; Founded 1924
18 holes, 5729 yards, S.S.S. 68
† Welcome WD except Tues.
Ⅰ WD £18; WE £24.
⌁ Welcome Thurs by prior arrangement; from £30.
🍽 Catering and bar facilities.
� Hillcrest; Everglades.

6A 165 Wilmslow
Warford Lane, Mobberley, Knutsford, Cheshire, WA16 7AY
🖥 www.wilmslowgolfclub.ukf.net
🖥 wilmslowgolfclub@ukf.net
☎ 01565 873620, Fax 872172, Sec 872148
From the A34 Wilmslow-Alderley Edge road take the B5085 signposted for Knutsford; Warford Lane is three miles.
Parkland course.
Pro John Nowicki; Founded 1889
Designed by Alexander Herd
18 holes, 6607 yards, S.S.S. 72
† Welcome by arrangement.

Ⅰ WD £45; WE £55.
⌁ Welcome Tues and Thurs by prior arrangement; packages for golf and catering available; minimum 24; from £40.
🍽 Full clubhouse facilities.

6A 166 Wirral Ladies
93 Bidston Road, Prenton, Merseyside, CH43 6TS
☎ 0151 6521255, Pro 6522468
On A41 adjacent to M53 Junction 3.
Heathland course.
Pro Angus Law; Founded 1894
Designed by H Hilton
18 holes, 5185 (mens), 4948 (ladies) yards, S.S.S. 65 (mens), 69 (ladies)
Ⅰ Practice area.
† Welcome.
Ⅰ WD £25.50; WE £25.50.
⌁ Welcome by arrangement.
🍽 Full facilities.
� Bowler Hat.

6A 167 Withington   ☏
Palatine Road, Manchester, Lancs, M20 2UE
🖥 withingtongc@lineone.net
☎ 0161 4459544, Fax 4455210, Pro 4454861
S of Manchester on B5166.
Parkland course.
Pro Bob Ling; Founded 1892
18 holes, 6364 yards, S.S.S. 71
† Welcome by arrangement.
Ⅰ Terms on application.
⌁ Welcome by prior arrangement; 27-hole packages available; from £42.
🍽 Full clubhouse facilities.

6A 168 Wolstanton
Hassam Parade, Newcastle, Staffs, ST5 9DR
☎ 01782 622413, Fax 622718, Pro 622718, Rest/Bar 616995
0.5 miles off A34, 3 miles from Newcastle, turn right at McDonalds.
Parkland course.
Pro Simon Arnold; Founded 1904
18 holes, 5807 yards, S.S.S. 68
† Welcome WD; with member at WE.
Ⅰ WD £20.
⌁ Welcome WD except Tues; catering packages can be arranged.

⦿ Clubhouse facilities.
🛏 Friendly Hotel on A34 at Newcastle.

6A 169 **Woodside**

Knutsford Road, Cranage, Holmes Chapel, Crewe, Cheshire, CW4 8HT
☎ 01477 532 388
Off M6 at Junction 18.
9 holes (18 tees).
† Pay and play.
Ⅰ WD £5.
🍴 Limited facilities.
⦿ Limited.

6A 170 **Worfield**

Roughton, Bridgnorth, Shropshire, WV15 5HE

🔗 www.worfieldgolf.co.uk
✉ enquiries@worfieldgolf.co.uk
☎ 01746 716541, Fax 716302,
Sec 716372, Rest/Bar 716357
3 miles outside Bridgnorth on A454, Wolverhampton road.
Parkland course.
Pro Stephen Russell; Founded 1991
Designed by T Williams/D Gough
18 holes, 6801 yards, S.S.S. 73
Ⅰ Practice area.
† Welcome WD; after 1pm at WE.
Ⅰ WD £20; WE £25.
🍴 Welcome by arrangement; packages arranged through secretary/manager; terms on application.
⦿ Full clubhouse facilities.
🛏 Old Vicarage, Bridgnorth.

6A 171 **Wrekin** ☎

Ercall Woods, Wrekin, Telford, Shropshire, TF6 5BX
✉ wrekingolfclub@lineone.net
☎ 01952 244032, Fax 252906,
Pro 223101, Sec 244032
1 mile from J7 M54; take the B5061 to Golf Links Lane.
Parkland course.
Pro Keith Housden; Founded 1905
18 holes, 5570 yards, S.S.S. 67
† Welcome WD.
Ⅰ WD £22; WE £30.
🍴 Welcome WD.
⦿ Clubhouse facilities.

Derbyshire, Nottinghamshire, Lincolnshire

The trio of Lord Alfred Tennyson, herb sausages and Margaret Thatcher ought to say something about Lincolnshire, but as to what it is I haven't the faintest idea. The golf courses seem to be an altogether more eloquent description of the character of this county.

On the coast, just up the road from Skegness, is Seacroft Golf Club which is one of the most pleasant surprises in golf. You can park your car in a car park a little way from the course but it is rather easier to stick it on the road behind the first tee. It is an unprepossessing beginning not altogether alleviated by the sight of the club buildings, begun in 1904 and apparently still unfinished.

But the course is an unexpected wonder. The front nine, with the exception of the sixth, heads south towards the Gibraltar Point nature reserve. A road to the right threatens out of bounds on several holes – in fact there are fourteen holes where out of bounds to the right is a possibility – but often that is the least of the golfer's worries. The inward nine is even better, with two excellent par threes and a par five that is perhaps the signature hole. From the tee you can see the outline of Hunstanton across the Wash. Take it in whilst you can, because once started on this dog leg par five, with thorn trees and bushes left and right and a well bunkered ridge across the fairway, you will need all your wits about you.

Driving inland from Seacroft past fields that seem a cross between the fens and Romney marshes eventually you will reach Woodhall Spa. At the home of the English Golf Union everything is thoroughly well prepared. The Hotchkin is the better of the two courses, although a few have never emerged from its bunkers. At around the time in the mid nineties when Woodhall was getting a second course, Forest Pines was opened and in just a few years has become one of Lincolnshire's best.

On past Stamford lies Luffenham Heath. Its members will say that it is not in Lincolnshire at all, but in Rutland. The wood panelled clubhouse is full of royal portraits, maybe because it lies within a conservation area. There is plenty of gorse, heather and shrubbery into which to stick your ball from the tee and the slippery, contoured greens maintain the challenge.

Notts Golf Club is more usually called Hollinwell, a name derived from Holy Well. It lies within the boundaries of Sherwood Forest so it is not surprising that there should be a fair bit of oak and silver birch about. It is a stiff test but does not quite have the romance that you might suspect from a course with a rock called Robin Hood's Chair behind its second green.

Sherwood Forest is the preferred venue of some in the county. It is not quite so exacting as Hollinwell, but it feels more intimate and has a memorable back nine. If the first nine was as good, Sherwood Forest would be indisputably the county's best. Coxmoor is also highly rated and Worksop is renowned as the home territory of Lee Westwood. Part of Lindrick, the venue of the 1957 Ryder Cup, is in Nottinghamshire, but for the most part it is in Yorkshire.

Derbyshire is not quite such lush land for golf and there are so many good walks to be had that it might be better not to spoil them. But Cavendish, designed by Alister Mackenzie of Augusta fame, is worth a visit with its recessed tees, meandering greens and huge swales. So too is Kedleston Park, although it is not the finest of James Braid's work and isn't always in the best of nick.

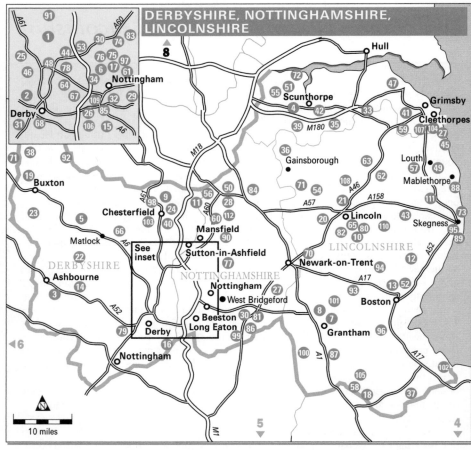

Belton Park Golf Club

Belton Lane, Londonthorpe Road, Grantham, Lincs. NG31 9SH

Founded in 1890 in the mature parkland of Belton House, this 27 hole course with streams, ponds, trees and a herd of deer provides an excellent, but fair test of golf.

Contact: Brian McKee for suitable tee times 01476 563911 • Trevor Ireland for society details 01476 567399

Green Fees: £36 per day, £30 per round, £42/£36 at weekends • Location: 1.5 miles NE of Grantham

---

6B 1 **Alfreton**
Highfields, Wingfield Rd, Oakthorpe, Alfreton, Derbys, DE5 7DH
☎ 01773 832070
On Matlock Road 1 mile W of Alfreton. Parkland course.
Founded 1892
11 holes, S.S.S. 66
† Welcome WD; with member at WE.
Ⅰ WD £18.
⌂ Welcome by prior arrangement; max 36; terms available on application.
⦿ Clubhouse facilities.
⇲ Swallow, South Normanton.

6B 2 **Allestree Park**
Allestree Hall, Allestree Park, Derby, Derbys, DE22 2EU
☎ 01332 550616, Fax 541195, Sec 552971, Rest/Bar 552971
4 miles N of Derby; 1 mile N of A38/A6 Junction.
Undulating parkland course.
Pro Leigh Woodward
Founded 1947
18 holes, 5806 yards, S.S.S. 68
† Welcome.
Ⅰ Terms on application.
⌂ Welcome by prior arrangement; various 18, 27, 36-hole packages available; catering; golf clinics; terms on application.
⦿ Clubhouse facilities.
⇲ International, Hotel Derby.

6B 3 **Ashbourne**
The Clubhouse Wyaston Road, Ashbourne, Derbys, DE6 1NB
🖳 www.ashbournegolfclub.co.uk
✉ sec@ashbournegc.fsnet.co.uk
☎ 01335 342078, Fax 347930, Pro 347960, Sec 343457
On A515 2 miles W of Ashbourne. A52 Derby-Leek road, turn off on Old Derby road.
Parkland course.
Pro Andrew Smith; Founded 1886/1999 redeveloped
Designed by Frank Pennink
18 holes, 6365 yards, S.S.S. 72
Ⅰ Practice round.
† Welcome WD.
Ⅰ WD £20; WE £30.

⌂ Welcome WD; by arrangement with professional; prices on application.
⦿ Clubhouse catering and bar.
⇲ Green Man; Hanover International both Ashbourne.

6B 4 **Ashby Decoy**
Burringham Rd, Scunthorpe, Lincs, DN17 2AB
🖳 www.ashbydecoy.co.uk
✉ ashby.decoy@btclick.com
☎ 01724 866561, Fax 271708, Pro 868972, Rest/Bar 842913
From M181 turn right at first three roundabouts; course is 400 yards on left course.
Pro A Miller; Founded 1936
Designed by Members
18 holes, 6250 yards, S.S.S. 70
† Welcome WD except Tues; with a member WE.
Ⅰ Summer WD £18; Winter WD £13.
⌂ Welcome WD except Tues by prior arrangement; various packages on application; from £22-£37.
⦿ Full clubhouse facilities.
⇲ Royal; Wortley, both Scunthorpe.

6B 5 **Bakewell**
Station Road, Bakewell, Derbys, DE45 1GB
☎ 01629 812307, Rest/Bar 812307
0.75 miles from Bakewell Square; cross River Wye on A619 Sheffield-Chesterfield Road; up Station Rd turning right before Industrial estate.
Hilly parkland course.
Founded 1899
Designed by George Low
9 holes, 5122 yards, S.S.S. 65
† Welcome WD; Ladies priority Thurs; WE by prior arrangement.
Ⅰ Prices on application.
⌂ Welcome by arrangement.
⦿ Meals and bar except Mon.
⇲ Rutland Arms.

6B 6 **Beeston Fields**
Old Drive, Beeston Fields, Nottingham, NG9 3DD
🖳 www.beestonfields.co.uk

✉ beestonfieldsgolfclub@supernet.com
☎ 0115 9257062, Fax 9254280, Pro 9220872
1 mile from Beeston, 5 miles W of Nottingham on S side of A52.
Parkland course.
Pro Alun Wardle; Founded 1923
Designed by Tom Williamson
18 holes, 6404 yards, S.S.S. 71
Ⅰ Practice area.
† Welcome WD (after 3pm Tues); some restrictions at WE.
Ⅰ WD £26-£36; WE £31.
⌂ Welcome Mon and Wed by prior arrangement; packages available for catering contact steward; separate dining room.
⦿ Clubhouse facilities.
⇲ Priory Hotel.

6B 7 **Belton Park** ♛
Belton Lane, Londonthorpe Rd, Grantham, Lincs, NG31 9SH
🖳 www.beltonpark.co.uk
✉ greatgolf@beltonpark.co.uk
☎ 01476 567399, Fax 592078, Pro 563911, Rest/Bar 563355
From A607 Grantham-Sleaford Road; turn right to Londonthorpe; course 1 mile on left.
Parkland course.
Pro Brian McKee; Founded 1890
Designed by T Williamson/Dave Thomas and Peter Alliss
Ⅰ Practice range, 2 practice areas.
† Welcome with handicap certs except Tues.
Ⅰ WD £30, WE £36.
⌂ Welcome WD except Tues; by prior arrangement; terms on application.
⦿ Full clubhouse facilities.
⇲ Angel & Royal/Kings/Marriot.

6B 8 **Belton Woods Hotel** ♛
Belton, Nr Grantham, Lincs, NG32 2LN
🖳 www.deveronline.co.uk
✉ belton.woods@deveronline.co.uk
☎ 01476 593200, Fax 574547, Pro 514332, Sec 514332, Rest/Bar 593200
2 miles E of A1 via Gonerby Moor; 2 miles N of Grantham on A607 Lincoln Road.

A fine parkland, 9 hole golf course situated on the edge of the Peak District, Derbyshire.
9 Holes - PAR 36. 18 Holes - PAR 72.
- Superb floodlit under cover driving range • A warm welcome to visitors and societies
- Buggy, trolleys and golf clubs available for hire • Modest green fees
- Golfing competitions can be arranged together with full hospitality facilities.

Pools Head Lane, Brailsford, Ashbourne, Derbyshire DE6 3BU   Tel: **01335 360096**

Parkland course with mature trees and ancient woodland.
Pro Steven Sayers
36 holes and a par-3 9-hole, 6831/6623 yards, S.S.S. 73
⚐ Practice range, 24 bays floodlit.
† Welcome; bookings taken 10 days in advance.
⌷ WD £27; WE £30.
⌲ Welcome WD by prior arrangement; packages available; company days organised; reductions for residents; banqueting facilities for 240; health and sports leisure centres; conference facilities; also Spitfire 9-hole course 1184 yards par 3.
🍽 Full bar and restaurant facilities.
⌁ Belton Woods on site.

6B 9 Birch Hall
Sheffield Rd, Unstone Green, Sheffield, S18 5DH
☎ 01246 291979, Rest/Bar 291087
Off A61.
Moorland course.
Pro Pete Ball; Founded 1992
Designed by David Tucker
18 holes, 6505 yards, S.S.S. 73
⚐ Practice area.
† Welcome; prior arrangement at WE.
⌷ WD £10; WE £10.
⌲ Welcome WD and afternoons at WE; catering on application; from £10.
🍽 Clubhouse facilities.
⌁ Sandpiper.

6B 10 Blankney
Blankney, Lincoln, Lincs, LN4 3AZ
☎ 01526 320263, Fax 322521,
Pro 320202
Course is on the B1188 10 miles S of Lincoln.
Parkland course.
Pro Graham Bradley; Founded 1904
Designed by Cameron Sinclair (updated Design)
18 holes, 6638 yards, S.S.S. 73
† Welcome by prior arrangement.
⌷ WD £24; WE £30.
⌲ Welcome by prior arrangement with General Manager; from £24.
🍽 Clubhouse facilities available.
⌁ Dower House; Golf Hotel.

6B 11 Bondhay Golf & Country Club
Bondhay Lane, Whitwell, Worksop, Notts, S80 3EH
☎ 01909 723608, Fax 720226
Just off A619; 5 minutes from M1 J30.
Parkland course.
Pro Michael Ramsden; Founded 1991
Designed by Donald Steel
18 holes, 6765 yards, S.S.S. 72
⚐ 15-bay floodlit covered range.
† Welcome; advance booking.
⌷ Winter WD £17; WE £22; Summer WD £17; WE £22.
⌲ Welcome by prior arrangement; catering packages by arrangement; function rooms available; also family course; from £4.
🍽 Full bar and restaurant facilities available.
⌁ Vandykes, Whitwell, Beeches, Rotherham; Lion Hotel, Worksop.

6B 12 Boston
Cowbridge, Honcastle Rd, Boston, Lincs, PE22 7EL
🖳 www.bostongc.co.uk
📧 steveshaw@bostongc.co.uk
☎ 01205 350589, Fax 367526,
Pro 362306, Rest/Bar 352533
Course is on the B1183 two miles N of Boston.
Parkland course with water on 8 holes.
Pro Nic Hiom; Founded 1900
Designed by BS Cooper; Extended by Donald Steel
18 holes, 6490 yards, S.S.S. 71
† Welcome by arrangement.
⌷ WD £22.50; WE £27.50.
⌲ Welcome WD except Tues; packages available for 18-36 holes; phone for details.
🍽 Clubhouse facilities.
⌁ New England; White Hart; Kings Arms all Boston.

6B 13 Boston West
Hubbert's Bridge, Boston, Lincs, PE20 3QX
🖳 www.bostonwestgolfclub.co.uk
📧 info@bostonwestgolfclub.co.uk
☎ 01205 290670, Fax 290725,
Pro 290540

At junction of A1121/B1192, 2 miles W of Boston.
Parkland course.
Pro Simon Collinwood/Paul Creasey; Founded 1995
Designed by KMB
18 holes, 6353 yards, S.S.S. 71
⚐ 20 bay covered, floodlit range; 6 hole Academy course.
† Welcome.
⌷ Terms on application.
⌲ Welcome at all times; golf and catering packages can be arranged; terms on application.
🍽 Full catering facilities.
⌁ Boston Lodge.

6B 14 Brailsford
Pools Head Lane, Brailsford, Ashbourne, Derbys, DE6 3BU
☎ 01335 360096
Signposted off A52 just before Ashbourne. 6 miles from Derby city centre along the A52 on the left hand side.
Parkland course.
Pro David McCarthy; Founded 1994
9 holes, 6292 yards, S.S.S. 70
⚐ Practice range 15 bays floodlit; Under coverpractice bunker and putting green; new clubhouse.
† Welcome.
⌷ POA.
⌲ Welcome by prior arrangement; reductions for groups of 16 or more of 20%; terms on application.
🍽 Full catering facilities and bar.
⌁ Mackwith Hotel, Mundy Arms Hotel.

6B 15 Bramcote Hills Golf Course
Thoresby Rd, off Derby Rd, Bramcote, Nottingham, Notts, NG9 3EP
☎ 0115 9281880
Leave M1 Junction 25, take A52 towards Nottingham, past Bramcote Leisure Centre; left after 0.25 miles.
Parkland course.
Founded 1981
18 holes, 1501 yards, S.S.S. 31
† Welcome; pay and play.
⌷ WD £6.50; WE and BH £7.00; Discounts for juniors, OAPs and students (£5.50 all week).

⚐ Welcome.
◉ None.
🛏 Novotel.

6B 16 Breedon Priory

The Clubhouse, Green Lane, Wilson,
Nr Derby, DE73 1LG
☎ 01332 863081, Sec 864046
On A453 3.5 miles W of M1 Junction
23A.
Parkland course.
Pro Jim Broughton; Founded 1991
Designed by D Snell
18 holes, 5777 yards, S.S.S. 70
† Welcome.
⌇ Prices on application.
⚐ Welcome by prior arrangement;
catering and golf packages available;
terms on application.
◉ Full clubhouse facilities. Golf
Simulator.

6B 17 Bulwell Forest

Hucknall Rd, Bulwell, Nottingham,
NG6 9LQ
☎ 0115 9770576, Fax 9763172,
Pro 9763172, Sec 9608435
On A611 close to M1 Junction 26.
Heathland course.
Pro Lee Rawlings
Founded 1870/1902
Designed by John Dolman
18 holes, 5561 yards, S.S.S. 67
† Welcome; restrictions at WE.
⌇ WD £11; WE £13.
⚐ Welcome WD; after 11am Tues;
2pm Sat and 12 noon Sun; full day
packages available; £25.
◉ Clubhouse catering facilities.
🛏 Moat House; Gateway both
Nottingham.

6B 18 Burghley Park

St Martins Without, Stamford,
PE9 3JX
✉ burghley.golf@lineone.net
☎ 01780 753789, Fax 753789
On B1081 1 mile S of Stamford.
Parkland course.
Pro Glenn Davies; Founded 1890
18 holes, 6236 yards, S.S.S. 70
⌇ Practice area.
† Welcome WD with handicap
certificates.
⌇ WD £25 day pass.
⚐ Welcome WD by prior
arrangement; full golf and catering
package including insurance; £42.
◉ Clubhouse facilities.
🛏 The George at Stamford; Garden
House; Lady Annes; Crown; Royal
Oak, Duddington.

6B 19 Buxton & High Peak ☎

Waterswallows Rd, Fairfield, Buxton,
Derbys, SK17 7EN
🖳 www.buxtonandhighpeakgolfclub.
co.uk
✉ sec@bhpgc.fsnet.co.uk
☎ 01298 26263, Fax 26333,
Pro 23112, Rest/Bar 23453
On A6 Manchester-Derby Road just N
of Buxton.
Parkland course.
Pro Gary Brown; Founded 1887
Designed by J Morris
18 holes, 5966 yards, S.S.S. 69
⌇ Driving range located next door.
† Welcome by prior arrangement.
⌇ WD £24; WE £30.
⚐ Welcome by prior arrangement; full
golf and catering packages available;
£40.
◉ Full clubhouse facilities.
🛏 Palace Hotel; Hawthorn Farm.

6B 20 Canwick Park ☎

Washingborough Road, Lincoln, Lincs,
LN4 1EF
🖳 www.canwickpark.co.uk
✉ info@canwickpark.co.uk
☎ 01522 542912, Fax 526997,
Pro 536870, Sec 542912
On B1190 Washingborough Road,
2 miles E of Lincoln.
Parkland course.
Pro SJ Williamson; Founded 1893/1975
Designed by Hawtree & Partners
18 holes, 6257 yards, S.S.S. 69
† Welcome WD; after 3pm at WE.
Between 10am and 12 pm and 2-4pm
£12 per round.
⌇ WD £20; WE £21; reduced green
fees at certain times; phone for details.
⚐ Welcome by prior arrangement;
packages available for catering and
golf; from £17.
◉ Clubhouse catering facilities.
🛏 Travel Inn; Branston Hall; Grand
Lincoln.

6B 21 Carholme

Carholme Road, Lincoln, LN1 1SE
🖳 www.carholme-golf-club.co.uk
✉ info@carholme-golf-club.co.uk
☎ 01522 523725, Fax 533733,
Pro 536811, Rest/Bar 523725
On A57 Worksop Road, 1 mile from
Lincoln city centre.
Parkland course.
Pro Richard Hunter; Founded 1906
18 holes, 6215 yards, S.S.S. 70
† Welcome by prior arrangement
except Sun.
⌇ Summer £18 per round £22 per
day. Winter £11 per round £13 per day.

⚐ Welcome by prior arrangement;
catering and golf packages available;
terms on application.
◉ Bar and restaurant (except Mon).
🛏 Delph GH.

6B 22 Carsington Water

Carsington, Wirksworth, Derbys
☎ 01403 784864
8 miles NE of Ashbourne off B5035.
Parkland course.
9 holes, 3000 yards, S.S.S. 33
† Welcome.
⌇ Pay and play £9.
⚐ Terms on application.
◉ Limited.

6B 23 Cavendish ☎

Gadley Lane, Buxton, Derbys,
SK17 6XD
☎ 01298 23494, Fax 79708,
Pro 25052, Sec 79708
On outskirts of Buxton off the ring road
in direction of A53 Leek.
Moorland/parkland course.
Pro P Hunstone; Founded 1925
Designed by Dr Alister MacKenzie
18 holes, 5721 yards, S.S.S. 68
⌇ Practice area.
† Everyone welcome.
⌇ WD/WE £26-£35.
⚐ Welcome by prior arrangement;
minimum 16; 27 holes £25; for catering
contact stewardess.
◉ Full clubhouse facilities available.
🛏 Leewood; Buckingham; Palace;
Portland, all Buxton.

6B 24 Chesterfield ☎

Walton, Chesterfield, Derbys, S42 7LA
☎ 01246 279256, Fax 276622,
Pro 276297, Rest/Bar 232035
Course is 2 miles W of town centre on
A632 to Matlock.
Parkland course.
Pro Mike McLean; Founded 1897
18 holes, 6261 yards, S.S.S. 70
† Welcome WD and Sun pm; with
member at WE.
⌇ WD £28 per round, £36 per day.
WE Sun pm £30 or with member WD
£14, WE £18.
⚐ Welcome WD by prior application;
packages available; from £36 inc. meals.
◉ Full clubhouse facilities.
🛏 Chesterfield Hotel; Swallows,
Normanton, Ibis Hotel, Chesterfield.

6B 25 Chevin

Golf Lane, Duffield, Derbys,
DE56 4EE

☎ 01332 841864, Fax 844228,
Pro 841112, Rest/Bar 842842
On A6 5 miles N of Derby outside
Duffield.
Hilly parkland course.
Pro Willie Bird; Founded 1894
Designed by W Braid
18 holes, 6057 yards, S.S.S. 69
⚑ Practice area.
♦ Welcome WD except before
9.30am and between 12.30pm and
2pm; WE with member.
⚑ WD £26; day ticket £32.
⚐ Welcome WD by prior
arrangement with Sec.
⦿ Full facilities, except Mon.
⛳ Strutt Arms adjacent.

6B 26 Chilwell Manor
Meadow Lane, Chilwell, Nottingham,
Notts, NG9 5AE
☎ 0115 9258958, Fax 9257050,
Sec 9257050, Rest/Bar 9257050
4 miles W of Nottingham on A6005
near Beeston.
Parkland course.
Pro Paul Wilson; Founded 1906
18 holes, 6395 yards, S.S.S. 70
♦ Welcome after 9am WD; after
11am WE.
⚑ WD £18; WE £20.
⚐ Welcome Mon, Wed, Fri. Full
clubhouse facilities available.
⛳ Post House; Novotel; Village.

6B 27 Cleethorpes　　　　☎
Kings Road, Cleethorpes, N E Lincs,
DN35 0PN
☎ 01472 816110, Fax 814060,
Pro 814060, Sec 816110,
Rest/Bar 812059
2 miles SE of Cleethorpes.
Mature coastal course.
Pro Paul Davies; Founded 1894
Designed by Harry Vardon (now vastly
altered)
18 holes, 6356 yards, S.S.S. 70
⚑ Practice area.
♦ Visitors welcome Mon, Thurs, Fri
and Sun.
⚑ WD £20; WE £25.
⚐ Welcome by prior arrangement.
⦿ Full facilities.
⛳ Kingsway; Wellow.

6B 28 College Pines　　　　☎
Worksop College Drive, Worksop,
Nottingham, S80 3AP
🖳 www.collegepinesgolfclub.co.uk
☎ 01909 501431, Fax 481227,
Pro 501431, Sec 501431,
Rest/Bar 488785

Half mile S of Worksop on B6034; just
off A57 Worksop by-pass.
Heathland course.
Pro Charles Snell; Founded 1994
Designed by David Snell
18 holes, 6801 yards, S.S.S. 72
⚑ 20 grass bays.
♦ Welcome by prior arrangement.
⚑ WD £13; WE £19.
⚐ Packages available.
⦿ Bar food/Restaurant.
⛳ Lion Hotel, Worksop Travel Lodge.

6B 29 Cotgrave Place
Stragglethorpe, Nr Radcliffe On Trent,
Nottingham, NG12 3HB
☎ 0115 9333344
Off A52 5 miles SE of Nottingham.
Parkland course with lake features.
Pro R Smith; Founded 1992
Designed by P Alliss/J Small
2 x 18 holes, 6303 yards, S.S.S. 70
⚑ Floodlit driving range.
♦ Welcome.
⚑ WD £22; £21; WE £25.
⚐ Welcome by prior arrangement;
catering and golf packages available
by prior arrangement; banqueting
facilities available; prices on
application.
⦿ Full clubhouse facilities available.
⛳ Hilton; Moat House; Langar Hall.

6B 30 Coxmoor
Coxmoor Rd, Sutton-In-Ashfield, Notts,
NG17 5LF
🖳 www.coxmoor.freeuk.com
✉ coxmoor@freeuk.com
☎ 01623 557359, Fax 557359,
Pro 559906, Rest/Bar 559878
Course is on the A611 1.5 miles S of
Mansfield.
Heathland course.
Pro D Ridley; Founded 1913
18 holes, 6589 yards, S.S.S. 72
⚑ Practice area.
♦ Welcome WD; with member at
WE.
⚑ WD £40-£50.
⚐ Welcome WD except Tues, by
prior arrangement; golf and catering
available.
⦿ Clubhouse, catering and bar
facilities.
⛳ Cockliffe House Hotel, Arnold;
Renaissance, South Normanton.

6B 31 Derby
Wilmore Road, Sinfin, Derby,
DE24 9HD
☎ 01332 766323, Fax 769004,
Pro 766462

2 miles from city centre off Wilmore Rd.
Parkland course.
Pro John Siddons; Founded 1923
18 holes, 6163 yards, S.S.S. 69
⚑ Practice green.
♦ Welcome by prior arrangement.
⚑ Terms on application.
⚐ Welcome by prior arrangement;
packages available; terms on
application.
⦿ Full clubhouse facilities available.
⛳ International, Derby.

6B 32 Edwalton Municipal
Edwalton Village, Nottingham, Notts,
NG12 4AS
☎ 0115 9234775
Off A606 from Nottingham at Edwalton
Hall, on Welling Lane.
Municipal parkland course; also 9-hole
par 3.
Pro J Staples; Founded 1981
Designed by Frank Pennink
9 holes, 3336 yards, S.S.S. 36
♦ Welcome.
⚑ WD £6.50; WE (am) £7.20. Loyalty
card holders WD £5.50; WE (am)
£6.20. Pensioners £3.90.
Unemployed/Students £4.00.
⚐ Welcome WD.
⦿ Lunches and meals available.
⛳ Many in local area.

6B 33 Elsham　　　　☎
Barton Rd, Elsham, Brigg, Lincs,
DN20 0LS
🖳 www.elshamgolfclub.co.uk
✉ elshamgolfclub@lineone.net
☎ 01652 680291, Fax 680308,
Pro 680432
3 miles N of Brigg on B1206 Road; 3
miles from J5 M180.
Parkland course.
Pro Stewart Brewer; Founded 1900
18 holes, 6426 yards, S.S.S. 71
♦ Welcome WD; with member at WE.
⚑ WD £24 (18 holes), £30 (36)
⚐ Welcome WD; full packages of golf
and catering available; from £40.
⦿ Full clubhouse catering facilities
available.
⛳ Arties Mill, Castlethorpe; Red Lion
Hotel, Redbourne; Jolly Miller, Wrawby.

6B 34 Erewash Valley
Golf Club Road, Stanton-by-Dale,
Ilkeston, Derbys, DE7 4QR
🖳 www.erewashvalley.co.uk
✉ secretary@erewashvalley.co.uk
☎ 0115 932 3258, Fax 944 0061,
Pro 932 4667, Sec 932 2984,
Rest/Bar 944 00613258

Course is 3 miles from the M1 Junction 25.
Parkland course.
Pro Mike Ronan; Founded 1905
Designed by Hawtree
18 holes, 6557 yards, S.S.S. 71
⚑ Practice ground.
✦ Welcome WD and pm.
⌁ WD £30.50; WE 40.50.
⌁ Welcome Mon, Wed, Fri by prior arrangement.
⍟ Restaurant and bar facilities.
⌸ Post House; Novotel.

6B 35 **Forest Pines**
Ermine Street, Nr Brigg, Lincs,
DN20 0AQ
⌨ www.forestpines.co.uk
✉ golfsales@forestpines.co.uk
☎ 01652 650756, Fax 650495
Take M180 Junction 4 and then A15 towards Scunthorpe; club at first roundabout.
Forest course.
Pro David Edwards; Founded 1996
Designed by John Morgan
27 holes; Forest 6859 yards; Pines 6670 yards; Beeches 6393 yards.
⚑ Grass driving range & practice ground, chipping area & putting green.
✦ Welcome.
⌁ WD/WE £36 round, £46 day.
⌁ Very welcome.
⍟ Full catering facilities.
⌸ 114-bed 4 star hotel on site.

6B 36 **Gainsborough**
The Belt Road, Thonock,
Gainsborough, Lincs, DN21 1PZ
✉ emma@gainsboroughgc.co.uk
☎ 01427 613088, Fax 810172,
Pro 612278
Signposted off A631 Gainsborough-Grimsby Rd.
US Style course with lakes and many bunkers.
Pro Stephen Cooper; Founded 1997 (Karsten Lakes) 1894/1985 (Thonock Park)
Designed by N Coles (Karsten Lakes) B Waites (Thonock Park)
Karsten Lakes 18; Thonock Park 18 holes, Karsten Lakes 6900; Thonock Park 6266 yards, S.S.S. Karsten Lakes 70; Thonock Park 70
⚑ 12 floodlit bays + Ping fitting centre.
✦ Welcome 7 days per week).
⌁ Karsten Lakes £30; Thonock Park £25; rates apply 7 days.
⌁ Welcome (WD for Thonock Park); packages for golf and catering can be arranged; snooker tables; menus

available for societies in restaurant; prices on application.
⍟ Full catering and bar service including coffee shop and restaurant.
⌸ Hickman Hill, Gainsborough.

6B 37 **Gedney Hill**
West Drove, Gedney Hill, Nr Spalding,
Lincs, PE12 0NT
☎ 01406 330922, Fax 330323,
Pro 330922
On B1166 6 miles from Crowland.
Links style course.
Pro David Hutton; Founded 1989
Designed by C Britton
18 holes, 5285 yards, S.S.S. 66
⚑ 10 Driving bays and a practice green.
✦ Welcome.
⌁ WD £6.50; WE £11.
⌁ Welcome by prior arrangement; catering available; snooker; terms on application.
⍟ Clubhouse catering.

6B 38 **Glossop & District**
Hurst Lane, off Sheffield Rd, Glossop,
Derbys, SK13 9PU
☎ 01457 865247, Pro 853117
Off A57 1.5 miles outside Glossop; turn at Royal Oak pub.
Moorland course.
Pro Daniel Marsh; Founded 1894
11 holes, 5800 yards, S.S.S. 68
⚑ Practice area.
✦ Welcome; restrictions on Sat.
⌁ Terms on application.
⌁ Welcome by prior arrangement; terms on application.
⍟ Clubhouse facilities.
⌸ Wind in the Willows, Glossop.

6B 39 **Grange Park**
Butterwick Rd, Messingham,
Scunthorpe, N Lincs, DN17 3PP
✉ info@grangepark.uk.com
☎ 01724 762945, Pro 762945
5 miles S of Scunthorpe between Messingham and E Butterwick; 4 miles S of M180 Junction 3.
Parkland course.
Pro Jonathan Drury; Founded 1991
Designed by Ray Price
18 holes, 6146 yards, S.S.S. 69
⚑ Practice range floodlit; also par 3 9-hole course (£3). 20 bays.
✦ Welcome at all times.
⌁ WD £10.50; WE £12.50.
⌁ Welcome by prior arrangement; packages available; terms on application.
⍟ Full clubhouse facilities.

⌸ Caravan park on site – booking advisable.

6B 40 **Grassmoor Golf Centre**
North Wingfield Rd, Grassmoor,
Chesterfield, Derbys, S42 5EA
⌨ www.grassmoorgolf.co.uk
✉ enquiries@grassmoorgolf.co.uk
☎ 01246 856044, Fax 853486
2 miles S of Chesterfield near M1 J29.
Moorland course.
Pro Gary Hagues; Founded 1990
Designed by Hawtree.
18 holes, 5723 yards, S.S.S. 69
⚑ Practice range 25 bays floodlit
✦ Welcome WE; by prior arrangement.
⌁ WD £12; WE £15.
⌁ Welcome.
⍟ Full facilities.
⌸ Chesterfield

6B 41 **Grimsby**
Littlecoates Rd, Grimsby, NE Lincs,
N34 4LU
☎ 01472 342823, Fax 342630,
Pro 356981, Sec/Mgr 342630
1 mile W of Grimsby town centre; turn left off A18 at first roundabout; course is 0.75 miles on left.
Pro Richard Smith; Founded 1922
18 holes, 6057 yards, S.S.S. 70
⚑ Practice ground.
✦ Welcome if member of a golf club; Ladies Day Tues.
⌁ WD £22-£28; WE £28.
⌁ Welcome Mon and Fri by prior arrangement.
⍟ Full facilities.
⌸ Post House.

6B 42 **Holme Hall**
Holme Lane, Bottesford, Scunthorpe,
DN16 3RF
⌨ www.holmehallgolf.co.uk
✉ tracey.curtis@btconnect.com
☎ 01724 851816, Fax 862078,
Pro 851816, Sec 862078,
Rest/Bar 282053/859185
Close to M180 Junction 4 for Scunthorpe East.
Heathland course.
Pro R McKiernan; Founded 1908
18 holes, 6404 yards, S.S.S. 71
✦ Welcome WD; only with member at WE.
⌁ WD £25 per round, £35 per day.
Members and guests only at WE.
⌁ Welcome WD by arrangement; on application; from £25.
⍟ Clubhouse facilities.
⌸ Club can provide list.

6B 43 **Horncastle**
West Ashby, Horncastle, Lincs,
LN9 5PP
☎ 01507 526800, Pro 526800,
Sec 526800, Rest/Bar 526800
Off A158 W of Horncastle.
Parkland course with water hazards.
Pro EC Wright; Founded 1990
Designed by Ernie Wright
18 holes, 5717 yards, S.S.S. 70
⏳ Practice range, 24 bays floodlit.
⬧ Everyone welcome.
⬩ WD £18 per round, £25 per day.
WE/Bank holidays £20 per round, £27
per day.
⬩ Welcome; packages for golf and
catering available; from £10.
🍽 Clubhouse facilities.
⬩ Admiral Rodney.

6B 44 **Horsley Lodge**
Smalley Mill Road, Horsley, Derbys,
DE21 5BL
🖧 www.horsleylodge.co.uk
📧 enquiries@horsleylodge.co.uk
☎ 01332 780838, Fax 781118
Course is off the A38 four miles N of
Derby.
Meadowland course.
Pro Graham Lyall; Founded 1990
Designed by Peter McEvoy
18 holes, 6400 yards, S.S.S. 71
⏳ Driving range.
⬧ Welcome WD, after 3pm WE.
⬩ WD/WE £42; half-price for
members; guests; hotel guests and
holders of Derbyshire union card £15.
⬩ Welcome Tues; Thurs or Fri by
prior arrangement; packages available;
conference facilities; from £22.
🍽 Clubhouse and à la carte
restaurant available; bars in 1840
clubhouse.
⬩ Horsley Lodge on site.

6B 45 **Humberston Park**
Humberston Ave, Humberston,
NE Lincs, DN36 4SJ
📧 chriscrookes@lineone.net
☎ 01472 210404
Off Humberstone Ave behind the
Cherry Garth Scouts Field.
Parkland course; leased by consortium
of 8 members.
Founded 1970
9 holes, 3672 yards, S.S.S. 58
⏳ Putting green.
⬧ Welcome.
⬩ WD 18 holes £9, 9 holes £7; WE
18 holes £11, 9 holes £8; discounts for
guests.
⬩ Welcome by arrangement.
🍽 Bar facilities and snacks.

6B 46 **Ilkeston Borough (Pewit)**
West End Drive, Ilkeston, Derbys,
DE7 5GH
☎ 0115 9307704, Sec 9327021,
Rest/Bar 9304550
0.5 miles E of Ilkeston.
Municipal meadowland course.
Founded 1920
9 holes, 4072 yards, S.S.S. 60
⬧ Everyone welcome.
⬩ 18 holes WD £6.95; WE £6.95; 9
holes WD £4.00; WE £4.00.
Concession rates Mon-Frid. £3.20 for
18 holes. Junior rate £2.35 all week for
18 holes.
⬩ Welcome weekends only by prior
arrangement.
⬩ The Post House Motel, Sandiacre,
near M1 motorway.

6B 47 **Immingham**   ℃
Church Lane, Immingham, Grimsby,
NE Lincs, DN40 2EU
🖧 www.immgc.com
📧 admin@immgc.com
☎ 01469 575298, Fax 577636,
Pro 575493
2 miles off M180 behind St Andrew's
Church.
Flat parkland course.
Pro Nick Harding; Founded 1975
Designed by Hawtree & Son (front 9);
F Pennink (back 9)
18 holes, 6215 yards, S.S.S. 70
⏳ Practice area.
⬧ Welcome WD; restrictions WE.
⬩ WD £12; WE £18. Societies
welcome.
⬩ Packages available; special winter
packages; book in advance/ring for
details; company days welcome.
🍽 Full clubhouse facilities.
⬩ Stallingborough Grange;
Ashbourne Hotel.

6B 48 **Kedleston Park**
Kedleston, Quarndon, Derby,
DE22 5JD
🖧 www.kedlestonparkgolf.com
📧 secretary@
kedlestonpark.sagehost.co.uk
☎ 01332 840035, Fax 840035,
Pro 841685, Sec 840335,
Rest/Bar 840634
4 miles N of Derby; from A38 follow
signs to Kedleston Hall.
Parkland course.
Pro Paul Wesselingh; Founded 1947
Designed by James Braid and
Morrison & Co
18 holes, 6675 yards, S.S.S. 72
⬧ Welcome by arrangement.
⬩ WD/WE £40.

⬩ Welcome Mon and Fri; catering
packages can be arranged; from £40.
🍽 Full catering facilities.
⬩ Kedleston Hotel; Midland Hotel;
Mundy Arms.

6B 49 **Kenwick Park**   ℃
Kenwick, Nr Louth, Lincs, LN11 8NY
🖧 www.louthnet.co.uk
📧 golfatkenwick@nascr.net
☎ 01507 605134, Fax 606556, Pro
607161, Sec 605134, Rest/Bar 608210
1 mile S of Louth.
Rolling parkland course.
Pro Eric Sharp; Founded 1992
Designed by Patrick Tallack
18 holes, 6782 yards, S.S.S. 73
⏳ 8 bays; members and guests only.
⬧ Welcome by prior arrangement.
⬩ WD £27; WE £35.
⬩ Welcome by prior arrangement;
catering and golf packages can be
arranged; terms on application.
🍽 Clubhouse facilities.
⬩ Kenwick Park Hotel on site.

6B 50 **Kilton Forest**
Blyth Rd, Worksop, Notts, S81 0TL
☎ 01909 486563, Fax 486563,
Sec 479199, Rest/Bar 479199
Course is one mile from Worksop on
the Blyth Road.
Parkland course.
Pro Stuart Betteridge; Founded 1978
18 holes, 6424 yards, S.S.S. 71
⏳ Chipping and putting area.
⬧ Welcome; bookings required at WE.
⬩ WD £10; WE £13.
⬩ Welcome by prior arrangement;
catering packages available; terms on
application.
🍽 Restaurant and bar facilities.
⬩ Regency; Lion both Worksop.

6B 51 **Kingsway**
Kingsway, Scunthorpe, N Lincs,
DN15 7ER
☎ 01724 840945
Between Berkeley and Queensway
roundabouts S of A18.
Undulating parkland course.
Pro Chris Mann; Founded 1971
Designed by RD Highfield
9 holes, 1915 yards, S.S.S. 59
⬧ Welcome.
⬩ WD £3.70; WE £4.35
⬩ None.

6B 52 **Kirton Holme**
Holme Rd, Kirton Holme Nr Boston,
Lincs, PE20 1SY

☎ 01205 290669
Off A52 4 miles W of Boston.
Parkland course.
Founded 1992
Designed by DW Welberry
9 holes, 5778 yards, S.S.S. 68
† Pay and play.
⌐ WD £5; WE £6.
⌐ Welcome by prior arrangement;
maximum 30; meals available; terms
on application.
🍽 Full clubhouse facilities.
⌐ Poacher Inn.

6B 53 Leen Valley ☎
Wigwam Lane, Hucknall, Notts,
NG15 7TA
⌐ www.jackbarker.co.uk
✉ leen-jackbarket@btinternet.com
☎ 0115 9642037, Fax 9642724
On B6011 off A611 from Hucknall.
Parkland course; was Hucknall GC.
Pro John Lines; Founded 1994
Designed by Tom Hodgetts
18 holes, 6251 yards, S.S.S. 72
⌐ Practice putting green; 9-hole par
3 course also available.
† Welcome anytime.
⌐ WD £10; WE £15.
⌐ Welcome; packages available inc
WE.
🍽 Full clubhouse facilities.
⌐ Premier Lodge Hucknall.

6B 54 Lincoln
Torksey, Lincoln, LN1 2EG
⌐ www.lincolngc.co.uk
✉ info@lincolngc.co.uk
☎ 01427 718721, Fax 718721,
Pro 718273, Rest/Bar 718210
Course is on the A156, 7 miles S of
Gainsborough, 10 miles W of Lincoln.
Inland links course.
Pro A Carter; Founded 1891
18 holes, 6438 yards, S.S.S. 71
⌐ Large practice area.
† Welcome.
⌐ WD £28; WE £30.
⌐ Welcome WD by prior
arrangement; catering packages
available.
🍽 Full clubhouse facilities.
⌐ Hume Arms.

6B 55 The Lincolnshire
Near Crowle, Scunthorpe, DN17 4BU
☎ 01724 711619, Fax 712248
Rest/Bar 711621
Off A1161 Crowle to Goole Road from
M180 Junction 2.
Parkland course.
Founded 1994
18 holes, 6400 yards, S.S.S. 71
† Everyone welcome.

⌐ Summer WD £12.00, WE £15.00;
Winter WD £12.00, WE £15.00.
⌐ Welcome at all times.
🍽 Full facilities available.
⌐ Red Lion, Epworth.

6B 56 Lindrick
Lindrick Common, Worksop, Notts,
S81 8BH
⌐ www.lindrickgolfcourse.co.uk
✉ lgc@ansbronze.com
☎ 01909 485802, Fax 488685,
Pro 475820, Sec 475282
On A57 4 miles NW of Worksop.
Heathland course; 1957 Ryder Cup;
1960 Curtis Cup.
Pro John R King; Founded 1891
Designed by Tom Dunn; Willie Parks
and H Fowler
18 holes, 6606 yards, S.S.S. 72
⌐ Practice range; 2 practice areas.
† Welcome WD except Tues.
⌐ WD £50 (18 holes), £60 (day); WE
£60.
⌐ Welcome by prior arrangement;
packages available; from £50.
🍽 Full clubhouse facilities.
⌐ Red Lion; Todwick.

6B 57 Louth Golf Club
Crowtree Lane, Louth, Lincs, LN11 9LJ
✉ louthgolfclub1992@btinternet.com
☎ 01507 602554, Fax 608501,
Pro 604648, Sec 603681,
Rest/Bar 611087
W of Louth, close to Hubbards Hills.
Undulating parkland course.
Pro A J Blundell; Founded 1965
Designed by CK Cotton
18 holes, 6430 yards, S.S.S. 71
⌐ Practice ground.
† Welcome by arrangement.
⌐ WD £20; WE £30.
⌐ Welcome by prior arrangement;
discounts for groups of more than 25;
catering packages available.
🍽 All day catering and bar facilities.
⌐ Masons Arms; Beaumont; Priory;
Kings Head; Brackenborough Arms
Hotel.

6B 58 Luffenham Heath
Ketton, Stamford, Lincs, PE9 3UU
⌐ www.luffenhamheath.co.uk
✉ jringleby@theluffenhamheathgc
.co.uk
☎ 01780 720205, Fax 722146,
Pro 720298, Sec 720205 x1, Rest/Bar
720205 x4
On A6121 5 miles W of Stamford.
Heathland course.
Founded 1911
Designed by James Braid

18 holes, 6315 yards, S.S.S. 70
† Welcome by arrangement.
⌐ WD/WE £40 round, £50 day.
⌐ Welcome by prior arrangement with
Sec; packages and catering available
on application; terms on application.
🍽 Full clubhouse facilities.
⌐ The George at Stamford; Monkton
Arms, Glaston.

6B 59 The Manor Golf
Laceby Manor, Laceby, Grimsby, Lincs,
DN37 7EA
✉ judith@manorgolf.com
☎ 01472 873468, Fax 271266,
Sec 873469, Rest/Bar 873470
On A16 0.5 miles past Oaklands Hotel.
Parkland course.
Pro Neil Laybourne; Founded 1992
Designed by Sir Charles Nicholson and
Rushton
18 holes, 6343 yards, S.S.S. 70
⌐ Practice area.
† Welcome by arrangement.
⌐ WD £18 WE £20.
⌐ Welcome by prior arrangement;
terms on application.
🍽 Full clubhouse facilities.
⌐ Oaklands.

6B 60 Mansfield Woodhouse
Leeming Lane North, Mansfield
Woodhouse, Notts, NG19 9EU
☎ 01623 623521
On A60 Mansfield-Worksop road, 2
miles N of Mansfield.
Public parkland course.
Pro L Highfield; Founded 1973
Designed by F Horseman and
A Highfield
9 holes, 4892 yards, S.S.S. 65
† Welcome except before 11am Sat.
⌐ £3.80 9 holes, £5.80 18.
⌐ None.
🍽 Clubhouse bar facilities.

6B 61 Mapperley
Central Ave, Plains Rd, Mapperley,
Nottingham, NG3 6RH
☎ 0115 9556672, Fax 9556670,
Pro 9556673, Sec 9556672,
Rest/Bar 9556672
Off B684 3 miles NE of Nottingham.
Undulating parkland course.
Pro Jason Barker; Founded 1907
18 holes, 6307 yards, S.S.S. 70
† Welcome by prior arrangement.
⌐ WD £20; WE £25.
⌐ Welcome by arrangement with
secretary; packages available; terms
on application.
🍽 Full clubhouse facilities.
⌐ Many in Nottingham.

Lincoln Golf Club
TORKSEY · LINCOLN · LN1 2EG

- 6438 yards, SSS 71
- Venue for Lincolnshire Amateur Championship and Lincolnshire County Championships
- Putting green
- Large practice area
- 3-hole pitch and putt
- Golf shop

Founded in 1891, Lincoln is a mature, testing, championship standard course built on sandy subsoil offering a variety of holes from links-style to parkland with mature trees and some water features.
We offer golfing packages in summer and winter, including a wide range of excellent snacks and meals.

Manager: Derek B Linton Tel/fax: 01427 718721.
Pro: Ashley Carter Tel/fax: 01427 718273. E-mail: info@lincolngc.co.uk
Web page: www.lincolngc.co.uk

6B 62 Market Rasen & District
Legsby Road, Market Rasen, Lincs, LN8 3DZ
☎ 01673 842319, Pro 842416, Sec 842319, Rest/Bar 842319
On A361 1 mile E of Market Rasen.
Heathland course.
Pro AM Chester; Founded 1922
Designed by Hawtree Ltd
18 holes, 6209 yards, S.S.S. 70
✝ Welcome with handicap certs; with member at WE.
⌇ WD £20 per round. £30 per day.
⌁ Welcome Tues and Fri; packages for catering available; from £11.
🍽 Full clubhouse facilities.
↩ Limes Hotel.

6B 63 Market Rasen Race Course
Legsby, Market Rasen, Lincs, LN8 3EA
☎ 01673 843434
At Market Rasen racecourse; follow signs to golf course from entrance.
Founded 1989
Designed by Racecourse/Peter Alliss
9 holes, 2377 yards, S.S.S. 45
✝ Welcome.
⌇ Terms on application.
⌁ Welcome with advance booking.

6B 64 Marriott Breadsall ₢
Moor Rd, Morley, Derbys, DE7 6DL
🖳 www.marriotthotel.com/emags
✉ golf.breadsallpriory@marriotthotel.co.uk
☎ 01332 832235, Fax 836036
3 miles NE of Derby off A61 towards Breadsall.
Parkland and moorland course.
Pro Darren Steeles
Founded 1977
Designed by Donald Steele.
Championship Priory course: 18 holes, 6120 yards, S.S.S. 69. Moorland: 18 holes, 6028 yards, S.S.S. 68.
⌇ 6 interior bays, 6 external bays.

✝ Welcome. Bookings 01332 836016.
⌇ Terms on application.
⌁ Welcome by prior arrangement; packages available; tennis swimming pool; gym and leisure facilities; terms on application.
🍽 Full hotel and clubhouse facilities; 5 bars and 2 restaurants.
↩ On site, Marriott Breadsall Priory.

6B 65 Martin Moor
Martin Moore Course, Martin Lane, Blankney, Lincs, LN4 3BE
☎ 01526 378243
On B1189 2 miles E of Metheringham.
Parkland course.
Founded 1992
Designed by S Harrison
9 holes, 6325 yards, S.S.S. 70
⌇ Practice ground.
✝ Welcome.
⌇ WD/WE £6.50 for 9. £9 for 18.
⌁ Welcome by prior arrangement; packages available; terms on application.
🍽 Bar snacks.
↩ Eagle Lodge; Golf Hotel; Petwood Hotel all Woodhall Spa.

6B 66 Matlock
Chesterfield Rd, Matlock, Derbys, DE4 5LZ
☎ 01629 582191, Fax 582135, Pro 584934, Rest/Bar 582142
On Chesterfield Road 1, mile from Matlock.
Moorland course.
Pro Mark Whithorn; Founded 1906
Designed by Tom Williamson
18 holes, 5996 yards, S.S.S. 69
✝ Welcome WD by prior arrangement.
⌇ WD £25; WE N/A.
⌁ Welcome by prior arrangement; catering available.

🍽 Clubhouse facilities.
↩ Red House, Darley Dale.

6B 67 Maywood
Rushy Lane, Risley, Draycott, Derbys, DE72 3SW
☎ 0115 9392306, Pro 9490043, Rest/Bar 9392306
Course is off the A52 to Risley from the M1 Junction 25 at the Post House Hotel.
Wooded course with water features.
Pro Simon Sherrat; Founded 1990
Designed by Peter Moon
18 holes, 6424 yards, S.S.S. 72
✝ Everyone welcome.
⌇ WD £15; WE £20.
⌁ Welcome by prior arrangement; full day's golf and coffee light lunch and 4-course evening meal; from £30.
🍽 Full bar and catering facilities available.
↩ Post House; Novotel; Risley Park.

6B 68 Mickleover ₢
Uttoxeter Rd, Mickleover, Derbys, DE3 5AD
☎ 01332 513339, Fax 512092, Pro 518662, Sec 512092, Rest/Bar 513339
Course is on the A516/B5020 three miles W of Derby.
Undulating parkland course.
Tim Coxon; Founded 1923
18 holes, 5708 yards, S.S.S. 68
✝ Welcome.
⌇ WD £22; WE £30.
⌁ Welcome Tues and Thurs; packages can be arranged; from £22.
🍽 Clubhouse facilities.
↩ Mickleover Court; International Derby.

6B 69 Millfield
Laughterton, Torksey, Nr Lincoln, Lincs, LN1 2LB

☎ 01427 718473, Fax 718473
On A113 between A57 and A158 8
miles from Lincoln; 10 miles from
Gainsborough.
Inland links course.
Pro Richard Hunter; Founded 1984
18 holes, 6001 yards, S.S.S. 71
† Welcome.
[WD £7; WE £7.
⌁ Welcome WD by prior
arrangement; tennis, bowls; second
18-hole course (4500 yards par 65)
and a 9-hole course (1500 yards par
3); terms on application.
🍴 Light refreshments; bar meals
available.
🛏 Holiday chalets & log cabins on site.

6B 70 **New Mills Golf Club**
Shaw Marsh, High Peak, Derbys,
SK22 4QE
🖧 www.newmillsgolfclub.co.uk
✉ carltcross@aol.com
☎ 01663 743485, Fax 743485,
Pro 746161, Sec 744305
1 mile off A6, through New Mills Town
Flat, moorland.
Founded 1907.
18 holes, 5604 yards.
† Yes, by prior arrangement.
[WD £20 approx; WE £25.
⌁ Yes.
🍴 Bar/Restaurant.
🛏 In New Mills Town Centre.

6B 71 **Newark**   ☏
Kelwick, Coddington, Newark, Notts,
NG24 2QX
☎ 01636 626282, Fax 626497,
Pro 626492, Sec 626282
On A17 between Newark and Sleaford
just past Coddington roundabout.
Parkland course.
Pro Peter Lockley; Founded 1901
18 holes, 6457 yards, S.S.S. 71
⚑ Practice ground.
† Welcome with handicap certs;
Ladies Day Tues.
[WD £22; WE £27.
⌁ Welcome WD by prior
arrangement; catering packages;
snooker; indoor coaching facilities;
terms on application.
🍴 Bar and meals.
🛏 George Inn, Leadenham;
Travelodge.

6B 72 **Normanby Hall**
Normanby Park, Normanby,
Scunthorpe, N Lincs, DN15 9HU
☎ 01724 720226, Fax 853183,
Rest/Bar 720252

5 miles N of Scunthorpe adjacent to
Normanby Hall.
Municipal parkland course.
Pro Chris Mann; Founded 1978
Designed by HF Jiggens; Hawtree and
Sons
18 holes, 6548 yards, S.S.S. 71
⚑ Practice range; practice area.
† Welcome; telephone for bookings.
[WD £8.00; WE £10.00.
⌁ Welcome by prior arrangement
with the local council.
🍴 Full facilities including banqueting
at Normanby Hall.
🛏 Royal; Wortley House.

6B 73 **North Shore**   ☏
North Shore Rd, Skegness, Lincs,
PE25 1DN
🖧 www.north-shore.co.uk
✉ golf@north-shore.co.uk
☎ 01754 763298, Fax 761902,
Pro 764822
Just off A52 Inglemels. 1 mile N of
Skegness town centre on the outskirts.
Parkland/links course.
Pro John Cornelius; Founded 1910
Designed by James Braid
18 holes, 6257 yards, S.S.S. 71
† Welcome.
[WD £22; WE £31.
⌁ Welcome by prior arrangement;
packages and hotel rates available;
from £33.
🍴 Full clubhouse catering and bar
facilities.
🛏 On site North Shore.

6B 74 **Norwood Park**   ☏
Norwood Park, Southwell, Notts,
NG25 0PF
🖧 www.norwoodpark.org.uk
✉ mail@norwoodgolf.co.uk
☎ 01636 816626, Fax 815702
Half a mile W of Southwell on the road
to Kirklington leading from A617.
Parkland course set in the grounds of
a stately home.
Pro Paul Thornton; Founded 1999
Designed by Clyde B Johnston
18 holes, 6805 yards, S.S.S. 72
⚑ 8.
† Welcome at any time.
[9 holes: WD £9.50, WE £14; 18
holes: WD £17, WE £24.
⌁ Welcome by prior arrangement.
🍴 Snacks available.
🛏 The Saracen's Head.

6B 75 **Nottingham City**
Lawton Drive, Bulwell, Nottingham,
NG6 8BL

☎ 0115 927 6916, Fax 2767,
Pro 2767, Rest/Bar 927 8021
2 miles from M1 Junction 26, follow
signs to Bulwell.
Municipal parkland course; private club.
Pro Cyril Jepson; Founded 1910
Designed by H Braid
18 holes, 6218 yards, S.S.S. 70
† Welcome.
[WD £12; WE £15.
⌁ Welcome by prior arrangement; 18
and 36-hole packages with catering
available; terms on application.
🍴 Clubhouse facilities.
🛏 The Gateway; Station Hotel.

6B 76 **Notts**
Hollinwell, Derby Rd, Kirkby-in-
Ashfield, Notts, NG17 7QR
✉ nottsgolfclub@
hollinwell.fsnet.co.uk
☎ 01623 753225, Fax 753655,
Pro 753087
Course is three miles from the M1
Junction 27 off the A611.
Heathland course with gorse/heather;
lake at Hollinwell.
Pro Alasdair Thomas; Founded 1901
Designed by Willie Park Jnr
18 holes, 7098 yards, S.S.S. 75
⚑ Covered driving range.
† Welcome by prior arrangement.
[WD £55-£80.
⌁ Welcome WD except Fri morning
by prior arrangement.
🍴 Clubhouse facilities.
🛏 Pine Lodge, Mansfield; Swallow,
S Normanton; The Holly Lodge,
Ravenshead.

6B 77 **Oakmere Park**   ☏
Oaks Lane, Oxton, Notts, NG25 0RH
🖧 www.oakmerepark.co.uk
✉ enquiries@oakmerepark.co.uk
☎ 0115 9653545, Fax 9655628
Course lies between Blidworth & Oxton.
Parkland course; also Commanders
course: 9 holes, 6573 yards, par 72.
Pro Daryl St John Jones; Founded 1977
Designed by Frank Pennink
27 holes, 6612 yards, S.S.S. 72
⚑ 18 bays.
† Welcome.
[WD £18; WE £24.
⌁ Welcome; restrictions at WE;
packages available; terms on
application.
🍴 Full clubhouse facilities.
🛏 Moat House, Nottingham.

6B 78 **Ormonde Fields**   ☏
Nottingham Rd, Codnor, Ripley,
Derbys, DE5 9RG
☎ 01773 742987

NEWARK GOLF CLUB
Founded 1901

On the Notts/Lincs border only 3 miles from the
A1, Newark Golf Club is set within its own
peaceful grounds away from main roads.

A tree-lined, parkland course with easy walking over 6458 yards with a large practice area
and putting green. The large clubhouse with restaurant serves wholesome food, in pleasant
surroundings, with good wines and beers. There is a spike bar plus a snooker table. The well-
stocked pro's shop provides golfers with all their requirements. The halfway house is adjacent
to the clubhouse with toilets and small kitchen. Societies and groups are very welcome
during the week. The Secretary can be contacted on **01636 626282** for any further details.

On A610 towards Ripley, 2 miles from
M1 Junction 26.
Undulating course.
Pro Peter Buttifant
Founded 1906
18 holes, 6011 yards, S.S.S. 69
† Welcome WD; by prior
arrangement WE.
[WD £17.50; WE £22.50.
⚷ Welcome by arrangement.
🍽 Full facilities.

6B 79 **Pastures** ℭ
Merlin Way, Mickleover, Derby, Derbys,
DE3 5UJ
☎ 01332 521074, Sec 516700,
Rest/Bar 521074
Course is on the A516 four miles W of
Derby.
Undulating meadowland course.
Founded 1969
Designed by Frank Pennink
9 holes, 5004 yards, S.S.S. 65
† Welcome with handicap certs.
[Prices on application.
⚷ Welcome by prior arrangement;
packages include lunch and evening
meal; from £22.
🍽 Limited catering.

6B 80 **Pottergate**
Moor Lane, Branston, Near Lincoln,
Lincs, LN4 1JA
☎ 01522 794867, Pro 794867,
Sec 794867, Rest/Bar 794867
On B1188 in Branston.
Parkland course.
Pro Lee Taske
Founded 1993
Designed by W Bailey
9 holes, 5164 yards, S.S.S. 65
† Everyone welcome.
[Prices on application.
⚷ Everyone welcome.
🍽 Bar and snacks available.
🛏 Moor Lodge, Branston.

6B 81 **Radcliffe-on-Trent**
Dewberry Lane, Cropwell Rd,
Radcliffe-on-Trent, Notts, NG12 2JH
🖳 www.radcliffentrentgc.co.uk
📧 les.rotgc@talk21.com
☎ 0115 933 3000, Fax 911 6991,
Pro 933 2396, Sec 933 3000,
Rest/Bar 911 7052
From A52 follow signs to Cropwell Butler.
Wooded parkland course.
Pro Craig George; Founded 1909
Designed by Tom Wilkinson
18 holes, 6381 yards, S.S.S. 71
🏌 2 large practice grounds.
† Welcome by arrangement.
[WD £24; WE £30.
⚷ Welcome Wed only; packages
available; from £23.
🍽 Full clubhouse catering and bar
facilities.
🛏 Westminster Hotel.

6B 82 **RAF Waddington**
Waddington, Lincoln, Lincs, LN5 9NB
☎ 01522 720271, Sec 957716854
Off A15 at Bracebridge Heath 3 miles
S of Lincoln. On RAF airfield.
Founded 1972
9 holes, 5558 yards, S.S.S. 69
† Must be accompanied by RAF
Waddington member.
[Prices on application.
⚷ By arrangement with captain or
sec; terms available on application.
🍽 Terms on application.
🛏 Moor Lodge; Mill Lodge.

6B 83 **Ramsdale Park Golf
Centre**
Oxton Road, Calverton, Notts,
NG14 6NU
🖳 www.ramsdaleparkgc.co.uk
📧 info@ramsdaleparkgc.co.uk
☎ 0115 9655600, Fax 9654105
Club is off the A614 betwwen
Mansfield and Nottingham.

Undulating course.
Pro Robert Macey; Founded 1992
Designed by Hawtree & Son
18 holes, 6546 yards, S.S.S. 71.
18 hole par 3 course, S.S.S. 54
🏌 26 bays.
† Pay and play.
[WD £17; WE £22.
⚷ Welcome by prior arrangement;
packages and catering available; also
par 3 course; prices on application.
🍽 Clubhouse facilities.
🛏 Many in local area.

6B 84 **Retford**
Ordsall, Retford, Notts, DN22 7UA
📧 retfordgolfclub@lineone.net
☎ 01777 711188, Fax 710412,
Pro 703733
Off A620 midway between Worksop
and Gainsborough.
Parkland course.
Pro C Morris; Founded 1920
18 holes, 6409 yards, S.S.S. 72
🏌 Practice ground.
† Welcome by prior arrangement
WD, visitors after 12.30 at WE; BH by
prior arrangement.
[Winter WD and WE £15; £14 with
a member; Summer WD £22 per
round; £30 for the day.
⚷ Welcome WD by prior
arrangement; golf and catering
packages available; prices on
application.
🍽 New clubhouse facilities.
🛏 West Retford; The Mill House both
Retford; Ye Olde Bell, Barnby Moor.

6B 85 **Riverside**
Trentside, Lenton Lane, Notts, NG7 2SA
☎ 0115 9862220
2 miles from city centre off A52
Ruddington road.
Parkland course.
3 x Pro, call for info

9 holes, 2001 yards, S.S.S. 31
⌇ Practice area.
† Welcome.
⌇ WD £6.80; WE £7.50.
⌁ Packages available.
⍾ Full bar and restaurant facilities.

6B 86 Ruddington Grange ♛
Wilford Road, Ruddinton, Nottingham,
Notts, NG11 6NB
⊹ www.ruddingtongrange.com
✉ info@ruddingtongrange.com
☎ 0115 9846141, Fax 9405165,
Pro 9211951, Sec 9214139
Off A52 Grantham Road S of
Nottingham.
Parkland course.
Pro Robert Simpson; Founded 1988
Designed by Eddie McCausland; David
Johnson; John Small
18 holes, 6543 yards, S.S.S. 72
† Welcome.
⌇ WD £19; WE £26.
⌁ Welcome WD by arrangement.
⍾ Full facilities and function room.
⌁ Cottage, Ruddington.

6B 87 Rutland County
Hardwick Farm, Great Casterton,
Stamford, Lincs, PE9 4AQ
⊹ www.rutlandcountygolf.co.uk
✉ pat@rutlandcounty.freeserve
.co.uk
☎ 01780 460239, Fax 460437,
Pro 460239, Sec 460330,
Rest/Bar 460330
4 miles N of Stamford on A1.
Inland Links course.
Pro Fred Fearn; Founded 1992
Designed by Cameron Sinclair
18 holes, 6401 yards, S.S.S. 71
⌇ 20.
† Welcome with prior arrangement.
⌇ WD £25; WE £30.
⌁ Packages available.
⍾ Bar and restaurant.

6B 88 Sandilands ♛
Roman Bank, Sandilands, Sutton-on-
Sea, Mablethorpe, Lincs, LN12 2RJ
☎ 01507 441432, Fax 441617
Course is on the A52 three miles S of
Mablethorpe.
Links course.
Founded 1901
18 holes, 5995 yards, S.S.S. 69
† Welcome; some WE restrictions.
⌇ Winter WD £12-£15, WE £15;
Summer WD £15-£20, WE £18-£25.
⌁ Welcome by prior arrangement.
⍾ Clubhouse facilities.
⌁ Grange and Links.

6B 89 Seacroft
Drummond Road, Skegness, Lincs,
PE25 3AU
⊹ www.seacroft-golfclub.co.uk
✉ richard@seacroft-golfclub.co.uk
☎ 01754 763020, Fax 763020,
Pro 769624, Sec 763020,
Rest/Bar 763020
S of Skegness towards Seacroft and
Gibraltar Point nature reserve.
Links course.
Pro Robin Lawie; Founded 1895
Designed by Tom Dunn
18 holes, 6479 yards, S.S.S. 71
† Welcome with handicap certs.
⌇ WD £32.50; WE £37.50.
⌁ Welcome by prior arrangement;
deposit required; catering and golf
days can be arranged.
⍾ Full clubhouse facilities.
⌁ Crown; Vine; Links.

6B 90 Sherwood Forest
Eakring Rd, Mansfield, Notts,
NG18 3EW
✉ sherwood@forest43.freeserve.co.uk
☎ 01623 626689, Fax 420412, Pro
627403, Sec 626689, Rest/Bar 623327
Off A617 at Oak Tree Lane to
roundabout; second exit; 1 mile to
junction; right; club is 500 yards.
Heathland course.
Pro Ken Hall; Founded 1895
Designed by HS Colt; Redesigned:
James Braid
18 holes, 6849 yards, S.S.S. 74
† Welcome by prior arrangement
with Sec; members' guests only at WE.
⌇ WD £40-£55.
⌁ Terms on application.
⍾ Full clubhouse facilities.
⌁ Pine Lodge; Swallow; Fringe.

6B 91 Shirland Lower Delves
Shirland, Nr Alfreton, Derbys, DE55 6AU
☎ 01773 834935, Sec 832515
Course is off the A61 Chesterfield
Road; turn opposite the church in
Shirland village.
Parkland course with views over
Derbyshire countryside.
Pro Neville Hallam; Founded 1977
18 holes, 6072 yards, S.S.S. 69
⌇ Practice area.
† Welcome WD; by prior
arrangement at WE.
⌇ WD £18; WE £25.
⌁ By prior arrangement with
professional; golf and catering packages
can be arranged; terms on application.
⍾ Full clubhouse facilities.
⌁ Riber Hall; Swallow Hotel; Higham
Farm.

6B 92 Sickleholme
Saltergate Lane, Bamford, Sheffield,
S33 OBN
☎ 01433 651306, Fax 659498,
Rest/Bar 651252
On A625 14 miles W of Sheffield.
Undulating parkland course.
Pro Patrick Taylor; Founded 1898
18 holes, 6064 yards, S.S.S. 69
⌇ Practice area.
† Welcome by prior arrangement;
except Wed am.
⌇ WD £29; WE £32.
⌁ Welcome by prior arrangement;
golf and catering packages can be
arranged; from £32.
⍾ Restaurant and bar facilities
available.
⌁ George; Plough, both Hathersage;
Yorkshire Bridge, Bamford.

6B 93 Sleaford ♛
Willoughby Rd, South Rauceby,
Sleaford, Lincs, NG34 8PL
✉ sleafordgolfclub@btinternet.com
☎ 01529488273, Fax 488326
2 miles W of Sleaford at South
Rauceby, S of the A153 Sleaford to
Grantham Road.
Inland links with trees and scrubland.
Pro James Wilson; Founded 1905
Designed by Tom Williamson
18 holes, 6443 yards, S.S.S. 71
⌇ Practice area.
† Welcome by prior arrangement.
⌇ Prices on application.
⌁ Welcome WD by prior
arrangement; packages can be
arranged; terms on application.
⍾ Restaurant and bar facilities.
⌁ Carre Arms; Lincolnshire Oak; Tally
Ho Motel.

6B 94 South Kyme ♛
Skinners Lane, South Kyme, Lincoln,
LN4 4AT
⊹ www.skgc.co.uk
✉ southkymegc@hotmail.com
☎ 01526 861113, Fax 861080,
Pro 861113, Sec 861113,
Rest/Bar 861113
Course is on the B1395 four miles off
the A17. Midway between Boston,
Sleaford and Woodhall Spa.
Fenland course.
Pro Peter Chamberlain (Dir of Golf);
Founded 1990
Designed by Graham Bradley
18 holes, 6597 yards, S.S.S. 71
⌇ Practice ground and 6-hole course.
† All welcome.
⌇ WD £20; WE £24; check for
seasonal special offers.

THE SHERWOOD FOREST GOLF CLUB LTD

EAKRING ROAD, MANSFIELD, NOTTS NG18 3EW

Secretary:	Ms. A. Miles	Tel: 01623 626689
Professional/Golf Mgr.	Mr. K. Hall	Tel: 01623 627403
Catering Department:		Tel: 01623 623327
		Fax: 01623 420412

Full catering service available with dining for up to 100 persons at one sitting. Course is heathland, set in the very heart of Robin Hood country, and was designed by James Braid. Yellow markers distance is 6294 yds. S.S.S. 71. White markers distance is 6714 yds. S.S.S. 73. Championship Tees 6849 yds. S.S.S. 74.

The course was founded in 1895 and was the **Midland region Qualifying Round for the Open Championship 1990 - 1995**; **British Open Amateur Seniors Championship 1997**, and the **English Open Amateur Seniors Championship 2001**. The club will also host the **English Boys' Championship (Carris Trophy)** in 2006.

Green fees on application to the Golf Manager.
Within a few miles of places of interest - such as the Major Oak (Robin Hood's larder).
Newstead Abbey, Thoresby Hall, Clumber Oark, and 14 miles from the centre of Nottingham.

🏌 Discount available for parties of 8 or more.
🍴 Clubhouse facilities (Restaurant & Bar snacks available).
🍴 The Finch Hatton Arms, Ewerb y (01529 460363).

6B 95 Southview
Burgh Rd, Skegness, Lincs, PE25 2LA
📧 spence.golfshop@spalding2000.freeserve.co.uk
☎ 01754 760589
On the A158 on the outskirts of Skegness signposted to Southview Leisure Park.
Parkland course.
Pro Peter Cole; Founded 1990
9 holes, 4816 yards, S.S.S. 64
† Welcome.
[WD £6 per day; WE £6 per round.
🏌 Welcome at all times; tuition; swimming; sauna; sunbeds; snooker.
🍴 Full bar & catering in leisure park.
🍴 North Shore; Crown; Links.

6B 96 Spalding
Surfleet, Spalding, Lincs, PE11 4EA
☎ 01775 680474, Fax 680988,
Sec 680386, Rest/Bar 680234

Off A16 Spalding to Boston Road, 4 miles N of Spalding.
Parkland course.
Pro John Spencer; Founded 1907
Designed by Spencer/Price/Ward extension 1993
18 holes, 6478 yards, S.S.S. 71
🏌 Practice ground; driving range.
† Welcome by prior arrangement.
[WD £25; WE £30.
🏌 Welcome Tues pm and Thurs; packages can be arranged; from £20.
🍴 Full catering and bar facilities except Tues.

6B 97 Springwater
Moor Lane, Calverton, Notts, NG14 6FZ
☎ 0115 9652129,
Rest/Bar 9654946
Off A6097 between Lowdham and Oxton. Extended 1998.
Parkland course.
Pro Paul Drew; Founded 1991
18 holes, 6224 yards, S.S.S. 71
🏌 6 bays, floodlit.
† Welcome.
[Pay and play; WD £15; WE £20.
🏌 Packages available.
🍴 Full clubhouse facilities.

6B 98 Stanedge
Walton Hay Farm, Stanedge, Chesterfield, Derbys, S45 0LW
☎ 01246 566156, Sec 566156
5 miles W of Chesterfield off the A632 and the B5057, near the Red Lion Pub.
Moorland course.
Founded 1934
9 holes, 5786 yards, S.S.S. 69
🏌 Practice area.
† Welcome WD (Fri before 2pm); WE with a member.
[WD £15.
🏌 Welcome by arrangement with Sec; catering packages can be arranged; terms on application.
🍴 Snacks at the bar.
🍴 Chesterfield Hotel; Olde House; both Chesterfield.

6B 99 Stanton-on-the-Wolds
Stanton-on-the-Wolds, Keyworth, Notts, NG12 5BH
☎ 0115 937 4885, Fax 4885,
Pro 937 2390
Off A606 8 miles SE of Nottingham.
Parkland course.
Pro Nick Hernon; Founded 1906
Designed by Tom Williamson

18 holes, 6369 yards, S.S.S. 71
⚲ Practice range, Practice area; chipping green.
♦ Welcome WD; WE with a member.
⌊ WD £20.
⟳ Welcome by prior arrangement with Sec.
🍴 Full bar and catering facilities.

6B 100 Stoke Rochford
Stoke Rochford, Grantham, Lincs, NG33 5EW
⚘ www.stokerochfordgolfclub.co.uk
☎ 01476 530275, Fax 530237, Pro 530218, Sec 01572 756305
6 miles S of Grantham off Northbound A1.
Parkland course.
Pro Angus Dow; Founded 1926/1936
Designed by Major Hotchkin/C. Turner
18 holes, 6256 yards, S.S.S. 70
♦ Welcome by prior arrangement.
⌊ WD £22-£30, £12 with a member; WE £28-£40, £14 with a member.
⟳ Welcome by prior arrangement; catering packages available; snooker; terms on application.
🍴 Full clubhouse bar and restaurant facilities.
⟿ Many in Grantham.

6B 101 Sudbrook Moor
Charity Street, Carlton Scroop, Near Grantham, Lincs, NG32 3AT
⚘ www.sudbrookmoor.co.uk
☎ 01400 250796, Pro 250796, Sec 250796, Rest/Bar 250876
On A607 6 miles NE of Grantham.
Meadowland course in picturesque valley.
Pro Tim Hutton; Founded 1986
Designed by Tim Hutton
9 holes, 4800 yards, S.S.S. 64
⚲ Driving range.
♦ Pay and play.
⌊ Winter WD £7, WE £9; Summer WD/WE £9.
⟳ Pay and play.
🍴 Coffee shop only.

6B 102 Sutton Bridge ℃
New Rd, Sutton Bridge, Spalding, Lincs, PE12 9RQ
☎ 01406 350323, Pro 351422
Off A17 Long Sutton to King's Lynn road at Sutton Bridge.
Parkland course.
Pro Alison Johns; Founded 1914
9 holes, 5822 yards, S.S.S. 69
♦ Welcome WD only.
⌊ WD £18.

⟳ Welcome WD by prior arrangement; minimum group 6; catering can be arranged.
🍴 Bar and restaurant facilities.
⟿ The Anchor Inn & numerous other small inns in the area.

6B 103 Tapton Park Municipal
Murray House, Crow Lane, Chesterfield, Derbys, S41 0EQ
☎ 01246 273887, Fax 558024, Pro 239500
Signposted in Chesterfield centre.
Municipal parkland course.
Pro Andrew Carnall; Founded 1934
18 holes, 6005, S.S.S. 69; 9 holes, 2613 yards, par 34
⚲ Pitch & putt course, practice area.
♦ Welcome; can book 6 days in advance.
⌊ WD £6.80; WE £8.40.
⟳ Welcome by prior arrangement; packages available; terms on application.
🍴 Bar and restaurant facilities available. Function room available.

6B 104 Tetney
Station Rd, Tetney, Grimsby, Lincs, DN36 5HY
☎ 01472 211644, Fax 211644, Rest/Bar 811344
Off A16 at Tetney; 1.5 miles down Station Rd.
Parkland course.
Pro Jason Abrams; Founded 1994
Designed by The Caswell Family & Stuart Grant
18 holes, 6245 yards, S.S.S. 69
⚲ Driving range, 12 bays.
♦ Welcome.
⌊ WD £10; WE £10.
⟳ Welcome, packages available for all-day catering and golf; from £25.
🍴 Bar and restaurant facilities available.

6B 105 Toft Hotel
Toft, Nr Bourne, Lincs, PE10 0XX
☎ 01778 590616, Rest/Bar 590614
6 miles E of Stamford on A6121.
Undulating parkland course with water features.
Pro Mark Jackson; Founded 1988
Designed by Derek and Roger Fitton
18 holes, 6486 yards, S.S.S. 71
♦ Welcome; tees bookable 14 days ahead.
⌊ WD £20; WE £25.
⟳ Welcome by arrangement.
🍴 Full bar and restaurant facilities and function room in hotel.

⟿ On site Toft Hotel; golfing packages available.

6B 106 Trent Lock Golf Centre
Lock Lane, Sawley, Long Eaton, Notts, NG10 2FY
☎ 0115 9464398, Fax 9461183, Pro 9464398, Rest/Bar 9461184
2 miles from M1 Junction 25.
Parkland course.
Pro Mark Taylor; Founded 1991
Designed by E.W. McCausland
18 holes, 5900 yards, S.S.S. 68; 9 holes 2911, par 36
⚲ Practice range; 24 bays floodlit.
♦ Welcome; must book at WE.
⌊ WD £10; WE £12. £5 for the 9-hole, no bookings.
⟳ Welcome by prior arrangement; from £24.95.
🍴 Bar snacks; restaurant; private functions room.

6B 107 Waltham Windmill
Cheapside, Waltham, Grimsby, NE Lincs, DN37 0HT
☎ 01472 824109, Fax 828931, Pro 823963
In village of Waltham.
Parkland course.
Pro Nigel Burkitt; Founded 1997
Designed by Jim Payne
18 holes, 6442 yards, S.S.S. 71
⚲ Practice ground.
♦ Welcome.
⌊ WD £20; WE £27.
⟳ Welcome WD by prior arrangement; restrictions at WE; packages available.
🍴 Catering bar and function room.
⟿ Brackenborough Arms.

6B 108 Welton Manor ℃
Hackthorn Rd, Welton, Lincs, LN2 3PD
☎ 01673 862827
Off A46 Lincoln-Grimsby road.
Undulating parkland course.
Pro Gary Leslie; Founded 1995
18 holes, 5601 yards, S.S.S. 67
⚲ Driving range, 10 bays floodlit.
♦ Welcome; pay and play.
⌊ WD £12; WE £15.
⟳ Welcome any time by prior arrangement.
🍴 Bar, restaurant and function facilities.
⟿ Four Seasons.

6B 109 Wollaton Park
Lime Tree Avenue, Wollaton Park, Nottingham, NG8 1BT

www.wollatonparkgolfclub.com
wollatonparkgc@aol.com
☎ 0115 978 4834, Fax 970 0736,
Sec 978 7574, Rest/Bar 978 7585
Off slip road from A52 at junction with
Nottingham ring road.
Parkland course.
Pro John Lower; Founded 1927
Designed by T Williamson
18 holes, 6445 yards, S.S.S. 71
† Welcome.
⌐ WD £35; WE £40.
⌐ Welcome by prior arrangement on
Tues and Fri; golf and catering
packages available on application to
secretary; from £30.
⍟ Clubhouse catering facilities
available.
⌐ Innkeepers Lodge, Nottingham.

6B 110 **Woodhall Spa**
The Broadway, Woodhall Spa, Lincs,
LN10 6PU
www.englishgolfunion.org
booking@englishgolfunion.org
☎ 01526 352511, Fax 351817,
Pro 351803
Course is on the B1191, 19 miles SE
of Lincoln.

Heathland course.
Pro Campbell C Elliott; Founded 1905
Designed by Col SV Hotchkin
Pro course: 18 holes, 7080 yards,
S.S.S. 75; Bracken course: 18 holes,
6735 yards, S.S.S. 74
⌁ Driving Range; teaching Academy;
Pitch and putt.
† Welcome by prior arrangement;
discount for EGU members.
⌐ WD £45; WE £45. EGU £30 on
bracken course.
⌐ Welcome by prior arrangement;
golf and catering by arrangement.
⍟ Full clubhouse facilities.
⌐ Golf; Petwood Hotel; Eagle
Lodge.

6B 111 **Woodthorpe Hall**
Woodthorpe, Alford, Lincs, LN13 0DD
www.woodthorpehall.co.uk
info@woodthorpehall.co.uk
☎ 01507 450000
Course is off the B1371 three miles N
of Alford.
Parkland course.
Founded 1986
18 holes, 5140 yards, S.S.S. 65
⌁ Practice nets.

† Welcome.
⌐ WD £10; WE £10.
⌐ Welcome WD by prior
arrangement; four weeks' notice
needed; packages can be arranged for
a minimum of 8; from £20.
⍟ Inn on site.

6B 112 **Worksop**
Windmill Lane, Worksop, Notts,
S80 2SQ
☎ 01909 472696, Fax 477732,
Pro 477731 x2, Sec 477731 x1,
Rest/Bar 477731 x3
Off the B6034 road to Edwinstowe off
the A57.
Heathland course with woods and
gorse.
Pro C Weatherhead
Founded 1914
Designed by Tom Williamson.
18 holes, 6660 yards, S.S.S. 73
† Welcome by prior arrangement.
⌐ WD £35; WE £45.
⌐ Welcome WD by prior
arrangement; catering packages can
be arranged; terms on application.
⍟ Full clubhouse facilities.
⍟ Lion Hotel, Worksop.

Lancashire, Isle of Man, Cumbria

The Mersey beat is the toughest and most famous cluster of golf courses in England. Royal Birkdale is the Open Championship venue amongst them. On a still day it is a challenge, on a normal day it can be a nightmare. The only easy thing about Birkdale is that most of the stances are flat.

Some of the surrounding courses can be just as hard. In attempting to qualify for the 1998 Open Jose Coceres, a winner on both sides of the Atlantic, shot 105 at Hesketh. Hillside is a very fine course, the last of Tony Jacklin's hurrahs when he won the PGA there in 1982. Birkdale is visible from its eleventh tee. Nearby Southport & Ainsdale is good enough to have hosted two Ryder Cups. And Formby is simply a joy.

The host of the 2004 Curtis Cup, the motto at Formby is not "segregation" but "self determination" an ethos evident in the independent existence of The Ladies Club, the only club in the UK that is owned and run by women.

Formby can be a ferociously hard test when the wind is up, but it is also one of the fairest. There are an unusual variety of heathland holes, pine clad holes and linksy holes and the surprises continue when the visitor enters the bar to be confronted by a huge hippopotamus head.

Along the coast from Blackpool lies another astonishingly rich piece of golfing country. Royal Lytham and St Annes, the venue of the 2001 Open, is a masterpiece. Set on a scrubby piece of land with no views of the sea and flanked by a railway and red Victorian houses, it is not the world's most beautiful course, but it demands some of its most beautiful golf. Seve Ballesteros rated the twelfth as the best par three in Britain, Jack Nicklaus thought the fifteenth one of the most difficult par fours in the world and the seventeenth would feature on many an all time top eighteen holes. Up the road is Fairhaven, where Les Dawson was a member, often said to have a bunker for every day of the year, Lytham Green Drive and St Annes Old Links.

The Isle of Man's foremost course is Castletown. On a clear day you can see the Cumbrian Hills, but this is an exposed primal course consisting of gorse, bracken, rough, rocks and beach with scarcely a tree in sight. The fifth hole is the first big challenge and it usually comes from the hotel manager who will offer a wager of a bottle of champagne for a par. He seldom loses. The tenth hole is known as the racecourse because it was the original site of the derby. On the seventeenth the golfer is faced with a drive across the Irish Sea which is a long carry in anyone's language.

Cumbria has a number of decent courses. Silloth-on-Solway was built by the North British railway company as a way of encouraging people to take the train. It is well worth the journey and perhaps Richard Branson should consider taking up such a scheme with Virgin. Brampton, sometimes called Talkin Tarn, has the Newcastle to Carlisle railway running along the side of its third hole, but is a fell course of rare beauty. Other courses have the scenery but not necessarily the quality of golf.

7 1 Accrington & District ☎
Devon Avenue, Oswaldtwistle, Accrington, Lancs, BB5 4LS
🖳 www.accrington-golf-club.fsnet.co.uk
📧 acgolf@globalnet.co.uk
☎ 01254 232734, Fax 233423, Pro 231091, Sec 381614, Rest/Bar 232734
On A679 5 miles from Blackburn
Parkland-moorland course.
Pro Bill Harling; Founded 1893
Designed by James Braid
18 holes, 6060 yards, S.S.S. 69
✏ Practice ground.
† Welcome.
🔓 WD £24; Fri, Sat, Sun, BH £30.
↻ Welcome by arrangement.
🍽 Full facilities except Mon & Thurs.
🛏 County; Dunkenhalgh Hotel.

7 2 Allerton Municipal Golf Course
Allerton Road, Mossley Hill, Liverpool, Merseyside, L18 3JT
☎ 0151 4287490, Fax 4287490, Pro 4281046, Rest/Bar 4288510
From end of M62 S on to Queens Drive, on to ring road to Yewtree Road, signposted on Allerton Road.
Parkland course; also 9-hole.

Pro B Large; Founded 1923
18 holes, 5494 yards, S.S.S. 67
✏ Beginners 9-hole course.
† Welcome.
🔓 Terms on application.
↻ Welcome WD and WE pm by arrangement with the professional; terms on application.
🍽 No facilities; light refreshments available.
🛏 Redbourne; Grange.

7 3 Alston Moor ☎
The Hermitage, Alston, Cumbria, CA9 3DB
☎ 01434 381675
Course is on the B6277 1.5 miles S of Alston; signposted from top of town.
Parkland and fell course.
Founded 1906/1969
Designed by Members
10 holes, 5518 yards, S.S.S. 67
† Welcome.
🔓 WD £9; WE £11.
↻ Welcome by prior arrangement; packages for golf and catering can be provided; prices on application.
🍽 Bar and catering facilities from May to October.
🛏 Secretary can provide details.

7 4 Appleby ☎
Brackenber Moor, Appleby in Westmorland, Cumbria, CA16 6LP
🖳 www.applebygolfclub.org.uk
☎ 017683 51432, Fax 52773, Pro 52922
Course is on the A66 two miles E of Appleby.
Moorland course.
Pro James Taylor; Founded 1903
Designed by Willie Fernie of Troon
18 holes, 5901 yards, S.S.S. 68
✏ Practice ground.
† Welcome.
🔓 WD £20 per round, £22 per day; WE £24 per round, £27 per day.
↻ Welcome by prior arrangement.
🍽 Full catering and bar except Tuesdays when menu is limited.
🛏 Tufton Arms; Royal Oak; Appleby Manor; The Gate.

7 5 Ashton & Lea ☎
Tudor Avenue, off Blackpool Road, Lea, Preston, PR4 0XA
🖳 www.ukgolfer.org
📧 ashtonleagolf@supernet.com
☎ 01772 735282, Fax 735762, Pro 720374
Course is on the A5085 three miles W of Preston.

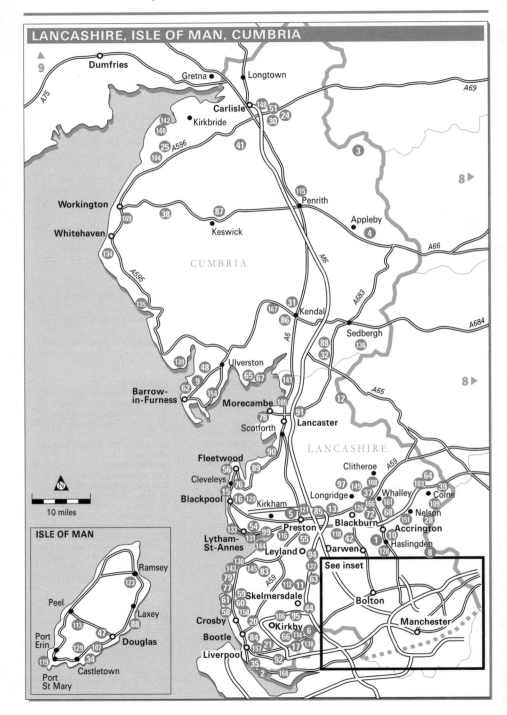

LANCASHIRE, ISLE OF MAN, CUMBRIA

KEY

1	Accrington & District	36	Chorley	71	Greenmount	106	Mossock Hall	140	Silverdale
2	Allerton Municipal	37	Clitheroe	72	Haigh Hall	107	Mount Murray	141	Solway Holiday Village
3	Alston Moor	38	Cockermouth	73	Harwood	108	Mytton Fold	142	Southport & Ainsdale
4	Appleby	39	Colne	74	Haydock Park	109	Nelson	143	Southport Municipal
5	Ashton & Lea	40	Crompton & Royton	75	Heaton Park	110	North Manchester	144	Southport Old Links
6	Ashton-in-Makerfield	41	Dalston Hall	76	Heron's Reach	111	Oldham	145	Stand
7	Ashton-under-Lyne	42	Darwen	77	Hesketh	112	Ormskirk	146	Standish Court
8	Bacup	43	Davyhulme Park	78	The Heysham	113	Peel	147	Stonyhurst Municipal
9	Barrow	44	Dean Wood	79	Hillside Golf Club	114	Pennington	148	Stonyhurst Park
10	Baxenden & District	45	Deane	80	Hindley Hall	115	Penrith	149	Swinton Park
11	Beacon Park	46	Denton	81	Horwich	116	Penwortham	150	Towneley
12	Bentham	47	Douglas	82	Houghwood	117	Pike Fold	151	Tunshill
13	Blackburn	48	Dunnerholme	83	Hurlston Hall	118	Pleasington	152	Turton
14	Blackley	49	Dunscar	84	Huyton & Prescot	119	Port St Mary Golf	153	Ulverston
15	Blackpool North Shore	50	Duxbury Park	85	Ingol		Pavilion	154	Walmersley
16	Blackpool Park	51	Eden	86	Kendal	120	Poulton-le-Fylde	155	Werneth (Oldham)
17	Blundells Hill	52	Ellesmere	87	Keswick	121	Preston	156	West Derby
18	Bolton	53	Fairfield Golf & Sailing	88	Kirkby Lonsdale	122	Prestwich	157	West Lancashire
19	Bolton Old Links		Club	89	Knott End	123	Ramsey	158	Westhoughton
20	Bootle	54	Fairhaven	90	Lancaster	124	Regent Park (Bolton)	159	Westhoughton Golf
21	Bowring	55	Fishwick Hall	91	Lansil	125	Rishton		Centre
22	Boysnope Park	56	Fleetwood	92	Lee Park	126	Rochdale	160	Whalley
23	Brackley	57	Flixton	93	Leigh	127	Rossendale	161	Whitefield
24	Brampton	58	Formby	94	Leyland	128	Rowany	162	Whittaker
25	Brayton Park	59	Formby Golf Centre	95	Liverpool Municipal	129	Royal Birkdale	163	Wigan
26	Breightmet	60	Formby Hall		(Kirkby)	130	Royal Lytham & St	164	William Wroe
27	Brookdale	61	Formby Ladies	96	Lobden		Annes	165	Wilpshire
28	Burnley	62	Furness	97	Longridge	131	Saddleworth	166	Windermere
29	Bury	63	Gathurst	98	Lowes Park	132	St Annes Old Links	167	Woolton
30	Carlisle	64	Ghyll	99	Lytham Green Drive	133	St Bees	168	Workington
31	Carus Green	65	Grange Fell	100	Manchester	134	Seascale	169	Worsley
32	Casterton	66	Grange Park	101	Manor (Bolton)	135	Sedbergh	170	Worsley Park Marriot
33	Castle Hawk	67	Grange-over-Sands	102	Marland Golf Course	136	Shaw Hill Hotel G & CC		
34	Castletown Golf Links	68	Great Harwood	103	Marsden Park	137	Sherdley Park		
35	Childwall	69	Great Lever & Farnworth	104	Maryport	138	Silecroft		
		70	Green Haworth	105	Morecambe	139	Silloth on Solway		

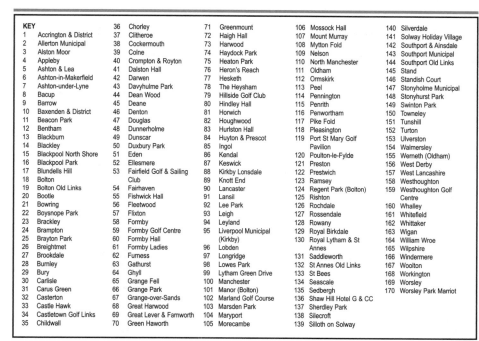

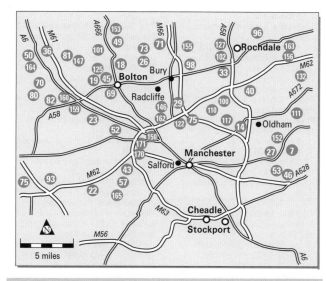

7 6 Ashton-in-Makerfield

Garswood Park, Liverpool Road, Ashton in Makerfield, Wigan, Lancs, WN4 0YT

✉ ainm.golfclub@tiscali.co.uk
☎ 01942 719330, Fax 719330, Pro 724229, Rest/Bar 727267

Off A58 from M6 0.5 miles to course. (between Junctions 23 and 24)
Parkland course.
Pro Peter Allan; Founded 1902
Designed by FW Hawtree
18 holes, 6205 yards, S.S.S. 70
† Welcome WD except Wed; WE only with member.
⌣ WD £28.
⌔ Welcome Mon, Tues and Thurs, Fri by prior arrangement.
◉ Full facilities.
⌁ Thistle, Holiday Inn, Haydock.

7 7 Ashton-under-Lyne

Gorsey Way, Ashton-under-Lyne, Lancs, OL6 9HT
☎ 0161 3301537, Fax 3306673, Pro 3082095

3 miles from town centre.
Semi-parkland course.
Pro Colin Boyle; Founded 1913
18 holes, 6209 yards, S.S.S. 70
† Welcome by prior arrangement; guests of members only at WE.

Parkland course with water features.
Pro M Greenough
Founded 1913
Designed by J Steer
18 holes, 6334 yards, S.S.S. 71
† Welcome by prior arrangement.
⌣ WD £26; WE £30.

⌔ Welcome by prior arrangement; Training/conference rooms available; packages include golf and catering; from £40.
◉ Full clubhouse facilities available.
⌁ Travel Inn, Lea; Marriott, Broughton.

⌶ WD £25; play only allowed with a member on Sun, £10.
⌁ Welcome Tues, Thurs and Fri; packages for golf and catering available; terms on application.
⦿ Clubhouse facilities.
⇦ Broadoak Hotel.

7 8 Bacup
Maden Road, Bacup, Lancs, OL13 8HY
☎ 01706 873170, Fax 877726
Off A671 7 miles N of Rochdale, 0.5 miles from Bacup centre.
Meadowland course.
Founded 1911
9 holes, 6008 yards, S.S.S. 67
† Welcome Wed, Thurs and Fri, and after competitions at WE.
⌶ Prices on application.
⌁ Welcome Wed, Thurs and Fri by prior arrangement.
⦿ Full clubhouse facilities available.
⇦ Royal, Waterfoot.

7 9 Barrow ⌾
Rakesmoor Lane, Hawcoat, Barrow in Furness, Cumbria, LA14 4QB
⌨ barrowgolf@supanet.com
☎ 01229 825444, Pro 825444, Sec 825444, Rest/Bar 825444
From M6 Junction 36 take A590 to Barrow; 3 miles before town follow Industrial route turning left into Bank Lane.
Parkland course.
Pro A Whitehall; Founded 1922
18 holes, 6200 yards, S.S.S. 70
† Welcome with handicap certs and by prior arrangement.
⌶ WD/WE £20 day.
⌁ Welcome by prior arrangement with the administrator; packages include a full day's golf and catering; snooker table; from £26.
⦿ Full clubhouse facilities.
⇦ Club can recommend local hotels.

7 10 Baxenden & District
Top-O'-The Meadow, Wooley Lane, Baxenden, Accrington, Lancs, BB5 2EA
⌕ www.baxendengolfclub.co.uk
⌨ baxgolf@hornmail.com
☎ 01254 234555
Take M65 Accrington exit and follow the signs for Baxenden; course signposted in village.
Moorland course.
Founded 1913
9 holes, 5717 yards, S.S.S. 68
† Welcome WD; with member only WE.

⌶ Prices on application.
⌁ Welcome WD by prior arrangement with the Secretary; packages include coffee, light lunch, 3-course meal and 27 holes of golf; from £27.
⦿ Bar and snacks available; meals to order.
⇦ Syke Side House; Haslingden.

7 11 Beacon Park
Beacon Lane, Dalton, Wigan, Lancs, WN8 7RU
☎ 01695 622700, Fax 622700, Pro 622700, Sec 726298, Rest/Bar 625551
Off A577 in Up Holland.
Parkland course.
Pro Gary Nelson; Founded 1982
Designed by Donald Steel
18 holes, 5931 yards, S.S.S. 69
⌶ Practice range, 24 bays floodlit.
† Pay and play.
⌶ Terms on application.
⌁ Welcome by prior arrangement; payment required 10 days in advance; terms on application.
⦿ Clubhouse facilities.
⇦ Lancashire Lodge.

7 12 Bentham
Robin Lane, Bentham, Lancaster, Lancs, LA2 7AG
⌕ www.benthamgolfclub.co.uk
⌨ secretary@benthamgolfclub.co.uk
☎ 015242 62455, Fax 62455, Rest/Bar 61018
Between Lancaster and Settle on B6480 13 miles E of M6 Junction 34.
Parkland course.
Pro Alan Watson; Founded 1922
18 holes,6100 yards, S.S.S. 69
† Everyone welcome.
⌶ WD/WE £25.
⌁ Welcome by arrangement.
⦿ Bar snacks and meals.
⇦ Whoop Hall, Kirkby Lonsdale.

7 13 Blackburn ⌾
Beardwood Brow, Blackburn, Lancs, BB2 7AX
⌨ sec@blackburngolfclub.com
☎ 01254 51122, Fax 665578, Pro 55942, Sec 51122, Rest/Bar 51122
Off A677 at W end of Blackburn.
Parkland course.
Pro A Rodwell; Founded 1894
18 holes, 6144 yards, S.S.S. 70
⌶ Practice ground, putting green, indoor practice area.
† Welcome by prior arrangement.

⌶ WD £26; WE £30; guests of members £10 all week; juniors with member £7.50, without member £10.
⌁ Welcome WD except Tues; catering and golf packages can be arranged; terms on application.
⦿ Clubhouse facilities except Mondays

7 14 Blackley ⌾
Victoria Avenue East, Blackley, Manchester, M9 7HW
☎ 0161 6432980, Fax 6538300, Pro 6433912, Sec 6547770, Rest/Bar 6432980
5 miles N of City centre.
Parkland course.
Pro Craig Gould; Founded 1907
Designed by Gaunt & Marlet
18 holes, 6217 yards, S.S.S. 70
† Welcome WD; with member at weekend.
⌶ WD £15 with member, £24 without.
⌁ Welcome WD except Thurs; golf and catering packages available; from £20.
⦿ Full clubhouse catering facilities available.
⇦ Bower Hotel, Chadderton, The Royal Toby.

7 15 Blackpool North Shore ⌾
Devonshire Road, Blackpool, Lancs, FY2 0RD
⌕ www.wbnscg.com
⌨ office@bnscg.com
☎ 01253 352054, Fax 591240, Pro 354640, Sec 325054 x6, Rest/Bar 351017
From M55 Junction 4 take Preston New Road to Whitegate Drive and Devonshire Road.
Moorland course with upper seaside elements.
Pro Brendan Ward; Founded 1904
Designed by Harry Colt
18 holes, 6431 yards, S.S.S. 71
⌶ Practice green.
† Welcome by prior arrangement; tees reserved for members until 9.30am & 12.30-1.30pm; not before 2pm Thurs and 4pm Sat.
⌶ WD £30; WE and BH £35.
⌁ Welcome WD except Thurs; golf and catering packages available; terms on application.
⦿ Catering and bar facilities daily.
⇦ Many in Blackpool.

7 16 Blackpool Park
North Park Drive, Blackpool, Lancs, FY3 8LS

☎ 01253 393960, Fax 397916, Pro 391004, Sec 397916, Rest/Bar 396683
2 miles E of Blackpool signposted off M55.
Parkland course.
Pro B Purdie; Founded 1925
Designed by Dr MacKenzie
18 holes, 6192 yards, S.S.S. 69
⌇ Practice nets, practice putting green, practice chipping.
† Welcome; tee reservations through Blackpool Borough Council.
⌊ WD £13; WE £15.
⌁ Welcome by prior arrangement with Blackpool Borough Council; terms on application.
⌽ Clubhouse facilities.
⌐ Many in Blackpool.

7 17 Blundells Hill
Blundells Lane, Rainhill, Liverpool, Merseyside, L35 6NA
⌸ www.blundellshill.co.uk
✉ info@blundellshill.demon.co.uk
☎ 0151 4309551, Fax 4265256, Pro 4300100, Rest/Bar 4269040
From M62 Junction 7 take A57 towards Prescot; turn left after garage; then 2nd left into Blundells Lane.
Parkland course.
Pro R Burbidge; Founded 1994
Designed by S Marnoch
18 holes, 6256 yards, S.S.S. 70
† Welcome by arrangement.
⌊ WD £25, WE £30.
⌁ Welcome Mon to Thurs; catering and golf packages for a minimum of 12 people; £33-£42.
⌽ Full clubhouse facilities.
⌐ Ship Inn, Rainhill; The Hilton, St Helens; The Village, Whiston; Hillcrest, Cronton.

7 18 Bolton
Chorley New Road, Lostock, Bolton, Lancs, BL6 4AJ
✉ boltongolf@lostockpark.fsbusiness.co.uk
☎ 01204 843278, Fax 843067, Pro 843073, Sec 843067 office/fax
3 miles W of Bolton, Junct. 6 of M61.
Parkland course.
Pro Bob Longworth; Founded 1891/1912
18 holes, 6237 yards, S.S.S. 70
† Welcome between 10am-12noon and after 2pm.
⌊ WD £34-£37; WE £40-£44.
⌁ Welcome Mon, Wed, Thur and Fri; discount available for groups over 10; packages for golf and catering available; terms on application.
⌽ Clubhouse facilities.

⌐ Devere Whites Hotel, Reebok Stadium.

7 19 Bolton Old Links ♟
Chorley Old Road, Bolton, Lancs, BL1 5SU
⌸ www.boltonoldlinks.co.uk
✉ mail@boltonoldlinks.co.uk
☎ 01204 842307, Fax 842307, Pro 843089, Rest/Bar 840050
On B6226 N of A58 from J5 on M61.
Moorland course.
Pro Paul Horridge; Founded 1891
Designed by Dr A MacKenzie
18 holes, 6469 yards, S.S.S. 71
⌇ Practice ground; indoor practice facilities.
† Welcome except on competition days; phone in advance to make booking
⌊ WD £30; WE £40.
⌁ Welcome WD by prior arrangement.
⌽ Full clubhouse facilities available except Mon (possible by prior arrangement).
⌐ Crest; Pack Horse; Last Drop; Moat House.

7 20 Bootle
Bootle Golf Course, Dunnings Bridge Road, Bootle, Merseyside, L30 2PP
☎ 0151 9281371, Fax 9491815, Rest/Bar 9286196
On A565 5 miles from Liverpool.
Municipal seaside links course.
Pro Alan Bradshaw; Founded 1934
Designed by F Stephens
18 holes, 6242 yards, S.S.S. 70
† Welcome.
⌊ WD £7.20; WE £9.20.
⌁ Welcome by prior arrangement.
⌽ Full clubhouse facilities available.
⌐ The Park Hotel.

7 21 Bowring Park Golf Course
Roby Road, Huyton, Liverpool, Merseyside, L36 4HD
☎ 0151 4891901
6 miles N of Liverpool.
Municipal parkland course.
Founded 1913
18 holes, 6147 yards, S.S.S. 70
† Welcome.
⌊ Adults WD £7.20, WE £8; OAP WD £3.55, WE £3.85; juniors WD £2.25, WE £3.60.
⌁ Welcome by prior arrangement.
⌽ Snacks; bar for members only.

7 22 Boysnope Park
Liverpool Road, Barton Moss, Eccles, Manchester, Lancs, M30 7RF

⌸ www.boysnopegolfclub.co.uk
☎ 0161 707 6125, Fax 707 3622, Pro 0701 86685
Off M60 at J11 on A57 towards Irlam.
Parkland course.
Pro Scott Currie; Founded 1998
18 holes, 6506 yards, S.S.S. 71
⌇ Driving range (0161 787 8687)
† Welcome.
⌊ WD £12; WE £14.
⌁ Welcome by prior notice.
⌽ Limited to snacks.

7 23 Brackley
Bullows Road, Little Hulton, Worsley, Manchester, Lancs, M38 9TR
✉ brackleygolfclub@aol.com
☎ 0161 790 6076, Sec 01942 876329
9 miles from Manchester on A6; turn right at White Lion Hotel into Highfield Rd; left into Captain Fold Rd; left into Bullows Rd.
Parkland course.
Founded 1976
9 holes, 6006 yards, S.S.S. 69
† Welcome; book at WE.
⌊ WD £5; WE and BH 9 holes £5, 18 holes £9; OAP WD £4; juniors WD £3.
⌁ Welcome by prior arrangement; from £p per head.
⌽ None.

7 24 Brampton (Talkin Tarn) ♟
Tarn Road, Brampton, Cumbria, CA8 1HN
☎ 016977 2255, Fax 41487, Pro 2000, Sec 2255, Rest/Bar 2255
1.75 miles from Brampton on B6413 Castle Carrock Road.
Moorland course.
Pro Stewart Wilkinson; Founded 1907
Designed by James Braid
18 holes, 6407 yards, S.S.S. 71
⌇ Practice ground/Driving range for irons only.
† Welcome; tee booked 9.30am-10.30am Mon, Wed, Thurs.
⌊ WD £22; WE £30.
⌁ Welcome by prior arrangement WD; limited at WE.
⌽ Full facilities in refurbished clubhouse.
⌐ Details of local guest houses and hotels offering reduced fees from club or pro.

7 25 Brayton Park Golf Course
Brayton, Aspatria, Carlisle, Cumbria, CA7 3PY
☎ 016973 20840, Fax 20854
Off A596 W of Carlisle.
Parkland course.

Royal Birkdale

Although Birkdale started life in 1889 as a mewling baby of nine holes, it wasn't until 1951 that the Home Office granted it royal status, three years before Birkdale hosted its first Open Championship. It had been due to host the Open in 1940, but a mad Austrian with a daft moustache and vegetarian ways put a stop to any of that.

The winner of Birkdale's first Open was the Australian Peter Thomson, a feat that he would repeat eleven years later when the best of the Americans were now present. Understandably Thomson is a fan of the course, writing, "Birkdale lacks nothing. It is a man-size course but not a monster. It is testingly narrow but not absurd, and certainly not artificial. The turf is superb and the greens at their best have that superlative glassy smoothness that only championship venues provide. By every standard it is as modern as supersonic planes".

Not everyone would agree. There are those who think that Birkdale is too flat and the fairways too lush to be representative of classic links golf. They are obviously looking out of a different clubhouse than Lee Trevino who said that Birkdale looked like the moon, although Trevino was referring more to the sandhills and the greens than the fairways.

And like so many great links Birkdale has two courses. There was the one that Johnny Miller fiddled his way around in 1976 and there was the one that Mark O'Meara played in 1998 when for the middle two days of the Championship you had to be lashed to your caddie in order to stay upright.

The conditions were pretty bad in practise as well. David Duval retired hurt after hitting five shots on the range and waited for the wind to die down. "You may be here until next year", came the advice. Tiger Woods asked when the weather would warm up and was informed by a member, "You never know. Last year summer fell on a Tuesday". By Saturday the conditions were even worse and after the defending champion Justin Leonard had come in with an 82 he said, "I'm going to take my score back to my home club, post it and see if I can get my handicap up a little bit. The good part is that now I can go back to my room, watch the leaders this afternoon and laugh my head off". It's not just the spectators who love to watch the pros suffer the misfortunes that they go though on a daily basis.

Such variable conditions mean that Birkdale has provided more than its share of stories. Dai Rees was a runner-up twice here, a position that was also memorably claimed by Mr Lu in 1971 and by a then unknown Seve Ballesteros, courtesy of that extraordinary chip between the bunkers on the final hole, in 1976. It was at Birkdale that Jack Nicklaus conceded a three foot putt and a tied match to Tony Jacklin on the final green of the 1969 Ryder Cup, before adding, "I don't think you would have missed that putt but in the circumstances I would never give you the opportunity". Twenty-four years later Hale Irwin would miss a two-inch putt by hitting a one-handed air shot and go on to finish one stroke behind the champion Tom Watson. In 1991 Ian Baker-Finch won the Championship and was destroyed by his achievement. And it was at Birkdale that the amateur Justin Rose holed an impossible wedge shot with his final stroke of the 1998 Championship to provoke what would be described as the biggest roar in the history of the Championship.

You have to hand it to the most recent of England's royal courses. There is clearly something special about Birkdale.
– **Mark Reason**

Pro Graham Batey; Founded 1978
Designed by Barry Ward
9 holes, 5042 yards, S.S.S. 64
♦ Welcome.
[WD £5 for 9 holes £7 for 18.
↷ Welcome by prior arrangement;
terms on application.
|◉| Bar Restaurant.
↩ Kelsey; Wheyrigg; Green Hill.

7 26 Breightmet
Red Lane, Red Bridge, Bolton, Lancs,
BL2 5PA
☎ 01204 527381, Sec 399275
Off Bury Road in Bolton.
Moorland/parkland course.
Founded 1911
9 holes, 6416 yards, S.S.S. 72
♦ Welcome by prior arrangement;
some restrictions Sat and Wed.
[WD £20; WE £25.
↷ Welcome WD; some Suns;
packages include full day's golf and
catering; snooker; £30-£35.
|◉| Full clubhouse facilities.
↩ In Bolton town centre.

7 27 Brookdale　　　　　℃
Medlock Road, Failsworth,
Manchester, Lancs, M35 9WQ
🖧 www.brookdalegolfclub.co.uk
📧 info@brookdalegolfclub.co.uk
☎ 0161 6814534, Fax 6886872,
Pro 6812655, Sec 6854534
From Manchester take A62 turning
right at Ashton Rd East; 1 mile turn
right into Failsworth Rd; 0.25 miles into
Medlock Road.
Parkland course.
Pro Tony Cupello; Founded 1896
18 holes, 5874 yards, S.S.S. 68
✐ Practice area.
♦ Welcome WD only.
[WD £22.
↷ Welcome Wed, Thurs, Fri;
packages incl. golf & catering from £34.
|◉| Clubhouse facilities.
↩ Smokies Park; Bower Hotel; Avant
Hotel.

7 28 Burnley　　　　　℃
Glen View Road, Burnley, Lancs,
BB11 3RW

🖧 www.burnleygolfclub.org.uk
📧 burnleygolfclub@onthegreen.co.uk
☎ 01282 421045, Fax 451281, Pro
455266, Sec 451281
Glen View road is off Manchester
Road
Moorland course.
Pro Paul McEvoy; Founded 1905
18 holes, 5969 yards, S.S.S. 69
♦ Welcome with handicap certs.
[WD £20; WE £25.
↷ Welcome everyday except Sat;
handicap certs required; 36 holes of
golf plus meals; £30 (£36 Sun).
|◉| Full facilities.
↩ Rosehill House Hotel.

7 29 Bury
Unsworth Hall. Blackford Bridge,
Manchester Road. Bury, Lancs,
BL9 9TJ
☎ 0161 766 4897, Fax 796 3480,
Pro 766 2213
On A56 1.5 miles from M62 Junction 17
Undulating semi-moorland course.
Pro D Proctor; Founded 1890
Designed by Dr A Mackenzie
18 holes, 5927 yards, S.S.S. 69
♦ Welcome except on club
competition days.
[WD £28; WE £32.
↷ Welcome Wed-Fri; packages
include full day's golf and catering £38.
|◉| Full clubhouse facilities.
↩ Red Hall; Rostrevor.

7 30 Carlisle　　　　　℃
Aglionby, Carlisle, Cumbria, CA4 8AG
📧 secretary@carlislegolfclub.org
☎ 01228 513029, Fax 513303, Pro
513241, Sec 513303
Course is on the A69 0.25 miles E of
M6 Junction 43.
Parkland course (Open Championship).
Pro Graeme Lisle; Founded 1908,
moved 1940
Designed by MacKenzie Ross
18 holes, 6223 yards, S.S.S. 70
✐ Practice area.
♦ Welcome except Tues and Sat.
[WD £30-£40; Sun £45.
↷ Welcome Mon, Wed, Fri by prior
arrangement; packages available;
club can administer competitions;

private dining facilities; terms on
application.
|◉| Full clubhouse facilities.
↩ Cumbrian Hotel, Carlisle; Crown
Hotel, Wetherall.

7 31 Carus Green
Burneside Road, Kendal, Cumbria,
LA9 6EB
🖧 www.carusgreen.co.uk
☎ 01539 721097, Fax 721097
From roundabout at N end of Kendal
follow A591 to Burnside.
Pro David Turner.
Designed by W Adamson
18 holes, 5961 yards, S.S.S. 68
✐ 16 bay floodlit.
♦ Welcome; some WE restrictions.
[Terms on application.
↷ Ring for details.
|◉| Full clubhouse catering.

7 32 Casterton　　　　　℃
Sedbergh Road, Casterton, Kirkby
Lonsdale, S Cumbria, LA6 2LA
🖧 www.castertongolf.co.uk
📧 castertongc@hotmail.com
☎ 01524 271592, Fax 274387
On A683 Sebergh Road.
Picturesque undulating parkland
course.
Pro Roy Williamson; Founded
1946/1993
Designed by W Adamson
9 holes, 5726 yards, S.S.S. 68
♦ Welcome by prior arrangement;
weekend reservations essential.
[WD £10; WE £14.
↷ Welcome by arrangement;
maximum 40; terms available on
application.
|◉| Full catering available.
↩ Pheasant, Casterton; Whoop Hall,
Kirkby Lonsdale.

7 33 Castle Hawk
Chadwick Lane, Heywood Rd,
Rochdale, Lancs, OL11 3BY
📧 teeoff@castlehawk.freeserve.co.uk
☎ 01706 640841, Fax 860587, Pro
633855, Rest/Bar 710020
Leave Rochdale on the Manchester
Road towards Castleton; turn right for

the course directly before Castleton station.
Undulating parkland/meadowland course.
Pro Frank Accleton
Founded 1965
Designed by T Wilson
18 holes, 5398 yards, S.S.S. 68
9 holes, 3036 yards, S.S.S. 55
♦ Welcome.
[Mon-Sat £9 Sun £11. Paying guests unable to play 9-hole course on Sat.
⌒ Welcome by prior arrangement.
⦿ Restaurant and bar facilities.
⌁ Royal Toby.

7 34 Castletown Golf Links
Fort Island, Castletown, Derbyhaven, Isle of Man, IM9 1UA
⌨ www.castletowngolflinks.co.uk
☎ 01624 822220, Fax 829661, Pro 822221, Sec as above or 07624 483336
3 miles from airport.
True links course.
Pro Murray Crowe
Founded 1892
Designed by MacKenzie Ross
18 holes, 6707 yards, S.S.S. 72
♦ Practice ground.
♦ Welcome; residents have priority at WE.
[WD £35; WE £40.
⌒ Welcome by prior arrangement; discounts for residents; catering packages available; snooker, sauna, indoor pool; from £35.
⦿ Full club and hotel catering restaurant and bar facilities.
⌁ On site hotel.

7 35 Childwall
Naylor's Rd, Liverpool, Merseyside, L27 2YB
☎ 0151 4870654, Fax 4870882, Pro 4879871
5 miles from Liverpool, 2 miles from M62 Junction 6.
Parkland course.
Pro Nigel Parr
Founded 1913
Designed by James Braid
18 holes, 6470 yards, S.S.S. 71
♦ Practice ground.
♦ Welcome WD except Tues between 9.45am and 2pm.
[WD £26; WE £35.
⌒ Welcome WD except Tues by prior arrangement.
⦿ Bar and restaurant facilities available.
⌁ Village; Derby Lodge.

7 36 Chorley
Chorley Road, Heath Charnock, Chorley, Lancs, PR6 9HX
⌨ www.chorleygolfclub.co.uk
✉ secretary@ chorleygolfclub.freeserve.co.uk
☎ 01257 480263, Fax 480722, Pro 481245
Course is on the A673 100 yds south of the A6 Junction at Skew Bridge traffic lights.
Heathland course.
Pro Mark Bradley
Founded 1897
Designed by JA Steer
18 holes, 6307 yards, S.S.S. 70
♦ Welcome WD by prior arrangement.
[WD £32.
⌒ Welcome Mon to Fri by prior arrangement.
⦿ Full bar and restaurant facilities available.
⌁ Yarrow Bridge; Parkville; Hartwood Hall; Gladmar.

7 37 Clitheroe
Whalley Road, Pendleton, Clitheroe, Lancs, BB7 1PP
⌨ www.clitheroegolfclub.com
✉ secretary@clitheroegolfclub.com
☎ 01200 422292, Fax 422292, Pro 424242, Rest/Bar 442494
2 miles S of Clitheroe on the Clitheroe-Whalley Road.
Parkland course.
Pro JE Twissell; Founded 1891/1932
Designed by James Braid
18 holes, 6323 yards, S.S.S. 71
♦ Practice area.
♦ Welcome by prior arrangement.
[WD from £32; full day from £37; WE £45.
⌒ Welcome by prior arrangement; packages can be arranged for golf and catering from £34.
⦿ Full clubhouse facilities.

7 38 Cockermouth
Embleton, Cockermouth, Cumbria, CA13 9SG
⌨ www.cockermouthgolf.co.uk /login.htm
✉ secretary@cockermouthgolf .co.uk
☎ 017687 76223, Fax 76941, Sec 76941
3 miles E of Cockermouth.
Fell land course.
Founded 1896
Designed by James Braid
18 holes, 5496 yards, S.S.S. 67
♦ Welcome by prior arrangement.

[Summer WD £18, WE £22; Winter WD £12, WE £16.
⌒ Welcome; terms on application; from £15.
⦿ Clubhouse facilities.
⌁ Trout; Derwent Lodge, both Cockermouth.

7 39 Colne
Law Farm, Skipton Old Road, Colne, Lancs, BB8 7EB
☎ 01282 863391, Fax 870547
From end of M65 E travel 1 mile to r/bout, then take first exit left for course.
Moorland course with trees.
Founded 1901
Designed by club members
9 holes, 6053 yards, S.S.S. 69
♦ Practice ground, practice green, putting green.
♦ Welcome except competition days; 2 balls only on Thurs.
[WD £16; WE £20.
⌒ Welcome WD; snooker; function room; terms on application; from £16.
⦿ Full clubhouse facilities except Mons.
⌁ The Oaks, Burnley; The Old Stone Trough, Colne.

7 40 Crompton & Royton
High Barn Street, Royton, Oldham, Lancs, OL2 6RW
☎ 0161 624 2154, Fax 652 4711, Sec 624 0986, Rest/Bar 624 9867
Off A627 at Royton centre.
Moorland course.
Pro David Melling
Founded 1908
18 holes, 6214 yards, S.S.S. 70
♦ Welcome; restrictions at WE and on Tues and Wed.
[WD £25; WE £35; reductions for guests of members.
⌒ Welcome Mon, Thurs and Fri; terms on application.
⦿ Clubhouse facilities.
⌁ Peraquito, Oldham.

7 41 Dalston Hall
Dalston, Carlisle, Cumbria, CA5 7JX
☎ 01228 710165
From M6 Junction 42 to Dalston Village; course 0.5 miles on right.
Parkland course.
Founded 1990
Designed by David Pearson
9 holes, 5103 yards, S.S.S. 65
♦ Welcome; tee booking required at WE and after 4pm WD.
[WD 9 holes £6.50, 18 holes £10; WE 9 holes £7.50,18 holes £13.

Welcome by arrangement; packages on application.
Bar and restaurant.
Dalston Hall caravan park on site; Dalston Hall Hotel adjacent.

7 42 Darwen
Winter Hill, Duddon Avenue, Darwen, Lancs, BB3 0LB
admin@darwengolfclub.com
01254 704367, Fax 773833, Pro 776370, Rest/Bar 701287
1.5 miles from Darwen centre.
Moorland/parkland course.
Pro W Lennon; Founded 1893
Established 1893.
18 holes, 6076 yards, S.S.S. 71
Welcome.
Prices on application.
Welcome by prior arrangement; terms on application.
Clubhouse facilities.
Whitehall Hotel & CC.

7 43 Davyhulme
Gleneagles Road, Urmston, Manchester, Lancs, M41 8SA
0161 7482260, Fax 7474067, Pro 7483931
Course is eight miles S of Manchester adjacent to Trafford Hospital in Davyhulme.
Parkland course.
Pro Dean Butler; Founded 1910
18 holes, 6237 yards, S.S.S. 70
Two practice putting greens, practice area with green and bunker, two indoor practice nets, tuition available, group and individual; pro shop caters for society prizes (giftware/glassware, etc).
Welcome WD and WE.
WD £24-£30; WE £33.
Welcome Mon, Tues, Thurs by arrangement.
Full facilities.
The Manor Hey Hotel; The Tulip.

7 44 Dean Wood
Lafford Lane, Upholland, Skelmersdale, Lancs, WN8 0QZ
office@dwgc.fsnet.co.uk
01695 622219, Fax 622245, Pro 627480, Rest/Bar 622980
1.5 miles from M6 Junction 26 following Up Holland signs.
Hilly parkland course.
Pro Stuart Danchin; Founded 1922
Designed by James Braid
18 holes, 6137 yards, S.S.S. 70
Practice area; practice nets.
Welcome by prior arrangement.

WD £30; WE £33 per day.
Welcome Mon, Thurs and Fri; terms on application.
Clubhouse facilities.
Holland Hall; Travel Inn.

7 45 Deane
Broadford Road, Bolton, Lancs, BL3 4NS
01204 61944, Fax 651808, Sec 651808
Course is one mile from Junction 5 on the M61.
Undulating parkland course.
Pro David Martindale; Founded 1908
18 holes, 5652 yards, S.S.S. 67
Welcome by arrangement.
WD £24; WE £28.
Welcome Tues, Thurs, Fri by prior arrangement; full day package of golf and catering; £35.
Clubhouse facilities.
Beaumont Hotel.

7 46 Denton
Manchester Road, Wilton Paddock, Denton, Manchester, Lancs, M34 2GG
dentongolfclub@btinternet.com
0161 336 3218, Fax 4751, Pro 2070
5 miles SE of Manchester off A57; also close to M60 Denton roundabout, Junction 24.
Parkland course.
Pro Michael Hollingworth; Founded 1909
18 holes, 6541 yards, S.S.S. 71
Welcome WD; WE only with a member.
WD £25; WE £30.
Welcome Wed to Fri.
New clubhouse facilities.
Stable Gate Travelodge; Diamond Hotels.

7 47 Douglas Golf Club
Pulrose Road, Douglas, Isle of Man, IM2 1AE
01624 675952, Pro 661558
1 mile from Douglas town centre, clubhouse near power station cooling tower.
Municipal parkland course.
Pro Mike Vipond; Founded 1927
Designed by Dr A MacKenzie
18 holes, 5922 yards, S.S.S. 68
Welcome; advisable to phone in advance.
WD £8; WE £13.
Welcome by prior arrangement.
Full meals and bar snacks throughout season.
Contact local tourist board.

7 48 Dunnerholme
Duddon Road, Askam-in-Furness, Cumbria, LA16 7AW
01229 462675
Take A590 to Askam, turn left over railway into Duddin Rd, continue down towards the seashore over cattle grid.
Links course.
Founded 1905
10 holes, 6154 yards, S.S.S. 70
Welcome except before 4.30pm Sun.
Prices on application.
Welcome by prior arrangement; few restrictions.
Bar and catering facilities.
Railway; White Water; Clarence; Wellington; Abbey House.

7 49 Dunscar
Longworth Lane, Bromley Cross, Bolton, Lancs, BL7 9QY
secretary@dunscargolfclub .fsnet.co.uk
01204 303321, Fax 303321, Pro 592992, Rest/Bar 598228
Off A666 3 miles N of Bolton.
Moorland course.
Pro Gary Treadgold; Founded 1908
Designed by George Lowe
18 holes, 6085 yards, S.S.S. 69
Practice facilities.
Welcome by prior arrangement.
WD £25; WE £35.
Welcome by prior arrangement; terms on application.
Clubhouse facilities.
Egerton House; Last Drop.

7 50 Duxbury Park
Duxbury Hall Road, Chorley, Lancs, PR7 4AT
01257 265380, Fax 241378, Sec 241634, Rest/Bar 277049
1.5 miles S of Chorley on A5106 from A6.
Municipal parkland course.
Pro Simon Middleham
Founded 1970
18 holes, 6390 yards, S.S.S. 71
Welcome; booking system.
Terms on application.
Welcome WD by prior arrangement.
Limited at club; facilities available close by.
Hartwood Hall; Kilhey Court.

7 51 Eden
Crosby-on-Eden, Carlisle, Cumbria, CA6 4RA
www.edengolf.co.uk
edengolf@aol.com

☎ 01228 573003, Fax 818435, Rest/Bar 573013
From M6 Junction 44 take A689 to Low Crosby and Crosby-on-Eden.
Parkland course.
Pro Steve Harrison; Founded 1991
Designed by G Eannop & Sons.
18 holes, 6368 yards, S.S.S. 72
Ⅰ 16 bay floodlit.
✝ Welcome; prior booking advisable.
Ⅼ Winter WD £22; WE £28; Summer WD £28; WE £32.
✐ Welcome by prior arrangement; discounts are available for larger groups; practice area; driving range; catering packages; terms available on application.
IOI Full clubhouse bar and restaurant facilities.
⌐ Wall Foot Hotel; Crosby Lodge; Crown Hotel.

7 52 Ellesmere ℭ
Old Clough Lane, Worsley, Manchester, M28 7HZ
✉ honsec@ellsmeregolf.fsnet.co.uk
☎ 0161 790 8591, Fax 790 7322, Sec 799 0554, Rest/Bar 790 2122
Off A580 adjacent to M60 ring road.
Parkland course.
Pro Terry Morley; Founded 1913
18 holes, 6265 yards, S.S.S. 70
✝ Welcome except on competition days and BH.
Ⅼ WD £25 round; WE £30 day.
✐ Welcome Mon, Tues and Fri; Wed also in winter: 27 holes of golf plus catering; from £35.
IOI Full clubhouse facilities available.
⌐ Novotel, Worsley.

7 53 Fairfield Golf & Sailing Club
Boothdale, Booth Road, Audenshaw, Manchester, Lancs, M34 5GA
⌨ www.fairfieldgolf.co.uk
✉ secretary@fairfieldgolf.co.uk
☎ 0161 301 4528, Fax 4254, Pro 370 2292
On A635 5 miles E of Manchester.
Parkland course around reservoir.
Pro SA Pownell; Founded 1892
18 holes, 5664 yards, S.S.S. 68
✝ Welcome WD; Thurs ladies day; some weekend restrictions; telephone in advance.
Ⅼ WD £20; WE £25..
✐ Welcome by prior arrangement with the secretary; terms on application
IOI Full facilities by prior arrangement.
⌐ Village, Hyde; York, Ashton-under-Lyne.

7 54 Fairhaven
Lytham Hall Park, Blackpool Road, Ansdell, Lytham-St-Annes, Lancs, FY8 4JU
✉ nugent@fairhaven-golfclub.co.uk
☎ 01253 736976, Fax 731461, Sec 736741, Rest/Bar 734787
Course is on the B5261 two miles from Lytham.
Semi links; Open Championship qualifying course.
Pro Brian Plucknett; Founded 1895
Designed by James Braid
18 holes, 6883 yards, S.S.S. 73
Ⅰ Practice area.
✝ Welcome by arrangement; restrictions at WE.
Ⅼ WD £35; WE £40.
✐ Welcome by arrangement.
IOI Full facilities except Mon; banqueting room.
⌐ Clifton Arms; Grand; Dalmeney; Fearnlea.

7 55 Fishwick Hall ℭ
Glenluce Drive, Farringdon Park, Preston, Lancs, PR1 5TD
⌨ www.fishwickhallgolfclub.co.uk
✉ fishwickhallgolfclub@supanet.com
☎ 01772 798300, Fax 704600, Pro 795870, Sec 798300, Rest/Bar 798300
From M6 Junction 31 take A59 past Tickled Trout; Glenluce Drive is first left at top of the hill.
Undulating meadowland/parkland course.
Pro Martin Watson; Founded 1912
18 holes, 6045 yards, S.S.S. 69
✝ Welcome.
Ⅼ WD £26; WE £31.
✐ Welcome by prior arrangement.
IOI Full catering facilities.
⌐ Tickled Trout.

7 56 Fleetwood
Princes Way, Fleetwood, Lancs, FY7 8AF
☎ 01253 873661, Fax 773573, Pro 873661, Sec 773573, Rest/Bar 873114
Off A587 0.5 miles from Fleetwood, follow signs for Fleetwood Freeport.
Links course.
Pro S McLaughlin; Founded 1932
Designed by Edwin Steer
18 holes, 6557 yards, S.S.S. 71 Par 72
Ⅰ Practice area.
✝ Welcome WD; some restrictions WE.
Ⅼ WD £30; WE £40. Day tickets WD £36; WE £40.
✐ Welcome by prior arrangement; discounts available for larger groups; from £24.

IOI Full clubhouse facilities.
⌐ North Euston; New Boston; Briardene.

7 57 Flixton
Church Road, Urmston, Manchester, Lancs, M41 6EP
☎ 0161 748 2116, Fax 748 2116, Pro 07836 665571, Rest/Bar 749 8834
Course is on the B5213 five miles SW of Manchester.
Parkland course.
Pro Danny Proctor; Founded 1893
9 holes, 6410 yards, S.S.S. 71
✝ Welcome by prior arrangement.
Ⅼ WD £16; WE £16.
✐ Welcome by prior arrangement; packages available; terms on application.
IOI Clubhouse facilities.

7 58 Formby
Golf Road, Formby, Liverpool, Lancs, L37 1LQ
⌨ www.formbygolfclub.co.uk
✉ info@formbygolfclub.co.uk
☎ 01704 872164, Fax 833028, Pro 873090
1 mile W of A565 adjacent to Freshfield Station.
Championship links course.
Pro Gary Butler; Founded 1884
Designed by Willie Park
18 holes, 6993 yards, S.S.S. 72
Ⅰ Practice area.
✝ By prior arrangement only.
Ⅼ WD £85 per round; WE £95.
✐ By prior arrangement only; terms on application.
IOI Full clubhouse facilities.
⌐ Dormy accommodation.

7 59 Formby Golf Centre
Moss Side, Formby, Liverpool, Merseyside, L37 0AF
☎ 01704 875952
Just off the Formby by-pass.
Parkland course.
Pro Mike Mawdsley; Founded 1985
9 pitch and putt holes, 1510 yards, S.S.S. 54
Ⅰ Practice range, 20 bays floodlit, putting green.
✝ Welcome; pay and play.
Ⅼ 9 or 18 holes £4.
IOI Coffee, tea and light refreshments.

7 60 Formby Hall
Southport Old Road, Formby, Liverpool, Merseyside, L37 0AB
☎ 01704 875699, Fax 832134, Pro

875699, Sec 875699, Rest/Bar 875699
Off Formby by-pass opposite
Woodvale Aerodrome.
Parkland course with 11 lakes.
Pro David Lloyd; Founded 1996
Designed by PSA/Alex Higgins
18 holes, 6731 yards, S.S.S. 72
🏌 Practice range, 31 bays floodlit;
academy.
† Welcome WD; restrictions at WE.
⌑ WD £35; WE £40.
⌒ Welcome by prior arrangement;
corporate days available; from £40.
🍴 5 bars and 2 restaurants open
from 7.30am-11pm.
🛏 Treetops; many B&B's can be
recommended.

7 61 Formby Ladies
Golf Road, Formby, Liverpool,
Merseyside, L37 1YH
☎ 01704 873493, Fax 873493,
Pro 873090, Rest/Bar 874127
Course is off the A565 five miles S of
Southport.
Seaside links course.
Pro Gary Butler; Founded 1896
18 holes, 5374 yards, S.S.S. 71
† Welcome by arrangement.
⌑ WD £40; WE £45.
⌒ Welcome by arrangement; full golf
and catering available; terms on
application.
🍴 Bar snacks available.
🛏 Treetops; selection in Southport.

7 62 Furness
Furness Golf Club, Central Drive,
Walney Island, Barrow-In-Furness,
Cumbria, LA14 3LN
☎ 01229 471232
Off A590 to Walney Island; 0.5 miles
after end of bridge.
Seaside links course.
Pro Andrew Whitehall; Founded 1872
18 holes, 6363 yards, S.S.S. 71
† Welcome by prior arrangement;
some restrictions apply on Wed & WE.
⌑ WD £20; WE £25.
⌒ Welcome by prior arrangement;
must be members of recognised golf
clubs; discounts for groups of more
than 10; from £17.
🍴 Clubhouse facilities.
🛏 White House; Infield GH.

7 63 Gathurst
Miles Lane, Shevington, Wigan, Lancs,
WN6 8EW
📧 mail@gathurstgolfclub/ltd.uk
☎ 01257 255235, Fax 255953,
Pro 255882, Rest/Bar 252861

1 mile S of M6 Junction 27.
Parkland course.
Pro D Clarke; Founded 1913
Designed by N Pearson
18 holes, 5778 yards, S.S.S. 69
🏌 Practice area.
† Welcome WD except Wed; WE
with member.
⌑ WD £27.
⌒ Welcome WD except Wed; 27
holes, full day's catering; from £33.
🍴 Bar and restaurant facilities
available.
🛏 Almond Brook Moathouse.

7 64 Ghyll
Ghyll Brow, Barnoldswick, Lancs,
BB18 6JQ
☎ 01282 842466
A56 to Thornton-in-Craven turn left on
B6252; 1 mile on left opposite Rolls
Royce factory.
Scenic parkland course.
Founded 1907
9/11 holes, 5770 yards, S.S.S. 67
† Welcome except Tues am; Fri after
4.30 or Sun.
⌑ Prices on application.
⌒ Welcome as with visitors;
reductions for parties of more than 8;
from £14.
🍴 Bar catering by arrangement.
🛏 Stirk House, Gisburn; Tempest,
Elslack.

7 65 Grange Fell
Grange Fell Road, Grange-over-
Sands, Cumbria, LA11 6HB
☎ 01539 532536, Sec 534098
From Junction 36 of the M6 follow the
signs to Barrow until Grange turn-off;
through the town in direction of
Cartmel.
Parkland course.
Founded 1952
9 holes, 5292 yards, S.S.S. 66
† Welcome.
⌑ WD £15; WE £20.
⌒ None.
🛏 Netherwood; Grange, both in
Grange-over-Sands; Aynsome, Cartmel.

7 66 Grange Park
Prescot Road, St Helens, Merseyside,
WA10 3AD
🌐 www.uk.golfer.org
📧 gpgc@ic24.net
☎ 01744 26318, Fax 26318, Pro
28785, Rest/Bar 22980
M62 Junction 7.
Heathland course.
Pro Paul Roberts; Founded 1891

18 holes, 6422 yards, S.S.S. 71
† Welcome WD except Tues;
restrictions at WE.
⌑ WD £26 WE £33.00.
⌒ Welcome WD except Tues;
packages including all-day food and up
to 36 holes of golf available; from
£39.00.
🍴 Full clubhouse facilities.
🛏 Hilton; Haydock Thistle; Haydock
Moathouse; St Helens.

7 67 Grange-over-Sands
Meathop Road, Grange-over-Sands,
Cumbria, LA11 6QX
🌐 www.grange-over-sandsgolfclub
.co.uk
📧 dwright@ktdinternet.com
☎ 015395 33180, Fax 33754, Pro
35937, Sec 33754, Rest/Bar 33810
Off A590 course is located just before
entering town just as you get to 30mph
sign.
Parkland course.
Pro Andrew Pickering; Founded 1919
Designed by A MacKenzie
18 holes, 5958 yards, S.S.S. 69
🏌 Practice area.
† Welcome with handicap certs.
⌑ WD £20, £25 for the day; WE £25,
£30 for the day.
⌒ Welcome by appointment;
packages available; prices on
application.
🍴 Full clubhouse facilities.
🛏 Grange Hotel; Graythwaite Manor;
Clare House.

7 68 Great Harwood
Harwood Bar, Whalley Road, Great
Harwood, Blackburn, Lancs, BB6 7TE
☎ 01254 884391
Easy access from Clitheroe by-pass.
Parkland course.
Founded 1896
9 holes, 6456 yards for 18 holes,
S.S.S. 71
† Welcome WD; restrictions at WE.
⌑ WD £16; WE £22.
⌒ Welcome by prior arrangement,
catering packages can be arranged;
snooker; prices on application.
🍴 Clubhouse facilities.
🛏 Dunkenhalgh, Clayton-le-Moors.

7 69 Great Lever & Farnworth
Off Plodder Lane, Farnworth, Bolton,
Lancs, BL4 0LQ
☎ 01204 656137, Fax 652780, Pro
656650, Rest/Bar 656493
From M61 Junction 4 take Watergate
Lane to Plodder Lane.

Parkland course.
Pro Tony Howarth; Founded 1917
18 holes, 6044 yards, S.S.S. 69
🏌 Practice area.
🏌 Welcome WD with handicap certs;
restrictions at WE.
🏌 WD £16.50; WE £27.
🏌 Welcome WD by arrangement; full
day packages available for golf and
catering except Mon; £29.50.
🍴 Full facilities except Mon.

7 70 Green Haworth

Green Haworth, Accrington, Lancs,
BB5 3SL
🌐 www.greenhaworth.
freeserve.co.uk
✉ golf@greenhaworth
.freeserve.co.uk
☎ 01254 237580, Sec 382510
From Accrington town centre take main
road to Blackburn then left on
Willows Lane; follow road for 2-3
miles; signposted after Red Lion
Hotel.
Moorland course.
Founded 1914
9 holes, 5556 yards, S.S.S. 68
🏌 Welcome WD; some restrictions
apply on Wed; Sat by prior
arrangement.
🏌 WD £15; Sat £20.
🏌 Societies allowed on the course by
prior arrangement.
🍴 Full facilities; restaurant can be
pre-booked.

7 71 Greenmount

Greenhalgh Fold Farm, Greenmount,
Bury, Lancs, BL8 4LH
☎ 01204 883712, Pro 888616
Leave M66 at Bury, follow signs to
Tottington, once in Tottington centre,
turn right at Carmelios, 1st left.
Undulating parkland course.
Pro Jason Seed; Founded 1920
9 holes, 4980 yards, S.S.S. 64
🏌 Welcome WD; with member at
WE, Tues ladies day.
🏌 Prices on application.
🏌 Welcome WD except Tues by prior
arrangement.
🍴 Full service except Mon; function
suite available.
🛏 Red Hall; Old Mill; Red Lion,
Victoria.

7 72 Haigh Hall

Haigh Country Park, Aspull, Wigan,
Lancs, WN2 1PE
☎ 01942 833337, Fax 831081,
Pro 831107, Sec 01942 833337

Take J27 off M6 and B5239 to
Standish; course 6 miles NE of Wigan.
Municipal parkland course.
Pro Ian Lee; Founded 1973
18 and a 9-hole course, 6500 yards,
S.S.S. 71
🏌 6.
🏌 Welcome any time by
arrangement; phone bookings via Pro.
🏌 Prices on application.
🏌 Welcome with prior arrangement
with the professional.
🍴 Full restaurant and cafe service.
🛏 Brocket; Oak; Almond Brook;
Moathouse.

7 73 Harwood

Springfield, Roading Brook Road,
Bolton, Lancs, BL2 4JD
🌐 www.harwoodgolfclub.co.uk
✉ secretary@harwoodgolfclub.co.uk
☎ 01204 524233, Fax 524233,
Pro 362834, Rest/Bar 522878
4 miles NE of Bolton on B6196.
Parkland course.
Pro Colin Maroney; Founded
1926/1998
Designed by Whole New Concept
18 holes, 5851 yards, S.S.S. 69
🏌 Practice area.
🏌 Welcome WD; with member at WE.
🏌 WD/WE £20 visitors; £12 guests.
🏌 Welcome by arrangement; terms
on application to secretary.
🍴 Clubhouse facilities.
🛏 Last Drop, Bromley Cross; The
Bolholt Hotel & Conference Leisure
Centre.

7 74 Haydock Park

Haydock Park Golf Club Co Ltd,
Newton Lane, Newton Le Willows,
Merseyside, WA12 0HX
✉ haydockparkgolfclub
@onetel.net.uk
☎ 01925 224389, Fax 228525, Pro
226944, Sec 228525, Rest/Bar 291020
1 mile E of the M6 off A580.
Parkland course.
Pro Peter Kenwright; Founded 1877
18 holes, 6058 yards, S.S.S. 69
🏌 Practice area, putting green.
🏌 Welcome WD except Tues.
🏌 WD £30.
🏌 Welcome WD except Mon and
Tues; from £42.
🍴 Full clubhouse facilities.
🛏 Kirkfield; Post House; Thistle.

7 75 Heaton Park

Middleton Road, Heaton Park, Prestwich,
Manchester, Lancs, M25 2SW

☎ 0161 654 9899, Fax 653 2003
M60 Junction 19.
Undulating parkland course.
Pro Gary Dermott; Founded 1912
Designed by JH Taylor
18 holes, 5755 yards, S.S.S. 68
🏌 Driving range, par 3 course, golf
academy.
🏌 Welcome; pre book all tee times.
🏌 WD £10; WE £12.50; special
twilight rates.
🏌 Welcome by prior arrangement.
🍴 Bar and catering in cafe.
🛏 Heaton Park Hotel.

7 76 Heron's Reach

De Vere Hotel, East Park Drive,
Blackpool, Lancs, FY3 8LL
✉ db.golfshop@
deverehotels.com
☎ 01253 766156, Fax 798800, Pro
766156, Sec 766156, Rest/Bar 838866
From M55 Junction 4, follow signs for
Blackpool on A583; at fourth set of
lights turn right into South Park Drive;
follow signs for zoo.
Parkland course with links
characteristics.
Pro Richard Bowman; Founded 1993
Designed by Peter Alliss and Clive
Clark
18 holes, 6628 yards, S.S.S. 72
🏌 Practice range, 18 bays floodlit.
🏌 Welcome WD/WE after 10am.
🏌 WD £40; WE £45.
🏌 Welcome all year round by prior
arrangement; packages available;
leisure club; swimming pool; tennis;
squash courts.
🍴 Full facilities; nineteen bar; 3
restaurants.
🛏 De Vere Blackpool on site.

7 77 Hesketh

Cockle Dick's Lane, off Cambridge
Road, Southport, Merseyside,
PR9 9QQ
🌐 www.ukgolfer.org/clubs/hesketh
✉ hesketh@ukgolfer.org
☎ 01704 536897, Fax 539250,
Pro 530050, Rest/Bar 531055/530226
Course is on the A565 one mile N of
Southport.
Seaside links course with some
parkland.
Pro John Donoghue
Founded 1885
Designed by JOF Morris
18 holes, 6655 yards, S.S.S. 72
🏌 Welcome by prior arrangement.
🏌 WD £40-£50; WE £50.
🏌 Welcome by prior arrangement;
inclusive packages for catering and

golf available for groups of 12 or more; from £50.
🍽 Bar and dining facilities.
🛏 Prince of Wales; Scarisbrick.

7 78 The Heysham ♌

Trumacar, Park Middleton Road, Middleton, Morecambe, Lancs, LA3 3JH
💻 www.heyshamgolfclub.com
📧 secretary@heyshamgolf
.freeserve.co.uk
☎ 01524 852000, Fax 853030, Sec 851011, Rest/Bar 859154
Off A683 5 miles from M6 Junction 34.
Parkland course with wooded areas.
Pro Ryan Done; Founded 1929
Designed by Alec Herd
18 holes, 6258 yards, S.S.S. 70
⚐ 8-bay range; practice areas.
🚩 Welcome with handicap certs.
⌇ Prices on application.
🕹 Welcome by arrangement with Sec; discounts for groups of 8 or more; from £22.
🍽 Full clubhouse facilities.
🛏 Strathmore, Morecambe.

7 79 Hillside Golf Club

Hastings Road, Southport, Merseyside, PR8 2LU
💻 www.ukgolfer.org
📧 hillside@ukgolfer.org
☎ 01704 569902, Fax 563192, Pro 568360, Sec 567169, Rest/Bar 568682
Course is on the A565 three miles S of Southport.
Outstanding championship links course.
Pro B Seddon; Founded 1911/1923
Designed by Fred Hawtree
18 holes, 6850 yards, S.S.S. 74
⚐ Practice ground.
🚩 Restricted WD, no visitors Sat or BH; contact Sec.
⌇ WD £60-£75; Sun £75 (one round only).
🕹 Restricted; contact Sec; special approval needed for groups of more than 24; terms on application.
🍽 Full bar and restaurant seating 100
🛏 Scarisbrick; Prince of Wales; Metropole.

7 80 Hindley Hall

Hall Lane, Hindley, Wigan, Lancs, WN2 2SQ
☎ 01942 255131, Fax 253871, Pro 255991
Off A6 from M61 Junction 6 then take Dicconson Lane; after 1 mile into Hall Lane; club just after lake.

Moorland course.
Pro Neil Brazell; Founded 1895
18 holes, 5913 yards, S.S.S. 68
⚐ Practice area.
🚩 Welcome if member of a club; check with Sec in advance.
⌇ WD £20; WE £27.
🕹 Welcome by prior arrangement; terms on application.
🍽 Clubhouse facilities.
🛏 Georgian House.

7 81 Horwich

Victoria Road, Horwich, Bolton, Lancs, BL6 5PH
☎ 01204 696980
Close to M61 Junction 6.
Parkland course.
Founded 1895
9 holes, 5286 yards, S.S.S. 67
🚩 Welcome with member or by prior arrangement with Sec..
⌇ Terms on application.
🕹 Welcome WD and occasional Sun by prior arrangement.
🍽 Full bar and catering facilities.
🛏 Swallowfield; Holiday Inn Express; The De Vere Whites Hotel.

7 82 Houghwood

Billinge Hill, Crank Road, St Helens, Merseyside, WA11 8RL
📧 houghwoodgolf@btinternet.com
☎ 01744 894754, Fax 894754, Pro 894444
From M6 Junction 26 follow signs to Billinge; course 1 mile from Billinge Hospital.
Parkland course with USGA standard greens.
Pro Paul Dickenson; Founded 1996
Designed by N Pearson
18 holes, 6202 yards, S.S.S. 70
⚐ Practice area; new snooker room.
🚩 Welcome.
⌇ WD £25; WE £35; Deals available.
🕹 Welcome by arrangement; from £17-£30.
🍽 Bar and restaurant facilities.
🛏 Post House, Haydock; Stakis, St Helens.

7 83 Hurlston Hall ♌

Hurlston Lane, Moorfield Lane, Scarisbrick, Ormskirk, Lancs, L40 8JD
💻 www.hurlstonhall.co.uk
📧 hurlstonhall@btinternet.com
☎ 01704 840400, Fax 841404, Pro 841120, Sec 840400, Rest/Bar 840400

On A570 8 miles from M58 6 miles from Southport and 2 miles from Ormskirk.
Parkland course with two brooks.
Pro John Esclapez; Founded 1994
Designed by Donald Steel
18 holes, 6746 yards, S.S.S. 72
⚐ Practice range, 18 bays floodlit, 2 teaching bays.
🚩 Welcome by prior arrangement; handicap certs may be required.
⌇ Summer WD £35, WE £40; Winter WD £22, WE £27.
🕹 Registered golf societies welcome by prior arrangement with club office; packages including 36 holes, catering and gourmet dinner can be arranged; satellite TV; golf academy; terms on application.
🍽 Full catering facilities available with 90-seat restaurant; balcony and patio.
🛏 Beaufort Hotel; Scarisbrick; Prince of Wales.

7 84 Huyton & Prescot

Hurst Park, Huyton Lane, Huyton, Liverpool, Merseyside, L36 1UA
☎ 0151 4893948, Fax 4893948, Pro 4892022, Sec 4893948, Rest/Bar 4891138
Course is 10 miles from Liverpool just off the M57.
Parkland course.
Pro John Fisher
Founded 1905
18 holes, 5839 yards, S.S.S. 68
⚐ Practice bay.
🚩 Welcome WD; WE with member £13.
⌇ WD £24.
🕹 By arrangement WD.
🍽 Full facilities.
🛏 Derby Lodge; Hillcrest; Bell Tower.

7 85 Ingol ♌

Tanterton Hall Road, Ingol, Preston, Lancs, PR2 7BY
💻 www.ingolgolfclub.co.uk
📧 ingol@golfers.net
☎ 01772 734556, Fax 729815, Pro 769646
Leave M6 Junction 32 and turn towards Preston; follow signs for Ingol.
Parkland course.
Pro Ryan Grimshaw; Founded 1980
Designed by Cotton, Pennink, Lawrie & Partners
18 holes, 6294 yards, S.S.S. 70
⚐ Practice grounds.
🚩 Welcome.

꜀ Winter WD £16, WE £20 (2003); Summer WD £25, WE £30 (2004).
꜄ Welcome by arrangement but not before 1.30pm on Sun; from £18-39.
🍽 Full facilities; bar and function rooms.
🚪 Marriott Broughton Park; Barton Grange.

7 86 Kendal ☏
The Heights, High Tenterfell, Kendal, Cumbria, LA9 4PQ
🖳 www.cumbria.com/kendalgcl
☎ 01539 723499, Fax 733708, Sec 733708, Rest/Bar 739363
To Kendal on A6 signposted in town.
Moorland course; redesigned in late 1998.
Pro Peter Scott; Founded 1891
18 holes, 5800 yards, S.S.S. 68
† Welcome any time except Sat competition days; by prior arrangement WE.
꜀ WD £22 round, £26 day; WE £27.50 round, £32.50 day.
꜄ Welcome anytime subject to availability and by prior arrangement; from £27.
🍽 Full facilities except Mon.
🚪 County.

7 87 Keswick ☏
Threlkeld Hall, Threlkeld, Keswick, Cumbria, CA12 4SX
🖳 www.keswickgolfclub.com
📧 secretary@keswickgolfclub.com
☎ 017687 79324, Sec 79324, Rest/Bar 79013, Pro 79010 (tee bookings)
Course is off the A66 four miles E of Keswick.
Moorland/parkland course.
Pro Garry Watson; Founded 1975
Designed by Eric Brown
18 holes, 6225 yards, S.S.S. 72
† Welcome, even most WE.
꜀ WD £20; WE £25.
꜄ Welcome by prior arrangement with Sec; some WE available; packages for 12 or more; prices on application.
🍽 Bar and dining facilities.
🚪 The Horse and Farrier; Lodore Swiss; Keswick; Borrowdale; Wordsworth; Middle Ruddings; see website.

7 88 Kirkby Lonsdale ☏
Scalebar Lane, Barbon, Carnforth, Lancs, LA6 2LJ
🖳 www.klgolf.dial.pipex.com
📧 kl.golf@dial.pipex.com
☎ 015242 76365, Fax 76503, Pro 76366, Rest/Bar 76367
On A683 Sedbergh Road 3 miles from Kirkby Lonsdale.
Parkland course.
Pro Chris Barrett
Founded 1991
Designed by Bill Squires
18 holes, 6538 yards, S.S.S. 72
꜀ Practice ground.
† Welcome.
꜀ WD £26; WE £32.
꜄ Welcome by arrangement
🍽 Clubhouse facilities.
🚪 Whoop Hall, Cowan Bridge; Pheasant, Casterton; Crooklands Hotel, Crooklands.

7 89 Knott End ☏
Wyreside, Knott End-on-Sea, Poulton, Lancs, FY6 0AA
📧 knottendgolfclub.co.uk.
☎ 01253 810576, Fax 813446, Pro, 811365, Rest/Bar 810254
A588 to Knott End.
Links course.
Pro Paul Walker; Founded 1911
Designed by James Braid
18 holes, 5843 yards, S.S.S. 68
꜀ Practice ground and net.
† Welcome WD not before 9.30am or between 12.30pm-1.30pm.
꜀ WD £23; WE £26.
꜄ Welcome by prior arrangement; terms on application
🍽 Full facilities.
🚪 Bourne Arms; Springfield House Hotel.

7 90 Lancaster
Ashton Hall, Ashton-with- Stodday, Lancaster, Lancs, LA2 0AJ
🖳 www.lancastergc.co.uk
📧 sec@lancastergc.co.uk
☎ 01524 751247, Fax 752742, Pro 751802, Rest/Bar 751105
On A588 2 miles S of Lancaster.
Parkland course.
Pro David Sutcliffe; Founded 1933
Designed by James Braid
18 holes, 6500 yards, S.S.S. 71
† Welcome by prior arrangement with handicap certs.
꜀ WD £32 round, £40 day.
꜄ Welcome by prior arrangement on WD; handicap certs required; catering and golf packages available; from £48.
🍽 Full clubhouse facilities.
🚪 Dormy House with accommodation for 18 on site,11 bedrooms en-suite.

7 91 Lansil
Caton Road, Lancaster, Lancs, LA1 3PE
☎ 01524 39269, Sec 39269, Rest/Bar 39269
Junction 34 off M6 head to Lancaster A683 2nd left turn after Holiday inn.
Parkland/meadowland course.
Founded 1947
9 holes, 5608 yards, S.S.S. 67
† Welcome but not before 1pm Sun.
꜀ WD £12; WE £12.
꜄ Welcome WD by arrangement; catering packages organised with steward.
🍽 Meals and bar snacks available.
🚪 Holiday Inn & Lancaster Town House.

7 92 Lee Park
Childwall Valley Road, Liverpool, Merseyside, L27 3YA
☎ 0151 4873882, Fax 4984666, Rest/Bar 4879861
On B5171 off A562 next to Lee Manor High School.
Parkland course.
Founded 1955
Designed by Frank Pennink
18 holes, 6108 yards, S.S.S. 70
† All welcome.
꜀ WD £20; WE £30.
꜄ Welcome Mon, Thurs and Fri by prior arrangement with Sec; terms on application.
🍽 Bar snacks and meals.
🚪 Gateacre Hall.

7 94 Leigh
Broseley Lane, Culcheth, Warrington, Cheshire, WA3 4BG
🖳 www.leighgolf.co.uk
📧 golf@leighgolf.fsnet.co.uk
☎ 01925 762943, Fax 765097, Pro 762013, Rest/Bar 763130
Off B5217 in Culcheth village.
Parkland course.
Pro Andrew Baguley
Founded 1906
Designed by James Braid
18 holes, 5884 yards, S.S.S. 68
꜀ Practice range: 3 practice areas; 2 putting greens.
† Welcome.
꜀ WD £30; WE £40.
꜄ Welcome Mon, except BH, and Tues; catering packages available; snooker room; from £25.
🍽 Full clubhouse facilities.
🚪 Greyhound, Leigh; Thistle, Haydock.

7 94 Leyland
Wigan Road, Leyland, Lancs,
PR25 5UD
🖥 www.leylandgolfclub.com
✉ manager@leylandgolfclub.com
☎ 01772 436457, Pro 423425
On A49 0.25 miles from M6 Junction
28.
Meadowland course.
Pro Colin Burgess
Founded 1924
18 holes, 6123 yards, S.S.S. 69
🏌 Practice area adjacent to first tee;
Brand new clubhouse opens June
2002.
† Welcome WD; WE only with a
member.
💷 WD £25; WE £25.
⌁ Welcome by prior arrangement
with Sec; packages available on
request.
🍽 Full facilities.
🛏 Jarvis.

7 95 Liverpool Municipal
Ingoe Lane, Liverpool, Merseyside,
L32 4SS
☎ 0151 5465435
M57 J6, 300 yards on right of
B5192.
Municipal meadowland course.
Pro David Weston
Founded 1966
18 holes, 6706 yards, S.S.S. 72
🏌 Practice ground.
† Welcome.
💷 WD £7.30; WE £8.30.
⌁ Welcome every day; tee booking
required 1 week in advance.
🍽 Bar and cafeteria.
🛏 Golden Eagle.

7 96 Lobden
Lobden Moor, Whitworth, Rochdale,
Lancs, OL12 8XJ
☎ 01706 343228, Fax 643241,
Sec 643241
Take A671 from Rochdale to
Whitworth
Moorland course.
Founded 1888
9 holes, 5697 yards, S.S.S. 68
† Welcome except Sat.
💷 WD £10; WE £12.
⌁ Welcome by prior arrangement;
terms on application.
🍽 By arrangement with steward.

7 97 Longridge
Fell Barn, Jeffrey Hill, Longridge,
Preston, Lancs, PR3 2TU
🖥 www.longridgegolfclub.co.uk
✉ secretary@longridgegolfclub
.fsnet.co.uk.co.uk
☎ 01772 783291, Fax 783022,
Pro 783022
From M6 Junction 31a follow signs to
Longridge.
Moorland course with panoramic
views.
Pro Stephen Taylor; Founded 1877
18 holes, 5969 yards, S.S.S. 69
🏌 Practice area/pitching area + new
Par 3 course.
† Welcome.
💷 Prices on application.
⌁ Welcome by written prior
arrangement with Sec; summer and
winter packages available.
🍽 Full facilities available except
Mon.
🛏 Shireburn Arms; Gibbon Bridge;
Black Moss GH.

7 98 Lowes Park
Hill Top, Lowes Road, Bury, Lancs,
BL9 6SU
✉ lowes@parkgc.fsnet.co.uk
☎ 0161 7641231, Fax 7639503,
Sec 7639503, Rest/Bar 7641231
On A56 1 mile N of Bury; turn at
Sundial Inn into Lowes Road.
Moorland course.
Founded 1930
9 holes, 6006 yards, S.S.S. 69
🏌 Small practice area.
† Welcome by prior arrangement.
💷 Prices on application.
⌁ Welcome by prior arrangement;
package deals available; ladies only on
Wed; terms available on application.
🍽 Full clubhouse facilities except
Mon.
🛏 Red Hall, Walmersley Road,
Ramsbottom.

7 99 Lytham Green Drive
Ballam Road, Lytham St Annes, Lancs,
FY8 4LE
🖥 www.ukgolfer.com
✉ green@greendrive.fsnet.co.uk
☎ 01253 737390, Fax 731350, Pro
737379, Rest/Bar 376087
1 mile from Lytham centre.
Parkland course.
Pro Andrew Lancaster; Founded 1913
Designed by J Steer.
18 holes, 6194 yards, S.S.S. 69
🏌 Large practice area.
† Welcome WD by prior arrangement.
💷 WD £32-£40.
⌁ Welcome WD except Wed; coffee
on arrival, soup and sandwiches, 3-
course meal, 27 holes of golf; £40.
🍽 Full clubhouse facilities available.

🛏 Clifton Arms, Lytham; Fernlea, St
Annes; Lindum, St Annes.

7 100 Manchester
Hopwood Cottage, Rochdale Road,
Middleton, Manchester, Lancs, M24 6QP
🖥 www.mangc.co.uk
✉ mgc@zen.co.uk
☎ 0161 643 3202, Fax 9174,
Pro 2638, Rest/Bar 2718/655 3073
From A627 (M) take the A664 for
Middleton.
Parkland-moorland course.
Pro Brian Connor; Founded 1882
Designed by HS Colt
18 holes, 6519 yards, S.S.S. 72
🏌 Practice area and driving range
available to members and guests.
† Welcome by arrangement.
💷 WD £25; WE £45.
⌁ Welcome by prior arrangement;
packages of golf and catering available
on application; £40-£50.
🍽 Full clubhouse facilities.
🛏 Norton Grange; Royal Toby.

7 101 Manor
Moss Lane, Kearsley, Bolton, Lancs,
BL4 8SF
✉ manorsports@netscapeonline.co.uk
☎ 01204 701027, Fax 796914
1 mile from M62 Junction 17.
Parkland course.
Founded 1995
18 holes, 4914 yards, S.S.S. 66
🏌 Driving range next door.
† Welcome; pay and play.
💷 WD £8; WE £10.
⌁ Welcome by arrangement.
🍽 Bar and restaurant; function
suites.
🛏 Clifton Park Country House.

7 102 Marland Golf Course
Springfield Park, Rochdale, Lancs,
OL11 4RE
🖥 http://users.macunlimited.net
/dwillspga
☎ 01706 649801, Pro 649801
3 miles from M62.
Parkland course.
Pro David Wills
Founded 1927
18 holes, 5237 yards, S.S.S. 66
† Welcome.
💷 WD £8.75; WE £10.75.
⌁ Welcome by prior arrangement
with the Professional; WE booking in
advance, WD pay and play.
🍽 None.
🛏 Royal Toby, Rochdale; Albany,
Heywood.

7 103 Marsden Park
Townhouse Road, Nelson, Lancs,
BB9 8DG
🖳 www.pendleleisuretrust.co.uk
☎ 01282 661912, Fax, 661944
From M65 Junction 13, take B5446
onto Leeds Road and right at second
roundabout.
Semi-parkland course.
Founded 1969/1976
Designed by CK Cotton & Partners
18 holes, 5833 yards, S.S.S. 68
⌁ Practice area.
† Pay and play.
⌑ WD Adults £13, OAPs £7.50,
juniors £4.50; 9 holes £13,WE £15; 9
holes £13; twilight (after 6pm) £9.
⌔ Welcome by prior arrangement;
golf and catering packages available
from £20.
🍽 Clubhouse facilities and meeting
room.
🛏 The Oaks, Burnley; Great
Marsden, Nelson.

7 104 Maryport
Bank End, Maryport, Cumbria,
CA15 6PA
🖳 maryportgcltd@onetel.net.uk
☎ 01900 812605, Fax 815626,
Sec 815626, Rest/Bar 812605
N of Maryport turn left off A596 on to
the B5300 (Silloth Road).
Seaside course, 9 holes links, 9 holes
parkland.
Founded 1905
18 holes, 6088 yards, S.S.S. 69
⌁ Practice area.
† Welcome.
⌑ WD £18; WE £23 summer. Winter
fees are WD £14 WE £18.
⌔ Welcome by prior arrangement;
discounts available for groups of nine
or more.
🍽 Full clubhouse facilities.
🛏 Ellenbank; Skinburness Hotel.

7 105 Morecambe
Marine Road East, Morecambe, Lancs,
LA4 6AJ
🖳 morecambegolf@btconnect.com
☎ 01524 412841, Fax 400088,
Pro 415596, Rest/Bar 418050
On road to Morecambe from A6.
Parkland/links course.
Pro Simon Fletcher; Founded 1905
Designed by Dr Alister MacKenzie
18 holes, 5750 yards, S.S.S. 69
† Welcome by arrangement.
⌑ Prices on application.
⌔ Welcome by prior arrangement;
terms on application.
🍽 Full clubhouse facilities.

7 106 Mossock Hall ☏
Liverpool Road, Bickerstaffe, Ormskirk,
Lancs, L39 0EE
🖳 mossockhall@hotmail.com
☎ 01695 421717, Fax 424961, Pro
424969
From M58 Junction 3 take first left to
Stanley Gate Pub; turn left and follow
road for 2 miles; club on right.
Meadowland course.
Pro Phil Atkiss; Founded 1996
Designed by Steve Marnoch
18 holes, 6375 yards, S.S.S. 70
† Welcome by prior arrangement
with professional.
⌑ WD £30; WE £35.
⌔ Welcome by prior arrangement
with golf course manager.
🍽 Full catering facilities including
restaurant; catering for private
functions.

7 107 Mount Murray Hotel ☏
and CC
Santon, Ballacutchel Road. Mount
Murray, Douglas, Isle of Man, IM4 2HT
🖳 www.mountmurray.com
🖳 hotel@mountmurray.com
☎ 01624 661111, Fax 611116,
Pro 695308, Sec 695308
On the Castletown road 2 miles from
Douglas.
Parkland course.
Pro Andrew Dyson; Founded 1994
Designed by Bingley Sports Turf
Research
18 holes, 6715 yards, S.S.S. 73
⌁ Chipping area, 24 bays floodlit, 2
putting greens.
† All Welcome.
⌑ WD £25; WE £30.
⌔ Welcome by prior arrangement;
hotel's facilities (gym, etc) tennis courts
and squash courts available for use.
🍽 Bistro and restaurant facilities
available.
🛏 On site Mount Murray Hotel (golf
packages available).

7 108 Mytton Fold ☏
Whalley Road, Langho, Blackburn,
Lancs, BB6 8AB
🖳 www.myttonfold.co.uk
☎ 01254 245392, Fax 248119,
Pro 245392, Rest/Bar 240662
9 miles N of Blackburn off A59.
Parkland course.
Pro Alex Twist; Founded 1994
18 (Championship course) holes, 6217
yards, S.S.S. 70
† Welcome by prior arrangement.
⌑ WD £16; WE £17.
⌔ Welcome by prior arrangement.

🍽 Full hotel facilities.
🛏 Mytton Fold.

7 109 Nelson ☏
King's Causeway, Brierfield, Nelson,
Lancs, BB9 0EU
🖳 nelsongc@onetel.net.uk
☎ 01282 614583, Fax 606226, Pro
617000, Sec 611834
On B6248 off A682 at Brierfield from
M65 Junction 12.
Moorland course.
Pro Nigel Sumner; Founded 1902
Designed by Dr A MacKenzie
18 holes, 6006 yards, S.S.S. 69
⌁ Practice field.
† Welcome.
⌑ WD £30; WE £35.
⌔ Welcome by prior arrangement;
catering and golf packages available;
from £25.
🍽 Full clubhouse facilities available.
🛏 Higher Trapp Country House;
Oaks Hotel.

7 110 New North Manchester
Rhodes House, Manchester Old Road,
Middleton, Manchester, Lancs, M24
4PE
🖳 www.nmgc.co.uk
🖳 secretary@nmgc.co.uk
☎ 0161 6439033, Fax 6437775,
Pro 6437094, Sec 6439033,
Rest/Bar 6432941
0.25 mile from Junction 19 off M60.
Moorland/parkland course.
Pro Jason Peel; Founded 1894
Designed by H Braid
18 holes, 6542 yards, S.S.S. 72
⌁ Small practice area.
† Welcome WD; by arrangement WE
through course pro.
⌑ WE £30; WE £35; discounts for 12+.
⌔ Welcome WD; terms on
application.
🍽 Full catering and bar service.
🛏 Bower, Oldham; Birch, Heywood.

7 111 Oldham
Lees New Road, Oldham, Lancs,
OL4 5PN
☎ 0161 624498, Pro 6268346,
Sec 624498, Rest/Bar 6244986
Off A669 turning right at Lees.
Moorland/parkland course.
Pro Richard Heginbotham; Founded
1891
18 holes, 5122 yards, S.S.S. 65
† Welcome by prior arrangement.
⌑ WD £18; £10 with member; WE
and BH £24; £13 with member.
⌔ Welcome by arrangement;
packages for all day golf and catering;
terms on application.

MARSDEN PARK Townhouse Road, Nelson, Lancs. BB9 8DG
Phone: 01282 661912 • Fax: 01282 661944 • Web: www.pendleleisuretrust.co.uk
From M65 Junction 13 take B5446 onto Leeds Road and right at second roundabout.
Semi Parkland Course, 18 holes, 5833 yards, S.S.S. 68.
Visitors welcome • golf and catering packages available from £20.00
Clubhouse facilities and meeting room • practice area • pay and play
2004 prices - WD Adults £13.00; Seniors £7.50; Juniors £4.50; 9 holes £10.50 • WE £15.50; 9 holes £13.00; twilight £9.00 after 6 pm

---

🍽 Full facilities.
🛏 Many hotels in 2-mile radius.

7 112 Ormskirk
Cranes Lane, Lathom, Ormskirk,
Lancs, L40 5UJ
🖥 www.ukgolfer.org
✉ ormskirk@ukgolfer.org
☎ 01695 572112, Fax 572227,
Pro 572074, Sec 572227,
Rest/Bar 572781
2 miles E of Ormskirk.
Parkland course.
Pro Jack Hammond; Founded 1899
18 holes, 6480 yards, S.S.S. 71
♦ Welcome.
🏌 WD £40; WE & Wed £45.
🗓 Welcome by prior arrangement;
terms on application.
🍽 Full facilities.
🛏 Briars Hall, Lathom.

7 113 Peel
Rheast Lane, Peel, Isle of Man,
IM5 1BG
☎ 01624 843456, Fax 843456,
Pro 844232, Sec 843456,
Rest/Bar 842227
On A1 signposted on outskirts of Peel.
Moorland course.
Pro Murray Crowe; Founded 1895
Designed by A Herd
18 holes, 5874 yards, S.S.S. 69
♦ Welcome WD; WE by
arrangement. Also available practice
ground and putting green.
🏌 WD £18; WE & Bank Holidays £25
🗓 Welcome on application to Sec;
packages on request.
🍽 Meals and snacks to order; bar.
🛏 Stakis, Douglas.

7 114 Pennington
St Helens Rd, Leigh, Lancs, WN7 3PA
☎ 01942 682852, Fax 682852, Pro
682852
Off A572 to S of Leigh.
Parkland course with ponds and
streams.
Pro Tim Kershaw; Founded 1975
9 holes, 2895 yards, S.S.S. 34
♦ Welcome.

🏌 WD £3.50; WE £4.60.
🗓 Welcome by prior arrangement.
🍽 Snack bar.
🛏 Thistle, Haydock.

7 115 Penrith
Salkeld Road, Maidenhill, Penrith,
Cumbria, CA11 8SG
☎ 01768 891919, Fax 891919,
Rest/Bar 865429
From Junction 41 on the M6 follow the
signs for Penrith and turn left when
entering town.
Parkland course.
Pro Garry Key; Founded 1890
18 holes, 6047 yards, S.S.S. 69
🏌 8 bays.
♦ Welcome by arrangement.
🏌 WD £26; WE £31.
🗓 Welcome by prior arrangement
with Sec; golf and catering packages
available; terms on application.
🍽 Clubhouse facilities.
🛏 George, Penrith.

7 116 Penwortham
Blundell Lane, Penwortham, Preston,
Lancs, PR1 0AX
🖥 www.ukgolfer.org
✉ penworthamgolfclub@supanet.com
☎ 01772 744630, Fax 740172,
Pro 742345, Rest/Bar 743207
Off A59 1.5 miles W of Preston.
Parkland course.
Pro Steve Holden; Founded 1908
18 holes, 6056 yards, S.S.S. 69
🏌 Practice area.
♦ Welcome WD except Tues & WE.
🏌 WD £25 for a round and £30 for
the day; WE £33.
🗓 Welcome WD except Tues by
prior arrangement; tee available
between 10am-12.30pm and after
2pm; golf and catering packages
available; from £41.
🍽 Full clubhouse facilities.
🛏 Carleton; Forte Posthouse, both
Preston.

7 117 Pike Fold
Hills Lane, Unsworth, Bury,
Manchester, BL9 8QP

☎ 0161 7663561, Fax 7963569,
Pro 7663561, Rest/Bar 7667653
4 miles N of Manchester off Rochdale
Road.
Undulating meadowland course.
Pro Andrew Cory; Founded 1909
9 holes, 6307 yards, S.S.S. 72
🏌 Practice green.
♦ Welcome Mon-Sat; members only
Sun.
🏌 Mon-Sat £20.
🗓 Welcome by appointment; catering
packages by arrangement with
Manager.
🍽 Full facilities by prior arrangement.
🛏 Villiage Hotel.

7 118 Pleasington   ℭ
Pleasington Lane, Pleasington,
Blackburn, Lancs, BB2 5JF
🖥 www.pleasington-golf.co.uk
✉ jean@pleasington-golf.co.uk
☎ 01254 202177, Fax 201028,
Pro 201630, Sec 202177,
Rest 207346
3 miles SW of Blackburn; from A674
turn north on to road signposted
Pleasington Station.
Undulating heathland/parkland course.
Pro GJ Furey; Founded 1891
18 holes, 6423 yards, S.S.S. 71
♦ Welcome by prior arrangement
Mon, Wed, Fri and WE.
🏌 WD £38, WE £42.
🗓 Welcome Mon, Wed, Fri.
🍽 Full clubhouse facilities.
🛏 The Millstone Hotel, Mellor,
Blackburn.

**7 119 Port St Mary Golf
Pavilion**
Kallow Point Road, Port St Mary, Isle
of Man, IM9 5EJ
☎ 01624 834932, Sec 497387
Just outside Port St Mary; course
signposted.
Public seaside links course.
Pro Murray Crowe; Founded 1936
Designed by George Duncan
9 holes, 5770 yards, S.S.S. 68
🏌 Putting green; croquet; tennis.
♦ Welcome but not before 10.30am
at WE.

WD £13.50; WE £14.
Welcome by arrangement; discounts for 10 or more players.
Bar, cafe and restaurant.
Port Erin; Bay View.

7 120 Poulton-le-Fylde
Myrtle Farm, Breck Road, Poulton-le-Fylde, Lancs, FY6 7HJ
☎ 01253 892444, Fax 892444, Sec 893150, Rest/Bar 893150
0.5 miles N of Poulton town centre.
Municipal meadowland course.
Pro Lewis Ware; Founded 1974
9 holes, 6056 yards, S.S.S. 70
Tuition available.
Welcome.
WD £8.50; WE £10.
Welcome by prior arrangement; packages available.
Bar and catering facilities.
Singleton Lodge.

7 121 Preston   ♔
Fulwood Hall Lane, Fulwood, Preston, Lancs, PR2 8DD
☎ 01772 700011, Fax 794234, Pro 700022, Rest/Bar 700436
From M6 J32 turn towards Preston and after 1.5 miles into Watling St Rd and then into Fulwood Hall Road.
Parkland course.
Pro Andrew Greenbank; Founded 1892
Designed by James Braid
18 holes, 6312 yards, S.S.S. 71
Welcome WD; some restrictions Tues; WE with member only.
WD £27-£32.
Welcome WD except Tues; golf and catering packages can be arranged; parties of more than 48 by special arrangement only; from £30.
Bar and restaurant facilities.
Broughton Marriott; Barton Grange.

7 122 Prestwich
Hilton Lane, Prestwich, Manchester, Lancs, M25 9XB
☎ 0161 7732544, Fax 7731404, Pro 7731404, Rest/Bar 7732544
On A6044 1 mile from Junction with A56.
Parkland course.
Pro Simon Wakefield; Founded 1908
18 holes, 4799 yards, S.S.S. 65
Practice green.
Welcome WD if carrying handicap certs.
WD £20.
Welcome on WD by prior arrangement with professional; 27-hole

golf and catering packages available; from £29.95.
Full clubhouse facilities.
Village Hotel.

7 123 Ramsey
Golf Professionals Shop, Ramsey Golf Club Brookfield Avenue, Ramsey, Isle of Man, IM8 2AH
✉ ramseypro@iofm.net
☎ 01624 814736, Fax 814736, Pro 814736, Sec 812244, Rest/Bar 813365
12 miles N of Douglas; 5 mins from town centre.
Parkland course.
Pro Andrew Dyson; Founded 1890
Designed by James Braid
18 holes, 5960 yards, S.S.S. 69
Practice area.
Welcome; please telephone in advance.
WD £22; WE £28.
Welcome by arrangement.
Lunches and full facilities available.
Grand Island.

7 124 Regent Park Municipal Golf Course
Links Road, Lostock, Bolton, Lancs, BL6 4AF
☎ 01204 844170, Pro 495201, Sec 844170, Rest/Bar 844170
1 mile from M61 Junction 6.
Municipal parkland course.
Pro Bob Longworth; Founded 1932
18 holes, 6130 yards, S.S.S. 69
Welcome; restrictions on Sat.
WD £;9.50 WE £11.50.
Welcome WD by arrangement.
Bar, restaurant, take away.
Forte Crest; Swallowfield.

7 125 Rishton
Station Road, Rishton, Blackburn, Lancs, BB1 4HG
🖳 www.rishton-golf-club.co.uk
✉ rishtongc@onetel.net
☎ 01254 884442, Fax 887711, Sec 07710 371118/01254 57727
3 miles E of Blackburn signposted from church in village.
Meadowland course.
Founded 1928
Designed by Peter Alliss/Dave Thomas.
9 holes, 6097 yards for 18 holes, S.S.S. 69
Welcome WD; WE with a member.
WD £10 with member; £17 without member; WE £12 (with member only).
Welcome with prior arrangement with Sec.

Bar & catering available except Mon.
Dunkenhalgh; Wickets Hotel, Rishton.

7 126 Rochdale
Edenfield Road, Rochdale, Lancs, OL11 5YR
☎ 01706 643218, Fax 861113, Pro 522104, Rest/Bar 646024
On A680 3 miles from M62 Junction 20.
Parkland course.
Pro Andrew Laverty; Founded 1888
18 holes, 6050 yards, S.S.S. 69
Welcome by arrangement.
Prices on application.
Welcome by prior arrangement; terms on application.
Full clubhouse facilities.

7 127 Rossendale   ♔
Ewood Lane, Haslingden, Rossendale, Lancs, BB4 6LH
☎ 01706 831686, Fax 228669, Pro 213616, Sec 831339
16 miles from Manchester off the M66.
Meadowland course.
Pro Stephen Nicholls; Founded 1903
18 holes, 6293 yards, S.S.S. 71
Practice green.
Welcome except Sat.
WD £25.50; members only Sat; Sun £30.
Welcome by prior arrangement.
Full facilities; banqueting facilities; brand new clubhouse.
Red Hall; Sykeside, Haslingden.

7 128 Rowany
Rowany Drive, Port Erin, Isle Of Man, IM9 6LN
✉ rowany@iommail.net
☎ 01624 834072, Fax 834072, Pro 834108, Rest/Bar 834108
4 miles W of Castletown; located at end of Port Erin promenade.
Parkland/seaside course.
Pro Founded 1895
18 holes, 5803 yards, S.S.S. 69
Outdoor practice area.
Welcome.
WD £16; WE £20.
Welcome by arrangement with the Manager.
Full bar, snacks and restaurant facilities.
Cherry Orchard; The Ocean Castle.

7 129 Royal Birkdale
Waterloo Road, Southport, Merseyside, PR8 2LX

Royal Lytham and St Annes

It wasn't until 1926 that Lytham and St Annes was granted the royal title. The club president of the time was described as "noble, aimless, irascible, bullying, dauntless, extravagant, generous, scorning craftiness or thrift, golden-hearted, golden-fisted, fast to his friends, sadistical and successful". So was it this giant of a man, with golden beard and blue eyes, who once cabled his trustees from the other side of the world "Sell Blackpool" that swayed the royal title? Of course it wasn't. As is the way with such things it was his wife Mrs Violet Clifton who almost certainly had a quiet word in Queen Mary's ear over one of their many teas together at Buckingham Palace.

Just a few weeks later the great Bobby Jones turned up on the shores of Lancashire, played a miraculous long iron from sand on the penultimate hole of the Championship and caused his partner Al Watrous to three-putt from the shock of it all. Watrous said at the time, "There goes a hundred thousand bucks" as all his future financial endorsements and opportunities slipped through his fingers.

Peter Thomson, who won his fourth Open Championship at Lytham in 1958, has described the course as "the strictest test of golfer's ability on the Championship roster, a torture route from start to finish" and "A very common flat piece of land, but beautifully bunkered. It has a wonderful finishing hole, a masterpiece. Any student of architecture should come to study this". Since those words another fourteen bunkers have been added bringing the total to 196 and counting.

Lytham certainly looks common. The opening holes have a shabby railway line running alongside and much of the rest of the course is surrounded by ugly, red Victorian houses. It lacks the spectacular views of Turnberry over the sea because it is set very slightly inland. Vistas were for houses, not for golf courses.

Lytham has two courses. There is the one that Tom Lehman played in 1996 when he finished the tournament on 13 under par. And there is the one that Seve Ballesteros played in 1979 when he was the only golfer to finish under par. They are both played over the same eighteen holes but the more demanding of the two involves God cranking up a gigantic wind machine.

At under 7,000 yards Lytham is not a severe test of long driving although the amateur David Dixon very nearly drove the final hole when David Duval won the Championship here in 2001. Lytham requires precision even if four out of the final five holes can be brutal when the prevailing wind is up and about.

With a list of winners that takes in Bobby Jones, Bobby Locke, Peter Thomson, Bob Charles, Gary Player, Seve Ballesteros, Tom Lehman and David Duval it is obvious that Lytham requires a hell of a talent, a hell of a short game or the Christian name Robert in order to play it successfully.

If Lytham has two courses, then there are also two ways to play it. You can do as Thomson and Player and Lehman and Duval did and endeavour to keep the ball in play at all costs. Or you can do as Seve did in 1979, smashing the ball into the car park and accident and emergency unit and then performing the most delicate surgery in order to recover.

The later Peter Dobereiner wrote of Seve's swordsmanship, "The dust of that brutal assault has not yet settled. Debris will continue to fall. It will take awhile for the spectators of the violence to recover; we are dazed like witnesses to a nearby explosion ... not a scratch on us, but the medics know we are candidates for a cup of sweet, strong tea and a quiet lie-down. Tranquility will come later". –
Mark Reason

🖳 www.royalbirkdale.com
🖥 secretary@royalbirkdale.com
☎ 01704 567920, Fax 562327,
Pro 568857, Sec 567920,
Rest/Bar 567920
Course is 1.5 miles south of Southport on the A565.
Open Championship venue 1998; links course.
Pro Brian Hodgkinson; Founded 1889
Designed by Hawtree & Taylor
18 holes, 6690 yards, S.S.S. 73
♦ Handicap certs required; not Sat; limited Fri and Sun am.
〖 WD £125; WE £150.
⌁ Welcome Mon, Wed and Thurs by prior arrangement.
🍽 Full catering facilities.
🛏 Local tourist board can provide detailed list.

7 130 Royal Lytham & St Annes
Links Gate, Lytham St Annes, Lancs, FY8 3LQ
🖳 www.royallytham.org
🖥 bookings@royallytham.org
☎ 01253 724206, Fax 780946,
Pro 720094
1 mile from centre of Lytham.
Links course; Open Championship venue 2001.
Pro Eddie Birchenough; Founded 1886
18 holes, 6682 yards, S.S.S. 74
〗 Balls from Pro shop only.
♦ Welcome Mon and Thurs only; WE Dormy guests only; limited availability for others.
〖 WD £110 round, £165 day.
⌁ Welcome by prior arrangement.
🍽 Full catering and bar facilities available.
🛏 Dormy House on site: 9 single, 4 twin-bedded rooms (no en suite facilities).

7 131 Saddleworth
Mountain Ash, Ladcastle Road, Uppermill, Oldham, Lancs, OL3 6LT
🖳 www.saddleworthgolfclub.org.uk
🖥 secretary@saddleworthgolfclub .org,uk
☎ 01457 873653, Fax 820647,
Pro 810412, Rest/Bar 872059
5 miles from Oldham, signposted off the A670 Ashton-Huddersfield Road at the bend where road crosses railway.
Scenic moorland course.
Pro Robert Johnson; Founded 1904
Designed by Dr A Mackenzie
18 holes, 6118 yards, S.S.S. 69
♦ All welcome.
〖 WD £23; WE £30.

⌁ Welcome WD by prior arrangement; package deals from £36 inclusive of 3- course meal.
🍽 Full facilities.
🛏 La Pergola, Denshaw.

7 132 St Annes Old Links
Highbury Road East, Lytham St, Annes, Lancs, FY8 2LD
🖳 www.coastalgolf.co.uk
🖥 secretary@coastalgolf.co.uk
☎ 01253 723597, Fax 781506,
Pro 722432, Sec 723597,
Rest/Bar 721826 Bar,
Catering 712863
Course is off the A584 coast road at St Anne's.
Championship links course.
Pro Daniel Webster; Founded 1901
Designed by Sandy Herd
18 holes, 6684 yards, S.S.S. 72
〗 Practice ground.
♦ Welcome except before 9.30am or between 12 noon-1.30pm WD.
〖 WD £45 day, £30 pm; Sun/BH £50.
⌁ Welcome by prior arrangement WD only; packages available; menus on request; separate changing rooms; snooker; from £58.
🍽 Full clubhouse dining and bar facilities.
🛏 Contact local tourist board.

7 133 St Bees
Peck Mill, St Bees, Cumbria, CA27 0EJ
☎ 01946 824300, Sec 822515
Course is on the B5345 four miles S of Whitehaven.
Seaside course.
Founded 1942
9 holes, 5122 yards, S.S.S. 65
♦ Welcome except on comp days.
〖 Prices on application.
⌁ Welcome by arrangement with the school.
🍽 No facilities.
🛏 Queens.

7 134 Seascale
The Banks, Seascale, Cumbria, CA20 1QL
🖳 www.seascalegolfclub.org
🖥 seascalegolfclub@aol.com
☎ 01946 728202, Fax 728202, Pro 721779
Course is off the A595 at NW edge of Seascale.
Links course.
Pro Shean Rudd; Founded 1893
Designed by Willie Campbell
18 holes, 6416 yards, S.S.S. 71

〗 Practice area for members and green fee paying visitors only.
♦ Welcome.
〖 WD £24-29; WE £27-£32. Winter £14; 2 fore 1.
⌁ Welcome by prior arrangement; discounts of 10 per cent for 12 or more and 15 per cent for 20 or more; from £20.
🍽 Clubhouse facilities.
🛏 Lutwidge Arms, Holmnook; Calder House, Seascale; Horse & Groom, Gosforth.

7 135 Sedbergh Golf Club
Dent Road, Sedbergh, Cumbria, LA10 5SS
🖥 sedbergc@btinternet.com
☎ 01539 621551, Fax 621551
1 mile from Sedbergh on road to Dent and 5 miles E of M6 Junction 37.
Mature parkland course in Yorkshire Dales National Park.
Founded 1896
Designed by W.G.Squires
9 holes, 5624 yards, S.S.S. 68 White, 67 Yellow, 70 Red (Ladies)
〗 Practice ground.
♦ Welcom; prior arrangement at WE.
〖 WD £18; WE £20.
⌁ Welcome by prior arrangement; various packages can be arranged; from £30.
🍽 Catering facilities.
🛏 George & Dragon, Dent; Bull, Sedbergh; Sec can assist with stay and play breaks.

7 136 Shaw Hill Hotel Golf ☎ & Country Club
Shaw Hill, Whittle Le Woods, Chorley, Lancs, PR6 7PP
🖥 info@shaw-hill.co.uk
☎ 01257 269221, Fax 261223, Pro 279222, Sec 791164, Rest/Bar 226825
Course is one mile N of M61 Junction 8 and two miles from M6 Junction 28.
Parkland course with water hazards.
Pro David Clarke; Founded 1925
Designed by T McCauley
18 holes, 6239 yards, S.S.S. 73
♦ Welcome WD only with handicap certs; residents of hotel only at WE.
〖 Prices available on application; subject to weather conditions and time of year.
⌁ Welcome WD with handicap certs; golf and catering packages can be arranged; terms on application.
🍽 Bar, restaurant and à la carte menus available.
🛏 Club has 30 rooms; leisure centre with extensive facilities (available for guests of hotel).

7 137 Sherdley Park
Sherdley Road, St Helens,
Merseyside, WA9 5DE
☎ 01744 813149/817967, Fax
817967, Rest/Bar 815518
M62 Junction 7 A570 Signposted St
Helens at second roundabout third exit;
second left into park.
Public undulating parkland course.
Pro Daniel Jones; Founded 1973
Designed by PR Parkinson
18 holes, 5974 yards, S.S.S. 69
🏌 Practice range, 12 bays floodlit.
† Welcome.
⌷ Prices on application; concessions
for pensioners and juniors.
♿ Welcome by prior arrangement;
terms on application.
🍴 Bar and cafeteria.
🛏 Hilton, St Helens.

7 138 Silecroft
Silecroft, Millom, Cumbria, LA18 4NX
☎ 01229 774342, Fax 774342
On A5093 three miles N of Millom
through Silecroft village towards shore.
Seaside course.
Founded 1903
9 holes, 5896 yards, S.S.S. 68
† Welcome WD; restricted access
WE and BH.
⌷ WD £15; WE £20.
♿ Welcome by arrangement.
🍴 Limited; Miners Arms provides
food.
🛏 Bankfield; Miners Arms.

7 139 Silloth on Solway
Station Road, Silloth, Wigton, Cumbria,
CA7 4BL
🖥 www.sillothgolfclub.co.uk
📧 sillothgolfclub@lineone.net
☎ 016973 31304, Fax 31782, Pro
32404, Sec 31304, Rest/Bar 32442
From Wigton follow B5302 to Silloth.
Championship links course; 1997;
British women's strokeplay; R&A
Regional Open Qualifier.
Pro Johnathan Graham; Founded 1892
Designed by Willie Park Jnr
18 holes, 6618 yards, S.S.S. 73,
visitors' yellow tees 6070 yards, S.S.S.
70
† Welcome by prior arrangement.
⌷ WD £32 per day; WE £43 per
round.
♿ Welcome by prior arrangement; full
day packages of golf and catering
available; Mon catering only by prior
arrangement; from £48.50.
🍴 Full bar and catering facilities,
except Mon.
🛏 Wheyrigg Hall, Wigton; Golf Hotel;

Queens; Skinburness, all Silloth-on-
Solway.

7 140 Silverdale
Red Bridge Lane, Silverdale,
Carnforth, Lancs, LA5 0SP
☎ 01524 701300, Fax 702074,
Sec 702074
3 miles NW of Carnforth by Silverdale
station.
Heathland/parkland course.
Founded 1906
18 holes, 5535 yards, S.S.S. 68
† Welcome by prior arrangement;
some Sun summer restrictions.
⌷ WD £20; WE £25.
♿ Welcome by prior arrangement
with Sec, WD and WE packages
available; from £35.
🍴 Clubhouse facilities.
🛏 Silverdale Hotel, Longlands.

7 141 Solway Holiday Village Golf Centre
Solway Holiday Village, Skinburness
Drive, Silloth, Wigton, Cumbria,
CA7 4QQ
☎ 016973 31236, Fax 32553
Easy to locate in village of Silloth.
Scenic parkland course.
Founded 1988
9 holes, 4001 yards, S.S.S. 3
† Welcome.
⌷ WD and WE £5 for daily pass.
♿ Welcome by arrangement.
🍴 Bar and restaurant.
🛏 Self-catering log chalets & c/vans.

7 142 Southport & Ainsdale
Bradshaws Lane, Ainsdale, Southport,
PR8 3LG
🖥 www.sandagolfclub.co.uk
📧 secretary@sandagolfclub.co.uk
☎ 01704 578000, Fax 570896,
Pro 577316
Courseon A565 3 miles S of Southport,
0.5 miles from Ainsdale station.
Links course.
Pro Jim Payne; Founded 1906
Designed by James Braid
18 holes, 6583 yards, S.S.S. 73
† Welcome WD between 10am-12
noon and 1:00pm-4.00pm.
⌷ WD £60-£75; WE £75 for a round.
♿ Welcome WD; terms on
application; from £50.
🍴 Full clubhouse facilities.

7 143 Southport Municipal
Park Road West, Southport,
Merseyside, PR9 0JS

☎ 01704 530133, Pro 535286
N end of Promenade.
Public seaside course.
Pro Bill Fletcher; Founded 1914
18 holes, 5953 yards, S.S.S. 69
† Welcome.
⌷ WD £6.50; WE £9.90.
♿ Welcome by prior booking at least
six days in advance.
🍴 Meals and bar facilities.
🛏 Scarisbrick; Prince of Wales.

7 144 Southport Old Links
Moss Lane, Churchtown, Southport,
Merseyside, PR9 7QS
📧 secretary@solgc.freeserve.co.uk
☎ 01704 228207, Fax 505353
Off Manchester Rd into Roe Lane then
into Moss Lane; close to town centre.
Parkland course with Links
characteristics.
Pro Gary Copeman; Founded 1926
9 holes, 6378 yards, Par 72, S.S.S. 71
† Welcome except Wed before
3.30pm and Sunday.
⌷ WD £25; WE £30.
♿ Welcome by prior arrangement;
terms on application.
🍴 Full facilities except Mon.
🛏 Whitworth Falls (01704 530074).

7 145 Stand   ⚷
Ashbourne Grove, Whitefield,
Manchester, Lancs, M45 7NL
📧 mark.dance@bt.com
☎ 0161 7662214, Fax 7963234,
Sec 7663197, Rest/Bar 7662388
1 mile N of M60 ring road Junction 17.
Undulating parkland course.
Pro Mark Dance; Founded 1904
Designed by Alex Herd
18 holes, 6426 yards, S.S.S. 71
† Welcome WD; restricted WE and
Tues due to ladies day.
⌷ WD/WE £30 + 50p for insurance.
♿ Welcome Wed and Fri; winter
packages.
🍴 Full facilities except Mon.
🛏 Hawthorn; Travel Inn.

7 146 Standish Court
Rectory Lane, Standish, Wigan, Lancs,
WN6 0XD
🖥 www.standishgolf.co.uk
📧 info@standishgolf.co.uk
☎ 01257 425777, Fax 425888,
Pro 425777, Rest/Bar 425777
5 mins off M6 Junction 27 following
signs for Standish village.
Parkland course.
Pro Blake Toone; Founded 1995
Designed by Patrick Dawson
18 holes, 5750 yards, S.S.S. 66

† Welcome by arrangement.
Ⓛ Mon/Tues £8; Wed-Fri £12; WE £16.
⌁ Welcome by prior arrangement; full day packages available from £15-£35.
Ⓘ Full clubhouse facilities available.
⌁ Kilhey Court; Wigan Moat House.

7 147 Stonyholme Municipal
St Aidans Rd, Carlisle, Cumbria, CA1 1LF
☎ 01228 625511, Fax 625511, Rest/Bar 625512
Course is off the A69 one mile W of M6 Junction 43.
Flat meadowland course.
Pro Stephen Ling; Founded 1974
Designed by Frank Pennink
18 holes, 5787 yards, S.S.S. 69
Ⓘ Practice area; practice range, 16 bays floodlit and 9-hole short course adjacent.
† Welcome.
Ⓛ WD £8.30; WE £10.40; day tickets available all week.
⌁ Welcome by prior arrangement.
Ⓘ Clubhouse facilities.
⌁ Post House; numerous B&Bs in the area.

7 148 Stonyhurst Park
c/o The Bayley Arms, Avenue Rd, Hurst Green, Clitheroe, Lancs, BB7 9QB
☎ 01254 826478, Fax 826797
On B6243 Clitheroe-Longridge road.
Parkland course.
Founded 1979
9 holes, 5529 yards, S.S.S. 67
† Welcome except WE; contact The Bayley Arms.
Ⓛ WD £15.
⌁ Limited and by prior arrangement only.
Ⓘ None.
⌁ The Bayley Arms.

7 149 Swinton Park
East Lancashire Road, Swinton, Manchester, Lancs, M27 5LX
🖳 www.spgolf.com
✉ info@spgolf.com
☎ 0161 7940861, Fax 2810698, Pro 7938077, Rest/Bar 7941785
On A580 5 miles from Manchester on East Lancs.
Parkland course.
Pro Jim Wilson; Founded 1926
Designed by Braid & Taylor
18 holes, 6726 yards, S.S.S. 72
† Welcome WD except Thurs; no WE.
Ⓛ WD £30.
⌁ Welcome by arrangement Mon, Tues, Wed and Fri.

Ⓘ Bar and restaurant facilities; function and conference rooms.
⌁ Large selection in Manchester city centre.

7 150 Towneley
Todmorden Road, Burnley, Lancs, BB11 3ED
☎ 01282 438473/421517, Sec 414555, Rest/Bar 451636
From M65, Junction 9, follow signs for Halifax.
Parkland course.
Founded 1932
Designed by Burnley Council
The Towneley course:18 holes, 5811 yards, S.S.S. 69; The Brunshaw course: 9 holes, par 3
Ⓘ Small practice ground, two tennis courts, two bowling greens, 18-hole pitch and putt.
† Welcome.
Ⓛ WD 9 holes £5.30, 18 holes £9.55; WE 9 holes £6.10, 18 holes £10.60.
Concessions for OAPs during week.
Concessions for unemployed and school children during week.
⌁ Welcome by prior arrangement; catering can be arranged with steward; from £8, not at WE during Summer.
Ⓘ Bar and restaurant facilities available
⌁ Alexander.

7 151 Tunshill
Tunshill Lane, Milnrow, Rochdale, Lancs, OL16 3TS
☎ 01706 342095
From M62 Junction 21 take road to Milnrow and follow Kiln Lane out of town to narrow lane for clubhouse.
Moorland course.
Founded 1901
9 holes, 5743 yards, S.S.S. 68
† Welcome WD except Tues evening; by prior arrangement WE
Ⓛ Terms on application.
⌁ Welcome WD by prior arrangement; terms available on application.
Ⓘ Restaurant and bar facilities.
⌁ John Milne, Milnrow.

7 152 Turton   ⚏
Chapeltown Road, Bromley Cross, Bolton, Lancs, BL7 9QH
🖳 www.turtongolfclub.co.uk
☎ 01204 852235, Pro 07816 284799
4 miles NW of Bolton behind Last Drop Hotel and country club, Last Drop Village.
Moorland course.
Pro Mark Saunders; Founded 1908

Designed by James Braid
18 holes, 6124 yards, S.S.S. 69
† Welcome except Wed 11.30am-3pm and WE only by prior arrangement.
Ⓛ WD £20; WE £25.
⌁ Welcome by arrangement.
Ⓘ Full catering facilities.
⌁ Last Drop; Egerton House.

7 153 Ulverston
Bardsea, Ulverston, Cumbria, LA12 9QJ
✉ ulverston@bardseapark. freeserve.co.uk
☎ 01229 582824, Fax 588910, Pro 582800
From M6 Junction 36 follow signs for Barrow on A590 and take A5087 to Bardsea.
Parkland course.
Pro MR Smith; Founded 1895/1909
Designed by A Herd
18 holes, 6201 yards, S.S.S. 71
Ⓘ Practice chipping green, practice grounds adjacent to course.
† Welcome by prior arrangement.
Ⓛ WD £30; WE £35.
⌁ Welcome by prior arrangement; packages for golf and catering can be arranged; terms on application.
Ⓘ Full clubhouse catering and bar facilities.
⌁ The Fisherman's Arms; The Swan; Lonsdale House.

7 154 Walmersley   ⚏
White Carr Lane, Bury, Lancs, BL9 6TE
☎ 0161 7647770, Fax 01706827618, Pro 7639050, Rest/Bar 7641429
Off A56 3 miles N of Bury.
Moorland course.
Pro P Thorpe; Founded 1906
18 holes, 5341 yards, S.S.S. 67
† Welcome.
Ⓛ WD £20; WE £20.
⌁ Welcome Wed-Fri; 27 holes golf, coffee, light lunch and 4-course meal; from £26.
Ⓘ Full clubhouse facilities.
⌁ Red Hall, Bury.

7 155 Werneth (Oldham)
Green Lane, Oldham, Lancs, OL8 3AZ
🖳 www.wernethgolfclub.co.uk
✉ sales@the-golf-centre.co.uk
☎ 0161 624 1190, Pro 628 7136
Course is five miles from Manchester, take the A62 to Hollinwood and then the A6104.
Moorland course.

Pro Roy Penney; Founded 1909
Designed by Sandy Herd.
18 holes, 5364 yards, S.S.S. 66
🏌 Practice ground and green.
🚶 Welcome WD; guests of members
only at WE.
💷 WD £18.50.
🛒 Welcome Mon, Wed and Fri by
arrangement.
🍽 Lunch & meals served except Mon.
🛏 Smokeys, Oldham.

7 156 West Derby ☏
Yew Tree Lane, Liverpool, Merseyside,
L12 9HQ
🖥 www.ukgolfer.org
📧 pmilne@westderbygc
.freeserve.co.uk
☎ 0151 2281540, Fax 2590505,
Pro 2205478, Sec 2541034
Follow signs for Knotty Ash to
roundabout and then into Blackmoor
Drive, right into Yew Tree Lane.
Flat parkland course with trees.
Pro Andrew Witherup; Founded 1896
18 holes, 6277 yards, S.S.S. 70
🚶 Welcome WD; except Tues.
💷 WD £28.50; WE £37.
🛒 Welcome WD except Tues; full golf
and catering packages available.
🍽 Bar and restaurant.
🛏 Derby Lodge, Huyton; Bell Tower,
Knowsley.

7 157 West Lancashire ☏
Hall Road West, Liverpool,
Merseyside, L23 8SZ
🖥 www.westlancashiregolf.co.uk
📧 golf@westlancashiregolf.co.uk
☎ 0151 924 1076, Fax 931 4448,
Pro 924 5662
M57 to Aintree then A5036 to Seaforth
and A565 to Crosby; signposted close
to Hall Rd Station.
Links course.
Pro Gary Edge; Founded 1873
Designed by CK Cotton/D Steel
18 holes, 6767 yards, S.S.S. 73
🏌 Practice ground; tuition available;
equipment for hire.
🚶 WD (except Tue), most Sat, some
Sun.
💷 WD £60 round, £75 day; WE £80
round, £95 day.
🛒 Welcome WD except Tues;
packages available.
🍽 Full clubhouse facilities.
🛏 Liverpool.

7 158 Westhoughton
School Street, Westhoughton, Bolton,
Lancs, BL5 2BR
☎ 01942 811085, Fax 811085,
Pro 840545, Sec 608958

Course is off School Lane, adjacent
to the Parish Church in
Westhoughton.
Parkland course.
Pro Jason Seed
Founded 1929
9 holes, 5772 yards, S.S.S. 68
🏌 Practice area.
🚶 Welcome.
💷 WD £18; WE £18; £10 with a
member.
🛒 Welcome; packages of 18 holes,
available with catering; from £25.
🍽 Full clubhouse facilities
available.
🛏 Large selection available in
Bolton.

**7 159 Westhoughton Golf
Centre**
Wigan Road, Westhoughton, Nr
Bolton, Lancs, BL8 2BX
🖥 www.ukgolfer.org/courses
/hartcommon
📧 hartcommon@ukgolfer.org
☎ 01942 813195
M61 Junction 5; travel through
Westhoughton towards Hindley.
Parkland course; home to Hart
Common GC.
Pro Gareth Benson; Founded 1996
Designed by Mike Shattock
18 holes, 6188 yards, S.S.S. 70
🏌 Practice range, 26 bays floodlit
covered; also 9-hole par 3 course.
🚶 Welcome.
💷 Prices on application.
🛒 Welcome by prior arrangement;
terms on application.
🍽 Clubhouse facilities; restaurant
open daily (not Mon).

7 160 Whalley ☏
Portfield Lane, Clerk Hill Road,
Whalley, Clitheroe, Lancs, BB7 9DR
🖥 www.whalleygolfclub.com
☎ 01254 822236, Pro 824766
Course is off the A671 one mile SE of
Whalley following the signs for
Sabden.
Parkland course.
Pro Jamie Hunt; Founded 1912
9 holes, 6258 yards, S.S.S. 70
🏌 Practice ground.
🚶 Welcome except Thurs pm and
Sat in summer.
💷 WD £16; WE £20.
🛒 Welcome by arrangement with
secretary; catering and packages on
application; from £15.
🍽 Clubhouse facilities.
🛏 Higher Trapp, Simonstone; Old
Stone Manor, Mytton.

7 161 Whitefield ☏
Higher Lane, Whitefield, Manchester,
Lancs, M45 7EZ
☎ 0161 3512700, Fax 3512712,
Pro 3512709, Rest/Bar 3512710
On A665 near Whitefield exit from M60.
Parkland course.
Pro Paul Reeves; Founded 1932
18 holes, 6045 yards, S.S.S. 69
🏌 Practice putting green and practice.
🚶 Welcome by arrangement.
💷 WD £25; WE £35.
🛒 Welcome WD except Tues; also
some Sat afternoons; groups of more
than 12 should contact club for rates.
🍽 Full clubhouse facilities.
🛏 The Village; Travel Lodge.

7 162 Whittaker
Shore Lane, Littleborough, Lancs,
OL15 0LH
☎ 01706 378310, Sec 842541
On Blackstone Edge Old Road, 1.5
miles out of Littleborough; turn right at
High Peak Hamlet.
Moorland course.
Founded 1906
9 holes, 5606 yards, S.S.S. 67
🏌 Practice ground.
🚶 Welcome except Tues pm and Sun.
💷 Prices on application.
🛒 Welcome by prior arrangement
with Sec; limited catering on
application with Sec; limited catering
on application; prices on application.
🍽 Bar can be arranged.

7 163 Wigan
Arley Hall, Arley Lane, Haigh, Wigan,
Lancs, WN1 2UH
🖥 www.wigangolfclub.co.uk
📧 ted@temsley.fsnet.co.uk
☎ 01257 421360, Sec 01942 244429
From M6 J27 through Standish on
B5239; turn left at Canal Bridge lights
and course is opposite Crawford Arms.
Parkland course.
Founded 1898
18 holes, 6020 yards, S.S.S. 70
🚶 Welcome except Tues and Sat.
💷 WD £30 18 holes, £40 all day; WE
£30 18 holes, £40 all day.
🛒 Welcome by prior arrangement;
special packages available; terms on
application.
🍽 Full catering.
🛏 Bellingham; Brockett Arms; Kilhey
Court.

7 164 William Wroe
Penny Bridge Lane, Urmston,
Manchester, Lancs, M41 5DX

☎ 0161 7488680, Fax 7488680,
Pro 0161 9288542
Leave M63 Junction 4 and take B5124
then B5158 to Flixton; 12 miles SW of
Manchester.
Municipal parkland course.
Pro Scott Partington; Founded 1974
18 holes, 4395 yards, S.S.S. 64
† Welcome: bookings taken 7 days
in advance.
Ⅰ WD £8.30; WE £11.50 and bank
holidays.
↻ Welcome with booking.
◉ Clubhouse facilities.
↩ Manor Hey.

7 165 Wilpshire
Whalley Road, Wilpshire, Blackburn,
Lancs, BB1 9LF
☎ 01254 248260, Fax 246745,
Pro 249558
Course on A666 4 miles N of Blackburn.
Moorland/parkland course.
Pro Walter Slaven; Founded 1890
18 holes, 5802 yards, S.S.S. 69
† Welcome WD; by arrangement WE.
Ⅰ WD £25.50; WE £30.50.
↻ Welcome by prior appointment.
◉ Full facilities.
↩ County; Swallow, Salmesbury.

7 166 Windermere   ☜
Cleabarrow, Windermere, Cumbria,
LA23 3NB
☙ www.windermere-golf-club@org.uk
✉ windermeregc@btconnect.com
☎ 015394 43123, Fax 43123,
Pro 43550, Rest/Bar 47715
On B5284 1.5 miles from Bowness
towards Kendal.
Undulating parkland course.
Pro Stephen Rook; Founded 1891
Designed by George Low

18 holes, 5132 yards, S.S.S. 65
† Welcome by arrangement.
Ⅰ WD £25; WE £30.
↻ Welcome by arrangement;
packages can be arranged; from £25.
◉ Bar and Licensed Restaurant.
↩ The Wild Boar Hotel (golf
discounts available).

7 167 Woolton
Doe Park Speke Road, Woolton,
Liverpool, Merseyside, L25 7TZ
☎ 0151 4862298, Fax 4861664,
Pro 4861298, Rest/Bar 4861601
6 miles from city centre on road to
Liverpool Airport.
Parkland course.
Pro Alan Gibson; Founded 1901
18 holes, 5724 yards, S.S.S. 68
† Welcome.
Ⅰ WD £24; WE £35.
↻ Welcome; packages can be
arranged; terms available on
application.
◉ Clubhouse facilities.
↩ Redbourne.

7 168 Workington
Branthwaite Road, Workington,
Cumbria, CA14 4SS
☎ 01900 603460, Fax 607122,
Pro 67828
Off A595 2 miles SE of Workington.
Undulating meadowland.
Pro Adrian Drabble; Founded 1893
Designed by James Braid/Howard
Swan
18 holes, 6247 yards, S.S.S. 70
ℐ Practice ground.
† Welcome if carrying handicap
certs.
Ⅰ Summer WD £20, WE and BH
£25; Winter WD £15, WE and BH £20.

↻ Welcome by prior arrangement
with Pro.
◉ Full facilities, 7 days/week if booked.
↩ Washington Central; Westlands
(adjacent to course), Melbreak Hotel.

7 169 Worsley
Stableford Avenue, Eccles,
Manchester, Lancs, M30 8AP
☎ 0161 7894202, Fax 7893200
Follow signs to Monton Green, Eccles
from M60, Junction 13 then to
Stableford Ave.
Parkland course.
Pro C Cousins; Founded 1894
Designed by James Braid
18 holes, 6252 yards, S.S.S. 70
† Welcome by prior arrangement.
Ⅰ WD £30; WE £35.
↻ Welcome Wed and Thurs; tees
available 10.15am and 1.35pm.
◉ Clubhouse facilities.
↩ Wendover, Monton.

7 170 Worsley Park Marriott   ☜
Marriott Worsley Park Hotel and
Country Club, Walkden Road, Worsley,
Manchester, M28 2QT
✉ golf.worsleypark@
marriotthotels.co.uk
☎ 0161 975 2043
Junction M13 off M62 to Worsley.
Signposted Marriott Hotel.
Set in 200 acres of mature parkland.
Pro David Screeton.
18 holes, 6611 yards, S.S.S. 71
† Welcome WD; restricted WE.
Ⅰ WD £60; WE £80.
↻ Welcome Mon-Fri.
◉ Restaurant, brasserie, sports and
spikes bar.
↩ Marriott Worsley Park Hotel &
Country Club

8A

Yorkshire

Strange that such a great golfing county should not possess a single royal course. And strange how one man's life can touch so many others. Dr Alister Mackenzie was a Cambridge medic who went on to become a field surgeon in the Boer War. Subsequently he became an adviser to the British government on camouflage and then in 1914 won first prize in a *Country Life* golf design competition. He went on to influence the architecture of courses as far ranging as Augusta, Cypress Point, Royal Melbourne, even Titirangi in New Zealand, a name that means "fringe of heaven".

There are a few fringes of heaven in the Leeds area where Mackenzie made his home. He had a hand in the Leeds courses of Alwoodley, Moortown, Sand Moor and further down the road at York he also designed Fulford.

He was particularly fond of Alwoodley where he became the club's first secretary in the days when they had a liveried butler. It is a course of great variety, a difficult finish and a par five eight that Henry Longhurst rated one of the best in the country. Sand Moor is quite a hilly course with some fine par threes and Moortown is notable as the venue of the first Ryder Cup to be played in Britain. It also boasts a *Tin Cup* type story when a competitor in the Brabazon chipped back to the eighteenth green via the open window of the bar.

The one famous course in this cluster not to bear the fingerprints of Mackenzie is Moor Allerton, the first Robert Trent Jones course in Britain. It has fine views over the Vale of York and typically cavernous bunkers, rolling greens and an assortment of lakes.

Completing the York, Leeds triangle are the courses around Harrogate. Pannal is an exposed moorland course of quality, Harrogate, overlooked by Knaresborough castle, is well thought of, but the pick is perhaps Ilkley. Situated in a valley below the moor, a river runs through it and is a vibrant feature of the opening seven holes. River, Bridge and Island are the names of the first three holes in acknowledgement of the influence of the Wharfe. Colin Montgomerie honed his game here thus joining Ian McGeechan, player and coach of Scotland and the Lions, as a Scottish sportsman with a large debt to Yorkshire.

To the north Ganton, lying in the Vale of York, is one of England's most treasured courses. It is the only inland course to have hosted the Amateur Championship and in 2003 the Walker Cup was played here, with Great Britain and Ireland coming back for an historic third consecutive victory. No matter how far a Briton, Irishman or American got ahead of his opponent, he always knew that he still had to overcome the severity of Ganton's finish.

Just to the north east of Ganton is Scarborough which has two good courses in the North Cliff and the South Cliff, the latter yet another Mackenzie design.

In truth the south of Yorkshire is not particularly blessed by outstanding golf courses. Woodsome Hall, near Huddersfield, has a good course that could not possibly live up to the historic clubhouse. Rotherham has a mansion for its clubhouse guarded by a vast beech, an equally impressive oak by the first tee and a user friendly golf course.

Part of Lindrick also lies in South Yorkshire, but for a golfing trip of rich diversity you really need to be heading north.

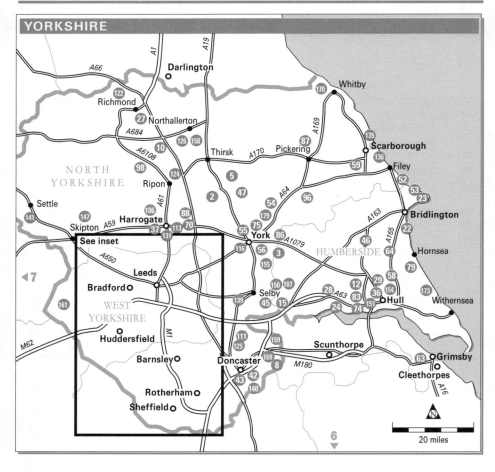

YORKSHIRE

KEY									
1	Abbeydale	23	Bridlington Links	47	Easingwold	71	Headingley	95	Low Laithes
2	Aldwark Manor	24	Brough	48	East Bierley	72	Headley	96	Malton & Norton
3	Allerthorpe Park	25	Calverley	49	Elland	73	Hebden Bridge	97	Marsden
4	Alwoodley	26	Castle Fields	50	Fardew	74	Hessle	98	Masham
5	Ampleforth College	27	Catterick	51	Ferrybridge 'C'	75	Heworth	99	Meltham
6	Baildon	28	Cave Castle Hotel	52	Filey	76	Hickleton	100	Mid Yorkshire
7	Barnsley	29	Cherry Burton	53	Flamborough Head	77	Hillsborough	101	Middleton Park
8	Bawtry Golf and Country	30	City Golf (153)	54	Forest of Galtres	78	Hollins Hall Golf Centre	102	Moor Allerton
	Club (6)	31	City of Wakefield	55	Forest Park	79	Hornsea	103	Moortown
9	Beauchief	32	Clayton	56	Fulford	80	Horsforth	104	Normanton
10	Bedale	33	Cleckheaton & District	57	Fulneck	81	Howley Hall	105	Northcliffe
11	Ben Rhydding	34	Cocksford	58	Ganstead Park	82	Huddersfield (Fixby)	106	Oakdale
12	Beverley & East Riding	35	Concord Park	59	Ganton	83	Hull	107	The Oaks
13	Bingley St Ives	36	Cottingham	60	Garforth	84	Ilkley	108	Otley
14	Birley Wood	37	Crimple Valley	61	Gott's Park	85	Keighley	109	Oulton Park
15	Boothferry Park	38	Crookhill Park	62	Grange Park	86	Kilnwick Percy	110	Outlane
16	Bracken Ghyll	39	Crosland Heath	63	Great Grimsby	87	Kirkbymoorside	111	Owston Park
17	Bradford	40	Crows Nest Park	64	Hainsworth Park	88	Knaresborough	112	Painthorpe House Golf
18	Bradford Moor	41	Dewsbury District	65	Halifax	80	Leeds (Cobble Hall)		& Country Club
19	Bradley Park	42	Doncaster	66	Halifax Bradley Hall	90	Leeds Golf Centre	113	Pannal
20	Brandon	43	Doncaster Town Moor	67	Hallamshire	91	Lees Hall	114	Phoenix
21	Branshaw	44	Dore & Totley	68	Hallowes	92	Lightcliffe	115	Phoenix Park
22	Bridlington	45	Drax	69	Hanging Heaton	93	Lofthouse Hill	116	Pike Hills
		46	Driffield	70	Harrogate	94	Longley Park	117	Pontefract & District

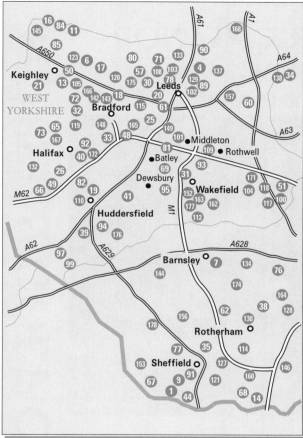

8A 1 Abbeydale

Twentywell Lane, Sheffield, S Yorks, S17 4QA
www.abbeydalegolf.co.uk
abbeygolf@compuserve.com
0114 2360763, Fax 23607632,
Pro 2365633, Sec, 2360763 x21,
Rest/Bar 2360763 x25
Course is off the A621 five miles S of Sheffield.
Parkland course
Pro Nigel Perry; Founded 1895
Designed by Herbert Fowler.
18 holes, 6261 yards, S.S.S. 71
⸙ Welcome by arrangement but not before 9.30am or between 12 noon and 1.30pm.
Ⅼ WD £35; WE £40.
⸙ Welcome by prior arrangement; terms on application.
⋈ By prior arrangement; bar and restaurant facilities.
⋈ Beauchief; Sheffield Moat House.

8A 2 Aldwark Manor

Aldwark, Alne, York, YO61 1UF
01347 838353, Fax 833991,
Pro 838353, Sec 838353,
Rest/Bar 838146
Course is off the A1 five miles SE of Boroughbridge; 13 miles NW of York off the A19.
Easy walking parkland around River Ure.
Founded 1978
18 holes, 6187 yards, S.S.S. 70
⸙ Practice green x 2; putting green
⸙ Welcome WD; some WE restrictions.
Ⅼ WD £25; WE £30.
⸙ Welcome WD; some restrictions; various packages available from £32.
⋈ Full catering in the Victorian Manor House built in 1856; minimum 12; private dining rooms available; full restaurant and bar facilities.
⋈ Aldwark Manor (60 bedrooms).

8A 3 Allerthorpe Park

Allerthorpe Park, Allerthorpe, York, Yorks, YO42 4RL
01759 306686, Fax 304308
Off the A1079 York-Hull road 2 miles W of Pocklington.
Parkland course
Founded 1994
Designed by J G Hatcliffe & Partners.
18 holes, 5506 yards, S.S.S. 66
⸙ Welcome.
Ⅼ WD £20; WE £20.
⸙ Welcome by prior arrangement; terms on application.
⋈ Clubhouse facilities.

8A 4 Alwoodley
Wigton Lane, Alwoodley, Leeds,
W Yorks, LS17 8SA
⌨ www.alwoodley.co.uk
✉ via website
☎ 0113 268 1680, Fax 293 9458,
Pro 268 9603, Rest/Bar 293 9457
On A61 5 miles N of Leeds.
Heathland/moorland course
Pro John Green; Founded 1907
Designed by Dr A MacKenzie & H Colt.
18 holes, 6666 yards, S.S.S. 72
♣ Practice ground.
♦ Welcome by prior arrangement;
terms on application.
♦ WD £65; WE £85.
♦ Welcome by prior arrangement;
terms on application.
♦ Bar and restaurant facilities;
catering available by prior
arrangement.
♦ Harewood Arms; Holiday Inn,
Bramhope.

8A 5 Ampleforth College
Gilling East, York, Yorks, YO5 5AE
☎ 01653 628555
Entrance oppostie church in the centre
of Gilling East.
Parkland course
Founded 1972
Designed by Ampleforth College
9 holes, 5567 yards, S.S.S. 69
♦ Welcome but restrictions between
2pm-4pm for pupils on WD.
♦ WD £9; WE £12.
♦ Club will consider applications.
♦ None; public house next door.
♦ Worsley Arms, Hovingham.

8A 6 Baildon ☎
Moorgate, Baildon, Shipley, Yorks,
BD17 5PP
⌨ www.baildongolfclub.com
✉ sec@baildongolfclub.freeserve
.co.uk
☎ 01274 584266, Pro 595162,
Sec 584266
3 miles N of Bradford off the Bradford-
Ilkley road.
Moorland course laid out as links course
Pro Richard Masters; Founded 1896
Designed by T Morris – modified by J
Braid.
18 holes, 6231 yards, S.S.S. 70
♣ Large practice area
♦ Welcome by prior arrangement.
♦ WD £20; WE £24.
♦ Welcome by prior arrangement;
discounts for larger groups; terms on
application.
♦ Clubhouse facilities, catering
packages available.
♦ Many in local area.

8A 7 Barnsley
Wakefield Road, Staincross, Nr
Barnsley, S Yorks, S75 6JZ
✉ barnsleygolfclub@hotmail.com
☎ 01226 382856, Fax 382856,
Pro 380358, Sec 382856,
Rest/Bar 382856
Course is on A61 three miles from
Barnsley.
Undulating meadowland course.
Pro Shaun Wyke; Founded 1928
18 holes, 5951 yards, S.S.S. 69
♣ Practice range 50 yards from
club/driving range next door
♦ Welcome.
♦ WD £10.50; WE £12.50.
♦ Welcome by prior arrangement;
terms on application. All bookings are
via the professional.
♦ Bar meals.
♦ Queens; Ardsley Moat House.

8A 8 Bawtry Golf and Country Club
Cross Lane, Austerfield, Doncaster,
Yorks, DN10 6RF
☎ 01302 710841, Fax 710841,
Pro 710841
Take A614 towards Fourn; Cross Lane
is on right at first roundabout.
Parkland course.
Pro Hayden Selby-Green/Steve Pool;
Founded 1974
Designed by E & M Baker Ltd
18 holes, 6900 yards, S.S.S. 73
♣ 10 bays floodlit and practice green.
♦ Welcome.
♦ WD £14 WE £18; per day WD £18
or WE £22.
♦ Welcome by prior arrangement;
terms on application. Includes WE.
♦ Clubhouse facilities.
♦ Crown, Bawtry. Mount Pleasent
Doncaster.

8A 9 Beauchief
Abbey Lane, Sheffield, S Yorks, S8 0DB
☎ 01142 367274, Pro 367274
From M1 Junction 33 towards city
centre and follow signs A612 to
Bakewell for 4 miles, turning left into
Abbeydale Road at lights.
Parkland course.
Pro Mark Trippett; Founded 1925
18 holes, 5469 yards, S.S.S. 66
♦ Municipal pay and play.
♦ WD £8.50; WE £11.
♦ Meals served daily.
♦ Beauchief adjacent to court.

8A 10 Bedale ☎
Leyburn Road, Bedale, N Yorks,
DL8 1EZ
⌨ www.bedalegolfclub.com
✉ bedalegolfclub@aol.com
☎ 01677 422451, Fax 427143,
Pro 422443, Sec 422451,
Rest/Bar 422568
From A1 take A684 through Bedale;
course 400 yards from town centre.
Parkland course
Designed by Hawtree.
Pro Tony Johnson; Founded 1894
18 holes, 6610 yards, S.S.S. 72
♦ Welcome with handicap certs.
♦ WD £23/round, £28/day; WE
£30/round.
♦ Welcome by prior arrangement;
catering & golfing packages available;
terms available on application.
♦ Clubhouse facilities.
♦ Nags Head, Pickhill; White Rose,
Leeming Bar; Buck Inn, Thornton
Watlass; Hartforth Hall, Hartforth; Croft
Spa, Croft on Tees; Swinton Park,
Masham; Solberge Hall, Northallerton;
Litle Holtby, Leeming Bar; Constable
Burton Hall, Leyburn; Kings Head,
Bedale; The Lodge, Leeming.

8A 11 Ben Rhydding
High Wood, Ben Rhydding, Ilkley,
W Yorks, LS29 8SB
⌨ benrhyddinggc.freeserve.co.uk
☎ 01943 608759, Sec 816067
From A65 to Ilkley turn up Wheatley
Lane and then into Wheatley Grove,
left on to High Wood, club signposted.
Moorland course; mix of light park/links.
Founded 1890/1947
Designed by W Dell
9 holes, 4711 yards, S.S.S. 64
♣ 2.
♦ Welcome WD; limited access with
member at WE.
♦ WD £12; WE £17.
♦ Very limited; access to small
parties; terms available on
application.
♦ Very limited/self catering.
♦ Local tourist office can supply
details.

8A 12 Beverley & East Riding ☎
Anti Mill, Westwood, Beverley, E Yorks,
HU17 8RG
☎ 01482 867190, Fax 868757,
Pro 869519, Sec 868757
On B1230 Walkington road 0.5 miles
W of town centre.
Common pastureland.
Pro Alex Ashby; Founded 1889
Designed by Dr JJ Fraser
18 holes, 5972 yards, S.S.S. 69
♦ Welcome.
♦ WD £15; WE £20.
♦ Welcome WD; catering packages
can be arranged.

🍽 Clubhouse facilities.
🚗 Lairgate, Beverley.

8A 13 Bingley St Ives ☂
The Golf Clubhouse, St Ives Estate, Harden, Bingley, BD16 1AT
🖥 www.bingleystives.co.uk
✉ bingleyst-ives@harden.co.uk
☎ 01274 562436, Fax 511788, Pro 562506, Sec 562436
Course is close to A650 Keighley to Bradford road and B629 Bingley to Denholme.
Parkland/moorland/woodland course.
Pro Ray Firth; Founded 1932
Designed by A MacKenzie
18 holes, 6482 yards, S.S.S. 71
🏌 Good practice facilities.
† Welcome by arrangement.
🍸 WD £25; WE £30.
🍀 Welcome by prior arrangement; all day golf and catering packages available; from £36.
🍽 Professional facilities and separate restaurant.
🚗 Contact club.

8A 14 Birley Wood
Birley Lane, Sheffield, S Yorks, S12 3BP
✉ birleysec@hotmail.com
☎ 0114 2647262, Fax 2647262, Pro 2394285, Sec 2653784
Course is off the A616 four miles S of Sheffield.
Public open course.
Pro Peter Ball; Founded 1974
18 holes, 5734 yards, S.S.S. 68
† Welcome.
🍸 WD £9.50; WE £11.00.
🍀 Welcome by prior arrangement with Sheffield International Venues.
Please book through the manager.
🍽 Catering at Fairways Inn adjacent to course.

8A 15 Boothferry Park
Spaldington Lane, Howden, Goole, E Yorks, DN14 7NG
☎ 01430 430364, Pro 430364, Rest/Bar 430371
On B1228 between Howden and Bubwith off M62 Junction 37.
Meadowland with ponds and ditches.
Pro N Bundy; Founded 1981
Designed by Donald Steel
18 holes, 6651 yards, S.S.S. 72
† Welcome at all times.
🍸 WD £10; WE £15. Summer rates.
Please telephone for Winter rates.
🍀 Welcome by prior arrangement with the professional; packages can be

arranged; terms on application.
🍽 Clubhouse facilities.
🚗 Cave Castle.

8A 16 Bracken Ghyll ☂
Skipton Road, Addingham, Yorks, LS29 0SL
🖥 www.brackenghyll.co.uk
✉ office@brackenghyll.co.uk
☎ 01943 831207, Fax 839453, Pro 831207, Sec 831207, Rest/Bar 830691
Off A65 Skipton road in Addingham.
Undulating parkland course.
Pro Andrew Hall; Founded 1993
Designed by OCM Associates
18 holes, 5525 yards, S.S.S. 67
† Welcome by prior arrangement.
🍸 WD £20; WE £24.
🍀 Welcome; catering and golf packages available; video tuition; indoor practice area; terms on application.
🍽 Full clubhouse facilities.
🚗 Craiglands; Devonshire Country House; Rombalds, Ilkley.

8A 17 The Bradford Golf Club ☂
Hawksworth Lane, Guiseley, Leeds, W Yorks, LS20 8NP
✉ manager@ bradfordgolfclub.sagehost.co.uk
☎ 01943 875570, Fax 875570, Pro 873719, Sec 875570, Rest/Bar 873817
Course is off the A6038 3.5 miles NE of Shipley.
Moorland/parkland course.
Pro Sydney Welden; Founded 1891
Designed by Fowler and Simpson
18 holes, 6303 yards, S.S.S. 71
🏌 Driving range (members and greenfee-paying visitors only).
† Welcome WD by prior arrangement; not Sat; limited Sun.
🍸 WD £30; WE £35.
🍀 Welcome WD by prior arrangement; catering packages available; terms available on application.
🍽 Full clubhouse facilities.
🚗 Marriott Hollins Hall; Chevin Lodge. Others available on request.

8A 18 Bradford Moor
Scarr Hall, Pollard Lane, Bradford, W Yorks, BD2 4RW
☎ 01274 771716, Sec 01274 771693
2 miles from Bradford town centre on Harrogate Rd.
Moorland course.
Founded 1906

9 holes, 5900 yards, S.S.S. 68
† Welcome WD.
🍸 WD £10.
🍀 Welcome WD by prior arrangement; catering and golf packages available; from £16.
🍽 Clubhouse facilities.

8A 19 Bradley Park
Bradley Road, Huddersfield, HD2 2PJ
✉ parnellreilly@tinyworld.co.uk
☎ 01484 223772, Fax 451613, Pro 223772, Sec 223772, Rest/Bar 223774
M62 Junction 26 in direction of Huddersfield; right at first lights.
Parklands course.
Pro Parnell Reilly; Founded 1973
Designed by Donald Steel
18 holes, 6284 yards, S.S.S. 70
🏌 18 floodlit; 9-hole par 3 course.
† Welcome anytime, must book for WE/BH.
🍸 WD £14; WE £16.
🍀 Welcome WD; catering packages can be arranged; from £10.
🍽 Clubhouse facilities.

8A 20 Brandon
Holywell Lane, Shadwell, Leeds, W Yorks, LS17 8EZ
☎ 0113 2737471, Sec 2737471
1 mile from N Leeds ring road at Roundhay Park.
Parkland course.
Founded 1967
Designed by George Eric Allamby
18 holes, 4800 yards, S.S.S. 62
† All welcome.
🍸 WD £6.50; WE £7.50.
🍀 Welcome WD by prior arrangement; 10 days' notice required; from £6.50.
🍽 Clubhouse snack facilities available.
🚗 White House; Rydal Bank.

8A 21 Branshaw ☂
Branshaw Moor, Oakworth, Keighley, W Yorks, BD22 7ES
☎ 01535 643235, Pro 647441, Rest/Bar 643235
Course is on the B6143 two miles SW of Keighley.
Moorland course.
Pro Simon Jowitt; Founded 1912
Designed by James Braid
18 holes, 5870 yards, S.S.S. 69
† Welcome WD; restrictions at WE.
🍸 WD £20; WE £30.
🍀 Welcome WD by prior arrangement.

🍽 Clubhouse catering facilities available.
🛏 Three Sisters, Haworth; Newsholme Manor, Oakworth.

8A 22 **Bridlington** ♛
Belvedere Road, Bridlington, E Yorks, YO153NA
🖥 www.bridlingtongolfclub.co.uk
📧 enquiries@bridlingtongolfclub.co.uk
☎ 01262 672092, Fax 606367, Pro 674721, Sec 606367, Rest/Bar 672092
Off A165 S of town on Bridlington-Hull road.
Open parkland course.
Pro ARA Howarth; Founded 1905
Designed by James Braid
18 holes, 6638 yards, S.S.S. 72
† Welcome by prior arrangement.
℃ WD £20; WE £35 (subject to review).
↻ Welcome by prior arrangement; golf and catering packages available; terms on application.
🍽 Full clubhouse facilities available.
🛏 Club can provide list on request.

8A 23 **Bridlington Links**
Flamborough Road, Marton, Bridlington, E Yorks, YO15 1DW
☎ 01262 401584, Fax 401702, Pro 401584, Sec 401584, Rest/Bar 401584
Course is on the B1255 just N of Bridlington towards Flamborough Head.
Clifftop links course.
Pro Steve Raybould; Founded 1993
Designed by Howard Swan
18 holes, 6719 yards, S.S.S. 72
🏌 24 covered floodlit.
† All welcome.
℃ WD £12; WE £15 (This includes lunch in winter months).
↻ Welcome; summer and winter packages available; driving range; short course; terms available on application.
🍽 Full clubhouse facilities.
🛏 Rags Hotel; Manor Court; Sewerby Grange; North Star, Flamborough.

8A 24 **Brough** ♛
Cave Road, Brough, E Yorks, HU15 1HB
🖥 www.brough-golfclub.co.uk
📧 dgt@brough-golfclub.co.uk
☎ 01482 667374, Fax 669823, Pro 667483, Sec 667291
Off A63, 10 miles W of Hull.

Parkland course.
Pro G W Townhill
Founded 1893
18 holes, 6134 yards, S.S.S. 69
† Welcome WD except Wed; WE by prior arrangement.
℃ WD £32; WE £45.
↻ Welcome by prior arrangement; full golf and catering packages available; terms available on application.
🍽 Full clubhouse facilities.
🛏 Beverley Arms; Walkington Manor; Holiday Inn; Jarvis.

8A 25 **Calverley**
Woodhall Lane, Pudsey, Yorks, LS28 5QY
☎ 0113 2569244, Fax 2564362, Sec 2569244
Close to M1 & M62 motorways 4 miles from Bradford, 7 miles from Leeds.
Parkland course.
Pro Neil Wendel-Jones; Founded 1980
18 holes, 5590 yards, S.S.S. 67
🏌 Large practice ground + 9-hole course.
† Welcome; restrictions Sat and Sun am.
℃ WD £12; WE £16.
↻ Welcome by arrangement; catering packages available for groups; terms available on application.
🍽 Full clubhouse facilities.
🛏 Marriott.

8A 26 **Castle Fields**
Rastrick Common, Rastrick, Brighouse, W Yorks, HD6 3HI
☎ 01484 713276, Sec 713276
On A643 1 mile out of Brighouse.
Parkland course.
Founded 1903
6 holes, 2406 yards, S.S.S. 50
† Welcome only as a guest of a member.
℃ WD £5.50; WE £7.50.
↻ Welcome only by prior arrangement with Sec.
🍽 Facilities at local Inns within 0.25 miles.

8A 27 **Catterick** ♛
Leyburn Road, Catterick Garrison, N Yorks, DL9 3QE
☎ 01748 833671, Fax 833268, Pro 833671, Sec 833268, Rest/Bar 833401
On B6136 6 miles SW of Scotch Corner.
Parkland/moorland course.
Pro Andy Marshall; Founded 1930

Designed by Arthur Day (1938)
18 holes, 6329 yards, S.S.S. 71
† Welcome by prior arrangement.
℃ Terms on application.
↻ Welcome by prior arrangement; packages can be arranged; 2 practice areas; billiards room; satellite TV.
🍽 Lounge bar, restaurant, bar snacks, snooker room.
🛏 Several.

8A 28 **Cave Castle Hotel**
South Cave, Brough, E Yorks, HU15 2EU
🖥 www.ccgc.co.uk
☎ 01430 421286, Pro 421286, Rest/Bar 422245
10 miles from Kingston upon Hull.
Parkland course.
Pro Stephen MacKinder; Founded 1989
18 holes, 6524 yards, S.S.S. 71
† Welcome.
℃ WD £15; WE £20.
↻ Welcome WD and after 1.30pm at WE; special packages available; conference facilities for 250; à la carte restaurant; practice facilities; terms on application.
🍽 Full hotel facilities/clubhouse.
🛏 Cave Castle.

8A 29 **Cherry Burton**
Leconfield Road, Cherry Burton, Beverley, Yorks, HU17 7RB
☎ 01964 550924
On the B1248 close to Beverley.
Parkland course.
Founded 1993
Designed by W Adamson
9 holes, 6480 yards, S.S.S. 71
🏌 Practice area.
† Welcome.
℃ WD £9; WE £10.
↻ Welcome by prior arrangement.
🍽 Bar and catering facilities available.
🛏 Beverley; Lairgate.

8A 30 **City Golf**
Redcote Lane, Leeds, W Yorks, LS4 2AW
☎ 0113 2633030, Fax 2633044
1.5 miles W of Leeds town centre off Kirkstall Road.
Parkland course.
Founded 1996
9 holes, 1800 yards, par 30
† Welcome.
℃ WD £5; WE £5.
↻ Welcome with prior booking.
🍽 Full facilities.

8A 31 **City of Wakefield**

Lupset Park, Horbury Road, Wakefield, W Yorks, WF2 8QS
☎ 01924 360282, Pro 360282, Sec 367442, Rest/Bar 367442
Course is on the A642 two miles W of Wakefield.
Parkland course.
Pro Roger Holland; Founded 1936
Designed by JSF Morrison
18 holes, 6319 yards, S.S.S. 70
† Everybody welcome.
▯ WD £10 round; WE £12 round.
⚐ Welcome on WD by prior arrangement; packages can be arranged through the stewardess; terms on application.
▮●▮ Clubhouse facilities.
⌑ Cedar Court, Forte Post House, Wakefield.

8A 32 **Clayton**

Thornton View Road, Clayton, Bradford, W Yorks, BD14 6JX
☎ 01274 880047
On A647 from Bradford following signs for Clayton.
Moorland course.
Founded 1906
9 holes, 5467 yards, S.S.S. 67
† Welcome WD and Sat unless comps.
▯ WD £10; WE £12.
⚐ Welcome by arrangement with Sec; catering packages by arrangement; snooker; terms on application.
▮●▮ Bar and bar snacks.
⌑ Pennine Hilton.

8A 33 **Cleckheaton & District**

Bradford Road, Cleckheaton, W Yorks, BD19 6BU
▤ info@cleckheatongolf.fsnet.co.uk
☎ 01274 851267, Fax 871382, Sec 851266, Rest/Bar 874118
On A638 from M62 Junction 26 towards Bradford.
Parkland course.
Pro Mike Ingham; Founded 1900
18 holes, 5860 yards, S.S.S. 68
† Welcome.
▯ WD £25; WE £30.
⚐ Welcome WD by arrangement; catering packages by arrangement; terms on application.
▮●▮ Clubhouse catering and bar facilities.
⌑ Novotel.

8A 34 **Cocksford**

Stutton, Tadcaster, N Yorks, LS24 9NG
☎ 01937 834253, Fax 834253, Rest/Bar 530346
Course is in village of Strutton close to the A64.
Parkland course with Cock Beck running through it.
Pro Graham Thompson; Founded 1991
Designed by Townend/Brodigan
27 holes, 5632 yards, S.S.S. 69
† Welcome by arrangement.
▯ WD £17; WE £23.
⚐ Welcome by prior arrangement; 27 holes golf; all-day catering high season only; 3rd nine added in 1995 to form Plews and Quarry high courses; £29.
▮●▮ Clubhouse facilities, including bistro and Sparrows restaurant all year round.
⌑ Club have cottages to rent.

8A 35 **Concord Park**

Shiregreen, Sheffield, S Yorks, S5 6AE
▤ concordparkgc@tiscali.co.uk
☎ 0114 2577378, Fax 2347792, Pro 2577378, Sec 2347792, Rest/Bar 5577378
Course is off the A6135 3.5 miles N of Sheffield. M1 J34 (5 mins)
Parkland course.
Pro Warren Allcroft; Founded 1952
18 holes, 4872 yards, S.S.S. 64
▯ 20 bays, floodlit and under cover.
† Welcome any timet.
▯ WD £7.50; WE £8.
⚐ Welcome; from £7.50.
▮●▮ Full clubhouse facilities.

8A 36 **Cottingham**

Woodhill Way, Cottingham, E Yorks, HU16 5RZ
☎ 01482 846030, Fax 845932, Pro 842394, Sec 846030, Rest/Bar 846032
Off A164 4 miles off the M62/A63.
Parkland course.
Pro Chris Gray; Founded 1994
Designed by J Wiles/T Litten
18 holes, 6034 yards, S.S.S. 69
▯ Two storey; £2 for 50 balls.
† Welcome by prior arrangement.
▯ WD £16; WE £24.
⚐ Welcome by prior arrangement; WD and WE packages available; from £30.
▮●▮ Fully licensed bar and restaurant.
⌑ Willerby Manor; Jarvis Grange.

8A 37 **Crimple Valley**

Hookstone Wood Road, Harrogate, Yorks, HG2 8PN
☎ 01423 883485

Course is off the A61 one mile S of town centre.
Parkland course.
Founded 1976
Designed by R Lumb
9 holes, 250 yards, S.S.S. 64
† Public pay and play.
▯ WD £7; WE £8 (9 holes).
⚐ Welcome by arrangement.
▮●▮ Fully licensed bar and restaurant.

8A 38 **Crookhill Park**

Carr Lane, Conisbrough, Nr Doncaster, S Yorks, DN12 2AH
☎ 01709 862979, Sec 863566, Rest/Bar 862974
Off A630 Doncaster to Rotherham road.
Parkland course.
Pro R Swaine; Founded 1976
18 holes, 5849 yards, S.S.S. 68
† Welcome by prior arrangement.
▯ WD £9.25; WE £10.50.
⚐ Welcome by prior arrangement with the professional; discounts available depending on group size; terms on application.
▮●▮ Clubhouse facilities.

8A 39 **Crosland Heath**   ♟

Felks Stile Road, Crosland Heath, Huddersfield, HD4 7AF
☎ 01484 653216, Fax 461079, Pro 653877, Sec 653262
Take A62 Huddersfield-Oldham road and follow signs for Countryside Leisure.
Moorland course
Pro John Eyre; Founded 1913
18 holes, 6004 yards, S.S.S. 69
▯ Practice fields.
† By prior arrangement only; handicap certs required.
▯ Terms on application.
⚐ Welcome except Sat by prior arrangement; catering packages by arrangement; terms on application.
▮●▮ Full facilities available except Mon.
⌑ Dryclough, Crosland Moor; Durker Roods, Meltham.

8A 40 **Crow Nest Park**   ♟

Coach Road, Hove Edge, Brighouse, W Yorks, HD6 2LN
⌨ www.crownestgolf.co.uk
▤ brownest@btconnect.com
☎ 01484 401121, Fax 720975, Pro 01484 401121, Rest/Bar 01484 401152
Off M62 at Brighouse follow signs for Bradford; turn left at Ritz.
Parkland course.
Pro Paul Everitt; Founded 1985

EASINGWOLD *Golf Club*
EGC

Stillington Road, Easingwold YO61 3ET

Tel: Club: **01347 821486**
Pro: **01347 821964**
Secretary: **01347 822474** (tel/fax)

www.easingwold-golf-club.co.uk
E-mail:
brian@easingwold-golf-club.fsnet.co.uk

Founded and constructed in 1930 as a nine hole course by a handful of crusading citizens and extended to 18 holes in 1976, Easingwold Golf Course is today one of the most popular courses in Yorkshire. Facetiously described by some as Easy Easingwold, but not by the serious and discerning golfer. It is a beautiful wooded and scenic course, but with more than it's share of difficulties for the wayward player. The adage: "Keep it straight!" was never more apt than here.

Entirely surrounded by farmland and rich in wildlife Easingwold Golf Course is particularly attractive and is located 12 miles North of York on the A19 at the South end of Easingwold.

Designed by W Adamson
9 holes, 6020 yards, S.S.S. 69
8 bays, floodlit, with power tees.
Welcome.
WD /WE £12 (9 holes); WD/WE £24 (18 holes).
Welcome; golf and catering packages available; terms on application.
Clubhouse facilities available.
Lane Head.

8A 41 Dewsbury District
The Pinnacle, Sands Lane, Mirfield, W Yorks, WF14 8HJ
www.dewsburygolf.co.uk
dewsburygolf@btconnect.com
01924 492399, Fax 492399, Pro 496030, Rest/Bar 491928
Course is two miles W of Dewsbury off the A644; 3 miles from the M62 J25.
Parkland/moorland course.
Pro N Hirst; Founded 1891
Designed by T Morris/P Alliss
18 holes, 6360 yards, S.S.S. 71
Practice ground – extensive.
Welcome WD and after 3.00pm WE.
WD £17; WE £15
Welcome WD and Sun after 2.30pm; full packages of 36 holes of golf and catering available; at £38.
Full clubhouse facilities.

8A 42 Doncaster
278 Bawtry Road, Bessacarr, Doncaster, S Yorks, DN4 7PD
gbdoncaster.g.c@ic24.net
01302 865632, Fax 865994, Pro 868404
On A638 between Doncaster and Bawtry.
Undulating heathland course.
Pro Graham Bailey; Founded 1894
18 holes, 6220 yards, S.S.S. 70
Welcome.
WD £27.50; WE £33.00.

Welcome WD by prior arrangement with Sec; packages by arrangement; terms available on application.
Full clubhouse facilities.
Punches; Danum.

8A 43 Doncaster Town Moor
Bawtry Road, Belle Vue, Doncaster, S Yorks, DN4 5HU
01302 533778, Pro 535286, Sec 533778, Rest/Bar 533167
Next to Doncaster Rovers FC and close to racecourse.
Moorland course.
Pro Steve Shaw; Founded 1895
18 holes, 6001 yards, S.S.S. 69
Practice ground.
Welcome; restrictions Sun.
WD £17; WE £18.
Welcome by arrangement; full days golf and catering by arrangement, prices on application.
Clubhouse facilities.
Royal St Ledger; Earl of Doncaster.

8A 44 Dore & Totley
Bradway Rd, Sheffield, S Yorks, S17 4QR
www.doreandtotleygolf.co.uk
dtgc@lineone.net
0114 2360492, Fax 2353436, Pro 2366844, Sec 2369872, Rest/Bar 2360492
6 miles S of Sheffield on the B6054 for Bradway.
Parkland course.
Pro Gregg Roberts; Founded 1913
18 holes, 6256 yards, S.S.S. 70
Welcome by prior arrangement except Sat; restrictions on Sun & Wed.
WD £26; WE £26.
Welcome except Wed and Sat; summer and winter packages can be arranged through Pro; terms on application.
Full clubhouse facilities.

8A 45 Drax
Drax, Nr Selby, N Yorks, YO8 8PQ
01405 860533
Corse is off the A1041 six miles south of Selby opposite Drax power station.
Tree-lined parkland course.
Founded 1989
9 holes, 5510 yards, S.S.S. 67
Only with a member.
Not available.
At Drax Sports and Social Club.

8A 46 Driffield
Sunderlandwick, Beverley Road, Driffield, E Yorks, YO25 7AD
01377 253116, Fax 240599, Pro 241224, Sec 253116, Rest 255211 Bar 240448
Off A164 Beverley to Driffield road off the first main roundabout.
Mature parkland course.
Pro Kenton Wright; Founded 1934
18 holes, 6215 yards, S.S.S. 70
Welcome with club or society handicap certs WD 9.30am-12noon & 1.30pm-30m; WE between 9.30am-11am.
WD £20; WE £30 per round.
Welcome by prior arrangement with handicap certs; catering packages available; practice area; terms on application.
Clubhouse facilities.
Bell, Driffield.

8A 47 Easingwold
Stillington Road, Easingwold, York, N Yorks, YO61 3ET
www.easingwolfgolfclub.co.uk
brian@easingwold-golf-club.fsnet.co.uk
01347 821486, Fax 822474, Pro 821964, Sec 822474, Rest/Bar 822078
On A19 12 miles N of York; 1 mile down Stillington road at S end of Easingwold.

Parkland course.
Pro J Hughes; Founded 1930
Designed by Hawtree
18 holes, 6712 yards, S.S.S. 72
↑ Large practice area.
✝ Welcome by prior arrangement.
↕ WD £28; WE £35.
♂ Welcome by prior arrangement;
golf & full catering packages; from
£41.95.
◯ Clubhouse facilities.
↪ The George.

8A 48 East Brierley
South View Road, Bierley, Bradford,
W Yorks, BD4 6PP
☎ 01274 681023, Sec 683666,
Rest/Bar 680450
4 miles S of Bradford.
Parkland course.
Founded 1904/28
9 holes, 4692 yards, S.S.S. 63
✝ Welcome. Except Sun.
↕ WD £14; WE £17.
♂ Welcome by prior arrangement;
terms on application.
◯ Full catering facilities.

8A 49 Elland
Hammerstone, Leach Lane, Elland,
W Yorks, HX5 0TA
☎ 01422 372505, Pro 374886
From M62 Junction 24 in direction of
Blackley.
Parkland course.
Pro N Kryzwicki; Founded 1910
9 holes, 5498 yards, S.S.S. 67
✝ Welcome.
↕ Terms on application.
♂ Welcome Tues, Wed, Fri; catering
packages available.
◯ Clubhouse facilities.
↪ Rock Hotel, Holywell Green.

8A 50 Fardew
Nursery Farm, Carr Lane, East
Morton, Keighley, W Yorks, BD20 5RY
✉ fardewgc@btclick.com
☎ 01274 561229, Fax 561229
1.25 miles from Bingley, then to E
Morton.
Parkland course.
Pro Ian Bottomley; Founded 1993
Designed by W Adamson
9 holes, 6208 yards, S.S.S. 70
↑ Open practice ground.
✝ Pay and play.
↕ WD £14; WE £16 (18 holes); £2
per 18 holes reduction if booked in
advance.
♂ Welcome by prior arrangement;
terms on application.

◯ Café.
↪ Beeches, Keighley.

8A 51 Ferrybridge 'C'
Ferrybridge 'C' P.S. Golf Club,
Knottingley, WF11 8SQ
☎ 01977 884165
On Castleford-Knottingley road 200
yards from A1.
Parkland course.
Founded 1976
Designed by NE Pugh
9 holes, 5138 yards, S.S.S. 65
✝ Welcome as guest of a member.
↕ Terms on application.
♂ Welcome by arrangement.
↪ Darrington Hotel; Golden Lion.

8A 52 Filey ☎
West Ave, Filey, N Yorks, YO14 9BQ
🖥 www.fileygolfclub.com
✉ secretary@fileygolfclub.com
☎ 01723 513293, Fax 514952,
Pro 513134, Sec 513293,
Rest/Bar 513293
1 mile S of Filey.
Links/parkland course.
Pro Gary Hutchinson
Founded 1897
Designed by J Braid
18 holes, 6112 yards, S.S.S. 69
↑ Practice facilities.
✝ Welcome by arrangement.
↕ WD £25; WE £30.
♂ Welcome with prior arrangement;
catering packages available; from
£22 (winter).
◯ Clubhouse facilities.
↪ White Lodge; Hallam.

8A 53 Flamborough Head ☎
Lighthouse Road, Flamborough,
Bridlington, E Yorks, YO15 1AR
🖥 www.flamboroughheadgolfclub
.co.uk
✉
secretary@flamboroughheadgolfclub
.co.uk
☎ 01262 850333, Pro 850222,
Sec 850683
5 miles NE of Bridlington situation on
Flamborough headland.
Clifftop course.
Pro Paul Harrison; Founded 1931
18 holes, 6189 yards, S.S.S. 69
↑ Practice area.
✝ Welcome.
↕ WD £20; WE £25.
♂ Welcome by arrangement; full day
golf and catering available.
◯ Clubhouse facilities.
↪ North Star, Flamborough.

8A 54 Forest of Galtres ☎
Moorlands Road, Skelton, York, Yorks,
YO32 2RF
🖥 www.forestofgaltresgolfclub.co.uk
✉ secretary@forestofgaltresgolfclub
.co.uk
☎ 01904 766198, Fax 769400,
Pro 766198, Sec 769400,
Rest/Bar 750287
Just off A19 Thirsk road through
Skelton; 1.5 miles from B1237 York
ring road.
Parkland in ancient Forest of Galtres.
Pro Phil Bradley; Founded 1993
Designed by S Gidman
18 holes, 6412 yards, S.S.S. 70
↑ Driving range and practice area.
✝ Welcome.
↕ WD £20; WE £27.
♂ Welcome by prior arrangement
only; discounts for groups of 12 or
more; from £27.
◯ Full clubhouse facilities.
↪ Beechwood Close; Jacobean
Lodge; Fairfield Manor.

8A 55 Forest Park
Stockton on Forest, York, YO32 9UW
☎ 01904 400425, Pro 400425,
Rest/Bar 400425
Course is 2.5 miles from E end of York
by-pass.
Flat parkland course.
Founded 1991
18 holes, 6660 yards, S.S.S. 72; 9
holes 6372 yards
↑ Open and covered ranges.
✝ Welcome.
↕ WD £20; WE £25.
♂ Welcome; all-day golf and catering
packages available; also 9-hole West
Course: 6372 yards, par 70; from £31.
◯ Full clubhouse facilities.
↪ B&B in Stockton-on-Forest.

8A 56 Fulford ☎
Heslington Lane, York, Yorks,
YO10 5DY
☎ 01904 413579, Fax 416918,
Pro 412882, Sec 413579,
Rest/Bar 411503
Off A19 1 mile S of York following
signs to University.
Parkland/heathland course.
Pro Martin Brown; Founded 1906
Designed by Major C MacKenzie
18 holes, 6775 yards, S.S.S. 72
✝ Welcome by arrangement.
↕ WD £45; WE £55.
♂ Welcome by prior arrangement;
not Tues am; packages can be
arranged through manager; terms on
application.

GANSTEAD PARK

GOLF CLUB

LONGDALES LANE
CONISTON
HULL
HU11 4LB

A warm welcome is given to all golfers
visiting our course many of whom return
year after year.

We offer an appealing, easy walking,
parkland course suitable for visiting parties.

Weekend packages available.

Contact Secretary on: 01482 817754 or Pro on: 01482 811121
e-mail: secretary@gansteadpark.co.uk
www.gansteadpark.co.uk

🍽 Full clubhouse facilities.
🛏 Pavilion; Hilton; Poste House; The Swallow; The Viking.

8A 57 Fulneck
The Clubhouse, Fulneck, Pudsey,
W Yorks, LS28 8NT
☎ 0113 2565191, Sec 256519,
Rest/Bar 2565191
Between Leeds and Bradford; at
Pudsey cenotaph turn left then turn
right at T-junction and take the first left
at Bankhouse lane.Turn left at the
Bankhouse Pub.
Undulating wooded parkland course.
Founded 1892
9 holes, 5456 yards, S.S.S. 66
🏌 Welcome all week. Prior booking
for Saturdays.
🍸 £15 per day all week, £8 with a
member.
⛳ Welcome by prior arrangement
with Sec; catering packages by
arrangement; terms available on
application.
🍽 By arrangement.
🛏 Stakis Hotel, Tong village.

8A 58 Ganstead Park   ☎
Longdales Lane, Coniston, Hull,
E Yorks, HU11 4LB
🖥 www.gansteadpark.co.uk
📧 secretary@gansteadpark.co.uk
☎ 01482 817754, Fax 817754,
Pro 811121, Sec 817754, Rest/Bar
811280
On A165 Hull-Bridlington road at
Ganstead.
Parkland course with water.
Pro Mike Smee; Founded 1976
Designed by Peter Green
18 holes, 6801 yards, S.S.S. 73
🏌 Welcome by prior arrangement.
🍸 Terms on application.
⛳ Welcome by prior arrangement;
special packages can be arranged;
terms on application.

🍽 Full clubhouse facilities.
🛏 Kingstown, Hedon; Tickton
Grange, Beverley; Gardeners Arms,
Skirlaugh.

8A 59 Ganton
Ganton, Scarborough, N Yorks,
YO12 4PA
🖥 www.gantongolfclub.com
📧 secretary@gantongolfclub.com
☎ 01944 710329, Fax 710922,
Pro 710260, Sec 710329,
Rest/Bar 712806
On A64 11 miles W of Scarborough.
Heathland/links championship course.
Pro Gary Brown; Founded 1891
Designed by Dunn, Vardon, Colt, CK
Cotton
18 holes, 6734 yards, S.S.S. 73
🏌 13 acre practice range and short
game area.
🏌 Welcome by prior arrangement.
🍸 WD round or day £65; WE round
or day and public holidays £75.
⛳ Welcome by prior agreement;
packages can be organised; terms on
application.
🍽 Full clubhouse facilities.
🛏 Crescent, Scarborough; Ganton
Greyhound; Blue Bell, Wearethorpe.

8A 60 Garforth
Long Lane, Garforth, Leeds, LS25 2DS
🖥 www.garforthgolfclub.co.uk
📧 garforthgcltd@lineone.net
☎ 0113 2862021, Pro 2862063,
Sec 2863308
6.5 miles E of Leeds off A642.
Parkland course.
Pro Ken Finlater; Founded 1913
Designed by Dr Alistair Mackenzie.
18 holes, 6304 yards, S.S.S. 70
🏌 Welcome WD.
🍸 WD on application.
⛳ Welcome WD by prior
arrangement; terms available on
application.

🍽 Full facilities.
🛏 Hilton.

8A 61 Gott's Park
Armley Ridge Road, Leeds, W Yorks,
LS12 2QX
☎ 0113 2311896, Rest/Bar 2310492
3 miles W of the city centre.
Parkland course.
Founded 1933
18 holes, 4978 yards, S.S.S. 65
🏌 Welcome.
🍸 WD £7.25; WE £8.75.
⛳ Welcome by arrangement.
🍽 Cafe facilities; bar in evenings and
WE.

8A 62 Grange Park
Upper Wortley Road, Rotherham,
S Yorks, S61 2SJ
☎ 01709 558884, Pro 559497
On A629 2 miles W of Rotherham.
Municipal parkland; private clubhouse
Pro Eric Clark; Founded 1971
18 holes, 6421 yards, S.S.S. 71
🏌 36 two-tier floodlit covered.
🏌 Welcome.
🍸 WD £9; WE £11.
⛳ Welcome by prior arrangement
with Sec; special catering and golf
packages available; terms on
application.
🍽 Full bar and catering facilities
Tues-Sun; limited Mon.
🛏 Swallow.

8A 63 Great Grimsby Golf Centre
Cromwell Road, Grimsby, DN31 2BH
☎ 014722 50555, Fax 67447,
Pro 50555
From A180 follow signs for Auditorium
and Leisure centre.
Parkland course.
Pro Stephen Bennett; Founded 1995
9 holes, 4652 yards, S.S.S. 32

🏌 Practice ground/27 driving bays.
🚩 Public pay and play.
⛳ WD £5.50; WE £6.50.
☞ None.
🍽 Limited.
🛏 Millfields Hotel, Grimsby.

8A 64 Hainsworth Park
Brandesburton, Driffield, E Yorks,
YO25 8RT
✉ hainsworth@hemscott.net
☎ 01964 542362
Just off A165 8 miles N of Beverley.
Parkland course.
Pro Paul Binnington; Founded 1983
18 holes, 6362 yards, S.S.S. 69
🚩 Welcome by prior arrangements.
⛳ Terms on application.
☞ Welcome by prior arrangement;
day tickets available (WD £20, WE
£25); from £14.
🍽 Full catering and restaurant
facilities.
🛏 Burton Lodge on course.

8A 65 Halifax
Union Lane, Ogden, Halifax, W Yorks,
HX2 8XR
☎ 01422 244171, Pro 240047,
Rest/Bar 248108
Course is on the A629 four miles from
Halifax.
Moorland course.
Pro Michael Allison
Founded 1895
Designed by WH Fowler, James
Braid
18 holes, 6037 yards, S.S.S. 70
🚩 Welcome WD; limited at WE.
⛳ WD £25; WE £35.
☞ Welcome WD by prior
arrangement with Sec; packages
available with catering; fees by prior
arrangement.
🍽 Full clubhouse facilities.
🛏 Windmill Court; Holdsworth House;
Moorlands.

8A 66 Halifax Bradley Hall
Stainland Road, Holywell Green,
Halifax, W Yorks, HX4 9AN
☎ 01422 374108, Pro 370231
On B6112 off A629 Halifax-
Huddersfield Road.
Moorland/parkland course.
Pro Peter Wood; Founded 1905/24
18 holes, 6213 yards, S.S.S. 70
🚩 Welcome with handicap certs.
⛳ WD £25; WE £30.
☞ Welcome with handicap certs and
by prior arrangement; golf and catering
packages; £33.

🍽 Full clubhouse facilities.
🛏 Rock Inn, Holywell Green.

8A 67 Hallamshire
The Clubhouse, Sandygate, Sheffield,
S Yorks, S10 4LA
☎ 0114 2301007, Fax 2302153,
Pro 2305222, Sec 2302153
3 miles W of Sheffield off A57 at
Crosspool.
Moorland course.
Pro Geoff Tickell; Founded 1897
Designed by Various including Dr A
MacKenzie
18 holes, 6359 yards, S.S.S. 71
🚩 Welcome; some restrictions at
WE.
⛳ Terms on application.
☞ Welcome by arrangement with
Sec; packages available; terms on
application.
🍽 Full clubhouse facilities.
🛏 Beauchef; Trust House Forte.

8A 68 Hallowes
Hallowes Lane, Dronfield, Sheffield,
S Yorks, S18 1UA
☎ 01246 413734, Fax 413753,
Pro 411196, Rest/Bar 410394
Take A61 Sheffield-Chesterfield road
into Dronfield and turn sharp right
under railway bridge.
Undulating moorland course.
Pro Philip Dunn
Founded 1892
18 holes, 6342 yards, S.S.S. 71
🚩 Welcome WD. Visitors
accompanied by members WE.
⛳ WD £30, WE £15 with member.
☞ Welcome WD by arrangement; day
ticket WD £35; catering by arrangement;
terms available on application.
🍽 Full clubhouse facilities.
🛏 Chantry.

8A 69 Hanging Heaton
White Cross Road, Bennett Lane,
Dewsbury, W Yorks, WF12 7DT
☎ 01924 461606, Fax 430100,
Pro 467077, Sec 430100
On A653 Dewbury-Leeds road 0.75
miles from town centre.
Parkland course.
Pro G Moore; Founded 1922
9 holes, 5902 yards, S.S.S. 69
🚩 Welcome WD; with member at
WE.
⛳ WD £11 with member £16 without.
☞ Welcome by arrangement with
Sec; full day packages available; terms
on application.
🍽 Full clubhouse facilities.

8A 70 Harrogate ☎
Forest Lane Head, Harrogate, N Yorks,
HG2 7TF
🖥 www.harrogate-gc.co.uk
✉ secretary@harrogate-gc.co.uk
☎ 01423 863158, Fax 860073,
Pro 862547, Sec 862999,
Rest/Bar 863158
On A59 betwen Knaresborough and
Harrogate.
Parkland course.
Pro Paul Johnson
Founded 1892
Designed by Sandy Herd; revised by
Dr A McKenzie
19 holes, 6241 yards, S.S.S. 70
🏌 Practice ground available.
🚩 Welcome by arrangement.
⛳ WD £36 per round/day; WE £40.
☞ Welcome by prior arrangement;
packages can be arranged; min 12.
🍽 Bar and restaurant.
🛏 Local tourist board can provide
brochures.

8A 71 Headingley
Back Church Lane, Adel, Leeds,
LS16 8DW
☎ 0113 2679573, Fax 2817334,
Pro 2675100, Sec 2679573,
Rest/Bar 2673052
Course is off the A660 Leeds to Otley
road.
Undulating parkland course.
Pro Neil Harvey
Founded 1892
18 holes, 6298 yards, S.S.S. 70
🏌 Practice area.
🚩 Welcome by prior arrangement.
⛳ WD £30; WE £40.
☞ Welcome by arrangement with the
manager; day ticket WD £35; snooker;
terms available on application.
🍽 Full facilities.
🛏 Village Hotel.

8A 72 Headley
Headley Lane, Thornton, Bradford,
W Yorks, BD13 3LX
☎ 01274 833481, Fax 833481
4 miles W of Bradford on B6145 in
Thornton village.
Moorland course.
Founded 1907
9 holes, 5253 yards, S.S.S. 64
🏌 Practice range and green
🚩 Welcome WD.
⛳ WD £15.
☞ Welcome by arrangement with
Sec; special golf and catering
packages available.
🍽 Dining room and bar.
🛏 Guide Post.

8A 73 Hebden Bridge

Wadsworth, Hebden Bridge,
HX7 8PH
☎ 01422 842896, Sec 843453
In Hebden Bridge, cross Keighley road,
up Birchcliffe Hill to top, turn left then
immediately right.
Upland course on edge of moor.
Founded 1930
9 holes, 5242 yards, S.S.S. 65
♦ Welcome by prior arrangement.
[WD £12; WE £15.
♦ Welcome, preferably on Wed; from
£12.
◎ Clubhouse facilities.
◄ Carlton; White Lion.

8A 74 Hessle

Westfield Road, Raywell, Cottingham,
Hull, E Yorks, HU16 5YL
♣ www.hessle-golf-club.co.uk
✉ secretary@hessle-golf-club.co.uk
☎ 01482 650171, Fax 652679,
Pro 650190, Rest/Bar 659187,
Bar Caterers 659457
Course is 3 miles SW of Cottingham
off the A164.
Undulating meadowland; new course
1975.
Pro Grahame Fieldsend
Founded 1898
Designed by Peter Alliss & Dave
Thomas
18 holes, 6604 yards, S.S.S. 72
♦ Welcome except Tues 9.am-1pm
or before 11.30am at WE.
[WD £25; WE £32.
♦ Welcome by prior arrangement
with Sec; catering packages by
arrangement except Mon; terms on
application.
◎ Catering except Mon.
◄ Grange Park; Willoughby Manor.

8A 75 Heworth

Muncaster House, Muncastergate,
York, Yorks, YO31 9JX
☎ 01904 422389, Fax 422389,
Pro 422389, Sec 426156
On A1036 York to Malton road 1.5
miles NE of York city centre.
Parkland course.
Pro S Burdett
Founded 1911
11 holes, 6141 yards, S.S.S. 69
♦ Practice area.
♦ Welcome.
[WD £15; WE £20, £11 with
member.
♦ Welcome by prior arrangement;
full catering packages available
except Mon; terms available on
application.

◎ Full clubhouse bar and catering
except Mon.

8A 76 Hickleton ☎

Lidget Lane, Hickleton, Nr Doncaster,
S Yorks, DN5 7BE
♣ www.hickletongc.co.uk
☎ 01709 896081, Fax 896083,
Pro 888436, Sec 896081,
Rest/Bar 896081
On B6411 Thurnscoe road off the A635
Barnsley road; 4.5 miles from A1 (M)
Junction 37.
Parkland course.
Pro Paul Audsley; Founded 1909
Designed by Huggett, Coles & Dyer
18 holes, 6418 yards, S.S.S. 71
♦ Welcome by prior arrangement.
[WD £20; WE £27.
♦ Welcome by prior arrangement;
summer packages available; terms on
application.
◎ Bar, with cask beers, and
restaurant available.
◄ Ardsley House, Barnsley;
Doncaster Moat House.

8A 77 Hillsborough

Worrall Road, Sheffield, S Yorks,
S6 4BE
♣ www.hillsboroughgolfclub.co.uk
✉ louis.horsman@line1.net
☎ 0114 2349151, Fax 2349151,
Pro 2332666, Sec 2349151,
Rest/Bar 2349151
Off A6102 Sheffield to Manchester
road NW of the city just past Sheffield
Wed's football ground, turning right at
Horse and Jockey pub.
Undulating wooded parkland and
heathland.
Pro Louis Horsman; Founded 1920
Designed by T Williamson
18 holes, 6216 yards, S.S.S. 70
♦ Welcome WD and after 2pm at
WE.
[WD £30; WE £35.
♦ Welcome by prior arrangement
with Sec; larger groups can negotiate
rates; snooker; catering packages;
driving range; terms on application.
◎ Full restaurant and bar service.
◄ Queens Ground, Hillsborough;
Grosvenor, Tankersley Manor,
Tankersley.

8A 78 Hollins Hall Golf ☎
Course

Marriott Hollins Hall and Country Club,
Baildon, Shipley, W Yorks, BD17 7QW
♣ www.marriotthotels.com/lbags
☎ 01274 530053

On A6038, main road from Shipley to
Otley. 10 miles from Leeds, 6 miles
from Bradford.
First 9 holes flat, 2nd 9 holes hilly.
18 holes, blue 6671, white 6354,
yellow 6051, red 5433 yards
♦ Yes.
[£35.
♦ Yes.
◎ Café/restaurant.
◄ Hollins Hall Hotel.

8A 79 Hornsea ☎

Rolston Road, Hornsea, E Yorks,
HU18 1XG
♣ www.hornseagolfclub.cwc.net
✉ hornseagolfclub@aol.com
☎ 01964 532020, Fax 532080,
Pro 534989, Rest/Bar 534524
Follow signs to Hornsea Free Port.
Club is 200 yards past port.
Parkland course.
Pro Stretton Wright; Founded 1898
Designed by Harry Vardon/Dr
McKenzie/J Braid
18 holes, 6421 yards, S.S.S. 72
♦ Practice area.
♦ Welcome WD and after 3pm Sat
and 2pm Sun.
[WD £26 or £34 for the day; Sat
£34 and Sun £26 per round.
♦ Welcome by prior arrangement;
packages available prices on
application.
◎ Full clubhouse facilities.
◄ Burton Lodge, Brandesburton;
Merlstead, Hornsea.

8A 80 Horsforth ☎

Layton Rise, Horsforth, Leeds,
W Yorks, LS18 5EX
♣ www.horsforthgolfclubltd.co.uk
✉ secretary@horsforthgolfclubltd.co.uk
☎ 0113 2586819, Fax 2589336,
Pro 2585200, Rest/Bar 2581703
Off A65 towards Ilkley 6 miles from city
centre.
Upland/parkland course.
Pro Dean Stokes/Simon Booth;
Founded 1906
Designed by Alistair McKenzie
18 holes, 6205 yards, S.S.S. 70
♦ Large practice ground.
♦ Welcome WD; WE by prior
arrangement.
[WD £26; WE £36. Mon-Fri 2 for 1
on golf and Daily Telegraph.
♦ Welcome WD by prior
arrangement; full packages of golf and
catering available.
◎ Full clubhouse facilities and off-site
meeting facilities.
◄ The Parkway.

8A 81 Howley Hall ☏
Scotchman Lane, Morley, Leeds,
W Yorks, LS27 0NX
www.howleyhall.co.uk
office@howleyhall.co.uk
☎ 01924 350100, Fax 350104,
Pro 350102, Rest/Bar 350107
Course is on the B6123 0.75 miles
from junction with the A650 at Halfway
House pub.
Parkland course.
Pro Gary Watkinson; Founded 1900
18 holes, 6346 yards, S.S.S. 71
† Welcome.
 WD £30; WE £40.
 Welcome by prior arrangement;
catering packages available on
application; from £29.
 Full clubhouse facilities.

8A 82 Huddersfield (Fixby) ☏
Fixby Hall, Lightridge Road,
Huddersfield, W Yorks, HD2 2EP
www.huddersfield-golf.co.uk
secretary@huddersfield-golf
.co.uk
☎ 01484 426203, Fax 424623,
Pro 426463, Sec 426203,
Rest/Bar 420110
From M62 Junction 24 follow signs to
Brighouse; turn right at traffic lights.
Parkland course.
Pro Paul Carman; Founded 1891
Designed by Herbert Fowler,
amendments by Hawtree.
18 holes, 6467 yards, S.S.S. 71
† Welcome; handicap certs required.
 WD £37; WE £47.
 Welcome WD except Tues; full
packages available; from £45.
 Full clubhouse bar, restaurant and
conference facilities.
 Cedar Court.

8A 83 Hull
The Hall, 27 Packman Lane, Kirkella,
Hull, E Yorks, HU10 7TJ
☎ 01482 658919, Fax 658919,
Pro 653074, Sec 658919,
Rest/Bar 653026
5 miles W of Hull.
Parkland course.
Pro David Jagger; Founded 1904
Designed by James Braid
18 holes, 6246 yards, S.S.S. 70
† Welcome by prior arrangement;
with member at WE.
 WD £26.50 per round, £32 per full
day.
 Welcome by prior arrangement;
terms available on application.
 Full clubhouse facilities.
 Willerby Manor; Grange Park.

8A 84 Ilkley ☏
Nesfield Road, Myddleton, Ilkley,
W Yorks, LS29 0BE
www.ilkleygolfclub.co.uk
honsec@ilkleygolfclub.co.uk
☎ 01943 600214, Fax 816130,
Pro 607463, Rest/Bar 607277
15 miles N of Bradford.
Parkland course.
Pro John Hammond; Founded 1890
Designed by Alistair Mackenzie
18 holes, 6262 yards, S.S.S. 70
† Welcome by arrangement;
handicap certs required.
 WD £42; WE/BH £50.
 Welcome by arrangement.
 Full clubhouse facilities.
 Devonshire Arms Country Hotel.

8A 85 Keighley ☏
Howden Park, Utley, Keighley,
W Yorks, BD20 6DH
www.keighleygolfclub.com
manager@keighleygolfclub.com
☎ 01535 604778, Fax 604833,
Pro 665370, Rest/Bar 603179
1 mile W of Keighley on the old
Keighley-Skipton road.
Parkland course.
Pro Mike Bradley; Founded 1904
18 holes, 6141 yards, S.S.S. 70
† Welcome except before 9.30am
and between 12 00pm-1.30pm WD;
Ladies day Tues; not Sat; by prior
arrangement Sun.
 WD £32; WE and BH £36.
 Welcome by prior arrangement
with the manager; day rates available;
catering by arrangement; terms on
application.
 Full bar and catering facilities
available every day; à la carte menu.
 Dales Gate.

8A 86 Kilnwick Percy ☏
Pocklington, E Yorks, YO42 1UF
☎ 01759 303090, Pro 303090,
Sec 303090, Rest/Bar 303090
1 mile E of Pocklington off the
B1246.
Parkland course.
Pro Joe Townhill; Founded 1994
Designed by John Day
18 holes, 6218 yards, S.S.S. 70
† Welcome any time.
 WD £18; WE £20; full day: WD
£25, WE £28.
 Welcome by prior arrangement;
terms on application.
 Snack menu, full catering service
available for societies by prior
arrangement.
 Yorkway Motel.

8A 87 Kirkbymoorside ☏
Manor Vale, Kirkbymoorside, York,
YO62 6EG
www.kirkbymoorsidegolf.co.uk
enqs@kirkbymoorsidegolf.co.uk
☎ 01751 431525, Fax 433190,
Pro 430402, Sec 431525
Course is on the A170 N of
Kirkbymoorside.
Parkland course; club moved to site
1953.
Pro John Hinchcliffe; Founded 1905/53
Designed by TK Cotton
18 holes, 6207 yards, S.S.S. 69
† Welcome after 9.00am.
 WD £22/round/ £28/day; WE £32.
 Welcome by prior arrangement;
packages available for golf and
catering; £29.50.
 Full clubhouse facilities available.
 George & Dragon; Kings Head,
both Kirkbymoorside.

8A 88 Knaresborough
Butterhills, Boroughbridge Road,
N Yorks, HG5 0QQ
knaresboroughgolfclub
@btopenworld.com
☎ 01423 862690, Fax 869345,
Pro 864865, Sec 862690,
Rest/Bar 863219
On A6055 Boroughbridge Road 2 miles
outside Knaresborough.
Parkland course with extensive trees.
Pro Gary J Vickers; Founded 1920
Designed by Hawtree & Son
18 holes, 6354 yards, S.S.S. 70
 Extensive practice facilities and
tuition available.
† Welcome after 9.30am WD and
noon WE; during winter season visitors
must be accompanied by a member on
WE.
 WD £28.50; WE £35.50.
 Welcome by prior arrangement
between April 1 and Oct 31; parties of
12 or more welcome; full day golf and
catering packages available from £40.
 Full restaurant and bar facilities.
 Ashley House Hotel, Harrogate.

8A 89 Leeds (Cobble Hall) ☏
Elemete Lane, Leeds, W Yorks, LS8 2LJ
www.leedsgolfclub.com
☎ 0113 2658775, Fax 2323369,
Pro 2658786, Sec 2659203
On A58 Leeds-Wetherby road.
Parkland course, views of Rounday
Park.
Pro Simon Longster; Founded 1896
18 holes, 6092 yards, S.S.S. 69
† Welcome WD by prior
arrangement.

WD £30; £35 for day.
Welcome by prior arrangement; packages available; terms on application.
Full catering facilities.
Holiday Inn, special rates available.

8A 90 Leeds Golf Centre
Wike Ridge Lane, Shadwell, Leeds, W Yorks, LS17 9JW
www.leedsgolfcentre.com
0113 2886000, Fax 2886185, Pro 2886000, Sec 2886000, Rest/Bar 2886160
Just off A61 Harrogate Road, 5 miles N of Leeds.
Open heathland course.
Pro N Harvey, M Pinkett; Founded 1993
Designed by Donald Steel
18 holes, 6482 yards off the white 5963 yards off the yellow, S.S.S. 71
20 covered floodlit.
Everyone welcome.
WD £15; WE £20.
Welcome; restricted numbers at WE; golf and catering packages are available; also the 12-hole Oaks course and corporate tuition sessions.
Full facilities.
Harewood Arms; Weetwood Hall, both Leeds; Ramada Jarvis, Wetherby.

8A 91 Lees Hall
Hemsworth Road, Norton, Sheffield, S8 9LI
0114 2554402, Fax 2552900, Pro 2507868, Sec 2552900, Rest/Bar 2551526
3 miles S of Sheffield.
Parkland course.
Pro Simon Berry; Founded 1907
18 holes, 6171 yards, S.S.S. 70
Welcome.
WD £20; WE £30.
Welcome WD by prior arrangement; catering packages by arrangement; snooker; terms on application.
Full facilities except Mon.
Grosvenor; Holiday Inn; Sheffield Moat House.

8A 92 Lightcliffe
Knowle Top Road, Lightcliffe, Halifax, W Yorks, HX3 8SE
01422 202459, Pro 204081, Sec 204081
Course is on the A58 Leeds-Halifax road.
Parkland course.
Pro Robert Kershaw; Founded 1907
9 holes, 5826 yards, S.S.S. 68

Practice green.
Welcome except on Wed and competition days.
WD £10; WE £15.
Welcome by prior arrangement; terms on application.
Full clubhouse facilities.
Trust House, Brighouse.

8A 93 Lofthouse Hill
Leeds Road, Lofthouse, Wakefield, WF3 3LR
www.lhgc.co.uk
01924 823703, Fax 823703, Pro 823703, Sec 823703, Rest/Bar 823703
Course is off the A61 four miles from Wakefield.
Parkland course.
Pro Derek Johnson; Founded 1994
Designed by BJ Design
18 holes, 5933 yards, S.S.S. 68
8 floodlit.
Welcome.
WD/WE £10.
Welcome.
Bar and catering facilities available.
Stanley View Guest House.

8A 94 Longley Park
Maple Street, Off Somerset Road, Huddersfield, W Yorks, HD5 9AX
01484 426932, Pro 422303, Sec 426932, Rest/Bar 426932
0.5 miles from Town centre.
Parkland course.
Pro Nick Leeming; Founded 1911
9 holes, 5269 yards, S.S.S. 66
Welcome WD; restricted WE.
WD £13; WE £16.
Welcome by arrangement except Thurs and Sat; catering by arrangement; terms available on application.
Full facilities except Mon.
George, Huddersfield

8A 95 Low Laithes
Parkmill Lane, Flushdyke, Ossett, W Yorks, WF5 9AP
www.lowlaithes.com
01924 273275, Fax 266067, Pro 274667, Sec 266067, Rest/Bar 273275/ 267517
Close to M1 Junction 40 off A638 towards Dewsbury; turn right at end of slip road.
Parkland course.
Pro Paul Browning
Founded 1925
Designed by MacKenzie

18 holes, 6463 yards, S.S.S. 71
Welcome WD after 9.30am and not between 12.30pm-1.30pm; WE by prior arrangement with the club Professional.
WD £22 per round, £25 per day. WE £36.
Welcome WD by prior arrangement; package includes 27 holes and full catering; £33.
Full clubhouse facilities.
Post House; Mews House, both Ossett.

8A 96 Malton & Norton
Welham Park, Malton, N Yorks, YO17 9QE
www.maltonandnortongolfclub.co.uk
maltonandnorton@btconnect.com
01653 697912, Fax 697912, Pro 693882, Sec 697912, Rest/Bar 692959
From York take the A64 to the centre of Malton, right at traffic lights and right at rail crossing; club is 0.75 miles.
Parkland course.
Pro Sl Robinson; Founded 1910
Designed by Hawtree & Son
27 (3 loops of 9) holes, Welham: 6456. Park: 6251. Derwent: 6295 yards; S.S.S. Welham: 71. Park 70. Derwent 70
Driving range.
Welcome.
WD £25; WE £30.
Welcome by prior arrangement; full catering packages available. All day catering package available from £17.50.
Full clubhouse facilities.
Many in local area.

8A 97 Marsden
Mount Rd, Hemplow, Marsden, Huddersfield, W Yorks, HD7 6NN
stephen.bousted@tesco.net
01484 844253, Pro 843300, Sec 01457 874158, Rest/Bar 844253
Course is off the A62 eight miles from Huddersfield.
Moorland course.
Pro Ron Johnson; Founded 1920
Designed by Dr A MacKenzie
9 holes, 5702 yards, S.S.S. 68
Welcome WD.
WD £10.
Welcome WD by arrangement; packages available; terms on application.
Clubhouse facilities except Tues.
Durker Roods, Meltham.

8A 98 **Masham**

Burnholme, Swinton Rd, Masham,
Ripon, N Yorks, HG4 4HT
☎ 01765 689379
Off A6108 10 miles N of Ripon.
Meadowland course.
Founded 1895
9 holes, 6068 yards, S.S.S. 70
♦ Welcome WD; with a member at
WE.
♦ WD £15 (18 holes), £20 for day, up
to 3 guests with member only £10 each.
♦ Welcome by arrangement with
Sec; catering packages available; from
£15.
♦ Full clubhouse facilities.
♦ Swinton Park Hotel; Kings Head;
Bay Horse; White Bear; Bruce Arms,
all in Masham.

8A 99 **Meltham**

Thick Hollins Hall, Meltham,
Huddersfield, W Yorks, HD9 4DQ
☎ 01484 850227, Fax 859051,
Pro 851521
On B6107 6 miles SW of
Huddersfield.
Parkland course.
Pro PF Davies; Founded 1908
21 holes, 6305 yards, S.S.S. 70
♦ Welcome except Wed and Sat.
♦ WD £25; WE £30.
♦ Welcome by prior arrangement; full
catering packages available; terms on
application.
♦ Full clubhouse facilities.
♦ Durker Roods Hall.

8A 100 **Mid Yorkshire**

Havercroft Lane, Darrington, Nr
Pontefract, Yorks, WF8 3BP
☎ 01977 704522, Fax 600823,
Pro 600844, Sec 704522,
Rest/Bar 704522
400 yards on A1 S from the M62/A1
intersection.
Parkland course.
Pro James Major; Founded 1993
Designed by Steve Marnoch
18 holes, 6466 yards, S.S.S. 71
♦ 22 floodlit.
♦ Welcome WD; restrictions on WE
mornings.
♦ WD £15 per round, day tickets
available. WE £25.
♦ Welcome WD; WE between 1pm-
4.30pm by prior arrangement;
conference facilities; catering packages
by arrangement; golf clinic; terms on
application.
♦ Bar and restaurant facilities
available.
♦ Darrington.

8A 101 **Middleton Park**

Ring Road, Beeston, Leeds, W Yorks,
LS10 3TN
✉ lynn@ratcliffel.fsnet.co.uk
☎ 0113 2700449, Pro 2709506
3 miles S of city centre.
Public parkland course.
Pro Jim Pape; Founded 1932
Designed by Leeds City Council
18 holes, 4947 yards, S.S.S. 69
♦ Welcome WD; book at WE.
♦ WD/WE £10.60.
♦ Welcome by arrangement.
♦ Limited.

8A 102 **Moor Allerton** ☎

Coal Road, Wike, Leeds, W Yorks,
LS17 9NH
⌨ www.moorallertongolfclub.co.uk
✉ enquiries@magc.co.uk
☎ 0113 2661154, Fax 2371124,
Pro 2665209, Sec 2661154,
Rest/Bar 2682225
5 miles from Leeds off A61 Harrogate
road.
Parkland course.
Pro Richard Lane; Founded 1923
Designed by Robert Trent Jones, Sr.
27 holes (3 x 9 loops), High: 6841.
Lakes: 6470. Blackmoor: 6673 yards;
S.S.S. High: 74. Lakes 72. Blackmoor:
73.
♦ 7.
♦ Very welcome by prior
arrangement.
♦ WD £49; WE £65.
♦ Welcome by prior arrangement; tee
times reserved for groups of 12 or
more; reductions Nov-March. Special
Twilight packages and Winter Warmers.
♦ Full clubhouse facilities for parties
up to 200.
♦ Club can provide list of
recommended hotels and preferred
rates.

8A 103 **Moortown**

Harrogate Road, Leeds, W Yorks,
LS17 7DB
⌨ www.moortown-gc.co.uk
✉ secretary@moortown-gc.co.uk
☎ 0113 268 6521, Fax 0986,
Pro 3636, Rest 8746, Bar 1682
On A61 Harrogate road 1 mile past
outer ring road.
Moorland course.
Pro Martin Heggie; Founded 1909
Designed by Dr A MacKenzie
18 holes, 6995 yards off the blue, 6757
yards off the white, S.S.S. 73
♦ Welcome by prior arrangement.
♦ WD £65; WE and BH £75 (round
or day).

♦ Welcome by prior arrangement.
♦ Full clubhouse restaurant and bar
facilities.
♦ Harewood Arms and others in
Leeds area.

8A 104 **Normanton**

Hatfield Hall, Aberford Road, Stanley,
Wakefield, WF3 4JP
⌨ www.normantongolf.co.uk
✉ fhoulgate@freenet.co.uk
☎ 01924 200900, Fax 200009,
Pro 200900, Sec 377943,
Rest/Bar 377943
Off M62 Junction 30; A642 1,7 miles
towards Wakefield turn right.
Parkland course.
Pro Frank Houlgate; Founded 1903
18 holes, 6205 yards, S.S.S. 71
♦ Mon–Fri.
♦ WD £26; unlimited 2 for 1
available.
♦ Welcome WD by prior
arrangement.
♦ Full facilities.
♦ Oulton Hall.

8A 105 **Northcliffe**

High Bank Lane, Shipley, W Yorks,
BD18 4LJ
⌨ www.northcliffegolfclubshipley.
co.uk
✉ northcliffe@bigfoot.com
☎ 01274 584085, Fax 584148,
Pro 587193, Sec 596731,
Rest/Bar 584085
On A650 W of Bradford to Saltaire
roundabout.
Undulating parkland course.
Pro M Hillas; Founded 1920
Designed by James Braid/Harry
Vardon
18 holes, 6113 yards, S.S.S. 71
♦ 6.
♦ Welcome by prior arrangement.
♦ WD £25; WE £30.
♦ Welcome by prior arrangement; full
day's catering and golf package; £40.
♦ Full clubhouse facilities.
♦ Bankfield Hotel, Bingley.

8A 106 **Oakdale**

Oakdale, Harrogate, Yorks, HG1 2LN
⌨ www.oakdale-golfclub.com
✉ sec@oakdale-golfclub.com
☎ 01423 567162, Fax 536030,
Pro 560510, Sec 567162,
Rest/Bar 502806
Turn into Kent Road from Ripon Road
in Harrogate.
Undulating parkland with panoramic
views.

Pro Clive Dell; Founded 1914
Designed by Dr A MacKenzie
18 holes, 6456 yards, S.S.S. 71
♦ Welcome.
� Terms on application.
⚸ Welcome WD by prior
arrangement; catering packages by
arrangement; terms available on
application.
🍴 Full facilities except Mon
lunchtime.
🛏 Crown; Majestic; Studley; Old
Swan; Balmoral; Cedar Court.

8A 107 The Oaks

Aughton Common, Aughton, York,
Yorks, YO42 4PW
🖳 www.theoaksgolfclub.co.uk
📧 oaksgolfclub@hotmail.com
☎ 01757 288577, Fax 288232,
Pro 288007 same no for tee booking,
Sec 288577, Rest/Bar 288001
On the B1228 1 mile N of Bubwith.
Wooded parkland course with 6
lakes.
Pro Jo Townhill; Founded 1996
Designed by J Covey
18 holes, 6743 yards, S.S.S. 72
⛳ 6.
♦ Public welcome weekdays.
Members and their guests only at
weekends. Accommodation available.
⌳ WD £25.
⚸ Welcome WD by arrangement;
packages of golf and catering
available; from £34.
🍴 Full bar and catering service; à la
carte restaurant.
🛏 Holiday cottages available.

8A 108 Otley

West Busk Lane, Otley, W Yorks,
LS21 3NG
🖳 www.otley-golfclub.co.uk
📧 office@otley-golfclub.co.uk
☎ 01943 465329, Fax 850387
Off A6038 on the outskirts of the
market town of Otley between Leeds
and Bradford.
Parkland course.
Pro Steven Tomkinso
Founded 1906
18 holes, 6245 yards, S.S.S. 70
♦ Welcome except Sat.
⌳ WD £30; WE £37.
⚸ Welcome WD by prior
arrangement with Sec; packages by
arrangement with Sec; terms on
application.
🍴 Full clubhouse bar and catering
facilities.
🛏 Chevin Lodge, Otley; Jarvis
Parkway, Leeds; The Grove, Ilkley.

8A 109 Oulton Park

Pennington Lane, Rothwell, Leeds,
LS26 8EX
☎ 0113 2823152, Fax 2826290,
Pro 2823152
Off M62 Junction 30, take the A642
to Rothwell, left at the second
roundabout.
Parkland course.
Pro Steve Gromett
Founded 1990
Designed by Peter Alliss & Dave
Thomas
27 holes, 6470 yards, S.S.S. 71
⛳ 22.
♦ Welcome by prior arrangement.
⌳ WD £11; WE £14.50.
⚸ Welcome WD by arrangement; full
golf and catering packages available;
also a 3169 yards par 35 9-hole
course; terms available on
application.
🍴 Full clubhouse restaurant and bar
facilities.
🛏 5-star Oulton Hall on site.

8A 110 Outlane

Slack Lane, Outlane, Huddersfield,
W Yorks, HD3 3YL
☎ 01422 374762, Fax 311789,
Pro 374762, Sec 311789
From M62 take A640 to Rochdale, left
under the motorway through Outlane
village.
Moorland/parkland course.
Pro DM Chapman
Founded 1906
18 holes, 6015 yards, S.S.S. 69
♦ Welcome by prior arrangement.
⌳ WD £19; WE £29.
⚸ Welcome by prior arrangement;
package details available from Mrs
Caroline Hirst; terms available on
application.
🍴 Full clubhouse facilities.
🛏 Old Golf House, Outlane.

8A 111 Owston Park

Owston Lane, Owston, Nr Carcroft,
Doncaster, S Yorks, DN6 8EF
🖳 www.foremostonline.com
☎ 01302 330821
5 miles off A19 near Doncaster.
9-hole play and play.
Founded 1988
Designed by Mike Parker
9 holes, 6148 yards, S.S.S. 71
⛳ Putting green.
♦ Welcome; pay and play.
⌳ WD £4.60; WE £4.85, OAP/Jun
under 16 £3.90 WD/WE.
⚸ No facilities.
🍴 Very limited.

8A 112 Painthorpe House

Golf & Country Club, Painthorpe Lane,
Crigglestone, Wakefield, WF4 3HE
☎ 01924 255083, Fax 252022, Sec
254737
Close to M1 Junction 39.
Undulating parkland course.
Founded 1961
9 holes, 4548 yards, S.S.S. 62
♦ Welcome; after 13.30 Sun.
⌳ WD £6; WE £7.
⚸ Welcome by arrangement; terms
on application.
🍴 Extensive facilities including four
bars, two ballrooms and a function
room.

8A 113 Pannal

Follifoot Road, Pannal, Harrogate,
Yorks, HG3 1ES
🖳 www.pannalgc.co.uk
📧 secretary@pannalgc.co.uk
☎ 01423 871641, Fax 870043,
Pro 872620, Sec 872628,
Rest/Bar 872629
Off A61 Leeds-Harrogate road 3 miles
S of Harrogate.
Moorland/parkland course.
Pro David Padgett; Founded 1906
Designed by Sandy Herd
18 holes, 6622 yards, S.S.S. 72
⛳ 12.
♦ Welcome by prior arrangement
only.
⌳ WD £41; WE £51.
⚸ Welcome by prior arrangement;
catering can be arranged; terms on
application.
🍴 Full clubhouse bar and catering
facilities.
🛏 Majestic, Harrogate.

8A 114 Phoenix

Pavilion Lane, Brinsworth, Rotherham,
S Yorks, S60 5PA
☎ 01709 363688, Fax 363788, Pro
382624
From M1 J24 towards Bawtry for
approx. 1 mile.
Undulating meadowland course.
Pro M Roberts; Founded 1932
18 holes, 6181 yards, S.S.S. 70
⛳ 20 covered.
♦ Welcome.
⌳ Terms on application.
⚸ Welcome WD by prior
arrangement; packages for golf and
catering available; from £24.
🍴 Full catering facilities.

8A 115 Phoenix Park

Phoenix Park, Dick Lane, Thornbury,
Bradford, W Yorks, BD3 7AT
☎ 01132 561694

Off A647 Bradford to Leeds road at Thornbury roundabout.
Undulating parkland course.
9 holes, 4646 yards, S.S.S. 66
⚑ Welcome WD only.
Ⅰ Terms on application.
⌾ Welcome by prior arrangement; terms on application.
⎆ Catering available by prior arrangement.

8A 116 **Pike Hills** ☏
Tadcaster Road, Askham Bryan, York, Yorks, YO23 3UW
✉ thesecretary@pikehills.fsnet.co.uk
☎ 01904 706566, Fax 700797, Pro 708756, Sec 700797, Rest/Bar 704416
On A64 4 miles W of York on eastbound carriageway.
Parkland course.
Pro I Gradwell; Founded 1904
18 holes, 6146 yards, S.S.S. 69
⚑ Welcome WD; only with member at WE.
Ⅰ WD £22.
⌾ Welcome by prior arrangement; packages include full catering and 36 holes of golf; £35.
⎆ Full clubhouse facilities.

8A 117 **Pontefract & District**
Park Lane, Pontefract, W Yorks, WF8 4QS
🖳 www.pdgc.co.uk
✉ manager@pdgc.co.uk
☎ 01977 792241, Fax 792241, Pro 706806, Mgr 792241, Rest/Bar 798886
Course is on the B6134 off the M62 Junction 32.
Parkland course.
Pro Nicholas Newman; Founded 1904
18 holes, 6232 yards, S.S.S. 70
⚑ Welcome WD; by prior arrangement WE.
Ⅰ WD £22 round, £28 day; WE £32.
⌾ Welcome WD except Wed; packages available; terms on application.
⎆ Full facilities.
⎌ Red Lion; Wentbridge House; Park Side Inn.

8A 118 **Pontefract Park**
Park Road, Pontefract, W Yorks
☎ 01977 723490
Close to Pontefract racecourse 0.5 miles from M62.
Public parkland course.
9 holes, 4068 yards, S.S.S. 62
⚑ Welcome.

Ⅰ WD £3.20; WE £3.20 (9 holes).
⌾ None.
⎆ None.

8A 119 **Queensbury**
Brighouse Road, Queensbury, Bradford, W Yorks, BD13 1QF
☎ 01274 882155, Fax 882155, Pro 816864,
Sec 882155, Rest/Bar 882155
From the M62 Junction 26 take the A58 towards Halifax for 3.5 miles then turn to Keighley for three miles; also via the A647, 4 miles from Bradford.
Undulating parkland course.
Pro Dave Delaney; Founded 1923
9 holes, 5024 yards, S.S.S. 65
⚑ Everyone welcome.
Ⅰ WD £15; WE £30.
⌾ Welcome by prior arrangement; packages available; function facilities; terms on application.
⎆ Full bar and à la carte restaurant service.
⎌ Novotel.

8A 120 **Rawdon**
Buckstone Drive, Rawdon, Leeds, W Yorks, LS19 6BD
☎ 0113 2506040, Pro 2505017, Sec 2506044
On A65 6 miles from Leeds turning left at Rawdon traffic lights.
Undulating parkland course.
Pro Craig Shackelton; Founded 1896
9 holes, 5982 yards, S.S.S. 69
⚑ Welcome WD.
Ⅰ Terms on application.
⌾ Welcome WD by prior arrangement; golf and catering packages available; 3 all-weather and 4 grass tennis courts.
⎆ Full facilities except Mon.
⎌ Peas Hill; Robin Hood; Travel Lodge.

8A 121 **Renishaw Park**
Golf House, Mill Lane, Renishaw, Sheffield, S Yorks, S21 3UZ
☎ 01246 432044, Fax 432116, Pro 435484, Rest/Bar rest ext 23 bar ext 22
1.5 miles W of the M1 Junction 30 on the A6135.
Parkland course.
Pro J Oates; Founded 1911
Designed by Sir G Sitwell and Edward Lutyens
18 holes, 6262 yards, S.S.S. 70
⚑ Welcome by arrangement.
Ⅰ WD £28; WE £42

⌾ Welcome by arrangement; packages on application.
⎆ Full clubhouse facilites.
⎌ Sitwell Arms.

8A 122 **Richmond** ☏
Bend Hagg, Richmond, N Yorks, DL10 5EX
☎ 01748 825319, Fax 821709, Pro 822457, Sec 823231, Rest/Bar 825319
From A1 Scotch Corner follow the Richmond road to lights in town; turn right.
Parkland course; extended to 18 in 1892.
Pro Paul Jackson; Founded 1892
Designed by Frank Pennink
18 holes, 5886 yards, S.S.S. 68
Ⅰ Large practice area.
⚑ Welcome, after 3.30pm on Sun.
Ⅰ WD £22; WE £25/round. WD £24; WE £30/day.
⌾ Welcome by prior arrangement; reduced rates for groups of 24+.
⎆ Full bar and restaurant facilities everyday.
⎌ Turf Hotel; Black Lion; Kings Head.

8A 123 **Riddlesden** ☏
Howden Rough, Riddlesden, Keighley, W Yorks, BD20 5QN
☎ 01535 602148, Sec 607646
From A650 Bradford road turn into Scott Lane.
Moorland course.
Founded 1927
18 holes, 4295 yards, S.S.S. 63
⚑ Welcome.
Ⅰ WD £12; WE £16.
⌾ Welcome on WD by prior arrangement; terms available on application.
⎆ Clubhouse facilities.
⎌ Dalesgate Hotel.

8A 124 **Ripon City**
Palace Road, Ripon, N Yorks, HG4 3HH
☎ 01765 601987, Pro 600411, Sec 603640, Rest/Bar 603640
Course is on A6108 1 mile N of Ripon.
Undulating parkland course.
Pro Tim Davis; Founded 1908
New 9 holes designed by ADAS
18 holes, 6120 yards, S.S.S. 69
⚑ Welcome with handicap certs preferred.
Ⅰ WD £20; WE £30.
⌾ Welcome by arrangement; packages available for groups of more than 20.

Full clubhouse facilities.
Nags Head; Kirkgate House both Thirsk.

8A 125 Owston Hall Hotel and GC – "The Robin Hood Golf Course"
Owston Hall, Owston, Nr Carcroft, Doncaster, S Yorks, DN6 9JF
www.owstonhall.com
enquiries@owstonhall.com
01302 722800, Bookings 722231, Fax 728885, Pro 722231, Sec 722231, Rest/Bar 722800
6 miles N of Doncaster on B1220 off the A19.
Parkland course; championship course, "Home to the PGA Euro-Pro Tour".
Pro Jason Laszkowicz; Founded 1988/1996
Designed by W Adamson
18 holes, 6937 yards, S.S.S. 72
Practice ground, short game area.
Welcome.
WD £16; WE £22.
Welcome by prior arrangement; full catering packages available for 12 or more players; free golf cart available for groups of more than 20; function room with facilities for 60-100 people.
Full restaurant and bar facilities in 18th century clubhouse.
Accommodation and health suite on site.

8A 126 Romanby
Yafforth Road, Northallerton, N Yorks, DL7 0PE
01609 778855, Fax 779084
Course is on the B6271 Northallerton-Richmond road one mile NW of Northallerton.
Parkland course.
Pro Tim Jenkins; Founded 1993
Designed by W Adamson
18 holes; 6663 yards, S.S.S. 72; plus 6 hole academy course
12.
Welcome.
WD £20; WE £25.
Welcome 7 days; Premier Tee and Silver Tee packages available; from £26.50.
Full clubhouse bar and restaurant facilities.
Golden Lion.

8A 127 Rother Valley
Mansfield Road, Wales Bar, Sheffield, Yorks, S31 8PE

0114 2473000, Fax 2476000
Course is between Sheffield and Rotherham off the M1 Junction 31; follow the signs for Rother Valley country park.
Parkland with water features.
Pro Jason Ripley; Founded 1996
Designed by M Roe/M Shattock.
18 holes, 6602 yards, S.S.S. 72
Welcome.
WD £11 (£7.50 Mon); WE £16.
Welcome at all times; packages include catering, golf and use of driving range; par 3 course; £10-£30.
Restaurant and bar facilities available.

8A 128 Rotherham
Thrybergh Park, Doncaster Road, Thrybergh, Rotherham, S Yorks, S65 4NU
www.rotherhamgolf.co.uk
gerry@rotherhamgolf.plus.com
01709 850466, Fax 859517, Pro 850480
On A630 Doncaster to Rotherham Road.
Parkland course.
Pro Simon Thornhill; Founded 1903
18 holes, 6324 yards, S.S.S. 70
Welcome by arrangement with Pro or Sec.
Terms on application.
Welcome except Wed by prior arrangement with Sec; minimum 16; discounts for groups of 40 or more; snooker; terms on application.
Full facilities.
The Courtyard; Moat House; Limes; Brecon.

8A 129 Roundhay
Park Lane, Leeds, Yorks, LS8 2EJ
0113 266 2695, Fax 266 1686, Pro 266 1686, Sec 266 4225
4.5 miles from city centre on A58 to Wetherby.
Parkland with mature trees.
Pro Jim Pape; Founded 1922
9 holes, 5322 yards, S.S.S. 65
Municipal pay and play.
WD £9.50; WE £10.50.
Welcome by arrangement with Pro; packages available on application; from £8.50.
Catering available in restaurant in evenings Tues-Sat; bar.
Beechwood.

8A 130 Roundwood
Off Green Lane, Rawmarsh, Rotherham, S Yorks, S62 6LA

01709 826061, Fax 523478, Sec 525208
Course is off the A633 2.5 miles N of Rotherham.
Parkland course.
Founded 1977
18 holes, 5713 yards, S.S.S. 67
Welcome except WD mornings.
WD £15; WE £20.
Welcome WD by prior arrangement; packages available; terms on application.
Bar facilities; catering Wed to Sat.

8A 131 Rudding Park
Follifoot, Harrogate, N Yorks, HG3 1DJ
www.ruddingpark.com
golf@ruddingpark.com
01423 872100, Fax 873011, Pro 873400
Off A658 Harrogate by-pass 2 miles S of Harrogate.
Parkland course.
Pro Mark Moore, Neil Moore, Rob Hobkinson, Dave Fountain; Founded 1995
Designed by Hawtree
18 holes, 6883 yards, S.S.S. 73
18 covered.
Welcome with handicap certs.
Winter (20 March): £17 Mon-Thurs, £21 Fri-Sun. Summer (March-Oct): £28.50 Mon-Thurs, £35 Fri-Sun.
Welcome with prior arrangement; packages available; terms on application.
Full clubhouse facilities.
Rudding Park.

8A 132 Ryburn
The Shaw, Norland, Sowerby Bridge, W Yorks, HX6 3QP
01422 831355, Sec 843070
3 miles S of Halifax.
Hilly moorland course.
Founded 1910
9 holes, 4907 yards, S.S.S. 65
Welcome WD; WE by arrangement.
WD £14; WE 20.
Welcome by prior arrangement; terms on application.
Catering and bar facilities.
The Hobbit Inn.

8A 133 Sand Moor
Alwoodley Lane, Leeds, W Yorks, LS17 7DJ
www.sandmoorgolf.co.uk
sandmoorgolf@btclick.com
0113 268 5180, Fax 266 1105, Pro 268 3925, Rest/Bar 268 1685/269 2718
6 miles from centre of Leeds on the A61 N.

Undulating parkland/moorland course.
Pro Frank Houlgate; Founded 1926
Designed by A MacKenzie
18 holes, 6414 yards, S.S.S. 71
⚐ Welcome WD, except 12 noon-
1.30pm, Tues 9.30am-10.30am and
Thurs 8.30am-12 noon.
⌑ WD £40.
⚲ Welcome WD by prior
arrangement; catering packages by
arrangement; terms available on
application.
◉ Full facilities.
⬱ Harewood Arms; Parkway; Forte
Crest.

8A 134 **Sandhill**
Middlecliffe Lane, Little Houghton,
Barnsley, S72 0HW
☎ 01226 753444, Fax 753444,
Rest/Bar 755079
Off A635 Barnsley-Doncaster road
near Darfield.
Parkland course.
Founded 1993
Designed by John Royston
18 holes, 6257 yards, S.S.S. 70
⌑ 18 floodlit.
⚐ Welcome.
⌑ WD £12; WE £16.
⚲ Welcome WD: not before 10am
Sat or 12 noon Sun; packages
available; terms on application.
◉ Full clubhouse facilities available.
⬱ Ardsley Moat House.

8A 135 **Scarborough North Cliff**
North Cliff Ave, Burniston Road,
Scarborough, YO12 6PP
⌕ www.ncgc.co.uk
✉ info@ncgc.co.uk
☎ 01723 360786, Fax 362134,
Pro 365920, Sec 367086
2 miles N of town centre on coast rd.
Seaside/parkland course.
Pro Simon Dellor; Founded 1928
Designed by James Braid
18 holes, 6425 yards, S.S.S. 71
⚐ Welcome except before 10am Sun.
⌑ WD £24; WE £28.
⚲ Welcome by prior arrangement
with Sec; packages for groups
between 8 and 40; catering packages
by arrangement; terms available on
application.
◉ Full facilities.
⬱ Park Manor; Headlands.

8A 136 **Scarborough South Cliff** ☏
Deepdale Avenue, Scarborough,
YO11 2UE

⌕ www.scarboroughgolfclub.co.uk
☎ 01723 360522, Fax 374737,
Pro 365150, Sec 374737
1 mile S of Scarborough on the main
Filey road.
Parkland/seaside course.
Pro Tony Skingle; Founded 1903
Designed by Dr A MacKenzie
18 holes, 6039 yards, S.S.S. 69
⌑ Large practice area.
⚐ Welcome.
⌑ Prices on application.
⚲ Welcome WD and WE by prior
arrangement; packages available;
terms on application.
◉ Full facilities.
⬱ Crown; St Nicholas; Southlands;
Mount House; Bradley Court.

8A 137 **Scarcroft**
Syke Lane, Scarcroft, Leeds, W Yorks,
LS14 3BQ
⌕ www.scarcroftgc.co.uk
✉ scarcroftgc@btconnect.com
☎ 0113 2892311, Pro 2892780,
Sec 2892311, Rest/Bar 2892263
Off A58 Leeds to Wetherby road
turning left at Bracken Fox public
house.
Parkland course.
Pro Darren Tear; Founded 1937
Designed by Robert Blackburn
18 holes, 6426 yards, S.S.S. 71
⌑ Driving range under construction.
⚐ Welcome; some WE restrictions.
⌑ WD £30; WE £40; party over 20
people call for price.
⚲ Welcome by prior arrangement;
packages available for all-day golf and
catering for groups of 20 or more; £40.
◉ Full clubhouse facilities.
⬱ Jarvis, Wetherby; Harewood Arms,
Harewood.

8A 138 **Scarthingwell**
Scarthingwell, Tadcaster, Yorks,
LS24 9PF
☎ 01937 557878, Fax 557909,
Pro 557864
Course is on the A162 three miles from
the A1 between Tadcaster and
Ferrybridge.
Parkland course.
Pro Steve Footman; Founded 1993
Designed by I Webster
18 holes, 6771 yards, S.S.S. 72
⚐ Welcome but prior booking
essential.
⌑ WD £16; WE £20.
⚲ Welcome by prior arrangement;
individual packages can be arranged;
summer and winter packages
available; terms on application.

◉ Full clubhouse facilities.
⬱ Hilton, Garforth; Selby Fork Hotel.

8A 139 **Selby**
Mill Lane, Brayton, Selby, N Yorks,
YO8 9LD
⌕ www.selbygolfclub.co.uk
✉ selbygolfclub@hotmail.com
☎ 01757 228622, Fax 228622,
Pro 228785, Sec 228622, Rest/Bar
228590, 228226
3 miles SW of Selby; 1 mile W of A19
at Brayton village.
Links course.
Pro Nick Ludwell; Founded 1907
Designed by JH Taylor & Hawtree Ltd,
Donald Steel & Co
18 holes, 6374 yards, S.S.S. 71
⚐ Welcome WD with handicap certs;
WE with member.
⌑ WD £30 per round, £35 for day.
⚲ Welcome Mon, Thurs and Fri by
prior arrangement; catering packages
by arrangement; snooker; terms on
application.
◉ Full facilities.
⬱ Londesbro; Selby Fork Motel; The
Owl.

8A 140 **Serlby Park**
Serlby, Doncaster, S Yorks,
DN10 6BA
☎ 01777 818268, Sec 818268,
Rest/Bar 818268
3 miles S of Bawtry.
Parkland course.
Founded 1906
Designed by Viscount Galway
9 holes, 5376 yards, S.S.S. 66
⚐ Welcome only with member.
⌑ Guests with members only.
⚲ Welcome only by prior
arrangement with Sec; terms on
application.
◉ Clubhouse facilities.
⬱ Crown, Bawtry; Mount Pleasant,
between Bawtry and Doncaster; Olde
Bell, Barnaby Moor.

8A 141 **Settle**
Buckhaw Brow, Settle, Yorks,
BD24 0DH
⌕ www.settlegolfclub.com
☎ 01729 825288, Sec 825288,
Rest/Bar 825288
Course is on Kendal Road one mile
beyond town.
Parkland course.
Founded 1895
Designed by Tom Vardon
9 holes, 6089 yards, S.S.S. 72
⚐ Welcome except Sun.

 WD £15; WE £15.
 Welcome by prior arrangement; terms on application.
 Clubhouse facilities available for limited catering.
 Falcon Hotel, Settle; Royal Oak, Settle.

8A 142 The Shay Grange Golf Centre

Long Lane, off Bingley Road, Bradford, W Yorks, BD9 6RX
☎ 01274 491945, Fax 491547
Course is off the A650 Bradford road at Cottingley.
Parkland course.
Pro Peter Tupling; Founded 1996
Designed by Tim Colclough
9 holes, 3380 yards, S.S.S. 58
 32.
 Pay and play.
 WD £7; WE £8.
 Welcome by prior arrangement; discounts available including golf and meals at our bistro.
 Limited.
 Jarvis Bankfield.

8A 143 The Shipley ☏

Beckfoot Lane, Cottingley Bridge, Bingley, W Yorks, BD16 1LX
 www.shipleygc.co.uk
 professional@shipleygc.co.uk
☎ 01274 563212, Fax 567739,
Pro 563674 ext 21, Sec 568652,
Rest/Bar 563674 ext 22
On A650 6 miles N of Bradford.
Parkland course.
Pro JR Parry; Founded 1896
Designed by Colt, Alison and Dr MacKenzie
18 holes, 6235 yards, S.S.S. 70
 Large practice area.
 Welcome except Tues before 3pm and Sat after 3.30pm.
 WD £35/day; WE/BH £40.
 Welcome Mon, Wed, Thurs, Fri; packages available; terms on application.
 Full clubhouse facilities available.
 The Ramada Jarvis Bank Field Hotel.

8A 144 Silkstone

Field Head, Silkstone, Barnsley, S Yorks, S75 4LD
☎ 01226 7980328, Pro 790128
On A628 1 mile from M1.
Undulating meadowland.
Pro Kevin Guy; Founded 1893
18 holes, 6069 yards, S.S.S. 70
 Welcome WD.

 Terms on application.
 Welcome WD by prior arrangement; packages available; terms on application.
 Full facilities except Mon.
 Ardsley Moat House; Brooklands Motel.

8A 145 Silsden

High Brunthwaite, Silsden, Keighley, W Yorks, BD20 0NH
 www.silsdengolfclub.co.uk
 info@silsdenglfclub.co.uk
☎ 01535 652998, Fax 654273, Sec 01943 864263
4 miles from Keighley on A6034 to Silsden, turn E at canal.
Moorland/meadowland course.
Founded 1913
18 holes, 5062 yards, S.S.S. 64, Par 67
 Welcome; WE restrictions.
 Terms on application.
 Terms on application.
 Clubhouse facilities.
 Steeton Hall.

8A 146 Sitwell Park ☏

Shrogswood Road, Rotherham, Yorks, S60 4BY
 www.sitwellgolf.co.uk
 secretary@sitwellgolf.co.uk
☎ 01709 541046, Fax 703637,
Pro 540961, Sec 541046,
Rest/Bar 700799
From M1 Junction 33; take 2nd exit at roundabout until signposted; also from M18 Junction 1.
Parkland course.
Pro Nick Taylor; Founded 1913
Designed by Dr A MacKenzie
18 holes, 6229 yards, S.S.S. 70
 Welcome.
 WD £25; WE £30.
 Welcome by prior arrangement with the Secretary; discounts for parties of 30; terms available on application. Snooker and billiard tables.
 Clubhouse facilities.
 Campanile; Beefeater; The Brecks.

8A 147 Skipton ☏

Short Lee Lane, Skipton, N Yorks, BD23 3LF
 www.skiptongolfclub.co.uk
 enquiries@skiptongolfclub.co.uk
☎ 01756 795657, Fax 796665,
Pro 793922, Sec 795657, Rest/Bar 793922
Course is on the A65 one mile N of Skipton.
Undulating parkland with panoramic views.

Pro Peter Robinson; Founded 1896
18 holes, 6076 yards, S.S.S. 69
 0.5 miles away.
 Welcome; some restrictions Tues and WE.
 Terms on application.
 Welcome WD by prior arrangement with Sec; packages available; snooker room; £23.
 Dining, banqueting and bar. Members and golfers only.
 Hanover, Skipton; Devonshire Arms, Bolton Abbey; Stirk House, Gisburn.

8A 148 South Bradford

Pearson Road, Odsal, Bradford, BD6 1BJ
☎ 01274 679195, Fax 690643, Sec 690643, Pro 673346
From Odsal roundabout take Stadium Road and then Pearson Road.
Undulating meadowland course.
Pro Paul Cooke; Founded 1906
9 holes, 6076 yards, S.S.S. 69
 Welcome WD.
 WD £18. 9 Hole course £12.
 Welcome Tues-Fri by prior arrangement; terms available on application.
 Full facilities except Mon.
 Guide Post.

8A 149 South Leeds ☏

Gipsy Lane, Off Middleton Ring Road, Leeds, W Yorks, LS11 5TU
 www.southleedsgolfclub.sagenet .co.uk
 sec@slgc.freeserve.co.uk
☎ 0113 2700479, Pro 2702598, Sec 2771676
Close to M1 Junction 45 and M62 Junction 28.
Undulating parkland course.
Pro Laurie Turner; Founded 1914
Designed by Dr A MacKenzie
18 holes, 5769 yards, S.S.S. 68
 Welcome WD; WE only with member.
 WD £14; WE £20.
 Welcome by prior arrangement; packages can be arranged depending on numbers; terms on application.
 Clubhouse facilities.
 Oulton Hall; Leeds International Hilton.

8A 150 Spaldington

Spaldington Lane, Howden, E Yorks, DN14 7NG
☎ 01757 288262, Pro 01430 432484, Rest/Bar 01430 432484

Take B1228 out of Howden towards
Bubwith and then head for
Spaldington.
Parkland course.
Pro A Pheasant; Founded 1995
Designed by PMS Golf
9 holes, 3482 yards, S.S.S. 29
⚑ 20 floodlit.
† Welcome.
� WD £4; WE £4.
⌁ Welcome.
🍽 Snacks.
🛏 The Wellington Hotel, Howden.

8A 151 Springhead Park
Willerby Road, Hull, E Yorks,
HU5 5JE
☎ 01482 656309, Sec 654875,
Rest/Bar 656309
From A62 follow signs from Humber
Bridge to Beverley to major roundabout
and then signs to Willerby.
Parkland course.
18 holes, 6401 yards off the white,
S.S.S. 71
† Municipal course; open to the
public with a green fee ticket.
� WD £10.50; WE £12.50.
⌁ Welcome by prior arrangement
with Sec; terms available on
application.
🍽 Clubhouse facilities.
🛏 Trusthouse Forte, North Ferraby.

8A 152 Springmill
Queens Drive, Osset, W Yorks
☎ 01924 272515
1 mile from Osset towards Wakefield.
Public parkland course.
9 holes, 2330 yards
† Welcome.
� Terms on application.

8A 153 Stocksbridge & District
30 Royd Lane, Townend, Deepcar,
Sheffield, Yorks, S36 2RZ
🖥 www.
stocksbridgeanddistrictgolfclub.com
✉ secretary@
stocksbridgeanddistrictgolfclub.com
☎ 0114 2882003, Pro 2882779
Close to M1 Junction 36.
Moorland course.
Pro Roger Broad; Founded 1924
18 holes, 5097 yards, S.S.S. 65
† Welcome WD.
� WD £21; WE £31.
⌁ Welcome WD by prior
arrangement; packages include 36
holes of golf and all day catering;
£25.
🍽 Stewardess 0114 2887479

🛏 Tankersley Manor; The Wentworth;
Ardsley House; Hallam Towers;
Grosvenor.

8A 154 Sutton Park
Salthouse Road, Hull, Yorks, HU8 9HF
☎ 01482 374242, Fax 701428,
Pro 0614781
A165 E to Salthouse Road.
Parkland course.
Pro Dennis Taylor; Founded 1935
18 holes, 6296 yards, S.S.S. 70
⚑ 32 (and 18 pitch and putt holes).
† Welcome by prior arrangement.
� Terms on application.
⌁ Welcome by prior arrangement;
terms on application.
🍽 Bar facilities.

8A 155 Swallow Hall
Swallow Hall, Crockery Hill, York,
YO19 4SG
🖥 www.swallowhall.co.uk
✉ jtscores@hotmail.com
☎ 01904 448889, Fax 448219,
Sec 448889
Off A19 S of York; after 1.5 miles turn
left to Wheldrake.
Public parkland course.
Founded 1991
18 holes, 3092 yards, S.S.S. 57
⚑ 7.
† Welcome.
� WD £10; WE £12.
⌁ Welcome by arrangement.
🍽 Full catering facilities.

8A 156 Tankersley Park
High Green, Sheffield, S Yorks, S35 4LG
🖥 www.pgagolfshop.co.uk
✉ iankirk5@aol.com
☎ 0114 2468247, Fax 2457818,
Pro 2455583
From M1 Junction 35A entrance 400
yards.
Parkland course.
Pro Ian Kirk; Founded 1907
Designed by Hawtree
18 holes, 6212 yards, S.S.S. 70
† Welcome, not at WE essential.
� WD £27; WE £36.
⌁ Welcome by prior arrangement on
WD; catering packages available;
terms on application.
🍽 Full catering facilities available; not
on Mondays; bar open every day.
🛏 Tankersley Manor; Norfolk Arms.

8A 157 Temple Newsam
Temple Newsam Road, Leeds,
W Yorks, LS15 OLN

☎ 0113 2645624, Pro 2647362
On A64 York road 5 miles from Leeds.
Then take A63.
Undulating parkland course.
Pro Adrian Newbold; Founded 1923
Designed by Lady Dorothy
36 holes, 6094 yards, S.S.S. 69
⚑ Practice area for 60 people.
† Welcome.
� Terms on application.
⌁ Welcome by arrangement;
packages available; terms on
application.
🍽 Full facilities; carvery WE.
🛏 Windmill; Mercury.

8A 158 Thirsk & Northallerton
Thornton-&-Street, Thirsk, N Yorks,
YO7 4AB
🖥 www.thirskandnorthallertongolfclub
.com
✉ simon@thirskandnorthallerton.com
☎ 01845 522170, Fax 525115,
Pro 526216, Sec 525115
Near A19 & A168 2 miles N of Thirsk.
Parkland course.
Pro Robert Garner; Founded 1914/1997
Designed by W Adamson
18 holes, 6495 yards, S.S.S. 70
† Welcome WD; only with member
at WE.
� WD £22; WE £28.
⌁ Welcome WD by prior
arrangement; catering packages
available.
🍽 Full clubhouse facilities.
🛏 Golden Fleece; Three Tuns.

8A 159 Thorne
Kirton Lane, Thorne, Doncaster,
S Yorks, DN8 5RJ
☎ 01405 815173, Fax 741899,
Pro 812084, Sec 812084
From M18 Junction 6 to Thorne;
signposted.
Parkland course.
Pro Edward Highfield; Founded 1980
Designed by Richard Highfield
18 holes, 5366 yards, S.S.S. 65
⚑ Practice area.
† Welcome.
� WD £9.50; WE £10.50; Jun £6.50;
Twilight £6.50.
⌁ Welcome by prior arrangement;
£50 deposit required which is refunded
on the day; terms on application.
🍽 Clubhouse facilities.
🛏 Belmont.

8A 160 Tinsley Park
High Hazel Park, Darnall, Sheffield,
S Yorks, S9 4PE

☎ 0114 2037435, Rest/Bar 2610004
Course is on the A57 from Junction 33
on the M1.
Parkland course.
Pro APR Highfield; Founded 1921
18 holes, 6084 yards, S.S.S. 69
♦ Welcome.
⌊ WD £8.50; WE £10.00.
⌒ Welcome by arrangement with the
local council.
⦿ Full facilities.
⤳ Royal Victoria.

8A 161 Todmorden

Rive Rocks, Cross Stone Rd,
Todmorden, OL14 8RD
☎ 01706 812986, Fax 812986
1.5 miles along Halifax road.
Moorland course.
Founded 1895
9 holes, 5902 yards, S.S.S. 68
♦ Welcome WD; WE by
arrangement.
⌊ WD £15; WE £20.
⌒ Welcome WD by prior
arrangement.
⦿ Clubhouse facilities.
⤳ Scaite Cliffe Hall; Brandschatter
Berghoff.

8A 162 Wakefield Golf Club

Woodthorpe Lane, Sandal, Wakefield,
WF2 6JH
▦ wakefieldgolfclub
@woodthorpelane.freeserve.co.uk
☎ 01924 255104, Fax 242752,
Pro 255380, Sec 258778
Course is on the A61 three miles S of
Wakefield.
Parkland course.
Pro Ian Wright; Founded 1891
Designed by Alex Herd
18 holes, 6653 yards, S.S.S. 72
♦ Welcome by prior arrangement.
⌊ WD £30; WE £40.
⌒ Welcome by application to Sec;
catering packages by arrangements;
snooker; terms on application.
⦿ Full facilities.
⤳ Cedar Court; The Chasley.

8A 163 Waterton Park

The Balk, Walton, Wakefield, WF2 6QL
▦ www.waterton.co.uk
☎ 01924 259525, Fax 256969,
Pro 255557, Rest/Bar 255855
Course is close to M1 Junction 39
following signs for Barnsley and A61;
left to Wakefield and then to Shay Lane.
Parkland on Waterton Hall, 26-acre
lake.
Pro Nick Wood; Founded 1995

Designed by S Gidman
18 holes, 6843 yards, S.S.S. 72; 73 for
women.
⌇ Practice range.
♦ Welcome as members' guests
only. Limited pay and play on WD.
⌊ Not available.
⌒ None.
⦿ Bars and dining room in the
exclusive club house.
⤳ Waterton Park.

8A 164 Wath

Abdy Lane, Rawmarsh, Rotherham,
S Yorks, S62 7SJ
☎ 01709 878609, Fax 877097, Pro
878609 x21, Sec 878609 x20,
Rest/Bar 878609 x22
Off A633 in Wath, 7 miles N of
Rotherham.
Parkland course.
Pro Chris Bassett; Founded 1904
18 holes, 6086 yards, S.S.S. 69, par 70
♦ Welcome WD; only with a member
WE.
⌊ WD £24, unlimited day £29.
⌒ Welcome by prior arrangement;
special packages available for golf and
catering; terms on application.
⦿ Full facilities.
⤳ Moat House, Rotherham.

8A 165 West Bowling ☎

Newall Hall, Rooley Lane, Bradford,
W Yorks, BD5 8LB
☎ 01274 724449, Pro 728036,
Sec 393207
At Junction of M606 and Bradford ring
road.
Parkland course.
Pro Ian Marshall; Founded 1898
18 holes, 5769 yards, S.S.S. 68
♦ Welcome WD; restrictions at WE.
⌊ WD £22; WE £30.
⌒ Welcome Wed, Thurs, Fri by
arrangement with the manager;
catering by arrangement; snooker;
terms on application.
⦿ Full facilities.
⤳ Novotel; Norfolk Gardens; Guide
Post; Tong Village; Victoria.

8A 166 West Bradford ☎

Chellow Grange Road, Haworth Road,
Bradford, W Yorks, BD9 6NP
▦ westbradfordgc@supanet.com
☎ 01274 542767, Fax 482079,
Pro 542102
Course is off the B6144 three miles
NW of Bradford city centre.
Parkland course.
Pro Nigel Barber; Founded 1900

18 holes, 5723 yards, S.S.S. 68
♦ Welcome WE before 3 pm.
⌊ WD £21; WE £21.
⌒ Welcome by arrangement;
packages including catering and golf
with reduced green fees available;
terms on application.
⦿ Full clubhouse facilities.

8A 167 West End (Halifax)

Paddock Lane, Highroad Well, Halifax,
W Yorks, HX2 ONT
▦ www.westendgc.co.uk
▦ info@westendgc.co.uk
☎ 01422 341878, Fax 341878,
Pro 363294, Rest/Bar 369844
2 miles W of Halifax off Burnley-
Rochford road.
Parkland course.
Pro David Rishworth; Founded 1906
Designed by Members
18 holes, 5937 yards, S.S.S. 69
♦ Welcome by prior arrangement.
⌊ WD £25; WE £30.
⌒ Welcome by prior arrangement
with Sec; packages available; from
£25.
⦿ Clubhouse facilities.
⤳ Windmill Court, Halifax.

8A 168 Wetherby ☎

Linton Lane, Wetherby, Yorks,
LS22 4JF
▦ www.wetherbygolfclub.com
▦ info@wetherbygolfclub.fsnet
.co.uk
☎ 01937 580089, Fax 581915,
Sec 580089, Rest/Bar 582527
Course is one mile W of A1 S of Linton
village.
Parkland course.
Pro David Padgett; Founded 1910
18 holes, 6235 yards, S.S.S. 70
⌇ Driving range.
♦ Welcome Tues afternoons; all day
Mon, Wed, Thurs, Fri.
⌊ WD £28 per round.
⌒ Welcome by prior arrangement;
packages available; discounts for
groups of 40; terms available on
application.
⦿ Full clubhouse facilities.
⤳ Jarvis Resort; Wood Hall.

8A 169 Wheatley

Armthorpe Road, Doncaster, S Yorks,
DN2 5QB
▦ wheatleygolfclub@route56.co.uk
☎ 01302 831655, Fax 812736,
Pro 834085, Sec 831655 ext 21,
Rest/Bar 831655 ext 24 (bar), ext 25
(kitchen)

Close to Doncaster racecourse following the ring road S; opposite large water tower.
Undulating parkland; relocated 1933.
Pro Steve Fox; Founded 1913/1933
Designed by George Duncan
18 holes, 6405 yards, S.S.S. 71
† Welcome.
[WD £27; WE £38.
↻ Welcome WD by prior arrangement; day ticket (WD £25); catering by prior arrangement; from £20.
|●| Full facilities.
⌂ Balmoral; Earl of Doncaster; Punches.

8A 170 **Whitby**
Sandsend Road, Low Straggleton, Whitby, N Yorks, YO21 3SR
⌨ www.ukgolfer.org
✉ whitby-golf-club@compuserve.com
☎ 01947 602768, Fax 600660, Pro 602719, Sec 600660, Rest 602768
On A174 coast road between Whitby and Sandsend.
Seaside course.
Pro Tony Mason; Founded 1892
18 holes, 6134 yards, S.S.S. 69
† Welcome by prior arrangement.
[WD £22; WE £28.
↻ Welcome by prior arrangement; winter and summer packages available for groups of 8 or more; from £21.50.
|●| Full facilities.
⌂ Seacliffe; White House; Arundel.

8A 171 **Whitwood**
Altofts Lane, Whitwood, Castleford, W Yorks, WF10 5PZ
☎ 01977 604215, Pro 512835, Rest/Bar 512835
Course is 0.5 miles towards Castleford off M62 Junction 31.
Parkland course.
Pro Richard Golding; Founded 1986
Designed by Steve Wells (Wakefield Council)
9 holes, 6282 yards, S.S.S. 70
† Welcome; booking system available.
[WD £5.90; WE £8.
↻ Welcome by arrangement with the Pro; terms on application.
|●| Available at local inn.
⌂ Bridge Inn.

8A 172 **Willow Valley Golf & Country Club**
Highmoor Lane, Clifton, Brighouse, W Yorks, HD6 4JB
⌨ www.wvgc.co.uk
✉ golf@wvgc.co.uk

☎ 01274 878624
From M62 Junction 25 take A644 to Brighouse; turn right at first roundabout.
American parkland style course.
Pro Julian Howarth; Founded 1993
Designed by J Gaunt
18 holes and 9 holes, 7021 yards for 18 holes and 2039 yards for 9 holes, S.S.S. 72
⚑ 24 floodlit.
† Welcome.
[WD £23; WE £28.
↻ Welcome WD; packages available for groups of 12/16 or more; from £32.00
|●| Full clubhouse facilities.
⌂ Black Horse Inn; Holiday Inn Clifton, Brighouse.

8A 173 **Withernsea**
Chestnut Ave, Withernsea, E Yorks, HU19 2PG
☎ 01964 612258, Sec 612078
25 miles E of Hull on main road to Withernsea.
Seaside links course.
Pro G Harrison; Founded 1907
9 holes, 6207 yards, S.S.S. 72
† Welcome; after 2pm Sun.
[WD £10; WE £10.
↻ Welcome by prior arrangement; catering packages can be arranged; from £10.
|●| Clubhouse facilities.
⌂ Kings Town Hotel, Headon.

8A 174 **Wombwell (Hillies)**
Wentworth View, Wombwell, Barnsley, S Yorks, S73 0LA
⌨ www.wombwellgolfclub.co.uk
☎ 01226 754433, Fax 758635, Sec 757788
4 miles SE of Barnsley.
Meadowland course.
Founded 1981
9 holes, 4190 yards, S.S.S. 60
⚑ Practice nets.
† Welcome.
[WD £6.30; WE £7.80.
WD £4.40; WE £5.20 (9 holes)
↻ Welcome by prior arrangement; from £6.30.
|●| Bar service only.
⌂ Ardsley House.

8A 175 **Woodhall Hills**
Woodhall Road, Calverley, Pudsey, W Yorks, LS28 5UN
☎ 0113 2564771, Sec 2554594
Take A647 Leeds-Bradford road to Pudsey roundabout; follow signs to

Calverley; 0.25 miles past Calverley Golf Club.
Parkland course.
Pro Warren Lockett; Founded 1905
18 holes, 6184 yards, S.S.S. 70
† Welcome.
[WD £20.50; WE £25.50.
↻ Welcome by arrangement with secretary/manager; golf and catering packages available for groups of 20 or more; from £31.
|●| Full clubhouse facilities available.
⌂ Cedar Court, Bradford.

8A 176 **Woodsome Hall**
Fenay Bridge, Huddersfield, W Yorks, HD8 0LG
☎ 01484 602739, Fax 608260, Pro 602034, Rest/Bar 602971
From either M62 Junction 24 or 26 towards Huddersfield then A629 towards Sheffield turning right at Farnley Tyas/Honley signs.
Parkland course.
Pro Mike Higginbottom; Founded 1922
Designed by J Braid
18 holes, 6096 yards, S.S.S. 69
† Welcome except Tues.
[WD £30; WE £40.
↻ Welcome by prior arrangement except Tues and Sat; handicap certs required; menus for catering packages available from club; TV lounges; halfway bar available; deposit required; terms available on application.
|●| Full catering and bar facilities; jacket and tie required.
⌂ Hanover International; Huddersfield Hotel.

8A 177 **Woolley Park**
Woolley Park, New Road, Woolley, Wakefield, W Yorks, WF4 2JS
⌨ www.woolleypark.co.uk
✉ info@woolleypark.co.uk
☎ 01226 380144, Fax 390295, Pro 380144, Sec 382209, Rest/Bar 380144
From Junction 38 on the M1 follow the signs for Woolley Hall; from the A61 Wakefield to Barnsley road take the Woolley signs from the crossroads.
Parkland course.
Pro Jon Baldwin; Founded 1995
Designed by M Shattock
18 holes, 6636 yards, S.S.S. 72
⚑ Token available from pro shop – open 7 days a week.
† Welcome.
[Terms on application.
↻ Welcome by prior arrangement; packages available; terms on application.

🍴 Clubhouse catering facilities.
🛏 Hotel Saint-Pierre.

8A 178 **Wortley**

Hermit Hill Lane, Wortley, Sheffield,
S35 7DF
💻 wortley.golfclub@virgin.net
☎ 0114 2888469, Fax 2888488,
Pro 2886490, Rest/Bar 2885294
Course is off the A629 through Wortley
village.
Undulating wooded parkland course.
Pro Ian Kirk; Founded 1894
18 holes, 6035 yards, S.S.S. 69
🚶 Welcome by prior arrangement.
💰 WD £28; WE £35.
🏌 Welcome Mon, Wed and Fri by

prior arrangement; catering by
arrangement except Mon; terms on
application.
🍴 Clubhouse facilities available
except Mon.
🛏 Ardsley Moat House; Brooklands,
both Barnsley; Tankersley Manor;
Wortley Hall.

8A 179 **York Golf Club**   ☎

Lords Moor Lane, Strensall, York,
Yorks, Y05 5XF
🖥 www.yorkgolfclub.co.uk
☎ 01904 491840, Fax 491852,
Pro 490304, Sec 491840
3 miles N of A1237 York ring road from
Earswick/Strensall roundabout.

Tree-lined heathland course.
Pro A Hoyle; Founded 1890
Designed by JH Taylor (1904)
18 holes, 6302 yards, S.S.S. 70
🚶 Welcome by prior arrangement;
with member on Saturdays only.
Visitors allowed on Sun.
💰 WD £33.
🏌 Welcome except Tues am and Sat;
packages can include 18, 27 or 36
holes of golf; some Sun available;
catering available.
🍴 Bar and catering facilities.
🛏 Accommodation guide sent on
request.

Northumberland, Durham, Cleveland, Tyne & Wear

Stephen Keppler is one end of the strange history of Seaton Carew. He looks like an extra out of *Lock, Stock and Two Smoking Barrels*, talks with a hybrid accent of cockney and the American deep south, earns a living as a club pro in Atlanta and made a splash by qualifying for the 2001 USPGA where he only just missed the cut. His bizarre journey via the British Walker Cup team began when he won the Boys Amateur Championship at Seaton Carew in 1978.

At the other end of Seaton Carew's history is a Dr Duncan McCuaig from St Andrews who, finding the local land reminiscent of his home course, began biffing a ball around it. His activity led in 1874 to the foundation of the Durham and Yorkshire Golf Club, later renamed Seaton Carew.

It is a fine links with an industrial backdrop of chimneys and chemical plants. Donald Steel called the 17th green, which is shaped like a scallop shell, "as notable an instrument of torture as man can devise".

Hartlepool Golf Club, similarly threatened by the North Sea, and Cleveland, a club formed in the local Lobster Inn, are good neighbouring courses although some object to the rampant air pollution of the area.

There are several good courses to the west of Hartlepool including Barnard Castle, defined by its becks and hills, and Bishop Auckland, a course built on Church of England land. But the most famous of them is Brancepeth Castle where Leonard Crawley, a former English Amateur

Champion, golf correspondent and driver of large motor vehicles, was an admiring member.

On land that was once a deer park Brancepeth presents many challenges, not least a wobbly bridge constructed by the Royal Engineers. Eight holes on the course are affected by ravines. The ninth hole, 200 plus yards across an exposed ravine, was described by Darwin as of "terrifying grandeur". At least the soul can find solace in views of the castle and the 12th century church of St Brandon.

Just south of Newcastle is Beamish Park, a parkland design influenced by Henry Cotton, and to the north of the city is the Northumberland. Lying largely within the rails of the racetrack the course is of sufficient quality (a Harry Colt and James Braid design) to have hosted the English Amateur and the Women's Commonwealth. It is on the short side unless your golf ball repeatedly ricochets back over your head from the rails, in which instant it plays rather long.

To the west of Newcastle is Slaley Hall, a former host of European tour events. The building has been modernised to create a pretty comfortable hotel, but the golf itself consists of a big course with a small character. Rather typical of its excess is the ninth hole which has a mass of features and a dearth of personality.

Heading further up the north east coast is Seahouses, a lovely meld of dunes, coves and marshland, and just before the Scottish border is Berwick-upon-Tweed. A fair links it is distinguished by views of Holy Island from amidst the dunes.

8B 1 Allendale

High Studdon, Allenheads Road,
Allendale, Hexham, Northumberland,
N47 9DH
🖳 www.allendale-golf.org
📧 nostalgiaplus@supanet.com
☎ 01434 685051, Fax 683926
On B6295 1.5 miles S of Allendale in
the direction of Allenheads.
Hilly parkland course.
Founded 1907/1992
Designed by Members/English Golf
Union/Sports Council
9 holes, 5044 yards, S.S.S. 65
† Welcome except August Bank
Holiday Mon.
⌞ Prices on application.
⌁ Welcome by arrangement;
corporate days welcome; catering by
arrangement; terms available on
application.
🍽 Clubhouse facilities available.
🛏 Kings Head; Allenheads Inn.

8B 2 Alnmouth Golf Club

Foxton Hall, Lesbury, Alnmouth,
Northumberland, NE66 3BE
🖳 www.alnmouthgolfclub.com
📧 secretary@alnmouthgolfclub.com
☎ 01665 830231, Fax 830992,
Pro 830043
5 miles SE of Alnwick.
Parkland course.
Pro Lindsey Hardy; Founded 1869
Designed by HS Colt
18 holes, 6429 yards, S.S.S. 71
† Welcome (not Fri/Sat); Dormy
House guests welcome at all times.
⌞ WD £27.40-£33; WE £35
⌁ Welcome (not Fri/Sat); day
packages available; from £29.
🍽 Clubhouse catering facilities
available.
🛏 Foxton Hall has its own Dormy
Housel – all rooms en suite

8B 3 Alnmouth Village

Marine Road, Alnmouth,
Northumberland, NE66 2RZ
🖳 www.golfuk.co.uk
📧 golfingspence@aol.com
☎ 01665 830370, Sec 603797
On A1068 from Alnmouth.
Undulating links course.
Founded 1869
9 holes, 6078 yards, S.S.S. 70
⌐ Practice ground.
† Welcome; restrictions on
competition days.
⌞ WD £15, WE £20; Juniors £7.50.
⌁ Welcome with handicap certs;
catering packages by arrangement;
from £15.

🍽 Catering available except
Tues.
🛏 Marine House Hotel; Red Lion;
Hope and Anchor.

8B 4 Alnwick

Swansfield Park, Alnwick,
Northumberland, NE66 2AB
📧 mail@alnwickgolfclub.co.uk
☎ 01665 602632, Sec 602499
From A1 S signposted to Willowburn
Ave and then into Swansfield Park
Road.
Parkland course.
Founded 1907/1993
Designed by G Rochester/A Rae
18 holes, 6250 yards, S.S.S. 70
† Welcome by prior arrangement
with the starter (01665 602632).
⌞ WD £18-£25; WE and BH £20-
£25.
⌁ Welcome between April 1 and Oct
1 by prior arrangement; packages
available in season of unlimited golf
and full day's catering; minimum 4; £25
🍽 Full clubhouse facilities available.
🛏 White Swan; Plough Hotel; Oaks
Hotel.

8B 5 Arcot Hall

Dudley, Cramlington, Northumberland,
NE23 7QP
🖳 www.arcothallgolfclub.com
📧 arcothall@tiscali.co.uk
☎ 01912 362794, Fax 170370,
, Pro 362794 x3, Sec 362794 x2,
Rest/Bar 362794 x5
Course is 1.5 miles off the A1 near
Cramlington.
Parkland course; formerly at Benton,
Pro Graham Cant
Founded 1909/48
Designed by James Braid
18 holes, 6389 yards, S.S.S. 70
† Welcome WD; restrictions WE.
⌞ WD £28; WE £32.
⌁ Welcome by prior arrangement on
WD; packages available; from £26.
🍽 Lounge bar and restaurant
facilities.
🛏 Holiday Inn; Swallow, Gosforth
Park.

8B 6 Backworth

Backworth Welfare, The Hall,
Backworth, Shiremoor, NE27 OAH
☎ 0191 2681048, Sec 2808107
Course on the B1322 one mile from
the A19/A191 Junction at Shiremoor
crossroads.
Parkland course.
Founded 1937

9 holes, 5930 yards, S.S.S. 68
† Welcome WD except Tues 11am-
3pm; restrictions at WE.
⌞ WD £12; WE £16.
⌁ Welcome by prior arrangement
with Sec; packages can be negotiated
depending on numbers; terms on
application.
🍽 Full bar and restaurant facilities
available.
🛏 Rex; Park; Stakis Wallsend;
Grand.

8B 7 Bamburgh Castle   ⛳

The Wynding, Bamburgh,
Northumberland, NE69 7DE
🖳 www.bamburghcastlegolfclub.org
📧 bamburghcastlegolfclub@
hotmail.com
☎ 01668 214378, Fax 214607,
Pro 214378, Sec 214321,
Rest/Bar 214378
Course is five miles E of the A1 via the
B1341 or the B1342 into Bamburgh
village.
Seaside course.
Founded 1904
Designed by George Rochester
18 holes, 5621 yards, S.S.S. 67
† Welcome by prior arrangement
except on competition days and BH.
⌞ WD £30 per round £40 per day.
WE £35 per round £40 per round.
⌁ Welcome by prior written
arrangement with Sec; full catering
packages available, except Tues; from
£32.
🍽 Full catering available except
Tues.
🛏 Victoria; Mizen; Sunningdale; Lord
Crewe.

8B 8 Barnard Castle

Harmire Road, Barnard Castle,
DL12 8QN
🖳 www.barnardcastlegolfclub.org
📧 pro@barnardcastlegolfclub.org
☎ 01833 638355, Fax 695551,
Pro 631980, Rest/Bar 637237
Course is on the B6278 one mile N
of town signposted Middleton in
Teesdale.
Parkland course.
Pro Darren Pearce; Founded 1898
Designed by AS Watson
18 holes, 6406 yards, S.S.S. 71
† Welcome by prior arrangement.
⌞ WD £20; WE £27.
⌁ Welcome WD by prior
arrangement; catering packages
available; from £18.
🍽 Restaurant and bar facilities.
🛏 Jersey Farm Hotel; Morris Arms

8B 9 Beamish Park

The Clubhouse, Beamish, Stanley,
Co Durham, DH9 0RH

🖳 www.beamishgolfclub.co.uk
📧 bpgc@beamishparkgc.fsbusiness
.co.uk
☎ 0191 3701382, Fax 3702937,
Pro 3701984

From A1 take B693 towards Stanley
and follow the signs for Beamish
museum.
Tree-lined parkland course.
Pro Chris Cole; Founded 1907/50
Designed by Henry Cotton (part)/W
Woodend
18 holes, 6218 yards, S.S.S. 70
🕴 Welcome by arrangement.
🍺 WD £22; WE £25.
⛳ Welcome by arrangement; on
application.
🍽 Full clubhouse facilities.
🛏 Beamish Hall Hotel.

8B 10 Bedlingtonshire

Acorn Bank, Hartford Road,
Bedlington, Northumberland,
NE22 6AA

🖳 www.bedlingtongolfclub.com
📧 secretary@bedlingtongolfclub.com
☎ 01670 822457, Fax 823048

Off A189 Ashington road 10 miles N of
Newcastle.
Parkland course.
Pro Marcus Webb; Founded 1972
Designed by Frank Pennink
18 holes, 6813 yards, S.S.S. 73
🎯 Practice ground.
🕴 Welcome by arrangement.
🍺 WD £18; WE £26.
⛳ Welcome by prior arrangement
with secretary; packages can be
arranged; terms available on
application.
🍽 Full clubhouse facilities.
🛏 Swan Inn, Choppington; Half Moon
Inn, Stakeford; Holiday Inn, Seaton
Born.

8B 11 Belford ☎

South Road, Belford, Northumberland,
NE70 7DP

🖳 www.belfordgolfclub.co.uk
📧 belfordgolfclub@tiscali.co.uk
☎ 01668 213433, Fax 213919,
Sec 213587, Rest/Bar 213433

Just off A1 midway between Alnwick
and Berwick on Tweed.
Parkland course.
Founded 1993
Designed by Nigel W Williams
9 holes, 6304 yards, S.S.S. 70
🎯 6 indoor, 4 outdoor.
🕴 Welcome.

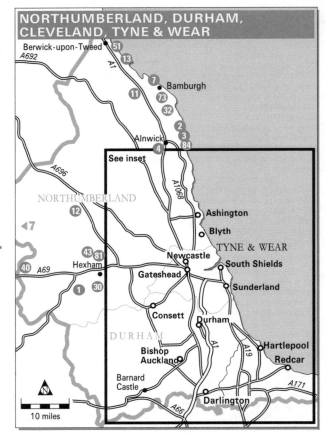

KEY
1	Allendale	16	Bishop Auckland	33	Durham City
2	Alnmouth	17	Blackwell Grange	34	Eaglescliffe
3	Alnmouth Village	18	Blyth	35	Elemore
4	Alnwick	19	Boldon	36	Garesfield
5	Arcot Hall	20	Brancepeth Castle	37	George Washington County
6	Backworth	21	Burgham Park		Hotel & GC
7	Bamburgh Castle	22	Castle Eden & Peterlee	38	Gosforth
8	Barnard Castle	23	Chester-le-Street	39	Hall Garth Golf & Country
9	Beamish Park	24	City of Newcastle		Club
10	Bedlingtonshire	25	Cleveland	40	Haltwhistle
11	Belford	26	Close House	41	Hartlepool
12	Bellingham	27	Consett & District	42	Heworth
13	Berwick-upon-Tweed	28	Crook	43	Hexham
	(Goswick)	29	Darlington	44	High Throston
14	Billingham	30	De Vere Slaley Hall	45	Hobson Municipal
15	Birtley	31	Dinsdale Spa	46	Houghton-le-Spring
		32	Dunstanburgh Castle	47	Hunley Hall

🍺 WD £15; WE £18.
⛳ Welcome by prior arrangement;
some WE available; packages include
27 holes plus all-day catering; from £23.
🍽 Full clubhouse facilities.
🛏 Blue Bell; Purdy Travel Lodge.

8B 12 Bellingham Golf Club ☎

Boggle Hole, Bellingham, Hexham,
Northumberland, NE48 2DT

🖳 www.bellinghamgolfcourse.co.uk.
📧 secretarybellinghamgc@
hotmail.co.uk.

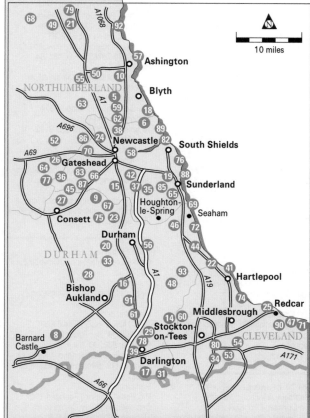

NORTHUMBERLAND

DURHAM

CLEVELAND

Ashington

Blyth

Newcastle

South Shields

Gateshead

Sunderland

Houghton-le-Spring

Seaham

Consett

Durham

Hartlepool

Bishop Aukland

Redcar

Middlesbrough

Stockton-on-Tees

Barnard Castle

Darlington

10 miles

48	Knotty Hill Golf Centre	64	Prudhoe	81	Tynedale
49	Linden Hall	65	Ramside	82	Tynemouth
50	Longhirst Hall	66	Ravensworth	83	Tyneside
51	Magdalene Fields	67	Roseberry Grange	84	Warkworth
52	Matfen Hall	68	Rothbury	85	Wearside
53	Middlesbrough	69	Ryhope	86	Westerhope
54	Middlesbrough Municipal	70	Ryton	87	Whickham
55	Morpeth	71	Saltburn-by-the-Sea	88	Whitburn
56	Mount Oswald	72	Seaham	89	Whitley Bay
57	Newbiggin-by-the-Sea	73	Seahouses	90	Wilton
58	Newcastle United	74	Seaton Carew	91	Woodham Golf & Country
59	Northumberland	75	South Moor		Club
60	Norton Golf Course	76	South Shields	92	Wooler
61	Oak Leaf Golf Complex	77	Stocksfield	93	Wynard Club
	(Aycliffe)	78	Stressholme Golf Centre		
62	Parklands Golf Club	79	Swarland Hall		
63	Ponteland	80	Teesside		

☎ 01434 220530, Fax 220160,
Sec 220530, Rest/Bar 220152
Off the B6320 16 miles NE of Hexham
and the A69, on the outskirts of
Bellingham.

Rolling parkland with natural hazards.
Founded 1893/1996
Designed by E Johnson/I Wilson (96)
18 holes, 6093 yards, S.S.S. 70
🏌 6 floodlit bays.

✝ Welcome; prior booking is
advisable.
⌐ WD £22; WE £27.
↻ Welcome every day by prior
arrangement; catering and golfing
packages available; from £19.50.
🍽 Full catering and bar facilities
available.
🛏 George; Riverdale Hall; Beaumont;
Cheviott.

8B 13 Berwick-upon-Tweed ☎

Goswick, Berwick-upon-Tweed,
Northumberland, TD15 2RW
🖥 www.goswicklinksgc.co.uk
📧 goswickgc@btconnect.com
☎ 01289 387256, Fax 387334,
Pro 387380
3.5 miles from A1; 5 miles S of
Berwick-upon-Tweed.
Links course.
Pro Paul Terras; Founded
1890/alterations1964
Designed by James Braid/F Pennink
18 holes, 6852 yards, S.S.S. 72
🏌 Practice area
✝ Welcome; restrictions before
9.30am and between 12 noon-2pm at
WE.
⌐ WD £28; WE £35.
↻ Welcome WD & WE; packages
include full day's golf and catering for
minimum 10; prices on application.
🍽 Full clubhouse catering and bar
facilities.
🛏 Blue Bell, Belford; Mizen Head,
Bamburgh; Haggerston Castle Holiday
Park.

8B 14 Billingham

Sandy Lane, Billingham, Cleveland,
TS22 5NA
📧 billinghamgc@onetel.net.uk
☎ 01642 533816, Fax 533816,
Pro 557060, Rest/Bar 554494
E of A19 near Billingham Town Centre.
Parkland course.
Pro Mike Ure; Founded 1967
Designed by Frank Pennink
18 holes, 6333 yards, S.S.S. 71
🏌 Practice ground.
✝ Welcome.
⌐ WD £25; £15 with member.
↻ Welcome by prior arrangement
with Sec; terms available on
application.
🍽 Full clubhouse facilities.
🛏 Billingham Arms.

8B 15 Birtley

Birtley Lane, Birtley, Co Durham,
DH3 2LR

☎ 0191 4102207, Sec 4102207,
Rest/Bar 4102207
Course is six miles S of Newcastle off
the A6127.
Parkland course.
Founded 1921
9 holes, 5660 yards, S.S.S. 67
† Welcome WD; with member at
WE.
Ⱡ WD £14.
⌁ Welcome WD by prior
arrangement; terms on application.
🍽 Bar facilities.
🛏 George Washington County; local
B&Bs can be recommended.

8B 16 Bishop Auckland ☏

High Plains, Durham Rd, Bishop
Auckland, Co Durham, DL14 8DL
🖳 www.bagc.co.uk
🖂 enquiries@bagc.co.uk
☎ 01388 661618, Fax 607005
0.5 miles N of town on Durham road.
Parkland course.
Pro David Skiffington; Founded 1894
Designed by James Kay
18 holes, 6399 yards, S.S.S. 70
† Welcome WD except Tues.
Ⱡ Prices on application.
⌁ Welcome by prior arrangement;
special packages for including 27 holes
golf and all-day catering; prices on
application.
🍽 Full clubhouse facilities.
🛏 The Castle; The Park Head.

8B 17 Blackwell Grange ☏

Briar Close, Blackwell, Darlington,
DL3 8QX
🖂 secretary@blackwellgrange.demon
.co.uk
☎ 01325 464464, Fax 464458,
Pro 462088, Sec 464458, Rest/Bar
464464
1 mile S of Darlington on A66.
Parkland course.
Pro Joanne Furby; Founded 1930
Designed by Frank Pennink
18 holes, 5621 yards, S.S.S. 67
† Welcome.
Ⱡ WD £20; WE £30.
⌁ Welcome WD except Wed;
catering packages available; from £20.
🍽 Full clubhouse facilities.
🛏 Blackwell Grange, Darlington.

8B 18 Blyth ☏

New Delaval, Blyth, Northumberland,
NE24 4DB
🖂 blythgc@lineone.net
☎ 01670 540110, Pro 356514,
Sec 540110

At W end of Plessey Road.
Parkland course.
Pro Andrew Brown; Founded 1905/1976
Designed by Hamilton Stutt & Co
18 holes, 6430 yards, S.S.S. 72
† Welcome WD.
Ⱡ WD £19; WE £24.
⌁ Welcome WD by prior
arrangement; 3 packages available for
society and company days; minimum
10; from £21.
🍽 Full clubhouse catering and bar
facilities.
🛏 Large number in Whitley Bay.

8B 19 Boldon

Dipe Lane, East Boldon, Tyne & Wear,
NE36 0PQ
☎ 0191 5365835, Fax 5190157,
Sec 5365360
Course is on the A184 one mile E of
the A19/A1 Junction.
Parkland course.
Pro Sean Richardson/Phillip Carlaw;
Founded 1912
18 holes, 6338 yards, S.S.S. 70
† Welcome WD with restrictions;
after 3.30pm only at WE.
Ⱡ WD £18; WE £22.
⌁ Welcome by arrangement; catering
packages available; snooker; from £18.
🍽 Bar snacks and restaurant
facilities.
🛏 Friendly.

8B 20 Brancepeth Castle ☏

Brancepeth Village, Durham,
Co Durham, DH7 8EA
🖳 www.brancepeth-castle-golf.co.uk
🖂 brancepethcastle@btclick.com
☎ 0191 3780075, Fax 3783835,
Pro 3780183, Sec 3780075,
Rest/Bar 3783393
On A690 4 miles W of Durham; left at
the crossroads before Brancepeth.
Parkland course.
Pro D Howdon; Founded 1924
Designed by HS Colt
18 holes, 6375 yards, S.S.S. 71
† Welcome by prior arrangement.
Ⱡ WD£29; WE £30.
⌁ Welcome WD by prior
arrangement; special rates for groups
of more than 12 and 30; banqueting
facilities available; formal dinners can
be arranged; starter available; video
service for lessons; prices on
application.
🍽 Full clubhouse catering and bar
facilities; formal dinner and banquet
can be arranged.
🛏 The Whitworth Hall Hotel;
Waterside GH, Royal Hotel, Durham.

8B 21 Burgham Park ☏

Burgham Park Golf and Leisure Club
Ltd, Near Felton, Morpeth,
Northumberland, NE65 8QP
🖂 sburghamgolf@btopenworld.com
☎ 01670 787898, Fax 787164,
Pro 787978
6 miles N of Morpeth off the A1 at
Longhorsley road (C137).
Parkland course.
Pro S McNally; Founded 1994
Designed by A Mair
18 holes, 6751 yards, S.S.S. 72
Ⱡ 10.
† Welcome.
Ⱡ Terms on application.
⌁ Welcome except on competitions
days; catering packages available;
terms on application.
🍽 Full catering and bar facilities.
🛏 Northumberland Arms, Felton; Blue
Bell, Belford.

8B 22 Castle Eden ☏

Castle Eden, Hartlepool, Cleveland,
TS27 4SS
🖳 www.
btinternet.com/~derek.livingstone2
🖂 derek.livingston@
btinternet.com
☎ 01429 836220, Fax 836510,
Pro 836689, Sec 836510,
Rest/Bar 836220
10 miles S of Sunderland; take slip
road off A19 towards Blackhall; 0.25
miles.
Parkland course.
Pro Peter Jackson; Founded 1927
Designed by Henry Cotton (back 9)
18 holes, 6282 yards, S.S.S. 70
† Welcome by prior arrangement.
Ⱡ WD £25; WE £35.
⌁ Golfing parties and societies
welcome. Contact Sec for information.
🍽 Full clubhouse facilities.
🛏 Castle Eden Inn.

8B 23 Chester-le-Street ☏

Lumley Park, Chester-Le-Street, Co
Durham, DH3 4NS
🖂 clsgc@ukonline.co.uk
☎ 0191 3883218, Fax 3881220,
Pro 3890157, Sec 3883218
Close to A167 0.5 miles E of Chester-
le-Street close to Lumley Castle and
Durham CCC ground.
Parkland course.
Pro David Fletcher; Founded 1908
Designed by JH Taylor (original 9)/T
Ray
18 holes, 6437 yards, S.S.S. 71
† Welcome by prior arrangement.
Ⱡ WD £23; WE £28.

Welcome by prior arrangements; coffee and catering available depending on numbers; terms on application. Not WE.
Full clubhouse facilities.
Lumley Castle.

8B 24 City of Newcastle
Three Mile Bridge, Gosforth, Newcastle upon Tyne, NE3 2DR
www.cityofnewcastlegolfclub.com
info@cityofnewcastlegolfclub.com
0191 2851775, Fax 2840700, Pro 2855481
Course is on the B1318 three miles N of Newcastle.
Parkland course.
Pro Steve McKenna; Founded 1892
Designed by Harry Vardon
18 holes, 6523 yards, S.S.S. 71
Welcome.
WD £25 round, £32 day; WE £30.
Welcome by prior arrangement most days; packages application on request from £22.
Full clubhouse facilities.
Swallow, Gosforth Park.

8B 25 Cleveland Golf Club
Majuba Road, Redcar, Cleveland, TS10 5BJ
www.clevelandgolfclub.co.uk
secretary@clevelandgolfclub.co.uk
01642 471798, Fax 471798, Pro 483462, Rest/Bar 481757
Off A174 following signs for Teeside and Redcar.
Links course.
Pro Craig Donaldson
Founded 1897
18 holes, 6696 yards, S.S.S. 72
Welcome.
WD £20; WE £22.
Welcome; packages can be arranged depending on numbers; terms on application.

Clubhouse bar and catering facilities.
Regency; Park.

8B 26 Close House
Close House, Heddon-on-the-Wall, Newcastle upon Tyne, NE16 5TQ
01661 852953, Sec 4886515
Course is off the A69 nine miles W of Newcastle.
Parkland/woodland course.
Founded 1965
Designed by Hawtree
18 holes, 5571 yards, S.S.S. 67
Members' guests all year; casual visitors June-Aug.
Terms on application.
Welcome WD by prior arrangement; packages available to include all-day catering; corporate days by arrangement.
Catering and bar facilities in the Mansion House.
Copthorne; Novotel, both Newcastle; Holiday Inn, Seaton Burn.

8B 27 Consett & District
Elmfield Road, Consett, Co Durham, DH8 5NN
01207 502186, Fax 505060, Pro 580210, Sec 505060
Course is on the A691 14 miles N of Durham.
Parkland course.
Pro Stuart Ord
Founded 1911
Designed by Harry Vardon
18 holes, 6080 yards, S.S.S. 69
Welcome by prior arrangement with Pro.
WD £18; WE £26.
Welcome by prior arrangement with Sec; all-day menu available for £11; from £18.
Full clubhouse facilities.
Derwent Manor (formerly Royal Derwent); Raven.

8B 28 Crook
Low Job's Hill, Crook, Co Durham, DL15 9AA
01388 762427, Sec 767926, Rest/Bar 767926
On A690 9 miles W of Durham.
Parkland course, hilly in parts.
Founded 1919
18 holes, 6102 yards, S.S.S. 69
Welcome by prior arrangement.
Prices on application.
Welcome WD by prior arrangement; packages on application; from £14.
Clubhouse facilities.
Helme Park.

8B 29 Darlington
Haughton Grange, Darlington, Co Durham, DL1 3JD
www.darlington-gc.co.uk
darlingtongolfclub@virgin.net
01325 355324, Fax 488126, Pro 484198
Between A1(M), A19 and A66 at N end of Darlington.
Parkland course.
Pro Craig Dilley; Founded 1908
Designed by MacKenzie
18 holes, 6181 yards, S.S.S. 69
9-acre practice. Buggies for hire.
Welcome WD.
WD £20.
Welcome by prior arrangement; packages and special rates for larger groups; from £30.
Full clubhouse facilities.
White Horse; Kings Head, both Darlington; Eden Arms, Rushyford.

8B 30 De Vere Slaley Hall
Slaley, Hexham, Northumberland, NE47 0BY
www.deveregolf.co.uk
slaley.hall@devere-hotels.com
01434 673350, Fax 673152, Pro 673154

Off A69; 23 miles from Newcastle.
Wooded, heath and parkland course.
Pro Mark Stancer
Founded 1989
Designed by Dave Thomas (Hunting
Course) and Neil Coles (Priestman
Course)
Hunting: 18 holes, 7088 yards, S.S.S.
74; Priestman: 18 holes, 6951 yards,
S.S.S. 72.
† Welcome any day.
⌊ WD/WE £22.50.
⌒ Welcome WD for groups of 12+;
from £22.50. Residential breaks from
£69.60. Customised golf days
available.
⦿ Bar clubhouse.
⊸ Bedrooms on site.

8B 31 **Dinsdale Spa**
Neasham Road, Middleton-St-
George, Darlington, Co Durham,
DL2 1DW
☎ 01325 332222, Fax 332297,
Pro 332515, Sec 332297
Off the A67 near Teeside Airport
midway between Middleton St George
and Neasham.
Parkland course.
Pro Neil Metcalfe
Founded 1910
18 holes, 6090 yards, S.S.S. 69
⌇ Practice ground.
† Welcome when tee times allow.
⌊ WD £25; WE with member £15;
second guest £17.50.
⌒ Welcome by prior arrangement
with Sec; catering packages available;
from £20.
⦿ Full clubhouse bar and catering
facilities.
⊸ Croft Spa; Davenport.

8B 32 **Dunstanburgh Castle** ℭ
Embleton, Elnwick, Northumberland,
NE66 3XQ
🖧 www.dunstanburgh.com
✉ golfclub@dunstanburgh.com
☎ 01665 576562, Fax 576562
7 miles NE of Elnwick off the A1; follow
signs to Embleton.
Seaside links course.
Founded 1900
Designed by James Braid
18 holes, 6298 yards, S.S.S. 70
† Welcome.
⌊ WD £20; WE £24/£29 day ticket.
⌒ Welcome by prior arrangement;
packages available; separate dining
facilities; from £16.
⦿ Full clubhouse facilities.
⊸ Sportsmans Inn; Dunstanburgh
Castle, both Embleton.

8B 33 **Durham City** ℭ
Littleburn Lane, Langley Moor,
Durham, DH7 8HL
🖧 www.durhamcitygolf.co.uk
✉ durhamcitygolf@lineone.net
☎ 0191 378 0069, Fax 4265,
Pro 0029, Sec 386 4434
Course is off the A690 two miles SW of
Durham.
Parkland course.
Pro Steve Corbally; Founded 1887
Designed by CC Stanton
18 holes, 6326 yards, S.S.S. 70
† Welcome by prior arrangement.
⌊ WD £24; WE £30.
⌒ Welcome WD; packages available;
terms on application.
⦿ Full catering; limited service Mon.

8B 34 **Eaglescliffe** ℭ
Yarm Road, Eaglescliffe, Stockton-on-
Tees, Cleveland, TS16 0DQ
✉ eaglescliffegcsec@tiscali.co.uk
☎ 01642 780238, Fax 780238,
Pro 790122, Rest/Bar 780098
On A135 Stockton to Yarm.
Undulating parkland course.
Pro Graeme Bell; Founded 1914
Designed by James Braid, modification
by H Cotton
18 holes, 6275 yards, S.S.S. 70
† Welcome.
⌊ WD £26-£35; WE £36-£50.
⌒ Welcome WD by prior
arrangement; packages include 18/27
holes of golf and 3-course meal; prices
on application.
⦿ Full clubhouse facilities.
⊸ Parkmore; Sunnyside; Clairville.

8B 35 **Elemore**
Easington Lane, Houghton-le-Spring,
Tyne and Wear
☎ 0191 5173057, Fax 5173054
5 miles E of Durham City; W of
Easington Lane.
Parkland course.
Founded 1994
Designed by Jonathan Gaunt
18 holes, 5947 yards, S.S.S. 69
† Pay and play.
⌊ WD £9; WE £12.
⌒ Welcome by prior arrangement;
terms on application.
⦿ Bar and function room.
⊸ Fox and Hounds, Hetton-le-Hole.

8B 36 **Garesfield**
Chopwell, Tyne And Wear,
NE17 7AP
☎ 01207 561309, Fax 561309,
Pro 563082, Rest/Bar 561278

On B6315 to High Spen off A694 from
A1 at Rowlands Gill.
Undulating wooded parkland course.
Pro David Race; Founded 1922
Designed by William Woodend
18 holes, 6458 yards, S.S.S. 72
† Welcome .
⌊ Terms on application.
⌒ Welcome by prior arrangement
except Mon and Sat; catering
packages can be arranged with the
steward; terms on application.
⦿ Full clubhouse facilities except
Mon.
⊸ Towneley Arms, Rowlands Gill.

8B 37 **The George** ℭ
Washington County Hotel
& CG
Stonecellar Road, Washington, Tyne
and Wear, NE37 1PH
☎ 0191 4029988, Fax 4151166,
Pro 4178346, Sec 4168341
Course is signposted from the A1(M)
and the A194.
Parkland course.
Pro David Patterson; Founded 1990
18 holes, 6604 yards, S.S.S. 72
⌇ 20.
† Welcome by prior arrangement;
special rates for hotel guests.
⌊ WD £20; WE £20.
⌒ Welcome by prior arrangement;
special rates for groups of more than
15; hotel packages; leisure club; pool;
spa; terms on application.
⦿ Full clubhouse and hotel facilities.
⊸ 105-bedroom George Washington
Country Hotel on site.

8B 38 **Gosforth**
Broadway East, Gosforth, NE3 5ER
☎ 0191 2853495, Fax 2846274,
Pro 2850553, Sec 2853495,
Rest/Bar 2856710
Off A6125 3 miles N of Newcastle.
Parkland course with stream feature.
Pro Grahame Garland; Founded 1906
18 holes, 6024 yards, S.S.S. 69
† Welcome by prior arrangement.
⌊ WD/WE £25.
⌒ Welcome WD by prior
arrangement; catering packages
available; discounts for groups of more
than 12; from £25.
⦿ Full clubhouse facilities.
⊸ Swallow Gosforth Park; Novotel.

8B 39 **Hall Garth Golf &**
Country Club
Coatham Mundeville, Nr Darlington,
Co Durham, DL3 3LU

www.corushotels.co.uk/hallgarth
☎ 01325 320246, Fax 310083,
Pro 300400, Sec 300400,
Rest/Bar 300400
From A1 (M) Junction 59 take A167
towards Darlington; top of hill.
Parkland course.
Founded 1995
Designed by B Moore
9 holes, 6607 yards, S.S.S. 72
† Welcome.
Ⓛ WD £8; WE £10.00.
⌔ Welcome; packages available;
terms on application.
◉ Bar and restaurant facilities on
site; hotel on site.
⌁ Hall Garth, 16th century country
house with leisure facilities.

8B 40 Haltwhisle ☂

Banktop, Greenhead, Via Carlisle,
Cumbria, CA6 7HN
☎ 016977 47367, Fax 011434
344311, Sec 01434 344000
Off A69 N of Haltwhisle turn right at
Greenhead.
Parkland course.
Founded 1967
Designed by Members
18 holes, 5660 yards, S.S.S. 69
† Welcome except after 5pm Wed
and Fri and before 3pm on Sun.
Ⓛ WD £12; WE £15.
⌔ Welcome by prior arrangement;
packages include 27 holes of golf and
all-day catering; from £20.
◉ Bar and catering facilities
available.
⌁ Greenhead Hotel.

8B 41 Hartlepool

Hart Warren, Hartlepool, Cleveland,
TS24 9QF
www.hartlepoolgolfclub.co.uk
☎ 01429 274398, Fax 274129,
Pro 267473
Course is off the A1086 at N edge of
Hartlepool.
Seaside links course.
Pro Graham Laidlaw; Founded 1906
Designed by James Braid (in part)
18 holes, 6215 yards, S.S.S. 70
𝄽 Practice area.
† Welcome; restricted to members'
guests Sun.
Ⓛ WD £26; WE £40.
⌔ Welcome WD by prior
arrangement; catering packages
available from the steward; snooker;
terms on application.
◉ Full clubhouse facilities, except
Mon.
⌁ Staincliffe; Marine; Travel Inn.

8B 42 Heworth

Gingling Gate, Heworth, Tyne and
Wear, NE10 8XY
☎ 0191 496 4424, Pro 438 4223,
Sec 469 9832
Course is close to the A1 (M) SE of
Gateshead.
Parkland course.
Founded 1912
18 holes, 6421 yards, S.S.S. 71
† Welcome but not before 10am at
WE.
Ⓛ WD/WE £18.
⌔ Welcome by prior arrangement;
catering packages by arrangement;
dining room; from £17-£22.
◉ Bar and restaurant.
⌁ George Washington.

8B 43 Hexham ☂

Spital Park, Hexham, Northumberland,
NE46 3RZ
www.hexhamgolfclub.ntb.org.uk
✉ hexham.golf.club@talk21.com
☎ 01434 603072, Fax 601865,
Pro 604904, Sec 603072
Course is on the A69 one mile W of
Hexham.
Undulating parkland course.
Pro Martin Foster; Founded 1907
Designed by Harry Vardon
18 holes, 6301 yards, S.S.S. 70
𝄽 Practice ground.
† Welcome by arrangement.
Ⓛ WD £30; WE £40.
⌔ Welcome except WE by
arrangement; packages available; from
£25.
◉ Clubhouse catering and bar.
⌁ Beaumont.

8B 44 High Throston

Hart Lane, Hartlepool, Cleveland,
TS26 OUG
☎ 01429 275325, Sec 268071
From A19N take A179 to Hartlepool.
Parkland course with USGA standard
green.
Pro Graham Bell (available upon
request); Founded 1996
Designed by J Gaunt
18 holes, 6247 yards, S.S.S. 70
𝄽 Practice green and putting green.
† Welcome.
Ⓛ WD £16; WE and BH £19.
⌔ Welcome by prior arrangement.
◉ Hot food and drinks.
⌁ Raby Arms.

8B 45 Hobson Municipal

Burnopfield, Newcastle-upon-Tyne,
NE16 6BZ

☎ 01207 271605, Fax 271069,
Pro 271605, Sec 570189,
Rest/Bar 270941
On main Newcastle-Consett road
opposite Hobson Industrial estate.
Parkland course.
Pro JW Ord; Founded 1980
18 holes, 6403 yards, S.S.S. 71
† Pay and play.
Ⓛ WD £12; WE £16.
⌔ Welcome by arrangement with the
Pro; packages available; terms on
application.
◉ Catering and bar facilities.
⌁ Towneley Arms.

8B 46 Houghton-le-Spring

Copt Hill, Houghton-le-Spring, Tyne
and Wear, DH5 8LU
☎ 0191 5847421, Fax 5840048,
Pro 5847421, Sec 5840048,
Rest/Bar 5841198
On B1440 Houghton-le-Spring to
Seaham Harbour road 0.5 miles from
Houghton-le-Spring.
Hillside testing; semi heathland.
Pro Kevin Gow; Founded 1908
18 holes, 6443 yards, S.S.S. 71
† Welcome after 9am; WE
restrictions.
Ⓛ WD £20-£30; WE £28-£33.
⌔ Welcome by prior arrangement;
golf and catering packages available;
from £30.
◉ Catering and bar facilities
available.
⌁ White Lion; Ramside Hall; Rainton
Lodge.

8B 47 Hunley Hall ☂

Brotton, Saltburn-by-the-Sea, N Yorks,
TS12 2QQ
www.hunleyhall.co.uk
✉ enquiries@hunleyhall.co.uk
☎ 01287 676216, Fax 678250,
Pro 677444
From A19 take A174 to Brotton into St
Margaret's Way.
Coastal.
Pro Andrew Brook; Founded 1993
Designed by J Morgan
27 holes, 6918 yards, S.S.S. 73
𝄽 12 floodlit bays.
† Welcome.
Ⓛ WD £25; WE £35.
⌔ Welcome Mon to Sat; packages for
18 and 27 holes of golf and catering
available; from £26, terms on
application.
◉ Restaurant and bars; members
bar; spike bar; all-day catering
available.
⌁ Accommodation on site; 2 Star.

8B 48 Knotty Hill Golf Centre
Sedgefield, Stockton-on-Tees,
TS21 2BB
🖥 www.knottyhillgolfcentre.co.uk
📧 khgc21@btopenworld.com
☎ 01740 620320, Fax 622227,
Sec 620320, Rest/Bar 620320
Course is on the A177 one mile from
Sedgefield, and four miles from the A1
(M) Junction 60.
Naturally undulating parkland course.
Founded 1991
Designed by C Stanton
𝄢 21 bays.
† All welcome. Grass tee area, 2
putting greens, 2 chipping areas &
practice bunker.
⌇ WD £12; WE £13 – prices for both
courses.
⌁ Welcome WD; terms on
application; restrictions WE.
🍴 Full clubhouse facilities available.
🏨 Hardwick Hall, Sedgefield.

8B 49 Linden Hall   ☏
Linden Hall Hotel, Longhorsley,
Morpeth, Northumberland,
NE65 8XF
🖥 www.lindenhall.co.uk
📧 golf@lindenhall.co.uk
☎ 01670 500011, Fax 500001,
Rest/Bar 500033
From A1 take A697 to Coldstream until
reaching Longhorsley; course half mile
on right.
Parkland course.
Pro David Curry; Founded 1997
Designed by J Gaunt
18 holes, 6846 yards, S.S.S. 73
𝄢 Practice range, 12 bays.
† Welcome with handicap certs.
⌇ WD £30; WE £35.
⌁ Welcome by prior arrangement;
packages for golf and catering
available; corporate days arranged;
leisure club, gym in hotel; prices on
application.
🍴 Grill room, conservatory and 2
bars.
🏨 Linden Hall on site.

8B 50 Longhirst Hall   ☏
Longhirst Hall, Longhirst,
Northumberland, NE61 3LI
🖥 www.longhirstgolf.co.uk
📧 enquiries@longhirstgolf.co.uk
☎ 01670 858519, Pro 791768, Sec
862449, Rest/Bar 791505
From A1 take signs to Hebron Cockle
Park; after 2 miles at T junction turn
left and follow signs for Longhirst Hall;
2 miles N of Morpeth.
Parkland course.
Pro Graham Kent; Founded 1997
18 holes, 6572 yards, S.S.S. 72

𝄢 Practice.
† Welcome.
⌇ Seniors £20; juniors £10.
⌁ Welcome by prior arrangement;
packages include golf, catering and, if
required, hotel and self-catering
accommodation; group and corporate
days can be arranged for any size.
🍴 Full facilities in clubhouse and The
Hall.
🏨 Longhirst Hall 75-room hotel on
site and self-catering at Micklewood
Village on site.

8B 51 Magdalene Fields   ☏
Berwick-upon-Tweed, Northumberland,
TD15 1NE
🖥 www.magdalene-fields.co.uk
📧 mail@magdalene-fields.co.uk
☎ 01289 306384, Fax 306384,
Sec 306130
5 minutes walk from centre of town in
direction of coast.
Seaside course with parkland fairways.
Founded 1903
18 holes, 6527 yards, S.S.S. 71
† Welcome by prior arrangement.
⌇ WD £20; WE £22.
⌁ Welcome WD; restrictions Sat and
Sun; catering packages available; from
£19.
🍴 Bar and restaurant.
🏨 Queen's Head, Berwick.

8B 52 Matfen Hall   ☏
Matfen Hall, Matfen, Near Newcastle
upon Tyne Northumberland, NE20 ORH
🖥 www.matfenhall.com
📧 info@matfenhall.com
☎ 01661 886400, Fax 886055,
Pro 886400, Rest/Bar 886500
Just off B6318 Military road 15 miles W
of Newcastle.
Parkland course.
Pro John Harrison; Founded 1994
Designed by M James/A Mair/J Gaunt
18 holes, 6569 yards, S.S.S. 71
𝄢 Open air practice facilities
including short game area.
† Welcome.
⌇ Winter WD £15, WE £20; Summer
WD £30, WE £40.
⌁ Welcome by prior arrangement;
golf and catering packages available;
par 3 course; practice range; terms on
application. Society and Company calls
are welcome.
🍴 Full bar and restaurant facilities
available.
🏨 Matfen Hall Country House Hotel.

8B 53 Middlesbrough
Brass Castle Lane, Marton,
Middlesbrough, TS8 9EE

🖥 www.middlesbroughgolfclub.co.uk
📧 enquiries@middlesbroughgolfclub
.co.uk
☎ 01642 311515, Fax 319607,
Pro 311766, Sec 311515,
Rest/Bar 316430
1 mile W of A172 5 miles S of
Middlesbrough.
Parkland course.
Pro Don Jones; Founded 1908
Designed by James Braid
18 holes, 6278 yards, S.S.S. 70
𝄢 3 practice grounds and putting
green; short game academy; driving
nets.
† Welcome except Tues and Sat.
⌇ Prices on application.
⌁ Welcome by prior arrangement;
packages of golf and catering available;
terms available on application.
🍴 Full facilities; restaurant service
available at 24 hours notice.
🏨 Blue Bell Hotel, Acklam.

8B 54 Middlesbrough Municipal
Ladgate Lane, Middlesbrough, TS5 7YZ
🖥 www.middlesbrough.gov.uk
☎ 01642 315533, Fax 300726,
Pro 300720
Access to the course from the A19 via
the A174 to Acklam.
Undulating parkland course.
Pro Alan Hope; Founded 1977
Designed by Middlesbrough Borough
Council
18 holes, 6333 yards, S.S.S. 70
† Welcome but must arrange starting
time.
⌇ WD £10.90; WE £13.50, Twilight
£6.25; Winter WD £8; WE £10; Twilight
£5.
⌁ Welcome by prior arrangement;
terms on application.
🍴 Catering available; lunches.
🏨 Blue Bell.

8B 55 Morpeth   ☏
The Common, Morpeth, NE61 2BT
🖥 www.morpethgolf.co.uk
☎ 01670 504942, Fax 504942,
Pro 515675, Sec 504942,
Rest/Bar 504942
On A197 1 mile S of Morpeth.
Parkland course.
Pro Martin Jackson; Founded 1906
Designed by Harry Vardon (1922)
18 holes, 6104 yards, S.S.S. 69
𝄢 Practice area.
† Welcome by prior arrangement
after 9.30am.
⌇ WD £22.50; WE £27.50.
⌁ Welcome WD by prior
arrangement with Sec; packages for

golf and catering available; terms on application.
🍽 Snacks, bar lunches, dinner available; no catering on Mon during winter.
🛏 Waterford Lodge; Queens Head; Linden Hall.

8B 56 Mount Oswald
Mount Oswald Manor, South Road, Durham, Co Durham, DH1 3TQ
🖥 www.mountoswald.co.uk
✉ information@mountoswald.co.uk
☎ 0191 3867527, Fax 3860975
On A1050 SW of Durham.
Partly wooded parkland course.
Founded 1924
18 holes, 5984 yards, S.S.S. 69
ℐ Practice area.
† Welcome every day; Sun after 10am.
ℒ WD £12.50; WE and BH £15.
⤢ Welcome by prior arrangement; special rates for 12 or more; WE available; function room for 80; other smaller private rooms; packages for golf and catering; from £24.
🍽 Full clubhouse catering.
🛏 Three Tuns.

8B 57 Newbiggin-by-the-Sea Clubhouse
Newbiggin-by-the-Sea, Northumberland, NE64 6DW
☎ 01670 817344, Fax 520236
Off A197 following signs for Newbiggin-by-the-Sea from A189 from Newcastle.
Seaside links course.
Founded 1884
18 holes, 6516 yards, S.S.S. 71
ℐ Remote practice area.
† Welcome after 10am except on competition days.
ℒ WD £16; WE £20.
⤢ Welcome by prior arrangement with Sec; catering packages available.
🍽 Full clubhouse facilities.
🛏 Beachcomber.

8B 58 Newcastle United
60 Ponteland Road, Cowgate, Newcastle-upon-Tyne, Northumberland, NE5 3JW
🖥 www.nujc.co.uk
✉ info@nujc.co.uk
☎ 0191 2864693, Fax 2864323, Pro 2869998, Sec 2864323
2 miles W of the city centre.
Mooreland course.
Founded 1892
Designed by Tom Morris
18 holes, 6612 yards, S.S.S. 71

† Welcome WD; not on WE competition days.
ℒ Prices on application. WD £22 per day. Motorised buggies and bar meals available. Special rates for societies.
⤢ Welcome by arrangement; catering packages by arrangement; snooker; terms available on application.
🍽 Bar and snacks.
🛏 Gosforth Park.

8B 59 Northumberland
High Gosforth Park, Newcastle-upon-Tyne, Tyne and Wear, NE3 5HT
☎ 0191 236 2498, Fax 236 2036, Rest/Bar 236 22009
Off A1 5 miles N of Newcastle.
Parkland course.
Founded 1898
Designed by HS Colt/James Braid
18 holes, 6683 yards, S.S.S. 72
ℐ Large practice area.
† Welcome by arrangement.
ℒ WD/WE £40.
⤢ Welcome by arrangement.
🍽 Full clubhouse facilities.
🛏 Swallow, Gosforth Park; Marriott.

8B 60 Norton Golf Course
Junction Road, Stockton-on-Tees, Cleveland, TS20 1SU
☎ 01642 676385, Fax 608467, Sec 674636, Rest/Bar 612452
From A177 2 miles N of Stockton roundabout.
Parkland course.
Founded 1989
Designed by T Harper
18 holes, 5855 yards, S.S.S. 71
† Public pay and play.
ℒ WD £11.50; WE £13.50.
⤢ Welcome by prior arrangement; packages available both for WD; bookings much be made more than 7 days in advance; from £19.
🍽 Full catering facilities.
🛏 Swallow, Stockton.

8B 61 Oak Leaf Golf Complex (Aycliffe)
School Aycliffe Lane, Newton Aycliffe, Co Durham, DL5 6QZ
☎ 01325 310820, Fax 310820, Pro 310820, Sec 316040
Take A1 (M) to A68 and then turn into Newton Aycliffe; course on left.
Parkland course.
Pro Ernie Wilson
18 holes, 5818 yards off the white; 5308 yards off the yellow, S.S.S. 68 off the white; 66 off the yellow
ℐ 18 bays floodlit.

† Everyone welcome; no restrictions.
ℒ WD £10.50; WE £13; concessions for under-18s and over-60s. WD £7.50 WE £10.50.
⤢ Welcome at off-peak times; deposit required; sports and leisure complex; terms on application.
🍽 Bar and restaurant facilities available.
🛏 Redworth Arms, Redworth; Eden Arms; Gretna Hotel.

8B 62 Parklands Golf Club
High Gosforth Park, Newcastle-upon-Tyne, NE3 5HQ
☎ 0191 236 4480, Fax 236 3322
Course is off the A1 three miles N of Newcastle.
Parkland course.
Pro Brian Rumney; Founded 1971
18 holes, 6060 yards, S.S.S. 69
ℐ 45 floodlit.
† Welcome.
ℒ WD £17; WE £20.
⤢ Welcome by prior arrangement; catering packages available; terms on application.
🍽 Bar and restaurant facilities available.
🛏 Marriott Gosforth Park.

8B 63 Ponteland
Bell Villas, Ponteland, Newcastle-upon-Tyne, Tyne and Wear, NE20 9BD
☎ 01661 822689, Fax 860077, Pro 01661822689 ext 18, Sec 822689 ext 10, Rest/Bar 822689 ext 21
On A696 2 miles N of Newcastle Airport.
Parkland course.
Pro Alan Robson-Crosby; Founded 1927
Designed by Harry Ferney
18 holes, 6524 yards, S.S.S. 71
† Welcome Mon-Thurs; Fri, Sat, Sun as members' guest.
ℒ WD £25.00; WE £10.00 per day with a member.
⤢ Welcome on Tues and Thurs; catering packages can be arranged; from £22.50.
🍽 Full clubhouse facilities.

8B 64 Prudhoe
Eastwood Park, Prudhoe, Northumberland, NE42 5DX
☎ 01661 832466, Fax 830710, Pro 836188, Sec 835168
Course is on the A695 12 miles W of Newcastle.
Parkland course.
Pro John Crawford; Founded 1930

18 holes, 5862 yards, S.S.S. 69
⚐ Practice ground.
† Welcome except on competition days.
⚑ Prices on application £20 per day.
⚘ Welcome WD by arrangement; terms on application.
⚑ Bar snacks and meals available.
⚒ Beaumont, Hexham.

8B 65 **Ramside**
Ramside Hall Hotel, Carrville, Durham, DH1 1TD
☎ 0191 386 9514, Fax 386 9519
On A690 Sunderland road 400m from A1 (M) Junction 62.
Parkland course; 3 x 9 loops.
Pro Robert Lister; Founded 1996
Designed by Stephen Marnoch Jonathan Gaunt
27holes/3 loops of 9 holes, 1-18 holes 6851 yards off the blue, S.S.S. 73 off the blue
⚐ 16.
† Welcome by prior arrangement. 3 x 9 loops: Bishops Cathedral; Cathedral Princess; Prince Bishops.
⚑ WD £28; WE £35.
⚘ Welcome by prior arrangement; full society and corporate packages available; terms on application.
⚑ Full bar and restaurant facilities; hotel restaurant and bar also.
⚒ On site Ramside Hall.

8B 66 **Ravensworth**
'Angel View', Long Bank, Gateshead, NE9 7NE
⚎ www.ravensworthgolfclub.co.uk
✉ ravensworth.golfclub@virgin.net
☎ 0191 4876014, Pro 4913475
Course is off the A1, ¼ mile from Angel of the North.
Moorland/parkland course.
Pro not yet decided; Founded 1906
18 holes, 5966 yards, S.S.S. 69
† Welcome.
⚑ Prices on application.
⚘ Welcome WD by prior arrangement; catering packages available; terms on application.
⚑ Full facilities available.
⚒ Swallow Hotel, Gateshead.

8B 67 **Roseberry Grange**
Grange Villa, Chester-le-Street, Durham, DH2 3NF
☎ 0191 370 0660, Fax 2047, Sec 2047
3 miles W of Chester-le-Street close to A1(M) Junction.
Parkland course.

Pro Alan Hartley; Founded 1987
18 holes, 6023 yards, S.S.S. 69
† Welcome WD; by prior arrangement WE.
⚑ WD £11.50; WE £15.
⚘ Welcome; terms on application.
⚑ Full clubhouse facilities.
⚒ Lumley Castle; Beamish Park.

8B 68 **Rothbury**
Old Race Course, Rothbury, Morpeth, Northumberland, NE65 7TR
☎ 01669 621271, Sec 630378
Off A697 at Weldon Bridge following the signs for Rothbury; 15 miles N of Morpeth.
Flat course alongside river.
Founded 1891
Designed by J B Radcliffe
9 holes, 5779 yards, S.S.S. 67
† Welcome WD; restrictions apply at WE.
⚑ WD £13; WE £18.
⚘ Welcome WD by arrangement; catering packages available during the day; by arrangement for evening meals; bar closed between 3pm-7.30pm; reductions for larger groups; from £11.
⚑ Clubhouse facilities.
⚒ Queens Head; Newcastle Hotel, both Rothbury.

8B 69 **Ryhope**
Leechmore Way, Ryhope, Sunderland, Durham, SR2 0DH
☎ 0191 5237333, Sec 5536373
Turn off the A19 at Ryhope village towards Hollycarrside.
Being re-designed.
Pro Brian and Roger Janes; Founded 1991
Designed by Sunderland Borough Council
16 holes, 6001 yards, S.S.S. 69
† Welcome.
⚑ WD £6, WE £7; £1 discount for over-60s; £2 discount for cheaper; £1 discount for ladies.

8B 70 **Ryton**   ♋
Dr Stanners, Clara Vale, Ryton, Tyne and Wear, NE40 3TD
☎ 0191 4133253, Fax 4131642, Sec 4133737, Rest/Bar 4133737
Course is off the A695 signposted Crawcrook.
Parkland course.
Founded 1891
18 holes, 5950 yards, S.S.S. 69
† Welcome WD; by prior arrangement WE.

⚑ Prices on application.
⚘ Welcome; discounts for groups of more than 16; WE available; catering packages; prices available on application.
⚑ Clubhouse facilities.
⚒ Ryton County Club; Hedgefield; Marriott Gateshead.

8B 71 **Saltburn-by-the-Sea**
Hob Hill, Saltburn-by-Sea, Cleveland, TS12 1NJ
⚎ www.saltburngolf.co.uk
✉ infor@saltburngolf.co.uk
☎ 01287 622812, Fax 625988, Pro 624653
On A1268 1 mile from Saltburn.
Parkland course.
Pro Mike Nutter; Founded 1894
18 holes, 5897 yards off the white, S.S.S. 68, par 70 off the white
† Welcome; restrictions Sun and Thurs; limited Sat.
⚑ WD £24; WE £30.
⚘ Welcome by prior arrangement; catering available except Mon; terms on application.
⚑ Full clubhouse facilities; limited Mon catering but could cater for larger parties on Mon.
⚒ Royal Oak.

8B 72 **Seaham**
Dawdon, Seaham, Co Durham, SR7 7RD
☎ 0191 5812354, Pro 5130837, Sec 5811268
2 miles NE of the A19.
Heathland course.
Pro Glyn Jones; Founded 1911
Designed by Dr A MacKenzie
18 holes, 6017 yards, S.S.S. 67
† Welcome.
⚑ Prices on application.
⚘ Welcome; terms available on application.
⚑ Full clubhouse facilities.

8B 73 **Seahouses**
Beadnell, Seahouses, Northumberland, NE68 7XT
⚎ www.seahousesgolf.co.uk
✉ secretary@seahousesgolf.co.uk
☎ 01665 720794, Fax 721994, Sec 720794, Rest/Bar 720794
On the B1340 S of Seahouses village.
Links course; upgraded to 18 in 1976.
Founded 1913/1976
18 holes, 5542 yards, S.S.S. 67
⚐ Putting green.
† Welcome; groups of more than four must book in advance.

WD £18 round;.WE/BH £25 round, £30 day

Welcome by prior arrangement everyday except Sun; packages for catering, golf and local hotels available; prices available on application.

Full catering service except Mon when limited food is available; full bar and catering in summer.

Sunningdale; Beadnell Towers; Sportsman; Blue Bell, Belford.

8B 74 Seaton Carew
Tees Road, Seaton Carew, Hartlepool, TS25 1DE

01429 266249, Fax 261040, Pro 890660, Sec 261040 (Bookings 296496)

Course is off the A178 three miles S of Hartlepool.
Championship links course.
Pro Mark Rogers; Founded 1874
Designed by Duncan McCuaig
Old: 18 holes, 6613 yards, S.S.S. 72; Brabazon: 18 holes, 6855 yards, S.S.S. 73; Micklem: 18 holes, S.S.S. 71

Practice area.
Welcome WD; WE restricted.
WD £35; WE £45 per day.
Welcome by prior arrangement; catering by arrangement.
Full facilities.
Staincliffe; Marine.

8B 75 South Moor Golf Club
The Middles, Craghead, Stanley, Co Durham, DH9 6AG

01207 232848, Fax 284616, Pro 283525, Sec 232848, Rest/Bar 232848

Off the A693 6 miles W of Chester-le-Street on B6532 1 mile S of Stanley.
Moorland course.
Pro Shaun Cowell; Founded 1923
Designed by Dr A MacKenzie
18 holes, 6445 yards, S.S.S. 71

Welcome with handicap certs.
WD £15; WE £26.
Welcome WD between 9.30am-11am and 2pm-3.30pm; WE between 10am-11am and 2pm-3.30pm; catering packages available; snooker table; from £15.
Full clubhouse facilities.
Lambton Arms; Lumley Castle; South Causey; Harperley Hotel

8B 76 South Shields
Cleadon Hills, South Shields, Tyne and Wear, NE34 8EG
www.ssgc.co.uk

thesecretary@southshields-golf.freeserve.co.uk
0191 456 8942, Fax 8942, Pro 0110, Rest/Bar 0475
Close to A19 and A1 (M) near Cleadon Chimney.
Heathland links course.
Pro Gary Parsons; Founded 1893
Designed by McKenzie/Baird
18 holes, 6264 yards, S.S.S. 71

Welcome.
WD £22; WE £27.
Welcome by prior arrangement; terms on application.
Clubhouse catering and bar facilities available.
Sea Hotel.

8B 77 Stocksfield
New Ridley, Stocksfield, Northumberland, NE43 7RE
www.sgcgolf.co.uk
info@sgcgolf.co.uk
01661 843041, Fax 843046
2 miles from Stocksfield on the New Ridley Road, off the A695 Hexham-Prudhoe Road.
Woodland/parkland course.
Pro David Mather
Founded 1913
Designed by Frank Pennink
18 holes, 5945 yards, S.S.S. 69

Welcome except Wed and Sat.
WD £30; WE £35.
Welcome by arrangement; special packages with or without catering for 18/27/36 holes available; some reductions for larger groups; from £18.
Full clubhouse facilities.
Beaumont, Hexham; Royal Derwent, Allensford.

8B 78 Stressholme Golf Centre
Snipe Lane, Darlington, DL2 2SA
01325 461002
2 miles S of Darlington.
Parkland course.
Pro Ralph Gibens; Founded 1976
18 holes, 6229 yards, S.S.S. 71

15 bays; floodlit.
Welcome.
WD £11; WE £13.
Welcome by arrangement with professional; terms on application.
Clubhouse facilities.
Blackwell Grange.

8B 79 Swarland Hall
Coast View, Swarland, Morpeth, Northumberland, NE65 9JG
01670 787010, Rest/Bar 787940

Course is one mile W of the A1 eight miles S of Alnwick.
Parkland course.
Pro Wayne Tyrie; Founded 1993
18 holes, 6628 yards, S.S.S. 72

Practice.
Welcome.
WD £13; WE £18. Full Day £18 WD, WE £23.
Welcome; packages available for golf and catering; 10 percent discount for parties of more than 12; from £12
Full dining and bar facilities available.
The Oaks Hotel, Alnwick.

8B 80 Teesside
Acklam Road, Thornaby, Stockton, Cleveland, TS17 7JS
www.teessidegolfclub.com
teesside@golfclub76.freeserve .co.uk
01642 616516, Fax 676252, Pro 673822, Sec 616516, Rest/Bar 676249
Off A1130 Thornaby-Acklam Road.
Parkland course.
Pro Ken Hall; Founded 1901
18 holes, 6535 yards, S.S.S. 71

Welcome by arrangement; before 4.30pm WD after 11.30am WE.
WD £26; WE £26.
Welcome WD by prior arrangement; minimum group 10, max 35; from £22.
Full clubhouse facilities.
Swallow, Stockton; Golden Eagle, Thornaby.

8B 81 Tynedale
Tyne Green, Hexham, Northumberland, NE46 3HQ
www.tynedale-golf-club.co.uk
enquiries@tynedale-golf-club.co.uk
01434 608154
From A69 Hexham road turn into Countryside Park; course 0.5 miles on S of river Tyne.
Parkland course.
Founded 1907
9 holes, 5403 yards, S.S.S. 67

Welcome; except before 12 Sun
Prices on application.
Welcome by prior arrangement; discounts for groups of more than 10; prices on application.
Full clubhouse facilities.
Beaumont; County; Royal.

8B 82 Tynemouth
Spital Dene, Tynemouth, North Shields, Tyne and Wear, NE30 2ER
secretary@tynemouthgolfclub.com

☎ 0191 257 4578, Fax 259 5193,
Sec 257 3381
On A695.
Parkland course.
Pro John McKenna
Founded 1913
Designed by Willie Park
18 holes, 6359 yards, S.S.S. 71
† Welcome WD after 9.30am; after
12.30pm Sun; limited Sat.
ℂ WD/WE 2.5.
⤳ Welcome WD by prior arrangement;
catering packages available; terms
available on application.
🍽 Lunches, teas and snacks available.
⌁ Park Hotel, Tynemouth.

8B 83 Tyneside
Westfield Lane, Ryton, Tyne and Wear,
NE40 3QE
☎ 0191 413 2177, Fax 413 2742,
Pro 413 1600, Sec 413 2742,
Rest/Bar 4138357
7 miles W of Newcastle off A695 S of
river.
Parkland course.
Pro Malcolm Gunn
Founded 1879
Designed by HS Colt (1910)
18 holes, 6033 yards, S.S.S. 69
𝟙 Large practice area.
† Welcome.
ℂ WD£25; WE.£30
⤳ Welcome by prior arrangement;
reductions for groups of 18 or more;
catering packages available; prices on
application.
🍽 Full clubhouse catering and bar
facilities.
⌁ Ryton Park; Hedgefield Inn;
Copthorne, Newcastle; Marriott,
Gateshead; Ravensdene, Gateshead.

8B 84 Warkworth
The Links, Warkworth, Morpeth,
Northumberland, NE65 0SW
☎ 01665 711596
Off A1068 at Warkworth; 10 miles N of
Morpeth.
Seaside links course.
Founded 1891
Designed by Tom Morris
9 holes, 5986 yards, S.S.S. 69
𝟙 Practice.
† Welcome except Tues and Sat.
ℂ WD £12; WE £20.
⤳ Welcome by prior arrangement;
catering packages available by
arrangement with stewardess; from
£12.
🍽 Bar and catering facilities in
season; by arrangement in winter.
⌁ Warkworth House; Sun.

8B 85 Wearside
Coxgreen, Sunderland, Tyne and
Wear, SR4 9JT
🖰 www.wearsidegolf.com
✉ secretary@wearsidegolf.com
☎ 0191 534 2518, Fax 534 6186,
Pro 534 4269
Course is off the A183 towards
Chester-le-Street; turn right signposted
Coxgreen to a T junction; then turn left.
Meadowland/parkland course.
Pro Doug Brolls; Founded 1892
Designed by H Vardon.
18 holes, 6373 yards, S.S.S. 70
𝟙 Practice + 4-hole par 3 practice
course.
† Welcome except on comp. days.
ℂ WD £20; WE £26.
⤳ Welcome on application to Sec;
catering packages available; from £25.
🍽 Full clubhouse facilities.
⌁ Seaburn.

8B 86 Westerhope
Whorlton Grange, Westerhope,
Newcastle-upon-Tyne, NE5 1PP
☎ 0191 2867636, Pro 2860594,
Rest/Bar 2869125
On the B6324 5 miles W of Newcastle;
close to the Jingling Gate public house.
Wooded parkland course.
Pro N Brown; Founded 1941
Designed by Alexander Sandy Herd
18 holes, 6444 yards, S.S.S. 71
† Welcome.
ℂ Terms on application.
⤳ Welcome by prior arrangement;
catering packages available; prices on
application.
🍽 Full clubhouse facilities.
⌁ Airport Moat House; Holiday Inn;
Novotel, all Newcastle.

8B 87 Whickham
Hollinside Park, Whickham, Newcastle-
upon-Tyne, Tyne and Wear, NE16 5BA
✉ enquiries@whickhamgolfclub.co.uk
☎ 0191 4887309, Fax 4881576,
Pro 4888591, Sec 4881576
Off the A1 at Whickham; follow signs
for Burnopfield, club 1.3 miles.
Parkland course.
Pro Graeme Lisle; Founded 1911
18 holes, 5878 yards, S.S.S. 68
† Welcome.
ℂ WD £20; WE £25.
⤳ Welcome WD by arrangement with
Sec; discounts for larger groups;
catering packages; from £15.
🍽 Full catering facilities.
⌁ Gibside Arms, Whickham; Beamish
Park; County; Copthorne; Derwent
Crossing, all Newcastle.

8B 88 Whitburn
Lizard Lane, South Shields, Tyne and
Wear, NE34 7AF
🖰 www.golf_whitburn.co.uk
✉ wgcsec@ukonline.co.uk
☎ 0191 529 2144, Fax 529 4944,
Pro 529 4210, Sec 529 4944
Off coast road mid-way between
Sunderland and South Shields.
Parkland course.
Pro David Stephenson; Founded 1932
18 holes, 5900 yards, S.S.S. 68
𝟙 Practice area.
† Welcome WD; by prior
arrangement WE.
ℂ WD £22; WE £27.
⤳ Welcome WD by prior arrangement;
restrictions Tues; limited availability WE;
discounts for groups of 11 or more;
catering packages available by prior
arrangement; from £20.
🍽 Full clubhouse facilities.
⌁ Seaburn; Roker; Little Haven,
South Shields.

8B 89 Whitley Bay
Claremont Road, Whitley Bay, Tyne
and Wear, NE26 3UF
🖰 www.whitleybaygolfclub.co.uk
✉ secretary@whitleybaygolfclub.co.uk
☎ 0191 2520180, Fax 2970030,
Pro 2525688, Rest/Bar 2520180
N of Town centre.
Simulated links course.
Pro Gary Shipley; Founded 1890
18 holes, 6529 yards, S.S.S. 71
† Welcome WD.
ℂ WD £24.
⤳ Welcome by prior arrangement;
discounts available for larger groups;
catering packages available; from £30.
🍽 Clubhouse catering facilities.
⌁ The Grand, Tynemouth; Park;
Windsor, both Whitley Bay; Stakis
Wallsend.

8B 90 Wilton
Wilton, Redcar, Cleveland, TS10 4QY
☎ 01642 465265, Fax 452730,
Pro 452730, Sec 465265,
Rest/Bar 465886
Off A174 Whitby-Redcar road through
Lazenby following signs for Wilton
Castle.
Parkland course.
Pro Pat Smillie; Founded 1952/66
18 holes, 6153 yards, S.S.S. 69
𝟙 Under future development.
† Welcome if carrying handicap certs.
ℂ WD £22; WE £24.
⤳ Mon, Wed and Fri and some
Sundays and BH. Catering on
arrangement with secretary.

Full clubhouse facilities.

Post House, Thornaby; Marton Way; Blue Bell, both Middlesbrough.

8B 91 **Woodham Golf & Country Club** ☏

Burnhill Way, Newton Aycliffe, Durham, DL5 4PN

☎ 01325 320574, Fax 315254, Pro 315257, Rest/Bar 301551

Off the A167 to Woodham village in Newton Aycliffe.

Parkland course.

Pro Peter Kelly; Founded 1983

Designed by J Hamilton Stutt

18 holes, 6771 yards, S.S.S. 72

† Welcome by prior arrangement.

⌇ WD £18; WE £29.

⌔ Welcome by prior arrangement; some WE available; minimum 12 players; catering packages by arrangement; buggy hire available; practice area; from £18.

Full bar and restaurant facilities available.

Eden Arms, Rushyford.

8B 92 **Wooler** ☏

Dod Law, Doddington, Wooler, Northumberland, NE71 6EA

☎ 01668 281791

Course is East of the B6525 Wooler-Berwick Rd; signposted from Doddington Village.

Moorland course.

Founded 1976

Designed by Club Members

9 holes, 6372 yards, S.S.S. 70

† Welcome.

⌇ Terms on application.

⌔ Welcome by prior arrangement with Sec; catering can be arranged terms on application.

Bar and Catering facilities available.

Wheatsheaf; Black Bull; Ryecroft Tankerville Arms.

8B 93 **The Wynard Club** ☏

Wynyard Park, Billingham, TS22 5QJ

☎ 01740 644399, Fax 644599

On A689 at Wynyard Park between A1 and A19.

Parkland course with mature woodlands.

Pro Chris Mounter; Founded 1996

Designed by Hawtree & Son

18 holes, 7100 yards, S.S.S. 73

⌲ Floodlit driving range; practice ground; David Leadbetter Golf Academy

† Welcome.

⌇ Terms on application.

⌔ Corporate and society days; full corporate golf day organisation and packages available; terms on application.

Full restaurant and bar facilities.

Club can supply list of local hotels.

Lothian, Borders, Dumfries & Galloway

Scotland likes to do things its own way and golf is no different. The early Scottish clubs were precisely that. To begin with they did not have a private golf course but were gentlemen's clubs that came together to arrange matches, fix bets and to wine and dine together. Two amongst this pioneering band were the Royal Burgess Golfing Society of Edinburgh and Royal Musselburgh.

But the most influential was the Honourable Company of Edinburgh Golfers, architects of the first rules of the game and owners of one of golf's most famous courses. Muirfield has perhaps the most astonishing array of champions of any Open venue. The inclusive list reads Harry Vardon, James Braid (twice), Ted Ray, Walter Hagen, Henry Cotton, Gary Player, Jack Nicklaus, Lee Trevino, Tom Watson, Nick Faldo (twice), Ernie Els and, er, Alf Perry. Partly because it is flatter and greener than many links, Nicklaus considered Muirfield the fairest of all the Open courses.

Tell that to Tony Jacklin. In the third round of the 1972 Open Trevino went on a run of birdies that included a thinned bunker shot on the sixteenth that hit the flag halfway up and fell down into the hole. In the final round Trevino made a complete mess of the seventeenth, said "I've thrown it away," and then chipped in for a par. Jacklin played the hole classically, three putted from nowhere and was never the same man again.

The course is an unusual design in that the first nine are played clockwise round the boundary circle and the second nine are played mainly anti-clockwise around an inner ring. Muirfield has been voted the finest course in the world.

It is the elite amongst an extraordinary little cluster of courses. Gullane has three courses, Nos 1, 2 and 3, and a view of Muirfield. As long ago as 1650 the local weavers used to play matches against each other on Gullane Hill, a wonderful piece of land that still has no need of winter rules.

The No 1 is the premier course. The greens are almost beyond compare, as is the panoramic view from the seventh tee. Just up the road are Longniddry, Kilspindie and Luffane New. Luffane may be over one hundred years old but in this part of the world that is considered ingenue.

Just along the coast lies North Berwick, one of the world's most venerable courses with old-fashioned virtues like stone walls and redans. Furthest east in this most extraordinary stretch of golfing terrain is Dunbar, founded over 200 years ago and with one of the meanest holes around. The par three sixteenth is called the Narrows. The name has something to do with the fact that it is 25 yards wide with an out of bounds wall to the left and a beach to the right.

Travelling inland the heart of the Borders has more to do with rugby than golf, but the Roxburghe is a new course that is fast establishing a reputation. Nearer to the capital Dalmahoy, the venue of the 1992 Solheim Cup, caters to all sorts of extravagant tastes including clay pigeon shooting and polo.

On the western side of the country Portpatrick and Powfoot are fine golfing flankers either side of Southerness, a course designed by Mackenzie Ross whilst he was resurrecting Turnberry just after the war. Almost opposite to Silloth-on-Solway, Southerness is a championship challenge that has hosted the Scottish Amateur.

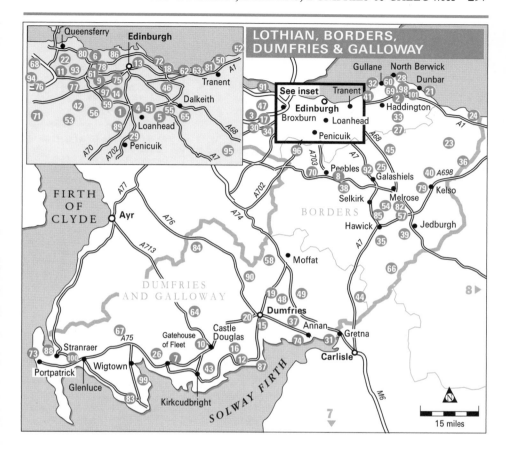

9A 1 **Baberton** ☎
50 Baberton Avenue, Juniper Green,
Midlothian, EH14 5DU
🖧 www.baberton.co.uk
📧 babertongolfclub@btinternet.com
☎ 0131 4534911, Fax 4534678,
Pro 4533555, Sec 4534911,
Rest/Bar 453 3361
On A70 5 miles W of central
Edinburgh.
Parkland course.
Pro Ken Kelly; Founded 1893
Designed by Willie Park
18 holes, 6129 yards, S.S.S. 70
🕴 Welcome by prior arrangement
with the professional or club manager.
🏌 Terms available on application to
the club.
🍴 Welcome by prior arrangement;
catering packages available; from
£22.
🍽 Full clubhouse facilities.
🛏 Braid Hills, Edinburgh.

9A 2 **Bass Rock**
6 Harperdean Cottages, Harperdean,
Haddington, E Lothian, EH41 3SQ
☎ 01620 822082
🏌 Club plays at North Berwick.

9A 3 **Bathgate**
Edinburgh Road, Bathgate, West
Lothian, EH48 1BA
🖧 www.bathgategolfclub.visps.com
📧 bathgategolfclub@lineone.net
☎ 01506 630505, Fax 636775,
Pro 630553, Rest/Bar 652232
Club lies two mins E of town centre
and station.
Parkland course.
Pro S Strachan; Founded 1892
Designed by Willie Park
18 holes, 6328 yards, S.S.S. 70
🏌 Practice facilities.
🕴 Welcome.
🏌 WD £20; WE £35.

🍴 Welcome by prior arrangement; full
day's catering package £12.
🍽 Full clubhouse facilities.
🛏 Hillcroft; Dreadnought; Kaimpark;
Hilton, Livingston.

9A 4 **Braid Hills**
Braid Hills Approach, Edinburgh,
Midlothian, EH10 6JY
☎ 0131 4529408, Pro 4476666
Course is on A702 from City centre.
Hillside course with panoramic views.
Founded 1897
18 holes, 5865 yards, S.S.S. 68
🕴 Welcome.
🏌 WD £12; WE £14.
🍴 Welcome by prior arrangement; in
summer two courses (second course:
4832 yards, S.S.S 64); in winter they
amalgamate as one; from £12.
🍽 Clubhouse facilities.
🛏 Braid Hills.

KEY		34	Harburn	68	Niddry Castle
1	Baberton	35	Hawick	69	North Berwick
2	Bass Rock	36	Hirsel	70	Peebles
3	Bathgate	37	Hoddom Castle	71	Polkemmet Country Park
4	Braid Hills	38	Innerleithen	72	Portobello
5	Broomieknowe	39	Jedburgh	73	Portpatrick (Dunskey)
6	Bruntsfield Links	40	Kelso	74	Powfoot
7	Cally Palace Hotel	41	Kilspindie	75	Prestonfield
8	Cardrona Hotel	42	Kingsknowe	76	Pumpherston
9	Carrickknowe	43	Kirkcudbright	77	Ratho Park
10	Castle Douglas	44	Langholm	78	Ravelston
11	Cogarburn	45	Lauder	79	The Roxburghe
12	Colvend	46	Liberton	80	Royal Burgess Golfing
13	Craigentinny	47	Linlithgow		Society of Edinburgh
14	Craigmillar Park	48	Lochmaben	81	Royal Musselburgh
15	Crichton Royal	49	Lockerbie	82	St Boswells
16	Dalbeattie	50	Longniddry	83	St Medan
17	Deer Park Golf &	51	Lothianburn	84	Sanquhar
	Country Club	52	Luffness New	85	Selkirk
18	Duddingston	53	Marriott Dalmahoy	86	Silverknowes
19	Dumfries & County	54	Melrose	87	Southerness
20	Dumfries & Galloway	55	Melville	88	Stranraer
21	Dunbar	56	Merchants of Edinburgh	89	Swanston
22	Dundas Park	57	Minto	90	Thornhill
23	Duns	58	Moffat	91	Torphin Hill
24	Eyemouth	59	Mortonhall	92	Torwoodlee
25	Galashiels	60	Muirfield – Honourable	93	Turnhouse
26	Gatehouse-of-Fleet		Co of Edinburgh Golfers	94	Uphall
27	Gifford Golf Club	61	Murrayfield	95	Vogrie
28	Glen	62	Musselburgh	96	West Linton
29	Glencorse	63	Musselburgh Old Course	97	West Lothian
30	Greenburn	64	New Galloway	98	Whitekirk
31	Gretna	65	Newbattle	99	Wigtown & Bladnoch
32	Gullane	66	Newcastleton	100	Wigtownshire County
33	Haddington	67	Newton Stewart	101	Winterfield

9A 5 Broomieknowe

Golf Course Road, Bonnyrigg,
Midlothian, EH19 2HZ
🖳 www.broomieknowe.com
📧 administrator@
broomieknowe.com
☎ 0131 663 9317, Fax 6632152,
Pro 6602035, Rest/Bar 6637844
Club is off the A7 at the Eskbank Road
roundabout 5 miles from Edinburgh
Parkland course.
Pro Mark Patchett; Founded 1905
Designed by James Braid; Alterations
by Hawtree/Ben Sayer
18 holes, 6150 yards, S.S.S. 70
 † Welcome.
 Ⅰ WD £19; WE £25.
 ↻ Welcome WD by prior
arrangement; day tickets available for
£28, catering available; group
discounts available.
 🍴 Clubhouse facilities.
 ↩ Dalhousie Castle.

9A 6 Bruntsfield Links ℧

32 Barton Avenue, Davidsons Mains,
Edinburgh, EH4 6JH
🖳 www.sol.co.uk/b/bruntsfieldlinks/
📧 secretary@bruntsfield.sol.co.uk
☎ 0131 3361479, Fax 3365538,
Pro 3364050, Sec 3361479,
Rest/Bar 3362006

Off A90 Forth Bridge road 3 miles NW
of Edinburgh city centre; 6 miles from
the airport.
Mature parkland course with stunning
views of the Firth of Forth.
Pro Brian MacKenzie; Founded
1761/1898
Designed by Wille
Park/MacKenzie(22)/Hawtree(74)
18 holes, 6407 yards, S.S.S. 71
 Ⅰ 6 bays.
 † Welcome by prior arrangement
with Sec or Pro.
 Ⅰ WD £45; WE £50 round.
WD60; WE 65 day.
 ↻ Welcome with prior written
arrangement; packages available for
lunch, high tea or dinner in the club's
magnificent dining room; jacket and tie
required in clubhouse; from £45.
 🍴 Full catering and Bar facilities
available.
 ↩ Many in Edinburgh area.

9A 7 Cally Palace Hotel

Gatehouse of Fleet, Castle Douglas,
Kirkcudbrightshire, DG7 2DL
🖳 www.callypalace.co.uk
📧 info@callypalace.co.uk
☎ 01557 814 341, Fax 814 522
33 miles W of Dumfries on A75;
signposted from Gatehouse.

Parkland course.
Founded 1994
Designed by Tom Macaulay
18 holes, 6062 yards, S.S.S. par 71
 † Hotel guests only.
 Ⅰ Applicable to guests only.
 🍴 Full hotel facilities.
 ↩ On site Cally Palace.

9A 8 Cardrona Hotel Golf & ℧
Country Club

Cardrona, By Peebles, EH45 6LZ
🖳 www.cardrona-hot.com
📧 golf.cardrona@madonald-hotels
.co.uk
☎ 01896 833600, Fax 833766,
Pro 833701
From A720 Ring Road, turn off towards
Penicuik on A703. Turn left at
Leadburn to Peebles (A703). At r/bout
in Peebles, left on A72 towards
Galashiels. Hotel is 3 miles on right.
Parkland course.
Pro Fraser Hall; Founded 2002
Designed by Dave Thomas
18 holes, 6900 yards, S.S.S. 73
 Ⅰ Driving range; putting green.
 † Welcome.
 Ⅰ WD £50; WE £70.
 ↻ Welcome.
 🍴 Catering and bar facilities.
 ↩ 4 star hotel on site.

9A 9 Carrickknowe

Glendevon Park, Edinburgh, EH12 5VZ
🖳 www.edinburghleisure.co.uk
📧 golf@edinburghleisure.co.uk
☎ 0131 337 1096
Opposite the Holiday Hotel on
Balgreen Road.
Parkland course.
Founded 1933
18 holes, 6055 yards, S.S.S. 68
 † Welcome.
 Ⅰ WD £10; WE £12.50.
 ↻ Welcome.
 🍴 Catering by request.

9A 10 Castle Douglas

Abercromby Road, Castle Douglas,
Kirkcudbrightshire, Dumfries &
Galloway, DG7 1BA
☎ 01556 502801, Sec 502099
On A713 towards Ayr 400 yards from
the town clock.
Parkland course.
Founded 1905
9 holes, 5408 yards, S.S.S. 66
 † Welcome.
 Ⅰ WD £ 12; WE £12.
 ↻ Welcome; bar meals can be
arranged; from £ 12.

9A · LOTHIAN, BORDERS, DUMFRIES & GALLOWAY · 299

Bar meals available.
Kings Arms; Imperial; Douglas Arms.

9A 11 Cogarburn
Newbridge, Midlothian, EH28 8NN
☎ 0131 333 4110
Close to Edinburgh Airport sliproad off
A8 Glasgow Road.
Parkland course.
Founded 1975
12 holes, 5070 yards, S.S.S. 64
♦ Welcome by prior arrangement
with Sec.
↕ WD £12; WE £16.
♦ Welcome by prior arrangement
with Sec; catering can be arranged in
new clubhouse; from £10.
Full catering and bar facilities
available.
Barnton; Royal Scot.

9A 12 Colvend
Colvend, Dalbeattie,
Kirkcudbrightshire, Dumfries &
Galloway, DG5 4PY
www.colvendgolfclub.co.uk
secretary@colvendgolfclub.co.uk
☎ 01556 630398, Fax 630495,
Sec 610878, Rest/Bar 630398
On A710 Solway coast road 6 miles
from Dalbeattie.
Parkland course.
Founded 1905
Designed by Willie Fernie 1905;
D Thomas (1985); J Soutar extension
to 18 (1997)
18 holes, 5220 yards, S.S.S. 67
♦ Everyone welcome.
↕ WD/WE £22 (per day).
♦ Welcome by prior arrangement;
tee reservations require £5 per head
deposit; catering packages available.
Full catering and bar facilities
available.
Cairngill; Clonyard; Baron's Craig;
Pheasant.

9A 13 Craigentinny
143 Craigentinny Ave, Edinburgh,
EH17 6RG
☎ 0131 5547501, Sec 6574815,
Rest/Bar 6524815
Club is one mile from Meadowbank
Stadium.
Links course.
Pro Tom Steele; Founded 1891
18 holes, 5179 yards, S.S.S. 66
♦ Public links course.
↕ WD £10.00; WE £11.50.
♦ Welcome by prior arrangement
with Council; details available on
application.

Catering facilities available at
club.
Local hotels and guesthouses
within half a mile.

9A 14 Craigmillar Park
1 Observatory Road, Edinburgh,
Midlothian, EH9 3HG
craigmillarparkgc@lineone.net
☎ 0131 6670047, Fax 6620371,
Pro 6672850, Sec 6670047,
Rest/Bar 6672837
From A68 Princes Street turn right at
Cameron Toll; course 100 yards on
right.
Parkland course.
Pro Scott Gourlay; Founded 1895
Designed by James Braid
18 holes, 5851 yards, S.S.S. 69
♦ Welcome WD and Sun after 2pm.
↕ WD £20, WE £30.
♦ Welcome WD by prior arrangement
with Sec; separate facilities; catering
packages available.
Full catering facilities.

9A 15 Crichton Royal
Bankend Road, Dumfries,
Dumfriesshire, DG1 4TH
☎ 01387 247894, Fax 257616,
Sec 247894, Rest/Bar 247894
1 mile from Dumfries near Crichton
Royal Hospital.
Wooded parkland course.
9 holes, 3084 yards
♦ Welcome by prior arrangement,
but must avoid competition days.
↕ £12.
♦ Welcome by advance notice; terms
on application.
Clubhouse facilities.

9A 16 Dalbeattie
60 Maxwell Park, Dalbeattie,
Kirkcudbrightshire, DG5 4LS
www.dalbeattiegc.co.uk
arthurhowatson@aol.com
☎ 01556 611421, Sec 610311
Course is 1 mile from Dalbeattie on the
B794 (Haugh of Urr road), 10 miles
SW of Dumfries.
Parkland course.
Founded 1894
9 holes, 5710 yards, S.S.S. 68
♦ Practice range and putting green;
buggies for hire.
♦ No restrictions.
↕ £16 18 holes, £20 day.
♦ Welcome at all times.
Clubhouse facilities.
The Kings Arms, The Square,
Dalbeattie.

9A 17 Deer Park Golf &
Country Club
Golf Course Road, Camps Rigg,
Livingston, West Lothian, EH54 8AB
deerpark@muir/group.co.uk
☎ 01506 446699, Fax 435608,
Pro 446688
Leave M8 at Junction 3 and follow signs
to Knightsbridge; club is signposted.
Parkland course.
Pro Brian Dunbar; Founded 1978
Designed by Charles Lawrie
18 holes, 6192 yards, S.S.S. 72
♦ Everyone welcome.
↕ WD £24; WE £36.
♦ Welcome by prior arrangement
both WD and WE; catering packages
available; from £32.
Full clubhouse and country club
facilities.
Travel Lodge, Deer Park; Houston
House; Hilton.

9A 18 Duddingston
Duddingston Road West, Edinburgh,
Midlothian, EH15 3QD
www.duddingston-golf-club.com
☎ 0131 6611005, Fax 6614301,
Pro 6614301, Sec 6617688,
Rest/Bar 6617688
2 miles from city centre near A1 turning
right at Duddingston crossroads.
Parkland course.
Pro Alastair McLean; Founded 1895
Designed by Willie Park Jnr
18 holes, 6473 yards, S.S.S. 72
♦ Welcome WD.
↕ WD £30.
♦ Welcome Tues and Thurs by prior
arrangement; catering packages can
be arranged; terms on application.
Full clubhouse facilities.
Many in Edinburgh.

9A 19 Dumfries and County
Edinburgh Road, Dumfries,
Dumfriesshire, DG1 1JX
www.dumfriesandcounty-gc.
fsnet.co.uk
dumfries@aol.com
☎ 01387 253 585, Fax 253585,
Pro 268918, Sec 253585,
Rest/Bar 249921
On A701 Moffat to Edinburgh road 1
mile NE of town centre.
Parkland course; The Wee Yin; 90
yards, 14th.
Pro Stuart Syme; Founded 1912
Designed by Willie Fernie
18 holes, 5918 yards, S.S.S. 69
♦ Welcome WD between 9.30am-
11am; 2pm-3.30pm; WE Sat; Sun after
10am.

WD/WE £28 round; WD/WE £3 day.
🏌 Welcome by prior arrangement with pro; separate facilities; catering packages available.
🍽 Club bar and dining room.
🛏 Cairndale; Station; Moreig; Balmoral; Edenbank; Imperial.

9A 20 **Dumfries and Galloway**
2 Laurieston Avenue, Dumfries, Dumfriesshire, DG2 7NY
🖥 www.dggc.co.uk
✉ info@dggc.co.uk
☎ 01387 263848, Fax 263848, Pro 256902, Sec 263848, Rest/Bar 253582
On A75 W of Dumfries.
Parkland course.
Pro Joe Fergusson; Founded 1880
Designed by Willie Fernie
18 holes, 6309 yards, S.S.S. 71
🚶 Welcome except competition days; prior booking essential in summer.
🏌 WD £25; WE £30.
🏌 Welcome by prior arrangements; catering packages available except Mon; from £25.
🍽 Full facilities available; except Mon.
🛏 Cairndale; Station.

9A 21 **Dunbar**
East Links, Dunbar, East Lothian, EH42 1LL
🖥 www.dunbar-golfclub.co.uk
✉ secretary@dunbargolfclub.sol.co.uk
☎ 01368 862317, Fax 865202, Pro 862086, Sec 862317, Rest/Bar 862317
0.5 miles E of Dunbar; 30 miles E of Edinburgh off A1.
Links course.
Pro Jacky Montgomery; Founded 1794/1856
Designed by Tom Morris
18 holes, 6426 yards, S.S.S. 71
🚶 Welcome WD by prior arrangement 9.30am-12.30pm & 2pm onwards except Thurs; WE 10am-12 noon and after 2pm.
🏌 Terms upon application.
🏌 Welcome by prior arrangement WD; catering packages available; from £30.
🍽 Full clubhouse facilities.
🛏 Cruachan Guest House; Barns Ness Hotel.

9A 22 **Dundas Parks**
South Queensferry, Lothian, EH30 9SS
🖥 www.dundasparks.co.uk
☎ 0131 3315603
Course is one mile south of S Queensferry on the A8000.

Parkland course.
Founded 1957
9 holes, 6024 yards, S.S.S. 69
🏌 Practice range.
🚶 Welcome by arrangement.
🏌 Terms on application.
🏌 Welcome by prior arrangement; terms on application.

9A 23 **Duns** ☏
Harden Rd., Trinity Park, Duns, Berwickshire, TD11 3HN
☎ 01361 882194, Sec 882717
Course is one mile W of Duns off the A6105 Greenlaw – Duns road, taking the junction signposted Longformacus.
Parkland/upland course.
Founded 1894/1921
Designed by AH Scott
18 holes, 6209 yards, S.S.S. 70
🚶 Welcome.
🏌 WD £14; WE £17.
🏌 Welcome by prior arrangement with Sec; some WE tee-times available; all day golf; limited clubhouse facilities but snack meals can be arranged April – October; from £15.
🍽 Full facilities.
🛏 Barniken House.

9A 24 **Eyemouth**
The Clubhouse, Gunsgreenhill, Eyemouth, TD14 5SF
✉ eyemouthgolfclub@global.net
☎ 01890 750551, Pro 750004
One mile off the A1 on the A1107 E of Burmouth.
Seaside parkland course.
Pro Paul Terras; Founded 1884/1994
Designed by James Baine
18 holes, 6472 yards, S.S.S. 72
🚶 Welcome any day.
🏌 WD £22; WE £27.
🏌 Welcome by prior arrangement; special catering packages available.
🍽 Full clubhouse facilities.
🛏 Press Castle; Cul-Na-Sithe; Dunlaverock House; Ship; Dolphin; Churches Hotel.

9A 25 **Galashiels** ☏
Ladhope Recreation Ground, Galashiels, Selkirkshire, TD1 2NJ
☎ 01896 753724, Sec 755525
On A7 to Edinburgh 0.5 miles N of town centre.
Hilly parkland course.
Founded 1883
Designed by James Braid
18 holes, 5240 yards, S.S.S. 67
🚶 Welcome.
🏌 Under review.

🏌 Welcome by prior arrangement with Sec; package deals available; terms available on application.
🍽 Full clubhouse facilities.
🛏 Abbotsford Arms; Kingsknowes; Kings.

9A 26 **Gatehouse-of-Fleet**
Laurieston Rd, Gatehouse-of-Fleet, DG7 2PW
☎ 01644 450260, Sec 01557 450260
From A75 into Gatehouse-of-Fleet follow signs for Laurieston; course 0.5 miles.
Parkland course with stunning views.
Founded 1921
9 holes, 5042 yards, S.S.S. 66
🚶 Welcome. Membership available (£90 per annum 2001 rate).
🏌 WD £10; WE £10.
🏌 Welcome by prior arrangement; local hotels can provide catering arrangements; terms on application.
🍽 None at course.
🛏 Masonic Arms; Murray Arms.

9A 27 **Gifford Golf Club** ☏
Edinburgh Road, Gifford, Haddington, East Lothian, EH41 4JE
🖥 www.giffordgolfclub.com
✉ secretary@giffordgolfclub.fsnet.co.uk
☎ 01620 810 591 (starter – Apr-Sep), Sec 810 267
Off A1 4 miles from Haddington.
Undulating parkland course in Lammermuir foothills.
Founded 1904
Designed by Willie Watt
9 holes, 6255 yards, S.S.S. 70
🚶 Welcome.
🏌 WD £15, £25 day ticket; WE £15. 9 holes £10.
🍽 Full facilities at village hotels; clubhouse.
🛏 Goblin Ha'; Tweeddale Arms.

9A 28 **Glen** ☏
East Links, Tantallon Terrace, North Berwick, East Lothian, EH39 4LE
🖥 www.glengolfclub.co.uk
☎ 01620 892726, Fax 895288, Pro 894596, Rest/Bar 892221
Signposted from A198 1 mile E of town centre.
Seaside links course.
Founded 1906
Designed by James Braid
18 holes, 6243 yards, S.S.S. 70
🚶 Welcome.
🏌 WD £28; WE £38.
🏌 Welcome by prior arrangement; catering packages available.

🍽 Full clubhouse facilities.
🛏 Marine; Belhaven; Golf.

9A 29 **Glencorse**
Milton Bridge, Penicuik, Midlothian,
EH26 0RD
☎ 01968 677189, Fax 674399,
Pro 676481, Rest/Bar 677177
On A701 Peebles road 9 miles S of
Edinburgh.
Parkland course with stream of 10
holes.
Pro C Jones; Founded 1890
Designed by Willie Park
18 holes, 5217 yards, S.S.S. 66
✝ Welcome; restrictions on comp
days.
⌇ WD £20; WE £26.
⌁ Welcome Mon-Thurs and Sun
afternoon by prior arrangement;
packages for golf and catering also
available for parties of 10 or more;
from £18.
🍽 Full clubhouse catering and bar
packages.
🛏 Royal Hotel, Penicuik.

9A 30 **Greenburn** ♛
6 Greenburn Rd, Bridge Street,
Fauldhouse, Bathgate, West Lothian,
EH47 9HG
☎ 01501 771187, Rest/Bar 770292
4 miles S of M8 Junction 4 and 5.
Parkland/moorland course.
18 holes, 6046 yards, S.S.S. 70
⌇ Practice area.
✝ Welcome by prior arrangements;
WE 9am-10am and 2pm-3pm.
⌇ WD £17; WE £20.
⌁ Welcome WD by prior
arrangement; catering packages
available; terms on application.
🍽 Full clubhouse facilities.
🛏 Hillcroft.

9A 31 **Gretna**
Kirtle View, Gretna, Dumfriesshire,
DG5 5HD
☎ 01461 338464
Course is 0.5 miles W of Gretna on S
side of the A75; 1 mile from the
M74/A75 Junction.
Parkland course.
Founded 1991
Designed by Nigel Williams/Bothwell
9 holes, 6430 yards, S.S.S. 71
⌇ Driving range.
✝ Welcome except on comp. days.
⌇ WD £8: WE £10.
⌁ Welcome by prior arrangement
catering packages by arrangement
terms on application.

🍽 Catering available by prior
arrangement.
🛏 Many Hotels in local area.

9A 32 **Gullane** ♛
West Links Road, Gullane, East
Lothian, EH31 2BB
🖥 www.gullanegolfclub.com
✉ manager@gullanegolfclub.com
☎ 01620 842255, Fax 842327,
Pro 843111
Leave the A1 N to the A198; 22 miles
east of Edinburgh.
300-year-old seaside links course; Two
qualifying courses.
Pro Alasdair Good; Founded
1882/1898/1910
Course 1: 18 holes, 6466 yards, S.S.S. 72
Course 1: 18 holes, 6244 yards, S.S.S. 71
Course 3: 18 holes, 5252 yards, S.S.S. 66
⌇ Practice ground available to all
those playing golf.
✝ Welcome with handicap certs by
prior arrangement.
⌇ WD £70, WE £85 (Course 1); WD
£29, WE £35 (Course 2); WD £17, WE
£24 (Course 3).
⌁ Welcome by prior arrangement;
corporate days can be arranged; also
conference day packages with exclusive
use of the first-class accommodation in
the Members' clubhouse for seminars
and conferences for groups of 12-24;
Heritage of Golf Museum; coaching
clinics; terms available on application.
🍽 Full clubhouse catering facilities in
the Members' clubhouse.
🛏 Club can provide a list in Gullane,
North Berwick and Aberlady.

9A 33 **Haddington** ♛
Amisfield Park, Whittinghame Drive,
Haddington, East Lothian, EH41 4PT
🖥 www.haddingtongolf.co.uk
✉ info@haddingtongolf.co.uk
☎ 01620 822727, Fax 826580,
Pro 822727, Sec 823627,
Rest/Bar 826058
Three quarters of a mile E of
Haddington just off the A1; 17 miles E
of Edinburgh.
Parkland course.
Pro John Sandilands; Founded 1865
18 holes, 6335 yards, S.S.S. 70
⌇ Large practice area.
✝ Welcome, WE pre-booking essential.
⌇ WD £21; WE £30 Discounts for
group bookings of 8+.
⌁ Welcome; full day's golf; catering
packages available in the season by
arrangement Oct-Mar; from £30.
🍽 Full catering & bar facilities Apr-Sep.
🛏 Plough, Maitlandfield;The George.

9A 34 **Harburn**
West Calder, West Lothian, EH55 8RS
✉ harburn@whsmithnet.co.uk
☎ 01506 871131, Fax 870286,
Pro 871582, Sec 871131,
Rest/Bar 871256
Course is on the B7008 2 miles of West
Calder 5 miles from M8 Junction 4.
Parkland course.
Pro Stephen Mills.; Founded 1933
18 holes, 5921 yards, S.S.S. 68
✝ Welcome except on competition days.
⌇ WD £25; Fri £30; WE £35.
⌁ Welcome except on competition
days; packages for Mon-Thurs; Fri, Sat
and Sun available including day's golf,
lunch and high tea; separate changing
facilities; from £37.50.
🍽 Full clubhouse facilities.
🛏 Bankton House; Livingston Hilton.

9A 35 **Hawick** ♛
Vertish Hill, Hawick Golf Club House,
Hawick, Roxburghshire, TD9 0NY
☎ 01450 372293, Sec 374947
Just S of Hawick on A7.
Parkland course.
Founded 1877.
18 holes, 5933 yards, S.S.S. 69
⌇ Practice area.
✝ Welcome; restrictions until after
3.30pm on some Sats; not before
10.30am Sun.
⌇ WD £20; WE £20.
⌁ Welcome by arrangement; catering
packages in season; separate facilities;
terms on application.
🍽 Full clubhouse facilities in summer.
🛏 Kirkland; Mansfield House; Emsfield.

9A 36 **Hirsel**
Kelso Rd, Coldstream, Berwickshire,
TD12 4NJ
🖥 www.hirselgc.co.uk
✉ bookings@hirselgc.co.uk
☎ 01890 882678, Fax 882233
On A697 through Coldstream; golf club
is signposted.
Parkland course.
Founded 1949
18 holes, 6111 yards, S.S.S. 70
⌇ Practice area.
✝ Welcome.
⌇ WD £26; WE £32.
⌁ Welcome by prior arrangement;
catering and golf packages available;
more than 10 players must book in
advance; 2-10 must book up to 10
days in advance; no starts before
10am; terms on application.
🍽 Full clubhouse facilities.
🛏 Tillmouth park; Collingwood Arms;
Cross Keys.

Royal Burgess Golfing Society of Edinburgh

As its name suggests, The Royal Burgess Golfing Society of Edinburgh has a history that is long, distinguished and ever-so-slightly complicated. "Which story do you want to hear?" asks club archivist Philip Knowles, "After all we have had three courses, seven clubhouses and three different names in our time".

That time-span is now almost 270 years – the original Golfing Society of Edinburgh having started its golf on the city's Bruntsfield Links in 1735 – making Royal Burgess the oldest golf club in Britain. They moved to Musselburgh links in 1874 and arrived at Barnton, just north of the city, in 1894. And they have been there ever since, becoming first The Edinburgh Burgess Golfing Society and then acquiring Royal status in 1929, on the command of King George V. The Society's royal connection continues and the Duke of York has been an honorary member since 1991.

The club remains rightly proud of its history and status but, like any good 270-year-old organisation, has had to modernise. An ambitious extension to the clubhouse has just been completed, offering a vast changing area and a new "casual" bar (the first time gentlemen have not been required to wear a shirt and tie for post-match drinks) while maintaining the grandeur of the old clubhouse and even commemorating a couple of Edinburgh's golfing legends in a spectacular stained glass window. John "Fiery" Carey and James Binnie, two legendary Edinburgh caddies now look down on members and guests as they enter the club with the uncompromising attitude that you would expect from two men who clearly had "the knowledge" of Edinburgh golf.

Head up the clubhouse stairs and past Fiery and Binnie to take your best view of the course and watch as some set out eagerly up the hill at the first and others parade themselves with chests puffed out down the par-four 18th having driven the 247 yards required to reach the green. There is certainly a feel-good finish here. Indeed the course measures just 6,486 yards and is the same plot of land that Tom Morris designed this course on at the turn of the century. Still visible in the turf are Old Tom's original bunkers that used to run all the way across the fairway in front of several greens.

Today's technology has dramatically altered the difficulty of the Burgess. Their club motto remains "Far and Sure" – but big hitting really is not imperative. However you do still have to be sure. Holes 10–12 best illustrate the nature of the course. The 10th (380 yards, par four) requires a decent hit into a hill, which will then leave the only "blind" approach shot of the round, up the hill and around to the right. At the back of the elevated green stands a grand house, befitting a Royal course. The 11th (348 yards, par four) takes you back down the hill and right again. A well-struck drive will not only look glorious against a blue sky but should leave you with a wedge into the green. Then the 12th offers the second-shortest par-four of the round (314 yards), made reasonably intimidating to the higher handicapper by its narrow fairway lined with trees.

Last year, three golfers were so "sure" that they set a course record of 61 (two of them playing together) and calls to toughen up the rough swiftly followed; to which the Burgess responded. Certainly, they are not afraid to modernise here. They never have been. Bernard Darwin, writing in 1910, recounts a tale of the "Sabbath Breakers" of Bruntsfield Links, travelling through town in their Sunday best, with a set of clubs hidden about their carriage as they sneaked away from Edinburgh to enjoy a day in nearby Barnton. – **Jim Bruce-Ball**

9A 37 Hoddom Castle

Hoddom, Lockerbie, Dumfriesshire,
DG11 1AS
🖰 www.hoddomcastle.co.uk
📧 hoddomcast;e@aol.com
☎ 01576 300251, Fax 300757,
Sec 300244, Rest/Bar 300727
Course is 3 miles from the A74 and 2
miles SW of Ecclefechan on the B752;
M74 Junction 6.
Pay and play inland course.
Designed by D Rothwell.
9 holes, 2274 yards, S.S.S. 33
† Welcome.
🎫 £9.
🏌 Limited.
🍴 Snacks.

9A 38 Innerleithen

Leithen Water, Innerleithen,
Peeblesshire, EH44 6NL
☎ 01896 830951, Sec 830050
0.75 miles from town centre down
Leithen Road.
Heathland/parkland course.
Founded 1886
Designed by Willie Park
9 holes, 6056 yards, S.S.S. 69
† Welcome.
🎫 WD £11; WE £13.
🏌 Welcome but groups of more than
six should book; maximum 42; from £11.
🍴 Facilities available by prior
arrangement.
🍴 Corner House; Traquar Arms.

9A 39 Jedburgh

Dunion Road, Jedburgh,
Roxburghshire, TD8 6LA
☎ 01835 863587
0.75 mile W of Jedburgh on Hawick
road.
Undulating parkland course.
Founded 1892
9 holes, 5555 yards, S.S.S. 67
† Welcome except on competition
days; WE booking advisable.
🎫 Terms on application.
🏌 Welcome with at least 2 weeks'
notice; catering and bar facilities
available between May and
September; from £20 for full food/golf
package.
🍴 Available in season.
🍴 Royal; Jedforest.

9A 40 Kelso   ☏

Racecourse Rd., Kelso,
Roxburghshire, TD5 7SL
☎ 01573 223009, Sec 223259
1 mile N of Kelso inside National Hunt
Racecourse.

Flat parkland course.
Founded 1887
Designed by James Braid
18 holes, 6046 yards, S.S.S. 70
† Welcome.
🎫 WD £16; WE £20.
🏌 Welcome by prior arrangement;
includes all day golf; catering packages
available; notice needed for Mon or
Tues; from £20.
🍴 Clubhouse facilities; closed Mon-
Wed in winter.
🍴 Cross Keys; Queen's Head.

9A 41 Kilspindie

The Clubhouse, Aberlady, Longniddry,
East Lothian, EH32 0QD
🖰 www.golfeastlothian.com
📧 kilspindie@btconnect.com
☎ 01875 870358, Fax 870358,
Pro 870695, Rest/Bar 870216
Off A198 North Berwick road
immediately E of Aberlady; private road
leads to the club.
Traditional Scottish links.
Pro Graham Sked; Founded 1867
Designed by Ross & Sayers; Extended
by Willie Park
🏌 Putting green, practice
bunker/green, driving nets.
† Welcome by prior arrangement
with the club.
🎫 WD £28.50; WE £35.
🏌 Welcome by prior arrangement;
catering packages available; terms on
application.
🍴 Full catering facilities with bar and
dining room.
🍴 Kilspindie House.

9A 42 Kingsknowe   ☏

Lanark Road, Edinburgh, Midlothian,
EH14 2JD
☎ 0131 4411144, Fax 4412079,
Pro 4414030, Sec 4411145
On A70 on the SW ouskirts of
Edinburgh.
Undulating parkland.
Pro Andrew Marshall; Founded 1908
Designed by Alex Herd, James Braid,
JC Stutt
18 holes, 5979 yards, S.S.S. 69
† Welcome by prior arrangement
with Pro.
🎫 WD £21; WE £30.
🏌 Welcome by prior application to
sec; full day's golf and catering
available; separate changing; from
£18.
🍴 Full clubhouse catering and bar
facilities.
🍴 Orwell Lodge; Edinburgh Post
House.

9A 43 Kirkcudbright   ☏

Stirling Crescent, Kirkcudbright,
Kirkcudbrightshire, DG6 4EZ
📧 kbtgolfclub@lineone.net
☎ 01557 330314, Fax 330314
Off A711 road from the A75 Dumfries-
Stanraer Road.
Parkland course.
Founded 1893
18 holes, 5739 yards, S.S.S. 69
† Welcome; some restrictions
Tues/Wed.
🏌 Welcome by prior arrangement; full
day £25; from £20.
🍴 Clubhouse facilities.
🍴 Royal; Selkirk; Commercial.

9A 44 Langholm

Whitaside, Arkinholm Terrace,
Langholm, Dumfriesshire, DG13 0JR
🖰 www.langholmgolfclub.co.uk
📧 golf@langholmgolfclub.co.uk
☎ 013873 81247, Sec 80408
Off the A7 Edinburgh-Carlisle road in
centre of Langholm; follow signs to the
course.
Hillside course.
Founded 1892
9 holes, 6180 yards, S.S.S. 70
† Welcome.
🎫 WD £10; WE £10.
🏌 Welcome by prior arrangement;
catering available by prior
arrangement; £10.
🍴 Clubhouse facilities.
🍴 Eskdale; Buck: Crown.

9A 45 Lauder

Galashiels Rd., Lauder, Scottish
Borders, TD2 6RS
🖰 www.lauder-golfclub.org.uk
📧 secretary@lauder-golfclub.org.uk
☎ 01578 722526, Fax 722526
On A68 30 miles S of Edinburgh; 0.5
miles outside Lauder.
Heathland course.
Founded 1896
Designed by W. Park of Musselburgh
9 holes, 6050 yards, S.S.S. 69
† Welcome except before noon Sun
and 5.30pm-7.30pm Wed.
🎫 WD £10; WE £10.
🏌 Welcome by prior arrangement;
golf only available; from £10.
🍴 Catering can be arranged with
local hotels.
🍴 Lauderdale; Eagle; Black Bull.

9A 46 Liberton   ☏

Gilmerton Road, Edinburgh,
Midlothian, EH16 5UJ

☎ 0131 6643009, Fax 6660853,
Pro 6641056, Rest/Bar 664 8580
Exit Edinburgh city by-pass at
Gilmerton A7 Junction; course 3 miles
towards city.
Parkland course.
Pro Ian Seith; Founded 1920
18 holes, 5170 yards, S.S.S. 65
† Welcome.
[WD £20; WE £30.
☝ Welcome WD by prior written
arrangement; 36 holes of golf, coffee,
lunch, high tea; max 40; £33.
🍴 Full clubhouse facilities.

9A 47 Linlithgow ☏
Braehead, Golf Course Rd, Linlithgow,
W Lothian, EH49 6QF
🖥 www.linlithgowgolf.co.uk
💻 linlithgowgolf@talk21.com
☎ 01506 671044, Fax 842764,
Pro 844356, Sec 842585
Approx 10 miles from Edinburgh on
M9.
Undulating parkland course.
Pro Steve Rossie; Founded 1913
Designed by Robert Simpson of
Carnoustie
18 holes, 5729 yards, S.S.S. 68
🏌 Practice area.
† Welcome except Sat and
competition days.
[WD £20 (£10 winter); WE £25
(£10 winter).
☝ Welcome by arrangement with
Sec; catering packages available
except Wed/Sat, from £17.25.
🍴 Full clubhouse facilities.
🛏 Star & Garter; Westfort.

9A 48 Lochmaben
Castlehillgate, Lochmaben, Lockerbie,
Dumfriesshire, DG11 1NT
🖥 www.lochmabengolf.co.uk
💻 lochmabengc@aol.com
☎ 01387 810552
Course is 4 miles from the A74 at
Lockerbie on the A709 road to
Dumfries.
Parkland course.
Founded 1926
Designed by James Braid
18 holes, 5377 yards, S.S.S. 67
🏌 Practice area.
† Welcome; on competition days by
prior arrangements.
[WD £20; WE £25.
☝ Welcome by prior arrangement;
catering packages available; caddie
car and buggy hire.
🍴 Full clubhouse facilities.
🛏 Crown Hotel; Queens, Sommerton
House.

9A 49 Lockerbie ☏
Corrie Rd., Lockerbie, Dumfriesshire,
DG11 2ND
🖥 www.lockerbiegolf.com
💻 enquiries@lockerbiegolf.com
☎ 01576 203363, Fax 203363,
Sec 203363, Rest/Bar 203363
Leave M74 at Lockerbie and course is
signposted.
Tree-lined parkland course with pond
in play on 3 holes.
Founded 1889
Designed by James Braid (original 9)
18 holes holes, 5463 yards, S.S.S. 67
† Welcome; prior booking is advisable.
[WD £18; WE £20.
☝ Welcome by prior arrangement; 36
holes of golf; morning coffee, light lunch;
evening meal (£35 Sat); from £30.
🍴 Full clubhouse facilities.
🛏 Queens; Kings; Ravenshill;
Dryfesdale.

9A 50 Longniddry
Links Road, Longniddry, East Lothian,
EH32 0NL
🖥 www.longniddrygolfclub.co.uk
💻 secretary@longniddrygolfclub
.co.uk
☎ 01875 852141, Fax 853371,
Pro 852228, Sec 852141,
Rest/Bar 852 623
On B6363 in Longniddry village from
the A1.
Parkland and links course.
Pro John Gray; Founded 1921
Designed by Harry Colt
18 holes, 6260 yards, S.S.S. 70
🏌 Practice area.
† Welcome WD; WE by arrangement.
[WD £37.5o; WE £48.
☝ Welcome by prior arrangement
and with handicap certs; catering
packages can be arranged with the
clubmaster; tee times between 9.30am
and 4pm; deposit of £10 per person
required; credit cards accepted; max
40; from £50 for two rounds.
🍴 Full clubhouse facilities.
🛏 Kilspindie house; Maitlandfield;
Greencraigs.

9A 51 Lothianburn ☏
Biggar Road, Edinburgh, Midlothian,
EH10 7DU
☎ 0131 4455067, Pro 4452288,
Rest/Bar 4452206
On A702 Biggar to Carlisle road, 200
yards from City by-pass at Lothianburn
exit.
Hilly course.
Pro Kurt Mungall; Founded 1893/1928
Designed by James Braid (1928)

18 holes, 5662 yards, S.S.S. 68
† Welcome WD up to 4.30pm; WE
with member.
[WD £16.
☝ Welcome WD by prior
arrangement with Sec; discounts
available for more than 16 in a party;
catering packages by prior
arrangement; from 13.
🍴 Clubhouse facilities.
🛏 Braid Hills.

9A 52 Luffness New
Aberlady, East Lothian, E32 0QA
💻 lngc@talk21.com
☎ 01620 843114, Fax 842933,
Sec 843336, Rest/Bar 843114
1 mile outside Aberlady on the A198
Gullane road.
Links course.
Founded 1894
Designed by Tom Morris (1894)
18 holes, 6122 yards, S.S.S. 70
🏌 Practice range: 5-hole course.
† Welcome WD only.
[WD £45.
☝ Welcome WD by prior arrangement;
full day's golf £65; catering by prior
arrangement; from £45.
🍴 Smoke room; dining room; lunch
daily except Mon; high tea/dinner by
arrangements (min 10).
🛏 Marine, N Berwick; Golf, Greywalls
(Gullane).

9A 53 Marriott Dalmahoy ☏
Kirknewton, Midlothian, EH27 8EB
🖥 www.marriott.co.uk/edigs
💻 golf.dalmahoy@marriotthotel.co.uk
☎ 0131 335 8010, Fax 335 3577
Course is on the A71 seven miles W of
Edinburgh.
Rolling parkland course.
Pro Neal Graham; Founded 1927
Designed by James Braid
2 x 18 holes; East: 6651 West: 5168
yards; S.S.S. East:72 West 68
🏌 Practice range, 12 bay all-weather
floodlit.
† Welcome WD and WE by prior
arrangement and with handicap certs.
[WD £55 (East), £35 (West); WE
£70 (East), £40 (West).
☝ Welcome WD by prior
arrangement, corporate days can be
organised; catering and residential
packages available; leisure facilities,
including indoor heated pool, spa,
sauna, tennis, gym, health and beauty
saloon; terms on application.
🍴 Facilities in the Long Weekend
Restaurant.
🛏 Marriott Dalmahoy.

9A 54 Melrose

Dingleton, Melrose, Roxburghshire
TD6 9HS
☎ 01896 822855, Sec 822788
2 miles N of St Boswell off the A68
Newcastle to Edinburgh Road; half a
mile S of Melrose.
Undulating wooded parkland course.
Founded 1880
9 holes, 5562 yards, S.S.S. 68
♦ Welcome WD; Sat very limited;
most Sundays available; Tues ladies
priority.
Ⅼ WD £20, WE £20.
⚘ Welcome by arrangement, catering
can be arranged.
🍽 Available by prior arrangement.

9A 55 Melville

South Melville, Lasswade, Midlothian,
EH18 1AN
♨ www.melvillegolf.co.uk
✉ golf@melville.co.uk
☎ 0131 6638038, Fax 6540814,
Sec 6540224
Off the Edinburgh city by-pass on the
Galashiels A7 road.
Parkland course.
Pro Gary Carter
Founded 1995
Designed by P Campbell/G Webster
9 holes, 4310 yards, S.S.S. 62
Ⅰ 34 bays; 22 covered, 12 outdoor.
Ⅼ 9 holes: WD £9, WE £11; 18 holes:
WD £16, WE £20.
⚘ Welcome by prior arrangement.
🍽 Snacks available.
⚐ Melville Cstle; Laird & Dog;
Dalhousie Castle.

9A 56 Merchants of Edinburgh ☏

Merchants of Edinburgh, 10 Craighill
Gardens, Edinburgh, Midlothian,
EH10 5PY
♨ www.merchantsgolf.com
✉ admin@merchantsgolf.com
☎ 0131 447 1219, Pro 446 9833,
Pro 447 8709, Sec 447 1219,
Rest/Bar 447 1219
Course is off the A701 S of
Edinburgh.
Hilly parkland course.
Pro Neil Colquhoun
Founded 1907
18 holes, 4889 yards, S.S.S. 64
♦ Welcome WD before 4pm.
Ⅼ WD £19.
⚘ Welcome WD before 4pm by prior
booking. Packages arranged.
🍽 Full bar and catering facilities,
seven days.
⚐ Braid Hills.

9A 57 Minto ☏

Minto Village, by Denhom, Hawick,
Roxburghshire, TD9 8SH
♨ www.mintogolf.co.uk
✉ pat@mintogolfclub.freeserve.co.uk
☎ 01450 870220, Fax 870126,
Sec 375841
5 miles NE of Hawick leaving A698 at
Denholm.
Parkland course.
Founded 1928
18 holes, 5453 yards, S.S.S. 67
Ⅰ Practice area and putting green.
♦ Welcome by prior arrangement.
Ⅼ WD £22; WE £27.50.
⚘ Welcome by prior arrangement;
packages available; from £22.
🍽 Full clubhouse facilities.
⚐ Contact the Scottish Tourist
Board.

9A 58 Moffat ☏

Coatshill, Moffat, Dumfriesshire,
DG10 9SB
♨ www.moffatgolfclub.co.uk
✉ moffatgolfclub@onetel.net.uk
☎ 01683 220020, Fax 221802
Leave M74 at Beattock. Junc 15; take
A701 to Moffat for 1 mile; club is
signposted.
Moorland course with tree plantations,
spectacular views.
Founded 1884
Designed by Ben Sayers
18 holes, 5263 yards, S.S.S. 67
Ⅰ Nets.
♦ Welcome except Wed after 3 pm.
Ⅼ WD £19.50, WE £27.
⚘ Welcome by prior arrangement
except Wed; includes 2 rounds of golf,
morning coffee; snack lunch; evening
dinner; from £32.
🍽 Full clubhouse facilities.
⚐ Beechwood Country; Moffat
House; Annandale Arms; Balmoral;
Buccleuch; Star; Black Bull.

9A 59 Mortonhall ☏

231 Braid Road, Edinburgh,
Midlothian, EH10 6PB
♨ www.mortonhallgc.co.uk
✉ clubhouse@mortonhallgct.co.uk
☎ 0131 4476974, Fax 4478712,
Pro 4475185, Sec 4476974,
Rest/Bar 4472411
On A72 2 miles S of the city.
Moorland course.
Pro Malcolm Leighton; Founded 1892
Designed by James Braid and Fred
Hawtree
18 holes, 6502 yards, S.S.S. 72
♦ Welcome by prior arrangement.
Ⅼ £35; £45 for the day.

⚘ Welcome by prior arrangement;
catering packages available; terms on
application.
🍽 Bar and catering facilities available.
⚐ Braid Hills.

9A 60 Muirfield (Honourable Company Of Edinburgh Golfers)

Muirfield, Gullane, East Lothian,
EH31 2EG
☎ 01620 842123
Course is on the A198 to the NE of
Gullane.
Links course; staged 14 Open
Championships since 1892.
Founded 1744
Designed by Tom Morris
18 holes, 6970 yards, S.S.S. 73
♦ Welcome only Tue and
Thur.
Ⅼ WD £90.
⚘ Welcome on Tues and Thurs only
by prior arrangement; no more than
12 golfers allowed; must have
handicap certs; 18 handicap
maximum for men; terms available
on application.
🍽 Full catering and bar service
available (ladies may not lunch in
clubhouse).
⚐ Greywalls; Kilspindie House.

9A 61 Murrayfield

43 Murrayfield Road, Edinburgh,
EH12 6EU
☎ 0131 337 3478, Fax 3130721,
Pro 3373479
2 miles W of city centre.
Parkland course.
Pro James Fisher; Founded 1896
18 holes, 5764 yards, S.S.S. 69
♦ Welcome only with member.
Ⅼ Terms on application.
⚘ Limited.
🍽 Bar snacks; dining room; meals
served daily except Mon.
⚐ Ellersly House; Murrayfield.

9A 62 Musselburgh ☏

Monktonhall, Musselburgh, Midlothian,
EH21 6SA
♨ www.themusselburghgolfclub.com
✉ secretary
@themusselburghgolfclub.com
☎ 0131 665 2005, Fax 4435,
Pro 7055
On B6415 to Musselburgh from the
end of the A1 Edinburgh By-pass.
Parkland course.
Pro Fraser Mann; Founded 1938
Designed by James Braid
18 holes, 6614 yards, S.S.S. 73

† Welcome by prior arrangement.
𝌆 WD £25; WE £30.
🗘 Welcome by prior arrangement; catering packages available; terms on application.
🍽 Bar and restaurant facilities available.
🛏 Kings Manor; Woodside.

9A 63 Musselburgh Old Course ☎
10 Balcarres Road, Musselburgh, East Lothian, EH21 7SD
🖳 www.musselburgholdlinks.co.uk
📧 mocgc@breathemail.net
☎ 0131 665 6981, Fax 5438, Sec 4861
Course is seven miles E of Edinburgh on the A199 at Musselburgh racecourse.
Seaside links course.
9 holes, 5774 yards, S.S.S. 69
† Welcome WD, prior booking essential.
𝌆 Terms on application.
🗘 Welcome by prior arrangement; terms on application.
🍽 Catering facilities.

9A 64 New Galloway
High Street, New Galloway, Castle Douglas, Kirkcudbrightshire, DG7 3RN
🖳 www.nggc.com
☎ 01644 420737, Fax 450685, Sec 450685
Course is of the A713 to New Galloway.
Moorland course.
Founded 1902
Designed by G Baillie
9 holes, 5006 yards, S.S.S. 67
† Welcome.
𝌆 WD/WE £15 per day.
🗘 Welcome by prior arrangement with Sec; catering packages can be organised from £10.
🍽 Bar and snack facilities available.
🛏 Kenmure Arms; Cross Keys; Ken Bridge.

9A 65 Newbattle ☎
Abbey Road, Dalkeith, Midlothian, EH22 3AD
📧 mail@newbattlegolfclub.co.uk
☎ 0131 663 1819, Fax 654 1810, Pro 660 1631, Rest/Bar 663 2123
On A7 7 miles SW of Edinburgh; taking Newbattle exit at Eskbank roundabout.
Undulating parkland course.
Pro Scott McDonald; Founded 1896
Designed by H S Colt.
18 holes, 6025 yards, S.S.S. 70
† Welcome WD up to 4pm.
𝌆 WD £20 round, £30 day.

🗘 Welcome Mon-Fri by prior arrangement between 9.30am and 4pm; catering packages available; terms on application.
🍽 Full clubhouse facilities.
🛏 Lugton; Eskbank.

9A 66 Newcastleton ☎
Holm Hill, Newcastleton, Roxburghshire, TD9 0QD
☎ 013873 75608
On A7 25 miles N of Carlisle; 10 miles from Canonbie/Newcastleton Junction.
Hilly course.
Founded 1894
Designed by J Shade (74)
9 holes, 5491 yards, S.S.S. 70
† Welcome.
𝌆 WD £10; WE £10.
🗘 Welcome by prior arrangement; packages can be arranged with local hotel; from £10.
🍽 Facilities at Liddlesdale Hotel.
🛏 Liddlesdale; Grapes.

9A 67 Newton Stewart ☎
Kirroughtree Avenue, Minnigaff, Newton Stewart, Wigtownshire, DG8 6PF
☎ 01671 402172
Course is close to the A75 Carlisle-Stranraer rd; one mile from town centre.
Parkland/hill course.
Founded 1896/1992
18 holes, 5887 yards, S.S.S. 69
𝌆 Practice range.
† Welcome.
𝌆 WD £22 (winter £10); WE £25 (winter £10).
🗘 Welcome by prior arrangement; catering by prior arrangement with the steward; terms available on application.
🍽 Full clubhouse facilities available.
🛏 Glencalm; Crown.

9A 68 Niddry Castle
Castle Road, Winchburgh, Broxburn, West Lothian, EH52 6RQ
🖳 www.niddrycastlegc.co.uk
☎ 01506 891097
Course is on the B9080 in centre of village; five miles from the Newbridge interchange.
Parkland course.
Founded 1982
Designed by Derek Smith
9 holes, 5518 yards, S.S.S. 67
† Welcome WD; by arrangement at WE.
𝌆 WD £13; WE £19.
🗘 Welcome WD by prior arrangement; full catering packages by arrangement; £12.

🍽 Full clubhouse facilities.
🛏 Tally-Ho, Winchburgh.

9A 69 North Berwick
New Club House, Beach Road, North Berwick, East Lothian, EH39 4BB
🖳 www.topweb.free-online.co.uk/nb
📧 northberwickgc@aol.com
☎ 01620 895040, Fax 893274, Pro 893233, Sec 895040, Rest/Bar 894766
In North Berwick take the last left turn before the town centre.
Links course.
Pro D Huish; Founded 1832
18 holes, 6420 yards, S.S.S. 72
† Welcome by prior arrangement.
𝌆 WD £50; WE £70.
🗘 Welcome by prior arrangement; catering packages can be arranged; terms on application.
🍽 Full clubhouse catering facilities available.
🛏 Marine Hotel; many B&Bs in the area.

9A 70 Peebles ☎
Kirkland Street, Peebles, Peeblesshire, EH45 8EU
🖳 www.peeblesgolfclub.co.uk
📧 secretary@peeblesgolfclub.co.uk
☎ 01721 720197, Fax 724441
Located on the NW side of Peebles off A72; signposted; 23 miles S of Edinburgh.
Undulating parkland course.
Founded 1892
Designed by James Braid; Alterations by HS Colt
18 holes, 6160 yards, S.S.S. 70
† Welcome by prior arrangement with the club.
𝌆 WD £32; WE £39 (group discounts available).
🗘 Welcome by prior arrangement except on Sat; new clubhouse opened in 1997; catering packages available by arrangement; terms on application.
🍽 Full clubhouse facilities available.
🛏 Peebles Hotel Hydro; Park; Kingsmuir; Greentree.

9A 71 Polkemmet Country Park
Park Centre, Polkemmet Country Park, Bathgate, West Lothian, EH47 0AD
☎ 01501 743905, Rest/Bar 744441
Park is on the N side of the B766 midway between Harthill and Whitburn.
Parkland course.
Founded 1981
Designed by W Lothian District Council
9 holes, 6531 yards

† Welcome; no restriction.
Ⅼ WD £4.75; WE £5.55.
⌁ Welcome.
🍽 Bar and restaurant facilities available.
🛏 Eillcroft, Whitburn; Holiday Inn; Dreadnought, both Bathgate.

9A 72 Portobello

Stanley Street, Edinburgh, Midlothian, EH15 1JJ
☎ 0131 6694361
On A1 E of Edinburgh, off Milton Road.
Parkland course.
Founded 1826
9 holes, 4504 yards, S.S.S. 64
† Welcome.
Ⅼ WD £4.50 WE £5.00.
⌁ Welcome by prior arrangement.
🛏 Kings Manor.

9A 73 Portpatrick Dunskey ♌

Golf Course Road, Portpatrick, Stranraer, Wigtownshire, DG9 8TB
🖳 www.portpatrickgolfclub.com
🖥 enquiries@portpatrickgolfclub.com
☎ 01776 810273, Fax 810811, Sec 810817, Rest/Bar 810819
Follow A77 or A75 to Stranraer and then follow signs for Portpatrick; on entering village turn right at the War Memorial.
Links style clifftop course.
Founded 1903
Designed by Dunskey Estate/W M Hunter of Prestwick
18 holes, 5913 yards, S.S.S. 67
🏌 Practice range.
† Welcome with handicap certs.
Ⅼ WD £25; WE £39.
⌁ Welcome by prior arrangement; handicap certs required; catering packages available; weekly tickets £120; day rates; also dinvin course: 1504 yards, par 3; from £10.
🍽 Full clubhouse facilities; meals until 9pm daily.
🛏 Fernhill; Portpatrick; Downshire; Harbour House.

9A 74 Powfoot

Cummertrees, Powfoot, Annan, Dumfriesshire, DG12 5QE
🖳 www.powfoot.com
🖥 bsutherland@ powfootgolfclub.fsnet.co.uk
☎ 01461 700276, Fax 700276, Pro 700327, Sec 700276
Course is off A75 to Annan/Dumfries taking the second turning for Annan until signs for Cummertrees and Powfoot on the B724; 3 miles later sharp left after railway bridge.

Links course.
Pro Gareth Dick; Founded 1903
Designed by James Braid
18 holes, 6266 yards, S.S.S. 71
† Welcome except Sat and after 1pm on Sun.
Ⅼ WD £25; WE £27; BH £28.
⌁ Welcome by prior arrangement; terms on application.
🍽 Full clubhouse facilities.
🛏 Powfoot Golf Hotel; Cairndale Hotel, Dumfries, Imperial Hotel, Castle Douglas.

9A 75 Prestonfield ♌

6 Priestfield Road North, Edinburgh, Midlothian, EH16 5HS
🖳 www.prestonfield.co.uk
☎ 0131 667 9665, Pro 667 8597, Sec 667 9665
Close to Commonwealth Games pool.
Parkland course.
Pro John McFarlane; Founded 1920
Designed by Peter Robertson
18 holes, 6212 yards, S.S.S. 70
† Welcome by arrangement.
Ⅼ WD £22; WE £33.
⌁ Welcome WD starting from 9.30am and 2pm; catering packages available; terms on application.
🍽 Full catering except Mon.
🛏 Prestonfield House; March Hall; Rosehall.

9A 76 Pumpherston

Drumshoreland Road, Pumpherston, Livingston, West Lothian, EH53 0LH
🖳 www.pumpherstongolfclub.com
☎ 01506 432869, Fax 438250, Pro 433337, Sec 433336, Rest/Bar 433338
400 yards E of the village cross.
Undulating parkland course.
Founded 1895
Designed by Graham Webster.
18 holes
† Welcome with a member.
Ⅼ WD £18 round, £25 day; WE £22 round, £33 day.
⌁ Welcome WD by prior arrangement; max party 24; bar snack and meals to order; terms on application.
🍽 Clubhouse facilities.

9A 77 Ratho Park

Ratho, Newbridge, Midlothian, EH28 8NX
🖳 www.rathoparkgolfclub.com
🖥 secretary.rpgc@btconnect.com
☎ 0131 335 0068, Fax 333 1752, Pro 333 1406, Rest/Bar 335 0069
Adjacent to Edinburgh Airport 8 miles W of Edinburgh.
Parkland course.

Pro Alan Pate
Founded 1928
Designed by James Braid
18 holes, 5960 yards, S.S.S. 68
† Welcome by prior arrangement with the Pro.
Ⅼ WD £25; WE £35.
⌁ Welcome Tues, Wed, Thurs by prior arrangement; packages for golf and catering available for groups of 12 or more; terms available on application.
🍽 Full clubhouse bar and restaurant facilities. No catering on Mondays.

9A 78 Ravelston

24 Ravelston Road, Blackhall, Edinburgh, Midlothian, EH4 5NZ
☎ 0131 3152486
From city centre turn left at Blackhall Junction then across the crossroad and turn right 100 yards further on.
Parkland course.
Founded 1912
Designed by James Braid
9 holes, 5200 yards, S.S.S. 65
† Welcome WD.
Ⅼ Wd £7.50.
⌁ Small groups welcome by prior arrangement; from £15.
🍽 Snacks and bar facilities.
🛏 Garden Court Holiday Inn.

9A 79 The Roxburghe

Heiton, Kelso, Roxburghshire, TD5 8JZ
🖳 www.roxburghe.net
🖥 golf@roxburghe.net
☎ 01573 450333, Fax 450611
On A698 between Jedburgh and Kelso.
Woodland/parkland course.
Pro Craig Montgomerie; Founded 1997
Designed by Dave Thomas
18 holes, 7111 yards, S.S.S. 75
🏌 Practice range and short game area.
† Welcome by prior arrangement.
Ⅼ WD/WE £60; day ticket £80.
⌁ Welcome by prior arrangement; catering packages by prior arrangement.
🍽 Spikes bar; full facilities available in hotel.
🛏 The Roxburghe Hotel (on site).

9A 80 Royal Burgess Golfing Society of Edinburgh

181 Whitehouse Rd, Edinburgh, Midlothian, EH4 6BY
🖳 www.royalburgess.co.uk
🖥 secretary@royalburgess.co.uk
☎ 0131 339 2075, Fax 339 3712, Pro 339 6474, Rest/Bar 339 2012

Royal Musselburgh

Royal Musselburgh does have a sting in the tail, the club's strokesaver is kind enough to point out to guests before they embark on a round at the sixth oldest golf club in the world. But will they listen? The real majesty of this course only really shows itself on the back nine, starting with a sweeping par-four up and over a hill to a green nestled in the most secluded corner of the course (Morrison's Haven). Then three more thought-provoking par-fours must be negotiated – and enjoyed: don't forget to pause and relish the view as you walk off the raised green at the 12th and on to the elevated tee at 13.

The 13th is regarded as the toughest on the course, chiefly because of its length (452 yards) and to walk off with a bogey is no disgrace, but the par-three 14th can put an even bigger number on your scorecard – if you misjudge your tee shot. The trick, probably, is to play this course only once – because when you stand on the tee at "The Gully" for the first time you have no idea what awaits an errant shot, and are unable to psyche yourself out.

The par-four 15th plays longer than its 440 yards because of the dead ground a tee shot has to cover before reaching the top of the hill on the fairway. The line should be up the left-hand side of the fairway because of the slight dog-leg nature of the hole, but too far left and the trees await.

The worst is probably then over and another fantastic par-three then awaits (the members here rate their short holes as fine as any on the Lothian coast), followed by a par-four 17th which is reminiscent of much of the front nine. Anything right off the tee at 18 heads towards the clubhouse. It is not the place to be but you can appreciate the splendour of Prestongrange, the 12th century building that the club has used as its home since 1925.

Royal Musselburgh Golf Club celebrated its 230th birthday this year, although some contest that the club is older. Historians of the club can only be certain that 1774 was the first year that the silver cup, the oldest trophy in golf, was first presented by the gentlemen golfers of Musselburgh to the Golf Club. Like the Honourable Company of Edinburgh Golfers, the Royal Burgess Golfing Society and Bruntsfield Golf Club, Royal Musselburgh began life on the Musselburgh Levenhall links, where Mrs Forman would serve golfers drinks from her "Inn" on the course. From there it moved to Prestongrange, just outside Edinburgh.

The Duke of Connaught granted Musselburgh Golf Club royal status in 1876, two years after its centenary. The Duke had visited the nearby pit at Carberry Colliery with the then club president Sir Archibald Hope and weeks later accepted an invitation to become Honorary President of the club. Later that year, the Duke agreed that the club could then call itself Royal.

Life proceded smoothly at Prestongrange from the 1920s until the 1940s when financial problems gripped the club and nearly closed it down. The hard times were precipitated by the death of the Duke of Connaght in 1942, then the Second World War came and, afterwards, serious debt. Interestingly the nearby mining community came to the rescue and, in 1958, the Coal Industry Social Welfare Organisation took over the course administration. There has always been a close bond between the club and the coal board and the successful union between Royal Musselburgh and the CISWO continues today – **Jim Bruce-Ball**

18 holes, par 70, 6237 yards

Royal Musselburgh Golf Club

Prestongrange House, Prestonpans, East Lothian EH32 9RP

Tel/Fax: **01875 810276**   Web: **www.royalmusselburgh.co.uk**

This parkland course was designed by James Braid and, in contrast to many of East Lothian's courses, offers golfers views of Edinburgh and Arthur's Seat. The golfing challenge comes on the homeward stretch where a series of par 4s are well protected by trees. The 5th oldest club in the world, the magnificent clubhouse has a superb collection of golfing memorabilia.

Special features: the par 3 14th, 'The Gully', penalises short approach shots with a 30 feet drop just in front of the putting surface.

Course is on the W side of Edinburgh on the Queensferry road, 100 yards from the Barnton Junction.
Parkland course.
Pro Steven Brian; Founded 1735
Designed by Tom Morris
18 holes, 6486 yards, S.S.S. 71
† Welcome by prior arrangement; no lady members.
 By prior arrangement.
 Welcome by prior arrangement; catering by arrangement; terms available on application.
 Clubhouse lunches and bar snacks.
 Barnton; Royal Scot.

9A 81 Royal Musselburgh ☏
Royal Musselburgh Golf Club, Prestongrange House, Prestonpans, East Lothian, EH32 9RP
 www.royalmusselburgh.co.uk
 royalmusselburgh@btinternet.com
 01875 810276, Fax 810276, Pro 810139, Rest/Bar 813671
Course is on the B1361 North Berwick Road.
Parkland course.
Pro John Henderson; Founded 1774
Designed by James Braid
18 holes, 6237 yards, S.S.S. 70
 Practice area only.
† Welcome by prior arrangement.
 WD £25; WE £35.
 Welcome WD except Fri afternoons by prior arrangement; catering can be arranged; £35 per day for golf; round £25.
 Full catering facilities available.
 Marine Hotel; Golf Inn.

9A 82 St Boswells
Braeheads Road, St Boswells, Melrose, Roxburghshire, TD6 0DE
☎ 01835 823527
Off the A68 in St Boswells.
Parkland course.

Founded 1899
Designed by William Park, altered by John Shade (1956)
9 holes, 5250 yards, S.S.S. 66
† Welcome by prior arrangement.
 WD £18; WE £20.
 Welcome by prior arrangement if more than six in party; catering can be arranged in advanced; from £15.
 Bar and light snacks available at WE; other times by prior arrangement.
 Buccleuch Arms.

9A 83 St Medan
Monreith, Newton Stewart, Wigtownshire, DG8 8NJ
☎ 01988 700358
Off the A747 3 miles S of Port William following the A714 from Newton Stewart.
Links course.
Founded 1905
9 holes, 4454 yards, S.S.S. 63
† Welcome.
 18 holes £15, day £22 (WD or WE).
 Welcome by prior arrangement; terms on application.
 Clubhouse facilities.

9A 84 Sanquhar
Old Barr Rd, Sanquhar, Dumfriesshire, DG4 6JZ
☎ 01659 50577, Sec 58181
Course is off the A76, 0.5 miles from Sanquhar.
Parkland course.
Founded 1894
9 holes, 5594 yards, S.S.S. 68
† Welcome.
 WD £10; WE £12.
 Welcome by arrangement; catering by arrangement; snooker; bowls; darts; from £10.
 Clubhouse facilities.
 Blackaddie; Glendyne; Nithsdale.

9A 85 Selkirk ☏
The Hill, Selkirk, Selkirkshire, TD7 4NW
☎ 01750 20621, Pro 20621, Sec 20621, Rest/Bar 20621
Course is 0.5 miles S of Selkirk on the A7.
Heathland course.
Founded 1883
Designed by Willie Park
9 holes, 5575 yards, S.S.S. 68
 Ashkirk (4 miles south Selkirk A7).
† Welcome WD by prior arrangement except Mon pm; WE by prior arrangement.
 Terms on application.
 Welcome WD; some WE; catering packages prior arrangement; terms on application.
 Bar open evenings and WE during the summer; at other times by arrangement.
 Heatherlie; Woodburn; Glen, all Selkirk.

9A 86 Silverknowes
Silverknowes Road, Edinburgh, Midlothian, EH4 5ET
☎ 0131 3363843
W end of Edinburgh off Cramond Foreshore.
Municipal links course.
Founded 1958
18 holes, 6097 yards, S.S.S. 70
† Welcome by prior arrangement.
 WD £10.00; WE £12.50.
 Welcome by prior arrangement; terms on application.
 Commodore, adjacent.

9A 87 Southerness
Southerness, Kirkbean, Dumfries, Dumfriesshire, DG2 8AZ
 www.southernessgolfclub.com
 admin@southernessgc.sol.co.uk
☎ 01387 880677, Fax 880644, Sec 880677, Rest/Bar 880677

Course on A710 15 miles S of Dumfries.
Links course on Solway firth.
Founded 1947
Designed by MacKenzie Ross
18 holes, 6566 yards, S.S.S. 73
  † Welcome by prior arrangement;
handicap certs required.
  ⌐ WD £35; WE £45.
  ⌐ Welcome by prior arrangement;
packages available; from £45.
  ⍾ Full catering facilities.
  ⌐ Cairndale; Clonyard; Cavens
House; Paul Jones Hotel.

9A 88 **Stranraer**   ☎
Stranraer, Chreachmore, Leswalt,
Stranraer, DG9 0LF
  ⌐ www.stranraergolfclub.net
  ⌐ stranraergolf@btclick.com
  ☎ 01776 870245, Fax 870445
On A718 to Kirkcolm 3 miles from
Stranraer.
Parkland/seaside course; on present
site since 1953.
Founded 1905/1953
Designed by James Braid
18 holes, 6308 yards, S.S.S. 72
  † Welcome except at members'
times; not before 9.15am or between
12.30pm-1.30pm and 5-6pm.
  ⌐ WD £25; WE £30.
  ⍾ Welcome by prior arrangement;
some restrictions apply as to visitors;
catering can be arranged; separate
locker rooms; terms on application.
  ⍾ Full catering and bar service.
  ⌐ North West Castle; Craignelder
Hotel; Torrs Warren Hostel.

9A 89 **Swanston**   ☎
11 Swanston Road, Edinburgh,
Midlothian, EH10 7DS
  ☎ 0131 4452239, Fax 4452239,
Pro 4454002
S side of the city on the lower slopes
of Pentland Hills.
Hillside course.
Pro Stu Pardoe; Founded 1927
Designed by Herbert More
18 holes, 5004 yards, S.S.S. 65
  † Welcome WD; some WE
restrictions.
  ⌐ WD £15; WE £17.50.
  ⍾ Welcome by prior arrangement;
catering and golf packages available;
from £15.
  ⍾ Full facilities.
  ⌐ Braid Hills.

9A 90 **Thornhill**
Blacknest, Thornhill, Dumfriesshire,
DG3 5DW

  ⌐ coordinatorthirngillgc@btinternet
.com
  ☎ 01848 330546, Pro 331779,
Sec 331779
Off A76 at Thornhill 14 miles N of
Dumfries.
Moorland/parkland course.
Pro James Davidson; Founded 1893
18 holes, 6085 yards, S.S.S. 70
  † Welcome by prior arrangement.
  ⌐ To be decided.
  ⍾ Welcome by prior arrangement;
catering packages arranged through
the steward; terms on application.
  ⍾ Full clubhouse facilities.
  ⌐ George; Buccleuch; Trigony.

9A 91 **Torphin Hill**
Torphin Road, Edinburgh, Midlothian,
EH13 0PG
  ⌐ www.torphinhillgc.sagenet.co.uk
  ⌐ info@torphinhillgc.sagenet.co.uk
  ☎ 0131 441 1100, Pro 4061,
Sec 7166
SW of Colinton Village.
Hilly course.
Pro Jamie Browne; Founded 1895
18 holes, 4580 yards, S.S.S. 67
  † Welcome except before 2pm at WE.
  ⌐ WD £12; WE £20.
  ⍾ Welcome WD by prior
arrangement; terms on application.
  ⍾ Clubhouse facilities.
  ⌐ Braid Hills.

9A 92 **Torwoodlee**   ☎
Edinburgh Road, Galashiels,
Selkirkshire, TD1 2NE
  ⌐ www.torwoodleegolfclub.org.uk
  ⌐ secretary@torwoodleegolfclub
.org.uk
  ☎ 01896 752660, Fax 752260,
Sec 752260, Rest/Bar 752260
2 miles outside Galashiels on the main
Edinburgh Road.
Parkland course.
Founded 1895
Designed by Willie Park (new layout,
John Garner)
18 holes, 6087 yards, S.S.S. 68
  † Welcome by prior arrangement.
  ⌐ Terms on application.
  ⍾ Welcome by prior arrangement;
packages for golf and catering
available; from £25.
  ⍾ Full clubhouse facilities.
  ⌐ Kingsknowe; Galashiels; Burts,
Melrose; Millers, Melrose.

9A 93 **Turnhouse**
154 Turnhouse Road, Edinburgh,
Midlothian, EH12 0AD

  ⌐ www.turnhousegc.com
  ⌐ info@turnhouse.com
  ☎ 0131 3391014, Pro 3397701
Course is on the A9080 W of city near
the airport.
Parkland/heathland course.
Pro John Murray; Founded 1897
Designed by James Br aid.
18 holes, 6153 yards, S.S.S. 69
  † Welcome by arrangement WD only.
  ⌐ From £22.
  ⍾ Welcome by prior arrangement WD
only; catering packages available
everyday for 12 or more; terms on
application.
  ⍾ Full facilities every day.
  ⌐ Royal Scot; Posthouse; Stakis.

9A 94 **Uphall**
Houston Mains, Uphall Golf Club,
Uphall, West Lothian, EH52 6JT
  ⌐ uphallgolfclub
@businessunmetered.com
  ☎ 01506 856404, Fax 855358,
Pro 855553
On A899 200 yards W of Uphall; 0.5
miles from M8 Junction 3; 15 miles W
of Edinburgh.
Tree-lined parkland course.
Pro Gordon Law; Founded 1895
18 holes, 5592 yards, S.S.S. 67
  † Welcome by prior arrangement
except on competition days.
  ⌐ WD £17; WE £22.
  ⍾ Welcome by prior arrangement;
catering packages available; disabled
facilities.
  ⍾ Full bar and catering facilities
available.

9A 95 **Vogrie**
Vogrie Estate Country Park,
Gorebridge, Midlothian, EH23 4NN
  ☎ 01875 821716, Sec 8217986
Off A68 Jedburgh Road.
Parkland course.
Founded 1989
9 holes, 5060 yards, S.S.S. 66
  † Public pay and play.
  ⌐ Terms on application.
  ⍾ Welcome; some restrictions; terms
on application.
  ⍾ Tea room in park.

9A 96 **West Linton**   ☎
Medwyn Road, West Linton,
Peeblesshire, EH46 7HN
  ⌐ www.wlgc.co.uk
  ⌐ secretarywlgc@btinternet.com
  ☎ 01968 660463, Pro 660256,
Sec 660970, Rest/Bar 660589
Course is off the A702 at West Linton.

Moorland course.
Pro I Wright; Founded 1890
Designed by Braid/Millar/Fraser
18 holes, 6132 yards, S.S.S. 69
♦ Welcome WD and after 1pm on non-competition WE.
⌐ Terms on application.
♂ Welcome WD by prior arrangement with Sec; catering packages available; from £25.
⦿ Full clubhouse facilities.
↝ Gordon Arms.

9A 97 West Lothian ☎
Airngath Hill, Linlithgow, West Lothian, EH49 7RH
☎ 01506 826030, Fax 826030, Pro 825060
Take A706 from Linlithgow to Bo'ness for 2.5 miles, and then turn right to the golf club.
Parkland course.
Founded 1892
Designed by W Park (1892), J Adams (1923), F Middleton (1975)
18 holes, 6046 yards, S.S.S. 71
♦ Welcome WD; WE by prior arrangement.
⌐ WD £17; WE £22.
♂ Welcome WD and non-competition WE by prior arrangement; terms available on application.
⦿ Full clubhouse facilities available.
↝ Richmond Park; Earl O'Moray.

9A 98 Whitekirk ☎
Whitekirk, N Berwick, Lothian, EH39 5PR
⌐ www.whitekirk.com
▤ countryclub@whitekirk.com
☎ 01620 870300, Fax 870330
Course is mile and a half from North Berwick on the A198.
Links course.
Pro Paul Wardell; Founded 1995
Designed by Cameron Sinclair.
18 holes, 6526 yards, S.S.S. 71
⌐ Golf Academy; practice range.
♦ Welcome.
⌐ WD £22/£35, WE £35/£50.
♂ Welcome; £35/£65 (special WD offers available).
⦿ Full clubhouse meals available.

9A 99 Wigtown & Bladnoch
Lightlands Terrace, Wigtown, Dumfries & Galloway, DG8 9EF
☎ 01988 403354
On A746 0.25 miles from town centre.
Parkland course.
Founded 1960
9 holes, 5462 yards, S.S.S. 67
♦ Welcome.
⌐ WD £15; WE £15.
♂ Welcome by prior arrangement; packages with local hotels; terms on application.
⦿ Clubhouse facilities.
↝ Conifers Leisure Park.

9A 100 Wigtownshire County ☎
Mains Of Park, Glenluce, Newton Stewart, Wigtownshire, DG8 0NN
⌐ www.wigtowncountygolfclub.com
▤ enquiries@wigtownshiregolfclub.com
☎ 01581 300420
On the A75 8 miles E of Stranraer.
Links course.
Founded 1894
Designed by G Cunningham/C Hunter
18 holes, 5843 yards, S.S.S. 68
♦ Welcome.
⌐ WD £22; WE £24
♂ Welcome by prior arrangement; discounts for groups of 10 or more.
⦿ Clubhouse facilities.
↝ Glenbay; Kelvin, both Glenluce; North West Castle, Stranraer.

9A 101 Winterfield ☎
North Road, Dunbar, East Lothian, EH42 1AU
☎ 01368 862280, Fax 863562, Pro 863562, Sec 863562, Rest/Bar 862280
Off A1 to Dunbar; club 0.5 miles from High Street.
Links course.
Pro Kevin Phillips; Founded 1935
18 holes, 5169 yards, S.S.S. 64
♦ Welcome; WE by prior arrangement.
⌐ WD £15; WE £17.
♂ Welcome by prior arrangement with Pro; packages available for 18 or 36 holes of golf plus catering; from £15.
⦿ Full clubhouse facilities.
↝ Bayswell; Hillside; Goldenstones; Craigengelt; Royal Mackintosh.

Strathclyde

It has been said, with only a slight exaggeration, that you can walk from Ayr to Glasgow without ever leaving a golf course. If there really was a fairway to heaven then it would lie on the Ayrshire coast where there are more great golf courses per square mile than anywhere else in the world (although inhabitants of the Melbourne sand belt might challenge that assertion). How peculiar then that it was not until 1978 that Troon became the first club in the West of Scotland to be granted the royal title, the only one to be bestowed in the reign of the present monarch.

A day at Troon is rather pricey and the second course is something of an anticlimax – one American commentator wryly said that it was a lot of money to play in a car park – but the welcome is excellent and the marshals politely diligent in ensuring that the pace of play is maintained above a steady crawl. After the 1973 Open here Lee Trevino said, "Someone once said that nobody 'murders' Troon. The way I played they couldn't even arrest me for second degree manslaughter". Eleven years earlier Jack Nicklaus, playing in his first Open, took a ten at the eleventh hole where a railway lurks behind the stone wall by the green. The second nine really can be that difficult, but from the regular tees the course is manageable for an amateur golfer on top of his game. In 2003 Gary Wolstenholme won his second Amateur Championship here and he is one of the shortest hitters to play at that level of the game.

To the south of Troon are the two courses at Turnberry of which the more famous is the Ailsa, although the Arran is not to be sniffed at. It is remarkable that there is any golf going on here at all. In the Second World War the grass had become concrete airstrips used to train the RAF Coastal Command.

Turnberry was the scene of the 1977 Open when Tom Watson and Jack Nicklaus spent the final two rounds exchanging birdies on a hole-by-hole basis. It is also the setting of the most photographed scene in golf, the drive from the ninth tee set out on a rocky promontory. On a summer's evening Turnberry just makes you want to sigh.

Moving north to Ayr itself Belleisle is an excellent public course and rather more affordable than some of its more famous neighbours. But Prestwick feels like home. The venue of the first twelve Open Championships, Prestwick was the perfect host to the 2001 Amateur Championship. Anyone who wants to learn about the history of golf must play Prestwick, a barren enchantment of dunes, sleepers and railway tracks.

North of Troon there is an extraordinary trio of courses that are next door to one another. At one end of Western Gailes a golfer can hit a shot over the railway onto Kilmarnock (Barassie) and at the other end he can knock it onto Glasgow Gailes. To the north are Irvine and Largs. A new addition to the cluster is Dundonald, a fearsome test in the making.

Across the sea are Machrie on the Isle of Skye and Machrihanish on the Mull of Kintyre. Machrie is a testing links with the enticement of an after-round whisky by the peat fire. Machrinahish vies with Prestwick for the finest opening hole in Scottish golf. The golfer has to decide how much of the beach to carry with his drive, the beachcomber has to decide where to shelter.

The grandest recent addition to golf in the region is Loch Lomond where Retief Goosen won the 2001 World Invitational a month after becoming US Open Champion and where Sergio Garcia was fined for being rather rude about the greens.

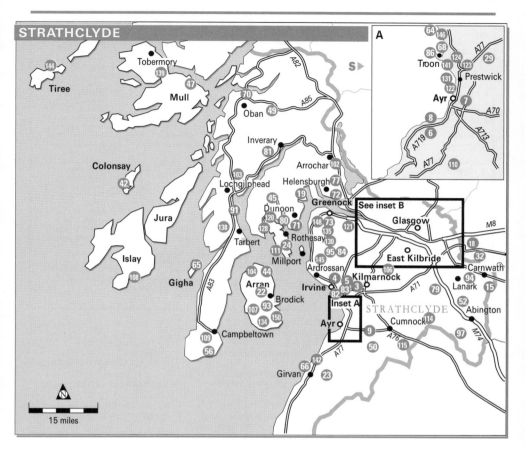

STRATHCLYDE

Tobermory
Tiree
Mull
Oban
Inverary
Colonsay
Lochgilphead
Arrochar
Helensburgh
Greenock
Dunoon
Rothesay
Jura
Islay
Tarbert
Millport
Gigha
Ardrossan
Kilmarnock
Arran
Irvine
Brodick
STRATHCLYDE
Cumnock
Campbeltown
Ayr
Girvan

A
Troon
Prestwick
Ayr

See inset B
Glasgow
East Kilbride
Carnwath
Lanark
Abington

Inset A

15 miles

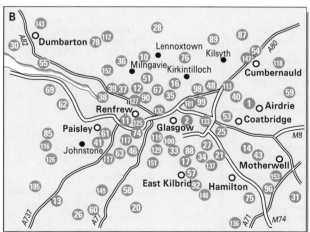

B
Dumbarton
Lennoxtown
Kilsyth
Milngavie
Kirkintilloch
Cumbernauld
Renfrew
Airdrie
Paisley
Glasgow
Coatbridge
Johnstone
East Kilbride
Hamilton
Motherwell

9B 1 Airdrie
Rochsoles, Airdrie, Lanarkshire,
ML6 0PQ
☎ 01236 762195, Pro 754360
Course is N of Airdrie on Glenmavis
road.
Parkland course.
Pro Jamie Carver; Founded 1877
Designed by James Braid
18 holes, 6004 yards, S.S.S. 69
† Welcome by letter of introduction.
⌐ WD £15; WE £15.
↗ Welcome WD by prior
arrangement with Sec; catering
packages can be arranged; snooker;
from £15.
⌐ Full clubhouse facilities.
⌐ Tudor; Kenilworth.

9B 2 Alexandra Park
Alexandra Park, Sannox Gdns,
Glasgow, G31 8SE

KEY				
1 Airdrie	31 Carluke	63 Fereneze	95 Largs	126 Ranfurly Castle
2 Alexandra Park	32 Carnwath	64 Gailes Golf Course	96 Larkhall	127 Renfrew
3 Annanhill	33 Cathcart Castle	65 Gigha	97 Leadhills	128 Rothesay
4 Ardeer	34 Cathkin Braes	66 Girvan	98 Lenzie	129 Rouken Glen
5 Auchenharvie Golf	35 Cawder	67 Glasgow	99 Lethamhill	130 Routenburn
Complex	36 Clober	68 Glasgow (Gailes)	100 Linn Park	131 Royal Troon
6 Ayr Belleisle	37 Clydebank & District	69 Gleddoch Country Club	101 Littlehill	132 Ruchill
7 Ayr Dalmilling	38 Clydebank Municipal	70 Glencruitten	102 Loch Lomond	133 Sandyhills
8 Ayr Seafield	39 Clydebank Overtoun	71 Gourock	103 Lochgilphead	134 Shiskine
9 Ballochmyle	40 Coatbridge	72 Greenock	104 Lochranza	135 Skelmorlie
10 Balmore	41 Cochrane Castle	73 Greenock Whinhill	105 Lochwinnoch	136 Strathaven
11 Barshaw	42 Colonsay	74 Haggs Castle	106 Loudoun Gowf Club	137 Strathclyde Park
12 Bearsden	43 Colville Park	75 Hamilton	107 Machrie Bay	138 Tarbert
13 Beith	44 Corrie	76 Hayston	108 Machrie Hotel & Golf	139 Tobermory
14 Bellshill	45 Cowal	77 Helensburgh	Links	140 Torrance House
15 Biggar	46 Cowglen	78 Hilton Park	109 Machrihanish	141 Troon Municipal
16 Bishopbriggs	47 Craignure	79 Hollandbush	110 Maybole	142 Turnberry Hotel
17 Blairbeth	48 Crow Wood	80 Innellan	111 Millport	143 Vale of Leven
18 Blairhead Golf Course	49 Dalmally	81 Inveraray	112 Milngavie	144 Vaul
19 Blairmore & Strone	50 Doon Valley	82 Irvine	113 Mount Ellen	145 West Kilbride
20 Bonnyton	51 Douglas Park	83 Irvine Ravenspark	114 Muirkirk	146 Western Gailes
21 Bothwell Castle	52 Douglas Water	84 Kilbirnie Place	115 New Cumnock	147 Westerwood Hotel Golf
22 Brodick	53 Drumpellier	85 Kilmacolm	116 Old Course Ranfurly	& Country Club
23 Brunston Castle	54 Dullatur	86 Kilmarnock (Barassie)	117 Paisley	148 Whinhill
24 Bute	55 Dumbarton	87 Kilsyth Lennox	118 Palacerigg	149 Whitecraigs
25 Calderbraes	56 Dunaverty	88 Kirkhill	119 Pollok	150 Whiting Bay
26 Caldwell	57 East Kilbride	89 Kirkintilloch	120 Port Bannatyne	151 Williamwood
27 Cambuslang	58 East Renfrewshire	90 Knightswood	121 Port Glasgow	152 Windyhill
28 Campsie	59 Easter Moffat	91 Kyles of Bute	122 Prestwick	153 Wishaw
29 Caprington	60 Eastwood	92 Laglands	123 Prestwick St Cuthbert	
30 Cardross	61 Elderslie	93 Lamlash	124 Prestwick St Nicholas	
	62 Erskine	94 Lanark	125 Ralston	

☎ 0141 5561294, Pro 7700519
Course is off the M8 before Blochairn.
Wooded parkland course.
Pro Alistair Bake
Founded 1818
Designed by Graham McArthur
9 holes, 4016 yards, S.S.S. 61
† Welcome.
Ⅼ Terms on application.
⚲ Welcome.
🍽 None.
🛏 Millennium Hotel; Kelvin Park; Stakis Ingram Hotel; Central; Courtyard.

9B 3 **Annanhill**

Irvine Road, Kilmarnock, Ayrshire, KA1 3RT
☎ 01563 521644, Sec 525557
One mile N of Kilmarnock on the A71 Irvine Road.
Parkland course.
Founded 1957
Designed by J McLean
18 holes, 6269 yards, S.S.S. 70
† Welcome by prior arrangement.
Ⅼ WD £12; WE £17.
⚲ Welcome by prior arrangement; catering packages can be arranged in advance; terms available on application.
🍽 Full clubhouse facilities available.
🛏 Howard Park; Portman.

9B 4 **Ardeer**

Greenhead, Stevenston, Ayrshire, KA20 4JX
🖥 www.ardeergolfclub.co.uk
☎ 01294 464542, Fax 456316, Pro 601327, Sec 465316
Follow A78 signs for Largs and Greenock on High Road by-passing Stevenston; turn right in Kerelaw road for course.
Parkland course.
Founded 1880
18 holes, 6409 yards, S.S.S. 71
† Welcome except Saturdays.
Ⅼ WD £22; WE £30.
⚲ Welcome Sun-Fri; full day's golf (£50 on Sun); discounted packages available for groups of 12 or more; discounted from £35.
🍽 Full clubhouse catering facilities available.

9B 5 **Auchenharvie Golf Complex**

Moorpark Road West, Stevenston, Ayrshire, KA20 3HU
☎ 01294 603103, Pro 603103, Rest/Bar 469051
Take the A78 to Ardrossan, take A738 to Stevenson.
Parkland course.
Pro Paul Rodgers; Founded 1981
Designed by Michael Struthers
9 holes, 5203 yards, S.S.S. 65

∤ Driving range floodlit.
† Welcome.
Ⅼ Adult £7.50/9 holes; Junior/Senior £4.
⚲ Welcome by prior arrangement; from £5.25.
🍽 Clubhouse bar.
🛏 Redburn Hotel.

9B 6 **Ayr Belleisle**

Belleisle Park, Doonfoot Road, Ayr, Ayrshire, KA7 4DU
☎ 01292 441258, Fax 442632, Sec 441258, Rest/Bar 442331
Follow the signs for Burns Cottage Drive on the A719 1.5 miles S of Ayr. Parkland course/on same site as Ayr Seafield.
Pro David Gemmel; Founded 1927
Designed by James Braid & Stutt
18 holes, 6431 yards, S.S.S. 71
† Public pay and play.
Ⅼ Prices on application.
⚲ Welcome; 7-day advance booking system; catering by prior arrangement in local hotels; separate locker room.
🍽 Facilities available.
🛏 Belleisle.

9B 7 **Ayr Dalmilling**

Dalmilling, Westwood Ave, Ayr, Ayrshire, KA8 0QY
☎ 01292 263893, Fax 610543

On A77 1 mile N of Ayr near racecourse.
Parkland course/meadowland.
Pro Philip Cheyney; Founded 1960
18 holes, 5724 yards, S.S.S. 67
† Welcome by prior arrangement.
£ WD £13; WE £16.50.
⚐ Welcome by at least 7 days' prior arrangement; catering packages involving snacks/lunches/high tea available; terms available on application.
⚑ Full clubhouse facilities available.

9B 8 Ayr Seafield
Belleisle Park, Ayr, Ayrshire, KA7 4DU
☎ 01292 441258, Fax 442632
Course is 1.5 miles S of Ayr on the A719 following signs for Burns Cottage Drive.
Parklands/seaside course; on same site as Ayr Belleisle.
Pro David Gemmel; Founded 1927
Designed by J Braid
18 holes, 5481 yards, S.S.S. 68
⨍ Practice range.
† Welcome.
£ WD £11; WE £11.
⚐ Welcome by prior arrangement; seven-day booking system in operation; catering can be arranged in the local hotels; from £11.
⚑ Limited.
⚑ Belleisle.

9B 9 Ballochmyle
Ballochmyle, Mauchline, Ayrshire, KA5 6LE
☎ 01290 550469, Fax 553657
On B705 off A76 1 mile S of Mauchline; following signs for Ballochmyle Hospital.
Inland/parkland course.
Founded 1937
18 holes, 5972 yards, S.S.S. 69
† Welcome except Sat.
£ Terms on application.
⚐ Welcome every day except Sat; tee times available between 9am-10am and 2pm-3pm WD; Sun 10am-10.45am and 2.30pm-3.15pm; Catering packages available; terms on application.
⚑ Full clubhouse facilities.
⚑ Royal; Dumfries Arms.

9B 10 Balmore
Balmore, Torrance, Glasgow, G64 4AW
⚐ www.balmoregolfclub.co.uk
✉ secretary@balmoregolfclub.co.uk
☎ 01360 620240, Pro 624123, Sec 620284

6/7 miles N of Glasgow on A807 off A803.
Parkland course.
Pro Kevin Craggs; Founded 1906
Designed by Harry Vardon
18 holes, 5542 yards, S.S.S. 67
⨍ Practice area.
† Welcome by introduction of a member.
£ Terms on application.
⚐ Terms on application.
⚑ Full clubhouse facilities.

9B 11 Barshaw
Barshaw Park, Glasgow Road, Paisley, Renfrewshire
☎ 0141 8892908
1 mile before Paisley Cross off the A737.
Meadowland course.
Founded 1920
18 holes, 5703 yards, S.S.S. 67
† Welcome.
£ WD £7.70; WE £7.70; concessions apply.
⚐ Limited.
⚑ Limited.
⚑ Water Mill; Brablock

9B 12 Bearsden
Thorn Road, Bearsden, Glasgow, Lanarkshire, G61 4BP
☎ 0141 942 2351, Sec 586 5300, Rest/Bar 942 2351
1 mile N of Bearsden Cross on Thorn Road.
Parkland course.
Founded 1891
9 holes, 6014 yards, S.S.S. 69
† Welcome only as the guest of a member.
£ Terms on application.
⚐ Welcome only by prior arrangement; terms available on application.
⚑ Full facilities.

9B 13 Beith ⚋
Threepwood Road, Beith, Ayrshire, KA15 2JR
⚐ www.beithgolfclub.co.uk
✉ bgc-secretary@hotmail.com
☎ 01505 503166, Fax 506814, Sec 506814, Rest/Bar 503166
1st left southbound on Beith by-pass A737.
Hilly parkland course.
Founded 1896
Designed by the Members
18 holes, 5625 yards, S.S.S. 68
† Welcome.
£ WD £20; WE £25.

⚐ Welcome by written prior arrangement; catering packages by arrangement; from £24.
⚑ Full catering facilities.

9B 14 Belshill ⚋
Community Rd, Orbiston, Bellshill, Lanarkshire, ML4 2RZ
☎ 01698 745124, Fax 292576
Between Belshill and Strathclyde Country Park close to M74 Junction 5 for the A725 Junction on the A8.
Parkland course.
Founded 1905
18 holes, 6315 yards, S.S.S. 70
† Welcome by prior arrangement; no Saturday visitors.
⚐ No Sunday visitors; all inclusive packages available for 18 and 36 holes; from £18.
⚑ Full catering facilities.
⚑ Bothwell Bridge; Moorings House; Silvertrees.

9B 15 Biggar
The Park, Broughton Road, Biggar, Lanarkshire, ML12 6QX
☎ 01899 220618, Pro 220319, Sec 220566
Off the A702 0.5 miles from the town centre.
Parkland course.
Founded 1895
Designed by Willie Park
18 holes, 5537 yards, S.S.S. 67
† Welcome by prior arrangement.
£ WD £8; WE £14.
⚐ Welcome by prior arrangement; packages for golf and catering may be available in 1998; terms on application.
⚑ Full clubhouse facilities available.
⚑ Elphinstone; Clydesdale; Tinto.

9B 16 Bishopbriggs
Brackenbrae Road, Bishopbriggs, Glasgow, Lanarkshire, G64 2DX
⚐ www.scottishholidays.net
✉ bgcsecretary@dial.pipex.com
☎ 0141 7721810, Fax 7622532, Pro ,Sec 7728938, Rest/Bar 7721810
On A803 4 miles N of Glasgow turning 200 yards short of the Bishopbriggs cross.
Parkland course.
Founded 1906
Designed by James Braid
18 holes, 6041 yards, S.S.S. 69
† Welcome by prior arrangement with the club.
£ Terms on application.

Welcome WD; apply to Secretary at least 1 month in advance; terms on application.

Catering facilities.

9B 17 **Blairbeth**
Blairbeth Golf Club, Fernbrae Avenue, Rutherglen, Glasgow, Lanarkshire, G73 4SF

www.blairbeth.com
committee@blairbethgc.fsnet.co.uk
0141 634 3355, Sec 634 3325
1 mile S of Rutherglen off Stonelaw Rd.
Parkland course.
Founded 1910/57
18 holes, 5537 yards, S.S.S. 68
Welcome either as a member's guest or by prior arrangement with club.
Terms on application.
Terms on application.
Clubhouse facilities.
Kings Park.

9B 18 **Blairhead Golf Club**
Ben Har Road, Shotts, Lanarkshire, ML7 5BJ
0150 182 0431, Fax 5868, Pro 2658, Sec 5868
Take M8 to Junction 5; then A7057 to Shotts; 1.5 miles to course.
Parkland course.
Pro John Strachan; Founded 1895
Designed by James Braid
18 holes, 6125 yards, S.S.S. 70
Practice range available.
Welcome WD; Sat after 4.30pm and Sun by prior arrangement.
WD £14 single round £22 full day; WE £16 single round £28 full day.
Welcome WD; full day's golf and catering included in packages; visitors' locker room; £30.
Full clubhouse facilities. Please contact clubhouse for further information.
Golden Circle; Bathgate; Travelodge Newhouse; Hillcroft Whitburn.

9B 19 **Blairmore & Strone**
Blairmore, by Dunoon, Argyll, PA23 8TJ
01369 840676
On A880 0.75 miles N of Strone and 5 miles N of Dunoon.
Undulating moorland and parkland course with panoramic views of the Clyde.
Founded 1896
Designed by J Braid
9 holes, 4224 yards, S.S.S. 62
Welcome; some restrictions Sat and Mon evening.
WD £8; WE £10.

Welcome by prior arrangement with Secretary; from £8.
Bar facilities available in the Summer.

9B 20 **Bonnyton**
Kirtonmoor Road, Eaglesham, Glasgow, G76 0QA
01355 302781, Fax 303151, Pro 302256
1 mile S of Eaglesham; 10 miles S of Glasgow.
Moorland course.
Pro Kendal McWade; Founded 1957
18 holes, 6255 yards, S.S.S. 71
Welcome by arrangement.
Terms on application.
Welcome Mon and Thurs by prior arrangement; catering packages can be arranged; terms available on application.
Full clubhouse facilities.
The Hilton, East Kilbride.

9B 21 **Bothwell Castle**
Blantyre Road, Bothwell, Glasgow, Lanarkshire, G71 8PJ
01698 853177, Fax 854052, Pro 852052, Sec 854052
3 miles N of Hamilton on the A9071 from the M74 Junction 5.
Parkland course.
Pro Adam McCloskey; Founded 1922
18 holes, 6243 yards, S.S.S. 70
Welcome WD 9.30am to 3.30pm.
WD £22.
Welcome by written prior arrangement; catering packages by arrangement; from £22.
Full clubhouse facilities.
Silvertrees; Bothwell Bridge.

9B 22 **Brodick**
Brodick, Brodick, Isle of Arran, KA27 8DL
peter@fatpro.freeserve.co.uk
01770 302349, Pro 302513
1 mile N of Pier.
Parkland/links course.
Pro Peter McCalla; Founded 1897
18 holes, 4736 yards, S.S.S. 64
Welcome by prior arrangement.
WD £18; WE £20.
Welcome by prior written arrangement; catering packages available; from £14.
Full clubhouse facilities.

9B 23 **Brunston Castle**
Bargany, Dailly, by Girvan, Ayrshire, KA26 9RH

www.brunstoncastle.co.uk
golf@brunstoncastle.co,uk
01465 811471, Fax 811545
Off the A77 at Girvan then on to B741 to Dailly.
Parkland course.
Pro Leon Dowman; Founded 1992
Designed by Donald Steel
18 holes, 6662 yards, S.S.S. 73
15 bays all floodlit.
Welcome.
Wd £28; WE £32.
Welcome by prior arrangement with the club Pro; package includes full day's golf; company days; pro-ams; 10 per cent discount for larger groups; £5 per person deposit required; from £40.
Full clubhouse facilities with restaurant.
Brunston Castle Holiday Resort; Malin Court, Turnberry; Ardlochan Hotel, Maidens.

9B 24 **Bute**
St Ninians, 32 Marine Place, Rothsay, Isle of Bute PA20 0LF
www.butegolfclub.com
secretary@butegolfclub.com
01700 502158
In Stravanan Bay off A845 Rothesay-Kilchattan Bay road.
Links course.
Founded 1888
9 holes, 4994 yards, S.S.S. 64
Welcome, but not before 11.30 pm on Sat.
From £8; details available on application.
Kingarth; St Blanes.

9B 25 **Calderbraes**
57 Roundknowe Road, Uddingston, Glasgow, Lanarkshire, G71 7TS
01698 813425
Close to start of M74; 4 miles from Glasgow.
Hilly parkland course.
Founded 1891
9 holes, 5186 yards, S.S.S. 67
Nevada Bobs (within 1 mile).
Welcome on WD.
WD £13 day ticket.
Welcome WD by prior arrangement; maximum 20; catering packages available; from £12.
Full bar and catering facilities available.
Redstones.

9B 26 **Caldwell**
Caldwell Golf Club, Uplawmoor, G78 4AU

🖰 www.caldwellgolfclub.i8.com
📧 caldwellgolfclub@aol.com
☎ 01505 850329, Fax 850604,
Pro 850616, Sec 850366
Off A736 5 miles SW of Barrhead; 12
miles NE of Irvine.
Moorland course.
Pro Stephen Forbes; Founded 1903
18 holes, 6228 yards, S.S.S. 70
† Welcome WD but advisable to
check in advance.
⌊ Terms on application.
⌁ Welcome WD except Thur by prior
arrangement; catering by arrangement;
terms on application.
🍽 Clubhouse facilities.
↩ Uplawmoor; Dalmeny Park.

9B 27 Cambuslang
30 Westburn Drive, Cambuslang,
Glasgow, Lanarkshire, G72 7NA
☎ 0141 164 1310
Off main Glasgow to Hamilton road at
Cambuslang.
Parkland course.
Founded 1892
9 holes, 5942 yards, S.S.S. 69
† Welcome by written application to
secretary, come with members.
⌊ Terms on application.
⌁ Apply in writing to secretary;
catering by arrangement; terms on
application.
🍽 Full clubhouse facilities.
↩ Cambus Court.

9B 28 Campsie
Crow Road, Lennoxtown, Glasgow,
G65 7HX
☎ 01360 310244, Pro 310920
Course is on the B822 to the N of
Lennoxtown.
Hillside/parkland course.
Pro Mark Brennan; Founded 1897
Designed by W Auchterlonie
18 holes, 5509 yards, S.S.S. 68
† Welcome WD; WE by prior
arrangement after 4 pm.
⌊ WD £20; WE £25.
⌁ Welcome by prior arrangement
with Sec.; full day's golf; catering: by
prior arrangement; from £30 to £37.50.
🍽 Clubhouse facilities.
↩ Glazert Country House Hotel,
Lennoxtown.

9B 29 Caprington
Ayr Road, Caprington, Kilmarnock,
Ayrshire, KA1 4UW
☎ 01563 523702
Course is on the Ayr road S of
Kilmarnock.

Parkland course.
18 holes, 5781 yards, S.S.S. 68
† Welcome.
⌊ Terms on application.
⌁ Apply to secretary.
🍽 Clubhouse facilities.

9B 30 Cardross
Main Road, Cardross, Dumbarton,
Dunbartonshire, G82 5LB
🖰 www.cardross.com
📧 golf@cardross.com
☎ 01389 841213, Fax 842162,
Pro 841350, Sec 841754
On A814 to Helensburgh 18 miles from
Glasgow.
Parkland course.
Pro Robert Farrell; Founded 1895
Designed by James Braid
18 holes, 6469 yards, S.S.S. 71
⫶ Driving new; short practice area;
putting green.
† Welcome WD.
⌊ WD £30 round, £45 day.
⌁ Welcome WD By Prior
Arrangement.
🍽 Full clubhouse facilities.
↩ Cameron House; Kirkton House.

9B 31 Carluke
Mauldslie Road, Carluke, Lanarkshire,
ML8 5HG
📧 admin-carlukegolf@supanet.com
☎ 01555 770574, Pro 751053,
Rest/Bar 771070
Access from both M74 and M8; from
the M74 leave at J7 and take the
Lanark turn until the lights at Garron
Bridge; then left on to the A71 and
then on to the B7011; club is 2.5 miles.
Parkland course.
Pro Ricky Forrest; Founded 1894
18 holes, 5899 yards, S.S.S. 69
† Welcome WD 9am-4pm.
⌊ WD £23 but variable in the
summer months.
⌁ Welcome by prior arrangement;
maximum 24; from £23-£33.
🍽 Full clubhouse facilities.
↩ Popinjay; Cartland Bridge.

9B 32 Carnwath
Carnwath Golf Club, 1 Main Street,
Carnwath, Lanark, Lanarkshire,
ML11 8JX
☎ 01555 840251, Fax 841070
5 miles NE of Lanark.
Undulating parkland course.
Founded 1907
18 holes, 5953 yards, S.S.S. 69
† Welcome except Sat or after
4pm.

⌊ WD £22; WE £34.
⌁ Welcome WD except Tues and
Thurs by prior arrangement; catering
by arrangement.
🍽 Every day except Tues and Thurs.
↩ Tinto, Symington.

9B 33 Cathcart Castle
Cathcart Castle Golf Club, Mearns
Road, Clarkston, Glasgow,
Lanarkshire, G76 7YL
📧 secretary@cathcartcastle.com
☎ 0141 6389449, Fax 63817201,
Pro 6383436
Course is on B767 1 mile from Clarkston.
Undulating parkland course.
Pro Stephen Duncan; Founded 1895
18 holes, 5832 yards, S.S.S. 68
† Tourists welcome by prior
arrangement.
⌊ WD £30; WE £30.
⌁ Welcome Tuesdays and Thursdays
by arrangement with secretary; day
ticket £35; catering by prior
arrangement; from £25.
🍽 Clubhouse facilities.
↩ Redhurst; Busby.

9B 34 Cathkin Braes
Cathkin Road, Rutherglen, Glasgow,
G73 4SE
📧 golf@cathkinbraes.freeserve.co.uk
☎ 0141 634 6605, Fax 630 8196,
Pro 634 0650
On B759 SE of Glasgow between
A749 and B766.
Moorland course.
Pro Stephen Bree; Founded 1888
Designed by James Braid
18 holes, 6208 yards, S.S.S. 71
⫶ Practice facilities.
† Welcome WD.
⌊ WD £25.
⌁ Welcome WD by prior
arrangement; packages from £25.
🍽 Full catering facilities.
↩ Stuart; Bruce; Burnside; Busby.

9B 35 Cawder
Cadder Road, Bishopbriggs, Glasgow,
Lanarkshire, G64 3QD
🖰 www.cawdergolfclub.org.uk
📧 secretary@cawdergolfclub.org.uk
☎ 0141 761 1281, Fax 1285,
Pro 772 7102
Course is off the A803 Glasgow-
Kirkintilloch road 0.5 miles E of
Bishopbriggs.
Parkland course.
Pro Ken Stevely; Founded 1933
Designed by Donald Steel (Cawder);
James Braid (Keir)

Cawder: 18 holes, 6295 yards, S.S.S. 71; Keir: 18 holes, 5870 yards, S.S.S. 68
♦ Welcome WD by prior arrangement with secretary.
ℾ WD £30.
⚷ Welcome WD by prior arrangement with secretary; day ticket £40; catering packages by arrangement; from £26.
⦿ Full catering facilities.
↩ Crow Wood House.

9B 36 Clober ☏
Craigton Road, Milngavie, Glasgow, G62 7HP
🖳 www.clober.co.uk
✉ secretary@clober.co.uk
☎ 0141 9561685, Fax 9561416, Pro 9566963, Sec 9561685, Rest/Bar 956 1685
7 miles NW of Glasgow.
Parkland course.
Pro Campbell Elliot; Founded 1952
Designed by Lyle family
18 holes, 4963 yards, S.S.S. 66
♦ Welcome WD until 4pm.
ℾ WD £16.
⚷ Welcome WD by prior arrangement; catering packages available; terms available on application.
⦿ Full clubhouse facilities.
↩ Burnbrae, West Highland Gate.

9B 37 Clydebank & District
Hardgate Golf Club, Glasgow Road, Hardgate, Clydebank, Dunbartonshire, G81 5QY
🖳 www.clydebankanddistrictgolfclub.co.uk
✉ eightaday@yahoo.com
☎ 01389 383833, Fax 383831, Sec 383831, Pro 383835
Off A82 turning right at Hardgate; ten miles W of Glasgow.
Parkland course.
Pro P R Jamieson; Founded 1905
18 holes, 5825 yards, S.S.S. 68
♦ Welcome WD.
ℾ WD £15.
⚷ Welcome WD by prior arrangement; terms available on application.
⦿ Full clubhouse facilities.
↩ West Hills; Boulevard; Radnor; Duntocher; West Highways.

9B 38 Clydebank Municipal
Overtoun Road, Dalmuir, Clydebank, G81 3RE
☎ 0141 9528698, Rest/Bar 9528698

Eight miles W of Glasgow.
Municipal parkland course.
18 holes, 5349 yards, S.S.S. 67
♦ Welcome except between 11am-2pm at WE.
ℾ Terms on application.
⚷ Contact local district council; terms on application.
⦿ Snack and cafe facilities available.
↩ Radnor.

9B 39 Clydebank Overtoun
Overtoun Road, Clydebank, Dunbartonshire, G81 3RE
☎ 0141 9526372
Course is five minutes from Dalmuir station.
Municipal parkland course.
Pro Ian Toy; Founded 1928
18 holes, 5349 yards, S.S.S. 66
♦ Welcome.
ℾ WD £6.55; WE £7.
⚷ Welcome by arrangement; limited facilities.
⦿ Café only.

9B 40 Coatbridge
Townhead Road, Coatbridge, Lanarkshire, ML5 2HX
☎ 01236 421492
In Coatbridge town.
Public parkland course.
Pro George Weir; Founded 1971
18 holes, 6026 yards, S.S.S. 69
⚸ Practice range, 18 bays floodlit.
♦ Welcome.
ℾ WD £5.10; £7.60.
⚷ Welcome by prior arrangement.
⦿ Full facilities.

9B 41 Cochrane Castle ☏
Scott Avenue, Johnstone, Renfrewshire, PA5 0HF
☎ 01505 320146, Fax 325338, Pro 328465
Half a mile off Beith Road in Johnstone.
Parkland course.
Pro Alan Logan; Founded 1895
Designed by Charles Hunter of Prestwick; altered by James Braid
18 holes, 6194 yards, S.S.S. 71
♦ Welcome WD; with member at WE.
ℾ WD £22 per round. £30.00 per day.
⚷ None.
⦿ Full clubhouse facilities available.
↩ Bird in Hand; Lynnhurst, both Johnstone.

9B 42 Colonsay
Isle of Colonsay, Argyll, PA61 7YP
🖳 www.colonsay.org.uk

☎ 01951 200316, Fax 200353, Sec 200369
Two miles W of Scalasaig pier; car ferry two-and-a-half hour journey from mainland.
Natural machair course.
Founded 1880
18 holes, 4775 yards, S.S.S. 72
♦ Welcome.
ℾ WD £10; WE £10.
⦿ All facilities at Colonsay Hotel; courtesy car provided to course.
↩ The Colonsay Hotel.

9B 43 Colville Park
New Jerviston House, Merry Street, Motherwell, Lanarkshire, ML1 4UG
☎ 01698 263017, Fax 230418, Pro 265779, Sec 265378
One mile NE of Motherwell railway station.
Parkland course.
Pro Alan Forrest; Founded 1923
Designed by James Braid
18 holes, 6265 yards, S.S.S. 70
♦ Welcome only as the guest of a member.
ℾ WD £3; WE £3.
⚷ Welcome by written prior arrangement; catering packages can be arranged; maximum 36; £20.
⦿ Full clubhouse facilities available.
↩ Old Mill; Moorings; Silvertrees.

9B 44 Corrie
Sannox, Isle of Arran, KA27 8JD
☎ 01770 810223
Seven miles N of Brodick on A84 coast road.
Picturesque undulating course.
Founded 1892
9 holes, 3896 yards, S.S.S. 61
♦ Welcome except for some Thurs and Sat afternoons.
ℾ Adult £14; Junior £7; day tickets only.
⚷ Welcome by prior arrangement; catering by arrangement; maximum normally 12.
⦿ Catering available in season April until October.

9B 45 Cowal
Ardenslate Road, Kirn, Dunoon, Argyll, PA23 8NN
🖳 www.cowalgolfclub.co.uk
☎ 01369 705673, Fax 705673, Pro 702395, Sec 705673, Rest/Bar 702426
From the Shore road turn up Kirn Brae.
Heath/parkland course.
Pro Russell Weir; Founded 1891

Designed by James Braid
18 holes, 6063 yards, S.S.S. 70
♦ Welcome.
⌑ WD £24; WE £34.
⌲ Welcome; packages include
transport, catering and 18 holes of golf;
from £38.
🍽 Full clubhouse catering available.
🛏 Local tourist office can provide
details.

9B 46 Cowglen ☎

301 Barrhead Road, Glasgow,
Lanarkshire, G43 1AU
✉ r.jamieson-accountant@fsmail.net
☎ 01505 503000, Fax 01505 503000,
Pro 0141 649 9401, Rest/Bar 0141
649 6003
S side of Glasgow following signs for
Burrell Collection,M77 2mns from the
end of Barrhead Junction.
Undulating parkland course.
Pro Simon Payne; Founded 1906
18 holes, 5976 yards, S.S.S. 69
♦ Welcome on WD,competition free
days.
⌑ WD/WE £25.50 (excl. Sat).
⌲ Welcome by prior arrangement
with secretary; catering packages
available; from £22.
🍽 Clubhouse facilities.
🛏 Tinto, Thistle close to city centre.

9B 47 Craignure

Scallastle, Craignure, Isle of Mull,
PA65 6AY
✉ mullair@btinternet.com
☎ 01680 3004402, Fax 300402
Course in one mile from Oban/Mull
ferry terminal.
Links course built on estuary of
Scallastle River.
Founded 1895/1979
Designed by Howitt/Phillips.
9 holes, 5357 yards, S.S.S. 66
♦ Welcome except on competition
days.
⌑ Terms on application.
⌲ Welcome by arrangement; weekly
ticket (from £45) available.
🍽 Limited clubhouse facilities.

9B 48 Crow Wood

Garnkirk House, Cumbernauld Road,
Muirhead, Glasgow, G69 9JF
☎ 0141 7792011, Fax 7799148,
Pro 7791943, Sec 7794954
Off A80 Stirling road midway between
Stepps and Muirhead five miles N of
Glasgow.
Parkland course.
Pro Brian Moffat; Founded 1925

Designed by James Braid
18 holes, 6168 yards, S.S.S. 70
♦ Welcome WD.
⌑ Prices on application.
⌲ Welcome WD only by prior
arrangement; catering can be
arranged.
🍽 Full clubhouse facilities.
🛏 Garfield House, Stepps; Crow
Wood House, Muirhead; The Travel
Lodge.

9B 49 Dalmally

'Orchy Bank', Dalmally, Argyll,
PA33 1AS
☎ 01838 200370
Two miles W of Dalmally Village on
A85.
Parkland course.
Founded 1987
Designed by C McFarlane Barrow
9 holes, 4514 yards, S.S.S. 63
♦ Welcome.
⌑ WD £10; WE £10.
⌲ Welcome by prior arrangement;
bar snacks and meals can be
arranged; £8.
🍽 By prior arrangement; bar facilities.
🛏 Glen Orchy Lodge.

9B 50 Doon Valley

Hillside, Patna, Ayr, Ayrshire, KA6 7JT
☎ 01292 531607, Sec 550411
On A713 Ayr to Castle Douglas road
ten miles S of Ayr.
Undulating parkland course.
Founded 1927
Designed by Course redesigned by E
Ayrshire Council
9 holes, 5895 yards, S.S.S. 70
⌑ Practice area and practice green.
♦ Welcome WD; WE by
arrangement.
⌑ WD/WE £10/round.
⌲ Welcome WD; WE by prior
arrangement; day ticket for golf;
catering available by arrangement.
🍽 Bar open evenings WD; all day
WE.
🛏 Kirkton Inn (01292 560241).

9B 51 Douglas Park

Hillfoot, Bearsden, Glasgow, G61 2JT
🖥 www.douglasparkgolfclub.net
✉ secretary@douglasparkgolfclub.net
☎ 0141 942 2220, Fax 0985,
Pro 1482, Sec 0985, Rest/Bar 2220
Course is six miles N of Glasgow
adjacent to Hillfoot station off Milngavie
road.
Undulating parkland course.
Pro DB Scott; Founded 1897

Designed by Willie Fernie.
18 holes, 5962 yards, S.S.S. 69
⌑ Bearsden Driving Range (within ½
mile).
♦ Welcome only as members'
guests; occasional overseas visitors if
course is quiet.
⌑ WD £23.
⌲ Welcome Wed and Thurs only; full
day's golf £31; catering can be
arranged.
🍽 Full catering and licensed bar
available.
🛏 Burnbrae; West Highland Gate
(both within 1 mile).

9B 52 Douglas Water

Ayr Road, Rigside, Lanark, ML11 9NY
☎ 01555 880361
Course is on the A70 seven miles SW
of Lanark.
Undulating parkland course.
Founded 1922
Designed by Striking Coal Miners 1921
9 holes, 5890 yards, S.S.S. 69
♦ Welcome except on competition
days.
⌑ Terms on application.
⌲ Welcome by prior arrangement
with secretary; terms available on
application.
🍽 Very limited.

9B 53 Drumpellier ☎

Drumpellier Ave, Coatbridge,
Lanarkshire, ML5 1RX
🖥 www.drumpellier.com
✉ administrator@drumpelliergc
.freeserve.co.uk
☎ 01236 424139, Fax 428723,
Pro 432971
Course is on the A89 eight miles E of
Glasgow.
Parkland course.
Pro Jamie Carver; Founded 1894
Designed by W Fernie
18 holes, 6227 yards, S.S.S. 70
♦ Welcome WD.
⌑ £30 round, £40 day.
⌲ Welcome WD by prior
arrangement; catering packages
available.
🍽 Full clubhouse catering facilities.
🛏 Centre Lodge, Coatbridge.

9B 54 Dullatur ☎

Glen Douglas Dirve, Dullatur, Glasgow,
Lanarkshire, G68 0AR
☎ 012367 23230, Fax 27271
One and a half miles from
Cumbernauld Village.
Parkland course.

Pro Duncan Sinclair; Founded 1896
Designed by J Braid
Antonine: 18 holes, 5940 yards, S.S.S.
69; Carrickstone: 18 holes, 6204 yards,
S.S.S. 70
† Welcome except on comp days.
[Available upon application.
⌐ Packages available on request.
⏺ Full clubhouse facilities available.

9B 55 Dumbarton

Broadmeadows, Dumbarton,
Dunbartonshire, G82 2BQ
⌐ www.dumbartongolfclub.co.uk
✉ secretary@dumbartongolfclub
.co.uk
☎ 01389 765995, Fax 765995,
Sec 765995, Rest/Bar 732830
Course is off the A82 fifteen miles NW
of Glasgow.
Meadowland course.
Founded 1888
18 holes, 6017 yards, S.S.S. 69
† Welcome WD.
[WD £25.
⌐ Welcome by arrangement; catering
by arrangement; terms on application.
⏺ Full clubhouse facilities available.
⤳ The Abbots Ford Hotel & The
Dumbuck Hotel.

9B 56 Dunaverty

Southend By Campbeltown,
Campbeltown, Argyll, PA28 6RW
☎ 01586 830677
Course is on the B842 ten miles S of
Campbeltown.
Undulating seaside course.
Founded 1889
18 holes, 4799 yards, S.S.S. 63
† Welcome.
[From £13.
⌐ Limited availability; strictly by prior
arrangement; day tickets start at £22
WD; £25.00 WE.
⏺ Snacks available.
⤳ Argyll.

9B 57 East Kilbride

Chapelside Road, Nerston, Glasgow,
Lanarkshire, G74 4PF
☎ 013552 20913, Pro 22192,
Sec 47728
Course is in Nerston 10 miles SE of
Glasgow.
Parkland course.
Pro Willie Walker; Founded 1900/67
Designed by Fred Hawtree
18 holes, 6419 yards, S.S.S. 71
† Welcome WD by prior
arrangement with secretary.
[WD £25.

⌐ Welcome WD by prior written
arrangement; catering packages
available; pool room; from £20.
⏺ Full clubhouse facilities.
⤳ Hilton; Bruce; Stuart; Crutherland
House.

9B 58 East Renfrewshire ℃

Loganswell, Pilmuir, Newton Mearns,
Glasgow, Lanarkshire, G77 6RT
✉ david@eastrengolfclub.co.uk
☎ 01355 500256, Pro 500206,
Sec 0141 333 9989,
Rest/Bar 500256
Course is on the A77 Glasgow to
Kilmarnock road two miles S of
Newton Mearns.
Moorland course.
Pro Stewart Russell; Founded 1922
Designed by James Braid
18 holes, 6097 yards, S.S.S. 70
[Free practice area.
† Welcome by arrangement with Pro.
[WD £40 or £50 for a day ticket.
⌐ Welcome Tues and Thurs by
arrangement with secretary; catering
and bar facilities by prior arrangement
with the club stewardess.
⏺ Full clubhouse facilities.

9B 59 Easter Moffat ℃

Mansion House, Plains, Airdrie,
Lanarkshire, ML6 8NP
☎ 01236 842289, Pro 843015,
Sec 842878
Two miles E of Airdrie on the old
Edinburgh-Glasgow road.
Moorland/parkland course.
Pro Graham King; Founded 1922
18 holes, 6240 yards, S.S.S. 70
† Welcome.
[WD £20; no visitors WE.
⌐ Welcome WD by prior
arrangement; day tickets £20; catering
by prior arrangement; from £15.
⏺ Clubhouse facilities.
⤳ Tudor Hotel, Airdrie.

9B 60 Eastwood ℃

Muirshield Loganswell, Newton
Mearns, Glasgow, G77 6RX
⌐ www.eastwoodgolfclub.org
✉ secretary@
eastwoodgolfclub.demon.co.uk
☎ 01355 500280, Fax 500280,
Pro 500285, Sec 500280,
Rest/Bar 500261
Off A77 from Glasgow; three miles S of
Newton Mearns.
Moorland/parkland course.
Pro Iain Darroch; Founded 1893
Designed by G Webster

18 holes, 6071 yards, S.S.S. 69
[Practice area.
† Welcome WD.
[WD £24 £30 for full day.
⌐ Welcome WD by prior
arrangement; catering packages by
arrangement; from £24.
⏺ Clubhouse facilities.
⤳ Redhurst, Fenwick.

9B 61 Elderslie ℃

63 Main Road, Elderslie, Johnstone,
Renfrewshire, PA5 9AZ
⌐ www.eldersliegolfclub.net
✉ annanderson@eldersliegolfclub
.freeserve.co.uk
☎ 01505 323956, Fax 344346,
Pro 320032, Sec 323956,
Rest/Bar 322835
On A737 between Paisley and
Johnstone.
Undulating parkland course.
Pro Rickey Bowen; Founded 1909
Designed by James Braid
18 holes, 6175 yards, S.S.S. 70
† Welcome WD.
[WD £24; £32 for two rounds.
⌐ Welcome Mon, Wed and Fri by
prior arrangement; day ticket £32;
catering by arrangement; snooker;
from £20.
⏺ Full clubhouse facilities.
⤳ The Glasgow Airport.

9B 62 Erskine

Bishopton, Renfrewshire, PA7 5PH
☎ 01505 862302, Pro 862108
Off Erskine Toll Bridge and turn left
along B815 for 1.5 miles.
Parkland course.
Pro Peter Thomson; Founded 1904
18 holes, 6241 yards, S.S.S. 70
† Welcome if introduced by or
playing with a member.
[Terms on application.
⌐ Welcome by prior arrangement;
catering by prior arrangement only;
terms on application.
⏺ Meals served to members or their
guests only.
⤳ Erskine; Crest.

9B 63 Fereneze ℃

Fereneze Avenue, Barrhead, Glasgow,
Renfrewshire, G78 1HJ
☎ 0141 881 1519, Fax 881 7149,
Pro 880 7058, Sec 881 7149
9 miles SW of Glasgow near Barrhead
station.
Moorland course.
Pro Haldane Lee; Founded 1904
18 holes, 5962 yards, S.S.S. 71

✝ Welcome by prior arrangement or with member.
ⵊ Terms on application.
⚲ Welcome WD only by prior arrangement; catering by arrangement; terms available on application.
🍽 Full clubhouse facilities available; WD evening meals by prior arrangement.
🛏 Dalmeny Park.

9B 64 Gailes Golf Course and Range
Killermont, Bearsden, G61 2TW
⛳ www.glasgowgailes-golf.com
☎ 01294 311258
From Glasgow – M77/A77 S, A71 to Irvine, straight off at next junction Harbourside, signposted from there.
Flat.
18 holes, 7000 yards
✝ Yes.
ⵊ WD £42 per round, £50 per day; WE £55 per round, £60 per day.
⚲ Yes.
🍽 Yes.
🛏 Thistle Hotel, Irvine.

9B 65 Gigha
Isle of Gigha, PA41 7AA
☎ 01583 505242
Short ferry sailing from Kintyre Peninsular to the Isle of Gigha. Course is short walk from ferry terminal.
Parkland course.
Founded 1988
Designed by Members
9 holes, 5042 yards, S.S.S. 65
✝ Practice area.
✝ Welcome.
ⵊ Daily/round £10.
⚲ Welcome; day ticket £10; meals and bar at Gigha Hotel; from £10.
🍽 Meals and bar available at the Gigha Hotel.
🛏 Gigha; Tayinloan.

9B 66 Girvan
Girvan, Ayrshire, KA26 9HW
☎ 01465 714346, Rest/Bar 714272
Course is off A77 Stranraer to Ayr rd.
Seaside links/parklands course.
Founded pre 1877
Designed by James Braid
18 holes, 5064 yards, S.S.S. 64
✝ Practice area.
✝ Welcome by prior arrangement.
ⵊ Prices on application.
⚲ Welcome by prior arrangement; catering available.
🍽 Catering by arrangement.
🛏 Turnberry Hotel.

9B 67 Glasgow
Killermont, Bearsden, Glasgow, G61 2TW
☎ 0141 942 1713, Fax 0770, Pro 8507, Sec 2011
6 miles NW of Glasgow near Killermont Bridge taking the A81 Maryhill Road.
Parkland course.
Pro Jack Steven; Founded 1787/1905
Designed by Tom Morris Snr
18 holes, 5977 yards, S.S.S. 69
✝ Welcome by prior arrangement.
ⵊ WD £55; WE not available.
⚲ None.
🍽 Lunches and high teas by application.
🛏 Grosvenor; Burnbrae; Black Bull; Pond.

9B 68 Glasgow (Gailes)
Gailes, By Irvine, Ayrshire, KA11 5AE
☎ 01294 311258, Fax 0141 9422011, Pro 01294 311561, Sec 0141 942 2011, Rest/Bar 01294 311258
2 miles S of Irvine on A78.
Championship seaside links.
Pro Jack Steven; Founded 1787/1892
Designed by Willie Park, Jnr
18 holes, 6513 yards, S.S.S. 72
✝ Welcome by prior arrangement with secretary or if introduced by a member.
ⵊ WD £42; WE £47.
⚲ Welcome by prior arrangement with secretary only; WD day tickets £52; catering by prior arrangement; from £42.
🍽 Full clubhouse facilities.
🛏 Hospitality Inn, Irvine; Marine, Troon.

9B 69 Gleddoch Country Club
Old Greenock Road, Langbank, Port Glasgow, Renfrewshire, PA14 6YE
☎ 01475 540304, Fax 540459, Pro 540704
M8 to Greenock; first turning to Langbank Houston on B789.
Parkland/moorland course.
Pro Keith Campbell; Founded 1975
Designed by Hamilton Stutt
18 holes, 6357 yards, S.S.S. 71
✝ Welcome by arrangement with Pro.
ⵊ WD £30; WE £40; day tickets start at £40.
⚲ Welcome; catering packages by arrangement; terms on application.
🍽 Clubhouse facilities.
🛏 Glenddoch House.

9B 70 Glencruitten
Glencruitten Road, Oban, Argyll, PA34 4PU
☎ 01631 562868, Club Shop 564115, Sec 564604
1 mile from the town centre.
Parkland course.
Founded 1908
Designed by James Braid
18 holes, 4250 yards, S.S.S. 63
✝ Practice area.
✝ Welcome.
ⵊ WD £17; WE £20.
⚲ Welcome by prior arrangement; discounts available.
🍽 Full clubhouse facilities.

9B 71 Gourock
Cowal View, Gourock, Renfrewshire, PA19 1HD
⛳ www.gourockgolfclub.com
✉ secretary@gourockgolfclub.com
☎ 01475 631001, Fax 633307, Pro 636834
2 miles uphill from Gourock station.
Moorland course.
Pro James Mooney; Founded 1896
Designed by James Braid/Henry Cotton
18 holes, 6408 yards, S.S.S. 72
✝ Small practice area.
✝ Welcome by prior arrangement with Pro shop.
ⵊ WD £20; WE £27.
⚲ Welcome by prior arrangement; day tickets available WD £27; WE £29; catering by prior arrangement.
🍽 Bar lunches and high teas; dinners by arrangement.
🛏 Jarvis Ramada, Cloch Road, Gourock.

9B 72 Greenock
Forsyth Street, Greenock, Renfrewshire, PA16 8RE
☎ 01475 720793, Sec 791912
1 mile SW of the town on the main road to Gourock on the A8.
Moorland course.
Pro Paul Morrison; Founded 1890
Designed by James Braid
27 holes, 5838 yards, S.S.S. 69
✝ Welcome by prior arrangement with secretary.
ⵊ Terms on application.
⚲ Welcome by prior arrangement with secretary.
🍽 Full clubhouse facilities.
🛏 Tontine.

9B 73 Greenock Whinhill
Beith Road, Greenock, Renfrewshire, PA16 9LN

☎ 01475 724694, Pro 721064
Off Largs Road.
Parkland course.
Founded 1911
Designed by W Fernie
18 holes, 5504 yards, S.S.S. 68
† Welcome.
⌊ WD £6.50; WE £6.50.
⟳ None welcome.
⦿ By prior arrangement.
↪ Stakis Gantock.

9B 74 Haggs Castle

70 Dumbreck Road, Glasgow,
Lanarkshire, G41 4SN
✉ haggscastlegc@lineone.net
☎ 0141 427 0480, Fax 1157,
Pro 3355, Sec 1157
Course is close to Junction 1 off the
M77.
Parkland course.
Pro C Elliott; Founded 1910
Designed by Peter Alliss & Dave
Thomas
18 holes, 6426 yards, S.S.S. 71
† Welcome on WD by prior
arrangement.
⌊ WD £40.
⟳ Welcome WD only by arrangement
with secretary; catering by
arrangement; terms on application.
⦿ Full clubhouse facilities.
↪ Sherbrooke Castle, Pollokshields.

9B 75 Hamilton

Riccarton, Ferniegair, Hamilton,
Lanarkshire, ML3 7UE
✉ grahamchapman
@hamiltongolfclub.co.uk
☎ 01698 282872, Fax 459537,
Pro 282324, Sec 459537
Off A74 between Larkhall and Hamilton.
Parkland course.
Pro Deek Wright; Founded 1892
Designed by James Braid
18 holes, 6264 yards, S.S.S. 70
⌊ Practice area.
† Welcome on WD by prior
arrangement.
⌊ WD £30 (18 holes); £40 day ticket.
⟳ By arrangement with secretary;
catering packages by arrangement;
terms on application.
⦿ Clubhouse facilities.

9B 76 Hayston

Campsie Road, Kirkintilloch, Glasgow,
Lanarkshire, G66 1RN
🖥 www.haystongolf.com
✉ secretary@haystongolf.com
☎ 0141 7761244, Fax 7769030,
Pro 7750882, Sec 7750723

7 miles N of Glasgow.
Parkland course.
Pro Steve Barnett; Founded 1926
Designed by James Braid
18 holes, 6042 yards, S.S.S. 70
⌊ Practice area.
† Welcome by prior arrangement on
WD only.
⌊ Available upon application.
⟳ Welcome Tues and Thurs by prior
arrangement; day tickets from £37;
maximum 24; catering by arrangement.
⦿ Full clubhouse facilities.
↪ Kincaid House.

9B 77 Helensburgh ☎

25 East Abercromby Street,
Helensburgh, Dunbartonshire, G84 9JD
✉ thesecretary@helensburghgolfclub
.org,uk
☎ 01436 674176, Fax 671170,
Pro 675505, Sec 674173
Follow A82 to Helensburgh; signposted
in town.
Moorland course.
Pro David Fotheringham; Founded 1893
Designed by James Braid
18 holes, 6104 yards, S.S.S. 70
† Welcome WD.
⌊ WD £25 round, £35 all day.
⟳ Welcome by prior arrangement; all
day golf plus food £46.
⦿ Full clubhouse dining facilities.
↪ Commodore, Helensburgh;
Camerous House, Balloch.

9B 78 Hilton Park

Stockiemuir Road, Milngavie, Glasgow,
G62 7HB
✉ info@hiltonparkgolfclub.freeserve
.co.uk
☎ 0141 9565124, Fax 9564657,
Pro 9565125, Sec 9564657,
Rest/Bar 9565124
On A809 8 miles N of Glasgow.
Moorland course.
Pro Billy McCondichie; Founded 1927
Designed by James Braid
36 holes, 6054/5497 yards, S.S.S.
70/73
† Welcome WD by prior
arrangement.
⌊ WD £24, £32 full day.
⟳ Welcome WD; day rate of approx.
£30; catering by arrangement; from £20.
⦿ Full catering facilities available.
↪ Kirkhouse; County Club.

9B 79 Hollandbush

Acretophead, Lesmahagow, Lanark,
Lanarkshire, ML11 0JS
🖥 www.hollandbushgolfclub.co.uk

✉ mail@hollandbushgolfclub.co.uk
☎ 01555 893484, Fax 893484,
Pro 893646, Sec 893484,
Rest/Bar 893546
Off Junction 9 M74 at Lesmahagow
and Coalburn.
Parkland course on edge of moorland.
Founded 1954
Designed by K Pate/J Lawson
18 holes, 6318 yards, S.S.S. 70
⌊ Practice range available.
† Public municipal course.
⌊ WD £8.20; WE £9.30.
⟳ Welcome.
⦿ Full clubhouse facilities but not on
Mon.
↪ Shawlands; Popinjay.

9B 80 Innellan

Knockamillie Road, Innellan, Argyll
☎ 01369 830242
4 miles S of Dunoon.
Parkland course.
Founded 1891
9 holes, 4878 yards, S.S.S. 63
† Welcome anytime except Mon
evening.
⌊ Terms on application.
⟳ Welcome by prior arrangement;
catering by arrangement; terms on
application.
⦿ By prior arrangement.
↪ Esplanade; Slatefield; Rosscalm.

9B 81 Inveraray

North Cromalt, Inveraray, Argyll
☎ 01499 302079, Sec 302073
SW corner of town on Lochgilphead
Road.
Parkland course.
Founded 1993
Designed by Watt Landscaping
9 holes, 5700 yards, S.S.S. 68
† Welcome except competition days.
⌊ WD £15; WE £15.
⟳ Welcome by prior arrangement;
golf only; catering available by special
arrangement with local hotels; from
£10.
⦿ None.
↪ George Hotel; Argyll Hotel.

9B 82 Irvine

Bogside, Irvine, Ayrshire, KA12 8SN
☎ 01294 275979, Pro 275626
On the road from Irvine to Kilwinning,
turn left after Ravespark academy and
carry straight on for 0.5 miles over the
railway bridge.
Links course.
Pro Jim McKinnon; Founded 1887
Designed by James Braid

18 holes, 6408 yards, S.S.S. 73
♦ Welcome; but not before 3pm at WE.
ℾ WD £50; WE £60.
⟳ Welcome by prior arrangement with secretary; catering packages by prior arrangement; from £30.
⦿ Full clubhouse facilities.
⟿ Hospitality Inn; Golf Hotel.

9B 83 Irvine Ravenspark
13 Kidsneuk Lane, Irvine, Ayrshire, KA12 8SR
☎ 01294 271293, Pro 276467
On A78 midway between Irvine and Kilwinning.
Municipal parkland course.
Pro Peter Bond; Founded 1907
18 holes, 6429 yards, S.S.S. 71
♦ Welcome; not before 2.30pm on Sat.
ℾ WD £9; WE £13.
⟳ Welcome WD; by prior arrangement; from £15.50.
⦿ Full clubhouse facilities.
⟿ Thistle; Annfield; Redburn; Golf Inn.

9B 84 Kilbirnie Place ℭ
Largs Rd, Kilbirnie, Ayrshire, KA25 7AJ
☎ 01505 683398, Sec 684444
On the main Largs Road on the outskirts of Kilbirnie.
Parkland course.
Founded 1922
18 holes, 5517 yards, S.S.S. 69
♦ Welcome WD.
ℾ WD £17 WE £25.
⟳ Welcome by prior arrangement; from £18.
⦿ Full facilities.

9B 85 Kilmalcolm
Porterfield Road, Kilmacolm, Renfrewshire, PA13 4PD
✉ secretary@ kilmalcolmgolf.sagehost.co.uk
☎ 01505 872139, Fax 874007, Pro 872695
From M8 Glasgow airport follow the main signs to Irvine; turn off second junction and follow A761 to Kilmalcolm.
Moorland course.
Pro Iain Nicholson; Founded 1890
Designed by James Braid
18 holes, 5961 yards, S.S.S. 69
♦ Welcome; booking essential for WE.
ℾ WD £20.50; WE £20.50 will be changing.
⟳ Welcome WD by prior arrangement; packages and prices depend on numbers; terms on application.

⦿ Full clubhouse facilities.
⟿ Many in Glasgow, Renfrew and Paisley.

9B 86 Kilmarnock (Barassie)
Hillhouse Road, Troon, Ayrshire, KA10 6SY
🖳 www.kbgc.co.uk
🖳 barassiegc@lineone.net
☎ 01292 313920, Fax 318300, Pro 311322
Course is two miles N of Troon directly opposite Barassie railway station.
Championship links course.
Pro Gregor Howie; Founded 1887
Designed by Theodore Moone.
27 holes, 6484 yards, S.S.S. 74
♦ Welcome WD except Wed; not before 8.30am or between 12.30pm – 1.30pm.
ℾ WD £58, WE £60.
⟳ Welcome WD except Wed by arrangement; catering can be arranged in advanced with club caterer; dining room; television lounge; also 9-hole course available, 2888 yards, par 34.
⦿ Full clubhouse dining and bar; jacket and tie must be worn in dining room.
⟿ Gailes Hotel and Restaurant (01294 204040).

9B 87 Kilsyth Lennox
Tak-Ma-Doon, Kilsyth, Glasgow, Lanarkshire, G65 0HX
☎ 01236 824115, Sec 823213
Course is on the A80 12 miles from Glasgow.
Moorland/parkland course.
Founded 1907
18 holes, 5912 yards, S.S.S. 70
♦ Welcome by prior arrangement with secretary or starter.
ℾ WD £14; WE £16.
⟳ Welcome by arrangement with secretary; from £16.
⦿ Clubhouse facilities.

9B 88 Kirkhill
Greenlees Road, Cambuslang, Glasgow, Lanarkshire, G72 8YN
☎ 0141 6413083, Fax 6418499, Pro 6417972, Sec 6418499, Rest/Bar 6413083
Follow East Kilbride road from Burnside, take first turning on left past Cathkin by-pass roundabout.
Meadowland course.
Pro Duncan Williamson; Founded 1910
Designed by James Braid
18 holes, 6030 yards, S.S.S. 70
♦ Welcome by arrangement.

ℾ WD £20; WE £22.
⟳ Welcome by prior arrangement; catering by prior arrangement with caterer; from £15.
⦿ Full facilities by prior arrangement; snacks and bar meals available.
⟿ Kings Park; Burnside; Stuart; Bruce.

9B 89 Kirkintilloch
Todhill, Campsie Road, Kirkintilloch, Glasgow, G66 1RN
☎ 0141 7761256, Fax 7752424, Sec 7752387
1 mile from Kirkintilloch on road to Lennoxtown.
Parkland course.
Founded 1895
Designed by James Braid
18 holes, 5860 yards, S.S.S. 69
♦ Welcome with letter of introduction.
ℾ WD £20 round, £30 day.
⟳ Welcome by prior arrangement; day ticket £30; catering by arrangement.
⦿ Clubhouse facilities; restrictions Mon and Tues.
⟿ Garfield, Stepps.

9B 90 Knightswood
Lincoln Avenue, Knightswood, G13
☎ 0141 959 6358
From city centre go W along Great Western Road through Knightswood past cross then left into Lincoln Ave.
Flat parkland course.
Founded 1920
9 holes, 5586 yards, S.S.S. 64
♦ Welcome, except Fri morning.
ℾ WD/WE £3.90.
⦿ Limited.
⟿ Charing Cross Tower Hotel; The Grovesnor; Jury's Pond

9B 91 Kyles of Bute ℭ
The Moss, Kames, Tighnabruaich, Argyll, PA21 2AB
☎ Sec 01700 811603
Course is on the B3836 on the road from Dunoon via Tighnabruaich, to B8000 to Millhouse.
Undulating moorland course.
Founded 1907
9 holes, 4748 yards, S.S.S. 64
♦ Welcome all times except Wed evenings and Sun 9.30am – 1pm.
ℾ WD £10 per day WE £10 per day.
Annual membership £100.
⟳ Welcome by arrangement with secretary.
⦿ Snacks when available.
⟿ Royal; Kames; Kilfinan.

9B 92 Laglands
Auldhouse Road, East Kilbride,
Glasgow, Lanarkshire, G75 9DW
☎ 01352 48172, Sec 0141 6442623
Course is three miles SE of East
Kilbride.
18 holes, 6202 yards, S.S.S. 70
† Welcome.
[Terms on application.
⌁ Terms on application.

9B 93 Lamlash
Lamlash, Isle of Arran, KA27 8JU
⊕ www.lamlashgolfclub.co.uk
☎ 01770 600296, Fax 600296,
Sec 600272
Course is three miles S of pier terminal
at Brodick.
Undulating heathland course.
Founded 1889
Designed by W Auchterlonie/W Fernie
18 holes, 4640 yards, S.S.S. 64
⫟ Practice putting green.
† Welcome.
[£14 but this is only available after
4pm; Day ticket WD £18, WE £22.
⌁ Welcome; full catering available.
⊓ Full clubhouse facilities.
⌑ Glenisle; Lilybank; Marine.

9B 94 Lanark   ☎
The Moor, Whitelees Rd, Lanark,
S Lanarkshire, ML11 7RX
▤ lanarkgolfclub@talk21.com
☎ 01555 663219, Fax 663219,
Pro 661456
Take A73 or A72 to Lanark; turn left in
town for Whitelees road.
Moorland course.
Pro Alan White; Founded 1851
Designed by T Morris
18 holes, 6306 yards, S.S.S. 71
† Welcome WD; with member at
WE.
[WD £30. Full day £40.
⌁ Welcome by prior arrangement on
WD; larger groups welcome Mon-
Wed; maximum of 12 people Thurs &
Fri; catering by arrangement.
⊓ Full clubhouse facilities.
⌑ Cartland Bridge; Popinjay; Tinto.

9B 95 Largs
Irvine Rd, Largs, Ayrshire, KA30 8EU
⊕ www.largsgolfclub.co.uk
▤ secretary@largsgolfclub.co.uk
☎ 01475 673594, Fax 673594,
Pro 686192, Sec 673594, Rest/Bar
687390
Course is on the A78 one mile S of
Largs.
Parkland/woodland course.

Pro Kenneth Docherty; Founded 1891
18 holes, 6115 yards, S.S.S. 71
† Welcome by arrangement.
[WD £30 per round, £40 per day;
WE £40.
⌁ Welcome Tues and Thurs by prior
arrangement; packages available for
18 and 36 holes of golf plus catering;
from £30.
⊓ Full clubhouse facilities.
⌑ Priory House; Haylie; Queens.
Moorings Hotel.

9B 96 Larkhall
Burnhead Rd, Larkhall, Lanarkshire,
NLI9 3AA
☎ 01698 881113, Sec 889597
Take M8 to Larkhall exit then head SW
on B7019.
Municipal parkland course.
Founded 1909.
9 holes, 6423 yards, S.S.S. 71
† Welcome.
[WD £3.50; WE £3.80.
⌁ Welcome by prior arrangement;
limited catering is available; from
£3.50.
⊓ Bar.

9B 97 Lead Hills
2 Gowan Bank, Leadhills, Biggar,
Lanarkshire, ML12 6XR
☎ 01659 74356, Fax 74356,
Sec 74272
On B797 in Leadhills village 6 miles
from A74 at Abingdon.
Moorland course, highest in Scotland.
Founded 1935
9 holes, 4100 yards, S.S.S. 62
† Welcome.
[Details available on request.
⌁ Welcome catering organised in
local hotel; from £5.
⊓ Local hotel.
⌑ Hopetoun Arms.

9B 98 Lenzie   ☎
19 Crosshill Rd, Lenzie, Glasgow,
G66 5DA
⊕ www.lenziegolfclub.co.uk
▤ scotdavidson@
lenziegolfclub.demon.co.uk
☎ 0141 776 1535, Pro 777 7748,
Sec 812 3018, Rest/Bar 776 1535
10 miles NE of Glasgow; leave M8 at
Stirling Junction then head for
Kirkintilloch.
Parkland course.
Pro J McCallum; Founded 1889
18 holes, 5984 yards, S.S.S. 69
⫟ Practice area and greens.
† Welcome by prior arrangement.

[WD £24 round, £30 day.
⌁ Welcome by prior arrangement
with the club Sec; catering packages
available by prior arrangement;
professional can assist on society days
with golf clinic etc, from £28.
⊓ Full clubhouse facilities available.
⌑ Moddiesburn; Garfield; Stepps.

9B 99 Lethamhill
Cumbernauld Rd, Glasgow, G33 1AH
☎ 0141 7706220, Fax 7700520,
Pro 7707135, Sec 7706220
On A80 adjacent to Hogganfield Loch.
Municipal parkland course.
Pro Gary Mctagart
18 holes, 5836 yards, S.S.S. 70
† Welcome.
[WD £7.70; WE £7.70.
⌁ Welcome.
⊓ Limited.

9B 100 Linn Park
Simshill Rd, Glasgow, G44 5EP
☎ 0141 633 0377
Off M74 S of Glasgow.
Public parkland course.
Founded 1925
Designed by Glasgow Parks
18 holes, 5005 yards, S.S.S. 65
† Welcome.
[Details upon application.
⌁ Welcome by prior application from
£5.50.
⊓ Clubhouse facilities available for
changing only.

9B 101 Littlehill
Auchinairn Rd, Bishopbriggs, Glasgow,
G74 1UT
☎ 0141 7721916, Sec 770 0519
3 miles N of city centre.
Public parkland course.
Founded 1924
Designed by James Braid
18 holes, 6228 yards, S.S.S. 70
† Welcome.
[WD/WE £7.85; concessions apply.
⌁ Apply to Council for full details.
⊓ Clubhouse facilities available;
except Mon; no catering on winter WE.

9B 102 Loch Lomond
Rossdhu House, Luss by Alexandria,
Dunbartonshire, G83 8NT
⊕ www.lochlomond.com
☎ 01436 655555, Fax 655500
On the A82 on the W bank of Loch
Lomond.
Championship parkland course
Scottish Open.

Pro Colin Campbell; Founded 1994
Designed by Tom Weiskopf and Jay
Morrish
18 holes, 7060 yards, S.S.S. 72
† Private; as the guest of a member
only.
⌐ WD £150; WE £150.
↷ None.
🍽 First-class clubhouse facilities
available.
🛏 Cameron House.

9B 103 Lochgilphead
Blarbuie Rd, Lochgilphead, Argyll,
PA31 8LE
☎ 01546 602340
Follow signs for Argyll and Bute
Hospital from the centre of
Lochgilphead.
Challenging parkland course.
Founded 1891/1963
Designed by Dr Ian MacCammond
9 holes, 4484 yards, S.S.S. 63
† Welcome.
⌐ WD/WE £15.
↷ Welcome; weekly ticket of £45
reductions for groups registered with
the club: from £12.
🍽 Bar facilites.
🛏 Stag, Argyll.

9B 104 Lochranza
Lochranza, Isle of Arran, KA27 8HL
🖧 www.lochranzagolf.com
📧 office@lochgolf.demon.co.uk
☎ 01770 830273, Fax 830600
Course is in Lochranza opposite
distillery.
Grassland course with rivers/trees 3
holes on seashore.
Founded 1899; redesigned 1991
Designed by Iain M Robertson
18 holes, 5470 yards, S.S.S. 70
† Welcome between April and Late
October. Pay & Play; no membership.
⌐ £15 round, £20 day.
↷ Welcome by prior arrangement.
Available packages can include
accomodation, meals, ferry, distillery
visit and golf.
🍽 Snacks available.
🛏 Hotel/guest house packages
available.

9B 105 Lochwinnoch ☎
Burnfoot Rd, Lochwinnoch,
Renfrewshire, PA12 4AN
🖧 www.lochwinnochgolf.co.uk
📧 admin@lochwinnochgolf.co.uk
☎ 01505 842153, Fax 843668,
Pro 843029, Sec 842153,
Rest/Bar 842153

On A760 10 miles S of Paisley.
Parkland course.
Pro Gerry Reilly; Founded 1897
18 holes, 6025 yards, S.S.S. 71
† Welcome WD before 4pm.
⌐ WD £20; WE £20.
↷ Welcome by prior arrangement
WD; catering packages available.
Please contact course secretary for
details.
🍽 Clubhouse facilities.
🛏 Lindhurst.

9B 106 Loudoun Golf Club ☎
Galston, Ayrshire, KA4 8PA
🖧 www.loudoungowfclub.biz
📧 secretary@loudgowf.sol.co.uk
☎ 01563 821993, Fax 820011,
Sec 821993, Rest/Bar 820551
On A71 5 miles E of Kilmarnock.
Parkland course.
Founded 1909
18 holes, 6016 yards, S.S.S. 68
† Welcome WD only by prior
arrangement.
⌐ WD £21 per round.
↷ Welcome WD by prior
arrangement; catering packages can
be arranged; from £11.
🍽 Full catering facilities.
🛏 Loudoun Mains; Newmilns; Fox
Bar Kilmarnock.

9B 107 Machrie Bay
Machrie, Isle of Arran, KA27 8DZ
🖧 www.twemsleywaitrose.com
📧 pwemsley@waitrose.com
☎ 01770 850232, Sec 860380
9 miles W of Brodick.
Links course.
Founded 1900
Designed by William Fernie
9 holes, 2200 yards, S.S.S. 62
⌿ Practice area.
† Welcome.
⌐ WD £10; WE £45.
↷ Welcome by prior arrangement.
🍽 Catering – teas, coffees, snacks,
meals.

9B 108 Machrie Hotel and ☎
Golf Links
Port Ellen, Isle of Islay, Argyll,
PA42 7AN
🖧 www.machrie.com
📧 machrie@machrie.com
☎ 01496 302310, Fax 302404,
Sec 302212
Ferry from Kennacraig (2hrs) or plane
from Glasgow (30 mins).
Traditional links course.
Founded 1891

Designed by Wille Campbell/Donald
Steel
18 holes, 6292 yards, S.S.S. 70
⌿ 6 hole par 3 course adjacent to
main course.
† Welcome residents recieve
discounts.
⌐ £35.
↷ Welcome by prior arrangment; day
rates available; also accomodation and
golf packages can be arranged; hotel
can also advise on air packages from
Glasgow; conference facilities; own
beach; Salmon and Trout fishing
snooker from £20.
🍽 Full clubhouse catering and bar
facilities with à la carte restaurant.
🛏 Machrie Hotel.

9B 109 Machrihanish
Machrihanish, Campbeltown, Argyll,
PA28 6PT
🖧 www.machgolf.com
📧 secretary@machgolf.com
☎ 01586 810213, Fax 810221,
Pro 810277
Course is five miles W of
Campbeltown on the B843.
Natural links course.
Pro Ken Campbell; Founded 1876
Designed by Tom Morris
18 holes, 6225 yards, S.S.S. 71
† Welcome by prior arrangement.
⌐ WD £35; WE £45.
↷ Welcome by prior arrangement
with club Pro; some WE available;
catering by prior arrangement; some
air packages available;
accommodation packages also on
offer.
🍽 Full clubhouse facilities.
🛏 See club for details

9B 110 Maybole
Memorial Park, Maybole, Ayrshire,
KA19
☎ 01292 616666
Course is nine miles S of Ayr on main
Stranraer road.
Hillside course with splendid views.
Founded 1905
9 holes, 5304 yards, S.S.S. 66
† Welcome.
⌐ Available upon application.
↷ Welcome.
🛏 Many available in local area;
Abbotsford.

9B 111 Millport
Golf Rd, Millport, Isle of Cumbrae,
KA28 0HB
🖧 www.millportgolfclub.co.uk

📧 secretary@millportgolfclub.co.uk
☎ 01475 530311, Fax 530306,
Pro 530305, Sec 530306
10 mins ferry crossing from Largs in
Ayrshire; 4 miles from the Ferry
Terminal.
Heathland course.
Pro Haldane Lee; Founded 1888
Designed by James Braid
18 holes, 5828 yards, S.S.S. 69
🏌 Practice area.
† Welcome.
Ⅰ WD £20; WE £25.
⌁ Welcome by prior arrangement;
catering packages by arrangement.
🍴 Full facilities.

9B 112 **Milngavie**
Laighpark, Milngavie, Glasgow,
G62 8EP
☎ 0141 9561619;, Fax 9564252
Off A809 NW of Glasgow; club can
provide detailed directions.
Moorland course.
Founded 1895
Designed by J Braid
18 holes, 5818 yards, S.S.S. 68
† Welcome on WD by prior
arrangement.
Ⅰ WD £22.
⌁ Welcome by prior arrangement;
packages ranging from £9 can be
arranged including 4-course dinner;
from £20.
🍴 Full clubhouse facilities available.
🍸 Black Bull; Burnbrae; both
Milngavie.

9B 113 **Mount Ellen**   ☎
Johnstone Rd, Johnstone House,
Gartcosh, Glasgow, G69 8EY
☎ 01236 872277, Fax 872249
From M8 N and A89 take B752 N to
Gastosh on to B804 in direction of
Glenboig.
Parkland course.
Pro Iain Bilsborough; Founded 1905
18 holes, 5525 yards, S.S.S. 66
† Welcome WD only.
Ⅰ WD £24.
⌁ Welcome by prior arrangement;
terms on application.
🍴 Full clubhouse facilities.
🍸 Garsfield Housel; Stepps;
Moodiesburn House; Moodiesburn.

9B 114 **Muirkirk**
Cairn View, Muirkirk, Strathclyde,
KA18 3QW
☎ 01290 661556, Fax 661556
13 miles W of Junction 12 on M74 on
A70.

Pay and play.
Founded 1991
9 holes, 5366 yards, S.S.S. 67
† Welcome at all times.
Ⅰ £8.00 seniors £5, juniors £3.
⌁ Societies welcome at WE by
arrangement with secretary.
🍴 Limited.
🍸 The Coachouse Inn, and various
B&Bs.

9B 115 **New Cumnock**
Lochill, New Cumnock, Ayrshire,
KA18 4BQ
☎ 01290 338848
On the A76 1 mile to the NW of New
Cumnock.
Parkland course.
Founded 1901
Designed by W Fernie
9 holes, 5332 yards, S.S.S. 68
† Welcome; tickets available from
the Loch side Hotel next to course.
Ⅰ From £8 adult day £6 for children;
£4 winter price £8 standard.
⌁ None.
🍴 Limited; Lochside Hotel next door.
🍸 Lochside Hotel.

9B 116 **Old Course Ranfurly**   ☎
Ranfurly Place, Bridge of Weir,
Renfrewshire, PA11 3DE
🖥 www.oldranfurly.com
📧 seretary@oldranfurly.com
☎ 01505 613612, Fax 613214,
Pro 613612, Sec 613214,
Rest/Bar 613612
Course is five miles W of Glasgow
Airport.
Heathland course.
Pro Derek McIntosh; Founded 1905
Designed by W Park Jnr
18 holes, 6061 yards, S.S.S. 70
† Welcome by prior arrangement WD;
as the guest of a member only at WE.
Ⅰ WD £20.
⌁ Welcome by written prior
arrangement WD; day ticket of £30
available; from £20.
🍴 Full clubhouse facilities available.
🍸 Normandy; Renfrew; Glyn Hill,
Paisley.

9B 117 **Paisley**
Braehead, Paisley, PA2 8TZ
🖥 www.paisleygc.com
📧 paisleygc@onetel.net.uk
☎ 0141 8843903, Fax 8843903,
Pro 8844114, Rest/Bar 8842292
Leave M8 J 27 follow signs for Paisley
town centre. Turn left into Causeyside
Street, follow road for 1.5 miles. Turn

right at Glenburn road and left into
Braehead Road. Golf club top of hill.
Moorland course.
Pro Gordon Stewart; Founded
1895/1951
Designed by J Stutt
18 holes, 6466 yards, S.S.S. 72
† Welcome WD before 4pm.
Ⅰ WD £24 per round, £35 per day
ticket. Members and their guests
welcome at WE.
⌁ Welcome by prior arrangement
WD; day ticket £35; golf and catering
package can be provided.
🍴 Full clubhouse facilities available.

9B 118 **Palacerigg**
Palacerigg Country Park,
Cumbernauld, G67 3HU
🖥 www.palaceerigggolfclub.co.uk
📧 palacerigg_golfclub@lineone.net
☎ 01236 734969, Fax 721461,
Pro 721461
Take A80 to Cumbernauld and follow
signs for Country Park.
Wooded parkland course.
Pro John Murphy
Founded 1974
Designed by Henry Cotton
18 holes, 6444 yards, S.S.S. 71
† Welcome.
Ⅰ WD £5.10; WE £7.40.
⌁ Welcome WD by prior
arrangement; range of packages
available; full day's golf and catering;
from £25.
🍴 Full clubhouse facilities available;
restrictions Mon/Tues.
🍸 Castlecarry; Moodiesburn;
Cumbernauld Travel Inn.

9B 119 **Pollok**
90 Barrhead Road, Glasgow,
G43 1BG
🖥 www.pollokgolf.com
📧 pollock.gc@lineone.net
☎ 0141 6321080, Fax 6491398,
Sec 6324351, Rest/Bar 6324451
Course lies four miles S of the city of
Glasgow off M77 Junction 2 on B736.
Wooded parkland course.
Founded 1892
Designed by James Douglas.
18 holes, 6257 yards, S.S.S. 70
† Welcome WD; WE by
arrangement.
Ⅰ WD £35 round, £45 day; WE £40
round, £50 day.
⌁ Welcome by prior arrangement
with the Secretary, £32 per day Mon-
Fri, £40 Sat and Sun.
🍴 Full clubhouse catering facilities.
🍸 Albany; Macdonald.

9B 120 Port Bannatyne

Bannatyne Mains Rd, Port Bannatyne,
Isle of Bute, PA20 0PH
☎ 01700 504544, Sec 505152
Course is two miles N of Rothesay on
the Isle of Bute above the village of
Port Bannatyne.
Hilly seaside course.
Founded 1912
Designed by James Braid
13 holes, 5085 yards, S.S.S. 65
† Welcome.
ʃ WD llow/high season £8/9; WE
£12/16.
♂ Welcome by prior arrangement;
reductions for groups of 30-39 to £10;
for more than 40.
⚑ New clubhouse. Ardmory House;
Royal; Ardbeg.

9B 121 Port Glasgow

Devol Farm Industrial Estate, Port
Glasgow, Inverclyde, PA14 5XE
☎ 01475 704181
On M8 towards Greenock SW of
Glasgow in the town of Port
Glasgow.
Undulating course.
Founded 1895
18 holes, 5712 yards, S.S.S. 68
† WD until 3.55pm; WE by
introduction after 4pm Sat.
ʃ WD £15, day pass £20.
♂ Welcome by prior arrangement on
non-competition days; catering by prior
arrangement; terms available on
application.
🍽 Clubhouse facilities.
⚑ Clune Brae; Star.

9B 122 Prestwick

2 Links Rd, Prestwick, Ayrshire,
KA9 1QG
🔗 www.prestwickgc.co.uk
✉ bookings@prestwickgc.co.uk
☎ 01292 477404, Fax 477255,
Pro 479483
1 mile from Prestwick Airport adjacent
to Prestwick Station.
Links course; hosted first Open
Championship in 1860.
Pro Frank Rennie
Founded 1851
Designed by Tom Morris
18 holes, 6544 yards, S.S.S. 73
† Welcome by arrangement.
ʃ WD £90; day ticket £130.
♂ Welcome by prior arrangement;
terms on application.
🍽 Full clubhouse facilities; dining
room men only; Cardinal room.
⚑ Parkstone; Fairways; Golf View;
North Beach.

9B 123 Prestwick St Cuthbert

East Rd, Prestwick, Ayrshire,
KA9 2SX
🔗 www.stcuthbert.co.uk
✉ secretary@stcuthbert.co.uk
☎ 01292 477101, Fax 671730
Take A77 to Whitletts roundabout and
then follow signs for Heathfield Estate.
Parkland course.
Founded 1899
Designed by Stutt & Co
18 holes, 6470 yards, S.S.S. 71
† Welcome WD but booking
essential; only with member at WE.
ʃ WD/WE £29.
♂ Welcome by prior arrangement;
day ticket £38; meal packages can be
arranged with prior notice; from £12.
🍽 Full clubhouse facilities.
⚑ St Nicholas; Golf.

9B 124 Prestwick St Nicholas

Grangemuir Rd, Prestwick, Ayrshire,
KA9 1SN
🔗 www.prestwickstnicholas.com
✉ secretary@prestwickstnicholas.com
☎ 01292 477608, Fax 473900, Pro,
473904, Sec 477608, Rest/Bar 473902
From Prestwick town centre take the
road to Ayr; turn right at Grangemuir
road Junction; proceed under railway
bridge to course.
Links course.
Founded 1851/1892
Designed by C Hunter & J Allan
18 holes, 5952 yards, S.S.S. 69
† Welcome WD and Sun afternoon;
prior booking essential.
ʃ WD £36; WE £41.
♂ Welcome WD and some Sun
afternoons by prior arrangement;
catering by prior arrangement.
🍽 Full clubhouse refurbishment
completed spring 1998.
⚑ Parkstone.

9B 125 Ralston

Strathmore Ave, Ralston, Paisley,
Renfrewshire, PA1 3DT
☎ 0141 8821349, Fax 8839837,
Pro 8104925, Rest/Bar 8821470
Course is off the main Paisley to
Glasgow road.
Parkland course.
Pro Colin Monro; Founded 1904
18 holes, 6113 yards, S.S.S. 69
† With members only on WD.
ʃ WD £18.
♂ Welcome by prior arrangement;
catering by arrangement; terms on
application.
🍽 Full clubhouse facilities.
⚑ Abbey.

9B 126 Ranfurly Castle

Golf Road, Bridge of Weir,
Renfrewshire, PA11 3HN
🔗 www.ranfurlycastle.com
✉ secranfur@aol.com
☎ 01505 612609, Fax 610406,
Sec 612609
From the M8 take the Irvine road to
Bridge of Weir; turn left at Prieston
road and at top of the rise the
clubhouse is on right.
Spacious heathland course.
Pro Tom Eckford; Founded 1889
Designed by Andrew Kirkaldy & Willie
Auchterlonie
18 holes, 6284 yards, S.S.S. 71
† Welcome WD.
ʃ WD £25.
♂ Welcome weekdays except
Wednesdays. £25 per round. £35 per
day.
🍽 Full clubhouse bar and restaurant
service.
⚑ Glynhill; Renfrew; Stakis Glasgow
Airport.

9B 127 Renfrew

Blythswood Estate, Inchinnan Road,
Renfrew, PA4 9EG
🔗 www.renfrew.scottishgolf.com
✉ secretary@renfrew.scottishgolf
.com
☎ 0141 8866692, Fax 8861808
Leave the M8 at Junction 26 then take
the A8 to Renfrew turning to the club at
the Normandy Hotel.
Parkland course.
Founded 1894
Designed by John Harris
18 holes, 6818 yards, S.S.S. 73
† Visitors are welcome.
ʃ WD £35.00.
♂ Welcome Mon Tues and Thurs by
arrangement; catering by arrangement;
day ticket £35. Single round £30.
🍽 Full clubhouse bar and catering
facilities.
⚑ Dean Park; Glynhill; Normandy
Hotel.

9B 128 Rothesay

Canada Hill, Rothesay, Isle of Bute,
PA20 9HN
✉ pro@rothesaygc.fsnet.co.uk
☎ 01700 503554, Fax 503554,
Pro 503554, Sec 504585,
Rest/Bar 502244
30 minutes by steamer from Wemyss
Bay.
Undulating parkland/moorland course.
Pro Jim Dougal; Founded 1892
Designed by James Braid/Ben Sayers
18 holes, 5486 yards, S.S.S. 67
ʃ Practice area.nets.

Royal Troon

Royal Troon is the most recent of the royal courses, receiving the honour in its centenary year, 1978. It is the course of winners like Arnold Palmer and Lottie Dod, of losers like Gene Sarazen and Greg Norman, and of locals like Gordon Brown, Colin Montgomerie.

It is also a course built on sand. Gary Player once asked Norman J Ferguson, the greenkeeper, how deep the sand was in the bunkers. Ferguson recollected his reply by saying, "I told him as far as I knew it stretched from here to Australia as I had never seen anything to prove different". Player was not amused.

Sometimes the sand is hospitable. In the Second World War a bunker behind the fifth green became the home address of a refugee caddie known as Kilwinning and Gordon Brown, the sadly deceased former British Lions rugby player and member of Royal Troon, once spoke of another bunker that provided a bed for the night.

He said, "My father-in-law was walking home one night when he was a teenager and took a short cut across Royal Troon. He ran home and woke up his dad shaking with fright. He said that he had just seen a bear and got a clip round the ear for telling lies. Insisting on his tale the next morning he went back out with his father and there lying in a bunker beside the 11th green was a gypsy fellow with a dancing bear sound asleep beside him".

But Troon's bunkers are not usually so kindly. Bobby Clampett, all youthful curls and twirls, had a huge lead after five holes of the third round at the 1982 Open. He then visited three bunkers as he tacked his way up the sixth hole, put an eight on his card and was hardly heard of again until he took up commentating. Seven years later Greg Norman, who had opened with six consecutive birdies on his way to a remarkable 64 on the final day, would lose a play-off to Mark Calcavecchia after driving 350 yards into a hitherto unreached bunker on the 18th hole.

But before you even get to the sand, you have to have big enough shoes to stand up in a gale. Gene Sarazen missed qualification by a shot at the 1923 Open after shooting an 85 on a day when the storm was so furious that the fishermen were not allowed out in their boats. Fifty years later Sarazen returned to a calmer Troon.

The Postage Stamp is the shortest hole in Championship golf and it is almost one of the most treacherous. A professional by the splendid name of Aubrey Boomer once said of it, "The green is garrisoned by an archipelago of bunkers and looks even smaller than it actually is as you stand trembling and uncertain on the tee".

Yet on the first day of the 1973 Open the 71-year-old Sarazen had a hole in one at the Postage Stamp and extraordinarily on the second day, after missing the green with his tee shot, holed from the bunker for a two. Serendipity.

In the final round of the '89 Open Mark Calcavecchia went from bush to bush as he played the eleventh hole and was so disgusted by the time he reached the green that he didn't bother cleaning his ball, but just went up and hit the darned thing. The 30-footer disappeared for a par. On the very next hole Calcavecchia chipped in on the full from a grassy bank. More serendipity.

If there's a hand that shapes the destiny of man, it appears to wear a golf glove and hover in the skies above Troon.
– Mark Reason

† Visitors most welcome. Prior arrangement advised at weekends.

⌐ Terms on application.

⌐ Welcome by prior arrangement; catering by prior arrangement; from £15.

⌐⦿⌐ Full clubhouse facilities in the season April-October.

⌐ Club will supply comprehensive list of local hotels.

9B 129 Rouken Glen

Stewarton Rd, Thornliebank, Glasgow, G46 7UZ

☎ 0141 638 7044, Fax 6115

5 miles S of Glasgow.

Parkland course.

Pro Kendal McReid; Founded 1922

18 holes, 4800 yards, S.S.S. 64

Designed by James Braid

⌐ Practice range, 18 bays floodlit.

† Welcome.

⌐ Terms on application.

⌐ Welcome by prior arrangement; terms on application.

⌐⦿⌐ Snacks.

⌐ The MacDonalds.

9B 130 Routenburn

Largs, Ayrshire, KA30 8SQ

☎ 01475 673230, Pro 687240, Sec 672757, Rest/Bar 606475

1 mile N of Largs turning left at first major turning on the Greenock road.

Seaside hill course.

Pro Greig McQueen; Founded 1914

Designed by James Braid

18 holes, 5680 yards, S.S.S. 68

† Welcome WD by prior arrangement.

⌐ WD/WE £15.50.

⌐ Welcome WD by prior arrangement; catering packages by prior arrangement; terms on application.

⌐⦿⌐ Full facilities except Thurs.

⌐ Brisbane Hotel; Willowbank Hotel.

9B 131 Royal Troon

Craigend Rd, Troon, Ayrshire, KA10 6EP

⌐ www.royaltroon.com

⌐ bookings@royaltroon.com

☎ 01292 311555, Fax 318204, Pro 313281

3 miles from A77 and Prestwick Airport.

Championship links course; host of 2004 Open.

Pro Brian Anderson; Founded 1878

Designed by Willie Fernie

18 holes, 7150 yards, S.S.S. 75

⌐ 12 bays and practice area.

† May-Oct, Mon, Tues and Thurs only; maximum handicap 20 (men), 30 (ladies).

⌐ LOld Course, Portland Course: WD £185 (incl 2-course lunch).

⌐ Welcome by prior arrangement; price includes lunch and coffee; also Portland course: 18 holes 6274 yards par 71.

⌐⦿⌐ Full bar and restaurant service.

⌐ Marine; Piersland House; Lochgreen and others.

9B 132 Ruchill

Brassey Street, Maryhill, Glasgow, G20

☎ 0141 7700519, Pro 7707135, Sec 7706220

From Glasgow city centre,100 yards off M8, Junction 12.

Municipal parkland course.

Pro G Taggart; Founded 1928

18 holes, 5836 yards, S.S.S. 68

⌐ Practice pitch and putt.

† Public.

⌐ Pay and play.

⌐ Contact city council.

9B 133 Sandyhills

223 Sandyhills Rd, Glasgow, G32 9NA

☎ 0141 778 1179 (bar), Sec 1179

E side of Glasgow from Tollcross road turn left at Killin Stand right into Sandyhills Road.

Parkland course.

Founded 1905

18 holes, 6237 yards, S.S.S. 70

† Welcome by prior arrangement. Terms on application.

⌐ Welcome by prior arrangement; catering packages available; terms on application.

⌐⦿⌐ Full clubhouse catering facilities available.

⌐ Hilton; Moat House; Marriott, all in Glasgow.

9B 134 Shiskine

Blackwaterfoot, Isle of Arran, KA27 8HA

☎ 01770 860226, Fax 860205, Pro 860226

Course is 300 yards off the B880 in Blackwaterfoot.

Seaside course with magnificent views.

Founded 1896

Designed by Willy Ferney

12 holes, 2990 yards, S.S.S. 42

† Welcome; handicap certs required in July and August period.

⌐ WD £15; WE £19.

⌐ Welcome by prior arrangement with club manager; packages available with Kinloch Hotel accommodation and golf; day tickets available (WD £25; WE £30); also weekly and fortnightly tickets; tennis and bowls.

⌐⦿⌐ Tea room lunches high teas from April-Oct; bar at Kinloch Hotel 500 yds.

⌐ Kinloch Hotel.

9B 135 Skelmorlie ☏

Skelmorlie, Ayrshire, PA17 5ES

☎ 01475 520152

1 mile from Wemyss Station.

Parkland/moorland course.

Founded 1891

Designed by James Braid

18 holes, 5104 yards, S.S.S. 65

† Welcome by prior arrangement except Sat.

⌐ Terms on application.

⌐ Welcome by prior arrangement except Sat catering by prior arrangement terms available on application.

⌐⦿⌐ Full clubhouse facilities.

⌐ Haywood.

9B 136 Strathaven

Overton Avenue, Glasgow Road, Strathaven, ML10 6NL

⌐ www.strathavengc.com

⌐ info@strathavengc.com

☎ 01357 520421, Fax 520539, Pro 521812, Sec 520421, Rest/Bar 520421

On A723 East Kilbride road on outskirts of the town.

Tree-lined undulating parkland course.

Pro Stuart Kerr; Founded 1908

Designed by William Fernie of Troon

Extended to 18 holes by JR Stutt

18 holes, 6250 yards, S.S.S. 71

† Everyone welcome weekdays. Not weekends.

⌐ WD until 4pm £26 per round. WD £86 per day.

⌐ Welcome Tues by prior arrangement with Sec; catering by prior arrangement; club can organise morning coffee hot and cold snacks lunches high teas and dinners; Packages start from £12.

⌐⦿⌐ Full clubhouse facilities available.

⌐ Strathaven; Springvale.

9B 137 Strathclyde Park

Mote Hill, Hamilton, Lanarkshire, ML3 6BY

☎ 01698 429350, Pro 285511

1.5 miles from M74 close to Hamilton Ice rink.

Public parkland course.
Pro William Walker
9 holes, 6350 yards, S.S.S. 70
🏌 Practice range available.
� Welcome.
£ WD £3.30 WE £3.90.
⟳ Welcome; catering by prior
arrangement; from £3.
🍽 Catering by prior arrangement.
⟿ Travelodge.

9B 138 Tarbert
Kilberry Rd, Tarbert, Argyll, PA29 6XX
☎ 01880 820565
1 mile from A83 to Campbeltown from
Tarbert on B8024.
Hilly seaside course.
9 holes, 4460 yards, S.S.S. 63
� Welcome by prior arrangement.
£ From £8.
⟳ Welcome WD; day ticket for £15;
from £10.
🍽 Full clubhouse facilities available.
⟿ Stonefield Castle; West Loch.

9B 139 Tobermory
Erray Rd, Tobermory, Isle of Mull,
PA75 6PR
🖳 www.tobermoreygolfclub.com
✉ secretary@tobermorygolfclub.com
☎ 01688 302338, Fax 302140,
Sec 302338, Rest/Bar 302387
Signposted in Tobermory.
Cliff top heathland course with views
over Sound of Mull.
Founded 1896
Designed by David Adams (1935)
9 holes, 4890 yards, S.S.S. 64
🏌 Practice range and net.
� Welcome; advance booking
system.
£ £15 dayl Juniors (under 18) half
price (2003).
⟳ Welcome by prior arrangement.
🍽 Clubhouse facilities available Apr-
Oct.

9B 140 Torrance House
Strathaven Rd, East Kilbride, G75 0QZ
☎ 01355 249720, Sec 248638
Course is on the A726 on outskirts of E
Kilbride travelling South to Strathaven.
Municipal parkland course.
Founded 1969
Designed by Hawtree and Sons
18 holes, 6476 yards, S.S.S. 71
🏌 Practice range 1 mile from club.
� Welcome; advance booking
system.
£ Terms on application.
⟳ Welcome by prior arrangement by
calling 01355 80627; catering

packages by prior arrangement from
£16.
🍽 Full clubhouse facilities available.

9B 141 Troon Municipal
Harling Drive, Troon, Ayrshire,
KA10 6NE
🖳 www.golfsouthayrshire.co.uk
☎ 01292 312464, Fax 312578,
Pro 315566
100 yards from the railway station.
Links course.
Pro Gordon Mckenley; Founded 1905
Darley: 18 holes, 6360 yards, S.S.S. 71
Lochgreen: 18 holes, 6822 yards,
S.S.S. 72; Fullerton: 18 holes, 4689
yards,
S.S.S. 63
🏌 Practice areas available.
� Welcome.
£ Terms on application.
⟳ Welcome by prior arrangement;
catering by arrangement; terms on
application.
🍽 Full clubhouse facilities.
⟿ Anchorage Hotel; Marine Hotel;
South Beach Hotel.

9B 142 Turnberry Resort ℭ
Turnberry Hotel, Turnberry, Ayrshire,
KA26 9LT
🖳 www.turnberry.co.uk
✉ monty.turnberry@westin.com
☎ 01655 331000, Fax 331706,
Pro 334043
On A77 15 miles SW of Ayr.
Championship seaside links.
Pro David Fleming; Founded 1897
Designed by MacKenzie Ross (Ailsa)
18 holes, 6976 yards, S.S.S. 72
🏌 12 long game 4 short game.
� Booking essential.
£ WD £80; WE £80. Subject to
variation in April 2002.
⟳ Only welcome if society is resident
in the hotel.
🍽 Full clubhouse restaurant and bar;
first-class hotel facilities.
⟿ Turnberry Hotel.

9B 143 Vale of Leven ℭ
Northfield Rd, Bonhill, Alexandria,
Dumbartonshire, G83 9ET
🖳 www.valeoflevengolfclub.org.uk
✉ secretary@valeoflevengolfclub
.org.uk
☎ 01389 752351, Fax 489950,
Pro 498930
Off A82 Glasgow to Dumbarton road at
signs marked Bonhill & Alexandria.
Moorland course with views of Loch
and Ben Lomond.

Pro Barry Campbell
Founded 1907
18 holes, 5162 yards, S.S.S. 66
� Welcome except Sat.
£ WD £16; WE £20.
⟳ Welcome by prior arrangement;
catering packages by prior
arrangement with club secretary.
🍽 Full clubhouse and bar facilities
available.
⟿ Balloch; Duck Bay Marina;
Lomond Park; Tullichewan.

9B 144 Vaul
Scarinish, Isle of Tiree, Argyll,
PA77 6XH
☎ 01879 220729
On the E end of the Island 3 miles
from the pier and 5 miles from the
airport; 40-minute flight from Glasgow;
50 miles W of Oban by ferry.
Links course.
Founded 1920
9 holes, 5674 yards, S.S.S. 68
� Welcome.
£ WD £5; WE £5.
⟳ Welcome by prior arrangement;
weekly and fortnightly tickets available;
from £10.
🍽 Catering at Lodge Hotel.
⟿ Lodge; Glassary GH; Kirkapol GH.

9B 145 West Kilbride
33-35 Fullerton Drive, Seamill,
W Kilbride, Ayrshire, KA23 9HT
🖳 www.westkilbride.com
✉ golf@westkilbride.com
☎ 01294 823911, Fax 829573,
Pro 823042, Rest/Bar 823128
On A78 Androssan to Largs road at
Seamill.
Flat seaside links course alongside
Firth of Clyde.
Pro Graham Ross
Founded 1893
Designed by Tom Morris
18 holes, 6452 yards, S.S.S. 70
🏌 Practice area.
� Welcome WD after 9.30am.
£ WD £38.
⟳ Welcome Tues and Thurs only by
prior arrangement; catering to be
arranged in advance with the caterer;
from £38.
🍽 Full clubhouse facilities.
⟿ Seamill Hydro.

9B 146 Western Gailes
Gailes, Irvine, Ayrshire, KA11 5AE
🖳 www.westerngails.com
✉ enquiries@westerngailes.com
clubmanager@westerngailes.com

☎ 01294 311357/311649 (all reservations and enquiries), Fax 312312, Sec 01435 40354
Course is on the A78 five miles N Troon. Championship links; final Open qualifying course.
Founded 1897
18 holes, 6714 yards, S.S.S. 73
🏌 Small practice area.
♦ Welcome WD except Thurs, Tues and Sat.
£ WD £90. incl lunch; £90 Sun.
↻ Welcome by prior arrangement WD except Thurs and Tues; day tickets from £125; catering by arrangement.
🍽 Clubhouse catering and bar.
↝ The Gailles Lodge (01294 204040).

9B 147 Westerwood Hotel ☉
St Andrews Drive, Cumbernauld, G68 0EW
📧 westerwood@morton-hotel.com
☎ 01236 457171, Fax 738478, Pro 725281, Sec 725281
Signposted off the A80 13 miles from Glasgow.
Parkland course.
Pro Allen Tate; Founded 1989
Designed by Seve Ballesteros and Dave Thomas
18 holes, 6616 yards, S.S.S. 72
🏌 Practice range available.
♦ Welcome.
£ WD £13.50; WE £15.
↻ Welcome by prior arrangement; packages available; hotel leisure facilities; residents discounts; from £22.50.
🍽 Full clubhouse catering facilities available.
↝ Westerwood Hotel on site.

9B 148 Whinhill
Beith Road, Greenock, Renfrewshire
☎ 01475 724694, Sec 724694
Just outside Greenock on Old Largs Road.
Parkland course.
18 holes, 5434 yards, S.S.S. 68
♦ Welcome.
£ Terms on application.
↻ None.
🍽 Small clubhouse for members only.

9B 149 Whitecraigs
72 Ayr Rd, Giffnock, G46 6SW
📧 wcraigsgc@aol.com
☎ 0141 6394530, Fax 616 3648, Pro 6392140, Rest/Bar 6391795
Course is on the A77 seven miles S of Glasgow.
Parkland course.
Pro Alistair Forrow; Founded 1905
18 holes, 6013 yards, S.S.S. 70
♦ Welcome on WD but booking is essential.
£ WD £40; including coffee high tea and light snacks.
↻ Welcome Wed only; catering by arrangement; day tickets from £50; from £35.
🍽 Full clubhouse facilities available.
↝ The Redhurst Hotel.

9B 150 Whiting Bay
Golf Course Rd, Whiting Bay, Isle of Arran, KA27 8QT
☎ 01770 700487
8 miles S of Brodick.
Undulating heathland course.
Founded 1895
18 holes, 4405 yards, S.S.S. 63
♦ Welcome.
£ WD £13; WE £17; after 4pm all rounds are £10.
↻ Welcome by prior arrangement with Sec; discounts available for groups of 10 or more; from £13.
🍽 Clubhouse catering and bar facilities.
↝ Cameronia; Grange House; Kiscadale; Royal.

9B 151 Williamwood
Clarkston Rd, Netherlee, Glasgow, G44 3YR
📧 secretary@ williamwoodgc.fsnet.co.uk
☎ 0141 637 1783, Fax 571 0166, Pro 673 2715
5 miles S of Glasgow.
Wooded parkland course.
Pro Stewart Marshall; Founded 1906
Designed by James Braid
18 holes, 5878 yards, S.S.S. 69
🏌 Practice area.
♦ Welcome.
£ WD £27, day pass £37.

↻ Welcome WD by arrangement; catering by arrangement; terms on application.
🍽 Full clubhouse facilities available.
↝ Redhurst Clarkston; The Busby Hotel, Busby.

9B 152 Windyhill ☉
Baljaffray Rd, Bearsden, Glasgow, G61 4QQ
🖥 www.windyhill.co.uk
☎ 0141 942 2349, Fax 5874, Pro 7157
1 mile N of Bearsden.
Parkland course.
Pro Chris Duffy; Founded 1908
Designed by James Braid
18 holes, 6254 yards, S.S.S. 70
🏌 Practice area.
♦ Welcome WD.
£ WD £20.
↻ Welcome by prior arrangement; discounts available for larger groups; catering available by arrangement; £25.
🍽 Full bar and restaurant facilities.
↝ Jury's Pond Hotel; Glasgow Travel Lodge.

9B 153 Wishaw
55 Clelend Road, Lower Main Street, Wishaw, Lanarkshire, ML2 7PH
📧 jwdouglas@btconnect.com
☎ 01698 375480, Fax 375480, Pro 358247, Rest/Bar 372869
Course is 15 miles SE of Glasgow; five miles from the M74 Motherwell Junction.
Parkland course.
Pro Stuart Adair; Founded 1897
Designed by James Braid
18 holes, 5999 yards, S.S.S. 69
🏌 Practice range available.
♦ Welcome WD until 4pm; not Sat and by prior arrangement Sun.
£ WD £20 round, £30 day.
↻ Welcome WD; Sun only by special arrangement; day's golf; catering packages by prior arrangement.
🍽 Full clubhouse facilities available.
↝ Commercial Hotel.

Tayside, Central Region, Fife

If Ayrshire is heavenly then Fife is sacred ground. On that note there has been a great deal of blaspheming about St Andrews in recent years along the lines that modern equipment has emasculated it and the longer players can just blast left most of the way round. There is something in this, but should anyone be lucky or persuasive enough to get a start time on the Old Course after dawn they will hardly turn it down.

Fortified by finnan-haddock Henry Longhurst used to regard the journey to St Andrews, the home of the Royal and Ancient, as the most romantic rail journey in the world. But these days Leuchars is as far as you can get. Longhurst wrote an article beseeching Barbara Castle not to close St Andrews station. It ended "You can't let them do it, Barbara. You can't, really" until he was forced to add the postscript, "Sadly, and as ultimate proof that nothing is sacred in this world, she did".

Nicklaus said that there were three types of Open, one in Scotland, one in England and one at St Andrews. However much technology has changed it, the Old Course is still sacred ground, but the New, the Dukes, the Eden and the Jubilee all also take a fair bit of playing.

Yet for all its history the R&A isn't the oldest royal club in Britain. That distinction belongs to Royal Perth, honoured in 1833, a club that plays its golf on the North Inch, a quirky course with two par threes under 100 yards.

Moving back into the 21st century and a 15-minute drive along the coast from St Andrews, a new course has sprung up called Kingsbarns. The British tried to build a links on this land but failed, so the Americans supplied the necessary initiative instead. They have made a brilliant job of it.

Further round the coast Leven and Lundin links are the sort of neighbours we would all like to have and Crail is an old friend of many. To the north of St Andrews Scotscraig is a brutally hard course with some ferocious bunkers.

Inland Ladybank is a much more soothing proposition amidst the gorse and pines, as is Buchanan Castle, over towards Glasgow. Buchanan Castle was the home to the belligerent Ryder Cup golfer Eric Brown who won all his singles matches in the fifties. Typically he described another course in the region as "a bloody goat track but a sporty one".

The course was Crieff and from it you can see Gleneagles where the 2014 Ryder Cup will be played. It is a beautiful spot amidst the Grampians and the Trossachs and has three courses, the Kings, the Queens and the Monarch. Those with a taste for scenery and elevated tees will enjoy Gleneagles.

Dundee's leading course is probably Downfield which Peter Thomson considered to be one of the best inland courses he had ever played. Blairgowrie, Glenbervie, King James VI and Montrose, a course used by the Royal Montrose Golf Club, are all worth noting in the region, but it is Montrose's neighbour to the south that bestrides them like a colossus. Plonked on a harsh piece of land open to the weather Carnoustie welcomes visitors and then spends several hours berating them about the quality of their golf.

The final three holes must represent one of the most daunting finishes in the world. The 16th is 230 yards to a small heavily bunkered green, the 17th fairway is an island amidst the twists of the Barry Burn and the eighteenth is *mon dieu et sacre bleu*. Since his collapse at the 1999 Open Jean van de Velde has returned to play the hole in a mere five strokes – with a putter.

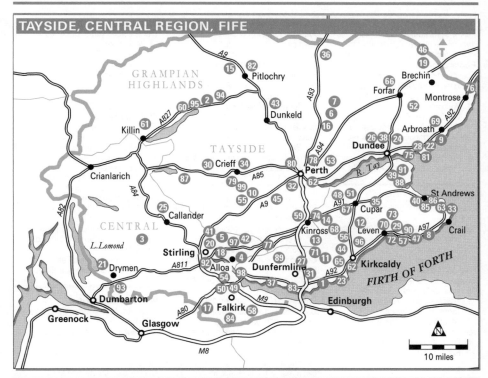

TAYSIDE, CENTRAL REGION, FIFE

9C 1 **Aberdour**

Seaside Place, Aberdour, Fife, KY3 0TX
☎ 01383 860688, Fax 860050,
Pro 860256, Sec 860080
In Aberdour village on coast route to
Burntisland.
Parkland/seaside course with views of
River Forth.
Pro David Gemmell

Founded 1896
Designed by Peter Robertson & Joe
Anderson
18 holes, 5460 yards, S.S.S. 66
† Welcome by prior arrangement.
Ⅰ Mon-Sat: £20; Sun: £35.
✎ Welcome except Sat by prior
arrangement; day ticket from £30;
catering by arrangement with the

clubmaster; maximum parties of 24 on
Sun; from £35.
🍽 Full clubhouse catering.
🛏 Woodside.

9C 2 **Aberfeldy**

Taybridge Rd, Aberfeldy, Perthshire,
PH15 2BH

☎ 01887 820535
Follow signs from A9 at Ballinluig through the centre of Aberfeldy for Weem and first right at Wades Bridge.
Parkland course.
Founded 1895
Designed by Souters
18 holes, 5283 yards, S.S.S. 66
♦ Welcome.
[WD £18; WE £24.
⌁ Welcome by prior arrangement; catering by arrangement; terms on application.
🍽 Full facilities.
🛌 Palace; Crown, both Aberfeldy.

9C 3 **Aberfoyle**
Braeval, Aberfoyle, Stirlingshire, FK8 3UY
☎ 01877 382493, Sec 01360 550847
1.5 miles from Aberfoyle on the main Stirling road.
Parkland course.
Founded 1890
Designed by James Braid
18 holes, 5218 yards, S.S.S. 66
♦ Welcome; some restrictions at WE.
[Terms on application.
⌁ Welcome by prior arrangement; restrictions on numbers; from £12.
🍽 Full clubhouse facilities.
🛌 Rob Roy Motor Inn; Forth Inn.

9C 4 **Alloa** ☏
Schawpark, Sauchie, Clackmannanshire, FK10 3AX
✉ alloagolf@schawpark.fsbusiness.co.uk
☎ 01259 722745, Fax 218796, Pro 724745
On the A908 1 mile N of Alloa; 8 miles E of Stirling.
Undulating parkland course.
Pro Bill Bennett
Founded 1891
Designed by James Braid
18 holes, 6229 yards, S.S.S. 71
🏌 2 practice areas; putting greens; driving net.
♦ Welcome.
[Prices on application.
⌁ Welcome WD by arrangement; catering available by prior arrangement; snooker room; from £23.
🍽 Full clubhouse facilities.
🛌 Harviestoun; Royal Oak; Dunmar House; Claremont Lodge.

9C 5 **Alva**
Beauclerc St, Alva, Clackmannanshire, FK12 5LH
☎ 01259 760431

Course is on the A91 Stirling to St Andrews road; follow signs for Alva Glen as the club car park is at entrance to Glen Hillside.
Sloping fairways/plateau greens.
Founded 1901
9 holes, 4846 yards, S.S.S. 64
♦ Welcome.
[Terms on application.
⌁ Welcome by prior arrangement; facilities limited; no pro shop no equipment for hire; terms on application.
🍽 Bar snacks only; clubhouse open for 7pm each night and from noon at WE.
🛌 Alva Glen.

9C 6 **Alyth**
Pitcrocknie, Alyth, Perthshire, PH11 8HF
🖳 www.alythgolfclub.co.uk
✉ enquiries@alythgolfclub.co.uk
☎ 01828 632668, Fax 633491, Pro 632411, Sec 632268
Course is one mile SE of Alyth on the B954.
Parkland course with views over Angus & Perthshire.
Pro Tom Melville; Founded 1894
Designed by Tom Morris/James Braid.
18 holes, 6205 yards, S.S.S. 71
♦ Welcome by prior arrangement.
[WD £22; WE £33.
⌁ Welcome by prior arrangement; catering available by arrangement; Pro can assist with golf clinics; day and weekly tickets; from £22.
🍽 Full clubhouse facilities.
🛌 Lands of Loyal; Alyth; Lossett.

9C 7 **Alyth Strathmore**
Leroch, Alyth, Perthshire, PH11 8NZ
🖳 www.strathmoregolf.com
✉ enquiries@strathmoregolf.com
☎ 01828 633322
Course is five miles E of Blairgowie on the A926.
Founded 1996
18 holes, 6454 yards, S.S.S. 72
🏌 10 floodlit bays and practice area.
♦ Welcome; pay and play.
[Terms on application.
⌁ Welcome; corporate days available.
🍽 Full clubhouse facilities.
🛌 Lands of Loyal; Alyth; Lossett.

9C 8 **Anstruther** ☏
Marsfield, Shore Rd, Anstruther, Fife, KY10 3DZ
☎ 01333 310956, Fax 312283, Sec 312283
Turn off main road at Craw's Nest Hotel.
Seaside course.

Founded 1890
9 holes, 4588 yards, S.S.S. 63
♦ Welcome.
[WD £12; WE £15.
⌁ None.
🍽 Snacks and lunches.
🛌 Craw's Nest.

9C 9 **Arbroath**
Elliot, Arbroath, Angus, DD11 2PE
☎ 01241 872069, Pro 875837
Take A92 from Dundee N and turn right 2 miles before Arbroath.
Seaside links course.
Pro Lindsay Ewart; Founded 1903
Designed by James Braid
18 holes, 5856 yards, S.S.S. 69
♦ Welcome; not before 9.30am WE.
[WD £18; WE £24.
⌁ Welcome by prior arrangement; catering by arrangement; terms on application.
🍽 Full clubhouse facilities.
🛌 Seaforth; Cliffburn; Viewfield.

9C 10 **Auchterarder**
Orchil Rd, Auchterarder, Perthshire, PH3 1LS
🖳 www.auchterardergolf.co.uk
✉ secretary@auchterardergolf.co.uk
☎ 01764 662804, Fax 664423, Pro 663711
Course is off the A9 next to Gleneagles Hotel.
Wooded heathland course.
Pro Gavin Baxter; Founded 1892
Designed by Bernard Sayers
18 holes, 5775 yards, S.S.S. 68
♦ Welcome by prior arrangement or with a member.
[POA.
⌁ Welcome by prior arrangement with Sec; catering and golf packages by arrangement.
🍽 Full catering and bar facilities available.
🛌 Cairn Lodge; Colliearn House; Duchally.

9C 11 **Auchterderran**
Woodend Rd, Cardenden, Fife, KY5 0NH
☎ 01592 721579, Sec 720080
Course is on the main Lochgelly to Cardenden road at the N end of Cardenden.
Parkland course.
Founded 1904
9 holes, 5250 yards, S.S.S. 66
♦ Welcome, but prior booking advisable.
[From £9.

⌁ Welcome by arrangement; catering by prior arrangement; from £9.
🍽 Bar and snacks facilities available; meals cooked to order.
⌁ Bowhill; Central.

9C 12 Balbirnie Park
Markinch, Glenrothes, Fife, KY7 6NR
✉ craigfdonnerley@aol.com
☎ 01592 612095, Fax 612383,
Pro 752006, Sec 752006
2 miles E of Glenrothes off A92 on A911.
Scenic parkland course.
Pro Craig Donnerley; Founded 1983
18 holes, 6210 yards, S.S.S. 70
⚑ Practice area.
† Welcome by arrangement.
⌁ WD £27; WE £33.
⌁ Welcome by prior arrangement; catering packages by arrangement; terms on application.
🍽 Full clubhouse; all-day catering.
⌁ Balbirnie House.

9C 13 Ballingry
Lochore Meadows Country Park, Crosshill, by Lochgelly, Ballingry, Fife, KY5 8BA
🌐 www.lochore-meadows.co.uk
✉ info@lochore-meadows.co.uk
☎ 01592 414300
W of M90 between Lochgelly and Ballingry.
Parkland course.
Founded 1981
9 holes, 6484 yards, S.S.S. 71
† Welcome.
⌁ WD £10 (18) £7 (9); WE £13 (18) £9 (9).
⌁ Welcome by prior arrangement; angling, wind-surfing; terms on application.
🍽 Catering in café in park centre.
⌁ Navitie House.

9C 14 Bishopshire
Kinnesswood by Kinross, Tayside, KY13
☎ 01592 780203
Course is three miles E of Kinross off the M90.
Upland course.
Founded 1903
Designed by W. Park
10 holes, 4784 yards, S.S.S. 64
† Welcome.
⌁ Terms on application.
⌁ Limited by arrangement; catering by arrangement or at local hotels; from £6.
🍽 Available at the Lomond Hotel 400 yards away.
⌁ Lomond; Scotlandwell Inn.

9C 15 Blair Atholl
Blair Atholl, Perthshire, PH18 5TG
☎ 01796 481407, Fax 481751
Course is on the A9 five miles N of Pitlochry.
Parkland course.
Founded 1896
9 holes, 5710 yards, S.S.S. 68
† Welcome except competition days.
⌁ WD £15; WE £17.
⌁ Welcome by prior arrangement; catering by arrangement; from £13.
🍽 Clubhouse facilities.
⌁ Atholl Arms; Tilt.

9C 16 Blairgowrie
Perthshire, PH10 6LG
🌐 www.theblairgowriegolfclub.co.uk
✉ office@theblairgowriegolfclub.co.uk
☎ 01250 872622, Fax 875451,
Pro 873116
1 mile S of Blairgowrie off the A93; 15 miles N of Perth.
Heathland course with pine, silver birch, bloom.
Pro Charles Dernie
Founded 1889
Designed by Thomas/Alliss
Landsdown: 18 holes, 6802 yards, S.S.S. 74. Rosemount: 18 holes, 6580 yards, S.S.S. 73. Wee Course: 9 holes, 2327 yards, S.S.S. 63 (designed by Old Tom Morris in 1889).
† Welcome by prior arrangement; some restrictions apply Wed, Fri and WE.
⌁ Prices on application.
⌁ Welcome with same restrictions as visitors; catering packages by arrangement; terms on application.
🍽 Full clubhouse facilities.
⌁ Kinloch House; Moorfield House; Altamount House; Angus Hotel; Rosemount Golf Hotel; Ballathie House Hotel; Dalmore Hotel.

9C 17 Bonnybridge
Larbert Rd, Bonnybridge, Stirlingshire, FK4 1NY
☎ 01324 812323, Rest/Bar 812822
Course is on the B816 three miles W of Falkirk.
Undulating moorland course.
Founded 1925
9 holes, 6128 yards, S.S.S. 70
† Welcome with a member or by letter of introduction.
⌁ WD £16; WE £16.
⌁ None.
🍽 Meals at WE; bar facilities; limited in winter.
⌁ Royal.

9C 18 Braehead
Cambus, by Alloa, Clackmannanshire, FK10 2NT
🌐 www.braehead.gc.btinternet.co.uk
✉ braehead.gc@btinternet.com
☎ 01259 722078, Fax 214070,
Pro 722078, Sec 725766,
Rest/Bar 725766
On A907 Stirling-Alloa Road about 1.5 miles W of Alloa.
Parkland course.
Pro Jamie Stevenson; Founded 1891
18 holes, 6086 yards, S.S.S. 69
Designed by Robert Tait.
⚑ Practice range.
† Everyone welcome.
⌁ WD £20; WE £30; summer rate full weekday £30, full weekend day £40.
⌁ Welcome all week by prior arrangement; catering packages by arrangement; from £30 per day.
🍽 Full catering facilities.
⌁ Royal Oak; Dunmar House.

9C 19 Brechin Golf and Squash Club ☏
Trinity, by Brechin, Angus, DD9 7PD
☎ 01356 622383, Pro 625270
1 mile outside Brechin on the A90 road to Aberdeen.
Rolling parkland course.
Pro Stephen Rennie; Founded 1893
18 holes, 6096 yards, S.S.S. 70
⚑ Practice range.
† Welcome; restrictions Sat and Sun 10am-12 noon & 2.30pm-4.30pm.
⌁ WD £20; WE £25.
⌁ Welcome WD by prior arrangement; packages for eight or more include all catering and 2 rounds of golf; £30.
🍽 Full clubhouse facilities.
⌁ Glenesk Hotel, Edzell.

9C 20 Bridge of Allan
Sunnlaw, Bridge of Allan, Stirlingshire
🌐 www.boagc.com
☎ 01786 832332
3 miles N of Stirling.
Undulating course; one of toughest par 3s in Scotland.
Founded 1895
Designed by Old Tom Morris
9 holes, 5120 yards, S.S.S. 66
† Welcome WD and Sun.
⌁ WD on application.
⌁ By prior arrangement; terms on application.
🍽 Bar facilities.
⌁ Royal.

9C 21 Buchanan Castle ☏
Drymen, Glasgow, G63 0HY

Royal & Ancient Golf Club of St Andrews

St Andrews is probably the most famous course in the world. Famous for the Swilken Burn, crossed by the Swilken Bridge – and famous for the Valley of Sin beyond it. It is famous for the bunkers – 112 of them, including the Hell bunker at the 14th, and the Road Bunker at the 17th. And it is famous for its enormous double greens, that still surprise many visitors as they square up to putts of almost 100 yards on a regular basis. But more than this, St Andrews is famous for being the home of golf, and this year it celebrates its 250th birthday.

The club was founded in the spring of 1754, by 22 Scottish lawyers, politicians, soldiers and noblemen. They convened in the Fife town to devise a competition to be played over the Old Course. They called themselves the Society of St Andrews Golfers.

Minutes from that famous meeting 250 years ago record that: "the noblemen and gentlemen above named being admirers of the ancient and healthfull exercise of the golf and the same time having the interest and prosperity of the ancient city of St Andrews at heart, being the *alma mater* of the golf, did in the year of our lord 1754 contribute for a silver club ... to be played for on the links of St Andrews upon the 14th day of May said year and yearly in time coming".

The R&A, though, is not the world's oldest club – that honour belongs to its Edinburgh neighbour the Royal Burgess, which dates back to 1735 and is featured elsewhere in this guide – and it is also younger than the Honourable Company of Edinburgh Golfers, which was founded in 1744. Indeed, the R&A's silver club competition imitated the Honourable Company's silver club competition which was first played in Leith. The R&A was formally constituted in 1766 and was made up of Scotland's clubbable types who would meet to play golf, drink and dine. At some of their functions, the consumption of alcohol was regarded as obligatory. Tea drinkers were fined. When the novelist Tobias Smollett visited Leith, he described the golfers he met there as "gentlemen of independent fortunes ... [who] never went to bed without having each the best part of a gallon of claret in his belly".

In 1814 members at St Andrews had to pay their first subscription, and four years later King William IV authorised the club's royal patronage. They were now the Royal and Ancient Golf Club of St Andrews – and they required a clubhouse to befit their status. Forty years later, they got one. In 1854, 100 years after the competition for the silver club, the stately building that overlooks the Old Course, opened for members' use.

Professional golf was just around the corner, but contrary to many visitor's belief, St Andrews was not the first Open venue – nor was it especially keen to host the event for the first time in 1873 – 13 years after Prestwick had hosted first competition. It was Prestwick who approached the R&A to contribute to the cost of a new trophy (a claret jug to replace the championship belt for which the Tom Morrisses had been battling it out for over a decade). Eventually, the R&A, Prestwick and the Honourable Company paid £10 each for the trophy and prize money was raised to £20 for the event. Tom Kidd was the first man to win the jug – and claim the £11 prize money.

In September 1897 the R&A were asked to take responsibility for the rules. Until then, clubs had made their own rules but by the end of the nineteenth century, there were 1,000 clubs in the UK and some conformity was required. The R&A, with its distinguished membership of lawyers, soldiers and politicians, made the rules. From that moment forth, the Royal and Ancient Golf Club of St Andrews was "the home of golf". – **Jim Bruce-Ball**

buchanancastle@sol.co.uk
☎ 01360 660307, Fax 660993,
Pro 660330, Sec 660307,
Rest/Bar 660369
Course is on the A811 Glasgow to
Aberfoyle road; entrance just before
Drymen.
Secluded parkland course with
stunning views.
Pro Keith Baxter; Founded 1936
Designed by James Braid
18 holes, 6059 yards, S.S.S. 69
♦ Practice range.
♦ Welcome by arrangement.
♦ WD/WE £34.
♦ Welcome Thurs and Fri by prior
arrangement; full day's golf £44;
catering by arrangement with Club
master; casual visitors welcome.
♦ Full clubhouse facilities.
♦ Buchanan Arms; Winnock Hotel.

9C 22 Buddon Links
Links Parade, Carnoustie Angus,
Tayside, DD7 7JE
♦ www.carnoustiegolflinks.co.uk
administrator@carnoustiegolflinks
.co.uk
☎ 01241 853249, Fax 852720,
Pro 411999, Sec 853789
10 miles E of Dundee on A92.
Links course.
Pro Lee Vannett
Designed by Alan Robertson, Old Tom
Morris
18 holes, 5420 yards, S.S.S. 67
♦ Nets.
♦ Welcome; some weekend
restrictions.
♦ £25.
♦ By arrangement.
♦ Contact local clubs.

9C 23 Burntisland
Burntisland, Fife, KY3 9LQ
♦ www.burtisheadgolfhouseclub
.co.uk
☎ 01592 872116, Fax 873247,
Pro 873116, Rest/Bar 874083
Course is on the B923 0.5 miles E of
Burntisland.
Parkland course.
Pro Paul Wytrazek; Founded 1897
Designed by J Braid
18 holes, 5965 yards, S.S.S. 70
♦ Welcome except competition days.
♦ WD £17; WE £25; concessions
apply for juniors.
♦ Welcome except on comp days;
contact manager for starting times;
£10 per head deposit; catering
packages by arrangement; terms on
application.

♦ Full clubhouse bar and catering:
facilities 8am-8pm.
♦ Inchview; Kingswood.

9C 24 Caird Park
Mains Loan, Dundee, Tayside, DD4 9BX
☎ 01382 453606, Sec 461460,
Pro 459438
Course is reached via Kingsway to the
NE of the town.
Parkland course.
Pro Jack Black; Founded 1926
18 holes, 6352 yards, S.S.S. 70
♦ Public.
♦ Available on request – tel 438871.
♦ Book through Dundee City Council
leisure and parks dept; terms on
application.
♦ By prior arrangement; bar and
lounge facilities.
♦ Swallow; Kingsway.

9C 25 Callander
Aveland Rd, Callander, Perthshire,
FK17 8EN
callandergc@nextcall.net
☎ 01877 330090, Fax 330062,
Pro 330975
Course is off the A84 at the E end of
Callander.
Parkland course.
Pro Allen Martin; Founded 1890
Designed by Tom Morris (1890);
Redesigned by W Fernie
18 holes, 5151 yards, S.S.S. 65
♦ Small practice range.
♦ Welcome by prior arrangement.
♦ POA.
♦ Welcome by prior arrangement;
catering packages by arrangement;
from £26 for a day ticket.
♦ Full catering facilities.
♦ Abbotsford Lodge; Myrtle Inn;
Dreadnought.

9C 26 Camperdown (Municipal)
Camperdown Park, Dundee, Tayside,
DD2 4TF
☎ 01382 623398, Starter Box 432688
At Kingsway Junction of the Coupar-
Angus Road.
Parkland/wooded course.
Pro Roddy Brown; Founded 1959
Designed by Eric Brown
18 holes, 6561 yards, S.S.S. 72
♦ Welcome; pay and play.
♦ WD £20, WE £20 (approx.).
♦ Welcome by prior arrangement; on
application; from £20 (approx.).
♦ Clubhouse facilities.
♦ The Swallow. Travel Lodge
(directly outside).

9C 27 Canmore
Venturefair Ave, Dunfermline, Fife,
KY12 0PE
☎ 01383 724969, Fax 731649,
Pro 728416
Course is on the A823 one mile N of
Dunfermline.
Undulating parkland course.
Pro David Gemmel; Founded 1897
18 holes, 5432 yards, S.S.S. 66
Designed by Ben Sayers.
♦ Welcome WD; Sat after 4pm; not
on competition days.
♦ WD £16 and £22 for a day ticket;
WE £21 and £32 for a day ticket.
♦ Welcome by prior arrangement;
catering and day rates by
arrangement; from £12.
♦ Full clubhouse facilities.
♦ Several in Dunfermline.

9C 28 Carnoustie Golf Links
Links Parade, Carnoustie, Angus,
DD7 7JE
♦ www.carnoustiegolflinks.co.uk
administrator@
carnoustiegolflinks.co.uk
☎ 01241 853789, Fax 852720,
Pro 411999, Sec 853789, Rest/Bar
411999
Course is on the A930 12 miles NE of
Dundee.
Open Championship links.
Pro Colin Sinclair; Founded 1842
Designed by A Robertson; Tom Morris;
James Braid
Three 18-hole courses, 5420/6020/
6941 yards, S.S.S. 75
♦ Welcome by prior arrangement;
WE restrictions.
♦ WD up to £80; WE up to £80.
♦ Welcome by prior arrangement;
catering by arrangement; also
Burnside course: 18 holes 6020 yards;
£30 per round. Buddon links: 18 holes,
5420 yards; £25 per round.
♦ Full clubhouse facilities.

9C 29 Charleton
Colinsburgh, Fife, KY9 1HG
♦ www.carlton.co.uk
bonde@charlton.co.uk
☎ 01333 340505, Fax 340583
0.5 miles W of Colinsburgh on B942.
Parklands course.
Pro Andy Huddon; Founded 1994
Designed by Johnny Salversson
18 holes, 6343 yards, S.S.S. 71
♦ 12 bays; nets.
♦ Welcome; pay and play course.
♦ WD £20; WE £24; day tickets. WD
£32; WD £38.
♦ Rates for groups of 15 or more.

🍽 Restaurant; bar.
🛏 Victoria hotel.

9C 30 Comrie
Laggan Braes, Comrie, Perthshire,
PH6 2LR
🖳 www.comriegolf.co.uk
📧 renquiries@comriegolf.co.uk
☎ 01764 670055
On A85 7 miles W of Crieff; course
signposted from village.
Founded 1891
9 holes, 6040 yards, S.S.S. 70
† Welcome; restrictions after 4.30pm
Mon and Tues.
Ⅰ WD details on application.
⟋ Welcome by arrangement; catering
by arrangement; from £10.
🍽 Light refreshments; coffee; teas.
🛏 Royal; Earnbank.

9C 31 Cowdenbeath
Seco Place, Cowdenbeath, Nr
Dunfermline, Fife, KY4 8PD
☎ 01383 511918, Sec 611251
6 miles E of Dunfermline.
Parkland course.
Founded 1990/1998
18 holes, S.S.S. 70
Ⅰ Practice range.
† Welcome.
Ⅰ WD £14; WE £22.
⟋ Welcome by arrangement; catering
by prior arrangement; from £10.
🍽 Bar and snacks available.
🛏 Halfway House; Kingseat.

9C 32 Craigie Hill ☎
Cherrybank, Perth, Perthshire,
PH2 0NE
📧 chgc@fairieswell.freeserve.co.uk
☎ 01738 624377, Fax 620829,
Pro 622644, Sec 620829
1 mile W of Perth with easy access
from A9 and M90.
Hilly course with wonderful views.
Pro Ian Muir; Founded 1911
Designed by W Ferne and J Anderson
18 holes, 5386 yards, S.S.S. 67
† Welcome; bookings required on Sun.
Ⅰ Terms on application.
⟋ Welcome WD and some Sun by
prior arrangement; catering by
arrangement; from £18.
🍽 Full facilities. Not Mon.
🛏 Lovat.

9C 33 Crail Golfing Society
Balcomie Clubhouse, Fifeness, Crail,
KY10 3XN
🖳 www.golfagent.com/clubsites/crial

📧 crialgolfs@aol.com
☎ 01333 450686, Fax 450416,
Pro 450960, Sec 451414,
Rest/Bar 450278
Course is 11 miles SE of St Andrews
on the A917. Seventh oldest club in
world; moved from Sauchope in 1895.
Links course
Pro Graeme Lennie; Founded
1786/1895
Designed by Tom Morris
† Welcome.
Ⅰ WD £30; WE £35.
⟋ Full catering facilities.
🍽 Full service with views over course
and N Sea.
🛏 Club can supply detailed list.

9C 34 Crieff
Perth Rd, Crieff, Perthshire, PH7 3LR
☎ 01764 652397, Fax 653803,
Pro 652909
Course is on the A85 on the E edge of
Crieff.
Parkland ferntower course.
Pro David Murchie; Founded 1891
Designed by Old Tom Morris/R
Simpson (1914)/J Braid (1924)/J Stark
& J Freeman (1980)
27 holes, 6450 yards, S.S.S. 72
† Welcome.
Ⅰ WD from £23; WE from £30. June,
July, August, Sept WD £26, WE £35.
⟋ Welcome; catering by
arrangement; from £20.
🍽 Full clubhouse facilities.
🛏 Crieff Hydro; Murray Park; Foulford
Inn.

9C 35 Cupar ☎
Hilltarvit, Cupar, KY15 5JT
📧 secretary@cupargolfclub.freeserve
.co.uk
☎ 01334 653549, Fax 653549
25 miles on Ceres Rd; SE outskirts of
Cupar; 9 miles from St Andrews.
National Trust parkland course; oldest
9-hole course in country.
Founded 1855
Designed by Alan Robertson
9 holes, 5074 yards, S.S.S. 65
† Welcome except Sat.
Ⅰ WD £15; WE £15.
⟋ Welcome; discounts available;
private room; catering by arrangement;
from £12.
🍽 Snacks and meals.
🛏 Eden House.

9C 36 Dalmunzie
Spittal of Glenshee, Blairgowrie,
Perthshire, PH10 7QG

🖳 www.dalmunzie.com
📧 reservations@dalmunzie.com
☎ 01250 885226, Fax 885226,
Rest/Bar 885224
On A93 Blairgowrie to Braemar Rd; 18
miles N of Blairgowrie.
Hilly upland course.
Founded 1922
Designed by Alister MacKenzie
9 holes, 2099 yards, S.S.S. 30
† Everyone welcome.
Ⅰ WD/WE £12.
⟋ Welcome by arrangement;
discounts of 10 per cent for more than
10 on WD; terms available on
application.
🍽 Facilities in hotel.
🛏 Dalmunzie House.

9C 37 Dollar ☎
Brewlands House, Dollar,
Clackmannanshire, FK14 7EA
🖳 http://mysite.freeserve.com/
dollargolfclub
📧 dollar.gc@brewlandshouse
.freeserve.co.uk
☎ 01259 742400, Fax 743497
In Dollar, signposted, 0.5 miles off the
A91.
Hillside course; 2nd Brae is 97 yards.
Founded 1890
Designed by Ben Sayers
18 holes, 5242 yards, S.S.S. 66
† Welcome except competition days.
Ⅰ WD £13.50; WE £22.
⟋ Welcome by prior arrangement;
packages (WD £30 WE £35) include
36 holes of golf and full day's catering;
maximum 36.
🍽 Full clubhouse facilities.
🛏 Castle Campbell Hotel.

9C 38 Downfield
Turnberry Ave, Dundee, Tayside,
DD2 3QP
🖳 www.downfieldgolf.co.uk
📧 downfieldgc@aol.com
☎ 01382 825595, Fax 813111,
Pro 889246, Sec 825595
Follow Kingsway to A923; right into
Faraday St then first left to Harrison
Road; left at Dalmahoy Drive and
sharp left to club.
Championship parkland course;
Qualifying course for 1999 Open.
Pro Kenny Hutton; Founded 1932
Designed by James Braid
18 holes, 6803 yards, S.S.S. 73
† Welcome WD; restrictions at WE.
Ⅰ Terms on application.
⟋ Welcome by arrangement; special
packages available for golf and
catering; terms on application.

🍽 Full clubhouse facilities.
🛏 Gourdie Croft; Swallow, both Dundee; Invercarse Hotel.

9C 39 Drumoig Hotel and Golf Course
Leuchars, St Andrews, Fife, KY16 0BE
🖥 www.drumoigleisure.com
📧 drumoig@sol.co.uk
☎ 01382 541800, Fax 542211
From Forth Rd bridge exit M90 at Junction 2A Follow A92 to Glenrothes then remain on this road following signs for Tay Bridge when you reach Forgan roundabout go right onto the St Andrews road. Drumoig is down the hill on the left hand side.
Parkland course.
Founded 1996
18 holes, 6376 yards, S.S.S. 70
ⅼ Onsite practice facility.
† Welcome all week.
ⅼ WD £28; WE £33.
⌁ Special rates for 8 or more.
🍽 Full facilities.

9C 40 The Duke's Course (St Andrews)   ₢
St Andrews, Fife, KY16 9SP
🖥 www.oldcoursehotel.co.uk
☎ 01334 474371
Five minutes drive from the centre of St Andrews.
Classic Scottish parkland course.
Founded 1995
Designed by Peter Thomson
18 holes, 7271 yards, S.S.S. 75
ⅼ 10 bays and practice area.
† Welcome.
ⅼ £50 – £55.
⌁ Welcome any time.
🍽 Clubhouse facilities include bar restaurant and Boardroom for private dining and meetings.
🛏 Old Course Hotel Golf Resort & Spa.

9C 41 Dunblane New
Perth Rd, Dunblane, Stirlingshire, FK15 0LJ
🖥 www.dngc.co.uk
📧 secretary@dngc.co.uk
☎ 01786 821521, Fax 825281, Pro 81521, Sec 821527
Course is six miles N of Stirling on the old A9 at the Fourways roundabout.
Parkland course.
Pro Bob Jamieson; Founded 1923
Designed by James Braid and Cecil Hutchison
18 holes, 5957 yards, S.S.S. 69
† Welcome WD; restrictions at WE.
ⅼ Terms on application.

⌁ Welcome Mon, Thurs and Fri by prior arrangement; catering packages by arrangement; tennis and squash adjacent; terms available on application.
🍽 Full clubhouse facilities.
🛏 Dunblane Hilton Hydro; Stirling Arms.

9C 42 Dunfermline   ₢
Pitfirrane, Crossford, Dunfermline, Fife, KY12 8QW
📧 pitfirrane@aol.com
☎ 01383 723534, Pro 729061
On S of A994 2 miles W of Dunfermline on the road to the Kincardine Bridge.
Parkland course.
Pro Steven Craig; Founded 1887
Designed by JR Stutt & Sons
18 holes, 6126 yards, S.S.S. 70
ⅼ Buggy hire.
† Welcome WD and Sun between 0930-1630; not Sat.
ⅼ WD £25; Sun £35.
⌁ Welcome WD and Sun by arrangement; day ticket WD from £35; Sun from £35; catering by arrangement.
🍽 Bar and restaurant facilities.
🛏 Keavil; Pitfirran Arms; The Maltings.

9C 43 Dunkeld & Birnam
Fungarth, Dunkeld, Perthshire, PH8 0HU
📧 richbrrnc@aol
☎ 01350 727524, Fax 728660
Course is on the A923 one mile N of Dunkeld.
Heathland course with panoramic views.
Founded 1892
18 holes, 5511 yards, S.S.S. 67
† Welcome.
ⅼ WD £22; WE £27.
⌁ Welcome by prior arrangement; catering packages by prior arrangement; from £8.50.
🍽 Full bar and catering facilities.
🛏 Royal Dunkeld; Stakis Dunkeld House Resort.

9C 44 Dunnikier Park
Dunnikier Way, Kirkcaldy, Fife, KY1 3LP
📧
raymondjohnston@blueyonder.co.uk
☎ 01592 261599
Leave A92 at Kirkcaldy West roundabout and join B981 for 1 mile.
Parkland course.

Pro Gregor Whyte; Founded 1963
Designed by R Stutt
18 holes, 6601 yards, S.S.S. 72
† Welcome; invitation needed for clubhouse.
ⅼ Terms on application.
⌁ Welcome by prior arrangement with Sec; catering packages by arrangement; terms on application.
🍽 Full catering facilities.
🛏 Dunnikier House; Dean Park.

9C 45 Dunning
Rollo Park, Dunning, Perth, PH2 0RG
☎ 01764 684747, Sec 684987
Off A9 9 miles SW of Perth on B9141.
Parkland course.
Founded 1952
9 holes, 4894 yards, S.S.S. 64
† Welcome except on WE.
ⅼ WD £14 £16 WE.
⌁ Welcome WD and most Sun; WD price £14; from £10.
🍽 Soft and hot drinks in clubhouse; meals by prior application; in village hotels.
🛏 Kirks Hotel and Dunning Hotel.

9C 46 Edzell   ₢
High St, Edzell, by Brechin, Angus, DD9 7TF
🖥 www.edzellgolfclub.net
📧 secretary@edzellgolfclub.net
☎ 01356 648462, Fax 648094, Pro 648462, Sec 647283
Take B996 off the A90 at the N end of the Brechin by-pass.
Parkland course.
Pro Alastair Webster; Founded 1895
Designed by Bob Simpson
18/9 holes, 6348/4144 yards, S.S.S. 71/61
ⅼ Practice range, driving range, 9 bays, floodlight.
† Welcome.
ⅼ WD £25; WE £31.
⌁ Welcome; some restrictions; by prior arrangement with Sec; catering by prior arrangement; driving range; terms available on application.
🍽 Full clubhouse bar and restaurant facilities.
🛏 Glenesk; Panmure, both Edzell.

9C 47 Elie Sports Club
Elie, Fife, KY9 1AS
☎ 01333 330955, Sec 330508, Rest/Bar 331132
Course is on the A917 10 miles S of St Andrews.
Seaside course.
Pro Robin Wilson; Founded 1900

Designed by James Baird
9 holes, 4160 yards, S.S.S. 64
⊺ Six covered bays & six outdoor
bays.
† Welcome.
⌐ Day ticket WD £10; WE £10.
⌐ᗏ Welcome by prior arrangement;
packages available; terms on
application.
🍽 Clubhouse facilities.
⌐ᗏ Old Manor; Lundin Links; Victoria
Hotel.

9C 48 Elmwood ⊺

Stratheden, Nr Cupar, Fife, KY15 5RS
ᕀ www.elmwoodgc.co.uk
✉ clubhouse@elmwoodgc.co.uk
☎ 01334 658780, Fax 658781
Signposted both from A91 and A94,
one mile W of Cupar and only 9 miles
from St Andrews.
Parkland course.
Pro Graeme McDowall; Founded 1997
18 holes, 6000 yards, S.S.S. 68, Par
70
⊺ Practice area.
† Welcome at all times.
⌐ WD £18; WE £22.
⌐ᗏ Welcome at all times with
discounts for groups over 12 and 20.
🍽 Clubhouse with full licensed
restaurant, open to all visitors and non-
golfers.

9C 49 Falkirk ⊺

136 Stirling Rd, Camelon, FK2 7YP
ᕀ www.falkirkcarmuirsgolfclub.co.uk
✉ carmuirsfgc@virgin.net
☎ 01324 611061, Fax 639573,
Pro 612219, Sec 639573
On A9 1.5 miles N of Falkirk.
Parkland course.
Pro Stewart Craig; Founded 1922
Designed by James Braid
18 holes, 6230 yards, S.S.S. 70
⊺ Practice area.
† Welcome WD; not Sat.
⌐ WD £20 round, £30 day.
⌐ᗏ Welcome WD and Sun by prior
arrangement; catering by arrangement;
£30.
🍽 Full clubhouse facilities.
⌐ᗏ Stakis Park Hotel.

9C 50 Falkirk Tryst ⊺

86 Burnhead Rd, Larbert, FK5 4BD
☎ 01324 562415, Fax 562054,
Pro 562091, Sec 562054, Rest/Bar
570436
On A88 5 miles N of Falkirk close to
the A9 Falkirk-Stirling road.
Links course.

Pro Steven Dunsmore; Founded 1885
18 holes, 6053 yards, S.S.S. 69
† Welcome WD by prior
arrangement.
⌐ WD £22.
⌐ᗏ Welcome WD by prior
arrangement; catering packages by
arrangement; from £22.
🍽 Full facilities.
⌐ᗏ Stakis Park; Airth Castle; Airth;
Plough; Stenhousemuir; Commercial
Larbert.

9C 51 Falkland

The Myre, Falkland, Cupar, Fife,
KY15 7AA
☎ 01337 857404
In the Howe of Fife near to Freuchie
and Auchtermuchty.
Parkland course.
Founded 1976
9 holes, 4988 yards, S.S.S. 65
† Welcome but restricted on
competition days.
⌐ WD £7.50; WE £10 (under review).
⌐ᗏ Welcome by prior arrangement;
packages available; terms on
application.
🍽 Full facilities (restricted at present)
– phone for arrangements.
⌐ᗏ Hunting Lodge.

9C 52 Forfar

Cunninghill, Arbroath Rd, Forfar,
Angus, DD8 2RL
ᕀ www.forfargolfclub.com
✉ forfargolfclub@uku.co.uk
☎ 01307 462120, Fax 468495,
Pro 465683, Sec 463773
From A90 to Forfar centre; course is
one mile E of town on the A932
Arbroath road.
Parkland course.
Pro Peter McNiven; Founded 1871
Designed by James Braid
18 holes, 6066 yards, S.S.S. 70
† Welcome by prior appointment.
⌐ Terms on application.
⌐ᗏ Welcome between 10am-11.30am
and 2.30pm-4pm except Sat morning;
day tickets available; catering by
arrangement.
🍽 Full clubhouse facilities available.
⌐ᗏ Chapelbank Forfar.

9C 53 Glenalmond

Glenalmond, Perth, Perthshire,
PH1 3RY
☎ 01738 842003, Fax 842014
Moorland course; part of Glenalmond
College.
Founded 1923

Designed by James Braid
9 holes, 4801 yards, S.S.S. 68
† No casual visitors. Members only.
⌐ Terms on application.

9C 54 Glenbervie ⊺

Stirling Rd, Larbert, Stirlingshire,
FK5 4SJ
ᕀ www.glenberviegolfclub.com
✉ secretary@glenberviegolfclub
.fsnet.co.uk
☎ 01324 562505, Fax 551504,
Pro 562725, Rest/Bar 562983
M876 J2 left on to A9; club 300 yards.
Parkland course.
Pro David Ross; Founded 1932
Designed by James Braid
18 holes, 6423 yards, S.S.S. 71
† Welcome WD.
⌐ WD £30.
⌐ᗏ Welcome Tues and Thurs by prior
arrangement; packages for 18/36 holes
of golf and catering; from £40.
🍽 Full clubhouse facilities.

9C 55 Gleneagles Hotel ⊺

Auchterarder, Perthshire, PH3 1NF
☎ 01764 662231
Halfway between Perth and Stirling on
the A9.
Inland links/moorland course.
18 holes, 6471 yards, S.S.S. 69
⊺ Practice range for members and
residents only.
† Welcome.
⌐ WD from £75 and up to £100.
Reduced rates for residents.
⌐ᗏ Welcome; catering packages by
arrangement; also 9-hole par 3 course;
country club for residents; health spa;
clay target shooting school; equestrian
centre; terms on application.
🍽 Full clubhouse bar and grill
facilities; full hotel restaurant
conference centre and bars.
⌐ᗏ Gleneagles Hotel.

9C 56 Glenrothes

Golf Course Rd, Glenrothes, Fife,
KY6 2LA
☎ 01592 758686
Leave M90 at Junction 3; A92 for
Glenrothes; follow signs for Whitehill
Industrial Estate.
Parkland course.
Founded 1958
Designed by JR Stutt
18 holes, 6444 yards, S.S.S. 71
† Welcome.
⌐ Available on request.
⌐ᗏ Welcome by prior arrangement;
catering available by arrangement with

steward; groups of 12-40 only; day tickets available; terms on application.
🍽 Full bar and catering facilities.
🛏 Holiday Inn; Rescobie Hotel.

9C 57 Golf House
Elie, Leven, Fife, KY9 1AS
✉ sandy@golfhouseclub.freeserve.co.uk
☎ 01333 330327, Fax 330895, Pro 330955, Sec 330301
Course is on the A915 12 miles S of St Andrews.
Links course; Ladies club: Elie & Earlsferry GC.
Pro Robin Wilson; Founded 1875
18 holes, 6241 yards, S.S.S. 70
⚐ 3 Driving range bays and practice green.
† Welcome after 10am; ballot in July & August; no Sun visitors May-Sept.
⚑ WD £38, £50 per day; WE £48, £60 per day.
⚐ Welcome except in July and August; day rates.
🍽 Full catering and bar.
🛏 Craw's Nest Anstruther.

9C 58 Grangemouth
Polmonthill, by Falkirk, Stirlingshire, FK2 0YE
☎ 01324 503840, Pro 503040, Rest/Bar 711500
M9 J4; follow signs to Polmonthill.
Parkland course.
Pro Greg McFarlane; Founded 1973
Designed by Sportwork
18 holes, 6314 yards, S.S.S. 70
† Welcome.
⚑ WD £15; WE £19.
⚐ Welcome by prior arrangement; catering by prior arrangement; from £14.00.
🍽 Clubhouse facilities available.
🛏 Inchrya; Grange; Lea Park.

9C 59 Green Hotel
2 The Muirs, Kinross, KY13 7AS
🖥 www.green-hotel.com
✉ golf@green-hotel.com
☎ 01577 863407, Fax 863180, Pro 865125, Rest/Bar 862237
Course is opposite Green Hotel, Kinross (J6 on M90).
Parkland course.
Pro A Crerar; Founded 1991
Designed by Sir David Montgomery
Red: 18 holes, 6256 yards, S.S.S. 71
Blue: 18 holes, 6384 yards, S.S.S. 72
† Welcome.
⚑ WD £22 round, £22 day; WE £33 round, £45 day (Red and Blue).

⚐ Welcome; catering in hotel or clubhouse by arrangement.
🍽 Full facilities at hotel and clubhouse.
🛏 Green Hotel.

9C 60 Kenmore Golf Course ♺
Kenmore, Aberfeldy, Perthshire, PH15 2HN
🖥 www.taymouth.co.uk
✉ info@taymouth.co.uk
☎ 01887 830226, Fax 8290591, Pro 830226, Sec 830226, Rest/Bar 830775
On A827 through Kenmore village.
Slightly undulating parkland course.
Pro Finlay Menzies; Founded 1992
Designed by R Menzies
9 holes, 6052 yards, S.S.S. 69
† Welcome.
⚑ WD £15; WE £16.
⚐ Welcome by arrangement; catering packages available; £22.
🍽 Full service.
🛏 Kenmore.

9C 61 Killin ♺
Killin, Perthshire, FK21 8TX
🖥 www.killingolfclub.co.uk
✉ info@killingolfclub.co.uk
☎ 01567 820312, Sec 01764 683778
W end of Loch Tay on A827 Killin to Aberfeldy road.
Parkland course; 5th/14th is The Dyke 96 yards.
Founded 1911
Designed by John Duncan of Stirling
9 holes, 5016 yards, S.S.S. 65
† Welcome.
⚑ WD/WE £18.
⚐ Welcome by prior arrangement; full packages available; from £12.
🍽 Full catering and bar facilities.
🛏 Bridge of Lochay; Killin; Clachaig.

9C 62 King James VI ♺
Moncreiffe Island, Perth, Perthshire, PH2 8NR
🖥 www.kingjamesvi.co.uk
☎ 445132 (fax), Pro 632460, Sec 445132
In the centre of the River Tay; access by footpath from Tay Street or Shore Road.
Parkland course; one of only two courses on river island in the world.
Pro A Coles; Founded 1858/1897
Designed by Tom Morris
18 holes, 6038 yards, S.S.S. 68
⚐ Practice ground, putting green, nets.
† Welcome by prior arrangement but not Sat.

⚑ Terms on application.
⚐ Welcome by prior arrangement with the Pro; catering by arrangement; from £18.
🍽 Full facilities.
🛏 Salutation; Royal George; Isle of Skye.

9C 63 Kinghorn
Macduff Crescent, Kinghorn, Fife, KY3 9RE
☎ 01592 890345
Off A92 3 miles W of Kirkcaldy.
Undulating links course.
Founded 1887
Designed by layout recommended by Tom Morris
18 holes, 5166 yards, S.S.S. 66
† Welcome.
⚑ WD £9; WE £12.
⚐ Welcome by prior written arrangement; groups of 12-30; catering packages by arrangement; from £9.
🍽 Full catering facilities.
🛏 Kingswood; Longboat.

9C 64 Kingsbarns Links
Kingsbarns, Fife, KY16 8QD
🖥 www.kingsbarns.com
✉ info@kingsbarns.com
☎ 01334 460860, Fax 460877, Rest/Bar 460867
6 miles SE of St Andrews on the A917.
Links course.
Pro David Scott; Founded 2000
Designed by Kyle Phillips
18 holes, 6174 yards
⚐ Driving range with complimentary balls.
† Pay and play – book in advance.
⚑ £125 (June-Nov).
⚐ Welcome by appointment.
🍽 Full Catering facilities and Bar.
🛏 Hotels in Crail & St Andrews.

9C 65 Kirkcaldy ♺
Balwearie Rd, Kirkcaldy, Fife, KY2 5LT
☎ 01592 260370, Fax 205240, Pro 203258
On A92 at W end of town.
Parkland course.
Pro A Caira; Founded 1904
Designed by Tom Morris
18 holes, 6038 yards, S.S.S. 69
† Welcome; some restrictions Sat.
⚑ WD £24; WE £30.
⚐ Welcome by prior arrangement; restrictions Sat; day rates and catering packages available; from £16.
🍽 Full clubhouse facilities.
🛏 Parkway Hotel; Dunnikier House.

Royal Montrose

Scottish golf is steeped in history and nowhere more so than at Montrose where the royal and ancient game has been played since the middle of the 16th century. Today, this attractive Angus burgh features two fine courses, the 6,495 yard Medal and the 4,830 yard Broomfield – both excellent examples of how the game used to be played before it spread inland.

The Medal course at Montrose is a classic links which deserves to be celebrated much more than it is. It might not exude the charm of the Old Course, or provide as daunting a challenge as nearby Carnoustie, but it still offers a superb test, good enough to stage the Scottish Amateur Championship, the Scottish Professional Championship and numerous Open Qualifiers.

Details about the origins of golf in Montrose are somewhat sketchy but what we do know is that James Melville (1556–1614), an eminent theologian and a former Moderator of the Church of Scotland, learned to "use the glubb for goff" there as a six year old. Sir Robert Gordon of Gordonston also wrote about the links of "Montrois" in 1628 and in 1629 it spawned the first recorded golf widow.

The unfortunate woman was none other than Mistress Magdalene Carnegie who married James Graham, a son of the 1st Marquis of Montrose, in November of that year. His diary shows that on the morning of the wedding he played golf with his future brother-in-law, the Laird of Lusse. He enjoyed another round after the ceremony and continued to wear out the links on a regular basis until 1650 when he was hung, drawn and quartered as a traitor, having backed the wrong side in the English Civil War.

Graham came to a sticky end but golf in his home town continued to prosper. On January 1st, 1810, The Montrose Golf Club was instituted, making it the ninth or tenth oldest club in the world. Thirty-five years later it became Montrose Royal Albert Golf Club when His Royal Highness, Prince Albert, became the club's patron.

It is a wonder that Prince Albert continued to be the patron of the club after receiving another letter of monstrous obsequiousness. The letter is packed with phrases such as "deepest respect", "the medium of this address" (a letter), "loyal and heartfelt congratulations", "respectfully expressing our grateful thanks", "gracious condescension" and so on. The request was that the Prince might turn up for a speech, but (in the words of the club's historian) he was probably so bored by their refusal to take 'yes' for an answer, that he turned the club down.

In 1986, the Royal Albert Club merged with the Victoria Club and the captain wrote to the palace asking that the club could change its name to the Royal Montrose Club. Permission was duly granted and the club's present Patron is His Royal Highness, Prince Andrew, Duke of York.

During the middle of the nineteenth century, Montrose links could claim to have more holes than any other course. Whereas Musselburgh had seven to nine holes and St Andrews had just introduced 18, Montrose had no less than 25 and they were all used in 1866 for an open event that attracted two past Open champions, Willie Park and Andrew Strath, but was won by Glaswegian, Tom Doleman, with a score of 112.

Nowadays, of course, convention dictates there are just 18 holes. The current layout owes much to the design capabilities of Willie Park who was brought in to modernize the layout in 1903. In the 1920s a shorter second course, the Broomfield, was established and today both are administered by the local Links Trust with representation from the local clubs. – **Colin Callander**

Crusoe Hotel
2 Main Street, Lower Largo, Fife KY8 6BT • **STB ★★★**

The birthplace of Robinson Crusoe

Great Waterside location with it's own harbour just 10 minutes from St Andrews. We are in the heart of golf country with Lundin Links, Elie, Crail, Ladybank and St Andrews all within 15 minutes drive. Two bars and popular local restaurant help to make this a great location for a golf break. B&B from £30.00 per person.

Tel: **01333 320759** • E-mail: **relax@crusoehotel.co.uk** • Web: **crusoehotel.co.uk**

9C 66 Kirriemuir
Northmuir, Kirriemuir, Angus, DD8 4LN
🖳 www.kirriemuirgc@aol.com
☎ 01575 573317, Fax 574608,
Sec 572144
N of Kirriemuir and accessible from
A90 Dundee-Aberdeen road.
Parkland course.
Pro Karyn Dallas; Founded 1908
Designed by James Braid
18 holes, 5510 yards, S.S.S. 67
† Welcome WD.
Ⅰ POA.
⟳ Welcome by prior arrangement;
day tickets available; catering and
hospitality packages available; £5 pp
deposit required; from £16.
🍽 Full catering packages.
⬛ Airlie Arms; Thrums: Castleton
Park; Chapelbank.

9C 67 Ladybank
Annsmuir, Ladybank, Fife, KY15 7RA
🖳 www.ladybankgolf.co.uk
🖳 ladybank@aol.com
☎ 01337 830814, Fax 831505,
Pro 830725, Rest/Bar 830320
In Ladybank half mile from A91/A92
intersection on A92 towards Kirkcaldy.
Heathland course.
Pro Martin Gray; Founded 1879
Designed by Tom Morris
18 holes, 6601 yards, S.S.S. 72
Ⅰ Practice area.
† Welcome WD and some Sun by
arrangement; handicap certs preferred.
Ⅰ WD £45; WE £50. April to Oct ,
day ticket £55.
⟳ Welcome WD by prior
arrangement with the secretary;
catering packages available; names
and handicaps of all players required 7
days before arrival; dining room for 70;
from £30.
🍽 Full clubhouse bar and catering
facilities.
⬛ Club can provide a list of local
hotels.

9C 68 Leslie
Balsillie, Leslie, Fife, KY6 3EZ
☎ 01592 620040
Leave M90 at Junctions 5 or 7; Leslie
11 miles.

Undulating course.
Founded 1898
9 holes, 4940 yards, S.S.S. 64
† Welcome.
Ⅰ WD £8.50; WE £10.50.
⟳ Welcome by arrangement; catering
by arrangement; from £8.50.
🍽 Clubhouse facilities.
⬛ Greenside; Rescobie.

9C 69 Letham Grange Resort ℧
Colliston, by Arbroath, Angus, DD11 4RL
🖳 lethamgrange@sol.co.uk
☎ 01241 890377, Fax 890725
Follow Letham Grange signs in
Arbroath from Dundee-Arbroath road.
Parkland course.
Pro Steven Moir; Founded 1987
Designed by Donald Steel
2 x 18 holes, 6968 yards, S.S.S. 73
Ⅰ Practice facilities.
† Welcome; some restrictions at WE.
Ⅰ WD £35 WE £40 (Old); WD £18,
WE £22.50 (Glens); combination rates
available from £40.
⟳ Welcome by prior arrangement;
catering packages available; contact
Ben Greenhill at club; from £25.
🍽 Full clubhouse facilities.
⬛ 4-star Letham Grange.

9C 70 Leven Golfing Society
PO Box 14609, Links Rd, Leven, Fife,
KY8 4HS
🖳 lgs@bosinternet.com
☎ 01333 426096, Fax 424229,
Sec 424229, Rest/Bar 426096
Enter Leven on A915 from Kirkcaldy
and follow signs to the Beach.
Seaside links course.
Founded 1820
18 holes, 6427 yards, S.S.S. 70
† Welcome; not before 9.30am WD;
10.30am WE.
Ⅰ WD £32; WE £37.
⟳ Welcome by prior arrangement;
catering packages by arrangement;
snooker table; from £32.
🍽 Full catering facilities.
⬛ Caledonian Hotel.

9C 71 Lochgelly
Cartmore Road, Lochgelly, Fife, KY5 9PB

☎ 01592 780174, Pro 782589,
Sec, 01383 512238, Rest/Bar 780174
On A910 2 miles NE of Cowdenbeath.
Parkland course.
Pro Martin Goldie; Founded 1896/1911
18 holes, 5454 yards, S.S.S. 67
† Everyone welcome.
Ⅰ WD £12; WE £23 for a full day.
⟳ Welcome by prior arrangement;
terms on application.
🍽 By arrangement only. Always
available.

9C 72 Lundin
Golf Rd, Lundin Links, Fife, KY8 6BA
🖳 www.lundingolfclub.co.uk
🖳 secretary@lundingolfclub.co.uk
☎ 01333 320202, Fax 329743,
Pro 320051
On seaward side of the village on
East Neuk Coast Road from Kirkcaldy.
Seaside links course.
Pro David Webster
Founded 1868
Designed by James Braid
18 holes, 6371 yards, S.S.S. 71
† Welcome between 9am-3.30pm
Mon-Thurs; 9am-3pm Fri; after 2.30pm
Sat; some limited tee times on
Sundays.
Ⅰ WD £40; WE £50.
⟳ Welcome by prior arrangement
with Sec; WD ticket of £40; full catering
available.
🍽 Full facilities.
⬛ The Old Manor; The Lundin Links;
The Crusoe.

9C 73 Lundin Ladies
Woodielea Road, Lundin Links, Fife,
KY8 6AR
🖳 www.lundinladies.co.uk
🖳 secretary@lundinladies.co.uk
☎ 01333 320832, Sec 320832
10 miles East of Kirkcaldy on A915 on
N side of road in village of Lundin
Links.
Parkland course.
Founded 1891
Designed by James Braid
9 holes, 4730 yards, S.S.S. 67
† Visitors welcome including men.
Green fees may vary between summer
and winter.

⟋ Terms on application.
⟲ Block bookings available except Wed April-August; contact clubhouse for further information.
🍴 Tea and Coffee available.
🛏 Lundin Links; Old Manor Hotel.

9C 74 Milnathort

South St, Milnathort, Kinross, KY13 9XA
✉ milnathortgolf@ukgateway.net
☎ 01577 864069
1 mile N of Kinross leaving M90 at Junction 6(N)/Junction 7(S).
Undulating course with trees.
Founded 1910
9 holes, 5993 yards, S.S.S. 69
⟋ Practice range.
† Everyone welcome.
⟋ WD £12; WE £14.
⟲ Welcome by prior arrangement; catering by arrangement with clubmaster; from £16.
🍴 Clubhouse facilities.
🛏 Jolly Beggars; Thistle; Royal.

9C 75 Monifieth

Medal Starters Box, Princes St, Monifieth, Angus, DD5 4AW
☎ 01382 532678, Fax 535553, Pro 532945
5 miles E of Dundee on coast.
Links course.
Pro Ian McLeod; Founded 1850
18 holes, 6655 yards, S.S.S. 72
⟋ Practice range.
† Welcome.
⟋ WD £30; WE £36.
⟲ Welcome; composite tickets available with Ashludie Course (18 holes, 5123 yards, par 68).
🍴 Clubhouse facilities.
🛏 Panmure packages available; Woodlands.

9C 76 Montrose Links Trust ☎

Traill Drive, Montrose, Angus, DD10 8SW
🖳 www.montroselinks.co.uk
✉ secretary@montroselinks.co.uk
☎ 01674 672634/672932, Fax 671800
Turn off Dundee-Aberdeen A90 at Brechin and take the A935 to Montrose.
Links course.
Pro Jason Boyd
Founded 1562
Designed by Willly Park Jnr
Medal: 36 holes, 6544 yards, S.S.S. 72. Broomfield 4830 yards, S.S.S. 63.
⟋ Practice area and putting green.

† Welcome; but not before 2.45pm Sat or 10am on Sun (Medal); no restrictions on Broomfield.
⟋ Medal course: WD £38 round, £48 day, £42 composite day; WE £42-£56 day, £48 comps. Broomfield course: `WD £18; WE £20.
⟲ Welcome by prior arrangement; same restrictions as for visitors; facilities available at the 3 clubs adjacent to courses (Montrose Caledonia GC 01674 672313; Montrose Mercantile GC 672408; Royal Montrose 672376); also Broomfield course.
🍴 Catering available at member clubs.
🛏 Park Hotel; Links Hotel; George Hotel.

9C 77 Muckhart ☎

Drumburn Rd, Muckhart, by Dollar, Clackmannanshire, FK14 7JH
☎ 01259 781423, Fax 781544, Pro 781493
Off A91 6 miles E of Alloa; S of Muckhart; signposted.
Heathland course on rising ground.
Pro Keith Salmoni; Founded 1908/1971
27 holes, 6034 yards, S.S.S. 69
⟋ Practice area.
† Welcome.
⟋ WD £20; WE £25.
⟲ Welcome; catering by arrangement; £10 addition for playing 9-hole course.
🍴 Full catering and bar facilities.
🛏 Glenfargh.

9C 78 Murrayshall

Murrayshall Country House Hotel, Scone, Perthshire, PH2 7PH
🖳 www.murrayshall.co.uk
✉ info@murrayshall.co.uk
☎ 01738 554804, Fax 552595, Rest/Bar 551171
On A94 Cupar-Angus road 4 miles from Perth by Scone.
Parkland course/Woodland course.
Pro Alan Reid; Founded 1981/2000
Designed by J Hamilton Stutt
18 holes, 6441 yards, S.S.S. 72
18 holes, 5362 yards, S.S.S. 69
⟋ 18,11 of which are covered.
† Everyone welcome.
⟋ WD £30; WE £35.
WD £20; WE £25.
⟲ Welcome; packages by arrangement; from £22.
🍴 Full facilities + hotel bar/restaurants.
🛏 Murrayshall on site.

9C 79 Muthill

Peat Road, Muthill, by Crieff, Perthshire, PH5 2DA

🖳 www.muthillgolfclub.co.uk
✉ muthillgolfclub@lineone.net
☎ 01764 681523, Fax 681557, Sec 681523
From Crieff course is on right before Muthill at Bowling Green.
Undulating parkland course.
Founded 1911
Designed by members
9 holes, 4700 yards, S.S.S. 63
† Everyone welcome.
⟋ WD £15; WE £18.
⟲ Welcome but booking essential.
🍴 Meals but no bar.
🛏 The Village Inn.

9C 80 North Inch

35 Kinnoull Street, Perth, PH1 5GD
☎ 01738 476476, Fax 475210, Pro 636481
N of Perth adjacent to Gannochy Trust Sports Complex.
Tree-lined course running alongside river.
Pro Stewart Gow
18 holes, 5178 yards, S.S.S. 65
† Welcome.
⟋ WD £4.20; WE £5.25.
⟲ Welcome by prior arrangement; some summer restrictions apply.
🍴 Catering at Bell's Sports Complex.

9C 81 Panmure

Burnside Road, Barry, Carnoustie, DD7 7RT
🖳 www.panmuregolfclub.co.uk
✉ secretary@panmuregolfclub.co.uk
☎ 01241 855120, Fax 859737, Pro 852460, Sec 855120, Rest/Bar 853120
Off A930 2 miles W of Carnoustie.
Seaside course.
Pro Neil MacKintosh; Founded 1845
18 holes, 6317 yards, S.S.S. 71
⟋ Practice range.
† Welcome except Tues am and Sat before 4pm.
⟋ WD £48; WE £48 or £64 per day.
⟲ Welcome by arrangement; catering packages by arrangement; day ticket £64.
🍴 Full facilities.
🛏 Carlogie; Panmure; Station; Woodlands; Carnoustie Hotel.

9C 82 Pitlochry

Golf Course Rd, Pitlochry, Perthshire, PH16 5QY
☎ 01796 472792, Fax473947, Rest/Bar 472334
A9 to Pitlochry then via Atholl Rd, Larchwood Rd to Golf Course road.

Undulating course.
Pro Mark Pirie; Founded 1908
Designed by Willie Fernie of Troon;
Modernised by Major Cecil Hutchinson
18 holes, 5811 yards, S.S.S. 69
  † Welcome by arrangement with the
Pro. Terms on application.
  ⌦ Welcome by arrangement; catering
by arrangement with Steward; terms
on application.
  ⌖ Outings welcome by arrangement;
with Pro; terms on application.
  ⦿ Full clubhouse facilities.

9C 83 Pitreavie (Dunfermline) ☎

Queensferry Rd, Dunfermline, Fife,
KY11 8PR
  ☎ 01383 722591, Fax 722591,
Pro 723151
M90 N of Forth Road Bridge; 3rd exit
signposted Dunfermline; club 3 miles.
Parkland course.
Pro Paul Brookes; Founded 1922
Designed by Dr A MacKenzie
18 holes, 6032 yards, S.S.S. 69
  ⌁ Practice area.
  † Welcome.
  ⌦ WD £19; WE £26.
  ⌖ Welcome; catering by
arrangement; terms on application.
  ⦿ Full clubhouse facilities.
  ⟿ Pitbauchlie House; King Malcolm.

9C 84 Polmont ☎

Manuelrigg Maddiston, by Falkirk,
Stirlingshire, FK2 0LS
  ☎ 01324 711277, Fax 712504,
Sec 713811
4 miles S of Falkirk 1st right after Fire
Brigade HQ.
Undulating parkland course.
Founded 1904
9 holes, 6092 yards, S.S.S. 69
  † Welcome except on Sat.
  ⌦ WD £8; WE £14.
  ⌖ Welcome by prior arrangement;
catering by arrangement with Sec;
from £14.
  ⦿ Clubhouse facilities.
  ⟿ Inchyra Grange; Polmont.

9C 86 St Andrews Bay ☎

St Andrew s, Fife, KY16 8PN
  ⌨ www.standrewsbay.com
  ✉ info@standrewsbay.com
  ☎ 01334 472664, Fax 471115
A917 from St Andrews to Crail. 2 miles
on left.
Seaside course.
Designed by Sam Torrance and Bruce
Devlin.

Torrance: 7029 yards, S.S.S. 73;
Devlin: 7039, S.S.S. 74
  ⌁ Grass range; not covered.
  † Yes.
  ⌦ £30 over winter, going into season.
  ⌖ Yes.
  ⦿ 1 restaurant/buffet à la carte, bar
with light meals all day.
  ⟿ On site.

9C 87 St Fillans

South Loch Earn Rd, St Fillans,
Perthshire, PH6 2NJ
  ⌨ www.st-fillans-golf.com
  ✉ stfillansgolf@aol.com
  ☎ 01764 685312, Fax 685312,
Sec 820422
On A85 at E end of the village.
Parkland course.
Founded 1903
Designed by W Auchterlonie
9 holes, 6043 yards, S.S.S. 69
  † Welcome.
  ⌦ WD £15; WE £20.
  ⌖ Welcome by arrangement;
maximum 24; catering by
arrangement.
  ⦿ Catering facilities; no bar.
  ⟿ Achray; Four Seasons; Drummond
Arms.

9C 88 St Michaels ☎

Leuchars, Fife, KY16 0DX
  ⌨ www.st michaels.co.uk
  ✉ stmichaelsgc@btclick.com
  ☎ 01334 839365, Fax 838789,
Sec 838666
5 miles from St Andrews on main road
to Dundee.
Undulating parkland course.
Founded 1903
18 holes, 5802 yards, S.S.S. 68
  † Welcome except before 12 noon
on Sun.
  ⌦ 7 days £25.
  ⌖ Welcome by written prior
arrangement; restrictions apply on
Sun; 36 holes of golf and full catering.
  ⦿ Full facilities.
  ⟿ St Michaels Inn; many in St
Andrews.

9C 89 Saline

Kinneddar Hill, Saline, Fife, KY12 9LT
  ☎ 01383 852591
Course is five miles NW of
Dunfermline.
Hillside course.
Founded 1912
9 holes, 5304 yards, S.S.S. 66
  † Welcome except Sat.
  ⌦ WD £9; WE £11.

9C 85 St Andrews

St Andrews Links Management
Committee, Pilmour Cottage, St
Andrews, Fife, KY16 9JA
  ☎ 01334 466666, Fax 477036,
Pro 475757, Sec 475757, Bar/Rest
473107
60 miles north of Edinburgh via
A91 to St Andrews; turning to
course is on the left before the
town; by rail to Leuchars on
Edinburgh-Dundee main line.
  ⌦ Apply for details.
  ⌖ Welcome; terms on application.
  ⦿ Clubhouse facilities and in
local hotels.
  ⟿ Full range in St Andrews from
B&B to international standard.

Old Course
18 holes, 6566 yards, S.S.S. 72
Most famous Championship links
in the world.
Founded 1400
Designed by Nature and
Tom Morris, A Robertson,
A MacKenzie
  † Welcome with handicap certs;
no play on Sun.

Balgove Course
9 holes, 1530 yards
Founded 1974
  † Welcome; children under 16
reduced prices.
  ⌦ WD £7; WE £7.

Eden Course
18 holes, 6112 yards, S.S.S. 70
Founded 1914
Designed by HS Colt
  † Public.

Jubilee Course
18 holes, 6805 yards, S.S.S. 72
Founded 1897/1989
Designed by J Angus/ Donald
Steel (1989)
  † Welcome.

New Course
18 holes, 6604 yards, S.S.S. 72
Founded 1895
Designed by Old Tom Morris
  † Welcome.

Strathtyrum Course
18 holes, 5094 yards, S.S.S. 65
Founded 1993
Designed by Donald Steel
  † Welcome.

Royal Perth

King James IV of Scotland (1473–1513) was a man who left an indelible mark on his country. Jimmy the Numeral, as American golf writer Dan Jenkins once famously labelled him, inherited the throne when he was a mere 15 years of age but that did not preclude him from practising dentistry and founding a Royal College of Surgeons in Scotland long before such an institution existed south of the border. He was also the first monarch to insist on compulsory education for his country's noblemen but arguably his most lasting contribution to Scottish society came in 1502 when he lifted a longstanding ban on playing the game of golf.

The ban had been implemented by King James II in 1457 and reinforced by King James III in 1471 in the vain hope that it would leave the local populace more time to practise their archery. However, there is ample evidence to suggest that it never worked and at the start of the 16th century James IV bowed to public pressure and legalised the royal and ancient game.

James might well also have had personal interest in mind when he legalised the game because records show that a couple of days after the announcement he purchased some clubs from a local bowmaker. That makes this enlightened monarch the first named golfer in history and by association also made Perth the oldest dated golfing location in the world.

No documentation exists to tell us where James and his cronies practised the game but what we do know is that by the 18th century golf was played on both the North and South Inches in the town.

The Perth Golfing Society was formed in 1824 and nine years later it was accorded royal status by William IV – the first club anywhere to be given the Royal accolade.

During the 19th century the city of Perth developed into something of a centre of excellence as far as the game of golf was concerned. Contemporary professionals of the calibre of Allan Robertson, Willie Park, Andra' Kirkaldy and Tom Morris Snr all made frequent visits to take part in money matches and in 1864 13-year-old Tom Morris Jnr travelled to the town to make his competitive debut in a match against Willie Greig.

Golf was blossoming in Perth but it would be wrong to suggest that its progress was altogether uninterrupted. In 1861, for example, the Town Council decided to plant trees on the North Inch as an amenity for the public. That engendered the wrath of local golfers who marched on the Inch and uprooted all the trees.

The Council chose not to enforce its tree planting policy and the golf course survived. Over the years, there have been numerous different layouts on the Inch but today's version measures a manageable 5,154 yards and features a beguiling combination of generous fairways and dramatic views of the River Tay and beyond.

One odd description says that "It looks not unlike Clapham Common". In a much earlier description the Rev. T. D. Miller wrote, "To a stranger, at the first glance, the Inch seems sadly lacking in hazards. In the park part there is ample scope for the wildest of drives. But it is when we leave the Inch and gain the peninsula that the real sport begins". – **Colin Callander**

⚲ Welcome WD and Sun only;
maximum 24; catering packages by
prior arrangement; terms on
application.
🍽 Full catering.
🛏 Saline Castle; Campbell;
Pitbauchly.

9C 90 Scoonie
North Links, Leven, Fife, KY8 4SP
🖳 www.scooniegolfclub.com
🖂 manager@scooniegolfclub.com
☎ 01333 307007, Fax 307008
10 miles SW of St Andrews.
Parkland course.
Founded 1951
18 holes, 4979 yards, S.S.S. 65
� Welcome by arrangement with
Secretary except Sat, or via the website.
⌐ WD on application.
⚲ Welcome by appointment with
Secretary; groups of 12-30; catering by
arrangement; terms on application.
🍽 Full clubhouse facilities.
🛏 Caledonian.

9C 91 Scotscraig ☎
Golf Rd, Tayport, Fife, DD6 9DZ
🖂 scotscraig@scottishgolf.com
☎ 01382 552515, Fax 553130,
Pro 552855
On B946 3 miles from S end of Tay
Road Bridge.
Links course.
Pro Stuart Campbell; Founded 1817
18 holes, 6550 yards, S.S.S. 72
♜ Welcome WD and by prior
arrangement at WE.
⌐ WD £44; WE £50.
⚲ Welcome by prior arrangement;
packages by arrangement; day tickets
WD £54; WE £60.
🍽 Full catering facilities.
🛏 Seymour; Scores; Rusacks; Russell;
Sandford.

9C 92 Stirling
Queens Rd, Stirling, Stirlingshire,
FK8 3AA
🖳 www.stirlinggolfclub.tv
🖂 enquiries@stirlinggolfclub.tv
☎ 01786 464098, Fax 460090, Pro
471490, Rest/Bar 460099
On A811 1 mile W of town.
Parkland course.
Pro Ian Collins; Founded 1869
Designed by J Braid/H Cotton
18 holes, 6438 yards, S.S.S. 71
⌐ Practice area.
♜ Welcome WD; some WE
restrictions.
⌐ WD £28; WE £28; £40 day ticket.

⚲ Welcome WD by prior
arrangement; day ticket £40; catering
by arrangement; pool table.
🍽 Full clubhouse facilities.
🛏 Golden Lion.

9C 93 Strathendrick
Glasgow Rd, Drymen, Stirlingshire,
G63 0AA
🖂 marrisonpe@aol.com
☎ 01360 660695, Fax 600567,
Sec 600567
Off A811 1 mile S of Drymen; 17 miles
NW of Glasgow.
Hilly moorland course.
Founded 1901
9 holes, 4982 yards, S.S.S. 64
♜ Welcome WD 8.30am-2.30pm
May-Sept.
⌐ WD £12.
⚲ Limited access by prior
arrangement; terms on application.
🍽 None.
🛏 Buchanan Arms; Winnock.

9C 94 Strathtay
Lyon Cottage, Strathtay, Perthshire,
PH9 0PG
☎ 01887 840211
4 miles W of Ballinlug on A827, off A9
20 miles north of Perth.
Inland course.
9 holes, 4082 yards, S.S.S. 61
♜ Welcome, no restrictions.
⌐ WD£12; WE/BH £15.
⚲ Welcome by prior arrangement;
packages available.
🍽 Full clubhouse facilities.
🛏 Riverside Hotel, Grandtully.

9C 95 Taymouth Castle ☎
Kenmore, by Aberfeldy, Tayside,
PH15 2NT
☎ 01887 830228, Fax 830228,
Rest/Bar 830397
Course 5 miles W of Aberfeldy on A827.
Parkland course.
Pro Gavin Dott
Founded 1923
Designed by James Braid
18 holes, 6066 yards, S.S.S. 69
♜ Welcome.
⌐ WD £22 WE £26.
⚲ Welcome by prior arrangement;
special packages for parties 16+.
🍽 Full clubhouse facilities.
🛏 Kenmore.

9C 96 Thornton ☎
Station Road, Thornton, Fife,
KY1 4DW

🖳 www.thorntongolfclubfife.co.uk
🖂 johntgc@ic24.net
☎ 01592 771111, Fax 774955,
Sec 771111, Rest/Bar 771161
1 mile off the A92 road at the
Redhouse roundabout midway
between Kirkcaldy and Glenrothes.
Parkland course.
Founded 1921
Designed by Members
18 holes, 6170 yards, S.S.S. 69
♜ Welcome.
⌐ Midweek round £20; midweek
day £30; WE round £30; WE day
£40.
⚲ Welcome; catering packages by
arrangement.
🍽 Full clubhouse facilities.
🛏 Rescobie; Weatherlodge, both
Glenrothes; Royal; Dean Park, all
Kirkcaldy.

9C 97 Tillicoultry
Alva Road, Tillicoultry, FK13 6BL
🖂 tilligc@stirling.co.uk
☎ 01259 750124
9 miles E of Stirling on the A91.
Undulating parkland course.
Founded 1899
Designed by Peter Robertson
9 holes, 5475 yards, S.S.S. 67
♜ Welcome by arrangement.
⌐ WD £12; WE £18.
⚲ Welcome by arrangement with
Sec; catering by prior arrangement;
terms on application.
🍽 Restaurant and bar facilities.

9C 98 Tulliallan
Alloa Rd, Kincardine on Forth,
FK10 4BB
🖳 www.tulliallan-golf-club.co.uk
🖂 enquires@tulliallangc.f9.co.uk
☎ 01259 730396, Fax 733950,
Pro 730798, Sec 730396, Rest/Bar
733953/733952
0.5 miles N of the Kincardine Bridge on
the Alloa road.
Parkland course.
Pro Stephen Kelly
Founded 1902
18 holes, 5965 yards, S.S.S. 69
⌐ Driving range.
♜ Welcome by arrangement.
⌐ WD £17.50; WE £22.
⚲ Welcome by prior arrangement
except Sat; day tickets WD: £30;
WE: £40; WD maximum group of 40;
Sun max group of 24; from £20;
catering available with booking in
advance.
🍽 Full clubhouse facilities.
🛏 Radisson Hotel, Airth Castle.

9C 99 Whitemoss
Whitemoss Road, Dunning, Perthshire,
PH2 0QX
☎ 01738 730300, Fax 774955
1 mile off the A9; 2 miles past the
Gleneagles Hotel.
Parkland course.

Founded 1994
Designed by IGolf
18 holes, 5995 yards, S.S.S. 69
✝ Welcome by arrangement.
⌷ WD £15; WE £18.
⟡ Welcome by prior arrangement;
Catering packages available by prior

arrangement; catering packages
available by prior arrangement; day
tickets £25.
▐ Full facilities.
⟿ Colon Hotel, The Smiddy Haugh.

Highlands, Grampian

When Tom Watson pitched up at Royal Dornoch in 1981 he intended to play eighteen holes, pack his bag and move on. Unable to tear himself away he played a second and then a third round before declaring, "This is the most fun I have had playing golf in my whole life". That is not a bad endorsement from a man who two years later would win his fifth Open Championship.

In 2002 Royal Dornoch celebrated its 125th anniversary although there are records of golf being played on the links as early as 1616. Donald Ross, the most famous of all American golf architects, was the pro and head greenkeeper here for a while and touches of his style linger on. The most famous hole is the fourteenth hole called "Foxy", a double dogleg with a tilting green, but void of bunkers. Harry Vardon called it "the most memorable hole in golf".

The fact that Dornoch is further north than Moscow might deter some, but it is easily accessible from Inverness airport and not as cold as you might think. Remoteness and tranquillity are part of the charm unless you are unlucky enough to be around when Guy Ritchie and Madonna are having one of their bashes.

Andrew Carnegie, of steel and music hall fame, was reputedly asked to play at Dornoch. The club has a shield in his name. But legend has it that he thought he ought to learn to play the game first so he had Skibo constructed, a course that was redesigned by Donald Steel at the start of the nineties. It is now the Carnegie Club, a fine course but prohibitively expensive.

Other notable courses at the northern extremity of Scotland are Brora, where a midnight competition is held in June, Tain, a heather and links course that offers good value, and Golspie, a course full of underfoot variety.

Back through Inverness on the south side of the Moray Firth is Nairn where the 1999 Walker Cup was held. Colin Montgomerie won the 1987 Scottish Amateur here and named his design company accordingly. The likes of Willie Whitelaw and Harold McMillan were staunch advocates of the course and area, which was known as the Brighton of the North. It is not the longest links in the world, but the glassy greens will find out anyone who has been a victim of their putter.

Inland of Inverness, close to the shores of Loch Ness, is Boat of Garten. The course is a test of accuracy and concentration as the mind is apt to be distracted by the beauty of the Cairngorms and River Spey.

East of Nairn lies Moray, the Old is better than the New, with views over the Firth, and Cruden Bay, formerly a golfing resort in the days of the railway.

The Balgownie course at Royal Aberdeen with its valleyed fairways between the dunes was described by Bernard Darwin as "much more than a good golf course – a noble links". Founded in 1780 it is one of the oldest clubs in the world, although the game was played much earlier than that. The Aberdeen register of 1565 lists golf as "an unlawful amusement".

Anyone who has seen *Local Hero* but not visited this part of Scotland will still recognise the beauty of this coastline and beauty is perhaps the greatest recommendation of the area's two lesser renowned royal courses. Duff House Royal, designed by Alister Mackenzie, is the better test of golf. Royal Tarlair is a much more mundane layout but has more spectacular scenery. But neither can be said to be up there with Dornoch or Aberdeen.

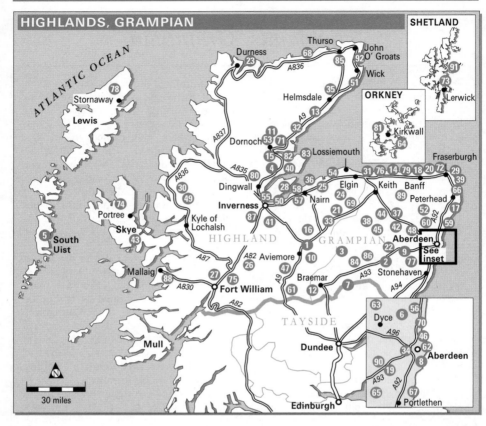

HIGHLANDS, GRAMPIAN

SHETLAND

ORKNEY

ATLANTIC OCEAN

Stornaway

Lewis

South Uist

Skye

Portree

Kyle of Lochalsh

Mallaig

Mull

Durness

Thurso

John O' Groats

Wick

Helmsdale

Dornoch

Lossiemouth

Fraserburgh

Dingwall

Inverness

Elgin

Keith

Banff

Peterhead

Nairn

Aberdeen

See inset

Aviemore

Braemar

Stonehaven

Fort William

Dyce

Aberdeen

Dundee

Portlethen

Edinburgh

Lerwick

Kirkwall

HIGHLAND

GRAMPIAN

TAYSIDE

30 miles

KEY

1	Abernethy	19	Deeside	37	Huntly	56	Murcar	75	Spean Bridge
2	Aboyne	20	Duff House Royal	38	Insch	57	Nairn	76	Spey Bay
3	Alford	21	Dufftown	39	Inverallochy	58	Nairn Dunbar	77	Stonehaven
4	Alness	22	Dunecht House	40	Invergordon	59	Newburgh-on-Ythan	78	Stornoway
5	Askernish	23	Durness	41	Inverness	60	Newmachar	79	Strathlene Buckie
6	Auchmill	24	Elgin	42	Inverurie	61	Newtonmore	80	Strathpeffer Spa
7	Ballater	25	Forres	43	Isle of Skye	62	Northern	81	Stromness
8	Balnagask (Nigg Bay)	26	Fort Augustus	44	Keith	63	Oldmeldrum	82	Tain
9	Banchory	27	Fort William	45	Kemnay	64	Orkney	83	Tarbat
10	Boat of Garten	28	Fortrose and	46	King's Links	65	Peterculter	84	Tarland
11	Bonar Bridge & Ardgay		Rosemarkie	47	Kingussie	66	Peterhead	85	Thurso
12	Braemar	29	Fraserburgh	48	Kintore	67	Portlethen	86	Torphins
13	Brora	30	Gairloch	49	Lochcarron	68	Reay	87	Torvean
14	Buckpool (Buckie)	31	Garmouth & Kingston	50	Loch Ness	69	Rothes	88	Traigh Golf Course
15	Carnegie Club	32	Golspie	51	Lybster	70	Royal Aberdeen	89	Turriff
16	Carrbridge	33	Grantown-on-Spey	52	McDonald	71	Royal Dornoch	90	Westhill
17	Cruden Bay	34	Hazlehead	53	Monk's Walk	72	Royal Tarlair	91	Whalsay
18	Cullen	35	Helmsdale	54	Moray	73	Shetland	92	Wick
		36	Hopeman	55	Muir of Ord	74	Skeabost		

9D 1 Abernethy
Nethybridge, Inverness-Shire, PH25 3EB
🖧 www.abernethygolfclub.com
📧 info@abernethygolfclub.com
☎ 01479 821305, Fax 821305,
Sec 872479
On B970 Grantown-on-Spey to Boat of
Garten road.
Undulating course with views of Spey
valley.
Founded 1893
9 holes, 4986 yards, S.S.S. 66
⚲ Practice green.
† Welcome with restrictions applying
on Sun.
⌇ WD £13; WE £16.
⚷ Welcome by arrangement with
Sec; packages available; terms on
application.
🍴 Full clubhouse facilities in
season.
↩ Nethybridge; Mountview;
Heatherbrae.

9D 2 Aboyne ☎
Formaston Park, Aboyne,
Aberdeenshire, AB34 5HP
🖧 www.aboynegolf.com
📧 aboynegolf@btinternet.com
☎ 013398 86328, Fax 87592,
Pro 86328, Sec 87078,
Rest/Bar 86328
Course is off the A93 from Aberdeen;
take first turning on right after entering
village.
Undulating parkland course.
Pro Steven Moir; Founded 1883
18 holes, 5944 yards, S.S.S. 68
† Welcome.
⌇ WD £20; WE £25.
⚷ Welcome by prior arrangement;
day tickets available (WD £25, WE
£30); catering packages by
arrangement between April and
October; from £12.
🍴 Full facilities during summer.
↩ Huntly Arms.

9D 3 Alford ☎
Montgarrie Road, Alford, AB33 8AE
🖧 www.golf.alford.co.uk
📧 info@alford-golf-club.co.uk
☎ 019755 62178, Fax 64910,
Sec 62178, Rest/Bar 62178
On A944 in the village of Alford 25
miles W of Aberdeen.
Parkland course.
Founded 1982
Designed by David Hurd
18 holes, 5483 yards off the white,
S.S.S. 65
† Welcome; some restrictions on
club comp days.

⌇ WD £13; WE £20.
⚷ Welcome by prior arrangement;
day tickets available (WD £19; WE
£26); shotgun starts can be organised
for a minimum of 50 players; catering
packages by prior arrangement; from
£13.
🍴 Full clubhouse facilities available.
↩ Kildrummy Castle; Forbes Arms.

9D 4 Alness ☎
Ardross Rd, Alness, Ross-Shire
☎ 01349 883877
Course is on the A9 10 miles N of
Dingwall.
Founded 1904
Designed by John Sutherland
18 holes, 5000 yards, S.S.S. 64
† Welcome except 4.30pm-7.30pm
Mon.
⌇ Terms upon application.
⚷ Welcome by prior arrangement;
catering by prior arrangement; terms
on application.
🍴 By prior arrangement.
↩ Commercial Hotel.

9D 5 Askernish
Lochboisdale, Askernish, South Uist,
Western Isles, HS81 5SY
☎ 01878 700401
Take the ferry from Oban to
Lochboisdale; course is 5 miles N of
Lochboisdale.
Links course; most Western course in
Scotland.
Founded 1891
Designed by Tom Morris
18 holes, 5242 yards, S.S.S. 67
† Welcome.
⌇ WD £10; WE £10.
⚷ Welcome; terms available on
application.
🍴 By prior arrangement.
↩ Lochboisdale Hotel.

9D 6 Auchmill
Bonny View road, Auchmill, AB16 7FQ
☎ 01224 715214
5 miles N of Aberdeen.
Municipal parkland course.
18 holes, 5560 yards, S.S.S. 69
† Welcome.
⌇ On application.
⚷ Only with prior arrangement
through Council.
🍴 Limited.

9D 7 Ballater ☎
Victoria Road, Ballater, Aberdeenshire,
AB35 5QX

☎ 013397 55567, Fax 55057,
Pro 55658
42 miles W of Aberdeen on the A93.
Heath/parkland course.
Pro Billy Yule; Founded 1892
Designed by James Braid/H Vardon
18 holes, 6112 yards, S.S.S. 69
† Welcome by arrangement.
⌇ Terms on application.
⚷ Welcome by arrangement; catering
and day rates; from £18.
🍴 Bar and catering facilities.
↩ Club can provide comprehensive
list.

9D 8 Balnagask (Nigg Bay)
St Fitticks Rd, Balnagask, Aberdeen
☎ 01224 876407, Sec 871286,
Rest/Bar 871286
2 miles SE of the city.
Municipal seaside course.
Founded 1903
Designed by Hawtree & Son
18 holes, 6065 yards, S.S.S. 69
⚲ 9-hole pitch and putt.
† Welcome.
⌇ WD £9; WE £11.25.
⚷ Welcome by prior arrangement
with the council.
🍴 By arrangement with the council.
↩ Caledonian.

9D 9 Banchory ☎
Kinneskie Rd, Banchory,
Kincardineshire, AB31 5TA
📧 crighton@
banchorygolf club.uk.org
☎ 01330 822365, Fax 822491,
Pro 822447
Course is 100 yards off the A93 the
main Aberdeen to Braemar road.
Parkland course; 16th hole Doo'cot is
88 yards.
Pro David Naylor; Founded 1905
18 holes, 5781 yards, S.S.S. 68
† Welcome; all times bookable.
⌇ WD £20 (18 holes) day ticket £27;
WE £23 (18 holes).
⚷ Welcome; catering packages by
prior arrangement; terms on
application.
🍴 Full catering lounge and dining
room facilities.
↩ Burnett Arms; Tor-na-coille;
Banchory Lodge.

9D 10 Boat of Garten ☎
Inverness-Shire, PH24 3BQ
🖧 www.boatgolf.com
📧 boatgolf@enterprise.net
☎ 01479 831282, Fax 831523,
Rest/Bar 831731

Royal Aberdeen

Founded in 1790, the Royal Aberdeen club, or Balgownie Links as the actual course is named, is widely recognised as possessing one of the finest outward nines in the world. Year after year, some of golf's most knowledgeable architects come to look and learn.

With only 350 members and a traditional gentlemanly clubhouse, Royal Aberdeen is a classic old-style golf club of log fires and whisky. In 1872 Prince Leopold became the Patron, but its royal status was granted 31 years later by King Edward VII.

The club disregards pub-type accessories such as pool tables or one-armed bandits. It is enough to have a natural links course that meanders out through a valley and back along a plateau and that is free of the ravages of the local footballers who prompted the club to find new land in 1888.

Although the course runs essentially out and back along the North Sea shore, individual holes switch direction subtly, changing the angle of the wind and bringing variety and balance to a testing examination of golf at any level.

What makes the outward nine so special is the blend of holes, with some of the tees placed on the landward side, others on the seaward side, plus the wonderful dune formations, good greens and stunning views.

After an opening hole conspicuous by two well-positioned bunkers that can play havoc with club selection, the golfer is faced by the longest hole on the course. The second is a classic par five at 507 yards that was simply meant to be a golf hole and nothing else. Stand on the tee and watch how the fairway stretches through the dunes. An accurate drive is essential. Then try to thread your second up through the valley. If you negotiate that, a tricky pitch awaits you to a green guarded by bunkers right and left.

The third is a strong par three from an elevated tee on the seaward side and any high handicappers who manage to carry the bunker on to the green deserve considerable praise. Don't be deceived by the fifth that, although relatively short at 290 off the yellow tees, has a strategically positioned bunker to prevent players slamming their tee shot with a driver.

The wind plays such a big part here that the golf course is always shifting. "You can never go out there and think you can hit a certain club on a certain hole", said Royal Aberdeen professional Ronnie MacAskili. "The golf course changes all the time. The slightest breeze makes the course very angry and it tests you right from the word go which makes the outward nine so interesting. You have to be right on the ball, if you'll excuse the pun. I've been here for 27 years and every time I go out, the course throws up a new challenge."

If you get to the turn with your confidence intact, you shouldn't have too many problems coming back. No par fives await you, but beware the blind drive on the tenth where anyone who overshoots the green is left with an awkward downhill chip or putt. The eighteenth is a superb finishing hole with an elevated tee into a bunkered valley followed by an elevated green.

Because Royal Aberdeen is on a sand base and drains quickly, winter rules normally apply for just two months of the year, with only frost forcing closure. When that happens, play invariably switches to the club's second, far shorter Silverbum course – part links, part parkland – which is a fair test in itself.

Although the whiff of helicopters flying to and from the North Sea oil rigs have become a regular and not always welcome feature at Balgownie, most players have managed to adapt over the years. Besides, the choppers provide an additional excuse for that bad round! – **Andrew Warshaw**

2 miles E of A9 30 miles S of
Inverness.
Heathland course.
Pro James Ingram; Founded 1898
Designed by James Braid
18 holes, 5967 yards, S.S.S. 69
  🏌 Practice area.
  † Welcome WD 9.30am-6pm; WE
10am-4pm.
  👤 WD £29; WE £34.
  ⛳ Welcome by prior arrangement;
day tickets available; catering by
arrangement; separate changing
rooms available.
  🍽 Full clubhouse facilities.
  🛏 The Boat.

9D 11 Bonar Bridge Ardgay
Market Stance, Migdale Rd, Bonar
Bridge, Sutherland, IV24 3EJ
  📧 bonarardgaygolf@aol.com
  ☎ 01863 766199, Fax 766738,
Sec 766750
Off A836 at Bonar Bridge 0.5 miles up
Migdale Rd; 12 miles W of Dornoch.
Parkland course.
Founded 1904
9 holes, 5162 yards, S.S.S. 65
  † Welcome.
  👤 WD £14 day ticket (2003)
  ⛳ Welcome by prior arrangement;
terms available on application.
  🍽 Clubhouse facilities in season.

9D 12 Braemar   ♔
Cluniebank Rd, Braemar,
Aberdeenshire, AB35 5XX
  ☎ 013397 41618, Sec 01224 704471,
Rest/Bar 013397 41618
Signposted from the village centre; turn
left opposite Fife Arms Hotel.
Parkland course.
Founded 1902
Designed by Joe Anderson
18 holes, 4935 yards, S.S.S. 64
  † Welcome.
  👤 WD £14; WE £17.
  ⛳ Welcome; packages include 36
holes of golf and catering; from £20;
WE £32.
  🍽 Full clubhouse facilities.
  🛏 Invercauld Arms; Fife Arms;
Moorfield House.

9D 13 Brora
43 Golf Rd, Brora, Sutherland,
KW9 6QS
  🖥 www.broragolf.co.uk
  📧 secretary@broragolf.co.uk
  ☎ 01408 621417, Fax 622157
On A9 N of Inverness; turn right over
bridge in centre of Brora.

Traditional links course.
Founded 1891
Designed by James Braid
18 holes, 6110 yards, S.S.S. 69
  🏌 Practice range.
  † Welcome.
  👤 WD £28, WE £33 (per round –
winter rates on request.
  ⛳ Welcome by prior arrangement; on
application.
  🍽 Full clubhouse facilities.
  🛏 Royal Marine; Links.

9D 14 Buckpool (Buckie)
Barhill Rd, Buckie, Banffshire,
AB56 1DU
  🖥 www.buckpoolgolf.com
  📧 golf@buckpoolgolf.com
  ☎ 01542 832236
Turn off the A98 at Buckpool.
Links course.
Founded 1933/65
Designed by Hawtree & Taylor
18 holes, 6257 yards, S.S.S. 70
  † Welcome.
  👤 WD £15; WE £20.
  ⛳ Welcome by prior arrangement;
packages include 36 holes of golf with
full catering; WE discounts for groups
of more than 10.
  🍽 Full clubhouse facilities.
  🛏 Marine, Buckie; Cluny, Buckie; Old
Coachhouse, Buckie.

9D 15 Carnegie Club
Skibo Castle, Dornoch, Sutherland,
IV25 3RQ
  🖥 www.carnegieclub.co.uk
  📧 sharon.stewart@carnegieclubs
.com
  ☎ 01862 894600, Fax 894601,
Pro 881260, Sec 894660
Take A9 towards Wick from Inverness;
first left after Dornoch Bridge
signposted Meikle Ferry North;
continue for 1 mile and turn right at
Green Sheds.
Championship links course; new 9-
hole parkland course (members
course).
Pro David Thompson; Founded 1994
Designed by Donald Steel
18 holes, 6671 yards, S.S.S. 72
  🏌 Driving range bays.
  † WD by arrangement only.
  👤 £100 per person golf only; £140
per person inc lunch.
  ⛳ WD only; includes soup,
sandwiches and house wine.
  🍽 Full facilities in the club.
  🛏 Morangie House; Mansfield House,
both Tain; Royal Golf; Burghfield, both
Dornoch.

9D 16 Carrbridge
Inverness Rd, Carrbridge, Inverness-
shire, PH23 3AU
  ☎ 01479 841623, Sec 841412
Off A9 25 miles S of Inverness.
Parkland course/heathland course.
Founded 1980
Designed by local enthusiasts
9 holes, 5402 yards, S.S.S. 69
  † Welcome.
  👤 WD £16; WE £18.
  ⛳ Limited to small groups.
  🍽 Tea coffee and snacks from April-
October.

9D 17 Cruden Bay
Aulton Rd, Cruden Bay, Peterhead,
Aberdeenshire, AB42 0NN
  🖥 www.crudenbaygolfclub.co.uk
  📧 cbaygc@aol.com
  ☎ 01779 812285, Fax 812945,
Pro 812414
Course is off the A90 10 miles from
Peterhead; or from Aberdeen off the
A90 and then the A975.
Championship links course.
Pro Robbie Stewart; Founded 1899
Designed by Tom Morris & Archie
Simpson
27 holes, 6395 yards, S.S.S. 72
  🏌 Practice range; 10 covered bays.
  † Welcome; restrictions until after
9.30am Mon; after 10.30am Tues and
at WE (Main); Welcome (St Olaf).
  👤 WD £55, WE £65 (Main); WD £15,
WE 15, £20 (St Olaf) – 2003 rates.
  ⛳ Welcome WD except Wed by prior
arrangement; handicap certs needed;
minimum 16 players; catering by prior
arrangement; from £25 (Main);
welcome (St Olaf).
  🍽 Full clubhouse facilities.
  🛏 Club can provide list.

9D 18 Cullen
The Links, Cullen, Buckie, Banffshire,
AB56 4WB
  🖥 www.cullengolfclub.co.uk
  📧 cullengolfclub@btinternet.com
  ☎ 01542 840685
Off the A98 at the W end of the town
on the Moray Firth coastline.
Traditional links course with natural
rock landscaping.
Founded 1879.
Designed by Tom Morris (original 9
holes); Charles Neaves
18 holes, 4610 yards, S.S.S. 62
  † Welcome WD; some restrictions on
WE and July/August.
  👤 Terms on application.
  ⛳ Welcome by prior arrangement;
restrictions on Wed and Sat; day

Royal Dornoch

Long before a golf club was formed at Dornoch in 1877, the game was played along the seashore and frowned upon by the authorities because they wanted the local subjects to practise a different sort of marksmanship. Good soldiers were needed more than good golfers.

Today Royal Dornoch, which has staged both the Amateur and Scottish Amateur, is rated among the best courses in the world. It has a deserved reputation as one of the hidden gems of the game, being far removed from Scotland's main centres of population and, until the last 30 years, relatively inaccessible.

Dress code is more flexible than at many elite clubs, though if you get caught with your hat on in the bar, it will cost you a round of drinks. Most people aren't warned until they are standing at the counter!

In terms of romance and scenery, it is simply unique with a local population of just 1,200 and a mesmerising flow of holes, contours and colours. Prince Andrew (royal status was granted by King Edward VII in 1906) and Ben Crenshaw are among the honorary members, while Tom Watson, who headed north for a quick practice round before winning the third of his five Opens at Muirfield, ended up playing three times in a day. He called it "the most enjoyment I've ever had on the golf course".

Royal Dornoch is fun yet also a supreme test of skill and concentration for your average handicapper, which is one reason why certificates are required: 24 maximum for men, 39 for women. Is this a rare example of men being discriminated against by a golf club?

American golfers love the peaceful-ness and serenity of Dornoch despite being, forced either to carry their bags or use trollies. Only two buggies are provided, each for players with a proven medical ailment. After a relatively uncomplicated opening hole, the par three second is a killer round the green, which is 45 yards from front to back, surrounded by steep bankings and two monster bunkers with horribly deep faces. Watson said that the second to the second at Dornoch was the hardest shot he had ever played.

Although Dornoch is a haven of tranquility most of the time and one of the few links courses where you can see the sea from every hole, it does have one off-putting factor. Every few minutes fighter jets roar overhead, threatening your concentration as they fly in and out of the nearby bombing base in a constant stream of training exercises.

Dornoch has no official signature hole, but the seventh, looking back along the beach and the North Sea where dolphins frolic, has arguably the best view while the fourth, a 427-yard par four, has a landing area off the tee of only about 30 yards, the drive having to carry rough, bunkers and hollows.

The famous fourteenth is a double dog-leg and the only hole without a single bunker. Instead, the ultra thin green is 48 yards wide, but only 24 yards deep and sits across the line of play. No wonder the hole is named "Foxy".

Dornoch is generally fair, rewards good shots and won't have you searching for a ball that you swear was sweetly and accurately struck. There is a downside, however. You can easily go round without losing a single ball, only to discover you haven't played anywhere near your handicap.

Hitting fairways is relatively straight-forward, but at Dornoch pitching and chipping is everything. You are just as likely to be faced by a fifty-yard chip as a five-yard chip because of the size and speed of the greens. Just ask Tom Watson.

– **Andrew Warshaw**

The Royal Dornoch Golf Club Welcomes you

The Championship Course, rated 16th amongst the world's top courses is a classic links challenging the golfer's skills in the traditional manner.

The Struie Links, extended in 2003 by 5 new holes to 6276 yards Par 72 is, with its own character, suitable for all abilities.

Tel Reservations: **(01862) 810219**
Fax: **(01862) 810792**
Secretary: **(01862) 811220**
e-mail: **bookings@royaldornoch.com**
Web site: **http://www.royaldornoch.com**

---

tickets available; catering packages by arrangement; from £10.
🍽 Clubhouse catering and bar.
🍸 Cullen Bay; Royal Oak; Bayview; Three Kings; Grant Arms; Seafield Arms; Waverley.

9D 19 Deeside
Golf Rd, Bieldside, Aberdeen, Aberdeenshire, AB15 9DL
🖥 www.deesidegolfclub.com
💻 admin@deesidegolfclub.com
☎ 01224 869457, Pro 861041, Rest/Bar 861792
Course on A93 three miles W of Aberdeen.
Parkland course.
Pro FJ Coutts; Founded 1903
18 holes, 6424 yards, S.S.S. 70; 9 holes, 5083 yards, S.S.S. 67
† Welcome after 9am WD and 4pm Sat; handicap cert required.
� WD £45; WE £60.
🌿 Welcome Thurs only by arrangement; catering packages by arrangement; terms available on application.
🍽 Full facilities.
🍸 Cults; Narcliffe at Pitfodels.

9D 20 Duff House Royal
The Banyards, Banff, Banffshire, AB45 3SX
🖥 www.theduffhouseroyalgolfclub. co.uk
💻 duff_house_royal@btinternet.co.uk
☎ 01261 812062, Fax 812224, Pro 812075, Sec 812062, Rest/Bar 812062
On A98.
Parkland course.
Pro R Strachan; Founded 1909
Designed by Dr A & Major CA MacKenzie
18 holes, 6161 yards, S.S.S. 70
† Welcome except before 11am and between 12.30pm-3.30pm WE and in July/August.
� WD £26; WE £32.
🌿 Welcome by prior arrangement; catering and day packages by application; terms on application.
🍽 Full facilities.
🍸 Banff Springs; County; Fife Lodge.

9D 21 Dufftown
Tomintoul Road, Dufftown, Keith, Banffshire, AB55 4BS
🖥 www.dufftowngolfclub.com
💻 marion_dufftowngolfclub@ yahoo.com
☎ 01340 820325, Fax 820325
On B9009 1 mile S of Dufftown.
Moor/parkland course.
Founded 1896
Designed by members
18 holes, 5308 yards, S.S.S. 67
† Welcome.
� £15 per round; £20 for the day.
🌿 Welcome by prior arrangement; discounts for groups of more than 12; catering by prior arrangement; from £12.
🍽 Full clubhouse facilities.
🍸 Fife Arms, Dufftown; Craigellachie Hotel; Minmore House Hotel.

9D 22 Dunecht House
Dunecht, Skene, Aberdeenshire, AB3 7AX
Course on B994 to Dunecht.
Inland wooded course.
Founded 1925
9 holes, 6270 yards, S.S.S. 70
† Members only.
� Terms on application.

9D 23 Durness ☎
Balnakeil, Durness, Sutherland, IV27 4PN
💻 mackenziedurness@aol.com
☎ 01971 511364, Fax 511321
57 miles NW of Lairg on A838; turn left in village square.
Links/parkland course.
Founded 1988
Designed by F Keith; L Ross; I Morrison
9 holes, 5555 yards, S.S.S. 69
† Welcome.
� Terms on application.
🌿 Welcome; terms available on application.
🍽 Clubhouse facilities.
🍸 Cape Wrath; Parkhill; Rhiconich.

9D 24 Elgin ☎
Hardhillock, Birnie Road, Elgin, Moray, IV30 8SX
🖥 www.elgingolfclub.com
💻 secretary@elgingolfclub.com
☎ 01343 542338, Fax 542341, Pro 542884
On A941 Birnie road, 1 mile S of Elgin town centre.
Parkland course.
Pro Kevin Stables; Founded 1906
Designed by John MacPherson
18 holes, 6411 yards, S.S.S. 71
☐ 16.
† Everyone welcome.
☐ £28/round any day of the week.
🌿 Welcome by prior arrangement with Sec David Black; discounts for larger groups; full catering available.
🍽 Clubhouse bar and catering.
🍸 Sunninghill; Laichmoray; Eight Acres; Mansion House.

9D 25 Forres ☎
Muiryshade, Forres, IV36 2RD
🖥 www.forresgolfclub.fsnet.co.uk
💻 sandy@forresgolfclub.fsnet .co.uk
☎ 01309 672250, Fax 672250, Rest/Bar 672949
On A96 26 miles E of Inverness; 1 mile S of Forres.
Parkland course.
Pro Sandy Aird;
Founded 1889
Designed by James Braid
18 holes, 6141 yards, S.S.S. 69
† Welcome by prior arrangement with the Professional.
☐ WD £24; WE £24.
🌿 Welcome by prior arrangement; maximum number 60; terms on application.
🍽 Full clubhouse facilities.
🍸 Ramnee; Cluny Banil; Camsbrooke; Knockholme.

9D 26 Fort Augustus
Markethill, Fort Augustus, Inverness-shire, PH32 4DT
☎ 01320 366660
0.75 miles S of Fort Augustus on A82.
Moorland course.
Founded 1905
Designed by Dr Lean
9 holes, 5452 yards, S.S.S. 67

† Welcome.
[WD £10; WE £10.
⌒ Welcome by prior arrangement; on application; from £8.
|●| Limited.
⌐ Lovat Arms; Richmond House.

9D 27 Fort William
North Rd, Torlundy, Inverness-shire, PH33 6SN
⊞ www.fortwilliamgolf.co.uk
✉ jdungolf@aol.com
☎ 01397 704464, Fax 705893
On A82 2 miles N of Fort William.
Parkland course.
Founded 1975
Designed by JR Stutt
18 holes, 6217 yards, S.S.S. 71
† Welcome.
[WD/WE £22 round, £30 day.
⌒ Welcome by arrangement; golf packages only.
|●| Bar snacks available.
⌐ Milton; Moorings.

9D 28 Fortrose & Rosemarkie   ☎
Ness Rd East, Fortrose, Ross-shire, IV10 8SE
⊞ www.fortrosegolfclub.co.uk
✉ secretary@fortrosegolfclub.co.uk
☎ 01381 620529, Fax 621328, Pro 620733,
Off A832 to Fortrose off the A9 at Tope roundabout.
Links course on headland; stunning views.
Founded 1888
Designed by James Baird
18 holes, 5883 yards, S.S.S. 69
† Welcome.
[WD £35; WE £40.
⌒ Welcome by prior arrangement with Sec; day tickets available (WD £35, WE £40); from £20.
|●| Clubhouse facilities.
⌐ Royal; Kinkell House.

9D 29 Fraserburgh   ☎
Philorth, Fraserburgh, Aberdeenshire, AB43 8TL
⊞ www.fraserburghgolfclub.net
✉ fburghgolf@aol.com
☎ 01346 516616, Rest/Bar 518287
S of first roundabout when entering Fraserburgh and then first right.
Links course.
Founded 1779
Designed by James Braid
27 holes, 6308 yards, S.S.S. 71
† Everyone welcome.
[WD £20; WE £25.

⌒ Welcome by prior arrangement; catering packages by arrangement; also 9-hole course, 4800 yards, par 66; from £8.
|●| Bar and dining room facilities available.
⌐ Station; Tufted Duck, both Fraserburgh.

9D 30 Gairloch
Gairloch, Ross-shire, IV21 2BE
✉ secretary@gairlochgc.freeserve.net
☎ 01445 712407
On A832 60 miles W of Inverness.
Seaside course with stunning views; 7th hole An Dun, is 91 yards.
Founded 1898
Designed by Captain AW Burgess
9 holes, 4514 yards, S.S.S. 64
⫢ Practice area with bunker.
† Welcome.
[WD £15; WE £15.
⌒ Welcome by prior arrangement; weekly ticket: £49; by prior arrangement; refreshments.
|●| Clubhouse facilities.
⌐ Gairloch; Myrtle Bank Millcroft; Old Inn, Creag Mor.

9D 31 Garmouth & Kingston   ☎
Spey St, Garmouth, Fochabers, Morayshire, IV32 7NJ
✉ garmouthgolfclub@aol.com
☎ 01343 870388, Fax 870388
3 miles N of A96 at Mosstodloch cross roads.
Links/parkland course.
Founded 1932
Designed by George Smith
18 holes, 5935 yards, S.S.S. 69
† Welcome by prior arrangement.
[Terms on application.
⌒ Welcome by prior arrangement; catering by arrangement; games room; terms on application.
|●| Bar and dining room facilities.
⌐ Garmouth; Gordon Arms Fochabers.

9D 32 Golspie   ☎
Ferry Rd, Golspie, Sutherland, KW10 6ST
⊞ www.golspie-golf-club.co.uk
✉ info@golspie-golf-club.co.uk
☎ 01408 633266, Fax 633393, Rest/Bar 634187
On A9 to Golspie.
Links course.
Founded 1889
Designed by James Braid
18 holes, 5990 yards, S.S.S. 68

† Welcome.
[WD/WE £25 round, £35 day.
⌒ Welcome by prior arrangement; discounts for groups; catering by arrangement; prior booking essential.
|●| Bar and catering facilities.
⌐ Sutherland Arms; Golf Links; Ben Bhraggie; Stags Head.

9D 33 Grantown-on-Spey
Golf Course Rd, Grantown-on-Spey, Morayshire, PH26 3HY
⊞ www.grantownonspeygolfclub.co.uk
✉ secretary@grantownonspeygolfclub.co.uk
☎ 01479 872079, Fax 873725
On NE of town signposted off the Grantown-Nairn/Forres road.
Parkland/woodland course.
Founded 1890
Designed by James Braid/A C Porown/Willie Park
18 holes, 5710 yards, S.S.S. 68
⫢ Practice range.
† Welcome except before 10am at WE.
[WD £20; WE £25 per round.
WD £25; WE £30 per day.
⌒ Welcome by prior arrangement except before 10am at WE; catering by arrangement.
|●| Full bar and catering facilities.

9D 34 Hazlehead
Hazlehead Park, Aberdeen, AB15 8BD
☎ 01224 910711, Sec 310711
Course is four miles NW of the city centre.
Municipal moorland courses.
Pro Alistair Smith
18 holes, 6304 yards, S.S.S. 68
† Welcome.
[WD £9; WE £25.
⌒ Apply to council; 2 other courses; 18 holes 6045 yards, S.S.S. 68; 9holes 2770 yards S.S.S. 34 terms on application.
|●| Available nearby.
⌐ Treetops; Belverdere Queens.

9D 35 Helmsdale
Golf Rd, Helmsdale, Sutherland, KW8 6JA
☎ 01431 821063
Off A9 in village of Helmsdale.
Moorland course.
Pro R Sutherland; Founded 1895
9 holes, 3720 yards, S.S.S. 60
† Welcome.
[Terms on application.
⌒ Welcome by application.
|●| None.
⌐ Navidale; Bridge; Belgrave.

9D 36 Hopeman Golf Club ☏
Hopeman, Moray, IV30 5YA
www.hopeman-golf-club.co.uk
hopemangc@aol.com
☎ 01343 830578, Fax 830152
On B9012 7 miles N of Elgin.
Seaside links-type course.
Founded 1906
Designed by Charles Neaves
18 holes, 5590 yards, S.S.S. 67
† Welcome except some Sat
competition days.
[WD £16; WE £21; concessions
apply.
↻ Welcome by prior arrangement
with Sec; catering packages by
arrangement; pool table; terms
available on application; trollies and
buggies for hire.
🍽 Full catering facilities.
🛏 Station.

9D 37 Huntly ☏
Cooper Park, Huntly, Aberdeenshire,
AB54 4SH
www.huntlygc.co.uk
huntlygc@tinyworld.co.uk
☎ 01466 792643, Pro 794181
On A96 0.5 miles from the town centre
through school arch.
Parkland course.
Pro Sendy Aird; Founded 1892
18 holes, 5399 yards, S.S.S. 66
† Welcome.
[WD £15; WE £20.
↻ By arrangement with Sec; catering
by arrangement; snooker; darts; terms
on application.
🍽 Clubhouse facilities.
🛏 Commercial; Station.

9D 38 Insch
Golf Terrace, Aberdeenshire
☎ 01464 820363
Off A96 28 miles NW of Aberdeen.
Parkland course with water hazards
extended 1997.
18 holes, 5395 yards, S.S.S. 67
† Welcome.
[Terms on application.
↻ By arrangement with Sec; catering
by arrangement; snooker darts terms
on application.
🍽 Clubhouse facilities.
🛏 Commercial; Station.

9D 39 Inverallochy
White Link Inverallochy, Nr
Fraserburgh, AB43 8XY
☎ 01346 582000, Sec 582324
4 miles SE of Fraserburgh.
Seaside links course.

Founded 1888
18 holes, 5101 yards, S.S.S. 66
† Welcome by prior arrangement
except before 10am at WE.
[WD £12; WE £15. Winter WD £8,
WE £10.
↻ Welcome by prior arrangement;
catering by arrangement; terms on
application.
🍽 Catering and licensed bar.
🛏 Tufted Duck.

9D 40 Invergordon ☏
King George St, Invergordon, Ross-
shire, IV1 0BD
☎ 01349 852715
Course is off the B817 from the A9 to
Invergordon.
Parkland course; extended to 18 holes
1996.
Founded 1893
Designed by J Urquhart; Extended by
A Rae 1996
18 holes, 6030 yards, S.S.S. 69
ℐ Practice area.
† Welcome.
[WD £15; WE £15; £20 per day.
£10 in winter.
↻ Welcome by prior arrangement with
Clubhouse manager; day ticket £15;
catering by arrangement; from £12.
🍽 Bar and bar meals service.
🛏 Kincraig; Marine.

9D 41 Inverness ☏
Culcabock Rd, Inverness, IV2 3XQ
www.invernessgolfclub.co.uk
igc@freeuk.com
☎ 01463 233422, Fax 239882,
Pro 231989, Sec 239882,
Rest/Bar 233422
1 mile W of A9 near Raigmore
Hospital.
Parkland course.
Pro Alistair Thomson; Founded 1883
Designed by J J Fraser/G Smith/
alterations at later date James Braid
18 holes, 6256 yards, S.S.S. 70
ℐ Practice area.
† Welcome; restrictions on Sat comp
days.
[WD £33 per round; £42 per day.
↻ Welcome by prior arrangement;
limited; terms on application.
🍽 Full restaurant and bar.
🛏 Marriot; Craigmonie; Inverness
Thistle.

9D 42 Inverurie ☏
Blackhall Rd, Inverurie, AB51 5JB
www.inveruriegc.co.uk
administrator@inveruriegc.co.uk

☎ 01467 620193, Fax 621051,
Pro 620193, Sec 624080
17 miles W of Aberdeen off the A96.
Slightly wooded parkland course.
Pro John Logue; Founded 1923
Designed by G Smith and JM Stutt
18 holes, 5711 yards, S.S.S. 68
† Welcome.
[WD £16; WE £20.
↻ Welcome by prior arrangement;
some discounts for larger groups;
catering packages by arrangement;
from £16.
🍽 Full bar and catering.
🛏 Strathburn; Kintore Arms.

9D 43 Isle of Skye
Sconser, Isle of Skye, IV48 8TD
☎ 01478 650414, Fax 650414
On A87 between Skye Bridge and
Portree.
Parkland course.
Founded 1964
Designed by Dr F Deighton
9 holes, 4677 yards, S.S.S. 64
† Welcome.
[Terms on application.
↻ Welcome by arrangement with
Sec; discounts for groups of 15 or
more; from £10.
🍽 Snacks/tea-room; other catering by
arrangement.
🛏 Sligachan Hotel.

9D 44 Keith
Fife Park, Keith, Banffshire, AB55 3DF
☎ 01542 882469
A96 to Keith; course 0.5 miles.
Parkland course.
Founded 1965
18 holes, 5802 yards, S.S.S. 68
† Welcome.
[Terms on application.
↻ Welcome by prior arrangement;
day tickets available; catering packages
by arrangement; pool table; from £10.
🍽 Clubhouse facilities.
🛏 Fife Arms; Grampian; Royal; Ugie
House, all in Keith.

9D 45 Kemnay ☏
Monymusk Road, Kemnay,
Aberdeenshire, AB51 5RA
www.kemnaygolfclub.co.uk
administrator@kemnaygolfclub.co.uk
☎ 01467 642225, Fax 643715,
Sec 643746, Rest/Bar 642060
On A96 15 miles N of Aberdeen; turn
on to B994.
Parkland course.
Pro Ronnie McDonald; Founded
1908

Designed by Greens of Scotland Ltd (new Course)
18 holes, yellow yard 6001, Fight peg 6362, S.S.S. 60; Yellow pag and 71 Fight peg
† Welcome except on competition days.
⌷ WD £20; WE £24.
⌁ Welcome by prior arrangement; day tickets available; catering by arrangement; from £17.
⍟ Full clubhouse facilities available.
⟿ Park Hill Lodge; Grant Arms; Burnett Arms.

9D 46 King's Links
Golf Rd, King's Links, Aberdeen, AB24 5QB
☎ 01224 632269
Close to Pittodrie Stadium in the E of the city.
Municipal seaside course.
18 holes, 6384 yards, S.S.S. 71
† Welcome.
⌷ Terms on application.
⌁ Welcome by prior arrangement; day tickets (WD £20, WE £25); reductions for 20 or more golfers; from £16.
⍟ Clubhouse facilities.
⟿ Silverfjord; Scot House.

9D 47 Kingussie
Gynack Rd, Kingussie, Inverness-shire, PH21 1LR
☎ 01540 661600, Fax 662066, Rest/Bar 661374
Off A9 and turn in to club at Duke of Gordon Hotel.
Scenic hilly course.
Founded 1891
Designed by Vardon & Herd
18 holes, 5555 yards, S.S.S. 67
† Welcome.
⌷ WD £16; WE £18.
⌁ Welcome by prior arrangement; day tickets (WD £20, WE £25); reductions for 20 or more golfers; from £16.
⍟ Clubhouse facilities.
⟿ Silverfjord; Scot House.

9D 48 Kintore ☏
Balbithan, Kintore, Inverurie, Aberdeenshire, AB51 0UR
🖳 www.kintoregolfclub.net
✉ kintoregolfclub@lineone.net
☎ 01467 632631, Fax 632995
Off A96 12 miles N of Aberdeen.
Undulating moorland course.
Founded 1911
18 holes, 6019 yards, S.S.S. 69
⌁ Practice nets; buggie/trolley hire.

† Welcome except Mon & Wed 4.30pm-6pm and after 4.30pm Fri.
⌷ Terms on application.
⌁ Welcome by prior arrangement; catering by arrangement; day tickets available; terms available on application.
⍟ Full clubhouse facilities.
⟿ Torryburn; Thainstone.

9D 49 Lochcarron
East End, Lochcarron
☎ 01520 722229
0.5 miles E of Lochcarron.
Parkland/links course.
Founded 1908
9 holes, 3578 yards, S.S.S. 60
† Welcome except Sat 2-5pm.
⌷ WD £7.50; WE £7.50.
⌁ Welcome by prior arrangement only; catering by arrangement at village hotel; weekly ticket £20; from £7.50.
⍟ No clubhouse facilities; catering at local hotels.
⟿ Rockvilla Hotel.

9D 50 Loch Ness ☏
Fairways Leisure, Castle Heather, Iverness, IV2 6AA
🖳 www.golflochness.com
✉ info@golflochness.com
☎ 01463 7713335, Fax 712695, Pro 713334
From A9 take Inshes/Culloden turnoff then at roundabout take Sir Walter Scott Drive. Course is on left after 2nd r/bout and accessed via 3rd r/bout.
Parkland course.
Pro Martin Piggot; Founded 1908
Designed by Caddies Golf Course Design
White: 18 holes, 6797 yards, S.S.S. 72
Yellow: 18 holes, 6493 yards, S.S.S. 71
⌁ 20 bay covered and floodlit driving range; putting green
† Welcome.
⌷ WD £25; WE £30.
⌁ Welcome.
⍟ Full bar and catering.
⟿ GH to 5-star hotels within 10 min.

9D 51 Lybster
Main St, Lybster, Caithness, KW3 6BL
☎ 01593 721308, Sec 721316
On A9 13 miles S of Wick.
Moorland course; smallest in Scotland.
Founded 1926
9 holes, 3796 yards, S.S.S. 62
† Welcome; honesty box.
⌷ WD £8; WE £8.

⌁ Welcome except Sat evening (club comp).
⟿ The Port and Arms Hotel.

9D 52 McDonald
Hospital Rd, Ellon, Aberdeenshire, AB41 9AW
🖳 www.mcdonaldgolfclub.co.uk
✉ mccdonald.golf@virgin.net
☎ 01358 720576, Fax 720001, Pro 722891, Rest/Bar 723741
Course is off the A90 16 miles N of Aberdeen.
Parkland course.
Pro Ronnie Urquhart; Founded 1927
18 holes, 5991 yards, S.S.S. 70
† Welcome by prior arrangement.
⌷ WD £16; Sat £18; Sun £18.
⌁ Welcome by prior arrangement; day tickets available (WD £22, Sat £26, Sun £26).
⍟ Full clubhouse facilities.
⟿ Buchan Hotel; New Inn; Station Hotel.

9D 53 Monk's Walk, Skibo Castle
The Carnegie Club, Skibo Castle, Dornoch, Sutherland, IV25 3RQ
🖳 www.carnegieclubs.com
✉ skibo@carnegieclubs.com
☎ 01862 894600
Up A9, over Dornoch bridge, turn left towards Clashmore.
Flat links course.
† Yes, Mon-Fri.
⌷ £130 for 18 holes + lunch.
⌁ Yes, still £130 pp.
⍟ Yes.
⟿ Skibo Castle.

9D 54 Moray
Stotfield Rd, Lossiemouth, Moray, IV31 6QS
🖳 www.moraygolf.co.uk
✉ secretary@moraygolf.co.uk
☎ 01343 812018, Fax 815102, Pro 813330
At Lossiemouth turn off from A96, 6 miles N of Elgin, on the coast.
Links course.
Pro Alistair Thomson; Founded 1889
Designed by Tom Morris
2x18 holes, old 6617 new 6004 yards, S.S.S. new 69 old 73
⌁ Large practice range, private driving range nearby; golf carts.
† Welcome by arrangement.
⌷ WD £30; WE £35 (New); WD £40 WE £50 (Old).
⌁ Welcome by prior arrangement; some discounts available for larger

Duff House Royal

In the minds of most golf fans, the greatest legacy left to the game by Dr Alister Mackenzie is Augusta National Golf Club, a course he jointly designed with Bobby Jones in 1932, and where the first Major Championship of each season, the Masters, is contested every April.

However, in the north east of Scotland, patrons of Duff House Royal Golf Club in Banff might feel slightly differently as their superb golf course also features the hand of Mackenzie, the only difference being that theirs came first.

The original plans for Duff House Royal were laid down by the five times Open champion and prolific designer James Braid in 1909 but the course was redesigned to the layout recognised today by Mackenzie in 1923.

In an area where superb links golf courses abound, the beautifully manicured parkland layout is a pleasant change while at the same time being a demanding test for golfers of all abilities. The main features of the relatively flat course are the large, signature two-tier Mackenzie greens which form part of most of the putting surfaces.

From the elevated first tee, there is a wide-ranging view across the adjoining first and 18th fairways in similar fashion to the opening and closing holes of the Old Course at St Andrews.

Five par fours start the course, the toughest perhaps being the fourth which features a huge two-tiered green which can make a three or four club difference between front and back, while the fifth demands an arrow-straight drive to avoid the trees on the right.

After the first short hole, the sixth, comes three along the river Deveron, the 460 yard seventh a genuine stroke index one hole, while the short ninth demands one of the most accurate tee shots of the round if the big bunker guarding the front of the green is to be crossed without going over the putting surface and down the bank towards the water.

The most picturesque hole on the back nine is the par five 12th which bends uphill right to left before reaching a large plateau green, from where the hole takes its name, and from where magnificent views of the 18th Century Duff House and grounds are available.

Anyone amassing a decent card cannot afford to relax however as the finishing stretch is demanding, starting with the two long par fours, the 14th and 15th which run in opposite directions, the 242 yard par three 16th with the river on the right and a raft of bunkers on the left of the green, and the 462 yard 17th where the drive and approach shots have to be threaded through a narrow strip of land between the Deveron on the right and the out of bounds on the left. The 18th has a generous fairway but the out of bounds on the road to the right is an ever present danger.

The pro's shop presumably does a roaring trade, because back in the 17th century one Franceis Broun was hanged for stealing golf balls in the area. Over two hundred years later Banff Golf Club was formed and in 1925 it was granted the royal title by the Duchess of Fife on its amalgamation with the Duff House Club.

– **Nick Alexander**

groups; day tickets WD £40, WE £45 (New); WD £55, WE £70 (Old).
🍽 Full clubhouse facilities.
🛏 Stotfield; Skerry Brae; Laverock Bank.

9D 55 **Muir of Ord** ☏
Great North Rd, Muir of Ord, Ross-shire, IV6 7SX
🖧 www.golfhighland.co.uk
✉ muirgolf@supanet.com
☎ 01463 870825, Fax 871867
15 miles N of Inverness.
Moorland/parkland course with links-type fairways.
Founded 1875
Designed by James Baird
18 holes, 5557 yards, S.S.S. 68
† Welcome but not before 11am at WE and on competition days.
⌾ WD £18; WE £20.
⌁ Welcome by prior arrangement; discounts available for groups of more than 15; daily and weekly tickets available; snooker and pool tables; from £14.
🍽 Bar and catering facilities.
🛏 Ord Arms; Priory.

9D 56 **Murcar** ☏
Bridge of Don, Aberdeen, AB22 8BD
🖧 www.murcar.co.uk
✉ golf@murcar.co.uk
☎ 01224 704354, Fax 704354, Pro 704370, Rest/Bar 705345
On A92 3 miles from Aberdeen on road to Fraserburgh.
Links course.
Pro Gary Forbes; Founded 1909
Designed by Archie Simpson
Murcar Championship:18 holes, 6314 yards, Par 71;Strabathie: 9 holes, 5,369 yards, Par 70.
⚐ Practice area.
⌾ Murcar: WD £50 round £70 day; WE/BH £60 round £80 day; Strabathie: WD £10 9 holes, £25 day; WE/BH £15 9 holes, £35 day.
⌁ Welcome WD with prior arrangement with Sec.
🍽 Full clubhouse facilities.
🛏 Mill of Mundurno.

9D 57 **Nairn**
Seabank Rd, Nairn, IV12 4HB
✉ bookings@nairngolfclub.co.uk
☎ 01667 453208, Fax 456328, Pro 452787, Rest/Bar 452103
Off A96 at Nairn Old Parish Church.
Championship links;1990 Walker Cup venue.

Pro Robin Fyfe; Founded 1887
Designed by Tom Morris; James Braid; A Simpson
18 holes (9 hole Newton course), 6430 yards, S.S.S. 71
⚐ Practice ground.
† Welcome by prior arrangement.
⌾ WD £70; WE £70.
⌁ Welcome by prior arrangement; handicap certs required; catering packages by arrangement.
🍽 Full clubhouse facilities.
🛏 Golf View; Newton; Altonburn; Windsor Hotel.

9D 58 **Nairn Dunbar**
Lochloy Rd, Nairn, IV12 5AE
🖧 www.nairndunbar.com
✉ secretary@nairndunbar.com
☎ 01667 452741, Fax 456897, Pro 453964
0.5 miles E of Nairn on A96.
Links course.
Pro D Torrance; Founded 1899
18 holes, 6765 yards, S.S.S. 74, S.R. 139
⚐ 300 yard practice facility.
† Welcome (advance reservation advisable).
⌾ WD £39; WE £48.
⌁ Welcome but booking essential. Group rates are negotiable.
🍽 Full clubhouse facilities available.
🛏 Golf View; Links; Claymore.

9D 59 **Newburgh-on-Ythan** ☏
Beach Road, Newburgh, Aberdeenshire, AB41 6BE
🖧 www.newburgh-on-ythan.co.uk
✉ secretary@newburgh.co.uk
☎ 01358 789058, Fax 788104, Pro 789058, Sec 789084
From A90 12 miles N of Aberdeen to A975 to Newburgh.
Links course; new 9 holes added 1996.
Founded 1888/1996
Designed by Greens of Scotland (Aberdeen)
18 holes, 6162 yards, S.S.S. 72
⚐ Practice area available.
† Welcome.
⌾ Terms available on application.
⌁ Welcome by prior arrangement; full day's golf and catering packages available; terms available on application.
🍽 Full clubhouse facilities.
🛏 Udny Arms; Ythan Hotel.

9D 60 **Newmachar** ☏
Swailend, Newmachar, Aberdeen, AB21 7UU

☎ 01651 863002, Fax 863055, Pro 863222
12 miles N of Aberdeen off A947 Aberdeen-Banff road.
Parkland course.
Pro Gordon Simpson; Founded 1990
Designed by Dave Thomas
Hawkshill: 18 holes, 6623 yards, S.S.S. 73
Swailend: 18 holes, 6388 yards, S.S.S. 70
⚐ Practice range 12 bays.
† Welcome but handicap certs are required.
⌾ WD £30 WE £40 (Hawkshill); WD £15 WE £20 (Swailend).
⌁ Welcome by prior arrangement; from £30 (Hawkshill); from £15 (Swailend).
🍽 Full clubhouse facilities available.
🛏 Dunavon House; Kirkhill; Marriott Dyce.

9D 61 **Newtonmore**
Golf Course Rd, Newtonmore, Highland, PH20 1AT
🖧 www.newtonmoregolf.com
✉ secretary@newtonmoregolf.com
☎ 01540 673878, Fax 670147, Pro 673611, Rest/Bar 673328
2 miles S of Newtonmore off the A9.
Parkland course.
Pro Bob Henderson; Founded 1893
Designed by James Braid
18 holes, 6031 yards, S.S.S. 69
† Welcome.
⌾ WD £20; WE £24.
⌁ Welcome by prior arrangement with Sec; day tickets available; catering packages by arrangement; pool table.
🍽 Full clubhouse facilities; except Tuesdays, no catering exceptions made for large parties.
🛏 Glen; Balavil Sports; Lodge; Mains.

9D 62 **Northern**
Golf Rd, Kings Links, Aberdeen, AB24 5QB
☎ 01224 636440, Fax 622679
E of City. Down at the sea.
Municipal seaside course.
Founded 1887
18 holes, 6270 yards, S.S.S. 69
⚐ 18 all floodlit.
† Welcome.
⌾ POA.
⌁ Welcome by arrangement; terms on application.
🍽 Full facilities at WE; by arrangement WD.

9D 63 **Oldmeldrum** ☏
Kirk Brae, Oldmeldrum, Aberdeenshire, AB51 0DJ

☎ 01651 872648, Fax 873555,
Pro 873555
On A947 from Aberdeen.
Parkland course; extended to 18 holes in 1994.
Pro Hamish Love; Founded 1885
18 holes, 5988 yards, S.S.S. 69
🏌 Driving range.
† Welcome by prior arrangement.
Γ WD £18; WE £22.
⚲ Welcome by prior arrangement with pro; catering packages by arrangement; from £14.
🍴 Full facilities.
🛏 Meldrum House; Meldrum Arms; Redgarth; Cromlet Hill B&B.

9D 64 Orkney
Grainbank, Kirkwall, Orkney, KW15 1RD
☎ 01856 872457
W boundary of Kirkwall.
Parkland course.
Founded 1889
18 holes, 5411 yards, S.S.S. 67
† Welcome.
Γ WD £15; WE £15 per day in summer. in winter £5 per day.
⚲ Welcome; day's golf; snacks and meals can be arranged at lunchtime during the summer; games room; from £10.
🍴 Full clubhouse facilities.

9D 65 Peterculter   ☎
Oldtown, Burnside Rd, Peterculter, Aberdeen, AB14 0LN
🖳 www.petercultergolfclub.co.uk
🖂 info@petercultergolfclub.co.uk
☎ 01224 735245, Fax 735580,
Pro 734994, Rest/Bar 735245
Take the A93 to Royal Deeside into Peterculter turning left before Rob Roy Bridge.
Undulating scenic parkland course on banks of River Dee.

Pro Dean Vannet; Founded 1989
Designed by E Lappin/Greens of Scotland
18 holes, 5947 yards, S.S.S. 68
† Welcome.
Γ WD £20; WE £24.
⚲ Welcome WD by prior arrangement; day tickets (WD £27, WE £30); catering by prior arrangement; from £12.
🍴 Full clubhouse facilities.

9D 66 Peterhead   ☎
Craigewan Links, Peterhead, Aberdeenshire, AB42 1LT
🖂 phdgc@freenetname.co.uk
☎ 01779 472149, Fax 480725,
Sec 480725, Rest/Bar 472149
On A92 and A975 30 miles N of Aberdeen.
Seaside links course.
Founded 1841
Designed by Willie Park and James Braid
18 holes, 6173 yards, S.S.S. 71
† Welcome; some Sat restrictions apply.
Γ WD £24 per round, £34 per day; WE £30 per round, £40 per day. 9-hole course: £14 for adults, £7 for juniors.
⚲ Welcome by arrangement with Sec; restrictions Sat; catering packages by arrangement; also 9-hole course, 2400 yards, S.S.S. 60; from £16.
🍴 Clubhouse with full facilities.
🛏 Palace; Waterside Inn.

Piperdam Golf Club
(See advertisement on this page)

9D 67 Portlethen   ☎
Badentoy Rd, Portlethen, Aberdeenshire, AB12 4YA

🖳 www.portlethengolfclub.com
🖂 info@portlethengc.fsnet.co.uk
☎ 01224 781090, Fax 781090,
Pro 782571, Rest/Bar 782575
On the A90 six miles S of Aberdeen.
Parkland course.
Pro Muriel Thomson; Founded 1989
Designed by Donald Steel
18 holes, 6670 yards, S.S.S. 72
† Welcome WD 9.30am-3pm; not Sat; Sun after 1pm.
Γ WD £15; WE £22.
⚲ Welcome by prior arrangement with admin dept; catering packages available; buggy hire.
🍴 Full clubhouse facilities.
🛏 Travel Inn.

9D 68 Reay
The Clubhouse, Reay, by Thurso, Caithness, KW14 7RE
🖳 www.reaygolfclub.co.uk
🖂 info@reaygolfclub.co.uk
☎ 01847 811288, Sec 568333
11 miles W of Thurso.
Seaside links course.
Founded 1893
Redesigned by Braid.
18 holes, 5884 yards, S.S.S. 68
† Welcome except competition days.
Γ £20 per round or day.
⚲ Welcome by prior arrangement with Sec; catering by prior arrangement; from £15.
🍴 By arrangement.
🛏 Forss House, Forss; Park Hotel, Thurso; Melvich Hotel; see website.

9D 69 Rothes
Blackhall, Rothes, Aberlour, Banffshire, AB38 7AN
☎ 01340 831443, Fax 831443,
Sec 831676
10 miles S of Elgin on A941 at S end of the town.

Royal Tarlair

When you leave the town of Macduff on the Moray Firth coast of Scotland and head east towards Fraserburgh on the A98, the first sight that greets you to your left is the spectacular vista of Royal Tarlair Golf Club. Perched precariously on the cliff tops it would appear a mountain goat might be more in order as a companion than a caddie, but once out on the course, the swirling wind is not the only bracing element as the undulating course represents a delight for golfers of all abilities and a challenge for the more serious of breaking the standard scratch score of 68.

On a clear day the panoramic views are breathtaking, both out over the rolling waves of the North Sea and down the coastline to the distant village of Pennan, made famous by the film *Local Hero*.

Over 80 years ago, the local heroes were the trustees of the late Duke of Fife, who granted the site on generous terms to the architect, leading professional of the day Mr George Smith of Lossiemouth, who was of the opinion that it would make one of the finest courses in the north of Scotland.

A meeting was called in November 1923, with the late Colonel JJ George in the chair, and a committee was formed. With the aid of an unemployment grant and £1070 from a two-day bazaar held in August 1925 and opened by Lord Carnegie, it was thought the financial situation was sound. It was.

Officially opened in 1926 and given the Royal designation by the then HRH Princess Royal later the same year, the layout and surrounding area have been subjected to several changes over the decades, all of which have improved the overall experience.

The course never disappoints whatever the weather and changes to the clubhouse, which underwent a major refurbishment recently, means the club now provides the facilities expected in most quality golf clubs.

Most of the golfers who venture out to tackle Royal Tarlair return to talk of two things. The first is the famous par three 13th hole, named Clivet, a tee shot every golfer should experience at least once in their lifetime. The exhilarating hole offers the golfer the opportunity to test their nerve and resolve to the limit as the tee shot is played over a yawning gully to a green whose backdrop is the North Sea itself. Not a tee shot for the faint-hearted especially when played into the prevailing wind. The second thing every-one talks about is the quality of the greens which have helped many putts find their way to the bottom of the cup over the years.

Maybe those greens are irrigated by the underground spring of Tarlair, although nobody has been able to find it since the First World War when a German mine drifted ashore and blew it up.

Like Duff House Royal, the club occupies land that once belonged to the Duke of Fife and originally rented the leasehold of the land. But in 1926 the club was granted the royal title by the grand old Duchess of Fife. – **Nick Alexander**

Parkland course.
Founded 1990
Designed by John Souter
9 holes, 4972 yards, S.S.S. 65
† Everyone welcome.
⌇ WD £12; WE £15.
⌁ Welcome by prior arrangement;
packages for golf and catering can be
arranged; terms available on
application.
🍽 Full bar and restaurant facilities.
🛏 Ben Aigen; Eastbank; Craigellachie
Hotel, Craigellachie.

9D 70 Royal Aberdeen
Links Road, Bridge of Don, Aberdeen,
AB23 8AT
🖥 www.royalaberdeengolf.com
📧 admin@royalaberdeengolf.com
☎ 01224 702571, Fax 826591,
Pro 702221
2 miles N on the main road from
Aberdeen on the A90 to Fraserburgh.
Seaside links course.
Pro R MacAskill; Founded 1780
Designed by Robert Simpson and
James Braid
18 holes, 6502 yards, S.S.S. 73
† Welcome WD; WE restrictions.
⌇ WD £75 round, £100 day; WE £85
round.
🍽 Dining room; lounge and bar.
🛏 Atholl; Marcliffe; Udny Arms.

9D 71 Royal Dornoch
Golf Rd, Dornoch, Sutherland,
IV25 3LW
🖥 www.royaldornoch.com
📧 bookings@royaldoornoch.com
☎ 01862 810219, Fax 810792,
Pro 810902, Sec 811220,
Rest/Bar 810371
Course is 45 miles N of Inverness off
the A9.
Championship and recreactional links
course.
Founded 1877
Designed by Tom Morris; John
Sutherland; George Duncan
Championship course: 18 holes, 6514
yards, S.S.S. 73; Struie Course: 18
holes, 6276 yards, S.S.S. 70.
† Welcome with handicap certs
(championship course).
⌇ WD £69; WE £79.
⌁ Welcome by prior arrangement;
handicap certs required; catering by
prior arrangement; and combination
tickets with Struie course also
available; from £80.
🍽 Full clubhouse facilities.
🛏 Club can provide a list of local
hotels GH and B&Bs.

9D 72 Royal Tarlair ☏
Buchan St, Macduff, Aberdeenshire,
AB44 1TA
🖥 www.royaltarliar.co.uk
📧 info@royaltarliar.co.uk
☎ 01261 832897, Fax 833455
Course is on the A98 48 miles from
Aberdeen.
Parkland course.
Founded 1923
Designed by George Smith
18 holes, 5866 yards, S.S.S. 68
† Welcome.
⌇ £15 round. Per day £20.
⌁ None.
🍽 Full catering and bar.
🛏 Banff Springs.

9D 73 Shetland
Dale, Gott by Lerwick, Shetland Is
☎ 01595 840369
3 miles N of Lerwick.
Undulating moorland course.
Founded 1891
Designed by Fraser Middleton
18 holes, 5776 yards, S.S.S. 69
† Welcome.
⌇ WD from £12; WE from £12.
⌁ Welcome by arrangement; weekly
tickets available; from £12.
🍽 Bar and snacks.
🛏 Lerwick; Grand; Queens.

9D 74 Skeabost
Skeabost Bridge, Isle of Skye,
IV51 9NP
☎ 01470 532322
40 miles from Kyle of Lochalsh.
Parkland course.
Founded 1984
9 holes, 3224 yards, S.S.S. 60
† Welcome.
⌇ WD £10; WE £10.
🍽 Bar and restaurant in the hotel
April-Oct.
🛏 Skeabost (26 beds).

9D 75 Spean Bridge
Station Rd, Spean Bridge, Fort William,
PH34 4EU
☎ 01397 704954
8 miles N of Fort William on A82.
Inland course.
9 holes, 2203 yards, S.S.S. 63
† By arrangement only.
⌇ £8.
⌁ By arrangement only.

9D 76 Spey Bay ☏
Spey Bay, Fochabers, Moray,
IV32 7PJ

☎ 01343 820424
Turn off the A96 near Fochabers
Bridge follow the B9104 Spey Bay
road to coast.
Links course.
Founded 1907
Designed by Ben Sayers
18 holes, 6092 yards, S.S.S. 69
⌇ Practice range.
† Welcome but booking advisable on
Sundays.
⌇ WD £10; WE £13.
⌁ Welcome by application; day
packages available; tennis;
petanque; putting; terms available on
application.
🍽 Full facilities; meals and bar all
day; bar lunches in winter.
🛏 Spey Bay.

9D 77 Stonehaven ☏
Cowie, Stonehaven, Aberdeenshire,
AB39 3RH
☎ 01569 762124, Fax 765973
N of Stonehaven on A92; signposted at
the mini roundabout near the Leisure
Centre.
Parkland course on cliffs overlooking
Stonehaven Bay.
Founded 1888
Designed by A Simpson
18 holes, 5103 yards, S.S.S. 65
† Welcome except before 4pm Sat
and on competition days.
⌇ WD £15; WE £20.
⌁ Welcome WD and Sun; catering
available by prior application to
Secretary; terms available on
application.
🍽 Full facilities. everyday except
Mondays.
🛏 Heugh; County; Station; Crown.

9D 78 Stornoway
Castle Grounds, Stornoway, Isle of
Lewis, HS2 0XP
🖥 www.stornowaygolfclub.co.uk
📧 admin@stornowaygolfclub.co.uk
☎ 01851 702240
0.5 miles outside Stornoway in the
grounds of Lews Castle.
Parkland course.
Founded 1890
Designed by JR Stutt
18 holes, 5252 yards, S.S.S. 66
† Welcome except on Sun.
⌇ £15 round; £25 day; £45 week.
⌁ Welcome by prior written
arrangement with Secretary; special
rates available by application; from
£12.
🍽 Bar and bar snacks.
🛏 Caberfeidh; Royal; Seaforth.

9D 79 Strathlene Buckie ☎
Portessie, Buckie, Banffshire,
AB56 2DJ
📧 strathgolf@ukonline.co.uk
☎ 01542 831798, Fax 831798
Off the Elgin-Banff coast route 2 miles
E of Buckie Harbour.
Undulating moorland/seaside course.
Pro Brian Slorach; Founded 1877
Designed by Alex Smith
18 holes, 5977 yards, S.S.S. 69
⚑ 14 bay driving range; golf training
facility included.
† Welcome except before 9.30am
and between 12 noon-2pm at WE.
⚐ Terms on application.
⚑ Welcome by prior arrangement;
catering by arrangement; day and
weekly tickets available; terms on
application.
🍽 Full facilities; one bar and meals.

9D 80 Strathpeffer Spa ☎
Golf Course Road, Strathpeffer, Ross-
shire, IV14 9AS
🖱 www.strathpeffergolf.co.uk
📧 mail@strathpeffergolf.co.uk
☎ 01997 421219, Fax 421011,
Rest/Bar 421219
5 miles N of Dingwall.
Upland course.
Founded 1888
Designed by W Park
18 holes, 4813 yards, S.S.S. 64
⚑ Small practive area.
† Welcome except before 10am Sun.
⚐ Available on application.
⚑ Welcome by prior arrangement;
packages available for golf and
catering.
🍽 Full facilities.
🛏 Ben Wyvis; Highland; Holly
Lodge.

9D 81 Stromness
Ness, Stromness, Orkney, K16 3DU
☎ 01856 850772
Situated at the S end of town bordering
Hoy Sound.
Parkland course.
Founded 1890
18 holes, 4762 yards, S.S.S. 63
† Welcome.
⚐ WD £12; WE £12.
⚑ Welcome; catering packages by
arrangement; tennis; pool table; darts
and bowls; terms available on
application.
🛏 Stromness; Royal.

9D 82 Tain Golf Club ☎
Chapel Road, Tain, Ross-shire,
IV19 1JE
🖱 www.tain-golfclub.co.uk
📧 info@tain-golfclub.co.uk

☎ 01862 892314, Fax 892099
35 miles N of Inverness on A9; 0.25
miles from Tain.
Links course.
Founded 1890
Designed by Tom Morris
18 holes, 6404 yards, S.S.S. 71
† Everyone welcome.
⚐ WD £33 per round, £40 per day;
WE £40 per round, £50 per day.
⚑ Welcome by prior arrangement;
discount of 20% for groups over 12;
catering by arrangement; terms
available on application.
🍽 Full facilities.
🛏 Morangie; Mansfield House, both
Tain; Royal; Carnegie Lodge, both
Tain.

9D 83 Tarbat
Rock Cottage, Rock Field Village,
Portmahomack, Ross-Shire,
IV20 1SL
📧 christina@
portmahomack.fsnet.co.uk
☎ 01862 871486
9 miles E of Tain on the B9165 off A9.
Seaside links course.
Founded 1909
Designed by J. Sutherland
9 holes, 5082 yards, S.S.S. 65
⚑ Practice ground.
† Welcome; some restrictions on Sat.
⚐ Day ticket: WD £12; WE £12.
⚑ Welcome by prior arrangement
with Sec; catering by arrangement;
local hotels provide full meal and bar
service.
🍽 Limited facilities; see local hotels.
🛏 Castle; Caledonian; Oyster
Catcher.

9D 84 Tarland
Aberdeen Rd, Tarland, Aboyne,
Aberdeenshire, AB34 4YN
☎ 01339 881413
5 miles NW of Aboyne; 30 miles W of
Aberdeen.
Parkland course.
Founded 1908
Designed by Tom Morris
9 holes, 5875 yards, S.S.S. 68
† Welcome.
⚐ WD £12; WE £15.
⚑ Welcome by prior arrangement;
terms on application.
🍽 Full facilities June-Sept; otherwise
by arrangement.
🛏 Aberdeen Arms; Commercial.

9D 85 Thurso ☎
Newlands of Geise, Thurso, Caithness,
KW14 7XF

☎ 01847 893807
2 miles SW from centre of Thurso on
B870.
Parkland course.
Founded 1893
Designed by W Stuart
18 holes, 5853 yards, S.S.S. 69
† £20 per day; 2 for 1 vouchers
accepted all year.
⚐ Terms on application.
⚑ Welcome by prior arrangement;
terms on application.
🍽 Full facilities.

9D 86 Torphins
Bog Rd, Torphins, Aberdeenshire,
AB31 4JU
📧 stuart@macgregors.fsnet.co.uk
☎ 01339 882115, Sec 882402
Signposted in village; 6 miles W of
Banchory on A980.
Parkland course with Highland views.
Founded 1896
9 holes, 4738 yards, S.S.S. 64
⚑ Practice facilites, putting and nets.
† Welcome.
⚐ WD £13, WE £14; 9 holes £7.
⚑ Welcome by prior arrangement.
🍽 Full facilities at WE.
🛏 Learney Arms.

9D 87 Torvean
Glenurquhart Rd, Inverness,
Inverness-shire, IV3 8JN
📧 info@torveangolfclub.com
☎ 01463 225651 (office), Fax
711417, Starter/Shop 711434, Rest/Bar
225651
On A82 Fort William road approx
1 mile from Inverness town centre.
Parkland course.
Founded 1962
Designed by T Hamilton
18 holes, 5784 yards, S.S.S. 68
† Welcome; tee bookings advisable.
⚐ WD £15; WE £18 aprox, call to
confirm.
⚑ Welcome by arrangement with
Highland Council.
🍽 Club chef.
🛏 Lochness House Hotel.

9D 88 Traigh Golf Course
Traigh, Arisaig, by Mallaig, Arisaig,
Inverness-Shire, PH39 4NT
☎ 01687 450337, Sec 450645
On the B8008 Fort William to Mallaig
road.
Links course.
Founded 1905
Designed by John Salvesen
9 holes, 4912 yards, S.S.S. 65

† Welcome.
[Terms on application.
🍽 Clubhouse snacks.
🛌 Arisaig Hotel: Glasnacardoch House; West Highland.

9D 89 **Turriff**　　　　ⓣ
Rosehall, Turriff, Aberdeenshire, AB53 4HD
🖳 www.turriffgolfclub.com
📧 secretary@turriffgolf.sol.co.uk
☎ 01888 562982, Fax 568050, Pro 563025
On B9024 1 mile up Huntly road.
Meadowland/parkland course.
Pro John Black; Founded 1896
18 holes, 6107 yards, S.S.S. 69
🏌 Practice ground.
† Welcome except before 10am WE; handicap certs required.
[WD £18; WE £24.
↺ Welcome by arrangement with Sec; day tickets available (WD £20, WE £28).
🍽 By prior arrangement.
🛌 Union; White Heather; Banff Springs.

9D90 **Westhill**　　　　ⓣ
Westhill Heights, Aberdeenshire, AB32 6RY

📧 wgolfclub@aol.com
☎ 01224 740159, Fax 749124, Pro 740159, Sec 742567, Rest/Bar 743361
Course is on A944 6 miles from Aberdeen.
Parkland/moorland course.
Pro George Bruce; Founded 1977
Designed by Charles Lawrie
18 holes, 5849 yards, S.S.S. 69
🏌 Practice green; practice area; practice bunker.
† Welcome except Sat.
[WD £14; WE £20.
↺ Welcome WD and Sun by prior arrangement; catering packages by special arrangement; terms on application.
🍽 Bar facilities.
🛌 Broadstreik Inn; Westhill Inn.

9D 91 **Whalsay**
Skaw Taing, Island of Whalsay, Shetland, ZE2 9AL
☎ 01806 566483
At N end of Island.
Moorland course.
Founded 1975
18 holes, 6009 yards, S.S.S. 68
† Welcome; restrictions on competition days.

[WD £10; WE £10.
↺ Welcome by prior arrangement; packages available; terms on application.
🍽 Bar and catering facilities available.
🛌 Hotels on Shetland.

9D 92 **Wick**
Reiss, Wick, Caithness, KW1 4RW
☎ 01955 602726, Sec 602935
Course is on the A9 three miles north of Wick.
Links course.
Founded 1870
Designed by McCulloch
18 holes, 5976 yards, S.S.S. 70
† Welcome.
[WD £15; WE £15.
↺ Welcome by prior arrangement catering by prior arrangement.
🍽 Bar an limited catering facilities available.
🛌 Mackays.

It has been claimed that the Blorenge and the river Usk are "the purple headed mountain and the river running by" of Cecil Alexander's hymn *All Things Bright and Beautiful*. Although it's more likely that Alexander wrote the words in her native Ireland, you can understand how the myth of Wales arose.

The Monmouthshire, with views of the Blorenge and the Usk, Royal St David's and Aberdovey on the West coast, Nefyn and District, perched on the cliffs, Cradoc and Llandrindod Wells, at the foothills of the Brecon Beacons and Cambrian Mountains, Ashburnham, overlooking Carmarthen Bay, the list just goes on and on. Wales has a preponderance of spectacularly beautiful golf courses.

Darwin wrote of Aberdovey "It is the course that my soul loves best in the world. About this one course in the world I am a hopeless and shameful sentimentalist and I glory in my shame". The sixteenth is a wonderful risk and reward hole with a railway line running alongside. In response to an angry train driver who had just been pinged by his drive, one living member said, "If you had been on time, I'd have missed you".

A few miles to the north Royal St David's nestles in the shadow of Harlech castle and Snowdon. Actually, "nestle" is not really a word that many associate with St David's. When people stagger in after grappling with gale force winds and a sequence of gargantuan dunes, after a struggle to even reach some of the fairways, the language is a bit fresher than "nestle". It has been said that St David's is the hardest par 69 in the world and not many would disagree.

Royal Porthcawl, the host of the 1995 Walker Cup, has the reputation of being Wales's top course. It is quite an accolade because there are so many to choose from. Not so very far from Porthcawl, Southerndown is a wonderful anachronism. There is a fascinating variety of holes, right from the contradictory opening par four of short yardage and long carries, that goes up a hill without an apparent end. The course is very well mowed by sheep although the recycled material they leave behind can cause awkward lies. And being in Wales, there are superb views, this time of the Bristol Channel.

Celtic Manor, the new, flash kid on the block has done a great deal to promote golf in Wales after being awarded the 2010 Ryder Cup. But the decision had more to do with rewarding a sponsor of the European Tour than favouring a great golf course.

Of Wales's golfing hotels, many people have a soft spot for St Pierre, the first post war championship course to be built in Britain. It is incredible now to think that the cost of the construction, the land and the manor house (where the crown jewels were stashed during the Battle of Agincourt) was just £30,000. It has many childhood memories for me, but then it is that sort of place. Wasn't it here that Bernhard Langer climbed up a tree to play a chip shot onto the green?

Wales is full of myth. At the Glamorganshire the card reads, "Slow play is deplored". It was here that between the wars a member won a bet by taking 68 minutes to play eighteen holes. We all fancy we could do that, but could we score 63 in the process.

Tenby, the oldest constituted club in Wales, Borth & Ynslas, Conwy, Prestatyn, Pyle & Kenfig, Pennard, they all have courses worth the playing and stories worth the telling.

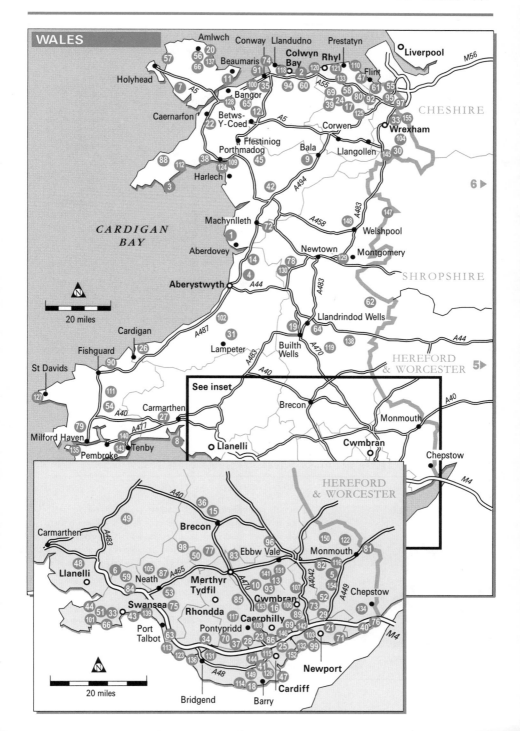

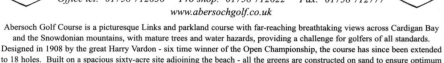

Abersoch Golf Club

Golf Road, Abersoch, Pwllheli, Gwynedd LL53 7EY

Office tel: 01758 712636   Pro shop: 01758 712622   Fax: 01758 712777

www.abersochgolf.co.uk

Abersoch Golf Course is a picturesque Links and parkland course with far-reaching breathtaking views across Cardigan Bay and the Snowdonian mountains, with mature trees and water hazards, providing a challenge for golfers of all standards. Designed in 1908 by the great Harry Vardon - six time winner of the Open Championship, the course has since been extended to 18 holes. Built on a spacious sixty-acre site adjoining the beach - all the greens are constructed on sand to ensure optimum conditions for golfers in all conditions. With a sheltered position and a mild climate, Abersoch is the ideal course all year round. To make your visit as comfortable as possible, we also have a full catering service, all-day bar facilities and special golfing weekend breaks including accommodation. Enjoy a warm welcome at Abersoch!

---

10 1 Aberdovey ☎
Station Road, Aberdovey, Gwynedd, LL35 0RT
⌨ www.aberdoveygolf.co.uk
☎ 01654 767493, Fax 767027,
Pro 767602, Sec 767493,
Rest/Bar 767210
On A493 W of Aberdovey, adjacent to station.
Links course.
Pro John Davies; Founded 1892
Designed by Braid/Fowler/Swan.
18 holes, 6445 yards, S.S.S. 71
🏌 Practice area.
🏌 Welcome with handicap certs.
🍴 WD £36; WE £41.50.
⛳ Welcome by prior arrangement; handicap certs needed; terms on application.
🍽 Clubhouse facilities.
🛏 Trefeddian; Penhelig; Brodawel.

10 2 Abergele ☎
Tan-y-Gopa Rd, Abergele, Conwy, LL22 8DS
⌨ www.abergelegolfclub.co.uk
📧 secretary@abergelegolfclub .freeserve.co.uk
☎ 01745 824034, Fax 824772, Pro 823813, Rest/Bar 826716
A55 at Abergele/Rhuddlan exit; through town; first left past the police station.
Parkland course.
Pro IR Runcie; Founded 1910
Designed by Hawtree & Sons/ David Williams & Associates.
18 holes, 6595 yards, S.S.S. 72
🏌 Welcome by arrangement.
🍴 Terms on application.
⛳ Welcome by arrangement; members have priority until 10.15am and until 2pm in the afternoon; 27 holes of golf, light lunch, 3-course meal; terms on application.
🍽 Full clubhouse facilities.
🛏 Kinmel Manor; Esplanade Hotel, Llandudno.

10 3 Abersoch ☎
Golf Road, Abersoch, Gwynedd, LL53 7EY
⌨ www.abersochgolf.co.uk
📧 admin@abersochgolf.co.uk
pro@abersochgolf.co.uk
☎ 01758 712636, Fax 712777
6 miles from Pwllheli; first left through the village.
Seaside links course.
Pro Alan Jones; Founded 1907
Designed by Harry Vardon
18 holes, 5671 yards, S.S.S. 68
🏌 Welcome with handicap certs.
🍴 WD £25; WE £30.
⛳ Welcome by prior arrangement.
🍽 Full facilities.
🛏 Deucoch; Carisbrooke, Nanhoron.

10 4 Aberystwyth ☎
Bryn-y-Mor Road, Aberystwyth, Ceredigion, SY23 2HY
⌨ www.aberystwythgolfclub.com
📧 aberystwythgolf@talk21.com
☎ 01970 615104, Fax 626622, Pro 625301, Sec 615104, Rest/Bar 615104
N end of the promenade behind the seafront hotels; access road adjacent to cliff railway; 1 mile from the town centre.
Undulating meadowland course.
PGA Professional on site; Founded 1911
Designed by Harry Vardon
18 holes, 6119 yards, S.S.S. 71
🏌 Welcome; some WE restrictions. 2 Practice grounds & putting green.
🍴 WD £20; WE £25.
⛳ Welcome by prior arrangement; packages available.
🍽 Bar and restaurant facilities.
🛏 Apply to Sec for details.

10 5 Alice Springs
Kemys Commander, Usk, Monmouthshire, NP15 1JU

☎ 01873 880708, Fax 881075, Pro 880914
3 miles N of Usk and 8 miles N of Abergavenny on B4598.
Parkland course.
Pro Mike Davis
Founded 1986
Designed by Keith R. Morgan
Monnow Course: 18 holes; Usk Course: 18 holes, Monnow Course: 5544; Usk Course: 5953, S.S.S. Monnow Course: 69; Usk Course: 70
🏌 Welcome; book at any time- Mon to Sun.
🍴 WD £15; WE £17.
⛳ Welcome by prior arrangement; packages available; driving range.
🍽 Full catering and bar facilities; terms on application.
🛏 Cwrt Bleddybn; The Three Salmons Hotel, Usk; The Rat Trap.

10 6 Allt-y-Graban
Allt-y-Graban Rd, Pontlliw, Swansea, W Glam, SA4 1DT
☎ 01792 885757/883279
From M4 Junction 47 take the A48 to Pontlliw.
Parkland course.
Founded 1993
Designed by FG Thomas
9 holes, 4453 yards, S.S.S. 63
🏌 Practice green.
🏌 Welcome.
🍴 18 holes WD £10; WE £12.
⛳ Welcome; minimum 10; catering by arrangement; from £6.
🍽 Clubhouse facilities.
🛏 Forest Motel; The Fountain Inn.

10 7 Anglesey ☎
Station Road, Rhosneigr, Gwynedd, LL64 5QX
⌨ www.theangleseygolfclub.com
📧 info@theangleseygolfclub.com
☎ 01407 810219, Fax 811202, Pro 811202, Sec 811127

8 miles SE of Holyhead; on A4080 off
A5 between Gwalchmai and
Bryngwran.
Links course with dunes and heather.
Pro mathew Parry; Founded 1914
18 holes, 6300 yards, S.S.S. 68
✝ Welcome.
Ⅰ Terms on application.
◔ Welcome by prior arrangement;
packages and reductions available for
more than 10 players; terms on
application.
🍽 Clubhouse bar and catering
facilities.
🛏 Treaddur Hotel; Trecastell; Maelog
Lake; Gadleys Country House; Eryl Mor.

10 8 Ashburnham
Cliff Terrace, Burry Port,
Carmarthenshire, SA16 0HN
☎ 01554 832269, Fax 832269,
Pro 833846, Rest/Bar 832466
4 miles from Llanelli; 9 miles from M4.
Championship links.
Pro RA Ryder; Founded 1894
2 x 18 holes, Championship: 6936;
Medal: 6627 yards, S.S.S.
Championship course:74; Medal
course:73
✝ Welcome by prior arrangement.
Ⅰ WD £27.50 per round; WE £32.50
per round.
◔ Welcome WD by prior
arrangement.
🍽 Full facilities except Mondays.
🛏 Ashburnham; Stradey Park Hotel;
Diplomat Hotel.

10 9 Bala Golf Club   ☎
Penlan, Bala, Gwynedd, LL23 7YD
☎ 01678 520359, Fax 521361
Off the main Bala-Dolgellau road.
Upland course with spectacular
views.
Pro Tony Davies; Founded 1973
10 holes, 5031 yards, S.S.S. 64
✝ Welcome; some WE restrictions.
Ⅰ WD £15; WE £20.
◔ Welcome by prior arrangement;
terms on application.
🍽 Bar with snacks available.
🛏 The Plas Coch Hotel, special
packages available.

10 10 Bargoed
Heolddu, Bargoed, CF81 9GF
☎ 01443 830143, Fax 830608
Pro 836411, Sec 830608
10 miles north of Caerphilly.
Part moorland/mountain course.
Founded 1912
18 holes, 6049 yards, S.S.S. 70

✝ Welcome WD; with member only
at WE.
Ⅰ WD £18. With a member only at
weekends.
◔ Welcome by prior arrangement.
🍽 Bar facilities and evening meals.
🛏 Meas Manor; Park; Baverstocks.

10 11 Baron Hill
Beaumaris, Anglesey, N Wales, LL58
8YW
🖳 www.baronhill.co.uk
✉ golf@baronhill.co.uk
☎ 01248 810231, Fax 810231
A545 from Menai Bridge to Beaumaris;
Turn left on entering Beaumaris.
Heathland course.
Founded 1895
9 holes, 5596 yards, S.S.S. 68
Ⅰ 1 practice net, 1 practice green.
✝ Welcome by arrangement with
Secretary or steward; club
competitions on Sundays. Ladies day
Tue morning.
Ⅰ WD £15; WE £15.
◔ Welcome by prior arrangement;
bar and catering packages available;
terms on application.
🍽 Clubhouse facilities.
🛏 Bull's Head; Bishop's Gate;
Bulkeley.

10 12 Betws-y-Coed
The Clubhouse, Betws-y-Coed,
Gwynedd, LL24 0AL
☎ 01690 710556
Off A470 or A5 opposite Midland Bank
in village centre.
Parkland course.
Founded 1971
9 holes, 4998 yards, S.S.S. 64 men's
course; 4427 yards, S.S.S. 66
women's course,
S.S.S. 64
✝ Everyone welcome.
Ⅰ Summer: WD £15; WE £20. Winter
WD £10 WE and bank holidays £15
winter.
◔ Welcome by prior arrangement;
catering and bar packages available;
terms on application.
🍽 Full clubhouse facilities.
🛏 Glan Aber; Gwydir; Waterloo;
Royal Oak, Fairhaven.

10 13 Blackwood
Lon Pennant, Cwmgelli, Blackwood,
Gwent, NP12 1EL
☎ 01495 223152, Sec 222121
Course is 0.25 miles N of Blackwood
on the A4048 Blackwood-Tredegar
road.

Parkland course.
Founded 1914
9 holes, 5304 yards, S.S.S. 66
✝ Welcome WD; with a member at
WE.
Ⅰ WD £14; WE £18.
◔ Welcome by prior arrangement;
terms on application.
🍽 Bar and catering facilities.
🛏 Maes Manor.

10 14 Borth and Ynyslas   ☎
Borth, Dyfed, Ceredigion, SY24 5JS
🖳 www.borthgolf.co.uk
✉ secretary@borthgolf.co.uk
☎ 01970 871202, Fax 871202,
Pro 871557
8 miles S of Machynlleth; 4 miles N of
Aberystwyth on A487.
Links course.
Pro JG Lewis; Founded 1885
Designed by H Colt
18 holes, 6116 yards, S.S.S. 70
Ⅰ Practice ground.
✝ Welcome by arrangement.
Ⅰ All week £28 per round.
◔ Welcome; minimum 10 in summer,
6 in winter; catering packages
available.
🍽 Bar and catering facilities.
🛏 Golfing packages, Belle View,
Royal Hotel, Aberystwythl.

10 15 Brecon
Newton Park, Llanfaes, Brecon,
Powys, LD3 8PA
☎ 01874 622004
50 yards, from A40 on W of town.
Parkland course.
Founded 1902
Designed by J Braid
9 holes, 5476 yards, S.S.S. 66
✝ Welcome.
Ⅰ WD £12; WE £15.
◔ Welcome by arrangement; catering
packages available; terms on
application.
🍽 Catering facilities available.
🛏 Peterstone Court.

10 16 Bryn Meadows Golf &
Country Club.
Maesycwmmer, Ystrad Mynach,
Caerphilly, CR82 7SN
🖳 www.brynmeadows.co.uk
☎ 01495 225590, Fax 228272, Pro
221905, Sec 225590, Rest/Bar 225590
Off A469 15 miles from Cardiff.
Parkland course.
Pro Bruce Hunter; Founded 1973
Designed by E Jefferies & B Mayo
18 holes, 6156 yards, S.S.S. 70

Caer Beris Manor
Hotel and Restaurant

Builth Wells, Powys LD2 3NP

Tel: (01982) 552601
Fax: (01982) 552586

e-mail: caerberismanor@btinternet.com   www.caerberis.co.uk

First built in 1093, Caer Beris Manor has been transformed over the past few years into a three star real 'Country House Hotel'. Visiting golfers are welcome at Builth Wells 18 hole course which is adjacent to the hotel. The beautiful parkland setting makes playing a delight. Residents enjoy concessions on green fees. Also nearby are 18 hole courses at Llandrindod and Cradoc as well as 9 hole courses at Knighton and Brecon.

---

† Welcome.
[WD £15; WE £25.
⌁ Welcome WD by arrangement; special golf packages; function rooms; gym; indoor pool; Jacuzzi; pool table.
🍽 Full facilities; bar and à la carte restaurant.
🛏 On site hotel Bryn Meadows.

---

10 17 Bryn Morfydd Hotel ✆
Llanrhaeadr, Denbighshire, Clwyd, LL16 4NP
☎ 01745 890280, Fax 890488
Off A525 between Denbigh and Ruthin.
Founded 1982/92
Designed by Alliss/Thomas (Duchess course)
Dukes course:18; Duchess course: 9 holes, Dukes course: 5800; Duchess course: 2000 yards, S.S.S. Dukes course: 68; Duchess course: 27
⌇ Practice nets and putting green.
† Welcome.
[WD £15; WE £20.
⌁ Welcome by arrangement; packages available; from £25.
🍽 Full clubhouse and hotel facilities.
🛏 3-star hotel on site.

---

10 18 Brynhill ✆
Port Rd, Barry, S Glam, CF62 8PN
☎ 01446 720277, Fax 720422
M4 Junction 33 take signs for Barry and Cardiff Airport on to the A4050.
Undulating meadowland course.
Pro Michael Herbert; Founded 1921
Designed by GK Cotton
Summer: 18; Winter: 18 holes, Summer: 5997; Winter: 5732 yards, S.S.S. Summer: 70; Winter: 69
† Welcome except Sun; handicap certs may be required.
[WD £20; WE £25.
⌁ Welcome WD by prior arrangement; from £17.
🍽 Bar and catering facilities; lunches, afternoon teas and dinners.
🛏 Mount Sorrel; International; Copthorne.

---

10 19 Builth Wells ✆
Golf Clubs Road, Builth Wells, Powys, LD2 3NF

🖥 www.builthwellsgolfclub.co.uk
📧 builthwellsgolfclub1@ btinternet.com
☎ 01982 553296, Fax 551064, Pro 551155
On A483 Builth-Llandovery road just after River Irfon bridge on outskirts of Builth.
Parkland course; no par 5s.
Pro Simon Edwards; Founded 1923
18 holes, 5376 yards, S.S.S. 67
† Welcome with handicap certs.
[WD £17; WE £23.
⌁ Welcome; packages and reductions; terms on application.
🍽 Clubhouse bar and catering.
🛏 Pencerrig House; Caerberis Manor; Greyhound Hotel; Cedars GH.

---

10 20 Bull Bay ✆
Bull Bay, Amlwch, Anglesey, LL68 9RY
🖥 www.bullbaygc.co.uk
📧 ian@bullbaygc.co.uk
☎ 01407 830960, Fax 832612, Pro 831188, Rest/Bar 830213
On A5025 via Benllech and course is 1 mile beyond Amlwch.
Clifftop heathland course, most northern course in Wales.
Pro John Burns; Founded 1913
Designed by Herbert Fowler of Walton Heath
18 holes, 6276 yards, S.S.S. 70
⌇ Practice area and putting green.
† Welcome by prior arrangement.
[WD £22; WE £27.
⌁ Welcome; meals can be provided all day except Mon.
🍽 Clubhouse facilities.
🛏 Trecastell; Bull Bay; Lastra Farm Hotel.

---

10 21 Caerleon
Broadway, Caerleon, Newport, Gwent, NP18 1AY
☎ 01633 420342, Fax 420342, Pro 420342, Sec 420342, Rest/Bar 420342
3 miles from M4 Junction 25 for Caerleon.
Parkland course.
Pro M Phillips; Founded 1974
Designed by Donald Steel
9 holes, 5800 yards, S.S.S. 68

⌇ Practice range 12 Bays floodlit.
† Everyone welcome.
[WD: 18 holes £6.20; 9 holes £4.15; WE: 18 holes £7.70; 9 holes £5.20.
⌁ Welcome by arrangement; terms on application.
🍽 Snacks and bar.
🛏 Priory.

---

10 22 Royal Town of ✆
Caernarfon Golf Club
Aberforeshore, Llanfaglan, Gwynedd, LL54 5RP
🖥 www.caernarfongolfclub.co.uk
📧 caerngc@talk21.com
☎ 01286 678359, Fax 672535, Sec 673783, Rest/Bar 673976
A470 from A55 at Caernarfon towards Porthmadog; at new road bridge turn right, club 1.5 miles.
Parkland course.
Pro Aled Owen; Founded 1907/1981
18 holes, 5891 yards, S.S.S. 68
† Welcome.
[WD £22; WE £30/£245; Mon £15.
⌁ Welcome; special rates for 10 or more players; full facilities available; terms on application.
🍽 Full catering and bar facilities.
🛏 Celtic Royal; Seiont Manor; Bryn Eisteddfod,all Caernarfon; Eryl Mor, Bangor; Esplanade, Llandudno.

---

10 23 Caerphilly
Pencapel, Mountain Rd, Caerphilly, CF83 1HJ
☎ 029 208 83481, Fax 63441, Pro 69104, Sec 63441
On A469 7 miles from Cardiff; 250 yards from rail and bus stations.
Steep wooded mountainside course.
Pro Joel Hill; Founded 1905
Designed by Fernie (original 9)
18 holes, 5728 yards, S.S.S. 69
⌇ Practice green and bunkers.
† Welcome WD; WE only with a member.
[WD £26.
⌁ Limited numbers, by prior arrangement only.
🍽 Bar and dining room.
🛏 Mount; Greenhill; Moat House; Cedar Tree.

10 24 Caerwys 9 of Clubs

Caerwys, Mold, Flintshire, CH7 5AQ
☎ 01352 720692, Sec 721222,
Rest/Bar 720379
1.5 miles S of the A55 midway
between St Asaph and Holywell.
Undulating parkland course.
Founded 1988
Designed by Eleanor Barlow
9 holes, 3080 yards, S.S.S. 60
† Welcome.
[WD £7; WE £9.
☞ Welcome by prior arrangment.
⏲ Light refreshments.
☞ Self catering accommodation.

10 25 Cardiff

Sherborne Ave, Cyncoed, Cardiff,
CF23 6SJ
🖳 www.cardiffgc.co.uk
✉ cardiff.golfclub@virgin.net
☎ 029 2075 3320, Fax 206 80011,
Pro 207 54772, Rest/Bar 207 53067
3 miles N of Cardiff, 2 miles W of
Pentwyn, on A48(M) M4 Junction 29.
Undulating parkland course.
Pro Terry Hanson; Founded 1922
18 holes, 6013 yards, S.S.S. 70
† Welcome.
[WD £40; WE £45.
☞ Welcome by prior arrangement; Fri
only; terms on application; snooker
room available.
⏲ New clubhouse facilities.
☞ Post House, Pentwyn & Holiday Inn.

10 26 Cardigan ☯

Gwbert-on-Sea, Cardigan, Ceredigion,
SA43 1PR
🖳 www.cardigangolf.co.uk
✉ golf@cardigan.fsnet.co.uk
☎ 01239 621775, Fax 621775,
Pro 615359, Rest/Bar 612035
3 miles N of Cardigan.
Links/parkland course with view of
River Teifi and Cardigan Bay.
Pro C Parsons; Founded 1895
Designed by Grant/Hawtree
18 holes, 6687 yards, S.S.S. 72
† Welcome.
[WD £22.50; WE and BH £27.50.
☞ Welcome by prior arrangement;
packages and catering available;
satellite TV; pool table; squash courts;
discounts available, please contact sec
for details.
⏲ Clubhouse facilities.
☞ Cliff Hotel; Gwbert Hotel.

10 27 Carmarthen ☯

Blaenycoed Rd, Carmarthen,
Carmarthenshire, SA33 6EH

🖳 www.cumlaingolfclub.com
☎ 01267 281214, Fax 281493,
Pro 281493, Sec 281588
4.5 miles N of town.
Upland course.
Pro Pat Gillis; Founded 1907
Designed by JH Taylor
18 holes, 6245 yards, S.S.S. 71
† Welcome; ladies day Tues.
[Winter: WD £15; WE £20;
Summer: WD £20; WE £25.
☞ Welcome WD; packages and
discounts available; terms on
application.
⏲ Full clubhouse facilities.
☞ Falcon; Ivy Bush; Forge Motel.

10 28 Castell Heights

Blaengwynlais, Caerphilly, Mid-
Glamorgan, CF8 1NG
☎ 029 2088 6666, Fax 2086 3243,
Sec 2086 1128
4 miles from M4 Junction 32 on the
Tongwynlais-Caerphilly road.
Mountainside course.
Pro Sion Bebb; Founded 1982
9 holes, 5376 yards, S.S.S. 66
🏌 Practice range; 6 bays.
† Welcome; dress codes apply.
[WD/WE £5.50.
☞ Welcome by arrangement; advised
to phone Sec.
⏲ Bar and bar snacks.
☞ The Friendly Hotel.

10 29 The Celtic Manor Resort ☯

Coldra Woods, Newport, NP18 1HQ
🖳 www.celtic-manor.com
✉ postbox@celtic-manor.com
☎ 01633 413000, Fax 412910,
Pro 410312
M4 J4 just 5 mins from Severn Bridge.
Three championship courses in 1400
acres of panoramic undulating
parkland course.
Pro Kevin Carpenter; Founded 1995
Designed by Robert Trent-Jones Jnr
(Wentwood Hills 1999) & Robert Trent-
Jones Snr (Roman Road 1995, Coldra
Woods 1996)
Wentwood Hills: 7403 yards, par 72,
S.S.S. 77 (PGA European Tours venue
– Wales open); Roman Road: 18
holes, 6685 yards, par 69, S.S.S. 72;
Coldra Woods: 4001 yards, par 39
🏌 The Golf School: two-tier floodlit
driving range, coaching with video
graphics; short play areas; practice
range. Superb clubhouse with luxury
locker rooms.
† Everyone welcome.
[Please call reservations for prices
or visit the website.

☞ Welcome by prior arrangement;
corporate and society packages
available.
⏲ 4 restaurants on site. 3 bars, also
full catering facilities available.
☞ 400-room 32-suite 5-star hotel with
1500-delegate Convention Centre.

10 30 Chirk ☯

Chirk, Nr Wrexham, Flintshire,
LL14 5AD
🖳 www.jackbarker.com
✉ chirkgolf@lineone.net
☎ 01691 774407, Fax 773878, Pro
774407, Sec 774407, Rest/Bar 774243
Course is five miles S of Wrexham just
off the A5.
Parkland course; 2 holes greater than
600 yards.
Pro Mark Maddison; Founded 1991
18 holes, 7045 yards, S.S.S. 73
🏌 Practice range, 15 undercover
floodlit bays; practice bunker.
† Everyone welcome.
[Terms on application.
☞ Welcome; full clubhouse facilities;
terrace; buggies; driving range; also 9-
hole Mine Rock course par 3.
⏲ Clubhouse facilities; spike bar;
restaurant; snacks and meals.
☞ Golden Pheasant, Glyn Cieriog;
The Royal Hotel, Llangollen.

10 31 Cilgwyn

Llangybi, Lampeter, Ceredigion,
SA48 8NN
☎ 01570 493286
Course is 4 miles N of Lampeter on
the A485.
Parkland course.
Founded 1905/1977
9 holes, 5309 yards, S.S.S. 67
† Welcome.
[WD £10: WE £15.
☞ Welcome minimum of 10 players
bar and restaurant packages available
from £8.
⏲ Clubhouse facilities.
☞ Falcondale; Black Lion, both
Lampeter.

10 32 Clay's Golf Centre

Bryn Estyn Road, Wrexham, LL13 9UB
☎ 01978 661406, Fax 661417,
Pro 661406, Sec 661406,
Rest/Bar 661416
From A483 Wrexham-Chester road
take A534 for Nantwich and Wrexham
Industrial Estate; 2 miles turn to golf
centre.
Parkland course; new 9-hole pitch and
putt course.

Pro D Larvin; Founded 1991
Designed by RD Jones
18 holes, 5794 yards, S.S.S. 68
⚐ 16.
† Welcome all times.
⚑ WD £14; WE £19.
⚬ Welcome by prior arrangement;
minimum 12; deposit required; practice
balls; 18-27 holes of golf; light lunch; 3-
course dinner; terms on application.
🍴 Full catering facilities available.
⚐ Cross Lane, Marchweil; Holt
Lodge, Wrexham.

10 33 **Clyne** ♣

118/120 Owls Lodge Lane, Mayals,
Swansea, SA3 5DP
🖳 www.clynegolfclub.com
🖥 clynegolfclub@supanet.com
☎ 01792 401989, Fax 401078,
Pro 402094, Sec 401989,
Rest/Bar 403534
From the M4 to Swansea; exit for
Mumbles at Blackpill, head for Gower
and then take first right into Owls
Lodge Lane.
Moorland course.
Pro Johnathan Clewett; Founded 1920
Designed by HS Colt/Harris
18 holes, 6334 yards, S.S.S. 71
⚐ Practice area; chipping green;
putting green.
† Welcome with handicap certs.
⚑ WD £26; WE £32.
⚬ Welcome WD except Tues;
catering packages and reductions for
more than 20 players; from £21.
🍴 Clubhouse facilities.
⚐ Marriott, Swansea; St Anne's,
Mumbles.

10 34 **Coed-y-Mwstwr Golf Club**

The Club House, Coychurch, Near
Bridgend, CF35 6AF
🖳 www.coed-y-mwstwr.co.uk
🖥 coed-y-mwstwr@lineone.net
☎ 01656 864934, Fax 864934
From M4 Junction 35 turn towards
Bridgend and then into Coychurch.
Parkland course.
Founded 1994
Designed by Chapman Warrel
12 holes, 6144 yards, S.S.S. 70
⚐ 2.
† Welcome with handicap certs;
dress codes apply.
⚑ Prices on application.
⚬ Welcome by prior arrangement;
packages available; terms on
application.
🍴 Clubhouse facilities.
⚐ Coed-y-Mwstwr.

10 35 **Conwy (Caernarvonshire)**

Beacons Way, Morfa, Conwy,
Gwynedd, LL32 8ER
🖳 www.conwygolfclub.co.uk
🖥 secretary@conwygolfclub.co.uk
☎ 01492 593400, Fax 593363, Pro
593225, Sec 592423, Rest/Bar 593400
Just off A55 at Conwy.
Links course.
Pro Peter Lees; Founded 1890
18 holes, 6647 yards, S.S.S. 72
† Welcome with handicap certs
standard golf dress code.
⚑ Winter WD £22, WE £25; Summer
WD £30, WE £36; juniors £8 all yr.
⚬ Welcome with prior arrangement
through Sec; catering available winter
package coffee and biscuits 18 holes of golf
and 3 course meal WD £26, WE £30;
summer packages also available; snooker
room; dartboards; function room; Pro is a
commentator.
🍴 Clubhouse facilities.
⚐ Royal; Esplanade; The
Risborough; all Llandudno; The Castle,
Conwy.

10 36 **Cradoc**

Penoyre Park, Cradoc, Brecon, Powys,
LD3 9LP
🖳 www.cradoc.co.uk
🖥 secretary@cradoc.co.uk
☎ 01874 623658, Fax 611711,
Pro 625524, Sec 623658,
Rest/Bar 624396
Take B 4520 road to Upper Chapel
past Brecon Cathedral and turn left to
Cradoc village.
Parkland course.
Pro Richard W Davies; Founded 1967
Designed by C.K.Cotton
18 holes, 6301 yards, S.S.S. 72
⚐ 12.
† Welcome by prior arrangement.
⚑ WD £20; WE £25.
⚬ Welcome by prior arrangement
with secretary; packages available;
terms on application.
🍴 Clubhouse facilities available.
⚐ Peterstone Court; Llangoed Hall;
Castle of Brecon; Lansdown; The
George Hotel.

10 37 **Creigiau** ♣

Llantwit Road, Creigiau, Cardiff,
CF15 9NN
🖥 manager@creigiaugolf.co.uk
☎ 029208 90263, Fax 90706
4 miles NW of Cardiff towards Llantrisant.
Parkland course.
Pro Ian Luntz; Founded 1926
18 holes, 6063 yards, S.S.S. 70
⚐ Practice area for members only.
† Welcome WD except Tues (ladies
day) when prior booking is required;

members only at weekends.
⚑ WD £30.
⚬ Welcome by prior arrangement;
min 20 max 40 (Wed & Fri).
🍴 Bar and full catering facilities.
⚐ Friendly Hotel; Miskin Manor; Park;
Royal; Angel; Hilton; St Davids; Celtic
Manor.

10 38 **Criccieth**

Ednyfed Hill, Criccieth, Gwynedd,
LL52 0PH
☎ 01766 522154, Pro 522154,
Sec 523385, Rest/Bar 522154
On A497 4 miles from Portmadoc;
turn right past Memorial Hall; course
0.5 miles.
Meadowland course.
Founded 1904
18 holes, 5787 yards, S.S.S. 68
† Welcome.
⚑ WD £13/16; WE £18.
⚬ Welcome by prior arrangement.
🍴 bar and catering facilities.
⚐ George IV; Bron Eifion; Marine;
Lion.

10 39 **Denbigh** ♣

Henllan Rd, Denbigh, LL16 5AA
🖥 secretary@denbighgolfclub
.fsbusiness.com
☎ 01745 816669, Fax 814888, Pro
814159, Sec 816669, Rest/Bar 816664
Course is 0.5 mile from Denbigh on the
B5382.
Parkland course.
Pro Mike Jones; Founded 1922
Designed by John Stockton
18 holes, 5712 yards, S.S.S. 68
† Welcome by prior arrangement.
⚑ WD £27 for day, £20 per round;
WE £32, for day, £27 per round.
⚬ Welcome; packages and catering
available; call for details.
🍴 Clubhouse facilities available.
⚐ Talardy Park; Oriel House, both St
Asaph.

10 40 **Dewstow**

Caerwent, Monmouthshire, NP26 5AH
🖳 www.dewstow.com
🖥 info@dewstow.com
☎ 01291 430444, Fax 425816,
Pro 430444, Sec 430444,
Rest/Bar 430444
Off A48 between Newport and
Chepstow.
Parkland course/Valley course.
Pro Johnathan Skeuse; Founded
1988
2 x 18 holes, 6176 yards, S.S.S. 69
Park course/70 Valley course

⌁ Practice range, 26 bays floodlit and covered.
† Everyone welcome.
[WD £17; WE £20 summer rates. Various deals in winter. Please consult professional shop for details.
⚘ Welcome WD; some restrictions at WE; packages available; from £21.
⦿ Full bar and restaurant facilities.
⚑ Beaufort; Old Course.

10 41 Dinas Powis
Golf House, Old Highwalls, Dinas Powis, CF64 4AJ
☎ 029 205 12727, Fax 205 12727, Pro 205 13682, Rest/Bar 14128/12157
Centre of Dinas Powys, 5 miles from Cardiff.
Parkland course; 90 yards 7th.
Pro Gareth Bennett; Founded 1914
18 holes, 5872 yards, S.S.S. 69
⌁ Practice area.
† Welcome with handicap certs; dress codes apply.
[WD £25; WE £30 (£12/£14 with member).
⚘ Welcome by prior arrangement and with handicap certs; terms on application.
⦿ Clubhouse facilities.
⚑ Many in Cardiff.

10 42 Dolgellau ✆
Pencefn Road, Dolgellau, Gwynedd, LL40 2ES
⚏ www.dolgellaugolf.com
☎ 01341 422603, Fax 422603, Sec 422603, Rest/Bar 422603
0.5 miles N of Dolgellau.
Parkland course.
Founded 1911
9 holes, 4671 yards, S.S.S. 63
⌁ Practice range; club and trolley hire.
† Always welcome.
[WD £15; WE £18; two-for-one vouchers.
⚘ Welcome by prior arrangement; catering packages available; from £13.
⦿ Clubhouse facilities.
⚑ Royal Ship Hotel, Dolgellau.

10 43 Earlswood
Jersey Marine, Neath, West Glamorgan, SA10 6JP
☎ 01792 321578, Pro 816159, Sec 812198
Signposted off B 4290 road off the A483 Neath-Swansea road.
Parkland course.
Pro Mike Day; Founded 1993
Designed by Stan Gorvett
18 holes, 5174 yards, S.S.S. 68

† Everyone welcome.
[WD/WE £9.
⚘ Welcome by prior arrangement; £9 per person standard rate for groups.
⦿ By arrangement with secretary.
⚑ Many in Swansea area.

10 44 Fairwood Park ✆
Blackhills Lane, Upper Killay, Swansea, SA2 7JN
☎ 01792 297849, Fax 297849, Pro 299194, Sec 297849, Rest/Bar 203648
Turn into Blackhills Lane opposite Swansea Airport.
Parkland championship course.
Pro Gary Hughes; Founded 1969
Designed by Hawtree & Co.
18 holes, 6650 yards, S.S.S. 73
† Welcome by prior arrangement.
[WD £25; WE £30.
⚘ Welcome by prior arrangement; terms on application.
⦿ Clubhouse facilities.
⚑ Winston Hotel Bishopston; Langrove Hotel, Parkmill; Hillcrest, Mumbles.

10 45 Ffestiniog
Clwb Golff Ffestiniog, Y Cefn, Ffestiniog, Gwynned
⚏ ffestinioggolfclub.aol.com
☎ 01766 762637, Sec 831829
On the B4391 1 mile from Ffestiniog.
Scenic mountain course.
Founded 1893
9 holes, 5032 yards, S.S.S. 65
† Welcome; some WE restrictions.
[WD £10; WE £10.
⚘ Welcome by prior arrangement.
⦿ Clubhouse facilities by arrangement; bar.
⚑ Abbey Arms; The Pengwren.

10 46 Flint
Cornist Park, Flint, Flintshire, CH6 5HJ
⚏ www.flintgolfclub.netfirms.com
☎ 01352 732327
Course is one mile S from the centre of Flint.
Parkland course.
Founded 1965
Designed by H Griffith
9 holes, 5980 yards, S.S.S. 69
† Welcome.
[WD £10; WE £10. Closed on Sundays to non-members.
⚘ Welcome WD by arrangement; up to 27 holes of golf.
⦿ 3-course meal from £12.
⚑ Clubhouse facilities.

10 47 Glamorganshire ✆
Lavernock Rd, Penarth, CF64 5UP
⚏ glamgolf@btconnect.com
☎ 029 207 01185, Fax 01185, Pro 07401, Rest/Bar 07048
5 miles SW of Cardiff just off M4 J33.
Parkland course.
Pro Andrew Kerr-Smith; Founded 1890
Designed by W East & T Simpson
18 holes, 6056 yards, S.S.S. 70
⌁ Practice ground with net buggies and clubs for hire.
† Welcome by arrangement; dress codes apply.
[WD £35; WE £40.
⚘ Welcome Thurs and Fri only; catering packages available; reductions for more than 20; from £25.
⦿ Clubhouse facilities.
⚑ Walton House Hotel; Raisdale both Penarth.

10 48 Glyn Abbey ✆
Trimsaran, Kidwelly, Carmarthenshire SA17 4LB
⚏ www.glynabbey.co.uk
⚏ martin@glynabbey.co.uk
☎ 01554 810278, Fax 810889
On B4317 between carway and Trimsaran, 6 miles NW of Llanelli, 3 miles from Kidwelly.
Pro Darren Griffiths; Founded 1992
Designed by Dr Martin.Hawtree
18 holes, 6173 yards, S.S.S. 70
⌁ Open driving range; 6 bay covered range under construction
† Welcome.
[WD £15; WE £20.
⚘ Welcome.
⦿ Fully licensed clubhouse with all day catering.

10 49 Glynhir
Glynhir Rd, Llandybie, Ammanford, Carmarthenshire, SA18 2TF
☎ 01269 850472, Fax 851365, Pro 851010, Sec 851365
3.5 miles from Ammanford; off A483 towards Llandello.
Parkland course.
Pro Duncan Prior; Founded 1967
Designed by FW.Hawtree
18 holes, 6026 yards, S.S.S. 70
⌁ Covered, 4 bay driving range
† Welcome except Sun with handicap certs.
[WD £16; WE £22.
⚘ Welcome by arrangement; Tues and Fri; terms on application.
⦿ Clubhouse facilities.
⚑ The Mill at Glynhir (next to course); Cawdor Arms; White Hart Inn; Plough Inn, all Llandello.

10 50 Glynneath
Penycraig, Glynneath, SA11 5UH
www.glynneathgolfclub.co.uk
neil.evans9@lineone.co.uk
☎ 01639 720452, Pro 720872,
Rest/Bar 722726
From A465 road at Glynneath take
B4242 for 1.5 miles to
Pontneathvaughan.
Parkland and wooded hilltop course.
Pro Neil Evans; Founded 1931
Designed by Cotton
18 holes, 5656 yards, S.S.S. 68
† Welcome; no restrictions.
⌐ WD £17; WE £22; Mon £10.
⌐ Welcome; catering and bar snacks
available.
🍽 Clubhouse facilities.
🚩 Baverstock; Tynewydd Hotel,
Penderyn.

10 51 Gower
Cefn Goleu, Three Crosses, Gowerton,
Swansea, SA4 3HS
www.gowergolf.co.uk
arichards@gowergolf.co.uk
☎ 01792 872480, Fax 872480,
Pro 879905, Rest/Bar 875535
Follow the A484 towards Gowerton
and then take the B4295 to
Penclawdd; after one mile turn to
Three Crosses.
Parkland course with lakes.
Pro Alan Williamson; Founded 1995
Designed by Donald Steel
18 holes, 6441 yards, S.S.S. 71
ƒ All-weather practice facility.
† Welcome.
⌐ Terms on application.
⌐ Welcome by prior arrangement;
maximum 100; from £12.
🍽 Bar and catering facilities
available.
🚩 Accommodation at club.

10 52 Greenmeadow
Treherbert Road, Croesyceiliog,
Cwmbran, Gwent, NP44 2BZ
www.greenmeadowgolf.com
info@greenmeadowgolf.com
☎ 01633 869321, Fax 868430,
Pro 862626
Off A4042 5 miles N of M4 Junction 26.
Parkland course.
Pro Dave Woodman; Founded 1978
18 holes, 6078 yards, S.S.S. 70
ƒ Practice range; 26 bays covered
and floodlit.
† Welcome.
⌐ Terms on application.
⌐ Welcome by prior arrangement;
packages available; professional clinics;
tennis courts; private function rooms.

🍽 Full clubhouse catering facilities.
🚩 Parkway; Commodore.

10 53 Grove   ℭ
South Cornelly, Nr Porthcawl, Mid
Glamorgan, CF33 4RP
☎ 01656 788771, Fax 788414, Pro
788300, Sec 788771, Rest/Bar 788771
Off M4 Junction 37 near the
Glamorgan Heritage Coast at
Porthcawl.
Parkland course with water features.
Pro Leon Warne; Founded 1997
18 holes, 6128 yards, S.S.S. 70
† Welcome; bookings essential.
⌐ Terms on application.
⌐ Welcome by prior arrangement.
🍽 Bar and restaurant; function
rooms.
🚩 Green Acre Motel, 17 bedrooms all
ensuite, indoor pool, restaurants, bars
with beautiful views over the welsh hills.

10 54 Haverfordwest   ℭ
Arnolds Down, Haverfordwest,
Pembrokeshire, SA61 2XQ
www.haverfordwestgolf.
homestead.com
haverfordwestgc@btconnect.com
☎ 01437 763565, Fax 764143,
Pro 768409
1 mile E of Haverfordwest on A40.
Parkland course.
Pro Alex Pile; Founded 1904
18 holes, 5973 yards, S.S.S. 69
† Welcome by prior arrangement.
⌐ POA.
⌐ Welcome by arrangement; catering
packages available; terms on
application.
🍽 Bar; bar snacks and dining room.
🚩 Wolfcastle Country Club.

10 55 Hawarden
Groomsdale Lane, Hawarden,
Deeside, Flintshire, CH5 3EH
www.hawardengolfclub.co.uk
secretary@hawardengolfclub.co.uk
☎ 01244 531447, Fax 536901, Pro
520809
Off A55 at Ewloe towards Hawarden;
Groomsdale Lane opposite police
station after playing fields.
Undulating parkland course.
Pro Alec Rowlands; Founded 1911/1950
18 holes, 5894 yards, S.S.S. 68
† Welcome; members comp day
Sat.
⌐ WD £18; Sun £25.
⌐ Welcome by prior arrangement
with Sec.
🍽 Bar and full catering facilities;

meals by arrangement.
🚩 St David's Park, Ewloe.

10 56 Henllys Hall
Beaumaris, Anglesey, Gwynedd,
LL58 8HU
☎ 01248 810412, Fax 811511
4 miles from A55.
Parkland course with Snowdonia views
and water features.
Pro Peter Maton; Founded 1997
Designed by Roger Jones
18 holes, 6098 yards, S.S.S. 71
ƒ Practice area.
† Welcome by prior arrangement.
⌐ Terms on application.
⌐ Welcome by prior arrangement;
catering and hotel packages; terms on
application; sun room; fitness centre;
tennis court; swimming pool; leisure
centre.
🍽 Full hotel facilities; bar and
restaurant.
🚩 Henllys Hall on site.

10 57 Holyhead   ℭ
Trearddur Bay, Holyhead, Anglesey,
LL65 2YL
☎ 01407 763279, Fax 763279, Pro
762022, Rest/Bar Bar 762119 Rest
765113
A55 to Holyhead, carry on to
roundabout, 1 mile from Trearddur Bay.
Undulating heathland.
Pro Steve Elliott; Founded 1912
Designed by James Braid
18 holes, 6060 yards, S.S.S. 70
ƒ Practice range 0.5 miles away; 10
bays.
† Welcome; advised to book in
advance.
⌐ Terms on application.
⌐ Welcome by arrangement.
🍽 Full bar and catering facilities.
🚩 On site dormy house hotel;
Trearddur Bay; Anchorage; Beach.

10 58 Holywell
Brynford, Nr Holywell, Flintshire,
CH8 8LQ
holywell_golf_club@lineone.net
☎ 01352 713937, Fax 07092369597,
Pro 710040
From A55 at Holywell exit take A5026
then take Brynford signs.
Natural moorland/links type course
around quarries.
Pro Matt Parsley; Founded 1906
18 holes, 6164 yards, S.S.S. 70
ƒ Practice area and buggies for hire.
† Welcome; dress codes apply.
⌐ WD £18; WE £23.

⚲ Welcome by arrangement with Sec; catering packages available; snooker; reduced rates for groups of 20; from £15.
🍴 Full catering facilities and bar.
🛏 Club can recommend hotels.

10 59 Inco
Clydach, Swansea, W Glamorgan, SA6 5QR
☎ 01792 842929, Rest/Bar 841257
Course is two miles N of the M4 Junction 45.
Parkland course with river and trees featured.
Founded 1965
18 holes, 6064 yards, S.S.S. 69
⚑ Practice green, practice nets.
🚶 Welcome.
🔖 WD £18, WE £23 (summer rates).
⚲ Welcome by prior arrangement.
🍴 Full catering service available.

10 60 Kinmel Park Golf Complex
Bodelwyddan, Denbighshire, LL18 5SR
☎ 01745 833548
Just off A55 between St Asaph and Abergele.
Parkland course.
Pro Peter Stebbings; Founded 1988
Designed by Peter Stebbings
9 holes, 3100 yards, S.S.S. 58
🚶 Pay and play.
🔖 WD £4; WE £4.50.
⚲ Welcome; Peter Stebbing's Golf Academy; snack bar and refreshments; terms on application.
🍴 Bar.

10 61 Kinsale
Llanerchymor, Holywell, Flintshire, CH8 9DX
☎ 01745 561080
Off A548 coast road at turning for Maes Pennant.
Parkland course.
Pro Alan Norwood; Founded 1994
Designed by Ken Smith
9 holes, 6005 yards, S.S.S. 70
⚑ Practice range, 12 Bays floodlit.
🚶 Welcome; pay and play.
🔖 WD and WE: 9 holes £7.50; 18 holes £11.00; special price for juniors every day but Sun.
⚲ Welcome by arrangement.
🍴 Full clubhouse facilities.
🛏 Kinsale Hall.

10 62 Knighton ♿
The Ffrydd, Knighton, Powys, LD7 1DL

☎ 01547 528646. Sec 528046
SW of Knighton off the A488 Shrewsbury-Llandrindod Wells road at junction with A4113.
Upland course.
Founded 1913
Designed by Harry Vardon
9 holes, 5338 yards, S.S.S. 66
🚶 Welcome; advised to book in advance for weekends.
🔖 WD £10; WE £12.
⚲ Welcome by prior arrangement; terms on application.
🍴 Clubhouse facilities.
🛏 Red Lion; Knighton Hotel.

10 63 Lakeside
Water St, Margam, Port Talbot, SA13 2PA
☎ 01639 899959, Fax 892767, Rest/Bar 883486
0.5 miles from M4 Junction 38 off A48 to Margam Park.
Parkland course.
Pro M Wootton; Founded 1992
Designed by M Wootton/DT Thomas
18 holes, 4580 yards, S.S.S. 63
⚑ Driving range.
🚶 Welcome.
🔖 WD/WE £10.
⚲ Welcome except Sun; golf and meal; £15.
🍴 Catering available.
🛏 Twelve Knights; Seabank; Esplanade.

10 64 Llandrindod Wells ♿
Llandrindod Wells, Powys, LD1 5NY
🖥 www.lwgc.co.uk
✉ secretary@lwgc.co.uk
☎ 01597 822010, Fax 823873, Pro 822247, Sec 823873, Rest/Bar 822010
Signposted in the town.
Moorland course.
Pro Phil Davies; Founded 1905
Designed by Harry Vardon
18 holes, 5759 yards, S.S.S. 69
⚑ 8 bay driving range.
🚶 Welcome.
🔖 Prices on application.
⚲ Welcome by prior arrangement with Sec; terms on application.
🍴 Clubhouse facilities.
🛏 Metropole; Montpellier; Llanerch; Commodore; Penybont; Pencerrig.

10 65 Llanfairfechan
Llannerch Road, Llanfairfechan, Conwy, LL33 0EB
☎ 01248 680144, Sec 680524
Course is south of the A55 in Llanfairfechan.

Parkland course.
Founded 1972
9 holes, 3119 yards, S.S.S. 57
⚑ Practice nets.
🚶 Welcome.
🔖 WD £10; WE £10. All day
⚲ Welcome by prior arrangement; catering by arrangement; terms on application.
🍴 Some catering and bar facilities evenings and weekends.
🛏 Split Willow.

10 66 Llangefni (Public)
Llangefni, Anglesey, LL77 8YQ
☎ 01248 722193, Pro 722193
On the outskirts of Llangefni towards Amlwch.
Parkland course.
Pro Paul Lovell; Founded 1983
Designed by Hawtree & Sons
9 holes, 1467 yards, S.S.S. 28
🚶 All Welcome.
🔖 WD £3.20; WE £3.50; children and OAPs £1.80 & WE £2.00.
⚲ Welcome by prior arrangement.
🍴 In local café.

10 67 Llangland Bay
Llangland Bay, Swansea, SA3 4QR
🖥 www.llanglandbaygolfclub.com
✉ golf@llanglandbay.sagehost.co.uk
☎ 01792 361721, Fax 361082, Pro 366186, Sec 361721, Rest/Bar 366023
Take Junction 42 of M4 heading west towards Swansea. Take A483 to Swansea. From Swansea take the main road to Mumbles. Follow signs to Caswell and Langland from Mumbles.
Seaside parkland course.
Pro Mark Evans; Founded 1904
Designed by various designers
18 holes, 5857 yards, S.S.S. 69
🚶 Welcome; must have current handicap certificate.
🔖 Terms on application.
⚲ Welcome by prior arrangement; maximum 36; catering packages available by prior arrangement; winter packages available; terms on application. Handicap certificates essential.
🍴 Clubhouse facilities except Mondays.
🛏 St Annes Hotel; Wittenberg Hotel.

10 68 Llanishen
Cwm, Heol Hir, Lisvane, Cardiff, CF14 9UD
☎ 029 207 55078, Fax 55078, Pro 55076, Rest/Bar 52205

5 miles N of Cardiff 1 mile N of Llanishen.
Parkland course.
Pro RA Jones; Founded 1905
18 holes, 5338 yards, S.S.S. 67
† Welcome WD; WE only with a member.
[WD/WE £32 (£16 with member).
⌁ Welcome Thurs; catering available.
⦿ Clubhouse facilities.
⌁ Cardiff Bay; Angel; Manor House; New House.

10 69 Llannerch Park
North Wales Golf Range and Course, St Asaph, Denbighshire, LL17 0BD
☎ 01745 730805, Pro 730805
On A525 between St Asaph and Trefnant.
Parkland course.
Pro Michael Jones; Founded 1988
9 holes, 1587 yards, S.S.S. 30
⌇ 14.
† Public pay and play.
[WD £3.00; WE £3.00.
⌁ Societies welcome. Pre arrangement for groups would be appreciated.
⦿ Refreshments.
⌁ The Oriel House; The Trefnant Hotel; The Bryn Glas.

10 70 Llantrisant & Pontyclun
off Ely Valley Road, Talbot Green, Mid-Glam, CF72 8AL
✉ lpgc@barbox.net
☎ 01443 222148, Pro 228169, Sec 224601
M4 J34 then A4119 to Talbot Green.
Parkland course.
Founded 1927
18 holes, 5328 yards, S.S.S. 66
⌇ Driving range nearby.
† Welcome except Sun; terms on application.
[WD £20; WE £25.
⌁ Welcome; menus available at all times; from £15.
⦿ Bar and restaurant facilities.
⌁ Miskin Manor.

10 71 Llanwern
Tennyson Avenue, Llanwern, Newport, NP6 2DY
✉ royherbert@btopenworld.com
☎ 01633 412029, Fax 412029, Pro 413233, Rest/Bar 413278
1 mile from M4 jct 24.
Parkland course.
Pro Stephen Price; Founded 1928
18 holes, 6177 yards, S.S.S. 69
† Welcome.

[WD non-members £25 guests of member £15.
⌁ Welcome WD by prior arrangement.
⦿ Catering available.
⌁ Stakis Country Court; Hilton National; Holiday Inn; Travel Inn; Celtic Manor.

10 72 Llanyrafon
Llanfrechfa Way, Cwmbran, NP44 8HT
☎ 01633 874636
S to Pontypool off the M4 Junction 26.
Parkland course.
Pro Dave Woodman; Founded 1981
9 holes, 2566 yards, S.S.S. 54
⌇ Practice area.
† Welcome.
[WD £3.10; WE £3.60; under 16s and over 60s: WD £2.20 WE £2.30.
⌁ Welcome by arrangement.
⦿ Refreshments.

10 73 Machynlleth
Newtown Road, Machynlleth, Powys, SY20 8DU
☎ 01654 702000
0.5 miles out of town on the A480 Newtown road.
Parkland course.
Founded 1904
Designed by James Braid
9 holes, 5726 yards, S.S.S. 67
⌇ Practice area and putting green.
† Welcome; Thurs 12-3 ladies; Sun 8-11.30 men.
[WD/WE £15.
⌁ Welcome; 10% reduction for groups of 8 or more; terms on application. Catering available on application to the secretary in writing.
⦿ Clubhouse facilities.
⌁ Wynnstay, Plas Dolguog; Maenllwyd Guest House.

10 74 Maesdu
Hospital Rd, Llandudno, Gwynedd, LL30 1HU
☎ 01492 876016, Fax 871570, Pro 875195, Sec 876450
A55 to Conwy-Deganwy exit, then A546 to clubhouse.
Parkland course.
Pro Simon Boulden; Founded 1915
Designed by Tom Jones
18 holes, 6545 yards, S.S.S. 72
⌇ Practice range, clubs and buggies for hire.
† Welcome by arrangement.
[WD £25 round, £30 day; WE £35 round pm (restricted am).
⌁ Welcome everyday; maximum 36 at WE; 50 in week; no concessions; from £25.

⦿ Catering and bar facilities.
⌁ Royal; Esplanade; Risboro.

10 75 Maesteg
Mount Pleasant, Neath Rd, Maesteg, CF34 9PR
✉ ijm@fsmail.net
☎ 01656 734106, Fax 731822
Adjacent to B4282 main Maesteg to Port Talbot road 0.5 miles from Maesteg.
Hilltop course with forest views down the valley.
Founded 1912
Designed by James Braid (1945)
18 holes, 5939 yards, S.S.S. 69
⌇ Practice ground.
† Welcome.
[WD £17; WE £20.
⌁ Welcome by prior arrangement.
⦿ Bar meals available; restaurant.
⌁ Heronstone, Bridgend; Abervon, Port Talbot; Greenacres GH, Maesteg.

10 76 Marriott St Pierre Hotel Golf & CC ♔
St Pierre Park, Chepstow, Monmouthshire, NP16 6YA
🖳 www.marriott.com
✉ reservations.stpierre@marriotthotels.co.uk
☎ 01291 625261, Fax 635227, Pro 635205
Course 2 miles from Chepstow on A48.
Parkland course.
Pro Craig Dun; Founded 1962
Designed by Bill Cox
18 holes on championship course, 18 holes on amateur course, 6538 champ/5569 amat yards, S.S.S. 68 amat/74 champ
⌇ 13.
† Everyone welcome.
[Terms on application.
⌁ Welcome WD; WE residents only; catering packages available; function rooms available; terms available on application.
⦿ Long Weekend Café Bar; The Orangery restaurant.
⌁ On site Marriott hotel.

10 77 Merthyr Tydfil ♔
(Cilsanws), Cloth Hall Lane, Cefn Coed, Merthyr Tydfil, Mid-Glam, CF48 2NU
☎ 01685 723308
Course is two miles N of Merthyr on Cilsanws Mountain in Cefn Coed.
Mountain top heathland course.
Founded 1908
Designed by V Price/R Mathias (new holes); old holes – not known.

Royal Porthcawl

Donald Steel put it rather well. "It can represent the best and the worst, heaven and hell. However, few courses reward the good old fashioned virtues of control and flight better than Porthcawl".

Tiger Woods will know exactly what Steel is on about. In 1995, Royal Porthcawl became the first club in Wales to host the Walker Cup. Woods was on the American team. In the opening round of singles, Woods was up against Gary Wolstenholme who in the modern idiom is about as short as it is possible to be.

Wolstenholme cheerfully admits that he never tires of relating the tale of his victory over Woods. He says, "You can win matches by intimidating your opponent if you keep hitting fairways and greens the whole time. The famous win against Tiger was an example".

Standing on the eighteenth tee the pair were all square. After the drives, as usual Tiger was way out in front. Wolstenholme had a five-wood left which he coaxed down to the edge of the green. With nothing more than a seven-iron in his hands Woods then tugged his second shot out of bounds in the direction of the clubhouse. "Great Britain and Ireland wins the match, one up". As Steel observed and Wolstenholme confirmed, Porthcawl rewards the man who can control his ball.

Yet the course had rather humbler origins than its modern reputation might suggest. Founded in 1891, it consisted of nine holes on a piece of land called Lock's Common. The golfers shared it with cattle and needed the permission of the local parish vestry to use the land. Consent was given for half-a-crown and several jugs later a song was composed called, "Who sold the Lock's Common for a gallon of drink".

Eventually eighteen holes were completed nearer to the shoreline although, despite its setting, Royal Porthcawl is not a typical links course. The good news is that there is a lack of the huge sandhills that can cause so much grief at places like Ballybunion. The bad news is that there is an absence of huge sandhills, allowing the wind to tear across the course unchecked. Yet the triangular layout of the course at least makes all wind directions eminently playable.

The par five fifth was considered by Henry Cotton to be one of the great holes in golf. It is not overly long at 476 yards, but the second or third shot is uphill to a green generous in its length and wretchedly parsimonious in its width. A boundary wall flanks the green to the left and there is a huge grassy knoll and a cavernous bunker to the right. If you are lucky enough to find the green, but unlucky enough to be beyond the pin, you will need to attach crampons to the golf ball in order to make the subsequent putt stop.

The opening trio of holes are amongst the best in golf, each one a par four, each one posing different questions, each one threatening the same result – a ball on the beach. It is possible to see the ocean from every one of Porthcawl's eighteen holes, but it is only at the start that the view is a threatening one.

Royal Porthcawl is a bewitching combination of links and moorland golf, of rolling fairways and befuddling greens. The granting of royal status was as precarious as those greens. In 1908 the application for royal status seemed to have been rejected out of hand by the Home Secretary. Yet six months later, on 30 March 1909, another letter arrived bestowing royal status. What happened in the intervening months to cause such a sudden about turn? Like the true line of so many putts at Royal Porthcawl, it remains a matter of conjecture. – **Mark Reason**

18 holes, 5622 yards, S.S.S. 69
† Welcome except on Sun competition days.
Ⓘ WD £10; WE £15.
⌁ Welcome by prior arrangement; meals available; terms available on application.
🍽 Clubhouse facilities.
🛏 Mount Dolu Lodge.

10 78 Mid-Wales Golf Centre
Maesmawr, Caersws, Nr Newtown, Powys, SY17 5SB
🔗 www.midwalesgolfcentre.co.uk
☎ 01686 688303
6 miles W of Newtown.
Farmland course.
Founded 1992
Designed by Jim Walters
9 holes, 2554 yards, S.S.S. 54
▮ Practice range 12 bays floodlit and covered.
† Welcome.
Ⓘ WD £8; WE £10.
⌁ Welcome by prior arrangement.
🍽 Light snacks and bar.
🛏 Maesmawr Hall.

10 79 Milford Haven ☏
Woodbine House, Hubberston, Milford Haven, SA73 3RX
🔗 www.mhgc.co.uk
☎ 01646 692368, Fax 697870, Pro 697870, Sec 697822
0.75 miles W of town on road to Dale.
Meadowland course.
Pro Dylwn Williams; Founded 1913
Designed by David Snell
18 holes, 6035 yards, S.S.S. 70
▮ 4.
† Everyone welcome.
Ⓘ WD £15; WE £20.
⌁ Welcome at all times; terms on application.
🍽 Restaurant and bar facilities.
🛏 Lord Nelson; Sir Benfro; Little Haven.

10 80 Mold
Cilcain Rd, Pantymwyn, Mold, Flintshire, CH7 5EH
🔗 www.moldgolfclub.co.uk
✉ info@moldgolfclub.co.uk
☎ 01352 741513, Fax 741517, Pro 740318
3 miles from Mold; leave on Denbigh road; turn left after 400 yards (next to Bluebell public house) and follow road for 2.5 miles.
Undulating parkland course.
Pro Mark Jordan; Founded 1909
Designed by Hawtree
18 holes, 5528 yards, S.S.S. 67
† All welcome including weekends.
Ⓘ WD £18; WE £25.
⌁ Welcome by prior arrangement; catering packages by arrangement.
🍽 Full facilities.
🛏 The Holiday Inn (Chester West).

10 81 Monmouth ☏
Leasbrook Lane, Monmouth, Monmouthshire, NP25 3SN
🔗 www.monmouthgolfclub.co.uk
✉ sec.mongc@barbox.net
☎ 01600 712212, Fax 772399, Sec 07770 592355
Signposted from the Monmouth-Ross on Wye (A40) road.
Undulating parkland course.
Pro Mike Waldron; Founded 1896
18 holes, 5698 yards, S.S.S. 69
▮ Practice area; putting green.
† Welcome anytime except Sun morning before 11.30am.
Ⓘ WD £19; WE £22.
⌁ Welcome by prior arrangement with the secretary; packages available; from £18.
🍽 Clubhouse facilities.
🛏 Several recommended in vicinity.

10 82 Monmouthshire ☏
Llanfoist, Abergavenny, Monmouthshire, NP7 9HE

🔗 www.monmouthshiregolfclub.co.uk
✉ secretary@mgcabergavenny.fsnet.co.uk
☎ 01873 852606, Fax 850470, Pro 852532
2 miles SW of Abergavenny.
Parkland course; three successive par 5s.
Pro Brian Edwards; Founded 1892
Designed by James Braid
18 holes, 5806 yards, S.S.S. 70
† Welcome by arrangement.
Ⓘ WD £30; WE £35.
⌁ Welcome Mon and Fri by prior arrangement; for groups of 16-35 £25; 36+ £20; terms on application.
🍽 Full clubhouse facilities.
🛏 The Bear Hotel, Crickhowell; The Manor, Crickhowell.

10 83 Morlais Castle
Pant, Dowlais, Merthyr Tydfil, CF48 2UY
🔗 www.morlaiscastle-golfclubgolfclub.co.uk
✉ info@mcgc.fsnet.co.uk
☎ 01685 722822, Fax 388700, Pro 388700
Follow signs for Brecon Mountain Railway.
Moorland course.
Pro H Jarrett; Founded 1900
18 holes, 6320 yards, S.S.S. 71
▮ Practice ground; buggies and clubs for hire.
† Welcome.
Ⓘ WD £16; WE £20.
⌁ Welcome WD by prior arrangement with Sec.
🍽 Full catering and bar facilities in new clubhouse.
🛏 Treganna; Travel Lodge.

10 84 Morriston ☏
160 Clasemont Rd, Morriston, Swansea, SA6 6AJ
☎ 01792 771079, Fax 795628, Pro 772335, Sec 796528

3 miles N of Swansea city centre on
A4067.
Parkland course.
Founded 1919
18 holes, 5755 yards, S.S.S. 68
⚑ Practice area.
♦ Welcome.
⚑ WD £18; WE £30.
⚘ Welcome by prior arrangement
only.
🍽 Lunches and bar facilities
available.
⛨ The Holiday Inn; Dolphin; Forest
Motel; Jarvis.

10 85 Mountain Ash ☏
The Clubhouse, Cefn Pennar,
Mountain Ash, Mid-Glam, CF45 4DT
☎ 01443 472265, Fax 479628,
Pro 478770, Sec 479459
Off A470 Cardiff to Abercynon road at
Mountain Ash; follow signs to Cefn
Pennar.
Mountain heathland course.
Pro Darran Clark; Founded 1908
18 holes, 5553 yards, S.S.S. 67
♦ Welcome.
⚑ WD £20; WE £30.
⚘ Welcome; special packages
available from sec.; terms on application.
🍽 Clubhouse facilities.
⛨ Baverstocks, Aberdare.

10 86 Mountain Lakes ☏
Blaengwynlais, Nr Caerphilly, Mid-
Glam, CF83 1NG
📧 info@golfclub.co.uk
☎ 029 20861128, Fax 20863243,
Pro 20886666, Sec 20861128,
Rest/Bar 20886686
4 miles from M4 Junction 32 on
Tongwynlais-Caerphilly road.
Mountain-Parkland course.
Pro S Bebb; Founded 1989
Designed by B Sandow/J Page
18 holes, 6343 yards, S.S.S. 73
⚑ Practice range, 15 bays.
♦ Welcome.
⚑ WD £18; WE £18.
⚘ Welcome by prior arrangement;
terms on application; from £19.
🍽 Restaurant and bar facilities.
⛨ New Country House.

10 87 Neath
Cadoxton, Neath, SA10 8AH
☎ 01639 643615, Pro 633693
2 miles from Neath in Cadoxton.
Mountain course.
Pro EM Bennett; Founded 1934
Designed by James Braid
18 holes, 6490 yards, S.S.S. 72

♦ Welcome WD.
⚑ WD £20.
⚘ Welcome by arrangement with
Sec; terms on application.
🍽 Full clubhouse facilities.
⛨ Castle Neath.

10 88 Nefyn & District ☏
Morfa Nefyn, Pwllheli, Gwynedd,
LL53 6DA
📧 www.gnefyn-golf-club.com
📧 nefyngolf@tesco.net
☎ 01758 720966, Fax 720476,
Pro 720102, Rest/Bar 721626/720218
1 mile W of Nefyn; 18 miles W of
Caernarfon.
Seaside clifftop course on Llyn
Peninsula.
Pro John Froom; Founded 1907
26 holes, 6548 yards, S.S.S. 71
⚑ Practice area.
♦ Welcome by prior arrangement;
handicap certs preferred; dress codes
apply.
⚑ WD £27, day pass £33; WE £32,
day pass £38.
⚘ Welcome by prior arrangement
except for 2 weeks in August; 10 per
cent reduction for groups of 12 or
more; snooker table; terms on
application.
🍽 Full clubhouse facilities; restaurant
and bar.
⛨ Nanhoron Nefyn.

10 89 Newport
Great Oak, Rogerstone, Newport,
Gwent, NP10 9FX
☎ 01633 892643, Fax 896676,
Pro 893271, Rest/Bar 894496
3 miles from Newport M4 Junction 27
on B4591.
Parkland course.
Pro Paul Mayo; Founded 1903
Designed by Ross/Fernie.
18 holes, 6431 yards, S.S.S. 71
♦ Welcome by prior arrangement.
⚑ WD £40; WE £45.
⚘ Welcome Wed; Thurs; Fri and
some Sun; handicap certs required;
discounts available at off-peak times;
from £35.
🍽 Full clubhouse facilities.
⛨ Celtic Manor, Newport.

10 90 Newport (Pembs) ☏
Newport, Pembrokeshire, SA42 0NR
☎ 01239 820244
Follow signs for Newport Sands from
Newport.
Seaside course.
Pro Julian Noott; Founded 1925

Designed by James Braid
9 holes, 5815 yards, S.S.S. 68
⚑ Driving bays (2 open and 2
covered).
♦ Welcome.
⚑ Terms on application.
⚘ Welcome by prior arrangement;
terms on application.
🍽 Full bar and restaurant facilities.
⛨ Self-catering flats on site.

10 91 North Wales ☏
72 Bryniau Rd, West Shore,
Llandudno, Gwynedd, LL30 2DZ
📧 www.northwales.uk.com/nwgc
📧 golf@nwgc.freeserve.co.uk
☎ 01492 875325, Fax 873355,
Pro 876878, Rest/Bar 875342
2 miles from A55 on A546
Llandudno/Deganwy road.
Links course.
Pro Richard Bradbury; Founded 1894
Designed by Tancred Cummins
18 holes, 6287 yards, S.S.S. 71
♦ Welcome.
⚑ WD £26; WE and BH £36.
⚘ Welcome with handicap certs;
practice area and snooker; terms on
application.
🍽 Full bar and restaurant facilities.
⛨ Many in Llandudno.

10 92 Northop Country ☏
Park Golf Club
Nr Chester, Flintshire, CH7 6WA
📧 www.devereonline.co.uk
📧 northop@devere-hotels.com
☎ 01352 840440, Fax 840445
Off A55 at Northop/Connahs Quay exit
(J33A); entrance is on slip road.
Parkland course.
Pro Matthew Pritchard; Founded 1994
Designed by John Jacobs
18 holes, 6735 yards, S.S.S. 73
⚑ Driving range.
♦ Welcome by prior arrangement.
⚑ All week £40.
⚘ Welcome by arrangement WD;
catering packages available; corporate
days arranged; tennis; gym; sauna.
🍽 Full restaurant facilities; bar;
terrace.
⛨ St Davids Park, Ewloe (01244
520800).

10 93 Oakdale
Llwynon Lane, Oakdale, Gwent,
NP12 0NF
📧 rossholeinone@aol.com
☎ 01495 220044
M4 Junction 28 then A467 to Crumlin
and B4251 to Oakdale.

NORTH WALES GOLF CLUB

Enjoy the infinite variety of this traditional championship links course with its natural beauty, undulating fairways and excellent greens. The course is situated by the seas with panoramic views of the Conwy Estuary, Anglesey and the Great Orme.

Come and enjoy 'The North Wales' experience.

Tel: Manager: 01492 875325 • Professional: 01492 876878

Parkland course.
Founded 1990
Designed by Ian Goodenough
9 holes, 2688 yards, S.S.S. 56
⚐ Practice range, 18 bays floodlit.
⚑ Welcome.
⚐ WD £5; WE £5 (second 9 £3);
basket of range balls £1.30.
⚐ Welcome by prior arrangement.
⚐ Snacks in clubhouse.
⚐ The Maes Manor; The Woodhouse.

10 94 Old Colwyn

Woodland Avenue, Old Colwyn, Clwyd,
LL29 9NL
☎ 01492 515581
Off A55 at Old Colwyn exit towards Old
Colwyn.
Undulating meadowland course.
Founded 1907
Designed by James Braid
9 holes, 5263 yards, S.S.S. 66
⚑ Welcome WD; by prior
arrangement at WE.
⚐ WD £10; WE £15.
⚐ Welcome by arrangement;
reductions for 10 or more players;
menus by arrangement; terms on
application.
⚐ Full clubhouse facilities.
⚐ Bodelwyddan Castle has reduced
rates for golfers; Lyndale.

10 95 Old Padeswood ♛

Station Rd, Padeswood, Mold, Clwyd,
CH7 4JL
⚐ www.oldpadeswood.co.uk
✉ oldpad@par72.fsbusiness.co.uk
☎ 01244 547701, Fax 545082,
Pro 547401, Sec 554414, Rest/Bar
547701
On A5118 between Penyfford and Mold
close to A55.
Meadowland course in valley.
Pro Tony Davies; Founded 1933/1978
Designed by Arthur Joseph
18 holes, 6685 yards, S.S.S. 72
⚐ Practice range.
⚑ Welcome.
⚐ WD £25; WE £30.
⚐ Welcome WD; restaurant; bar.
⚐ Full clubhouse facilities.
⚐ Many in Chester Wrexham and
Mold.

10 96 Old Rectory Hotel And Conference Centre

Llangattock, Crickhowell, Powys,
NP8 1PH
⚐ www.theoldrectoryhotelcrichowell
.co.uk
✉ ftu@theoldrectoryhotelcrichowell
.co.uk
☎ 01873 810373
A40 to Crickhowell.
Parkland course.
Founded 1968
9 holes, 2600 yards, S.S.S. 54
⚑ Welcome.
⚐ WD £7.50; WE £7.50.
⚐ Terms on application; bars meals
and restaurant available.
⚐ Bar and restaurant.
⚐ On site hotel; 20 en suite rooms.

10 97 Padeswood & Buckley ♛

The Caia, Station Lane, Padeswood,
Mold, Flintshire, CH7 4JD
✉ padeswoodgc@compuserve.com
☎ 01244 550537, Fax 541600,
Pro 543636, Sec 550537,
Bar 550537 Rest 546072
Off Penyfford-Mold road A5118 at Old
Padeswood turning; club 50 yards
further on.
Parkland course alongside River Alyn.
Pro DV Ashton; Founded 1933
Designed by Heap and Partners
18 holes, 5888 yards, S.S.S. 69
⚑ Welcome; members only at
weekends; dress codes apply.
⚐ WD £20 per round or £25 per day.
summer April-October Sat £25 per
round. £13 per person per round
weekdays.
⚐ Welcome WD; packages include
28 holes of golf; coffee on arrival.
⚐ Light lunch and dinner; prices on
application; full clubhouse facilities and
restaurant.
⚐ St David's Park; Ewloe; Beaufort
Park; New Brighton.

10 98 Palleg

Palleg Rd, Lower Cwmtwrch, Swansea
✉ palleg@golf-club.freeserve.co.uk
☎ 01639 842193, Fax 845661
Course is off the Swansea-Brecon
road.

Meadowland course.
Pro Sharon Roberts; Founded 1930
Designed by CK Cotton
9 holes, 6418 yards, S.S.S. 72 (18
holes from May 2004)
⚑ Welcome with handicap certs WD;
with member at WE.
⚐ WD £13.
⚐ Welcome by prior arrangement;
terms on application.
⚐ Clubhouse facilities.
⚐ Y Stycle, Upper Cwmtwrch; Dab-
yr-Ogof Caves; Abercrane; Goufch
Arms B&B.

10 99 Parc Golf Club

Church Lane, Coedkernew, Newport,
Gwent, NP1 9TU
☎ 01633 680933, Fax 680955,
Pro 680933, Sec 681011,
Rest/Bar 681011
M4 Junction 28; on to A48 towards
Cardiff for 1.5 miles.
Parkland course.
Pro Darren Griffiths; Founded 1989
Designed by B Thomas & T Hicks
18 holes, 5619 yards, S.S.S. 68
⚐ Extensive tuition by Darren
Griffiths, Russell Jones and Barry
Thomas. Practice range; 38 bays
floodlit and carpeted; buggies and
clubs for hire.
⚑ Welcome WD; WE by prior
arrangement.
⚐ WD £15; WE £17.
⚐ Welcome by arrangement.
⚐ Full facilities; bar restaurant;
function room; conference suite.
⚐ Coach & Horses; Travel Lodge,
both Castleton.

10 100 Penmaenmawr ♛

Conway Old Rd, Penmaenmawr,
Conwy, LL34 6RD
☎ 01492 623330, Fax 622105
3 miles W of Conwy on A55 to
Dwygyfylchi.
Undulating parkland course.
Founded 1910
9 holes with 18 tees, 5350 yards,
S.S.S. 66
⚐ Practice area.
⚑ Welcome except Sat.
⚐ WD £12; Sun £18.

✑ Welcome by prior arrangement; inclusive package of 27 holes including lunch and dinner; from £25.
🍽 Bar and restaurant.
🛏 Caerlyr Hall.

---

10 101 Pennard ₡
2 Southgate Rd, Southgate, Swansea, W Glamorgan, SA3 2BT
🖳 www.pennardgolfclub.com
✉ pigeon01@globalnet.co.uk
☎ 01792 233131, Fax 234797, Pro 233451
8 miles W of Swansea via A4067 and B4436.
Links course.
Pro Mike Bennett; Founded 1896
Designed by J Braid
18 holes, 6231 yards, S.S.S. 72
⚑ Practice area; no buggies allowed on course; trolleys and clubs for hire.
🕴 Welcome; dress codes apply (no jeans or trainers) on course and in clubhouse.
Ⓛ WD £28; WE £36.
✑ Welcome by prior arrangement; minimum group 12; snooker; from £22.50.
🍽 Bar snacks; lunches and evening meals.
🛏 Winston, Bishopston; Fairy Hill, Reynoldston; Gower Golf Club, Three Crosses.

---

10 102 Penrhos Golf & CC ₡
Llanrhystud, Nr Aberystwyth, Cardiganshire, SY23 5AY
🖳 www.penrhosgolf.co.uk
✉ info@penrhos.co.uk
☎ 01974 202999, Fax 202100
9 miles S of Aberystwyth on A487; take Llanrhystud turning on to B4337; signs from village.
Parkland course.
Pro Paul Diamond; Founded 1991
Designed by Jim Walters
18 holes and 9-hole academy course, 6641 yards, S.S.S. 72
⚑ 3 bays and teeing off area.
🕴 Welcome except Sat/Sun am.
Ⓛ WD £20; WE £25.
✑ Welcome by arrangement; catering packages available; £18-£40.
🍽 Full clubhouse facilities.
🛏 On site motel; 15 en suite rooms; Marine; Conrah Country, both Aberystwyth; Plas Morfa Llanon.

---

10 103 Peterstone Golf & Country Club ₡
Peterstone Wentloog, Cardiff, CF3 2TN
🖳 www.peterstonelakes.com
✉ peterstone_lakes@yahoo.com
☎ 01633 680009, Fax 680563, Pro 680075
Take A48 towards Cardiff from M4 Junction 28 turning left to Marshfield; course 2.5 miles.
Links/parkland course.
Pro Darren Clark; Founded 1990
Designed by Bob Sandow
18 holes, 6555 yards, S.S.S. 72
🕴 Welcome.
Ⓛ WD £16.50; WE £22.50.
✑ Welcome Mon-Fri; full packages; corporate days; photographs; starter; half-way house; on-course competition; presentation evenings; terms on application.
🍽 Full bar and restaurant facilities; Fairways restaurant.
🛏 Wentloog; Travelodge; Moat House.

---

10 104 Plassey
The Plassey Golf Course, Eyton, Wrexham, LL13 0SP
🖳 www.plasseygolf.co.uk
☎ 01978 780020, Fax 781397
4 miles SE of Wrexham signposted from A483.
Parkland course.
Pro Simon Ward; Founded 1992
Designed by K Williams
9 holes, 2434 yards, S.S.S. 32
🕴 Apr-Sep: WD £950 (9 holes), £16 (18 holes); WE £11/£17/50. Oct-March: WD £6/50/£9, WE £7.50/£12.70. Reductions for juniors; bookinbg advisable
Ⓛ WD £7; WE £8 for 9 holes. WD £7; WE £12 for 18 holes.
✑ Unlimited access; terms on application. Practice area restricted to members.
🍽 Full facilities.
🛏 Cross Lanes Hotel.

---

10 105 Pontardawe
Cefn Llan, Pontardawe, Swansea, SA8 4SH
☎ 01792 863118, Fax 830041, Pro 830977
From M4 Junction 45 take A4067 to Pontardawe.
Moorland course.
Pro Gary Hopkins; Founded 1924
18 holes, 6038 yards, S.S.S. 70
⚑ Practice green.
🕴 Welcome WD with handicap certs.
Ⓛ WD £18.
✑ Welcome by arrangement; prices vary depending on numbers; catering by arrangement.

🍽 Full clubhouse facilities.
🛏 Pen-yr-Alt.

---

10 106 Pontnewydd
Upper Cwmbran, Gwent, NP44 1AB
✉ ct.phillips@virgin.net
☎ 01633 482170, Fax 838598, Sec 838598
Follow signs for Upper Cwmbran; W side of Cwmbran.
Meadowland course.
Founded 1875
18 holes, 5278 yards, S.S.S. 67
🕴 Welcome WD; WE as guest of a member.
Ⓛ WD £15 (£10 with member).
✑ Welcome by prior arrangement; terms on application.
🍽 Limited.
🛏 Parkway; Commodore.

---

10 107 Pontypool ₡
Lasgarn Lane, Trevethin, Pontypool, Gwent, NP4 8TR
✉ ponypoolgolf@btconnect.com
☎ 01495 763655, Fax 755564, Pro 755544
Off A4042 at St Cadoc's Church in Pontypool.
Mountain course.
Pro James Howard
Founded 1919
18 holes, 5963 yards, S.S.S. 69
🕴 Welcome by arrangement.
Ⓛ WD £20; WE £24.
✑ Welcome by prior arrangement; packages available; terms on application.
🍽 Full catering facilities except Mon.
🛏 Three Salmons; Glyn-yr-Avon, both Usk; Parkway, Cwnbran.

---

10 108 Pontypridd
Ty-Gwyn, Ty-Gwyn Road, The Common, Pontypridd, Mid-Glam, CF37 4DJ
☎ 01443 402359, Fax 491622, Pro 491210, Sec 409904
12 miles NW of Cardiff E of Pontypridd off A470.
Mountain course.
Pro Wade Walters; Founded 1905
Designed by Bradbeer
18 holes, 5881 yards, S.S.S. 66
🕴 Welcome with handicap certs.
Ⓛ Terms on application.
✑ Welcome by arrangement with the Pro; packages available; terms on application.
🍽 Clubhouse facilities.
🛏 Lechwen Hall; The Millfield Hotel.

PRESTATYN GOLF CLUB

Marine Road East, Prestatyn, Denbighshire, LL19 7HS.

Telephone/Fax: **01745 854320**

E-mail: **prestatyngcmanager@freenet.co.uk**

Website: **www.prestatyngc.co.uk**

Established in 1905 P.G.C is one of only three Championship courses on the North Wales Coast. The Club welcomes visitors weekdays and Sundays, quality catering available.

Details of green fees and special offers available on request.

---

10 109 Porthmadog ☎
Morfa Bychan, Porthmadog, Gwynedd, LL49 9UU
☎ 01766 514124, Fax 514638, Pro 513828, Rest/Bar 512037
1 mile W of Porthmadog High Street after turning towards Black Rock Sands.
Parkland/links course.
Pro Pete Bright; Founded 1905
Designed by James Braid
18 holes, 6400 yards, S.S.S. 71
⚐ Two practice grounds.
† Welcome by arrangement.
ⵎ WD £25; WE £30.
⚘ Welcome by prior arrangement; discounts for groups of more than 16; catering available; terms on application.
⚐ Clubhouse facilitiesl large restaurant, lounge bar; Spike bar; snooker room.
⚐ Tydden Llwyn; Royal Sportsman.

---

10 110 Prestatyn ☎
Marine Rd East, Prestatyn, Denbighshire, LL19 7HS
⚐ www.prestatyngc.co.uk
⚐ prestatyngcmanager @freenet.co.uk
☎ 01745 854320, Fax 888327, Pro 852083, Sec 888353
Off A548 coast road to Prestatyn.
Championship links.
Pro ML Staton; Founded 1905
Designed by S Collins
18 holes, 6808 yards, S.S.S. 73
⚐ Practice areas.
† Welcome except Sat and Tues morning.
ⵎ WD £25; WE £30.
⚘ Welcome except Sat and Tues am by prior arrangement; 27 holes; lunch and dinner.
⚐ Clubhouse facilities.
⚐ Talardy St Asaph; Traeth Ganol; Sands; Prestatyn; Craig Park; Dyserth.

---

10 111 Priskilly Forest Golf Club
Castlemorris, Haverfordwest, Pembrokeshire, SA62 5EH
⚐ www.priskilly-forest.co.uk
⚐ jevans@priskilly-forest.co.uk
☎ 01348 840276, Fax 840276
On B4331 towards Mathry off A40 at Letterstone.
Picturesque mature parkland course.
Pro S Parsons; Founded 1992
Designed by J.Walters
9 holes, 5874 yards, S.S.S. 69
⚐ Practice area.
† Welcome.
ⵎ Prices on application.
⚘ Welcome by arrangement; limited catering facilities.
⚐ Licensed bar and tea rooms.
⚐ Priskilly Forest Country House WTB 4-star GH on site.

---

10 112 Pwllheli ☎
Golf Rd, Pwllheli, Gwynedd, LL53 5PS
⚐ www.pwllheligolfclub.co.uk
⚐ admin@pwllheligolfclub.co.uk
☎ 01758 612520, Fax 701644, Gen Mgr 701644
Turn into Cardiff Road in town centre; bear right at the first fork; signposted.
Parkland/links course.
Pro Stuart Pilkington; Founded 1900
Designed by Tom Morris; extended James Braid
18 holes, 6200 yards, S.S.S. 69
⚐ Practice ground.
† Welcome.
ⵎ WD £25; WE £30.
⚘ Welcome most days by prior arrangement.
⚐ Full facilities.
⚐ Caeau Capel; Nefyn; Bryn Eisteddfod Clynnogfawr; Nanhoron Morfa.

---

10 113 Pyle & Kenfig
Waun-y-Mer, Kenfig, Bridgend, S Wales, CF33 4PU

⚐ www.pyleandkenfiggolfclub .co.uk
⚐ secretary@pyleandkenfidgolfclub .co.uk
☎ 01656 783093 and 771613, Fax 772822, Pro 772446
M4 Junction 37 in direction of Porthcawl, call for directions.
Links/downland course.
Pro Robert Evans; Founded 1922
Designed by H Colt
18 holes, 6741 yards, S.S.S. 73 (white tees)
⚐ Practice area.
† Welcome.
ⵎ WD £45; Sun £65.
⚘ Welcome by arrangement; prices vary according to numbers; terms on application.
⚐ Full bar and catering facilities.
⚐ Fairways; Atlantic; Seabank, all Porthcawl; Rose & Crown, Nottage.

---

10 114 Radyr ☎
Drysgol Rd, Radyr, Cardiff, CF15 8BS
⚐ www.radyrgolf.co.uk
⚐ manager@radyrgolf.co.uk
☎ 029 2084 2408, Fax 3914, Pro 2476
4 miles from M4 Junction 32; 8 miles from Cardiff.
Parkland course.
Pro R Butterworth; Founded 1902
18 holes, 6078 yards, S.S.S. 70
† Welcome by prior arrangement.
ⵎ WD £38; WE £38.
⚘ Welcome with prior arrangement; catering packages available; separate facilities for parties of 35-40; dining room for 125+; terms on application.
⚐ Full dining and bar facilities.
⚐ Quality Inn.

---

10 115 RAF St Athan
Clive Road, St Athan, Vale of Glamorgan, CF62 4jd
⚐ sec@stanthangolfclub

☎ 01446 751043, Fax 751862
First right after St Athan village on Cowbridge road.
Parkland course.
Founded 1976
9 holes, 6542 yards, S.S.S. 72
⌁ Practice green.
✝ Welcome except Sun.
⌶ WD £12; Sat £16.
⌁ Welcome by arrangement with Sec.
⏲ Full facilities available; except Mon.

10 116 Raglan Parc ☏
Parc Lodge, Raglan, Monmouthshire, NP25 2ER
✉ golf@raglanparcfreeserve.co.uk
☎ 01291 690077, Fax 690075, Pro 0778680-7629, Sec 690077, Rest/Bar 690077
0.5 miles from Raglan at junction of A40 and A449.
Undulating parkland course.
Pro Gareth Gage; Founded 1994
18 holes, 6604 yards, S.S.S. 72
✝ Welcome; booking advisable.
⌶ WD £15; WE £18.
⌁ Welcome by prior arrangement.
⏲ Light lunch and 3-course meal; from £25; Bar snacks and light meals.
⏘ The Beaufort; The Country Court; Travelodge.

10 117 Rhondda
Golf House, Penrhys, Mid-Glamorgan, CF43 3PW
✉ rhonddagolf@aol.com
☎ 01443 433204, Fax 441384, Pro 441385, Sec 441384, Rest/Bar 433204
On Penrhys road between Rhondda Fach and Rhondda Fawr.
Mountain course.
Pro Gareth Bebb; Founded 1910
18 holes, 6205 yards, S.S.S. 70
⌁ 22.
✝ Welcome WD; restrictions WE.
⌶ WD £15; WE £20.
⌁ Welcome by arrangement; function room available; terms on application.
⏲ Full clubhouse bar and catering facilities.
⏘ Heritage Park.

10 118 Rhos-on-Sea
Penrhyn Bay, Llandudno, Conwy, LL30 3PU
☎ 01492 549641, Pro 548115
From A55 take Old Colwyn exit and follow coast road to Penrhyn Bay;

course is between Rhos-on-Sea and Llandudno.
Pro Mike Macara; Founded 1899
Designed by JJ Simpson
18 holes, 6064 yards, S.S.S. 69
✝ Welcome.
⌶ WD £22; WE £30.
⌁ Welcome everyday but only by prior arrangement; catering terms on application – phone 01492 549641.
⏲ Full clubhouse facilities.
⏘ On site dormy house hotel.

10 119 Rhosgoch ☏
Rhosgoch, Builth Wells, Powys, LD2 3JY
⚏ www.rhosgoch-golf.co.uk
☎ 01497 851251, Fax 851251, Sec 851251, Rest/Bar 851251
Off B4594 at turning to Clyro, between Erwood and Kington.
Parkland course.
Founded 1984
Designed by Herbie Poore
9 holes, 4995 yards, S.S.S. 66
✝ Everyone welcome.
⌶ WD £8; WE £10.
⌁ Welcome by prior arrangement; terms on application.
⏲ Bar and snacks.
⏘ Clyro Court, The Swan Hotel, The Kilvert Hotel.

10 120 Rhuddlan
Meliden Rd, Rhuddlan, Denbighshire, LL18 6LB
⚏ www.rhuddlangolfclub.co.uk
✉ golf@rhuddlangolfclub.fsnet.co.uk
☎ 01745 590217, Fax 590472, Pro 590898, Sec 590217, Rest/Bar 591978
Course is off the A55 three miles N of St Asaph.
Parkland course.
Pro Andrew Carr; Founded 1930
Designed by Hawtree & Co.
18 holes, 6471 yards, S.S.S. 71 off the whites, 70 off the yellows
✝ Welcome; only with a member on Sun.
⌶ WD £24; Sat £30.
⌁ Welcome WD by arrangement.
⏲ Lunch and dinner daily; bar facilities.
⏘ Plas Elwy; Kinmel Manor (packages available for both).

10 121 Rhyl
Coast Rd, Rhyl, Denbighshire, LL18 3RE
☎ 01745 353171, Fax 353171

1 mile from station on A548 Prestatyn road.
Seaside links course.
Pro Tim Leah; Founded 1890
9 holes, 6220 yards, S.S.S. 70
⌁ Practice area.
✝ Welcome.
⌶ WD £20; WE £25.
⌁ Welcome by prior arrangement; discount of 20 per cent for parties of more than 20 players; full catering packages available; snooker; from £1.
⏲ Full catering facilities.
⏘ Grange; Marina; Garfields.

10 122 The Rolls of Monmouth
The Hendre, Monmouth, Monmouthshire, NP25 5HG
⚏ www.therollsgolfclub.co.uk
✉ enquiries@therollsgolfclub.co.uk
☎ 01600 715353, Fax 713115, Sec 715353, Rest/Bar 715353
4 miles NW of Monmouth on the B4233.
Parkland course.
Founded 1982
18 holes, 6733 yards, S.S.S. 73
✝ All welcome by arrangement.
⌶ Prices on application.
⌁ Welcome by prior arrangement; special offers on Mon.
⏲ Lunch 18 holes; prices on application; full catering facilities available.

10 123 Royal Porthcawl
Rest Bay, Porthcawl, Mid Glam, CF36 3UW
⚏ www.royalporthcawl.com
✉ royalporthcawl@aol.com
☎ 01656 782251, Fax 771687, Pro 773702, Rest/Bar 782251
M4 Junction 37 and follow signs for Porthcawl/Rest bay.
Championship Links course.
Pro Peter Evans; Founded 1891
Designed by Charles Gibson
18 holes, 6685 yards, S.S.S. 74
⌁ Practice range.
✝ Welcome Mon pm, Tues, Thurs, Fri. Handicap Certs required.
⌶ WD £70– £90; WE £80–£100.
⌁ Welcome by arrangement restaurant and bar facilities.
⏲ Full restaurant and bar facilities.
⏘ Club has own Dormy house from £45 pp.

10 124 Royal St David's ☏
Harlech, Gwynedd, LL46 2UB
⚏ www.royalstdavids.co.uk
✉ secretary@royalstdavids.co.uk

☎ 01766 780361, Fax 781110,
Pro 780857, Rest/Bar 780203
On the A496 Lower Harlech road
under the Castle.
Championship links.
Pro John Barnett; Founded 1894
18 holes, 6571 yards, S.S.S. 74
† Welcome; booking essential.
⌷ WD £40; WE £50.
↻ Welcome; booking essential; £10
deposit per player 2 months before
visit.
🍽 Full catering facilities.
🛏 Rum Hole; St David's, both
Harlech.

---

10 125 Ruthin Pwllglas ☏
Ruthin Pwllglas, Ruthin, Denbighshire,
LL15 7AR
☎ 01824 702296
On A494 2.5 miles S of Ruthin; right
fork before Pwllglas village.
Parkland/meadowland course.
Pro Michael Jones; Founded 1906
Designed by David Lloyd Rees
10 holes, 5418 yards, S.S.S. 66
† Welcome.
⌷ WD £12.50; WE £18.00.
↻ Welcome by prior arrangement.
🍽 Bar and catering facilities by prior
arrangement.
🛏 Ruthin Castle; The Whitstay; The
Anchor; The Manor House; The Eagles.

---

10 126 St Andrews Major
Coldbrook Rd East, Nr Cadoxton,
Barry, S Glamorgan, CF6 3BB
💻 www.standrewsmajorgolfclub.co.uk
☎ 01446 722227, Fax 748953,
Pro 712164, Sec 722227
From M4 Junction 33 follow signs to
Barry and Cardiff Airport turn left to Sully.
Parkland course.
Pro Iestyn taykor; Founded 1993
Designed by MRM Leisure
18 holes, 5862 yards, S.S.S. 70
⌿ 12 Bay driving range, floodlit.
† Welcome, pay and play course +
membership.
⌷ 9 holes: WD/WE £10. 18 holes:
WD £16, WE £18.
↻ Welcome packages available 18
holes and 2 course meal £20.
🍽 Full bar and restaurant facilities;
Sun lunches.
🛏 Copthorne; The International;
Mount Sorrell; Travel Lodge.

---

10 127 St David's City
Whitesands, St David's,
Pembrokeshire, SA62 6PT
☎ 01437 721751

Course is two miles W of St David's
following the signs for Whitesands Bay.
Links course; most westerly Welsh
course.
Founded 1902
9 holes, 5582 yards, S.S.S. 70
† Welcome; some restrictions Fri
pm.
⌷ Day tickets: WD £15 (winter £10);
WE £15 (winter £10).
↻ Welcome by arrangement.
🍽 At the Whitesands Bay Hotel
adjacent to course.
🛏 Whitesands Bay; Old Cross; St
Nons; Warpool Court.

---

10 128 St Deiniol
Pen y Bryn, Bangor, Gwynedd,
LL57 1PX
💻 www.st-deiniol.co.uk
✉ secretary@stdeiniol.fsbusiness
.co.uk
☎ 01248 353098, Fax 370297
From A5/A55 intersection (J11) follow
A5122 for 1 mile to E of Bangor.
Undulating parkland course; views of
Menai and Snowdonia.
Founded 1906
Designed by James Braid
18 holes, 5654 yards, S.S.S. 67
† Welcome; phone in advance for
weekends.
⌷ WD £16; WE £20.
↻ Welcome by appointment;
packages vary; terms on application.
🍽 Full clubhouse facilities; no
catering Mon by prior arrangement.
🛏 Eryl Mor.

---

10 129 St Giles
Pool Rd, Newtown, Powys, SY16 3AJ
☎ 01686 625844, Fax 625844
1 mile E of Newtown on A483.
Riverside/parkland course.
Pro DP Owen; Founded 1895
9 holes, 6012 yards, S.S.S. 70
⌿ Practice putting area.
† Welcome.
⌷ Terms on application.
↻ Welcome by arrangement;
packages include refreshments.
🍽 By prior arrangement.

---

10 130 St Idloes
Penrallt, Llanidloes, Powys, SY18 6LG
☎ 01686 412559, Pro 412559,
Sec 650712, Rest/Bar 412559
Off A470 at Llanidloes; 1 mile down
B4569.
Undulating course; superb views from
hill plateau.
Founded 1906

Designed by Members
9 holes, 5540 yards, S.S.S. 66
† All welcome, ring for information.
⌷ WD £12.50; WE £15.50.
↻ Welcome; packages available;
terms on application.
🍽 Clubhouse facilities.
🛏 Mount Inn; Unicorn; Lloyds; also
lots of B&Bs.

---

10 131 St Mary's Golf Club
St Mary's Hill, Pencoed, S Glamorgan
💻 www.stmaryshotel.com
✉ reservations-stmarys@btopenworld
.com
☎ 01656 861100, Fax 863400,
Pro 868900
Off Junction 35 of M4.
Parkland courses.
Pro John Peters.
18 hole championship, 5291 yards, Par
68; 12 hole, 2838 yards
⌿ 15 bay floodlit driving range.
† Welcome by prior arrangement.
⌷ 18 holes: WD £20; WE £25.
12 holes: WD £6.50; WE £12.
↻ Welcome; packages available.
Country club; floodlit driving range.
🍽 Bar, spike bar, restaurant,
conference facilities.
🛏 24 luxury rooms on site.

---

10 132 St Mellons ☏
St Mellons, Cardiff, CF3 8XS
💻 www.stmellonsgolfclub.co.uk
✉ stmellons@golf2003.fsnet.co.uk
☎ 01633 680408, Fax 681219,
Pro 680101, Rest/Bar 680401
Close to M4 Junctions 28 (W); 30 (E);
15 mins from Celtic Manor
Parkland course.
Pro Barry Thomas; Founded 1964
18 holes, 6275 yards, S.S.S. 70
† Welcome WD; members only at WE.
⌷ WD £27.50.
↻ Welcome Tues and Thurs;
packages vary according to numbers;
terms on application.
🍽 Clubhouse facilities.
🛏 St Mellons Hotel; Travel lodge.

---

10 133 St Melyd
The Paddock, Prestatyn, Denbighshire,
LL19 9NB
💻 www.stmelydgolf.co.uk
✉ info@stmelydgolf.co.uk
☎ 01745 854405, Fax 856908
On A547 on the main Prestatyn to
Meliden road.
Undulating parkland course.
Pro Andrew Carr; Founded 1922
9 holes, 5839 yards, S.S.S. 68
† Welcome except Thurs (Ladies
day) and Sat.

Royal St David's

God and man must have stayed up very late together and drunk an awful lot of coffee in order to knock up a backdrop of Snowdonia, Cardigan Bay and Harlech Castle. The set designers have done Royal St David's proud.

Visually it is an awesome golf course. It also requires a great deal of playing. David Huish, the professional at North Berwick, called it "the most difficult par 69 in the world". One of the problems is that it is not a traditional out and back links. There are pockets of holes facing in all directions. So whatever the direction of the wind it will slap you in the face somewhere on the course.

The finish to Royal St David's – with the exception of the eighteenth which some consider a rather mundane par three, an overstated view because of what precedes it – is majestic. The fifteenth is a superb par four of over four hundred yards, influenced on both sides by some towering dunes. The sixteenth tee is the highest on the course. A spectacular drive is inevitable and if well hit will leave a short second that is hard to gauge. The seventeenth, reflecting some of the holes in the second half of the front nine, curiously relies more on its heathland nature for protection. Just to complicate things further each of the three holes points in a different direction.

The founding fathers of the course were Harold Finch-Hatton, an exotic boomerang-wielding adventurer and brother to the Finch-Hatton of *Out of Africa* fame, and William Henry More, who would become one of the finest club secretaries the game has ever known. Among his many sensible dicta are, "Cultivate the arithmetical skill and memory of a ready-money bookmaker – without his repartee... And when the handicap lists are up rejoice exceedingly if there be general grumbling. You may rest assured that justice has been done".

Not everything ran smoothly. Like one or two other clubs, the patronage of the Prince of Wales, the future Edward VII, encouraged the club to prematurely assume the royal title in 1901. But seven years later royal status was officially granted, so not too much offence could have been taken.

More had much bigger hurdles to overcome in his years as secretary. David Lloyd George, in the days when he was Chancellor of the Exchequer, was accused by one member of having failed to pay his green fee.

But perhaps the most bizarre incident of all was the instigation of a local rule on account of the original greenkeeper's bibulous nature. Because the afore-mentioned was often to be found comatose from drink and stretched out in a pink hunting jacket on various parts of the course, it was decided that a ball coming to rest near his figure could be dropped two club lengths away without penalty.

Perhaps More's greatest contribution was to make a phone call to facilitate Robert Graves's commission with the Welch Royal Fusiliers. It was through this association that Graves, a reluctant member who resigned from the golf club and gave up the game because "I found it made for my temper", came to write *Goodbye To All That*.

At times the more recent members can understand Graves's frustration with the game. There is a crow that has a habit of making off with golf balls. Even more serious have been the drainage problems although David Morkill, the current in the line of articulate secretaries, is perhaps the only man who could have explained a drainage project that seemed to involve American mud, the Archimedes Screw and half the contents of Tracey Island.

Come rain or shine, St David's is worthy of its monarchical and canonised status. – **Mark Reason**

WD £18; WE and BH £22.
Welcome except Thurs and Sat;
18 holes and 3-course meal £24.
Full facilities except Tues.
Nant Hall; Graig Park.

10 134 **Shirenewton Golf Club**
Shirenewton, Nr Chepstow, Gwent,
NP6 6RL
lee.paget@aol.com
01291 641471, Fax 641472,
Rest/Bar 641642
Off M4 take A48 towards Newport, on
reaching Chirk take road to
Shirenewton (2.5 miles).
Parkland course.
Pro Tim Morgan; Founded 1995
Designed by M Weeks/Tony Davies
18 holes, 6607 yards, S.S.S. 72
Practice range.
Welcome.
WD £15; WE £18.
Welcome by prior arrangement.
Full facilities.
On site.

10 135 **South Pembrokeshire**
Military Rd, Pembroke Dock,
Pembrokeshire, SA72 6SE
01646 621453, Fax 621453,
Pro 682442
Main A477 road from Carmarthen to
Pembroke dock; 100 yards after town
boundary sign turn right to Pembroke.
Follow brown golf course direction
signs
Parkland course.
Pro J Tilson; Founded 1970
18 holes, 6100 yards, S.S.S. 72
6.
Welcome.
WD £17; WE £23.
Welcome by prior arrangement;
catering packages available; some
discounts for larger groups; from £16.
Clubhouse facilities.
Coach House; Cleddau Bridge;
Kings Arms.

10 136 **Southerndown**
Ogmore-by-Sea, Bridgend, CF32 0QP
www.southerndowngolfclub.com
southerndowngolf@btconnect.com
01656 880476, Fax 880317,
Pro 880326, Sec 880476,
Rest/Bar 880326
4 miles from Bridgend on the coast
road to Ogmore-by-Sea.
Links/downland course.
Pro Denis McMonagle; Founded 1906
Designed by W Herbert Fowler
18 holes, 6417 yards, S.S.S. 72

Welcome.
WD £40; WE £60.
Welcome WD by prior
arrangement; handicap certs required.
Full facilities.
Sea Lawns; Sea Bank; Heronston;
Great House.

10 137 **Storws Wen**
Brynteg, Anglesey, LL78 8JY
01248 852673, Fax 853843,
Pro 852673, Sec 852673,
Rest/Bar 852673
2 miles from Benllech on B5108;
course is 1.5 miles on right before the
California Hotel.
Parkland course.
Founded 1996
Designed by K Jones
9 holes, 5002 yards, S.S.S. 65
Welcome.
WD: 9 holes, £10; 18 holes £13;
WE: 9 holes £13; 18 holes £18.
Welcome by arrangement;
packages available.
Clubhouse facilities.
Fully furnished WTB 4-star self-
catering accommodation on site.

10 138 **Summerhill Golf Club** ☎
Hereford Road, Clifford, Hay-on-Wye,
HR3 5EW
01497 820451
On B4352 from Hay towards toll
bridge.
Parkland course.
Pro Andy Gealy; Founded 1994
9 holes, 5858 yards, S.S.S. 70
Welcome.
Terms on application.
Welcome by prior arrangement;
private function room; catering
packages.
Full facilities.
Kilvert; Swan.

10 139 **Swansea Bay**
Jersey Marine, Neath, W Glamorgan,
SA10 6JP
01792 812198, Fx 841153,
Pro 816159
From A483 take B4290 to Jersey
Marine.
Links course.
Pro Mike Day; Founded 1892
18 holes, 6605 yards, S.S.S. 73
Welcome with handicap certs;
dress code applies.
WD £17; WE £24.
Welcome by arrangement;
packages by arrangement; terms on
application.

Full clubhouse facilities.
Many in Swansea area.

10 140 **Tenby** ☎
The Burrows, Tenby, Pembrokeshire,
SA70 7NP
www.tenbygolfclub.co.uk
tenbygolfclub@ukk.co.uk
01834 842978, Fax 842978,
Pro 844447, Sec 842978
On A477 to Tenby, W of town.
Championship links course.
Pro Mark Hawkey; Founded 1888
18 holes, 6224 yards, S.S.S. 71
Practice area.
Welcome with handicap certs.
WD £30, WE £35 per round.
Welcome by arrangement; catering
packages by arrangement.
Full facilities.

10 141 **Tredegar and Rhymney**
Cwmtysswg, Rhymney, NP22 3BQ
golfclub@tredegarandrhymney
.fsnet.co.uk
01685 840743, Sec 843400,
Rest/Bar 840743
On B4256 1.5 miles from Rhymney.
Undulating mountain course.
Founded 1921
18 holes, 5332 yards, S.S.S. 67
Welcome.
Prices on application.
Welcome except Sun am.
Bar and snacks; meals by prior
arrangement.
Red Lion, Tredegar.

10 142 **Tredegar Park**
Parc-y-Brain Road, Rogerstone,
Newport, NP10 9TG
secretary.tpgc@breathemail.net
01633 895219, Fax 897152,
Pro 894517, Sec 894433
Near the 14 locks canal centre.
Parkland course.
Pro M Morgan; Founded 1923
Designed by James Braid
18 holes, 6564 yards, S.S.S. 72
Practice ground; clubs for hire.
Welcome with handicap certs and
member.
WD £15; WE £20.
Welcome by prior arrangement;
minimum group 16; from £35.
Restaurant and bar facilities.
Rising Sun.

10 143 **Trefloyne**
Trefloyne Park, Penally, Tenby,
Pembrokeshire, SA70 7RG

☎ 01834 842165, Fax 841165
Off A4139 Tenby to Pembroke road at
Penally.
Parkland course.
Pro S Laidler; Founded 1996
18 holes, 6635 yards, S.S.S. 71
⚐ Practice ground; buggies and
clubs for hire.
⚑ Welcome.
⚐ WD £21; WE £26.
⚐ Welcome by prior arrangement;
clubhouse facilities; minimum 8.
⚐ Catering by arrangement; light
refreshments; licensed bar.

---

10 144 Vale of Glamorgan ☎
Hensol Park, Hensol, S Glamorgan,
CF7 8JY
☎ 01443 665899, Rest/Bar 667800
From M4 Junction 34 follow signs to
Pendoylan.
Parkland course.
Pro Peter Johnson; Founded 1993
Designed by P Johnson
18 + 7 holes, 6401 yards, S.S.S. 71
⚐ Practice range, 20 floodlit bays;
buggies and clubs for hire; tuition.
⚑ Welcome WD; with member at
WE; standard dress.
⚐ WD £30.
⚐ Welcome by arrangement with
Adrian Davies; full society packages;
function room; Vale of Glamorgan
health and racket club; computer
analysis; £25-£39.
⚐ Full clubhouse facilities and bar;
Hotel restaurant 'Lakes Brasserie' and
'Hogan's Bar'.
⚐ On site hotel 143 rooms.

---

10 145 Vale of Llangollen
The Club House, Holyhead Road,
Llangollen, Denbighshire, LL20 7PR
☎ 01978 860613, Fax 860906,
Pro 860040, Sec 860906
1.5 miles E of Llangollen on the A5.
Parkland course set on valley floor.
Pro David Vaughan; Founded 1908
Designed by Members
18 holes, 6656 yards, S.S.S. 73
⚐ Practice area.
⚑ Welcome with handicap certs.
⚐ WD £30; WE £40.
⚐ Welcome WD; 30 holes of golf with
club catering; from £30.
⚐ Clubhouse facilities.
⚐ Bryn Howel; Tyn-y-Wern; Wild
Pheasant All Llangollen.

---

10 146 Virginia Park
Virginia Park, Caerphilly, Mid-Glam,
CF8 3SW

☐ cwithy@fsnet.co.uk
☎ 02920 863919, Pro 850650
In centre of town next to Caerphilly
recreation centre.
Parkland course.
Pro Peter Clark; Founded 1992
9 holes, 4772 yards, S.S.S. 66
⚑ Welcome.
⚐ WD: 9 holes £7.50 18 holes £14;
WE: 9 holes £7.50.
⚐ Welcome by arrangement.
⚐ Full bar and refreshments.

---

10 147 Welsh Border Golf Complex
Bulthy Farm, Bulthy, Middletown, Nr
Welshpool, Powys, SY21 8ER
☐ neil@coco.freeserve.co.uk
☎ 01743 884247, Fax 884247,
Sec 884247, Rest/Bar 884247
Via A458 Shrewsbury/Welshpool road
following sign from Middletown.
Parkland course.
Pro Mike Kendall; Founded 1991
Designed by Andrew Griffiths
2 separate 9-hole courses, 6012 yards,
S.S.S. 69
⚐ 10.
⚑ Welcome; dress codes apply for
Long course.
⚐ Long: WD/£12; short £8.
⚐ Welcome by prior arrangement.
⚐ Bar and restaurant facilities.
⚐ Rowton Castle.

---

10 148 Welshpool ☎
Golfa Hill, Welshpool, Powys,
SY21 9AQ
⚐ www.welshpoolgolfclub.co.uk
☐ welshpool.golfclub@virgin.net
☎ 01938 850249
On the A458 out of Welshpool towards
Dolgellau.
Mountain course.
Pro Bob Barlow; Founded 1931
Designed by James Braid
18 holes, 5708 yards, S.S.S. 70
⚐ Golf carts for hire.
⚑ Welcome.
⚐ Summer: WD/WE/BH £25.50;
Winter: WD/WE/BH £15.50
⚐ Welcome by prior arrangement;
WD packages available from £18.
⚐ Clubhouse facilities.
⚐ Golfa; Royal Oak, both Welshpool.

---

10 149 Wenvoe Castle ☎
Wenvoe, Cardiff, CF5 6BE
⚐ www.wenvoecastlegolfclub.com
☐ wenvoe.castlegc.golfclub@virgin.net
☎ 029 205 94371, Fax 94371,
Pro 93649, Rest/Bar 91094

Follow Signs for Cardiff Airport from
M4 Junction 33.
Parkland course.
Pro J Harris; Founded 1936
Designed by J Braid
18 holes, 6422 yards, S.S.S. 71
⚐ Two practice facilities; putting
green.
⚑ Welcome WD only.
⚐ WD £32.
⚐ Welcome WD; special rates for 16
or more.
⚐ Clubhouse facilities.
⚐ The Copthorne.

---

10 150 Wernddu Golf Centre ☎
Old Ross Rd, Abergavenny,
Monmouthshire, NP7 8NG
☎ 01873 856223, Fax 852177
1.5 miles NE of Abergavenny on
B4521 off A465.
Parkland course; 18th is 615 yards.
Pro Tina Tetley; Founded 1992
Designed by J Watkins
18 holes, 5413 yards, S.S.S. 67
⚐ Practice range, 26 bays floodlit; 9
hole pitch & put.
⚑ Welcome.
⚐ WD £15; WE £15.
⚐ Welcome; maximum 24; terms on
application; from £16.
⚐ Bar snacks.
⚐ Angel.

---

10 151 West Monmouthshire
Golf Road, Nantyglo, Gwent, NP23 4QT
☎ 01495 310233, Fax 311361,
Pro 310233, Sec 310233,
Rest/Bar 310233
A465 Heads of Valley road, western
valley A467 to Semtex roundabout;
follow Winchestown signs.
Mountain heathland course; highest in
England and Wales.
Founded 1906
18 holes, 6300 yards, S.S.S. 69
⚑ Welcome; with member Sun.
⚐ WD £15; Sat £15.
⚐ Welcome WD by prior
arrangement; package includes meals;
from £20.
⚐ Full clubhouse facilities available.
⚐ Nearby Guest Houses available.

---

10 152 Whitchurch (Cardiff) ☎
Pantmawr Rd, Whitchurch, Cardiff,
CF14 7TD
☐ secretary@
whitchurchcardiffgolfclub.com
☎ 029 206 20958, Fax 205 29860,
Pro 206 14660, Sec 206 20985,
Rest/Bar 205 29893/205 29877

Along A470 towards Cardiff from M4
Junction 32 First turning left.
Parkland course.
Pro Eddie Clark; Founded 1914
18 holes, 6258 yards, S.S.S. 71
✝ Welcome WE (if no major
competitions).
⌶ WD £35; WE £40.
⟆ Welcome Thurs; reductions for
groups over 60 and between 24-40;
minimum 24; 24-40 £22; 41-60 £25;
61+ £28.
🍽 Full clubhouse facilities available.
🛏 Quality Inn; Friendly Hotel; Masons
Arms.

10 153 Whitehall
The Pavilion, Nelson, Treharris,
Mid-Glam, CF46 6ST
☎ 01443 740245
Off A470 at Treharris and Nelson exit.
Mountain course.
Founded 1922
Designed by local enthusiasts
9 holes, 5666 yards, S.S.S. 69

✝ Welcome WD; with captain's
permission at WE.
⌶ WD £15; WE £20.
⟆ Welcome by arrangement with
Sec; catering packages by
arrangement.
🍽 Clubhouse facilities.
🛏 Llechwen Hall, Pontypridd.

10 154 Woodlake Park   ♼
Glascoed
Pontypool, Monmouthshire, NP4 0TE
🖳 www.woodlake.co.uk
✉ golf@woodlake.co.uk
☎ 01291 673933, Fax 673811,
Pro 671135
3 miles W of Usk overlooking
Llandegfedd reservoir.
Undulating parkland course.
Pro Leon Lancey; Founded 1993
Designed by MJ Wood/HN Wood
18 holes, 6284 yards, S.S.S. 72
⫞ Practice range, nets available.
✝ Welcome WD; with booking at WE.
⌶ WD £22.50; WE £30.

⟆ Welcome by prior arrangement;
catering and golf packages available;
snooker; pool table; from £20.
🍽 Full clubhouse bar and restaurant
facilities.
🛏 Three Salmons; Rat Trap; New
Court and Greyhound Inn, all Usk.

10 155 Wrexham
Holt Road, Wrexham, N Wales,
LL13 9SB
☎ 01978 261033, Fax 364268,
Pro 351476, Sec 364268, Rest 358705
Course is two miles NE of Wrexham
on the A534.
Sandy parkland course.
Pro Paul Williams; Founded 1906/1924
Designed by James Braid
18 holes, 6233 yards, S.S.S. 70
✝ Welcome with handicap certs.
⌶ WD £22; WE £27.
⟆ Welcome WD except Tues, 27
holes of golf, coffee on arrival, light
lunch, evening meal; £35.
🍽 Full clubhouse catering facilities.

Butch Harmon, the erstwhile coach of Tiger Woods, could find a new job on the Irish Tourist Board. He says, "I actually think the courses in Ireland are a little better than those in Scotland. My favourite golf course in the world is Royal County Down and the front nine of Royal County Down may be the best nine holes in golf. I also love where Darren Clarke is from – Royal Portrush is a great golf course".

Portrush is a severe test of driving and by the time the golfer reaches the aptly named Purgatory and Calamity Corner he can be broken on its wheel. In 1951 it became the only Irish club to have hosted an Open Championship, when Max Faulkner's victory preceded a drought of British winners that would last until Tony Jacklin's win in 1969.

Harry Colt considered the course his masterpiece and Darwin wrote that the famous architect had built himself a monument more enduring than brass. Fred Daly, Ireland's only Open Champion to date, caddied here in his youth and Joe Carr, the most loved of Irish golfers, stood on the ninth tee ten up with ten to play in the final of the Amateur Championship.

On the other side of Belfast is Royal County Down, a course that Old Tom Morris laid out at a cost "not to exceed four pounds". Is it better than Portrush? Is Monet better than Manet? Is Rupert Brooke better than Wilfred Owen? Are these pointlessly subjective questions?

County Down is situated in the shadow of the Mountains of Mourne and lined with heather and gorse and huge sand dunes. Tom Watson said that the first eleven holes were the finest consecutive holes of links golf that he had ever played. The modernists are not fond of the amount of blind shots that they are required to play, but then they also tend to complain if they have a bad lie in a bunker.

Royal Portrush and Royal County Down are the great courses of Northern Ireland, but there are also plenty of good ones. Portstewart and Castlerock are close by Portrush on the northern coast. In early days Portstewart went against the usual golfing trend by banning a railway station in order to discourage the vulgar hordes. It is more welcoming these days and will soon become the second club in Ireland to have 54 holes. Castlerock is a difficult exposed links with a famous fourth called "leg of mutton" with an out of bounds on either side and a stream across.

In Belfast itself are Balmoral, the home club of Daly, Shandon Park, host to the Gallaher Ulster Open in the sixties, Malone, a parkland course re-sited in the sixties, and Belvoir Park, where Philip Walton won the Irish Professional Championship in his great Ryder Cup year of 1995. Royal Belfast, the oldest club in Ireland, is now just outside the city at Holywood after a couple of moves. Designed by Harry Colt, Royal Belfast's current course is probably better than either of its predecessors even if the new place has a reputation for exclusivity.

Clandeboye has 36 holes, a championship course and wonderful views over the Irish Sea and Belfast Lough, Bangor is yet another Braid design, Ardlass begins almost on the edge of a cliff and Warrenpoint is the home club of Ronan Rafferty. County Tyrone is surprisingly devoid of golf courses given its size but it does boast Dungannon, the home club of Darren Clarke, and Omagh, a fine course on the river Drumragh. Between Tyrone and Down, County Armagh has one or two decent parkland courses of which perhaps the pick is Portadown by the river Bann.

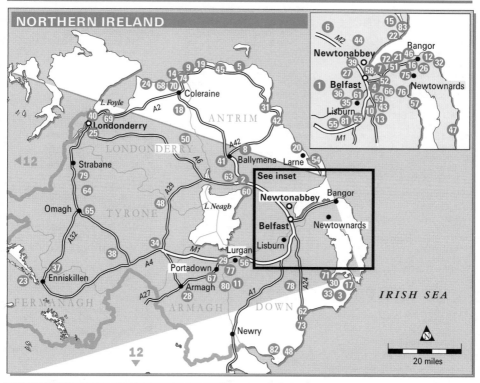

KEY
1 Aberdelghy	16 Blackwood	33 Downpatrick	50 Kilrea	67 Portadown
2 Allen Park	17 Bright Castle	34 Dungannon	51 Kirkistown Castle	68 Portstewart
3 Ardglass	18 Brown Trout	35 Dunmurry	52 The Knock	69 Radisson Roe Park Hotel
4 Ashfield	19 Bushfoot	36 Edenmore Golf Course	53 Lambeg	70 Rathmore
5 Ballycastle	20 Cairndhu	37 Enniskillen	54 Larne	71 Ringdufferin
6 Ballyclare	21 Carnalea	38 Fintona	55 Lisburn	72 Royal Belfast
7 Ballyearl Golf and	22 Carrickfergus	39 Fortwilliam	56 Lurgan	73 Royal County Down
Leisure Centre	23 Castle Hume	40 Foyle	57 Mahee Island	74 Royal Portrush
8 Ballymena	24 Castlerock	41 Galgorm Castle	58 Mallusk	75 Scrabo
9 Ballyreagh	25 City of Derry	42 Garron Tower	59 Malone Golf Club	76 Shandon Park
10 Balmoral	26 Clandeboye	43 Gilnahirk	60 Massereene	77 Silverwood
11 Banbridge	27 Cliftonville	44 Grace Hill	61 Mount Ober	78 Spa
12 Bangor	28 County Armagh	45 Greenisland	62 Mourne	79 Strabane
13 Belvoir Park	29 Craigavon	46 Helen's Bay	63 Moyola Park	80 Tandragee
14 Benone Par 3	30 Crossgar	47 Holywood	64 Newtownstewart	81 Temple
15 Bentra	31 Cushendall	48 Kilkeel	65 Omagh	82 Warrenpoint
	32 Donaghadee	49 Killymoon	66 Ormeau	83 Whitehead

11 1 Aberdelghy Golf Club
Bells Lane, Lambeg, Lisburn, Co
Antrim, BT27 4QH
🖳 www.mmsportsgolf.com
📧 info@mmsportsgolf.com
☎ 028 926 62738, Fax 926 03432
Beween Dunmurry and Lambeg off the
Belfast-Lisburn road.
Municipal parkland course.
Pro Ian Murdoch; Founded 1986
Designed by Alec Blair.
18 holes, 4553 yards, S.S.S. 62
⚑ 5 miles drive.

† Welcome except Sat am.
Ⓛ WD £7.20; WE £9.20.
⌂ Welcome except Sat am.
🍴 Snacks available.

11 2 Allen Park
45 Castle Rd, Antrim, Co Antrim, BT41
4NA
📧 antrimpark@antrim.gov.uk
☎ 028 944 29001
Inland course.
18 holes, 6683 yards, S.S.S. 70

Pro Paul Russell
⚑ Driving range, 20 bay, fully floodlit.
† Welcome.
Ⓛ Terms on application.
⌂ Packages available; terms on
application.

11 3 Ardglass   ☎
Castle Place, Ardglass, Co Down,
BT30 7TP
🖳 www.ardglassgolfclub.com
📧 info@ardglassgolfclub.com

☎ 028 448 41219, Fax 41841,
Pr0 41022
On B1 7 miles from Downpatrick; 30
miles S of Belfast.
Seaside course.
Pro Philip Farrell; Founded 1896
Designed by David Jones
18 holes, 6065 yards, S.S.S. 69
♦ Welcome WD; Sun afternoon.
⌐ WD £28; WE £40 (2003 rates).
⌁ Welcome by prior arrangement
WD and Sun am; packages on
application; £15.
⌾ Full facilities.
⌐ Burrendale; Slieve Danard; Burford
Lodge GH; Margaret's Cottage GH.

11 4 Ashfield

Freeduff, Cullyhanna, Co Armagh
BT35 0NA
⌐ http://freespace-virgin.net/
ashfield.golfing
⌐ ashfield.golfing@virgin.net
☎ 028 308 68180, Fax 68611
Parkland course.
Pro Eril Maney; Founded 1990
18 holes, 5620 yards, S.S.S. 67
♦ Driving range.
♦ Welcome.
⌐ WD £12; WE £15.
⌁ Terms on application.
⌾ Clubhouse facilities.

11 5 Ballycastle ♛

Cushendall Road, Ballycastle, Co
Antrim, BT54 6QP
⌐ www.ballycastlegolfclub.com
⌐ info@nballycastlegolfclub.com
☎ 028 20762536, Fax 20769909,
Pro 20762506
On A2 between Portrush and
Cushendall.
Mixture of parkland, links and heath.
Pro Ian McLaughlin; Founded 1890
18 holes, 5744 yards, S.S.S. 69
♦ Welcome by prior arrangement;
some WE restrictions.
⌐ WD £20; WE £30.
⌁ Welcome by prior arrangement;
WE restrictions; terms on application.
⌾ Full clubhouse facilities.
⌐ Marine.

11 6 Ballyclare ♛

25 Springvale Rd, Ballycare, BT39
9JW
☎ 028 933 22696, Fax 22696, Pro
34541, Rest/Bar 42352
1.5 miles N of Ballyclare at Five
Corners.
Parkland course.
Founded 1923

Designed by Tom McCauley
18 holes, 5745 yards, S.S.S. 71
♦ Practice range.
♦ Welcome.
⌐ WD £16; WE £22.
⌁ Welcome by prior arrangement;
minimum 20 players; catering by
arrangement; snooker; from £14-£18.
⌾ Bar and restaurant service.
⌐ Country House; Dunadry Inn;
Chimney Corner; Five Corners B&B;
Fairways B&B.

11 7 Ballyearl Golf and Leisure Centre

585 Doagh Rd, Newtownabbey,
Belfast, BT36 8RZ
⌐ www.newtownabbey.gov.uk
⌐ sbartley@newtownabbey.gov.uk
☎ 028 90848287, Fax 90844896,
Pro 90840899,
Rest/Bar 90843401
1 mile N of Mossley off B59.
Public parkland course.
Pro Richard Johnston.
9 holes, 2306 yards, S.S.S. 27
♦ Practice range, driving range, 27
bays, fully floodlit.
♦ Welcome.
⌐ WD £6 (non-members); WE £9
(non-members) 2 x 9, junior price WD
£3, WE £4.50. OAP £2.75 WD and
£3.25 WE.
⌁ Terms on application.
⌾ No facilities; vending machines
only.
⌐ Corrs Corner; Motel; Chimney
Corner.

11 8 Ballymena ♛

128 Raceview Rd, Ballymena, DT42
4HY
☎ 028 258 61487, Fax 61487,
Pro 61652, Rest 61207, Bar 62087
2.5 miles E of the town on the A42 to
Broughshane and Carnlough.
Heathland/parkland course.
Pro Ken Revie; Founded 1903
18 holes, 5299 yards, S.S.S. 67
♦ Practice area.
♦ Welcome except Tues and Sat.
⌐ WD £17; WE £22.
⌁ Welcome by prior arrangement
with the Hon Secretary.
⌾ Full clubhouse bar and restaurant.

11 9 Ballyreagh

2 Glen Rd, Portrush, Antrim, BT56 8LX
☎ 028 708 22028, Fax 22028
In Portrush.
Par 3 and pitch and putt courses
Pro Robert L Cockcroft; Founded 1979

Designed by Don Patterson
9 holes, 2800 yards, S.S.S. 33
♦ WD adults £5.25, juniors £3.50;
WE adults £6.25, juniors £5.25 (par 3
course).
⌐ £9.00.
⌁ Limited.

11 10 Balmoral

518 Lisburn Rd, Belfast, BT9 6GX
⌐ www.bbalmoralgolf.com
⌐ admin@balmoralgolf.com
☎ 028 90381514, Fax 90 666759,
Pro 90667747, Rest/Bar 90668540
2 miles S of Belfast city centre;
immediately beside the King's Hall on
the Lisburn road opposite Balmoral
Halt station.
Parkland course.
Pro Geoff Blakeley; Founded 1914
18 holes, 6276 yards, S.S.S. 70
♦ Welcome except Sat and after
3pm Sun.
⌐ WD £20; WE £30.
⌁ Welcome by prior arrangement
Mon and Thurs; special packages are
available.
⌾ Full clubhouse bar and restaurant.
⌐ Forte Crest; Europa; Plaza; York;
Balmoral; Beechlawn.

11 11 Banbridge ♛

116 Huntly Rd, Banbridge, Co Down,
BT32 3UR
⌐ www.banbridgegolf.freeserve.co.uk
⌐ info@banbridgegolf.freeserve.co.uk
☎ 028 40662211, Fax 40669400,
Pro 40626189, Rest/Bar 40662342
1 mile N of Banbridge.
Parkland course.
Founded 1913
18 holes, 5590/5341/4987 yards,
S.S.S. 67
♦ Driving range available through the
Pro shop.
♦ Welcome; dress code.
⌐ WD £17; WE £22.
⌁ Welcome by prior arrangement;
must be GUI recognised societies;
catering by arrangement; from £12.
⌾ Lounge and bar facilities available.
⌐ Bannville House; Bellmont Hotel;
Downshire Arms Hotel.

11 12 Bangor ♛

Broadway, Bangor, Co Down, BT20
4RH
⌐ david-ryan@btconnect.com
☎ 028 912 70922, Fax 914 53394,
Pro 914 62164
0.75 miles S of town centre.
Parkland course.
Pro Michael Bannon; Founded 1903
Designed by James Braid

BANBRIDGE GOLF CLUB 116 Huntley Road, Banbridge BT32 3UR

Situated in the heart of the beautiful Co. Down countryside, 25 miles south of Belfast with easy access from the main Belfast to Dublin Road, our excellent facilities include a challenging 18 hole mature parkland course, well-stocked Pro Shop, superb luxurious Clubhouse, restaurant and conference room. GUI Registered Societies welcomed (April - September); visiting golfers Liability Insurance included.

Tel: 028 4066 2211 (Office) • 028 4066 2342 (Caterer) • 028 4062 6189 (Golf Shop)
Fax: 028 4066 9400 • Email: info@banbridge-golf.freeserve.co.uk • Web: www.banbridge-golf.freeserve.co.uk

---

18 holes, 6410 yards, S.S.S. 71
⚐ Practice green.
♣ Welcome except Sat; ladies have priority Tues.
⚑ WD £25; WE £30. that includes £0.75 insurance charge.
⚘ Welcome by prior arrangement except Tues and Sat; catering by arrangement; £20 + catering.
🍽 Full bar and catering facilities.
⚔ Marine Court; Royal.

11 13 **Belvoir Park**
73 Church Rd, Newtownbreda, Belfast, BT8 7AN
⚐ www.belvoirparkgolfclub.com
✉ info@belvoirparkgolfclub.com
☎ 028 90491693, Fax 9064 6113,
Pro 9064 6714, Rest/Bar 90642817
4 miles from Belfast off the Ormeau road.
Parkland course.
Pro Maurice Kelly; Founded 1927
Designed by HS Colt
18 holes, 6516 yards, S.S.S. 71
⚐ Practice range.
♣ Welcome. prior bookings.
⚑ WD £33; WE £38.
⚘ Only 6 per month permitted by prior arrangement with the club Secretary.
🍽 Full facilities supplied by Brian McMillan.
⚔ La Mon House; Stormont.

11 14 **Benone Par 3 Course**
53 Benone Ave, Benone, Limavady, Derry, BT49 0IQ
☎ 028 777 50555
10 miles N of Limavady on A2.
Inland course.
9 holes, 1447 yards
⚐ Driving range.
♣ Pay and play.
⚑ £6.20.
🍽 Seasonal.

11 15 **Bentra**
1 Slaughterford Rd, Whitehead, Co Antrim, BT38 9TG
☎ 028 93378996, Rest/Bar 353666
5 miles N of Carrickfergus on Larne rd.
Municipal parkland course.

Founded 1842
9 holes, 6084 yards, S.S.S. 68
⚐ Practice range 200 yards 10 bays.
♣ Pay and play.
⚑ WD £8.50; WE £11.70.
⚘ Welcome; tee times can be reserved.
🍽 Bar snacks at Bentra roadhouse.

11 16 **Blackwood**   ⚓
150 Crawfordsburn Rd, Clandeboye, Bangor, BT19 1GB
☎ 028 91852706, Fax 91853785
On A2 towards Bangor from Belfast turn to Newtonards; course 1.5 miles.
Parklands.
Pro Debbie Hanna; Founded 1994
Designed by Simon Gidman
18 holes, 6392 yards, S.S.S. 70
⚐ Practice range 25 Floodlit Bay.
♣ Welcome; pay and play.
⚑ WD £19; WE £25.
⚘ Welcome by prior arrangement.
🍽 Bar snacks and restaurant.
⚔ Clandeboye Lodge.

11 17 **Bright Castle**
14 Coniamstown Rd, Bright, Co Down, BT30 8LU
☎ 028 44841319
5 miles S of Downpatrick.
Parkland course; 16th hole, par 6 is 735 yards.
Founded 1970
Designed by Arnold Ennis
18 holes, 7143 yards, S.S.S. 74
⚐ Brand new clubhouse due for completion Spring 2002.
♣ Welcome.
⚑ WD £11; WE and BH £14.
⚘ Welcome by prior arrangement; catering by arrangement.
🍽 Catering facilities.
⚔ Abbey Lodge.

11 18 **Brown Trout**   ⚓
209 Agivy Road, Aghadowey, Nr Coleraine, Co Londonderry, BT51 4AD
⚐ www.browntroutinn.com
✉ bill@browntroutinn.com
☎ 028 70868209, Fax 70868878
7 miles S of Coleraine on the intersection of A54 & B66.

Parkland course.
Pro Ken Revie; Founded 1973
Designed by Bill O'Hara Snr
9 holes, 5510 yards, S.S.S. 68
♣ Welcome.
⚑ WD £10; WE £15.
⚘ Welcome by prior arrangement; catering packages by prior arrangement; private room for meals and presentations; accommodation for small groups; society rates from £7.
🍽 Full catering and bar facilities.
⚔ Brown Trout Country Inn on site.

11 19 **Bushfoot**
50 Bushfoot Rd, Portballintrae, Co Antrim, BT57 8RR
✉ bushfootgolfclub@bt.com
☎ 028 20731317, Fax 20731852, Sec 20731317,
Rest/Bar 20732588
4 miles E of Portrush on the coast.
Seaside links course.
Founded 1890
9 holes, 5914 yards, S.S.S. 68
♣ Welcome except on competition days (Tue and Sat). Practice ground available.
⚑ WD £15; WE £19.
⚘ Welcome by prior arrangement. function room; snooker room.
🍽 Restaurant and Bar.
⚔ Bay View Hotel; Port Ballintrae.

11 20 **Cairndhu**   ⚓
192 Coast Rd, Ballygally, Larne, Co Antrim, BT40 2QG
✉ cairndhu@globalgolf.com
☎ 028 28583324
4 miles N of Larne on the Glens of Antrim coast road.
Parkland course.
Pro Bob Walker; Founded 1928
Designed by John S.F. Morrison
18 holes, 6700 yards, S.S.S. 69
♣ Welcome.
⚑ WD £20.00; Sat £30.00; Sun-£25.00.
⚘ Welcome by prior arrangement; discounts for groups of 20 or more; from £15.
🍽 Clubhouse facilities.
⚔ Highways; Londonderry Arms; Ballygally Holiday Apartments.

Royal Belfast

Think Royal courses and Northern Ireland and perhaps Portrush and County Down come to mind first before Belfast. But Royal Belfast Golf Club, founded on November 9th 1881, proudly proclaims itself as the oldest club in Ireland and points to this proving to be the inspiration for the growth of the game across the Irish Sea.

And while the growth has continued unabated the roots are, inevitably, traced back to Scotland.

The Royal Belfast members have one Thomas Sinclair to thank for being a prime mover in the creation of the club. Having played golf with friends at St. Andrews whilst visiting Scotland in the summer of 1881, Sinclair was smitten by the game.

On his return home he joined forces with experienced golfer George Baillie, a Scottish-born English schoolmaster.

Sinclair looked for a suitable site for a course close to Belfast and chose Kinnegar in Holywood (an area owned by Captain Harrison the first President of the club). Not men to sit back and idly dream, the original 18 members of the club worked with such enthusiasm that the course was laid out within seven weeks and on Boxing Day 1882 the first 18 hole competition was held.

The club is now at its third home. It moved in 1892, because of over-crowding on Saturdays, allied to the increasing use of the area as a rifle range. It remained on fifty acres of land at Carnalea near Bangor for 21 years and a nine hole course was created.

In 1925 the club again decided to move, primarily due to over-crowding, and purchased the mansion and surrounding 140 acres of land at Craigavad which remains its present home.

The club was granted the Royal title in 1885 after a visit from the Prince of Wales who became the club's first patron. This patronage has continued through the history of the club, the position currently being held by Prince Andrew, Duke of York.

The impressive Victorian clubhouse, with views across Belfast Lough, was built for a Belfast linen manufacturer and was eventually owned by the Lord Mayor of Belfast. The course was designed, as was Portrush by H. C. Colt, the eminent English course architect, with the assistance of Walker Cup player W. A. Murray.

Visitors are welcome at the club but Wednesdays, Thursday evenings and Saturdays before 4:30pm are reserved for members. Those wishing to play are advised to contact either the Secretary or Professional beforehand to check playing availability.

The club is situated seven miles from Belfast off the A2 road to Bangor.
– **Jon Ryan**

11 21 **Carnalea**

Station Rd, Bangor, Co Down, BT19
1EZ
☎ 028 912 70368, Fax 73989,
Pro 70122, Rest/Bar 914 61901
1.5 miles from Bangor adjacent to
Carnalea station.
Parkland course on shore of Belfast
Lough.
Pro Thomas Loughran; Founded 1927
18 holes, 5574 yards, S.S.S. 67
† Welcome; Sat after 2.30pm.
Ⓘ WD £17.50; WE £22.
⟲ Welcome except Sat; catering by
arrangement; from £20.
🍴 Bar and restaurant facilities.
💤 Royal; Marine Court;
Crawfordsburn Inn.

11 22 **Carrickfergus** ♒

35 North Rd, Carrickfergus, Co Antrim,
BT38 8LP
🖳 www.carrickfergusgc.com
📧 carrickfergusgc@talk21.com
☎ 028 93 363713, Fax 363023,
Pro 351803, Rest/Bar 362203
Odd A2 9 miles NE of Belfast on the
North Rd; 1 mile from Shore Road.
Parkland/meadowland course.
Pro Gary Mercer; Founded 1926
18 holes, 5623 yards, S.S.S. 68
† Welcome except Sat.
Ⓘ Terms on application.
⟲ Welcome WD by arrangement.
🍴 Full facilities.
💤 Coast Road; Dobbins; Glenavna;
Quality Inn.

11 23 **Castle Hume** ♒

Castle Hume, Blake Road, Enniskillen,
Co Fermanagh, BT93 7ED
🖳 www.castlehumegolf.com
📧 info@castlehumegolf.com
☎ 028 663 27077, Fax 27076
A few minutes' drive from Enniskillen
on the Belleek/Donegal road.
Parkland course.
Pro Shaun Donnelly; Founded 1991
18 holes, 6525 yards, S.S.S. 72
⚐ Driving range.
† Welcome.
Ⓘ WD £20/€30; WE £25/€37.
⟲ Welcome; minimum group of 12;
discounted fees for groups 12 or more:
WD £15; WE £20.
🍴 Bar and restaurant.
💤 Manor House; Killykevlin;
Ashberry; Railway.

11 24 **Castlerock** ♒

65 Circular Rd, Castlerock, Co
Londonderry, BT51 4TJ

☎ 028 708 48314, Fax 49440,
Pro 49424, Rest/Bar 48215
Off A2 6 miles W of Coleraine.
Links course.
Pro Ian Blair; Founded 1901
Designed by Ben Sayers
18 holes, 6737 yards, S.S.S. 72
⚐ Practice range.
† Welcome; arrange with office.
Ⓘ WD £35; WE £60.
⟲ Welcome by prior arrangement;
catering by prior arrangement; from
£25.
🍴 Full catering facilities.

11 25 **City of Derry** ♒

49 Victoria Rd, Londonderry, BT47 2PU
🖳 www.cityofderrygolfclub.com
📧 info@cityofderrygolfclub.com
☎ 028 71346369, Fax 71310008,
Pro 71311496
On main Londonderry-Strabane road
three miles from Craigavon Bridge.
Parkland course; also 9-hole pay and
play Dunhugh course.
Pro Michael Docherty; Founded 1912
18 holes, 6429 yards, S.S.S. 71
⚐ Practice range.
† Welcome WD before 4.30pm; WE
by prior arrangement.
Ⓘ WD £20; WE £25.
⟲ Welcome WD; WE availability.
🍴 Full facilities.
💤 Everglades; Broomhill House;
White Horse Inn; Waterfoot; Tower
City.

11 26 **Clandeboy** ♒

Tower Rd, Conlig, Newtownards, Co
Down, BT23 7PN
🖳 www.cgc-ni.com
📧 contact@cgc-ni.com
☎ 028 912 71767, Fax 914 73711,
Pro 912 71750, Bar 914 73706,
Rest 912 70992
In village of Conlig off the Belfast-
Bangor road at Newtownards.
Parkland course.
Pro Peter Gregory; Founded 1933
Designed by Baron von Limburger
36 holes, 5755 yards, S.S.S. 68 & 71
† Welcome; Sat & Sun restrictions.
Ⓘ WD £22; WE £27.50; (Ava); WD
£27.50; WE £33 (Dufferin).
⟲ Welcome WD except Thurs;
packages include golf and food; from
£20-£35 (Ava); from £30-£40
(Dufferin).
🍴 Full clubhouse dining and bar
facilities.
💤 The Clandeboy Lodge; Marine
Court Hotel.

11 27 **Cliftonville**

44 Westland Rd, Belfast, BT14 6NH
☎ 028 90744158, Pro 90228585,
Sec 90746595,
Rest/Bar 744158
From Belfast take Antrim road for two
miles then turn into Cavehill Rd and
left again at Fire Station.
Parkland course.
Pro Robbie Hutton; Founded 1911
9 holes, 5706 yards, S.S.S. 70
⚐ Practice range.
† Welcome except Tues afternoon
and Sat.
Ⓘ WD £13; WE £16.
⟲ Welcome by arrangement with
secretary J M Henderson.
🍴 Bar and Catering facilities.
💤 Lansdowne Court.

11 28 **County Armagh** ♒

The Demesne, 7 Newry Rd, Armagh,
Co Armagh, BT60 1EN
🖳 www.golfarmagh.co.uk
📧 info@golfarmagh.co.uk
☎ 028 375 25861, Fax 25861,
Pro 25864, Rest/Bar 11720/22501
Off Newry Rd 0.25 miles from the city.
Parkland course.
Pro Alan Rankin; Founded 1893
18 holes, 6212 yards, S.S.S. 69
⚐ Practice range.
† Welcome except 12 noon-2pm Sat;
12 noon-3pm Sun.
Ⓘ WD £15; WE £20 (may change
2004).
⟲ Welcome by arrangement except
Sat.
🍴 Full facilities except Mon.
💤 Charlemont Arms; Armagh City
Hotel.

11 29 **Craigavon Golf Ski Centre**

Turmoyra Lane, Silverwood, Lurgan,
Co Armagh, BT66 6NG
☎ 028 383 26606, Fax 383 47272
Playing facilities at Craigavon.
Founded 1984. Off Junction 10 of M1
motorway.
Parkland course.
Pro Jason Greenaway
Founded 1984
39 holes, 6188 yards for 18 holes,
S.S.S. 72
⚐ 11 covered bays, 7 open bays.
† Everyone welcome.
Ⓘ Mon-Fri adult £13.50, WE adult
£17; junior/senior citizen Mon-Fri £4;
WE junior/senior citizen £5.
⟲ Local rules will apply.
🍴 Cafe open 7 days per week.
Society meals available.

11 30 Crossgar
231 Derryboye Rd, Crossgar, Co.
Down, BT30 9DL
☎ 028 44831523
From Belfast 5 miles S of Saintfield
close to town of Crossgar.
Parkland course.
Founded 1993
Designed by John Cuffey
9 holes, 4538 yards, S.S.S. 63
† Welcome.
Ⅼ WD £10; WE £11. (9-hole £6 WD;
£7 WE).
⌀ Welcome by prior arrangement;
from £9.
⌂ Millbrook Lodge; Abbey Lodge.

11 31 Cushendall   ₢
Shore Road, Cushendall, Ballymena,
Co Antrim, BT44 0NG
☎ 028 21771318, Sec 21758366,
Rest/Bar 21771318
On main Antrim coast road 25 miles N
of Larne.
Parkland course.
Founded 1937
Designed by Daniel Delargy
9 holes, 4384 yards, S.S.S. 63
† Welcome; starting sheet
weekends; Thursday, Ladies Day.
Ⅼ WD £13; WE £18; £5 reduction of
playing with member.
⌀ Welcome on application to
secretary Mr S McLaughlin; catering
packages available in summer; from
£15.
⏀ Full catering in summer; bar
facilities.

11 32 Donaghadee   ₢
84 Warren Rd, Donaghadee, Co Down,
BT21 0PQ
✉ deegolf@frenet.co.uk
☎ 028 918 88697, Fax 88891,
Pro 82392
6 miles S of Bangor on the coast road.
Part links and inland course.
Pro Gordon Drew; Founded 1899
18 holes, 5570 yards, S.S.S. 69
† Welcome at all time (not Sat
before 4pm).
Ⅼ WD £22; WE £28.
⌀ Welcome Mon, Wed, Fri by prior
arrangement; discounts for groups of
24 or more catering packages
available by arrangement; from £20.
⏀ Clubhouse facilities.

11 33 Downpatrick   ₢
43 Saul Rd, Downpatrick, Co Down,
BT30 6PA
⬚ www.downpatrickgolfclub.org

✉ info@downpatrickgolfclub.com
☎ 028 446 15947, Fax 17502, Pro
15167, Rest/Bar 15244/12152
23 miles SE of Belfast off A24 and A7.
Parkland course.
Pro Robbie Hutton; Founded 1930
Designed by Hawtree & Sons
18 holes, 6299 yards, S.S.S. 69
† Welcome; some WE restrictions.
Ⅼ WD £20; WE £25.
⌀ Welcome by prior arrangement.
⏀ Full facilities.
⌂ Denvir; Abbey Lodge.

11 34 Dungannon   ₢
34 Springfield Lane, Mullaghmore,
Dungannon, Co Tyrone, BT70 1QX
⬚ www.dungannongolfclub.com
✉ info@dungannongolfclub.com
☎ 028 877 22098, Fax 27338,
Rest/Bar 29995
0.5 miles from Dungannon on
Donaghmore road.
Parkland course.
Founded 1890
18 holes, 6046 yards, S.S.S. 69
† Welcome; restrictions Tues
(ladies day).
Ⅼ WD £20; WE £25.
⌀ Welcome by prior arrangement
except Tues and Sat.
⏀ Full facilities.
⌂ Reahs Guesthouse; Stangmore
Country House.

11 35 Dunmurry   ₢
91 Dunmurry Lane, Dunmurry,
BT17 9JS
☎ 028 90610834, Fax 90602540,
Pro 90621314, Sec 90620834,
Rest/Bar 621402
Follow signs for Dunmurry from the
M1; turn left at first traffic lights.
Parkland course.
Pro J Dolan; Founded 1905
Designed by TJ McAuley
18 holes, 6080 yards, S.S.S. 69
† Welcome by prior arrangement.
Ⅼ WD £23; WE £33.
⌀ Welcome WD by written
arrangement; packages available; from
£16.
⏀ Full clubhouse facilities.
⌂ Beech Lawn.

**11 36 Edenmore Golf &
₢Country Club**
Edenmore House, 70 Drumnabreeze
Rd, Magheralin, Co. Armagh,
BT67 0RH
⬚ www.edenmore.com
✉ info@edenmore.com

☎ 028 926 11310, Fax 13310,
Sec 19241, Rest/Bar 19199
M2 west from Belfast to Moira exit.
Through Moira to Magheralin.
Signposted from Magheralin.
Parkland course.
Founded 1992
Designed by Frank Ainsworth
18 holes, 6244 yards, S.S.S. 71
ɟ Practice area; health & fitness
club; conference centre.
† Welcome except Sat am; priority
for members before 2pm on Sat.
Ⅼ WD £15; WE £20.
⌀ Welcome by prior arrangement;
packages on request; private dinners
for groups of 25-150.
⏀ Restaurant available 7 days.
⌂ White Gables.

11 37 Enniskillen   ₢
Castlecoole, Enniskillen, Co
Fermanagh, BT74 6HZ
⬚ www.enniskillengolfclub.com
✉ enquiries@enniskillengolfclub.com
☎ 028 66325250
1 mile from Enniskillen off Tempo Rd.
Parkland course.
Founded 1896
Designed by Dr Dixon & George
Mawhinney/TJ McAuley
18 holes, 6189 yards, S.S.S. 69
† Welcome.
Ⅼ WD £15; WE and BH £18.
⌀ Welcome by arrangement; catering
by arrangement with the steward;
snooker.
⏀ Full catering and bar facilities.
⌂ Fort Lodge; Ashbury; Killyhevlin;
Railway; Belmore Court.

11 38 Fintona   ₢
Ecclesville Demesne, Fintona, Co
Tyrone, BT78 2BJ
☎ 028 82841480, Fax 82841480,
Pro 82840777
9 miles SW of Omagh.
Parkland course.
Pro Paul Leonard; Founded 1904
9 holes, 5866 yards, S.S.S. 70
† Welcome WD.
Ⅼ WD £15; guests of members £10.
⌀ Welcome by prior arrangement;
packages available; groups of more
than 20 £10; under 20 £15.
⏀ Full facilities on request.
⌂ Silver Birches.

11 39 Fortwilliam   ₢
8A Downview Ave, Belfast, B15 4EZ
☎ 028 903 70770, Fax 71891,
Pro 70980, Rest/Bar 71557

Royal County Down

There can't be many championship courses around the world that Jack Nicklaus hasn't played but, until the summer of 2001, Royal County Down was one of them. For some reason the great man had never made it to Northern Ireland, but when he was invited to play in the Senior Open British Championship, his curiosity got the better of him. So it was that Nicklaus, Arnold Palmer and Gary Player teed it up on a misty July morning – an appropriate triumvirate for a course so steeped in history.

And he was not disappointed. Despite the odd grumble about the number of blind holes, he proclaimed it "a great golf course". "You can't take risks", he added. "You just have to hang in there and be defensive."

Founded in 1889, Royal County Down is a links in the finest tradition, evolving naturally out of the dune landscape and described by the late Peter Dobereiner as "thrilling, even without a club in your hand". With its splendidly old-fashioned clubhouse, it has clung to its history, changing little since Harry Vardon made a few changes before the First World War.

In 1908 Vardon said of the changes, "I have always thought Newcastle the best course in Ireland, and now it holds its own with all others". Presumably he wasn't the only one to hold that view because in the same year King Edward VII decided that "Newcastle" should become Royal County Down.

Since then the club has played host to 15 Irish Open Amateur Championships, two British Open Amateurs, two Home Internationals and, in 1968, the Curtis Cup. More recently the Senior British Open came to town as part of a three-year deal beginning in 2000.

The first three holes follow the shores of Dundrum Bay to a towering sandhill and offer a daunting challenge. The fourth is the first of four short holes, played from a lofty tee and requiring an intimidating 200-yard shot to a smallish green fortified by grassy swales and bunkers.

There are two fine dog-leg holes, the fifth and thirteenth, and arguments abound as to which is the better. The challenge at both is positioning the tee shot, at the fifth to have sight of the green and at the thirteenth to reach through the neck of the valley to overcome the dog-leg.

The sixth, with its tiny green, leads on to the second of the par threes at the seventh, the green falling away to a large bunker on the left. The 429-yard eighth requires not only a well-positioned tee shot, but a pinpoint second into a narrow green sloping away to trouble on either side. The ninth tee shot is blind, but what you don't see from the tee is compensated by what greets you at the brow of hill – surely one of golf's great views.

The tenth is the third short hole and, with the eleventh and twelfth, leads northwards to the dog-legged thirteenth with its green set in a amphitheatre of gorse. The fourteenth, the last short hole, is played from a raised tee into a well- bunkered green 200 yards away.

The course then heads home. The fifteenth requires two demanding strokes – a slight dog-leg and a green guarded by gorse on the left and a heather hollow on the right. The sixteenth is a short par four played over a valley. Most will go for the green and look for a birdie and, while this is feasible, the impetuous can be tempted.

The last two holes continue towards the clubhouse with the par five eighteenth providing a thrilling finale. Re-structured by Donald Steel in 1998 challenge for even the best players – fair when played sensibly, but quick to punish the impulsive.

Located at Newcastle in the south of County Down, the club is accessible from all parts of Ireland and the UK, with Belfast International Airport just an hour's drive away. – **Simon Hart**

3 miles from Belfast off Antrim road.
Parkland course.
Pro Peter Hanna; Founded 1891
Designed by Butchart
18 holes, 6030 yards, S.S.S. 69
♱ Welcome.
Ⅼ WD £22; WE £29.
⌁ Welcome by prior arrangement;
discounts for groups of more than 15;
catering packages available by
arrangement; from £18.
🍽 Clubhouse facilities.
🛏 Lansdowne Court; Chimney
Corner.

11 40 Foyle ☏
12 Alder Road, Londonderry, Co
Londonderry, BT48 8DB
🖳 www.foylegolfcentre.co.uk
🖂 mail@foylegolf.club24.co.uk
☏ 028 713 52222, Fax 53967,
Rest/Bar 52222 x210/211
2 miles N of Londonderry off Culmore
road.
Parkland course.
Pro Kieran McLaughlin; Founded 1994
Designed by F Ainsworth
18 holes, 6678 yards, S.S.S. 71
⛳ Practice range 25 bays covered
and floodlit; golf academy.
♱ Welcome.
Ⅼ WD £12; WE £15.
⌁ Welcome; bookings taken 12
months in advance; discount for
groups of 14 or more; packages with
hotels and catering available; also 9-
hole par 3 course; from £12.
🍽 Restaurant and bar facilities;
private function rooms.
🛏 Waterfoot Hotel & CC; Whitehorse
Inn; City Hotel.

11 41 Galgorm Castle ☏
Galgorm Rd, Ballymena, BT42 1HL
🖳 www.galgormcastle.com
🖂 golf@galgormcastle.com
☏ 2082 564 6161, Fax 565 1151,
Rest/Bar 565 0220
On outskirts of Ballymena off A42.
Parkland course.
Pro Phil Collins; Founded 1997
Designed by S Gidman
18 holes, 6736 yards, S.S.S. 72
♱ Welcome by prior arrangement.
Ⅼ WD £25; WE £30.
⌁ Packages; corporate days.
🍽 Full clubhouse facilities.
🛏 Galgorm Manor.

11 42 Garron Tower
St Macnissi's College, Carnlough, Co
Antrim, BT44 0JS

☏ 028 28885202
Playing facilities at Cushendall and
Ballycastle Golf Clubs.
Founded 1968

11 43 Gilnahirk
Manns Corner, Upper Braniel Rd,
Gilnahirk, Castlereagh, Belfast, BT5 7TX
☏ 028 90448477
3 miles from Belfast off Ballygowan
road.
Public moorland course.
Pro Kenneth Gray; Founded 1983
9 holes, 5924 yards, S.S.S. 68
♱ Welcome.
Ⅼ WD: 18 holes £8.50, 9 holes £5;
WE: 18 holes £10, 9 holes £6.
⌁ Welcome by prior arrangement.
🍽 No catering facilities.

11 44 Grace Hill ☏
141 Ballinlea Road, Stranocum,
Co Antrim BT53 8PX
🖳 www.gracehillgolfclub.co.uk
☏ 028 207 51209, Fax 51074
7 Miles from Ballymoney. Signposted
on A26 North at Ballymoney Bypass.
Take A2/B147 Stranocum/Ballintoy.
Parkland course with lakes
Founded 1995
Designed by Frank Ainsworth
18 hole championship course, 6531
yards, S.S.S. 73
⛳ Driving range.
♱ Welcome; best times WD; check
with clubhouse for WE.
Ⅼ WD £20; WE £25.
⌁ Welcome.
🍽 Bar and restaurant.
🛏 Variety of accommodation in close
proximity to course.

11 45 Greenisland
156 Upper Rd, Carrickfergus,
Co Antrim, BT38 8RW
☏ 028 90862236, Rest/Bar 90862236
8 miles N of Belfast; 2 miles from
Carrickfergus.
Parkland course.
Founded 1894
Designed by C Day
9 holes, 5624 yards, S.S.S. 69
♱ Everyone welcome.
Ⅼ WD £12; WE £18.
⌁ Welcome by prior arrangement; on
application; from £12.
🍽 Full clubhouse facilities.

11 46 Helen's Bay
Golf Rd, Helen's Bay, Bangor, Co
Down, BT19 1TL

🖂 pclarke@helensbaygc.com
☏ 028 91852601, Fax 91852815,
Sec 91852815, Rest/Bar 91852601
4 miles W of Bangor off the B20; next
to Crawfordsburn Country Park.
Parkland course on shores of Belfast
Lough.
Founded 1896
9 holes, 5181 yards, S.S.S. 67
♱ Welcome except Tues and Sat;
restrictions Thurs pm and Fri summer
am.
Ⅼ WD £17; Fri, Sun and BH £20.
⌁ Welcome by prior arrangement
Sun, Mon, Wed, Thurs morning and
Fri; Minimum 10 Maximum 40; private
room for dining or presentations;
catering packages available; from £12.
🍽 Full bar and restaurant facilities.

11 47 Holywood ☏
Nuns Walk, Demesne Rd, Holywood,
Co Down, BT18 9LE
☏ 028 90423135, Fax 90425040,
Pro 90425503, Rest/Bar 9042138
On A2 6 miles E of Belfast.
Undulating course.
Pro Paul Gray; Founded 1904
18 holes, 6028 yards, S.S.S. 68
♱ Welcome except Sat.
Ⅼ WD £15; Sun £20.
⌁ Welcome except Thurs, Sat and BH.
🍽 Bar and catering facilities.

11 48 Kilkeel ☏
Mourne Park, Kilkeel, Co Down, BT34
4LB
☏ 028 4762296, Fax 91765095
3 miles W of Kilkeel; 45 miles S of
Belfast.
Parkland course.
Pro Eddie Hackett; Founded 1948/1993
Designed by Lord Justice Babbington
18 holes, 6615 yards, S.S.S. 72
⛳ Practice range close to course.
♱ Welcome by prior arrangement.
Ⅼ WD £16; WE £20.
⌁ Welcome by arrangement; catering
on application; from £14.
🍽 Full clubhouse facilities.
🛏 Kilmurey Arms; Cronfield Arms;
Slieve Danard; Burrendale.

11 49 Killymoon ☏
200 Killymoon Rd, Cookstown, Co
Tyrone, BT80 8TW
🖂 kglc@btopenworld.com
☏ 028 867 63762, Fax 63762,
Pro 63460, Rest/Bar 62254
Off A29 0.5 miles S of Cookstown.
Parkland course.
Pro Gary Chambers; Founded 1889

Designed by Hugh Adair
18 holes, 5486 yards, S.S.S. 69
↑ Welcome except Sat after 4pm.
🍴 WD £20; WE £25.
⌁ Welcome except Thurs and Sat by prior arrangement; rates negotiable.
🍽 Full facilities.
🛏 Glenavon; Greenvale; Royal.

11 50 Kilrea
47A Lisnaerot Rd, Kilrea,
Co Londonderry BT51 5SF
☎ 028 295 40044
0.5 miles from Kilrea Village.
Parkland course.
Founded 1919
9 holes, 5494 yards, S.S.S. 68
↑ Welcome except after 4.30pm
Tues and Wed and Sat pm.
🍴 WD £10; WE £12.50.
⌁ Welcome by prior arrangement.
🍽 Full catering facilities.
🛏 Port Neal Lodge.

11 51 Kirkistown Castle ♛
142 Main Rd, Cloughey, Co Down,
BT22 1JA
🖳 www.kcgc.org
📧 kirkistown@supanet.com
☎ 028 42771233, Fax 4277 1699,
Pro 427 71004
A20 from Belfast to Kircubbin; follow signs to Newtonards and Portaferry; then B173 to Cloughey.
Links course.
Pro John Peden; Founded 1902
Designed by B Polley
18 holes, 5616 yards, S.S.S. 70
↑ Welcome.
🍴 WD £20.75; WE £27.75.
⌁ Welcome WD by prior arrangement; packages for groups of 16 or more.
🍽 Full facilities.
🛏 Portaferry.

11 52 The Knock ♛
Summerfield, Upper Newtownards Rd, Dundonald, BT16 2QX
📧 knockgolfclub@btconnect.com
☎ 028 904 83251, Fax 87277,
Pro 83251, Rest/Bar 82249
4 miles E of Belfast off the Upper Newtownards road.
Parkland course.
Pro Gordon Fairweather; Founded 1895
Designed by Cole, Mckenzie & Allison
18 holes, 6435 yards, S.S.S. 71
🏌 Practice green.
↑ Welcome every day except Sat.
🍴 WD £25; WE £40; £3 after 2pm
Sun.

⌁ Welcome Mon and Thurs; discounts for groups of more than 40; catering packages; from £20.
🍽 Full bar and restaurant facilities.
🛏 Stormont; Clandeboye; Strangford.

11 53 Lambeg
Aberdelghy, Bells Lane, Lambeg, Lisburn, Co Antrim, BT27 4QH
☎ 028 92662738
Off main Lisburn road at Bells Lane in Lambeg.
Parkland course.
Pro Ian Murdoch; Founded 1986
18 holes, 4528 yards, S.S.S. 62
↑ Welcome except Sat am.
🍴 WD £10; WE £12.
⌁ Welcome except Sat am.
🛏 Hotels in Belfast.

11 54 Larne
54 Ferris Bay Rd, Islandmagee, Larne, BT40 3RT
☎ 028 933 82228, Fax 82088,
Rest/Bar 82442
From Belfast N to Carrickfergus and 6 miles from Whithead; from Larne S along the coast road to Islandmagee.
Seaside course.
Founded 1894
Designed by Babington
9 holes, 6288 yards, S.S.S. 69
↑ Welcome except Sat.
🍴 WD £10; WE £18.
⌁ Welcome except Sat.
🍽 Full clubhouse facilities available.
🛏 Magheramorne House.

11 55 Lisburn ♛
68 Eglantine Rd, Lisburn, Co Antrim, BT27 5RQ
☎ 028 926 77216, Fax 926 03608,
Pro 926 77217, Rest/Bar 926 62186
Take Springfield roundabout exit from M1 in direction of Hillsborough.
Parkland course.
Pro Blake Campbell; Founded 1905/1973
Designed by Hawtree & Sons
18 holes, 6647 yards, S.S.S. 72
↑ Welcome WD before 3pm; Sat after 5.30pm; Sun with member.
🍴 WD: Adult £25 Juvenile £12.50; WE: Adult £30 Juvenile £15.
⌁ Welcome Mon and Thurs before 3pm; discounts for groups of 20 or more before 12.30; from £25.
🍽 Clubhouse facilities available.

11 56 Lurgan ♛
The Demesne, Lurgan, Co Armagh, BT67 9BN

🖳 www.lurgancgolfclub.co.uk
📧 lurgan@btclick.com
☎ 028 38322087, Fax 38325306,
Pro 38321068
Centre of Lurgan off Windsor Avenue past park and down road between Park Lake and Brownlow House.
Parkland course.
Pro Des Paul; Founded 1893
Designed by Frank Pennink
18 holes, 6257 yards, S.S.S. 70
↑ Welcome except Sat; Tues Ladies day; Wed competition day; visitors permitted certain times; restrictions Fri pm; best to ring in advance.
🍴 WD £15; WE £20.
⌁ Welcome by prior arrangement as guest policy; discounts for groups of 50 or more; catering packages available; from £15.
🍽 Restaurant and lounge bar.
🛏 Ashburn; Carngrove; Seagoe.

11 57 Mahee Island ♛
14, Mahee Island, Comber, Newtownards, Co Down, BT23 6ET
☎ 028 975 41234
Turn left 0.5 miles from Comber off Comber to Killyleagh road.
Parkland/seaside course.
Founded 1929
Designed by Mr Robinson
9 holes, 5564 yards, S.S.S. 68
↑ Welcome; restrictions Sats only.
🍴 WD £10; WE £15.
⌁ Welcome WD except Mon; Sun available; catering by prior arrangement; from £10.
🍽 By prior arrangement; no bar.

11 58 Mallusk
Newtownabbey, Co Antrim, BT36 2RF
☎ 028 90843799, Fax 321647
From Belfast on A8 to Antrim; course just before Chimney Corner Hotel.
Founded 1992.
9 holes, 4686 yards, S.S.S. 64
↑ Welcome except Sat before 11.30am.
🍴 WD £6.50; WE £9.
⌁ Welcome by prior arrangement.
🍽 None.
🛏 Chimney Corner.

11 59 Malone Golf Club ♛
240 Upper Malone Rd, Dunmurry, Belfast, BT17 9LB
📧 manager@malonegolfclub.co.uk
☎ 028 90612695, Fax 90431394,
Pro 90614917, Sec 90612758,
Rest/Bar 614916/612695
5 miles from Belfast city centre

Parkland course.
Pro Michael McGee; Founded 1895
Designed by Fred Hawtree/Comdr.
J Harris
18 holes, 6599 yards, S.S.S. 71
♦ Welcome; start sheet operates
Wed pm.
ℐ WD: non-members £33 guests of
members £15; WE: non-members £38
guests of members £17.
♫ Welcome Mon and Thurs by prior
arrangement; catering packages by
prior arrangement; also Edenderry
course: 9 holes 3160 yards par 72; £32.
⁙ Full clubhouse catering and bar
facilities.

11 60 Massereene   ☎
51 Lough Rd, Antrim, Co Antrim, BT41
4DQ
⊹ www.massereenegolfclub1895
.com
✉ massereenegc@utvinternet.com
☎ 028 944 28096, Fax 87661,
Pro 64074, Rest/Bar 28101
1 mile S of town; 3.5 miles from
Aldergrove Airport.
Parkland course.
Pro Jim Smyth; Founded 1895
Designed by F.W. Hawtree
18 holes, 6604 yards, S.S.S. 72
♦ Welcome WD and WE; Fri Ladies
day; Sat restrictions.
ℐ WD £25; WE £30.
♫ Welcome by prior arrangement;
from £20.
⁙ Full facilities.
⟿ Dunadry.

11 61 Mount Ober
24 Ballymaconaghy, Knockbracken,
Belfast, BT8 4SB
☎ 028 907 95666, Fax 05862,
Pro 01648, Sec 904 01811
Off Four Winds roundabout.
Parkland course.
Pro Steven Rourke; Founded 1985
18 holes, 5448 yards, S.S.S. 66
ℐ Practice range, floodlit bays.
♦ Welcome except Sat.
ℐ WD £14/50; WE £16.50.
♫ Welcome except Sat; catering
packages; function rooms; 10 percent
discount in Pro shop; from £11.
⁙ Full clubhouse facilities.
⟿ La Mon House; Stormont Hotel.

11 62 Mourne
36 Golf links Rd, Newcastle, Co Down,
BT33 0AN
☎ 01936723889
Playing facilities at Royal Co Down.

11 63 Moyola Park   ☎
Shanemullagh, Castledown,
Magherafelt, Co Londonderry,
BT45 8DG
✉ moyolapark@btconnect.com
☎ 028 794 68468, Fax 46826,
Pro 68830, Rest/Bar 68270
Course is off the A6 Belfast/Derry road
– at Magherfelt roundabout.
Mature parkland course.
Pro Bob Cockcrof
Founded 1976
Designed by Don Patterson
18 holes, 6491 yards, S.S.S. 71
♦ Welcome by arrangement.
ℐ WD £20; WE/BH £30.
♫ Welcome by prior arrangement
only; discounts available; packages by
arrangement.
⁙ Clubhouse facilities.
⟿ Rural College; Glenavon Hotel;
Walsh's Hotel, Maghera.

11 64 Newtownstewart   ☎
38 Golf Course Rd, Newtownstewart,
Co Tyrone, BT78 4HU
⊹ www.globalgolf.com/
m.newtownstewart
✉ newtown.stewart@lineone.net.
☎ 028 816 61466, Pro 816 62242
2 miles SW of Newtownstewart on B84.
Parkland course.
Founded 1914
Designed by Frank Pennik
18 holes, 5341 yards, S.S.S. 69
ℐ Practice range; buggies hire and
club hire available at the golf shop.
♦ Welcome.
ℐ WD £12; WE £17.
♫ Welcome if affiliated to the GUI;
catering packages by arrangement;
special society packages from £15 WD
£20 WE (meal inclusive).
⁙ Bar and restaurant facilities.
⟿ Mellon Country Inn, Silverburch.

11 65 Omagh
83a Dublin Road, Omagh, Co Tyrone,
BT78 1HQ
☎ 028 822 41442/43160,
Fax 822 43160, Rest/Bar 822 43160
On A5 about one mile from town
centre.
Parkland course.
Founded 1910
18 holes, 5650 yards, S.S.S. 70
♦ Welcome WD and WE; Tues
Ladies day.
ℐ WD £12 WE £18.
♫ Welcome WD and WE by prior
arrangement.
⁙ Clubhouse facilities.
⟿ Silverbirch; Hawthorne House.

11 66 Ormeau
50 Park Rd, Belfast, BT7 2FX
☎ 028 90641069, Fax 90640250,
Pro 90640999, Sec 90640700
Adjacent to Ormeau road alongside
Ravenhill Rd and Park Rd.
Parkland course.
Pro Bertie Wilson; Founded 1892
9 holes, 4862 yards, S.S.S. 65
♦ Welcome; Sat members only.
ℐ WD £9; WE £11.
♫ Welcome mainly Thurs and Sun;
packages available.
⁙ Full bar and catering facilities
available.
⟿ Stormont Hotel.

11 67 Portadown   ☎
192 Gilford Rd, Portadown, Craigavon,
Co Armagh, BT63 5LF
✉ portadowngc@btconnect.com
☎ 028 38355356, Pro 38334655,
Rest/Bar 38355356
3 miles from Portadown on Gilford
road.
Parkland course.
Pro Paul Stevenson; Founded 1908
18 holes, 5786 yards, S.S.S. 70
♦ Welcome by arrangement;
members only Tues (ladies) and Sat
(men).
ℐ WD £18; WE £23.
♫ Welcome by prior written
arrangement; green fees from £17;
catering packages by prior
arrangement; snooker squash and
indoor bowls available for members.
⁙ Bar and restaurant facilities.

11 68 Portstewart
117 Strand Road, Portstewart,
Co Londonderry, BT55 7PG
⊹ www.portstewartgc.co.uk
✉ bill@portstewartgc.co.uk
☎ 028 70832015, Fax 70834097,
Pro 70832601, Sec 70832015,
Rest/Bar 70834543
4 miles W of Portrush.
Links course.
Pro Alan Hunter; Founded 1894
18 holes, 6779 yards, S.S.S. 73
♦ Welcome WD on application.
ℐ Strand: WD £60 WE £80;
Riverside: WD £12 WE £17; Old: WD
£10 WE £14.
♫ Welcome WD by prior booking.
⁙ Full facilities in season. Limited
facilities on Mondays.

11 69 Radisson Roe Park   ☎
Roe Park, Limavady, Co Derry, BT49
9LB

Royal Portrush

With its spectacular views over the seas Royal Portrush has a thoroughly deserved reputation as one of the most scenic courses in Europe. Even the drive, about an hour from Belfast International airport, is dramatic along a road carved out of the cliffs. The course began life in 1888 as simply the County Club and in 1892 was granted the Royal prefix when the Duke of York was patron. Three years later the name was changed to the Royal Portrush Golf Club and the same year was the venue of the first professional tournament held in Ireland.

The course has strong links with the Open Championship; Fred Daly, the first Irishman to win the title, was a member of the club. Daly triumphed in 1947 at Hoylake and four years later his home club hosted the championship – the first time it had been held in Ireland.

The winner was the flamboyant Englishman Max Faulkner who, when asked for his autograph before he went out for the final round of the championship, famously wrote: "Max Faulkner, 1951 Open champion". He later recalled: "There was no way I was going to lose".

Faulkner's finest moment came in the third round at the 16th, when he hooked his tee shot within a few inches of the out-of-bounds fence. Spurning safety he took his three wood hoping to start the ball out of bounds, and fade it back into play.

The gallery watched spellbound, as the ball moved right, right and right again as it crossed the fence and bounded up the fairway on to the green. "It was", said Faulkner's American playing partner Frank Stranahan, "the greatest shot I've ever seen".

It was a sign of very different times that the final two rounds of the Open at Royal Portrush were played on the Friday, to allow the club professionals to get back to their shops.

A sense of this great golf course comes from the names of the holes – the 4th is named after Fred Daly, the 6th bears the name of the course architect Harry Colt and probably the most famous Portrush hole – the 210 yard par three 14th – leaves nothing to the imagination with its name – Calamity. If you have negotiated that safely there is no chance to relax as you stand on the next tee – Purgatory.

But savour the history and descriptions in the Giant's Grave, White Rocks, Himalayas, Dhu Varren and Feather Bed holes. Who could resist recounting a round in the bar after playing a course like that? – **Jon Ryan**

☎ 028 77760105
Course is on the A2 Londonderry-Limavady road 16 miles from Londonderry.
Parkland course.
Pro Seamus Duffy; Founded 1993
18 holes, 6309 yards, S.S.S. 71
🏌 Practice range 10 covered floodlit bays.
♤ Welcome.
🍸 WD £20; WE £20.
🏌 Welcome by prior arrangement; catering packages; from £15.
🍽 Restaurant and bar facilities.
🛏 Radisson Roe Park Hotel on site.

11 70 Rathmore
Bushmills Rd, Portrush, BT56 8JG
📧 dwilliamson555@btconnect.com
☎ 028 708 22996, Fax 22996, Rest/Bar 22285
Playing facilities at Royal Portrush.
Founded 1947.
Links.
18 holes, 6273 yards
♤ Details on request.
🍸 WD £30; WE £35.
🏌 Details on request.
🛏 Magherabuoy House; Royal Court.

11 71 Ringdufferin
Ringdufferin Rd, Toye, Killyleagh, Co Down, BT30 9PH
📧 jimlindsay@btinternet.com
☎ 028 44828812, Fax 44828812, Sec 44828812, Rest/Bar 44828812
2 miles N of Killyleagh on Comber road.
Parkland course.
Pro Roy Skillen; Founded 1992
Designed by F Ainsworth
18 holes, 5113 yards, S.S.S. 66
♤ Everyone welcome.
🍸 9 holes: WD £7 WE £8; 18 holes: WD £10 WE £12.
🏌 Welcome; catering by arrangement; from £6.
🍽 Clubhouse facilities.

11 72 Royal Belfast
Station Rd, Craigavad, Holywood, Co Down, BT18 0BP
🛜 www.royalbelfast.co.uk
📧 royalbelfastgc@btclick.com
☎ 028 904 28165, Fax 21404, Pro 28586, Rest/Bar 903 97792
2 miles E of Holywood on A2.
Parkland course.
Pro Chris Spence; Founded 1881
Designed by HC Colt/Donald Steel (1988)

18 holes, 6306 yards, S.S.S. 71
🏌 Practice area with two bay shed for bad weather.
♤ Welcome except Wed or Sat before 4.30pm.
🍸 WD £45 WE £55.
🏌 Welcome by arrangement.
🍽 Full facilities.
🛏 Culloden.

11 73 Royal County Down ☎
Newcastle, Co Down, BT33 0AN
🛜 www.royalcountydown.org
📧 golf@royalcountydown.org
☎ 028 43723314, Fax 4372 6281
On A24 30 miles S of Belfast.
Links course.
Pro Kevan Whitson; Founded 1889
Designed by Tom Morris Senior
36 holes, 7065 and 4708 yards, S.S.S. 74 and 63
♤ Welcome WD except Wed; other days by prior arrangement.
🍸 Championship: WD £90 WE £100; Annesley: WD £18; WE £28.
🏌 Welcome by arrangement with Sec for the Annsley links.
🍽 Full clubhouse facilities.

11 74 Royal Portrush
Bushmills Rd, Portrush, Co Antrim, BT56 8JR
☎ 028 70822311, Fax 70823139
1 mile from Portrush off A1.
Championship links; 1951 Open course.
Pro Gary McNeil; Founded 1888
Designed by H.S. Colt
18 holes, 6818 yards, S.S.S. 73
♤ Welcome WD between 9.10am-11.50am; Mon between 9.20am-11.50am.
🍸 Wed and Fri after 2pm; restrictions at WE. WD £70; WE and BH £80.
🏌 None.
🍽 Local hotels can provide meals.

11 75 Scrabo ☎
233 Scrabo Rd, Newtownards, Co Down, BT23 4SL
📧 scrabogc@compuserve.com
☎ 028 918 12355, Fax 22919, Pro 17848, Rest/Bar 15048
Off A20 10 miles E of Belfast; near Scrabo Tower.
Gorse/parkland course.
Pro Paul McCrystal; Founded 1907
18 holes, 5699 yards, S.S.S. 71
♤ Welcome WD except Wed.
🍸 WD £18; WE £23.
🏌 Welcome any day except Sat; not in June; from £13.

🍽 Full bar and restaurant.
🛏 Strangford Arms; George; La Mon House.

11 76 Shandon Park ☎
73 Shandon Park, Belfast, BT5 6NY
☎ 028 907 93730, Fax 904 02773, Pro 907 97859
3 miles from city centre via Knock dual carriageway.
Parkland course.
Pro Barry Wilson; Founded 1926
Designed by Brian Carson
18 holes, 6282 yards, S.S.S. 70
♤ Welcome WD and Sun.
🍸 WD £22; WE £27.
🏌 Welcome Mon and Fri only by prior arrangement; reductions available for groups of more than 24 and 40.
🍽 Meals and bar snacks.
🛏 Stormont.

11 77 Silverwood
Tormoyra Lane, Silverwood, Lurgan, Co Armagh, BT66 6NG
☎ 028 38326606, Fax 38347272
Playing facilities at Craigavon off M1 roundabout ar Largon.
Founded 1984
18 holes, 6188 yards, S.S.S. 72
🏌 Putting green.
♤ Welcome.
🍸 Terms on application.
🏌 Welcome.
🍽 Cafe.

11 78 Spa ☎
20 Grove Rd, Ballynahinch, Co Down, BT24 8PN
☎ 028 97562365, Fax 974158
0.5 miles from Ballynahinch; 11 miles S of Belfast.
Wooded parkland course.
Founded 1907/1987
Designed by F Ainsworth
18 holes, 6469 yards, S.S.S. 72
♤ Welcome except Sat.
🍸 WD £16; WE £20.
🏌 Welcome except Sat; discounts for parties of more than 16; catering packages by arrangement. No reduction on Sun.
🍽 Full clubhouse facilities.
🛏 White Horse; Millbrook.

11 79 Strabane ☎
33 Ballycolman Rd, Strabane, Co Tyrone, BT82 9PH
📧 strabgc@aol.com
☎ 028 713 82007, Fax 718 86514, Rest/Bar 713 82271

1 mile from Strabane on Dublin road beside church and schools.
Parkland course.
Founded 1908
Designed by Eddie Hackett
18 holes, 5854 yards, S.S.S. 69
♠ Welcome WD; WE by arrangement.
⌇ WD £15; WE £17.
⌁ Welcome by arrangement with Sec.
◉ Full facilities by arrangement only.
⌁ Fir Trees Hotel.

11 80 **Tandragee** ℭ
Market Hill Rd, Tandragee, Co Armagh, BT62 2ER
⚏ www.tandragee.co.uk
▤ office@tandragee.co.uk
☎ 0035 538 41272, Fax 388 40664, Pro 388 41761, Rest/Bar 388 41763
On B3 in Tandragee on the A27.
Parkland course.
Pro Paul Stevenson; Founded 1922
Designed by F. Hawtree
18 holes, 5747 yards, S.S.S. 71
♠ Welcome WD 10.30am-2pm and WE after 3pm.
⌇ WD £15; WE £20.
⌁ Welcome by prior arrangement; catering by prior arrangement; from £15.
◉ Full bar and restaurant facilities.
⌁ Carngrove; Seagoe; Bannview.

11 81 **Temple Golf and Country Club**
60 Church Rd, Boardmills, Lisburn, Co Down, BT27 6UP
⚏ www.templegolf.com
▤ info@templegolf.com
☎ 028 926 39213
On main Ballynahinch road out of Belfast.
Parkland course.
Founded 1994
9 holes, 5451 yards, S.S.S. 66
⌁ Practice area.
♠ Welcome except Sat am in summer.
⌇ WD £10; WE £14.
⌁ Welcome by arrangement; from £16.
◉ Full facilities.
⌁ Own en-suite bedrooms available.

11 82 **Warrenpoint** ℭ
Lower Dromore Rd, Warrenpoint, Co Down, BT34 3LN
▤ warrenpointgolfclub@tog21.com
☎ 028 417 53695, Fax 417 52918, Pro 417 52371, Rest/Bar 417 52219
5 miles from Newry on Warrenpoint road.
Parkland course.
Pro Nigel Shaw; Founded 1893
18 holes, 6161 yards, S.S.S. 70

♠ Welcome by prior arrangement.
⌇ WD £20; WE £27.
⌁ Welcome by prior arrangement.
◉ Full facilities.
⌁ Canal Court.

11 83 **Whitehead** ℭ
McCrea's Brae, Whitehead, Co Antrim, BT38 9NZ
☎ 028 933 70820, Fax 70825, Pro 70821, Rest/Bar 70822 (bar) 70823 (restaurant)
On the Co Antrim coast between Larne and Carrickfergus.
Parkland course.
Pro Colin Farr; Founded 1904/1975
Designed by AB Armstrong
18 holes, 6050 yards, S.S.S. 69
♠ Welcome WD; WE With a member.
⌇ WD £116; WE £21.
⌁ Welcome WD anytime and Sun 10.30an-12 noon by prior arrangement; catering by prior arrangement with chef.
◉ Full clubhouse facilities.
⌁ Coast Road, The Quality Inn.

REPUBLIC OF IRELAND

12

You wouldn't expect a republic to have too much to do with monarchy and that is the case with Eire. On the face of it they have three royal courses, but closer examination reveals just the one. It turns out that Royal Tara is entirely self-appointed due to its proximity to the seat of the Ancient Kings of Ireland and that The Curragh has the royal charter but chooses not to use it. That leaves Royal Dublin as the only royal course in a country that is crammed with the great and the good of golf.

Ireland really is a glutton for golf. Already stuffed full of great courses, it has spent the last few years attracting the likes of Arnold Palmer, Bernhard Langer, Christy O'Connor Jnr, Greg Norman, Peter McEvoy, Des Smyth, Philip Walton and Jack Nicklaus to build several more. It would be possible to fill this space with no more than a list of recommended names. But one sensible way to give an idea of the choice involved is to start in the north west corner and sweep anti-clockwise.

Donegal offers Ballyliffin, described by Nick Faldo as "the most natural golf course ever", Rosapenna and Donegal, where just the names of the Blue Stack Mountains and the Valley of Tears hint at the enchantment of the place. County Sligo has been described by Tom Watson as "a magnificent links" and Enniscrone by an admiring architect as "the last site for a great links development in the British Isles".

Westport is one of the most beautiful spots in Mayo and a venue for the Irish Close Championship, whilst in Galway Connemara has just been upgraded to championship standard and Galway Bay is that strange hybrid called "parkland by the sea".

Lahinch on the spectacular coast of Clare has been described as "the Irish St Andrews" and is a favourite of Phil Mickelson and just along the coast lies Doonbeg, designed by God and Greg Norman.

Like the country as a whole Kerry is spoiled for choice. Ballybunion has two monumental courses to the north; Tralee is a Palmer design with an open front nine and dune laden back nine in *Ryan's Daughter* country; and from the legendary links of Waterville they say that you can see Boston on a clear day. In the midst of them all is Killarney, inspired by an aristocratic figure who was known simply as Castlerosse. He had a tree plonked in the middle of the fifteenth green to attract publicity and declared, "When anyone sees Killarney, even if he is the basest heretic, he must believe in God".

Cork has Bantry Bay, the recently-opened and ruggedly splendid Old Head of Kinsale, and Fota Island where the Irish Open was played until recently and to which it will hopefully return.

Wicklow is the home of Pat Ruddy, the sort of bloke who gives golf courses a good name even in the circles of the most seethingly politically correct. This charming man is responsible for the extraordinary links called the European and was also persuaded to take a hand in the design of Druids Glen.

Huddled together in the arms of Dublin are Royal Dublin, the home club of Christy O'Connor; Portmarnock, of whose greens Darwin said, "Even on a raw Easter time they demand that the ball should be soothed rather than hit towards the hole"; Portmarnock Links "where nothing is overlooked but the sea"; and The Island. The final stop around the coastal tour is County Louth, a secluded gem at the mouth of the River Boyne.

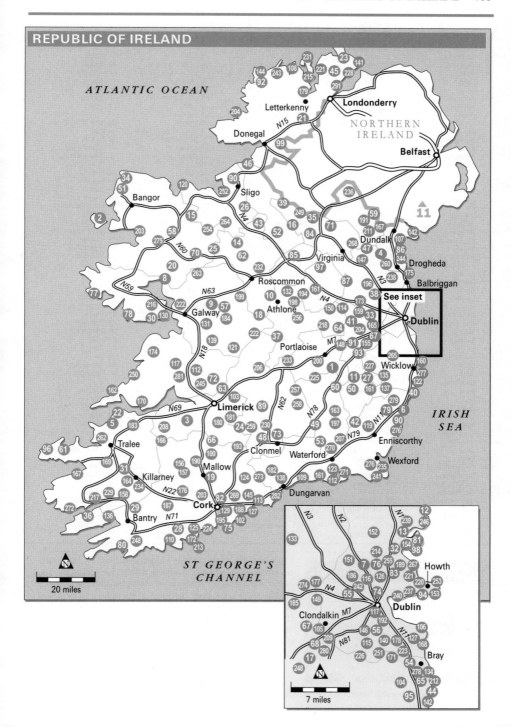

12 1 Abbeyleix
Stradbally Rd, Abbeyleix, Co Laois
☎ 00353 502 31450, Fax 30108,
Sec 31546, Rest/Bar 31450
Course is situated 0.5 miles off Main
Street.
Parkland course; Founded 1895.
Designed by Mel Flanagan
18 holes, 6017 yards, S.S.S. 70
† Welcome.
Ⅼ WD €15; WE €35.
⌲ Welcome.
⦿ By arrangement.
↵ Abbeyleix Manor Hotel, Abbeyleix;
Heritage Hotel; Killeshin Hotel;
O'Loughlins Hotel; Montague Hotel, all
Portlaoise (8 miles).

12 2 Achill Island
Keel Achill, Co Mayo
☎ 00353 98 43456
Via Castlebar or Westport.
Seaside course.
Founded 1952
Designed by P Skerrit
9 holes, 5378 yards, S.S.S. 66
† Welcome.
Ⅼ WD €15, WE €20.
⦿ Full clubhouse facilities available.
↵ Atlantic; McDowalls; Slievemore;
Strand; Gray's GH.

12 3 Adare Golf Club
Adare Manor Hotel & Golf Resort,
Adare, Co Limerick
⬚ www.adaremanor.com
✉ golf@adaremanorl.com
☎ 00353 613 96566, Fax 96124, Sec
96204
10 miles from Limerick on the Killarney
Road. Adare dual carriageway, and
follow to golf course.
Parkland course built round a castle
and friary ruins.
Pro (touring) Christy O'Connor Jnr
Founded 1995
Designed by Robert Trent Jones Sr
18 holes, 7138 yards, Par 72
Ⅰ Driving range.
† Welcome WE with member or by
prior arrangement.
Ⅼ WD €120, residents €100.
⌲ Welcome by prior arrangement;
catering packages can be supplied;
see website for hotel packages.
⦿ Clubhouse facilities available.
↵ Adare Manor hotel.

12 4 Ardee
Town Parks, Ardee, Co Louth
☎ 00353 41 6853227, Fax 6856137,
Pro 68 56747

0.25 miles N of town on Mullinstown
Road.
Parkland course.
Pro Scot Kirkpatrick; Founded 1911
Designed by Eddie Hackett
18 holes, 5500 yards, S.S.S. 69
Ⅰ Practice Range.
† Welcome WD.
Ⅼ WD €35; Sat €50.
⌲ Welcome Mon-Sat by prior
arrangement.
⦿ Full facilities available.

12 5 Ardfert ☾
Sackville, Ardfert, Tralee
☎ 00353 66 7134744, Fax 7134744
6 miles N of Tralee on R551.
Parkland course.
9 holes, 5702 yards, S.S.S. 38
Ⅰ Driving range.
† Welcome.
Ⅼ 9-hole €15; 18-hole; €23.
⌲ All welcome.
⦿ Catering available.

12 6 Arklow ☾
Abbeylands, Arklow, Co Wicklow
☎ 00353 402 32492,
Fax 91604
Signposted from town centre after
turning at bridge.
Links course.
Founded 1927
Designed by Hawtree & Taylor
18 holes, 5604 yards, S.S.S. 69
Ⅰ Practice range; practice bunkers
and nets.
† Welcome by arrangement.
Ⅼ WD €40.
⌲ Welcome by prior arrangement;
Welcome WD and Sat morning;
deposit of required; catering packages.
⦿ Bar and restaurant facilities.
↵ Arklow Bay.

12 7 Ashbourne ☾
Archerstown, Ashbourne, Co Meath
⬚ www.ashbournegolfclub.ie
✉ ashgc@iol.ie
☎ 00353 1 835 2005, Fax 835 2561,
Pro 835 9002, Rest/Bar 835 2005
On N2 12 miles from Dublin.
Parkland course with water features.
Pro John Dwyer; Founded 1991
Designed by Des Smyth
18 holes, 5872 yards, S.S.S. 70
Ⅰ Practice area.
† Welcome.
Ⅼ WD €35; WE €45.
⌲ Welcome WD; golf and catering
packages available; terms on
application.

⦿ Full bar and restaurant service.
↵ Ashbourne House.

12 8 Ashford Castle
Cong, Co Mayo
⬚ www.ashford.ie
✉ ashford@ashford.ie
☎ 003539 495 46003, Fax 46260
27 miles N of Galway on shores of
Lough Corrib.
Parkland course.
Pro Tom Devereux; Founded 1972
Designed by Eddie Hackett
9 holes, 4506 yards, S.S.S. 70
† Residents only.
Ⅼ WD/WE €60.
⌲ Welcome by prior arrangement
with pro.
⦿ Bar facilities.
↵ Ashford Castle; packages
available.

12 9 Athenry ☾
Palmerstown, Oranmore, Co Galway
✉ athenrygc@eircom.net
☎ 00353 91 794466
5 miles from Athenry off N6 Galway-
Dublin road.
Parkland course.
Pro Raymond Ryan; Founded 1902
Designed by Eddie Hackett
18 holes, 6200 yards, S.S.S. 70
† Welcome except Sun.
Ⅼ WD €26; WE €32.
⌲ Welcome by prior arrangement.
⦿ Full bar and catering facilities.

12 10 Athlone
Hodson Bay, Athlone, Co Roscommon
☎ 00353 902 92073, Fax 94080
3 miles N of Athlone on the
Roscommon Road.
Parkland course; All Ireland finals
course 1998.
Pro Martin Quinn; Founded 1892
Designed by J McAllister
18 holes, 5935 yards, S.S.S. 71
† Welcome; some restrictions Tues
and Sun.
Ⅼ WD €27; WE €30.
⌲ Welcome by prior arrangement;
discount for groups of more than 40;
catering packages available; terms on
application.
⦿ Full clubhouse facilities.
↵ Hodson Bay; Prince of Wales;
Shamrock; Royal Hoey.

12 11 Athy
Geraldine, Athy, Co Kildare
⬚ www.athygolfclub.com

✉ info@athygolfclub.com
☎ 00353 598 331729, Fax 634710
On T6 2 miles N of Athy.
Undulating parkland course.
Founded 1906
Designed by Jeff Howes.
18 holes, 6335 yards, S.S.S. 69
⌿ Driving range opposite.
† Welcome WD.
⌇ €25.
⌁ Welcome Sat mornings. 9am–1pm.
⦿ By arrangement with the steward.
⬱ Lenster Arms Hotel; Kilkea Castle.

12 12 Balbriggan
Blackhall, Balbriggan, Co Dublin
☎ 00353 1 8412229, Fax 8413927,
Sec 8412229, Bar 8412173
0.75 miles S of Balbriggan on the N1
Dublin-Belfast Road.
Parkland course.
Founded 1945
Designed by R Stilwell; J Paramour
18 holes, 5922 yards, S.S.S. 71
† Welcome WD except Tues.
⌇ WD €32.
⌁ Welcome by prior arrangement
with Sec; discounts for more than 30
players; from €31.
⦿ Full clubhouse facilities.

12 13 Balcarrick
Corballis, Donabate, Co Dublin
☎ 00353 1 8436228, Rest/Bar 843
6957
Founded 1972
18 holes, 6362 yards, S.S.S. 73
† Welcome.
⌇ WD €32; WE €40.

12 14 Ballaghaderreen
Aughalista, Ballaghaderreen,
Co Roscommon
☎ 00353 907 60295
3 miles from Ballaghaderreen.
Parkland course.
Founded 1937
9 holes, 5363 yards, S.S.S. 67
† Welcome.
⌇ €15 per day.
⌁ Welcome by prior arrangement.
⦿ Bar and snack facilities.

12 15 Ballina
Mossgrove, Shanaghy, Ballina,
Co Mayo
⬱ www.ballinagolfclub.com
✉ ballinagc@eircom.net
☎ 00353 96 21050
On the outskirts of Ballina on the
Bonniconlon Road.

Parkland course.
Founded 1910
Designed by Eddie Hackett
18 holes, 6103 yards, S.S.S. 69
† Welcome.
⌇ WD €20; WE €30.
⌁ Welcome; reductions for groups of
12 or more; from €20 WD and €27
WE.
⦿ Full clubhouse facilities.
⬱ Downhill; Bartra House.

12 16 Ballinamona
Mourne Abbey, Mallow, Cork
☎ 00353 222 9314, Fax 9314
Parkland links
Founded 1997.
Designed by J O'Keeffe & Associates
18 holes, 6200 yards, Par 72
† Welcome all day, every day.
⌇ €25.
⌁ Welcome.
⬱ Accommodation with 3 mins.

12 17 Ballinamore
Creevy, Ballinamore, Co Leitrim
☎ 00353 78 44346
1.5 miles NW of Ballinamore.
Parkland course.
Founded 1939
Designed by Arthur Spring
9 holes, 4782 yards, S.S.S. 68
† WD welcome; WE phone in
advance.
⌇ Terms on application; group rates
available.
⦿ Bar facilities.

12 18 Ballinascorney
Bohernabreena, Tallaght, Co Dublin
☎ 00353 1 451 2082
10 Miles SW of Dublin.
Parkland course.
Founded 1971
18 holes, 5648 yards, S.S.S. 67
† WD Welcome; WE phone in
advance.
⌇ WD €25; WE €35; group rates
available.
⦿ Bar facilities.

12 19 Ballinasloe   ℭ
Rossgloss, Ballinasloe, Co Galway
✉ ballinasloegolfclub@eircom.net
☎ 00353 905 42126, Fax 42538
2 miles off the N6 on the Portumna
Road.
Parkland course.
Pro Nigel Howley/Shane O'Grady;
Founded 1894
Designed by Eddie Connaughton

18 holes, 5865 yards, S.S.S. 70
⌿ Practice area.
† Welcome Mon-Sat.
⌇ WD €29; WE €25. Group rate:
€20.
⌁ Welcome Mon-Sat; catering
packages.
⦿ Bar and restaurant facilities.
⬱ Haydens; East County; Gullanes.

12 20 Ballinrobe   ℭ
Cloona Castle, Ballinrobe, Co Mayo
✉ bgcgolf@iol.ie
☎ 00353 92 41118, Fax 41889, Sec
09241118, Rest/Bar 42090
30 miles from Galway. 6 miles from
Ashford Castle Hotel.
Parkland course set in beautiful
scenery.
Founded 1895
Designed by Eddie Hackard
18 holes, 5540 yards, S.S.S. 73
⌿ 5 bays.
† Welcome; some restrictions on
Sun.
⌇ Terms on application.
⌁ Welcome WD by arrangement;
catering packages by arrangement;
fishing can be organised; terms on
application.
⦿ Bar and restaurant facilities.

12 21 Ballybofey &   ℭ
Stranorlar
Stranorlar, Ballybofey, Co Donegal
☎ 00353 74 31093
Course is signposted off the Strabane-
Ballybofey Road; 14 miles from
Strabane.
Parkland course.
Founded 1957
Designed by PC Carr
18 holes, 5437 yards, S.S.S. 69
† Welcome.
⌇ Terms on application.
⌁ Welcome by prior arrangement;
terms on application.
⦿ Bar facilities; meals by
arrangement.

12 22 Ballybunion
Sandhill Rd, Ballybunion, Co Kerry
⬱ www.ballybuniongolfclub.ie
✉ bbgolf@iol.ie
☎ 00353 68 27146, Fax 27387
20 miles N of Tralee.
Traditional links course.
Pro Brian O'Callaghan; Founded 1893
Designed by Simpson McKenna
2 x 18 holes, 6593 yards, S.S.S. 72
⌿ Practice facility with pitching green,
driving bays and putting greens.

Bearna Golf & Country Club

Corboley, Barna, Co. Galway, Ireland

Set amidst the celebrated beauty of West of Ireland landscape on the fringe of Connemara, and enjoying commanding views of Galway Bay, the Burren, the Aran Islands and rugged hinterlands, Bearna Golf Course is already being hailed as one of Ireland's finest. The inspired creativity of it's designer R J Browne in the siting of tees and sand-based greens throughout more than 100 hectares of unique countryside has resulted in generously proportioned fairways, many elevated tee-boxes, and some splendid carries. Water comes into play at 13 of the 18 holes, each one boasting unique features and which together test the golfer's total repertoire of skills. The final four holes especially provide a spectacular finish to a satisfying and memorable experience.

Golf Shop Tel: 091 - 592677 / 592756 • Bar/Restaurant Tel: 091 - 592866 / 592328 • Fax: 091 - 592674

Email: Info@bearnagolfclub.com • Web page: www.bearnagolfclub.com

---

† Welcome WD; limited at WE.
⌣ Telephone for 2004 prices.
⌁ Ring Sec to find out information.
🍽 Full catering facilities.
⤴ Club can provide detailed list; some golf packages available.

12 23 Ballyhaunis
Coolnaha, Ballyhaunis, Co Mayo
☎ 00353 907 30014
Course is two miles from Ballyhaunis on the N83.
Parkland course.
Pro David Carney; Founded 1929
9 holes, 5413 yards, S.S.S. 68
† Welcome Mon-Sat; with member Sun.
⌣ Terms on application.
⌁ Welcome Mon-Sat by prior arrangement; reductions for groups of more than 20; from €20.
🍽 Full catering facilities available.
⤴ Cill Aodain; Belmont.

12 24 Ballykisteen Golf & Country Club   ♛
Ballykisteen, Co Tipperary
⤴ www.tipp.ie/ballykgc.htm
☎ 00353 62 33333
3 miles from Tipperary on the Limerick Road. 20 mins from Limerick city.
Parkland course.
Founded 1994
Designed by Des Smyth
18 holes, 6765 yards, S.S.S. 73
⌁ Floodlight driving range, 12 bays.
† Welcome booking advisable.
⌣ Terms on application.
⌁ Welcome.
🍽 Bar and restaurant.

12 25 Ballyliffin   ♛
Ballyliffin, Carndonagh P.O,
Co Donegal
⤴ www.ballyliffingolfclub.com

☎ 00353 77 76119, Fax 76672
8 miles from Buncrana.
Seaside links course.
Founded 1947
39 holes, 6612 yards, S.S.S. 72
† Welcome.
⌣ WD €38; WE €42.
⌁ Welcome by prior arrangement; terms on application.
🍽 Bar snacks and meals.

12 26 Ballymote
Carrigans, Ballymote, Co Sligo
☎ 00353 71 89059, Rest/Bar 83089
Course is off the N4 15 miles S of Sligo Town.
Parkland course.
Founded 1993
9 holes, 5302 yards, S.S.S. 65
† Welcome.
⌣ Terms on application.
⌁ Welcome; discount for groups of more than 20.
🍽 At local restaurant.
⤴ Sligo Park; Tower Hotel, Sligo; Noreen Mullen GH; Eileen Cahill GH.

12 27 Baltinglass   ♛
Baltinglass, Co Wicklow
☎ 00353 508 81350, Sec 81031
40 miles S of Dublin.
Parkland course.
Founded 1928
Designed by Dr WG Lyons; Hugh Dark and Col. Mitchell
9 holes, 5554 yards, S.S.S. 69
† Welcome.
⌣ WD €16; WE €20.
⌁ Three welcome per month; terms on application.
🍽 By arrangement.
⤴ Carlow.

12 28 Bandon
Castlebernard, Bandon, Co Cork

☎ 00353 23 41111, Fax 44690
2 miles W of Bandon.
Parkland course.
Pro Paddy O'Boyle; Founded 1909
18 holes, 5663 yards, S.S.S. 69
† Welcome by prior arrangement.
⌣ WD €30; WE €35.
⌁ Welcome between March and October on WD.
🍽 Except Wed and Sat; catering packages available. Full bar and catering facilities.

12 29 Bantry Bay   ♛
Donemark, Bantry, Co Cork
⤴ www.bantrygolf.com
✉ info@bantrygolf.com
☎ 00353 27 50579/53773, Fax 53790, Sec 50579
2 km NW of Bantry on the Killarney Road.
Clifftop parkland course with views of Bantry Bay/Beara.
Founded 1975
Designed by E Hackett & C O'Connor Jnr
18 holes, 5910 yards, S.S.S. 72
† Welcome WD 8.30am-4.30pm; by arrangement WE and BH.
⌣ Off peak €35; peak €40; WE/BH €5 extra.
⌁ Welcome by prior arrangement; catering packages available.
🍽 Full catering facilities.
⤴ West Lodge; Bantry Bay; Reendesert; Ballylickey Manor; Seaview.

12 30 Bearna
Corboley, Barna, Co Galway
⤴ www.bearnagolfclub.com
✉ info@bearnagolfclub.com
☎ 00353 91 592677, Fax 59264
Turn right at traffic light in Barna village. Club is 2 miles from village on right-hand side.

Moorland course.
Founded 1996
Designed by Robert J. Brown
18 hole Par 72 Championship course.
⌁ Practice facilities.
✝ Welcome subject to availability.
⌐ WD €35; WE €45.
♂ Welcome.
⦿ Bar and restaurant.
⟿ Twelve Pins Hotel, Barna;
Connemara Coast Hotel, Furbo.

---

12 31 Beaufort ☏
Churchtown, Beaufort, Killarney,
Co Kerry
⬚ www.globalgolf.com
▤ beaufortgc@eircom.net
☎ 00353 64 44440, Fax 44752
7 miles W of Killarney off the N72.
Parkland course.
Pro Hugh Duggan
Founded 1995
Designed by Arthur Spring
18 holes, 6605 yards, S.S.S. 72
✝ Welcome.
⌐ WD €45; WE €55.
♂ Welcome; discounts available for
groups.
⦿ Full bar and catering.
⟿ Europe; Great Southern; Dunloe
Castle.

---

12 32 Beaverstown ☏
Beaverstown, Donabate, Co Dublin
⬚ www.beaverstown.com
▤ manager@beaverstown.com
☎ 00353 1 8436439, Fax 84350539,
Rest/Bar 84351371
15 miles N of Dublin; 3 miles from
Dublin Airport.
Parkland course.
Pro Anthony Schweppe
Founded 1984
Designed by Eddie Hackett; revised by
P McEvoy
18 holes, 5972 yards, S.S.S. 72
⌁ Practice nets; practice area;
putting green.
✝ Welcome WD and Sat.
⌐ WD €52; WE €68.
♂ Welcome by prior arrangement;
terms on application.
⦿ Full facilities.
⟿ Carnegie Court Swords.

---

12 33 Beech Park ☏
Johnstown, Rathcoole, Co Dublin
⬚ www.beechpark.ie
▤ info@beechpark.ie
☎ 00353 1 4580522, Fax 4588365
3km from Rathcoole village off the
Naas dual carriageway.

Parkland course.
Founded 1974
Designed by Eddie Hackett
18 holes, 5762 yards, S.S.S. 70
✝ Welcome Mon, Thurs and Fri; only
with a member at WE.
⌐ WD €38.
♂ Welcome Mon, Thurs and Fri;
catering packages available.
⦿ Full bar and catering.
⟿ Green Isle; City West; Bewleys;
Ambassador.

---

12 34 Belmullet
Carne, Belmullet, Co Mayo
☎ 00353 97 82292, Sec 81136
1.5 miles W of Belmullet.
Seaside links course.
Founded 1925
Designed by Eddie Hackett
18 holes, 6058 yards, S.S.S. 72
✝ Welcome.
⌐ March-Oct €40; Nov-Feb €25.

---

12 35 Belturbet
Erne Hill, Belturbet, Co Cavan
☎ 00353 4995 22287, Sec 22498
0.5 miles on the Cavan Road from
Belturbet.
Parkland course.
Founded 1950
9 holes, 5347 yards, S.S.S. 65
✝ Welcome.
⌐ Terms on application.
♂ Welcome by prior arrangement.
⦿ Full facilities.

---

12 36 Berehaven
Millcove, Castletownbere, Co Cork
⬚ www.beregolf.com
▤ beregolfclub@eircom.net
☎ 00353 277 0700, Fax1957
On the main Castletownbere Road 20
miles W of Glengarriff.
Links course.
Founded 1906/1993
9 holes, 5600 yards, S.S.S. 67
✝ Welcome.
⌐ WD €20; WE €25.
♂ Details of special rates available
on application, tennis, fishing,
swimming sailing available.
⦿ Clubhouse facilities.

---

12 37 Birr ☏
The Glenns, Birr, Co Offaly
☎ 00353 509 20082
2.5 miles W of Birr on the Banagher
Road.
Parkland course.
Founded 1893

18 holes, 5748 yards, S.S.S. 69
✝ Welcome; must book at WE.
⌐ WD €23; WE €32.; details of
seasonal offers available on
application.
♂ Welcome by prior arrangement;
discounts available depending on
numbers; catering packages available;
terms on application.
⦿ Full catering facilities.
⟿ Dooleys; County.

---

12 38 Black Bush ☏
Thomastown, Dunshaughlin, Co Meath
⬚ www.iol.ie/blackbush
▤ golf@blackbush.iol.ie
☎ 00353 1 8250021, Fax 8250400
0.5 miles E of Dunshaughlin on
Ratoath Road.
Parkland course.
Pro Shane O'Grady; Founded 1987
Designed by Robert Brown
27 holes, 6849 yards, S.S.S. 72 (A+B);
6434 yards, S.S.S. 70 (B+C)
⌁ Practice range. Driving range, 5
bays, floodlit.
✝ Welcome.
⌐ WD €30; WE €45 (including Fri).
♂ Welcome WD; catering packages
available; also 9-hole course; terms on
application.
⦿ Full catering facilities.

---

12 39 Blacklion
Toam, Blacklion, Co Cavan
☎ 00353 72 53024
Off the Sligo-Enniskillen Road at
Blacklion.
Parkland course.
Founded 1962
Designed by Eddie Hackett
9 holes, 5605 yards, S.S.S. 69
✝ Welcome.
⌐ Terms on application.
♂ Welcome by arrangement.
⦿ Full facilities.

---

12 40 Blainroe ☏
Blainroe, Co Wicklow
▤ blainroegolfclub@eircom.net
☎ 00353 404 68168, Fax 69369,
Pro 66470
3 miles S of Wicklow on coast road.
Parkland course by the sea.
Pro John Macdonald; Founded 1978
Designed by Hawtree & Sons
18 holes, 6070 yards, S.S.S. 72
✝ Welcome by prior arrangement.
⌐ WD €43; WE €45.
♂ Welcome by prior arrangement;
catering packages available.
⦿ Full clubhouse facilities.

12 41 **Bodenstown**
Bodenstown, Sallins, Co Kildare
☎ 00353 45 897096, Fax 898126
5 miles N of Naas.
Parkland course.
Founded 1973
36 holes, 6321 yards, S.S.S. 73
🏌 Welcome; members only on Old
Course at WE.
🍴 WD and WE €20.
⛳ Welcome by prior arrangement.
🍽 Full catering facilities.

12 42 **Borris**
Deer Park, Borris, Co Carlow
☎ 00353 503 73143
16 miles from Carlow off Dublin Road.
Parkland course.
Founded 1902
9 holes, 5596 yards, S.S.S. 69
🏌 Welcome.
🍴 WD and WE: €20.
⛳ Welcome; terms on application.
🍽 Bar and catering facilities
available.
🛏 Lord Bagenal; Seven Oaks;
Newpark.

12 43 **Boyle**
Knockadoo Brusna, Boyle, Co
Roscommon
☎ 00353 79 62594
2 miles S of Boyle on the N61
Roscommon Road.
Parkland course.
Founded 1911/1972
Designed by Eddie Hackett
9 holes, 4914 yards, S.S.S. 66
🏌 Welcome.
🍴 Available on application.
⛳ Welcome by prior arrangement;
discounts and catering packages
available.
🍽 Full bar and catering facilities.
🛏 Forest Park; Royal.

12 44 **Bray**
Greystones Rd, Bray, Co Wicklow
🖳 www.braygolfclub.com
💻 braygolfclub@eircom.net
☎ 00353 127 63200, Fax 63262
Off the N11 from Dublin.
Parkland course.
Pro Ciaran Carroll; Founded 1897
18 holes, 6456 yards, S.S.S. 72
🏌 Welcome WD except Tues.
🍴 Summer: WD €60; WE €70.
Winter: WD €45; WE €55.
⛳ Welcome by prior arrangement;
must be affiliated to GUI.
🍽 Limited facilities.
🛏 Woodlands Court, Bray.

12 45 **Buncrana**
Buncrana, Co Donegal
💻 buncranagc@eircom.net
☎ 00353 77 62279
Parkland course.
9 holes, 4250 yards, S.S.S. 62
🏌 Welcome.
🍴 Available on application.
⛳ Mon-Thurs by prior arrangement,
especially WE.
🍽 Under refurbishment.

12 46 **Bundoran**
Bundoran Golf Club, Bundoran,
Co Donegal
🖳 www.bundorangolfclub.com
💻 bundorangolfclub@eircom.net
☎ 00353 71 98 41302, Fax 42014
22 miles N of Sligo.
Links/parkland course.
Pro David Robinson; Founded 1894
Designed by Harry Vardon
18 holes, 5688 metres, S.S.S. 70
🏌 Welcome by arrangement; book for
weekends.
🍴 WD €40; WE €50.
⛳ Welcome by prior arrangement.
🍽 Limited on course to snacks; by
arrangement. Hotel on site for meals.
🛏 Great Northern Hotel on course;
Holyrood; Addingham; Fox's Lair;
Marlborough; Atlantic; Grand Central.

12 47 **Cabra Castle**
Kingscourt, Co Cavan
🖳 www.cabracastle.com
💻 cabrach@iol.ie
☎ 00353 4296 67030
6 miles S of Carrickmacross.
Parkland course.
Founded 1977
9 holes, 5308 yards, S.S.S. 68
🏌 Welcome; only with a member on
Sun. Free golf if hotel resident.
🍴 Terms on application.
⛳ Welcome by prior arrangement
except Sun. WE packages available.
🍽 Full facilities.
🛏 Cabra Castle Hotel.

12 48 **Cahir Park**
Kilcommon, Cahir, Co Tipperary
🖳 www.cahirparkgolfclub.com
💻 management@cahirparkgolfclub
.com
☎ 00353 52 41474, Fax 42717,
Sec/Mgr 41474 ext 1, Rest/Bar 41474
ext 3
1 mile S of Cahir on Clogheen Road.
Parkland course.
Founded 1965
Designed by Eddie Hackett

18 holes, 5446 yards, S.S.S. 69
🏌 Welcome; by prior arrangement at
WE.
🍴 WD €25; WE €30.
⛳ Welcome on Sat by prior
arrangement; catering packages can
be arranged with 72 hours notice;
terms on application.
🍽 Bar facilities.

12 49 **Callan**
Geraldine, Callan, Co Kilkenny
🖳 www.callangolfclub.com
💻 info@callangolfclub.com
☎ 00353 567 725136, Fax 056
55155, Pro 056 7725136, Sec 056
7755875, Rest/Bar 056 7725136
10 miles S of Kilkenny; 1 mile from
Callan.
Parkland course.
Pro John Odwyer; Founded 1929
Designed by Des Smyth
18 holes, 6450 yards, S.S.S. 70
🏌 Welcome.
🍴 WD €25; WE/BH €30.
⛳ Welcome WD and Sat am by prior
arrangement.
🍽 Full bar facilities, catering
available
🛏 The Old Charter House.

12 50 **Carlow**   ♛
Deerpark, Dublin Rd, Carlow,
Co Carlow
🖳 www.carlowgolfclub.com
💻 carlowgolfclub@tint.ie
☎ 00353 599 131695, Fax 40065
1 mile from Carlow station off Naas to
Dublin Road.
Undulating parkland.
Pro Andrew Gilburt; Founded 1899
Designed by Tom Simpson
18 holes, 5844 yards, S.S.S. 71
🏌 Welcome.
🍴 WD €45; WE €60.
⛳ Welcome WD by arrangement.
🍽 Full catering facilities.

12 51 **Carne Golf Links**   ♛
Carne, Belmullet, Co Mayo
🖳 www.carnegolflinks.com
💻 carnegolf@iol.ie
☎ 00353 97 82292, Fax 81477,
Rest/Bar 82123
1.5 miles W of Belmullet.
Seaside links course.
Founded 1992
Designed by Eddie Hackett
18 holes, 6119 yards, S.S.S. 72
🏌 Welcome.
🍴 March-Oct WD €40/day; WE
€50/round.

12 52 Carrickmines

Golf Lane, Carrickmines, Dublin 18
☎ 00353 1 2955972
8 miles S of Dublin.
Heath/parkland course.
Founded 1900
9 holes, 6063 yards, S.S.S. 69
† Welcome except Wed and Sat.
[18 holes: WD €33; WE €38.
9 holes: WD €19; WE €22.
⟳ None.
🍽 Limited.

12 53 Carrick-on-Shannon

Woodbrook, Carrick-on-Shannon,
Co Roscommon
📧 ckgc3@eircom.net
☎ 00353 719 667015
3 miles W of Carrick on N4.
Parkland course.
Founded 1910
Designed by Hawtree Ltd
18 holes, 5523 metres, S.S.S. 68
† Welcome.
[Terms on application.
⟳ Welcome by prior arrangement
with Sec.
🍽 Full bar and catering facilities.

12 54 Carrick-on-Suir

Garravoone, Carrick-on-Suir,
Co Tipperary
☎ 00353 51 640047
15 miles from Waterford.
Parkland course.
Founded 1939
Designed by Edward Hackett
18 holes, 6061 yards, S.S.S. 71
† Welcome Wed and WE; booking
advisable.
[WD €26; WE €30; reduced rates if
with a member; group rates available.
⟳ Welcome; catering packages;
private rooms; group discounts.
🍽 Full catering facilities.
⟿ Carraig.

12 55 Carton House

Maynooth, Co Kildare
🖳 www.carton.ie
📧 sales@carton.ie
☎ 00353 162 86271, Fax 86555
From Dublin city, take N4 motorway
west towards Galway/Sligo. From N4,
take Leixlip West exit and follow signs
to Carton House. Clus 14 miles west of
Dublin, 30 min drive from Dublin airport.
Pro David Fleming
O'Meara, founded 2002; Montgomerie,
founded 2003
Designed by Mark O'Meara and Colin
Montgomerie

O'Meara: 18 holes, 7006 yards, S.S.S.
74; Montgomerie: 18 holes, 7300
yards, S.S.S. 74
�𝐼 Golf Academy on site.
† Always welcome.
[Mon-Thur €110; Fri-Sun €125.
⟳ Always welcome Excellent group
rates for 12 or more golfers.
🍽 Clubhouse has full bar and
restaurant facilities.
⟿ Details of local accommodation are
available on request.

12 56 Castle

Woodside Drive, Rathfarnham, Dublin
📧 info@castlegc.ie
☎ 00353 1 4904207, Fax 4920264
Turn left after Terenure and take
second right.
Parkland course.
Pro David Kinsella; Founded 1913
Designed by HS Colt
18 holes, 6024 yards, S.S.S. 69
† Welcome WD, booking advisable.
[WD €60.
⟳ Welcome by prior arrangement
only.
🍽 Full facilities.

12 57 Castle Barna

Daingean, Co Offaly
🖳 www.castlebarna.ie
📧 info@castlebarna.ie
☎ 00353 506 53384, Fax 53077
Just off main Dublin-Galway road (N6)
at Tyrellspass. One hr from Dublin.
Parkland course.
Founded 1993
Designed by A Duggan
18 holes, 6200 yards, S.S.S. 69
�𝐼 Practice putting green.
† Welcome; restrictions Sun am.
[WD €22; WE €28.
⟳ Welcome by arrangement, society
special available; one round golf, steak
meal and B&B €75 pp.
🍽 Coffee shop and restaurant.
⟿ The Sportsman Inn; Tullamore
Court Hotel; Midway Park Hotel; The
Bridge House Hotel.

12 58 Castlebar ☎

Rocklands, Castlebar, Co Mayo
☎ 00353 94 21649
1.25 miles from town centre.
Parkland course.
Founded 1910
18 holes, 5698 yards, S.S.S. 70
† Welcome WD.
[Terms on application.
⟳ Welcome by prior arrangement.
🍽 By arrangement.

12 59 Castleblayney

Onomy, Castleblayney, Co Monaghan
☎ 00353 42 9749485
Almost in Castleblayney town centre.
Parkland course.
Founded 1984
Designed by Bobby Browne
9 holes, 4923 yards, S.S.S. 66
† Welcome.
[Available upon application.
⟳ Welcome by prior arrangement.
🍽 Full facilities.
⟿ Glencarn; Central.

12 60 Castlecomer ☎

Drumgoole, Castlecomer, Co Kilkenny
🖳 www.castlecomergolf.com
📧 castlecomergolf@eircom.net
☎ 00353 564 441139
On N7 10 miles N of Kilkenny 60 miles
from Dublin.
Parkland course.
Founded 1935
Designed by Pat Ruddy
18 holes, 6175 yards, S.S.S. 72
⟲ Practice area.
† Seven days by prior arrangement.
[WD €40; WE €50.
⟳ Welcome any day.
🍽 By prior arrangement.

12 61 Castlegregory Golf and Fishing Club

Stradbelly, Castlegregory, Kerry
🖳 www.castlegregory-golfclub.com
☎ 00353 667 139444, Fax 139958
2 miles W of Castlegregory.
9-hole links.
Founded 1989
Designed by Arthur Spring
9 holes, 5842 yards, S.S.S. 68
⟲ Practice area.
† Welcome.
[Terms on application.
⟳ Welcome by prior arrangement.
🍽 Limited Club facilities.

12 62 Castlerea

Clonalis, Castlerea, Co Roscommon
☎ 00353 907 20068
On main Dublin-Castlebar Road.
Parkland course.
Founded 1905
9 holes, 4974 yards, S.S.S. 66
† Welcome.
[Terms on application.
⟳ Welcome by prior arrangement;
catering packages by arrangement.

12 63 Castletroy ☎

Castletroy, Co Limerick

www.castletrougolfclub.ie
cga@iol.ie
☎ 00353 61 335753, Fax 335373,
Pro 330450
Course is 3 miles from Limerick on the
N7.
Parkland course.
Founded 1937
18 holes, 5854 metres, S.S.S. 70
♦ Welcome by prior arrangement.
▯ WD €40; WE €50.
♢ Welcome by prior arrangement.
🍽 Full catering facilities.
🛏 Castletroy Park; Kilmurry Lodge.

12 64 Castlewarden Golf & Country Club
Castlewarden, Straffan, Co Kildare
www.castlewardengolflcub.com
info@castlewarden.com
☎ 00353 1 4589254, Fax 4588972
Between Rathcoole and Kill.
Moorland course.
Founded 1989
Designed by Tommy Halpin;
Redesigned: RJ Browne (1992)
18 holes, 6690 yards, S.S.S. 72
▮ Practice area.
♦ Welcome Mon, Thurs and Fri.
▯ Mon-Thurs am €28, pm €38.
♢ Welcome Mon, Thurs, Fri and
some Sat mornings.
🍽 Full facilities.

12 65 Charlesland ☾
Greystones, Co Wicklow
www.charlesland.com
☎ 00353 1 2874350, Fax 2874360
Off the N11 Dublin-Wexford Road at
Delgany turning.
Seaside course.
Pro Pete Duignam; Founded 1992
Designed by E Hackett
18 holes, 6169 metres, S.S.S. 72
▮ Full practice facilities.
♦ Welcome every day.
▯ WD €45; WE €60.
♢ Welcome by prior arrangement;
discounts for group bookings; terms on
application.
🍽 Full facilities.
🛏 Charlesland – 12 bedroom, on site.

12 66 Charleville ☾
Smiths Rd, Ardmore, Charleville,
Co Cork
www.charlegolf.com
charlevillegolf@eircom.net
☎ 00353 63 81257, Fax 81274, Pro
21269
On main road from Cork to Limerick.
Parkland course.

Founded 1909
27 holes, 6430 yards, S.S.S. 70
♦ Welcome by prior arrangement.
▯ Terms on application.
♢ Welcome except Sun by prior
arrangement.
🍽 Bar and restaurant service
available.

12 67 Cill Dara
Kildare, Co Kildare
☎ 00353 455 21433, Fax 22945
1 mile E of Kildare.
Moorland course.
Pro Mark Bouyle; Founded 1920
9 holes, 5738 yards, S.S.S. 70
♦ Welcome.
▯ Terms on application.
♢ Welcome by prior arrangement;
catering packages available.
🍽 Clubhouse facilities.
🛏 Corragh Lodge.

12 68 City West Hotel
City West Country House Hotel,
Saggart, Dublin
☎ 00353 1 4010900, Fax 4010945
Off M50 at M7 for S of Ireland at City
West Business Park.
Parkland course.
Designed by Christie O Connor
18 holes, 6691 yards, S.S.S. 70
♦ Welcome.
▯ WD 38; WE €45. Residents: WD
€32; WE €38.
♢ Welcome, packages available.
Hotel and conference facilities.
🍽 Full catering facilities.

12 69 Clane
Clane, Co Kildare
☎ 00353 1 6286608
Playing facilities at Clongowes.
Founded 1976
9 holes
♦ Welcome except Sun.
▯ Terms on application.
♢ Welcome WD by prior
arrangement; catering packages by
arrangement.
🍽 By arrangement.

12 70 Claremorris ☾
Rushbrook, Castlemagarrett,
Claremorris, Co Mayo
www.ebookireland.com
claremorrisgc@ebookireland.com
☎ 094 93 71527, Fax 72919, Sec
71527, Rest/Bar 71527
1.5 miles from Claremorris on Galway
Road.

Parkland course.
Founded 1917
Designed by Tom Craddock.
18 holes, 6143 metres, S.S.S. 71
♦ Welcdome except Sun.
▯ WD €25; WE €30.
♢ Welcome WD by prior
arrangement; catering packages by
arrangement.
🍽 By arrangement.

12 71 Clones
Hilton Park, Clones, Co Monaghan
☎ 00353 47 56017
3 miles from Clones.
Parkland course.
Founded 1913
9 holes, 5206 yards, S.S.S. 67
♦ Welcome.
▯ WD and WE: €20.
♢ Welcome by prior arrangement
with the secretary; catering by
arrangement.
🍽 Clubhouse facilities.
🛏 Lennard Arms; Creighton;
Hibernian; Riverdale.

12 72 Clonlara
Clonlara Golf and Leisure, Clonlara,
Co Clare
☎ 00353 61 359807, Fax 342288
Course is 7 miles NE of Limerick on
the Corbally-Killaloe Road.
Woodland/parkland course.
Founded 1993
12 holes, 5187 yards, S.S.S. 69
♦ Welcome; pay and play.
▯ Mon-Thurs €13; Fri-Sun and BH
€15. Students over 16 €10, under €8.
OAP €10. Discounts do not apply Fri-
Sun or BH.
♢ Welcome by prior arrangement;
discounts for groups of 20 or more;
tennis; sauna; games room; fishing;
terms on application.
🍽 Bar facilities; catering by order.
🛏 Self-catering accommodation on
site.

12 73 Clonmel
Lyreanearla, Mountain Rd, Clonmel,
Co Tipperary
www.clonmelgolfclub.com
cgc@indigo.ie
☎ 00353 52 24050, Fax 83349,
Rest/Bar 83341
3 miles from Clonmel.
Parkland course.
Pro Robert Hayes; Founded 1911
Designed by Eddie Hackett
18 holes, 5845 yards, S.S.S. 71
▮ Across the road.

† Welcome.

⌇ WD €30; WE €35 (with member €25).

↻ Welcome from April to September (Saturdays); midweek outings welcome all year round.

⎰ Full clubhouse facilities available.

↝ Clonmel Arms; Minella; Hearns; Hanora's Cottage.

12 74 Clontarf ☎

Donnycarney House, Malahide Rd, Co Dublin

♨ www.clontarfgolfclub.ie

✉ info.cgc@indigo.ie

☎ 00353 1 8331892, Fax 8831933, Pro 8331877, Rest/Bar 8331520

2.5 miles NE of city centre off Malahide Road.

Parkland course.

Pro Mark Callan

Founded 1912

18 holes, 5317 yards, S.S.S. 67

† Welcome.

⌇ WD €50; WE €60.

↻ Welcome Tues or Fri; packages include catering; from €40.

⎰ Full clubhouse facilities available.

↝ Clontarf Castle.

12 75 Cobh

Ballywilliam, Cobh, Co Cork

☎ 00353 21 4812399, Fax 66915 6409

1 mile E of Cobh.

Public parkland course.

Pro Dermot O'Connor; Founded 1987

Designed by Bob O'Keeffe

9 holes, 4366 yards, S.S.S. 63

† Welcome WD; by prior arrangement WE.

⌇ €16.

↻ Welcome Mon-Sat.

⎰ Bar facilities.

12 76 Coldwinters

Newtown House, St Margaret's, Co Dublin

☎ 00353 1 8640324

On M50 Ballymun exit, then the Noel exit, for 1.5 miles come to a T junction turn left.

Parkland course; also 9-hole course 2163 metres par 31.

Pro Roger Yates; Founded 1993

18 holes, 5973 yards, S.S.S. 69

⫞ 23 bays, floodlit and undercover.

† Welcome; pay and play.

⌇ Terms on application.

↻ Welcome by prior arrangement.

⎰ Coffee shop on site.

↝ Many in Dublin.

12 77 Connemara Championship Links ☎

Ballyconneely, Clifden, Co Galway

♨ www.westcoastlinks.com

✉ links@iol.ie

☎ 00353 95 23502, Fax 23662

Signposted from Clifden.

Links course.

Pro Hugh O'Neill; Founded 1973

Designed by Eddie Hackett

27 holes, 6611 yards, S.S.S. 73

⫞ Practice area and putting green.

† Welcome.

⌇ WD €50; WE €55, low season WD €30, WE €35.

↻ Welcome; minimum parties of 20; catering packages available; terms on application.

⎰ Full bar and restaurant facilities.

↝ Rock Glen; Abbey Glen; Foyles; Alcock & Brown; Ballinahynch.

12 78 Connemarra Isles ☎

Annaghuane, Connemara, Connemara, Galway

☎ 00353 91 572498, Fax 572214

5 miles W of Costello.

Links.

9 holes, 5168 yards, S.S.S. 67

† Welcome.

↻ Terms on application.

⎰ Full facilities in thatched clubhouse.

12 79 Coollattin ☎

Coollattin, Shillelheh, Co Wicklow

♨ www.coollattingolfclub.com

✉ coollattingolfclub@eircom.net

☎ 00353 55 29125, Fax 29930, Sec 054 77314

12 miles SW of Aughrim.

Parkland course.

Pro Peter Jones

Founded 1922

18 holes, 6148 yards, S.S.S. 69

† Welcome WD.

⌇ WD €35; WE €45.

↻ Welcome WD by prior arrangement.

⎰ Full catering facilities available.

12 80 Coosheen

Coosheen, Schull, Co Cork

☎ 00353 28 28182

1 mile E of Schull.

Seaside parkland course.

Founded 1989

Designed by Daniel Morgan

9 holes, 4020 yards, S.S.S. 58

† Welcome.

⌇ WD and WE: €16.

↻ Welcome; from €16.

⎰ Full bar and restaurant.

↝ East End; West Cork; Westlodge.

12 81 Corballis

Dunabate, Co Dublin

✉ corballis@golfdublin.com

☎ 00353 1 8436583

N of Dublin on Belfast Road.

Links course.

Founded 1971

Designed by City Council

18 holes, 49951 yards, S.S.S. 64

† Public pay and play.

⌇ WD €14; WE €18.

↻ By arrangement.

⎰ Snack facilities.

↝ Waterside Hotel.

12 82 Cork ☎

Little Island, Cork, Co Cork

♨ www.corkgolfclub.ie

✉ corkgolfclub@eircom.net

☎ 00353 21 4353451, Fax 4353410

5 miles E of Cork City off N25.

Parkland/heathland course.

Pro Peter Hickey; Founded 1888

Designed by Alister MacKenzie

18 holes, 6119 yards, S.S.S. 72

† Welcome.

⌇ WD €80; WE € 90.

↻ Packages by arrangement from €60 WD; €65 WE.

⎰ Bar and catering facilities.

↝ Silver Springs; Jurys.

12 83 Corrstown ☎

Corrstown, Kilsallaghan, Co Dublin

♨ www.corrstowngolfclub.com

✉ info@corrstowngolfclub.com

☎ 00353 1 8640533, Pro 8643322

10 minutes from Dublin Airport; access from Swords Rd and Ashbourne Rd.

Parkland course.

Pro Pat Gittens

Founded 1992

Designed by E B Connaughton

27 holes, 5584 yards, S.S.S. 72

⫞ Driving range.

† Welcome Mon-Fri; after 1pm WE.

⌇ WD €50; WE €60.

↻ Welcome by prior arrangement.

⎰ Full bar and catering facilities.

↝ Forte Crest; Great Southern, both Dublin Airport; Forte Posthouse, Swords Road.

12 84 County Cavan ☎

Arnmore House, Drumelis, Cavan, Co Cavan

♨ www.cavangolf.ie

✉ cavangc@iol.ie

CONNEMARA
CHAMPIONSHIP GOLF LINKS
Ballyconneely, Clifden, Co. Galway

Connemara Championship Golf Links, designed by Eddie Hackett, is as tough a challenge as you are likely to find anywhere, with a par 72 seldom matched. The back nine has been described as "the equal of any in the world".

Club House Secretary Manager
Tel: +353 (0) 95 23502 or 23602. Fax: +353 (0) 95 23662
Email: links@iol.ie Website: www.connemaragolflinks.com

☎ 00353 4943 31541, Fax 31541, Pro 31388
1 mile from Cavan on Killeshandra Rd.
Parkland course.
Pro William Noble; Founded 1894
Designed by Peter McGrath.
18 holes, 5634 yards, S.S.S. 70
🏌 Driving range.
🏳 Welcome.
🍴 Terms on application.
🏌 Welcome; restrictions Wed & Sun.
🍽 Full catering facilities.
🛏 Farnham Arms; Kilmore.

12 85 County Longford
Glack, Longford
☎ 00353 43 46310, Fax 47082
E of Glack off the Dublin-Sligo N4 Rd.
Undulating parkland course.
Founded 1894
Designed by E Hackett
18 holes, 5494 yards, S.S.S. 67
🏳 Welcome.
🍴 Terms on application.
🏌 Welcome by prior arrangement.
🍽 Clubhouse catering facilities.

12 86 County Louth
Baltray, Drogheda, Co Louth
🖳 www.countylouthgolfclub.com
📧 reservations@countylouthgolfclub.com
☎ 00353 4198 81530, Fax 81531, Pro 81536
5 miles NE of Drogheda.
Links course.
Pro Paddy McGuirk; Founded 1892
Designed by Tom Simpson
18 holes, 6936 yards, S.S.S. 73
🏳 Welcome by prior arrangement.
🍴 WD €60; WE €80.
🏌 Welcome by prior arrangement; catering packages by arrangement;
🍽 Full bar and catering facilities.
🛏 Boyne Valley.

12 87 County Meath (Trim)
Newtownmoynagh, Trim, Co Meath
☎ 00353 46 31463
3 miles from Trim on the Longwood Road.
Parkland course.
Founded 1898

Designed by Eddie Hackett
18 holes, 6503 yards, S.S.S. 72
🏳 Welcome; restrictions Thurs, Sat and Sun.
🍴 Terms on application.
🏌 Welcome Mon-Sat by prior arrangement.
🍽 Full bar and catering facilities.

12 88 County Sligo
Rosses Point, Co Sligo
🖳 www.countysligogolfclub.ie
📧 cosligo@iol.ie
☎ 00353 71 77134, Fax 77460, Pro 77171, Sec 77186, Rest/Bar 77186
5 miles N of Sligo.
Links course.
Pro Jim Robinson; Founded 1894
Designed by Colt & Alison
27 holes, 6043 yards, S.S.S. 72
🏌 Practice area.
🏳 Welcome; Between 11.40 and 1pm at WE.
🍴 €55 Mon-Thur; €70 Fri, Sat and Sun.
🏌 Welcome by prior arrangement; special rates and packages for 20 or more players.
🍽 Full clubhouse facilities.
🛏 Tower Hotel; Sligo Park; Yeats Country Hotel.

12 89 County Tipperary Golf & Country Club
Dundrum, Co Tipperary
📧 dundrumh@iol.ie
☎ 00353 62 71717, Fax 71718, Pro 71717
6 miles W of Cashel.
Parkland course.
Founded 1993
Designed by Philip Walton
18 holes, 6955 yards, S.S.S. 72
🏳 Welcome.
🍴 WD €38; WE €45.
🏌 Welcome; information about group discounts available upon request.
🍽 Full catering and bar facilities.
🛏 Dundrum House on site.

12 90 Courtown
Kiltennel, Gorey, Co Wexford
☎ 00353 55 25166

Leave N11 at Gorey following the Road to Courtown Harbour.
Parkland course.
Pro John Coone; Founded 1936
Designed by Harris & Associates/ Henry Cotton
18 holes, 5898 yards, S.S.S. 71
🏳 Welcome; some restrictions Tues and WE.
🍴 May-Sept WD €36, WE €42; Oct-Apr WD €30, WE €36.
🏌 Welcome by prior arrangement with secretary/manager; reductions for groups of more than 20.
🍽 Full catering and bar facilities.
🛏 Marlfield; Courtown; Bayview.

12 91 Craddockstown
Craddockstown, Naas, Co Kildare
☎ 00353 45 97610
Parkland course.
Founded 1983
18 holes, 6134 yards, S.S.S. 72
🏳 Welcome.
🍴 Available upon application.

12 92 Cruit Island
Kincasslagh, Letterkenny, Co Donegal
☎ 00353 75 43296
6 miles from Dungloe opposite the Viking House Hotel.
Links course.
Founded 1986
9 holes, 4860 yards, S.S.S. 66
🏳 Welcome by prior arrangement.
🍴 €20 all times.
🏌 Welcome by prior arrangement Mon-Fri & Sat morning; from €15.
🍽 Full clubhouse facilities available.
🛏 Standhouse; Keadeen.

12 93 Curragh
Curragh, Co Kildare
☎ 00353 45 441714, Fax 442476, Pro, 441896, Sec 441714, Rest/Bar 441238
2 miles SE of Newbridge.
Parkland course.
Pro Gerry Burke; Founded 1883
Designed by David Ritchie
18 holes, 6035 yards, S.S.S. 71
🏳 Welcome by prior arrangement.
🍴 WD €32.

Welcome by prior arrangement Mon-Fri & Sat morning; from €40 (inc meal).

Full clubhouse facilities available.

Standhouse; Keadeen.

12 94 Deer Park Hotel
Deer Park Hotel, Howth, Co Dublin
www.deerpark-hotel.ie
sales@deerpark.iol.ie
00353 1 8322624, Fax 8326039
9 miles E of the City centre.
Parkland course.
Founded 1973
Designed by Fred Hawtree
18 holes, 6830 yards, Par 72; 9x2; 12-hole pitch & putt

Welcome; restrictions Sun am.

WD €17; WE €25.

Welcome WD by prior arrangement; catering packages available by prior arrangement; function rooms; welcome all days.

Full restaurant and bar facilities.

Deer Park on site.

12 95 Delgany
Delgany, Co Wicklow
00353 128 74536, Fax 73977, Rest/Bar 75426
Off N11 1 mile past Glenview Hotel.
Parkland course.
Pro Gavin Kavanagh; Founded 1908
Designed by H Vardon
18 holes, 5480 yards, S.S.S. 68

Practice area.

Welcome.

WD €40; WE €50.

Welcome by prior arrangement.

Full bar and catering facilities.

Glenview; Delgany Inn.

12 966 Delvin Castle
Delvin Castle, Delvin, Westmeath
00353 44 64315
On N52 in the village of Delvin.
Mature parkland with lakes.
Mature parkland with lakes.
Founded 1995
Designed by J Day
18 holes

Welcome; restrictions Wed and Sun.

Available upon request.

Welcome by prior arrangement.

Full bar and catering service available.

12 97 Dingle Links / Ceann Sibeal
Ballyferriter, Dingle, Co Kerry

www.dinglelinks.com
dinglegc@iol.ie
00353 66 915 6255, Fax 6409
1.5 Mile from Ballyferriter, 40 miles from Tralee/Kilarney.
Traditional links.
Pro Dermot O'Connor; Founded 1924
Designed by Eddie Hackett
18 holes, 6696 yards, S.S.S. 72

Putting green.

Welcome every day.

Winter WD €50, WD €60; Summer WD €65, WE €75.

Welcome; catering packages by arrangement; €40.

Full bar and restaurant service.

Skellig; Benners.

12 98 Donabate
Donabate, Balcarrick, Co Dublin
www.donabategolfclub.ie
00353 1 8436346, Fax 8434488
1 mile N of Swords on the Dublin-Belfast Road.
Parkland course.
Pro Hugh Jackson; Founded 1925
27 holes, 6534 yards, S.S.S. 73

Practice ground; putting green.

Welcome WE with a member.

WD €45; WE €55.

Welcome by prior arrangement.

Clubhouse catering facilities.

Watersite Hotel; The Bracken Court Hotel.

12 99 Donegal
Murvaghy, Laghey, Co Donegal
www.donegalgolfclub.ie
info@donegalgolfclub.ie
00353 749 734054, Fax 734377
8 miles from Donegal on the Ballyshannon Road.
Links course.
Pro Leslie Robinson; Founded 1960/73
Designed by Eddie Hackett
18 holes, 6547 yards, S.S.S. 75

Practice range, large practice ground.

Welcome.

Mon-Thurs €50; Fri-Sun and BH €65.

Welcome by prior arrangement; discounts for more than 16 golfers.

Full bar and restaurant facilities.

Sandhouse.

12 100 Doneraile
Doneraile, Co Cork
00353 22 24137, Sec 24379
Off T11 28 miles from Cork; 9 miles from Mallow.
Parkland course.

Founded 1927
9 holes, 5055 yards, S.S.S. 67

Welcome.

Terms on application.

Welcome by prior arrangement.

12 101 Dooks
Glenbeigh, Co Kerry
www.dooks.com
office@dooks.com
00353 6697 68205, Fax 68476
On the N70 between Killonglin and Glenbeigh.
Links course.
Founded 1889
Designed by Martin Hawtree
18 holes, 6300 yards, S.S.S. 68

Welcome.

WD/WE: €48; advisable to book for WE.

Welcome by prior arrangement; from €48.

Full clubhouse facilities.

Towers; Bianconi.

12 102 Douglas
Douglas, Co Cork
00353 21 895297
3 miles from Cork; 0.5 miles past Douglas village.
Parkland course.
Founded 1909
18 holes, 5664 yards, S.S.S. 69

Welcome; reservations needed at WE.

Terms on application.

Welcome by prior arrangement before start of the season.

Catering facilities.

12 103 Dromoland Castle
Newmarket-on-Fergus, Co Clare
www.dromoland.ie
golf@dromoland.ie
00353 61 368444, Fax 368498
14 miles from Limerick on N18 and 6 miles from Shannon on N19.
Parkland course.
Pro David Foley
Founded 1963
Designed by Ron Kirby
18 holes, 6808 yards, S.S.S. 72

Practice area; putting area.

Welcome.

Residents €70; Indiv WD/WE €100; group 12+ WD/WE €70.

Welcome by prior arrangement; catering packages available; leisure spa and health studios and swimming pool; from €120, please enquire.

Full clubhouse facilities.

Dromoland Castle.

12 104 Druids Glen
Newtonmountkennedy, Co Wicklow
☎ 00353 1 2873600, Fax 2873699,
Pro 2873211
Signposted on N11 from Dublin taking Newtonmountkennedy/Glengalaugh junction.
Parkland course; Euro Tour venue.
Pro Eamonn Darcy; Founded 1993
Designed by T Craddock & P Ruddy
18 holes, 7026 yards, S.S.S. 73
✍ Practice range, practice facilities and 3-hole academy.
† Welcome.
✏ WD and WE: €125.
⟳ Welcome every day by prior arrangement; minimum 20 players; catering packages by arrangement; from €82.50.
⦿ Full clubhouse bar and restaurant facilities.
⟿ The Druids Glen Marriott.

12 105 Dublin Mountain
Gortlum, Brittas, Co Dublin
☎ 00353 1 4582622
Undulating parkland course.
Founded 1993
18 holes, 5433 yards, S.S.S. 69

† Welcome.
✏ Terms on application.
⟳ Terms on application.
⦿ Clubhouse facilities.

12 106 Dun Laoghaire ☎
Eglinton Park, Tivoli Rd, Dun Laoghaire, Co Dublin
✉ dlgc@iol.ie
☎ 00353 1 2803916, Fax 2804868,
Pro 2801694, Sec 2803916
7 miles S of Dublin; 0.5 miles from Ferry port.
Parkland course.
Pro Vincent Carey; Founded 1910
Designed by HS Colt
18 holes, 5298 yards, S.S.S. 68
† Welcome except Thurs and Sat.
✏ WD and WE: €50.
⟳ Welcome by prior arrangement with the manager; discounts for groups of 30 or more; from €45.
⦿ Full clubhouse facilities.
⟿ Royal Marine; Rochestown; Killiney Castle.

12 107 Dundalk ☎
Blackrock, Dundalk, Co Louth

✉ dkgc@iol.ie
☎ 00353 4293 21731, Fax 22022
2 miles S of Dundalk taking the coast Road to Blackrock.
Parkland course.
Pro Leslie Walker; Founded 1904
Designed by Dave Thomas & Peter Alliss
18 holes, 6160 yards, S.S.S. 72
✍ Driving range.
† Welcome.
✏ WD/WE €55.
⟳ Welcome by prior arrangement; catering packages by arrangement;
⦿ Bar and restaurant facilities available.
⟿ Fairway.

12 108 Dunfanaghy
Dunfanaghy, Letterkenny, Co Donegal
☎ 00353 74 36335
On N56 from Letterkenny 0.5 miles E of Dunfanaghy.
Seaside links course.
Founded 1904
Designed by H Vardon
18 holes, 5006 yards, S.S.S. 66
† Welcome but notice is essential.
✏ WD €22; WE €27.

⌁ Welcome by prior arrangement; discounts for groups of more than 12 and 20; from €17 and €20 at WE.
⦿ Full clubhouse facilities available.
⌁ Arnolds; Carrig Rua; Port-n-Blagh; Shandon.

12 109 **Dungarvan** ☎
Knocknagranagh, Dungarvan, Co Waterford
⌂ www.dungarvongolfclub.com
✉ dungarvongc@eircom.net
☎ 00353 58 43310, Fax 44113, Pro 44707
2.5 miles E of Dungarvan on the N25 Waterford to Rosslare Road.
Parkland course.
Pro David Hayes; Founded 1924/1993
Designed by Maurice Fives
18 holes, 6785 yards, S.S.S. 73
⚑ Practice range 1 mile.
† Welcome; booking needed at WE.
⌇ WD €30; WE €40.
⌁ Welcome by prior arrangement; catering packages available.
⦿ Full clubhouse facilities available.
⌁ Clonea Strand; Gold Coast; Lawlors; Park.

12 110 **Dunmore**
Dunmore House, Muckross, Clonakilty, Co Cork
⌂ www.dunmorehousehotel.com
☎ 00353 23 33352, Fax 34686
Signposted 3 miles from Clonakilty.
Hilly Open course.
Founded 1967
Designed by E Hackett
9 holes, 4464 yards, S.S.S. 61
† Welcome. Except Sun and BH.
⌇ Details upon request.
⌁ Welcome by prior arrangement.
⦿ Bar and restaurant facilities in Dunmore House.

12 111 **Dunmore East Golf** ☎ **& Country Club**
Dunmore East, Co Waterford
⌂ www.dunmore-golf.com
✉ dunmoregolf@eircom.net
☎ 00353 51 383151, Fax 383151
10 miles from Waterford in the village of Dunmore East.
Seaside parkland course.
Pro James Nash; Founded 1993
Designed by William Henry Jones
18 holes, 6655 yards, S.S.S. 71
† Welcome.
⌇ WD €25; WE €30.
⌁ Welcome by prior arrangement; terms on application.
⦿ Full clubhouse facilities.

⌁ Ivory Lodge; The Fairways Golf Lodges.

12 112 **East Clare** ☎
Coolreigh, Bodyke, Co Clare
✉ eastclaregolfclub@tinet.ie
☎ 00353 61 921322, Fax 921717
15 miles E of Ennis.
Parkland course.
Founded 1992
Designed by A Spring
18 holes, 5922 yards, S.S.S. 71
† Welcome.
⌇ WD €25; WE €30.
⌁ Welcome; discounts for groups of 25 or more – call for details.
⦿ Bar and restaurant.
⌁ None.

12 113 **East Cork**
Gortacrue, Midleton, Co Cork
☎ 00353 21 4631687, Fax 4613695, Pro 463 3667
Leave Cork to Waterford road at Midleton; course is 2 miles on the Fermoy Road.
Pro Don MacFarlane; Founded 1970
Designed by Edward Hackett
18 holes, 5774 yards, S.S.S. 67
† Welcome with prior booking.
⌇ WD and WE: €25.
⌁ Welcome by prior arrangement; minimum 10 players.
⦿ Full clubhouse facilities.
⌁ Commodore; Middleton Park; Garryvoe.

12 114 **Edenderry**
Kishawanny, Edenderry, Co Offaly
☎ 00353 405 31072, Fax 33911
6 miles from Enfield.
Parkland course.
Founded 1947
Designed by E Hackett
18 holes, 6029 yards, S.S.S. 72
† Welcome.
⌇ WD €30; WE €35 (€18 with member).
⌁ Welcome except Thurs and Sun.
⦿ Clubhouse facilities.
⌁ Wells; Tullamore Court.

12 115 **Edmondstown**
Edmondstown Rd, Rathfarnham, Dublin 16
⌂ www.edmondstowngolfclub.ie
✉ info@edmondstowngolfclub.ie
☎ 00353 1 4932461, Fax 4933152, Pro 4941049, Sec 4931082, Rest/Bar 493 2461, 4933205
8 miles SW of City centre.

Parkland course.
Pro Andrew Crofton; Founded 1944
Designed by McEvoy Cooke
18 holes, 6011 metres, S.S.S. 73
⚑ Practice ground.
† Welcome but it is advisable to make reservations.
⌇ WD €55; WE €65.
⌁ Welcome; terms on application.
⦿ Full facilities.
⌁ Many in Dublin.

12 116 **Elm Green**
Castleknock, Dublin
⌂ www.golfdublin.com
☎ 00353 1 8200797
15 mins from Dublin Airport.
Public course.
Pro Arnold O'Connor; Founded 1992
18 holes, 6013 yards, S.S.S. 66
⚑ 25 bays.
† Welcome.
⌇ WD €65; WE €75.
⌁ Welcome.
⦿ Limited.
⌁ Local pubs available.

12 117 **Elm Park**
Nutley Lane, Donnybrook
✉ office@elmparkolfclub.ie
☎ 00353 1 2693438, Pro 2692650
2 miles from City centre.
Parkland course.
Pro Seamus Green; Founded 1925
Designed by Fred Davies
18 holes, 5355 yards, S.S.S. 68
† Welcome by prior arrangement.
⌇ Terms on application.
⌁ Welcome Tues.
⦿ Full facilities.

12 118 **Ennis** ☎
Drumbiggle, Ennis, Co Clare
☎ 00353 6568 29211, Fax 41848, Pro 20690, Sec 24074
1 mile from town centre.
Parkland course.
Pro Martin Ward; Founded 1912
18 holes, 5592 yards, S.S.S. 69
† Welcome.
⌇ WD and WE: €30.
⌁ Welcome by prior arrangement; minimum group 10.
⦿ Full clubhouse facilities.
⌁ Auburn Lodge; Old Ground; West County.

12 119 **Enniscorthy** ☎
Knockmarshal, Enniscorthy, Co Wexford
☎ 00353 54 33191

EDMONDSTOWN GOLF CLUB

EDMONDSTOWN ROAD, RATHFARNHAM, DUBLIN 16, IRELAND • **Tel:** + 353 1 493 1082 • **Fax:** + 353 1 493 3152

Website: www.edmondstowngolfclub.ie • *E-mail: info@edmondstowngolfclub.ie*

Edmondstown Golf Club is situated amongst the most delightful surroundings on the foothills of the Dublin mountains, and only 11km (7 miles) from Dublin's City centre. A testing parkland course, it lends itself to the golfer who desires a socially enjoyable round of golf on a well-maintained and manicured golf course.

Green Fees: €55 Monday to Friday • €65 Saturday, Sunday and Bank Holidays.

1 mile from town on the Newross-Waterford Road.
Parkland course.
Pro Martin Sludds; Founded 1926
Designed by E. Hackett
18 holes, 6115 yards, S.S.S. 72
† Welcome by prior arrangement.
↳ Mon-Thurs €25; Fri-Sun €34.
⌁ Welcome by prior arrangement with group rates available; terms on application.
⚐ Full facilities.
⌁ Murphy Floods.

---

12 120 Enniscrone   ♋
Enniscrone, Co Sligo
↳ www.enniscronegolf.com
⊟ enniscronegolf@eircom.net
☎ 00353 96 36297, Fax 36657, Pro 36666, Rest/Bar 36660
7 miles from Ballina.
Championship links course.
Pro Charlie McGoldrick; Founded 1918/31
Designed by E Hackett/ Donald Steel
27 holes, 6775 yards, S.S.S. 73
⌁ Practice area.
† Welcome by prior arrangement; timesheet operates every day.
↳ WD €50; WE €63.
⌁ Welcome by prior arrangement; minimum €45; green fee: WD €40; €45.
⚐ Full bar and catering.
⌁ Downhill House Hotel, Ballina; Atlantic, Benbulben, Castle Arms, all in Enniscrone.

---

12 121 Esker Hills G & CC   ♋
Tullamore, Co Offaly
↳ www.eskerhillsgolf.com
⊟ info@eskerhillsgolf.com
☎ 00353 506 55999, Fax 55021
2.5 miles W of Tullamore.
Undulating parkland course.
Founded 1996
Designed by C O'Connor Jnr
18 holes, 6618 yards, S.S.S. 70
† Welcome.
↳ WD €27; WE €37.
⌁ Welcome by arrangement; terms on application.
⚐ Coffee shop facilities.
⌁ The Bridge House Hotel. Tullamore Court.

12 122 The European Club
Brittas Bay, Co Wicklow
↳ www.theeuropeanclub.com
⊟ info@theeuropeanclub.com
☎ 00353 404 47415, Fax 47449
37 S of Dublin on N11.
Links course.
Founded 1993
Designed by Pat Ruddy
20 holes, 7368 yards, S.S.S. 72
⌁ Practice range, practice ground.
† Welcome by prior arrangement.
↳ Apr-Oct €125; Nov-Mar €75.
⌁ Welcome by prior arrangement; minimum group 24I from €60.
⚐ Full clubhouse facilities.
⌁ Tinakilly House; Grand, Wicklow; Arklow Bay; Woodenbridge, Arklow Bay; Marriott, Druids Glen.

---

12 123 Faithlegg   ♋
Faithlegg Golfclub, Co Waterford
☎ 00353 51 382241
6 miles from Waterford city centre on the banks of the Suir.
Parkland course.
Pro John Julie; Founded 1993
Designed by Patrick Merrigan
18 holes, 6674 yards, S.S.S. 72
⌁ Practice area.
† Welcome.
↳ Mon-Thurs €22 before 9am and €35 after; Fri-Sun €50.
⌁ Welcome by prior arrangement; packages available; terms on application.
⚐ Full bar and restaurant facilities.

---

12 124 Fermoy   ♋
Corrin, Fermoy, Co Cork
☎ 00353 25 31472
2 miles from Fermoy off Cork-Dublin Rd.
Undulating parkland course.
Founded 1893
Designed by Commander Harris
18 holes, 5795 yards, S.S.S. 70
† Welcome WD.
↳ Terms on application.
⌁ Welcome WD and Sat am.
⚐ By arrangement.

---

12 125 Fernhill
Carrigaline, Co Cork

☎ 00353 21 373103
Parkland course.
Founded 1994
18 holes
† Welcome.
↳ Terms on application.
⌁ Terms on application.

---

12 126 Forrest Little   ♋
Forest Little, Cloghran, Co Dublin
↳ www.forrestlittle.com
☎ 00353 1 8401763, Fax 8401000
0.5 miles beyond Dublin Airport on the Dublin-Belfast Road, take first left.
Parkland course.
Pro Tony Judd; Founded 1940
Designed by Fred Hawtree
18 holes, 5865 yards, S.S.S. 70
† Welcome WD.
↳ Terms on application.
⌁ Welcome, normally Mon & Thurs pm.
⚐ Full bar snacks and restaurant.

---

12 127 Fota Island
Fota Island, Carrigtwohill, Co Cork
↳ www.fotaislandgolfclub.ie
⊟ reservations@fotaisland.ie
☎ 00353 214 883700, Fax 883713, Pro 883710
Take N25 E from Cork City towards Waterford and Rosslare; after 9 miles take the exit for Cobh/Fota, course 0.5 miles.
Pro Kevin Morris; Founded 1993
Designed by Peter McEvoy and Christy O'Connor Jnr; redesigned by Jeff Howes.
18 holes, 6927 yards, S.S.S. 73
⌁ Driving range.
† Welcome.
↳ From €62–€98.
⌁ Group rates for min of 20 available on application; from €49.
⚐ Full facilities.
⌁ Midleton Park; Ashbourne House; Jury's Cork.

---

12 128 Foxrock
Torquay Rd, Dublin, Co Dublin
☎ 00353 1 2893992, Fax 2894943, Pro 2893414
About 6 miles from Dublin; turn right off T7 just past Stillergan on the

Leopardstown Road then left into
Torquay Road.
Parkland course.
Founded 1893
9 holes, 5667 yards, S.S.S. 69
♦ Welcome Mon-Wed am, Thurs, Fri
and Sun with a member.
Ⅼ €40, €15 with a member. Welcome
Mon and Thurs.
⦿ Snacks.

12 129 **Frankfield**
Frankfield, Douglas, Co Cork
☎ 00353 21 363124
10 miles S of Cork.
Parkland course.
Founded 1984
9 holes, 4621 yards, S.S.S. 65
♦ Welcome.
Ⅼ Terms on application.
⦿ Lunches.

12 130 **Galway**
Blackrock, Salthill, Co Galway
☎ 00353 91 522033, Fax 529783,
Pro 523038
3 miles W of Galway.
Tight tree-lined parkland course.
Pro Don Wallace; Founded 1895
Designed by A MacKenzie
18 holes, 5832 yards, S.S.S. 71
♦ Welcome.
Ⅼ WD €35; WE €45.
⟳ Welcome WD prior arrangement;
catering packages by arrangement.
⦿ Full catering facilities.
⇝ Salthill; Galway Bay; Jameson's;
Spinnacker.

12 131 **Galway Bay Golf &** ⏁
Country Club
Renville, Oranmore, Co Galway
☎ 00353 91 790500
From Galway take the coast road
through Oranmore; course is
signposted from there.
Founded 1993
Designed by Christy O'Connor Jnr
18 holes, 7190 yards, S.S.S. 72
Ⅰ Practice range; practice bays.
♦ Welcomwith handicap certs.
Ⅼ Apr-Oct: Mon-Thurs €55, Fri-Sun
€60, Nov- March: Mon-Thurs €25,
Fri-Sun €32.
⟳ Welcome by prior arrangement;
group rates available for groups of
over 20.
⦿ Restaurant; spikes bar; bar.

12 132 **Glasson Golf & CC** ⏁
Glasson, Athlone, Co Westmeath

☎ 00353 902 85120
6 miles N of Athlone on the N55.
Parkland course.
Founded 1994
Designed by C O'Connor
18 holes, 7120 yards, S.S.S. 72
♦ Welcome.
Ⅼ Terms on application.
⟳ Welcome by prior arrangement;
catering packages by arrangement.
⦿ Full clubhouse facilities.

12 133 **Glen of the Downs**
Coolnaskeagh, Delgany,
Co Wicklow
⥃ www.glenofthedownsc.com
✉ info@glenofthedowns.com
☎ 00353 1 2876240, Fax 2870063
Founded 1998
Designed by Peter McEvoy.
18 holes, 6443 yards, S.S.S.71
♦ Welcome every day
Ⅼ Summer: WD €65; WE €80.
Winter: WD €50; WE €65. Early Bird
and Winter Specials available.
⟳ Welcome every day.
⦿ Full facilities.
⇝ Glenview Hotel; Chester Hotel.

12 134 **Glebe**
Kildalkey Rd, Trim, Meath
✉ glebegc@eircom.net
☎ 00353 46 31926
1 mile from Trim.
Parkland pay and play course.
Designed by Eddie Hackett.
18 holes, 6466 yards, S.S.S. 73
Ⅰ Large practice area.
♦ Welcome.
Ⅼ WD €16; WE €19 (2003 rates).
⟳ By arrangement.
⦿ Snacks available.

12 135 **Glencullen**
Glencullen, Co Wicklow
☎ 00353 1 2940898
4 miles from Kilternan; follow signs for
Johnny Fox's pub.
9 holes, 5400 yards, S.S.S. 69
♦ Welcome.
Ⅼ Terms on application.
⦿ Snack facilities.

12 136 **Glengarriff**
Glengarriff, Co Cork
☎ 00353 27 63150
On T65 55 miles W of Cork.
Seaside course.
Founded 1936
9 holes, 4094 yards, S.S.S. 66
♦ Welcome.

Ⅼ Terms on application.
⟳ Welcome by prior arrangement
with discounts depending on group
size.
⦿ Full facilities.
⇝ Self-catering lodge
accommodation on site.

12 137 **Glenmalure**
Greenane, Rathdrum, Co Wicklow
☎ 00353 404 46679, Sec 46879
2 miles W of Rathdrum.
Parkland course.
Founded 1993
Designed by Pat Suttle
18 holes, 5850 yards, S.S.S. 66
♦ Welcome.
Ⅼ WD €25; WE €35.
⟳ Welcome by prior arrangement;
discounts depending on group
numbers.
⦿ Full facilities.

12 138 **Gold Coast Golf** ⏁
Ballinacourty, Dungarvan,
Co Waterford
☎ 00353 58 44055, Fax 44055,
Rest/Bar 42249
Located 3 miles from Dungarvan.
Parkland course by the sea.
Founded 1939. Amended 1997
Designed by Maurice Fives
18 holes, 6171 yards, S.S.S. 72
Ⅰ Practice range.
♦ Welcome by prior arrangement.
Ⅼ WD €35; WE €45.
⟳ Welcome by prior arrangement;
discounts depending on size of group
and date of visit.
⦿ Full facilities.
⇝ Gold Coast Hotel; Gold Coast
Holiday Homes; Clonea Strand.

12 139 **Gort**
Castlequarter, Gort, Co Galway
⥃ www.gortgolf.com
✉ info@gortgolf.com
☎ 00353 91 632244, Fax 632387,
Rest/Bar 630909
Off Kilmacduagh Road.
Parkland course.
Founded 1924/1996
Designed by C O'Connor Jnr
18 holes, 5974 yards, S.S.S. 71
♦ Welcome; some restrictions Sun
morning.
Ⅼ WD €25; WE €30.
⟳ Welcome by prior arrangement;
deposit of €100 in advance; catering
packages available.
⦿ Lunches and snacks available.
⇝ Lady Gregory, Gort.

GREYSTONES GOLF CLUB

Tel: 01-287 4136
www.greystonesgc.com
secretary@greystonesgc.com

Golf has been played at Greystones since 1895 and every technological age of the game, from gutta percha balls to the most recent space age innovations have been tested and resisted on the fairways there.

Major redevelopment of the course has taken place in recent years to the designs of leading architect Patrick Merrigan and the result is a pleasing blend of the most wonderful scenery, a veritable botanic delight in a county known as the garden of Ireland, with an amazing array of golf shots which arouse the tiger in every golfer.

The club has a great tradition of hospitality and it continues to offer the warmest welcome to visiting players into the new century whether they come alone or in groups. The facilities, which include an extensive modern clubhouse, are capable of dealing with the most sophisticated corporate outing or society meetings and group green fees are very keen. Interested in a little bit of golfing heaven.

Then telephone, e-mail or contact at:

GREYSTONES GOLF CLUB, WHITSHED, GREYSTONES, Co WICKLOW

---

12 140 Grange
Rathfarnham, Dublin
☎ 00353 1 4932889, Fax 4939490,
Pro 4932299, Sec 493 9490
7 miles S from city.
Parkland course.
Founded 1910
Designed by James Braid
18 holes, 5517 yards, S.S.S. 69
† Welcome WD except Tues and Wed afternoon.
⌇ WD €57.
⌇ Welcome Mon and Thurs by prior arrangement.
⦿ Full facilities.

12 141 Greencastle
Greencastle, Moville, Co Donegal
☎ 00353 7 781013
On L85 23 miles NE of Londonderry through Moville.
Public seaside course.
Founded 1892
Designed by Eddie Hackett
18 holes, 5211 yards, S.S.S. 67
† Welcome.
⌇ WD €20; WE €26.
⌇ Welcome by prior arrangement.
⦿ Bar and catering facilities.

12 142 Greenore ♛
Greenore, Co Louth
⌸ www.greenoregolf.com
⌷ greenoreglfclub@eircom.net
☎ 00353 4293 73678, Fax 83898,
Pro 83718, Sec 73212, Rest/Bar 73678 x22
15 miles out of Dundalk on the Newry Road.
Wooded seaside semi links course.
Founded 1896
Designed by Eddie Hackett
18 holes, 6647 yards, S.S.S. 71
⫞ Driving range.
† Welcome by prior arrangement.
⌇ WD €33; WE €45.
⌇ Welcome by arrangement.

⦿ Full facilities.
⌇ Apply to club.

12 143 Greystones ♛
Greystones, Co Wicklow
⌸ www.greystonesgc.com
⌷ secretary@greystonesgc.com
☎ 00353 1 2874136, Fax 2873749,
Pro 2875308, Rest/Bar 2876624
N11 out of Dublin towards Wexford.
Parkland course.
Pro Karl Holmes; Founded 1895
Designed by Paddy Merrigan.
18 holes, 5322 yards, S.S.S. 69
† Welcome Mon, Tue, Fri
⌇ WD €33; WE €38.
⌇ Welcome by arrangement.
⦿ Full facilities.
⌇ La Touche.

12 144 Gweedore
Derrybeg, Letterkenny, Co Donegal
☎ 00353 749 5531140
L82 from Letterkenny or T72 from Donegal.
Seaside course.
Designed by Eddie Hackett
9 holes, 6150 yards, S.S.S. 69
† Welcome.
⌇ Details available upon application.
⌇ Welcome at WE.
⦿ Lunches at WE.

12 145 Harbour Point ♛
Little Island, Cork, Co Cork
⌸ www.harbourpointgolfclub.com
⌷ hpoint@iol.ie
☎ 00353 214 353094, Fax 354408,
Pro 353719
6 miles E of Cork.
Parkland course.
Pro Morgan O'Donovan; Founded 1991
Designed by Paddy Merrigan
18 holes, 6063 yards, S.S.S. 72
† Welcome.

⌇ WD €33; WE €38.
⌇ Welcome; minimum nine; reductions for groups of more than 20 and 40.
⦿ Full facilities.
⌇ John Barley Corn; Ashbourne House; Midleton Park; Fitzpatricks Silver Springs.

12 146 Hazel Grove
Mt Seskin Rd, Jobstown, Tallaght, Dublin
☎ 00353 1 4520911
On the Blessington Road 2.5 miles from Tallaght.
Parkland course.
Founded 1988
Designed by Jim Byrne
11 holes, 5030 yards, S.S.S. 67
⫞ Practice area.
† Welcome except Tue and Sun morning.
⌇ Terms on application.
⌇ Welcome by prior arrangement; maximum 50 players; Sat morning maximum 40; catering packages available.
⦿ Bar function room.
⌇ Abberly Court.

12 147 Headfort ♛
Kells, Co Meath
⌷ hgcadmin@eircom.net
☎ 00353 469 240146, Fax 046 9249282, Pro 046 9240639, Rest/Bar 046 9241944
N3 from Dublin on Cavan route.
Parkland course.
Pro Brendan McGovern; Founded 1928
Designed by Christy O'Connor Jnr
36 holes, 5973 yards, S.S.S. 71
† Welcome.
⌇ WD €40; WE €45. New course: WD €55; WE €60.
⌇ Welcome by prior arrangement; catering package by arrangement.

🍽 Full facilities.
💬 Headfort Arms.

12 148 Heath
The Heath, Portlaoise, Co Laois
☎ 00353 502 46533, Fax 46866,
Pro 46622
4 miles NE of Portlaoise off the main
Dublin to Cork/Limerick Road.
Heathland course.
Pro Eddie Doyle; Founded 1930
18 holes, 5721 yards, S.S.S. 70
ℐ Practice range.
♱ Welcome WD; WE by prior
arrangement.
ℂ Terms on application.
⌁ Welcome by prior arrangement.
🍽 Full facilities.

12 149 Hermitage
Lucan, Co Dublin
☎ 00353 1 6268049, Pro 6268072
8 miles from Dublin; 1 mile from
Lucan.
Parkland course.
Pro Simon Byrne; Founded 1905
Designed by Eddie Hackett
18 holes, 6051 yards, S.S.S. 71
♱ Welcome WD.
ℂ WD €70; WE €80.
⌁ Welcome WD by arrangement; five
golf and meal packages; latest tee time
1.45pm; from €70.
🍽 Full clubhouse catering facilities.
💬 Finnstown; Bewley; Spa; Morans
Red Cow; Green Isle.

12 150 Highfield
Carbury, Co Kildare
☎ 00353 697 31021
In Carbury.
Parkland course.
Pro Peter O'Hagan; Founded 1992
18 holes, 5919 yards, Par 70, S.S.S.
68
ℐ 5 bays.
♱ Welcome.
ℂ WD €40; WE €30.
⌁ Welcome; booking is advisable.
🍽 Yes.

12 151 Hollystown
Hollystown, Dublin 15, Co Dublin
☎ 00353 1 8207444
8 miles off N3 Dublin-Cavan road at
Mulhuddart or off the main N2 Dublin-
Ashbourne road at Ward.
Parkland course.
Founded 1993
18 holes, 6303 yards, S.S.S. 72
ℐ Practice ground, driving range.

♱ Welcome.
ℂ WD €25; WE €35.
🍽 Coffee shop.

12 152 Hollywood Lakes   ☏
Hollywood, Ballyboughal, Co Dublin
🖳 www.hollywoodlakesgolf.com
📧 hollywoodlakes@eircom.net
☎ 00353 1 8433406, Fax 8433002,
Sec 8433407
15 minutes N of Dublin Airport via N1
and R129 to Ballyboughal.
ParklSid Baldwin; Founded 1991
Designed by Mel Flanagan
18 holes, 6246 yards, S.S.S. 72
ℐ Practice range; practice bar
♱ Welcome except Sat and Sun
before 2.00; booking advisable.
ℂ WD €35; WE €45.
⌁ Welcome by prior arrangement;
reductions for larger groups; catering
packages by arrangement; early bird
rates between 8am and 10am Mon-Fri;
from €25.
🍽 Full facilities.
💬 Grove; Grand; Airport; Carnegie
Court, Swords.

12 153 Howth   ☏
Carrickbrack Rd, Sutton, Dublin 13
🖳 www.howthgolfclub.ie
📧 secretary@howthgolfclub.ie
☎ 00353 1 8323055, Fax 8321793
Situated on Howth Head to the NE of
Dublin.
Heathland course.
Pro John McGuirk; Founded 1912
Designed by James Braid
18 holes, 5614 metres, S.S.S. 69
ℐ Practice ground.
♱ Welcome WD except Wed.
ℂ WD and WE: €50.
⌁ Welcome WD except Wed;
reductions on numbers over 10 by
arrangement.
🍽 Bar snacks, full catering for groups
by arrangement.
💬 Marine; Bailey Court.

12 154 The Island Golf Club
Corballis, Donabate, Co Dublin
🖳 www.theislandgolfclub.com
📧 reservations@theislandgolfclub
.com
☎ 00353 1 843 6205, Fax 843 6860,
Sec 843 6462, Pro 843 5002
Leave N1 1 mile beyond Swords at
Donabate signpost, then L91 for 3
miles and turn right at sign.
Traditional links course.
Pro Kevin Kelleher; Founded 1890
Designed by F Hawtree & Eddie

Hackett (over last 30yrs)
18 holes, 6206 metres, S.S.S. 73
ℐ Practice facilities.
♱ Welcome by prior arrangement.
ℂ All time €110.
⌁ Welcome by prior arrangement.
🍽 Full facilities.

12 155 The K Club   ☏
Kildare Hotel & Country club, Straffan,
Co. Kildare
☎ 00353 1 601 7300, Fax 6017399
22 miles from Dublin via N7 Naas
Road.
Parkland course.
Pro Ernie Jones; Founded 1991
Designed by Arnold Palmer
18 holes, 7159 yards, S.S.S. 74
ℐ Practice range available.
♱ Welcome by prior arrangement.
ℂ Apr-Oct €245; Nov-Mar €110.
⌁ Welcome groups of 16 or more;
catering packages by arrangement.
🍽 Full clubhouse facilities, bar, coffee
shop.
💬 Kildare Hotel & Country Club on
site, 5-star.

12 156 Kanturck – 18 Holes
Fairyhill, Kanturck, Co Cork
☎ 00353 29 50534, Sec 0872 217510
1 mile from Kanturck via Fairyhill Road
Parkland course.
Founded 1973
Designed by Richard Barry
18 holes, 5721 yards, S.S.S. 70
♱ Welcome but prior arrangement is
advisable.
ℂ WD €15; WE €20.
⌁ Welcome by prior arrangement
with the seretary; catering packages by
arrangement through the secretary;
group rates available.
🍽 Full facilities.
💬 Duhallow Park; Assolas.

12 157 Kanturck – 9 Holes
Fairyhill, Kanturck, Cork
☎ 00353 29 47238, Fax 50534
Course is three miles SW of Kanturck
on the R579.
Founded 1974
9 holes, 6026 yards, S.S.S. 69
♱ Welcome.
ℂ Terms on application.
🍽 Bar and catering facilities.

12 158 Kenmare   ☏
Killowen Rd, Kenmare, Co Kerry
🖳 www.kenmaregolfclub.com
📧 info@kenmoregolfclub.com

☎ 00353 64 41291, Fax 42061
Off the N22 Cork to Killarney Road and
then on to the R569.
Parkland course on the mouth of a
river; set in the mountains.
Pro Simon Duffield; Founded 1903
Designed by Eddie Hackett
18 holes, 6000 yards, S.S.S. 69
† Welcome but booking will be
necessary on weekends.
⌇ Details available on application.
⌀ Welcome by prior arrangement;
minimum 18 players; catering by
arrangement.
⦿ Only snacks are available;
restaurant next door.
⌁ Park; Kenmare Bay; Sheen Falls.

12 159 Kilcock
Gallow, Kilcock, Co Meath
☎ 00353 1 6284074
2 miles N of Kilcock.
Parkland course.
Founded 1985
Designed by Eddie Hackett
18 holes, 5801 yards, S.S.S. 70
† Welcome WD; WE by prior
arrangement.
⌇ WD €20; WE €25.
⌀ Welcome by prior arrangement.
⦿ Full catering.
⌁ Glenroyal, Maynooth; Johnstown
House, Enfield.

12 160 Kilcoole
Newcastle Road, Kilcoole, Co Wicklow
⌸ www.kilkoolegolfclub.com
✉ adminkg@eircom.net
☎ 00353 1 287 2066, Fax 201 0497
21 miles S of Dublin on Wicklow
Coast.
Parkland course.
Founded 1992
Designed by Brian Williams
9 holes
⌇ Welcome; booking essential; WD
€30, WE €35.
⌀ Welcome by prior arrangement.
⦿ Full clubhouse facilities available.
⌁ Latouche; Druids; Glen View
Marriott, Glenview.

12 161 Kilkea Castle   �'
Castle Dermot, Co Kildare
✉ kilkeagolfclub@eircom.net
☎ 00353 503 45555, Fax 45505
40 miles from Dublin.
Parkland course.
Founded 1994
Designed by McDadd & Cassidy
18 holes, 6097 metres, S.S.S. 71
† Welcome; by booking only.

⌇ Mon–Thurs €39 Fri–Sun and BH
€45.
⌀ Welcome by prior arrangement;
terms on application.
⦿ Full facilities.
⌁ Kilkae Castle Hotel.

12 162 Kilkee   �'
East End, Kilkee, Co Clare
⌸ www.kilkeegolfclub.ir
✉ kilkeegolfclub@eircom.net
☎ 00353 6590 56048
400 yards from town centre.
Clifftop course; Founded 1896
Designed by McAlister
18 holes, 5537 yards, S.S.S. 69
† Welcome.
⌇ Terms on application.
⌀ Welcome by prior arrangement;
restrictions in July and early August;
catering packages by arrangement.
⦿ Full facilities.

12 163 Kilkenny   �'
Glendine, Kilkenny, Co Kilkenny
⌸ www.kilkennygolfclub.com
✉ enquiries@kilkennygolfclub.com
☎ 00353 56 65400, Pro 65400 x18,
Sec 65400 x10
1 miles NW of Kilkenny off the
Castlecorner Road.
Parkland course.
Founded 1896
18 holes, 5857 yards, S.S.S. 70
† Welcome.
⌇ WD €35; WE €40.
⌀ Welcome but booking is essential.
⦿ Clubhouse facilities.

12 164 Killarney Golf Club   �'
Mahoney's Point, Killarney, Co Kerry
⌸ www.killarney-golf.com
✉ reservations@killarney-golf.com
☎ 00353 64 31034, Fax 33065,
Pro 31615, Rest/Bar 31034 x112
2 miles W of Killarney on the N70.
Parkland and lakeside course.
Pro Tony Covemy
Founded 1939
Designed by Sir Guy Campbell &
Henry Longhurst
3x18 holes – Killeen: 6474 metres,
S.S.S. 73; Mahoney's Point: 6164
metres, S.S.S. 72; Lackabane: 6410
metres, S.S.S. 72
⌀ Driving range.
† Welcome by prior arrangement.
⌇ WD and WE: €75.
⌀ Welcome with prior arrangement
and handicap certificates essential;
discounts for groups of 20 or more;
from €70.

⦿ Full clubhouse facilities.
⌁ Club can provide a detailed list.

12 165 Killeen
Kill, Co Kildare
☎ 00353 45866003
N7 to Kill village then head to Straffan.
Parkland course.
Founded 1991
18 holes, 4989 yards, S.S.S. 70
† Welcome.
⌇ WD €25; WE €32.
⌀ Welcome.
⦿ Full bar and catering.

12 166 Killeline
Cork Road, Newcastle West,
Co Limmerick
☎ 00353 69 61600
Cork road on the edge of Newcastle
West.
Parkland course.
Founded 1993
Designed by Kevin Dorian
18 holes, 6720 yards, S.S.S. 72
† Welcome.
⌇ Terms on application.
⌀ Welcome at all times by
arrangement; catering packages
available.
⦿ Full facilities. Bar and restaurant.
⌁ Courtney Lodge (very close);
Rathkeale House; Devon Inn.

12 167 Killin Park
Killin Park, Dundalk
☎ 00353 42 9339303
Parkland
3 miles NW of Dundalk on Castledown
Road.
Founded 1991
Designed by Eddie Hackett.
18 holes, 5388 yards, S.S.S. 65
† Welcome.
⌇ WD €18; WE €23.
⌀ Welcome by prior arrangement.
⦿ Snacks and bar; full meal by
arrangement.
⌁ The Derryhale, Fairways

12 168 Killiney   �ّ
Ballinclea Rd, Killiney, Co Dublin
✉ killineygollf@eircom.net
☎ 00353 1 2852823, Fax 2852861,
Pro 2856294
3 miles from Dun Laoghaire.
Parkland course.
Pro Paddy O Biol; Founded 1903
9 holes, 5655 yards, S.S.S. 70
† Welcome but booking is essential.
⌇ WD and WE: €38.

⚐ Welcome on most days, but prior arrangement is necessary.
🍴 Full clubhouse facilities.
🛏 Killiney Castle; Killiney Court.

12 169 Killorglin
Steelroe, Killorglin, Co Kerry
🖧 www.kilorglingolf.ie
📧 kilgolf@iol.ie
☎ 00353 6697 61979, Fax 61437
On the N70 Tralee Road 3km from the bridge at Killorglin.
Parkland course.
Pro Billy Dodd
Founded 1992
Designed by Eddie Hackett
18 holes, 6467 yards, S.S.S. 71
† Welcome.
⌷ Terms on application.
⚐ Welcome; terms on application.
🍴 Full clubhouse facilities.
🛏 Bianconi Inn; Riverside House; Grove Lodge; Fairways B&B; Laune Bridge; Fern Rock.

12 170 Kilrush ♻
Parknamoney, Kilrush, Co Clare
🖧 www.kilrushgolfclub.com
📧 info@kilrushgolfclub.com
☎ 00353 6590 51138, Fax 52633, Sec 087 623 7557
0.5 miles from Kilrush on N68 from Ennis.
Parkland course.
Pro Sean O'Connor; Founded 1934
Designed by Dr A Spring (extended in 1994)
18 holes, 5986 yards, S.S.S. 70
† Welcome.
⌷ WD €25; WE €30.
⚐ Welcome by prior arrangement; discount terms on application.
🍴 Full clubhouse facilities available all year round.
🛏 Halpins; Stella Maris; Bellbridge.

12 171 Kilternan Golf & ♻
Country Club
Kilternan Hotel, Enniskerry Road, Co Dublin
🖧 www.globalgolf.com
📧 kgc@kilternan-hotel.ie
☎ 00353 1 2955559, Fax 2955670, Sec 2952986/2952332
On N11 S of Dublin.
Hilly parkland course.
Pro Gary Headley; Founded 1988
Designed by E Hackett
18 holes, 5223 yards, S.S.S. 66
⌷ Driving nets, practice, putting green. Buggies and trolleys available.
† Welcome.

⌷ WD €27; WE €34.
⚐ Welcome by prior arrangement; leisure club; tennis courts; workout studios.
🍴 Clubhouse menu.

12 172 Kinsale ♻
Farrangalway, Kinsale, Cork
☎ 00353 47 74722, Fax 73114, Pro 73258
3 miles N of Kinsale on Cork Road. 3 miles NE of Kinsale.
Parkland course.
Pro Ger Broderick; Founded 1912
Designed by J Kenneally
18 holes, 6609 yards, S.S.S. 72
† Welcome.
⌷ WD €35; WE €50.
⚐ Welcome by prior arrangement; restricted to 11.30am-1.30pm only at WE; catering by arrangement.
🍴 Full clubhouse facilities.
🛏 Actons; Trident; Blue Haven.

12 173 Knockanally Golf & ♻
Country Club
Donadea, North Kildare
📧 golf@knockanally.com
☎ 00353 458 69322
3 miles off the main Dublin-Galway Road between Kilcock and Enfield.
Parkland course.
Pro Martin Darcy; Founded 1985
Designed by Noel Lyons
18 holes, 6424 yards, S.S.S. 72
† Welcome.
⌷ WD €30; WE €50.
⚐ Welcome by prior arrangement everyday.
🍴 Full clubhouse facilities.
🛏 The John's Town House Hotel.

12 174 Lahinch Golf Club
Lahinch, Co Clare
🖧 www.lahinchgolf.com
📧 info@lahinchgolf.com
☎ 00353 6570 81003, Fax 81592
34 miles from Shannon Airport.
Seaside course.
Pro Robert McCaver
Founded 1892
Designed by JD Harris/Donald Steel (Castle); Old course designed by Tom Morris (1892), redesigned by Dr A MacKenzie
Castle: 18 holes, 5138 yards, S.S.S. 70;
Old: 18 holes, 6633 yards, S.S.S. 71
† Welcome.
⌷ Terms on application.
⚐ Welcome but booking is essential; especially for Sun.
🍴 Full facilities.

12 175 Laytown & ♻
Bettystown
Bettystown, Co Meath
🖧 www.bettystowngolfclub.ntuinternet.com
📧 bettystowngolfclub@ntuinternet.com
☎ 00353 41 27563, Fax 28506, Pro 28793, Sec 27170, Rest/Bar 28630
45 miles N of Dublin Airport.
Links course.
Pro Robert Browne; Founded 1909
18 holes, 5668 yards, S.S.S. 69
† Welcome by prior arrangement.
⌷ Terms on application.
⚐ Welcome WD and some Sat; terms on application.
🍴 Full bar and catering facilities.

12 176 Lee Valley
Clashanure, Ovens, Co Cork
☎ 00353 21 7331721, Fax 7331695, Pro 331758
On main Cork-Killarney Road. M22.
Parkland course.
Pro John Savage; Founded 1993
Designed by Christy O'Connor Jnr
18 holes, 6715 yards, S.S.S. 72
† Welcome by prior arrangement.
⌷ April-Oct: WD €44, WE €54; Nov-March: WD €30, WE €38. Early Bird - April-Oct before 10.00am - €30.
⚐ Welcome by prior arrangement.
🍴 Full clubhouse facilities.
🛏 Blarney Park; Farran House.

12 177 Leixlip
Leixlip, Co Kildare
☎ 00353 1 6244978, Sec 6246185
Off N4 past Lucan.
Parkland course.
Founded 1994
Designed by E Hackett
18 holes, 6068 yards, S.S.S. 70
† Welcome.
⌷ Details upon application.
⚐ Welcome by prior arrangement; discounts for large groups.
🍴 Clubhouse facilities.
🛏 Becketts; Springfield; Spa.

12 178 Leopardstown Golf
Centre
Foxrock, Dublin
☎ 00353 1 2895341, Fax 2892569
5 miles S of Dublin.
Parkland course.
Pro Michael Allen, Steven O'Donnell
18 holes, 5384 yards, S.S.S. 66
⌷ 50 indoor and 50 outdoor.
† Welcome.
⌷ Terms on application.

⚲ Welcome, but booking in advance is essential.
🍽 Café and restaurant facilities.

12 179 Letterkenny
Barnhill, Letterkenny, Co Donegal
☎ 00353 7421150
On T72 2 miles N of Letterkenny.
Parkland course.
Founded 1913
Designed by E Hackett
18 holes, 6239 yards, S.S.S. 71
† Welcome.
 Terms on application.
⚲ Welcome by arrangement.
🍽 Bar and snacks available; meals by prior arrangement.

12 180 Limerick
Ballyclough, Co Limerick
⛯ www.limerickgc.com
☎ 00353 61 415146, Fax 319219, Pro 412492, Rest/Bar 414083
Course is south of the city on the Fedamore Road.
Parkland course.
Pro Lea Hurrington; Founded 1891
18 holes, 5938 yards, S.S.S. 71
† Welcome before 4pm WD except Tues.
 €50.
⚲ Welcome Mon, Thu, Fri Morning.
🍽 Full facilities.
⛲ Feltcourse Hotel.

12 181 Limerick County Golf ☏ & Country Club
Ballyneety, Co Limerick
⛯ www.limerickcounty.com
✉ lcgolf@iol.ie
☎ 00353 61 351881, Fax 351384, Pro 351881
5 miles S of Limerick towards Bruff/Kilmallock.
Parkland course.
Pro Donal McSweeney; Founded 1994
Designed by Des Smyth
18 holes, 6191 yards, S.S.S. 72
⫪ Practice range; driving range and golf school.
† Welcome.
 Mon-Tue €30; Wed-Fri €37; WE €50.
⚲ Welcome; deposit required; from €25.
🍽 Full facilities.
⛲ Castleroy Park; Woodlands; Jury's; Clarion.

12 182 Lismore
Lismore, Co Waterford

☎ 00353 58 54026
0.5 miles from Lismore on the Killarney Road.
Parkland course.
Founded 1965
Designed by Eddie Hackett
9 holes, 5291 yards, S.S.S. 67
† Welcome; some Sun reserved.
 Details available upon application.
⚲ Welcome by arrangement; terms on application.
🍽 Clubhouse facilities.

12 183 Listowel ☏
Feale View, Listowel, Kerry
☎ 00353 68 21592
In village of Listowel.
Parkland course.
9 holes, S.S.S. 70
† Welcome.
 Terms on application.
🍽 Snack bar facilities.

12 184 Loughrea
Loughrea, Co Galway
☎ 00353 91 841049
On L11 1 mile N of Loughrea.
Meadowland course.
Founded 1924
Designed by Eddie Hackett
18 holes, 5176 yards, S.S.S. 68
† Welcome.
 €20 daily.
⚲ Welcome by prior arrangement.
🍽 Clubhouse facilities.

12 185 Lucan
Celbridge Rd, Lucan, Co Dublin
✉ lucangolf@eircom.net
☎ 00353 1 6280246, Fax 6282929, Sec 6282106
Take the N4 from Dublin and turn off at Celbridge.
Parkland course.
Founded 1897
Designed by E Hackett
18 holes, 5994 yards, S.S.S. 71
† Welcome. Mon, Tues and Fri.
Other times with member.
 WD and WE: €45.
⚲ Welcome by arrangement.
🍽 Full bar and restaurant service.
⛲ Springfield; The Lucan Spa.

12 186 Luttrellstown Castle ☏
Castleknock, Dublin 15
⛯ www.luttrellstown.ie
✉ golf@luttrellstown.ie
☎ 00353 1 8089988, Fax 8089989
Leave N1 at M50 intersection following southbound signs; exit M50 at

Castleknock. 7 miles from Dublin city centre.
Parkland course.
Pro Edward Doyle; Founded 1993
Designed by Dr Nick Bielenberg/ Edward Connaughton
18 holes, 7000 yards, S.S.S. 74
⫪ Driving range.
† Welcome every day.
 Sun-Thur €85; Fri, Sat €95.
⚲ Welcome; special rates negotiable for groups; terms available on application.
🍽 Full clubhouse facilities.
⛲ Private 15th century castle on the estate.

12 187 Macroom
Lackaduv, Macroom, Co Cork
✉ macroomgc@iol.ie
☎ 00353 26 41072, Fax 41391
On main Cork/Killarney road; centre of town, through Castle Arch.
Parkland course.
Founded 1924
Designed by J Kennealy (new 9 holes)
18 holes, 5574 yards, S.S.S. 70
† Welcome; some WE restrictions.
 Details upon application.
⚲ Welcome by prior arrangement between March-October.
🍽 Full facilities.
⛲ The Castle Hotel.

12 188 Mahon
Clover Hill, Blackrock, Co Cork
☎ 00353 21 294280
2 miles SE of Cork.
Municipal parkland course.
Founded 1980
18 holes, 4217 yards, S.S.S. 62
† Welcome WD; WE by prior arrangement.
 WD €18; WE €19.
🍽 Bar snacks; lunch and dinner by arrangement.

12 189 Malahide ☏
Beechwood, The Grange, Malahide, Co Dublin
⛯ www.malahidegolfclub.ie
✉ malgc@clubi.ie
☎ 00353 1 8461611, Fax 8461270, Pro 8460002
8 miles N of Dublin; 1 mile S of Malahide.
Parkland course.
Pro John Murray; Founded 1892
Designed by Eddie Hackett
27 holes, 6066 yards, S.S.S. 72
† Welcome Mon, Thurs, Fri; limited WE availability.

☪ WD €50; WE €85.
⛳ Welcome Mon, Thurs, Fri and Sat morning; discounts available; catering by arrangement; from €22.
🍽 Full bar and restaurant facilities available.
🛏 Grand Hotel; Portmarnock Links; White Sands.

---

12 190 **Mallow**   ♛

Ballyellis, Mallow, Co Cork
📧 golfmall@golffree.indigo.ie
☎ 00353 22 21145, Fax 42501, Pro 43424
1.5 km from Mallow on the Killanvullen Road.
Parkland course.
Pro Sean Conway; Founded 1892/1947
Designed by Commander JD Harris
18 holes, 5960 yards, S.S.S. 72
† Welcome; booking advisable WE.
☪ WD €32; WE €38; booking required for tee-off time.
⛳ Welcome WD by prior arrangement; packages available.
🍽 Full clubhouse facilities.
🛏 Longueville House; Hibernian.

---

12 191 **Mannan Castle**

Donaghmoyne, Carrickmacross, Co Monaghan
📧 mannancastlegc@eircom.net
☎ 00353 4296 63308, Fax 63308
4 miles NE of Carrickmacross on the Crossmaglen Road.
Parkland course.
Founded 1994
Designed by F Ainsworth
18 holes, 6008 yards
† Welcome.
☪ WD €20; WE €30.
⛳ Welcome WD and Sat mornings.
Full clubhouse facilities.
🍽 Catering facilities.

---

12 192 **Milltown**

Lower Churchtown Rd, Milltown, Co Dublin
☎ 00353 1 4976090, Fax 4976008
3 miles S of the city centre via Ranelagh village.
Parkland course.
Pro John Harlet; Founded 1907
Designed by FE Davies
18 holes, 5638 yards, S.S.S. 69
† Welcome except Tues and Sat; with a member on Sun.
☪ €80 WD only; booking required.
⛳ Welcome by prior arrangement; catering packages by prior arrangement; private function room.

🍽 Bar and restaurant facilities.
🛏 Berkeley Court; Jury's; Herbert Park; Montrose.

---

12 193 **Mitchelstown**

Mitchelstown, Co Cork
🖥 www.mitchelstown-golf.com
📧 info@mitchelstown-golf.com
☎ 00353 25 24072
1 mile from Mitchelstown off the N8 Dublin to Cork Road.
Parkland course.
Founded 1908
Designed by David Jones
18 holes, 5773 metres, S.S.S. 71
† Welcome.
☪ WD €25; WE €30.
⛳ Welcome except Sun; catering packages available.
🍽 Full facilities.

---

12 194 **Moate**

Aghanargit, Moate, Co Westmeath
☎ 00353 902 81271, Fax 81267, Sec 36198
On Dublin-Galway Road.
Parkland course.
Pro Paul Power; Founded 1900
Designed by B Browne (1993 extension)
18 holes, 5960 yards, S.S.S. 70
† Practice area.
† Welcome.
☪ WD €20; WE €30 (€12 with member).
⛳ Welcome except after 12.30pm at WE; catering packages available; visitors locker room.
🍽 Full bar and catering facilities.
🛏 Grand.

---

12 195 **Monkstown**   ♛

Parkgariffe, Monkstown, Co Cork
☎ 00353 21 4841376, Sec 841376
11 miles E of Cork; turn right off the Rochestown Road at the Rochestown Inn.
Parkland course.
Pro Matt Murphy; Founded 1908/71
Designed by Peter O'Hare/Tom Carey
18 holes, 5669 yards, S.S.S. 70
† Practice ground.
† Welcome.
☪ Terms on application.
⛳ Welcome by prior arrangement.
🍽 Restaurant and bar facilities available.
🛏 Rochestown Park.

---

12 196 **Moor-Park**

Mooretown, Navan, Co Meath

☎ 00353 46 27661
Parkland course.
Founded 1993
18 holes, 5600 yards, S.S.S. 69
† Welcome.
☪ Terms on application.
🍽 Limited snack bars.

---

12 197 **Mount Juliet**

Thomastown, Co Kilkenny
🖥 www.mountjuliet.com
📧 golfinfo@mountjuliet.ie
☎ 00353 56 777 3064, Fax 3078, Pro 3071
Course is signposted in Thomastown off the main Dublin-Waterford Road.
Parkland course.
Pro Sean Cotter
Founded 1991
Designed by Jack Nicklaus
18 holes, 7264 yards, S.S.S. Blue (Championship) 75, White 73, Green 72, Orange 70, Red 73
† Practice ground with driving bays and 18-hole putting course.
† Welcome by prior arrangement.
☪ WD €140; WE €155.
⛳ Welcome by prior arrangement; minimum 20 people; Mon-Thurs €105; Fri, Sat, Sun €145.
🍽 Full facilities.
🛏 Mount Juliet.

---

12 198 **Mount Temple**

Mount Temple Village, Moate, Co Westmeath
☎ 00353 902 81545, Fax 81957
4 miles off the main N6 Dublin-Galway route in Mount Temple Village.
Combination of links and parkland course.
Founded 1991
Designed by Robert J Brown and Michael Dolan
18 holes, 5872 yards, S.S.S. 71
† Practice range; 3-hole practice area.
† Welcome; by arrangement at WE.
☪ WD €25; WE €32.
⛳ Welcome by prior arrangement; terms on application.
🍽 Catering and wine licence; pub 100 yards.
🛏 Hudson Bay; Prince of Wales; Royal Hoey; Shamrock Lodge; Bloomfield House.

---

12 199 **Mountbellew**

Shankhill, Mountbellew, Co Galway
🖥 www.gui.ie
☎ 00353 905 79259, Fax 79274, Sec 79274

Course is on the T4, 28 miles E of Galway.
Undulating meadowland course.
Founded 1929
18 holes, 5214 metres, S.S.S. 66
ℐ Practice area.
† Welcome.
ℐ Details available upon application.
⚲ Welcome by prior arrangement; terms on application.
🍽 Catering by arrangement; snacks.
🛏 The Malthouse.

12 200 Mountrath
Knockinina, Mountrath, Co Laois
☎ 00353 502 32558, Fax 56735
0.5 miles off the main Dublin-Limerick Road.
Undulating parkland course.
Founded 1929
18 holes, 5643 metres, S.S.S. 70
† Welcome; some WE restrictions.
ℐ WD and WE: €20.
⚲ Welcome WD by prior arrangement; discounts for larger groups; terms on application.
🍽 Full clubhouse facilities available.
🛏 Killeshin; Montague; Leix Co; Grants; Racket Hall.

12 201 Mullingar
Belvedere, Mullingar, Co Westmeath
☎ 00353 44 48366, Pro 41499
3.5 miles from Mullingar on the N52.
Parkland course.
Pro Mr John Burns
Founded 1894
Designed by James Braid
18 holes, 6468 yards, S.S.S. 70
† Welcome.
ℐ WD €32; WE €38.
⚲ Welcome by prior arrangement; packages available; terms on application.
🍽 Full clubhouse facilities.

12 202 Mulranny
Mulranny, Westport, Co Mayo
☎ 00353 98 36262
15 miles from Westport.
Links course.
Founded 1968
9 holes, 6255 yards, S.S.S. 69
† Welcome.
ℐ Terms on application.
⚲ Welcome by prior arrangement.
🍽 Full clubhouse facilities available.
🛏 Many in Westport.

12 203 Muskerry
Carrigrohane, Co Cork

☎ 00353 214 385297, Fax 516860, Pro 381445, Rest/Bar 396104
7 miles W of Cork near Blarney.
Parkland course.
Pro Martin Lehane; Founded 1897
18 holes, 5786 yards, S.S.S. 71
† Welcome WD except Wed afternoons; Thurs mornings and after 3.30pm Fri.
ℐ Terms on application.
⚲ Welcome by prior arrangement.
🍽 Full facilities.

12 204 Naas
Kerdiffstown, Naas, Co Kildare
☎ 00353 458 74644, Fax 96109
Between Johnstown and Sallins.
Parkland course.
Founded 1886
Designed by Arthur Spring
18 holes, 5660 yards, S.S.S. 69
† Welcome Mon, Wed, Fri and Sat.
ℐ WD €27; WE €35.
⚲ Welcome Mon, Wed, Fri and Sat morning.
🍽 Bar; meals by prior arrangement only.
🛏 The Ambassador, Killanahee; Habour View; Red House; Johnstown Inn.

12 205 Narin & Portnoo   ⚈
Portnoo, Co Donegal
✉ narinportnoo@eircom.net
☎ 00353 75 45107, Fax 45107
From Donegal via Ardara.
Links seaside course.
Founded 1930
18 holes, 5396 metres, S.S.S. 69
† Welcome; some summer restrictions.
ℐ WD €25; WE €30.
⚲ Welcome by prior arrangement.
🍽 Snacks and full bar facilities.
🛏 The Lake House Hotel

12 206 Nenagh Golf Club   ⚈
Beechwood, Nenagh, Co Tipperary
🖥 www.nenaghgolfclub.com
✉ nenaghgolfclub@eircom.net
☎ 00353 673 1476, Fax 4308, Pro 3242, Sec 4808
4 miles E of Nenagh.
Parkland course.
Founded 1892
Designed by Alister MacKenzie/ E Hackett/Patrick Merrigan
18 holes, 6009 metres, S.S.S. 72
ℐ Practice range; large practice ground.
† Welcome but by prior arrangement at WE.
ℐ Details available on application.
⚲ Welcome by prior arrangement.

🍽 Full facilities.
🛏 Abbeycourt Hotel, Nenagh.

12 207 New Ross
Tinneranny, New Ross, Co Wexford
☎ 00353 514 21433, Fax 20098
1 mile from town centre off Waterford Road.
Parkland course.
Founded 1905
18 holes, 5751 yards, S.S.S. 70
† Welcome; some Sun restrictions.
ℐ WD €20; WE €30.
⚲ Welcome by arrangement; no group discounts available.
🍽 Clubhouse facilities.

12 208 Newcastle West   ⚈
Ardagh, Co Limerick
✉ ncwgolf@eircom.net
☎ 00353 69 76500, Fax 76511
Off N21 2 miles beyond Rathkeale.
Parkland course.
Pro Tom Murphy
Founded 1939/94
Designed by Arthur Spring
18 holes, 6317 yards, S.S.S. 72
ℐ Driving range.
† Welcome.
ℐ Available on application.
⚲ Welcome with prior arrangement; catering packages by arrangement.
🍽 Bar and restaurant.
🛏 Courtenay Lodge; Rathkeale House; Devon Inn.

12 209 Newlands
Clondalkin, Dublin
☎ 00353 1 4593157, Pro 4593538
6 miles from city centre.
Parkland course.
Founded 1926
Designed by James Braid
18 holes, 5696 yards, S.S.S. 70
† Welcome.
ℐ WD and WE: €55.
⚲ Welcome WD.
🍽 Full facilities.

12 210 North West   ⚈
Lisfannon, Buncrana, Co Donegal
🖥 www.northwestgolfclub.tk
✉ nwgc@tinet.ie
☎ 00353 77 61715, Fax 63284
2 miles S of Buncrana.
Seaside links course.
Pro Seamus McBriarty
Founded 1892
18 holes, 5759 yards, S.S.S. 69
† Welcome.
ℐ Available upon request.

⟳ Welcome by prior arrangement WD and WE in the summer.
📶 Bar and restaurant.
⟲ Gateway Hotel.

---

12 211 Nuremore ℃
Carrickmacross, Co Monaghan
🖧 www.nuremore.com
📧 nuremore@eircom.net
☎ 00353 4296 61438, Fax 61853
1 mile S of Carrickmacross.
Parkland course.
Pro Maurice Cassidy
Founded 1964
Designed by Eddie Hackett
18 holes, 6246 yards, S.S.S. 74
† Welcome.
⌐ WD €35; WE €42.
⟳ Welcome by prior arrangement.
📶 Clubhouse and hotel facilities.
⟲ Nuremore Hotel and Country Club.

---

12 212 Old Conna ℃
Ferndale Road, Bray, Co Dublin
🖧 www.oldconna.com
☎ 00353 1 2826055, Fax 2825611,
Pro 2720022
12 miles from Dublin.
Parkland course.
Founded 1977
Designed by Eddie Hackett
18 holes, 5590 yards, S.S.S. 72
† Welcome but booking advisable.
⌐ €45. Discounts before 9:30am on WD and for those who with members.
📶 Bar and full meal service.
⟲ Royal Hotel; The Killiney Court.

---

12 213 Old Head Golf Links
Kinsale, Co Cork
🖧 www.oldheadgolflinks.com
📧 info@oldheadgolf.ie
☎ 00353 21 778444
20 miles S of Cork. Clifftop setting on Atlantic promontory.
Founded 1996
Designed by J Carr/R Kirby/P Morrigan
18 holes, 7200 yards, S.S.S. 72
ⵊ Driving range, putting and chipping green.
† Welcome.
⌐ WD/WE €250.
⟳ Welcome by prior arrangement; from €230.
📶 Bar and light meals; full restaurant service.

---

12 214 The Open Golf Centre
Newtown House, St Margaret's, Co Dublin
☎ 00353 1 8640324

4 miles from Dublin; adjacent to Dublin Airport.
Parkland course.
Pro Robin Machin; Founded 1993
Designed by Martin Hawtree
27 holes, 6570 yards
ⵊ Practice range 15 bays.
† Welcome.
⌐ WD €16; WE €24.
⟳ Welcome by prior arrangement; from €16.
📶 Full facilities.
⟲ Forte Crest.

---

12 215 Otway
Saltpans, Rathmullan, Co Donegal
☎ 00353 74 58319
15 miles NE of Letterkenny by Lough Swilly.
Links course.
Founded 1893
9 holes, 4234 yards, S.S.S. 60
† Welcome.
⌐ Terms on application.
⟳ Welcome.
⟲ Fort Royal; Rathmullan House; Pier Hotel.

---

12 216 Oughterard ℃
Gortreevagh, Oughterard, Co Galway
☎ 00353 91 82131
1 mile from Oughterard on N59.
Mature parkland course with elevated greens.
Founded 1973
Designed by Hawtree/Hackett
18 holes, 6089 yards, S.S.S. 69
† Welcome.
⌐ Terms on application.
⟳ Welcome WD.
📶 Bar snacks; full à la carte menu.

---

12 217 Parknasilla
Parknasilla, Sneem, Co Kerry
☎ 00353 64 45122
2 miles E of Sneem on the Ring of Kerry Road.
Undulating seaside course.
Pro Miles Watt; Founded 1974
9 holes, 4652 yards, S.S.S. 65
† Welcome.
⌐ Terms on application.

---

12 218 Portarlington ℃
Garryhinch, Portarlington, Co Offaly
🖧 www.portarlingtongolf.com
📧 portarlingtongc@eircom.net
☎ 00353 502 23115
On L116 between Portarlington and Mountmellick.
Parkland course.

Founded 1909
18 holes, 6004 yards, S.S.S. 71
† Welcome.
⌐ WD €20; WE €25.
⟳ Welcome; from WD€ 20; WE €27.
📶 Bar and restaurant facilities.
⟲ East End Hotel.

---

12 219 Portmarnock ℃
Portmarnock, Co Dublin
🖧 www.portmarnockgolfclub.ie
📧 secretary@portmarnockgolfclub.ie
☎ 00353 1 8462968, Pro 8462634, Rest/Bar 8461400 and 8462794
From Dublin along the coast road to Baldoyle and on to Portmarnock.
Seaside links course.
Pro Joey Purcell; Founded 1894
Designed by WC Pickeman and George Ross
27 holes, 6497 yards, S.S.S. 75
† Welcome.
⌐ WD €130; WE €160.
⟳ Welcome Mon, Tues, Thu and Fri by prior arrangement.
📶 Full facilities.
⟲ The Portmarnock Hote; The Grand Hotel.

---

12 220 Portmarnock Hotel & Golf Links
Strand Road, Portmarnock, Co Dublin
☎ 00353 1 846 0611, Fax 846 1077
On road out of Portmarnock, on right just before coast road to Malahide.
Seaside links.
Pro Paul Cuddy; Founded 1995
Designed by Bernhard Langer
18 holes, 6500 yards, S.S.S. 71
† Welcome.
⌐ Apr-Oct €100; Nov-Mar €60 WD, €85 WE; residents €80 summer; €52 winter.
⟳ Accommodation and golf packages available.
📶 Bar and restaurant.
⟲ Hotel on site.

---

12 221 Portsalon ℃
Portsalon, Fanad, Co Donegal
📧 portsalongoldclub@eircom.net
☎ 00 353 74 91 59459, Fax 59919
Course is 20 miles north of Letterkenny.
Links course.
Founded 1891
Designed by Pat Ruddy
18 holes, 6185 metres, S.S.S. 72
† Welcome by prior arrangement.
⌐ WD €35; WE/BH €40.
⟳ Welcome by prior arrangement.
📶 Full facilities.

Royal Dublin

Pretty, it is not; but a great, testing challenge. Royal Dublin, home of Christy O'Connor snr – "Himself", as he is known – is the classic links, straight out and back, built on a sandbank, now called Bull Island, which emerged after Captain William Bligh, the unfortunate captain of the *Bounty*, built a sea wall to provide shipping with a safe approach to the Port of Dublin in the early 1800s. And from this wind-whipped scrubland, they carved the course and moved in the club in 1889. Access to the course is over a charming wooden bridge, which immediately gives a sense of excitement and drama. For some it will be the gates of hell. It was for the troops who used it as a firing range in training during the First World War. The club were compensated to the tune of £10,000 for the destruction of the course, which enabled them to bring in HS Colt to redesign it. He raised many tees to give wonderful views of Dublin Bay and put in a drainage system which has become part of the hazards

Lulled by the simplicity of the first hole, the difficulties that lie ahead become apparent from the second. A 445-metre (this is Ireland, remember; about 495 yards) par-five from the back tee (430m from the more sensible white tees; and a tough par-four from the yellow), you need a really solid drive to make the fairway; and the wind, which is usually at your back may not be of great help. It is a horribly narrow sward, and two bunkers lurk on either side ready to swallow a good drive. The rough is that typical links-type mongrel grass, toughened by salinity and exposure which hides the ball well and is difficult to escape from. And you really need to be on the green – which is well guarded – with your third, for that will save you having to haul your bag all the way back to the third tee.

And that sets the tone for the outward nine: perhaps more of a psychological test, staring across that rugged rough, and keeping disciplined to avoid forcing the shot. For many, the three-iron may be the most sensible stick in the bag off the tee.

But, having said that, you will need a cracking drives of over 200 yards on the third; and on the fifth to a ribbon of a fairway where the right is out of bounds; the seventh and the eighth, where bunkers – usually with a hare nestling out of the wind – adorn the landing area.

If anything, the fairways seem to open up coming home; but remember, the wind usually will be coming at you; though it has been known to shift the other way, and on the day I was there, it came across the course. But homeward, it is 500 yards longer. And the drainage seems to play a greater part; on the 10th, it crosses the fairway 50m from the green, give the average amateur pause for thought: just how brave are you? For length, the 493m (539yd) 11th is a case in point. Getting to the green is hard enough, but given that the green itself is a massive 67m, on two levels; club selection for the approach can be an art, depending on the pin position.

And then there is the 18th; their famous dog-leg right: Actually, it's a 90-degree corner: the challenge, under the gaze of the gallery on the club-house balcony is whether to cut the corner, over "the garden". Derision awaits, either way.

But once in, there is a magnificent club-house in which to relax; with dining rooms and bars, and plenty of memorabilia. – **Mark Salter**

The Royal Dublin course will be undergoing extensive reconstruction over the winter of 2004 and some holes will be out of commission.

Portsalon Golf Hotel; Fort Royal; Rathmullan House.

12 222 **Portumna**
Ennis Rd, Portumna, Co Galway
✉ jfhines@eircom.net
☎ 00353 509 41059, Fax 41798, Pro 941051
1.5 miles from Portumna on Ennis Rd.
Parkland course.
Pro Richard Clarke; Founded 1913
Designed by Eddie Carrington
18 (extra 2 in development) holes, 5474 yards, S.S.S. 71
⚐ Practice area.
† Welcome.
⌇ €25.
⌔ Welcome by prior arrangement with Sec; special packages available; terms on application.
⦿ Restaurant and bar.
↩ Shannon Oaks.

12 223 **Powerscourt** ⟨⟨
Powerscourt Estate, Enniskerry, Co Wicklow
✉ golfclub@powerscourt.ie
☎ 003531 204 6033, Fax 276 1303, Rest/Bar 204 6042
12 miles south of Dublin just off N11 in Enniskerry.
Parkland course.
Pro Paul Tompson
Designed by Peter Macevoy (East)/ David McLay Kidd (West)
36 holes. East: 7063 yards, S.S.S. 72; West: 6941 yards, S.S.S. 72
† Welcome.
⌇ €110.
⌔ Welcome by arrangement.
⦿ Full bar and restaurant facilities.
↩ Five self-contained apartments.

12 224 **Raffeen Creek**
Ringaskiddy, Co Cork
☎ 00353 21 378430
1 mile from Ringaskiddy ferry.
Seaside/parkland course with water.
Founded 1988
Designed by Eddie Hackett
9 holes, 5098 yards, S.S.S. 68
† Welcome WD; WE afternoon only.
⌇ Terms on application; concs. apply.
⌔ Welcome by arrangement.
⦿ Bar food.

12 225 **Rathdowney**
Rathdowney, Portlaoise, Co Laois
☎ 00353 505 46170, Fax 46065
Off the N7 in Rathdowney.
Parkland course.

Founded 1930
Designed by Eddie Hackett
18 holes, 5894 yards, S.S.S. 71
† Welcome; some Sun restrictions.
⌇ WD €20; WE €25.
⌔ Welcome by prior arrangement with the secretary; bar and catering packages by prior arrangement; from €20.
⦿ Clubhouse facilities.
↩ Leix Co; Woodview GH.

12 226 **Rathfarnham**
Newtown, Rathfarnham
☎ 00353 1 4931201, Fax 4931561
Course is two miles from Rathfarnham.
Parkland course.
Pro Brian O'Hara
Founded 1899
Designed by John Jacobs
9 holes, 5833 yards, S.S.S. 70
† Welcome WD except Tues and WE.
⌇ WD and WE: €30.
⌔ Welcome by prior arrangement.
⦿ Lunch and dinners by prior arrangement.
↩ Free Rock.

12 227 **Rathsallagh Golf and** ⟨⟨ **County Club**
Dunlavin, Co Wicklow
✉ info@rathsallagh.com
☎ 00353 45 403316, Fax 403295, Pro 403316
Course is 32 miles SW of Dublin.
Parkland course.
Pro Brendan McDaid
Founded 1994
Designed by Peter McEvoy and Christy O'Connor Jnr
18 holes, 6160 yards, S.S.S. 71
⚐ Driving range.
† Welcome.
⌇ Jan-March: Mon-Thurs €40; Fri-Sun €50; April-Oct: Mon-Thurs €60; Fri-Sun €75.
⌔ Welcome by arrangement.
⦿ Full function room, bar and restaurant, full catering facilities.
↩ Rathsallagh Country House.

12 228 **Redcastle**
Redcastle, Moville, Co Donegal
☎ 00353 77 82073
Parkland course.
Founded 1983
9 holes, 6152 yards, S.S.S. 70
† Welcome.
⌇ WD €20; WE €26.
⌔ Welcome, but booking essential.
⦿ Full bar and restaurant.

12 229 **Ring of Kerry Golf and County Club**
Templenoe, Kenmare, Co Kerry
🖳 www.ringofkerrygolf.com
✉ reservations@ringofkerrygolf.com
☎ 00353 64 42000, Fax 42533
Take N70 Ring of Kerry road out of Kenmare. Club is less than 4 miles on right-hand side.
Parkland course.
Pro Adrian Whitehead; Founded 1998
Designed by Eddie Hackett
18 holes, 6869 yards, S.S.S. 73
⚐ Driving range; practice green.
† Welcome.
⌇ 18 holes: WD/WE €80, 36 holes: WD/WE €120.
⌔ Welcome; WD €50, WE €55.
⦿ Restaurant (a la carte) serving breakfast, luch, dinner; bar.
↩ Kenmare has many B&Bs, Guesthouses and 3 and 5 star hotels

12 230 **Rockwell**
Rockwell College, Cashel, Co Tipperary
☎ 00353 62 61444
Parkland course.
Founded 1964
9 holes, 3782 yards, S.S.S. 60
† Welcome by arrangement.
⌇ Terms on application.
⌔ Terms on application.
⦿ Limited facilities.

12 231 **Rosapenna** ⟨⟨
Rosapenna Hotel, Downings, Co Donegal
🖳 www.rosapenna.ie
☎ 00353 74 55301, Fax 55128
25 miles from Letterkenny.
Links course.
Pro Don Patterson; Founded 1893
Designed by Tom Morris (1893); redesigned by Braid & Vardon
18 holes, 6271 yards, S.S.S. 71
† Welcome.
⌇ WD €40; WE €45.
⌔ Welcome, but must have handicap certificates.
⦿ Full hotel bar and restaurant facilities.
↩ Rosapenna Hotel (4-star) on site.

12 232 **Roscommon**
Mote Park, Roscommon, Co Roscommon
☎ 00353 903 26382
Course is 0.25 miles from Roscommon Town.
Parkland course.
Founded 1904/1996

Designed by Eddie Connaughton
18 holes, 6040 yards, S.S.S. 70
† Welcome except Tuesdays and
Sundays.
�する ⟋ Dec-Feb: €15; March-Nov: €25.
⟋ Welcome by prior arrangement;
catering by arrangement.
🍽 Full bar and restaurant facilities
available.
⟋ Abbey; Royal; Regans; Gleesons.

12 233 **Roscrea**
Derryvale, Roscrea, Co Tipperary
☎ 00353 505 21130, Fax 23410
2 miles E of Roscrea on N7.
Parkland course.
Founded 1892
Designed by A. Spring
18 holes, 5708 yards, S.S.S. 70
† Welcome.
⟋ WD €20; WE €25.
⟋ Welcome by prior arrangement;
group discounts available.
🍽 Bar and restaurant facilities.
⟋ Rackett Hall Hotel; Grants Hotel.

12 234 **Ross**   ☎
Ross Rd, Killarney, Kerry
🖧 www.rossgolfclub.com
☎ 00353 64 31125, Fax 31860
0.5 miles from Killarney.
Parkland course with water features.
Pro Alan O'Mara
Founded 1995
Designed by Roger Jones
9 holes, 3300 yards, S.S.S. 72
† Welcome.
⟋ Terms on application.
⟋ Welcome.
🍽 Full clubhouse facilities with
spectacular views.
⟋ The Gleneagle.

12 235 **Rosslare**
Rosslare Strand, Co Wexford
🖧 www.rosslaregolf.com
✉ office@rosslaregolf.com
☎ 00353 53 32203, Fax 32263, Pro
32032, Sec 32203, Rest/Bar 32113
6 miles from the Rosslare ferry
terminal and 10 miles South of
Wexford.
Seaside links course.
Pro Johnny Young; Founded
1905/1992
Designed by Hawtree & Taylor (Old);
Christy O'Connor Jnr (New)
18 for old and 12 for the new holes,
6577 yards, S.S.S. 72
⟋ Driving range.
† Welcome.
⟋ WD €35; WE €50.

⟋ Welcome by prior arrangement;
catering packages by arrangement.
🍽 Full clubhouse facilities.
⟋ Kelly's Resort; Crosbie Cedars.

12 236 **Rossmore**
Rossmore Park, Cootehill Road,
Monaghan, Co Monaghan
✉ mcnicgolf@hotmail.com
☎ 0035 347 71222, Sec 81316
1.5 miles on the Cootehill Road out of
Monaghan town.
Parkland course.
Pro Gareth McShea; Founded 1916
Designed by Des Smyth
18 holes, 6200 yards, S.S.S. 68
† Welcome.
⟋ WD €25; WE €35.
⟋ Welcome; from €25 but discounts
are available for larger groups.
🍽 Full bar and restaurant facilities.
⟋ Four Seasons.

12 237 **Royal Dublin**
North Bull Island, Dollymount, Dublin 3
🖧 www.theroyaldublingolfclub.com
✉ mkennedy@theroyaldublingolfclub
.com
☎ 00353 1 8336346, Fax 8336504,
Pro 8336477, Sec 833 6346, Rest/Bar
8333370 and 8337153
NE from Dublin along the Coast Road
to Bull Wall across the wooden bridge.
Links course.
Pro Leonard Owens; Founded 1885
Designed by HS Colt
18 holes, 6900 yards, S.S.S. 73
† Welcome except Wed and Sat
before 4pm.
⟋ €120 all week.
⟋ Welcome but must book a year in
advance; catering by prior
arrangement.
🍽 Full clubhouse facilities, bar and
restaurant.
⟋ Marine; Hollybrook; Howth Lodge.

12 238 **Royal Tara**
Bellinter, Navan, Co Meath
🖧 www.royaltaragolfclub.com
✉ info@royaltaragolfclub.com
☎ 00353 469 025508, Fax 026684,
Pro 026009
Off N3 30 miles N of Dublin.
Parkland course.
Pro Adam Whiston; Founded 1906
Designed by Des Smyth Golf Design
27 holes, 6400 yards, S.S.S. 71
† Welcome by arrangement.
⟋ WD €35; WE €45.
⟋ Welcome Mon, Thurs, Fri and Sat
by arrangement.

🍽 Full bar and catering facilities.
⟋ "The Adrboyne, New Grange.

12 239 **Rush**
Rush, Co Dublin
✉ info@rushgolfclub.com
☎ 00353 1 8437548, Fax 8438177,
Sec 8148177
Off the Dublin-Belfast Road at Blakes
Cross.
Links course.
Founded 1943
9 holes, 5598 yards, S.S.S. 69
† Welcome WD only.
⟋ €32.
⟋ Welcome by prior arrangement.
🍽 Full facilities.

12 240 **St Annes**   ☎
North Bull Island, Dollymount
🖧 www.stanneslinksgolf.com
✉ info@stanneslinksgolf.com
☎ 00353 1 8336471, Fax 8334618,
Pro 8336471, Sec 833 6471
5 miles N of Dublin City.
Links course.
Pro Paddy Skerritt; Founded 1921
Designed by Eddie Hackett
18 holes, 5669 metres, S.S.S. 69
⟋ Practice area.
† Welcome, except Sun.
⟋ WD €45; WE €60.
⟋ Welcome; group rates available.
🍽 Full facilities.
⟋ Marine; St Lawrence; Forte
Posthouse; Grand; Sutton Castle.

12 241 **St Helen's Bay**   ☎
St Helen's, Kilrane, Rosslare Harbour,
Co Wexford
🖧 www.sthelensbay.com
✉ sthelens@iol.ie
☎ 00353 53 33234, Fax 33803
5 minutes from the Rosslare ferry-port
in the village of Kilrane.
Links/parkland course mixture.
Pro Liam Bowler; Founded 1993
Designed by Philip Walton
18 holes, 6091 yards, S.S.S. 72 + new
9 holes.
⟋ Driving range and teaching
academy.
† Welcome.
⟋ Terms on application.
⟋ Welcome by prior arrangement;
packages available; tennis;
accommodation on site; terms on
application.
🍽 Full clubhouse, dining and bar
facilities.
⟋ On-site cottage accommodation;
Great Southern; Rosslare; Ferrycarrig.

12 242 St Margaret's Golf & ☎ Country Club
St Margaret's, Co Dublin
🔗 www.stmargaretsgolf.com
✉ reservations@stmargaretsgolf.com
☎ 00353 186 40400, Fax 40289
4 miles W of Dublin Airport.
Parkland course.
Pro David O'Sullivan; Founded 1992
Designed by Ruddy & Craddock
18 holes, 6917 yards, S.S.S. 73
† Welcome.
⌐ April-Oct: Mon-Wed €60; Thurs
and Sun €70; Fri-Sat €75; Nov-March:
Mon-Wed €45; Thurs and Sun €55;
Sat €65.
⌐ Welcome by prior arrangement;
corporate days available.
🍴 2 bars and 1 restaurant.
🛏 Carnegie Court Hotel, Swords;
Ashbourne House, Swords; Holiday
Inn; Great Southern Hotel.

12 243 St Patricks
Hotel Carrigart, Carrigart, Donegal
🔗 www.carrigarthotel.com
☎ 00353 74 551141, Fax 55250
Seaside links course.
Founded 1996
Designed by E Hackett & Joanne
O'Herne
36 holes, 7046 yards, S.S.S. 72
† Welcome.
⌐ Welcome by prior arrangement,
short notice is fine.
🛏 Carrigart (full facilities with views
across Sheephaven Bay).

12 244 Seapoint ☎
Termonfeckin, Co Louth
🔗 www.seapointgolfclub.com
✉ golflinks@seapoint.ie
☎ 00353 4198 22333, Fax 22331,
Rest/Bar 98810
In Termonfeckin off the N1 Dublin to
Drogheda Road.
Championship links course.
Pro David Carroll; Founded 1993
Designed by Des Smyth; Declan
Branigan
18 holes, 7100 yards, S.S.S. 74
⌐ Driving range with a large practice
ground.
† Welcome.
⌐ Mon-Thurs €40; Fri €50; WE: €60.
⌐ Welcome WD by arrangement;
discounts for larger groups.
🍴 Bar and restaurant facilities.
🛏 Boyne Valley; Neptune Hotel.

12 245 Shannon ☎
Shannon Airport, Co Clare

☎ 00353 61 471849, Fax 471507
0.5 miles from Shannon Airport.
Woodland/parkland course.
Founded 1966
18 holes, 6186 yards, S.S.S. 72
† Welcome; WE booking advisable.
⌐ WD €35; WE €45.
⌐ Welcome by prior arrangement.
🍴 Bar snacks and meals.

12 246 Skerries
Hacketstown, Skerries, Co Dublin
🔗 www.skerriesgolfclubf.ie
✉ skerriesgolfclub@eircom.net
☎ 003531 849 1567, Fax 1591, Pro
0925, Rest/Bar 3135/1204
N of Dublin Airport off the Belfast
Road.
Parkland course.
Pro Jimmy Kinsella; Founded 1905
18 holes, 6081 yards, S.S.S. 72
† Welcome.
⌐ WD €50; WE €60.
⌐ Welcome on Mon and Thurs by
prior arrangement; terms on
application.
🍴 Full facilities.
🛏 Trusthouse Forte; Dublin Airport.

12 247 Skibbereen & West ☎
Licknavar, Skibbereen, Co Cork
🔗 www.skibbgolf.com
✉ bookings@skibbgolf.com
☎ 00353 28 21227, Fax 22994
2 miles from Skibbereen on the
Baltimore Road.
Parkland course.
Founded 1905
Designed by Eddie Hackett
18 holes, 6069 yards, S.S.S. 68
† Welcome.
⌐ Terms on application.
⌐ Welcome by prior arrangement.
🍴 Full clubhouse facilities.
🛏 West Cork; Eldon; Casey's;
Baltimore Harbour; Celtic Ross.

12 248 Slade Valley ☎
Lynch Park, Brittas, Co Dublin
✉ sladevalleygc@eircom.net
☎ 00353 1 4582183, Fax 4582784
8 miles W of Dublin off M7.
Undulating parkland course.
Founded 1970
Designed by WD Sullivan and
D O'Brien
18 holes, 5337 yards, S.S.S. 68
† Welcome WD; WE with a member.
⌐ WD €25; WE €40.
⌐ Welcome by prior arrangement
with Sec.
🍴 Full WE facilities.

🛏 Green Isle; Downshire House; City
West.

**12 249 Slieve Russell Hotel ☎
Golf & Country Club**
Ballyconnell, Co Cavan
🔗 www.quinn-hotels.com
✉ slieve-golf-club@quinn-hotels.com
☎ 00353 49 26444, Fax 26474,
Pro 25090
90 miles NW of Belfast.
Parkland course.
Pro Liam McCool; Founded 1992
Designed by Paddy Merrigan
18 holes, 6413 yards, S.S.S. 74
⌐ Floodlit 5 bays + practice green &
bunkers.
† Welcome; book in advance.
⌐ Terms on application.
⌐ Welcome by prior arrangement.
🍴 Full facilities.
🛏 159 bedrooms.

12 250 Spanish Point
Spanish Point, Miltown Malbay, Co Clare
☎ 00353 6570 84198
2 miles from Milton Malbay; 8 miles
from Lahinch.
Seaside course.
Founded 1896
9 holes, 3574 yards, S.S.S. 58
† Welcome.
⌐ Terms on application.
⌐ Welcome; booking is strongly
recommended.
🍴 Light snacks only.

12 251 Stackstown ☎
Kellystown Road, Rathfarnham, Dublin
16
✉ stackstowngc@eircom.net
☎ 00353 1 4941993, Fax 4933934,
Pro 4944561
Take exit 13 off the M50 follow the
road to Leopardstown and Ticknock
about 1 mile.
Set in the foothills of Dublin mountains
with panoramic views.
Founded 1976
Designed by Pat Ruddy
18 holes, 6171 yards, S.S.S. 71
† Welcome WD; WE by prior
arrangement.
⌐ WD €35; WE €45.
⌐ Welcome – 10-15% reduction.
🍴 Full bar and restaurant.

12 252 Strandhill
Strandhill, Co Sligo
☎ 00353 71 68188, Fax 68811
5 miles W of Sligo.

Links course.
Founded 1932
18 holes, 5516 yards, S.S.S. 68
† Welcome; booking is recommended.
Ɩ WD €35; WE €45.
⌁ Welcome by prior arrangement; from €35.
⦿ Full facilities.
⟿ Ocean View; Tower.

12 253 Sutton
Cush Point, Sutton, Dublin 13
⊞ www.suttongolfclub.org
▤ suttongc@indigo.ie
☎ 00353 1 8322965, Fax 8321603, Pro 8321703
7 miles NE of city centre.
Seaside links course.
Pro Nicky Lynch
Founded 1890
9 holes, 5226 yards, S.S.S. 67
† Welcome; restrictions Tues and Sat.
Ɩ WD €35; WE €45.
⌁ Welcome by prior arrangement.
⦿ Full restaurant. Conference facilities.
⟿ The Marine.

12 254 Swinford
Brabazon Park, Swinford, Co Mayo
▤ regantommy@eircom.net
☎ 00353 94 9251378 (also Fax)
1 km S of Swinford on the Kiltimagh Road.
Parkland course.
Founded 1922
9 holes, 5542 yards, S.S.S. 70
† Welcome.
Ɩ €15 per day.
⌁ Prices on application.
⦿ Full catering; lounge bar.
⟿ Cill Aodain; Breaffy; Welcome Inn.

12 255 Swords
Balheary Ave, Swords, Dublin
⊞ www.swordsopengolfcourse.com
▤ swordsgc@indigo.ie
☎ 00353 1 8409819/8901030, Fax 8409819
5 mins from Swords centre.
Parkland course.
Designed by Tommy Halpin.
18 holes, 5631 metres, S.S.S. 69
† Welcome.
Ɩ WD €15; WE €22 ; pay and play.
⌁ Welcome.
⦿ Snack bar.

12 256 Tara Glen
Ballymoney, Courtown, Co Wexford
☎ 00353 55 25413
Parkland course.
Founded 1993
9 holes, 6332 yards
† Welcome by prior arrangement.
Ɩ £20.
⌁ Welcome by prior arrangement.
⦿ Bar.

12 257 Templemore
Manna South, Templemore, Co Tipperary
☎ 00353 504 31400/329230.5 miles S of town centre off the N62.
Parkland course.
Founded 1972
9 holes, S.S.S. 70
⏳ Tennis courts (2), all weather/floodlit.
† Welcome.
Ɩ WD €12; WE €16.
⌁ Welcome. Catering can be arranged; terms on application.
⦿ Limited but available by prior arrangement.
⟿ Templemore Arms; Grants; Anner; Hayes; Munster.

12 258 Thurles ☎
Turtulla, Thurles, Co Tipperary
📧 thurlesgolfclub@eircom.net
☎ 00353 504 24599, Fax 24647,
Pro, 21983, Rest/Bar 21983
1 mile from Thurles towards the main
Cork-Dublin road.
Parkland course.
Pro Sean Hunt; Founded 1944
Designed by J McAllister
18 holes, 6465 yards, S.S.S. 71
⚐ Practice range 200 yards from
club.
† Welcome except Sun; Tues Ladies
Day.
⌁ €35.
⚐ Welcome except Sun & Tues. from
€25-€35.
🍴 Full facilities.
🛏 Anner; Hayes, Munster Hotel.

12 259 Tipperary
Rathanny, Tipperary
📧 tipperarygolfclub@eircom.net
☎ 00353 62 51119, Fax 52132
1 mile from the town on the Glen of
Aherlow Road.
Parkland course.
Founded 1896
18 holes, 6300 yards, S.S.S. 71
⚐ Driving range adjacent.
† Welcome; some Sun restrictions
apply.
⌁ WD €20; WE €25.
⚐ Welcome by prior arrangement.
🍴 Bar and full restaurant facilities.
🛏 Royal, Tipperary; Aherlow House
Hotel; Glen Hotel.

12 260 Townley Hall
Townley Hall, Tullyallen, Drogheda,
Co Louth
☎ 00353 4198 42229
Parkland course.
Founded 1994
18 holes, 4978 yards
† Welcome.
⌁ Details available upon application.

12 261 Tralee Golf Links
West Barrow, Ardfert, Co Kerry
🌐 www.traleegolfclub.com
📧 info@traleegolfclub.com
☎ 00353 6671 36379, Fax 36008
8 miles West from Tralee on the
Churchill Road.
Links course.
Pro David Power; Founded 1896/1984
Designed by Arnold Palmer Design
18 holes, 6192 metres, S.S.S. 73
⚐ Driving range.
† Welcome.

⌁ WD/WE €130.
⚐ Welcome by prior arrangement;
discounts available for larger groups.
🍴 Full restaurant, bar and clubhouse
facilities.
🛏 Mount Brandon; Grand;
Abbeygate.

12 262 Tramore
Newtown Hill, Tramore, Co Waterford
🌐 www.tramoregolfclub.com
📧 tragolf@iol.ie
☎ 00353 51 386170, Fax 390961,
Rest/Bar 381247/386583
Course is 7 miles S of Waterford on
coast road.
Parkland course.
Founded 1894
Designed by Tibbett (1936/37)
18 holes, 6055 yards, S.S.S. 72
⚐ Local one.
† Welcome; prior booking is
advisable.
⌁ Mon-Thur €40; Fri, Sat €55 (high
season; €35/€34 (mid-season – Apr-
Oct); €30/€35 (off season – Nov-Mar).
⚐ Welcome by prior arrangement.
🍴 Catering and bar facilities.
🛏 Grand; Majestic; O'Sheas.

12 263 Tuam ☎
Barnacurragh, Tuam, Co Galway
📧 tuamgolfclub@eircom.net
☎ 00353 93 28993, Fax 26003,
Pro 24091
1 mile outside Tuam on the Athenry
Road.
Parkland course.
Pro Larry Smyth; Founded 1904
Designed by Eddie Hackett
18 holes, 6045 yards, S.S.S. 71
⚐ Practice range.
† Welcome.
⌁ WD/WE €25.
⚐ Welcome by prior arrangement
except on Sat afternoon and Sun;
discounts for groups of more than 20;
deposit of €100 required; catering by
arrangement.
🍴 Full clubhouse bar and restaurant
facilities.

12 264 Tubbercurry
Ougham, Tubbercurry, Co Sligo
🌐 wwwtubbercurrygolfclub.com
📧 contact@tubbercurrygolfclub.com
☎ 00353 71 85849
0.5 miles from town on the Ballymote
Road.
Parkland course.
Founded 1991
Designed by Eddie Hackett

9 holes, 6079 yards, S.S.S. 69
⚐ Practice green and nets.
† Welcome; Sun by arrangement.
⌁ Details on application.
⚐ Welcome except Sun; discounts
available; catering by arrangement;
from €15.
🍴 Full bar and restaurant facilities.
🛏 Crawleys.

12 265 Tulfarris Hotel & ☎
Country Club
Blessington, Co Wicklow
☎ 00353 45 64612
6 miles from Blessington off N81.
Parkland course.
Founded 1989
Designed by Eddie Hackett
9 holes, 5612 yards, S.S.S. 69
† Welcome; some Sun restrictions.
⌁ Terms on application.
⚐ Welcome by prior arrangement;
terms on application.
🍴 Restaurant and bar facilities.

12 266 Tullamore ☎
Brookfield, Tullamore, Co Offaly
🌐 www.tullamoregolfclub.ie
📧 tullamoregolfclub@eircom.net
☎ 00353 506 21439, Fax 41806,
Pro 51757
3.5 miles S of Tullamore off the R451
to Kinnity from the N52.
Parkland course.
Pro Donah McArdle; Founded 1886
Designed by James Braid
18 holes, 6434 yards, S.S.S. 70
† Welcome but prior booking is
advisable.
⌁ WD €37; WE €48.
⚐ Welcome by prior arrangement;
terms on application.
🍴 Full bar and restaurant facilities.

12 267 Turvey Golf & CC ☎
Turvey Ave, Donabate, Dublin
🌐 www.turveygolfclub.com
📧 info@turveygolfclub.com
☎ 00353 1 8435179, Fax 8435179
Parkland course.
Designed by P McQuirk
18 holes, 6400 yards, S.S.S. 72
† Welcome.
⌁ WD €25; WE €31.
🍴 Snack bar.
🛏 12 room hotel.

12 268 Virginia
Virginia, Co Cavan
🌐 www.bichotels.com
☎ 00353 49 8548066

50 miles N of Dublin on the main
Dublin-Cavan Road.
Meadowland course.
Founded 1946
9 holes, 4139 metres yards, S.S.S. 62
- † Welcome.
- WD and WE: €15.
- Welcome by prior arrangement.
- Hotel on site.
- Park Hotel.

12 269 Water Rock
Midleton, Cork
☎ 00353 21 613499, Fax 633150
5 mins from Midleton.
Parkland course.
18 holes, 6223 yards, S.S.S. 70
- † Welcome.
- Terms on application.
- Clubhouse facilities.

12 270 Waterford ₢
Newrath, Waterford, Co Waterford
☎ 00353 51 876748, Fax 853405,
Pro 856568
On N9 from Dublin 1 mile from
Waterford or N25 from Rosslare.
Parkland course.
Founded 1912
Designed by Cecil Barcroft and Willie
Park
18 holes, 5722 yards, S.S.S. 70
- † Welcome.
- Terms on application.
- Welcome by arrangement with
secretary/manager; terms on application.
- Full clubhouse facilities available.
- Jury's; Tower; Granville; Bridge.

12 271 Waterford Castle Golf ₢
& Country Club
The Island, Ballinakill, Co Waterford
☎ 00353 518 71633, Fax 71634
2 miles from Waterford on the
Dunmore East Road.
Parkland course on island in River Suir.
Founded 1992
Designed by Des Smyth and Declan
Brannigan
18 holes, 6814 yards, S.S.S. 73
- Driving range – €2/bucket of balls
- † Welcome by arrangement.
- Low season: WD €35; WE €41;
high season: WD €41; WE€50.
- Welcome by arrangement.
- Clubhouse facilities.
- 00353 578 78203.

12 272 Waterville Golf Links
Ring of Kerry, Waterville, Co Kerry
- www.watervillegolflinks.ie

wvgolf@iol.ie
☎ 00353 66 74102
1 mile W of Waterville half-way through
the Ring of Kerry.
Links course.
Pro Liam Higgins; Founded 1889/1972
Designed by E Hackett
18 holes, 7484 yards, S.S.S. 74
- Practice range open to green fee
paying players and members.
- † Welcome.
- On request.
- Welcome by prior arrangement;
discount 10% for 20 or more players;
from €110.
- Full clubhouse facilities.
- Waterville House; Butler Arms; Bay
View.

12 273 West Waterford ₢
Coolcormack, Dungarvan, Co Waterford
- www.westwaterfordgolf.com
- info@westwaterfordgolf.com
☎ 00353 58 43216/41475, Fax
44343, Sec 41475, Rest/Bar 48875
3 miles W of Dungarvan off the N25 on
the Aglish Road.
Parkland course.
Founded 1993
Designed by Eddie Hackett
18 holes, 6712 yards, S.S.S. 72
- † Welcome.
- WD €30; WE €40.
- Welcome everyday by prior
arrangement.
- Full clubhouse facilities available
everyday.
- Lawlors; Park; Clonea Strand.

12 274 Westmanstown
Clonsilla, Dublin 15
☎ 00353 1 8205817, Fax 8205858,
Sec 0862446296
Course is off the Dublin Road in Lucan
village 1.25 miles following the signs
for Clonsilla.
Parkland course.
Founded 1988
Designed by Eddie Hackett
18 holes, 5826 yards off the blue, 5613
yards off the white, 4900 yards for
ladies, S.S.S. 70
- † Welcome but booking is essential
at WE. Cheaper with a member €15.
- WD €35; WE €40.
- Welcome by prior arrangement.
- Full clubhouse facilities available.
- The Spa Hotel; Westcounty; Travel
Lodge.

12 275 Westport ₢
Carrowholly, Westport, Co Mayo

www.golfwestport.com
wpgolf@eircom.net
☎ 00353 982 7070, Fax 7217, Pro
8262
2 miles from Westport.
Parkland course.
Pro Alex Mealia
Founded 1908
Designed by Hawtree & Son
18 holes, 6959 yards, S.S.S. 73
- † Welcome.
- Terms on application.
- Welcome by prior arrangement;
special packages available; terms on
application.
- Lounge bar and dining facilities
available.

12 276 Wexford
Mulgannon, Wexford
☎ 00353 53 42238, Pro 46300,
Sec 44611
In Wexford town.
Parkland course.
Founded 1960
Designed by J. Hamilton Stutt & Co
(original); Des Smyth (new)
18 holes, 5578 yards, S.S.S. 70
- † Welcome; restrictions Wed
evening and Thurs.
- WD €26; WE €32.
- Welcome by prior arrangement;
discounts for larger groups; terms on
application.
- Bar and snacks.

12 277 Wicklow ₢
Dunbur Rd, Wicklow, Co Wicklow
☎ 00353 404 67379, Pro 66122
On L29 32 miles from Dublin.
Seaside course.
Founded 1904
18 holes, 5695 yards, S.S.S. 70
- † Welcome but booking for WE is
strongly advisable.
- WD and WE: €35.
- Welcome by prior arrangement.
- Full clubhouse facilities.

12 278 Woodbrook ₢
Dublin Rd, Bray, Co Wicklow
- www.woodbrook.ie
- golf@woodbrook.ie
☎ 00353 1 2824799, Fax 2821950
Course is 11 miles south of Dublin on
the N11.
Parkland course.
Pro William Kinsella; Founded 1926
18 holes, 5996 yards, S.S.S. 71
- Practice area.
- † Welcome by arrangement; booking
essential for WE.

⌶ Oct-March: €55; April-Sept: WD €85, WE and BH €95.
⌔ Welcome Mon, Thurs and Fri by prior arrangement.
🍽 Full clubhouse facilities.
🛏 The Royal Hotel; The Glen View.

12 279 **Woodenbridge**

Woodenbridge Golf Club, Vale of Avoca, Arklow, Co Wicklow
🖱 www.woodenbridgegolfclub.com
📧 wgc@eircom.net
☎ 00353 402 35202, Fax 35754
45 miles S of Dublin on N11 to Arklow.
Parkland course.
Founded 1884
Designed by Patrick Merrigan
18 holes, 6400 yards, S.S.S. 70
⌶ Practice ground.
✝ Welcome except Thursdays and Saturdays.
⌶ WD €51; WE/BH €63.
⌔ Welcome WD by prior arrangement.
🍽 Full clubhouse facilities.

12 280 **Woodlands**

Coill Dubh, Naas, Co Kildare
☎ 00353 45 860777
On outskirts of Naas.
Parkland course.
Founded 1985
18 holes, 5202 yards, S.S.S. 71
✝ Welcome but booking is normally needed for weekends.
⌶ WD €16; WE €20.
⌔ Welcome with prior arrangement.
🍽 Bar food available and catering on request.

12 281 **Woodstock** ♆

Woodstock House, Shanaway Road, Ennis, Co Clare
🖱 www.woodstockgolfclub.com
📧 woodstock.ennis@eircom.net
☎ 00353 65 6829463,
Fax 6820304
In Ennis.
Parkland course.
Founded 1993
Designed by Dr Arthur Spring.

18 holes, 5879 yards, S.S.S. 71
✝ Welcome.
⌶ WD €35; WE €40.
⌔ Welcome by prior arrangement; terms of group rates on application.
🍽 Club house catering facilities; bar food available.
🛏 Woodstock House Hotel.

12 282 **Youghal** ♆

Knockaverry, Youghal, Co Cork
🖱 www.wyoughalgolfclub.net
📧 youghalgolfclub@eircom.net
☎ 00353 24 92787, Fax 92641, Pro 92590
On N25 between Rosslare and Cork.
Parkland course.
Pro Liam Burns; Founded 1898
Designed by Commander Harris
18 holes, 5646 yards, S.S.S. 70
✝ Welcome.
⌶ WD €25; WE €32.
⌔ Welcome by prior arrangement.
🍽 Full clubhouse facilities available.
🛏 Walter Raleigh; Devonshire Arms.

INDEX